The Discovery of the Unconscious

THE
Discovery
OF THE
Unconscious

THE HISTORY AND EVOLUTION
OF DYNAMIC PSYCHIATRY

Henri F. Ellenberger

 BasicBooks
A Division of HarperCollins*Publishers*

INTRODUCTION

THIS BOOK IS INTENDED TO BE a history of dynamic psychiatry based on a scientific methodology, with a detailed and objective survey of the great dynamic psychiatric systems, notably those of Janet, Freud, Adler, and Jung. An interpretation of facts and systems is proposed, on the basis of an evaluation of the socio-economic, political, and cultural background, as well as of the personality of the pioneers, their environment, and the role of certain patients.

The starting point of my study came about through reflection on the contrast between the evolution of dynamic psychiatry and that of other sciences. No branch of knowledge has undergone so many metamorphoses as dynamic psychiatry: from primitive healing to magnetism, magnetism to hypnotism, hypnotism to psychoanalysis and the newer dynamic schools. Furthermore, these various trends have gone through repeated waves of rejection and acceptance. However, acceptance has never been as un-equivocal as in the case of physical, chemical, or physiological discoveries, not to mention the fact that the teachings of the newer dynamic schools are to a great extent mutually incompatible. As another conspicuous feature, the current accounts of the history of dynamic psychiatry contain more errors, gaps, and legends than the history of any other science.

The aim of my research was threefold. The first task was retracing the history of dynamic psychiatry as accurately as possible, departing from the "hero-worship" perspective of certain former accounts, while keeping a rigorously impartial outlook and abstaining from any kind of polemics. The relevant methodology can be summed up in four principles: (1) Never take anything for granted. (2) Check everything. (3) Replace everything in its context. (4) Draw a sharp line of distinction between the facts and interpretation of facts. Whenever possible, I resorted to primary sources, such as archives, specialized libraries, and the testimonies of trustworthy witnesses. Secondary sources have been assessed in regard to their reliability. By means of extensive research pursued for a dozen years with this critical method, I was able to collect a great number of new facts, while many facts already known are placed in a new light. Many legends that have been repeated from author to author are shown to be erroneous.

My second task was to reconstruct and expound the great dynamic psychiatric systems. This implies that the development of each system had to be followed in chronological order from the very beginning. (The study of Janet had thus to start with the philosophical writings of his youth, that of Freud with his neuroanatomic writings, that of Adler with his early papers on social medicine, and that of Jung with the talks he gave to members of his student association.) Each system had to be shown in the light of its own principles. To make each system intelligible implied exploration of its sources and an effort to replace its originator in the context of his social setting and the network of his relationships with his contemporaries. To replace a work in its context is also the best means to assess its true originality.

My third task was to give an interpretation of the history of dynamic psychiatry and of the great dynamic systems. To that effect the history of dynamic psychiatry had to be recounted in a double perspective, that is, as the events appeared to contemporaries and as they appear to us in retrospect (many facts which seemed of little importance to contemporaries appear to us to have been crucial, and vice versa). This way of writing history entailed an extensive inquiry into the socio-economic, political, cultural, and medical background, as well as into the personalities of the pioneers and their environment, including their patients. The aim of this inquiry was to find an explanation of the paradoxical features in the evolution of dynamic psychiatry, and to throw some light upon the origin, sources, and meaning of the great dynamic psychiatric systems.

The present book begins with a survey of the ancestry of dynamic psychiatry. This survey has historical interest because a continuous chain can be demonstrated between exorcism and magnetism, magnetism and hypnotism, hypnotism and the great modern dynamic systems. It also has theoretical interest because we find in primitive healing evidences of subtle therapeutic techniques, many of which are similar to the most modern psychotherapeutic methods, whereas other ones are without known parallels today. Ten varieties of primitive healing are thus reviewed and compared with modern methods. Emphasis is laid also on those methods of psychic training which were taught by the Greco-Roman philosophical schools and amounted to varieties of psychotherapy, and on the religious cure of the "pathogenic secret." Here, too, a continuous line of evolution is shown between this type of healing and certain techniques of modern dynamic psychiatry.

Chapter 2 tells the story of the birth, evolution, and vicissitudes of dynamic psychiatry between Mesmer and Charcot, that is, from 1775 to 1893. A number of important new points are brought to light about Mesmer, Puységur, and Kerner. It is shown that the advent of spiritism in the years 1848 to 1853 meant a decisive turning point in the history of dynamic psychiatry, and that much of the teachings of the old magnetizers were forgotten after 1850 and partly rediscovered by Bernheim and Charcot around 1880. I utilized a biography of Charcot published in Russian by the physician Lyubimov, who had been Charcot's friend for twenty years; this important source had escaped the attention of all other historians before now.

The main innovation in Chapter 3 is the notion of the First Dynamic Psychiatry. It is shown that throughout the nineteenth century there existed a well-rounded system of dynamic psychiatry, in spite of inevitable fluctuations and divergencies between the rival groups of magnetists and hypnotists. The basic features of the first dynamic psychiatry were the use of hypnosis as an approach to the unconscious mind, the interest in certain specific conditions called "magnetic diseases," the concept of a dual model of the mind with a conscious and an unconscious ego, the belief in the psychogenesis of many emotional and physical conditions, and the use of specific psychotherapeutic procedures; the therapeutic channel was seen as being the "rapport" between hypnotist and patient. Magnetism and hypnotism produced a new type of healer whose characteristic features are described on the basis of autobiographies of ancient magnetists and on other documents never utilized by historians to this date. It is shown, further, that the cultural impact of the first dynamic psychiatry was far greater than is generally believed.

Chapter 4 is devoted to a new and original interpretation of the history and features of the first dynamic psychiatry. The paradoxical shifting from Mesmer's technique to that of Puységur, and from the latter to the authoritarian hypnotic therapy of the second half of the nineteenth century are explained as reflections of changes in the relationships between social classes. Other vicissitudes in the evolution of dynamic psychiatry are interpreted as manifestations of the struggles between great cultural trends: the Baroque, Enlightenment, Romanticism, Positivism. Striking similarities are shown between the basic concepts of Freud and Jung, on the one side, and certain concepts of Romantic philosophers and psychiatrists on the other, including the late-comers of Romanticism, Fechner and Bachofen. The impact of the socio-economic upheavals brought forth by the industrial revolution is also analyzed, as well as the influence exerted by Darwin and Marx upon dynamic psychiatry.

In the 1880's and 1890's it would have seemed that the first dynamic psychiatry had won its final triumph as many of its teachings were accepted by Charcot and Bernheim. However, this triumph was short-lived and followed by a swift decline. The aim of Chapter 5 is to find an interpretation of those paradoxical events by means of an inquiry into socio-economic upheavals and the cultural trends which gave a new orientation to the public mind. Among the trends that explain the orientation toward a new dynamic psychiatry, emphasis is laid upon the new "uncovering" psychology of Nietzsche and others, the neo-Romantic movement, the trend toward repsychologization of psychiatry, the rapid development of sexual psychopathology, the interest in dreams, the exploration of the unconscious (one great pioneer here was Flournoy). It is shown that the word "psychotherapy" had become fashionable around 1890 and that there was a demand for a new psychotherapy that would satisfy the intellectual needs of upper class patients.

Chapter 6 constitutes the first biographical study of Pierre Janet to be given in any language, on the basis of data provided by the community registers, the archives of the Paris Medical School, the Ecole Normale Supérieure, the Lyceums in Châteauroux and Le Havre, the Collège de France, and abundant information provided by Janet's two daughters and many persons who had been acquainted with him. Several legends concerning Janet are refuted. This chapter also gives for the first time a really all-encompassing survey of Janet's psychological system. Janet's priority in the discovery of the cathartic therapy is evidenced by means of numerous quotations, and attention is drawn to the fact that the first (and possibly only) case of diabolical possession treated and cured by dynamic psychotherapy was that of Janet's patient "Achilles" in 1890 and 1891. The reader will find a description of Janet's theories on psychological automatism, of his psychological analysis, of the great psychological synthesis he constructed from 1908 on, and of his ideas on the psychology of religion. Due credit is given to Janet's psychotherapy, which is rarely mentioned in any textbook.

So much has been published about Freud and psychoanalysis that it would seem impossible to bring anything really new to this field. Nevertheless the reader will find in Chapter 7 a number of previously unknown facts and fresh interpretations. Analyzing Freud's Jewish background, the author shows that there had been several groups of Austrian Jews with quite different conditions of life, and that these differences were reflected in the great variety of attitudes shown by their descendants, that is, the Austrian Jews in Freud's time. Regarding Freud's life, some new biographical material is brought forth. The author was able to utilize recently discovered material pertaining to the story of the Freud family in Freiberg, an episode of Freud's school years, a part of the recently discovered Freud–Silberstein correspondence, an evaluation of Freud's capacity as an officer (recently unearthed by Mrs. Renée Gicklhorn in the archives of the Austrian Ministry of War). A critical survey of the story of Freud's paper on male hysteria before the Viennese Society of Physicians on October 15, 1886, is given and shows that the common version of this episode is but a legend. Freud's self-analysis is interpreted as an occurence of a specific creative illness. The episode of Freud's journey to America in 1909 is illustrated with hitherto unpublished details. Freud's intervention in the so-called Wagner–Jauregg trial is reconstructed with the help of unpublished documents recently discovered by Mrs. Renée Gicklhorn. The present book includes the most complete collection of interviews of Freud on record. It also brings a review of the main interpretations of Freud's personality. A detailed survey of Freud's work is given in chronological sequence taking into account the cultural and scientific movement of the time. Freud's masters and those men who played an important role in the shaping of his thought are examined in the light of new data. Regarding Breuer, for instance, I utilized unpublished data provided by Breuer's family, notably the documents concerning the Breuer Foundation (*Breuer–Stiftung*) the very existence of which seems to have escaped the attention of other historians before now. Emphasis is laid on Moritz Benedikt as being one of the very important sources for Freud, whereas it is shown the Freud's relationship to Charcot was not that of disciple to master, but rather in the guise of an existential encounter. A careful scrutiny of facts already known and inquiries in the Viennese archives convinced me that the usual version of Anna O.'s disease is untenable, that her condition belonged to the great "magnetic diseases" of the past, but because the teachings of the old magnetists had been forgotten, the case was bound to be misunderstood. Much new material was discovered regarding Freud's sources, his relationships with some of his contemporaries, the context of his discoveries, and their impact.

The reader will find in Chapter 8 a critical account of Alfred Adler's family background and life history, based on extensive research in the Viennese archives and inquiries among members of the Adler family and several of his earlier disciples. It is shown that Adler's Jewish background was quite different from Freud's, which would explain the great differences in the attitudes of the two men in regard to the Jewish and Gentile worlds. It is shown also how Adler's family constellation was reflected in his later theories. Among other unfamiliar facts is the revelation of the pre-Freudian period in Adler's thought. After prolonged research, I was able to find a copy (probably the only surviving one) of Adler's first publication, his *Health Book for the Tailor Trade* (1898). A series of articles published by Adler in a little-known Austrian periodical were also unearthed. A scrutiny of the booklet and articles shows that the main tenets of Adler's future system were already present in these early works, in other words that Adler's individual psychology cannot be considered as "a distortion of psychoanalysis," but as a return to and elaboration of the ideas Adler had developed during the six years of his pre-psychoanalytic period. The evolution of Adler's thought is related step by step and its various facets are illustrated with examples drawn from among his little known writings, including interviews given to newspapers or magazines. A complete and

accurate description of Adler's methods of individual and collective psychotherapy and therapeutic education is given; many data scattered throughout individual psychological literature are gathered here and presented in
a systematic way. Several unknown sources of Adler are described—for
instance, the works of Russian writers.

Chapter 9 brings a great deal of fresh information about Carl Gustav
Jung. It begins with a description of his Swiss background and the extraordinary story of his grandparents. Memories of Jung's former schoolmate,
Gustav Steiner (recently published in the *Basler Stadtbuch*, a publication
hardly known outside Basel), proved invaluable for reconstruction of that
period of Jung's life and thought. I was able to identify the young medium
on whom Jung performed early experiments and to obtain new data about
this episode. I definitely refute the current stereotype that Jung's system is
merely a distortion of Freud's psychoanalysis. It is shown that several of
Jung's main ideas were already present in Jung's student days. Jung's self-
experiment of 1913 to 1919 is related on the basis of published and unpublished material and interpreted as an example of a creative illness. The
survey given of Jung's system is probably the most complete and all-
encompassing of any that has been written to date: not only did I utilize
the whole of Jung's published works, and the interviews he gave to newspapers and magazines, but I had access to the complete collection of
Jung's unpublished lectures and seminars. The evolution of Jung's thought
is described in its chronological sequence and progress. The account given
of Jung's psychotherapy is also the most complete given to this date. Various
little-known aspects of Jung's thought are referred to, such as his philosophy
of history and the extensive, unpublished commentaries he gave of
Nietzsche's *Zarathustra*. Hitherto unknown or overlooked sources of Jung's
ideas are pointed out, as well as Jung's influence in unsuspected fields (for
instance, the origin of the lie-detector, the origin of Alcoholics Anonymous,
and recent theories of national economy and political philosophy).

Chapter 10 is the key-stone, as it were, of the whole book. It aims at
giving a synthesis of the story of the birth and growth of the new dynamic
psychiatric systems from 1893 to 1945. The origin and development of each
system is shown year by year, in their interplay as well as in their relationships to other psychiatric and psychotherapeutic trends, and to the cultural
and political background. In this way it will appear to the reader that the
growth of psychoanalysis and of the newer dynamic systems was not so
much a revolution as a gradual evolution from the first dynamic psychiatry
to the newer ones. The story of dynamic psychiatry is thus intermingled
with that of events of the time: wars and political upheavals, literary and
artistic movements, international congresses, sensational trials, and even
psychiatric systems from 1882 to 1945. The origin and development of each
are emphasized, for instance Charcot's death and the publication of
psychiatric books or literary works that caused a sensation. It is shown that,

contrary to a current assumption, polemics around psychoanalysis hardly started before 1907, that is, before psychoanalysis took the shape of a movement. Several episodes of these polemics are singled out, particularly the Zurich polemic of 1912 (which has never been related by other historians before now); it is shown that the meaning of these polemics to people of that time was somewhat different from the aspect they acquired in retrospect. Attention is drawn to a variety of dynamic systems or psychotherapeutic techniques that played a great role in their time but are more or less forgotten today. Throughout this whole chapter a great number of unknown or little-known data are offered to the reader.

A short concluding chapter is devoted to classifying and defining the factors that caused and directed the evolution of dynamic psychiatry, namely, the socio-economic background; the succession of, and conflicts between, great cultural trends; the personality, family situation, life events, and neuroses of the founders; the phenomenon of "creative illness" (in regard to Freud and Jung); the role of the social class from which the founders drew their patients; the complex and ambiguous role of certain privileged patients (mostly hysterical women); the role of environment, colleagues, disciples, rivals, contemporary books and contemporary events.

PERSONAL
ACKNOWLEDGMENTS

THE RESEARCH THAT CONSTITUTES the substance of the present book was made possible by a grant of the National Institute of Mental Health that enabled me to spend four months in Austria, Germany, Switzerland, and France, interviewing people and collecting archival data, and that secured the salary of a research secretary for three years. A sojourn in England was made possible by a grant of the British Council, and a second research summer in Vienna and Zurich by a grant of the Direction of the Psychiatric Services in Quebec. The latter also paid the salary of a secretary for the completion of the book. I also received encouragement and a generous allotment of time from the University of Montreal.

Precious advice and information was received from Professor Werner Leibbrand of Munich, Professor Erwin Ackernecht of Zurich, and particularly Professor Erna Lesky of Vienna, who also lent me her *History of the Viennese Medical School* while this work was still unpublished.

The Viscount du Boisdulier provided me with a great deal of information from family archives about his illustrious ancestor, the Marquis de Puységur. First-hand information about Pierre Janet was supplied by his two daughters, Miss Fanny Janet and Mrs. Hélène Pichon-Janet, as well as by Professor Jean Delay and Mr. Ignace Meyerson. Mrs. Käthe Breuer gave me much information about her father-in-law, Dr. Joseph Breuer, and permission to utilize unpublished letters and other documents, among others, those of the Breuer Foundation.

Mr. Ernest Freud obligingly showed me the office and library of his father, as reconstructed in his home in Maresfield Gardens, London, and supplied information on various points. Dr. K. R. Eissler, director of the Freud Archive, gave the author valuable advice and kindly lent him the manuscript of his unpublished study on Freud's personality. First-hand memories about Freud and the early history of the psychoanalytic movement were received mainly from the late Reverend Oskar Pfister and Dr. Alphonse Maeder, both in Zurich. The stark discrepancy between the currently accepted version of certain events and the relation given of the same by these two old-timers was one of the incentives which brought me to a more critical attitude in my investigations. In my inquiries about Freud I was helped in the most generous way by Mrs. Renée Gicklhorn, in Vienna, who lent me the manuscript of her unpublished book on the so-called Wagner–Jauregg trial, as well as photocopies of several precious documents.

Reminiscenses about Alfred Adler were provided by Dr. Alexandra Adler and relatives in Austria, Germany and America. Dr. Hans Beckh–Widmanstetter introduced the author into the labyrinth of the Viennese archives, helped him in every possible way, pursued the research on his behalf afterwards, and gave him permission to utilize his unpublished study on Alfred Adler's childhood and youth. Further information was provided by Professor Viktor Frankl, Reverend Ernst Jahn, of Berlin-Stieglitz, and Professor and Mrs. Ansbacher, of Burlington, Vermont.

I had been personally acquainted with the late C. G. Jung and had interviewed him on all the points I found obscure in his teachings; I then wrote the draft of an account of Jung's theories, after reading which, Jung returned it to me with pencilled annotations. Thanks are also due to Mr. and Mrs. Franz Jung, Dr. von Sury, Dr. C. A. Meier, Miss Aniéla Jaffé, and those who allowed me to read Jung's unpublished lectures and seminars.

Information on various important points was provided by Dr. Charles Baudouin, Dr. Ludwig Binswanger, Dr. Oscar Diethelm, Dr. Henri Flournoy, Dr. Eugène Minkowski, Dr. Jacob Moreno, Dr. Gustav Morf, Mrs. Olga Rorschach, Dr. Leopold Szondi, and many others.

I have to acknowledge collectively the help of the librarians in the New York Public Library, the Library of Congress in Washington, the National Library of Medicine in Bethesda, Maryland, the Bibliothèque Nationale in Paris, the Library of the British Museum in London, the Swiss National Library in Bern, the University Libraries of Strasbourg, Nancy, Basel, Zürich, Geneva, Vienna, and Sofia, the Library of the Goetheanum in Dornach, Switzerland, the archive department of the Neue Zürcher Zeitung, Zurich, and last but not least—the Libraries of McGill University and of the University of Montreal.

Long as it is, this list is still incomplete and should at least include those students whose questions and remarks often incited me to look more closely at certain problems, thus confirming the truth of Rabbi Chanuna's sentence in the Talmud: "Much did I learn from my teachers, more from my colleagues, most from my students."

CONTENTS

ILLUSTRATIONS

The Discovery of the Unconscious

1

The Ancestry of
Dynamic Psychotherapy

ALTHOUGH THE SYSTEMATIC INVESTIGATION of the unconscious mind and of psychic dynamism is fairly new, the origins of dynamic psychotherapy can be traced back in time through a long line of ancestors and forerunners. Certain medical or philosophical teachings of the past, as well as certain older healing methods, offer a surprisingly high degree of insight into what are usually considered the most recent discoveries in the realm of the human mind.

For many years, accounts of cures performed among primitive peoples by medicine men, shamans, and the like aroused little attention among psychiatrists. Such accounts were regarded as queer stories, of interest only to historians and anthropologists. Medicine men were thought to be either grossly ignorant and superstitious individuals, able to cure only those patients who would have recovered spontaneously in any case, or dangerous impostors exploiting the credulity of their fellow men.

Today we have reached another, more positive evaluation. The development of modern psychotherapy has drawn attention to the mystery of the mechanism of psychological healing and shown how many of its details still puzzle us. Why is it that certain patients respond to a certain type of cure while others do not? We do not know; therefore, anything that might shed light on such problems is welcome.

Historical and anthropological research has brought forth important documents and revealed evidence of the use among primitive and ancient peoples of many of the methods used by modern psychotherapy, even though in a different form, as well as evidence of other subtle therapeutic techniques for which present-day parallels can hardly be found. The study of primitive healing thus is of interest not only to anthropologists and historians (as being the root from which, after a long evolution, psychotherapy developed) but is also of great theoretical importance to the study of psychiatry as the basis of a new science of comparative psychotherapy.

In this chapter we shall first discuss the discovery of primitive psycho-therapy and then present a survey of the main techniques of primitive healing that will lead to a comparison with modern psychotherapy. We will conclude with a brief sketch of the evolution from primitive healing to present-day dynamic psychotherapy.

The Discovery of Primitive Psychotherapy

One of the first scientists to understand the scientific relevance of primitive healing was the German anthropologist Adolf Bastian (1826–1905).[1] During his field work in Guyana, Bastian happened one day to suffer from severe headache and fever and he asked the local medicine man to treat him with his usual method. It is worthwhile to summarize the account of that experience:

> The medicine man bade his white patient to come to his lodge shortly after dusk and to bring with him his hammock and a few leaves of tobacco, which were put into a bowl of water placed on the floor of the lodge. The treatment was performed in the presence of about thirty natives who had gathered there. There was no window, no chimney; the door was closed and it was pitch-dark. The patient was ordered to lie down on his hammock and to keep still, not to raise his hand or head; he was warned that if he touched the ground with his foot, his life would be endangered. A young native boy who spoke English lay down on another hammock and translated as much as he could of the words spoken by the medicine man and by the *kenaimas* (demons or spirits). The medicine man began by conjuring up the *kenaimas*. It was not long before these manifested their presence by all kinds of noises, first low and soft, then louder and eventually becoming deafening. Each of them spoke with its own voice, which varied according to the alleged personality of the *kenaima*. Some of them were supposed to fly through the air; the patient could hear the rustling of their wings and feel a draft on his face. He even felt the touch of one of them and was agile enough to bite off a few fragments, which he later found to be leaves of boughs that the medicine man must have been swinging through the air.
>
> He could also hear the demons licking the tobacco leaves that were on the ground. The ceremony made a powerful impression on the patient, who gradually fell into a kind of hypnotic sleep, awakening slightly when the noise receded, but falling again into deeper insensitivity as soon as it increased. The ritual lasted for not less than six hours and was completed when the medicine man suddenly put his hand on the patient's face. But when the latter arose, his headache had not vanished. The medicine man, however, insisted upon the payment of his fee, contending that he had cured the patient. As a proof of the cure he showed him a caterpillar, which, he alleged, was the "disease" he had extracted from the patient when putting his hand on his forehead.
>
> Bastian commented on the fantastic achievement of this man who, for six whole hours, had displayed an intense activity and an unparalleled skill in ventriloquism. Unfortunately, Bastian, who apparently did not catch much of the words exchanged between the medicine man and the *kenaimas,* did not report about the meaning of the ceremony or about the personality of the medicine man, and does not seem to have inquired about the efficacy of such treatments among native

patients. He insisted upon the necessity of collecting similar data because, he said, primitive medicine was rapidly disappearing, and these data would be of the greatest value for medicine as well as for ethnology.

A great deal of scattered data relating to primitive medicine had, of course, already been published at that time. The arduous task of collecting and organizing this data was attempted by Bartels on the basis of extensive material.[2] He showed that a number of treatments used in primitive medicine are rational—for example, drugs, ointments, massage, diet, and others—and that they represent an earlier stage in the development of modern medicine, whereas many others are irrational procedures based on fallacious disease theories that have no counterpart in scientific medicine. Examples of these are the search for restoration of a supposedly lost soul, the extraction of the disease in the form of a foreign body (obviously produced through jugglery), the expulsion of evil spirits, and others. Bartels' compilation, however, was still only a mosaic of isolated facts drawn from widely different peoples. Since his time, our knowledge of primitive medicine has greatly increased. We are now in a better position to distinguish the specific features of primitive medicine among the many peoples of the world. But we must not lose sight of the fact that our knowledge will always remain fragmentary. Numerous primitive populations disappeared before any serious ethnological investigation could be conducted and of those that survived, many have retained only distorted remnants of their former customs and lore. Nevertheless, the data in our possession provide us with fairly accurate knowledge of the main features of primitive medicine, as can be seen, notably, in the books of Buschan[3] and Sigerist.[4]

Forest E. Clements distinguished five main forms of treatment that can be deduced from the disease theory through a "very simple cause-and-effect sort of reasoning." They are summarized in the Table 1–1.[5]

TABLE 1–1

DISEASE THEORY	THERAPY
1. Disease-object intrusion	Extraction of disease-object
2. Loss of the soul	To find, bring back, and restore the lost soul
3. Spirit intrusion	a. Exorcism b. Mechanical extraction of the foreign spirit c. Transference of the foreign spirit into another living being.
4. Breach of taboo	Confession, propitiation
5. Sorcery	Counter-magic.

Such forms of therapy are highly differentiated, and it is clear that many other procedures could have been devised on the basis of the same disease theories. For example, given the theory that disease results from the intrusion of a disease-object, there is no reason why the treatment should consist of the extraction of the disease-object through mouth-sucking rather than through any of the other possible means. However, a survey of the known facts shows that almost everywhere the disease-object is extracted only by this method. This peculiar fact brings us to the logical conclusion that we are dealing with a specific form of treatment that must have originated in one place and then spread to the rest of the world. As we shall see later, we can even attempt a reconstruction of the development of primitive medicine from the earliest prehistoric times to the present day.

As the many forms of primitive therapy became better known and reliable documents became available, psychiatrists began to show an interest in them. Charcot had been interested in psychopathological manifestations among primitive populations, and wanted to compare them with those of his hysterical patients in Paris. One of his associates, Meige,[6] gathered reports on possession and exorcism among the natives of Central Africa, and an African woman, who had arrived from her native land with severe hysterical symptoms, was examined and treated in Charcot's ward at the Salpêtrière[7] In 1932, Oskar Pfister commented on an account of a cure by a Navaho medicine man and attempted an interpretation in psychoanalytic terms.[8] Other similar studies were published by Freudian and Jungian analysts. Among anthropologists, Claude Lévi-Strauss vigorously emphasized the basic identity of certain age-old concepts of primitive medicine to certain new concepts of modern dynamic psychiatry.[9]

Loss and Restoration of the Soul

According to an ancient concept, disease occurs when the soul—spontaneously or by accident—leaves the body or is stolen by ghosts or sorcerers. The healer searches for the lost soul, brings it back, and restores it to the body to which it belongs.

The disease theory is widespread, but not universal. It is prevalent among some of the most primitive populations of the earth, such as the Negritos of the Malay Peninsula, the Pygmies of the Philippines, the Australians, and, generally speaking, those peoples who belong to what Graebner and Schmidt called the *Urkulturkreis*. However, this disease theory may also be found among populations of more advanced cultures, mainly in such areas as Siberia, where it is the foremost theory of disease, Northwest Africa, Indonesia, New Guinea, and Melanesia. But even in one given area there are many local varieties regarding the concepts relative to the nature of the soul, the causes and agents of soul loss, the destination of the lost soul, and the curability of the disease.[10]

This disease theory is connected with a specific concept of the soul that has been the object of Tylor's pioneer studies.[11] During sleep or fainting, the "soul" seems to separate itself from the body. In dreams and visions, the sleeper sees human shapes that differ from those of his conscious experience. These two notions are combined in the theory that man bears within himself a kind of duplicate, a ghost-soul whose presence in the body is a prerequisite to normal life, but that is able to leave the body temporarily and to wander about, especially during sleep. In the words of Frazer, "the soul of a sleeper is supposed to wander away from his body and actually to visit the places, see the persons, and perform the acts of which he dreams." During these wanderings the soul may meet with accidents and dangers of all kinds, which have been described by Frazer in his classic book *Taboo and the Perils of the Soul*.[12] The soul, for example, may lose its way, be injured, or be separated from the body if the sleeper is suddenly awakened, while the soul is far away. It may get caught and detained by evil spirits during its wanderings, and may also leave the body in a waking state, especially after a sudden fright. Finally, it may also be forcibly removed from the body by ghosts, demons, or sorcerers.

Logically, then, the treatment of the disease consists in finding, bringing back, and restoring the lost soul. However, the techniques, as well as the disease theory, vary widely. Sometimes the lost soul remains in the physical world, either far removed from or close to the patient; sometimes it wanders into the world of the dead or the spirits. The latter concept is found predominantly in Siberia, where a cure can be performed only by a shaman, that is, a man, who, during his long initiation, has been introduced into the world of the spirits and is thus able to function as a mediator between that world and the world of the living. Russian ethnologists have gathered many remarkable accounts of shamanism. One of them, Ksenofontov, states:

> When a human being has "lost his soul," the shaman works himself into ecstasy by means of a special technique; while he remains in that state, his soul travels to the world of the spirits. Shamans contend to be able, for instance, to track down the lost soul in the underworld in the same way as a hunter tracks down game in the physical world. They must often make a bargain with the spirits who have stolen the soul, propitiate them and bring them gifts. Sometimes they have to fight the spirits, preferably with the help of other spirits who are on their side. Even if they are successful, they must anticipate the vengeance of the evil spirits. Once they have recaptured the lost soul, they bring it back and restore it to the deprived body, thus achieving the cure.[13]

In other parts of the world, the healer need not go so far away, nor must he work himself into ecstasy. The technique may consist simply of conjurations and other magical operations. This is the case with the Quechua Indians of Peru. We are indebted to Dr. Federico Sal y Rosas for a detailed study on the soul-loss disease among that population.[14] From 1935 to 1957, Sal y Rosas noted 176 cases of *Susto* (the Spanish word for "fright") in Huaráz and the neighboring provinces. The Quechua word *Jani* designates the disease as well as the soul and the healing cure. Sal y Rosas emphasized that *Susto* is not a mere superstition, but a medical condition that can be approached both scientifically and anthropologically. The following is a summary of Sal y Rosas's account:

> The Quechua Indians believe that the soul (or perhaps part of it) can leave the body, either spontaneously or through being forced. The *Susto* disease can occur in two ways: either through fright caused, for instance, by thunder, the sight of a bull, a snake, and so on, or because of malevolent influences, not following upon fright (the latter being called "*Susto* without *Susto*"). Among the malevolent forces that can produce the abduction of the soul, the influence of the earth is considered supreme. The Quechuas show a great fear of certain slopes and caves, and especially of the old Incan ruins. Whether the *Susto* occurs following a fright or not, in both cases the power to be propitiated is the earth.
>
> How can the disease be designated as *Susto* when it was not preceded by a fright? It may be diagnosed as such when an individual loses weight and energy and becomes irritable, has disturbed sleep and nightmares, and especially when he falls into a state of physical and mental depression called *Michko*. The matter is then clarified by a *curandera*. This woman will rub the body of the patient from head to toe with a live guinea pig in such a way that the animal dies at the end of the operation. Then she will skin it and read her oracular diagnosis in the animal's blood, which is made to drip into a bowl of water, and from the lesions she discovers in the animal's organs.
>
> The healing ceremony begins with an operation called the *Shokma*, which is also performed by a *curandera*, who recites certain invocations while rubbing the patient from head to toe with a mixture of various flowers and leaves and the flour of several kinds of grain. The mixture is then collected and handed over to a male healer, a *curioso*, who now performs the essential parts of the rites.
>
> The *curioso* comes to the patient's house at midnight, wraps the mixture in a piece of the patient's clothing, and prepares him to receive the absent spirit. He then leaves the patient, who remains alone in the darkened house with the door open; he walks away, using the mixture to make a white line along the ground to enable the soul to find its way back; he goes either to the spot where the patient experienced his initial fright or to some dreaded place, such as an old grave or the ruin of an Incan fortress. There, using the mixture, he makes a cross on the ground, places himself at the center of the cross, and offers what remains of the mixture as a propitiatory sacrifice to the earth. He then solemnly calls the lost soul, repeating his call five times. At the end of the fifth invocation, he must perceive a special noise that indicates the presence of the lost soul before he can return to the house of the patient, carefully following the white track. The patient must be asleep; the healer cautiously lifts the blanket over the patient's feet, this being the place where the soul supposedly re-enters the body accompanied by a special rustle that is audible to the healer. At this moment, the patient is expected to dream that his soul returns to his body in the shape of a tame animal. The healer now leaves the house, either through another door or by walking backward. The patient's family is not allowed to return until the following morning, and in most cases, when they return, they find the patient cured. If not, the failure is ascribed to the fact that the patient

was not asleep when he ought to have been, or to some other defect in the procedure, and the operation will be repeated at another time.

Sal y Rosas compiled statistics on 176 patients, mostly children or adolescents afflicted with *Susto,* who underwent a medical examination. It was found that these patients belonged to two distinct groups: The first consisted of 64 emotionally disturbed individuals suffering from anxiety, depression, hysterical symptoms, and the like. The second group included 112 patients afflicted with physical diseases such as tuberculosis, malaria, postdysentery colitis, malnutrition, anemia, and so on, all further complicated by emotional disturbances.

A remarkable fact is the frequently successful outcome of the healing procedure. With praiseworthy honesty, Sal y Rosas writes: "I have personally observed many cases of typical or even atypical *Susto* abruptly improve or recover completely after one or two sessions of *Jani.* . . . Such a success achieved by a humble rural *curioso* or by a peasant woman, with their primitive and savage psychotherapy, contrasts with the failure of graduated physicians— among them the author of this article—in the cure of *Susto.*"

Among all primitive disease theories probably none is stranger to us than the idea of soul loss. Nothing is further from our principles of treatment than the restoration of a lost soul to a patient. And yet, if we ignore the cultural element and seek the roots of facts, we may find a common ground between those primitive concepts and ours. Do we not say that our mental patients are "alienated," "estranged" from themselves, that their ego is impoverished or destroyed? Could not the therapist who gives psychotherapy to a severely deteriorated schizophrenic patient by trying to establish a contact with the remaining healthy parts of the personality and to reconstruct the ego be considered the modern successor of those shamans who set out to follow the tracks of a lost soul, trace it into the world of spirits, and fight against the malignant demons detaining it, and bring it back to the world of the living?

Intrusion and Extraction of the Disease-Object

This theory maintains that disease is caused by the presence in the body of a harmful foreign substance, such as a piece of bone, a pebble, a splinter of wood, or a small animal. Certain peoples believe that disease is caused not by the object itself but by a special disease-essence contained in the object. Sometimes, the harmful disease-object is believed to have been shot into the body by a sorcerer.

This disease theory is widespread in America (excepting the eastern Eskimos), very common in eastern Siberia, Southeast Asia, Australia, New Zealand, and in several other parts of the world. It has also left many traces in European popular medicine and folklore. A striking fact is the connection between this disease theory and a peculiar kind of treatment: the medicine man uses his mouth to suck out the disease-object. Other methods, such as massage, are much less frequent.

It is obvious that the disease-object seemingly extracted by the medicine man is produced by means of a trick, which explains why some Europeans who watched such healing procedures declared that the medicine men were quacks and impostors. Yet, there is little doubt that these cures are often successful. It has also been pointed out that among certain populations the disease-object is of such a nature that a patient could not possibly believe that it had been extracted from his body. We face here a situation that frequently occurs in anthropology. In order to understand the meaning of a custom or belief, one must consider it within the sociological structure of the community. Similarly, we cannot understand this kind of therapy without knowing the natives' attitudes and beliefs in regard to the disease, the medicine man, and the treatment.

To clarify this point, we will briefly summarize a document published by Franz Boas in 1930. It is an autobiographical fragment, related to him by a Kwakiutl shaman and published in the original Kwakiutl, with an English translation.[15] Lévi-Strauss has drawn attention to the great interest of this document from the point of view of comparative psychotherapy.[16] What follows is a summary of Boas' reports of the adventures of Qaselid, a Kwakiutl shaman belonging to a tribe of Indians of the North Pacific coast of British Columbia:

The narrator, Giving-Potlatches-to-the-World, relates how he doubts the powers of the shamans, and in order to find out the truth, he tries to become admitted to one of their groups. Because of his acquaintance with two of them, he manages to watch a therapeutic performance and closely observes their healing techniques. The ceremony is being conducted by the shaman, Making-Alive, who is assisted by four other shamans and several song leaders, in the presence of a number of men, women, and children in the patient's house. After various rites, Making-Alive feels the patient's chest and wets his mouth; he then sucks the place where he has localized the sickness. After a while, he takes from his mouth something looking like a bloody worm, declaring that he has extracted the "disease," after which he sings his sacred song. At the end of the ceremony, Making-Alive presses his stomach, vomits blood, and catches in it a piece of shining quartz that he throws up in the air and declares to have shot into the stomach of Giving-Potlatches-to-the-World. This is the vocation. The narrator is then invited to become a shaman; he has the choice of accepting or refusing. He decides to accept, and soon thereafter receives, in a secret meeting of the shamanistic group, his first lesson in shamanism.

The four-year curriculum of that school included memorizing a number of magic songs pertaining to various kinds of diseases, the technique of "feeling" the disease (that is, palpation of the body, including some obstetrical techniques), practical exercises in simulated fainting, trembling, convulsions, vomiting of blood, and the therapeutic techniques. Our student learns how the shamans, before the healing ceremony, put some eagle down in a corner of their mouths, mix it with blood obtained either by biting their tongues or by rubbing their gums; after many magic songs and gestures, the shaman, with more or less effort, extracts the "disease" from the patient's body and shows it to the patient and the family in the form of a bloody earthworm. Our student also learns how he must pretend to spend the night among the graves and how the shamans utilize "dreamers," that is, spies who inconspicuously get information from the patients about their diseases and secretly report it to the shamans.

The narrator performs his first cure on a young man, Food-Owner, grandson of a chief. The patient had dreamed that he was cured by the new shaman candidate; this dream is sufficient indication, and he is requested to cure the patient. He uses the method of the bloody earthworm, and the patient claims to be cured. It is a big success for the candidate, who is given the name of Qaselid and acquires the reputation of being a great shaman. The patient was cured "because he strongly believed in his dream about me," states the narrator; but it seems that at this point, he begins to think of himself as really being a great shaman.

While on a visit to the nearby tribe of the Koskimo, Qaselid is invited to be a spectator at a therapeutic ceremony performed for the daughter of a chief, Woman-Made-to-Invite. Qaselid notices that the Koskimo shamans use a different technique; instead of extracting the disease in the form of a bloody earthworm, they simply show a little saliva, pretend that it is the "disease." Thus, the Koskimo shamans are worse quacks than the Kwakiutl shamans, who at least produce something tangible. At this point, the story takes an unexpected turn: the Koskimo shamans fail to cure Woman-Made-to-Invite. Qaselid requests and receives permission to try his method, he extracts and shows the alleged "disease" (the bloody earthworm), and the patient declares herself cured. The Koskimo shamans are ashamed, and Qaselid himself probably somewhat surprised to see that although both methods, the Kwakiutl and the Koskimo, are humbug, one of them nevertheless cures better than the other!

The Koskimo shamans invite Qaselid to a secret conference with them that takes place in a cave at the foot of a hill, amidst the trees of the forest. One of the shamans, Great-Dance, greets Qaselid in a friendly manner and explains to him their theory of disease and treatment. The disease, he says, is a man; when they capture his soul, the disease dies and the patient is cured; therefore, they have nothing to show to the people. They urge Qaselid to explain, in turn, why it is that the disease sticks to his hands. But Qaselid refuses to speak, saying that he is still only a novice shaman and that he is not allowed to speak until he has completed his four-year apprenticeship. The Koskimo fail to get him to speak, even though they send their daughters to him in the hope of seducing him.

After returning to his village, Qaselid is challenged by an old shaman of considerable repute to a competition in curing several patients. Qaselid sees that the old man uses another kind of trick: he pretends to incorporate the extracted disease into his head ring or into his rattle, which has the shape of a carved bird. Then, by virtue of the strength of the disease, these objects can, for a while, float in the air. Among the patients is a woman who declares that the old shaman has always unsuccessfully tried to cure her. Qaselid tries the method of the bloody earthworm, and the woman claims to be cured. In defiance of the old shaman, Qaselid sings his sacred song and distributes two hundred dollars among the spectators, so that they might know his name.

The old shaman is upset and sends his daughter to request a conference with Qaselid. "I pray that you try and save my life for me," he tells him, "so that I may not die of shame, for I am a plaything of our people on account of what you did last night." He urges Qaselid to explain his method to him. Qaselid demands a demonstration of the old shaman's tricks, to which the old man complies, but Qaselid refuses to speak in turn, despite the old man and his daughter's supplications. The next morning, the old shaman and his family have disappeared, and he is said to have gone "crazy" soon thereafter.

Qaselid continues to study the tricks of other shamans, while adding to his own therapeutic successes with the method of the bloody earthworm. At the end of the narrative, it is clear that he finds it more and more difficult to recognize the "real" shamans from the quacks. He is sure only of one who is a "real" shaman because he does not accept payment from his patients and because he has never been seen laughing; all others "pretend to be shamans." On the other hand, Qaselid reports his own successes without apparently remembering that he started his career with the intention to unmask the tricks that he now applies himself very successfully.

Setting apart the possible element of mythomania in the narrator, the story of that man who became a healer in spite of himself may help us to better understand the process of such a treatment. It is obvious that the action of sucking out the disease-object is but a part of an elaborate ceremony that includes other rites such as songs and magic gestures, and requires the help of assistants (the beat-drummers). The therapeutic session is carefully prepared and well structured. It takes place in the presence of men, women, and children and culminates in a dramatic climax, with the shaman showing the disease-object to the patient, his family, and the audience.

But this ceremony, in turn, can become efficient only within a psychological and sociological framework that includes: (1) The healer's faith in his own abilities, even if he knows that part of the technique depends on some kind of quackery. (2) The patient's faith in the healer's abilities, as shown in the case of Qaselid's first patient. (The success and reputation of a healer increase, of course, the public's faith in his abilities.) (3) The disease, the healing method, and the healer must all be acknowledged by the social group. The shaman is a member of an organization that has its training, its schools, its strict rules, its meeting places, its secret agents, as well as rivalries with other similar organizations.

To us, the thought of treating diseases by extracting and demonstrating a disease-object is as unthinkable as that of the recapture of a lost soul. However, is it not—even for a civilized patient—an impressive moment when the object of his disease is demonstrated to him, when a surgeon shows him, for instance, the tumor he has removed from his body; a dentist, the bad tooth; a practitioner, the expelled tapeworm?

The psychiatrist can show no such concrete object to his patient; but if we think of the meaning of the "transference neurosis," we could find some similarity to the process of the materialization of the disease. The neurosis is replaced by a "transference neurosis," the nature and origin of which are demonstrated to the patient and consequently cured.

Possession and Exorcism

According to this disease theory, the illness is due to evil spirits that have penetrated the patient's body and "taken possession" of it. Possession, however, is a broader concept than disease, since there are also numerous instances of artificial or ceremonial possession.

As a form of illness, possession is widespread, although it is not universal. It seems to be unknown among the Negritos of the Malay Peninsula, the Pygmies of the Philippines, the Australians, and others. It is not very common on the American continent. Its center of diffusion seems to have been in western Asia.

Given such a disease theory, at least three methods can be—and indeed have been—devised. The first consists in trying to expel the spirit mechanically, through bleeding, beating, or whipping the patient, or by means of noises and smells. The second consists in transferring the spirit into the body of another being, usually an animal (a method that can be associated with exorcism). The third—and by far the most frequently applied—method is *exorcism*, that is, the driving out of the spirit by conjurations or other psychic means. Exorcism has been one of the foremost healing procedures in the Mediterranean area and is still in use in several countries; it is of particular interest to us because it is one of the roots from which, historically speaking, modern dynamic psychotherapy has evolved.

Possession and exorcism have been the object of extensive studies, among which we can list a classic book by Oesterreich, which contains a great deal of carefully analyzed material.[17] Oesterreich emphasizes that possession, in spite of its infinite variety of aspects, universally displays the same basic features.

An individual suddenly seems to lose his identity to become another person. His physiognomy changes and shows a striking resemblance to the individual of whom he is, supposedly, the incarnation. With an altered voice, he pronounces words corresponding to the personality of the new individual. Not infrequently he becomes able to perform movements of astonishing amplitude and force. Possession ordinarily occurs in fits of varying frequency, duration, and intensity.

There are two different types of possession, the somnambulic and the lucid. The individual in somnambulic possession suddenly loses consciousness of his self and speaks with the "I" of the supposed intruder; after regaining consciousness, he remembers nothing of what "the other one" has said or done. In cases of lucid possession, the individual remains constantly aware of his self, but feels "a spirit within his own spirit," struggles against it, but cannot prevent it from speaking at times. In both forms possession is experienced as a kind of intrapsychic parasitism: just as a tapeworm can live in the body, so can a parasitic spirit live in the soul,

Catholic theology, incidentally, reserved the word *possession* for the somnambulic form and called the lucid form *obsession*, a word that has been adopted by psychiatry, though with another meaning.

A second important distinction is that which exists between spontaneous and artificial possession. Spontaneous possession occurs without or against the will of the subject; it is a specific mental condition from which the patient seeks relief with the help of the exorcist. Artificial possession is not a disease; it is a mental technique practiced voluntarily by certain individuals to achieve specific goals. The pythonesses of Delphi in ancient Greece, the Siberian shamans of today, and the spiritists in our Western civilization, all cultivate artificial types of possession in which the fit starts at will and ends spontaneously.

A third basic distinction is that which exists between overt and latent possession. Possession, whether somnambulic or lucid, is overt when the possessing spirit speaks spontaneously through the mouth of the possessed individual. It is latent when the patient is unaware of it; he may suffer from mental disease, or neurotic or physical disturbances for months and years, never suspecting that his troubles stem from an evil spirit. In such cases the exorcist's first task is to make the possession manifest by compelling the evil spirit to speak; only then can the exorcism be performed. The cure is ordinarily more easily obtained than with cases of overt possession. The procedure used to compel the evil spirit to manifest itself could be compared to what we call transference neurosis, though a rather dramatic and short-lived one: its effect is to bring forth an abreaction and healing of previous neurotic disturbances.

Exorcism is the exact counterpart of possession and a well-structured type of psychotherapy. Its basic characteristics are the following: The exorcist does not, ordinarily, speak in his own name, but in the name of a higher being. He must have absolute confidence in this higher being and in his own powers, as well as in the reality of the possession and of the possessing spirit. He addresses the intruder in a solemn way on behalf of the higher being whom he represents. He dispenses encouragement to the possessed individual and saves his threats and admonitions for the intruder. The exorcist's preparation for his task is long and difficult, often including prayer and fasting. The exorcism should, whenever possible, take place in a sacred spot, in a structured environment, and in the presence of witnesses, while at the same time avoiding crowds of the curious. The exorcist must induce the intruder to speak, and after lengthy discussions, a bargain may sometimes take place. Exorcism is a struggle between the exorcist and the intruding spirit—often a long, difficult, and desperate struggle that may continue for days, weeks, months, or even years before a complete victory can be achieved. Not infrequently does the exorcist meet with defeat; moreover, he is in danger himself of becoming infested with the very spirit he has just expelled from the patient.

Although the basic features of possession and exorcism are constant, an infinite variety of aspects exists from one country to another and from one epoch to another.

In Japan it often took on the aspect of *possession by an animal,* mostly the fox, which plays a considerable role in Japanese superstition and folk-lore. The following is a short account of the case of Kitsune-Tsuki (possession by the fox), as described by a German physician, Von Baelz.

An irascible and stubborn seventeen-year-old woman was recovering from severe typhoid fever. Female relatives were around her bed, sitting or rather kneeling according to the Japanese custom. Someone mentioned that a fox had been seen slipping into the house in the dusk; that was something ominous. The patient hearing this, felt a shattering throughout her body and became possessed. The fox had entered into her and talked several times a day from within her body. He soon acted as her master, upbraiding and tyrannizing the poor young woman.

After a few weeks, a reputed exorcist of the Nichiren sect was called and pronounced his exorcisms, but without success. The fox declared sarcastically that he was too clever to be taken in by such a trick. However, he was ready to leave the starving, sick body voluntarily, provided someone would give him a rich meal. How was that to be done? On a certain day at 4 o'clock someone had to go to a Fox Temple, about 12 kilometers away, and bring two pots of rice prepared in a certain way, roasted bean-cakes, many roasted mice and raw vegetables, that is, all the favorite dishes of supernatural foxes. Then the fox would leave the patient at exactly the same time. And so it happened. Exactly at 4 o'clock, at the moment when the dishes were placed out in the remote temple, the young woman breathed deeply and said: "He has gone." The possession was cured.[18]

This is an instance of spontaneous, lucid, overt possession by an animal spirit. We must consider the cultural and social background of the patient. Traditional Japanese superstition holds that the fox is endowed with super-natural powers; he is said to be able to take any shape at will, to serve those who use him to protect and avenge themselves, and to possess other individuals against their will. According to Kiyoshi Nozaki, Kitsune-Tsuki is at present restricted to certain regions and to lower-class women, usually nervous, hypersensitive persons who grow up in a superstitious environment and were eyewitness to similar cases.[19] This specific disease responds to a specific type of healer. The priests of the Nichiren sect were reputed to be the best exorcists (perhaps because of their own sincere belief in the fox and in his powers). As in many other instances of exorcism, the bargain here is also inherent in the procedure of expelling the possessing spirit: the fox agrees to withdraw, but not without obtaining some compensation.

Possession by an ancestor spirit exists in Madagascar in a ceremonial form, the Tromba cult.[20] The spirits of former kings or warriors are evoked in a ritual ceremony and incarnate themselves temporarily in certain persons who play the role of medium for these ceremonies. The "spirits" then talk to the population. But it may happen that some spectators spontaneously fall into possession, and this may be the beginning of a collective psychosis. Spontaneous possession also exists in Madagascar under another form, the *Bilo,* whose special kind of healing will be mentioned later.

The Tromba may be compared to the Haitian voodoo cult, in which the possessing spirits, or Loa, are often thought to be the spirits of ancient heroes or of voodoo deities. But here, too, ritual possession is sometimes the starting point of spontaneous possession of a morbid character.

Possession by a god is a characteristic feature of certain religions. Years ago, Von Baelz described, in Japan, the pilgrimage at Minobu, the chief temple of the Nichiren sect, where pilgrims sat for hours praying before the gigantic statues of ferocious-looking gods, ceaselessly repeating the same invocations, swaying their bodies back and forth until some of them suddenly saw the statue's eyes come to life and gaze at them. At that moment, they felt a serpent or tiger entering their bodies, they fell into convulsive fits, and were thus ready for exorcism. These are instances of artificial, voluntary possession; but here, too, suggestible spectators could be seized by involuntary, spontaneous possession. Other strange accounts of possession by Japanese gods have been made by Percival Lowell, who described this ritual possession as a means of maintaining a living relationship with the mythical protectors of the nation.[21]

Quite different is the possession by evil spirits, a dreaded manifestation likely to cast a veil of opprobrium over the possessed individual. Demoniac possession has been a frequent occurrence for many centuries in the Middle East and in Europe, and it is characteristic that its symptoms and the rites of exorcism are much the same among Jews, Christians, and Mohammedans. In Ethiopia and Egypt a more differentiated form is that of the *Zar* or possession by the *Djinns,* a manifestation that will be discussed later.

In the Middle East and in Europe the clinical manifestations of demoniac possession can be threefold: The first is severe mental illness, usually schizophrenia, which is molded by the pressure of belief and tradition into the shape of permanent possession. This has been well documented by Kriss and Kriss-Heinrich in their description of Greek sanctuaries and places of pilgrimage.[22] In the monastery of St. Gerasimos on the island of Cephalonia, the authors saw chronic and severe mental patients who had been confined there for years. Their hands and feet were in chains and they were in a state of great motor and verbal agitation. When a religious ritual was performed in their presence, their agitation increased and they proffered blasphemies and obscenities (which is to be understood as a desperate struggle for power between the authority of the Church and the will of the patients). The most genuine mental patient was pressured into playing the role of his illness in accordance with a pattern established by tradition and belief around him. In the above case, the psychotics believed they were possessed by demons and acted accordingly. In the words of Kriss and Kriss-Heinrich:

> This may be explained in that these patients have, in their youth, been impregnated with firm notions of what insanity is like, with the result that, when they themselves fall prey to mental illness, these notions then become a living reality.

Whether through spontaneous remission or through the effect of suggestion, quite a few of these patients did recover, and they experienced this recovery as a result of the Church's victory over the "power of darkness."

The second form, latent possession made manifest by means of a preliminary exorcism, has been used in many places to cure physical or mental illness. The demon, having become manifest, can then be expelled by a second exorcism that at the same time frees the patient from his illness. Knotz, an Austrian physician who practiced at the beginning of this century in Bosnia at a time when scientific medicine was still almost nonexistent in that part of the world, related how every year, on the day of St. John the Baptist, crowds of pilgrims made their way to an old Franciscan chapel where the Fathers spent the entire evening hearing their confessions.[23] On the morning of June 24, the fathers pronounced the ritual prayers and those pilgrims who manifested signs of possession were thereupon exorcised. The Fathers were thus able to heal hysterical women whom official medicine could not have helped. The same kind of exorcism was practiced by Father Gassner around 1775, and its historical importance will be shown in Chapter 2.

The third form, overt spontaneous possession, is now considered to be a more or less severe form of hysterical neurosis. It is, at the present time, not infrequent in some eastern Mediterranean regions. Hartocollis, who visited Cephalonia in 1953, gave a description of such cases and of the exorcism in which several features seem noteworthy.[24] The first is the sudden worsening of the mental disorders at the moment when the exorcist displays the holy relics. This manifestation can become so severe that some patients must be tied down for the duration of the exorcism. It is explained by the islanders as the rage of the demon, who anticipates his expulsion. (In modern language this would be called a resistance and short transference neurosis.) The inhabitants of Cephalonia also claim that the moment the demon is expelled a branch will fall in a mysterious way or a church window will break inexplicably, which is also ascribed to the expelled demon's rage. The more nasty and powerful the demon, the more likely he is to demonstrate his rage in such a manner. When the patient has been cured, he does not leave the island without presenting a gift to the monastery; it is, in Janet's words, "an act of termination," and it also enhances the patient's self-esteem.

The history of the Western world during the past twenty centuries abounds with stories of possession—either individual or collective, sometimes in epidemic form—and with stories of exorcism. Roskoff[25] has shown that the manifestation of possession as well as that of witch-hunting gradually disappeared, largely because of the influence of the Enlightenment, which dispelled belief in the devil, so that even religious circles ascribed less and less importance to him. It is no wonder then that the last manifestations of possession and exorcism are to be found in those settings that, for one reason or another, were opposed to the spirit of the Enlightenment: first, among traditionalists such as Father Gassner (of whom we will speak in Chapter 2); then among certain Romanticists—Justinus Kerner, for instance, who remained intrigued by such manifestations; third, among the pietists, who violently opposed the rationalist spirit of the Enlightenment; to them, the powers of darkness were a living reality that Christians have to face and fight at every moment of their existence.[26] Johann Christoph Blumhardt (1805–1880) was a product of that setting.

The case of Gottliebin Dittus and the Reverend Blumhardt is a typical example of possession and exorcism, patterned exactly on the model of those performed in the early Christian Church. It took place, however, in the middle of the nineteenth century—and was thus an instance of primitive healing in modern times and in a modern setting. Moreover, it is an exceptionally well-documented occurrence that has been the object of much study, from both the psychiatric and the religious points of view.

This celebrated exorcism took place in the small village of Möttlingen, Württemberg, during 1842 and 1843, shortly after Blumhardt had been appointed Lutheran pastor there. We will first give a summary of the possession and exorcism as related by Blumhardt in the official report he sent to his church authorities.

Gottliebin Dittus, twenty-eight years of age, had lost both parents in her childhood and was now living with three older siblings, all unmarried. Blumhardt's first impression of her at a casual encounter was unfavorable: He found something repulsive about her. In late April 1842, Blumhardt was told that Gottliebin was seeing visions of a woman who had died two years previously and who was holding a child in her arms; he was also told that the house in which Gottliebin lived with her siblings was haunted. Neighbors could hear strange and terrifying noises at night. One such night, the country physician and several witnesses remained in the house and confirmed the rumors. Blumhardt was called to the scene, where the young woman had lain unconscious for one entire day. On his advice, she was taken to stay with her cousin. The house ceased to be haunted, but the symptoms of possession, among other violent convulsions, appeared in Gottliebin. During one of Blumhardt's visits, her expression and voice changed and she began speaking with the voice of the dead woman. A dramatic dialogue took place between the pastor and the spirit, who claimed that she could find no rest in the nether world, nor could she pray, because she had in her lifetime murdered two small children and was now in the power of the devil. Blumhardt never doubted that he was facing the powers of darkness and decided that he would not eschew the struggle. He came repeatedly to see Gottliebin, whose symptoms became increasingly worse. She was soon possessed by three demons, then by seven and fourteen. They finally came by the hundreds and the thousands, proffering the worst blasphemies through her mouth. Allegedly pushed by the demons, Gottliebin gave blows to those who were near, but never to Blumhardt. The latter never once indulged in any ritual; his weapon, in accordance with the word of the Gospel, consisted in prayer and fasting. One day in February 1843, Gottliebin reported that during her most recent fit of loss of consciousness, her soul had flown around the earth and seen the demons causing an earthquake in some faraway country that, from her description, Blumhardt thought to be the West Indies. A few days later, the news of this catastrophe reached the village. Around the same time, Gottliebin began to vomit sand, pieces of glass, nails, and other objects. She was also losing enormous amounts of blood. Among the spirits who spoke through her mouth, many claimed to be the demons' victims and asked Blumhardt's permission to rest in his house or else in the church, to which he agreed after much hesitation, on the condition however that Jesus was to grant his permission first. Gottliebin was now beginning to feel Blumhardt's influence and to accept his orders. The final crisis occurred at Christmas in 1843. The demons tried one last and desperate assault. Not content with torturing Gottliebin, they now also attacked her brother and her sister Katharina; the brother's ordeal was soon over, and he recovered quickly; the demons also seemed to have lost interest in Gottliebin. Katharina, however, who had never before been troubled by them, now became their plaything and acted in much the same way as had Gottliebin in her worst moments. Finally, on December 28, 1843, after a desperate struggle between Blumhardt and the demoniac world, Katharina uttered a horrifying scream through the night, and at 2 A.M., she cried "Jesus is victor!" At 8 A.M. the following morning, the spirits had vanished and Katharina recovered. The power of darkness was broken, and Gottliebin was freed of spirits and demons.[27]

This case will be better understood when the background of the patient and that of the healer—as well as the peculiar social and cultural setting in which the incident occurred have been considered.

Unfortunately, little is known about the background of Gottliebin Dittus. Blumhardt's report states that she grew up in a deeply religious family that was at the same time very superstitious. She told Blumhardt that shortly after her birth, she had been stolen twice by an invisible spirit who had dropped her by the door when her frightened mother invoked the name of Jesus. This seems rather extraordinary, but at that time the belief that newborn infants could be stolen and exchanged by fairies, goblins, or devils was widespread in many rural areas of Europe.[28] She also told him of an aunt, who, she said, was a witch and who tried to entice her to follow in her footsteps. Gottliebin's possession and cure might thus be considered as an expression of the cultural conflict between the Church and superstition.

The background of Johann Christoph Blumhardt is much better known.

According to his biographers, he came from a needy, exceedingly pious home.[29] From early childhood he showed strong religious inclinations (having read the Bible twice at the age of twelve). A diligent student, he studied theology and worked in several parishes, during which time he wrote profusely on the history of Christian missions and other related subjects. In July 1838, at the age of thirty-three, he was appointed pastor at Möttlingen and married in September of that year. Blumhardt had always been convinced that the devil was a dreadful reality that played a major role in human affairs. Some of his ideas may seem strange to us. He thought, for instance, that the mortar used in the construction of the pyramids had been mixed by wizards who were helped by the devil. He was also convinced that sin was the root of most diseases, and he reproved the use of drugs extracted from venomous plants. He also thought that the use of sedative medications was dangerous to the spirit.[30] Ideas of that nature, however, were not uncommon among Romantic physicians and philosophers. On the other hand, Blumhardt was undoubtedly a highly intelligent and cultivated man, of heroic courage, and with the faith of an apostle.

The village of Möttlingen is located in a remote part of the Black Forest, in which superstition and the belief in witchcraft flourished. The Reverend Barth, Blumhardt's predecessor and also a pietist, had conducted an intensive religious-revival campaign without much success.[31] It is noteworthy that Gottliebin Dittus was said to have been his favorite parishioner. Blumhardt's appointment was considered as a relief by the population. During the two years of the exorcism, the inhabitants of the village took a lively and enduring interest in the daily vicissitudes of the struggle, and the eventual expulsion of the spirits and demons was felt to be the triumph of the whole community.

As a first result of Blumhardt's victory, the religious revival that had been vainly attempted by the Reverend Barth was now becoming a reality. One after the other, parishioners came to Blumhardt, confessing their sins and requesting his blessing. In an account he gave of this revival, we see how appalled he was at the number and gravity of the sins confessed to him, to which were added superstitious practices, witchcraft, and the practice of birth control.[32] It would seem that the Church authorities regarded Blumhardt with some anxiety and suspicion, and he was subjected to vehement attacks by certain of his colleagues.

Blumhardt himself had undergone a great change. He was now the man, who, with the sole means of prayer and fasting, had sustained a prolonged struggle against the powers of darkness and overcome them with the help of God. "Jesus is victor" became his motto. He had extraordinary prestige and respect in Möttlingen and its surroundings. Crowds flocked to him to confess their sins and to obtain relief from their ills through the power of his prayer. Four years later, friends helped him to acquire property in Bad Boll, where he continued his work, preaching, healing the sick, and corresponding extensively. At this point Gottliebin Dittus entered his household and became invaluable to him in his activities, particularly in his work with the mentally ill. Commenting on that fact, Viktor von Weizsäcker wrote:

> I deem one of the most remarkable examples of reciprocal action of helper and help-needing individuals the incident of the two-year struggle of old Blumhardt with Gottliebin Dittus. . . . This young woman would be considered today a case of the most severe hysteria. After two years of ceaseless struggle, she became a member of Blumhardt's household. . . . This solution meant a victory of Blumhardt over hysteria and a victory of Gottliebin over Blumhardt: he obtained the withdrawal of the demons, and she community of life with him. Truly, this victory was a compromise for both sides, but at the same time the step to a new level of life. . . .[33]

Several psychiatrists have attempted to interpret Blumhardt's healing of Gottliebin Dittus in modern terms. One of them, Michaelis, concluded that the incident could only in part be translated in terms of psychoanalysis or other modern dynamic doctrines; there remains a "transcendental" aspect above and beyond those modern doctrines.[34]

Another psychiatrist, Benedetti, who specializes in the psychotherapy of psychoses, wrote a study in which he underlined the striking similarities between that cure and the psychotherapy of severe schizophrenics. He says that Blumhardt discovered intuitively, more than a century ahead of others, the principle of such cures. In summary:

> Blumhardt's first reaction was one of hesitation and defence, a necessary prelude to regarding a case in its full seriousness. The main effort was directed toward himself (prayer and fasting), just as the therapist of psychoses must give primary attention to his "counter-transference." The healer then appeals to the patient, who responds with his first positive answer: this was the moment when Gottliebin accepted to repeat a few words of prayer pronounced by Blumhardt, which he rightly understood to be the decisive point in starting the cure. Blumhardt then throws himself into Gottliebin's demoniacal world, just as the modern therapist explores the inner world of his schizophrenic patient's delusions. The fact that the manifestations of possession kept getting worse is compared by Benedetti to the apparent worsening of psychotic symptoms through the effect of the patient's resistance. The patient tries to overcome the therapist, who must respond by frustrating such wishes, and this, says Benedetti, is exactly what Blumhardt did. Blumhardt also sharply differentiated his attitude toward the "victimized" spirits and evil spirits; in the same way, the therapist is very responsive to anything that comes from the healthy part of the patient's mind, while repudiating all sick manifestations. Blumhardt's acute psychological insight is shown in the fact that while resistance was taking increasingly absurd, exaggerated, and desperate forms, he was now setting conditions, testing his patient, and giving her orders. (We could add at this point that Blumhardt made full use of what existential

therapists call the *kairos,* that is, the elective point for decisive intervention or decision.) [35]

This memorable exorcism occurred at a time when the positivist and scientific outlook was penetrating all fields of life, and instances of demoniac possession were becoming extremely rare. Occasionally, possessed patients were brought to mental hospitals or to the Salpêtrière in Paris until the end of the nineteenth century. One of them happened to be treated there by Janet during the years 1890 and 1891, and it is worthwhile to compare the different approaches in the two treatments that were separated by only one half-century. We will see in Chapter 6 how Janet cured this patient, without, of course, resorting to exorcism, but by unraveling the "fixed subconscious idea" that was the root of the disturbance and by bringing it to the patient's awareness.

Dynamic psychotherapists today could hardly find anything more obsolete than the healing method of exorcism. However, some similarities do exist, as pointed out by Benedetti with regard to the psychotherapy of severe schizophrenia. Another comparison could be made with Maeder's own method of short psychotherapy, in which the patient's genuine desire for help is a first requisite, while very strong demands are made of the psychiatrist.[36] It is not just a matter of analyzing his own counter-transference, but of working on his own personality and of developing and maintaining in himself a genuine wish to help the patient. In that active procedure, the patient first calls for help (this is the "appeal process"); the therapist responds with his will and readiness to help and then calls for the self-healing tendencies within the patient. The latter answers by projecting onto the therapist the "archetype of the Saviour," with a gradual activation of his self-healing tendencies, although the therapist must sometimes induce this reaction with special techniques. This process should then eventually lead the patient to the capacity for constructive love, which, according to Maeder, is the criterion of the cure.

Healing Through Confession

Among certain primitive peoples, that a severe disease or even an acute psychogenic death can result from the infringement of a taboo is not a "disease theory," but an actual fact, confirmed by many reliable eye-witnesses. One instance, reported by a missionary in the French Congo, the Reverend Grébert, follows:

> In Samkita, a pupil by the name of Onguie was suddenly seized by convulsions and was carried into the dormitory, where he fainted. When we came back to see him, he was surrounded by boys; some were holding his rigid arms and legs, others were vainly trying to open his clenched fists at the risk of breaking his fingers. Frightened as they were, it did not occur to them to remove the foam

that was choking him. The little body was arched, but it soon relaxed. We were given a few hasty explanations: "He ate bananas that were cooked in a pot that had been used previously for manioc. Manioc is *eki* for him; his grandparents told him that if he ever ate any of it—even a tiny little bit—he would die." The violation of the ancestral command causes them such fright, such visceral anguish, such an organic collapse, that the sources of life are rapidly exhausted. "Look," they said pointing to the diaphragm that was shaking as if a small animal were struggling beneath the skin, "he has an *evur*, which is getting excited." There was no doubt about the seriousness of the case. Alas! no medication would pass through the obstructed throat. The poor child had lost consciousness and was beginning to rattle. A man of his tribe ran to the neighboring village to get the medication against *evur*, an egg mixed with certain other substances. We, in the meantime, were struggling against asphyxia by performing rhythmic tractions of the chest, but were unable to get hold of the tongue. It was all to no avail. The overtaxed heart ceased to beat, and the boy died in our arms.[37]

This is one of three cases reported by the Reverend Grébert. In two of them the patient died. The third patient was saved by European medicine, although with the utmost difficulty. Similar instances have been reported from Uganda and Central Africa, and the conspicuous fact is that, in such cases, Western medicine is almost powerless, whereas the medicine man is able to achieve a surprisingly rapid and complete recovery in patients on the verge of death.

In Polynesia there have been frequent reports of psychogenic deaths resulting from the violation of a taboo, although the features differ from those common in Africa. Death occurs in a less dramatic way, more slowly and quietly; the patient lies down, refusing nourishment, and dies within a few days.[38] What is important here is not so much the violation of a taboo, but rather that the violation has been exposed and made public and the offender has thus been made an object of shame.[39]

Many primitive populations believe that certain diseases result from the violation of taboos or from other offenses. However, innumerable variations exist as to the beliefs concerning the nature of such offenses, the curability of the resulting diseases, and the possible treatments. Confession of sins is not regarded everywhere as a method of treatment; when it does exist, it often entails more than just a method of treatment of disease.

A comprehensive survey of data relative to the confession of sins was made by Raffaele Pettazzoni, who emphasized that among most primitive populations the concept of "sin" is identical with that of "breach of taboo."[40] No distinction is made as to whether this breach was voluntary or not; even fortuitous events may be identified with sin, which is the case, for instance, among the Kikuyu, if an individual meets a certain kind of snake along his path. However, some primitive populations also take certain moral offenses into consideration, notably those of a sexual character. Among diseases most frequently believed to be the result of sin are painful and protracted childbirth and sterility in women. Confession of sins is usually public among primitive peoples; the secrecy of confession does not exist. Confession itself is often supplemented by certain eliminatory procedures, such as washing, vomiting, or bleeding.

The Aztecs of ancient Mexico often confessed to a priest, with adultery and drunkenness being the two main sins. Among the Mixtecs, confession of sins was commonly resorted to in cases of illness, and sins of theft and offenses against property were particularly taken into consideration. In the Incan kingdom, confession was a universal custom: dates were set for general confession to priests called the *ichuris*. The ceremony included invocation of the gods; confession, which followed a long list of possible sins; exhortation; and penitence. Here, too, confession was resorted to in case of illness; a father would confess when his child was sick and a husband when his wife was ill. When an Inca was sick, all the inhabitants of the kingdom had to confess. According to Pettazzoni, the reverse took place in China, where the Emperor confessed his sins in the event of a public calamity.

The concept of disease as a punishment for sin was predominant among the Semitic civilizations of the ancient Orient. Sin was then clearly defined as a voluntary offense against moral and religious laws. Many diseases, among them emotional and mental illness, were thought to be the result of sin. Confession also existed as a means of relief, and often of healing.

Many traces of this disease concept have survived until today. Popular beliefs about the terrible diseases resulting from the "sin" of masturbation have not yet disappeared. Reacting against such scientifically untenable concepts, psychiatry has radically excluded the word "sin" from its vocabulary. But it has been rediscovered by modern dynamic psychiatry, if not as "sin," then at least in the notion of "guilt feeling." The pathogenic action of guilt feelings and the therapeutic effect of confession even on physical diseases cannot be disregarded. A clinical observation published by Aldenhoven may be quoted in that regard:

A forty-two-year-old woman was admitted to the hospital on the fifth day of a pneumonia that had broken out while she was alone in her unheated apartment. By the time of her admission, she was in a critical condition, exhausted, with severe dyspnea, slight cyanosis, pulse 120, rectal temperature 40.0 C. (104.0 F.). The X-rays showed a pneumonia of the left upper lobe.

The following day her condition was worse, in spite of the medications. (This was before the era of antibiotics.) The same evening—the sixth of the disease —the pulse was like a thread, with a frequency of 150; the cyanosis increased, and the respiration became extremely superficial. The patient was covered with cold sweat, the look of her wide eyes expressed anguish, and she said repeatedly that she was going to die.

Dr. Aldenhoven visited her in the evening. An old friend of her family's was present in the room. Aldenhoven ordered a blood-letting of 180 cc. and an injection of camphor. He had the feeling that these measures might slightly prolong the patient's life, but would hardly check her gradual decline; pulse and breathing were fading away, the anxious look grew dimmer, the voice was hardly perceptible. The physician sat down at her bedside and told the patient that her sister, to whom she was very attached, would come the next morning. She whispered faintly: "I will die before morning . . . and it will be proper punishment!" —"Punishment?" asked the physician quietly, "well, then you will *not* die. We will see to it that you pay the penalty above the earth and not below." These words, which expressed a positive medical conviction, hit the mark. The patient felt herself understood. She asked the visitor to leave the room and told the physician that the pneumonia had befallen her at the place where she had been unfaithful to her husband (from whom she was now estranged and who was still a prisoner of war); now, disease and death represented punishment. Immediately following this confession, an astonishing change occurred in the clinical picture: the anxious look vanished from the patient's physiognomy, the pulse grew stronger and more relaxed, the respiration deepened and became more quiet, the cyanosis receded. One or two hours later, she had recovered to the point of being able to cheerfully drink her morning coffee. The further course of recovery developed without any noteworthy incident.[41]

Healing Through Gratification of Frustrations

The role of frustrated wishes in the etiology of disease has been known from time immemorial. "Hope deferred makes the heart sick, but the wish come true is a tree of life" (Proverbs XIII, 12). A Maori proverb says: "There is a well of dissatisfaction in the heart of man, and hence vexation and anxiety."[42]

For many centuries, medical textbooks contained descriptions of two conditions that are largely forgotten today: homesickness and lovesickness. The former, also called nostalgia, was experienced by soldiers or by other individuals who had left their own country; they missed home, day-dreamed about it incessantly, could concentrate on nothing else, and would often die unless they returned there, in which case a prompt and spectacular recovery took place.[43] Lovesickness was observed in young men or women hopelessly in love. They would slowly fade away and die unless they were united with the object of their love (which was often kept secret). Nineteenth-century psychiatry excluded these two conditions from its nosology and did not ascribe much importance to frustrated wishes as a psychogenic factor. Dynamic psychiatry has re-emphasized their meaning, which primitive medicine had at times well understood.

When the French Jesuits started their missionary work among the Indians of northeastern America in the seventeenth century, they were amazed to see the importance attached by the Hurons and the Iroquois to the gratification of an individual's wishes as expressed in his dreams. "It would be cruelty, nay murder, not to give a man the subject of his dream; for such a refusal might cause his death," wrote a Jesuit Father.[44] It was therefore a sacred duty to give a man what he had seen in his dream or to let him accomplish the action he had dreamed of—the more so when the individual was already sick. Nothing then could save him except the gratification of his heart's desire as revealed by his dreams.

One of the Jesuit missionaries, Father Raguenau, gave an excellent account of the beliefs and practices of the Hurons in that regard.[45] The Hurons distinguished three causes of disease: natural causes; sorcery; unfulfilled wishes. Of the unfulfilled wishes, some were known to the individual; others, called *ondinnonk,* were not known but could be revealed to him in his dreams. These dreams could however be forgotten, and certain wishes would not even appear in dreams. Diviners, called the *saokata,* were then able to determine those unconscious wishes by looking, for instance, into a jar filled with water. If the patient was mortally ill, the diviners would declare that the object of his wishes was impossible to obtain. When there were chances of recovery, they would enumerate objects supposedly desired by the patient, and a "festival of dreams" would be organized. A collection was made among the group, and the objects collected were given to the patient during a banquet that included dances and other manifestations of public rejoicing. There was no question of returning these objects to the donors. Thus, the patient would not only recover from his disease with all his wishes gratified, but would sometimes come out a rich man. On the other hand, some of the donors might become sick in turn and dream of receiving some compensation for their loss. A "festival of dreams" was thus a combination of therapy, public rejoicing, and property exchanges.

In other accounts, the Jesuit Fathers described the festival of dreams as a mad collective frenzy in which the dreamers ran about screaming and threatening the others, compelling them to guess their dreams and to give them one thing after another until they had guessed correctly.

There are also instances of what could be called symbolic realization: A Jesuit Father happened to visit an Iroquois community on the day of the festival of dreams. One of the Iroquois wanted to kill him under the pretext that he had dreamed of killing a Frenchman; however, he was given a Frenchman's coat and found it to be a good enough substitute.[46] Another story describes a young woman who was severely ill. Someone in the community dreamed that she would recover if her parents prepared a banquet with twenty heads of elk, a thing impossible to obtain at that time of year. An interpreter of dreams appropriately decided that the twenty head of elk could be replaced by twenty loaves of bread.[47]

This kind of therapy may seem unthinkable to us: Who would treat a patient by giving him all that he would wish for? However, the healing effects of the gratification of desires is perhaps underestimated today. Good fortune can, sometimes, still play the role of a therapist.

An historical instance is shown in the biography of François Magendie (1783–1855). When studying medicine between the ages of twenty-one and twenty-two, Magendie lived in the utmost poverty and was almost starving; he became ill, depressed, and disgusted with life. At this point, a lawyer unexpectedly came to see him and told him that he had inherited a sum of twenty thousand francs—which was, at that time, a very considerable amount. Magendie was cured instantly. He established a stable with fine horses and pedigree dogs and lived in such an extravagant manner that, one year later, no money was left —only the memory of a wonderful time. Magendie then returned to his medical studies and later became a great physiologist.

The psychodynamics of this case are made intelligible if we recall that Magendie belonged to a wealthy family that had lost its fortune during the French Revolution. His father, an admirer of Rousseau, had brought him up in a rather undisciplined way. Young Magendie was therefore at the same time frustrated and intolerant to frustration. His thoroughbreds and his dogs represented for him what the festival of dreams meant to an Iroquois.[48]

It is likely that the gratification of frustrated desires plays a decisive role in certain exorcisms and other therapeutic procedures. Bruno Lewin has shown that the vicarious gratification of sexual desires may account for the therapeutic successes of the Egyptian *Zar.*

The *Zar* ceremony is performed in Egypt among the lower social classes as a treatment for neurotic and hysterical women. It is organized by a woman called the *kudya* who is helped by three other women who sing, dance, and play the drum and the tambourin. Participation is restricted to women. After various rites, the patient is led into the room in a bride's attire. An animal is sacrificed, frankincense is burned, and the patient is undressed and clad in a white shirt. The *kudya* then begins to dance as if in a trance, her motions getting wilder, until she falls exhausted to the floor. After a while, the music starts again, at first in a slow and gentle mood; the *kudya* calls for the *djinn* who is supposed to be her lover. The music and dance become wild again, and the *kudya* in her trance succumbs to her imaginary lover with orgiastic movements and falls to the floor once more, inviting other demons to come. The patient joins the *kudya* in her wild dance, and the other women join in as well, until all of them throw off their clothes and, in their trance, are sexually possessed by the *djinns.* Dr. Lewin states that a large proportion of the patients are actually helped by such a ceremony. Some women go to a *Zar* every month. Most of them are frigid and unhappily married, and the *Zar* provide them with the only sexual gratification they can obtain.[49]

Sometimes the frustrated wishes are neither possessive nor libidinal drives, but rather drives toward self-realization. Dr. Louis Mars describes paranoiac reactions that occur in Haiti among active and ambitious individuals who are under the stress of increasing difficulties and repeated failures.[50] Such people feel persecuted and, in turn, begin to irritate and trouble others. The collective attitude in Haiti is noteworthy; the patient is listened to with sympathetic attention, and a position suited to his capacities is sought. The projections gradually recede, and the disturbed individual is reintegrated into his community.

Many people feel frustrated because their lives are dull and uninteresting and because they receive no consideration from their fellow men, including their own families. From certain accounts from Madagascar, it would seem that therapeutic procedures aim directly toward the gratification of such frustrated needs. Two accounts are summarized here:

> Le Barbier described the *Bilo* (a word that designates, at the same time, the disease, the patient, and the therapeutic ceremony): *Bilo,* he said, is "the queerest, strangest, and most imaginary disease, and the easiest to cure." The patients are nervous, hypersensitive to noise, unable to remain quiet. The local healer, or *ombiasa,* decides what day the "coronation" will take place. The hero of the ceremony is the patient himself, who is being addressed as "King," while his family is the "court" and the villagers his subjects. On the day of the ceremony, the patient is dressed in beautiful clothes and is shown respect and deference. Twice daily, songs and dances are performed for him, and he may join in if he so wishes. These celebrations are continued for fifteen to twenty days, until the patient is cured. An ox is then sacrificed, and the *Bilo* drinks of its blood.[51]
>
> In an account from another province of Madagascar, it is reported that after fifteen days of singing and dancing, the procedure culminates in the "elevation" of the *Bilo.* A platform of approximately 2½ meters (about 8 feet) in height is erected, on which the patient is placed with a small statue at his feet; a sacrifice is performed, and the patient is bathed and served a meal that he eats on the elevated platform.[52]

It is understandable how the patient's "ego" (in the colloquial meaning of this word) must be inflated when, for two entire weeks, he is addressed and treated like a king and then elevated onto a platform. No wonder the *Bilo* cure is often reported to be successful.[53] In a study on miraculous cures, Janet stresses that many of the patients thus cured had been sick because they lacked social recognition.[54] A miraculous cure, for them, was tantamount to a sudden increase in prestige and social recognition.

Ceremonial Healing

One of the main differences between modern scientific treatment and primitive healing is that the former is matter-of-fact, while the latter is usually performed as a ceremony. This is true for all of the methods that we have so far discussed. In some cases, it would seem that the ceremonies are not simply a secondary element of the healing procedure, but the main therapeutic agent.

There are many types of ceremonial healing. Hocart has shown that certain healing ceremonies are former initiation rites (or parts of them) that are obsolete as such but that have acquired a new meaning as healing methods.[55] Sometimes, the healing ceremony is a kind of re-enactment of the initial (pathogenic) trauma. Sometimes it is a re-enactment of the great myths of the tribe, such as the creation of the world or the stories of the gods.[56] In many ceremonial healings—with or without such re-enactments—the patient is integrated into a group (notably a healers' society, as among the Zuñi) or into the social setting to which he belongs: family, clan, tribe. Finally, the ceremony may be effective through the sheer beauty of the rites, the costumes, the music, and the dances.

Healing through the *re-enactment of the initial trauma* has been described among the Pomo, an Indian tribe from California. Freeland reports that the Pomo have several different kinds of doctors.[57] One of them, called the outfit doctor (or singing doctor), is the only one to make use of a so-called frightening method. If the origin of the disease is unknown, its symptoms unclear, its course of evolution protracted, the healer suspects that it was caused by an encounter between the patient and a spirit (an event that the patient may not recall). The medicine man consults with the family to find out what the patient was doing when he first became ill, and together they speculate as to the probable nature of the spirit. The medicine man then decides to reproduce the vision as closely as he can. He may dress up as a ghost or build a model of a monster. A realistic setting is devised, and the scene is suddenly revealed to the patient. If he reacts with great fear, the guess is considered to be correct. Ordinary treatments are used to bring the patient out of the state of collapse which follows this ordeal. The medicine man then takes off his ghost costume or destroys the model before the patient's eyes to relieve his mind of fear. Recovery is said to be rapid.

A patient was suffering from a chronic illness that had yielded to no treatment. The family remembered that he had been hunting in the mountains on the day he took sick. The medicine man's guess was that the patient had seen a water monster at a spring. He made a model of a large snake with several joints; it was six feet long and one foot wide, and could be moved and pulled by strings; the monster was then painted in white, red, and black. When the patient saw the terrifying apparition, he was seized with such fear that he took to attacking people around him; six persons were needed to hold him down, until he finally fainted. The medicine man then made him perspire, bathed him, and gave him a drink of water, and told him then that he had initially seen a water monster that had haunted him ever since. The man soon improved.

Another patient, a woman, had been frightened during the night and had fainted. A "singing doctor," who happened to be at hand, assumed that she must have seen a ghost. He rapidly disguised himself as a ghost and, with the help of her father, frightened the patient, after which he reassured her, explaining the story. The next day, she felt well again.

We would call such therapeutic procedures either psychic shock therapy or psychodrama.

A more elaborate procedure was found among the Zuñi, where the healing activity was not the prerogative of one man but of a number of medicine societies, that is, groups of healers who claimed to perform their cures through the agency of the gods of their societies. These gods were believed to enter the healers' bodies during the ceremony. Mathilda Stevenson wrote a detailed description of these societies and of their healing ceremonies.[58] These differ from one society to another, according to the myths of their respective gods.

As an example, Mrs. Stevenson described a ceremony, performed by one of the societies, for the cure of a sore throat. The members of the society gathered at sunset in the patient's room. The patient was on a rug in the center of the floor, reclining in the arms of his "fraternity father." Three theurgists, wearing the masks and costumes of the three gods of the society, entered the room through the roof, led by a female member bearing the insignia of the society and carrying a basket containing a sacred meal. The "gods" performed several dances and other rites around the patient, drawing lines with sacred pollen on his body. One of the rites consisted of the patient's expectorating through the mouth opening of the Great God's mask (handed to him by the theurgist and later returned to him). During the entire ceremony, a choir kept chanting to the accompaniment of certain instruments. After a long series of other rites, the "gods" left. The fraternity father then gave two cakes to the patient, who had to eat one and give the other one to a stray dog, after which the other members of the society left. A feast had been prepared for them by the patient's family.

There are several conspicuous facts in this treatment. (1) It is a collective treatment, organized and performed not by one man, but by a healing society. (2) It is a psychodrama: The three main healers, wearing the costumes and masks of the three gods, are assisted by the other members of the society, while the patient plays an active role in the rites. (3) It is a religious therapy, since the gods are brought near and their myths re-enacted. (4) It is also a "beauty therapy" because of the magnificence of the songs, the rites, and the costumes. (5) In part, it is a treatment through the transference of disease or evil to another being. (The sore throat is transferred to a stray dog.) (6) The patient is expected to join the society after his recovery (a procedure that modern psychiatry is beginning to rediscover: former alcoholics often join temperance societies; discharged mental patients join together in clubs).[59]

A still more elaborate form of ceremonial healing is found among the Navaho, an Indian tribe noted for its fine weaving, beautiful colored sand paintings, and music. They also have a highly elaborated mythology. Their ceremonial healings, in contrast to those of the Zuñi, are performed not by medicine societies but under the direction of a medicine man. The ritual is so complex that a medicine man requires several years to learn one of the "Nine Days' Chants," the major ceremonies, which are re-enactments of the great myths of the creation of the world and the feasts of the Navaho gods.

Often a Navaho falls into a state of anxious depression as the result of a bad dream, the illusion of having seen a ghost, or the fear of having offended a sacred animal. The patient may feel so ill that he sometimes allows himself to die of slow starvation. In such a case, a timely ceremonial cure performed by the right medicine man can be surprisingly effective and rapid.

A remarkable instance of such a case was observed and filmed in 1928 by Laura Adams Armer. The Reverend Oskar Pfister gave an illustrated account of that cure in the journal *Imago* and added a psychoanalytic commentary. [60]

The patient, a man of about fifty, dreamed that he saw his children dead. This upset him so that he fell into a severe depression. A star gazer was consulted a few weeks later. He worked himself into a trance, looked at the stars, and saw a bear; he then told the patient, "Search for the chanter who can sing the Mountain Chant; for you will surely die if you do not find him." The chanter was found and told the patient; "When you were a young boy, you saw a sick or a dead bear; or your mother saw it before you were born. This bear was sacred; it must now be reconciled." To achieve this, one of the Nine Days' Chants, the Male Form of the Mountain Chant, had to be performed.

Two huts were built; one, the "house of songs," or "medicine lodge" for the patient, the second for his wife and children. All the clan brothers came to help during the nine-day-long cure, while the women of the family helped with the cooking and service. The patient, the healer, and the other men started out by taking steam baths and by performing purification rites.

The songs, rites, and ceremonies performed during the nine days are so complex that it would take an entire book to describe in detail one ceremony alone. (A monograph on the Night Chant had been written by Washington Matthews.) [61] A dozen men gathered before the medicine lodge on the sixth, seventh, eighth, and ninth days and, under the direction of the healer, made beautiful pictures with colored sands on the ground. These drawings are as remarkable for their artistic value as for their mythological and symbolic meanings. The healer accompanied these rites with magic gestures and songs. Every day, at the end of the performance, the picture was destroyed, the colored sands gathered up and poured over the patient. At the end of the ninth day, about two thousand Navaho—men, women, and children—gathered around the family to sing the concluding songs of the Mountain Chant, and the ceremony was ended with a joyful religious dance. At this point, the patient felt himself cured. Information obtained two years later stated that the cure had been a complete success and that no relapse had occurred.

In his comments on this cure, the Reverend Oskar Pfister proposes a psychoanalytic interpretation: the bear is the symbol of the father. As a child, the patient had death wishes against his father, and he now feared that his children felt the same toward him; he retaliated with unconscious death wishes against his children and felt guilt about it. He had to be reconciled with the father by means of two surrogates (the star gazer and the medicine man), as well as with the entire community and the gods of the tribe. During the nine-day ceremony, he was first reconciled with his family and his clan brethren, then with a larger group, and finally, on the last evening, with the tribe as a whole. All these atonements and reconciliations occurred on an unconscious, symbolic level.

This interpretation may shed some light on the cure; however, there must be much more to it. Pfister himself adds that the intensive participation of an entire sympathetic community is reminiscent of certain religious cures at holy shrines. In the Navaho healing ceremonies, however, the patient is not only reconciled with the community and with the gods, but this gradual reconciliation is brought about through the re-enactment of the cosmogonic and other sacred myths. Furthermore, the Navaho are unparalleled in their overwhelming abundance of highly cultural performances inherent in such a cure: art, music, poetry, dance—a "beauty therapy" for which we find no counterpart in modern psychotherapy.

The only parallel to such ceremonial healings found in the Western world are the cures at holy shrines, many of which flourish in the Mediterranean area. One of the best known shrines is in Lourdes, a place famous for the impressive beauty of the site, the Spring and the Grotto, the majesty of the ritual, the pageantry of the processions, and "the perpetual prayer going on day and night, on the part of vast numbers of people—so that the very air is charged and vibrant with it."[62] Less noticeable, perhaps, is the gradual integration of pilgrims and patients into groups of increasingly large numbers. After a serious individual preparation (confession, prayer, exhortation) at his place of residence, the patient joins a group of pilgrims from his own parish. Several parish groups then merge into larger groups from one bishopric and the long and uncomfortable journey takes place in an atmosphere of glowing enthusiasm. The three days' stay in Lourdes is scheduled and timed with great exactness; the patient finds himself in an immense crowd in which, however, he never feels lost and is always well taken care of; Every parish, bishopric, or nation retains its individuality. But at the peak of the pilgrimage ceremonies, all these distinctions melt away, and the pilgrim feels himself fusing temporarily into a countless multitude, into one enormous soul that swarms with religious enthusiasm. A number of cures are reported to have taken place at this climax, just as Stevenson's patient was cured on the last evening of the Nine Days' Chant.

Healing Through Incubation

The procedures of primitive therapy are often so complex that it is not easy to classify them. This applies, for example, to incubation, which could be classified among other types of ceremonial healing because the essential part, the incubation, was both preceded and followed by various rites and ceremonies. However, it is appropriate to describe it separately because it obviously was the main therapeutic agent.

Incubation means "lying on the ground": The patient was expected to spend a night in a cave, lying on the ground. He would then have a dream of vision, which would cure him.

This type of therapy seems to have reached its highest point of perfection in ancient Greece in the Asklepeia, or temples of Asklepios (Esculapius), one of the gods of medicine. But its origin must have been much earlier. In ancient times, incubation apparently took place in a sacred cavern (later replaced by an underground chamber in the Asklepeia). There are other examples of the use of caverns for magic-religious purposes such as the oracle of Trophonius in ancient Greece.[63] Those who visited there had to undergo a special preparation, including the drinking of water from the "Fountain of Forgetfulness" and the "Fountain of Memory." In the cavern, they had frightening visions, which left them terror-stricken when they emerged. Priests then placed the visitors into the "Chair of Memory" so that they could recount what they had seen. The same awe surrounded the mysterious ceremonies of the Asklepeia; in which there were the same elaborate preparations, the same mysterious underground happenings, and the same expectation of receiving an oracle—in the Asklepeia a healing oracle in the form of a dream.

Among the many Asklepeia of which we have records, the best known are those of Epidauros, Pergamon, and Cos.[64] The temple of Asklepios was an important institution, as we know from accounts of ancient authors and from modern archeological research. The sick came from far away to seek cures in these holy places. Unfortunately, much about their methods is unknown to us, such as the meaning and use of a circular labyrinth, the *tholos,* which has been found in the ruins of several Asklepeia.

We may assume that the beautiful site of many Asklepeia, the journey, the period of waiting, the rumors about wonderful cures, all affected the patient. Before being admitted to the sanctuary, he underwent a given preparation, a purification including fasting, drinking the water of sacred fountains, and various other rites. The highlight of the treatment was the *incubation,* that is, the sleep in the sanctuary. The patient was clothed in a special gown adorned with purple stripes and sometimes wore a crown on his head. The sacred abode in which he had to spend the night was an underground place called the *abaton.* Its walls were covered with inscriptions telling of miracles that had taken place therein. In earliest times, the patient had to lay on the ground; this was later replaced by a couch called the *kline.* In contrast to the analytic couch of today, the *kline* was intended for sleeping and dreaming.

During the night the patient spent in the *abaton,* he might see apparitions, receive an oracle, or have visions or dreams.

An "apparition" meant that the patient, while still awake, saw the figure of a god, mostly Asklepios, who remained silent or who brought him a message; or he could hear voices, feel a wind blowing, or see a blinding light. These manifestations have been widely discussed and have been ascribed differently, either to the use of drugs, hypnosis, or to the humbug of the priests. An "oracle" meant that the patient had a dream in which he was given instructions by a god or a priest. A "vision" was a dream in which the patient was given foreknowledge of an event that would soon occur. A "dream proper" was a very special kind of dream that would *in itself* bring on the cure. It was not a dream that needed interpretation to unveil the advice it contained; the patient simply dreamed, and thereupon the disease disappeared! This is obviously a kind of psychotherapy that has no equivalent in our time and that deserves more attention. In a study of these phenomena, the Jungian analyst C. A. Meier mentions that a similar concept was expressed by Kieser, a pupil of Mesmer: "Where the inner feeling of the disease becomes personified and expresses itself in symbols, healing can occur."[65]

Healing Through Hypnosis

To what extent hypnosis was or is applied to therapeutic aims in primitive medicine is still a controversial question, in spite of the amount of data that has been gathered.[66] Hypnotic or semihypnotic states no doubt often occur in patients during many primitive healing procedures. Bastian states clearly in his account of his own experience in Guyana that he fell into a pleasant kind of hypnotic state. It is, however, not clear to what extent the hypnotic state in such cases is brought on voluntarily by the medicine man, and whether it is rather a side effect of the total procedure.

There is no doubt, either, that certain medicine men are able to make a conscious and purposeful use of hypnosis, as exemplified by the ceremonies surrounding the initiation of Australian medicine men. This would be the probable explanation for the descriptions given by these medicine men of the fantastic powers with which they were allegedly endowed. These descriptions are similar all over the continent, even into the farthest regions. According to Elkin, Australian medicine men are unanimous in telling that, during the final initiation, their bodies were opened, their organs removed and replaced by others, and the incisions healed without leaving any scars.[67] It is also said that these medicine men are able to produce collective hallucinations, such as visions of a magic cord. Elkin's statements have been confirmed by R. Rose, an investigator who received training in parapsychology.[68] These hallucinations are strikingly similar to those that have been reported from Tibet, and Elkin therefore assumes that the Australians and the Tibetans derive their secret knowledge from a common source.

Although these facts seem to indicate a knowledge of hypnosis among medicine men, they do not necessarily imply that hypnosis has ever consciously been used for therapeutic goals. The instance that most closely approximates modern hypnotic procedure is found in a document from an Egyptian scroll dating back to the third century A.D., published by Brugsch.[69] It relates how hypnosis was induced in a young boy through fixation of a luminous object and what he reportedly saw and heard while in the trance. This would indicate that hypnosis was used merely as a means of producing clairvoyance and not as a therapeutic device. It has been said that the terrifying visions in Trophonius's cavern and the healing visions in the Asklepeia were of a hypnotic nature; this is quite possible, but evidence is lacking.

Magical Healing

Many of the healing procedures we have reviewed so far have been called magic or contained certain magic elements; but magic covers a field much broader than medicine.

Magic can best be defined as an inadequate technique of power of man over nature and a fallacious anticipation of science.[70, 71] Through a pseudo-technique, the magician endeavors to achieve all that modern man is able to attain through adequate scientific means. But whereas science is "neutral" and can be applied toward good and evil ends, magic is usually more strongly divided into "bad" or "good" ("black" or "white"). The former supposedly creates disease, the latter allegedly cures it.

Magic has also been described as a system in which the features of social life are unduly projected onto the material world.[72] In its ignorance of the abstract, constant, and impersonal laws of the universe, magic replaces them with a system of rules similar to those of social life. The forces of nature are addressed with conjurations and incantations formed on the model of social requests and commandments. Rites are devised on the model of social ceremonies. In this manner, the magician is supposed to gain control over the forces of nature, such as the weather, the fecundity of animals, and the abundance of crops, and also to create and heal disease.

The practices of primitive medicine which are called magic constitute a heterogeneous group that can be divided into several subgroups:

1. There is sometimes a rational (although disguised) use of efficient drugs or poisons, even if most magic substances probably work as placebos.

2. Parapsychological powers such as clairvoyance and telepathy may be used occasionally.

3. Hypnotic manifestations probably play a part at times.

4. There is undoubtedly also an extensive use of tricks and jugglery.

5. Suggestion is probably by far the most important agent at work in the practice of magic. A magic procedure may actually attain its goal because the individual submitting to it firmly believes in its efficacy; the magician believes in his own power, and the entire community believes in the existence and efficacy of magic art because this art is felt to be necessary for social cohesion.[73]

The belief in magic is universal among primitive populations. It persisted among civilized peoples (mostly under the name of witchcraft) until a comparatively recent date, receding only under the influence of science. The power, not to say omnipotence, ascribed to magic among primitive populations is shown in the widespread belief that it is possible to kill a person through magic and to save him at the last moment before death through countermagic. This, in fact, is more than just a superstitious belief, and there are many reliable reports of such happenings in some parts of the world such as Australia and Melanesia.

Among other authors, H. Basedow described how, in central Australia, a person can be killed by means of a "pointing stick" or "pointing bone" used in conjunction with certain rites and conjurations. The death of the victim occurs within a few hours:

> A man who realizes that he is being "boned" by an enemy is, indeed, a pitiful sight. He stands aghast, his eyes staring at the treacherous pointer, his hands lifted as though to ward off the lethal medium which he imagines is pouring into his body. His cheeks blanch and his eyes become glassy, and the expression on his face becomes horribly distorted, like that of a person stricken with palsy. He attempts to shriek, but usually the sound chokes in his throat, and all one might see is froth around his lips. His body begins to tremble and his muscles twitch involuntarily. He sways backwards and falls to the ground, and appears for a short while to be in a swoon; but he soon begins to writhe as if in mortal agony and, covering his face with his hands, begins to moan. After a while, he composes himself somewhat and crawls to his wurley [hut]. From then on, he sickens and frets, refusing to eat and keeping aloof from the daily affairs of the tribe. Unless help is forthcoming in the shape of a counter-charm administered by the Nangarri or medicine man, his death is only a matter of a comparatively short time.[74]

The Nangarri who has been called to save the patient allows the presence of a number of relatives. He chants magic verses, locates the alleged seat of the evil, extracts it through the mouth-sucking method, and shows it to the family.

> The effect is astounding. The miserable fellow, until then well on the road to death, raises his head to gaze in wonderment at the object held by the Nangarri, which he imagines in all seriousness has been extracted from within his body. Satisfied with its reality, he even lifts himself up into a sitting position and calls for a drink of water. The crisis is over, and the patient's recovery is speedy and complete. Without the Nangarri's intervention, the "boned" fellow would have fretted himself to death for a certainty; but the sight of a concrete object, claimed by the recognized authority of the tribe to be the cause of the complaint, signifies recovery to him, and with its removal comes a renewed lease on life. The implicit faith a native cherishes in the magic powers of his tribal medicine man results in cures that exceed anything recorded by the faith-healing disciples of more cultured communities.[74]

Such examples help us to understand the meaning of magic medicine. If a magician is able, through collective suggestion, to cause the acute psychogenic death of his victim, and then to snatch him quickly from the brink of death, a magician is also able to produce a great number of suggested symptoms or diseases, and then to cure them. He should also be able to cure many sick people who simply *believe* or *suspect* they are the victims of magic. In such cases a further magical process is involved: diagnosing whether a person is bewitched or not, and if he is, finding out who is the instigator is a task often referred to a specialist, the diviner.

Magic healing can thus be divided into two main procedures. The first is countermagic. A disease supposedly caused by black magic is healed through the removal of the cause. This implies either the killing of the supposed sorcerer or the counteracting of his sorcery. Another application of countermagic is the prevention of magic actions through talismans or other means. The second procedure is the direct application of magic to the treatment of a disease, without implying that the disease was caused by magic.

There are many types of magicians and innumerable varieties of magical and countermagical practices. Much of it still survives in the popular medicine of civilized countries. A systematic investigation of magical medicine will no doubt help us to better understand those manifestations that we call suggestion and autosuggestion.

Rational Therapies in Primitive Medicine

It has too often been assumed that primitive medicine belonged to the realm of the irrational and the fantastic. We must not forget that the medicine man is dealing primarily with severe and extraordinary diseases and that there are usually other men, whom we may call lay doctors, who concern themselves with minor or obviously physical diseases. As shown by Bartels, a considerable part of primitive medicine represents a former stage of empirical medicine, such as the use of baths and sweating houses, massage, elementary surgery, and drugs. It is well known that modern pharmacopoeia derives a large number of its most active drugs from primitive medicine. Certain populations developed this type of rational and empirical therapy to a higher level than did others. One of the best studies of rational primitive medicine is that of G. W. Harley, who lived among the Mano tribe in Liberia.[75] He lists about one hundred conditions, of which only fifteen were treated by magical or other irrational methods. More than two hundred plants were used by medicine men in the form of infusion, decoction, and others.

R. W. Felkin, a young physician who had done missionary work in Uganda in 1884, published an account of a Caesarean section that he witnessed in 1879 in Katura, then a part of the Bunyoro Kingdom.[76] This description aroused considerable scepticism. Recent research, however, shows that medicine in the kindgom of Bunyoro had achieved other high accomplishments. As Davies has stated, some local geniuses apparently "had crossed the Rubicon that divides the magical world from that governed by experimental science."[77]

In regard to the treatment of mental diseases, the same could be said of the methods used by a native healer in Lapland that were reported by the ethnologist J. Qvistad.[78] For a mental patient this healer would prescribe a general rule of life: abstaining from alcoholic beverages, tobacco, and coffee; rising and retiring early; keeping occupied with light work. Someone should constantly attend the patient, without giving him the impression of his being watched. The patient should take no medication, but should bathe twice daily, in sea water in the morning and in fresh water at night. He was not to be tied if he became aggressive, rather he was to be put into a room from which every potentially harmful object had been removed. If he attacked somebody, he should be given a slap on his naked body with a leafless twig; one should speak to him sharply and show no fear. This Lapland healer was said to have cured many mentally disturbed patients.

Basic Characteristics of Primitive Healing

We have, thus far, made a survey of the chief methods of primitive healing and pointed out certain similarities among several of those methods and modern psychotherapeutic methods. But the differences between primitive healing and modern psychotherapy should not be minimized, nor should it be overlooked that throughout the innumerable varieties of primitive healing, certain basic features can be recognized.

1. The primitive healer plays a much more essential role in his community than do physicians today. Sigerist writes: "It is an insult to the medicine man to call him the ancestor of the modern physician. He is that, to be sure, but he is much more, namely the ancestor of most of our professions."[79] He is not only concerned with the welfare of his people (from making rain to providing victory in war); he is often a dreaded wizard, is sometimes the bard who knows of the origin of the world and of the history of his tribe. Long before any division of labor had been devised, the healer was the only man with professional status, along with the chief and the priest, and he sometimes held all three offices. More frequently, however, the different functions of the healer were divided among several persons. Certain tribes had several classes of healers: There may have been shamans endowed with great prestige who would only treat diseases caused by the loss of the soul, whereas the treatment of common physical disease was assigned to healers of a lower degree.

2. In the presence of a disease, especially a severe or dangerous one, the patient places his hopes and confidence in the *person* of the healer rather than in his medications and other healing teachniques. It would therefore seem that the healer's personality is the principal agent of the cure, in addition to any necessary skill or knowledge. Maeder distinguished three types of primitive healer: the first may be called the lay healer, that is, the one who treats with rational or would-be rational methods. The second is the magician, who acts through his prestige and suggestion. The third is the religious healer, onto whom, according to Maeder, the patient projects the "archetype of the Saviour," while the healer awakens and develops in the patient his own self-healing tendencies.[80]

3. The primitive healer is a very skilled and learned man, "a man of high

degree," as Elkin calls the Australian medicine man, who acquires his status through long and difficult training. Most primitive healers receive their training from other healers and are members of a group that transmits their secret knowledge and traditions. Many of them have to undergo an "initiatory illness." Actually, many primitive healers are subject to psychopathological manifestations. In that regard, Ackerknecht distinguishes three types of medicine men: (a) the noninspirational, whose visions and trances are induced by fasting, alcohol, and drugs; (b) the inspirational, who undergo ritual possession, that is, a variety of self-hypnosis somewhat similar to the trances of our Western mediums; (c) true shamans, that is, those who become shamans only after undergoing a peculiar state of severe mental illness.[81] Such are the shamans of certain South African tribes, tribes in Indonesia, and, above all, in Siberia. The initiatory illness of the Siberian shaman has been described by Russian ethnologists:

> Nioradzé relates how the young man who has received the calling withdraws from society; he spends his nights on the naked ground or even in the snow, observes long periods of fasting, suffers great hardships, and converses with the spirits; he presents the picture of a severely psychotic individual. However, contrasting with an ordinary mental illness, this one starts with a shamanistic vocation and, during the course of his illness, the patient undergoes professional initiation at the hands of other shamans; the illness ends the very moment the training is completed and the patient is himself proclaimed shaman.[82]

It is obvious that we are not dealing here with an ordinary mental illness, but rather with a kind of "initiatory illness" that could be classified into the wider group of "creative illnesses."[83] This group also includes the experiences of certain mystics, poets, and philosophers. We will later examine the role that this kind of illness may have played in the foundation of dynamic psychiatry.

4. The healer may or may not be proficient in the treatment of fractures, in the knowledge of drugs, in massage, and other empirical treatments that are often left to lay healers. But his most important methods of healing are of a psychological nature, whether it be a matter of treating a physical or a mental illness. In primitive societies, the distinction between body and mind is not as clear-cut as in our society, and the medicine man may well be considered to be a psychosomatician.

5. Primitive healing is almost always a public and a collective procedure. Usually, the patient does not go to the healer by himself, but is accompanied by relatives who remain present during treatment. As we have seen, the treatment is at the same time a ceremony conducted within a well-structured group, involving either the patient's entire tribe or members of a medicine society that the patient joins after being cured.

We have, so far, summarized the basic common features and reviewed the most important varieties of primitive healing. Forest E. Clements has attempted to reconstruct its historical evolution on the basis of a careful comparison of the areas of diffusion of the major disease theories.[84] His hypothesis in regard to their period of origin and the chronological order of their emergence is summarized in Table 1–2.

TABLE 1–2

DISEASE THEORY	PERIOD OF EMERGENCE	GEOGRAPHIC CENTER
1. Disease-object intrusion	Paleolithic (earlier)	Old World
2. Soul loss	Paleolithic (later)	Siberia
3. Spirit intrusion	End of Pleistocene	Western Asia
4. Breach of taboo	Relatively recent	Three centers simultaneously

The "sorcery" disease theory is the most widespread of all, and its chronology is uncertain.

Temple Healing and Philosophical Psychotherapy

At some unknown time around 4000 B.C., the first kingdoms and empires were founded in Asia. They lay the groundwork for the development of organized religions with colleges of priests and the constitution of systematized bodies of knowledge that were the prefiguration of science, a science founded on observation and deduction rather than measurement and experimentation—as in modern science.

Certain techniques of primitive medicine were taken over by the new temple medicine. (Exorcism is one example.) Others were probably worked out and developed in the temples (such as the cures in the Asklepeia). Lay medicine also underwent an autonomous development, but showed itself more proficient in the treatment of physical diseases than in the treatment of emotional conditions. Thus arose the separation of priestly medicine and medicine proper, the first being represented by the healing priest, the latter by the physician. Ackerknecht has convincingly shown that the true ancestors of the modern physician are the lay healers, that is, those men to whom the medicine man left the empirical and physical care of the patients), whereas "the medicine man is rather the ancestor of the priest, the physician's antagonist for centuries."[85] For many centuries the physician and the healing priest lived side by side: Cos was the cradle of Hippocrates and of his school, but was also famous for its Asklepeion. Galen, the foremost physician of the second century A.D., unhesitatingly resorted to the Asklepeion of Pergamon for certain matters. It would seem that psychological healing was more developed in the Asklepeia than in lay medicine.

Aside from temple medicine and early scientific medicine, a remarkable feature of these cultures was the elaboration of highly developed techniques of mental training—often with psychotherapeutic implications—on the basis of certain philosophical and religious teachings. Most famous among them is Yoga, an extraordinarily elaborated "mystical technique" that is common to most of the religious and philosophical schools in India.[86] Other physiological and psychotherapeutic techniques have come forth from Buddhism, such as those of the Zen sect.

In the Western world, certain techniques of mental training have also been associated with philosophical schools. It is often overlooked that in the Greco-Roman era the adoption of a philosophy did not imply merely the acceptance of a certain doctrine. The Pythagoreans, the Platonists, the Aristotelians, the Stoics, and the Epicureans, were not just adherents of "philosophical systems," but members of organized "schools," also called "sects," that imposed on them a specific method of training and a way of life.[87] Each one of them had a kind of central institute or headquarters, in addition to the local branches. The Pythagorean Institute in Crotona, in the south of Italy, was destroyed by the enemies of the association, but for centuries the Platonists, the Aristotelians, and the Epicureans had their respective institutes (the Academy, the Lyceum, the House and Garden of Epicurus) in Athens. These institutes comprised living quarters for prominent members, lecture rooms, libraries, and workshops for publishing. Each of these schools was organized in its own way under the leadership of a *scholarch,* who was the successor of the founder, with a hierarchy of older and younger members. Members, who had sometimes undergone a kind of philosophical conversion, had to pass through an initiation and maintain a certain mode of living that could extend to diet and dress. They either upheld the doctrines and observed the rules of the school or were expelled.

Each school transmitted what its founder had taught; his successors were often at variance with him, but there always was an "official" doctrine of the school. The doctrine not only comprised metaphysics, but logic, morals, physics, and other sciences as well. The more fundamental teaching was reserved for the disciples, but there were lectures and writings for the public. The schools often polemized against the nonphilosophers, other schools, and those who seceded from their own groups. Members of each school were tied together by their common beliefs, the practice of the same exercises, the same way of life, and the cult of the founder—of his memory, more often, probably, his legend, and his writings. This was particularly conspicuous among the Epicureans; wherever they had a local group, they met once a month for a banquet in honor of their founder. They kept his portrait in their gathering places and on their rings, and those who went to Greece never failed to visit the founder's house and his garden near Athens.

Each school taught and practiced a specific method of psychic training. The Pythagoreans, a community bound by strict discipline and obedience to the "master," followed severe dietary restrictions, exercises in self-control (for instance, a long period of silence was observed during the initiation), exercises in memory recall, and memorizing for recitation. They also studied mathematics, astronomy, and music. The Platonists searched together for truth, which was expected to emerge in conversations between teacher and disciples. The Aristotelian school was a kind of research institute of encyclopedic scope. The element of psychic training was stressed among the Stoics and the Epicureans.[88] The Stoics learned the control of emotions and practiced written and verbal exercises in concentration and meditation, a method that was taken over, centuries later, by Saint Ignatius of Loyola. They chose a given topic, for instance death, and the object was to dissociate it from all established opinions, fears, and memories that had become associated with it. Another practice was that of the "consolations," which was a friendly philosophical discourse told or written to a person in sorrow. The Epicureans, in their meditations, avoided facing evil directly; rather, they evoked past and future joys. They also resorted to an intensive memorization of a compendium of maxims, which they recited ceaselessly, aloud or mentally. There is no doubt that such practices also exerted a psychotherapeutic action in many individuals. It has been contended that Stoicism showed certain features that can be found in the Adlerian and existentialist schools of today, that some of the characteristics of Plato's Academy can be found in the Jungian School, whereas Epicurus aimed at the removal of anxiety and has been compared in that regard to Freud.[89]

These schools exerted a considerable influence on the life of the times. They strove to disseminate their teaching through lectures and books (the Epicurean House near Athens was also a publishing house), and they occasionally influenced politicians. Many of their disciples were teachers or physicians. In present-day perspective, these schools seem of equal importance, and chapters devoted to them in histories of philosophy are of similar length, but contemporaries were impressed by their very unequal success and membership. Stoics outnumbered the disciples of Plato and Aristotle, but by far the most popular were the Epicureans, who had large communities in almost all the cities of the Greco-Roman world.

Philosophical psychotherapy did not merely consist of the methods of collective education, discipline, and mental training that they taught on a collective level. They could also inspire methods for individual therapy, as evidenced by Galen's treatise *On the Passions of the Soul.*[90] Galen's method must be understood against the background of contemporary culture and mores. Brutality reigned in his time. Galen's own mother, he says, used to bite her servants, and Galen cites, as an example of moderation, his father, who, when he was angry with his servants, did not kick them, but waited until his anger subsided before having them beaten. Galen also tells that on a journey with a friend, two servants could not find one piece of luggage, whereupon his friend struck them with a sword and wounded them severely. Emperor Hadrian pierced the eye of one of his slaves in a fit of anger. It would seem that the Greeks and Romans of that time were prone to fits of uncontrolled behavior, issuing either from the "irascible" or from the "concupiscible" powers of the soul (in Galen's terminology). The existence of a mass of passive slaves upon which any outburst of passion could be discharged furthered that mode of behavior. This may also explain the extraordinary importance attributed by contemporary philosophers and moralists to the mastery of one's passions and the central place it occupies in Galen's treatise.

The method taught by Galen for mastering one's passions seems to have been borrowed mainly from the Stoics (though here as in medicine he was an eclectic). The first step consisted in abstaining from the crudest kind of emotional outburst, notably from kicking, biting, or wounding one's slaves. The second step was to find a mentor, a wise and older counselor who would point out your defects and dispense advice; Galen stresses the paramount importance of, and the difficulty in finding, such a man. The third step is to engage, with the help of one's mentor, in an unceasing effort to control one's passions. This training Galen considered feasible at any age, even at fifty, but it was wiser to start in early youth. There were also auxiliary methods, such as one in which the subject daily re-read and recited aloud the maxims of the Pythagorean school. As the years went by, the subject would reduce his standard of living to the mere necessities of life. He would, for instance, be content with two suits and two slaves. At that stage, when he had attained serenity and freedom even from grief, he would view passions as severe diseases of the soul and would then be able to help others. The method of the wise man in counseling his young disciple is illustrated in the above-mentioned treatise and in *On the Errors of the Soul*, in which Galen distinguishes two sources of errors: those of purely intellectual nature and those that derive from the passions.

Religious Healing and "Cure of Souls"

The Catholic Church took over, from formerly established religions, practices such as prayers, vows, pilgrimages (which certainly had a stimulating virtue at a time when people lived a monotonous life, rooted to one place), and gave great importance to the practice of confession made individually to a priest bound by absolute secrecy. There are reasons to believe that the common practice of confession exerted an influence upon the development of psychology, in the form of autobiographies such as St. Augustine's *Confessions* and of the psychological novel.[91] A body of psychological knowledge was acquired by the priests and was systematized to some extent in textbooks of moral theology, but the very nature and rigidity of the priestly secret of confession made that systematized knowledge rather abstract.[92]

Protestant reformers abolished compulsory confession, but it was among Protestant communities that a new practice and tradition arose, the "Cure of Souls" (*Seelsorge*). There were many aspects and varieties of "Cure of

Souls." One of them is of particular importance.[93] Certain Protestant ministers were considered as being endowed with a particular spiritual gift that enabled them to obtain the confession of a disturbing secret from distressed souls and to help those persons out of their difficulty. These clerical men maintained the tradition of absolute secrecy, though it was not imposed on them with the same rigidity as in the Catholic Church. For lack of an authentic historical example of such a healing, we will turn to a novel by Heinrich Jung-Stilling, *Theobald oder die Schwärmer,* published in 1785. In one of the main episodes of that novel, we find a detailed account of a "Cure of Souls," which most probably was inspired by a real occurrence that came to the novelist's attention.

A young unmarried woman, Sannchen, is afflicted with a peculiar kind of depression. Physicians attribute it to a "weakness of the nerves," call it hysteria, and treat the patient with medications without success. The anxious family then hears of a village pastor, Reverend Bosius, who is said to have a particular gift for "Cure of Souls" and they ask for his help. Reverend Bosius is described in the novel as a pious, learned, unassuming, and devoted man. As soon as he arrives he goes for a walk in the garden with Sannchen. His kindness impresses her favorably. He begins with a long, friendly talk about the love of God that is reflected in all of Nature, where every being is a thought of God. Now, what is the most beautiful of all the thoughts of God? It is love. And what is love? It is the drive of the lover to be united with the beloved. This brings Sannchen to tell him of her secret and thwarted love for Theobald and of a transgression that she has committed. Having heard her confession, Reverend Bosius exclaims: "Good Souls! How little you know about love!" Whereupon he starts to explain to her that under the guise of love she has been deceived by passion. Passion is nothing but "natural sexual drive" (*natürlicher Geschlechtstrieb*), that is, the natural instinct of animals that want to reproduce, however refined and sublimated it can look.

Following this first conversation, Reverend Bosius brings Sannchen to accept her fate, and now, with her agreement, he explains the situation to her parents; then he talks Theobald into agreeing to marry her, so that the first part of the novel is concluded with a quiet wedding of Theobald and Sannchen.[94, 95]

We will note that the pathogenic secret that Reverend Bosius came upon so rapidly was related to a love affair; it appears as if he knew from his past experience with his "Cure of Souls" that it must have been so. We note also that Reverend Bosius did not consider that he had fulfilled his task when he had just obtained the confession and given consolation. With the patient's permission, he played an active role in bringing about solutions to the patient's distressing problems. The whole procedure is somewhat reminiscent of a present-day short psychotherapy.

There came a time when the knowledge of the pathogenic secret and its treatment fell into the hands of laymen. When this happened is not known, but it may have been among the early magnetists (whom we will discuss in the following chapter). The notion of the burdening secret became known to these men soon after the discovery by Puységur of the state of "magnetic sleep" (later called hypnosis). The very first patient in whom Puységur induced magnetic sleep in 1784, Victor Race, informed him of a conflict he had with his sister and about which he would never dare speak in a normal state. He followed Puységur's advice in a normal state to his own satisfaction.[96] In 1786 the Count of Lutzelbourg published the story of one of his patients who was infatuated with a male friend, in whom he had the utmost confidence in a waking state.[97] However, in "magnetic sleep" he knew that his supposed friend was a traitor who had harmed him and explained to the magnetist what he had to do in order to pass on this knowledge from his "sleep" to his waking state. In the early period of magnetism, similar cases were reported everywhere; they became less frequent in the second half of the nineteenth century, but in the 1880's and 1890's, there were still hypnotists who knew how to relieve their patients of burdensome secrets told in hypnotic states.

The notion of the pathogenic secret gradually became known to a wider public. Evidence may be found in a series of literary works throughout the nineteenth century. A novel by Jeremias Gotthelf (pseudonym of the Swiss pastor Albert Bitzius), published in 1843, tells the story of a young man, the son of rich peasants, who is slowly dying in despair because he is secretly in love with a young maid whom his parents would not allow him to marry because she is an orphan and poor.[98] The family has arranged a marriage with a rich and arrogant bride. An experienced old fortuneteller guesses the secret and induces the family to break the engagement and marry the young man to his loved one: From that moment he is cured. In 1850, Nathaniel Hawthorne described, in his masterpiece *The Scarlet Letter,* how a pathogenic secret can be discovered by a wicked man and exploited in order to torture his victim to death.[99]

A remarkable story of a pathogenic secret and its cure was told in 1888 by Ibsen in his play *The Lady from the Sea.*

A neurotic woman, Ellida, suffers from a mysterious neurosis that must have some connection with the sea: Ellida spends an abnormal amount of time bathing and swimming in the fiord, though she claims to hate its "sick and sickening water," in contrast to the vivid water of the open sea. Whenever one speaks of the sea and seafarers, she becomes startled and shows a deep interest. She suggests to an artist the idea of painting a siren dying on the shore after the sea has receded. Talking with a sculptor, she immediately thinks of modeling Tritons, sirens, and Vikings. Speaking of her baby who died in infancy, she maintains that the color and glow of his eyes changed according to the various colors and aspects of the sea. She holds a theory that if mankind had chosen to live in the sea rather than on the earth, men would be better and happier, but mankind has taken the wrong way, it is too late to go back to the sea; a confused feeling of that error is the deepest root of human sorrow. Gradually, the secret emerges: Ellida was attracted (or maybe seduced) by a mysterious seafarer; she joined their rings in a single chain; he threw the chain into the sea and disappeared, saying that he would return one day to her. The mysterious seafarer returns and demands from Ellida the fulfillment of her promise, but in the meantime, she has married. Her husband leaves her the choice between himself and the stranger, though appealing to her sense of duty. She chooses her husband, and the writer gives us to understand that this free and responsible decision will bring about her healing.[100]

Ibsen's play stresses two aspects of the pathogenic secret: (1) the many symbolic ways in which it expresses itself involuntarily, and (2) the healing may not depend solely on the intervention of the psychotherapist, but on the free, responsible choice allowed the patient.

It seems that the first medical man who systematized the knowledge of the pathogenic secret and its psychotherapy was the Viennese physician, Moritz Benedikt.[101] In a series of publications that appeared between 1864 and 1895, Benedikt showed that the cause of many cases of hysteria and other neuroses resides in a painful secret, mostly pertaining to sexual life, and that many patients can be cured by the confession of their pathogenic secrets and by the working out of the related problems.

One may wonder to what extent modern dynamic psychiatry was influenced by the old notion of the pathogenic secret and its healing. As we shall see in later chapters, some of Janet's and Freud's cases pertain to unconscious pathogenic secrets (as it was with the magnetists and hypnotists). In his "Preliminary Communication" published jointly with Breuer in 1893, Freud mentions in a footnote that "we found the closest approach to our theoretical and therapeutic statements in occasionally published remarks of Benedikt." With the further development of psychoanalysis, the concept of the pathogenic secret became gradually absorbed into those of traumatic reminiscences, repression, and neurotic guilt feelings.

Among the pioneers of dynamic psychiatry, the one who devoted the most attention to this concept was C. G. Jung, who may have heard of it from his father, a Protestant minister.[102] Jung considered this treatment a preliminary part of the complete psychotherapeutic treatment. Among Freud's early disciples, Reverend Oskar Pfister, of Zurich, was the first to apply psychoanalysis to the Seelsorge. To those who have known him personally or carefully read his writings, it is clear that psychoanalysis was to Pfister to a certain extent a rediscovery and a perfecting of the traditional "Cure of Souls." Pfister always thought of his psychoanalytic practice as part of his pastoral work. For that reason one finds in his writings many accounts of short analytic therapies based on the rapid uncovering of more or less "repressed" unpleasant memories. The circle was now completed: The therapy of the pathogenic secret, which had started from the "Cure of Souls," had returned to it in a modernized form.

Scientific Psychotherapy

A new era was inaugurated at the end of the sixteenth and during the seventeenth centuries with the birth of modern science. Whereas in the early scientific era, knowledge had rested on observation and deduction, modern scientific knowledge is based on experimentation and measurement. Science strives toward the unification of human knowledge: There is only one science, of which the particular sciences are branches. This rules out the possibility of distinct schools existing side by side, each with its own doctrines and traditions in opposition to those of other schools. Thus, medicine became a branch of science, psychiatry a branch of medicine, and psychotherapy an application of psychiatry, based on scientific findings. In that perspective, the physician, including the psychiatrist, becomes more and more a technician and a specialist. Since science is all-inclusive knowledge, it cannot admit the validity of extrascientific healing—hence, the contempt of "official" medicine for all kinds of primitive and popular medicine, the latter containing remnants of primitive and early scientific medicine.[103]

The difference between primitive and scientific therapy can be summarized in Table 1–3.

TABLE 1–3

PRIMITIVE HEALING	SCIENTIFIC THERAPY
1. The healer is much more than a physician; he is the foremost personality of his social group.	1. The therapist is a specialist among many others.
2. The healer exerts his action primarily through his personality.	2. The therapist applies specific techniques in an impersonal way.
3. The healer is preponderantly a psychosomatician; he treats many physical diseases by psychological techniques.	3. There is a dichotomy between physical and psychic therapy. The accent in psychiatry is on the physical treatment of mental illness.
4. The healer's training is long and exacting, and often includes the experience of a severe emotional disease that he has to overcome in order to be able to heal other people.	4. The training is purely rational and does not take into consideration the personal, medical, or emotional problems of the physician.
5. The healer belongs to a school that has its own teachings and traditions diverging from those of other schools.	5. The therapist acts on the basis of a unified medicine, which is a branch of science and is not an esoteric teaching.

This parallel could be concluded by quoting Ackerknecht's remark that the medicine man "plays his role as the most irrational man in an irrational pattern," whereas the modern physician is "rationalizing even the irrational."[104]

Modern Dynamic Psychotherapy

The account of how dynamic psychiatry and psychotherapy slowly developed during the nineteenth century and broke through the turn of this century with Charcot, Janet, Freud, and his followers constitutes the subject of the present book.

Historically, modern dynamic psychotherapy derives from primitive medicine, and an uninterrupted continuity can be demonstrated between exorcism and magnetism, magnetism and hypnotism, and hypnotism and the modern dynamic schools.

By referring to the above table, we can see that certain features of modern dynamic therapy point to an unmistakable affinity with primitive healing. Psychoanalysts are often considered more prominent members of the community than the average "scientific" physician. A psychoanalyst's personality is his major therapeutic tool. Psychoanalytic training is incomparably more exacting than that of most other specialists and includes a long personal analysis aimed at working out the psychoanalyst's emotional problems. Dynamic psychotherapy produced a revival of psychosomatic medicine. Modern dynamic psychiatry is divided into a variety of "schools," each with its own doctrine, its own teaching, its own training. Does all this mean that dynamic psychotherapy is a regression in the direction of the past, or rather that the scientific approach proved insufficient to cover the entire personality of man and must be supplemented by other approaches? We will return to this problem at the end of this book.

Notes

1. Adolf Bastian, "Über psychische Beobachtungen bei Naturvölkern," *Schriften der Gesellschaft für Experimental-Psychologie zu Berlin,* II (Leipzig: Ernst Günther, 1890), 6–9.

2. Max Bartels, *Die Medizin der Naturvölker. Ethnologische Beiträge zur Urgeschichte der Medizin* (Leipzig: Th. Grieben, 1893).

3. Georg Buschan, *Über Medizinzauber und Heilkunst im Leben der Völker* (Berlin: Oswald Arnold, 1941).

4. Henry Sigerist, *A History of Medicine,* Vol. I (New York: Oxford University Press, 1951).

5. Forest E. Clements, "Primitive Concepts of Disease," *University of California Publications in American Archeology and Ethnology,* XXXII, No. 2 (1932), 185–252.

6. Henri Meige, *Les Possédées noires* (Paris: Schiller, 1894).

7. Georges Gilles de la Tourette, *Traité clinique et thérapeutique de l'hystérie* (Paris:

Plon-Nourrit, 1891), p. 121.

8. Oskar Pfister, "Instinktive Psychoanalyse unter den Navaho-Indianern," *Imago*, XVIII, No. 1 (1932), 81–109.

9. Claude Lévi-Strauss, "Sorciers et psychanalyse," *Courrier de l'Unesco*, IX (July–August 1956), 8–10.

10. William W. Elmendorf, "Soul Loss Illness in Western North America," *Selected Papers of the XXIXth International Congress of Americanists*, III (Chicago: University of Chicago Press, 1952), 104–114.

11. Edward B. Tylor, *Primitive Culture* (London: John Murray, 1871).

12. J. G. Frazer, *The Golden Bough*, Vol. II: *Taboo and the Perils of the Soul* (3rd ed., London: Macmillan, 1911).

13. G. V. Ksenofontov, in *Schamanen-Geschichten aus Sibirien*, trans. into German and ed. by Adolf Friedrich and Georg Buddrus (Munich: O. W. Barth, 1955). (Condensed excerpt.)

14. Federico Sal y Rosas, "El mito del Jani o Susto de la medicina indígena del Perú," *Revista Psiquiátrica Peruana*, I, No. 2 (1957), 103–132.

15. Franz Boas, "The Religion of the Kwakiutl Indians," Part II, Translations, *Columbia University Contributions to Anthropology* (New York: New York University Press, 1930), X, 1–4.

16. Claude Lévi-Strauss, "Le Sorcier et sa magie," *Les Temps modernes*, IV, No. 41 (1949), 121–138.

17. Traugott Konstantin Oesterreich, *Die Besessenheit* (Langenzalza: Wendt & Klauwell, 1921); Eng. trans., *Possession, Demoniacal and Other Among Primitive Races, in Antiquity, the Middle Ages, and Modern Times* (New York: Richard R. Smith, 1930).

18. Ludwig von Baelz, "Über Besessenheit," *Verhandlungen der deutschen Gesellschaft Naturforscher und Ärzte*, No. 79 (1906).

19. Kiyoshi Nozaki, *Kitsuné. Japan's Fox of Mystery, Romance and Humor* (Tokyo: The Hokuseido Press, 1961), pp. 211–227.

20. Henri Rusillon, *Un petit continent: Madagascar* (Paris: Société des Missions Évangéliques, 1933).

21. Percival Lowell, *Occult Japan, or the Way of the Gods* (Boston: Houghton Mifflin Company, 1895).

22. Rudolf Kriss and Hubert Kriss-Heinrich, "Peregrinatio Hellenika," *Veröffentlichungen des Oesterreichischen Museums für Volkskunde*, VI (Vienna, 1955), 66–82.

23. Quoted in Erwin Liek, *Das Wunder in der Heilkunde* (Munich: J. F. Lehmanns Verlag, 1930), pp. 67–70.

24. Peter Hartocollis, "Cure by Exorcism in the Island of Cephalonia," *Journal of the History of Medicine*, XIII (1958), 367–372.

25. Gustav Roskoff, *Geschichte des Teufels*, Vol. II (Leipzig: F. A. Brockhaus, 1869).

26. Justinus Kerner, *Nachricht von dem Vorkommen des Besessenseyns . . . .* (Stuttgart: J. C. Cotta, 1836).

27. This report has long been known only from incomplete, sometimes inaccurate copies that have been utilized by Blumhardt's biographers. The complete text was published in 1955, *Blumhardts Kampf* (Stuttgart-Sillenbuch: Verlag Goldene Worte, 1955).

28. Many instances of such beliefs can be found in the monograph by Gisela Piaschewsky, *Der Wechselbalg: Ein Beitrag zum Aberglauben der nordeuropäischen Völker* (Breslau: Maruschko and Berendt, 1935).

29. Friedrich Zündel, *Pfarrer Johann Christoph Blumhardt–Ein Lebensbild* (Zurich: S. Höhr, 1880).

30. Pierre Scherding, *Christophe Blumhardt et son père*. Publ. Faculté de Théologie Protestante de Strasbourg, No. 34 (Paris: Alcan, 1937).

31. *Ibid.*

32. Pfarrer Blumhardt, "Mittheilungen," *Evangelisches Kirchenblatt zunächst für Württemberg* (1845), pp. 113–122; 227–233; 241–254. (The author is indebted to the Württemberg National Library, Stuttgart, for a photocopy of this document.)

33. Viktor von Weizsäcker, *Seelenbehandlung und Seelenführung* (Gütersloh: C. Bertelsmann, 1926).

34. Edgar Michaelis, *Geisterreich und Geistesmacht. Der Heilungs- und Dämonenkampf J. Chr. Blumhardts* (Bern: Haupt, 1949).

35. Gaetano Benedetti, "Blumhardts Seelsorge in der Sicht heutiger psychotherapeutischer Kenntnis," *Reformatio*, IX (1960). 474–487; 531–539.

36. Alphonse Maeder, *Studien über Kurz-Psychotherapie* (Stuttgart: Klett, 1963).

37. Fernand Grébert, *Au Gabon*, 2nd ed., rev., enlarged (Paris: Société des Missions évangéliques, 1928), pp. 171–172.

38. Marcel Mauss, "Effet psychique chez l'individu de l'idée de mort suggérée par la collectivité (Australie: Nouvelle Zélande)," *Journal de psychologie normale et pathologique*, XXIII (1926), 653–669.

39. This difference between African and Polynesian facts was pointed out to the author in a conversation with the anthropologist Maurice Leenhardt.

40. Raffaele Pettazzoni, *La confessione dei peccati*, 3 vols. (Bologna: Nicola Zanichelli, 1929, 1935, 1936).

41. H. Aldenhoven, "Klinischer Beitrag zur Frage der Todesahnungen," *Psychotherapie*, II (1957), 55–59.

42. Quoted by G. Blake-Palmer, in "Maori Attitudes to Sickness," *The Medical Journal of Australia*, XLIII, No. 2 (1956), 401–405.

43. Fritz Ernst, *Vom Heimweh* (Zurich: Fretz & Wasmuth, 1949); M. Bachet, "Etude sur les états de nostalgie," *Annales Médico-Psychologiques*, CVIII, No. 1 (1950), 559–587; No. 2, 11–34.

44. Father Raguenau, *The Jesuit Relations and Allied Documents*, XLII (Cleveland: Burrows Brothers Co., 1899), 164.

45. Father Raguenau, in *The Jesuit Relations*, XXXIII (1898), 188-208. The interest of this account has been shown by Mark D. Altschule, *Roots of Modern Psychiatry* (New York: Grune & Stratton Inc., 1957).

46. Raguenau, *The Jesuit Relations*, XLII (1899), 158–160.

47. Raguenau, *The Jesuit Relations*, VIII (1897), 260–262.

48. Maurice Genty, "Magendie," in P. Busquet and M. Genty, eds., *Les Biographies médicales* (Paris: Baillière, 1936), IV, 113–144.

49. Bruno Lewin, "Der Zar, ein ägyptischer Tanz zur Austreibung böser Geister bei Geisteskrankheiten, und seine Beziehungen zu Heiltanzzeremonien anderer Völker und der Tanzwut des Mittelalters," *Confinia Psychiatrica*, I (1958), 177–200.

50. Louis Mars, "La Schizophrénie en Haïti," *Bulletin du Bureau d'Ethnologie*, No. 15 (March 1958).

51. C. le Barbier, "Notes sur le pays des Bara-Imamono," *Bulletin de l'Académie malgache*, Nouvelle série, III (1916–1917), 63–162.

52. E. Birkeli, "Folklore sakalava recueilli dans la région de Morondava," *Bulletin de l'Académie malgache*, Nouvelle série, VI (1922–1923), 185–364.

53. Another powerful incentive to the cure is the fact that if the patient is not cured after the *Bilo*, he is held responsible and made the object of public reproval, and may be expelled from the community. This point has been brought to the author's attention by the anthropologist Louis Molet.

54. Pierre Janet, *Les Médications psychologiques* (Paris: Alcan, 1919), I, 11–17.

55. A. M. Hocart, *The Life-Giving Myth and Other Essays* (New York: Grove Press, Inc., 1954), Chap. 20.

56. The therapeutic effect of the "return to the origins" and the re-enactment of the great cosmogonic myths has been well expounded by Mircea Eliade, *Mythes, rêves et mystères* (Paris: Gallimard, 1957), pp. 48–59.

57. L. S. Freeland, "Pomo Doctors and Poisoners," *University of California Publications in American Archeology and Ethnology*, XX (1923), 57–73.

58. Mathilda C. Stevenson, "The Zuñi Indians: Their Mythology, Esoteric Fraternities and Ceremonials," *Annual Report of the Bureau of American Ethnology*, XXIII (Washington: Smithsonian Institution, 1901–1902), 3–608.

59. *Ibid.*

60. Oskar Pfister, "Instinktive Psychoanalyse unter den Navaho-Indianern," *Imago*, XVIII, No. 1 (1932), 81–109.

61. Washington Matthews, "The Night Chant, a Navaho Ceremony," *Memoirs of the American Museum of Natural History*, Vol. VI; *Anthropology*, Vol. V (1902).

62. Ruth Cranston, *The Miracle of Lourdes* (New York: McGraw–Hill, Inc., 1955), p. 7.

63. Pausanias, *Description of Greece*, IV, Book 9 (Cambridge, Mass.: Harvard University Press, The Loeb Classical Library, 1955), Chap. 39, pp. 347–355.

64. Emma J. Edelstein and Ludwig Edelstein, *Asclepius. A Collection and Interpretation of the Testimonies*, 2 vols. (Baltimore: The Johns Hopkins Press, 1945). Karl Kerenyi, *Der göttliche Arzt* (Basel: Ciba Gesellschaft, 1948).

65. C. A. Meier, *Antike Inkubation und moderne Psychotherapie* (Zurich: Rascher-Verlag, 1949), pp. 59–65.

66. Otto Stoll, *Suggestion und Hypnotismus in der Völkerpsychologie* (2nd ed., Leipzig: Von Weit & Co., 1904).

67. A. P. Elkin, *Aboriginal Men of High Degree* (Sidney: Australasian Publishing Co., 1945).

68. Ronald Rose, *Living Magic. The Realities Underlying the Psychical Practices and Beliefs of Australian Aborigines* (New York: Rand McNally & Co., 1956).

69. Heinrich Brugsch, *Aus dem Morgenlande* (Leipzig: Ph. Reclam jun., Universal-Bibliothek, 1893), No. 3151–52, pp. 43–53.

70. Marcel Mauss et H. Hubert, "Esquisse d'une théorie générale de la magie," *L'année Sociologique*, Vol. VII (1902–1903).

71. J. G. Frazer, *The Golden Bough*, Vol. I, *The Magic Art and the Evolution of Kings*, (3rd ed. (London: Macmillan, 1911).

72. Louis Weber, *Le Rythme du progrès* (Paris: Alcan, 1913).

73. The role of collective suggestion in such occurrences has been well illustrated by Marcel Mauss, cf. n. 70; see also Claude Lévi-Strauss, "Le Sorcier et sa magie," *Les Temps Modernes*, IV, No. 41 (March 1949), 121–138.

74. Herbert Basedow, *The Australian Aboriginal* (Adelaide: F. W. Preece and Sons, 1925), pp. 174–182.

75. G. W. Harley, *Native African Medicine* (Cambridge, Mass.: Harvard University Press, 1941).

76. R. W. Felkin, "Notes on Labour in Central Africa," *Edinburgh Medical Journal*, XXIX (1884), 922–930.

77. J. N. P. Davies, "The Development of 'Scientific' Medicine in the African Kingdom of Bunyoro-Kitara," *Medical History*, III (1959), 47–57.

78. J. Qvistad, *Lappische Heilkunde* (Oslo: Instituttet for Sammenlignende Kultur-forskning, 1932), pp. 90–91.

79. Henry Sigerist, *A History of Medicine* (New York: Oxford University Press, 1951), I, 161.

80. Alphonse Maeder, *Studien über Kurz-Psychotherapie* (Stuttgart: Klett, 1963).

81. Erwin H. Ackerknecht, "Problems of Primitive Medicine," *Bulletin of the History of Medicine*, XI, No. 5 (1942), 503–521.

82. Georg Nioradzé, *Der Schamanismus bei den sibirischen Völkern* (Stuttgart: Strecker and Schröder, 1925).

83. Henri Ellenberger, "La Notion de maladie créatrice," *Dialogue, Canadian Philosophical Review*, III (1964), 25–41.

84. Forest E. Clements, "Primitive Concepts of Disease," *University of California Publications in American Archaeology and Ethnology*, XXXII, No. 2 (Berkeley, 1932), 185–252.

85. Erwin H. Ackerknecht, "Problems of Primitive Medicine," *Bulletin of the History of Medicine*, XI, No. 5 (1942), 503–521.

86. See among others the books by Mircea Eliade, *Yoga, Essai sur les origines de la mystique indienne* (Paris: Geuthner, 1936); *Techniques du Yoga* (Paris: Gallimard, 1948).

87. Details about the organization of Greek philosophical sects may be found in the

books by Léon Robin, *La Pensée grecque et les origines de l'esprit scientifique* (Paris: Renaissance du Livre, 1923), pp. 61–85; Paul Friedländer, *Platon; Seinswahrheit und Lebenswirklichkeit* (2nd ed., Berlin: de Gruyter, 1954); Norman W. Dewitt, *Epicurus and His Philosophy* (Minneapolis: University of Minnesota Press, 1958), pp. 89–120.

88. Paul Rabbow, *Seelenführung. Methoden der Exerzitien in der Antike* (Munich: Koesel, 1954).

89. R. de Saussure, "Epicure et Freud," *Gesundheit und Wohlfahrt*, XVIII (1938), 356–360.

90. Galen, *On the Passions and Errors of the Soul*, trans. by Paul W. Harkins, with an introduction and interpretation by Walther Riese. (Columbus: Ohio State University Press, 1961).

91. The French poet Alfred de Vigny contended that the psychological novel owes its origin to the Christian practice of confession. Louis Ratisbonne, éd., *Journal d'un poète* (Paris: Michel Lévy, 1867), p. 172.

92. As we shall see in a later chapter, the objective study of sexual psychopathology owes its origin to the work of Catholic moral theologians. See p. 296.

93. Henri F. Ellenberger, "The Pathogenic Secret and Its Therapeutics," *Journal of the History of the Behavioral Sciences*, II (1966), 29–42.

94. Heinrich Stilling (Jung-Stilling), *Theobald oder die Schwärmer, eine wahre Geschichte*, 2 vols. (Frankfurt and Leipzig, 1785), I, 287–302.

95. There is a condensed and often inaccurate English translation: Heinrich Stilling, *Theobald or the Fanatic. A True Story*, trans. by Rev. Samuel Schaeffer (New York: Saxton and Miles, 1846). In this English translation, the critical sentence reads as follows: "...in reality, it is nothing higher than a mere natural instinct, the bare excitement of the animal principles what people may refine, sublimate, and raise to the most elegant Platonism, as they will; under all its sublimations it still remains the same gross, low, inferior principle notwithstanding." This is a somewhat refined translation of the plain language used by Reverend Bosius in the original text and to which Sannchen answers with this exclamation: *"Herr Pfarrer! Sie beschämen mich!"* (You make me feel ashamed!)

96. A. M. J. Chastenet de Puységur, *Mémoires pour servir à l'histoire et à l'établissement du magnétisme animal* (1784).

97. Count of Lutzelbourg, *Extraits des journaux d'un magnétiseur attaché à la Société des Amis Réunis de Strasbourg* (Strasbourg: Librairie Académique, 1786), p. 47.

98. Jeremias Gotthelf, *Wie Anne Bäbi Jowäger haushaltet und es ihr mit den Doktorn ergeht*, 2 vols. (Solothurn, 1843–1844).

99. Nathaniel Hawthorne, *The Scarlet Letter* (1850). The Centenary Edition, Vol. I (Columbus: Ohio State University Press, 1962).

100. Henrik Ibsen, *The Lady from the Sea* (Fruen fra havet) (1888), trans. by Eleanor Marx-Aveling (London: Unwin, 1890).

101. See Chap. 5, p. 301; Chap. 7, p. 536; Chap. 10, p. 767.

102. See Chap. 9, p. 714.

103. O. V. Hovorka and A. Kronfeld, *Vergleichende Volksmedizin*, 2 vols. (Stuttgart: Stretcher and Schröder, 1908–1909).

104. Erwin H. Ackerknecht, "Problems of Primitive Medicine," *Bulletin of the History of Medicine*, XI, No. 5 (1942), 503–521.

2

The Emergence of
Dynamic Psychiatry

THE EMERGENCE OF DYNAMIC PSYCHIATRY can be traced to the
year 1775, to a clash between the physician Mesmer and the exorcist
Gassner.

Gassner, an immensely successful and popular healer, personified the
forces of tradition. He had mastered an age-old technique that he applied
in the name of the established religion, but the spirit of the times was
against him. Mesmer, a son of the "Enlightenment," had new ideas, new
techniques, and great hopes for the future. He was instrumental in defeating
Gassner and believed that the time was propitious for the onset of the
scientific revolution that he had in mind.

However, the overthrow of a declining tradition does not in itself in-
augurate a new one. Mesmer's theories were rejected, the organization he
had founded was short-lived, and his therapeutic techniques were modified by his disciples. Nonetheless, he had provided the decisive impulse
toward the elaboration of dynamic psychiatry, even though it would be a
century before the findings of his disciples were to be integrated into the
official corpus of neuropsychiatry by Charcot and his contemporaries.

Gassner and Mesmer

In the first months of 1775, crowds of people, rich and poor, noblemen
and peasants, including among them patients of all kinds, swarmed to
the small town of Ellwangen, in Württemberg, to see Father Johann Joseph
Gassner, one of the most famous healers of all time. He exorcized patients
in the presence of Catholic and Protestant church authorities, physicians,
noblemen of all ranks, members of the bourgeoisie, and sceptics as well
as believers. His every word and gesture and those of his patients were
recorded by a notary public, and the official records were signed by the
distinguished eyewitnesses. Gassner himself was a modest country priest;

53

but once he had donned his ceremonial garments, had taken his seat, and
had the patient kneeling before him, astonishing things would take place.
Numerous collections of official records have survived, as well as accounts
given by eyewitnesses. Among the latter was an Abbé Bourgeois, from
whose narrative we borrow the following details: [1]

> The first patients were two nuns who had been forced to leave their community
> on account of convulsive fits. Gassner told the first one to kneel before him,
> asked her briefly about her name, her illness, and whether she agreed that
> anything he would order should happen. She agreed. Gassner then pronounced
> solemnly in Latin: "If there be anything preternatural about this disease, I order
> in the name of Jesus that it manifest itself immediately." The patient started
> at once to have convulsions. According to Gassner, this was proof that the con-
> vulsions were caused by an evil spirit and not by a natural illness, and he now
> proceeded to demonstrate that he had power over the demon, whom he ordered
> in Latin to produce convulsions in various parts of the patient's body; he called
> forth in turn the exterior manifestations of grief, silliness, scrupulosity, anger,
> and so on, and even the appearance of death. All his orders were punctually
> executed. It now seemed logical that, once a demon had been tamed to that
> point, it should be relatively easy to expel him, which Gassner did. He then
> proceeded in the same manner with the second nun. After the séance had
> ended, Abbé Bourgeois asked her whether it had been very painful; she
> answered that she had only a vague memory of what had happened and that
> she had not suffered much. Gassner then treated a third patient, a high-born
> lady who had previously been afflicted with melancholia. Gassner called forth
> the melancholia and explained to the lady what she was to do in order to
> overcome it in case she was troubled by it again.

Who was the man whose almost miraculous healings attracted such
crowds? The life history of Johann Joseph Gassner (1727–1779) is not
well known. Among biographical accounts, one, by Sierke,[2] is strongly
prejudiced against him; another, by Zimmermann,[3] is better documented
but is biased in his favor; both are based mainly on contemporary pamphlets, not on archive material. Gassner was born in Braz, a village of
indigent peasants in Vorarlberg, a mountainous province of western Austria. He was ordained into the priesthood in 1750, and beginning in
1758 carried out his ministry in Klösterle, a small village in eastern
Switzerland. A few years later, according to Zimmermann, he began to
suffer from violent headaches, dizziness, and other disturbances that became worse whenever he began celebrating the Mass, preaching, or hearing
confession. This particular detail led him to suspect that "the Evil One"
might be at work; he resorted to the Church's exorcism, prayers, and his
troubles eventually disappeared. He then began to exorcise sick people
within his parish, apparently with much success, since patients started to
come to him from all the neighboring districts. In 1774 his fame was in-

creased after he had cured a high-born lady, the Countess Maria Bernardine von Wolfegg.

In the same year Gassner wrote a booklet in which he explained the principles of his healing method.[4] He distinguished two kinds of illnesses: natural ones, that belonged to the realm of the physician, and preternatural ones, that he classified into three categories: *circumsessio* (an imitation of a natural illness, caused by the devil); *obsessio* (the effect of sorcery); and *possessio* (overt diabolical possession), the least frequent of them. In all of these cases Gassner first told the patient that faith in the name of Jesus was an essential prerequisite to being healed and asked his consent for the use of *exorcismus probativus* (trial exorcism). He then solemnly entreated the demon to make manifest the symptoms of the disease; if the symptoms were produced, Gassner considered it proven that the disease was caused by the devil and proceeded to exorcize him. But if no symptoms appeared, he sent the patient to a doctor. In that manner he felt his position to be unimpeachable, both from the viewpoint of Catholic orthodoxy and from that of medicine.

Because of his sudden fame, Gassner received invitations from various places; including Constance, where he performed cures by exorcism without apparently succeeding in gaining the favor of Cardinal Roth, Bishop of Constance. But he found a powerful protector in the Prince Bishop of Regensburg, Count Fugger, who appointed him to an honorary office at his own court. Gassner thus took up residence in the old church-town of Ellwangen and lived there between November 1774 and June 1775. During this period he reached the peak of his activities; patients thronged to Ellwangen, and a storm of polemics raged around him. Dozens of pamphlets were published, either for or against him, in Germany, Austria, Switzerland, and even in France.

Gassner had the support of some ecclesiastical protectors in addition to that of the masses and of those who hoped to be cured by him. (His enemies added that he was particularly popular with the innkeepers and carriage drivers, who largely benefited from the fad.) One of his admirers was the celebrated Zurich pastor Lavater. Among his adversaries were the Catholic theologian Sterzinger, the Protestant theologian Semmler, and most of the representatives of the Enlightenment. Rumors were circulated that cases of possession were sure to occur wherever Gassner's visit was announced; imitators, among them even peasants and children, began exorcizing with his method.[5] In Vienna, animated controversies took place, both for and against him.

Why was there such an outburst of passion? This can be better understood by looking at the situation in Europe in 1775.

Politically, Europe had begun to leave behind the old feudal organization to move toward the development of national states. In contrast with unified nations such as France and England, Germany, under the nominal sovereignty of the Emperor, was an inextricable conglomerate of more than three hundred states of all sizes. Most of continental Europe was under the domination of the Austrian monarchy, which ruled not only over Austria proper but also over a dozen subjected nations. Vienna, an artistic and scientific center of the first order, was the seat of its brilliant court. A strong and rigid system of hereditary social classes prevailed everywhere: nobility, bourgeoisie, peasantry, and laborers, each class having its subclasses. The Church had a firm grip on the lower and middle classes. But Europe had come under the spell of a new philosophy, the Enlightenment, which proclaimed the primacy of Reason over ignorance, superstition, and blind tradition. Under the guidance of Reason, mankind was expected to proceed along a path of uninterrupted progress toward a future of universal happiness. In Western Europe the Enlightenment had developed radical tendencies that were to materialize later in the American and French revolutions. The remainder of Europe was ruled by "enlightened depotism," a compromise between the principles of Enlightenment and the interests of the ruling classes. Maria Theresa of Austria, Frederick II of Prussia, and Catherine the Great of Russia were the typical representatives of that system. In the Church, too, "enlightened" tendencies were gaining ground: the order of Jesuits was taken as scapegoat and abolished in 1773. The notorious witch hunts and processes had not yet completely disappeared (one of the last executions was to be that of Anna Göldi in Glarus, Switzerland, in 1782), but everything related to demons, possession, or exorcism was shunned. [6]

In view of this atmosphere, it becomes understandable why so much opposition arose against Gassner, and also why even his most faithful protectors were forced into positions of extreme caution. The Prince Bishop of Regensburg ordered an inquiry that took place in June 1775, after which Gassner was advised to reduce his activity and to exorcize only patients who had been sent to him by their respective church ministers. The University of Ingolstadt delegated a commission with representatives from its four faculties to make an inquiry. This inquiry was held on May 27, 1775, in Regensburg and had a rather favorable outcome. The Imperial Court in Vienna also took an active interest in the matter. [7]

In Munich the Prince-Elector Max Joseph of Bavaria also appointed an inquiry commission. This commission invited Dr. Mesmer, who claimed to have discovered a new principle called animal magnetism and who had just returned from a journey along the Rhine and to Constance, where he was said to have performed marvelous cures. Mesmer arrived in Munich, and, on November 23, 1775, gave demonstrations during which he elicited in patients the appearance and disappearance of various symptoms, even of convulsions, simply by a touch of his finger. [8] Father Kennedy, the Secretary of the Academy, was suffering from convulsions, and Mesmer showed that he was able to bring them forth in him and dispel them at will. On the following day, in the presence of court members and members of the Academy, he provoked attacks in an epileptic and claimed that he was able to cure the patient through animal magnetism. In effect this amounted to Gassner's procedure, without involving the use of exorcism. Mesmer declared that Gassner was undoubtedly an honest man, but that he was curing his patients through animal magnetism without being aware of it. We can imagine that, upon hearing of Mesmer's report, Gassner must have felt somewhat like Moses when the Egyptian wizards reproduced his miracles in the Pharaoh's presence. But unlike Moses, Gassner had not been permitted to witness Mesmer's performance or to reply to his report.

Meanwhile, the Imperial Court, which was decidedly not favorably disposed toward Gassner, had asked the Prince Bishop of Regensburg to dismiss him, and he was sent to the small community of Pondorf. In Rome, Pope Pius VI (Giovanni Angelo Braschi) had ordered an investigation into Gassner's activities. In the decree that followed, it was stated that while exorcism was a common and salutary practice of the Church, it was to be performed with discretion and with strict adherence to the prescriptions of the Roman ritual.

Gassner died in Pondorf on April 4, 1779. His tombstone bore a lengthy inscription in Latin, describing him as the most celebrated exorcist of his time.

No one ever questioned Gassner's absolute piety, his lack of pretentions, and his unselfishness. Unfortunately for him, he had come too late, and the controversies that had been raging around him had a much more important object: the struggle between the new Enlightenment and the forces of tradition. Gassner's downfall prepared the way for a healing method that retained no ties with religion and satisfied the requirements of an "enlightened" era. Curing the sick is not enough; one must cure them with methods accepted by the community.

Franz Anton Mesmer (1734–1815)

The fateful turning point from exorcism to dynamic psychotherapy was thus reached in 1775 by Franz Anton Mesmer, who has been at times compared to Columbus. Both Columbus and Mesmer discovered a new world, both remained in error for the remainder of their lives about the real nature of their discoveries, and both died bitterly disappointed men. Another point of similarity is the imperfect knowledge we have of the details of their lives.

None of Mesmer's disciples seems to have been interested in the story of his master's life. The first to inquire about it was Justinus Kerner,[9] who traveled to Meersburg, where Mesmer had died, and gathered firsthand documents and information about him. Recently, the research done by Tischner,[10] Schürer-Waldheim,[11] Bittel,[12] Wohleb,[13] Milt,[14] and

Vinchon[15] has shed some light on several periods of Mesmer's life, about which, however, large gaps still remain.

Franz Anton Mesmer was born on May 23, 1734, in Iznang, a small village on the German shore of Lake Constance, the third of nine children. His father was a game warden in the service of the Prince Bishop of Constance. Nothing is known of Franz Anton's childhood and youth; the first recorded fact of his life states that in 1752, at the age of 18, he was registered at the Jesuit Theological School in Dillingen. In 1754, Mesmer registered at the Jesuit University of Ingolstadt for his third year in theology. His activities and whereabouts during the years 1754 to 1759 are not known. It is likely that he spent them studying philosophy. He registered as a law student in Vienna in 1759 and changed to medicine the following year. Mesmer completed his medical studies in Vienna, where his dissertation on the influence of planets on human diseases won him his degree in 1766, at the age of thirty-three.

Mesmer's scholastic career was remarkable in several regards. It was certainly not unusual for the Church to notice an intelligent and diligent boy, and to provide him with the possibility of studying in ecclesiastical schools with a view toward a future clerical vocation. One of his brothers, Johann, later became a priest in a nearby community, and this is obviously how Franz Anton also began his studies. However it is most unlikely that the Church or his family continued supporting him when he changed from theology to philosophy, then to law, and finally from law to medicine. It is more probable that he found rich protectors, as he did in later periods of his life. He might also have been associated with secret societies.

In 1767 the young doctor married a wealthy widow of noble descent, Maria Anna von Posch, and established himself in Vienna as a physician.[16] A refined man of the world and a patron of the arts, he lived on a splendid estate of which Leopold Mozart said: "The garden is incomparable, with its avenues and statues, a theater, a birdhouse, a dove-cot, and a belvedere on the summit."[17] Friends who visited the house included the musicians Gluck, Haydn, and the Mozart family. (Wolfgang Amadeus Mozart's earliest opera, *Bastien und Bastienne,* had its first performance in Mesmer's private theater.) Mesmer was one of the first to play the glass-harmonica, a new musical instrument that had been perfected in America by Benjamin Franklin.

During the years 1773 to 1774, Mesmer treated in his own home a twenty-seven-year-old patient, Fräulein Oesterlin, who was afflicted with no less than fifteen seemingly severe symptoms. He studied the quasi-astronomical periodicity of her crises and became able to predict their recurrence. He then endeavored to modify their course. It had just become known that some English physicians were treating certain diseases with magnets, and it occurred to Mesmer to provoke an "artificial tide" in his patient. After making her swallow a preparation containing iron, he attached three specially conceived magnets to her body, one on her stomach, the two others on her legs. The patient soon began to feel extraordinary streams of a mysterious fluid running downward through her body, and all her evils were swept away for several hours. This happened, Mesmer reported, on July 28, 1774, a historical date.[18] He understood that these effects on the patient could not possibly be caused by the magnets alone, but must issue from an "essentially different agent," that is, that these magnetic streams in his patient were produced by a fluid accumulated in his own person, which he called animal magnetism. The magnet was but an auxiliary means of reinforcing that animal magnetism and giving it a direction.

Mesmer was forty years old when he made this discovery. He was to devote the rest of his life to its elaboration and to present it to the world.

As a result of this new method, Fräulein Oesterlin improved so greatly that she was able to marry Mesmer's stepson and become a healthy wife and mother. But the first disappointments were not long in coming. Father Hell, the astronomer who had provided Mesmer with magnets, claimed that the discovery was his, while Mesmer's medical friends strongly disapproved of his new research trend. Notwithstanding, Mesmer must have at that time become somewhat of a celebrity, because in June 1775, Baron Horeczky de Horka, a Hungarian nobleman, invited him to his castle in Rohow, Slovakia. The Baron was suffering from nervous spasms, which had persisted despite the efforts of Vienna's foremost physicians. Mesmer's stay in Rohow lasted about two weeks, of which an account was written by the Baron's house teacher Seyfert, who served as Mesmer's interpreter and, assuming that he was a quack, observed him keenly in order to unmask him.[19]

Shortly after Mesmer's arrival, several of the castle's inhabitants began to feel pains or peculiar sensations in their bodies as soon as they came near him. Even the sceptical Seyfert noticed that he was seized with an invincible sleepiness when Mesmer played music. It was not long before he became thoroughly convinced of Mesmer's extraordinary powers. He saw how Mesmer could elicit morbid symptoms in people around him, particularly in those whom he had magnetized. A lady who was singing lost her voice as soon as Mesmer touched her hand and recovered it when he made a gesture with his finger. As they were sitting together, Seyfert saw that Mesmer was able to influence people sitting in another room simply by pointing to their images reflected in a mirror, even though these people could see him neither directly nor indirectly in the mirror. At another time, when two musicians were playing the horn, Mesmer touched one of the instruments; immediately, a group of people—who could not see him—began to have symptoms that disappeared when Mesmer removed his hand. Meanwhile, the rumor had spread that an extraordinary healer had arrived at Rohow, and patients came from all the neighboring areas to see him. Mesmer magnetized many of them, while sending others to see their own doctors.

On the sixth evening, Mesmer announced that the Baron would have a crisis on the following morning—which actually happened. The crisis was unusually violent, and it was reported that the fever increased or decreased according to whether Mesmer came closer to the patient or drew away from him. A second, less violent crisis occurred a few days later, but the Baron found the treatment too drastic and Mesmer left Rohow, though not without healing, at the last minute, a peasant who had suddenly lost his hearing six weeks before.

Seyfert also relates his talks with Mesmer, who admitted that Gassner possessed magnetism to an extraordinary degree and that his own powers were not as great, wherefore he had to reinforce it by certain means. Seyfert had reasons to believe that Mesmer did so by wearing magnets on his body and by keeping them in his bed.

The following month, July 1775, Mesmer traveled to the shores of Lake Constance, his homeland, where he performed several sensational cures closely following in Gassner's footsteps. His stay in Rohow had apparently convinced him that he was able to outdo Gassner.[20] As we have seen, this glorious period of Mesmer's life culminated in his being called to Munich by the Prince-Elector, his demonstration of his own magnetic powers, his testimony about Gassner, and his nomination as a member of the Bavarian Academy of Sciences. When he returned to Vienna at the end of 1775, Mesmer must have been sure that his grandiose discovery would bring him lasting fame.

But the Viennese medical world was still indifferent or even hostile. Mesmer took several patients into his own home. One of them, Maria-Theresia Paradis, the eighteen-year-old daughter of a wealthy and influential civil servant, had been blind since the age of three and one-half. According to a biographer, she had been given the most refined education with the help of specially devised instruments, such as embossed maps to teach her geography, and Kempelen, the famous maker of automatons, had built her a printing machine with which she was able to write.[21] She moved around gracefully, could dance and perform needlework—but her greatest talent was music, which gained her the special attention and protection of the Empress Maria Theresa.[22] Vienna's foremost physicians had treated her for many years without results (she had even received more than three thousand electric discharges). But after a series of magnetic sessions with Mesmer, she declared that she was seeing. Her first visual perception was that of Mesmer; she found that the human nose had a strange, even frightening shape and expressed fear that it might hurt her eyes.[23] Her sight was gradually restored—or, this is what she said and what Mesmer announced—and her family expressed great delight. But her previous physicians denied the reality of the cure. A medical commission emphasized that the patient claimed to see only when Mesmer was present. An acute conflict arose between Mesmer and the Paradis family; the patient lost her sight for good. She returned home and pursued her career as a blind musician. Mesmer suggested that her cure was neither in her nor in her family's interest: she would have lost her fame as a blind musician, and perhaps also the generous financial support of the Empress.[24]

Soon afterward, in the latter part of the year 1777, Mesmer left Vienna. The reasons for his departure are unknown; his enemies later contended that he had been forced to leave. It had been assumed that he was disturbed by his failure in the case of Maria-Theresia Paradis and by the hostility of his colleagues. It may also be that the young patient had developed a strong attachment for him, and Mesmer a similarly strong attachment for her. (It is noteworthy that his wife remained in Vienna; he never saw her again.) But the true reason lies perhaps in Mesmer's oversensitive and unstable character, in his psychopathology.

According to his own account, Mesmer had undergone a depressive period.[25] He despaired of ever finding the truth. He would walk in the woods, talking to the trees, and for three months tried to think without the help of words. Gradually, he recovered his peace of mind and his self-confidence, and came to visualize the world in a completely new aspect. He now felt that it was his mission to make his great discovery known to the world. He left for Paris and arrived there in February 1778.

The atmosphere that Mesmer found in Paris was quite different from the one he had left in Vienna. The Austrian Empire was a stable state with an energetic government, a proficient administration, a watchful police. Paris was no less a cultural center than Vienna, but life there was strangely restless. Under a weak king and a frivolous queen the government was unstable and the financial situation catastrophic; enormous sums of money were engulfed in graft, speculation, and gambling. The ideas of Enlightenment developed a radical and antireligious tendency. The nobility was clinging obstinately to its exorbitant privileges, but paradoxically was showing a remarkable trend toward philanthropy and disinterested public service. In a disastrous war against England, France had lost India and Canada; now, partly out of feelings of revenge, the public was enthusiastic about the American War of Independence. There was, especially in Paris, a general tendency toward mass hysteria; the public went from one craze to another.[26]

It seems that Mesmer's fame had preceded him to Paris, where at that time a peculiar interest prevailed for distinguished foreigners. Mesmer was forty-three years of age, a tall, sturdy, handsome man whose imposing personality and worldly manners gained him easy access into French society, despite his strong German accent. For reasons not known, he soon parted with his first associate, the French surgeon Le Roux, and began magnetizing patients in a private residence in Créteil. He then settled in a private mansion on the Place Vendôme, where he received patients from the highest social circles and magnetized them for large fees. He was extremely eager to form contacts with representatives of the scientific bodies: Académie des Sciences, Société Royale de Médecine, Faculté de

Médecine. He gained at least one influential disciple in Dr. D'Eslon, private physician to the Count d'Artois, one of the King's brothers. Mesmer supplemented his efforts with publications written by himself[27] and by D'Eslon.[28]

In the meantime his practice had gradually increased. Before leaving Vienna, he had dispensed with the use of magnets and electricity as auxiliary means. In 1780 or 1781, having more patients than he was able to treat individually, he inaugurated a collective treatment, the *baquet,* which will be discussed later. Two of his clients showed him strong personal devotion: Nicolas Bergasse, a skillful lawyer with keen philosophical interests, who was politically active[29] and the banker Kornmann, whose young child Mesmer treated for a severe eye disease.[30]

Mesmer's system, as he expounded it in 27 points in the year 1779, can be summarized in four basic principles.[31] (1) A subtle physical fluid fills the universe and forms a connecting medium between man, the earth, and the heavenly bodies, and also between man and man. (2) Disease originates from the unequal distribution of this fluid in the human body; recovery is achieved when the equilibrium is restored. (3) With the help of certain techniques, this fluid can be channeled, stored, and conveyed to other persons. (4) In this manner, "crises" can be provoked in patients and diseases cured.

It is fairly easy to distinguish the various elements in what Mesmer and his disciples called the doctrine. The first and most immediate one was Mesmer's intuition of being the bearer of a mysterious fluid, animal magnetism, which he had noticed in himself for the first time when treating Fräulein Oesterlin. Mesmer described how he was able to provoke the appearance of symptoms in patients by his physical presence or by his gestures; he also reported that when he approached a man who was undergoing a bloodletting, the blood began flowing in a different direction. According to Mesmer, every human being possesses a certain amount of animal magnetism: Gassner possessed it to a very high degree, Mesmer had it somewhat less, and the sick have less than the healthy. An analogy could be drawn between this theory and the Polynesian concept of "mana," a universal, impersonal energy that can be stored in persons, objects, or places, and can be detected only through its objective effects.

The second element of the doctrine was the physical theories that were supposed to explain the nature and action of animal magnetism. Being a son of the Enlightenment, Mesmer was seeking a "rational" explanation and rejected any kind of mystical theory. On the other hand, since psychology was almost nonexistent at that time, he was naturally led to think of a physical concept, of something in the form of Newton's universal gravitation or of electricity. In his medical dissertation, Mesmer had already described a universal fluid pervading the cosmos, which he had named *gravitatio universalis.* Through this phenomenon, the influence of the sun, moon, and planets on the human body could be explained, as well as the periodical manifestations of certain diseases. He later called this fluid general agent. It was believed to exist in several forms: one was the influence of the magnet, another was electricity, and another was animal magnetism. This physical part of the doctrine was undoubtedly its weakest point and always remained unclear in Mesmer's mind because he was not a good systematizer.

A third element of Mesmer's system was the analogies given by the contemporary discoveries in the field of electricity. Mesmer imagined his fluid as having poles, streams, discharges, conductors, isolators, and accumulators. His *baquet,* an instrument that was supposed to concentrate the fluid, was an imitation of the recently invented Leyden jar. He also taught that there was a positive and a negative fluid that neutralized each other—an assumption that was never accepted by his disciples.

The fourth element of the doctrine was the theory of crises, obviously derived from Gassner's practice. Gassner believed the crisis to be the evidence of possession as well as the first step in the procedure of exorcism. For Mesmer, the crisis was the artificially procured evidence of the disease and the means to its cure. Crises, he said, were specific: in an asthmatic it would be an attack of asthma and in an epileptic it would be an epileptic fit. When the patient was repeatedly provoked, these crises became less and less severe. Eventually they disappeared, and this meant recovery.

These basic ingredients that Mesmer tried to synthesize in his doctrine led to his famous aphorism: "There is only one illness and one healing." No medication or therapeutic procedure ever cured a patient by itself; cures were achieved only through the effect of magnetism, although physicians had not been aware of it. Animal magnetism would now furnish mankind with a universal means of curing and preventing all illnesses, thus "bringing medicine to its highest point of perfection."

Mesmer's egocentricity led him to expect that medical schools would accept a theory that would cancel all that had been discovered since Hippocrates, and would cause the medical profession to become superfluous. Not surprisingly, the type of therapy performed by Mesmer was as repugnant to contemporary medicine as contemporary medicine was to him. Mesmer used no medication other than magnetic water. He would sit in front of his patient with his knees touching the patient's knees, pressing the patient's thumbs in his hands, looking fixedly into his eyes, then touching his hypochondria and making passes over his limbs. Many patients felt peculiar sensations or fell into crises. This was supposed to bring forth the cure.

Mesmer's collective method was still more extraordinary. An English physician, John Grieve, who was in Paris in May 1784, described in a letter his visit to Mesmer's house, noting that there were never less than two hundred patients at one time: [32]

I was in his home the other day and was witness to his method of operating. In the middle of the room is placed a vessel of about a foot and a half high which is called here a *baquet*. It is so large that twenty people can easily sit round it; near the edge of the lid which covers it, there are holes pierced corresponding to the number of persons who are to surround it; into these holes are introduced iron rods, bent at right angles outwards, and of different heights, so as to answer to the part of the body to which they are to be applied. Besides these rods, there is a rope which communicates between the *baquet* and one of the patients, and from him is carried to another, and so on the whole round. The most sensible effects are produced on the approach of Mesmer, who is said to convey the fluid by certain motions of his hands or eyes, without touching the person. I have talked with several who have witnessed these effects, who have convulsions occasioned and removed by a movement of the hand. . . .

The entire setting was intended to increase the magnetic influences: large mirrors reflected the fluid, which was conveyed by musical sounds emanating from magnetized instruments. Mesmer himself sometimes played on his glass-harmonica, an instrument that many people found to be shattering. The patients sat in silence. After a while some of them would experience peculiar bodily feelings, and the few who fell into crises were handled by Mesmer and his assistants in the *chambre des crises* (crisis room). Sometimes a wave of crises spread from one patient to another.

An even more extraordinary procedure was that of the magnetized tree, a kind of collective outdoor therapy for the poor.

Such therapeutic procedures seemed so extravagant that few physicians could escape from feeling that Mesmer was a quack. Professional resentment must have been increased by Mesmer's growing success and by the fabulous fees he demanded from his noble and wealthy patients.

In the middle of 1782, Mesmer seems to have understood that he had reached an impasse. For five years he had worked toward having his discovery acknowledged by the scientific societies, which he would then have sold at great profit to the French government so that he could apply and teach his method in a public hospital. But he was further than ever from his goal. In July 1782 he left for a sojourn in Spa—a health resort in what is today Belgium—with his devoted friends Bergasse and Kornmann. According to Bergasse's account, Mesmer received a letter stating that D'Eslon, pretending to replace him, had opened a practice of animal magnetism.[33] Mesmer was dismayed and furious at the "traitor" and visualized his own ruin. He was sure that after having stolen his secret, D'Eslon would also steal his clientele. The lawyer Bergasse and the financier Kornmann then formulated a new plan: they would organize a subscription to raise a large sum of money in order to buy Mesmer's discovery. The subscribers would be given possession of the "secret" and would be organized into a society that would educate students and spread Mesmer's teaching.

The project was a huge success. In spite of the enormous account of money demanded from the subscribers, they were found. Among them were the most illustrious names of the city and the court, names belonging to the most ancient aristocratic families such as Noailles, Montesquieu, and the Marquis de Lafayette, as well as prominent magistrates, lawyers, and physicians. The Bailli des Barres of the Order of Malta was to introduce magnetism to the Knights on the island.[34] However, growing difficulties arose between Mesmer and his disciples. Bergasse later published a documented account about these arduous negotiations of 1783 and 1784, which—if all the details were true—shows Mesmer as a fundamentally egocentric and suspicious man, moody, despotic, greedy, and at times even dishonest.

Nevertheless, the society (called Société de l'Harmonie)—a strange mixture of business enterprise, private school, and masonic lodge—was launched and flourished. Branches were founded in other French cities and towns. It secured a large fortune for Mesmer, in addition to his earnings from his magnetic practices. The society also published an epitome of Mesmer's doctrine[35] and transformed what had been one man's secret into the common knowledge of an enthusiastic group. Mesmer's despotism was often resented by his disciples, but animal magnetism was now an established institution in France, and it developed swiftly. The interest of the public, which had been focused on the American War of Independence and the peace treaty with England, was now released and turned toward Mesmer.

The year 1784 was as fateful for Mesmer as 1776 had been for Gassner: he encountered a peak of success, agitation, and then a rapid downfall.

In March 1784, as a result of the agitation around Mesmer, the King appointed a commission of inquiry consisting of members of the Académie des Sciences and the Académie de Médecine, and another commission consisting of members of the Société Royale. These commissions comprised the foremost scientists of their day: the astronomer Bailly, the chemist Lavoisier, the physician Guillotin, and the American ambassador Benjamin Franklin. The program of experiments had been devised by Lavoisier and was a model of the application of the experimental method.[36] The litigious point was not whether Mesmer cured his patients but rather his contention to have discovered a new physical fluid. The commissions' conclusion was that no evidence could be found of the physical existence of a "magnetic fluid." Possible therapeutic effects were not denied, but were ascribed to "imagination."[37] A supplementary and secret report was drafted for the King and pointed to the dangers resulting from the erotic attraction of the magnetized female patient to her male magnetizer.[38] One of the commissioners, Jussieu, disassociated himself from his colleagues and wrote a report suggesting that there certainly was an unknown efficient agent at work, probably "animal heat."[39] Mesmer was indignant because the commissioners had not come to him with their inquiries, but had gone to the "traitor" D'Eslon. Later, however, this circumstance proved fortunate for Mesmer: when the Public Ministry, on the basis of the commissioners' report, decided to prohibit the practice of animal magnetism, Bergasse succeeded in his efforts to have the interdiction lifted by Parliament—the highest judicial instance—on a legal technicality: the commissioners' report concerned D'Eslon's, not Mesmer's practice.

In any event, the reports do not seem to have seriously harmed the development of the magnetic movement. The Société de l'Harmonie developed its activities and similar societies were founded in various French cities. Simultaneously, however, the movement experienced an unprecedented number of setbacks: Mesmer was abundantly ridiculed in cartoons, popular songs, and satirical plays.[40] There was the unfortunate episode involving Court de Gébelin, a celebrated scholar who published an enthusiastic pamphlet about Mesmer after having been "cured" by him, whereupon he suffered a relapse and died in Mesmer's own home.[41] But public agitation was diverted from Mesmer a few months later by the new themes of Count Allesandrodi Cagliostro (Giuseppe Balsamo) and the scandal of the "Queen's necklace." Far more serious, as far as Mesmer was concerned, were the criticisms leveled against him by scientists and scholars. An anonymous author published a book, L'anti-magnétisme,[42] in which he traced in an objective manner the sources of Mesmer's doctrine and showed the connection between his healing method and that of Gassner. Another author, Thouret,[43] published an even more thorough study, taking Mesmer's 27 propositions one by one and showing that each of them had already been stated in much the same terms by authors such as Paracelsus, Van Helmont and Goclenius, and above all by Mead and Maxwell. Thouret concluded that Mesmer's theory, far from being a novelty, was an ancient system that had been given up for almost one century. Mesmer denied ever having read any of those authors (it had not yet become fashionable to call such sources by the name of "precursors"). Physicists, for their part, would not hear of the so-called magnetic fluid. A physician and physicist by the name of Marat declared that animal magnetism had no claim to being a physical theory.[44]

Still worse from Mesmer's point of view was the fact that he had hardly begun to unveil his doctrine when his disciples rebelled. They found it vague and incoherent, even though D'Eslon had already given some clear and limpid formulations of it. A Comité d'instruction was appointed to publish the doctrine in a form acceptable to the students.[45] Bergasse, who was playing a prominent role in the society, had found in Mesmerism the basis for a new world philosophy and expounded his theory in a work titled "Theory of the World and of Organized Beings."[46] It was published in limited numbers, and, in order to give it the aspect of a secret knowledge, 115 key words were replaced by symbols so that the uninitiated were unable to understand it. But this publication aroused Mesmer's wrath, and, following a sharp polemic between the two men, Bergasse left the society.

Meanwhile, many members had become disillusioned and they, too, defected. Worse perhaps, from Mesmer's viewpoint, was that one of his most faithful disciples, Puységur, of whom we shall speak later, though proclaiming his loyalty to Mesmer's teaching, discovered magnetic sleep, which was to give a new direction to the movement.

Another setback of a more personal nature was an incident that occurred on Good Friday (April 16, 1784) at the Concert Spirituel du Carême in the presence of the royal court and the elite of Parisian society. A blind young musician had arrived from Vienna to play the harpsicord—Maria-Theresia Paradis. Grimm reported that "all eyes turned toward Mesmer who had been unwise enough to come to the concert. He was well aware of being the center of attention and suffered one of the worst humiliations of his life."[47] His enemies promptly revived the old story that Mesmer had pretended to cure her but it was proven that he failed. Maria-Theresia spent the following six months in France, and her presence in Paris must have been very disturbing to Mesmer. In August of that year the Société de l'Harmonie in Lyons invited him to demonstrate his skill in the presence of Prince Henry of Prussia (a brother of King Frederick II). To his own consternation and to the dismay of his disciples, he failed utterly. It is likely that Mesmer reacted to those events as he had done in 1777: by falling into a depression and taking to flight.

In fact, Mesmer disappeared from Paris, having probably left at the beginning of 1785. His whereabouts were unknown to his disciples. Rumors circulated that he was living in England under an assumed name. The movement he had founded was developing more and more in the direction given it by Puységur.

Mesmer's activities during the following twenty years are largely unknown. Only part of his wanderings through Switzerland, Germany, France, and Austria have been traced.[48] It has been found that when he returned to Vienna in 1793, he was expelled as being politically suspect, and that, in 1794, his name was linked with an obscure political plot. He went to Switzerland, where he acquired Swiss citizenship, and settled in Frauenfeld, a small town near Lake Constance. He had lost part of his fortune but was still sufficiently wealthy to live as a man of leisure for the remainder of his life, in the style of a rich aristocrat. Recent research has revealed testimonies of people who knew him during that time. They describe him as a man of refined worldly manners, but as proud and egocentric, showing no interest in other people's ideas. He resented the world that had not accepted his discovery, the physicians who had rejected him, and his disciples who had distorted his teachings.

By that time Mesmer was so completely forgotten that most of his disciples did not even know that he was still alive. Wolfart, a German physician, finally went to visit him in 1812. A Romanticist and patriot, Wolfart was surprised that Mesmer expressed himself exclusively in French—in the

manner of the old German aristocracy. He published a German translation
of Mesmer's last book, which contained not only the ultimate outline of his
system but also a collection of his opinions on a great variety of subjects:
education, social life, public festivities, taxes, and prisons.[49] Unfortunately,
most of the papers that Mesmer entrusted to Wolfart were lost. Wolfart
was so careless that, when publishing Mesmer's book, he gave his Christian
name as Friedrich instead of Franz.

One or two years before his death, Mesmer moved to Meersburg, on the
shores of Lake Constance, and died there on March 5, 1815—a few miles
from his birthplace.

When Justinus Kerner visited Meersburg in 1854, he heard wondrous
stories from old people who had known the great man.[50] He was told that
when Mesmer went to the island of Mainau, flocks of birds would fly toward
him, following him wherever he walked, and settling around him when he
sat down. Mesmer, they added, had a pet canary in an open cage in his
room. Every morning the bird would fly to his master, perch on his head,
and wake him with his song. He would keep him company during his
breakfast, sometimes dropping lumps of sugar into his cup. With a slight
stroke of his hand, Mesmer would put the bird to sleep or wake it up. One
morning the bird remained in its cage: Mesmer had died during the night.
The canary sang and ate no more, and a few days later he was found
dead in his cage.

What was the true personality of this man, who, in his homeland, had
left the reputation of being a wizard? We cannot obtain a satisfactory
answer; too much about him is unknown. We know nothing of his childhood
nor of his emotional life, aside from his unhappy marriage. On the basis of
existing documents, several pictures can be drawn:

The first and best-known picture is given by his French disciples, especially
by Bergasse in his lengthy account filled with bitter resentment, written
after Mesmer had expelled him from the movement.[51] In these accounts
Mesmer is shown as a man dominated by the fixed idea that he had made
an epoch-making discovery that the world ought to accept immediately,
even before it could be fully revealed. He wanted to keep his secret to
himself as long as he pleased and to make it known only when it became
convenient for him. His doctrine of animal magnetism, however, should
remain his permanent and exclusive property; no one was allowed to
add, modify, of subtract anything without his permission. He demanded
absolute devotion from his disciples, although he did not feel the need to
reciprocate by showing them gratitude, and he broke with anyone who
manifested independent ideas. Mesmer felt as though he was living in a
world of enemies who were continually trying to steal, distort, or suppress
his discovery. He took indifference for hostility and contradiction for persecution. This picture of Mesmer is perhaps not very different from that
of several other great scientists. It is (in Jung's terms) the typical syndrome

of "psychological inflation" and must be considered a secondary development superimposed on a more basic personality structure.

Mesmer felt a mysterious power within himself, which was demonstrated by his sensational healings and by the strange occurrences at the castle of Rohow. But in addition to these probably temporary occurrences, he possessed to a high degree a "personal magnetism"—a compelling mixture of charm and authority. He was unequaled in the art of convincing people and obtaining great favors from them. This may also explain the mystery of his social climbing in an era of impermeable class differentiation and his ability to deal with princes and aristocrats on a basis of equality.

The fluctuations of his personal magnetism were perhaps subordinated to certain more basic psychopathological features: a morbid oversensitivity, moodiness, and alternating elations and depressions. During his periods of success he showed a restless, almost hypomanic, activity. It seems that he expressed at times what might be called paranoiac delusions of grandeur. (A Swiss physician, Egg, relates that Mesmer had told him in 1804 that running water was magnetized because he, Mesmer, had magnetized the sun twenty years before.)[52] But he was also subject to sudden fits of discouragement. Mesmer described the abnormal condition he suffered from at the end of 1776. It is quite possible that something similar occurred in 1785. Both these episodes were perhaps associated with his feelings that his magnetic powers were exhausted.

With his uncanny powers, Mesmer is closer to the ancient magician than to the twentieth-century psychotherapist. His victory over Gassner reminds one more of a contest between rival Alaskan shamans than of a modern psychiatric controversy. However, his doctrine contained the seeds of several basic tenets of modern psychiatry:

A magnetizer, Mesmer proclaimed, is the therapeutic agent of his cures: his power lies in himself. To make healing possible, he must first establish a rapport, that is a kind of "tuning in," with his patient. Healing occurs through crises—manifestations of latent diseases produced artificially by the magnetizer so that he may control them. It is better to produce several, steadily weaker ones than one severe crisis. In collective treatment the magnetizer should control the reactions of the patients on one another.

Mesmer grouped his disciples into a society in which physicians and lay magnetizers were on an equal footing. Its members, who had made heavy financial sacrifices, learned his doctrine, discussed the results of their therapeutic work, and maintained the unity of the movement.

It is an open question as to whether Mesmer was a precursor of dynamic psychiatry or its actual founder. Any pioneer is always the successor of previous ones and the precursor of others. There is no doubt, however, that the development of modern dynamic psychiatry can be traced to Mesmer's animal magnetism, and that posterity has been remarkably ungrateful to him.

Puységur and the New Magnetism

There always comes a time when the creation emancipates itself from the creator and takes its independent course of life.

Mesmer had hardly begun to unveil his doctrine when one of his most faithful disciples, the Marquis de Puységur, made a discovery that was to give a new course to the evolution of magnetism. In the opinion of certain historians, this discovery equals or even exceeds the importance of Mesmer's own work. Charles Richet has said "the name of Puységur must be put on the same rank as that of Mesmer. . . . Mesmer is no doubt the *initiator* of magnetism, but not its true *founder.*"[53] Without Puységur, he adds, magnetism would have been short-lived and would have left only the memory of a transient psychic epidemic around the *baquet.*

Among Mesmer's most enthusiastic disciples were the three brothers De Puységur, who belonged to one of the most illustrious families of the French nobility. In the course of the centuries, the family had given France many prominent men, particularly in the military field.[54] Their family belonged to that branch of the French aristocracy that was active in philanthropic affairs. All three brothers became Mesmer's students and played a role in the history of animal magnetism.[55]

The youngest brother, Viscount Jacques Maxime de Chastenet de Puységur (1755–1848), gained his reputation on the parade grounds in Bayonne: an officer, apparently stricken with apoplexy, had fallen to the ground. The Viscount magnetized him on the spot and healed him in the presence of all the troops. He is said to have been subsequently placed in charge of the treatment of the sick soldiers in his regiment.

The second brother, Antoine-Hyacinthe, called the Count de Chastenet (1752–1809), was a naval officer who had made investigations about the Guanches of the Canary Islands and brought some of their mummies back to Paris. It was he who introduced animal magnetism into Saint-Domingue, the rich and prosperous French slave colony. The white masters soon swarmed around the *baquets,* and the Negro slaves demanded and obtained a *baquet* for their own use.

The oldest brother, Amand-Marie-Jacques de Chastenet, Marquis de Puységur (1751–1825), an artillery officer who had distinguished himself at the siege of Gibraltar and taken part at an official mission to Russia, divided his time between his military life and his castle in Buzancy near Soissons, where he owned the immense property of his ancestors. As did many of his aristocratic contemporaries, he kept a *cabinet de physique,* where he tried various experiments with electricity. Sceptical at first about Mesmerism, he was converted to it by his brother Antoine-Hyacinthe and began to give individual and collective treatments on his estate.[56]

One of his first patients was Victor Race, a young peasant of twenty-three, whose family had been in the service of the Puységur family for several generations. Victor, who was suffering from a mild respiratory disease, was easily magnetized and, in that state, showed a very peculiar crisis. There were no convulsions, no disorderly movements, as was the case with other patients; rather, he fell into a strange kind of sleep in which he seemed to be more awake and aware than in his normal waking state. He spoke aloud, answered questions, and displayed a far brighter mind than in his normal condition. The Marquis, singing inaudibly to himself, noticed that the young man would sing the same songs aloud. Victor had no memory of the crisis once it had passed. Intrigued, Puységur produced this type of crisis again in Victor and tried it successfully on several other subjects. Once they were in that state, they were able to diagnose their own diseases, foresee its course of evolution (which Puységur called the *pressensation*), and prescribe the treatments.

The number of his patients became so great that Puységur soon organized a collective treatment. The public square of the small village of Buzancy, surrounded by thatched cottages and trees, was not far from the majestic castle of the Puységurs. In the center of that square stood a large, beautiful old elm tree, at the foot of which a spring poured forth its limpid waters. The peasants would sit on the surrounding stone benches. Ropes were hung in the tree's main branches and around its trunk, and the patients wound ends of the rope around the ailing parts of their bodies. The operation started with the patients' forming a chain, holding one another by the thumbs. They began to feel the fluid circulate among them to varying degrees. After a while, the master ordered the chain to be broken and the patients to rub their hands. He then chose a few of them and, touching them with his iron rod, put them into "perfect crisis." These subjects, now called physicians, diagnosed diseases and prescribed treatment. To "disenchant" them (that is, to wake them from their magnetic sleep), Puységur ordered them to kiss the tree, whereupon they awoke, remembering nothing of what had happened. These treatments were carried out in the presence of curious and enthusiastic onlookers. It was reported that within little more than one month, 62 of the 300 patients had been cured of various ailments.

The new type of treatment introduced by Puységur thus included two different manifestations: the first was the "perfect crisis" itself with its appearance of a waking state, its elective relationship with the magnetizer whose commands the subject executed, and the amnesia that followed it. The analogy of that magnetic sleep with natural somnambulism was soon recognized, hence the name "artificial somnambulism." (Only much later was Braid to give this condition its present name, "hypnosis.") The second aspect was the "lucidity" displayed by certain patients, that is, their capacity to diagnose diseases, predict their courses, and prescribe treatments for themselves as well as for others with whom they were placed in rapport.

Puységur soon learned from Victor himself of another psychotherapeutic use of the perfect crisis.[57] At that time, Victor was very concerned about a quarrel he had with his sister. He would never have dared talk about it to anyone; but when in magnetic sleep, he felt free to confide in the Marquis, who suggested to Victor to look after his own interests and to find a satisfactory solution. Victor then actually took steps to rectify his situation.

The role played by Victor Race in the history of magnetism deserves special attention. Not only was he one of Puységur's first patients, and the very first to fall into the perfect crisis—of which he became the prototype— but it was from him that the Marquis learned fundamental principles. At the beginning of 1785, Puységur took Victor to Paris where he used him for demonstrations. Twice he showed him to Mesmer, whose reaction is not known. A worsening occurred in Victor's condition, who explained during magnetic sleep that it resulted from his being exhibited to curious and often incredulous people. Puységur thus learned that magnetism should be used only for therapeutic purposes and not for experimentation and demonstrations. Furthermore, while experimenting with Victor, Puységur realized the vanity of Mesmer's teaching of the physical fluid and understood that the real agent in the cure was the magnetizer's will.[58]

The effect of Puységur's discoveries was considerable. The wonderful cures of Buzancy were imitated elsewhere. From remote villages came idyllic stories of peasants and servants healed at the foot of magnetized trees by philanthropic counts and marquises.[59] But above all, the new kind of magnetic treatment introduced by Puységur spread swiftly, much to Mesmer's displeasure who contended that magnetic sleep was but one of the many forms of crises, and he firmly upheld his doctrine of the physical fluid, although many of his disciples defected. From that day on a slowly growing rift occurred between the orthodox Mesmerists who clung to the crisis and the fluid theory, and the followers of Puységur who concentrated their attention on artificial somnambulism, adopting a psychological theory, and eventually simplifying the technique of mesmerization.

In August 1785, Puységur was ordered to take command of his artillery regiment stationed in Strasbourg.[60] The local Masonic society had asked him to teach the principles of animal magnetism to its members. Puységur gave a course, which he concluded with the following words:

> I believe in the existence within myself of a power.
> From this belief derives my will to exert it.
> The entire doctrine of Animal Magnetism is contained in the two words: *Believe* and *want.*
> I *believe* that I have the power to set into action the vital principle of my fellow-men; I *want* to make use of it; this is all my science and all my means.
> *Believe* and *want*, Sirs, and you will do as much as I.

In Strasbourg, Puységur organized the Société Harmonique des Amis Réunis, whose aim it was to train magnetizers and to set up centers for magnetic treatment. By 1789 it counted more than two hundred members including the elite of Alsacian aristocracy, who pledged to give their treatments gratuitously, to write accurate reports of all their experiences, and to submit them to the society. Under its supervision a number of treatment centers were set up throughout Alsace. The activity of the Strasbourg society is of particular interest because, unlike other French centers, it published annual reports listing the cures with short case histories including the names of the practitioner and the patient, and the nature of illness.[61] Collective treatments were no longer mentioned, either in the form of the *baquet* or in the form of the magnetized tree. It would seem that theoretical considerations played an unimportant role in the society's activities.

There is no way of knowing how the movement would have developed had it not been abruptly interrupted by the Revolution in 1789. The Société de l'Harmonie and all its branches disappeared. The peasants, instead of sitting at the foot of magnetized trees, gathered around "liberty trees" to listen to revolutionary speeches. Many of Mesmer's aristocratic disciples emigrated; others perished on the scaffold, as did several former members of the Royal Commissions: Bailly, Lavoisier, and his opponent Thouret. Bergasse narrowly escaped the guillotine and later became a mystical philosopher and a close friend of Czar Alexander. When Malta was taken by Bonaparte and subsequently by the English, the Mesmerian Knights were expelled. In Saint-Domingue, magnetism degenerated into a psychic epidemic among the Negro slaves, increasing their agitation, and the French domination ended in a blood bath. Later Mesmer boasted that the new republic—now called Haiti—owed its independence to him.

The Marquis de Puységur spent two years in prison, after which he was able to recover his castle, become the Mayor of Soissons, write literary works, and take up once again his research on magnetism. He investigated the hypothesis that severe mental illness might be a type of somnambulic distortion and that some day magnetism might be used in hospitals to cure the insane. He undertook the treatment of a twelve-year-old boy, Alexandre Hébert, who was at times seized with terrific fits of frenzied fury. The Marquis spent six months with the boy, leaving him neither day nor night, thus anticipating the later attempts at a psychotherapy of severe psychosis.[62]

After Napoleon's overthrow, a new generation of magnetizers, who had not known Mesmer, saw in Puységur their respected patriarch, and it was hardly noticed that the term "mesmerizing" actually meant using the procedure inaugurated by Puységur. Returning to Buzancy in April 1818, the sixty-seven-year-old Marquis learned that Victor Race, who was now fifty-eight years of age, was severely ill and continually talking about him. Puységur went to see Victor and magnetized him in the same thatched cottage in which he had done it for the first time thirty-four years earlier. He was struck by the fact that Victor, in his magnetic sleep, remembered every detail of his previous somnambulic life. Victor's health improved, and the Marquis returned to Paris. Victor, the dean of French *somnambules,* died shortly thereafter and was buried in the cemetery at Buzancy. The Marquis ordered an inscription to be put on his tombstone. [63]

On May 29, 1825, Charles X was solemnly crowned at Reims in a celebration performed according to an archaic ritual. Puységur, the descendant of one of the oldest French families, dwelt for the duration of the coronation in one of the ceremonial tents that had been pitched on the public square. Due probably to the high humidity, the seventy-four-year-old aristocrat became severely ill and was taken back to his castle at Buzancy, where he soon died, leaving the reputation of a thoroughly honest and generous, if somewhat uncritical man. [64] With his innate respect for rank and primacy, he had always proclaimed himself Mesmer's respectful disciple and never tried to supersede him in any way. His name gradually fell into oblivion; his writings became scarce. Charles Richet rediscovered Puységur in 1884 and showed that most of what his illustrious contemporaries believed to have discovered in the field of hypnosis was already contained in Puységur's writings.

Today, Buzancy is a charming little village amidst forests and fertile fields and meadows. The castle of the old and powerful Puységur family has almost entirely disappeared. The centuries-old elm tree survived until 1940; the Société des Amis de Mesmer was about to shoot a film of Mesmer's life, an episode of which centered around this tree, when a storm uprooted it. The farmers rushed to gather its pieces; some farmers took pieces of its bark which they carefully kept, ascribing to them certain prophylactic or curative properties. [65] The spring continues to pour forth its waters at the same place and it is believed to have certain marvelous virtues. The tomb of Victor Race in the small village cemetery has disappeared, and his descendants, who have been traced to the present day, are quite unaware of their ancestor's historical role. [66] The peaceful little church contains the graves of several of the Puységurs, including that of Amand-Marie-Jacques de Chastenet, Marquis de Puységur, one of the great forgotten contributors to the history of the psychological sciences.

The Diffusion of Mesmerism

The Mesmerist movement was very young and inexperienced when it lost its leader in 1785. However, it went on, slowly developing along new lines. The early magnetists did much therapeutic work and published good observations. But the strange phenomena of magnetic sleep overexcited their imaginations and turned their minds toward the search for the extraordinary. In 1787, Petetin in Lyons published the story of a hysterical woman who fell into a cataleptic state in which her sensory functions were displaced to the epigastrium, that is, she could see and hear only through her epigastrium. [67] In Germany, although he had been known there and had made demonstrations from as early as 1775 to 1776, Mesmer's name later became attached to the new magnetism inaugurated by Puységur. In

1786, the Margrave Karl Friedrich of Baden sent a delegation to the Mesmerist Society in Strasbourg and introduced animal magnetism into his states. In 1787, Professor Böckmann, a physicist from Karlsruhe, founded the Archiv für Magnetismus und Somnambulismus. The extraordinary states of magnetic lucidity were used to try to obtain preternatural revelations. Much was made of the case of a twenty-three-year-old young lady living in the small town of Rastadt (state of Baden), who, in magnetic sleep, explained the mysteries of the human soul, of the seven degrees of magnetic sleep, of Nature, and even of God and the Trinity. [68]

After the temporary arrest caused by the Revolution, the development of animal magnetism took a different course in France and in Germany.

In France, as we have seen, magnetism was taken up again around 1805 by Puységur, who published several works on it. Together with those of Mesmer, they were considered for at least one generation as the great classics on the subject. But, beginning around 1812, new men were introducing new concepts and new methods into the study of magnetism.

There was first the conspicuous Abbé Faria, a Portuguese priest who claimed to have come from India and to be a Brahmin. He opened a public course on lucid sleep in Paris in 1813 in which he criticized the theory of the physical fluid as well as that of the rapport and contended that the essential process of magnetization was due less to the magnetizer than to the subject. [69] He further taught that certain types of individuals were susceptible to magnetization and called them *natural epoptes*. His technique consisted in seating his patients in comfortable chairs and having them fixate his open and raised hand, after which he commanded in a loud voice: "Sleep!" The subjects then fell into magnetic sleep. While they were in that state, he produced visions in them as well as posthypnotic suggestions. Unfortunately for Faria, he was handicapped by his poor French and (according to Noizet) became the victim of the practical joke of an actor who had come to one of his sessions with the intention of ridiculing him, after which Faria became the laughingstock of Paris. His name survived mainly because Alexandre Dumas used it for a character in his novel *The Count of Monte Cristo*. Janet has shown that it was Faria, who, via Noizet and Liébeault, was the true ancestor of the Nancy School.

Deleuze met with success where Faria had failed, and the revival of magnetism in France is usually ascribed to him. He too gave a public course and published a clear and well-organized textbook. [70] Deleuze stated that the era of "prodigious healings" had gone with Mesmer and Puységur, and that the period of the elaborate and codified technique had set in. He also noted that the old quarrel between the "fluidists" (who believed in Mesmer's physical fluid), the "animists" (who believed in psychological phenomena), and the intermediate theory (held by those who believed in the physical fluid's being directed by the will) was a thing of the past; the practitioners had come into their own. He gave excellent descriptions of the phenomena occurring during artificial somnambulism, was sceptical about alleged preternatural manifestations, and warned against the various dangers inherent in magnetic treatment.

If Deleuze was predominantly a clinician and an empiricist, Alexandre Bertrand, who had a dual training as a physician and as an engineer, approached the phenomena of animal magnetism with a view toward exploring them in a scientific and experimental manner.[71] Janet, who held Bertrand's work in the highest esteem, considered him to be the true initiator of the scientific study of hypnosis.

Noizet, an officer in the French army, who had watched Faria's demonstrations, relates how he became acquainted in 1819 with Bertrand, who had started his research on magnetism, and how he convinced Bertrand of the fallacy of the fluid theory. They became friends, and both sent manuscripts to a competition proposed by the Berlin Academy; but the manuscripts were returned. Bertrand revised his in the form of his *Traité*, whereas it took Noizet thirty-five years to publish his in a limited edition.[72] Noizet's teaching was to be taken over by Liébeault, and in this manner, Faria's technique eventually became the general method applied by the Nancy School. Both Bertrand and Noizet emphasized the fact that the human mind conceives of thoughts and reasonings of which we are not aware and which can be recognized only through the effects they produce.

Among the French students of magnetism, there were also men such as Charpignon, Teste, Gauthier, Lafontaine, Despine, Dupotet, Durand (de Gros), and others who deserve the highest credit, although they are largely forgotten today. Janet protested against the name of "precursors," which has been disdainfully given to them. These men, he said (as well as Puységur and the early Mesmerists), were the actual founders of the science of hypnotism; they had described all its phenomena right from the start and nothing substantial had been added during the nineteenth century.

These men had understood, for example, that the rapport was the central phenomenon in magnetism and somnambulism and that its influence extended far beyond the actual séance. Posthypnotic suggestions had already been described in 1787 and were well known to Faria and Bertrand.[73] The reciprocal influence between the patient and the magnetizer was soon included in the concept of *rapport*.[74] Early magnetizers warned against the danger inherent in the powerful interpersonal attraction issuing from the rapport, although they knew that this influence also had its limitations. Tardif de Montrevel emphasized in 1785 that the subject in magnetic sleep was well able to resist any immoral commands that an unscrupulous magnetizer might give.[75] They investigated the vicissitudes of individual treatments, explained how to start and terminate them and warned of the dangers of too frequent séances and of too prolonged treatment.[76] They also investigated various types of "magnetic" conditions, including cases of dual personality. The influence of mind over body and the possibility of curing many organic diseases through magnetism were a matter of course for them. They often met with one another in work groups and carefully recorded a journal of their treatments.

In spite of all their merits, the wide experience they had gathered, their scrupulous honesty and the rational approach of the best among them, these men failed to promote the cause of magnetism. They made desperate and fruitless efforts to have magnetism acknowledged by the scientific authorities: the successive commissions appointed by the Académie des Sciences always concluded their investigations with a rejection.[77] Janet pointed out that most of them, instead of applying themselves to the study of the most elementary manifestations of magnetic sleep, fancied that they could demonstrate the validity of their doctrine by extraordinary phenomena. Moreover, not only were most of them laymen, but they chose uneducated, sensitive subjects, set them in trances and had them diagnose diseases and prescribe treatments. This was an illegal practice of medicine in the second degree, as it were, and it attracted the wrath of the medical profession. Finally, they were defenseless against a host of quacks who utilized the technique of magnetism for well-paying stage demonstrations, which sometimes resulted in psychic epidemics and brought magnetism into disrepute.

The development of Mesmerism in Germany took on a distinctive character because, in contrast with France, German universities showed a lively interest in animal magnetism and it was adopted by the Romanticists and the philosophers of Nature. In 1812 the Prussian government appointed an official commission of inquiry whose reports, published in 1816, were favorable, whereupon the universities of Berlin and Bonn instituted chairs of Mesmerism.[78]

The German Mesmerists included men of high intellectual distinction such as Gmelin, Kluge, the brothers Hufeland, Kieser, Nasse, Passavant, and Wolfart, who, in 1811, founded the journal *Askläpeion*[79] in which much space was devoted to magnetism. Wolfart traveled to Frauenfeld to visit Mesmer and brought back with him Mesmer's last unpublished book.

As did their French colleagues, the German Mesmerists understood the fundamental role of rapport in the treatment but gave it a more philosophical interpretation. In his textbook Kluge wrote that magnetizer and patient formed a "magnetic circle," that is, a closed world of two individuals, which had to be protected from noise, light, and outward interference.[80] Friedrich Hufeland compared the unit of magnetizer and patient to the relationship between the pregnant woman and the fetus, and taught that the magnetic treatment went through stages similar to those experienced by the fetus up to its birth—which corresponds to the end of the cure.[81]

The German Romanticists were interested in animal magnetism for two reasons: the first being the attraction of Mesmer's theory of a universal, physical "fluid." Romantic philosophers visualized the universe as a living organism endowed with a soul pervading the whole and connecting its

78   THE DISCOVERY OF THE UNCONSCIOUS

parts. Mesmer's physical fluid—had its existence been demonstrated—would have furnished evidence of the Romantic conception. The second reason was Puységur's discovery of magnetic somnambulism with its extra-lucid manifestations. Mesmer had already spoken of a "sixth sense" revealed in the sensitivity to the fluid; Puységur had added that this sixth sense provided humans with an ability of describing distant events and predicting future happenings. The Romanticists now assumed that somnambulic lucidity would enable the human mind to establish communications with the World Soul.

For those reasons, considerable attention was devoted to the phenomenology of magnetic somnambulism. Kluge, in his textbook on animal magnetism, distinguished six degrees of the magnetic state: (1) Waking state, with a sensation of increased warmth; (2) Half-sleep; (3) "Inner darkness," that is, sleep proper and insensitivity; (4) "Inner clarity," that is, consciousness within one's own body, extrasensory perception, vision through the epigastrium, and so forth; (5) "Self-contemplation": the subject's ability to perceive with great accuracy the interior of his own body and that of those with whom he is put into rapport; (6) "Universal clarity": the removal of veils of time and space and the subject perceives things hidden in the past, the future, or at remote distances.[82]

Very few subjects, however, proved able to attain the last three stages and particularly the sixth one, and it was believed that it was a scientific and philosophical task of the highest importance to find one of those rare subjects and to work systematically with him. Thus, whereas the French were seeking extra-lucid *somnambules* as auxiliary subjects for medical practice, the Germans utilized them in an audacious attempt at experimental metaphysics.

Among the extraordinary subjects who flourished in Germany during that time, none became as famous as Katharina Emmerich and Friedericke Hauffe. Katharina Emmerich (1774–1824), a poor peasant woman and former nun in Dülmen, Westphalia, had visions and bore the stigmata of the Passion. After having visited her, the poet Clemens Brentano decided to break with his former life, and appointed himself secretary to the Saint. He settled in Dülmen and lived there from 1819 until her death in 1824.[83] In her cataleptic states, Katharina visioned Christ's Passion and suffered greatly. Every night she had dreams that followed one another in regular sequence according to the cycle of the liturgic year and that showed the life of Christ and of his Holy Mother. Brentano visited Katharina every morning and wrote down her dreams and visions as she dictated them to him. With this material, he compiled two books that were a great success.[84] [85] Notwithstanding the poet's embellishments,[86] many people believed these revelations to be actual historical records.

The other subject, Friedericke Hauffe (1801–1829), was not a saint but a seeress. She was made famous by the poet-physician Justinus Kerner and she, in turn, brought him great fame. In spite of their shortcomings, Kerner's investigations of the seeress were a milestone in the history of dynamic psychiatry.

Justinus Kerner (1786–1862) was the son of a modest civil servant in the state of Württemberg. In his delightful autobiography,[87] he tells of his childhood in Ludwigsburg, a small town with a haunted house and the tower where Dr. Faust was said to have practiced black magic. Adjacent to his parents' home was the asylum for the insane, which he could see from his window. In his early childhood, he met the poet Schiller. At the age of twelve, he was cured of a nervous ailment by the magnetizer Gmelin and retained a lasting interest in the mysteries of the human mind. Some of Kerner's poems remain among the minor classics of German poetry. As a physician, he was first to describe a kind of food-poisoning today called botulism and supplemented his clinical observations with ingenious experiments on animals with the poisonous substance.[88] In 1819 he was appointed city physician in the small town of Weinsberg, in Württemberg, where he remained until his death in 1862. The Kerner house, celebrated for the refined hospitality shown toward its visitors, soon became a little Mecca for poets, writers, philosophers, and people of all ranks and classes —including kings and princes.[89] Kerner was a kind, generous, humorous, and learned man, a brilliant conversationalist, a lover of nature, animals, popular songs, and folklore, and had a keen interest in the mysterious and the occult.[90] He was the first to make an inquiry about Mesmer's life and to collect relevant biographical documents. Among his patients he encountered cases of possession, which he called a demonic-magnetic disease. His therapy in such cases was a curious mixture of exorcism and magnetism.[91] In his attitude toward possession, magnetic somnambulism, and allegedly supranormal manifestations, Kerner was, according to his friend David Strauss, less credulous than it has been assumed.[92] He looked upon such matters as a poet, wishing that they were true, but not firmly convinced of their verity.

November 25, 1826, was a crucial date in Kerner's life: it marked his acquaintance with Friedericke Hauffe, who was brought to him in a condition near death. On April 6, 1827, he took her into his home, where she remained until shortly before her death in 1829. Her story, as told by Kerner, may be summarized as follows: [93]

> Friedericke Hauffe, the daughter of a game-keeper, was born in the village of Prevorst in Württemberg. An uneducated person, she had read nothing but the Bible and a hymn book. As a child, she already had visions and premonitions. At the age of nineteen, her parents engaged her to a man she did not love. That same day, a preacher whom she admired very much was buried. During his funeral service, she "died to the visible world" and her "inner life" began. Shortly after her wedding, she took sick, imagining that she was lying in bed with the preacher's corpse. She entered into a series of "magnetic circles,"

while her physical illnesses became more and more severe: she suffered from convulsions, catalepsy, hemorrhages, and fever for which neither physicians nor healers could find a remedy. She was finally brought to Kerner, emaciated, deadly pale, her eyes shining, and her face wrapped in a white cloth like that of a nun. Kerner first tried to treat her with the customary medical remedies, but noticed that every medication he gave her—even the smallest dose—brought about exactly the reverse of the anticipated reaction. He then resorted to "magnetic passes," whereupon the patient gradually improved.

For the remainder of her stay in Weinsberg, Friedericke led a "bodiless life," that is, her vital forces were supposed to originate not from her organism but exclusively from her being magnetized at regular intervals, day after day. During a great part of the time, she found herself in a magnetic sleep in which, however, whe was "more awake than anybody" and revealed her remarkable capacities as a "seeress." Kerner undertook a very thorough investigation of her, recording her sayings and making systematic experiments with the help and advice of a group of philosophers and theologians.

None of the people who visited the "seeress" ever suspected her of being a fraud. Many were deeply impressed. The theologian David Strauss said that her features were delicate, noble, and illuminated, that she expressed herself slowly in a solemn, musical voice almost like in a recitative, and that she spoke the purest High German instead of the Swabian dialect commonly spoken by the people. Her voice was full of feeling when she gave advice and exhortation and told about the spiritual world.

It is claimed that the "seeress" gave evidence of her ability to see distant events and foretell future happenings. Physical phenomena, for example, the spontaneous displacement of objects, were also said to occur in her presence. She received messages from disincarnate spirits about personal and general matters. Thus, she was able to bring revelations concerning the nature of man and about a system of "magnetic circles": there were seven "sun circles" and one "life circle." These were apparently symbolic representations of spiritual conditions.

The "seeress" spoke frequently in an unknown language which Kerner and his friends found sonorous and magnificent. It was, she said, the original language of mankind, forgotten since the time of Jacob, but which could be recovered in certain circumstances. Since she spoke it fluently and translated it, some people around her became able to understand it. Unfortunately, Kerner did not compile its grammar and vocabulary but recorded only a few sentences such as: *O pasqua non ti bjat handacadi?* (Willst thou not give me thy hand, physician?) or *Bona finto girro* (The people must go). This language was written in a system of ciphers of which each one also represented a number. Friedericke constantly combined these and other numbers into a system of inner computation which ceaselessly and automatically went through her mind.

Kerner, who had noticed the patient's oversensitivity to many things, undertook a systematic study of the action of various substances on her: minerals, plants, products of animal origin, as well as the influence of the sun, the moon, electricity, sounds, and music on her organism.

In her magnetic trances, the "seeress" often prescribed medications which unfailingly cured her exactly when predicted. In one of her dreams, she devised an apparatus which she called a "nerve-tuner" (*Nervenstimmer*) and which Kerner built according to her instructions; it proved efficient. Cures by the "seeress" of several other people were also reported, but Kerner does not seem to have encouraged very much this aspect of her talents.

The seeress aroused enormous interest in Germany. Philosophers such as Görres, Baader, Schelling, G. von Schubert, Eschenmayer, and theologians such as David Strauss and Schleiermacher, came repeatedly to see her in Weinsberg and discussed her revelations quite seriously. Soon after her death, Justinus Kerner published a book, *Die Seherin von Prevorst,* [94] compiling his clinical observations and experiments on the subject. To these was added a theoretical study by Adam Carl August von Eschenmayer. The book had a prodigious success in Germany, and has been republished several times; it was the first monograph devoted to an individual patient in the field of dynamic psychiatry. It has been alleged that Kerner and his associates were fooled by a hysterical woman, but there is no evidence that Friedericke was dishonest and no reason to believe that Kerner distorted or embellished her sayings. He obviously made great efforts to be objective, separating his observations from his experimentations and from the philosophical interpretations, which he left to Eschenmayer. But it did not occur to them that the mere fact of observing a subject with certain expectations might have an influence on the development of her symptoms. *The Seeress of Prevorst* is still valuable as the record of an involuntary experiment on the performances of the "mythopoetic" functions of the unconscious, when given time and under favorable circumstances.

The interest raised by Kerner's observations of the "seeress" resulted in a flood of letters and reports concerning similar phenomena. Kerner and his friends published much of this material in the *Blätter von Prevorst* (1831–1839) and in the *Magikon* (1840–1853). These were probably the first periodicals devoted mainly to parapsychology.

During the last period of his life, Kerner lost his beloved wife and gradually became blind. He fell into a pronounced depression but remained creative all the while. As a pastime he used to make inkblots on a sheet of paper, fold it and elaborate the resulting figures, giving them fanciful shapes and writing verses under each of them. These pictures, he said, were ghosts and monsters to which he ascribed a place in *Hades* (the transitory home of the spirits). This book, published posthumously under the title *Klecksographien,* became a source of inspiration for Hermann Rorschach much later for his inkblot tests. [95]

As we shall see later, many Germans of the early nineteenth century were, like Kerner, deeply influenced by animal magnetism, but its influence declined rapidly after 1850 under the impact of positivism and scientific rationalism.

Outside of France and Germany the development of Mesmerism was much slower. It met with strong and obstinate opposition in England until a breakthrough occurred between 1840 and 1850. A Manchester physician, James Braid, was much impressed by demonstrations given in November 1841 by the French magnetizer Lafontaine. Sceptical at first, he repeated Lafontaine's experiments and was soon convinced. He rejected the fluid theory and proposed a new one based on brain physiology; he adapted Faria's and Bertrand's old technique of fixating the hand by fixating a luminous object. Under the more suitable term "hypnotism," he made magnetism acceptable to certain medical circles, who came to ascribe to Braid himself the discovery of these phenomena.[96] Unfortunately, he attempted to combine hypnotism with phrenology, which gave rise to much confusion. Independently of Braid, an English surgeon by the name of John Elliotson published a report about surgical operations that he had performed painlessly on patients who had been put into magnetic sleep.[97] Elliotson complained that he met with violent opposition on the part of the Royal Medical and Chirurgical Society. Almost simultaneously another English surgeon, Esdaile, who was practicing in India, reported on 345 major surgical interventions that he had performed with the sole help of Mesmeric anesthesia, a technique he found easier to apply to Hindus than to English patients.[98] He also used it as a general method of treatment. Some years later, he mentioned the existence of a Mesmeric disease, that is, an artificial but by no means slight condition in people who had become used to frequent magnetization.[99] Soon thereafter the discovery of ether anesthesia made this technique obsolete.

Magnetism also found followers in Scotland. An anonymous author reported a number of ingenious experiments and noted the peculiar attraction magnetized patients had for each other while under the influence of Mesmeric sleep.[100] He also reported excellent therapeutic results with a patient put into magnetic sleep for ten days. Enthusiasm for Mesmerism was such that a psychic epidemic broke out in Edinburgh and other towns of Scotland in the year 1851.[101]

The introduction of magnetism into the United States occurred at an early date. We may mention incidentally that Lafayette, who had been one of Mesmer's aristocratic students, was asked by him to be his ambassador to George Washington. But the practical introduction of magnetism in North America took place mostly via New Orleans, which at that time was still a French city and where a flourishing Mesmeric society soon developed. In all other parts of the United States, the diffusion on magnetism was slow but it steadily increased after 1840. Among its adherents, two at least deserve special mention. One was Phineas Parkhurst Quimby (1802–1866), a young watchmaker. He understood that the real agent of the cure was suggestion and practiced a kind of "mind cure." One of his patients was later to become known under the name of Mary Baker Eddy (1821–1910), the founder of Christian Science.[102] Another was Andrew Jackson

Davis, a young man, who, having himself magnetized daily, dictated in his trance an enormous book of revelations about the world of the spirits.[103] The book was a great success and paved the way for the propagation of spiritism, which was soon to follow.

It is remarkable how the history of Mesmerism went through a succession of positive and negative phases. The first phase was the grand years of Mesmer's activity in Paris from 1777 to 1785; the second took place after 1815 and in the early 1820's; the third one, beginning around 1840, culiminated in the 1850's. According to Janet,[104] at least nine journals devoted to magnetism appeared in France from 1815 to 1850. Mesmerist societies held meetings and congresses, conferred prizes and awards, and on May 23, 1850, organized a grand celebration on the occasion of Mesmer's birthday, which included concerts, banquets, and speeches.

But as Mesmer's disciples became more numerous, enthusiastic, and fanatic, the movement deviated more from its initial norm and fell into discredit: It mingled increasingly with wild speculation, occultism, and, at times, with quackery. At this point unexpected developments occurred, subsequent to the advent of spiritism. To follow these developments, we must turn to the United States of America.

The Impact of Spiritism

In the years 1840 to 1850 the United States was a vast but rapidly expanding country with an energetic if relatively small population of approximately 20 million inhabitants, the majority of whom were living in small "townships." The common man's average level of education was higher than in other countries, but there was no "educated upper class" to impose the pressure of a tradition and cultural norms. Every man claimed the right to think for himself and used this right with more vigor and freshness than intellectual discipline. Preachers and congregations often changed their beliefs, and religious sects were numerous. There was a general and permanent predisposition toward psychic epidemics, which arose unexpectedly, spread rapidly, and were accepted "almost to a man" in vast areas. Recent discoveries, for example, the telegraph, fired the imagination; nothing seemed too fantastic to be rejected without further examination. Thus, it happened that a seemingly trivial incident became the starting point for a psychological epidemic of unexpected amplitude—the rise and spread of Spiritism.[105]

If contemporary reports are to be believed, the story started in 1847 when a man in Hydesville near Arcadia, New York, began to be bothered by mysterious noises occurring in his house at night and left the house to a farmer, John Fox, who occupied it with his wife and two daughters, aged fifteen and twelve. The disturbances persisted. On the evening of March 31, 1848, the knocking repeated the noises purposely made by one of the daughters and then—in the presence of neighbors—questions asked by the mother were answered in a rudimentary code; it was revealed that a man had been murdered in that house and buried in the cellar. Crowds of curious people flocked to the Fox house during the following days. Mrs. Fox and her daughters went visiting; the knocking followed them everywhere and communicated with them, purporting to be the "spirits" of deceased people. Mrs. Fox and her daughters soon commercialized their séances with the spirits, and they had many imitators. The contagion spread rapidly over the United States; the code system for communication with the spirits was perfected. Physical phenomena were reported in February 1850. For example, tables began to move during the sessions, loud and extraordinary noises were heard, and a fluid made itself visible. An impassionate controversy developed. There were spiritist groups, pamphlets, journals, and congresses. Many Mesmerists were among the first and most active supporters of the new movement.

At the beginning of 1852 the wave of spiritism crossed the Atlantic, invading England and Germany. In April 1853 it swept over France, and soon reached all parts of the civilized world.

Meanwhile, it had been discovered that the manifestations depended to a large extent on the personalities of the participants: some people prevented the "spirits" from appearing, others helped them, and a privileged few could serve as "mediums," or intermediaries between the living and the dead. Some mediums were able to write automatically, speak in a trance, and allegedly call forth the occurrence of physical phenomena. Around 1860 "spirits" began manifesting themselves visually during the séances, and in 1862 photographs purportedly taken of them as well as casts of their hands were shown. This was followed by the period of the extraordinary mediums: Florence Cook, Stainton Moses, Slade, Home, and others.[106] It was said that, during Home's sittings, pianos were raised into the air, harps and accordions played without anyone touching them, and spirits were heard.[107] Home was seen touching fire, and it was even reported that he once went out through a window and returned through the window in the next room, having "flown" out and in at the third-floor level[108] Sir William Crookes, a well-known physicist, experimented with Home and Florence Cook; Crookes swore to have seen, in the latter's presence, the "materializations" of a beautiful woman who called herself Katie King. She let herself be photographed by Crookes and talked to him and his friends.[109]

The epidemic slowly receded, but many spiritist groups remained quite active. In Paris, Hippolyte Rivail, a former schoolteacher who had been a disciple of Pestalozzi in Switzerland, became a convert to spiritism, which he systematized in numerous works under the pseudonym Allan Kardec and to which he gave the form of an immensely successful lay religion. His *Book of the Spirits*[110] became according to Janet, "a guide not only for the spiritists, but also for the spirits."

The scientific study of these manifestations, which had been attempted in an uncritical manner by Crookes, Zöllner, and others, was now under-taken more systematically by Charles Richet. A new science, that of parapsychology, gradually emerged. In England, Myers and Gurney founded in 1882 the Society for Psychical Research, which gathered a great amount of carefully selected data. A cautious investigator, Myers admitted the hypothesis of survival after death and of communication with the spirits of the deceased, while Flournoy, in Geneva, thought that these phenomena could be explained by subliminal perception and cryptom-nesia.[111]

The advent of spiritism was an event of major importance in the history of dynamic psychiatry, because it indirectly provided psychologists and psychopathologists with new approaches to the mind. Automatic writing, one of the procedures introduced by the spiritists, was taken over by scientists as a method of exploring the unconscious. Chevreul, who had already in 1833 demonstrated that the movements of the divining rod and the pendulum were unconsciously directed by the performer's hidden thinking,[112] took up his old experiments again with a view of providing a rational explanation of turning-tables.[113] A new subject, the medium, became avail-able for experimental psychological investigations, out of which evolved a new model of the human mind.

Another incentive to the further development of dynamic psychiatry was the appearance of great professional hypnotizers who gave public sessions throughout Europe and who attracted large crowds to their spectacular performances. We have seen how Braid, in Manchester, came to experiment with hypnotism after having watched the magnetizer Lafontaine. Similarly, around 1880, several neurologists began to reconsider their attitudes toward hypnotism after seeing performances by Hansen in Germany and Donato in Belgium, France, and Italy.[114]

These new approaches to dynamic psychology led to a revival of interest in the ill-famed hypnotism and to its investigation by university physicians such as the physiologist Charles Richet.[115] Two schools then arose and made their contributions to the newer dynamic psychiatry: the Nancy School and the Salpêtrière School.

The Nancy School[116]

In the period from 1860 to 1880, magnetism and hypnotism had fallen into such disrepute that a physician working with these methods would irretrievably have compromised his scientific career and lost his medical practice. Janet[117] mentioned the strange story of a distinguished city prac-titioner who had secretly set up a hospital in a cottage in a neighboring village, where he kept a few patients on whom he performed interminable hypnotic treatments and investigations.

Among the very few who dared hypnotize openly was Auguste Ambroise Liébeault (1823–1904), from whom the Nancy School was to originate.

Liébeault was the twelfth child of a peasant family who was living in the province of Lorraine.[118] Through hard work, he became a country doctor in Pont-Saint-Vincent, a village not far from Nancy. He proved to be a remarkably successful practitioner, and within ten years his practice had earned him a small fortune. As a medical student, he had found an old book on magnetism and had successfully magnetized some patients. It is not known what made him decide to use this method after all the years in which it had been in such disfavor. Since his clients were reluctant, he offered them an alternative: he proposed to either treat them with magnetism gratuitously, or with "official" medicine for his usual fee. The number of patients who chose magnetism increased so rapidly that, four years later, Liébeault had an immense practice that brought him almost no income. He then decided to take a two-year leave from his professional life and retired to a house he had bought in Nancy, devoting all of his time to writing a book about his method.[119] Hypnotic sleep, he taught, is identical with natural sleep, the sole difference being that the former is induced by suggestion, by concentrating the attention on the idea of sleep. This is also the reason why the subject remains in *rapport* with the hypnotizer. According to Janet, Liébeault's ideas were derived mainly from Noizet and Bertrand. (Curiously enough, Liébeault much later became a believer in the theory of the magnetic fluid, which he had rejected for most of his life.) But he was a better hypnotizer than writer; the story goes that in ten years only one copy of his book was sold.[120] He then re-opened his medical practice, giving consultations from 7:00 A.M. until noon and taking only the fees that his patients voluntarily offered to pay.

Van Renterghem, who visited Liébeault at the time of his belated fame, described him as a small, talkative, and vivacious man, with a wrinkled face, a dark complexion, and the appearance of a peasant.[121] Liébeault, he said, received between twenty-five to forty patients every morning in an old shed with whitewashed walls and paved with large, flat stones. Every patient was treated publicly and with no concern for the surrounding noise. Liébeault hypnotized the patient by ordering him to look into his eyes, suggesting that he was getting increasingly sleepy. Once the patient was slightly hypnotized, Liébeault assured him that he was relieved of his symptoms. Most of his patients were poor people from the city and peasants from the neighborhood, whom he indiscriminately treated with the same method no matter what disease they suffered from—arthritis, ulcers, icterus, or pulmonary tuberculosis.

For more than twenty years, Liébeault was considered by his medical colleagues to be a quack (because he hypnotized) and a fool (because he did not charge any fees). Rumors of his therapeutic miracles reached Bernheim, who decided to pay him a visit in 1882 and was converted to his ideas. It is a rare occurrence indeed that a renowned professor adopts a heretofore ill-reputed method from an old man who is said to be a quack and a fool. Bernheim publicly became Liébeault's admirer, pupil, and devoted friend, and introduced his methods in his university's medical hospital. Liébeault suddenly acquired fame as a great medical man; his book was rescued from oblivion and was widely read.

Liébeault may be considered as the spiritual father of the Nancy School, but its actual leader was Hippolyte Bernheim (1840–1919).[122] An Alsatian and a French patriot, Bernheim left his hospital and university positions in Strasbourg when it was annexed by the Germans in 1871, and was appointed in Nancy. The old Lorraine capital was pulsating with new life as a result of the arrival of numerous Alsatian refugees, the creation of a new university in 1872, and the flowering of a new school of decorative arts led by Emile Gallé and Victor Prouvé, which was to spread and become, around 1900, the "modern style." Bernheim, whose reputation was already established through his research on typhoid fever, as well as heart and pulmonary diseases, was appointed titular professor of internal medicine at the new university in 1879. Three years later, in 1882, he tried out and adopted Liébeault's hypnotic method, although he unlike his teacher utilized it only when he thought that he had a good chance of success.

Van Renterghem described Bernheim as a short, blue-eyed man, who spoke in a soft voice but who had a very authoritarian way of handling his hospital ward and hypnotizing his patients. Bernheim taught that hypnosis was easier to induce in people accustomed to passive obedience such as old soldiers or factory workers, among whom he had his best therapeutic successes. He had poor results with people of the higher and wealthier classes.

Bernheim revealed the existence of Liébeault's work to the medical world shortly after Charcot read his celebrated paper on hypnotism at the Académie des Sciences.[123] This began an embittered struggle between the two men. In 1886, Bernheim published his textbook,[124] which was a great success and made him the leader of the Nancy School. In opposition to Charcot, he proclaimed that hypnosis was not a pathological condition found only in hysterics, but it was the effect of "suggestion." He defined suggestibility as "the aptitude to transform an idea into an act," a feature that every human being possessed to a different degree. Hypnosis, he said, was a state of enforced suggestibility induced by suggestion. Bernheim currently used hypnotism to treat many organic diseases of the nervous system, rheumatism, gastrointestinal diseases, and menstrual disorders. He vehemently denied the validity of Charcot's theory of hysteria and claimed that the hysterical conditions, demonstrated in the Salpêtrière were artifacts. As time went on Bernheim made less and less use of hypnotism, contending that the effects that could be obtained by this method were equally obtainable by suggestion in waking state, a procedure that the Nancy School now termed "psychotherapeutics."[125]

Bernheim, however, was an internist, not a psychiatrist, and he had no organized school around him. In its restricted sense the Nancy School consisted of a group of four men: Liébeault, Bernheim, the forensic medical expert Beaunis, and the lawyer Liégeois. The latter two were particularly preoccupied with the implications of suggestion in crime and criminal responsibility. In its wider sense the Nancy School was a loose group of psychiatrists who had adopted Bernheim's principles and methods. Among them were Albert Moll and Schrenck-Notzing in Germany, Krafft-Ebing in Austria, Bechterev in Russia, Milne Bramwell in England, Boris Sidis and Morton Prince in the United States, and a few others who deserve special mention.

Otto Wetterstrand, a fashionable Swedish physician, lived in Stockholm in a large and sumptuous apartment with a succession of salons decorated with the finest rugs and furniture. He was a blond and blue-eyed man of middle height, wore a moustache, and had a tic of the eyelids. He saw between thirty and forty patients every afternoon and hypnotized them in the presence of the others. He also had a private hospital staffed with nurses who were his former patients. He applied a method of treatment by prolonged hypnotic sleep and maintained his patients in this state between 8 and 12 days. His strange methods gave rise to a legend depicting him as an extraordinary modern wizard.[126] He was the actual initiator of the method of prolonged continuous sleep—a technique that Otto Wolff modified in 1898 by substituting a medication, Trional, for hypnosis.

In Holland, Frederik Van Eeden,[127] better known as a prominent Dutch poet, made some audacious experiments with hypnosis. He attempted to teach French to a ten-year-old girl whom he had hypnotized, a language that she did not know in her waking state. He then transferred this knowledge from her sleeping state to her waking state so that, to her amazement, she found herself able to understand and speak some French.[128] In 1887 he and Van Renterghem organized a psychotherapeutic clinic in Amsterdam that took the name of *Institut Liébeault.*[129]

In Switzerland, Auguste Forel, professor of psychiatry in Zurich and director of the Burghölzli mental hospital, visited Bernheim in 1887 and soon became one of the masters of hypnotism. Like Liébeault and Bernheim, he was very successful with the treatment of certain physical diseases. He organized an outpatient service of hypnotic therapy. His most original application of hypnotism was in the management of his mental hospital where the personnel, not the patients, were hypnotized. Forel hypnotized a number of male and female nurses, who volunteered, and suggested to them that their sleep in the wards for agitated patients would be sound in spite of the noise, but that they would waken as soon as a patient did something unusual or dangerous. It was said that this method was quite successful.[130]

Sigmund Freud was one of the many visitors to Nancy[131] and spent a few weeks there with Bernheim and old Liébeault in 1889. He was impressed with Bernheim's contention that the posthypnotic amnesia was not as complete as was generally assumed. Through concentration and with the help of skillful questioning, Bernheim could bring the patient to remember what he had experienced under hypnosis.[132]

Around 1900, Bernheim was considered by many to be Europe's foremost psychotherapist; but ten years later he was almost forgotten. Other, supposedly more modern, men had risen to fame, particularly Dubois in Berne, who Bernheim said with bitterness, had "annexed" his discovery in 1871 (in the same sense as the Germans had "annexed" Alsace and Lorraine). After having been Liébeault's respectful disciple for years, Bernheim now obviously considered him as his precursor and himself as the true founder of psychotherapy.[133] At least he had the comfort, shortly before his death, of seeing his native Alsace restored to France.

Charcot and the Salpêtrière School

Contrary to the Nancy School, the Salpêtrière School was strongly organized and headed by a powerful figure, that of the great teacher Jean-Martin Charcot (1835–1893), a neurologist who had come belatedly to the study of certain mental phenomena.

During the years 1870–1893, Charcot was considered to be the greatest neurologist of his time. He was the consulting physician of kings and princes, and patients came to see him "from Samarkand and the West Indies." But fame had come to him after long years of incessant and obscure toil, and few of those who marveled at Charcot's extraordinary success realized that it was a belated one reached after many years of toil.

No real biography of Charcot has been written as yet. Most accounts such as that by Guillain[134] are based on necrologies and depict for the most part the Charcot of the brilliant years. Valuable memories have been recorded by his disciple Souques,[135] and particularly by the Russian physician Lyubimov,[136] who had been acquainted with Charcot for the last twenty years of his life.

Charcot was born in Paris, the son of a carriage-builder who, it was said, made carriages of great beauty and who was reputed to be more of an artist than an artisan. Very little is known of Charcot's childhood and youth. It is said that he was a cold, silent, shy, and aloof young man who had a speech impediment. He wore a black moustache (the story goes that his first rich patient was referred to him on the condition that he shave off his moustache). As an *interne* (medical resident), the young Charcot was assigned for some time to the Salpêtrière, an old hospital, which, at that time, was mainly a medical poorhouse for four or five thousand old women. Charcot realized that this hospital sheltered numerous patients with rare or unknown neurological diseases and would be a great source for clinical research. He kept this in mind while slowly pursuing his career as an anatomo-pathologist. As a young doctor he was asked by one of his teachers to be physician and companion to a rich banker traveling to Italy, which gave him an opportunity to become acquainted with Italy's artistic wealth.[137] His medical career was rather slow and laborious. However, the turning point came in 1862, when, at the age of thirty-six, Charcot was appointed chief physician in one of the Salpêtrière's largest sections and took up his old plans with feverish activity. Case histories were taken, autopsies performed, laboratories opened, while, at the same time, he began to acquire a team of devoted collaborators. He was inspired by Duchenne (de Boulogne), a neurologist of outstanding capacity who had no official position and whom Charcot called his Master in Neurology.[138] Within the 8-year period from 1862 to 1870, Charcot made the discoveries that made him the foremost neurologist of his time.

In 1870, Charcot assumed the supplementary charge of a special ward, which the hospital administration reserved for a fairly large number of women patients suffering from convulsions. Some were epileptics, others were hysterics who had learned to imitate epileptic crises. Charcot strove to discover means for distinguishing between hysterical and epileptic convulsions. He also began to investigate hysteria with the same method he used for organic neurological diseases, and, with his disciple Paul Richer, gave a description of the full-blown hysterical crisis (the *grande hystérie*).[139]

In 1878, probably under the influence of Charles Richet, Charcot extended his interest to hypnotism, of which he undertook a purportedly scientific study (as he had done with hysteria), taking as his subjects several of the most gifted of his female hysterical patients. He found that these subjects developed the hypnotic condition through three successive stages: "lethargy," "catalepsy," and "somnambulism," each stage showing very definite and characteristic symptoms. Charcot read his findings to the Académie des Sciences at the beginning of 1882.[140] It was, Janet said, a *tour de force* to have hypnotism accepted by the same Académie that had condemned it three times within the past century under the name of magnetism. This resounding paper gave hypnotism a new dignity, and the heretofore shunned subject once again became the topic of innumerable publications.

Among Charcot's most spectacular achievements were the investigations on traumatic paralyses, which he conducted in 1884 and 1885.[141] In his time paralyses were generally considered to result from lesions of the nervous system caused by an accident, although the existence of "psychic paralyses" had been postulated in England by B. C. Brodie[142] in 1837 and by Russel Reynolds[143] in 1869. But how could a purely psychological factor cause paralysis without the patient's awareness of that factor and exluding the possibility of simulations?

Charcot had already analyzed the differences between organic and hysterical paralyses. In 1884 three men afflicted with a monoplegia of one arm following trauma were admitted to the Salpêtrière. Charcot first demonstrated that the symptoms of that paralysis, while differing from those of organic paralyses, coincided exactly with the symptoms of hysterical paralyses. The second step was the experimental reproduction of similar paralyses under hypnosis. Charcot suggested to some hypnotized subjects that their arms would be paralyzed. The resulting hypnotic paralyses proved to have exactly the same symptoms as the spontaneous hysterical paralyses and the posttraumatic paralyses of the three male patients. Charcot was able to reproduce these paralyses step by step, and he also suggested their disappearance in the reverse order. The next step was a demonstration of the effect of the trauma. Charcot chose easily hypnotizable subjects and suggested to them that in their waking state, as soon as they were slapped on the back, their arm would become paralyzed. When awakened, the subjects showed the usual posthypnotic amnesia, and as soon as they were slapped on the back, they were instantly struck with a monoplegia of the arm of exactly the same type as the posttraumatic monoplegia. Finally, Charcot pointed out that in certain subjects living in a state of permanent somnambulism, hypnotic suggestion was not even necessary. They received the paralysis of the arm after being slapped on the back without special verbal suggestion. The mechanism of posttraumatic paralysis thus seemed to be demonstrated. Charcot assumed that the nervous shock following the trauma was a kind of hypnoid state analogous to hypnotism and therefore enabling the development of an autosuggestion of the individual. "I do not think that in any physiopathological experimental research it would often be possible to reproduce more accurately the condition which one has set oneself the task to study," Charcot concluded.

Charcot placed the hysterical, posttraumatic, and hypnotic paralyses in the group of dynamic paralyses in contrast to organic paralyses resulting from a lesion of the nervous system. He gave a similar demonstration with regard to hysterical mutism and hysterical coxalgia. Here, too, he reproduced experimentally, by means of hypnotism, clinical pictures identical with the hysterical conditions. In 1892, Charcot distinguished "dynamic amnesia," in which lost memories can be recovered under hypnosis, from "organic amnesia" where this is impossible.[144]

In the last years of his life, Charcot realized that a vast realm existed between that of clear consciousness and that of organic brain physiology. His attention was drawn to faith healing, and in one of his last articles he stated that he had seen patients going to Lourdes and returning healed from their diseases.[145] He tried to elucidate the mechanism of such cures and anticipated that an increased knowledge of the laws of "faith healing" would result in great therapeutic progresses.

There are many descriptions and pictures of Charcot, but they pertain almost without exception to Charcot at his zenith around 1880 or the declining Charcot of the last years. The most lively ones were given by Léon Daudet, who had studied medicine at the Salpêtrière and whose father, the novelist Alphonse Daudet, had been Charcot's intimate friend. Here is a condensed excerpt of Léon Daudet's *Memoirs* describing Charcot: [146]

> Charcot was a small, stout, and vigorous man with a big head, a bull's neck, a low forehead, broad cheeks. The line of his mouth was hard and meditative. He was clean-shaven and kept his straight hair combed back. He somewhat resembled Napoleon and liked to cultivate this resemblance. His gait was heavy, his voice authoritative, somewhat low, often ironical and insisting, his expression extraordinarily fiery.
>
> A most learned man, he was familiar with the works of Dante, Shakespeare, and the great poets; he read English, German, Spanish, and Italian. He had a large library full of strange and unusual books.
>
> He was very humane; he showed a profound compassion for animals and forbade any mention of hunters and hunting in his presence.
>
> A more authoritarian man I have never known, nor one who could put such a despotic yoke on people around him. To realize this, one only had to see how he could, from his pulpit, throw a sweeping and suspicious glance at his students and hear him interrupt them with a brief, imperative word.
>
> He could not stand contradiction, however small. If someone dared contradict his theories, he became ferocious and mean and did all he could to wreck the career of the imprudent man unless he retracted and apologized.
>
> He could not stand stupidity. But his need for domination caused him to eliminate the more brilliant of his disciples, so that in the end he was surrounded by mediocre people. As a compensation, he maintained social relationships with artists and poets and gave magnificent receptions.
>
> It was one of his favorite ideas that the share of dream-life in our waking state is much more than just "immense."

Many references to Charcot can be found in the *Diary* of Edmond and Jules de Goncourt. These two brothers were known for their biting descriptions and seem to have been particularly antagonistic toward Charcot, whom they described as follows: [147]

> Charcot was an ambitious man, envious of any superiority, showing a ferocious resentment against those who declined invitations to his receptions, a despot at the university, hard with his patients to the point of telling them bluntly of their impending death but cowardly when he himself was ill. He was a tyrant with his children and compelled for instance his son Jean, who wanted to be a seafarer, to become a physician. As a scientist, Charcot was a mixture of

genius and charlatan. Most unpleasant was his indiscretion in talking of his patients' confidential matters.

The description given by the Russian physician Lyubimov is so vastly different that one can hardly believe it concerns the same person: [148]

Beside his extraordinary gift as a teacher, a scientist and an artist, Charcot was extremely humane, devoted to his patients and would not tolerate anything unkind being said about anyone in his presence. He was a poised and sensible man, very circumspect in his judgments, with a quick eye for distinguishing people's value. His family life was a harmonious and happy one; his wife, who was a widow with a daughter when he married her, helped him with his work and was active in charitable organizations. He gave great care to the education of his son Jean who had spontaneously chosen to be a physician and whose first scientific publications were a great joy for his father. He enjoyed the devotion of his students and of his patients, so that his patron saint's day, the Saint Martin, on November 11th, was celebrated with entertainments and rejoicing at the Salpêtrière.

One may wonder how Charcot gained the enormous prestige that he enjoyed in the years 1880 to 1890. Several reasons may be discerned.

First, the Salpêtrière was anything but an ordinary hospital. It was a city within a city in the seventeenth-century style, consisting of about 45 buildings with streets, squares, gardens, and an old and beautiful church. It was also a place of historical fame: Saint Vincent de Paul had carried out his charitable activities there. It had later been converted by Louis XIV into an asylum for beggars, prostitutes, and the insane, and was one of the places where the notorious September Massacres had taken place during the French Revolution and where Pinel had achieved his mental hospital reforms. It was also known from one episode in the classic novel *Manon Lescaut* by the Abbé Prévost. Its thousands of old women had inspired some of Baudelaire's poems. Before Charcot, the Salpêtrière had been little known to medical students, and physicians did not relish the thought of being appointed there. Charcot was now credited with being the scientific wizard who had turned this historical place into a Temple of Science.

That old-fashioned hospital with its antiquated buildings had no laboratories, no examination rooms, and no teaching facilities. With his iron will—and with the help of his political connections—Charcot built a treatment, research, and teaching unit. He had carefully chosen his collaborators; he installed consulting rooms for ophthalmology, otolaryngology, and so on, as well as laboratories and a photographic service. Later he added a museum for anatomo-pathology, an out-patient service where men were also admitted, and a large auditorium. Among Charcot's disciples were Bourneville, Pitres, Joffroy, Cotard, Gilles de la Tourette, Meige, Paul Richer, Souques, Pierre Marie, Raymond, Babinski. There is hardly one French neurologist of that time who had not been a student of Charcot. Charcot exerted an absolute domination on the school that was his creation. Each of his lectures was carefully recorded by students and published in one of the several medical journals he had founded. There came a time when no one could be appointed to the Paris medical faculty without his sanction. This patriotic feeling contributed to Charcot's fame: he and Pasteur were to the French a proof of France's scientific genius, challenging Germany's alleged scientific superiority.

Charcot personified what the French call a *prince de la science;* he was not only a man of high scientific reputation, but also a powerful and wealthy man. Through his marriage with a rich widow and the extremely high fees that he charged his patients, he was able to lead the life of a member of the wealthy class. Aside from his villa in Neuilly, he had acquired in 1884 a splendid residence on the Boulevard Saint-Germain, which had been decorated according to his own plans. It was a kind of private museum with Renaissance furniture, stained-glass windows, tapestries, paintings, antiques, and rare books. He was himself an artist who did excellent drawings and was an expert in painting on china and enamel. He was a keen connoisseur of the history of art and was a master of French prose who had a great knowledge of French literature.[149] Charcot also possessed a knowledge of English, German, and Italian, which was a rare accomplishment at that time. He displayed a particular admiration for Shakespeare, whom he often quoted in English, and for Dante, whom he quoted in Italian. Every Tuesday night he gave sumptuous receptions in his splendid home to the *Tout-Paris* of scientists, politicians, artists, and writers. He was known to be the physician and sometimes the confidant of kings and princes. Emperor Pedro II of Brazil, it was said, came to his home, played billiards with him, and attended his lectures at the Salpêtrière. Charcot was a very influential figure in English medical circles. At an international congress that took place in London in 1881, his demonstration on the tabetic arthopathies was received with a storm of applause. He had many admirers in Germany, although he declined invitations to congresses in that country after the Franco-Prussian war of 1870 to 1871. In Vienna he was well acquainted with Meynert and Moritz Benedikt. Charcot was very popular in Russia, where he had been called several times as consultant physician to the Czar and his family. Russian physicians welcomed him because he relieved them from their strong dependence on German scientists. According to Guillain, he arranged an unofficial encounter between Gambetta and the Grand Duke Nikolai of Russia, from which the Franco-Russian alliance was to issue.[150] Charcot traveled extensively; every year he made a carefully planned journey to a different European country, visiting the museums, making drawings, and writing travelogues.

Great as it was, Charcot's prestige was still enhanced by a halo of mystery that surrounded him. It had slowly grown after 1870 and reached its peak with his celebrated paper on hypnotism in 1882. He gained the reputation of being a great thaumaturgist. Instances of his quasi-miraculous cures are reported by Dr. Lyubimov:[151]

> Many patients were brought to Charcot from all over the world, paralytics on stretchers or wearing complicated apparatuses. Charcot ordered the removal of those appliances and told the patients to walk. There was, for instance, a young lady who had been paralyzed for years. Charcot bade her stand up and walk, which she did under the astounded eyes of her parents and of the Mother Superior of the convent in which she had been staying. Another young lady was brought to Charcot with a paralysis of both legs. Charcot found no organic lesion; the consultation was not yet over when the patient stood up and walked back to the door where the cabman, who was waiting for her, took off his hat in amazement and crossed himself.

In the eyes of the public, Charcot was the man who had explored the abysses of the human mind, hence his nickname "Napoleon of Neuroses." He had come to be identified with the discovery of hysteria, hypnotism, dual personality, catalepsy, and somnambulism. Strange things were said about his hold on the Salpêtrière's hysterical young women and about happenings there. Jules Claretie relates that during a patients' ball at the Salpêtrière, a gong was inadvertently sounded, whereupon many hysterical women instantaneously fell into catalepsy and kept the plastic poses in which they found themselves when the gong was sounded.[152] Charcot was also the man whose searching gaze penetrated the depths of the past and who retrospectively interpreted works of art, giving modern neurological diagnoses of cripples represented by painters.[153] He founded a journal, the *Iconographie de la Salpêtrière,* followed by the *Nouvelle Iconographie de la Salpêtrière,* which were probably the first journals to combine art and medicine. Charcot was also considered to have founded a scientific explanation for demoniacal possession, which, he assumed, was nothing but a form of hysteria. He also interpreted this condition retrospectively in works of art.[154] He was known for his collection of rare old works on witchcraft and possession, some of which he had reprinted in a book series titled "The Diabolical Library."

All these features contributed to the incomparable fascination exerted by Charcot's *séances* at the Salpêtrière. Tuesday mornings were devoted to examining new, heretofore unseen patients in the presence of physicians and students. They enjoyed watching Charcot display his clinical acumen, and the assurance and swiftness with which he was able to disentangle the most complicated case histories to arrive at a diagnosis, even of rare diseases. But the greatest attraction were his solemn lectures given on Friday mornings, each of which had been prepared with the utmost care. Long before the beginning of the lectures, the large auditorium was filled to capacity with physicians, students, writers, and a curious crowd. The podium was always decorated with pictures and anatomical schemata pertaining to the day's lecture. His bearing reminding one of Napoleon or Dante, Charcot entered at 10 A.M., often accompanied by an illustrious foreign visitor and a group of assistants who sat in the first rows. Amidst the absolute silence of the audience, he started speaking in a low pitch and gradually raised his voice, giving sober explanations that he illustrated with skillful colored chalk drawings on the blackboard. With an inborn acting talent, he imitated the behavior, mimicry, gait, and voice of a patient afflicted with the disease he was talking about, after which the patient was brought in. The patient's entrance was sometimes also spectacular. When Charcot lectured on tremors, three or four women were introduced wearing hats with very long feathers. The trembling of the feathers allowed the audience to distinguish the specific characteristics of tremors in various diseases.[155] The interrogation took the form of a dramatic dialogue between Charcot and the patient. Most spectacular were the lectures that he gave about hysteria and hypnotism. Another of Charcot's innovations was the use of photographic projections, a procedure that was unusual for medical teaching at the time. The lecture concluded with a discussion of the diagnosis and a recapitulation, stating the lecture's main points; both of which were models of lucidity and concision. It lasted two hours, but the audience never found it too long, even when the topic concerned rare organic brain diseases.[156] Lyubimov points to the difference between Charcot's lectures and those of Meynert, which he had also attended in Vienna and which left him exhausted and confused, whereas he left Charcot's lectures with a feeling of exhilaration.

It is easy to understand the spellbinding effect that Charcot's teaching exerted on laymen, on many physicians, and especially on foreign visitors such as Sigmund Freud, who spent four months at the Salpêtrière during 1885 and 1886. Other visitors were more sceptical. The Belgian physician Delboeuf, whose interest in Charcot's work had brought him to Paris in the same period as Freud, was soon assailed by the strongest doubts when he saw how carelessly experiments with hysterical patients were carried out. On his return to Belgium, he published a strongly critical account of Charcot's methods.[157]

Those visitors who came to see Charcot in Paris for a short period, and were envious of him, were often unaware that he was surrounded by a host of powerful enemies. He was stamped as an atheist by the clergy and the Catholics (one of the reasons being that he had replaced the nuns at the Salpêtrière by lay nurses), but some atheists found him too spiritual.

He was publicly accused of charlatanism by the magnetists.[158] He also had fierce enemies in political and society circles (as is obvious from the *Diary* of the Goncourt brothers). Among neurologists, some who had

remained his admirers as long as he stayed on the solid ground of neuropathology deserted him when he shifted to the study of hypnotism and
to spectacular experiments with hysterical patients. Lyubimov tells how
the German neurologist Westphal expressed deep concern about the new
turn taken by Charcot's research after he visited him in Paris. In America
Charcot was attacked on the same grounds by Bucknill. Beard, who
admitted that Charcot had made "serious mistakes," nonetheless respected
him "as a man of genius and a man of honour."[159] Charcot also had to
wage a continuous battle against the Nancy School in which he was
steadily losing ground to his opponents. Bernheim sarcastically proclaimed
that among thousands of patients whom he had hypnotized, only one displayed the three stages described by Charcot—a woman who had spent
three years at the Salpêtrière. Charcot also met with undying hatred on
the part of some of his medical colleagues and particularly on the part of
his former disciple Bouchard, an ambitious man twelve years his junior.
Worse still, a few of his seemingly loyal disciples duped him by showing
him more and more extraordinary manifestations that they rehearsed with
patients and then demonstrated to him. It is true that many of his disciples never participated in such activities, but no one apparently dared
warn him. He had been extremely cautious for a long time, but eventually
La Rochefoucauld's maxim came to apply to him: "Deception always goes
further than suspicion." According to Guillain, Charcot began to feel
strong doubts toward the end of his life and was thinking of again taking
up the entire study of hypnotism and hysteria, which death, however, prevented him from doing. A secret enemy, who was well acquainted with
Charcot's medical condition and who for years sent him anonymous letters
depicting his angina pectoris and announcing his impending death, most
likely belonged to the medical circle around Charcot.[160]

The extreme opinions prevailing about Charcot, the fascination he exerted on the one hand, and the fierce enmities he had made on the other,
made it difficult in his lifetime to form a true assessment of the value of
his work. Contrary to expectations, the passing of time has not made this
task much easier. It is therefore necessary to distinguish the various fields
of his activity. First, it is often forgotten that Charcot, as an internist and
anatomo-pathologist, made valuable contributions to the knowledge of
pulmonary and kidney diseases, and that his lectures on diseases of old-
age were for a long time a classic of what is now called geriatrics. Second,
in neurology, which was his second career, he made outstanding discoveries upon which his lasting fame will undisputedly rest: delineation of
disseminated sclerosis, amyotrophic lateral sclerosis ("Charcot's disease"),
locomotor ataxia and its peculiar arthropathies ("Charcot's joints"), his
work on cerebral and medullar localizations, and on aphasia.

On the other hand, it is most difficult to evaluate objectively what could
be called Charcot's "third career," that is, his exploration of hysteria and

hypnotism. As happens with many scientists, he lost control of the new ideas that he had formulated and was carried away by the movement he had created.

Pierre Janet has accurately described Charcot's methodological errors in that field.[161] The first was his excessive concern with delineating specific disease entities, choosing as model types those cases that showed as many symptoms as possible; he assumed that the other cases were incomplete forms. This method having proved fruitful for neurology, Charcot took it for granted that the same would hold true for mental conditions as well. He thus gave arbitrary descriptions of the *grande hystérie* and the *grand hypnotisme*. A second error was to oversimplify the descriptions of these disease entities in order to make them more intelligible to his students. A third fatal error was Charcot's lack of interest in his patients' backgrounds and in the ward life of the Salpêtrière. He hardly ever made rounds; he saw his patients in his hospital examination room while his collaborators, who had examined them, reported to him. Charcot never suspected that his patients were often visited and magnetized on the wards by incompetent people. Janet has shown that the alleged "three stages of hypnosis" were nothing but the result of training that Charcot's patients underwent at the hands of magnetizers. Seeing that the early history of magnetism and hypnotism was forgotten, Charcot—even more than Bernheim—believed that all that he found in his hypnotized patients were new discoveries.

Another fact, which from the start distorted Charcot's investigations in dynamic psychiatry, was the peculiar collective spirit that pervaded the Salpêtrière. This closed community sheltered not only crowds of old women, but comprised also special wards for hysterical patients, some of them young, pretty, and cunning: nothing could be more eminently propitious to the development of mental contagion. These women were the star attractions, utilized to demonstrate clinical cases to the students and also in Charcot's lectures, which were given in the presence of the *Tout-Paris*. Because of Charcot's paternalistic attitude and his despotic treatment of students, his staff never dared contradict him; they therefore showed him what they believed he wanted to see. After rehearsing the demonstrations, they showed the subjects to Charcot, who was careless enough to discuss their cases in the patients' presence. A peculiar atmosphere of mutual suggestion developed between Charcot, his collaborators, and his patients, which would certainly be worthy of an accurate sociological analysis.

Janet has pointed out that Charcot's descriptions of hysteria and hypnotism were based on a very limited number of patients. The *prima donna*, Blanche Wittmann, deserves more than an anecdotal mention. The role of patients in the elaboration of dynamic psychiatry has been all too neglected and would also be worthy of intensive investigation. Unfortunately, it is very difficult to gather relevant information in retrospect.

We know nothing of Blanche Wittmann's origin and background prior to her admission to the ward for hysterical patients at the Salpêtrière. According to Baudouin, she was young when she arrived there and rapidly became one of Charcot's most renowned subjects and was nicknamed *la reine des hystériques*.[162] She was often exhibited to demonstrate the "three stages of hypnosis," of which she was not only the type, but the proto-type, according to Frederick Myers who had seen her.[163] Baudouin states that she is the woman in full hysterical crisis, depicted between Charcot and Babinski in Brouillet's famous painting; she can also be recognized in several pictures in the *Iconographie de la Salpêtrière* and elsewhere. She was authoritarian, capricious, and unpleasant toward the other patients as well as the personnel.

For some unknown reason, Blanche Wittmann left the Salpêtrière for some time and was admitted at the Hôtel-Dieu, where she was investigated by Jules Janet, Pierre Janet's brother.[164] After achieving the "first stage of hypnosis," that is, lethargy, Jules Janet modified the usual technique and saw the patient in a quite new condition. A new personality, that of Blanche II, emerged, showing herself as much more balanced than Blanche I. The new personality disclosed that she had been permanently present and conscious, hidden behind Blanche I. She was always aware of everything that occurred during the many demonstrations when Blanche I had acted out the "three stages of hypnosis" and was supposed to be unconscious. Myers noted that "it is strange to reflect for how many years the dumbly raging Blanche II has thus assisted at experiments to which Blanche I submitted with easy complacence."

Jules Janet kept Blanche Wittmann in her second state for several months and found that she was remarkably (and apparently lastingly) im-proved by his treatment. What later happened to Blanche Wittmann has been succinctly reported by Baudouin. She returned to the Salpêtrière where she was given a job in the photography laboratory and later, when a laboratory of radiology was opened, she became employed there. She was still authoritarian and capricious, denied her past history, and became angry when asked about that period of her life. Since the dangers of radiology were not yet known, she became one of the first victims of the radiologist's cancer. Her last years were a calvary that she crossed without showing the least hysterical symptom. She had to suffer one amputation after another and died a martyr of science.

It was, however, Charcot's third career, that contributed more than any-thing else to his contemporary fame. The writer T. de Wyzewa, in an obituary he wrote on Charcot, said that in a few centuries his neurological work might be forgotten, but that he would stand in the memory of man-kind as one who had revealed to the world an unsuspected realm of the mind.[165] It is because of that breakthrough, and not his own literary works (which have remained unpublished) that Charcot exerted a power-ful influence on literature. As stated by de Monzie, he was the starting

point of a whole tradition of psychiatrically oriented writers, such as
Alphonse Daudet and his son Léon Daudet, Zola, Maupassant,
Huysmans, Bourget, Claretie, and later Pirandello and Proust, not to speak
of many authors of popular novels.[166] Charcot himself was the model for
a specific character in many novels and plays in the 1890's: the great
scientist of world-renown impavidly pursuing his uncanny research in the
abyss of the human mind.

An American visitor who saw Charcot at the beginning of 1893 noticed
that, while his intellectual strength was as lively as ever, his physical health
was greatly shaken.[167] He kept on working feverishly until August 15,
1893, when he left for a vacation with two of his favorite disciples, Debove
and Strauss, intending to visit the Vézelay cathedral. He died unexpectedly
in his hotel room the night of August 16, and was given a national funeral
in Paris on August 19. In spite of the deluge of praise that was lavished
on his memory, his fame soon waned. The publication of his complete works,
which had been planned in fifteen volumes, was abandoned after volume
IX had appeared in 1894. According to Lyubimov, Charcot had left
a considerable amount of literary works: memoirs, illustrated travelogues,
critical studies on philosophical and literary works, all of which he did not
want published in his lifetime. Lyubimov adds that Charcot's true personality
could not have been known before their publication. However, none of these
writings has ever been printed. Charcot's son Jean (1867–1936), who
had studied medicine to please his father, gave up this profession a few
years later and became famous as a seafarer and explorer of the South
Pole.[168] Charcot's precious library was donated by his son to the
Salpêtrière and gradually fell into the most pitiful state of neglect, as well
as did the Musée Charcot.[169]

> The evil that men do lives after them;
> The good is oft interred with their bones.

So it was with Charcot. It was not long before his glory was transformed into
the stereotype of the despotic scientist whose belief in his own superiority
blinded him into unleashing a psychic epidemic. One year after Charcot's
death, Léon Daudet, who had been a medical student on his ward, published a satirical novel, *Les Morticoles*, which gave fictitious names to
prominent physicians and ridiculed the Paris medical world.[170] Charcot
was depicted under the name of Foutange and Bernheim was called
Boustibras. Faked hypnotical séances at the "Hôpital-typhus" with
"Rosalie" (portraying Blanche Wittmann) were described in a caricaturistic
manner. Another malevolent account of Charcot's Salpêtrière was later
given by Axel Munthe in his autobiographic novel *The Story of San
Michele*.[171]

Jules Bois, who was well-acquainted with Charcot, relates that during
the last months of his life, the old man expressed his pessimism with regard

to the future of his work, which he felt would not survive him for long.[172]
In fact, before ten years had elapsed after his death, Charcot was largely
forgotten and disowned by most of his disciples. His successor, Raymond,
while giving lip service to Charcot's work on neuroses, himself belonged
to the organicist trend in neurology. One of Charcot's favorite disciples,
Joseph Babinski, who had made himself known during Charcot's lifetime
by his experiments in transferring hysterical symptoms with a magnet from
one patient to another,[173] now became the main protagonist of a radical
reaction against Charcot's concept of hysteria. Hysteria, he claimed, was
nothing but the result of suggestion, and it could be cured by "persuasion."[174]
The name "hysteria" itself was replaced by that of "pithiatisme," coined
by Babinski. Guillain reports that when he was a resident at the Salpêtrière
in 1899, that is, six years after Charcot's death, there were still a few
of Charcot's hysterical female patients who would, for a small remuneration, act out for the students the full-fledged attack of the *grande hystérie*.
But hysterical patients eventually disappeared from the Salpêtrière.[175]

As years went by, Charcot's neurological discoveries were taken for
granted and his name became associated with a regrettable episode in the
long history of the Salpêtrière. In 1925, his centennial was celebrated
in the Salpêtrière with a strong emphasis on his neurological achievements and a few rapid apologies about the *légère défaillance* (the
slight lapse), which his work on hysterical and hypnosis had been. Psychoanalysts, however, praised him in that regard as a precursor of Freud.
In 1928 a group of Paris surrealists, in their endeavor to counteract all
accepted ideas of their time, decided to celebrate the discovery of Charcot's
hysteria, "the greatest poetical discovery of the end of the nineteenth
century."[176]

Several years later, the author of the present book, then a medical
student at the Salpêtrière, met a very old woman patient who had
spent almost her entire life there and had known Charcot and his school.
She kept talking to herself and had hallucinations during which she was
hearing all these men speaking in turn. Those voices from the past, which
had never been recorded but still resounded in the disturbed mind of that
wretched old woman were all that survived of the glory that had been
Charcot's Salpêtrière.

Conclusion

We may now look back on the development of dynamic psychiatry from
Mesmer to Charcot.

There was little dynamic psychotherapy before Mesmer, aside from the
largely obsolete, nonmedical practice of exorcism. Medical men had
elaborated a theory of "imagination," that is, a "power of the mind" endowed with multiple and multiform—sometimes extraordinary—manifestations (among which spontaneous somnambulism attracted special interest).

Mesmer developed what he believed to be a scientific theory and a universal medical therapy. He aimed at provoking "crises," which were supposed to have diagnostic value and to be the weapon for the cure. His main discovery was that of the "rapport" between magnetizer and patient.

Puységur replaced the pseudo-physical theory of the "fluid" with the insight that unknown psychological forces were at work. His great clinical discovery was that of "magnetic sleep," or "artificial somnambulism," that is, a condition similar to spontaneous somnambulism, with the difference that it could be induced and stopped at will and utilized for the exploration of unknown psychic functions as well as for therapy. The concept of rapport was elaborated and now regarded as a psychological phenomenon and the channel for the psychotherapeutic action.

The great wave of spiritism in the nineteenth century resulted in the discovery of new approaches to the conscious mind, such as automatic writing. Besides "artificial somnambulism," a new condition, the mediumnistic trance, was explored. Charcot pointed to the existence of unconscious "fixed ideas" as nuclei of certain neuroses, a concept that was to be developed by Janet and Freud.

Thus, prior to those two great pioneers lay a whole century of dynamic psychiatry, during which a considerable amount of investigation had been carried out, even though it was not completely systematized. This first dynamic psychiatry will be the subject of the next chapter.

Notes

1. We follow the German translation of those letters, given by Eschenmayer, "Über Gassners Heilmethode," *Archiv für thierischen Magnetismus,* VIII, No. 1 (1820), 86–135.
2. Eugen Sierke, *Schwärmer und Schwindler zu Ende des achtzehnten Jahrhunderts* (Leipzig: S. Hirzel, 1874), pp. 222–287.
3. J. A. Zimmermann, *Johann Joseph Gassner, der berühmte Exorzist. Sein Leben und wundersames Wirken* (Kempten: Jos. Kösel, 1879).
4. Johann Joseph Gassner, *Weise, fromm und gesund zu leben, auch gottselig zu sterben, oder nützlicher Unterricht wider den Teufel zu streiten* (Stift Kempten, in der Hochfürstlichen Buchdruckerei, 1774).
5. J. A. Zimmermann, *op. cit.,* pp. 115–122.
6. The life and fate of that unfortunate woman have been made the subject of a historically well-documented novel by K. Freuler, *Anna Göldi, die Geschichte der letzten Hexe* (Frankfurt am Main: Büchergilde Gutenberg, 1945).
7. Haen, court physician to Empress Maria Theresa, was strongly opposed to Gassner, who, he contended, had cured but few patients, and that those healings were the result of either fraud, imagination, or the long journeys and the diet of the patients. See Antonii de Haen, *Dissertatio theologico-physica de miraculis* (Naples: Typis Vincentii Ursini, 1778), p. 131.
8. A. Mesmer, *Schreiben über die Magnetkur* (n.p., 1776), II, 44–46.

9. Justinus Kerner, *Franz Anton Mesmer aus Schwaben, Entdecker des thierischen Magnetismus* (Frankfurt: Literarische Anstalt, 1856).

10. Rudolf Tischner, "Franz Anton Mesmer, Leben, Werk und Wirkungen," *Münchner Beiträge zur Geschichte und Literatur der Naturwissenschaften und Medizin*, I, No. 9/10 (1928), 541–714.

11. F. Schürer-Waldheim, *Anton Mesmer. Ein Naturforscher ersten Ranges* (Vienna: Selbstverlag, 1930).

12. Karl Bittel, *Der berühmte Hr. Doct. Mesmer, 1734–1815. Auf seinen Spuren am Bodensee, im Thurgau und in der Markgraffschaft Baden, mit einigen neuen Beiträgen zur Mesmer-Forschung* (Überlingen: August Feyel, 1939).

13. Joseph Rudolph Wohleb, "Franz Anton Mesmer. Biographischer Sachstandbericht," *Zeitschrift für die Geschichte des Oberrheins*, Neue Folge, LIII, Heft 1 (1939), 33–130.

14. Bernhardt Milt, "Franz Anton Mesmer und seine Beziehungen zur Schweiz," *Mitteilungen der antiquarischen Gesellschaft in Zürich*, XXXVIII, No. 1 (1953), 1–139.

15. Jean Vinchon, *Mesmer et son secret* (Paris: Legrand, 1936).

16. Mesmer's life in Vienna has been traced and studied by F. Schürer-Waldheim, *Anton Mesmer. Ein Naturforscher ersten Ranges* (Vienna: Selbstverlag, 1930).

17. Quoted by Karl Bittel, *Der berühmte Hr. Doct. Mesmer, 1734–1815* (Überlingen: August Feyel, 1939).

18. Franz Anton Mesmer, *Schreiben über die Magnetkur an einen auswärtigen Arzt* (Vienna, 1775).

19. This document was discovered and published by Justinus Kerner, *Franz Anton Mesmer aus Schwaben* (Frankfurt: Literarische Anstalt, 1856), pp. 19–45.

20. Accounts of some of these cures have been found by Bittel in contemporary local newspapers and are published in his biographic study on Mesmer. (See note 12.)

21. Ludwig August Frankl, *Maria-Theresia von Paradis. Biographie* (Linz, 1876).

22. For more than one hundred and fifty years all authors who wrote about her said that she was the Empress's godchild. As with so many other details, this one has also been shown to be untrue by Hermann Ullrich, "Maria-Theresia Paradis und Dr. Franz Anton Mesmer," *Jahrbuch des Vereines für Geschichte der Stadt Wien*, XVII–XVIII (1961–1962), 149–188.

23. According to Justinus Kerner, *Franz Anton Mesmer aus Schwaben* (Frankfurt: Literarische Anstalt, 1856).

24. Mesmer's account of this episode has been related in his *Précis historique des faits relatifs au magnétisme animal jusques en avril 1781* (London, 1781). Maria-Theresia's father gave a somewhat different version, which has been published by Justinus Kerner, *op. cit.*, pp. 61–71.

25. Mesmer's own description of his emotional sufferings is contained in his *Précis historique* (London, 1781), pp. 21–23.

26. Life in Paris during those critical years has been admirably described in the letters that Melchior Grimm wrote to his German sovereign, *Correspondance littéraire, philosophique et critique adressée à un souverain d'Allemagne*, 5 vols., par le Baron de Grimm et par Diderot (Paris: F. Buisson, 1813). This correspondence contains several valuable reports about Mesmer.

27. Franz Anton Mesmer, *Mémoire sur la découverte du magnétisme animal* (Paris: Didot, 1779). Also his *Précis historique*, 1781.

28. D'Eslon, *Observations sur le magnétisme animal* (London and Paris: Didot, 1780).

29. His biography has been written by Louis Bergasse, *Un Défenseur des principes traditionnels sous la Révolution, Nicolas Bergasse* (Paris: Perrin, 1910). *Un Philosophe lyonnais, Nicolas Bergasse* (Lyon: Le Van, 1938).

30. The account of this celebrated cure is given by Mialle, *Exposé par ordre alphabétique des cures opérées en France par le magnétisme animal, depuis Mesmer jusqu'à nos jours* (Paris: Dentu, 1826), II, 81–82.

31. Franz Anton Mesmer, *Mémoire sur la découverte du magnétisme animal* (Paris: Didot, 1779).

32. Sir William Ramsey, *The Life and Letters of Joseph Black* (London: Constable & Co., 1918), pp. 84–85.

33. Nicolas Bergasse, *Observations de M. Bergasse sur un écrit du Dr. Mesmer, ayant pour titre: Lettre de l'inventeur du magnétisme animal à l'auteur des réflexions préliminaires* (London, 1785).

34. Eugène Louis, *Les Origines de la doctrine du magnétisme animal.* Thèse méd., Paris, 1898–1899, No. 111 (Paris: Société d'Editions Scientifiques, 1898).

35. Caullet de Veaumorel, ed., *Aphorismes de M. Mesmer dictés à l'assemblée de ses élèves . . . en 344 paragraphes* (Paris: Quinquet, 1785).

36. Antoine Lavoisier, "Sur le magnétisme animal," Vol. III, *Oeuvres de Lavoisier* (Paris: Imprimerie Nationale, 1865), pp. 499–527.

37. *Rapport des Commissaires chargés par le Roy de l'examen du magnétisme animal* (Paris, 1784).

38. This report was reprinted in: Claude Burdin and Frédéric Dubois, *Histoire académique du magnétisme animal* (Paris: Baillière, 1841).

39. A. L. de Jussieu, *Rapport de l'un des commissaires chargés par le Roy de l'examen du magnétisme animal* (Paris: Veuve Hérissant, 1784).

40. See particularly those by Jean-Baptiste Radet, *Les docteurs modernes. Comédie-parade. . . . , suivie du baquet de santé. . . .* (Paris: Brunet, 1784).

41. Paul Schmidt, *Court de Gébelin à Paris* (Paris: Fischbacher, 1908).

42. *L'anti-magnétisme, ou origine, progrès, décadence, renouvellement et réfutation du magnétisme animal* (London, 1784).

43. M. Thouret, *Recherches et doutes sur le magnétisme animal* (Paris: Prault, 1784).

44. Marat, *Mémoire sur l'électricité médicale* (Paris: Méquignon, 1784), p. 110.

45. Caullet de Veaumorel, *Aphorismes de M. Mesmer, dictés à l'assemblée de ses élèves* (Paris: Quinquet, 1785).

46. Nicolas Bergasse, *Théorie du monde et des êtres organisés, suivant les principes de M.* (Paris, 1784).

47. Quoted by Wohleb, *op. cit.*

48. This period of Mesmer's life has been partly elucidated by the research done by Karl Bittel, *Der berühmte Hr. Doct. Mesmer, 1734–1815* (Überlingen: August Feyel, 1939), *op. cit.*, and Bernhard Milt, "Franz Anton Mesmer und seine Beziehungen zur Schweiz," *Mitteilungen der antiquarischen Gesellschaft in Zürich*, XXXVIII (1953), 1–139.

49. Karl Christian Wolfart, ed., *Mesmerismus, Oder System der Wechselwirkungen, Theorie und Anwendung des thierischen Magnetismus* (Berlin: Nicolai, 1814).

50. Justinus Kerner, *Franz Anton Mesmer aus Schwaben* (Frankfurt: Literarische Anstalt, 1856).

51. Nicolas Bergasse, *Observations de M. Bergasse sur un écrit du Dr. Mesmer, ayant pour titre: Lettre de l'inventeur du magnétisme animal à l'auteur des réflexions préliminaires* (London, 1785).

52. Johann Heinrich Egg's memoirs of Mesmer were published in a local newspaper and reproduced by Bernhard Milt, "Franz Anton Mesmer und seine Beziehungen zur Schweiz," *Mitteilungen der antiquarischen Gesellschaft in Zürich*, XXXVIII (1953), 1–139.

53. Charles Richet, *L'Homme et l'intelligence. Fragments de philosophie* (Paris: Alcan, 1884), pp. 295, 543. [Italics inserted.]

54. Robert de Puységur, *Notice généalogique sur la famille Chastenet de Puységur* (Paris: Lemerre, 1904). Marquis de Blosseville, *Les Puységur. Leurs oeuvres de littérature, d'économie politique et de science* (Paris: Aubry, 1873).

55. The author is particularly grateful to the Viscount du Boisdulier, the direct descendant of the Marquis de Puységur, who provided abundant information about his illustrious ancestor and the Puységur family.

56. The description of these first sessions was given by an eyewitness, Clocquet, a tax-collector, and by Puységur himself in an anonymous pamphlet: (Puységur), *Détail des cures opérées à Buzancy près de Soissons, par le magnétisme animal* (Soissons, 1784).

57. A. M. J. Chastenet de Puységur, *Mémoires pour servir à l'histoire et à l'établissement du magnétisme animal* (n. p., 1784).

58. A. M. J. Chastenet de Puységur, *Mémoires pour servir à l'histoire et à l'établissement du magnétisme animal* (2nd ed.; Paris: Cellot, 1809), pp. 39–52.

59. Anon., *Nouvelles cures opérées par le Magnétisme Animal* (n.p., 1784).

60. A. M. J. Chastenet de Puységur, *Du magnétisme animal, considéré dans ses rapports avec diverses branches de la physique générale* (Paris: Desenne, 1807), pp. 108–152.

61. A copy of these precious and exceedingly rare publications can be found at the Bibliothèque Nationale et Universitaire in Strasbourg. Their titles are as follows: *Exposé des différentes cures opérées depuis le 25 d'août 1785, époque de la formation de la société, fondée à Strasbourg, sous la dénomination de Société Harmonique des Amis-Réunis, jusqu'au 12. du mois de Juin 1786, par différents membres de cette Société* (Strasbourg: Librairie Académique, 1787). *Suite des cures faites par différents magnétiseurs, membres de la Société Harmonique des Amis-Réunis de Strasbourg.* (Strasbourg: chez Lorenz et Schouler, 1787). Vol. II, *Annales de la Société Harmonique des Amis-Réunis de Strasbourg, ou cures que des membres de cette société ont opérées par le magnétisme animal.* (A Strasbourg, & chez les principaux libraires de l'Europe, 1789), Vol. III.

62. A. M. J. Chastenet de Puységur, *Les Fous, les insensés, les maniaques et les frénétiques ne seraient-ils que des somnambules désordonnés?* (Paris: Dentu, 1812).

63. M. S. Mialle, *Exposé par ordre alphabétique des cures opérées en France par le magnétisme animal, depuis Mesmer jusqu'à nos jours (1774–1826),* 2 vols. (Paris: Dentu, 1826), I, 202–204.

64. *Encyclopédie du XIXe Siècle,* 3rd ed. (Paris, 1872, Vol. XIX art. *Puységur.* Bureau de l'Encyclopédie du XIXe siècle).

65: These details have been contributed by Mr. Guillermot, Mayor of Buzancy.

66. Letter of G. Dumas, Directeur des Services d'Archives de l'Aisne, June 14, 1963.

67. Petetin, *Mémoire sur la découverte des phénomènes que présentent la catalepsie et le somnambulisme, symptomes de l'affection hystérique essentielle* (Lyon, 1785).

68. *Extrait du journal d'une cure magnétique. Traduit de l'allemand* (Rastadt: J. W. Dorner, 1787).

69. Abbé de Faria, *De la cause du sommeil lucide, ou Etude de la nature de l'homme.* Tome 1er (Paris: chez Mme. Horiac, 1819). This is the only one published of four volumes planned by Faria.

70. J. P. F. Deleuze, *Histoire critique du magnétisme animal* (Paris: Schoell, 1810).

71. A. Bertrand, *Traité du somnambulisme et des différentes modifications qu'il présente* (Paris: Dentu, 1823).

72. Général Noizet, *Mémoire sur le somnambulisme et le magnétisme animal* (Paris: Plon, 1854).

73. Mouillesaux, in 1787, ordered a woman patient, while she was in magnetic sleep, to visit another person the following day at a given hour; the patient executed the order. Quoted in Tischner, "Franz Anton Mesmer: Leben, Werk und Wirkungen." Münchner Beiträge zur Geschichte und Literatur der Naturwissenschaften und Medizin, I, No. 9/10 (1928), 541–714.

74. *"Réciprocité magnétique"* is mentioned as early as 1784 in a pamphlet against Mesmer by an anonymous author who was well acquainted with Mesmer's theories: *La Vision, contenant l'explication de l'écrit intitulé: Traces du magnétisme & la théorie des vrais sages* (Paris: Couturier, 1784).

75. Tardif de Montrevel, *Essai sur la théorie du somnambulisme magnétique* (London, 1785), pp. 43–45.

76. This was expounded in great detail by Deleuze and most contemporary authors.

77. Claude Burdin and Frédéric Dubois, *Histoire académique du magnétisme animal* (Paris: Baillière, 1841).

78. Wilhelm Erman, *Der tierische Magnetismus in Preussen vor und nach den Freiheitskriegen aktenmässig dargestellt* (Munich and Berlin: R. Oldenburg, 1925).

79. *Askläpeion, allgemeines medizin-chirurgisches Wochenblatt für alle Theile der Heilkunde und ihre Hülfswissenschaften* (Berlin, 1811).

80. Carl Alexander Ferdinand Kluge, *Versuch einer Darstellung des animalischen Magnetismus als Heilmittel* (Berlin, 1811), pp. 102–108.

81. Friedrich Hufeland, *Ueber Sympathie* (Weimar: Verlag des Landes-Industrie-Comptoirs, 1811).

82. Kluge, cf. n. 8.

83. René Guignard, *Un Poète romantique allemand, C. Brentano* (Paris: Les Belles-Lettres, 1933).

84. *Das bittere Leiden unseres Herrn Jesu Christi. Nach den Betrachtungen der gottseligen Anna Katharina Emmerich* (Sulzbach: Seidel, 1837).

85. *Leben der heiligen Jungfrau Maria. Nach den Betrachtungen der gottseligen Anna Katharina Emmerich* (Munich: Literarisch-artistische Anstalt, 1852).

86. P. Winfried Hümpfner, *Clemens Brentanos Glaubwürdigkeit in seinen Emmerich-Aufzeichnungen* (Würzburg: St. Rita-Verlag, 1923).

87. Justinus Kerner, *Das Bilderbuch aus meiner Knabenzeit. Erinnerungen aus den Jahren 1786–1804* (Braunschweig: Viehweg & Sohn, 1819).

88. Justinus Kerner, *Das Fettgift, oder die Fettsäure und ihre Wirkungen auf den thierischen Organismus* (Stuttgart-Tübingen: J. G. Cotta, 1822).

89. Theobald Kerner, *Das Kernerhaus und seine Gäste* (2nd ed.; Stuttgart and Leipzig: Deutsche Verlags-Anstalt, 1897).

90. Heinrich Straumann, *Justinus Kerner und der Okkultismus in der deutschen Romantik* (Horgen-Zürich and Leipzig: Münster-Presse, 1928).

91. Justinus Kerner, *Geschichte zweyer Somnambülen. Nebst einigen andern Denkwürdigkeiten aus dem Gebiete der magischen Heilkunde und der Psychologie* (Karlsruhe: Gottlieb Braun, 1824).

92. David Friedrich Strauss, "Justinus Kerner," *Gesammelte Schriften*, Vol. I (Bonn: E. Strauss, 1876).

93. Justinus Kerner, *Die Seherin von Prevorst. Eröffnungen über das innere Leben und über das Hineinragen einer Geisterwelt in die unsere*, 2 vols. (Stuttgart-Tübingen: Cotta, 1829).

94. *Ibid.*

95. Justinus Kerner, *Klecksographien. Mit Illustrationen nach den Vorlagen des Verfassers* (Stuttgart: Deutsche Verlags-Anstalt, 1857).

96. James Braid, *Neurhypnology, or The Rationale of Nervous Sleep Considered in Relation with Animal Magnetism* (London: J. Churchill, 1843).

97. John Elliotson, *Numerous Cases of Surgical Operations Without Pain in the Mesmeric State* (Philadelphia: Lea and Blanchard, 1843).

98. James Esdaile, *Mesmerism in India and its Practical Application in Surgery and Medicine* (Hartford: Silas Andrus & Son, 1847).

99. James Esdaile, *Natural and Mesmeric Clairvoyance with its Practical Application of Mesmerism in Surgery and Medicine* (London: Hippolyte Baillière, 1852).

100. *Mesmerism; Its History, Phenomena, and Practice: With Reports of Cases Developed in Scotland* (Edinburgh: Frazer & Co., 1843).

101. John Hughes Bennett, *The Mesmeric Mania of 1851, with a Physiological Explanation of the Phenomena Produced* (Edinburgh: Sutherland and Knox, 1851).

102. See Frank Podmore, *Modern Spiritualism* (London: Methuen, 1902), I, 154–176.

103. See his autobiography, Andrew Jackson Davis, *The Magic Staff* (New York: J. S. Brown & Co., 1857).

104. Pierre Janet, *Les Médications psychologiques* (Paris: Alcan, 1919), I, 27–29.

105. We follow mainly the account given by Frank Podmore, *Modern Spiritualism. A History and a Criticism*, 2 vols. (London: Methuen, 1902).

106. Robert Amadou, *Les Grands médiums* (Paris: Denoël, 1957).

107. Mrs. Daniel Dunglas Home, *D. D. Home. His Life and Mission* (London: Trubner, 1888).

108. The Earl of Dunraven, *Experiences in Spiritualism with D. D. Home* (London: Thomas Scott, Work Court in Holborn, 1869).

109. E. E. Fournier d'Albe, *The Life of Sir William Crookes* (London: T. Fisher Unwin, 1923).

110. Allan Kardec, *Le Livre des esprits, contenant les principes de la doctrine spirite* (Paris: Dentu, 1857).

111. Frederick Myers, *Human Personality and Its Survival of Bodily Death,* 2 vols. (London: Longmans, Green and Co., 1903).

112. Michel Chevreul, "Lettre à M. Ampère sur une classe particulière de mouvements musculaires," *Revue des Deux Mondes,* 2nd series, 1833 (II), 258–266.

113. Michel Chevreul, *De la Baguette divinatoire, du pendule dit explorateur et des tables tournantes, au point de vue de l'histoire, de la critique et de la méthode expérimentale* (Paris: Mallet-Bachelier, 1854).

114. A. Jacquet, *Ein halbes Jahrhundert Medizin* (Basel: Benno Schwalbe, 1929), p. 169.

115. Charles Richet, "Du somnambulisme provoqué," *Journal de l'Anatomie et de la Physiologie normales et pathologiques de l'homme et des animaux,* II (1875), 348–377.

116. We follow mainly the book of A. W. van Renterghem, *Liébeault en zijne School* (Amsterdam: Van Rossen, 1898). Excerpts have been published in French translation in *Zeitschrift für Hypnotismus,* IV (1896), 333–375; V (1897), 46–55, 95–127; VI (1897), 11–44.

117. Pierre Janet, *Les Médications psychologiques* (Paris: Alcan), I, 30.

118. See biographic notice in Liébeault, *Pour constater la réalité du magnétisme. Confession d'un hypnotiseur. Extériorisation de la force neurique ou fluide magnétique* (Paris: Libraire du Magnétisme, n.d.).

119. A. Liébeault, *Du sommeil et des états analogues, considérés surtout au point de vue de l'action du moral sur le physique* (Paris: Masson, 1866).

120. This is one of the many legends in the history of dynamic psychiatry. Liébeault had had readers in France, in Switzerland, and even in Russia, as shown by the book of Nikolay Grot, *Snovidyeniya, kak predmet nautshnavo analiza* (Kiev: Tipografia Fritza, 1878)–who frequently refers to Liébeault's theory of sleep.

121. A. W. van Renterghem, cf. n. 116.

122. Biographic and autobiographic notices can be found in *Jubilé du Professeur H. Bernheim, 12 novembre 1910* (Nancy, 1910). (The author is particularly indebted to Mlle. G. Koest, Head Librarian of the University Medical School in Nancy, for the loan of this extremely rare publication and for other documents pertaining to the Nancy School.)

123. H. Bernheim, *De la suggestion dans l'état hypnotique et dans l'état de veille* (Paris: Doin, 1884).

124. H. Bernheim, *De la suggestion et de ses applications à la thérapeutique* (Paris: Doin, 1886). Eng. trans., *Suggestive Therapeutics,* trans. from the 2nd rev. French ed. by Christian Herter (New York: Putnam's, 1897).

125. H. Bernheim, *Hypnotisme, suggestion, psychothérapie. Etudes nouvelles* (Paris: Doin, 1891).

126. See Poul Bjerre, *The History and Practice of Psychoanalysis,* trans. by Elizabeth Barrow (Boston: Badger, 1920), Chap. 2.

127. See his autobiography. Frederik van Eeden, *Happy Humanity* (New York: Doubleday & Co., Inc., 1912).

128. Frederik van Eeden, "The Theory of Psycho-Therapeutics," *The Medical Magazine,* I (1895), 230–257.

129. A. W. van Renterghem, "L'Evolution de la psychothérapie en Hollande," *Deuxième Congrès International de l'Hypnotisme, Paris, 1900* (Paris: Vigot, 1902), pp. 54–62.

130. Auguste Forel, *Rückblick auf mein Leben* (Zurich: Europa-Verlag, 1935).

131. In his report about the Nancy School, Van Renterghem mentions Freud and Breuer. A. W. van Renterghem, *Liébeault en zijne School* (Amsterdam: Van Rossen, 1898), p. 133.

132. This was not so new as Bernheim believed. As early as 1818, Löwenhielm (*Bibliothèque du magnétisme animal,* V, 228–240) claimed that by putting two fingers on the forehead of the subject, the latter was able to recall what he had experienced during the hypnotic state; various methods to the same effect had been commonly used by other magnetizers.

133. H. Bernheim, Ecole de Médecine de Nancy. Doctrine de la suggestion, in "Nancy et Lorraine," *Idées modernes,* III (1909), 139–149. See also: *Jubilé du Professeur H. Bernheim* (Nancy, 1910).

134. Georges Guillain, *J. M. Charcot (1835–1893). Sa Vie, son oeuvre* (Paris: Masson and Cie, 1955).

135. A. Souques, "Charcot intime," *Presse Médicale,* XXXIII, I, No. 42 (May 27, 1925), 693–698.

136. A. Lyubimov, *Profesor Sharko, Nautshno-biografitshesky etiud* (St. Petersburg: Tip. Suvorina, 1894).

137. Levillain, "Charcot et l'Ecole de la Salpêtrière," *Revue Encyclopédique* (1894), pp. 108–115.

138. Georges Guillain, "L'Oeuvre de Duchenne (de Boulogne)," *Etudes Neurologiques,* 3rd series (Paris: Masson and Cie, 1929), pp. 419–448. Paul Guilly, *Duchenne (de Boulogne)* (Paris: Legrand, 1936).

139. Paul Richer, *Etudes cliniques sur l'hystéro-épilepsie ou Grande Hystérie* (Paris: Delahaye et Lecrosnier, 1881), with many pictures.

140. J. M. Charcot, "Sur les divers états nerveux déterminés par l'hypnotisation chez les hystériques," *Comptes-Rendus hebdomadaires des séances de l'Académie des Sciences,* XCIV (1882), 1, 403–405.

141. J. M. Charcot, *Oeuvres complètes, Leçons sur les maladies du système nerveux* (Paris: Progrès Médical, 1890), III, 299–359.

142. Benjamin Collins Brodie, *Lectures illustrative of certain local nervous affections* (London: Longmans and Co., 1837).

143. Russel Reynolds, "Remarks on Paralyses and other Disorders of Motion and Sensation, Dependent on Ideas," *British Medical Journal,* II (1869), 483–485.

144. J. M. Charcot, "Sur un cas d'amnésie rétro-antérograde, probablement d'origine hystérique," *Revue de Médecine,* XII (1892), 81–96. With follow-up by Souques, *Revue de Médecine,* XII (1892), 267–400, 867–881.

145. J. M. Charcot, "La Foi qui guérit," *Archives de Neurologie,* XXV (1893), 72–87.

146. Léon Daudet, *Souvenirs des milieux littéraires, politiques, artistiques et médicaux de 1885 à 1905.* 2nd series: *Devant la douleur* (Paris: Nouvelle Librairie Nationale, 1915), pp. 4–15. See also, by the same author, *Les Oeuvres et les hommes* (Paris: Nouvelle Librairie Nationale, 1922), pp. 197–243. *Quand mon père vivait, Souvenirs inédits sur Alphonse Daudet* (Paris: Grasset, 1940), pp. 113–119.

147. Edmond et Jules de Goncourt, *Journal. Mémoires de la vie littéraire* (Paris: Fasquelle et Flammarion, 1956). (See particularly Vol. III.) (condensed excerpt).

148. A. Lyubimov, cf. n. 136 (condensed excerpt).

149. Henri Meige, "Charcot artiste," *Nouvelle Iconographie de la Salpêtrière,* XI (1898).

150. Georges Guillain, *J. M. Charcot, 1825–1893. Sa vie, son oeuvre* (Paris: Masson and Cie, 1955).

151. A. Lyubimov, cf. n. 136 (condensed excerpt).

152. Jules Claretie, *La Vie à Paris, 1881* (Paris: Havard, 1882), pp. 128–129.

153. J. M. Charcot and Paul Richer, *Les Difformes et les malades dans l'art* (Paris: Lecrosnier and Babé, 1889).

154. J. M. Charcot and Paul Richer, *Les Démoniaques dans l'art* (Paris: Delahaye and Lecrosnier, 1887).

155. Ch. Féré, "J. M. Charcot et son oeuvre," *Revue des Deux Mondes,* CXXII (1894), 410–424.

156. Levillain, "Charcot et l'École de la Salpêtrière," *Revue Encyclopédique* (1894), pp. 108–115.

157. Joseph Delboeuf, "De l'Influence de l'imitation et de l'éducation dans le somnambulisme provoqué," *Revue Philosophique,* XXII (1886), 146–171.

158. Bué, *Le Magnétisme humain. Congrès International de 1889* (Paris: Georges Carré, 1890), pp. 333–334, 338–339.

159. George M. Beard, *The Study of Trance, Muscle-Reading and Allied Nervous*

Phenomena in Europe and America, with a Letter on the Moral Character of Trance Subjects and a Defense of Dr. Charcot (New York: 1882).

160. G. Hahn, "Charcot et son influence sur l'opinion publique," *Revue des Questions Scientifiques,* 2nd series, VI (1894), 230–261, 353–359. C. Féré, cf. n. 155.

161. Pierre Janet, "J. M. Charcot, son oeuvre psychologique," *Revue Philosophique,* XXXIX (1895), 569–604.

162. A. Baudouin, "Quelques souvenirs de la Salpêtrière," *Paris-Médical,* XV (I), No. 21 (May 23, 1925), pp. X–III.

163. Frederick Myers, *Human Personality and Its Survival of Bodily Death,* 2 vols. (London: Longmans, Green and Co., 1903).

164. Jules Janet, "L'Hystérie et l'hypnotisme, d'après la théorie de la double personnalité," *Revue Scientifique (Revue Rose),* 3rd series, XV (1888), 616–623.

165. *Le Figaro,* August 17, 1893.

166. A. de Monzie, "Discours au centenaire de Charcot," *Revue Neurologique,* XXXII, No. 1, June 1925. (Special issue for Charcot's centennial.)

167. C. F. Withington, (Letter to the Editor), *Boston Medical and Surgical Journal,* CXXIX (1893), 207.

168. See (Anon.), *Jean-Baptiste Charcot* (Paris: Yacht-Club de France, 1937). Auguste Dupouy, *Charcot* (Paris: Plon, 1938).

169. Jean-Baptiste Charcot, "Discours pronocé à l'inauguration de la bibliothèque de son père," *Bulletin Médical,* XXI (November 23, 1907).

170. Léon Daudet, *Les Morticoles* (Paris: Charpentier, 1894).

171. Axel Munthe, *The Story of San Michele* (New York: Duffin, 1929), Chap. 17.

172. Jules Bois, *Le Monde invisible* (Paris: Flammarion, n. d.), pp. 185–192.

173. J. Babinski, *Recherches servant à établir que certaines manifestations hystériques peuvent être transférées d'un sujet à l'autre sous l'influence de l'aimant* (Paris: Delahaye et Lecrosnier, 1886).

174. In various articles culminating in J. Babinski, "Définition de l'hystérie" (Société de Neurologie de Paris, séance du 7 novembre 1901, sous la présidence du Prof. Raymond), *Revue Neurologique,* IX (1901), 1074–1080.

175. Georges Guillain, *J. M. Charcot,* p. 174.

176. Aragon et Breton, "Le Cinquantenaire de l'hystérie (1878–1928)," *La Révolution Surréaliste,* IV, No. 11 (March 15, 1928), 20–22.

3

The First Dynamic Psychiatry (1775-1900)

THE CUMULATIVE EXPERIENCE of several generations of magnetizers and hypnotists resulted in the slow development of a well-rounded system of dynamic psychiatry. These pioneers undertook with great audacity the exploration and the therapeutic utilization of unconscious psychological energies. On the basis of their findings, they elaborated new theories about the human mind and the psychogenesis of illness. This first dynamic psychiatry was an impressive achievement, even more so since it was brought about mostly outside of—if not directly in opposition to—official medicine.

Since the first dynamic psychiatry was not the work of a single man, there was—in contrast with many other systems—no rigid conceptual framework to direct its growth. The main tenets were given by Mesmer and Puységur. They were followed by a great number of laymen and physicians, working either individually or in various unsystematic and even rival groups or schools, mainly in France and Germany, and later also in England and North America. The evolution was not continuous: all during the nineteenth-century there were a number of waves, ebbs, and tides.

About 1880, a great upsurge was felt and the first dynamic psychiatry was given university acknowledgment with Charcot and Bernheim. A rapid development followed. During that period, a new dynamic psychiatry slowly emerged, and for some time the two systems existed together until about 1900, when the new schools came to the foreground with the ensuing decline of the first dynamic psychiatry. However, two facts should be emphasized: (1) In the new dynamic schools, much of that which seems to us to be most original was in fact rooted in the first dynamic psychiatry. (2) Although the new system seemed at times to be radically opposed to the first dynamic psychiatry, the latter was in reality not superseded, but rather supplemented, by the former.

The Main Features

Throughout the innumerable variations of the first dynamic psychiatry, several main characteristics have remained constant:

1. Hypnotism was adopted as the main approach, the *via regia* to the unconscious. Supplementary approaches were added during the latter part of the century (mediumnism, automatic writing, and crystal gazing).

2. Particular attention was devoted to certain clinical pictures (sometimes called magnetic diseases): spontaneous somnambulism, lethargy, catalepsy, multiple personality, and, toward the end of the century, interest came to focus more and more on hysteria.

3. A new model of the human mind was evolved. It was based on the duality of conscious and unconscious psychism. Later, it was modified to the form of a cluster of subpersonalities underlying the conscious personality.

4. New theories concerning the pathogenesis of nervous illness, which were based at first on a concept of an unknown fluid, were soon replaced by the concept of mental energy. In the latter part of the nineteenth century the concepts of the autonomous activity of split fragments of personality and of the mythopoetic function of the unconscious arose.

5. Psychotherapy relied mostly upon the use of hypnotism and suggestion, with special consideration given to the rapport between patient and magnetizer. New types of therapists arose: the magnetizer and, later, the hypnotist, who was but a variation of the former.

In this chapter, we will briefly consider the sources of the first dynamic psychiatry, give a survey of the main features enumerated above, and then look into the influence of the first dynamic psychiatry on the cultural life in those days.

The Sources of the First Dynamic Psychiatry

Among the many sources of the first dynamic psychiatry, three should be given special emphasis:

We have already described the manner in which animal magnetism evolved historically out of the old practice of exorcism, and we have seen how Mesmer's crisis was induced in exactly the same way as Gassner's *exorcismus probativus*; the evil was brought out as a first step toward its removal. Possession eventually disappeared, but it was replaced by the manifestation of multiple personality. Isolated cases of possession were observed, however, throughout the nineteenth century, as in southern Germany, and men such as Justinus Kerner treated the possessed with a method that was a curious mixture of magnetism and exorcism.[1]

Another very important source of the first dynamic psychiatry was the old concept of "imagination." At the time of the Renaissance, philosophers and physicians became very interested in a power of the mind, *Imaginatio,* a term that held a much broader meaning than it does today and included what we call suggestion and autosuggestion. Many once famous but now forgotten works were devoted to *Imaginatio.* In a chapter of his *Essays,* Montaigne summarizes some of the prevalent ideas of his day.[2] He ascribes to imagination the contagious effects of human emotions. Imagination, according to Montaigne, was a frequent cause of physical, emotional, and mental disease, and even of death, as well as all manifestations commonly attributed to magic. Imagination could cause conspicuous physical phenomena such as the appearance of the stigmata or even the transformation of one sex into another. But imagination could also be used toward the cure of physical and mental ailments. In the eighteenth century, the Italian Muratori wrote a treatise, *On the Power of Human Imagination,* which was widely read and quoted.[3] Among the many manifestations of imagination, he described dreams, visions, delusions, fixed ideas, antipathy (that is, phobias), and above all somnambulism. In the second half of the eighteenth century, somnambulism became the focal point of all discussions of imagination. Marvelous stories were published everywhere about sleep-walkers who would write, swim rivers, or walk over rooftops in full-moon nights and whose lives were endangered if they were suddenly called by their names and wakened. We can hardly realize today how incredible and fantastic Puységur's assertion must have seemed to his contemporaries, that somnambulism could be induced and stopped artificially almost at will and used in the investigation of the most hidden secrets of the human mind.

A third source was the knowledge of hypnotism itself, which, throughout human history, had been discovered, forgotten, and rediscovered.[4] Without going back as far as the ancient Egyptians or even the Renaissance students of natural magic, we see that Gassner healed many of his patients by hypnotizing them (this becomes obvious when reading the account given by Abbé Bourgeois). Mesmer himself, when magnetizing, was putting some of his patients into hypnotic sleep. The report of the commissioners mentioned that " . . . all of them were subdued in an astonishing way to the man who was magnetizing them; in spite of their drowsiness, they woke up at his voice, his glance or a sign of him." However, neither Gassner nor Mesmer had clearly understood the implications of what they were doing, and it was Puységur, who in 1784 discovered that the perfect crisis he had called forth in his patients was nothing but artificially induced somnambulism.

The Royal Road to the Unknown Mind: Hypnotism

From 1784 to about 1880, artificial somnambulism was the chief method of gaining access into the unconscious mind. First called the perfect crisis by Puységur, magnetic sleep, or artificial somnambulism, was given the name of hypnotism by Braid in 1843.[5]

The nature of that condition was disputed from the beginning. Mesmer refused to see in it more than one particular form of crisis. A polemic developed between the fluidists, who explained it in terms of the alleged magnetic fluid, and the animists, who contended that it was a psychological phenomenon. But the identity of the nature of spontaneous somnambulism and of mesmeric sleep was never seriously questioned during the entire nineteenth century.[6]

The main arguments in favor of that conception were later summarized by Janet.[7] First, the individuals who are subject to spontaneous somnambulism are also easily magnetized and hypnotized. Second, it is easy to establish a rapport with an individual who is in spontaneous somnambulism and to make him shift from this condition into one of typical hypnotic sleep. Third, a person who has had an attack of spontaneous somnambulism of which he remembers nothing in his waking state will recall it when hypnotized. The reverse is also true.

On the other hand, though, there is an essential difference between natural and artificial somnambulism, in that the latter is directed and under the strict control of a man, the magnetizer, who induces it, molds its manifestations, and terminates it at will.

From the very beginning, the peculiar relationship between the magnetizer and the magnetized was the object of much wonder and speculation. Puységur noticed that his subject Victor did not merely carry out all his orders exactly, but that he seemed to anticipate or to guess them. The question immediately arose as to whether the subject would oppose limitations to the magnetizer's will and whether he could be forced by the magnetizer to commit immoral or criminal acts. The rapport, the special relationship between the magnetizer and the subject, also impressed the early Mesmerists from the beginning. It became clear that the magnetized person was oblivious to all but the magnetizer and that he could perceive the outside world only through the latter. It was soon discovered that the rapport extended its influence beyond the session of magnetic sleep: a person who is put into magnetic sleep for the second time remembers all that happened during the first session. The magnetizer is thus calling forth in his subject a special life of its own, aside from the normal conscious life, that is, a second condition with its own continuity, under increasing dependency on the magnetizer.

One of the most conclusive and striking proofs that the influence of hypnotism extends into normal conscious life is given by the facts of posthypnotic amnesia and posthypnotic suggestion. The early Mesmerists noticed that the subject in his normal condition recollected nothing of what had happened during his magnetic sleep, and they rightly compared this state with that which follows attacks of spontaneous somnambulism. Soon thereafter they discovered that a subject would, in his wakeful state, execute an order given him during his hypnotic sleep. This phenomenon of posthypnotic suggestion was described as early as 1787[8] and was abundantly experimented with by Deleuze[9] and Bertrand,[10] and later by Bernheim and the Nancy School. The fact that posthypnotic amnesia is not absolute and that an individual can be brought, by certain procedures, to recall in his wakeful state what happened during the hypnotic session was also known at an early period and was never completely forgotten, until it was redis-covered by Bernheim.[11]

As to the means of inducing mesmeric sleep (which we shall henceforth designate by its later name of hypnosis), the early magnetizers made use of Mesmer's technique of the passes, but this technique was soon abandoned in favor of two others. The first was fascination (a method already known to the ancient Egyptians, to Cornelius Agrippa, and others). The patient was asked to look at a fixed or slightly moving point, either luminous or not, or simply to look fixedly into the eyes of the hypnotist. This was the method later popularized by Braid, and it was also used by the Salpêtrière School. This technique was combined with the verbal one by the Abbé Faria, who seated his subject in a comfortable chair and gave him the im-perative order: "Sleep!". Other hypnotists would give the order in a gentler, lower voice. Faria's technique was later adopted by Liébeault and the Nancy School. The first mesmerists used such methods as blowing on the subjects' eyes as a means of terminating the hypnotic state.

Magnetizers soon realized that other requisites of a more general nature were no less important. They well understood what we call today the hypnotic situation and that no person can be hypnotized against his will. The subject must be made comfortable, reassured, and told to relax. The element of autosuggestion in hypnosis was also well understood by those pioneers and was clearly elicited by Braid and later by the Nancy School. The role of mutual suggestion was also perceived by the early magnetists, who, following Mesmer's example, treated patients in groups. One or two subjects, who were already familiar with the procedure, were hypnotized first in the presence of the others. It had been noticed that a person could be made more receptive by the mere fact of seeing others hypnotized. This collective method had been widely applied from Mesmer to Bernheim and Charcot, and also by popular stage hypnotists.

Early magnetizers did not realize, however, to what extent the hypnotic condition is molded by the hypnotist and has to be learned by the sub-ject. Janet has made the latter point quite explicit.[12] If your subject has never heard of hypnotism, Janet said, it is unlikely that you will be able to induce him into the usual hypnotic condition; if he was ever subject to spon-taneous somnambulism or to convulsive crises, he will probably fall into his previous pattern of somnambulism or of convulsive crisis, or perhaps into some vague nervous state, unless the hypnotist explains what is expected of him and thus prepares him to play his role. This is also the reason why the hypnotic condition differs according to the particular hypnotist, the school to which he belongs, and the successive periods in the history of the first dynamic psychiatry. This is how the early mesmerists had unknowingly shaped a specific type of hypnotic condition, which they believed to be the standard of magnetic sleep. The hypnotic state, as developed by them, comprised many manifestations, some of them fairly common and not far removed from normal psychological states, others rare and extraordinary.

One of the first characteristics of magnetic sleep to strike the early mesmerists was the increased acuteness of perception displayed by the subjects. Hypnotized individuals are able to perceive stimuli that are normally neglected or below the threshold of perception. Puységur was surprised to hear Victor sing aloud tunes, which he, Puységur, was singing to himself. Apparently Victor recognized the songs through the involuntary movements of the marquis' lips, since most people move their lips when singing to themselves. This hypersensitivity extends to all fields of perception and can explain many instances of alleged clairvoyance under hypnosis. Not less remarkable is the increased capacity of the memory; the hypnotized person may remember old and seemingly forgotten incidents of his childhood and describe happenings during artificial or spontaneous somnambulism or during intoxication. This hypermnesia extends to things that had apparently remained unnoticed by the subject.

It was soon discovered that hypnotism opens a direct access to certain psychological processes. Not only is the subject able to display greater physical strength than he believes himself capable of in his normal waking state, but he may—spontaneously or at the command of the hypnotist—turn deaf, blind, hallucinated, paralyzed, spastic, cataleptic or anesthetic. The anesthesia may be so perfect that surgical operations have at times been performed without pain under hypnosis. It would seem that Récamier was the first to perform a surgical operation under magnetic anesthesia in 1821. It is surprising that so little attention has been given to findings that could have avoided much suffering. When Esdaile began applying systematic hypnotic anesthesia in surgical operations, he met with scepticism and hostility. On the other hand, application of mesmeric sleep toward the cure of physical ailments was common among mesmerists and was never completely forgotten. Mainly through Liébeault's influence, it was widely known by the end of the 1880's that many conditions could be cured or alleviated by hypnotic suggestion (neuralgias, rheumatism, gout, and dysmenorrhea). Experiments on physiological modifications produced under hypnosis were performed even before the middle of the nineteenth century by Charpignon and Du Potet.[13]

From the beginning, mesmerists were struck by their subjects' ability to display emotions and to enact roles with astonishing perfection, utmost apparent sincerity, and, it seemed to them, with more skill than experienced actors. We remember how Victor impressed Puységur by showing more vivacity and intelligence under hypnosis than in his waking state. This ability went so far that Du Potet spoke in 1849 of a metamorphosis of the personality, and this phenomenon has been the starting point of the still disputed problem of age-regression."[14]

Early magnetists paid so much attention to the objective manifestations of hypnosis that they did not inquire much into the subjective experience of being hypnotized. They assumed that the condition was a sleep, although one of a peculiar kind, since the subject could often be said to be more awake than in his waking state. They made no great effort to reconcile this apparent contradiction, the coexistence of sleep and wakefulness. No systematic inquiries were undertaken until almost the end of the century under the influence of the Nancy School. To this day, the best account of a hypnotized person is perhaps that given by Eugen Bleuler who had himself hypnotized by his colleague, Dr. von Speyr of Berne:

> Von Speyr utilized Liébeault's technique of fixation combined with verbal suggestion. Bleuler strove to cooperate with the hypnotist while keeping as much awareness as he could. He soon noticed that parts of his visual field were falling out, as it were. Then, these empty spots expanded and the rest of the visual field became veiled. Finally, he could perceive only the contrast of light and shadow. He felt as though his eyes were moist and they burned slightly, but he felt relaxed. A comfortable warmth invaded his body from the head down to his legs; he felt no desire to move or to do anything, and it seemed to him that his thoughts were quite clear. He heard the hypnotist tell him to move his arms; he tried to resist the order, but failed partly. The hypnotist then told him that the back of his hand was insensitive; Bleuler thought that this could not be true and that Von Speyr was joking when telling him that he was pricking it (which he was actually doing). He awoke as if from a slumber at the hypnotist's injunction. He found that he had no amnesia and remembered the post-hypnotic suggestion to the effect that he would wake up at exactly 6:15 the following morning. He tried without success to remain aware of the time during the night. At 6:15 A.M., he suddenly awoke: someone had just knocked at the door. Bleuler concluded from that experiment that the hypnotic process had involved his unconscious more than his conscious would let him believe. Two or three further sessions with Von Speyr and Forel produced the same results as the first one.[15]

It would be worthwhile to compare the subjective experiences of various types of individuals and of persons hypnotized by hypnotists belonging to different schools. A recent research by Stokvis points unequivocally to the element of unconscious role-playing, which is manifested in hypnosis.[16]

Among the numerous manifestations of mesmeric sleep, one that particularly impressed Puységur and his followers was the unexpected lucidity displayed by the subject. This extraordinary keenness of perception led the early hypnotists to search more and more in the realm of the marvelous. As seen in the preceding chapter, they found that the patient was able to diagnose not only his own ailments and predict its course and prescribe the remedy, but that he seemed able to do as much for people with whom he had been set in rapport. Furthermore, it was contended that some of the hypnotized subjects, the so-called *somnambules extra-lucides,* were able to read with their eyes covered, to read the thoughts of others, to find lost objects, and even to predict the future. We now know that these were the results of mutual suggestion developing between magnetizer and magnetized. But contrary to the assumption of the first magnetizers, it became evident that a hypnotized subject is perfectly able to lie, not only through suggestion, but of his own volition.

One of the most controversial issues of hypnotism was the phenomenon of age regression recognized early by some hypnotists and subject to scrutiny in the 1880's and 1890's. The hypnotized subject is told that he is going backward in time, for instance to his adolescence or childhood at a given moment of his past. His behavior, his movements, and his voice change accordingly. He seems to have forgotten everything that happened to him since the moment that he is reenacting, and he gives a detailed account of happenings at this period of his life. Is this "true regression," that is, reviviscence of what the subject actually experienced at that given age, or is it only an excellent histrionic imitation of what he believes to have experienced then? This was a much discussed problem. Colonel de Rochas, a once famous hypnotist, conducted these experiments to their extreme limits and even *ad absurdum.*[17] He thus obtained from his subjects an age regression not merely of an ordinary kind but also the re-enactment of their babyhood, their birth, of their fetal period. Then came a blackout, followed by the picture of the person's previous life, going backward from old age to childhood, infancy, birth, and fetal period, followed by a new blackout and the revival of the second previous life. De Rochas' subjects thus re-enacted several previous lives, always alternating the life of a man with the life of a woman. Descriptions of those previous lives were often plausible, but somewhat marred by anachronisms. Some believed that Colonel de Rochas had found an experimental confirmation of the doctrine of reincarnation. Further doubts arose when De Rochas started having young people enact the various stages of life ahead of them. Scepticism increased when he claimed to have called forth an externalization of sensitivity: he removed the sensitivity from the hypnotized subject and transferred it to some external object. Thus, when the subject was being pricked, he felt nothing; but when this material object was being pricked, the subject felt as though he himself had been pricked. During the entire nineteenth century, literature on magnetism and hypnotism was flooded with fantastic stories of that kind, and this was doubtlessly one of the main reasons for the opposition of scientific circles to the first dynamic psychiatry.

Another reason for the opposition to hypnotism was the awareness of certain inconveniences and dangers associated with its practice. First of all, grave concern was expressed over the fact that while under hypnosis, the subject seemed to be under the hypnotizer's spell, obeying even his sometimes unpleasant or ridiculous demands. As early as 1785, a controversy arose in Paris as to whether the woman subject would yield to an immoral order given by the magnetizer. Tardif de Montrevel contended that if an unscrupulous magnetizer tried to seduce a woman, she would awaken.[18] However, men like Deleuze, Gauthier, Charpignon, and others emphasized the need for great caution on the part of the magnetizer. Teste noted that the subject soon became able to detect the secret wishes of the magnetizer and warned against the dangers, not only of crude sexual seduction, but of falling into a sincere and true love relationship.[19] Reverend Debreyne, who was a medically trained priest and educator, remarked that the magnetizer was usually a healthy and strong man, the subject usually a pretty young woman (rarely an old or ugly one), and he had good reason to believe that seduction occurred frequently.[20] Another danger was the surrender of an important secret by the patient to the magnetizer. As we shall see later, the problem of immoral acts and crimes committed under hypnosis became the topic for impassioned discussions in the 1880's and 1890's.

Inexperienced or unwise hypnotists sometimes had great difficulty in rousing their patients out of hypnotic sleep. In an autobiographic account, Du Potet relates how, in his youth, he amateurishly magnetized two young ladies and became frantic when he saw them fall into a cataleptic state and for hours made desperate efforts to bring them out of this condition, until they finally awoke.[21] No less serious were the disturbances experienced by the subject after hypnotic sessions that had been either too long or too strenuous, especially after experiments involving clairvoyance and *extra-lucidité*. Another pathological manifestation was vigilambulism, a peculiar state of permanent half-somnambulism of persons who had been repeatedly hypnotized but who had not been submitted to the regular maneuvers that would terminate their magnetic sleep. Such people seem to be fully awake, but are liable to receive suggestions from anyone who will talk to them.

As soon as the phenomenon of posthypnotic suggestion was recognized, potential dangers became apparent and stories were told of individuals whom unscrupulous hypnotists had ordered to perform foolish acts after they awoke. We shall return to this point when dealing with the forensic implications of the first dynamic psychiatry. Bernheim emphasized the fact that pseudo-memories can be suggested under hypnosis. After waking up, the patient will believe that he saw or did something according to the hypnotist's suggestion.[22]

Deleuze and the early mesmerists also described the evils resulting from too frequent or too prolonged hypnotic sessions. Such subjects gradually became addicted to hypnosis; not only did their need for frequent hypnotization increase, but they became dependent on their particular magnetizer, and this dependency could often take on a sexual slant. This well-known fact was rediscovered by Charcot, who gave an account of a woman who had been hypnotized five times within three weeks and who could think of nothing but her hypnotist, until she ran away from her home to live with him.[23] Her husband took her back, but she fell into severe hysterical disturbances that necessitated her admission to a hospital. Prolonged treatment by hypnosis has also been accused of precipitating the outbreak of psychoses in predisposed subjects.

Finally, whole psychic epidemics were brought on by stage hypnotists and charlatans, especially among young people and school-age children who played at hypnotizing one another.[24]

Seeing that the phenomenon of hypnotism was the central one in the first dynamic psychiatry, it is not surprising that a great number of theories and speculations were formulated about its nature. One extreme opinion was that held by the sceptics who simply denied its existence or believed that it was at most a kind of autosuggestion. The extreme opposite view, held by the mystics, held that hypnosis was a link between the natural and the supernatural worlds, the means through which the individual human soul could gain access to the World Soul. Between those two extremes, there were all kinds of intermediate opinions. Mesmer and the fluidists thought of hypnosis as a physical fluid that circulated in the body of the magnetized or between the subject and the magnetizer. Later, these speculations were replaced by theories involving notions of nervous energy or the repartition of zones of excitation and inhibition within the brain. It is noteworthy that sexual theories were enunciated from the beginning. In a secret appendix to the Report of the Commissioners to King Louis XVI, it was stated that "crises" undergone by magnetized women were often of an obviously sexual nature.[25] Meynert based his opposition to hypnotism on the fact that the entire attitude of the woman toward the hypnotist was permeated with strong sexual undertones and the sexual emotions also played a part in hypnotized men.[26] As for the psychological theories first enunciated by Puységur and developed by Bertrand, they became accepted toward the end of the century. We shall return to this point.

It cannot be held against the early mesmerists that they did not organize a scientific investigation of hypnotism. Experimental psychology was nonexistent then and, as emphasized by Janet, Bertrand deserves praise for a truly objective and systematic investigation of hypnotism. Investigations were carried out at the same time by Deleuze and Noizet, and later by Despine, Charpignon, Du Potet, Durand (de Gros), and others. Janet notes that the essential manifestations of hypnotism were known from the beginning and that nothing of importance was added during the nineteenth century.

The great shortcoming in the study of hypnotism was that, from the start, hypnotists failed to understand the full implication of the rapport they established with their patient. They were well aware that, through the repetition of the hypnotic sessions, they were calling forth a new and hidden life in the subject's mind; but they did not recognize to what extent that secret life exerted a specific attraction on the hypnotist himself. Involuntarily, the hypnotist suggested to the patient more than he thought he did, and the patient returned to the hypnotist much of that which the latter secretly expected. A process of mutual suggestion may thus develop; the history of dynamic psychiatry abounds in fantastic myths and romances that evolved through the unconscious collaboration of hypnotist and hypnotized. We can thus understand why the entire nineteenth century was in turn attracted and repelled by the phenomenon of hypnotism. At first glance, it seemed to open an access to a new, mysterious realm of the soul—increased sensitivity, sharpened memory, new command of physiological processes, revelation of unsuspected abilities of the subject— all of which seemed to promise wonderful discoveries. But once the exploration was under way, the explorer many a time lost his way and became the plaything of an elusive and deceitful Fata Morgana.

Other Approaches to the Unknown Mind

During the entire nineteenth century, hypnosis remained the basic approach to the unconscious mind. However, in the second half of the century, it was supplemented by other techniques, some of which were variations of hypnosis, others were techniques of a new nature. Still others were a combination of classical hypnosis with new techniques.

From the beginning, mesmerists had considered artificial somnambulism as a kind of sleep (hence the word "hypnosis" coined by Braid from the Greek *hypnos,* sleep). They distinguished different levels of that sleep, depending on its depth. The deeper the sleep, the more remarkable the results that could be obtained from the hypnotized individual. It therefore seemed improbable at first when some hypnotists such as Du Potet maintained that patients could be brought to obey commands, to become paralyzed, or to have hallucinations, without being put to sleep, that is, the subject remained aware of happenings and remembered the events of the session afterwards. This technique was used on a large scale by the stage hypnotist Donato who termed it "fascination." In a milder form, it was commonly used by Bernheim and the Nancy School under the name of *suggestion à l'état de veille.*

Of far greater importance was a new technique that appeared as a result of the spiritistic wave of the mid-century. In the early 1850's, certain mediums began not only to write under the spirit's dictation but they even loaned, so to speak, their pens to the spirits. In Paris, the Baron de Guldenstubbe alleged to have thus produced autographed messages from Plato and Cicero. Most mediums, however, seemed content with taking down the spirit's dictation, which they received while in trance, and they were greatly surprised when awakened and shown what they had written. A fairly abundant literature of that kind was published during the second half of the century. Some psychologists such as Frederick Myers[27] and William James[28] understood that automatic writing provided a means of access to the unconscious. They applied it, giving that method the character of a scientific procedure. As we shall see later, Janet systematically applied automatic writing in the investigations of his patients' subconscious.

Another technique of access to the unconscious mind was elaborated on an age-old practice used by diviners and fortune-tellers, which consisted in gazing into mirrors, crystal balls, water (lekanomantia), and so forth. In the early 1850's, the magnetizer Du Potet drew a white chalk circle on a black floor and had his patients stare at it until they had great varieties of visions and hallucinations.[29] In the 1880's, Myers and other members of the Society for Psychical Research came to the conclusion that these methods, much like that of automatic writing, were a means for detecting subconscious material in the minds of their patients.

The advent of spiritism had brought forth a new type of individual: the medium. Much is common to both hypnotic sleep and to the self-induced trance of the medium, but material produced by the latter is more spontaneous and likely to be more original. It was a great step forward for dynamic psychiatry when Flournoy at the end of the nineteenth century, followed soon by C. G. Jung, undertook a systematic investigation of mediums.[30]

These methods were finally combined with each other and, at a later period, experiments were made with hypnotized individuals who were made to write automatically and gaze into mirrors. Subjects were even further hypnotized into a kind of second-degree hypnosis, and intensive efforts were being made everywhere in that direction by the end of the century. But, as we shall see later, the answers lay with the new schools of dynamic psychiatry.

Model Clinical Pictures: Magnetic Diseases

Many psychiatric systems have grown out of the study of one particular disease. Organicist psychiatry often chose general paresis or aphasia as a paradigm of mental disease to refer to in the study of other mental diseases. The first dynamic psychiatry evolved around one particular condition: spontaneous somnambulism, and its artificially induced counterpart, hypnosis. But it was not long before other conditions showing close affinities with somnambulism were discovered and classified with it in a group sometimes called magnetic diseases.

We shall not dwell on somnambulism, which had long been the focus of interest as the purest example of imagination's marvelous workings. Interest in somnambulism had spread far beyond the realm of medicine and had expanded into the fields of philosophy and literature. We need only cite

Shakespeare's unforgettable picture of Lady Macbeth re-enacting fragments of the scene of her crime at night, thus giving herself away in an act of self-betrayal. Kleist, in his *Kätchen von Heilbronn* (1868), also gave literary descriptions of somnambulism. From the psychiatric viewpoint, the problem of the individual's relationship between his sleepwalking and his normal state was greatly speculated about during the nineteenth century, and the problem of the individual's responsibility aroused special interest.

Another clinical condition, which at first sight seems to be very different from somnambulism, is "lethargy," a very deep and prolonged sleep that is otherwise devoid of any particular physical disturbance but which sometimes takes the shape of apparent death (hence the widespread fear of being buried alive). From the time of ancient Greek medicine until the nineteenth century there was much speculation about the nature and causes of lethargy. Sometimes considered a specific disease in its own right, sometimes a sub-form of hysteria, it had been noticed that lethargy occasionally occurred in sleepwalkers and that hypnotic maneuvers would at times induce lethargy instead of artificial somnambulism.

An even more mysterious and more speculated about condition was catalepsy. Famous cases were reported by Boissier de Sauvages, Lorry, and many others in the eighteenth century. In 1785, Petetin, a physician in Lyons, published a remarkable study of an eighteen-year-old young woman who had, for two months, been in extreme anguish over the condition of her severely sick child.[31] As soon as the child recovered, she was seized with violent pains in her epigastrium. She then had a nervous crisis during which she sang with a marvelous voice, and fell into a state of catalepsy with complete apparent loss of motion and sensitivity. She was, however, able to reply in some way to questions asked. Petetin undertook a series of experiments on this patient and found that she was insensitive in her whole body with the exception of her epigastrium, to which all her senses seemed to have been transferred. She could hear, see, and smell only through her epigastrium. She was able, furthermore, to perceive her internal organs and predict the symptoms that would appear the following day. Petetin connected this cataleptic condition with somnambulism on the one hand and with hysteria on the other, and advanced an explanation based on the distribution of electric fluids in the body. After Petetin, more critical studies were written by Bourdin[32] and by Puel,[33] who described as basic symptoms the cessation of all voluntary motion, the passiveness toward imposed movements, the *flexibilitas cerea,* and the prolongation of muscular attitudes imposed upon the subject, which in a normal state would be difficult or impossible to maintain for a prolonged period. The relationship between catalepsy and hysteria still remained controversial. Briquet saw that catalepsy was equally frequent in men and women, whereas hysteria was twenty times more frequent in women.[34] However, he added that catalepsy occurred more often in hysterical than in nonhysterical patients, and he therefore assumed that there must be an affinity between catalepsy and hysteria. On the other hand, hypnotists found that subjects they were hypnotizing not infrequently fell into catalepsy instead of somnambulism.

These three magnetic conditions, somnambulism, lethargy, and catalepsy had in common the fact that they all had unclear affinities with hysteria, they sometimes occurred in the same patient, and they could be induced through hypnotic maneuvers. Subsequently, two other conditions were added to this group of magnetic diseases and were termed "maniacal ecstasy" and "ecstatic visions," by Prichard.[35]

Maniacal ecstasy (or ecstatic madness) was described by Prichard as a hypnotic state with incoherence in the mind. Whereas the sleepwalker seems to have a coherent view of his actions, in maniacal ecstasy the patient confuses or imperfectly connects his thoughts; the patient looks like a maniac or a demented person. Many hypnotists observed such transient conditions, especially in the form of hallucinatory confusion, in patients they were hypnotizing or during one phase of hysterical attack.

What Prichard termed "ecstatic vision" is a kind of intensive daydream in a person, who, to all outward appearance, is living a normal life, so that the strangest interferences occur between normal life and daydreams. Once the paroxysm is over, the individual retains a vivid memory of it as well as the impression of having lived through a fantastic episode. In Prichard's words, "there are instances in which the impressions retained after a paroxysm of ecstasy are so connected with external events or objects and so blended with reality as to make up a most singular and puzzling combination, and this is perhaps the true rationale of many a strange and mysterious tale."

> Prichard tells of a clergyman who had been in indifferent health for some time when, standing one day at a street corner, he saw a funeral procession coming toward him. He waited and watched it pass him by, and then noticed his own name on the coffin and saw the procession entering his own home. This was the beginning of an illness which led to his death within a few days.
>
> In another case, a gentleman of about thirty-five, who was walking in London around St. Paul's Church, encountered a stranger who first invited him to have dinner in the neighborhood and then suggested a visit to the top of the Church's dome. There, the stranger pulled something like a compass from his pocket which later turned out to be a magic mirror and offered the gentleman to make him see in it anyone he wished, no matter the distance that separated them; thinking of his sick father, the gentleman actually saw him distinctly in the mirror, reclining in his armchair. Seized with terror, he requested his companion that they might immediately descend. But on taking leave, the stranger said to him, "Remember, you are the slave of the man of the mirror." For the following several months, the gentleman remained obsessed with the memory of that experience. Prichard thinks that he had actually gone to the top of St. Paul's in a state of ecstatic reverie and that he was afterwards unable to distinguish the real from the imaginary in those events.

Literary descriptions of ecstatic visions can be found in several works by Gérard de Nerval,[36] in Wilhelm Jensen's *Gradiva*,[37] and more recently in André Breton's *Les Vases communiquants*,[38] an autobiographic story supplemented by a psychological analysis of the phenomenon.

Model Clinical Pictures: Ambulatory Automatism

For a long time, attention was focused on those coordinated actions which a person performed in somnambulic sleep. It became clear, though, that similar actions could be performed during the daytime by individuals who seemed to be awake. However, as in somnambulism, these actions were cut off from the continuity of consciousness. The individual then suddenly came back to his usual consciousness and seemed utterly unaware of what he had done.

As an instance, we can cite the once-famous case of a young German shepherd, Sörgel, who was an epileptic. One day, when he was sent to the forest to gather wood, he met a man, killed him, cut his feet off, and drank his blood. He then returned to the village, quietly related what he had done, and returned a while later to his normal state of consciousness in which he seemed to recall nothing at all. The court, showing much more psychological understanding than some of today's judges, acquitted Sörgel on the grounds that he could not be held responsible for what had happened.[39]

Similar cases were much discussed during the nineteenth century and were sometimes interpreted as instances of transient multiple personality.

In the 1880's, Charcot became interested in such cases, to which he devoted several of his most brilliant lectures.[40] He classified the fugues (wandering states followed by amnesia) according to the etiology, describing traumatic, epileptic, and hysterical forms of ambulatory automatism.

To the first group belongs the case of a fifty-four-year-old Paris midwife who had been called to a patient on this particular night in 1885. She fell on the staircase, hurt her head badly, and lost consciousness for about fifteen minutes, after which she went to her patient, delivered the child, and then fell asleep. Being called by the woman three hours later, she was seized with violent shivers, came back to her former self and was at a loss to understand how the child had been delivered. She had completely lost the memory of what had followed her accident.

As an instance of epileptic ambulatory automatism, Charcot quotes the case of an epileptic doorkeeper in Paris who, after cashing the three-months rentals from all the tenants in the house, disappeared, wearing his slippers on his feet, and went to spend a week on the Côte d'Azur. Afterward he recovered his consciousness and became so upset that he gave himself up to the police, requesting to be arrested. A psychiatric expert, Dr. Motet, had a difficult time convincing the court that the man was not responsible for his action.

Another epileptic patient treated by Charcot had been employed as a deliveryman by a Paris furniture store for nineteen years. One day in 1889, after cashing 900 francs from clients, he disappeared. Seven days later, he suddenly recovered his former consciousness during a concert by a military band, finding himself in Brest with only 700 francs left in his pocket. He gave himself up to a military policeman who put him in jail. The same patient had had several other fugues. During one of them, he regained consciousness to find himself swimming in the Seine: it had happened that in his fugue state, he was traveling in the city train farther than his ticket allowed; as the train was crossing a bridge, he jumped through a window and flung himself into the river, where he recovered his former self.

Charcot includes in the group of hysterical ambulatory automatism the numerous cases for which no traumatic or epileptic etiology could be found. Some of those cases were remarkable because of the length of their duration and the consequent and coherent behavior of the patient from the moment he lost awareness to the moment when he suddenly came back to himself to perhaps find himself in unknown surroundings or in a remote country. One of the best known of such cases was that of one of Forel's patients, according to the account published by his disciple Naef.

In August of 1895, a thirty-two-year-old man, sitting in a Zurich café, was startled by a news item he read in a newspaper. It was reported that a certain Mr. N. who, a few months earlier, had left Switzerland for Australia, had disappeared and was feared dead as a victim of murder or of an epidemic infection. Stirred by this news, the man rushed to his boarding house, searched anxiously through the pockets of his clothes, and found a passport bearing the name of Mr. N. The idea that he himself was Mr. N. preyed on his mind, but he wasn't quite sure of it: there was a wide gap in his memory. All he remembered was that he had applied a year earlier for an overseas post, and he had extremely vague images of a long sea voyage. For the past weeks, he had led an inconspicuous and most secluded life in Zurich. In his distress, he went to see Dr. Forel who admitted him to the Burghölzli as a patient. Inquiries showed that Mr. N. had been appointed by the Swiss government to an official post in Australia, that he had left for that country in November of the previous year and had fulfilled his functions quite normally for six months. He had left his residence in May on an official duty for a Central Australian town, where he had been struck by an epidemic disease, and his track had been lost at this point. However, someone claimed to have recognized him later in an Australian seaport, and it was found that he had returned from Australia to Naples under an assumed name.

The patient was depressed, exhausted, and nervous. Attempts to stimulate his memory with requests for concentration on certain points, confrontations with his family, and with a man he had known in Australia, all remained fruitless.

Forel hypnotized Mr. N. and, starting with the patient's most recent memories, proceeded slowly and progressively backward in chronological order, beginning each hypnotic session with the last memories brought forth by the previous one. The patient thus gave a detailed description of his journey from Switzerland to Australia, his activities in that country, his trip to the town in Central Australia where he had met with difficult problems and was struck with fever. From there on, the hypnotic treatment proved considerably more difficult. However, the hypnotic resistances were gradually overcome so that an almost complete recovery from the amnesia could be achieved.[41]

We may note that the anterograde amnesia had started in May and had ceased at the time of the patient's return to Switzerland, whereas the retrograde amnesia extended backward up to the circumstances that had just preceded the patient's departure for Australia; it was as if the entire Australian episode had to be cut out from the patient's memory. On the other hand, there was no attempt to shape a secondary personality except for the fact that Mr. N. had taken an assumed name for his return trip by boat. (The case history does not mention under which name he lived in Zurich.)

We should also note that with most of these patients, epileptic as well as hysterical, the appearance and disappearance of the fugue state curiously responded to the needs of certain situations. Both of Charcot's patients fell into this condition immediately after cashing appreciable sums of money; they were unable to account for the way in which they had spent it. Having returned to awareness, they felt guilty and displayed a self-punitive behavior. Charcot's second patient returned to awareness just after his "second self" managed to escape most adroitly the consequences he might have met with for traveling beyond the station allowed by his ticket. The account given in regard to Forel's patient is very discreet, but one can deduce, after reading the full story, that the patient had personal reasons for leaving Australia. In such cases as well as in those of multiple successive personalities, nineteenth century authors have not sufficiently emphasized the conscious or unconscious personal motivations underlying these shifts of personality. Actually, the first case history in which these personal motivations were duly underlined was the one published by Raymond and Janet in 1895.[42]

Modern Clinical Pictures: Multiple Personality

By the end of the eighteenth century and during all of the nineteenth century, occurrences of divided personality became known, at first as very rare if not legendary happenings. After 1840, they were regarded in a more objective manner, and by 1880 this problem was among the most discussed by psychiatrists and philosophers.

The problem of the unity of personality had already been pondered over by St. Augustine in his *Confessions.*[43] Considering the change that had taken place in him since his conversion, Augustine remarked that his old pagan personality, of which nothing seemed to remain in his waking state, still must exist since it was revived at night and in his dreams. He wrote: "Am I not myself, o Lord, my God. And yet, there is so much difference betwixt myself and myself within the moment wherein I pass from waking to sleeping or return from sleeping to waking." This brings Augustine to discuss

the problem of the dreamer's moral responsibility for his dreams. Later
the analogous problem of the individual's responsibility for actions committed
by his "secondary personality" would become the subject of similar
investigation.

The phenomenon of possession, so frequent for many centuries, could
well be considered as one variety of multiple personality. We have already
mentioned the two forms of possession: lucid possession (in which the
subject feels within himself the two souls striving against each other), and
somnambulistic possession (in which the subject loses consciousness of his
own self while a mysterious intruder seems to take possession of his body
and acts and speaks with an individuality of which the subject knows nothing
when he returns to awareness). We may note the parallelism between these
two forms of possession and the two main forms of multiple personality.
Moreover, just as possession could be manifest or latent, multiple personality
can be manifest (that is, appear and develop spontaneously), or it may
appear only under the influence of hypnotic maneuvers or automatic writing.

It is possible that instances of multiple personality existed years ago along
with possession, but remained unnoticed. Historians have resorted to this
explanation in order to elucidate certain historical enigmas such as the case
of the mysterious "Friend of God of the Oberland," who appears to have
been but a somnambulic second personality of the mystic Rulman Merswin.[44]
Actually, it was only after the disappearance of the phenomenon of possession that case histories of multiple personality began to appear in
mesmerist writings and later also in medical literature. As early as 1791,
Eberhardt Gmelin published a case of *umgetauschte Persönlichkeit*
(exchanged personality):

> In 1789, at the beginning of the French Revolution, aristocratic refugees arrived
> in Stuttgart. Impressed by their sight, a twenty-year-old German young woman
> suddenly "exchanged" her own personality for the manners and ways of a French-
> born lady, imitating her and speaking French perfectly and German as would a
> French woman. These "French" states repeated themselves. In her French
> personality, the subject had complete memory of all that she had said and done
> during her previous French states. As a German, she knew nothing of her
> French personality. With a motion of his hand, Gmelin was easily able to make
> her shift from one personality to the other.[45]

Reil was much interested by this case, elaborated on it, and connected it
with the phenomenon of dreams. He quotes among others a dream reported
by Lichtenberg, a German writer, who dreamed that he was relating a sad
but true story to someone when a third person interrupted him to remind
him of an important point, which he, Lichtenberg, had forgotten. "Why did
his fantasy," asked Reil, "create a third person who surprised him and made
him feel ashamed, how can the ego divide itself into persons who, out of
himself, produce things of which he is not aware that they were in him, and

surprise him as outside wisdom?"[46] As Reil so well understood, this problem is basically the same as that of multiple personality.

Then came a period of vaguely reported, semilegendary cases. Erasmus Darwin reports one in a few lines:

> I was once concerned for a very elegant and ingenious young lady, who had a reverie on alternate days which continued nearly the whole day; and as in her days of disease she took up the same kind of ideas, which she had conversed about on the alternate day before, and could recollect nothing of them on her well days; she appeared to her friends to possess two minds. This case was also of the epileptic kind, and was cured, with some relapses, by opium administered before the commencement of the paroxysm.[47]

One of the most famous cases of multiple personality was that of Mary Reynolds, said to have been published by Dr. John Kearsley Mitchell[48] around 1815, and later published in a more extended form with a follow-up by the Rev. William S. Plumer.[49]

Mary Reynolds, the daughter of the Reverend William Reynolds, was born in England and was a child when the family migrated to the United States. They settled near Titusville, Pennsylvania; this was still a wild countryside, inhabited mainly by Indians and a few Whites, and wild beasts roamed freely. In the spring of 1811, at the age of about nineteen, Mary went into the fields with a book in her hand, and was later found lying on the ground having seemingly lost consciousness; she soon recovered it, but remained apparently blind and deaf for five or six weeks. Her hearing returned suddenly, and her sight was gradually restored. Three months later, she was found in a deep sleep that lasted for many hours and from which she awoke having lost all memory, even the use of speech. Her condition was like that of a new born infant. However, she rapidly regained her lost knowledge. Five weeks later, she woke up one morning in her natural state and expressed surprise at the change of seasons, unaware that anything abnormal had happened to her during the past weeks. A few weeks later, she again fell into a deep sleep, awoke in her second state and took up life again precisely where she had left it some time before; these alternations from one state to another continued for fifteen or sixteen years, but finally ceased when she had reached the age of thirty-five, leaving her permanently in her second state in which she remained without further change until her death in 1854.

The differences between the two personalities were quite striking. In her first state Mary was a quiet, sober, and thoughtful person with a tendency to depression, a slow thinker devoid of imagination. In her second state she was gay, cheerful, extravagant, fond of company, fun, and practical jokes, with a strong propensity for versification and rhyming. Her two handwritings differed entirely. In each state she knew of the other and feared to fall back into it, but for different reasons. In her second state she considered the other one as dull and stupid.

Her second state caused much worry to her family because she became restless and eccentric; she wandered off into the woods without concern for wolves and bears, and once attempted to catch a rattlesnake. She was also under the spell of a brother-in-law. Immediately upon falling asleep, she would tell of the events of the day and sometimes laugh merrily at the jokes she had made during the day.

The case of Mary Reynolds is usually quoted as an instance of complete separation between the two personalities. However, it is clear from Rev. Plumer's account that the separation was not always so complete. In her second state, before she had learned to read again and had no memory of the Scriptures, she told of her dreams that manifested a knowledge of the Bible as well as memories of her dead sister Eliza, of whom she had not the slightest recollection when awake.

This case was popularized by the book written by Macnish, *The Philosophy of Sleep,* and was widely quoted in France under the name *la dame de Macnish.*[50] In 1889, Dr. S. Weir Mitchell, the son of Dr. John Kearsley Mitchell, published a more complete account of Mary Reynold's story from the papers of his father. It would seem that certain readers did not realize that Mary Reynolds and the "lady of Macnish" were one, and for some time the two observations were erroneously quoted separately as two instances of dual personality; this, incidentally, demonstrates the vagueness of the first account given by the elder Dr. Mitchell.[51]

The truly objective study of multiple personality was inaugurated in France by the publication of the story of "Estelle" by Despine Sr. in the form of a detailed account amounting to a monograph.[52] Despine was a general practitioner who had been appointed Medical Inspector of the thermal station of Aix-en-Savoie. He occasionally practiced magnetic treatment.

In July of 1836, Estelle, an eleven-year-old Swiss girl, was brought to Despine by her mother and her aunt. Her physicians in Neuchâtel had diagnosed a severe paralysis resulting from a lesion of the spinal cord. Estelle, who had lost her father during an epidemic in 1832, was a spoiled child. In November 1834, while playing with a child of her age, she was slightly pushed and fell on her seat. From then on, she complained of pains that gradually increased to the point of becoming eventually excruciating. All other treatments having failed, she was sent to Aix. She traveled by coach for five days, lying flat on her back in a large flat willow basket padded with eiderdown. The windows of the coach were tightly shut and covered with curtains. She caused a sensation at every stop and large crowds gathered to see her being carried into the local inn. No one except her mother and aunt could touch her without causing her to scream. She was absorbed in daydreams, fantastic visions and hallucinations, and forgot from one moment to the next all that was happening around her.

It is clear that the sixty-year-old physician felt a strong attachment for the little patient. Throughout his book, he tells of his admiration for her intelligence and courage during her ordeals. Despine carefully began a program of hydrotherapeutic and electric treatments, which were followed by a slow improvement. In December, her mother happened to tell Dr. Despine that Estelle was being comforted every evening by a choir of angels. This was illuminating for the doctor who suddenly understood that Estelle's case was one of "ecstasis," a condition that could be cured by animal magnetism. Estelle at first obstinately refused to be magnetized but, on her mother's insistence, she finally accepted on her own terms, which were that she would submit to magnetism only when she wanted to and only insofar as she was willing, and that everything she said in somnambulic state would be repeated to her word by word. Magnetic treatment was started at the end of December 1836. Her mother wrote the diary of the cure, of which large excerpts are contained in Despine's book. Magnetic sleep was easy to induce and was always followed by amnesia. During her sleep, Estelle prescribed her own treatment and diet. Soon after the first sessions, a comforting angel appeared to her in her magnetic sleep whom she named Angeline and with whom she engaged in lively conversations (of which, of course, only Estelle's parts were recorded). It was now Angeline who directed the treatment. The diet prohibited all foods that Estelle disliked and ordained that she should have anything she desired, including snow. It was also forbidden to contradict her. The angel had said: "Let her act according to her whims; she will not take advantage of the situation."

Starting in January 1837, Estelle began leading a dual life. In her normal state she was still paralyzed. The slightest movement caused her intolerable pain. She had to be covered with cushions, blankets, eiderdown blankets; she loved her mother and demanded her constant presence; she addressed Despine respectfully with *vous*. In her magnetic state, she became able to move, started to walk, felt a craving for snow and could not tolerate her mother's presence; she addressed Despine in the familiar way with *tu*. Her ability to walk depended on the presence of gold on her body. Certain other substances had a negative influence on her.

At the end of January 1837, she began to fall spontaneously into magnetic states, which alternated every twelve hours with her so-called normal state; in the latter she was still unable to make a single step. In her magnetic state she would walk, run, and travel by carriage without tiring; she loved to play with snow and to eat it. However, she remained intolerant of certain things such as cats, the sight of which would throw her into catalepsy, from which a rub down with gold would bring her out. Despine was particularly struck with the difference between her two diets. In her normal state, the child could tolerate but few foods. During her magnetic state, she would eat abundantly of everything. It seemed as though she had two stomachs, one for the crisis condition and one for the waking condition.

At the beginning of March 1837, Despine was called away from Aix for a few days. As she had predicted, Estelle suffered hallucinations and disturbances during his absence, and the household had to bear up silently with all of her extravagances. At the end of March, Estelle predicted that she would visualize a big ball that would burst, upon which a great improvement would follow. This prophecy came true on April 14, when, for the first time, the patient was able to make a few steps in her waking state. There was also an improvement in her magnetic state. She was able to swim and make excursions in the mountains, although she kept her idiosyncrasies.

In June the gradual fusion of her normal and magnetic states slowly took place. On June 13 the patient was discharged from Despine's treatment and traveled slowly back to Neuchâtel with her mother. The news of her cure had already reached her home town, where local newspapers published her story, calling her *la petite ressuscitée,* "the little resurrected one." She gradually lost her idiosyncrasies to the point where she was even able to face a cat without falling into catalepsy.

Despine's remarkable study soon fell into oblivion, partly because he was a general practitioner, and partly because his book has never been reprinted and is now extremely rare. Janet repeatedly pointed out the importance of the case, which inspired his own research. One interesting facet of Estelle's story is the manner in which the cure was achieved. Estelle's "normal" condition was actually the pathological one, whereas her abnormal or magnetic condition was really the healthy one. Despine brought this latter condition to its fullest development, upon which the fusion between the two conditions took place and the healthy personality took the lead. The case history shows how Despine, in a first phase, established a rapport with the child who became dependent on him in her magnetized condition while turning antagonistic toward her mother; he thus freed Estelle from her morbid dependency upon her mother. The girl's strong dependency on Despine showed during his absence. It would seem that he gradually loosened this dependency to the point where she was able to return to Neuchâtel with her mother.

It would be interesting to know what happened to Estelle after her memorable cure. No mention is made of it in Despine's later works. However, since he once quoted Estelle's full name, it was possible to identify her. She belonged to a prominent family of Neuchâtel, Switzerland, and was the daughter of a Swiss merchant who had established himself in Paris, where she was born on March 18, 1825. After her cure, she spent most of her life in France, married in Le Havre, and died there on December 15th, 1862, without leaving any children.[53]

Classification and Forms of Multiple Personality

Seeing that more and more cases of multiple personality were published during the nineteenth century, it was felt to be increasingly necessary to distinguish their clinical varieties and to classify them. Among various types of classification, the more rational is probably the following:

1. Simultaneous multiple personalities
2. Successive multiple personalities
   a. mutually cognizant of each other
   b. mutually amnestic
   c. one-way amnestic
3. Personality clusters

We shall now undertake a short survey of these different types, citing for each type one or two of the most typical clinical examples, including recent cases whenever they are of particular interest.[54]

Simultaneous Multiple Personalities:

Personalities are called simultaneous when they are able to manifest themselves distinctly at one and the same moment. It should be recalled that one cannot speak of multiple personalities where there are simply two focuses of attention or two streams of consciousness concurrently (as may happen with religious mystics, poets, artists, inventors); or when a person is enacting a role on a stage. In a true multiple personality, each personality has the feeling of its own individuality at the exclusion of the other or others.

Such conditions are very rare. However, even a normal individual may experience similar feelings when shifting from sleep to a waking state and vice-versa. We remember how St. Augustine wondered about the shifts from his new Christian personality back to his old pagan one and about those in the opposite direction.

Flournoy mentions similar transient states in his medium Hélène Smith:

> It is a state of consciousness sui generis, which it is impossible to describe adequately and which can only be represented by the analogy of those curious states, exceptional in the normal waking life, but less rare in dreams when one seems to change one's identity and become someone else.
>
> Hélène has more than once told me of having the impression of *becoming* or *being* momentarily Leopold. This happens more frequently at night, or upon awakening in the morning. She has first a fugitive vision of her protector. Then it seems that little by little he is submerged in her; she feels him overcoming and penetrating her entire organism, as if he really became her or she him.[55]

In his account of his self-experiences with mescalin, Giovanni Enrico Morselli relates his feeling that a wild beast was merging with himself, or, in other words, he felt he was like the lycanthropist of old metamorphosed into a wild animal, of which he could even perceive the color.[56]

More complex are the phenomena of the upsurge of memories from a former life which at times occur with hallucinatory vividness in a person, who, at the same time, retains clear consciousness of his own identity and whereabouts. One such case is the curious story of Max Bircher's patient "Ikara":

> Ikara, a Zurich housewife, had lost her mother at the age of thirteen and had spent an unhappy childhood and youth. She was a very diligent, practical, and serious person, but led a secret fantasy life, which she concealed from her acquaintances. At the age of fifteen, she was struck by the sudden realization that she knew about childbirth as if from personal experience. At twenty-five, she began having very vivid reminiscences of events that had happened to a

person whom she identified with herself in a former life. She spent two years in Bircher's medical sanatorium, and he tells of about ten of these manifestations of interference from a former life. These reminiscences had an absolutely personal and vivid character, although pertaining to an altogether different way of life. In that previous life, Ikara was a sturdy woman living in a primitive hut on the edge of a forest amidst a savage people clothed in animal skins. Once, she told of her experience of having stolen a hen; she was devouring it raw and felt the taste of its blood in her mouth when angry men, brandishing big sticks at her, started to chase her. She sought refuge in a nearby cave—and the vision suddenly stopped. Dr. Bircher was convinced that these were actual reminiscences of a former life that this woman had lived in a prehistoric era. It is regrettable that he did not make a detailed investigation of this patient's personal background.[57]

The coexistence in consciousness of two personalities is an exceptional state that is unlikely to last for a long time. Even when the two personalities are cognizant of each other, one of them is always dominant (even though the other's presence is being felt in the background). Therefore, a case such as that of Cory's patient belongs to the first group of successive multiple personalities.

Successive Multiple Personalities, Mutually Cognizant

This type of multiple personalities does not seem to be frequent. One of the best examples is the case published by Charles E. Cory:

Cory describes the case of a twenty-nine-year-old woman whose personality had become split into A and B three years before, following the shock she had experienced at her father's suicide. For some time thereafter, she had been afflicted with motor disturbances, hallucinations, and a peculiar instability and changes of mood. One evening, while sitting at the piano, she felt as though someone inside her told her to take a deep breath and then tried to sing with her voice. Several weeks went by before personality B learned to "emerge completely and take possession of the body." Ever since, the two personalities have alternated but always remain conscious of one another.

A remains the normal, habitual personality and keeps her previous character. She is a bright and cultured woman of good background, but rather shy and inhibited. She sings poorly. She had a rigid upbringing at home as well as at the convent school and, in her education, a strict taboo had been maintained as to sexual questions. B is a seemingly older, bolder but dignified and serious-looking woman who claims to be the reincarnation of the soul of a Spanish singer. She sings well and with assurance and speaks English with a strong Spanish accent. At times she speaks a language that she pretends is Spanish but is actually a composite of bits of broken Spanish and of Spanish-sounding word formations. She is extremely egocentric, shows strong passions, and her main interest lies in the sexual instinct. She pretends to be a voluptuous, fascinating beauty and to have been a dancer, a courtesan, and the mistress of a nobleman.

A and B consider themselves as being on good terms with each other but as being completely separate persons, much as two friends would be. Each knows the other only insofar as the other will wish to be known and is willing to reveal about herself. Each, if interested, is conscious of the other and remembers what she does. They may look at the same thing or read the same book simultaneously. However, it would seem that B never sleeps, and she claims to know A's early life better than A herself. She also maintains that she is A's guardian angel and once hypnotized her. She is obviously the dominating personality.

Cory was able to hypnotize each personality separately. He found that under hypnosis, A remembered things of which she was unconscious in her normal state but which B had told him about without being hypnotized. Once, while in hypnosis, B unexpectedly fell into a delirium of fear and suffering: she had seen the body of a lover who had committed suicide. "Down in her subconscious, there is a house of horrors."

Cory's account contains some hints about possible psychogenetic factors. At the convent school, A had known three little girls who had come from Mexico and who spoke Spanish among themselves. Shortly after her father's death, she had met a man many years her senior who looked like a Spaniard and whose mother was actually Spanish. On the other hand, the patient had suffered from strong sexual repression and inner conflict. Cory notes that the "two selves were formed along the lines of the old conflict."

Finally, it should be emphasized that Cory's patient never suggested that B might be a reviviscence of a former life of A (as in Ikara's story). B was supposed to be the reincarnation of a spirit. It is noteworthy that B is friendly with a coterie of believers in spiritism who encourage her belief of being a returned spirit and over whom she exerts a tyrannical influence.[58]

Successive Multiple Personalities, Mutually Amnestic

In this group, personalities A and B know nothing about each other. This was the case with Gmelin's young patient, whose French personality knew nothing about the German one, nor the German about the French. Mary Reynolds is usually quoted as a typical instance of this group, but, as we have seen above, some knowledge of her first personality at times permeated her second personality. One should be cautious in the study of old case histories, which have not always been recorded with the care one would wish for today. One of the first reliably recorded instances of mutually amnestic personalities is that of Ansel Bourne, published by Hodgson[59] and examined by William James.[60]

Ansel Bourne was born in 1826. The son of divorced parents, he had spent an unhappy childhood and had later become a carpenter working in small Rhode Island towns. An atheist, he publicly declared, on October 28, 1857, that he would rather be deaf and mute than go to church. Moments later, he lost his hearing, speech, and sight. On November 11, he went to the church, showing a written message announcing his conversion. On the following Sunday, November 15, he rose up in church in the midst of several hundred worshippers and proclaimed that God had cured him of his infirmities. This alleged miracle brought him enormous prestige, and henceforth Bourne combined his carpenter trade with the activity of itinerant preacher. Years later, he lost his wife and re-married, but his second marriage was an unhappy one.

Thirty years after his conversion, Ansel Bourne one day disappeared from his home in Coventry, Rhode Island. He had gone to Providence, cashed $551.00 at the bank, paid a visit to his beloved nephew, and from there his track had been lost.

Two weeks later, a certain Albert Brown arrived at Norristown, Pennsylvania; he rented a little store, bought some merchandise and started a small business of stationery, confection, and small articles. The man led a rather inconspicuous and secluded life. On March 14, he woke up early in the morning and was completely disoriented. He had come back to his former personality of Ansel Bourne and was at a loss to understand what he was doing in this strange place. He called his neighbors, who thought that he had become mentally deranged. Finally, his nephew arrived, liquidated the stock of merchandise, and took his uncle back to Coventry. Ansel Bourne had no recollection whatever of what he had done during the two months he had spent living under the name of Albert Brown.

In 1890, Ansel Bourne was hypnotized by William James and brought back, under trance, to his secondary personality of Albert Brown. Brown knew nothing of Bourne, but gave a coherent account of what he had done during the two months of his existence. Wherever his statements could be checked by an objective enquiry, they were found to be true. Regarding his fugue, he was obviously dissatisfied with life and suffered from his second wife's nagging nature. He disappeared just after having cashed a large sum of money. His new identity (Albert Brown from Newton, N.H.) was a faint disguise of his true one (Ansel Bourne from New York, N.Y.). It is strange that in his secondary state, Albert Brown did not notice anything unusual about the papers, checkbook, and so on, bearing the name of Ansel Bourne, which he had with him all that time. It would be interesting to know the circumstances that preceded his return to his former personality and how much money he had left.

A more recent and better documented case of mutually amnestic personalities was published in 1933 by S. I. Franz:

In December 1919, the Los Angeles police picked up a man who was wandering through the streets in a dazed condition. The man, who was carrying British and French war medals with him, said that he remembered nothing of his life prior to 1915 and that he was concerned about the problem of his identity. An old Californian lady assured him that she recognized him as her lost son, but he could not recognize her as his mother. Franz tried to elucidate the case, both through official enquiries and through repeated interviews with the patient.

The man's papers were made out to Charles Poulting, from Florida, but he did not look like a native American. His accent was Irish. He thought that he might be Canadian and had an inexplicable interest for the state of Michigan. He had traveled extensively throughout the United States as well as abroad. His memories started with the month of February 1915, but there were also some important gaps after that date. He had fought in World War I in France, in Belgium, and in British East Africa. With intense emotion, he told

Franz about his war experiences in the African jungle and related how, after escaping from German captivity with another soldier, he had seen his companion devoured by leopards.

While Poulting was thus attempting to recover his memory, the police again found him in the streets, in March 1930, completely disoriented. To Franz, he declared that his name was Charles Poultney; he indicated the date and place of his birth, his address in Dublin as well as the names of his parents, siblings, wife, and two children. He was believed to have been in Dublin in September 1914. He had come to the United States in 1913 and had lived in Michigan. He could remember nothing of what had happened after September 1914. "He was a man of forty-two with memories and experiences of only twenty-seven years."

Franz tried to make Poultney recover the memories of the second part of his life, using maps of countries where he was known to have sojourned. Studying the map of British East Africa, Poultney suddenly became intensely emotional while pointing out a little town: there, he said, he had had a pet monkey who had been caught and devoured by a leopard. (From the dynamic point of view, the emotion was obviously displaced from the more terrifying memory of having seen his companion devoured by leopards in the same region.) This emotional abreaction was accompanied by a flood of memories, which now streamed ceaselessly. "In a few minutes, he had lived fifteen years. He had met and he had recognized himself."

The life story of the patient was thus cut into three parts of unequal lengths, which Franz, called personalities A, B, and C. Personality A (Poulting) extended from the patient's birth to September 1914. Personality B covered the period from September 1914 to February 1915. This fragment of personality had been blotted out, probably under the effect of a shell-shock on the battlefield in northern France. Personality C started in February 1915 and continued up to the time when Franz undertook the patient's treatment in 1930. At the beginning of the treatment, the patient knew only of personality C and had lost A and B. After this episode of mental confusion, he had recovered A, but had lost B and C. Franz succeeded in bringing together A and C, but not the missing link of B (hence the title of his book: *Persons One and Three*).[61]

Successive Multiple Personalities: One-Way Amnestic

This means that personality A knows nothing of personality B, but the latter knows not only itself but also personality A. The prototype of this variety of multiple personalities was given by Azam's celebrated patient Félida. Eugène Azam (1822–1899), a professor of surgery at the Bordeaux Medical School, was interested in hypnotism at the time when it was considered to be unscientific. From 1858 to 1893, he studied and followed at intervals a woman, Félida X., for whom he coined the term *dédoublement de la personnalité*. He read a number of papers about this patient to various medical societies and later compiled his observations, completed them with a follow-up and published them in 1887 with an introduction by Charcot.[62]

Félida, born in 1843, was the daughter of a captain of the merchant marine. He died when she was a baby, and Félida had a difficult childhood. Still a child, she had to earn her living as a seamstress. From her thirteenth year on, she developed severe hysterical symptoms. She was a sullen, taciturn girl and a hard worker, but she constantly complained about headaches, neuralgias and a great variety of symptoms. Almost every day, she had a "crisis": she would suddenly feel an acute pain in her temples, after which she would fall into a lethargic state of a few minutes' duration. When she awakened, she was a different person altogether, gay, vivacious, sometimes elated, and completely free of ailments. This condition usually lasted for a few hours and would then give way to a short lethargic state from which she returned to her ordinary personality. Azam states that in her normal condition, Félida was of average intelligence, but that she became more brilliant in her secondary condition. In the latter she was very well aware not only of her previous secondary states but also of her entire life. In her normal state, she knew nothing of the secondary condition except that which others told her about. Much less frequently, Félida had another type of crisis, which Azam called her third condition: fits of terrible anxiety with frightening hallucinations.

One day, Félida consulted Azam because of nausea and an enlarged abdomen. Azam diagnosed a pregnancy, but Félida protested that she did not understand how this could be possible. Thereupon, she shifted into her secondary condition and laughingly admitted that she knew of her pregnancy but did not worry about it. She married her boy friend, her baby was born, and she improved markedly. She stopped seeing Azam for a long time. All her previous symptoms returned with her second pregnancy.

Among Félida's symptoms, Azam described unusual disorders of the vegetative nervous functions which became increasingly worse in the subsequent years of her life. She was suffering from pulmonary and gastric hemorrhages without any sign of pulmonary or gastric lesion. During her sleep, blood flowed slowly but continuously from her mouth. Any part of her body could suddenly become swollen, for instance, one-half of her face.

Azam stated in 1876 that Félida, who was now thirty-two years old and managing a grocery store, showed basically the same symptoms. But the primary and the secondary personalities were now in inverse relation to each other, that is, the periods of secondary personality were much longer than the periods of normal personality. The latter became worse. In her secondary personality, Félida felt well, she was freer, cared more about her personal appearance, was more sensitive, and more affectionate toward her family. She remembered her entire life. During the short periods of her primary personality, she was deprived of a great part of her memories (since she remembered nothing of her other personality), she worked harder, but she was gloomy and nasty toward her husband. In every regard, this so-called normal condition proved less desirable than the secondary or abnormal one. Félida's eleven childbirths occurred without exception in her normal, that is, her bad condition. In both conditions, she considered her present one to be her normal state and the other to be abnormal.

In the following years, up to 1887, Azam continued to observe Félida and wrote several follow-up studies on her. The secondary condition became more and more the predominant one, although it never became exclusive. As long as Azam observed her, Félida had short relapses into her primary normal condition. The disorders of the vegetative nervous system worsened steadily to the extent that she had frequent hemorrhages through all the mucosae of her body, without any sign of serious disease.

The majority of cases of multiple personalities belong to this group of one-way amnestic. As we have seen, B knows everything about A, whereas A knows nothing about B. Moreover, S. W. Mitchell emphasized the fact that in all known cases, it was found that personality B is freer and more elated; personality A is inhibited, compulsive, and depressed. Myers, and then Janet, declared that it was incorrect, as did Azam, to call personality A normal and personality B abnormal. Actually, personality A is the sick person, and B may be considered a return to the formerly healthy personality, such as it was before the onset of the illness.

Among the numerous instances of multiple personalities of this group, we will select and summarize one other, Morselli's patient Elena, perhaps the most remarkable case of multiple personality ever published. Elena was under Morselli's observation and treatment for three years.[63] His account, published in an Italian journal, is a well-documented monograph of a case of this type.

In May 1925, a twenty-five-year-old piano teacher, Elena F., was admitted to Morselli's psychiatric clinic in Milan. She addressed him in perfect French. Morselli asked her why she, an Italian, did not speak to him in her native tongue. She replied with apparent surprise that she was speaking Italian. She had a feeling of something strange and uncanny around her and complained that people were reading her thoughts, and that she was hearing voices that were pronouncing terrible accusations against her. She also assured Morselli (contrary to the facts) that her father was dead. While Morselli was performing a neurological examination on her, she had a short lethargic state, and then, expressing herself in Italian, she was surprised to see Morselli whom she did not recognize.

From then on, the French and Italian speaking personalities alternated. In each of them, Elena believed that she was speaking Italian. In her French condition, she spoke Italian as a French person would, and vice-versa. Aside from these two personalities, she had delirious states from time to time with terrifying hallucinations in which she saw, for instance, her mother being killed by her father (similar states were also described by Azam as Félida's third condition.)

Elena's Italian personality knew nothing of her French counterpart, whereas the latter knew of both itself and the Italian personality. The French personality was overtly psychotic, the Italian personality much less sick.

Objective inquiries showed that Elena's father was a sixty-six-year-old industrialist, her mother a sixty-two-year-old severely neurotic and alcoholic woman. Life at home was intolerable because of violent scenes between the parents.

Elena had always been sickly; she had devoted her whole passion and energy to music. She showed an aversion for sexual matters and had had no known love affair. Pulmonary and other diseases had resulted in her spending much time in climatic resorts. The onset of mental disturbances had followed a stay with her father in a village on the shores of Lake Maggiore.

Morselli's therapy was guided by two principles: (1) Seeing that the Italian personality was the sounder, he tried to keep Elena in it as much as possible. He found out that he could make her shift at will from the French to the Italian condition by making her read aloud 50 verses by Dante. (2) He attempted a careful elucidation of her past with her without the use of hypnosis. Morselli was struck by his patient's apparent ignorance of the facts of sex life and by certain gaps in her memory: she could remember nothing about the weeks spent with her father in a place of which she could not even recall the name.

Gradually, Elena recovered her forgotten memories at the cost of terrifying emotional abreactions. She remembered having been the victim of her father's incestuous attacks (the reality of which was confirmed from other sources). Most horrifying for her was the memory of his attempts to put his tongue into her mouth. Her flight into a French personality was thus an attempt to repress the memory of her father's "tongue" and for his incestuous attacks in general.

The decisive progress thus achieved was followed by Morselli's efforts to unite the French and Italian speaking personalities and fuse into one another. The psychotic symptoms gradually disappeared. The treatment was thus proven effective, but, shortly after leaving the hospital in July 1927, Elena died of a kidney infection.

Personality Clusters

For quite a long time the only cases to be published were those of "dual personality." But it was later realized that the human mind was rather like a matrix from which whole sets of subpersonalities could emerge and differentiate themselves. Mesmerists discovered that by superimposing a hypnotic procedure on the already hypnotized patient, a third personality would sometimes appear, as different from the usual magnetic personality as was the latter from the normal individual in his waking state. Pierre Janet was one of the first to make systematic experiments with his subjects Lucie, Léonie, and Rose about those multiple hypnotic subpersonalities. He showed the important role of name-taking or name-giving: "Once baptized, the unconscious personality is more clear and definite; it shows its psychological traits more clearly."[64]

Personality clusters sometimes develop spontaneously, although it always remains open to question to what extent the investigator may, by conscious or unconscious suggestion, prompt the multiplication and development of these personalities. Among the best-known instances we will cite the case of Miss Beauchamp, to whom Morton Prince devoted a classical monograph.

Christine Beauchamp, born in 1875, was twenty-three years of age when Morton Prince became acquainted with her in 1898. At that time she was a student in a New England college, a well-educated but very timid person who spent all of her time reading books. She had a high sense of duty, was diligent, scrupulous, proud and secretive and showed a morbid reticence to talk about herself. She suffered from headaches, fatigue, and an inhibition of the will, for which reasons Morton Prince was consulted and took her in treatment. Prince knew that Miss Beauchamp had lost her mother at the age of thirteen, she had always been unhappy at home, and she had suffered a number of psychic traumas between the ages of thirteen and sixteen, to the point of having run away from home on one occasion.

In order to relieve her from her neurasthenic sufferings, Prince undertook to hypnotize her, which he found easy to do. Under hypnosis, she shed the artificial reserve of her waking state, but showed otherwise basically the same personality. A few weeks later, Prince was surprised to see that when hypnotized, she displayed one of two different states (which he called B II and B III, giving to the waking-state personality the name of B I). Whereas B II was Miss Beauchamp herself intensified, B III was quite the opposite: she was gay, lively, reckless, rebellious, and she often stuttered. B I (Miss Beauchamp in her normal state) knew nothing of her two hypnotic subpersonalities; B II knew B I but not B III. On the other hand, B III knew all about B I and B II. The second hypnotic subpersonality, B III, whom Prince called Chris, chose the name of Sally. She showed scorn and contempt for B I, whom she found stupid. However, Sally didn't have Miss Beauchamp's culture and did not speak French. It was not long before Sally manifested her existence indirectly in Miss Beauchamp's life by suggesting to her stupid words and actions; it was a kind of "acting out." A few months later, Sally appeared directly on the scene in the form of an overt alternating personality who knew everything about Miss Beauchamp, while the latter was constantly left puzzled and embarrassed, never knowing what practical jokes Sally had played on her in the intervals.

Later, a new personality emerged, B IV, the Idiot; it seemed to be a regressive personality. At this point, Prince found out that Miss Beauchamp had suffered a nervous shock at the age of eighteen. During the years 1898 to 1904, said Prince, all these personalities played "a comedy of errors which has been sometimes farcical and sometimes tragic." He had a difficult time dealing with them. However, he did succeed in amalgamating these personalities into one, the real Miss Beauchamp. The details of this treatment, which one might correctly call a group therapy, are more completely described in Prince's book *The Dissociation of a Personality.* [65]

Complicated as this case may appear, it is still less so than that of Doris, published by Walter Franklin Prince. [66] This case, far too long and complex to be analyzed here, involves several enigmas that are extremely difficult to explain, such as the fact that one of the subpersonalities (Sick Doris) was gradually absorbed by the primary personality (Real Doris), whereas another one (Margaret) slowly receded and disappeared without her memories, being integrated by Real Doris, and another one, Sleeping Real Doris, silently disappeared.

General Remarks about Multiple Personality

We have seen that students of multiple personalities described cases of increasing complexity, ranging from short fugues of ambulatory automatism to prolonged and extraordinarily complex and mysterious cases of multiple personalities. Several authors also endeavored to describe atypical and attenuated cases of multiple personality. The manifestations of the double were explained as being a kind of projection of the secondary personality. The French Binet[67] and the German Lucka[68] described phenomena of depersonalization and *fausse reconnaissance* as transient, extenuated forms of dual personality.

Several theories were elaborated to explain these phenomena. At first, the discussion took place between the associationists who spoke of mental split and loss of connection between the two main groups of associations, and the organicists who maintained the idea of organic modification of the brain. At a later period, toward the end of the nineteenth century, the factors of motivation, role-playing, regression, and progression of the total personality were brought to light, as we shall see later, especially by Flournoy. Gardner Murphy concluded that "most cases of multiple personalities appear essentially to represent the organism's effort to live, at different times, in terms of different systems of values."[69] Multiple personalities thus dramatically illustrate the fact that unity of personality is not given to the individual as a matter of course, but must be realized and achieved through the individual's persistent, and perhaps life-long efforts.

After 1910, there was a wave of reaction against the concept of multiple personality. It was alleged that the investigators, from Despine to Prince, had been duped by mythomaniac patients and that they had involuntarily shaped the manifestations they were observing. The new dynamic psychiatry showed little interest in the problems of multiple personality. At the present time, however, there seems to be a partial revival of interest in it. In Italy, Morselli[70] described two very remarkable cases, that of Elena, already quoted, and that of Marisa,[71] where EEG's were recorded and found different in the two personalities. In Switzerland, Binder published two cases of dual personality; in one of these cases the secondary personality sent anonymous letters and the primary personality participated in the tracing down of their author.[72] In the United States, there was the sensational case of Thipgen and Cleckley, which aroused much interest and was made into a film.[73]

Model Clinical Pictures: Hysteria

From a clinical point of view, the earliest focus of attention of the first dynamic psychiatry was somnambulism. Multiple personality took over in a later period, but toward the end of the nineteenth century, hysteria became more prominent, and it was at this point that a synthesis was reached between the teachings of hypnotists on the one hand and official psychiatry on the other.

For twenty-five centuries, hysteria had been considered a strange disease with incoherent and incomprehensible symptoms. Most physicians believed it to be a disease proper to women and originating in the uterus. Starting with the sixteenth century, some physicians claimed that its seat was in the brain and that it could occasionally be found in men also. A truly objective and systematic study of hysteria begins with the French physician Briquet, whose celebrated *Traité de l'Hystérie* was published in 1859.[74] As internist, Briquet had been appointed to head a hospital department of hysterical patients at the Hôpital de la Charité in Paris. It was not long before he discovered that these patients were much different from what they were believed to be and found that hysteria had never been properly investigated. Within ten years and with the help of his staff, he made an investigation of 430 hysterical patients. He defined hysteria as "a neurosis of the brain, the manifestations of it consisting chiefly in a perturbation of those vital acts which are concerned with the expression of emotions and passions." He found one case of male hysteria for twenty cases of female hysteria, which he ascribed to the greater impressionability of women. Briquet absolutely denied the then commonly held view of erotic craving or frustrations as being at the root of this disease (he found hysteria almost non-existent among nuns, but very frequent among Paris prostitutes). He attached much importance to hereditary factors (he found that 25 per cent of the daughters of hysterical women became hysterical themselves). He further found that hysteria was more common in the lower social classes than in the higher strata of society, more frequent in the country than in the city, and he concluded that hysteria was caused by the effect of violent emotions, protracted sorrows, family conflicts, and frustrated love, upon predisposed and hypersensitive persons. Charcot was later to take over the main lines of this concept of hysteria.

In the meantime, magnetizers and hypnotists had accumulated a great deal of data about hysteria and its relationship to somnambulism and and other magnetic diseases. There finally came a time when hysteria was considered to be a great synthesis of all these various conditions. This new concept was based on three arguments:

First, there was the frequent association of more than one of these conditions in nonhysterical and hysterical patients. It had long been known that lethargy, catalepsy, and ecstasis were frequently seen in hystericals. In 1787, Pétetin contended that catalepsy was but a subform of hysteria. During hysterical attacks the patient could show in turn phases of lethargy, catalepsy, somnambulism, ecstasis, and hallucinations. Multiple personalities were shown to occur frequently in hysterical individuals, and the shift from one personality to another was often introduced by an attack of lethargy or any other magnetic condition.

Second, conditions exactly similar to those clinical pictures could be provoked by hypnotization, hypnosis itself being recognized from the beginning as artificially induced somnambulism. But it had soon been shown that hypnotization could also produce such states as lethargy, catalepsy, ecstasis, certain types of hallucinations, and transient changes of personality. Moreover, it was under repeated sessions of hypnotism that the phenomenon of splitting of the personality had been discovered. Early magnetizers had already described the induced magnetic personalities who sometimes even adopted a Mesmeric name.[75]

Third, experience had shown that all of these conditions could, at least under favorable circumstances, be cured by hypnotism. Early magnetizers had already obtained seemingly miraculous cures by magnetizing hysterical patients, and, as we have seen, cures of severe hysterical paralyses by suggestion in the waking state gave Charcot the reputation of being a great medical wizard.

Meanwhile, the theory that hysteria derived from frustrated sexual desires was never completely given up: it remained current not only in the public mind but was also held by gynecologists and by many neurologists. As was already stated, Charcot's concept of hysteria was largely inspired by Briquet, who denied the sexual theory of hysteria. Charcot agreed with him in that he did not admit that hysteria was per se a sexual neurosis. Nevertheless, he recognized that the sexual element played an extremely important part in the life of his hysterical women patients, as can be seen from a perusal of the book on the *grande hystérie* by his disciple Paul Richer.[76] Hallucinations and actions of the patient during hysterical crises, Richer said, could be the re-enactment of a psychic trauma formerly experienced by the patient (as for instance taking flight before a rabid dog), but in most cases they referred to sexual events (either dramatic, such as an attempt of rape, or frankly erotic scenes, or love scenes of a more reserved nature). The same patient could at other times have hallucinations of an imaginary kind. The hysterical attack could also express the patient's secret wishes, as happened with one of Richer's women patients who had fallen in love with a man whom she had seen only once, and who expressed in her hysterical delirium her feelings for him that she concealed in her normal state.

Toward the end of the nineteenth century, attempts were made to combine the then current sexual theory of hysteria with that of dual personality emanating from the first dynamic psychiatry. Binet declared in 1887, "I believe it satisfactorily established, in a general way, that two states of consciousness, not known to each other, can co-exist in the mind of an hysterical patient." In 1889, he proclaimed, "The problem that I seek to solve is, to understand how and why, in hysterical patients, a division of consciousness takes place."[77] An American gynecologist, A. F. A. King, attempted to give an answer. The key to the problem, he said, is that there are two departments of physiological government in the individual, the "department of self-preservation" and the "department of reproduction."[78] Under certain circumstances, civilized life may deprive a woman of satisfaction in the "department of reproduction." The hysterical process expresses the automatic functioning of that need, and, seeing that this process does not reach its goal, it is bound to repeat itself over and over again, for months and for years.

In support of this theory, King gave a detailed phenomenological analysis of the hysterical crisis; first, he said, although "hundreds of cases of hysteria had been recorded in males," it is mostly a disease of women between puberty and menopause, and especially in women whose sexual wants remain ungratified; the attacks are more frequent in the spring and summer, in idle women than in those engaged in the struggle for existence. The attack never occurs when the patient is alone. The patient is seemingly unconscious, but not really so; during the attack, she does not seem too sick, "her beauty is not impaired," and many times she is particularly attractive to men. While she is in that condition, a gentle touch of the hand will produce violent pains, which disappear with a firm pressure and rough handling. When the attack is over, the woman invariably feels ashamed of it; she delights in evoking sympathy, but the more she is given, the worse her condition becomes. In short, one can say that "there is method in her madness"; everything seems to be directed and the woman "appears to be acting a part." Her entire attitude is reminiscent of that of a woman who exposes herself to be raped while seemingly rejecting the idea. The fact that the patient is unaware of the relationship between the attacks and her sexual needs is explained by the theory of dual personality. This concept of hysteria, as we shall later see, is remarkably similar to that which Moritz Benedikt was formulating in Vienna at the same time.

It is worth mentioning that this concept of hysteria also pervades Flaubert's description of the character Salammbô in his novel of the same title published in 1859. It is the picture of a hysterical maiden who suffers from erotic cravings, the nature of which she does not understand, but which dictate her feelings, attitudes, and actions. Her neurotic disturbances disappear after Salammbô, sacrificing herself for her country's sake, gives herself to the enemy chief.[79]

Charcot made the first synthesis between the two traditions, that of the hypnotists and that of official psychiatry. He adopted Briquet's theory of hysteria as being a neurosis of the brain in constitutionally predisposed individuals (sometimes men too) and of its psychogenetic origin. Charcot also assimilated hypnosis and hysteria and (without realizing it) took over from the old magnetizers the equation of somnambulism, lethargy, and catalepsy. He also correlated many instances of ambulatory automatism and of multiple personalities with hysteria.

Aside from this clinical synthesis, the mechanism of hysteria itself began to be explained in terms of concepts of the first dynamic psychiatry. Charcot occasionally described hysteria as being a permanent state of semisomnambulism. This concept was later elaborated by Sollier, who gave this condition the name of "vigilambulism." Another concept, hinted at by Binet and more completely developed by Janet, explained hysteria as a permanent state of dual personality. Actually, such concepts were not only the culmination of the first dynamic psychiatry, but, as we shall see later, also the starting point of the new systems of dynamic psychiatry, notably those of Janet, Breuer, Freud, and Jung.

Models of the Human Mind

The study and practice of magnetism and hypnotism had led to reflections about the constitution of the human mind. Two models evolved: First, a concept of the duality of the human mind (*dipsychism*) and, later, a notion of the human mind as a cluster of subpersonalities (*polypsychism*).

Dipsychism

The first magnetizers were immensely struck by the fact that, when they induced magnetic sleep in a person, a new life manifested itself of which the subject was unaware, and that a new and often more brilliant personality emerged with a continuous life of its own. The entire nineteenth century was preoccupied with the problem of the coexistence of these two minds and of their relationship to each other. Hence the concept of the "double-ego," or "dipsychism."

From the beginning, ideas diverged as to whether that other, or hidden, mind was to be considered "closed" or "open." According to the first conception, the hidden mind is "closed" in the sense that it contains only things, which, at one time or other, went through the conscious mind, notably forgotten memories or occasionally memories of impressions that the conscious mind had only fleetingly perceived, as well as memories of daydreams and fantasies. Some authors contended that this forgotten material could follow an autonomous development, independent of the conscious mind. The dipsychism theory was particularly developed by Dessoir, who wrote the once famous book *The Double Ego* (1890), in which he expounded the concept that the human mind normally consists of two distinct layers, each of which has its own characteristics.[80] Each of these two egos consist, in turn, of complex chains of associations. Dessoir called them *Oberbewusstsein* and *Unterbewusstsein*, "upper consciousness" and "under consciousness"; we get an inkling of the latter during dreams and clearer impressions during spontaneous somnambulism. Induced hypnosis is nothing but a calling forth of the secondary ego, which thus comes temporarily to the foreground. As for dual personality, Dessoir believed that the second personality had acquired such strength that it competed for predominance with the main personality. Everyone, he added, bears within himself the seeds of a dual personality. Subsequent authors supplemented that theory with rich material that included inspiration, mysticism, and mediumnistic manifestations.[81]

Other authors contended that the hidden unconscious mind was "open," virtually in communication with an extra-individual and mysterious realm. We recall that many early German magnetizers believed that magnetic sleep put some subjects in communication with the World Soul, hence their ability to see into the past and foretell the future. Some, such as the somnambulist Alexis in Paris, contended that the history of man is preserved in its entirety and that he, when in magnetic trance, possessed the faculty of traveling through time and space, thus being able to witness any event that had taken place at any time in the past. Alexis was reputed to have found countless lost objects because of this precious ability.[82] Others claimed that memories of previous lives were accessible to humans in mediumnistic trance or in hypnotic sleep. Even before the great spiritistic wave of the 1850's, there were magnetizers who contended that magnetic sleep rendered possible the communication with disincarnated spirits. Finally, some thought that the unconscious mind was able to comprehend superior realities, either directly or in the form of universal symbols.

Polypsychism

This word seems to have been coined by the magnetizer Durand (de Gros). He claimed that the human organism consisted of anatomical segments, each of which had a psychic ego of its own, and all of them subjected to a general ego, the Ego-in-Chief, which was our usual consciousness. In this legion each subego had a consciousness of its own, was able to perceive and to keep memories and to elaborate complex psychic operations. The sum total of these subegos constituted our unconscious life. Durand (de Gros) went so far as to say that, when undergoing surgery under anesthesia, certain of these subegos suffered atrociously, although the conscious ego remained totally ignorant of those sufferings. In hypnosis, the main ego was pushed aside and the hypnotizer gained a direct access to a number of the subegos.[83] The theory of polypsychism was taken up and given a philosophical elaboration by Colsenet, who linked it with Leibniz's concept of a hierarchy of monads.[84]

Magnetizers and others gathered numerous psychological data in favor of this theory. As early as 1803, Reil connected the phenomenon of dissociated personalities with a similar occurrence that is manifested in a certain type of normal dreams:

The actors appear, the roles are distributed; of these, the dreamer takes only one that he connects with his own personality. All the other actors are to him as foreign as strangers, although they and all their actions are the creation of the dreamer's own fantasy. One hears people speaking in foreign languages, admires the talent of a great orator, is astounded by the profound wisdom of a teacher who explains to us things of which we do not remember ever having heard.[85]

In such dreams we find the model of the complex cluster of personalities, with one of whom the dreamer identifies himself, although other person- alities have their independent course and are more knowledgeable than he. As we have seen in Chapter I, the shaman lived among a host of spirits, some friendly and subordinate, others hostile. The same is true of the possessed: He may be possessed, not only by one or by several spirits, but (as was the demoniac of Gadara) by a "legion" of them. Spiritism has familiarized us with the notion of a medium calling forth, in turn, a whole number of spirits, who are sometimes divided into groups in a kind of hierarchic order, as testified by the famous American medium, Mrs. Piper. A similar state existed in those complex instances of multiple personalities such as Miss Beauchamp and Doris Fisher, where we find a number of personalities, each of which had its role and all of which were linked together by a complex system of interpersonal relationships. Instances such as these made the theory of the double ego insufficient, and it was felt that a concept of polypsychism had to be resorted to. G. N. M. Tyrrell well expressed that concept of polypsychism to which both psychical research and the tradition of magnetism had pointed: "The personality is a multiplicity in unity of a kind which is almost impossible to express in words."[86] This multiplicity of personalities implies that they belong to ranges of varying depths and are also graded in some hierarchic order. "The lesson is surely that identity of selfhood is not dependent on numerical separateness in the way that we habitually think it is. . . . Selfhood has not the kind of unity which we associate with numerical separateness."

One cannot overemphasize the influence that these two models of the mind, dipsychism and polypsychism, exerted on the systems of the new dynamic psychiatry. Dipsychism in its closed variety was the model from which Janet drew his concept of the subconscious and Freud his first concept of the unconscious as being the sum total of repressed memories and tendencies. Jung's theory of the unconscious was soon of the open variety, in that the individual unconscious is open to the collective unconscious of the archetypes. Both Freud and Jung evolved from a dipsychical to a polypsychical model of the human personality. With Freud, this occurred when he replaced his former model of the conscious-unconscious with his later three-fold model of the ego-id-superego, whereas Jung evolved a still more complex system.

Concepts of Psychogenesis and Illness

One of the most constant contentions of the first dynamic psychiatry was that of the psychogenesis of many mental and physical conditions. The psychogenesis of illness was evidenced above all by those cures performed with the help of magnetizing and hypnotizing. Theories were also brought forth with regard to pathogenesis.

The Fluidic Theory

Mesmer believed that he discovered the existence of a universal physical fluid, whose equilibrium or disturbances explained health and disease. His disciples gave three explanations of illness: insufficiency, faulty distribution, or poor quality of the fluid. It was assumed that the magnetizer, through the channel of the rapport, transmitted his own stronger and better fluid to the patient, thus re-establishing the equilibrium in the patient. Certain magnetizers were able to make their patients visualize this fluid whose shape and color they described. Even after Puységur had demonstrated the psychological nature of the magnetic cure, the fluidic theory persisted side by side with the psychological theory during the entire nineteenth century. The fluidic theory sometimes reappeared in a modernized version, for instance, around 1880, with Reichenbach's theory of the "Od," and it has adherents even today who believe in the theory of brain waves being transmitted from the hypnotist to the subject.

After the theory of the fluid had been abandoned, psychological concepts were resorted to, such as the power of the will (Puységur), or later the idea of psychological forces or nervous energy. During the latter part of the nineteenth century, the view was commonly held by hypnotists and shared by many academic physicians that illness was the result of a lack of nervous energy. Despite its vagueness, this concept was ever present in the first dynamic psychiatry and was ready to be later developed by Janet, Freud, Jung, and others.

Ideodynamism

The phenomenon of hypnosis showed how the implantation of an idea during the somnambulic condition could lead to the autonomous evolution of that idea and its materialization in the form of the accomplishment of the posthypnotic suggestion. The first magnetizers marveled at this fact, which fitted well into the current dynamic associationistic theories of Herbart in Germany and of the philosophy of Laromiguière in France.[87] This quite naturally led to the assumption that certain morbid symptoms could be derived from ideas implanted in the mind through some kind of suggestion. This idea progressed in the second half of the nineteenth century. Liébeault wrote in 1873:

An idea induced during artificial somnambulism becomes a fixed idea and remains unconscious after awakening. . . . One sees it pursue its course despite the usual thinking activity with an impetus which nothing can stop. More than that, while the mind is occupied with the daily actions of normal life which the subject accomplishes consciously and of his own free will, some of the ideas suggested in that former passive state continue their hidden movement. No obstacle can hinder them in their fatal course. . . .[88]

In a lecture on hysterical paralysis given in May 1885, Charcot mentioned that it was a well-known fact that, through suggestion,

. . . an idea, a coherent group of associated ideas settle themselves in the mind in the fashion of parasites, remaining isolated from the rest of the mind and expressing themselves outwardly through corresponding motor phenomena. . . . The group of suggested ideas finds itself isolated and cut off from the control of that large collection of personal ideas accumulated and organized from a long time, which constitutes consciousness proper, that is the Ego.[89]

Charcot concluded that hysterical paralysis originated in the same manner, although spontaneously. This was the beginning of the concept that small, split-off fragments of the personality could follow an invisible development of their own and manifest themselves through clinical disturbances. Janet called this phenomenon subconscious fixed ideas and declared:

One would have to go through all the mental pathology and part of the physical pathology to show the disturbances produced by an idea excluded from personal consciousness. . . . The idea, like a virus, develops in a corner of the personality inaccessible to the subject, works subconsciously, and brings about all disorders of hysteria and of mental disease.[90]

Later, when Jung defined what he termed a "complex," he equated it with what Janet had called the *idée fixe subconsciente*.

The old theory of imagination, having been discarded by Mesmer and replaced by this fluidic theory, was considered obsolete during the nineteenth century. However, once the theory of the fluid had been rejected in turn, a new explanation had to be found for the various and mysterious appearances, disappearances, and metamorphoses of phenomena found in hypnotized patients, in magnetic diseases, and in hysterical patients. The older term "suggestion" met with new favor along with the notion of autosuggestion, and the two came to designate the entire realm previously covered by the notion of imagination.

Toward the end of the nineteenth century, magnetizers and physicians became increasingly aware of the fact that there was a tendency among hysterical and hypnotized individuals to simulate, more or less consciously, all kinds of symptoms and to set up situations in which they tried to involve the hypnotists or physicians. The word "mythomania," which was later coined by Dupré, was found to apply to a great number of hysterics. Actually, mythomania could be understood as one particular aspect of a wider concept, that of the mythopoetic function of the unconscious. With the exception of a few brilliant studies such as that by Fournoy about his medium Helen Smith, this mythopoetic function has not received the attention it deserves, and it is regrettable that the new systems of dynamic psychiatry have not yet filled this gap.

Psychotherapeutic Procedures

The nineteenth century was a great era for psychotherapy. In 1803 Reil, in his book *Rhapsodien,* presented a complete program of psychotherapeutic methods for the cure of mental diseases. Various methods of moral therapy were applied with varying degrees of success in countries such as France, England, and the United States. Magnetizers and hypnotist devoted considerable efforts to the cure of nervous diseases and physical ailments.

Mesmeric therapy, magnetizing with the use of passes, aimed at provoking a crisis. As we have seen, this crisis was simultaneously the calling forth of the symptoms and the first step toward their elimination. This actually was a variety of what we call today the cathartic therapy.

Starting with Puységur, *artificial somnambulism* became the great therapeutic weapon, which it remained up to the end of the century. It should be emphasized that hypnotism is able to exert its therapeutic effects in several ways. Sometimes the patient is relieved through the beneficial effect of hypnotic sleep itself, a sleep of which some patients gave wondrous descriptions. One of Bjerre's patients, for instance, told of a ". . . most wonderful sensation, a feeling of concentration of one's self with one's body as if one were isolated within one's self. Everything disappears, only the I-consciousness is left. This concentration is like the most absolute rest one can imagine."[91]

Bjerre assumed that "hypnosis is a temporary sinking back into that primary state of rest obtained during foetal life." Used in this way, hypnosis apparently acted as a powerful sedative.

Sometimes, but certainly not always, hypnotism acted through suggestion, that is, the direct implantation of an idea into the passive mind of the patient. However, this action has often been misunderstood. Hypnotic suggestions were not necessarily forced upon the subject. It is true that there has been a trend of imperative suggestion, which can be traced historically from Faria through Noizet to Liébeault and the Nancy School. Such imperative suggestions were found to work best with persons who occupied subordinate positions in life and were accustomed to obeying orders (soldiers and laborers,) or with people whose willpower was weak or who were eager to submit their will to that of the hypnotist. But even in such cases, the power of imperative suggestion had its limitations. When used with a person who was unwilling to submit, it was found that there was either no success at all, or else only a temporary removal of the symptom, which then reappeared or was replaced by another one.

Another type of hypnotic cure that has not received enough attention implies a kind of bargaining between the patient and the hypnotist. This is reminiscent of what often happened in exorcism, of the long discussions between the exorcist and the evil spirits, and the spirit's agreement to leave at a given time and under certain conditions. Something similar repeatedly occurred in the magnetic cure. During his somnambulic sleep, the patient would foretell the evolution of his symptoms and prophesy the exact date of his definitive cure. He would also prescribe his own treatment. It was by no means an easy task for the magnetizer to find the right compromise with the demands of his patient without exposing himself to being maneuvered by him. The story of Estelle is a characteristic example: while seemingly accepting her numerous fancies, Despine worked toward a constant and gradual recess of her symptoms, each recess having to be accepted by the patient. This type of hypnotic therapy was widespread during the first half of the nineteenth century, but was neglected later, largely because both the Salpêtrière and the Nancy Schools used the method of command in hypnotic cure. Nevertheless, even with Bernheim one finds at times some features of the former method.[92] There is, for example, the story of Bernheim's telling a woman afflicted with hysterical aphonia that she would shortly recover her voice and that she knew the date on which this would happen. The patient's answer was "in eight days"; in fact, eight days later, she was able to speak.

Toward the end of the nineteenth century, a new method of hypnotic cure began to be applied: the cathartic method, which consisted of finding out and attacking the unconscious root of the symptom. However, it remains open to question to what extent certain supposedly "cathartic" cures were achieved through a process of compromise between patient and doctor of which the doctor had been unaware.

Suggestion in waking state, the third great therapeutic procedure, was already being practiced at the beginning of the nineteenth century under the name of fascination. It became widely used in the 1880's with Liébeault, Bernheim, and the Nancy School. Suggestion is based on the concept of "ideodynamism," that is, in Berheim's words, "the tendency of an idea to materialize into an act." According to him, the hypnotic state was the result of a suggestion induced in view of facilitating another suggestion. Otherwise, there was no fundamental difference between suggestion under hypnosis and suggestion in the waking state. Toward the end of the nineteenth century, the word "suggestion" was used so loosely that it came to lose its meaning.

The Therapeutic Channel: The Rapport

Whatever the psychotherapeutic procedure, it showed the same common basic feature: the presence and utilization of the rapport. This term was used from the beginning by Mesmer and was handed down by generations of magnetizers and hypnotists to the beginning of the twentieth century, while the concept was gradually being developed and perfected. Mesmer seems to have borrowed the word from contemporary physics: In experiments that were popular at that time, people formed chains by touching each other, thus transmitting to one another the electrical current originating in a machine; to that end, they had been put in rapport with each other. In the same manner, Mesmer put his patients in direct rapport with the *baquet* or with each other. When magnetizing a patient, he considered himself to be a source of magnetic fluid with which the patient had to be put in rapport according to certain specifications. It is not clear to what extent Mesmer realized that the relationship he thus established with his patients was more than a physical one. Puységur did understand the psychological implications of the rapport. When reading the writings of the early magnetizers, one is struck by the tremendous importance that they ascribed to the rapport.

Actually, the phenomenon of the rapport was not quite as new as it would seem; it had already been known in the procedure of exorcism. Aldous Huxley notes that "the relationship between demoniac and exorcist is probably even more intimate than that between psychiatrist and neurotic."[93] The specific type of relationship between the confessor and the penitent was of course well known, and Noizet probably referred to it when he compared the magnetizer with the *directeur* (that is *directeur de conscience* or "spiritual guide").[94]

Beside these similarities, the magnetic rapport had certain characteristics of its own, which were the object of much study on the part of the early Mesmerists. What impressed them was the peculiar sensitivity of the magnetized toward the magnetizer and his ability to perceive the latter's thoughts and even his bodily sensations. That the reverse was also true was known and, as early as 1784, the term "magnetic reciprocity" was introduced.[95]

The possibility of erotic connotation in the magnetic rapport was also known from the beginning since, as we have seen, it was brought to the attention of the King in an appended secret Report of the Commissioners. We have also seen that the possibility of seduction was raised and that it was ruled out in 1785 by Tardif de Montrevel, although he did admit that some kind of platonic attachment might develop between magnetizer and magnetized.[96] In 1787 a novelist wrote that since the magnetizer was active while the magnetized was passive, a dangerous situation could easily develop if both the male magnetizer and the female magnetized were young.[97] In 1817 a certain Klinger wrote a curious Latin dissertation that contains a lengthy comparison between the *commercium magneticum* (the magnetic rapport) and the act of generation.[98] In Germany, the structure of the rapport was under scrutiny from the viewpoint of "sympathy," a concept elaborated by the promoters of the Philosophy of Nature. Friedrich Hufeland[99] stated that the magnetic rapport is the most intimate relationship that can exist between two human beings and the only one that bears comparison with that of the fetus in the mother's womb. According to Hufeland, each cure achieved through animal magnetism goes through the same phases as the yet unborn child in its mother's womb.

All French magnetizers studied the rapport in detail and distinguished it from the influence, the prolongation of the rapport between sessions. Aubin Gauthier carefully distinguished the magnetic crisis (induced somnambulism) from the magnetic state during which the magnetizer could still exert a certain effect upon his subject. Charpignon claimed that not infrequently did a subject receive, between his sessions, a vision of his magnetizer so clear and true to nature that he was not disturbed by it.[100] In Germany, Von Schubert noted the fascination exerted on the subject by anything that came from the magnetizer. Some patients would drink only something that had been touched by the magnetizer. Von Schubert further noted that these patients would adopt the medical theories that were in the magnetizer's mind and would give prescriptions in that sense toward their own cure.[101]

The German magnetizers Gmelin and Heinecken had also noticed that patients who had been magnetized by the same magnetizer felt an irresistible attraction to each other. An anonymous Scottish author observed exactly the same phenomena; patients whom he had magnetized were extremely attracted to one another, gave each other mesmeric names, and considered themselves as brothers and sisters. [102]

The notion of the rapport, which had been so strong and clear at the onset of the nineteenth century, became somewhat clouded at a later period, partly as a result of Braid's insistence on self-induced hypnosis and on the patient's role. Neither Charcot nor Bernheim paid much attention to the rapport. But after 1885 there was a renewal of interest following Janet's first experiments with "Léonie." Seeking a plausible explanation for this fact of mental suggestion, Ruault carefully analyzed the structure of the relationship between the hypnotist and his subject.[103] He found that the subject had his thoughts constantly fixed on the person of the hypnotist, during the sessions as well as in the intervals between them. During the sessions, the subject was hypersensitive to the hypnotist to the extent that he was able to perceive the latter's faintest signs. Through habit and training, a process of mutual understanding by signs developed between them, of which neither was aware. The subject became sensitive to the slightest shades of the hypnotist's thoughts without realizing how, and without the hypnotist's awareness. Moreover, the subject had been trained by the magnetizer and believed in him and in his supernatural powers. Ruault added that many magnetizers impressed upon their patients' minds that no one else would ever be able to magnetize them. Some of them even reiterated this suggestion at the end of each session or gave their patients a talisman that they were always to keep on their bodies. This is how the magnetizer's influence became sufficiently powerful so that he was able to magnetize his subjects from a distance, at times even involuntarily. This confirmed the magnetizer's belief in his own powers, increased his self-confidence, which in turn increased his hold over his various subjects.

In 1889, Janet briefly mentioned this topic in his *Automatisme psychologique*.[104] He emphasized the role of electivity in the rapport and the fact that the subject had a kind of negative hallucination for everything that was not connected directly with the magnetizer (in modern language a "scotoma"). The same factor was also stressed by Moll in 1892.[105] At the International Congress of Psychology in Munich in 1896, Janet brought forth a fully elaborated theory of the rapport and of somnambulic influence.[106] He had analyzed in detail what had occurred in his patients' minds in the intervals between hypnotic sessions and found that in a first phase (of influence proper), a vast improvement apparently occurred. A hysterical patient was freed of most of his symptoms; he felt happier, more active, and more intelligent, and did not think much about his hypnotist. This was followed by a second phase, that of somnambulic passion in which the symptoms receded, and the patient felt an increased need to see the hypnotist and to be hypnotized. This urge often assumed the form of passion. Depending on the case, this could develop into ardent love, jealousy, superstitious fear, or profound respect, and was accompanied by the feeling of having been accepted or rejected. The subject sometimes saw the hypnotist in dreams or in hallucinations. Janet discovered the very important fact that posthypnotic suggestions would be obeyed mainly during the period of somnambulic influence and much less during the phase of somnambulic passion. He stressed the therapeutic implications of these observations.

Janet enlarged this paper and published it again one year later, in 1897.[107] On the basis of experiments with thirty patients, he confirmed the fact that posthypnotic suggestions would be carried out as long as the somnambulic influence lasted. Furthermore, Janet analyzed the subject's feeling toward the hypnotist during somnambulic passion and found it to be a mixture, differing from one patient to another, of erotic passion, filial or maternal love, and other feelings in which there was always a certain kind of love. However, the main factor was the patient's *besoin de direction*, the need to be directed. The therapeutic implications were twofold: First, the therapist had to take complete command of the patient's mind. Once this was achieved, he had to teach the patient to do without him, which could be accomplished by gradually widening the intervals between sessions. The patient had also to be made aware of his own feelings.

Janet's investigations on somnambulic influence aroused considerable interest and stimulated other observations on the same topic. Sollier agreed with Janet's description and added another fact from his own experience: It was of great importance to the subject that the hypnotist know a great deal about him, particularly when there had been experiences of age regression.[108] The patient then felt as though the hypnotist had known him all his life.

Much had changed indeed since Mesmer's first electrical concept of the rapport, and this changing notion received complex psychological elaboration by magnetizers and hypnotists before it culminated in Janet's view of the influence as being a peculiar variety of feelings toward the hypnotist mixed with the patient's need to be directed by him, which could be used by the hypnotist as a powerful therapeutic weapon.

The Psychotherapist

Magnetizers and hypnotists constituted a new type of healer, having much in common and being at the same time very different from anything that had previously existed. Not only did both groups consider Mesmer and Puységur as their great founders, and not only did they share similar doctrines and techniques, but they also had their associations, their journals, and their professional ethics.

It is difficult for us today to imagine what they were like, what they thought, how they worked in their daily practice. We can however gain some insight into these questions by reading some of their old textbooks, such as those by Deleuze, Bertrand, Charpignon, and especially that by Aubin Gauthier.[109] The magnetizer, says Gauthier, must be in good health lest he transmit his own diseases to his patients; if he should become ill, he will have to "purify" himself before returning to his work. He must lead a "wise and well regulated" life, be sober, calm, reserved, kind and dignified, and not talk too much, as well as be rigorously honest and scrupulous. In order to become a magnetizer one has to take a training course and to read the works of Mesmer, Puységur, and all the classics on magnetism. Puységur's old principle that the magnetizer should never accept any fees for his treatment is no longer acceptable, Gauthier says, because a man who devotes so much of his time to the study of magnetism cannot possibly give free treatment. A magnetizer is even entitled to higher fees than a physician because he must possess all the qualities of a medically trained person, plus the knowledge of magnetism, and perfect health. He not only gives of his knowledge, as do physicians, but he also transmits his vital forces to his patients. For the patient, the choice of the right magnetizer is of paramount importance; certain magnetizers are more successful with some patients than with others. A magnetizer should never accept a patient if he is not prepared to carry the treatment through to the end, because it often can be dangerous to interrupt a treatment. Before beginning with the treatment, the question of fees should be settled between the magnetizer and the patient and the days and hours of treatment decided upon, after which the sessions must be punctually attended by the patient. The latter must keep no secrets from the magnetizer about his illness or about anything that might help to explain it. During treatment the patient will have to abstain from any kind of excess, keep to a moderate diet, and refrain from smoking. The duration of the treatment can vary from a week to six months or more, but there should never be more than two sessions a day. The magnetizer should keep a diary about every patient in which each session should be recorded. No woman should be hypnotized unless her husband or another witness is present. One basic rule is to abstain from any kind of experimentation with one's patients. Clinical happenings will provide the magnetist with sufficient experience to satisfy his scientific curiosity. Gauthier proposed a "magnetizer's oath" inspired by the Hippocratic one.

Another problem raised at that period was the claim of medical societies that only a medical doctor should be allowed to practice magnetism. Lay magnetizers violently opposed that claim. In 1831, the Paris Académie de Médecine ruled that lay magnetizers should be authorized to practice, but under medical control; their diaries would have to be submitted at regular intervals for inspection by physicians. However, this rule was hardly ever observed.

We have a number of interesting autobiographies of magnetizers, most of them written by itinerant or stage magnetizers. One of the most celebrated French magnetizers, the Baron Du Potet de Sennevoy, relates in his autobiography that he was born in 1796 into a ruined aristocratic family.[110] He admits to having been a poor pupil and a rebellious child. Having heard of magnetism, he tried it out on two young girls and became terror-stricken when he was unable for hours to bring them out of their magnetic condition. Nevertheless, this incident led him to believe that he possessed great magnetic powers. He left for Paris to study magnetism, but it was not long before he broke with his colleagues and founded his own school. A proud and arrogant man, Du Potet was convinced that "he was the incarnation of magnetism" and that he had a mission to fulfill. After introducing the technique of the "magic mirror," he gradually evolved toward magic and seems to have developed real delusions of grandeur.

The Count de Maricourt, another well-known magnetizer of that period, had spent his childhood in Naples where he was introduced to magnetism by an old Irish priest and an old Italian physician who both practiced it.

Maricourt's first attempts at magnetizing were almost as unfortunate as those of Du Potet. After returning to France, he witnessed a performance given by an itinerant magnetizer for the students in his college. One of the students had severe accidents after having been magnetized. However, young De Maricourt was not discouraged by these events. As soon as he arrived in Paris, he went to see the magnetizer Marcillet and his illustrious *somnambule* Alexis. He later adopted Du Potet's teachings and wrote a long comparison between puységurism (which implies magnetic sleep) and potetism (a state of fascination without sleep). He later became a spiritist and a student of the relationship between incarnate and disincarnate spirits.[111]

One delightful forgotten work is the autobiography of Charles Lafontaine.[112] Born in 1803, he also claimed to belong to one of France's most ancient and aristocratic families. His father occupied an important administrative post, and young Charles had started to work with him. However, wishing to become an actor, he left his family for Paris where he worked with theater companies for several years, experiencing many "ups" and "downs." Once, he accidentally magnetized a woman and discovered that she was a lucid *somnambule* and, at the same time, that he possessed great magnetic powers. He relates that the day he became a magnetizer, he was ostracized by his family, his friends, and his former acquaintances and was treated as an outlaw. He then devoted himself to magnetism, which became his sole interest in a life of constant wandering and struggle. He gave great stage performances, which were sometimes marred by riots in which the police had to intervene. He also treated numerous patients privately. According to his own account, wherever he went the blind would see again, the deaf would hear, and the paralyzed would walk. In the city of Rennes, he magnetized a woman and taught her a theatrical role that she then performed beautifully on the stage before a large audience and of which she could remember nothing in her waking state. He traveled to London where his success was so great that thieves became so afraid of him that he could safely visit the worst taverns. Following Lafontaine's visit to Manchester, a surgeon of that city by the name of Braid was converted to magnetism and later became known as the promoter of braidism. Lafontaine's book reads like an entertaining novel of adventures.

Another autobiography worthy of mention, although written in a bombastic style, is that of Auguste Lassaigne.[113] Born in Toulouse in 1819, Lassaigne worked at first in a factory, while reading fantastic stories and learning juggling (sleight-of-hand) in his spare time. His tricks brought him such success that he eventually decided to make his living by this skill. During one of his tours, he met a young lady of eighteen, Prudence Bernard, who was a natural somnambulist. He watched her being treated by a magnetizer, and his skepticism about magnetism was swept away; he soon became an apostle of that doctrine. He married Prudence and took her along on his tours, magnetizing her publicly since she was a lucid somnambulist. Lassaigne believed himself to be endowed with a sacred mission; he considered magnetism to be a sublime science able to touch upon the deepest mysteries of human nature. He admitted, however, that there might also be something very human about those mysteries. He noted that magnetism could produce "heavenly voluptuousness" in the magnetized woman and that these sensations will be infinitely more delightful if the magnetizer is loved by her. Of Prudence, he said that "in waking state she is a woman, in somnambulism she is an angel." He believed it was her destiny to bring France back to the True Faith and compared her to Joan of Arc. The book is full of bitter invectives against the enemies of magnetism. There are also curious statements about the influence of marriage on the relationship between the magnetizer and his somnambulist. The difficulties arising from a slight matrimonial disharmony result in the subsequent failure of the somnambulic experiment. "Magnetism," Lassaigne concluded, "is the Science of the future."

It must be understood that these autobiographies inform us only about one type of magnetizer. Actually, most magnetizers were quiet, reserved men, who, aside from their medical or other profession, practiced magnetism on a few patients and kept careful records of their observations which they discussed in small local societies. These were the men with whom Janet came in contact when he was a young professor in Le Havre. Janet repeatedly said that these were truly the men who had discovered all that which Charcot, Bernheim, and their contemporaries believed to have discovered.

The Cultural Impact of the First Dynamic Psychiatry

The first dynamic psychiatry exerted a great influence on philosophy, literature, and even the arts. Three main trends of that science emerged in turn: animal magnetism, spiritism, and the teachings of hypnotism and multiple personality.

As early as 1787, a writer, Charles de Villers, who had served as an artillery officer under Puységur, published a novel, *Le Magnétiseur amoureux*, in which he developed a philosophical theory deduced from the phenomenon of magnetism.

As early as 1790, animal magnetism had become so widespread in Germany that it was almost common practice to consult somnambulists for problems of disease and health, for practical advice, and sometimes for spiritual guidance. There was of course also much opposition to that trend and the enemies of mesmerism found it easy to make it a target for ridicule. In 1786 it was reported that an actress so convincingly feigned sickness and somnambulism that she deceived several physicians.[114] Frederick William II, King of Prussia and unworthy successor of Frederick the Great, was himself the victim of an extraordinary intrigue wrought around him by a number of cynical men in his court. They enrolled the help of a somnambulist, a hunchbacked woman who was instructed to feign a trance and to act as though her spirit was conferring with God Almighty. The alleged divine words that she transmitted to the King originated of course with the men who employed her. They thus obtained from the King whatever honors and fortunes they strove for, and influenced his political decisions until they came in conflict with the Countess Lichtenau, the King's mistress. The King then ceased to believe in the somnambulist, who subsequently fell from favor.[115]

Notwithstanding such incidents, mesmerism constantly progressed in Germany. From 1790 to 1820, it was not only professed by men such as Gmelin, Kluge, and Kieser, but it also gained a foothold at the universities of Bonn and Berlin. Well-known physicians such as Wolfart, Hufeland, and Reil were convinced of its validity. Among philosophers and writers, several remained sceptical; Goethe, for instance, never showed any interest in mesmerism. On the other hand, the promoters of the Philosophy of Nature hailed magnetism as an epoch-making discovery. Schelling saw in magnetic somnambulism a means for establishing a connection between man and the World Soul and for laying the basis of experimental metaphysics. Fichte was more critical, but, having watched demonstrations on somnambulists, he arrived at the conclusion of the relativity of the ego and saw that man's individuality could be altered, divided, or subjected to another man's will.[116] Schopenhauer, who had been deeply impressed by the public performances given by the magnetizer Regazzoni in 1854, repeatedly expressed his interest in magnetism in his writing.[117] "Although not from an economical or technical, but certainly from a philosophical point of view, Animal Magnetism is the most momentous (*inhaltsschwer*) discovery ever made, even if, for the time being, it brings more enigmas than it solves."[118]

The impact of magnetism was equally felt by Protestant and Catholic theologians and became particularly important to a group of Catholic mystical philosophers. Windischmann advocated a "Christian healing art," to be practiced by priests who would combine the sacraments of the Church with the science of magnetism.[119] Ennemoser recommended that children should be magnetized in their mother's womb as well as trees in the fields.[120] Ringseis made himself the promoter of a "Christian Germanic medicine."[121] We have already seen the tremendous interest aroused in philosophers and theologians by Friedericke Hauffe, the seeress of Prevorst, and that Clemens Brentano, after his conversion, spent five years in Dülmen, recording the revelations of Katharina Emmerich.

The same interest was reflected in the literature of the time. There is hardly one German Romantic poet who remained untouched by the influence of animal magnetism. The writer whose work is permeated by magnetism, more than anyone else's is E. T. A. Hoffmann. A complete textbook of magnetism could be compiled from his novels and short stories.[122]

Magnetic somnambulism is viewed by Hoffmann as the true penetration of one person into another and thus comparable to the phenomenon of possession. During somnambulism, the magnetized (the passive feminine part) is in sympathy with the magnetizer (the active masculine part), but there is more to it: the magnetizer is also a mediator (*ein Mittler*) between the magnetized and universal harmony. But the magnetic session is only one particular case of a more general phenomenon. People magnetize each other unconsciously and unintentionally; hence the formation of "magnetic chains" linking individuals to each other. The world is a system of wills where the weaker is dominated by the stronger. The unknown power, of which the magnetizer is a medium, is a two-fold one: it can be either good or evil. The evil magnetizer is a kind of moral vampire who destroys his subject. The magnetized is usually a weak, naive, credulous and hypersensitive personality. Therefore, the magnetic relationship can be either good (friendly, fatherly), or evil (demoniacal). The notions of dual personality and of the double are particularly noticeable in Hoffmann's work.

Hoffmann gave descriptions of magnetic cures, notably in a short story titled *Das Sanktus*.[123] Bettina, a singer, had lost her beautiful voice, to the despair of the *Kapellmeister* (conductor) and of the physician who was unable to cure her. He finds the illness mysterious: Bettina can talk aloud, but her aphonia reappears as soon as she tries to sing. She is making no progress at all. The illness started on Easter Sunday, when, after singing a few solos, she left the church as the tenor began singing the Sanctus. A magnetizer who saw that she was about to go away told her not to leave the church yet. From then on, she could sing no more. The magnetizer, who had unintentionally caused the illness, will now cure it. While Bettina listens in from behind the door, he tells the *Kapellmeister* the story of a woman who had lost her voice because of an impious act and who recovered it when she relieved her conscience. Returning three months later, the magnetizer finds Bettina cured. This story shows that a magnetic cure was not necessarily always the result of a suggestive order impressed upon the patient's mind, but that it could also stem from a more refined psychological procedure. Bettina's illness had been caused by an unfortunate suggestion made at a moment when she felt guilty; she is not aware of the cause of her condition. The magnetizer makes her indirectly aware of it, and this is already the mechanism of a cathartic cure.

As we have already seen, mesmerism met with more resistance and scepticism in France than in Germany. Many people dismissed it altogether, as did Napoleon when he spoke with Puységur: "If your somnambulist is so clever, let her foretell what I shall be doing eight days hence and which will be the winning numbers at tomorrow's lottery."[124] Magnetism was condemned by the Académie and despised by universities. Among psychiatrists, it was known that experiments performed in Pinel's and Esquirol's hospitals remained without results, and it was said that Georget had been deceived by a hysterical woman. Religious circles were either reluctant or positively hostile. However, in 1846, the celebrated Dominican preacher Father Lacordaire declared in one of his sermons in Notre-Dame Cathedral that he believed in magnetism, which, he felt consisted of "natural but irregular forces which cannot be reduced to scientific formulas and which are being used by God in order to confound contemporary materialism."[125] The influence of magnetism was much stronger among certain groups of spiritualistic, mystical, and esoteric philosophers, as well as in Romantic circles. Several of the more important writers also showed much interest in magnetism.

Balzac was a believer in magnetism, recommended it as a treatment, and occasionally practiced it himself; magnetism also plays a role in several of his works.[126] Paul Bourget has shown that the "theory of the will" contained in Balzac's novel *Louis Lambert* is identical with the magnetic fluid theory as interpreted by Deleuze.[127] In *Ursule Mirouet,* another of Balzac's works, a sceptical physician is introduced to a magnetizer working with a somnambulistic woman whose spirit can be sent anywhere in the world. At the physician's request, the somnambulist's spirit visits his house in a provincial town and relates what is happening there at the moment; she even tells him what his ward is saying in her prayers. On his return home, the physician finds that all the details related by the woman were factual. Alexandre Dumas believed that he was endowed with magnetic powers, and his villa was the scene of magnetic experiments.[128] In one of his historical novels, he depicts Cagliostro not as the imposter he really was, but as a great magician and magnetizer.[129] Flaubert, in one episode of his posthumously published novel *Bouvard et Pécuchet,* gives a comical picture of what magnetism could become in the hands of inexperienced self-taught persons. The two characters organize collective sessions around a magnetized pear tree, and they try to cure a sick cow through magnetism. But magnetism was more exploited by popular writers than by great ones.[129] A best seller of that time was a novel by Frédéric Soulié, *Le Magnétiseur.*[130] The villain, a German magnetizer, magnetizes a mentally ill woman and thus learns a secret incident, which she had witnessed in the past and which she has now forgotten in her normal waking state. The magnetizer will now exploit this secret for the purpose of blackmail.

In England, Robert Browning wrote a rather obscure poem, *Mesmerism* (1855), in which a magnetizer, from a distance, orders a woman to come to his house on a rainy night. He is appalled by the influence his mind can exert over another and prays that he may never misuse it.[131]

In the United States, interest in magnetism developed more slowly but it gained importance during the 1830's. We have already seen the connection between magnetism and the origins of Christian Science and of spiritism. Edgar Allan Poe was impressed by the doctrine of magnetism.

It has been assumed that he was the author of an anonymous book expressing belief in the reality of the magnetic fluid, which a somnambulist could supposedly see, "white as a light," sprinkling brilliant sparks.[132] Poe's story *The Facts in the Case of Mr. Valdemar* is well known: a dying man's spirit is being kept attached to his deceased body by a magnetizer who was a friend of his. Weeks later, when the spirit is at last released, the body falls into instantaneous decomposition.[133] Incidentally, this story crossed the Atlantic at a time when Poe was not yet known in France, which could explain why it was accepted at face value at several places and quoted by Mabru as an example of the inconceivable absurdities believed in by magnetizers.[134]

The topic of dual personality, which was to inspire so many writers during the second half of the century, appeared in literature under the form of the "double," a projected dual personality.[135] The prototype of this type of writing was E. T. A. Hoffmann's story *The Devil's Elixirs*:

> The monk Medard, having drunk a magic elixir that he found in his monastery, has his personality secretly transformed into that of a wicked man. Sent by his superiors on a duty to Rome, he commits crimes and escapes. But he meets his Double: a monk, coming from the same monastery, having committed the same crimes and suffering from the same guilt feelings. The Double drinks the remainder of the elixir, becomes insane and is committed to an asylum. Medard goes to the Court, and then takes up his criminal life again. The Double reappears, is charged with having committed Medard's crimes, is arrested and sentenced to death. But just before the execution, Medard confesses his guilt and escapes, followed by the Double who disappears. Medard recovers consciousness in a sanitarium in Italy, and after due penitence, he returns to his monastery where he again finds his peace of mind.[136]

This novel is remarkable as an anticipation of Jung's concept of the "shadow": Medard has projected his shadow (the evil side of his personality) onto another being, hence his wicked and erratic life. Once he has accepted his guilt and assimilated the shadow, he achieves a higher integration of his personality. The concept of the double is understood in a different way by Edgar Allan Poe in his story "William Wilson":

> The narrator has noticed another boy in his school who happens to have the same name and date of birth as himself, looks very much like him, but speaks in a lower voice. He dislikes that other boy and becomes so frightened at seeing him that he runs away from the school. He embarks on a life of debauchery, but at each crucial step, the double unexpectedly reappears and accuses him, until one day William Wilson kills him and hears the dying Double tell him that he has murdered himself and is therefore dead too.[137]

Here, the double is understood as the moral conscience in the classical sense of the fight between good and evil within man (as, later, in Oscar

Wilde's *The Picture of Dorian Gray*). A quite different notion of the double is given by Dostoevski in his novel *Dvoinik* (The Double):

> Golyatkin, a petty office clerk, begins to display erratic behavior, which draws the attention of his superiors and his colleagues. He suddenly meets a man who has exactly his physical features and wears similar clothes. On the following day, the double is introduced at the office as a new clerk who has the same name and date of birth as Golyatkin, speaks to him in a humble tone and begs Golyatkin to protect him. Golyatkin takes him into his apartment. But as things progress, the double becomes increasingly more arrogant with him, ousts him from his post, lives at his expense and takes his friends away from him. Golyatkin becomes more and more confused, until one day the double helps put him into the carriage which is to conduct him to the mental hospital.[138]

In that novel, the double is obviously understood as being the morbid personality of a man who is becoming psychotic, that uncanny "other self," which is weak at first but increasingly takes control over the healthy ego.

The great wave of spiritism, which began in the United States in 1848 and spread over Europe in the early 1850s, forced magnetism to the background for some time to come. Spiritistic experiments became fashionable, and great mediums were the attractions of the day. There was a flood of literature purportedly written by spirits or dictated from the other world. During his exile in Jersey, Victor Hugo held spiritistic sessions in his home at which his son Charles was probably the medium. Aeschylus, Shakespeare, and the spirits of other illustrious men dictated fine French verses, which resembled clever imitations of Hugo's own poetry.[139] The astronomer Flammarion, an enthusiastic believer in spiritism, published revelations by spirits of famous persons, among which was a *Genesis* supposedly dictated by the spirit of Galileo.[140] Some mediums who had rather mediocre educational backgrounds wrote novels that in some cases, and according to certain critics, were of an unexpectedly high level. The best-known example is probably that of Pearl Lenore Curran, a woman born of British parents in Illinois in 1883. Though an uncle of hers was a medium, she apparently was never interested in spiritism. In 1912, however, she began to experiment with the Ouija board. Gradually, the letters came to her with increasing speed, and then vivid mental pictures developed. Suddenly, on July 8, 1913, she received a communication from a personality calling herself Patience Worth, allegedly a woman who had lived on a Dorset farm in England in the seventeenth century, and who dictated to Mrs. Curran an enormous amount of literary compositions, including poems and novels. Several of those novels and a selection of poems were published.[141] This literary output was written in a variety of peculiar old English dialects, which had however never been spoken. These dialects (a different one in each work), as well as the historical knowledge contained in each novel baffled the experts. Casper S. Yost[142] and Walter

Franklin Prince,[143] who interviewed Mrs. Curran, considered her case to be an unusual instance of the creative powers of the subconscious mind.[144]

The practice of automatic writing naturally led to that of automatic drawing and was soon taken up by mediums and members of spiritistic groups.[145] The playwright Victorien Sardou attracted attention with his curious drawings allegedly showing pictorial scenes from the planet Jupiter and featured among others the houses owned by Zoroaster, the prophet Elijah, and Mozart on that planet. Fernand Desmoulins, a professional artist, in his trances made portraits of deceased persons with stupendous rapidity, even in the dark. The number of such automatic drawings was sufficiently large to allow esthetics of the spirits to be made an object of study. Jules Bois described the main features of these artistic productions from the unconscious as having a tendency to asymmetry, abundant and unnecessary details, the replacement of firm lines by "equivocal" ones, and irregularity in the output. He believed that mediumnistic art exerted a definite influence upon the art school of the Symbolists, which started about 1891.

The spiritistic wave slowly receded, and the fashion returned to magnetism in its modernized form of hypnotism and to the problem of multiple personality. The aspect that most impressed the public was that of seduction and crime under hypnosis. Charpignon devoted a serious study to that problem in 1860.[146] In the 1880's, the question attracted considerable attention because of the Nancy School's unanimous belief in the possibility of such crimes, and it was widely discussed in newspapers, magazines, and novels. The Salpêtrière School, however, refused to admit the possibility of such crimes, with the result that, whenever hypnotism was invoked in the genesis of crimes in the courts, it led to disputes between experts of the two schools. Bernheim did not, of course, assert that anyone could be hypnotized into committing a crime, but he believed that it could happen in certain circumstances—either in an amoral subject who would offer no resistance to a criminal suggestion or in a weak individual who would commit the crime in an impulsive way, such as an epileptic or, indirectly, in an individual to whom delusions of persecution had been suggested that would result in his committing the crime. It was also possible to suggest false memories to a subject and thus transform him into a false witness. Bernheim also believed that autosuggestion played an important role in many criminal cases. Certain criminals, he said, were the victims of autosuggestion and therefore not responsible.[147] In Germany, Schrenck-Notzing firmly believed in hypnotic criminogenesis and described a wide range of crimes that could be committed under the effect of hypnosis and suggestion.[148]

We can hardly realize today to what extent hypnotism and suggestion were invoked in the 1880's to explain countless historical, anthropological, and sociological facts such as the genesis of religions, miracles, and wars. Gustave Le Bon popularized a theory of collective psychology based on the assumption that the "collective soul" of the crowd could be compared to the hypnotized mind, and the leader to the hypnotist.[149] Entire educational systems were based on the concept of suggestion. Great interest was shown in subjects who, under hypnosis, played theatrical roles, or painted or sang beautifully.[150]

Hypnotism inspired a multitude of novels. Some took as their theme a crime committed in a normal state but confessed under hypnosis[151] or under the effect of a suggestion by the dying victim upon his murderer.[152] In other novels the criminal would hypnotize an innocent person into committing a crime under his direction, but the true criminal would be discovered if the psychiatric expert was clever enough to hypnotize the performer of the criminal act.[153] The most successful novel based on hypnotism was perhaps George du Maurier's best seller *Trilby*.[154] The daughter of an English lord, Trilby was raised in Paris as a seamstress and became an artist's model. A perfidious music teacher, Svengali, hypnotized her and trained her to become a brilliant singer, after which he married her. But she could sing only when in hypnotic trance while Svengali kept his eyes on her from a theater loge. When Svengali died of a heart attack at the beginning of a performance, Trilby, no longer hypnotized, was unable to sing, and her career ended catastrophically. Of no lesser interest is *Le Horla*, a short story written by De Maupassant when he was about to collapse into general paresis.[155] A man became anxiety-stricken when he realized that strange and unaccountable events took place in his house, as if mysterious invisible beings had invaded it. He left for Paris, where, watching a hypnotic session, he was bewildered seeing a hypnotized woman given an order that she punctually carried out the following day, not knowing why she did it. The man, recognizing that this was also what was happening in his own mind, was consternated: "Someone possesses my soul and governs it. Someone directs all my actions, all my movements, all my thoughts. I myself am nothing but a terrified, enslaved spectator of the things which I am accomplishing."

No less numerous were the novels inspired by the topic of multiple personality. In France a popular best seller of that time was a novel by Gozlan: *Le Médecin du Pecq*. During a somnambulic escape, a rich neurotic young man living in a sanitarium made a young woman pregnant, of which he was quite unaware in his waking state.[156] The physician disentangled his confusion by analyzing the dreams that the young man reported to him every morning. After 1880, novels about multiple personalities increased rapidly. Jules Claretie carefully gathered documents at the Salpêtrière before writing *L'Obsession,* the story of a painter who became obsessed with the knowledge that his secondary personality would at times take control over his body, and who never knew what mischief the other was liable to perform.[157] Finally the painter was cured by an Alsatian doctor who suggested to him the death and burial of the other. *Sister Marthe,* by Charles Epheyre, was another sensational novel of that time: During a vacation in the country, a young physician was asked to treat a young orphan who was about to become a nun.[158] He hypnotized Sister Marthe in order to cure her of her nervous symptoms, but another personality appeared: Angèle, who knew that she was the daughter of a rich man and heiress to a great fortune (which the Sister did not seem to suspect). Angèle was in love with the young doctor and wanted to elope with him. However, on the morning of the planned elopement, Sister Marthe's personality suddenly reappeared at the railway station and she was thrown into confusion. She then took her vows and died of tuberculosis soon thereafter. Few readers of the *Revue des Deux Mondes* suspected Epheyre to be the pseudonym of the well-known physiologist Charles Richet. Hennique's *Minnie Brandon* was another success. A young Frenchman was in love with a charming and distinguished young Englishwoman, Minnie, who, upon drinking the slightest amount of alcohol, unfortunately turned into a horrible shrew, Brandon.[159] The struggle between Minnie and Brandon was finally won by the latter, and the young man, to his deep sorrow, was forced to take leave of both. Still worse was the fate of the hero in Mintorn's novel *The Somnambulist*: a dignified Protestant minister, good husband and father, turned in his somnambulic state into a criminal who seduced and raped women, and killed children, while his normal personality was unsuspecting.[160] Paul Lindau wrote a famous theatrical success, *The Other*:[161] a judge was conducting an investigation about a crime and discovered that he, or rather his unsuspected second personality, was its author. But the greatest achievement of this kind of literature was probably Stevenson's novel *The Strange Case of Dr. Jekyll and Mr. Hyde*.[162] This book is of special interest because of the manner in which it was conceived and written. Stevenson stated that he had, over the years, developed an intensive dream life. In his dreams the "little people" would come to him and suggest ideas for his novels. This sharp distinction between his waking and his dreaming personalities may have suggested to him the theme of his novel. He added that many details of the novel were dictated by the "little people."[163] It is important to note that, besides a few good novels and plays, a multitude of popular novels and cheap literature, which are entirely forgotten today, were published in the 1880's involving the themes of somnambulism, multiple personality, and crimes under hypnosis, which certainly contributed to shaping the mentality of that period.

Actually, a gradual evolution led from such oversimplified themes to more subtle ones. We have seen that Binet, Lucka, and other authors insisted on the fact that there were not only dramatic cases of split personality but also all kinds of transitory stages between actual personality split and the normal occurrence of facets of personality. This trend was also reflected in literature. Some authors chose sudden switches from one facet of personality to another as themes for their novels. Paul Bourget wrote *L'Irréparable* in 1883, describing the story of a woman, who, before her marriage, had been uninhibited, carefree and gay, and who suddenly turned into a depressive and regretful person afterwards.[164] One of the novel's characters, a philosopher in the manner of Ribot, explained the metamorphosis to the reader. In his novel *Le Jardin secret*,[165] Marcel Prévost told the story of a woman who left her personality behind when she married. Thirteen years later, she happened to come across the diary of her maidenhood and thus rediscovered her previous personality. This discovery caused her mind to become active and made her more aware of the world around her. She found evidence of her husband's unfaithfulness and thought of divorcing him. But after a long inner conflict, she decided to remain with him and to reorganize her life. She kept her second personality, although on a higher level of awareness.

At the beginning of the twentieth century, literature began giving subtler descriptions of the many facets of human personality, of their interplay, and of the polypsychic structure of the human mind, as seen in the works of Pirandello, Joyce, Italo Svevo, Lenormand, Virginia Woolf, and above all in those of Marcel Proust. The classical occurrence of multiple personality was now almost obsolete; it was mentioned only once in Marcel Proust's work, during idle talk in Madame Verdurin's salon, when someone mentioned the case of an honest man who, in his secondary personality, turned into a scoundrel.[166] It is noteworthy that this very story had been published by Marcel Proust's father, Adrien Proust, as a significant psychopathological case.[167] What Marcel Proust indefatigably analyzed were the many manifestations of polypsychism, the multiple shades of personality within us. He considered the human ego as being composed of many little egos, distinct though side by side, and more or less closely connected. Our personality thus changes from moment to moment, depending on the circumstances, the place, the people we are with. Events touch certain parts of our personality and leave others out. In a well-known description, the narrator told how, after being informed of the death of a woman, Albertine, the news was being understood successively by various parts of the personality. The sum of our past egos is a generally closed realm, but certain past egos may suddenly reappear, bringing forth a revival of the past. It is then one of our past egos that is in the foreground, living for us. Among our many egos, there are also hereditary elements. Others (our social ego, for instance), are a creation of the thoughts and influence of other people upon us. This explains the continuous fluidity in the mind, which is due to these metamorphoses of personality. Marcel Proust's work is of particular interest because its subtle analyses were not influenced by Freud and the other representatives of the new dynamic psychiatry. His academic sources went no further than Ribot and Bergson. It would be quite feasible to extract from his work a treatise on the mind, which would give a plausible picture of what the first dynamic psychiatry would have become had it followed its natural course.

Professional philosophers focused their attention on the phenomena of hypnotism and multiple personality. Taine[168] and Ribot[169] were greatly impressed by them. Janet contends that Félida's story was the great argument used in France by the positivist psychologists against Cousin's school of dogmatic philosophical psychology. "But for Félida, it is not sure that there would be a professorship of psychology at the Collège de France."[170] Fouillée saw in the phenomena of hypnotism and somnambulism a confirmation of the doctrine of the *idées-forces*. However, one of his biographers suggests that hypnotism possibly inspired rather than confirmed this conception.[171] Bergson had a personal knowledge of hypnotism; he was a professor in Clermont-Ferrand from 1883 to 1888, and actively participated in hypnotic sessions organized privately by Moutin, a physician of that city.[172] Bergson himself made some remarkable experiments about unconscious simulation of hypnotized subjects.[173] Later in one of his main works, Bergson contended that the arts are a refined and spiritualized version of the means used by hypnotism.[174]

Literary critics also resorted to the phenomenon of multiple personality to explain certain enigmas. In his interpretation of Novalis, Spenlé made hypotheses on a duality of personality.[175] While still a child, Novalis developed a second personality of daydreaming and imagination. This personality grew, and while Novalis lived an apparently normal life as a mining engineer, he also proclaimed his poetic dream to be superior to any reality. Paul Valéry explained in a similar way the personality of Swedenborg, the great Swedish mystic: At the age of about forty Swedenborg's eyes were "opened to the spiritual world."[176] He lived simultaneously in two worlds, the real one and a "spiritual world" in which he was in continuous relationship with angels and spirits. As Valéry aptly remarked, this was not a confusing of two worlds as happens in delusion, but the superposition of two worlds between which Swedenborg could come and go as he pleased.

The phenomena of literary creation were of great concern to the first dynamic psychiatry; the concepts of the dual mind, of dipsychism and polypsychism, and of unknown powers of the mind were often resorted to.

Hypnotism provided a first model of the human mind as a double ego, a conscious but restricted ego that the individual believes to be the only one, and a subconscious, much wider ego, unknown to the conscious one, but endowed with unknown perceptive and creative powers. The phenomenon of inspiration could be explained as a more or less intermittent outburst into the conscious mind of psychic material, which had been stored in the subconscious mind. Francis Galton expressed a similar idea: "There seems to be a presence-chamber in my mind where full consciousness holds court, and where two or three ideas are at the same time in audience, and an antechamber full of more or less allied ideas, which is situated just beyond the full ken of consciousness."[177] A successful working of the mind implies a "large attendance," an orderly combination of ideas in the "antechamber," and a fluency of output. It happens sometimes that such accumulated material arises automatically in the mind; then, "dividuality replaces individuality, and one portion of the mind communicates with another portion as with a different person."

A more sophisticated conception was developed by Chabaneix,[178] who distinguished between several levels of diurnal and nocturnal subconscious and described various kinds of relationships between the subconscious and the conscious (intermittent or permanent, uncontrolled or controlled contact), and their bearing upon artistic, scientific, and literary creation.

The phenomenon of inspiration was also often compared to that of a second personality, which slowly develops underground and suddenly emerges for a while; hence the feeling of having the work dictated by some kind of unknown being, though not so conspicuously as with Mrs. Curran and "Patience Worth." C. G. Jung interpreted Nietzsche's *Zarathustra* as the result of a second personality, which had silently developed until one day it suddenly broke into the open.[179] In Nietzsche's own words:

> *Da, plötzlich, Freundin! wurde Eins zu Zwei*
> *Und Zarathustra gieng an mir vorbei . . .*
> (Then suddenly, friend, did one become two—
> and Zarathustra passed by me)

Another theory of literary creation centered around the polypsychic model of the human mind: Since the human mind is a cluster of subpersonalities, one can imagine that a great novelist, say Balzac, is able to give to many of them an identity, an occupation, personality traits, and to let them slowly develop in their own way. Speaking of the multitude of well-differentiated characters in Balzac's novels, Jules Romains supposes that every one of them was one of the writer's "embryonic personalities," that is, they were *not* unconscious or repressed personalities, but "complete psychological systems, organic and individualized, each one having in itself all that is necessary to supply, at the contact of vital occurrences and social conditioning, a complete destiny of man or woman."[180] Jean Delay also thinks that the novelist has this power of developing latent subpersonalities in himself and of transforming them into literary characters.[181] He also emphasizes the process of the "creation of a double": anyone keeping a personal diary tends to develop a dual personality that gradually emerges in that diary, so that a peculiar interpersonal relationship develops between the diarist and his fictitious second self. This second self may then at a given point come to life, so to speak, in the form of a literary character in whom the writer will bring out his secret problems, his "poisons" (as did Goethe with *The Sorrows of Werther,* and André Gide with *André Walter*).

The process of literary creation was finally approached from the notion of "cryptomnesia." That term, which seems to have been coined by Flournoy, designates a phenomenon that was well known to the magnetizers and hypnotists. In hypnotic trance, and especially in the form of hypnotic regression, an individual can give accounts of many facts that his normal waking self has completely forgotten. Our true, cryptic memory is thus immensely wider than our conscious memory. Other evidences of cryptomnesia have been forthcoming in dreams, in fever, or in other physical conditions.[182] Flournoy showed that the "romances of subliminal imagination" of his medium Helen Smith issued for a large part in "cryptomnesias" from books she had read as a child and later forgotten. Cryptomnesia provided an explanation for occurrences of literary pseudo-plagiarism. Jung, for instance, discovered that an entire paragraph of Nietzsche's *Zarathustra* originated in an article of the fourth volume of the *Blätter von Prevorst* (the journal edited by Justinus Kerner), a publication that Nietzsche was known to have perused as a youth. The unconscious nature of the plagiarism was made probable by the fact that the original text was clumsily distorted and inserted in a quite unnecessary manner in the story of *Zarathustra.*[183] Many other instances of pseudo-plagiarism have been recognized since then; it would even seem that certain authors are particularly prone to it. Here, too, Nietzsche may be mentioned. Lou Andreas Salomé assured that the entire substance of his *Genealogy of Morals* originated with Paul Rée who had been discussing his conception in a conversation with Nietzsche; Nietzsche carefully listened to Rée, making Rée's thoughts his own, and later became hostile to him.[184] According to H. Wagenvoort, Nietzsche had an exceptional capacity of assimilating with incredible swiftness the thoughts of others and to forget that he had done so.[185] Thus, when the thought occurred to him again, he did not recognize its foreign origin and believed the thought to stem from his own mind. This is how, says Wagenvoort, Nietzsche borrowed, the main concepts developed in his *Origin of Tragedy* from Michelet's book *La Bible de l'Humanité.* According to other literary historians, Nietzsche's main original concepts would stem from Emerson, by way of cryptomnesia.[186] In fact, cryptomnesia seems to be such a frequent occurrence that Paul Valéry came to consider it as the mainspring of literary creation, "A plagiarist is he who has imperfectly digested the substance of the thoughts of others: he allows the morsels to be recognizable."[187]

The Decline of the First Dynamic Psychiatry

The history of the first dynamic psychiatry shows a paradox: for an entire century (1784 to 1882), new discoveries struggled for recognition, and, after they were at long last acknowledged by "official medicine" with Charcot and Bernheim, they enjoyed a brilliant phase of success of less than twenty years, to be followed by a swift decline. The problem of these ups and downs puzzled many minds. Janet suggested that there are trends, not only in the style of life, but also in medicine. After 1882 the medical world became infatuated with hypnotism; publications on it reached the hundreds until a point of saturation was reached and the trend abandoned. This may be true; but there must also have been factors inherent to hypnotism that caused this rapid decline.

A perusal of the literature on hypnotism of that time shows what those factors might have been. Numerous hypnotists who had at first been enthusiastic about hypnotism, soon discovered important drawbacks. Not everybody was able to become a good hypnotist, nor was the best hypnotist able to hypnotize everyone. It became obvious that many patients pretended to be hypnotized when they were not. Benedikt, for instance, related that he had allowed some of his students to hypnotize patients in his out-patient service; these patients then said that they had been in hypnotic sleep, but to senior physicians they confessed that they had only pretended to be hypnotized in order to please the young doctors.[188] The same is reported to have occurred not only with Charcot (as seen above), but also with Forel, Wetterstrand, and other experienced hypnotists whose patients even pretended to be cured because they did not dare contradict their authoritarian physicians.

It also happened that subjects feigned hypnosis in order to feel free to relieve themselves of painful secrets, which they would have been embarrassed to reveal otherwise. This may have been so from the earliest beginnings of magnetism. We have already told the strange story of a man who was infatuated with a male friend in whom he had the utmost confidence in waking state, but who, in magnetic crisis, told the Count of Lutzelbourg that his supposed friend betrayed and harmed him, and explained what was to be done in order to pass on this knowledge from his "crisis" to his waking state.[189] Many similar instances could be quoted. Dr. Bonjour,[190] a Swiss psychotherapist, tells how he noticed in 1895 that certain patients would reveal, under hypnosis, painful things that they pretended not to know in waking state but who later admitted always having known them but had been too shy to talk about them.

A more serious drawback was the tendency to unconscious simulation, which developed in many hypnotized individuals and which led them to guess the hypnotist's will and to comply with it. Bernheim, for instance, said: "It is incredible with what acumen certain hypnotized subjects detect, as it were, the idea which they ought to carry into execution. One word, one gesture, one intonation puts them on the track."[191] Bergson who had done some research on alleged thought-reading in hypnosis, concluded that the patient who is ordered to carry out a *tour de force* "will act in good faith and do the same as would the least scrupulous and most skillful of charlatans, that he will unconsciously utilize means of which we hardly even suspect the existence."[192] The Belgian physician Crocq told how, after having obtained marvelous results with hypnotism, he eventually became aware of certain facts:

> I have practiced much hypnotic experimentation and have obtained seemingly wonderful results; this is why I have become extremely cautious. I have called forth in a most surprising manner the exteriorization of sensitivity, the visibility of magnetic and electrical effluvia, and I nearly became the victim of my subjects, so wonderfully successful were the experiments. But a careful scrutiny of facts convinced me that this was nothing but the effect of autosuggestion. One should not forget that the hypnotized subject strives with all the means at his disposal to gratify the wishes of his hypnotist and to carry out not only his orders, but his thoughts as well. The hypnotized scrutinizes the brain of the hypnotist, who usually does not beware of the subject's extraordinary sensitivity and does not realize that a sign, which is imperceptible in waking state, can become of the utmost importance for the hypnotized individual.[193]

Crocq added that the same held true for hysteria, and he warned: "If you want to be duped, then experiment with hysterical patients."

Delboeuf, another Belgian, who visited the Salpêtrière and the Nancy School in 1886, commented on the striking differences obtained by Charcot, by Bernheim, and by the stage hypnotist Donato.[194] Delboeuf concluded that not only was there an undeniable action of the hypnotist on his subject ("like master, like disciple"), but that there was to an even greater extent a suggestive action of the hypnotized on the hypnotist ("like disciple, like master"); the first subject hypnotized imprints upon the hypnotist a method and a given expectation of results, which lays the pattern for the hypnotist's method and results with fresh subjects. Furthermore, the hypnotist who has been trained in a given manner passes on his method and expectation of results to his disciples, which explains the origin of rival schools, each one having the monopoly of specific hypnotic phenomena. Incidentally, it is noteworthy that these findings of Delboeuf have been duplicated recently on the basis of new and independent research by Martin Orne.[195] No wonder that hypnotic situation has often been compared to a *folie à deux*, where "one does not know which of the two is crazier." In the last years of the nineteenth century, these negative reports accumulated to the point where a powerful reaction took place against the use of hypnotism and the contemporary theories of hysteria. Among the leaders of this reaction were men who had experimented for years with means such as metalloscopy, the action of medication at a distance, and the transfer of symptoms from one patient to another. Janet, who had been most cautious and had experimented with hypnotism and hysterical patients without falling into any of their pitfalls, was one of the few who carried on those teachings of the first dynamic psychiatry, which had been proven to be sound.

The rejection of the first dynamic psychiatry was as irrational and sudden as had been the fashion that had caused its rise to fame in the 1880's. It occurred in spite of great resistance on the part of certain adherents of the first dynamic psychiatry who were discovering new and promising facts. There were, for instance, the new methods of hypnotic catharsis, with which Janet experimented from 1886 on, and Breuer and Freud in 1893 and 1895, of which we will speak in other parts of this book. There was also a method devised by Oskar Vogt, to which he gave the name of "partial hypnosis."[196] This method required easily hypnotizable subjects, who were also able to retain their sharp critical sense under hypnosis. The subject was hypnotized and his attention kept focused on a sharply delineated fact or memory, which allowed him to explore the unconscious substratum of one particular present or past feeling, an association, a dream, or a psychopathological symptom. Incidentally, this particular form of hypnosis is remarkably similar to what Ainslie Meares described as the "Y-State."[197] Frederick Myers, who was well acquainted with the pitfalls and fallacies of hypnotism, hysteria, and dual personality, consistently emphasized the actual progress that those notions had brought about in our knowledge of the human mind and the further progress that could be expected in the future.[198] One point was that a secondary personality was not necessarily inferior to the main one, but sometimes meant, on the contrary, a marked improvement (an idea that was later to be developed by Jung). However, "the successive discoveries of intoxicants, narcotics proper, and anaesthetics, formed three important stages in our growing control over the nervous system," and the discovery of hypnosis was a further stage. Hypnosis affords to many people an expansion and freedom of the mind that they are unable to achieve in the waking state: "I maintain that the hypnotic trance (. . .) has some analogy to genius as well as to hysteria. I maintain that for uneducated subjects, it has been the highest mental condition which they have ever entered; and that, when better understood and applied to subjects of higher type, it may dispose to flows of thought more undisturbed and steady than can be maintained by the waking effort of our tossed and fragmentary days." The time might come when man will alternate not only between waking and sleeping, but where "other states may come to co-exist with these."

Finally, Myers recalled that there had been remarkable and permanent cures achieved under hypnosis. In regard to the future, he felt that our knowledge of these states could be expanded and used in three new ways: first by bringing forth moral improvement by imprinting "hypnotic suggestions of a salutary kind"; second by acquiring "a state of unsusceptibility to physical pain"; and third by gaining power through dissociating the elements of our being in novel ways. These predictions of Myers were to materialize in Coué's method of autosuggestion, in the technique of painless childbirth, and in Schultz's autogenous training.

But it is of course easier to reject *en bloc* a teaching that has incorporated errors than to undertake the difficult task of selecting the grain from the chaff, and, as Janet had to conclude, "hypnotism is dead . . . until the day it will revive."

Conclusion

The first dynamic psychiatry constituted a well-constructed body of knowledge, which, in spite of inevitable fluctuations, had been much more of an organic unit than is usually assumed. Common opinion states that the first dynamic psychiatry disappeared around 1900 to be replaced by wholly new systems of dynamic psychiatry. But a careful scrutiny of facts reveals that there was no sudden revolution but, on the contrary, a gradual transition from the one to the others, and that the new dynamic psychiatries took over far more from the first than has been realized. The cultural influence of the first dynamic psychiatry has been extremely persistent and still pervades contemporary life to an unsuspected degree.

The new dynamic psychiatries, having incorporated much from the first one, also assimilated a great deal of knowledge from other sources. The new dynamic psychiatries can be understood only if one first makes a survey of the entire sociological and cultural background throughout the nineteenth century. This will be the subject of the following chapter.

Notes

1. Justinus Kerner, *Geschichten Besessener neuerer Zeiten. Beobachtungen aus dem Gebiete kakodämonischer-magnetischer Erscheinungen* (...). *nebst Reflexionen von C. A. Eschenmayer über Besessenseyn und Zauber* (2nd enlarged ed.; Karlsruhe: G. Braun, 1835).

2. Montaigne, *Essais* (1581) (Paris: éd. Pléiade, 1940), pp. 110–120. Eng. trans., *The Essays.* Great Books of the Western World, Vol. 25 (Chicago: Encyclopedia Britannica, 1952), pp. 36–42.

3. Lodovico Antonio Muratori, *Della Forza della Fantasia Umana* (Venice: Presso Giambatista Pasquali, 1745).

4. Otto Stoll, *Suggestion und Hypnotismus in der Völkerpsychologie* (2nd ed.; Leipzig: Von Weit & Co., 1904).

5. James Braid, *Neurhypnology; or, the Rationale of Nervous Sleep, Considered in Relation with Animal Magnetism* (London: John Churchill, 1843).

6. According to Janet, this theory was held by Bertrand, Deleuze, Braid, Noizet, Liébeault, Charcot, and the Salpêtrière School. Actually, Puységur wrote of "somnambulisme magnétique" as early as 1809, *Suite des mémoires pour servir à l'histoire et à l'établissement du magnétisme animal* (2nd ed.; Paris: Cellot, 1809), p. 221.

7. Pierre Janet, *Les Médications psychologiques* (Paris: Alcan, 1919), I, 267–271.

8. Mouillesaux, quoted in Rudolf Tischner, "Franz Anton Mesmer. Leben, Werk und Wirkungen," *Münchner Beiträge zur Geschichte und Literatur des Naturwissenschaften und Medizin*, I, No. 9/10 (1928), 541–714.

9. J. P. F. Deleuze, *Instruction pratique sur le magnétisme animal* (Paris: Baillière, 1825), p. 118.

10. A. Bertrand, *Traité du somnambulisme* (Paris: Dentu, 1823), pp. 298–299.

11. Count de Lövenhielm, *Bibliothèque du magnétisme animal* (1818), V, 228–240.

12. Pierre Janet, *Les Médications psychologiques* (Paris: Alcan, 1919), I, 281–283.

13. J. Charpignon, *Physiologie, médicine et métaphysique du magnétisme* (Paris: Baillière, 1848), pp. 364–365.

14. Baron Du Potet, quoted by Pierre Janet in *Les Médications psychologiques* (Paris: Alcan, 1919), I, 141.

15. Eugen Bleuler, "Zur Psychologie der Hypnose," *Münchener medizinische Wochenschrift*, XXXVI (1889), 76–77.

16. Berthold Stokvis, "Selbsterleben im hypnotischen Experiment," *Zeitschrift für Psychotherapie*, VI (1956), 97–107.

17. Albert de Rochas, *Les Vies successives. Documents pour l'étude de cette question* (Paris: Chacornac, 1911).

18. Tardif de Montrevel, *Essai sur la théorie du somnambulisme magnétique* (London, November 1785).

19. Alphonse Teste, *Manuel pratique du magnétisme animal* (3rd ed.; Paris: Baillière, 1846), pp. 486–493.

20. P. J. C. Debreyne, *Pensées d'un croyant catholique* (Paris: Poussielgue-Rusand, 1844), pp. 340–457.

21. Baron Du Potet, *La Magie dévoilée, ou principes de science occulte* (3rd ed.; Paris: Vigot, 1893), pp. 1–58.

22. H. Bernheim, "Les Hallucinations rétroactives suggérées dans le sommeil naturel ou artificiel," *Premier Congrès International de l'Hypnotisme Expérimental et thérapeutique* (Paris, August 8–12, 1889) (Paris: Doin, 1890), pp. 291–294.

23. J. M. Charcot, *Leçons du mardi à la Salpêtrière. Policlinique, 1888–1889* (Paris: Progrès Médical, 1889), pp. 247–256.

24. In modern literature, see particularly J. H. Schultz, *Gesundheitsschädigungen nach Hypnose, Ergebnisse einer Sammelforschung* (Halle: C. Marhold, 1922).

25. Reprinted in Claude Burdin and Frédéric Dubois, *Histoire académique du magnétisme animal* (Paris: Baillière, 1841).

26. Theodor Meynert, *Klinische Vorlesungen über Psychiatrie auf wissenschaftlichen Grundlagen* (Vienna: W. Braumüller, 1889–1890), p. 197.

27. Frederick Myers, "Automatic Writing," *Proceedings of the Society for Psychical Research*, III (1885), 1–63; IV (1886–1887), 209–261.

28. William James, "Automatic Writing," *Proceedings of the American Society for Psychical Research*, I (1885–1889), 548–564.

29. Baron Du Potet, *La Magie dévoilée, ou principes de science occulte* (Paris: Pommaret et Moreau, 1852).

30. Théodore Flournoy, *Des Indes à la planète Mars* (Geneva: Atar, 1900). *Esprits et médiums* (Geneva: Kündig, 1909).

31. Pétetin, *Mémoire sur la découverte des phénomènes que présentent la catalepsie et le somnambulisme, symptômes de l'affection hystérique essentielle* (Lyon, 1785). *Mémoire sur la découverte des phénomènes de l'affection hystérique essentielle et sur la méthode curative de cette maladie*, 2nd Part (1785).

32. Claude-Etienne Bourdin, *Traité de la catalepsie* (Paris: Rouvier, 1841).

33. J. T. Puel, *De la catalepsie* (Paris: Baillière, 1856).

34. P. Briquet, *Traité clinique de thérapeutique de l'hystérie* (Paris: Baillière, 1859).

35. James Cowles Prichard, *A Treatise on Insanity and Other Disorders Affecting the Mind* (London: Sherwood, Gilbert and Piper, 1835), pp. 454–458.

36. Gérard de Nerval, *Octavie* (1842), in *Oeuvres*, ed. Pléïade (Paris: Gallimard, 1952), pp. 305–312.

37. Wilhelm Jensen, *Gradiva. Ein pompejanisches Phantasiestück* (Dresden and Leipzig: C. Reissner, 1903).

38. André Breton, *Les Vases communiquants* (Paris: Edition des Cahiers Libres, 1932).

39. Anselm Feuerbach, *Aktenmässige Darstellung merkwürdiger Verbrechen*, 2 vols. (Giessen: Heyer, 1828).

40. J. M. Charcot, *Leçons du mardi à la Salpêtrière* (Paris: Progrès Médical, 1889), pp. 317–322.

41. M. Naef, "Ein Fall von temporärer totaler theilweise retrograder Amnesie (durch Suggestion geheilt)," *Zeitschrift für Hypnotismus*, VI (1897), 321–354.

42. F. Raymond and Pierre Janet, "Les Délires ambulatoires ou les fugues." *Gazette des Hôpitaux*, LXVIII (1895), 754–762.

43. St. Augustine, *Confessions*, X, Paragraph 41. Great Books of the Western World, Vol. XVIII (Chicago: Encyclopedia Britannica, 1952), p. 81.

44. A. Jundt, *Rulman Merswin et l'ami de Dieu de l'Oberland. Un problème de psychologie religieuse* (Paris: Fischbacher, 1890).

45. Eberhardt Gmelin, *Materialen für die Anthropologie*, I (Tübingen: Cotta, 1791), 3–89.

46. J. C. Reil, *Rhapsodien über die Anwendung der psychischen Curmethode auf Geisteszerrüttungen* (Halle: Curt, 1803), pp. 71–78, 93–96.

47. Erasmus Darwin, *Zoonomia, or the Laws of Organic Life* (3rd ed.; London: J. Johnson, 1801), II, 131.

48. J. K. Mitchell is supposed to have published the story of Mary Reynolds in the *Medical Repository* in 1815 or in the following few years. Mrs. Alice D. Weaver, Librarian of the New York Academy of Medicine, went through the collection, and found no mention of any article or letter by Dr. Mitchell concerning the case of Mary Reynolds.

49. Reverend William S. Plumer, "Mary Reynolds: A Case of Double Consciousness," *Harper's New Monthly Magazine*, XX (1859–1860), 807–812.

50. Robert Macnish, "*The Philosophy of Sleep* (3rd ed.; Glasgow: W. R. M'Phun, 1836), p. 187.

51. Pierre Janet, *Les Névroses* (Paris: Flammarion, 1909), pp. 246–259.

52. Dr. Despine Père, *De l'Emploi du magnétisme animal et des eaux minérales dans le traitement des maladies nerveuses, suivi d'une observation très curieuse de guérison de névropathie* (Paris: Germer, Baillière, 1840).

53. The author is grateful to Mr. A. Schnegg, the Archivist of Neuchâtel, and to Mr. H. Jung, Swiss Consul in Le Havre, for these details.

54. Among the general surveys of multiple personality, the most important ones are, in chronological order, the following:

Théodule Ribot, *Les Maladies de la personnalité* (Paris: Alcan, 1888).

H. Bourru and P. Burot, *Variations de la personnalité* (Paris: Baillière, 1888).

J. M. Charcot, *Leçons du mardi à la Salpêtrière* (Paris: Progrès Médical, 1889).

Alfred Binet, *Les Altérations de la personnalité* (Paris: Alcan, 1892).

Max Dessoir, *Das Doppel-Ich* (Leipzig: Günther, 1892).

Frederick Myers, *Human Personality and Its Survival from Bodily Death*, 2 vols. (London: Longmans, Green & Co., 1903).

T. K. Oesterreich, *Phänomenologie des Ich* (Leipzig: Barth, 1910).

Morton Prince, *The Unconscious* (New York: Macmillan and Co., 1914), pp. 147–310.

T. W. Mitchell, "Divisions of the Self and Co-Consciousness," in *Problems of Personality: Studies Presented to Dr. Morton Prince*, Macfie Campbell, ed. (New York, 1925), pp. 191–203.

Pierre Janet, *L'Evolution psychologique de la personnalité* (Paris: Chahine, 1929), pp. 483–506.

W. S. Taylor and Mabel F. Martin, "Multiple Personality," *Journal of Abnormal and Social Psychology,* XXXIX (1944), 281–300.

Gardner Murphy, *Personality* (New York: Harper & Row, 1947), pp. 433–451.

55. Théodore Flournoy, *Des Indes à la planète Mars* (Geneva: Atar, 1900); Eng. trans., *From India to the Planet Mars* (New York: Harper & Row, 1900), p. 119.

56. G. E. Morselli, "Mescalina e Schizofrenia," *Revista de Psicologia,* XL–XLI (1944–1945), 1–23.

57. Max Bircher-Benner, *Der Menschenseele Not, Erkrankung und Gesundung* (Zurich: Wendepunkt-Verlag, 1933), II, 288–310.

58. Charles E. Cory, "A Divided Self," *Journal of Abnormal Psychology,* XIV (1919–1920), 281–291.

59. Richard Hodgson, "A Case of Double Consciousness," *Proceedings of the Society of Psychical Research,* VII (1891–1892), 221–255.

60. William James, *The Principles of Psychology,* 2 vols. (New York: Holt, 1890).

61. S. I. Franz, *Persons One and Three. A Study in Multiple Personalities* (New York: McGraw-Hill, Inc., 1933).

62. Etienne Eugène Azam, *Hypnotisme, double conscience et altération de la personnalité.* Préface de J. M. Charcot (Paris: J. B. Baillière, 1887).

63. G. E. Morselli, "Sulla dissoziazione mentale," *Rivista Sperimentale di Freniatria,* LIV (1930), 209–322.

64. Pierre Janet, *L'Automatisme psychologique* (Paris: Alcan, 1889), p. 318.

65. Morton Prince, *The Dissociation of a Personality* (New York and London: Longman's, Green and Co., 1906).

66. Walter Franklin Prince, "The Doris Case of Quintuple Personality," *Journal of Abnormal Psychology,* XI (1916–1917), 73–122. James H. Hyslop and Walter Franklin Prince, "The Doris Fisher Case of Multiple Personality," *Journal of the American Society of Psychical Research,* X (1916), 381–399, 436–454, 485–504, 541–558, 613–631, 661–678.

67. Alfred Binet, *La Suggestibilité* (Paris: Schleicher, 1900).

68. Emil Lucka, "Verdoppelungen des Ich," *Preussische Jahrbücher,* CXV, No. 1 (1904), 54–83.

69. Gardner Murphy, *Personality* (New York: Harper & Row, 1947), pp. 433–451.

70. G. E. Morselli, "Le personalita alternanti," *Revista de psicologia normale, patologica e applicata,* XLII (1946), 24–52.

71. G. E. Morselli, "Personalita alternante e patologia affetiva," *Archivio de psicologia, neurologia e psichitria,* XIV (1953), 579–589.

72. Hans Binder, "Das anonyme Briefschreiben," *Schweizer Archiv für Neurologie und Psychiatrie,* LXI (1948), 41–43, and LXII, 11–56. (Cases of Albert F. and Heinrich L.).

73. Corbett H. Thipgen and Hervey Cleckley, *The Three Faces of Eve* (New York: McGraw-Hill, Inc., 1957).

74. P. Briquet, *Traité clinique et thérapeutique de l'hystérie* (Paris: J. B. Baillière, 1859).

75. Anon., *Mesmerism; Its History, Phenomena, and Practice: with Reports of Cases Developed in Scotland* (Edinburgh: Fraser & Co., 1843), pp. 101–106.

76. Paul Richer, *Etudes cliniques sur l'hystéro-épilepsie ou grande hystérie (...).* (Paris: Delahaye et Lecrosnier, 1881).

77. Alfred Binet, *On Double Consciousness. Experimental Psychological Studies* (Chicago: Open Court Publishing Company, 1889–1890).

78. A. F. A. King, "Hysteria," *The American Journal of Obstetrics,* XXIV, No. 5 (May 1891), 513–532.

79. This has been well understood and commented upon by Jules de Gaultier, *Le Génie de Flaubert* (Paris: Mercure de France, 1913), pp. 101–110.

80. Max Dessoir: *Das Doppel-Ich* (Leipzig: Günther, 1890). (Subsequent enlarged editions were enriched with facts borrowed from Binet, Janet, Myers, Gurney, and others.)

81. Richard Hennig, "Beiträge zur Psychologie des Doppel-Ich," *Zeitschrift für Psychologie*, XLIX (1908), 1–55.

82. *Le Sommeil magnétique expliqué par le somnambule Alexis en état de lucidité.* Introduction by Henry Delaage (Paris: Dentu, 1856).

83. J. P. Durand (de Gros), *Polyzoïsme ou pluralité animale chez l'homme* (Paris: Imprimerie Hennuyer, 1868). J. P. Philips (pseudonym of Durand), *Electro-dynamisme vital* (Paris: J. B. Baillière, 1855). J. P. Durand (de Gros), *Ontologie et psychologie physiologiques* (Paris: J. B. Baillière, 1871).

84. Edmond Colsenet, *Etudes sur la vie inconsciente de l'esprit* (Paris: Baillière, 1880).

85. J. C. Reil, *Rhapsodien über die Anwendung der psychischen Curmethode auf Geisteszerrüttungen* (Halle: Curt, 1803), p. 93.

86. G. N. M. Tyrrell, *Personality of Man* (Baltimore: Penguin Books, Inc., 1947), pp. 158–160, 198.

87. According to G. de Morsier, the principle of ideodynamism was introduced into psychiatry by Esquirol who took it over from the psychology of the "faculties of the soul" taught by Laromiguière whose courses he had attended. See G. de Morsier, "Les Hallucinations," *Revue d'Oto-Neuro-Opthalmologie*, XVI (1938), 244–352.

88. A. A. Liébeault, *Ebauche de psychologie* (Paris: Masson, 1873), p. 176.

89. J. M. Charcot, *Leçons sur les maladies du système nerveux*, in *Oeuvres Complètes*, III, 335–337

90. Pierre Janet, *L'Automatisme psychologique* (Paris: Alcan, 1889), p. 436. p. 436.

91. Poul Bjerre, *The History and Practice of Psychoanalysis*. Eng. trans. (revised ed., Boston: Badger, 1920), pp. 198–217.

92. Hippolyte Bernheim, *De la suggestion et de ses applications à la thérapeutique* (Paris: Doin, 1886).

93. Aldous Huxley, *The Devils of Loudun* (New York: Harper & Row, 1952), p. 183.

94. Noizet, *Mémoire sur le somnambulisme et le magnétisme animal.* Adressé en 1820 à l'Académie Royale de Berlin (Paris: Plon, 1854), p. 96.

95. Anon., *La Vision, contenant l'explication de l'écrit intitulé: Traces du magnétisme, & la théorie des vrais sages. A Memphis* (Paris: Couturier, 1784), pp. 22, 26.

96. Tardif de Montrevel, *Essais sur la théorie du somnambulisme magnétique* (London, 1785).

97. Villers, *Le Magnétiseur amoureux* (Geneva, 1787).

98. J. A. Klinger, *De Magnetismo Animali* (Wirceburgi: Nitribit, 1817).

99. Friedrich Hufeland, *Über Sympathie* (Weimar: Verlag des Landes-Industrie-Comptoir, 1811), p. 110.

100. Charpignon, *Physiologie, médecine et métaphysique du magnétisme* (2nd ed.; Paris: Baillière, 1848).

101. Gotthilf Heinrich von Schubert, *Ansichten von der Nachtseite der Naturwissenschaft* (Leipzig: Weigel, 1808).

102. *Mesmerism, Its History, Phenomena, and Practice: with Reports of Cases Developed in Scotland* (Edinburgh: Fraser & Co., 1843), pp. 101–106.

103. Albert Ruault, "Le Mécanisme de la suggestion hypnotique," *Revue Philosophique*, XX (1886) (II), 676–697.

104. Pierre Janet, *L'Automatisme psychologique* (Paris: Alcan, 1889), pp. 283–290.

105. Albert Moll, "Der Rapport in der Hypnose," *Schriften der Gesellschaft für psychologische Forschung* (Leipzig: Abel, 1892), III, IV, 273–514.

106. Pierre Janet, "L'Influence somnambulique et le besoin de direction," *III. Internationaler Congress für Psychologie in München, 1896* (Munich: J. F. Lehmann, 1897), pp. 143–147.

107. Pierre Janet, "L'Influence somnambulique et le besoin de direction," *Revue Philosophique*, XLIII (1897), (I), 113–143.

108. Paul Sollier, *L'Hystérie et son traitement* (Paris: Alcan, 1901), p. 161.

109. Aubin Gauthier, *Traité pratique du magnétisme et du somnambulisme* (Paris: Baillière, 1845), pp. 20–75, 309–354.

110. Baron Du Potet, *La Magie dévoilée, ou principes de science occulte* (3rd ed.; Paris: Vigot, 1893), pp. 1–58.

111. R. Count de Maricourt, *Souvenirs d'un magnétiseur* (Paris: Plon, 1884).

112. Charles Lafontaine, *Mémoires d'un magnétiseur*, 2 vols. (Paris: Germer-B. Baillière, 1886).

113. Auguste Lassaigne, *Mémoires d'un magnétiseur, contenant la biographie de la somnambule Prudence Bernard* (Paris: Baillière et Dentu, 1851).

114. *Lichtenbergs Magazin für das Neueste aus der Physik und Naturgeschichte* (1786), IV, 201–203.

115. Henry Brunschwig, *La Crise de l'état prussien à la fin du 18e siècle et la genèse de la mentalité romantique* (Paris: Presses Universitaires de France, 1947), pp. 197–200.

116. Xavier Leon, *Fichte et son temps. II, Fichte à Berlin (1789–1813)*. 2nd part (Paris: Colin, 1927), pp. 280–282.

117. Wilhelm Gwinner, *Arthur Schopenhauer aus persönlichem Umgang dargestellt* (Leipzig: Brockhaus, 1922).

118. Arthur Schopenhauer, *Versuch über das Geistersehn und was damit zusammenhängt*, in *Parerga und Paralipomena I. Sämmtliche Werke*, IV (Leipzig: Reclam, n.d.), 304.

119. K. J. H. Windischmann, *Versuch über den Gang der Bildung in der heilenden Kunst* (Frankfurt: Andreä, 1809). *Ueber Etwas, das der Heilkunst Noth thut* (Leipzig: Cnobloch, 1824).

120. Joseph Ennemoser, *Der Magnetismus nach der allseitigen Beziehung seines Wesens, seiner Erscheinungen, Anwendung und Enträthselung* (Leipzig: Brockhaus, 1819). *Der Magnetismus im Verhältnis zur Natur und Religion* (Stuttgart and Tübingen: Cotta, 1842).

121. Johann Nepomuk von Ringseis, *System der Medizin* (Regensburg: Manz, 1841).

122. Paul Sucher, *Les Sources du merveilleux chez E. T. A. Hoffmann* (Paris: Librairie Felix Alcan, 1912).

123. E. T. A. Hoffmann, *Das Sanktus*, in *Sämtliche Werke*, ed. Rudolf Frank (Munich and Leipzig: Rösl, 1924), IX, 143–163.

124. Comte de Las Cases, *Le Mémorial de Ste-Hélène* (1823) (Paris: éd. Pléïade, 1956), 918.

125. Henri Dominique Lacordaire, *Conférences de Notre-Dame de Paris*, II (Paris: Sagnier & Bray, 1847), 467–470).

126. Fernand Baldensperger, *Orientations étrangères chez Honoré de Balzac* (Paris: Champion, 1927).

127. Paul Bourget, *Au Service de l'ordre* (Paris: Plon, 1929), I, 243.

128. Joseph Adolphe Gentil, *Initiation aux mystères secrets de la théorie et de la pratique du Magnétisme, suivie d'expériences faites à Monte-Cristo chez Alexandre Dumas* (Paris: Robert, 1849).

129. Alexandre Dumas, *Mémoires d'un médecin, Joseph Balsamo* (Paris: Fellens et Dufour, 1846–1848).

130. Frédéric Soulié, *Le Magnétiseur*, 2 vols. (Paris: Dumont, 1834).

131. See Jerome M. Schneck, "Robert Browning and Mesmerism," *Bulletin of the Medical Library Association*, XLIV (1956), 443–451.

132. Joseph Jackson, ed., *The Philosophy of Animal Magnetism by a Gentleman of Philadelphia* (Philadelphia, 1928).

133. Edgar Allan Poe, "The Facts in the Case of Mr. Valdemar," *The American Review* (December 1845). *Mesmerism in Articulo Mortis. An Astounding and Horrifying Narrative, Showing the Extraordinary Power of Mesmerism in Arresting the Progress of Death. By Edgar A. Poe, Esq., of New York* (London: Short & Co., 1846).

134. G. Mabru, *Les Magnétiseurs jugés par eux-mêmes. Nouvelle enquête sur le magnétisme animal* (Paris: Mallet-Bachelier, 1858), pp. 512–517.

135. A survey of relevant literature has been made by E. Menninger-Lerchenthal, *Der Doppelgänger* (Bern: Hans Huber, 1946), pp. 75–83.

136. E. T. A. Hoffmann, "Die Elixiere des Teufels," in *Sämtliche Werke*, Rudolf Frank, ed. (Munich and Leipzig: Rösl, 1924), IV, 13–365.

137. Edgar Allan Poe, *William Wilson*. First published in Burton's *Gentleman's Magazine* (October 1839).

138. Feodor Dostoevski, *Dvoinik*, first published in the periodical *Otechestvennyia zapiski* (1846). Engl. trans., *The Double*, in *The Short Novels of Dostoevski*, with an Introduction by Thomas Mann (New York: Dial Press, 1945).

139. Gustave Simon, *Les Tables tournantes de Jersey* (Paris: Conard, 1923).

140. Camille Flammarion, *Les Habitants de l'autre monde, révélations d'outre-tombe* (Paris: Ledoyen, 1862–1863).

141. Patience Worth, *The Sorry Tale: A Story of the Time of Christ* (New York: Holt, Rinehart and Winston, Inc., 1917). *Hope Trueblood* (New York: Holt, Rinehart and Winston, Inc., 1918). *The Pot upon the Wheel* (St. Louis: The Dorset Press, 1921). *Light from Beyond* (Brooklyn: Patience Worth Publishing Co., n.d.). *Telka. An Idyl of Medieval England* (New York: Patience Worth Publishing Co.; London: Routledge and Kegan Paul Ltd., 1928).

142. Casper S. Yost, *Patience Worth: A Psychic Mystery* (New York: Holt, Rinehart and Winston, Inc., 1916).

143. Walter Franklin Prince, *The Case of Patience Worth. A Critical Study of Certain Unusual Phenomena*, Boston Society for Psychical Research, 1927.

144. G. N. M. Tyrrell, *Personality of Man* (Baltimore: Penguin Books, Inc., 1947), pp. 134–143.

145. Jules Bois, *Le Miracle moderne* (Paris: Ollendorf, 1907), pp. 145–163.

146. Charpignon: *Rapports du magnétisme avec la jurisprudence et la médecine légale* (Paris: Baillière, 1860).

147. Quoted by Crocq, *L'Hypnotisme scientifique* (Paris: Société d'Editions Scientifiques, 1900), pp. 267–269.

148. Baron von Schrenck-Notzing, "La Suggestion et l'hypnotisme dans leurs rapports avec la jurisprudence." *IIe Congrès International d'Hypnotisme, Paris, 1900, compte-rendu* (Paris: Vigot, 1902), pp. 121–131.

149. Gustave Le Bon, *Psychologie des foules* (Paris: Librairie Felix Alcan), 1895.

150. Emile Magnin, *L'Art et l'hypnose* (Paris: Alcan, 1907).

151. Hector Malot, *Conscience* (Paris: Charpentier, 1888).

152. Gilbert Augustin Thierry, *Marfa. Le Palimpseste* (Paris: Dumont, 1887).

153. Jules Claretie, *Jean Mornas* (Paris: Dentu, 1885).

154. George du Maurier, *Trilby* (New York: Harper & Row, Publishers, 1894).

155. Guy de Maupassant, "Le Horla" (1886) in *Oeuvres Complètes*, XII (Paris: Louis Conard, 1927).

156. Léon Gozlan, *Le Médecin du Pecq*, 3 vols. (Paris: Werdet, 1839).

157. Jules Claretie, *L'Obsession—Moi et l'autre* (Paris: Lafitte, 1908).

158. Charles Epheyre, "Soeur Marthe," *Revue des Deux Mondes*, XCIII (1889), 384–431.

159. Léon Hennique, *Minnie Brandon* (Paris: Fasquelle, 1899).

160. William Mintorn, *Le Somnambule* (Paris: Ghio, 1880).

161. Paul Lindau, *Der Andere* (New York: I. Goldmann, 1893). French adaptation, *Le Procureur Hallers*, in *Petite Illustration*, No. 46 (Paris, January 1914).

162. Robert Louis Stevenson, *The Strange Case of Dr. Jekyll and Mr. Hyde* (London: Longmans and Co., 1886).

163. Robert Louis Stevenson, "A Chapter on Dreams," in *Across the Plains, with Other Memories and Essays* (New York: Scribner's Sons, 1892).

164. Paul Bourget, *L'Irréparable* (Paris: Lemerre, 1883).

165. Marcel Prévost, *Le Jardin secret* (Paris: Lemerre, 1897).

166. Marcel Proust, "Le Temps retrouvé," in *A la Recherche du temps perdu* (Paris: Gallimard, 1961), (III), 716.

167. Adrien Proust, "Automatisme ambulatoire chez un hystérique," *Bulletin Médical*, IV (1890) (I), 107–108.

168. Hippolyte Taine, *De l'Intelligence*, 2 vols. (Paris: Hachette, 1870).

169. Th. Ribot, *Les Maladies de la mémoire* (Paris: Baillière, 1885). *Les Maladies de la personnalité* (Paris: Alcan, 1885).

170. Pierre Janet, *The Major Symptoms of Hysteria* (New York: Macmillan, 1907), p. 78.

171. Elizabeth Ganne de Beaucoudrey, *La Psychologie et la métaphysique des idées-forces chez Alfred Fouillée* (Paris: Vrin, 1936), pp. 87–88.

172. Gilbert Maire, *Bergson, mon maître* (Paris: Grasset, 1935).

173. Henri Bergson, "Simulation inconsciente dans l'état d'hypnotisme," *Revue Philosophique*, XXII (1886), (II), 525–531.

174. H. Bergson, *Essai sur les données immédiates de la conscience* (Paris: Alcan, 1889).

175. E. Spenlé, *Essais sur l'idéalisme romantique en Allemagne* (Paris: Hachette, 1904).

176. Paul Valéry, "Svedenborg," *Nouvelle Revue Française*, CLVI (1936), 825–844. *Oeuvres*, éd. Pléïade (Paris: Gallimard, 1957), I, 867–883.

177. Francis Galton, "Antechamber of Consciousness," Reprinted in *Inquiries into Human Faculty* (London: Dent, 1907), pp. 146–149.

178. Paul Chabaneix, *Physiologie cérébrale. Le Subconscient chez les artistes, les savants et les écrivains* (Paris: Baillière, 1897).

179. C. G. Jung, *Zarathustra-lectures* (unpublished) (Zurich: C. G. Jung Institute, Spring 1934). These verses of Nietzsche are from a poem "Sils-Maria," probably dedicated to Lou Andreas-Salomé.

180. Jules Romains, *Souvenirs et confidences d'un écrivain* (Paris: Fayard, 1958), pp. 113–114, 235–239). *Saints de notre calendrier* (Paris: Flammarion, 1952), pp. 46–47.

181. Jean Delay, *La Jeunesse d'André Gide*, 2 vols. (Paris: Gallimard, 1956–1957).

182. Among many other instances, see Henry Freeborn, "Temporary Reminiscence of a Long-Forgotten Language During the Delirium of Broncho-Pneumonia," *The Lancet*, LXXX (1902) I, pp. 1685–1686.

183. C. G. Jung, *Zur Psychologie und Psychopathologie sogenannter occulter Phänomene* (Leipzig: Oswald Mütze, 1902).

184. Lou Andreas-Salomé, *Friedrich Nietzsche in seinen Werken* (Vienna: Carl Konegen, 1894), pp. 189–190.

185. H. Wagenvoort, "Die Entstehung von Nietzsches Geburt der Tragödie," *Mnemosyne*, Ser. 4, XII (1959), 1–23.

186. Régis Michaud, *Autour d'Emerson* (Paris: Bossard, 1924).

187. Paul Valéry, *Autres Rhumbs* (Paris: Gallimard, 1927). Reprinted in *Oeuvres*, éd. Pléïade, II (Paris: Gallimard, 1960), p. 677.

188. Moritz Benedikt, *Hypnotismus und Suggestion. Eine klinisch-psychologische Studie* (Leipzig and Vienna: Breitenstein, 1894), pp. 66–67.

189. Count de Lutzelbourg, *Extraits des journaux d'un magnétiseur attaché à la Société des Amis Réunis de Strasbourg* (Strasbourg: Librairie Académique, 1786), p. 47.

190. Dr. Bonjour, "La Psychanalyse," *Bibliothèque Universelle et Revue Suisse*. 125th année. Vol. 97 (1920), 226–239, 337–354.

191. H. Bernheim, "De l'action médicamenteuse à distance," *Revue de l'Hypnotisme* (1888), p. 164.

192. Henri Bergson, "Simulation inconsciente dans l'état d'hypnotisme," *Revue Philosophique*, XXII (1886), 525–531.

193. Crocq, 'Discussion d'une communication de Félix Régnault," *IIe Congrès International de l'Hypnotisme* (Paris: 1900), (Paris: Vigot, 1902), pp. 95–96.

194. J. Delboeuf, "De l'Influence de l'éducation et de l'imitation dans le somnambulisme provoqué," *Revue Philosophique*, XXXII (1886), No. 2, 146–171.

195. Martin T. Orne, "Implications for Psychotherapy Derived from Current Research on the Nature of Hypnosis," *American Journal of Psychiatry*, CXVIII (1962), 1097–1103.

196. Oskar Vogt, "Valeur de l'hypnotisme comme moyen d'investigation psychologique," *IIe Congrès International de l'Hypnotisme* (Paris, 1900), (Paris: Vigot, 1902), pp. 63–71.

197. Ainslie Meares, "The Y-State–An Hypnotic Variant," *International Journal of Clinical and Experimental Hypnosis*, VIII (1960), 237–241.

198. Frederick W. H. Myers, "Multiplex Personality," *The Nineteenth Century*, XX (1886), 648–666.

4

The Background of
Dynamic Psychiatry

WE HAVE REVIEWED the ancestry of dynamic psychiatry (Chapter 1), its birth around 1775 and its historical evolution from Mesmer to Charcot (Chapter 2), and we have made a general survey of the first dynamic psychiatry as an organic and coherent system (Chapter 3). We will now inquire into its social, economic, and cultural background in order to see to what extent the first dynamic psychiatry can be explained by conditions existing in Europe at the end of the eighteenth century, and how changes in these conditions during the nineteenth century led to the formation of new systems of dynamic psychiatry. The teachings of Janet, Freud, Adler, and Jung were to a varying extent the heirs of the first dynamic psychiatry, but they were themselves determined by social factors and by philosophical, scientific, and cultural trends that we will survey as briefly as so complex a matter will permit.

The Social Background

The advent of animal magnetism and the shift from Mesmer to Puységur cannot be properly understood without taking into account the social conditions prevailing in Europe at the end of the eighteenth century. One-hundred-eighty years are a short span of time in comparison with the recorded history of mankind; even so, it is extremely difficult for us to imagine the way of life and of feeling of those ancestors whose nationalities and languages we have inherited. However, let us picture to ourselves that we are traveling back in time to the Europe of the 1780's. How strange would everything seem to us. How foreign the way of life of our forefathers. We would, of course, have to forget the atom bomb, television, radio, airplanes, automobiles, the telephone, railways, and hundreds of inventions and commodities that we take for granted. Men and women of that time would look almost as alien to us as if they were of another race; they differed from

182

us even biologically: they were of shorter build, huskier, extremely tough (surgical anesthesia did not exist, sedatives and narcotics were hardly known; people were used to physical suffering and to the sight of it). Even the wealthy, amidst their luxuries, lived in conditions that would seem incredibly uncomfortable to us. The great majority of the population ate foods that were coarse and offered little variety. Public hygiene being rudimentary, they were afflicted with many more infectious diseases, to the extent that about one-fourth of the population carried the marks of smallpox. Plumbing did not exist; dirt lay about everywhere and people were accustomed to strong odors. Going back to that period, we would furthermore have to forget many of our most cherished ways of thinking, believing, and of relating to others. For the majority there was far less intellectual stimulation than today. One need only read a novel written then, say Goethe's *The Sorrows of Young Werther* and imagine living the life of one of its characters: such a way of life would seem intolerably boring to us (whereas our way of life would have struck them in all likelihood as a dangerous frenzy). The vast majority of the population lived in the countryside where wolves and wild beasts freely roamed. The towns were smaller, and even in large cities such as Vienna and Paris people led lives that we would consider "provincial," knowing each other and living in more closely connected units than we do today.

Our forefathers' outlook on life would seem no less strange to us. Their way of thinking was generally less precise than ours. They no doubt knew many curious things forgotten today, but they also had many ideas, superstitions, and prejudices that would appear absurd to us. Science, for instance, was a rather vague notion for most people. A few great pioneers such as Priestley and Lavoisier stood isolated amidst a crowd of amateur scientists. Physics was primarily used for stage demonstrations, amusement, or quackery, or was a hobby of the aristocrats and the wealthy bourgeois who owned a *cabinet de physique*. However, there was a pervading feeling that mankind was coming of age after long centuries of darkness, and this opinion was strengthened by an uninterrupted flow of discoveries. Franklin was hailed as the man who had tamed the thunderbolt, and Montgolfier as the one who had inaugurated the conquest of the air. Explorers brought back news of the discovery of new countries and new populations in the South Pacific and elsewhere. In 1771, after completing a circumnavigation of the world, the French navigator Bougainville published a narrative of his travels, exciting imaginations with his description of the alleged natural happiness and utmost sexual freedom among the natives of Tahiti.[1] Commenting on Bougainville's narrative, Diderot concluded that the benefits of civilization and morals (which he did not deny) had been acquired at the cost of man's natural happiness.[2] Civilized man, he said, is the prey of internal strife between the "natural man" and the "moral and artificial man": whether the one or the other prevails in this strife,

civilized man remains forever an unhappy creature—an idea that was
later to be taken over by Nietzsche and Freud. The American War of Independence and the establishment of the First Republic across the ocean
had aroused the enthusiasm of the French public, who pictured this new
nation to be modeled on Sparta or on the early Roman Republic. Court
de Gébelin (one of Mesmer's admirers) was believed to have deciphered
the oldest myths and reconstructed the primeval language of mankind. In
short, the "enlightened" public had the feeling of living in an age of marvels
in which nothing was impossible.

The political and social structure of society was no less different from
ours. Monarchy prevailed everywhere under various forms, with the exception of small republics such as the Swiss cantons, and it is hard to
imagine today how incredible was the notion that a large country such as
the British Colonies of North America had adopted a republican constitution. Kings, emperors, princes, and petty sovereigns enjoyed great respect from their subjects. However, they were forced to accept many
limitations to their power set by custom, law, or public opinion. One fundamental difference between people of that era and ourselves was the rigorous division of society into classes. Theoretically, there were a great many
of them; actually, there was one basic distinction, that of aristocrats and
commoners. The noblemen originally were the descendants of old feudal
families; but few families were really that old, and most aristocratic families
had acquired their nobility as a reward for services rendered to the state,
through public functions, or simply because they had bought properties at
high cost or public functions that included a title of nobility. Not only was
there a hierarchy in the aristocracy, but there was also a division between
military nobility and judicial nobility. Whatever these distinctions, there
were certain common features: all aristocrats had privileges in regard to
taxes, to the administration of justice, and to the schools to which they sent
their children. They could carry swords and hunt wherever they pleased.
But they also had very strict obligations, and a great number of lucrative
occupations were prohibited to them. Also, if they had the privilege of
carrying a sword, it was considered to be their natural duty to defend their
sovereign. Aristocrats also performed duties in the navy, diplomatic services,
and high church offices. The still existing medieval castles had become unfashionable and were a topic for legends and "black novels." The higher
nobility chose more and more to live in fine and peaceful mansions in the
countryside, owned city homes, and had as much contact as possible with
the court. This class had developed a new, extremely sophisticated kind of
social life, a mark of which was an exquisite politeness and the inimitable
subtleties of conversation in which the French excelled; hence the prevalence
of the French language and manners among the nobility in most of Europe.
Aristocrats of the upper ranks felt obliged to maintain a very high and
expensive standard of living. Enormous sums were thus often squandered

on luxuries and gambling. However, the nobility was experiencing a crisis, which was particularly noticeable in France.[3] An increasing number of young French noblemen no longer found sufficient outlet for their ambitions and their need for activity. Also, hostility against the aristocracy kept spreading among the bourgeoisie, who envied their privileges. The reaction of French nobility was varied: many clung desperately to their privileges and tried to enforce them. A fairly large number turned to philanthropic activities; some even affected Republican ideals and showed enthusiasm for the American War of Independence. Since activities open to them were limited, and as their social life did not absorb all of their energies, a number of them strove to find new outlets, such as colonial enterprises or scientific research which they took seriously, although for the most part their endeavors would be rated as amateurish today.

Among the commoners, the bourgeoisie was on the ascent and was becoming increasingly numerous and powerful. Its way of life was quite different from that of the aristocracy. A main virtue of the latter had consisted in its generous and ostentatious way of spending money, whereas the bourgeoisie considered thrift allied with hard work as the main virtue. The proletariat was almost nonexistent on the Continent (the Industrial Revolution, which had started in England in the 1760's, had not yet crossed the Channel). At the bottom of the social ladder were the peasants, by far the great majority of the population. The real conditions of the peasantry have been appraised differently: many historians give a bleak picture of them, emphasizing their miserable life and their sufferings. Others point to the great improvements that had taken place during the eighteenth century. The peasant's lot was no doubt a hard one, even considering the fact that life at that time was harder for everybody. Serfdom was still prevalent for millions in Russia and in some parts of Central Europe. Even in Western Europe it had not yet completely disappeared, enabling a German prince, the Landgrave of Hesse, to sell his male subjects as soldiers to foreign powers. At best, agricultural methods were primitive as compared to modern ones. Peasants were crushed with taxes and had to submit to compulsory work (which was called *Robot* work in Austria) for landlord or state. In most of Europe peasants were illiterate, spoke innumerable dialects, and hardly understood their country's official language. But (almost unknown to the rest of the population) the peasants had a well-developed subculture of their own, consisting of popular customs, medical practices, popular arts, a wealth of oral literature, and numerous traditions including belief in sacred wells and sacred trees.

The way of life of every class was thus very different, and the relationships between classes extremely complex. The relationship of servants and their aristocratic masters was of a peculiar quality, which is not easy to understand today. Noble families living on their country estates were in close relation with the same peasant families, generation after generation. The same man could be his landlord's peasant and temporarily become his domestic or his soldier when the master took command of his regiment. Such relationships could extend over many generations. This interrelation between the master and his servant was undoubtedly quite authoritarian. In Russia, it was customary for aristocrats to punish their peasants with the knout. Even in France, the custom of a master beating his servant or forgetting to pay him his wages still existed until shortly before that time. However there was frequently a strong mutual devotion and much frankness in speech between the noble master and servant. We can find such relationships depicted in plays by Molière, Marivaux, and Beaumarchais, and see how different they were from the relationships between a bourgeois master and his servant. With the aristocracy, it was a relationship of despotism and submission, but also of symbiosis with a peculiar mixture of respect and familiarity. With the bourgeoisie, it was a more impersonal relationship of exploitation and resentment.

Seen in today's perspective, the history of animal magnetism seems filled with paradoxes. It seems incredible that Mesmer could have undertaken to cure patients for very high fees by assembling them around a container filled with magnetized water, or that such a practice caused distinguished ladies to fall into nervous crises. It would be too easy to speak of charlatanism and collective hysteria. It is also hardly less strange that prominent members of the aristocracy paid Mesmer, a foreigner, enormous sums of money in order to acquire an alleged "secret" that would enable them to cure patients gratuitously, or that a man like Puységur magnetized a tree in order to cure patients around it. And finally, it remains to be explained how the first two waves of animal magnetism, one with Mesmer's, the other with Puységur's technique, were followed after the French Revolution by a third, in many regards different, method of applying magnetism. We believe, however, that the strangeness will disappear and the facts become understandable when viewed in the light of the sociological background as sketched above.

Mesmer's victory over Gassner was a three-fold one: it represented the victory of the Enlightenment over the declining spirit of the Baroque, the victory of science over theology, and the victory of the aristocracy over the clergy. In its initial phase, animal magnetism must be understood within the frame of reference of the aristocracy and its system of values. Not being born a nobleman, Mesmer, who had married a lady of the Viennese aristocracy, led the life of a wealthy patrician and sought his clients among the noblemen. From the then current point of view, it was quite natural that he should charge them high fees; indeed, it would have been absurd on his part not to take money from people who squandered it without a second thought in gambling and other similar pastimes.

In regard to his *baquet,* this was a naïve apparatus inspired by those recent physical discoveries that impassioned the amateurish aristocrats.

Believing that he had discovered a new physical fluid, it was natural that Mesmer tried to accumulate it in a container in the same manner as physicists accumulated electricity in the Leyden jar. Mesmer had shaped his physical theory in imitation of the then current theory of electricity, hence the notion of the rapport and of the chain formed by patients through whom the fluid supposedly ran. One may now ask why most of his patients believed that they were feeling physiological effects of that fluid; but we need only recall that placebo effects occur not only with drugs and medications but with any physical agent. Even the foremost scientist of that time had difficulty in appreciating the physiological effects of electricity. Bertrand, a physicist who became one of the best students of animal magnetism, told curious stories about the first experimenters who could feel terrible shocks from an electric discharge that we would consider as only slightly disagreeable, and how they were frightened to the point of spending two days in bed, while other physicists candidly performed very dangerous experiments, which sometimes led to their deaths.[4] It took quite some time until the true physiological effects of physical agents were understood.

Another question one could ask is why the distinguished ladies sitting around Mesmer's *baquet* felt the effect of the alleged magnetic fluid only in the form of crises. The explanation will seem logical to those who have heard of the *vapeurs,* which was the neurosis of society women of that time. There were actually two fashionable neuroses during the second half of the eighteenth century: One, hypochondriasis, affected distinguished gentlemen and consisted of fits of depression and irritability. The other was the *vapeurs,* the neurosis of distinguished ladies, who fainted and had varied sorts of nervous fits. These neuroses were described in detail in treatises that have been classics, such as the *Treatise on the Vapeurs* by Joseph Raulin[5] and that by Pierre Pomme.[6] Fashionable physicians treated the *vapeurs* with all kinds of "modern" devices such as hydrotherapy and electricity. It was therefore quite fashionable for those ladies to go to Mesmer, who had introduced a new therapeutic method and who furthermore enjoyed the prestige of being a foreigner (a peculiar kind of xenophilia pervading France at that time). The kind of crisis produced around the *baquet* was nothing but an attack of the *vapeurs.* We could thus say that these crises were an abreaction of the current neurosis, elicited by a suggestive therapy that its author considered to be a rational application of recent physical research. In Mesmer's view, the therapeutic successes he obtained around the *baquet* could be nothing but a confirmation of his theory; hence his indignation over the Report of the Commissioners whom he accused of being biased against him.

What was the reason behind the abrupt and radical shift that took place between Mesmer's techniques and concepts and those of Puységur in the year 1784? It would seem that here, too, an explanation can be found in the sociological background. Let us first recall that Amand-Marie Jacques

de Chastenet, Marquis de Puységur, was a descendant of one of the most
ancient families of French nobility, which, in the course of centuries, had
given many prominent men to France, particularly in the military field, and
that he himself had made a brilliant military career. Like many of his
aristocratic contemporaries, he kept a *cabinet de physique*, in which he
performed various experiments with electricity. He divided his time between
his military life and his castle in Buzancy, where he owned a large property
that had been in the family for many generations. The Marquis, as well
as his two brothers, evidently belonged to the progressive wing of French
aristocracy that steered its activity into philanthropic channels. This explains
why Puységur and his associates of the Société de l'Harmonie practiced
magnetism free of charge. In view of their rank, it was to them a matter of
course that they could not use their knowledge of magnetism for lucrative
purposes (since, as we remember, almost all lucrative activities were
prohibited to French noblemen). Also, they could not charge fees to their
own peasants. All of Mesmer's aristocratic disciples shared this view as did
the noblemen of Alsace.

Returning to Buzancy, we see that the Marquis did not organize his
collective treatment around a *baquet* as did Mesmer, but rather around a
tree that he had magnetized, a procedure that Mesmer had used very little.
To Puységur, the magnetization of the tree was a scientific procedure; but
for the peasants, the tree had a specific meaning and appeal, which can
be explained by the popular beliefs and customs. In his monumental work
The Folklore of France, Sébillot devotes a chapter to popular beliefs and
practices relating to trees:

Sébillot states that the forests and sacred trees were probably the most respected divinities of the old Gauls, and that for centuries Christian missionaries
and bishops encountered the greatest difficulties in eradicating tree-worship;
this cult eventually disappeared, due more to the uprooting of trees and the
reclaiming of the land for agricultural purposes than to the religious prohibitions.
However, the cult of certain trees continued in a more or less disguised fashion
up to modern times. As late as 1854, a survey showed that in the Département
de l'Oise alone there still were not less than 253 trees to which a more or less
secret or disguised cult was given. Among these were 74 elm trees and 27 oaks.
Furthermore, and up to the French Revolution, many trees were associated with
the rendering of justice, and many others were believed to be endowed with
prophylactic or therapeutic virtues. During the seventeenth century and even
later, sick people would often attach themselves to tree trunks with the help of
ropes or some other means in order to transfer their disease to the tree. Sébillot
enumerates a great number of other practices, some of which still persisted at
the beginning of the twentieth century. Seen in that light, the story of the
magnetized elm tree of Buzancy loses much of its paradoxical character. The
utilization of magnetized trees did not disappear after Puységur, but it seems
to have receded into the background. Gauthier's textbook on magnetism
contains a chapter on this subject, in which we notice that only certain species

of trees were considered fit for magnetization, these being precisely the same kind of trees that had been revered as sacred in the past.[8] Perhaps the last mention of a magnetic tree is to be found in Flaubert's posthumous novel *Bouvard and Pécuchet*.[9] The two eccentric characters of this novel organize a treatment around a magnetized pear tree (which to the informed reader was sheer nonsense, since no fruit trees were considered apt for magnetization.)[7]

How can it be explained that the same procedure of the passes called forth crises in the patient when used by Mesmer and magnetic sleep when used by Puységur? Mesmer had produced countless crises in his patients, but almost no magnetic sleep; but from 1784 on, cases of somnambulism could be counted by the thousands. Here also the answer will be found in the sociological background of the patients. As we have seen, when Mesmer magnetized the society woman, it was quite natural if she responded with the crisis, which reproduced one of her old vapor fits. But when peasants and servants were magnetized, another kind of pathology, related to their social class, was elicited. But why did the peasant Victor display unexpected abilities when put into magnetic sleep? The answer is no doubt to be found in the peculiar relationship between a French nobleman of the end of the eighteenth century and his peasant. The Race family had lived on the property of the Puységurs in the village of Buzancy and had served them for many generations. The Viscount du Boisdulier, a contemporary descendant of the Marquis de Puységur, provided the following information:

> The Race family has been at the service of the Puységur for many centuries. A painting representing a hunting picnic organized by the Maréchal de Puységur, the grandfather of the magnetizer, included two grooms, one of whom was a Race; one of his descendents, Gabriel, who is still living today, was at my mother's service as a game-keeper in 1914."[10]

In the account given by Puységur of the various episodes with Victor, we note the peculiar mixture of familiarity and respect, the tone of which, however, varied much depending on whether Victor was awake or in magnetic sleep. In the latter condition, he showed not only more alertness and intelligence, but also much more confidence in the Marquis, confiding his worries to him and asking for his advice. He was quite frank and did not refrain from criticizing the Marquis' errors in his handling of magnetism.

Puységur's magnetic treatment of Victor shows two remarkable features: the first was the appearance of a dual personality, the new one being less inhibited and more brilliant than the ordinary one. The second was the quality of dialogue or even bargaining between the magnetizer and the magnetized, which often gave the treatment the aspect of a "patient directed therapy." In Victor's case, as well as in all contemporary instances of magnetic sleep, we notice that the magnetized patient stated his own diagnosis, announced the evolution of his illness, and often prescribed his own therapy or at least discussed the one prescribed by the magnetizer. We believe that all these features again find an explanation in the sociological background.

Hypnosis has been defined as the quintessence of the relation of dependency of one individual upon another. It is a surrender of one's will to the will of another and is more likely to occur when there is a considerable psychological or social distance between two individuals, the one endowed with power and prestige, the other, passive and submissive. A critical observer, the physician Virey wrote in 1818:

> It is always landlords who operate upon their subalterns, never the latter upon their superiors; it would seem that magnetism always works downward, never upward. The officers who so eagerly magnetized in their garrisons no doubt accomplished marvels upon poor soldiers who felt much honoured that marqueses, counts, knights would be willing to gesticulate over them.[11]

These features were eminently present in the Buzancy cures. Puységur's hold on the subjects was powerful because his ancestors had ruled over this territory for centuries, and the peasants had always considered them as their rightful lords. Only thus can one understand the authority exerted by the Marquis over his subjects and his ability to win their confidence and gather them around the magnetized elm tree for treatment. His prestige was of course enhanced by the fact that he was close to the Royal Court, had a high military command, and kept a *cabinet de physique* where he performed mysterious experiments.

Why was the new personality that appeared in magnetic sleep more brilliant than the usual one? We are not dealing here with an isolated fact. It had also been observed many times in the manifestation of possession that the "spirit" allegedly speaking through the mouth of the possessed revealed himself to be a more brilliant personality than his "host." Mühlmann pointed to the fact that spirits that possessed an individual in a conquered country tended to speak in the language of the oppressor.[12] It has often been reported that hypnotized peasant girls or servants tend to speak a more correct language than in their normal condition. This phenomenon could be called identification with a higher social class. We are led to assume that there was a similar tendency among French peasants and servants before the French Revolution. An episode in the autobiography of Madame Roland is very significant:

> When she was a child, her mother had taken her to a castle where she had some business, and they had been asked to dinner with the servants. They were struck with the discovery of a world that they had never suspected. The maids affected in their clothing and manners the behavior of their mistresses, and the men servants also strove to imitate their masters, speaking of nothing but

marquis, counts and other distinguished people whose affairs they were discussing as though they had intimate knowledge of them. The dishes and service
were a close parallel to those of the masters, and the meal was followed by
games at which fairly large sums were at stake, in the best aristocratic style.[13]

In a like manner, and unknown to Puységur, there must have been
a deep-seated wish in Victor to be like his master or, in modern language,
to identify with him. It is also the social relationship between the
aristocratic master and his peasant that could explain why Puységur's
hypnotic treatment of Victor took the peculiar form of a bargaining therapy,
a feature that was so common at that time and was gradually to recede
after the Revolution.

The sociological implications of Puységur's style of magnetic treatment
are well illustrated by the reports on the cures recorded in Strasbourg in
1786 to 1788. We have seen that the Marquis, in August 1785, had founded
a prosperous branch of the Société de l'Harmonie and that several
treatment centers were opened in Alsace under his supervision. These
reports are of special interest because each case history bears the name,
rank, and profession of the magnetizer and often indications about the
patient as well. The volume, published in 1787, contains the reports of
82 cures, 53 of which had been performed by noblemen: Baron Klinglin
d'Esser, 26; Baronne de Reich, 13; Count de Lutzelbourg, 6; Flachon de
la Jomarière, 6; Baron de Dampierre, 1; Baron Krook, 1.[14] The report
published in 1788 surveys 104 cures; the names of the magnetizers are
given in 95 cures, of which 56 were performed by noblemen.[15] Among
the cured patients whose occupations are listed we find a majority of
peasants, artisans, and servants (serving mostly bourgeois or aristocratic
families).

The new school of animal magnetism that arose after the Napoleonic
era was different in many regards from those of the first two periods. The
change can be understood in the light of the social upheaval brought about
by the French Revolution with its overthrow of the nobility and rise of the
bourgeoisie. There were still a number of noblemen among the magnetizers
in France, but they were, for the most part, like the Baron du Potet, the
descendants of ruined families, and more and more bourgeois were
entering the profession. Whatever their social origin, magnetizers now had
to earn their living; it can readily be seen why the period of gratuitous
treatment was gone. With the shift from magnetism to hypnotism around
the middle of the century, the authoritarian structure was strengthened.
The *baquet* and the magnetized tree were now obsolete; the patient
directed and the bargaining method receded before the method of orders
given under hypnosis, a procedure which by the end of the century
came to be identified with hypnotism itself. Hypnotists came mostly from
the high and middle bourgeoisie, and their patients were for the most

part laborers, soldiers, and peasants. The bourgeois character now taken on by hypnotism may perhaps also account for the more rational and systematic approach given to the theoretical and didactic aspects of hypnotism. But as we shall see later, new social factors contributed by the end of the nineteenth century to the advent of new types of psychotherapy.

Meanwhile, new driving forces of economical and political nature had become manifest, and we will review them briefly in order to evaluate their influence on the development of dynamic psychiatry.

The Economic and Political Background

Together with the social factors, powerful economical and political factors had already brought about a transformation of life. Among them were the Industrial Revolution and the principle of nationalities.

The *Industrial Revolution,* the birth and development of large-scale industry, occurred in England between 1760 and 1830.[16] New, perfected machines using natural and artificial sources of energy (water, steam, electricity) increased production enormously while maintaining the same manpower needs. Traditional crafts gradually disappeared, and a new tide of economic life arose, centered around the concept of profit. It implied a wide economic competition that gradually transformed the world into a gigantic market, vigorously disputed by the big industries of the various nations, together with an expanding system of transportation and communication, which in turn led to the opening up of new markets. New factories sprung up everywhere, causing the peasants to leave the countryside, bringing about a wide-scale urbanization and proletarization of the masses, bitter social problems, and the rise of socialism. Simultaneously, a rapid increase of population in Europe was followed by a large-scale emigration to North America and the overseas countries. Throughout the entire world, the "frontier" was opened to the grasp of the white man, who came either as a settler, taking over new countries, or as a colonist, or trader, exploiting the countries and their peoples.[17]

The main aspect of political life was the trend toward the *establishing of national states.* Several national states had slowly risen from the ruins of feudalism and the old dream of European unity under the aegis of pope and emperor. By the end of the eighteenth century, Spain, England, and France had become unified national states, while Italy and Germany were still subdivided into many small sovereign states and the Austrian monarchy remained a vast conglomerate of peoples under the scepter of the Hapsburgs. As Napoleon's domination stirred the peoples of Europe against him, a revival of the national spirit began to be felt everywhere, and this movement continued after the downfall of the Emperor.[18] Many peoples who had been under foreign domination became aware of their national identity, which was closely connected with their national language.

The principle was proclaimed that every nation had the right to constitute a national state of its own. Since the nation was identified with the language, bitter linguistic wars ensued throughout central and southeastern Europe.

This situation had a strong impact on science and culture. For many centuries, Latin had been the common language of the Church, administration, and universities in all of Europe. Its supremacy, already challenged by the Reformation, was to be overthrown by the rise of nationalism. It remained, however, the official language of Parliament, state, and administration of Hungary until the 1840's, and every cultivated person in Western Europe was still expected to speak it fluently.[19] But in most countries, scientists had already begun to use their own national languages, and the use of Latin rapidly decreased after the advent of the French Revolution.

The reason for the disappearance of Latin as an international European language is not to be found in its scientific inadequacy: Newton, Harvey, and Linnaeus had published their discoveries in Latin. Mach suggests that the reason was that the nobility wanted to enjoy the fruits of literature and science without having to learn that scholarly language.[20] Condorcet proclaimed that through the use of their national language, the publications of French scientists would no longer be an inaccessible realm to the average Frenchman; he left it to the scientists to learn the languages of their foreign colleagues.[21] When the elite use the national language for philosophical and scientific purposes, he said, this language will necessarily become enriched and perfected; this in turn will give the people the advantage of having a more perfect linguistic tool at their disposal and with it an easier access to general culture. There is no doubt that the abandonment of Latin and the adoption of national languages gave an enormous impetus to the development of science in the Western European countries (such as the development of psychology and psychiatry), but science tended to be less universal than it had been hitherto and it became a national concern, sometimes even a political weapon.

The Cultural Background: The Enlightenment

The history of Western civilization is to a great extent that of a few great cultural movements, the Renaissance, Baroque, Enlightenment, and Romanticism, which succeeded each other from the end of the Middle Ages to the nineteenth century. Each of them not only showed specific features in its philosophy, literature, art, and science, but implied a new style of life and culminated in the formation of an ideal type of man.[22] Each movement had its center of origin in one country, of which it kept certain characteristics while spreading over the rest of Europe: the Renaissance and Baroque in Italy, the Enlightenment in France, Romanticism in Germany. These movements (as well as other less important ones) cannot be defined as strict chronological entities; they slowly spread from one country to another and overlapped each other.

The Renaissance developed in Italy during the fourteenth, fifteenth, and part of the early sixteenth centuries. It flourished at the court of princes and in city-states in a period of intensive struggles, when feudalism was beginning to be shaken by the rising bourgeoisie. It spread over France and elsewhere during the sixteenth century. Its main features were a passionate interest in ancient Greco-Roman culture, not merely as a source of information and teaching, but as a model of life, associated with a coming to awareness of the human personality, of its nature, and of its place in the universe.[23] In the arts the Renaissance strove toward the ideal of perfect proportion in its static form, and it discovered the laws of perspective and stressed their importance. Its ideal type of man was described by Baldassare Castiglione as being of noble birth, versed in bodily exercise, of a refined education including art, music, and literature, combining dignity with spontaneity and grace in manners, and being little concerned with religion. The Renaissance also exalted the shrewd politician, the mighty genius, and the great scholar.[24] From then on and until the end of the nineteenth century, it was considered a matter of course that an educated person should possess an excellent knowledge of Latin and Greek and of their literatures, as well as of the modern classics in the national languages. One cannot, therefore, understand men like Janet, Freud, and Jung without realizing that they had been immersed from childhood in an atmosphere of intensive classical culture and that this culture pervaded all their thinking. One negative aspect of the Renaissance was its contempt for the vulgar, the illiterate, and the "fool." But there was also a great interest in mental illness and, as we have seen, in the multiform manifestations ascribed to that peculiar faculty of the mind, *imaginatio*. The study of imagination, one of the legacies of the Renaissance to the following centuries, was to become a main source of early dynamic psychiatry.

At the time of the birth of dynamic psychiatry, the Renaissance was over, and the succeeding cultural trend, the Baroque, was still flourishing in Spain and Austria. The Baroque movement was related to the rise of centralized powers, in which the monarch endeavored to keep the nobility and the bourgeoisie closely attached to his person. The models of life were no longer sought in Greek and Roman antiquity, but around the idealized figures of great monarchs (such as the King of Spain, the French *Roi-Soleil*), in great empires, involving elaborate ceremonials, costumes, and furnishings. It was also closely connected with the movement of the Counter-Reformation. In the arts, instead of the static and perfectly proportioned ideal of the Renaissance, the Baroque sought movement, change, and growth. It often had a predilection for the boundless, the colossal, the disproportionate, and exaggerated ornamentation. Its ideal man was depicted by Baltasar Gracián as a man of noble birth and fine education, to whom religion and honor were sacred; he was striving above all toward inner greatness, though with ostentation, "the man of majestic qualities and achievements."[25] In an often bombastic style, Baroque literature related stories of heroes who faced incredible handicaps and obstacles and who were the pawns of fate. The Baroque was a period of great philosophical systems and of great discoveries in all branches of science. According to Sigerist the Baroque interest in movement and development was expressed in medicine with Harvey's discovery of blood circulation and with his studies in embryology.[26] In psychiatry, it tended toward the building of systems and elaborate classifications. Unfortunately, the Baroque was also one of the worst periods of witch hunting and belief in devilish possession. The birth of dynamic psychiatry at the end of the eighteenth century can be fully understood only when placed back into the cultural and historical perspective of the decline of the Baroque and the triumph of the Enlightenment. As we have seen, this is symbolized by the contestation in 1775 between Gassner, the devoted priest and convinced exorcist, and Mesmer, the enlightened layman and would-be scientist.

The third great cultural movement, the *Enlightenment,* has been defined by Troeltsch as "the spiritual movement which led to the secularization of thought and State."[27] According to Kant's well-known definition:

Enlightenment is the leaving behind by man of his self-caused minority. Minority is the impossibility of using one's own reason without the guidance of another. That minority is *self-caused* when it is due not to the lack of reasoning power but to the lack of decision and courage to make use of it without the guidance of another. *Sapere aude*! Have the courage to make use of your *own* reason! is thus the motto of the Enlightenment.[28]

The Enlightenment, which was closely connected with the rise and consolidation of the bourgeoisie, originated in France around 1730, spread rapidly over England and Germany, and culminated around 1785. It assumed different forms in each of those countries. In France, it became political and sometimes antireligious. In England it developed a special interest in economics. In Germany it kept within the bounds of established religion and was adopted by the ruling princes in the form of enlightened despotism, typically represented by Frederick II, King of Prussia; notwithstanding his despotic attitude, he thought of and proclaimed himself as the first servant of his people in contrast with the typical Baroque sovereign, Louis XIV, who said: "The State is I" (*L'Etat, c'est moi*). But everywhere the conviction reigned that mankind had finally come of age after an extremely long period of ignorance and servitude, and could now, under the control of reason, steer toward a future of unlimited progress.[29] The Enlightenment's most fundamental characteristic was the cult of reason, considered to be a permanent universal entity, which was the same for all men of all ages and all countries. Reason was opposed to ignorance, error, prejudice, superstition, imposed beliefs, the tyranny of passions, and the aberrations of fantasy. Following those ideas was the notion that man was a sociable being and society was created for man. The ideal type of man belonged to the aristocracy or to the bourgeoisie, and his life was directed in accordance with the requirements of reason and of society. In France, he was represented by the *honnête homme,* a sociable figure. In England, he was more public-minded and concerned with economic problems. The philosophy of the Enlightenment was optimistic and practical, and proclaimed that science could and had to be applied for the welfare of mankind. Progress was understood not only in its material sense but as a qualitative and moral progress, implying social reforms. A further feature of the Enlightenment was also its faith in and deep concern for education.

In science, the Enlightenment eliminated the principle of authority, and began to apply analysis, used theretofore in mathematics, to other branches of knowledge, including the study of the human mind, society, and politics. Psychology strove to analyze the basic elements of the mind: sensations and associations, and then to reconstruct, by synthesis, the whole fabric of the human mind. Likewise, men such as Rousseau tried to imagine the evolution of society, starting with separate individuals who gathered together and concluded among themselves a "social contract." Until then, science had progressed mainly through the individual work of great scientists living isolated from each other and entertaining an active correspondence with one another. The Enlightenment furthered the creation of a network of scientific societies, which published proceedings of their activities. The members, who often comprised many amateurs, considered it as their duty to attend the sessions and to communicate their findings.

The rational, practical, optimistic features of the Enlightenment converged in the preoccupation with reforms and aid to the underprivileged members of the great human family. The Enlightenment proclaimed the principles of religious freedom and of mutual tolerance among the various religions, as illustrated by Lessing in his celebrated play *Nathan der Weise* (1779). It fought for the emancipation of Protestants in Catholic countries, of Catholics in Protestant countries, and of Jews throughout Europe. There was a movement among Christians for the emancipation of Jews, and among Jewish communities for emancipation from the rigid fetters of Jewish traditional orthodoxy and way of life.[30] The movement for the abolition of serfdom and slavery also took its roots in the Enlightenment. Among Protestants a trend called rationalism, developed, which was well-defined by the title of Kant's treatise *Religion within the Bounds of Mere Reason.* The element of reason in faith was stressed rather than that of blind tradition or mystical *élan.*[31] Attempts were made to find rationalizations for miracles (that is, to find supposedly scientific explanations for Biblical miracles). Roskoff has shown that belief in the devil was gradually dispelled in religious circles influenced by the Enlightenment, which accounts in part for the gradual receding of witch trials.[32] In the realm of justice, the Enlightenment fought against the use of torture and other grievous abuses,

which were still current. The movement toward judicial and penal reform
is illustrated by Beccaria's famed treatise *Dei Delitti e delle Pene* (1764)
and Howard's philanthropic activity for the improvement of prisons and
hospitals.

The Enlightenment's enormous impact on medicine is generally little
known.[33] It inaugurated pediatrics, orthopedics, public hygiene, and pro-
phylaxy, among others, with its campaign for inoculation against smallpox.
It influenced psychiatry in many ways, beginning with its laicization.
Many symptoms, which had been considered to be the effects of witchcraft
or possession, came to be considered as forms of mental illness. Efforts
were being made to understand mental illness in a scientific manner.
The rapid progress of mechanics and physics suggested the adoption of
mechanistic models in physiology and the reduction of psychic life to the
activity of the nervous system. Owing to the emphasis given to the faculty
of reason, mental illness was considered as being essentially a disturbance
of reason. Its causes were believed to be either some physical lesion,
especially of the brain, or the effects of uncontrolled passions. Therefore,
representatives of the Enlightenment taught principles of what we would
call mental hygiene, based on the training of the will and the subordination
of passions to reason. Kant himself, in one of his books, wrote a chapter
entitled "Of the Power of the Mind to be Master of One's Morbid Feelings
Through Simple Decision," in which he gave rules for overcoming sleeplessness, hypochondriasis, and various physical ailments through proper diet,
proper breathing, and particularly through systematic work interspersed
with periods of full relaxation and the establishing of solid habits, especially
accomplishing frequent and conscious acts of the will.[34] The Enlightenment's interest in mental illness was also evidenced by the growing number
of treatises on that subject published in the second half of the eighteenth
century, some of which already featured an outline similar to that of
modern textbooks. But most important, the Enlightenment was the period
when efforts were first made toward the reform of mental hospitals, which
by the end of the century were carried out by men who were among the
most typical representatives of the Enlightenment: Chiarugi, Tuke, Daquin,
and Pinel. Concern for mental patients also spread outside the medical
world; people such as the Alsatian pastor Oberlin took mental patients
into their homes and treated them with a mixture of supportive and work
therapy.[35] It was also the spirit of the Enlightenment that inspired Itard
in his efforts for the special education of mentally defective children, the
Abbé de l'Epée for that of the deaf-mute, and of Haüy for the blind.

The historical and cultural importance of the Enlightenment cannot be
overestimated: it constitutes the backbone of modern Western civilization.
The principles of freedom of religion, thought, speech, the principles of
social justice, equality, the social state, the notion of public welfare as being
a normal function of the state rather than an act of charity, the principle of

compulsory and free education, and the positive achievements of the American and French revolutions, all sprang from the Enlightenment, as did the foundation of modern psychiatry.

But the Enlightenment also had its negative points. It tended to place all men in the same category and to underestimate differences of physical and mental make-up, and cultural traditions. It furthered a one-sided concept of the emotions as being a disturbance of the rational mind, without acknowledging them in their own right. While furthering historical methodology, it lacked historical perspective. In spite of its strong emphasis on reason, it was not yet sufficiently critical, and science was still in what Bachelard has called the pre-scientific era.[36] A curious mixture of rationalism and irrational speculation could be found in many scientists of the Enlightenment. There were, for instance, numerous speculations in the natural sciences. Newton's discovery of the universal law of gravitation fascinated scientists, who were on the search for the universal force: fire, phlogiston, electricity, and even animal magnetism. Another prevalent preoccupation was the search for the "primitive world," which was supposed to have existed at the origin of mankind, a world endowed with supreme knowledge and unfathomable wisdom. This world was believed to have been destroyed by some catastrophe, but that parts of its traditions had been secretly transmitted by a chain of a few initiated wise men. This primitive world was thought by some to have been located in submerged Atlantis, by others in Central Asia. Boulanger contended that human civilization had been destroyed several times but reconstructed each time by a handful of survivors. The most recent of these catastrophes, he said, was the Biblical flood, the intolerable memory of which had been repressed by mankind but had survived in countless myths throughout the world and which Boulanger endeavored to interpret (Christian baptism, for example, was to him a symbolic reminder of the waters of the flood).[37] According to another belief, the submerged wisdom of the primitive world had been written down in undeciphered hieroglyphics and kept in Ancient Egypt. A novel by the Abbé Terrasson, *Séthos,* depicted the life of Egypt's wise men and their mysterious rites.[38] Masonic rites were supposed to reproduce some of those ancient and mysterious rites. Antoine Court de Gébelin published a set of enormous and magnificent volumes, expounding in its most minute details a reconstitution of the primitive world, taken from Greek and other myths, and even reconstructing the primitive language of mankind from the analysis of existing languages.[39] Characteristically, Court de Gébelin became Mesmer's enthusiastic follower, and many believed that Mesmer had rediscovered one of the secrets of the primitive world.

We can see how the birth of dynamic psychiatry can thus be understood as a manifestation of the Enlightenment in both its rational and irrational aspects. Mesmer was fundamentally a representative of the Enlightenment.

He believed himself to be a scientist who had taken over where Newton had left off. His superficial knowledge of physics led him to build would-be physical theories, which were not much more speculative than those of many *physicien-amateurs*, while the general atmosphere also led many of his contemporaries to consider him a scientist. Puységur and the members of the Société de l'Harmonie revealed another facet of the Enlightenment—the philanthropic trend to place the discoveries of science and its benefits at the disposal of all mankind and not to restrict it to only those who could afford it. In Alsace, the Société de l'Harmonie opened a number of free out-patient services to anyone who needed magnetization. (This, to our knowledge, is the first historically recorded instance of psychiatric treatment available free of charge to the underprivileged.)

Thus, we see that magnetism was a creation of the Enlightenment. It is even more ironic that magnetism was soon to be taken over and reinterpreted in quite a different way by the following cultural trend, Romanticism. But the antagonism and the interplay between the Enlightenment and Romanticism could be followed throughout the history of dynamic psychiatry, from Mesmer to modern times. As we shall see in following chapters, Janet's teaching can definitely be traced to the traditions issuing from the Enlightenment, whereas Freud and Jung can be identified as late epigones of Romanticism.

The Cultural Background: Romanticism

Romanticism originated in Germany, achieved its highest development there between 1800 and 1830, and then declined, although it spread over France, England, and other countries. Its impact was such that it had lasting effects on European cultural life throughout the nineteenth century. In its strictest sense, Romanticism applied to a number of small and loosely connected groups of poets, artists, and philosophers of the beginning of the nineteenth century. In its largest sense, it applied to a vast movement that expressed itself in a characteristic outlook on life.[40]

Romanticism has often been considered a cultural reaction against the Enlightenment. Whereas the latter proclaimed the values of reason and of society, Romanticism had the cult of the irrational and of the individual. Mystical tendencies, which had been pushed into the background by the Enlightenment, were now released. A political theory considered Romanticism as a movement of national renovation in line with the principle of nationalities. This movement was stronger in Germany than elsewhere as a result of the unfortunate political circumstances that had prevailed there for centuries: Germany had suffered the Thirty Years' War, had been reduced to political impotence by Richelieu, Louis XIV, and Napoleon, and was divided into a multiplicity of small sovereign states, thus being a nation without a state. Even its language and culture had been endangered by an excessive foreign influence. Romanticism gave the feeling of its own

national identity back to Germany, contributing thus to its political renovation. Brunschwig correlated the rise of Romanticism to the demographic disequilibrium in Germany at the end of the eighteenth century.[41]
The urban population of Germany increased enormously and a new generation of young bourgeois and intellectuals, deprived of career opportunities
and facing a bleak present, adopted an irrational mentality, turned toward
the remote past or the remote future, and lived in a constant expectation
of miracles in religion, medicine, love, occupation, and daily life.

Whatever the explanations about its origin, several features of Romanticism are essential:

1. Foremost was its deep feeling for nature, in contrast with the Enlightenment, which was centered around Man and found its expression in
a much quoted verse by Pope: "The proper study of Mankind is Man."
Romanticism looked upon nature with a feeling of deep reverence, with
Einfühlung (feeling into or empathy), with a craving to penetrate into its
depths in order to discover man's true relationship with nature. This
feeling for nature was shown in Romantic lyric poetry as well as in the
speculations of the philosophy of nature. It was even found in the
physiologist's interest in the rhythm and periodicity in the human organism
and their relationship with the cosmic movements.

2. Behind the visible nature, the Romantic sought to penetrate the
secrets of nature's "fundament" (*Grund*), which he considered to be at the
same time the fundament of his own soul. The means to reach that fundament not only lay in the intellect but also in the *Gemüt*, that is, the most
intimate quality of emotional life. Hence, the interest that was shown by
Romanticism for all manifestations of the unconscious: dreams, genius,
mental illness, parapsychology, the hidden powers of fate, its interest in
the psychology of animals. Hence, it was also preoccupied with popular
tales and folklore, and the spontaneous expression of popular genius.
This also explains the enthusiasm for magnetism. This principle, also
called the night-side of Nature, contained the universal symbols as well
as the seed of things to be. The systematic study of myths and symbols was
started by thinkers such as Christian Gottlieb Heyne, Friedrich Schlegel,
Creuzer, and Schelling, for whom they were not mere historical errors or
abstract concepts, but living forces and realities.

3. Third was the feeling for "becoming" (*Werden*). Whereas the Enlightenment believed in eternal reason and its steady manifestation in the form of
mankind's progress, Romanticism held that all beings stemmed from seminal
principles, which developed in individuals, societies, nations, languages,
and cultures. Human life was not just a long period of maturity following
a shorter period of immaturity, but a spontaneous process of unfolding, a
series of metamorphoses (which C. G. Jung was later to call individuation).
The *Bildungsroman,* novels describing the process of intellectual and emotional development of an individual, became a favorite form of literature

and probably inspired psychiatrists to write down case histories in connection with the entire history of their patients.

4. Romanticism was concerned with particular nations and cultures, not just with society in general. The German Romantics not only restored the German language and culture to their rightful place, but eagerly studied a great number of other cultures with their folklores, popular tales, myths, literature, and philosophies. Their *Einfühlung* into other cultures is best-shown in the astonishing perfection of their translations of foreign authors, in which the Romantic poets succeeded, for instance, in making Shakespeare into a German national poet. Friedrich Schlegel proclaimed, "A truly free and educated person ought to be able to attune himself at will, philosophically or philologically, critically or poetically, historically or rhetorically, to the ancient or to the modern, in the way one tunes an instrument, at any time and to any degree."[42] Novalis also thought that "the perfect person must live equally in several places and in several people."[43]

5. Romanticism brought a new feeling for history, striving to conjure up, as it were, the spirit of past centuries. It was said that Romanticism achieved *Einfühlung* with every possible period of history, with the sole exception of the Enlightenment. But its predilection was for the Middle Ages, which it rediscovered in much the same way as the Renaissance had rediscovered Greco-Roman antiquity.

6. In contrast with the Enlightenment, Romanticism lays a strong emphasis upon the notion of the individual. In 1800 in his *Monologues*, Schleiermacher[44] emphasized the absolute uniqueness of each individual, a concept held by all Romantics. The typically Romantic concept of *Weltanschauung* (view of the world) indicates a specific way of perceiving the world particular to a nation, a historical period, or an individual. According to Max Scheler, that word was coined by Wilhelm von Humboldt, who claimed that the science of a certain period was always unconsciously determined by its *Weltanschauung*.[45] Whereas the Enlightenment had tended to consider society as a more or less voluntary, if not artificial, product of the human will, or of a social contract, Romanticism considered communal life as nature-given and independent of the will of man. The Romantics often worked or lived together as two friends, two brothers, brother and sister, or in small groups of friends who met at regular intervals to exchange views and ideas. In the relationship between the sexes, Romantics demanded, above all, an emotional and spiritual quality and loathed the idea of the Enlightenment's marriage of reason. In 1799, Friedrich Schlegel aroused much controversy with his autobiographic novel *Lucinde*,[46] in which he exalted the notion of lasting love—Romantic love—as a fusion of physical passion and spiritual attraction. Novalis expressed the view that love should impart "the drive to perfect oneself with the beloved one and help her to reach perfection,"[47] a notion anticipating that of C. G. Jung as we shall see in a later chapter.

As had the preceding cultural movements, Romanticism produced its ideal type of Man. Its main features were an extreme sensitiveness enabling Man to "feel into" Nature and to "feel with" other men, a rich inner life, belief in the power of inspiration, intuition, and spontaneity, and the importance ascribed to emotional life. Romantics were sometimes criticized for their tendency to easy enthusiasm and sentimentality. But Friedrich Schlegel and the early Romantics pointed to the virtue of "irony," in the Romantic sense of the term, a detached attitude toward one's own feelings, however intimate.[48] However, it often happened that Romantic men and women were afflicted with that malady of which Schlegel gave a picture in *Lucinde*—a *Sehnsucht,* a longing for something indefinable and extraordinary, the hero, in continuous unrest, roaming around aimlessly, leading an erratic life that brings him at last to the brink of collapse. Many Romantics were actually restless and lacking in self-discipline, giving the best of their talents to improvisation and conversations, and leaving behind unfinished works. Some died prematurely, either of physical disease like Novalis, in mental illness, like Hölderlin, or by suicide, like Kleist. The romantic malady appeared in England and France also and gave rise to brilliant literary descriptions by Châteaubriand and by Alfred de Musset.

When speaking of Romanticism, one usually thinks of its expression in literature, in music, and in the arts; but in Germany, Romanticism also pervaded the fields of philosophy, science, and medicine. In view of its particular importance in regard to later developments in dynamic psychiatry, we should take a closer look at the implications of Romanticism in those spheres.

Philosophy of Nature and Romantic Philosophy

A specific school of thought, that of *Naturphilosophie* (philosophy of nature) was founded as an offshoot of German Romanticism by the philosopher Friedrich Wilhelm von Schelling (1775–1854) and included among its adherents scientists as well as philosophers.[49]

The starting point of Schelling's philosophy was the contention that nature and spirit both sprang from the absolute and constituted and indissoluble unity. "Nature is visible Spirit, Spirit is invisible Nature." Therefore, nature cannot be understood in terms of mechanical and physical concepts only, but must be understood in terms of the underlying spiritual laws, which the philosophy of nature endeavored to elucidate. In visible nature, the organic and visible world arose from a common spiritual principle, the world soul (*Weltseele*), which out of itself and through a series of generations successively produced matter, the living nature, and consciousness in man. The organic nature and the various realms of the living world differed through their degree of perfection, but they obeyed the same laws. Therefore, the laws governing one of the realms could be discovered through the exploration of other realms and the use of analogy, which was the magic wand of Romantic philosophy.

One of the philosophy of nature's basic principles was the essential unity of man and nature; human life was regarded as a participation in a kind of cosmic movement within nature. The universe was an organized whole in which each part was connected to all others through a relation of sympathy.[50] Hence the interest shown by the philosophers of nature for Mesmer's theory of animal magnetism, which they interpreted according to their own theories.

Another basic principle of the philosophy of nature was the "law of polarities," pairs of antagonistic and complementary forces that might unite in the form of indifference. There were, according to Schelling, polarities within nature such as day and night, force and matter, gravity and light. The polarity male and female was ascribed a wide importance extending over the limits of the animated world. Schelling and his disciples sought polarities everywhere. Treatises of chemistry were written under the aspect of the polarity acid and base. Human physiology was interpreted in terms of the polarities waking and sleeping, vegetative sphere and animal sphere (Reil), brain and ganglion system (Von Schubert).[51] Polarities were often conceived as a dynamic interplay of antagonistic forces. The physiologist August Winkelmann,[52] in his *Introduction into Dynamic Physiology* (1802), stated that "Nature is the struggle of forces, the conflict of a positive and a negative force." He based an entire system of dynamic physiology on the concept of these conflicting polarities, such as that of the nervous system and the system of circulation.

Another basic concept of Romantic philosophy was that of the primordial phenomena (*Urphänomene*) and the series of metamorphoses deriving from them. Goethe, who had anticipated the approach of the philosophy of nature in many ways, applied these two concepts in his studies on the metamorphoses of plants.[53] The word "metamorphosis," as used by Goethe, designated neither a material transformation visible to the observer, nor a pure abstraction, but a supposed change in the "formative force" (as formulated by Agnes Arber).[54] Goethe thus believed in the *Urpflanze* (a primordial plant) as a model for all plants, of which each botanic species would partake to some degree. Curiously enough, Goethe came to believe that the *Urpflanze* existed and he searched for it, although in his original conception its actual existence was not necessary. What C. G. Carus called the genetic method was a way of connecting a primordial phenomenon with the metamorphoses that derived therefrom and finding laws governing their connection.[55] Among other *Urphänomene* was the myth of the Androgyne. In his *Symposium,* Plato had told in a figurative sense that the primordial human being possessed both sexes, which had later become separated from each other by Zeus and that, ever since, man and woman were searching for each other in an effort to reunite. This myth, taken over by Boehme, Baader, and others was well suited to express the Romantic idea of the fundamental bisexuality of the human being, and it was elaborated in many ways by the Romantics.[56] No less basic to them was the notion of the unconscious. This word no longer meant St. Augustine's forgotten memories or Leibniz's "unclear perceptions," but was the very fundament of the human being as rooted in the invisible life of the universe and therefore the true bond linking man with nature. Closely related to the notion of the unconscious was that of the "inner" or "universal sense" (All-Sinn) by which man, before the fall, was able to cognize nature. Imperfect though this sense had become, it still enabled us, said the Romantics, to gain some direct understanding of the universe, be it in mystical ecstasy, poetic and artistic inspiration, magnetic somnambulism, or dreams. The latter were also a central concern of these men, and there is hardly a Romantic philosopher or poet who did not express his ideas on dreams.[57]

The concepts and way of thinking of Romantic Philosophy may seem strange to us, who have become accustomed to the methods of experimental science. However, they unmistakably reappeared in the new dynamic psychiatry. Leibbrand said that "C. G. Jung's teachings in the field of psychology are not intelligible if they are not connected with Schelling." He also pointed to the influence exerted by Schelling's conception of myths on modern dynamic psychiatry. (It may also be said that Leibbrand has shown analogies between Schelling's concept of mental illness as a nonspecific reaction of the living substance and the modern theories of Selye and of Speransky.)[58] Jones has also observed that Freud's concepts of mental life were dominated by polarities (dualism of instincts, polarities of subject-object, pleasure-unpleasure, active-passive), and he adds that a peculiar feature of Freud's thinking, throughout his life, was "his constant proclivity to dualistic ideas."[59] This was a typically Romantic way of thinking. The Romantic philosophic concept of Urphänomen not only reappears in Jung's work under the name of "Archetype," but is to be found in Freud's as well. What are the Oedipus complex, the murder of the primordial father, if not Urphänomene, which are postulated for mankind as a whole and described in individuals under their various metamorphoses? To Freud, it did not matter whether the murder of the primordial father had actually been perpetrated or not, no more than it did concern Goethe whether the Urpflanze actually existed as a botanical species. Important only were the relationships that could be deduced from it in regard to human culture, religion, the social order, and the psychology of the individual. In the same way, the Romantic idea of the fundamental bisexuality of the human being found its way into the psychiatric systems of Freud and Jung. Jung's concept of animus and anima are but a later reincarnation of the Romantic Urphänomen, expressed in the myth of the Androgyne. Fundamentally Romantic also are the concepts of the unconscious, particularly as revived in Jung's "collective unconscious" and the emphasis on dreams and symbols. As we shall see in the following pages, there is hardly a single concept of Freud or Jung that had not been anticipated by the philosophy of nature and Romantic medicine.

In addition to these general features pertaining to the Romantic concepts of man and nature, each of the Romantic thinkers had his own system. Some such as Von Schubert, Troxler, and C. G. Carus showed remarkable anticipation of the teachings of the new dynamic psychiatry. Schopenhauer, although not exactly a Romantic, belonged to the same era and was definitely among the ancestors of modern dynamic psychiatry.

Gotthilf Heinrich von Schubert (1780–1860) was the author of a highly poetic vision of nature, which sometimes reminds the modern reader of Bergson and Teilhard de Chardin and is striking in its similarities with certain Freudian and Jungian concepts.[60] According to Von Schubert, man in an original primordial state, lived in harmony with nature, then severed himself from it through his *Ich-Sucht* (self-love), but will revert to it later in a perfected form. The intuition of this fact, he believed, was expressed by ancient agricultural religions in their representations of the mysteries of the death and resurrection of Isis, Adonis, and Mithra. Von Schubert gave a grandiose sketch of the evolution of the earth, the successive appearance of the mineral, vegetal, and animal kingdoms, and its crowning with man, the spirit-bringer, and of the interrelations of the mineral, vegetal, and animal kingdoms within the universe and human nature. According to Kern, Von Schubert gave a clear indication of what von Uexküll was to call the *Umwelt*.[61] Von Schubert distinguished three constitutive parts of the human being: *Leib* (the living body), soul, and spirit, and added that these undergo a process of "becoming." Human life was a series of metamorphoses; a sudden one will sometimes occur shortly before death, or after the middle of life has been reached. Thus, man is a "double star"; he is endowed with a second center, his *Selbstbewusstein*, which gradually emerges in his soul. In man, as in all living beings, the longing (*Sehnsucht*) for love cannot easily be separated from the longing for death (*Todessehnsucht*) which is the striving to return "home" to nature, but which also points to a future life.

In another work, *The Symbolism of Dreams*, Von Schubert declared that when man has fallen asleep, his mind starts thinking in a "picture language," in contrast to the verbal language of waking life.[62] For a while both languages may flow parallel or mingle, but in dreams proper only the picture language (*Traumbildsprache*) remains. It is a hieroglyphic language in the sense that it can combine many images or concepts into one picture. Dreams use a universal language of symbols, which is the same for men throughout the world, and applies to men of the past as it does for contemporary men. The picture language of dreams is "a higher kind of algebra"; it sometimes takes a poetic quality, sometimes an ironic one (as in dreams where the image of birth means in fact death, or where excrement means gold). At night the human mind sometimes becomes able to perceive visions of events to come, but dreams more often have an amoral and demonic character because the neglected, repressed, and strangled (*vergewaltigte*) aspects of personality come to the fore.

We may graphically summarize some of the similarities between Von Schubert's concepts and those of Freud and Jung in the following table:

SCHUBERT	FREUD	JUNG
Threefold nature of Man:		
Leib (living body)	Id	
Soul	Ego	
Spirit	Superego	
Ich-Sucht (self-love)	Narcissism	
Changes in the course of life		Individuation
Second center of the human soul		*Selbst* ("self")
Todessehnsucht (longing for death)	Death instinct	
Dream: word language and picture language	Same concept	
Hieroglyphics	Condensation	
Universal symbols	Universal symbols	Archetypes

Another philosopher of nature, the Swiss Ignaz Paul Vital Troxler (1780–1866) was a disciple of Schelling, a friend of Beethoven, an experienced physician and an educator who taught philosophy in Basel and Berne.[63] After a century of oblivion, he has been rediscovered and recently brought to light. Troxler taught that the human being is composed, not of the three principles body, soul, and spirit (as professed by other Romantics), but of four principles, arrived at through the distinction of *Körper* and *Leib, Körper* being the body as viewed by the anatomist or surgeon, *Leib* being the animated and sensitive body (which may be rendered by *soma*). The *Tetraktys* consists of two polarities: soma-soul, which are on an equal level and complement one another, and spirit-body, the latter being subordinated to the former. These four principles are held together by the *Gemüt*, which is the living center of the *Tetraktys* and, in Troxler's words, "The true individuality of Man, by means of which he is in himself most authentically, the hearth of his selfhood, the most alive centrepoint of his existence." The course of life is a successive emergence of higher degrees of consciousness. The young child first learns to distinguish between the ego and the non-ego and then between the soul and the soma. After the soul disengages itself from the soma, man may satisfy himself with a purely intellectual knowledge, but he is also given the freedom to choose to reach a third level of development, which is that of the spirit, thus opening himself to the divine light. The true aim of philosophy is to make the spirit into an organ of knowledge through which man may become aware of higher spiritual realities; what Troxler called anthroposophy. There are definite similarities between Troxler's doctrine of the development of the human mind and Jung's concept of individuation, as well as between Troxler's *Gemüt* and Jung's *Selbst* (self).

Carl Gustav Carus (1789–1869), a physician and painter, is noted for his work on animal psychology and on physiognomy, and particularly for his book *Psyche,* which was the first attempt to give a complete and objective theory on unconscious psychological life. The book begins with the following words:

> The key to the knowledge of the nature of the soul's conscious life lies in the realm of the unconscious. This explains the difficulty, if not the impossibility, of getting a real comprehension of the soul's secret. If it were an absolute impossibility to find the unconscious in the conscious, then Man should despair of ever getting a knowledge of his soul, that is a knowledge of himself. But if this impossibility is only apparent, then the first task of a science of the soul is to state how the spirit of Man is able to descend into these depths.[64]

Carus defines psychology as the science of the soul's development from the unconscious to the conscious. According to him, human life is divided into three periods: (1) A pre-embryonic period in which the individual merely exists as a tiny cell within the mother's ovary. (2) the embryonic period; through fecundation, in which the individual is suddenly wakened from his long sleep, and the formative unconscious develops. (3) After birth, in which the formative unconscious continues to direct the individual's growth and the function of his organs. Consciousness arises gradually, but it always remains under the influence of the unconscious and the individual periodically returns to it in his sleep.

Carus distinguishes three layers of the unconscious: (1) The *general absolute unconscious,* which is totally and permanently inaccessible to our consciousness. (2) The *partial absolute unconscious* to which belong the processes of formation, growth, and activity of the organs. This part of the unconscious exerts an indirect influence on our emotional life. Carus describes the "districts of the soul" such as respiration, blood circulation, liver activity; each of these districts has an emotional tonality of its own and contributes to the constitution of the vital feeling underlying emotional life. Conscious thoughts and feelings also exert a slow and mediate action on the partial absolute unconscious; this explains why a person's physiognomy can reflect his conscious personality. (3) The *relative or secondary unconscious* comprehending the totality of feelings, perceptions, and representations, which were ours at one time or other and which have become unconscious.

Carus ascribes the following characteristics to the unconscious: (1) The unconscious has "prometheic" and "epimetheic" aspects, it is turned toward the future and toward the past but does not know of the present. (2) The unconscious is in constant movement and transformation; conscious thoughts or feelings, when becoming unconscious, undergo continuous modification and maturation. (3) The unconscious is indefatigable; it does not need periodic rest, whereas our conscious life needs rest and mental restoration which it finds by plunging into the unconscious. (4) The unconscious is basically sound and does not know disease; one of its functions is "the healing power of Nature." (5) The unconscious works along its own ineluctable laws and has no freedom. (6) The unconscious possesses its own inborn wisdom; in it, there is no trial and error, no learning. (7) Without being consciously aware of it, we remain in connection through the unconscious with the rest of the world, particularly with our fellow-beings.

Carus distinguishes four forms of interpersonal relationships: (1) from the conscious to the conscious; (2) from the conscious to the unconscious; (3) from the unconscious to the conscious; (4) from the unconscious to the unconscious. He formulated the principle that the individual unconscious is related to the unconscious of all men.

There are, said Carus, three kinds of dreams, each one belonging to one of the three "life circles" (*Lebenskreise*): mineral, vegetal, and animal. It is noteworthy that he attempted to interpret dreams according to their form rather than to their content.

Carus' *Psyche* represents the life-work of a physician and keen observer of the human mind. It shows the shape reached by the theory of the unconscious at the end of the Romantic period, before the positivistic trend became dominant. Carus was the source of Von Hartmann and of the later philosophers of the unconscious, as well as of Scherner's theory of dreams. His notion of an autonomous, creative, compensatory function of the unconscious was to be emphasized half a century later by C. G. Jung.

Arthur Schopenhauer (1788–1860) had published his main work, *The World as Will and Representation* in 1819, long before Carus had published his *Psyche,* but it remained unnoticed by philosophers and critics alike for twenty years. Only after 1850 did Schopenhauer attain fame. He became the master of Wagner and Nietzsche, and his work achieved great success in the 1880's.[65] Kant distinguished the world of phenomena and the world of the thing in itself, which is inaccessible to our knowledge. Schopenhauer called the phenomena representations, and the thing in itself will, equating the will with the unconscious as conceived by some of the Romantics; Schopenhauer's will had the dynamic character of blind, driving forces, which not only reigned over the universe, but also conducted man. Thus, man is an irrational being guided by internal forces, which are unknown to him and of which he is scarcely aware. Schopenhauer compared consciousness to the surface of the earth, the inside of which is unknown to us. These irrational forces consist of two instincts: the instinct of conservation and the sexual instinct, the latter by far the more important of the two. He compares the sexual instinct to the innermost features (*innere Zug*) of a tree of which the individual is but a leaf, drawing its nourishment from the tree and participating in its nourishment.[66] "Man is incarnate sexual instinct,

since he owes his origin to copulation and the wish of his wishes is to
copulate." Sexual instinct is the highest affirmation of life, "the most
important concern of Man and animal". . . "In conflict with it, no motivation, however strong, would be sure of victory". . . "The sexual act is
the unceasing thought of the unchaste and the involuntary, the ever recur-
ring daydream of the chaste, the key of all intimations, an ever ready matter for fun, an inexhaustible source of jokes." But, it is "a delusion of the
individual, who believes to care for his welfare whereas he is fulfilling the
aim of the Species." This is an example of how we are deluded by the will.
The will conducts our thoughts and is the secret antagonist of the intellect.
The will can compel man to prevent the intrusion of thoughts that would
be unpleasant to him: that which is contrary to our wish we cannot perceive. In a famous paragraph about "insanity" (*Wahnsinn*), Schopenhauer
explained it with the occurrence of repression: "The Will's opposition to
let what is repellent to it come to the knowledge of the intellect is the spot
through which insanity can break through into the spirit." [67]

The similarities between certain essential teachings of Schopenhauer and
Freud have been shown by Cassirer,[68] Scheler,[69] and particularly by
Thomas Mann.[70] Mann, who during his youth had been deeply immersed
in the metaphysics of Schopenhauer, declares that, while becoming acquainted with Freud's psychoanalysis, he "was filled with a sense of recognition and familiarity." He felt that Freud's description of the id and the
ego was "to a hair" Schopenhauer's description of the will and the intellect, translated from metaphysics into psychology. Dream psychology,
the great importance given to sexuality and the whole complexus of thought
"is a philosophical anticipation of analytic conceptions, to a quite astonishing extent." Actually, if Freud's psychoanalysis has sometimes been
called a "pansexualism," that term would apply much more to Schopenhauer's teaching. The main difference is that Schopenhauer viewed the
sexual instinct above all as a trick of the will at the service of generation,
while Freud viewed that instinct in itself and seldom spoke of its relation
with procreation. Luis S. Granjel says that Schopenhauer and Freud have
three main points in common: an irrationalistic conception of man, the
identification of the general life impulse with the sexual instinct, and their
radical anthropological pessimism.[71] These similarities, according to
Granjel, cannot be explained only in terms of a direct influence of Schopenhauer upon Freud, but also in terms of the similarity in the personalities
of these two thinkers: a reaction against the contemporary bourgeois society on the part of those men who, for different reasons, were permeated
with resentment.

The speculations and findings of German romantic philosophy in the
first two-thirds of the nineteenth century culminated in 1869 in Eduard
von Hartmann's famous *Philosophy of the Unconscious*.[72] The will of
Boehme, Schelling, and Schopenhauer finally took the much more ap-

propriate name of unconscious. Von Hartmann's unconscious apparently acquired the qualities of Hegel's idée; thus it is a highly intelligent although blind dynamism underlying the visible universe. Von Hartmann described three layers of the unconscious: (1) the absolute unconscious, which constitutes the substance of the universe and is the source of the other forms of the unconscious; (2) the physiological unconscious, which like Carus' unconscious, is at work in the origin, development, and evolution of living beings, including man; (3) the relative or psychological unconscious, which lies at the source of our conscious mental life. The main interest of the *Philosophy of the Unconscious* lies not so much in its philosophical theories as in its wealth of supporting material. Von Hartmann collected numerous and relevant facts concerning perception, the association of ideas, wit, emotional life, instinct, personality traits, individual destiny, as well as the role of the unconscious in language, religion, history, and social life.

Romantic Medicine

Though Romantic medicine has often been regarded as a chaos of vague and confused speculations, it contained, according to Leibbrand, quite a number of valuable insights.[73] The nature of illness, to which they brought dozens of ingenious theories, was foremost in its preoccupations. Novalis, himself a sickly man, said that diseases should be the most important concern of man, that "they are perhaps the most interesting stimulant and food for our thinking and acting, and that we know very little about the art of utilizing them.[74] He added that there are two kinds of hypochondriasis, a common one and a sublime one, and that the latter could provide an approach to the investigation of the soul. This leads one to believe that Novalis had anticipated the concept of creative illness. Actually, there is no doubt that such a thing as creative illness exists from which a person emerges with a new vision of the world or with a new philosophy, as we have seen when speaking of the shamans and will see when speaking of Fechner, Nietzsche, Freud, and Jung.[75] Mental hygiene was also one of the Romantics' preoccupations, although, in contrast to the optimistic outlook of the Enlightenment, it had now acquired a somewhat pessimistic connotation. Feuchtersleben, in his book *Dietetics of the Soul*, says that every person harbors a frightful seed of insanity, and he advises; "Struggle, with the help of all cheerful and active forces, to hinder its awakening."[76] No means are more efficient to tame the emotions than gaining an understanding of them; also, one should immerse oneself into absorbing work, which demands the total commitment of all of one's forces. Any slackening means sickness or death.

The Romantics' interest in mental illness was furthered by the fact that in that period, numerous mental institutions were opened and began to be headed by specialized physicians who lived constantly with their patients. A specific kind of psychiatry developed in this milieu. Asylum physicians, being quite independent, could each develop views concerning the nature and treatment of mental illness, which may account for the originality and audacity of those pioneers, whether they belonged to the school of the *Physiker* (organicists) or to that of the *Psychiker* (who emphasized the psychological roots of mental illness). Some of those asylum physicians were strongly influenced by the Romantic tide. Unfortunately, it is difficult to explore this forgotten chapter of psychiatric history: the writings of these men have become scarce and are often written in obsolete terminology.[77] But whoever studies them is surprised to see to what extent they had anticipated notions that we believe today to be quite new. We will restrict ourselves to four of these pioneers: Reil, Heinroth, Ideler, and Neumann.

Johann Christian Reil (1759–1813) was a student of brain anatomy and one of the foremost clinicians of his time. Kirchhoff calls him "the conscious discoverer and founder of rational psychotherapy." The great interest and particularly the modern character of his work have been pointed out by Ernest Harms.[78] Under the title *Rhapsodies on the application of the psychic cure method to mental disorders*, Reil elaborates an entire program for the treatment of mental illness with existing methods as well as with others of which he proposes the introduction.

First, the name of the institutions must be changed: the notorious word *Tollhaus* (lunacy asylum) must be replaced by "hospital for psychic cure-methods" or such like, and placed under the threefold direction of an administrator, a physician, and a psychologist. The hospital must be located in a pleasant landscape and subdivided into pavilions and should have a farm on its grounds. It must be conceived in two sections which differ radically in their aim and construction: one, devoted to those patients who are obviously incurable, should aim not only at the protection of society, but should strive to make life as pleasant as possible for the patients and keep them occupied. The other, of a quite different character, should be devoted to the cure of mental illness and neurosis. Reil distinguishes three types of cures: chemical cures (which include dietetics and drug treatment); mechanical and physical cures (which include surgery); and psychic cures which, Reil emphasizes, is a branch of therapy in its own right as important as surgery or pharmacology. For those cases where a physical cause underlies the mental disturbance, appropriate medical cure will be given. Psychic cure must be based on a precise system of "practical empirical psychology." The cure method must be adapted to the specific needs of each patient while stemming from a general system. Reil distinguishes three classes of psychic means of cure: (1) Bodily stimulations aiming at a modification of the general bodily feeling. These stimulations, depending on the case, will be pleasurable or unpleasurable in order to correct what we call today the "vital tonus." (2) Sensory stimulations, including a whole gammut of procedures that would be called today "reeducation of perception." Every one of the senses is the object of reeducation through specific methods of training. Among these methods is that of the "therapeutic theater" in which the employees of the institution will play various roles, and where the patients will also be given parts in accordance with their specific conditions. (3) The method of "signs and symbols" is a kind of shool based on reading and writing. It also includes a variety of occupational therapies comprising physical work, exercise, and art therapy.[79]

Ernest Harms considers Reil's conception of mental illness "the most magnificent psychological biological philosophy I have ever encountered."[80] Reil did not believe that all mental diseases were entirely psychic: he gave due consideration to the organic substratum, but he maintained that there were also diseases of the psyche caused by a loosening or disintegration of the *Gemeingefühl,* that is the basic feeling of "centricity" of our mental life underlying the conscious ego. A large number of psychopathological manifestations are described within that frame of reference.

Johann Christian August Heinroth (1773–1843) is often ridiculed today as the man who proclaimed that the main cause of mental illness was sin. In fact, it would suffice to replace the term "sin" by that of "guilt feeling" to make him appear almost contemporary. Heinroth was a learned man, a foremost clinician, and the author of a complete theory of the human mind in health and sickness. Among his many works is his *Lehrbuch,* a textbook that begins with a description of the human mind in its normal state, and of the emergence of degrees of consciousness, first that of *Selbstbewusstein* (self-consciousness) through a confrontation with external reality; then that of *Bewusstsein* (consciousness) proper, through a confrontation with self-consciousness; and finally *Gewissen* (conscience), a "stranger within our ego."[81] Conscience originates neither in the external world nor in the ego, but in an *Über-Uns* (over-us), which Heinroth seems to equate with reason and a way to God. According to him, health is freedom and mental illness is a reduction or loss of freedom. This loss of freedom is a result of *Ich-Sucht* (self-love) and of the various passions. Delusion is a disturbance of the intellect, even though its cause lies in passion. The second volume of Heinroth's textbook contains a systematic description of his psychotherapeutic methods: The first step consists of determining to what degree a pathological state requires therapeutic help, and then to evolve a specific therapeutic plan that will consider not only the symptoms but also the sex, age, occupation, personality, and economic and social conditions of the patient. This plan of treatment should also extend to the patient's family and surroundings. One main concern is to abstain from any unnecessary or dangerous treatment. Heinroth then describes in a detailed and practical manner the various treatments that should be given to the excited and the depressed patients as well as to patients of all conditions. Once again, the reader marvels at the modern character of many of these concepts.[82]

Karl Wilhelm Ideler (1795–1860) developed Stahl's and Langermann's teaching of the paramount importance of passions as a cause of mental illness. A prolific writer, Ideler's published works include a textbook of about 1800 pages, the first part of which is devoted to a description of the human mind with special emphasis given to the emotional life.[83] Each emotional drive is capable of unlimited development, and every passion is the beginning of an emotional illness, so that psychotherapy should be started at this point.[84] A basic law, taken over by Ideler from Stahl, which he calls the Law of Life is that the human being is in a constant process of self-destruction and self-reconstruction, and, in order to keep a correct balance, he must constantly appropriate the needed elements from the external world. In the second part of his book, Ideler expounds the pathogenesis of mental diseases. He depicts in detail the origin of the various passions, their struggle against each other, and the destructive effect of solitude and of the ungratified need for activity. A large part in the psychogenesis of mental illness is ascribed to ungratified sexual feelings. Nature, Ideler says, has willed that the strongest feeling of which human beings are capable is sexual love, in order to increase their potentialities toward a freer and richer development. Hence the bitter struggle resulting from nongratification. He describes the disconsolate condition of the loving virgin who has to replace her need for warmth with frivolous social amusements. "Before demanding renunciation on her part, train her in self-control; let her strengthen herself with energetic action through the accomplishment of duty, and provide her with substitutes for the deprivation of the most beautiful and fervent emotions." Hysterical attacks, Ideler adds, are nothing but a struggle of the soul with itself. Mental disease, however, is never the result of one cause alone. Predisposition plays a part, as does the discrepancy between overwhelming desire and restricted reality. Hence, disgusted with reality, man takes flight into fantasy where he can revel in the measureless joy of his dream world, or justify to himself his sufferings in horrifyingly distorted images.[85] Ideler insists that the genesis of delusion can be traced back to earliest childhood (*bis in die früheste Kindheit*). With regard to treatment, he firmly believes in the possibility of a psychotherapy of psychoses. However, he contends that "the cure of delusion can be accomplished only by psychic self-activity which the physician should but stimulate and direct." This direction entails a well-organized hospital and the well-balanced and devoted personalities of the doctor and of his co-workers.

One of the last representatives of this psychiatric trend was Heinrich Wilhelm Neumann (1814–1884), whose textbook also starts with an original system of medical psychology.[86] There are no chance happenings in mental life, Neumann says. As does Ideler, he holds that life is a constant process of self-destruction and reconstruction—to the former belongs forgetting, to the latter memory. In the course of his development, man acquires an increasing capacity for self-control, which can be equated with the individual "degree of freedom." With regard to psychopathology, Neumann ascribes the greatest importance to disturbances of the drives (*Triebe*). Instinctual needs express themselves in the consciousness by what Neumann calls the *Aestheses,* which not only have the characteristics of sensation but also of a challenge toward the organism as a whole. *Aesthesis* also acts as a warning of a potential danger, teaching at the same time how the danger should be met. There are instances when the alarm is given but where the *Aesthesis* is "metamorphosed" in such a way that it fails to show how the danger is to be met. The result is anxiety (*Angst*). Neumann emphasizes the relationship between drive and anxiety: "The drive which cannot be gratified becomes anxiety," and he adds that anxiety originates only when vital functions are threatened and when the threat comes to our awareness.[87]

Among the many topics developed by Neumann is that of the clinical manifestations of the sexual instinct originating in mental patients. The following symptoms can be noted: interest for bodily cleanliness or uncleanliness, undoing of one's hair, perpetual washing of one's body or ("what I consider pathologically equivalent") absolute uncleanliness and smearing of one's body, dislike or tearing of clothes, uninhibited relieving oneself in the physician's presence, irritation at female personnel who are called names such as "whores" or accusations of a sexual nature made against female acquaintances, constant talk of marriages other than one's own, frequent spitting, morbid religiosity, and exaggerated interest for the divine service and the pastor. Neumann proclaimed that the physician should not treat diseases, but patients, and that he should treat both body and mind simultaneously. However, the specific cure of mental illness, he added, lies in psychic means.

From the brief discussions of Reil, Heinroth, Ideler, and Neumann we can see each one's originality of thought, and the same is true for a number of their contemporaries.[88] Within the framework of Romantic psychiatry, we find that these men all had a number of features in common. They distrusted psychiatric classifications. Diagnosis, Neumann said, has nothing to do with name-giving; it is finding a key that will make the symptoms intelligible. Each insisted upon the necessity of regarding every individual case as a specific one in its own right. All of them, following the tradition of Stahl and Langermann, distinguished physical and psychic causes of mental illness, but believed that psychic causes were sufficient to cause severe mental illness. However, they differed with regard to the respective importance of the various passions: Heinroth insisted upon the role of "sin" (actually guilt feelings), Guislain on the role of anxiety, Ideler and Neumann on the role of sexual impulses and frustrations.

Each of these men expounded a highly original system of medical psychology. Among other concepts, they developed that of the law of balance between psychic intake and output, thus acknowledging the role of overly intensive stimuli. We recall Neumann's concept of the *Aesthesis* and of the "metamorphoses," and of the connection between ungratified drives and anxiety.

They were all deeply impressed with therapy, particularly with psychotherapy, even for severe mental illness. Reil and Heinroth, devised elaborate systems of psychotherapeutic methods ranging from work to shock therapy, and even to what would today be called psychodrama (Reil).

Unfortunately these men lived in comparative isolation and apparently met with little or no understanding on the part of the public authorities. The mid-century was not over when new scientific concepts arose. The study of brain anatomy became of prime importance, and the work of these pioneers fell into disrepute or oblivion. But anyone acquainted with the work of Reil, Heinroth, Ideler, Neumann, and Guislain will recognize a return to these forgotten sources in many of the discoveries of Bleuler, Freud, Jung, and the newer dynamic psychiatry.

The Epigones of Romanticism: Fechner and Bachofen

After 1850, the philosophy of nature and Romanticism seemed to have completely disappeared. It was the period of positivism and the triumph of the mechanistic *Weltanschauung.* However, Romanticism produced belated representatives, including two who are of particular importance to us: Fechner and Bachofen.

Gustav Theodor Fechner, the son of a Protestant minister, studied medicine in Leipzig, where he remained until his death.[89] His first interest led him to experimental physics. He obtained an unpaid university position and earned his living writing scientific translations and compiling elementary textbooks and popular encyclopedias. From time to time he published brief literary pamphlets under the pseudonym of Dr. Mises. In one, *Comparative Anatomy of the Angels,* Fechner followed the curve of evolution of the animal kingdom, from the amoeba to man and then, by extrapolation, attempted to construct the ideal form of a still higher being, an angel.[90] He concluded that such beings must be spheric, must perceive universal gravitation in the same way as humans perceive light, and communicate with each other by means of a language of luminous signs, much as humans converse with each other by means of an acoustic language. In 1836, Fechner published *The Little Book of Life after Death* under his own name,[91] in which he wrote that human life is divided into three periods: from conception to birth, from birth to death, and after death. Embryonic life is a continuous sleep, present life an oscillation between sleep and waking state, life after death may be a continuous waking state.

In 1833 at the age of thirty-two Fechner married and obtained the post of professor of physics at Leipzig University. In Wundt's words, "from the moment he attained an independent position which would give him freedom for his own work, from that very moment his strength was broken.

His excessive work had exhausted him. He had difficulty in finishing his lectures." During the following six years from 1834 to 1840, Fechner pursued his occupation under considerable strain, and performed experiments on subjective visual phenomena on himself. His eyesight was damaged and in 1840, at the age of 39, Fechner collapsed and had to give up his professional activities for the following three years. In modern nosology Fechner's illness would be termed a severe neurotic depression with hypochondriacal symptoms, possibly complicated by a lesion of the retina resulting from looking directly into the sun. Actually, it can also be considered as an instance of what Novalis called sublime hypochondriasis, a creative illness from which a man emerges with a new philosophical insight and a transformation in his personality.

> During most of his illness, Fechner felt compelled to live in complete seclusion, remaining in a darkened room the walls of which were painted black or wearing a mask on his face so as to shut out the light. He was unable to tolerate most foods, felt no hunger, and ate very little, so that his physical condition became precarious. His cure, according to his own account, occurred in an unusual way. A lady friend of the family dreamed that she was preparing a dish of strongly spiced ham cooked in Rhine wine and lemon juice for him. The following day, she actually did prepare the dish and brought it to him, insisting that he should at least taste it. He did so reluctantly, and felt improved. From that day on, he regularly ate small quantities of this dish and felt his physical strength returning to him. He then started to force his mental faculties back into action, which for one year required a tremendous effort on his part. In his own words, he "felt like a rider trying to subdue a runaway horse." He then had a dream in which he saw the number 77, which he understood to mean that he would be cured on the seventy-seventh day, and, he says, this actually happened.
>
>   The three-year period of depression was followed by a shorter one of elation. Fechner enjoyed an increasing feeling of well-being, expressed ideas of grandeur, felt as though he had been chosen by God and was now able to solve all of the world's riddles. All of this culminated in his conviction that he had discovered a universal principle as fundamental for the spiritual world as Newton's principle of gravitation was for the physical world. Fechner called it *das Lustprinzip* (the principle of pleasure): his hypomaniac euphoria had been transformed into a philosophical concept. Opening his eyes in his garden for the first time after his three years of darkness, he was struck with the beauty of flowers; he understood that they had a soul, and this led to his book *Nanna, or the Soul of Plants.* [92]

After his recovery, Fechner lived in perfect health for the remainder of his life, but a noteworthy metamorphosis had taken place within him. Prior to his illness, he had been a physicist who (according to Wundt) despised the philosophy of nature. Now, he had himself become a philosopher of that school. He then exchanged his professorship of physics at

Leipzig University for that of philosophy. His first series of lectures was devoted to the principle of pleasure, and he published them in a small book[93] and in a philosophical journal.[94] Thereafter, Fechner never ceased to develop this concept and to apply it to new fields of psychology.

During the second half of his life, Fechner wrote many well-organized and original treatises, often in a beautiful, lyrical style. Under his old pseudonym of Dr. Mises, he published a collection of the riddles he had composed during his illness.[95] Under his real name, he wrote two of the most typical works of the philosophy of nature: *Nanna,*[96] probably the first monograph devoted to the psychology of plants, an eminently romantic branch of psychology. The following work, *Zend-Avesta,* whose title was borrowed from the sacred books of the ancient Persians, was apparently intended, in Fechner's mind, to be a Bible of the philosophy of nature.[97] Fechner contends that the earth is a living being, of a higher level than man, a level corresponding to that of the angels as he had hypothetically deduced them in his earlier *Comparative Anatomy of the Angels.* All forms of earthly life issue from the living being ("Could a dead mother bear living children?"); this is also the reason why all living creatures are so well adjusted to their physical environment and are complementary to each other. In this living kingdom, man occupies a privileged position: "he was made for the Earth as the Earth was made for him." Discussing the place of the earth within the solar system, Fechner introduces the principles of "stability" and of "repetition." The solar system maintains itself through the fact that identical positions and kinds of movements are periodically repeated; the stability thus takes the specific form of repetition. *Zend-Avesta* contains the first hints of the application of the principle of stability and repetition to human physiology and psychology, and the first mention of Fechner's "psychophysical law."

These philosophical works were published in a highly unfavorable period, since the philosophy of nature had become thoroughly unfashionable. However, Fechner never despaired of propagating his philosophy, but, says Wundt, he changed his tactics and turned to experimental psychology. For many years Fechner had been preoccupied with the relationship between the physical and the spiritual worlds. He felt that there had to be a general law governing this relationship, and he tried to discover what mathematical formula would be the most probable one for such a law. According to his own account, that formula, which he called the psychophysical law, occurred to him suddenly on the morning of October 22, 1850, in time to enable him to mention it briefly in his book *Zend-Avesta.* He now proceeded to devise a long series of experiments to ascertain whether this law was true, and was absorbed by this research for the following ten years. His findings were contained in the two volumes of the *Psychophysics* published in 1860, which aroused considerable interest and were the starting point of modern experimental psychology.[98]

In a critical survey of Darwin's theory on the evolution of the species, Fechner formulated his "principle of the tendency to stability," a universal finalistic principle contended to be complementary to the causal principle.[99] This was after the principle of pleasure and the "psychophysical basic law," the third great universal principle enunciated by him. In 1876, Fechner published his work on experimental aesthetics, an attempt to base aesthetics on experimental research, and to understand it from the viewpoint of the principle of pleasure-unpleasure.[100] He also applied that principle to the psychology of wit and jokes. In 1879, at the age of 78, he published *The Day-View in Contrast to the Night-View* in which his own pantheistic vision of the world (the "day-view") is opposed to the dry, disconsolate conception of contemporary materialistic scientism (the "night-view").[101]

In 1879 the first institute of experimental psychology was opened in Leipzig by Fechner's great follower Wilhelm Wundt. Leipzig, Fechner's adopted city, had become the center of the new science and students came there from all over the world. Fechner himself was by now a legendary figure, his bald head crowned with long white hair, his old-fashioned clothes, and his proverbial absent-mindedness. When Fechner died at the age of eighty-six, in 1887, he had won belated fame and was hailed as the father of experimental psychology.

By the end of the nineteenth century, it seemed that Fechner would be remembered only as a pioneer of experimental psychology and as the author of the "fundamental psychophysical law." Ironically, however, it was from Fechner's philosophy of nature that Freud borrowed several basic concepts that he incorporated into his metapsychology. Fechner's influence on psychoanalysis is evidenced by the fact that Freud quoted him in *The Interpretation of Dreams, The Wit and the Unconscious,* and *Beyond the Pleasure Principle.*[102] Freud took from Fechner the concept of mental energy, the "topographical" concept of the mind, the principle of pleasure-unpleasure, the principle of constancy, and the principle of repetition. A large part of the theoretical framework of psychoanalysis would hardly have come into being without the speculations of the man whom Freud called the great Fechner.

Johann Jakob Bachofen (1815–1887), the promulgator of the theory of matriarchy, was born in Basel, Switzerland, in 1815 into an old and wealthy patrician family.[103] Bachofen studied law in Berlin, Paris, and Cambridge, but a strong interest in archeology led him to Italy. There, examining the decorations on antique tombs and their representations of the cult of the dead, he began to think that this art contained the symbolic remnants of a forgotten world. After several years spent as a judge and professor of Roman law in Basel, Bachofen resigned from most of his positions in order to devote himself to his favorite studies. Deciphering the symbols of antique art and mythology, he concluded that they expressed the forgotten memory of a period of mankind that had left no historical records, when the power lay in the hands of women, not men. The correct interpretation of these symbols would enable us to reconstruct the social and political features as well as the *Weltanschauung* and the physiognomy of that period of matriarchy, and also of the still more primitive period that had preceded it. This is how Bachofen became, in Turel's words, "the historian of an epoch without history." In 1861, Bachofen published his capital work, *The Law of Mothers,* which met with either indifference or sharp criticism on the part of specialists.[104] Living in Basel, Bachofen, a dignified bewhiskered gentleman with ceremonious manners led the life of a *Privatgelehrter* (private scholar), dividing his time between writing books and studying in Italy and Greece. A bachelor, he had lived in his parents' house until the age of fifty, when he married a beautiful young cousin aged twenty. In his native city, he was considered a slightly eccentric old scholar. When he died in 1887, his fame had just begun to spread throughout the world.

Unknown to Bachofen, the theory of matriarchy had already been anticipated by Joseph François Lafitau (1681–1746), a Jesuit scholar who spent five years among the Iroquois.[105] Father Julien Garnier, who had spent sixty years of his life with the Algonquin, Huron, and Iroquois, told Lafitau all that he knew about their customs and social organization. Property and the real power belonged to women, who delegated part of their power in civilian and military matters to the chiefs. Lafitau compared this system with that of the ancient Lycians and several other ancient civilizations, and contended that gynecocracy had once been widespread among ancient Mediterranean and Asiatic populations. Another French scholar, the Abbé Desfontaines described, in a novel purporting to relate the adventures of Gulliver's son, an imaginary island of Babilary, where the power resided in the hands of women who used it in the same manner as do men in most contemporary civilizations.[106] The book contained an appendix allegedly written by a scholar, who, having read the story of Gulliver Junior, found that there was nothing on his island that was new to anyone who was acquainted with the history of the ancient Lycians and Scythians.

In Bachofen's view, matriarchy was more than merely a social and political system. It was a wider notion involving religion, *Weltanschauung,* and the totality of the culture, related to every possible aspect of life. Furthermore, Bachofen contended that the development of mankind had undergone three stages: "hetairism," matriarchy, and patriarchy, each of which had retained symbolic remains of the preceding one.

The first stage, hetairism, was one of sexual promiscuity, where women were defenseless and exposed to the brutality of men, and where children did not know their fathers. It was also the period of "tellurism," the symbol of which is the muddy swamp, and its divinity the goddess Aphrodite (Venus).

The second stage, matriarchy, was established after thousands of years of struggle. Women founded the family and agriculture, and wielded social and political power. The mothers favored a social system of general freedom, equality, and peaceful relations between citizens. The main virtue resided in love for the mother; matricide was considered the most heinous of all crimes. Matriarchy was also a materialistic civilization that praised education of the body above education of the intellect and where practical values prevailed and found their expression in the development of agriculture and the building of huge town walls. Its highest divinity was the goddess Demeter (Ceres). Among its symbolic features were the primacy of night. Time was computed according to the number of nights, battles were fought, counsel was given, justice was rendered, and cults were held during the night. Other features included primacy of the moon, the earth, the dead; preference was given to sisters over brothers; to the last-born over the older children; finally the preference for the left side over the right side.

Bachofen considered the shift from matriarchy to patriarchy a progress toward a higher stage of civilization. This transition took place after bitter struggles, of which Bachofen believed to have found numerous proofs in Greek mythology. There had also been temporary relapses from patriarchy to matriarchy (as before from matriarchy to hetairism). Bachofen interpreted the phenomena of Amazonism and the Dionysian cult from that point of view.

Amazonism, as expressed in the ancient legends of the Amazons, was a kind of feminine imperialism (said Turel), which occurred during the old struggle between hetairism and matriarchy, and later as a degeneration of matriarchy during its struggle against emerging patriarchy.

The cult of Dionysus, which had been an episode in the struggle between hetairism and matriarchy, occurred as a rebellion of women against patriarchy. The Dionysian system favored the fine arts, but in contrast to the chaste discipline that prevailed in Demeteric matriarchy, it brought forth moral corruption, and, under the pretense of emancipating women, it actually led them to be exploited by men. It was a system favored by tyrants.

Once the patriarchal system had been solidly established, the memory of matriarchy became so intolerable to men that it was "forgotten." (We recall that a similar occurrence of collective forgetting had already been invoked by Boulanger in his theory about the destruction of a former civilization by the flood). But the memory of matriarchy survived in the form of symbols and myths, and according to Bachofen indirectly inspired some of the great masterpieces of Greek literature. Aeschylus' trilogy, the *Orestia,* was interpreted by Bachofen as the symbolic representation of the victory of matriarchy, the revenge of the patriarchal principle, and the latter's final triumph. In the myth of Oedipus, Bachofen considers the sphinx to be the symbol of the old hetairistic stage. By killing the sphinx, Oedipus contributed to the establishment of matriarchy in Thebes under the scepter of Queen Jocasta, but the ensuing disaster meant the collapse of matriarchy, which was to be replaced by patriarchy.[107]

Bachofen described patriarchy as a complete reversal of the matriarchic political and social organization, and of its religious and philosophical principles. Patriarchy favors individual independence and isolates men from each other, but brings them to a higher spiritual level. Human beings first love their mother, and come to love their father only at a later stage. Motherhood implies a more direct and material relationship with the child because of pregnancy and breast feeding. Paternal love rises above such features and is a more abstract principle. This was expressed in law by the procedure of adoption and by the concept of "spiritual procreation." It was also expressed in the symbolic shifting from night to day, from noon to sun, from earth to sky, from left to right side. Patriarchy's highest divinity is Apollo, the god of light and the fine arts.

The lack of success of Bachofen's work was due in part to the poor organization of his book, his numerous digressions, and the long Latin and Greek quotations for which he gave no translation. Above all it was because of the fact that his theories shook the previously unchallenged notion that the patriarchal family had been a permanent institution throughout the history of mankind. In Basel, not even a scholar such as Jakob Burckhardt understood these theories. However, old Bachofen found an admirer in the young Nietzsche, who adopted his concepts of the Dionysian and Apollonian civilizations (with the difference that Nietzsche considered Dionysian civilization a virile rather than a feminine one).[108] In his first philosophic work, *The Origin of Tragedy,* Nietzsche explained the birth of Greek tragedy as resulting from the fusion of two streams, the "Dionysian" impetuous inspiration and the "Apollonian" principle of order and perfection (much as Freud later explained the origin of the work of art by the fusion of the principle of pleasure and the principle of reality).[109]

But historians, sociologists, and anthropologists alike ignored Bachofen for a long time, with a few exceptions such as Lewis Morgan, the father of American ethnology, who had already given an excellent description of the matriarchic system prevailing among certain American Indian tribes and upon discovering Bachofen's theories, quoted him abundantly in his book *Ancient Society.*[110] Morgan was instrumental in having scientific societies and the government of the United States send a gift of numerous books dealing with the American Indians to Bachofen. Bachofen's work later inspired the concept of *Kulturkreis,* popular among German anthropologists (Wilhelm Schmidt, Koppers, and Gräbner), and attempts of certain prehistorians to reconstruct past stages of culture, one of which was matriarchy. Friedrich Engels gave a socialistic interpretation of Bachofen's work in his *Origins of the Family*.[111] Mathilde and Mathias Vaerting endeavored to distinguish between a man-dominated and a woman-dominated society, and concluded that what we call the male and female characters correspond only to the character of the dominating and the dominated sex, so that, according to them, women in a woman-dominated society would have the so-called "male character," and vice-versa.[112] Another socialist theoretician, August Bebel, explained that women had been the first human beings to be enslaved[113] Meanwhile, Bachofen had also been interpreted by Elisée Reclus and by Bakunin in the sense of their anarchistic ideology, and he even became popular among suffragettes.

Unexpectedly, Bachofen's fame reached a wider public at the beginning of the twentieth century because of a group of Neo-Romantic poets, philosophers, and artists of Munich who called themselves the *Kosmiker*[114] They became enthusiastic about Bachofen's descriptions of previous cultures and about his method of interpreting symbols. They proclaimed him a prophet and named him the mythologist of Romanticism.[115] Chosen texts of his works were published under their influence, and his ideas, thus propagated, eventually reached wider circles. Although almost none of Bachofen's works has been translated into other languages, many of his concepts became popular and are to be found (in a more or less distorted form) in numerous publications by historians, ethnologists, sociologists, political writers, psychologists, and psychiatrists, mostly without reference to his name.

The influence of Bachofen's ideas reached psychiatric circles through various channels, and his influence on dynamic psychiatry has been immense. Turel pointed to certain similarities in the basic concepts of Bachofen and Freud.[116] Bachofen, he wrote, discovered the phenomenon of repression half a century before Freud. One could add that he had also found the phenomenon of reaction formation: he pointed out, in the pictures of battles with the Amazons, that the women warriors were always shown as defeated, wounded, and killed. Bachofen also asserted that, if the Romans destroyed Etruscan culture to its last remains, it was because of their excessive fear and hatred of Etruscan matriarchy. There is a great similarity, Turel says further, between Bachofen and Freud in their concepts of interpreting symbols. Both claim that there is a limit beyond which the memory of the individual or of mankind cannot reach, and this is where Bachofen reconstructs mankind's history by interpreting myths, and Freud the individual's history by interpreting symptoms. Baeumler pointed out that (long before Nietzsche and Freud) Bachofen had upset the system of values of nineteenth-century bourgeoisie by showing that the realm of sexual life was not originally subordinated to moral values, but that it had unsuspected dimensions and an elaborate symbolism of its own.[117]

The comparisons between Bachofen and Freud could be carried further. From thoughts sometimes expressed by Bachofen, it would seem that he had the notion that the stages of evolution he described for society as a whole were also valid for the individual. Should this thought be followed through and transposed from society to the individual, one would obtain the following picture:

BACHOFEN	FREUD
"Hetairic" period of primitive promiscuity	Infantile period of "polymorphous perversion"
Matriarchy: domination of the "Mothers", gynecocracy	Pre-oedipal, "incestuous" period, strong attachment to the mother
Dionysian period	Phallic stage
Myths of Orestes, and Oedipus, symbolizing the shifting from matriarchy to patriarchy	Oedipus complex
Patriarchy	Genital adult stage
Repression of the memory of matriarchy	"Infantile amnesia"
Myths	Screen memories, symptoms

Bachofen's concept of the origin of Amazonism could also be compared with Freud's theory of the origin of female homosexuality.

Bachofen's influence reached Alfred Adler through the intermediaries, Engels and Bebel. Adler contends that the present oppression of women by men was an overcompensation of the male against a previous stage of female domination. Man internalizes the notion of the ancestral struggle between the sexes. According to Adler, the neurotic, being handicapped by a fear of women, develops within himself a "virile protest," so that he is, in his neurosis, the plaything of that struggle between the male and female principles.

As for C. G. Jung, he most probably had read Bachofen's main works, and his teaching is filled with concepts that may at least partly be ascribed to Bachofen's influence, such as those of the Anima and Animus, the "old wise man," and the "magna mater."

Mid-Century Crisis

Powerful social, political, and cultural transformations took place during the nineteenth century. These transformations did not come about consistently, but rather in cycles of acceleration and deceleration. The greatest crisis occurred in the mid-century; its most conspicuous aspect was the revolution of 1848 and its subsequent repression that shook Europe. But it extended over all other fields of human activity, and its consequences were decisive even for the fate of dynamic psychiatry.

Many changes had taken place during the first half of the century. After its inception in England, the Industrial Revolution had expanded all over Europe and North America, resulting in an increase in the forces of production, industrial output, volume of commercial transactions, and in the creation of new means of transportation. Parallel to the Industrial Revolution was a considerable increase in the birthrate of the European population. The comparatively poor conditions in which the peasants lived caused many of them to migrate to the urban centers. The general process of urbanization was particularly marked in France. Paris absorbed the best of the economic, political, and intellectual life of the nation. The combined effect of urbanization and industrialization resulted in the emergence of a new social class: the proletarian "masses," who became the fertile ground for the spread of socialism. After Owen and Saint-Simon, who were the first pioneers of that doctrine, there came between 1830 and 1848 a new generation of men such as Proudhon, who were of generous inspiration but of often vague ideas, and who were later called utopian socialists. The *Communist Manifesto,* published in 1848 by Karl Marx and Friedrich Engels, marked a new turning point, and after 1860 the socialist movement identified more and more with the ideology and the movement created by those two men.

As a consequence of the demographic change, masses of Europeans streamed into the North American countries, and to Argentina, Australia, and Siberia. Countries unfit for mass immigration were opened up by the white man for their exploitation.[118] These industrial, demographic, and scientific developments and the rapid political and economic conquest of the earth gave the white man optimism, self-confidence, and aggressiveness which belonged to the Western culture of the second half of the nineteenth century.

The bourgeoisie, the leading class and creator and operator of large-scale industry was now becoming fearful of the new growing class, the proletariat. Socialism became the nightmare of the bourgeoisie.

The world was divided more and more into large sovereign, independent nations. England was the leading power and the center of the British Empire. France was second, while Germany and Italy were still striving for their national unity. Some concern was being expressed about the new rising nations, the United States and Russia. In 1840, Alexis de Tocqueville prophesied that they would suddenly emerge as the two leading powers who would some day dominate the world and share it between them.[119] In 1869, Bachofen foretold that the historian of the twentieth century would speak only about America and Russia, and that old Europe's role would be restricted to that of teacher to the new masters.[120] But such ideas were hardly taken seriously. The nationalistic ferment that had been stimulated by Romanticism was beginning to shake the great multinational empires, Austria, Russia, and Turkey. The revolution of 1848 gave further proof of the strength of national aspirations.

Meanwhile, a new philosophy had emerged that was to become increasingly popular, that of positivism. Its origin can be traced back to the French Encyclopedists of the eighteenth century and particularly to Condorcet, who contended that the progress of the human mind would be achieved through the progress of science. The new philosophy, which had been inaugurated at the dawn of the nineteenth century by Saint-Simon, was systematized by Auguste Comte, his disciple Littré in France, and by John Stuart Mill and Herbert Spencer in England. Positivism's basic principle was the cult of facts; the positivists did not search for the unknowable, the thing in itself, the absolute, but for the kind of certitude afforded by experimental science and for constant laws such as laws of physics. Positivism rejects any speculation akin to the philosophy of nature. Another feature of positivism is its interest in applied science and its search for the useful. Following the line of the Enlightenment, it is concerned with man as a social being. It was Auguste Comte who created the word "sociology" and who established the foundations of that science, which he divided into static and dynamic sociology.

These were the main tendencies that were slowly working their way through the first half of the century and were then precipitated by the mid-century crisis. Its most conspicuous aspect was the revolution of 1848. This revolution was a political movement with strong emotional overtones. It was greeted with such juvenile enthusiasm throughout Europe that it has been called the spring of the peoples.[121] It was the upsurge of democracy against conservatism, of socialism against the privileges of the bourgeoisie, of oppressed nations against government by foreign powers. In many regards it was a temporary revival of Romanticism and a conflict between generations. In Germany it took on the special aspect of a search for national unity, but the convocation of Parliament in Frankfurt was followed by a lamentable failure, with the result that the sought-after unity became a fact only later, through Bismarck and under the Prussian hegemony. Everywhere in continental Europe the revolution started in enthusiasm, was followed by a period of euphoria, and was then defeated, bringing with it the triumph of the political reaction. This resulted in a period of depression among the youth. Many among the most progressive and energetic of European youths, especially in Germany, felt weary of Europe (*Europa-müde*), and emigrated to the United States.

The widespread and collective psychological manifestations that accompanied and followed the 1848 revolution have not been made the object of a systematic investigation. Among its various facets was an increased importance of animal magnetism. In many places psychic epidemics occurred after stage demonstrations. At the same time the great wave of spiritism already mentioned in Chapter 2 swept over the United States and then over England and continental Europe. The connection between the spiritistic epidemics and the 1848 revolution was well understood by Littré, who wrote: "In our epoch of revolutions, considerable upheavals have often disturbed society, filling some with profound fears, others with unlimited hope. The nervous system has become more sensitive (. . .) Such are the circumstances which favoured the contemporary explosion."[122]

The mid-century crisis completed the defeat of Romanticism. The few epigones such as Fechner and Bachofen were sure to be misunderstood. The second half of the century belonged to science and to the belief in science. During the French Revolution and Napoleon's reign, scientists were called upon, perhaps for the first time, to contribute, by the way of their discoveries, to the defense of their countries. This is possibly what inspired certain bold proposals. In 1803, Henri de Saint-Simon proclaimed that science should be organized into a unified body of knowledge and that scientists should be organized into a hierarchic body modeled on the Catholic clergy, under the direction of a Council of Newton.[123] Johann Christian Reil proposed that science should be organized in a military manner as a state institution.[124] Scientists of the various specialties would work in a disciplined manner under the command of their hierarchic superiors and would devote themselves to research in practical and applied sciences. In their leisure time they would be allowed to do research in the pure sciences.

However, the type of scientific organization that prevailed in the nineteenth century was as far from the constructive chaos of the eighteenth century as from the regimented science proposed by Saint-Simon and Reil. Research was now being carried out mainly in universities. Although each university was independent from the others, a relationship between them was assured by a network of scientific societies and scientific journals. One decisive event was the foundation of the University of Berlin (1806), an extremely bold gesture at that time since Prussia had been defeated and ruined. The foundation of the university was intended as a first step toward the regeneration of the nation. It was organized on a high scientific level and at great cost under the leadership of Wilhelm von Humboldt.[125] The University of Berlin soon became the model upon which other German universities were organized and new ones created. It eventually became a standard for all of central Europe. Thus, German science made rapid strides and began to supersede France around the mid-century, and Germany became the world's leading scientific country.

Under the combined influences of positivist philosophy, the concentration of scientific research in universities, and the trend of cultural optimism, Western science was pervaded with an almost religious faith in science that reached more and more layers of the population. Science was considered to gratify man's disinterested thirst for knowledge above all. "Do you believe," asked Nietzsche, "that the sciences could have taken shape and become great if the magicians, the alchemists, the astrologers and the witches had not preceded them? They who had first to create, through their promises and deceitful pretences, the thirst, hunger and taste for hidden and forbidden powers!"[126]

This also meant that science had to prove its efficacy by protecting the life of man, and by overcoming and conquering nature for his benefit. Science was now also a synthesis of tried techniques and had to follow a rigorous methodology of practical efficiency. Furthermore, science was now considered as a unified body of various disciplines and as a treasure of knowledge common to all mankind, from which everyone could benefit as well as contribute. This ruled out the existence of secret sciences and also of those scientific "schools" dependent on specific philosophical systems such as had existed in ancient Greece. Following the tradition of the Enlightenment, positivism claimed that science would solve the riddles of the universe. Only one further step had to be taken before claiming that science would provide a substitute for religion.

It should be said, however, that it has never been easy to find a criterion for what science is and what it is not. Animal magnetism, phrenology, and homeopathy were hailed as wonderful scientific discoveries and as new branches of science. They had thousands of enthusiastic disciples, were at times taught in universities, but throughout the nineteenth century they were dismissed by the majority of scientists.

The universal belief in science often took the shape of a religious faith and produced the mentality that has been called scientism. The scientism trend went so far as to deny the existence of all that was not approachable by scientific methods, and it often merged with atheism. After 1850, a wave of popular books propagating the exclusive belief in science combined it with atheism and sometimes with an oversimplified teaching of materialism. Such were the works of Büchner, Moleschott, and Vogt, and later those of Haeckel.

Whether the belief in science did take that extreme form or whether it remained more moderate, the general optimism remained a characteristic feature until the end of the century and is well illustrated in the novels of Jules Verne, who depicts scientific wonders in a hopeful light. The scientist became a well-known character of society under the stereotype of the *savant*.[127] The *savant* of necessity belongs to a university (outside of which there was almost no science). But he was not just the scholar of former times, he was now a researcher as well as a professor. His most manifest feature was his disinterestedness. Science was to him a religion, and the discovery of truth the goal of that religion, which had its saints and its martyrs. The *savant* was of necessity also a hard worker, absorbed in his research to the point of being absent-minded. Though modesty was not always his chief virtue, he often looked timid, was a poor conversationalist, and had little time for social life (outside of that which was necessary for his legitimate academic ambitions). His emotional life was shrouded in secrecy, his wife was a modest and courageous person, concerned only with his welfare and that of the children, often unable to understand her husband's work but always standing by him. The *savant* believed in "pure" science and felt nothing but contempt for the industrial researcher whose work was applied to practical ends. It was of course known that science could be applied also toward the means of killing, but it was considered an amusing paradox when people such as the anarchist Bakunin[128] or Ernest Renan expressed the idea that science might some day be used for the oppression and destruction of mankind.[129]

The general faith in science was maintained, not only by the positivists' worship but also through the innumerable discoveries and inventions that ceaselessly came to increase that belief, following one another so rapidly that one could, so to speak, see the face of the earth modified under their impact. The progress of medicine and hygiene was changing the conditions of human life, the average length of which had never ceased to increase from the beginning of the nineteenth century. This progress had deep social and biological implications.[130] Finally, the discovery of surgical anesthesia between 1840 and 1850 not only made the progress of surgery possible but eliminated the experience of physical pain, which was furthered by the subsequent discovery of analgesics and sedatives. Man was no longer conditioned to pain as he had been previously, and he became more sensitive and also more fearful of pain.[131] Thus, man at the end of the century was not quite the same biological being as he had been at its beginning, and it is therefore not surprising that he did not have quite the same psychopathology.

The New Doctrines: Darwin and Marx

The great sociological and political changes that took place in the Western world during the nineteenth century and more particularly after 1850 resulted in a need for new ideologies. Romanticism seemed to have completely collapsed. The Enlightenment never regained the prestige it had enjoyed at the end of the eighteenth century; however, it did remain sufficiently strong to bring forth the emancipation of the serfs in Russia and the slaves in the European colonies and in the United States. However, the spirit of the Enlightenment was increasingly countered by new cultural trends. The philosophy of the Industrial Revolution, free enterprise, competition, the opening up of new countries and the fierce struggle for world markets, found a seemingly scientific rationalization in *Darwinism*, whereas *Marxism* provided a philosophical basis for the socialist parties that arose from the development of a growing industrial proletariat and the intensification of the class struggle. These two doctrines, Darwinism and Marxism, exerted an overwhelming influence after 1860, an influence that made itself felt in all areas, including dynamic psychiatry.

CHARLES DARWIN (1809–1882) Charles Darwin first made himself known as a gifted young scientist who, in his capacity of naturalist, participated in the circumnavigation made by the *Beagle,* a boat whose mission was to make geodesic and cartographic inquiries of coastal areas in the southern hemisphere.[132] The result of Darwin's observations during those five years of travel around the world (1831–1836) established him at once as one of the eminent naturalists of his time. A few years later his poor health forced him into seclusion on his property near London, where he devoted the few daily hours during which he felt well enough to work to the natural sciences. In October 1838, Darwin chanced to read Malthus' *Essay on the Principle of Population* in which the "struggle for existence" was conceived as a principle ruling the development of human populations. It occurred to Darwin that the "struggle for existence" could also provide an explanation for the natural selection from which the progress and transformation of natural species originate. He wrote brief outlines of that theory in 1842 and 1844. During the following twenty years he continued to write monographs on various subjects of geology and zoology, while slowly perfecting his theory on the evolution of species and collecting a great amount of relevant facts. He began to write his *magnum opus* in May 1856 and had completed half of it by June 1858 when he received a manuscript from Alfred Wallace in which the same theory of evolution of species through natural selection and struggle for existence was developed. Darwin's friends arranged for a joint presentation of Wallace's paper and excerpts of Darwin's sketch of 1844 at the Linnean Society in July 1858 and for a joint publication.[133] Thereupon, Darwin started writing a condensed version of his book, and in 1859 the publication of *The Origin of Species* brought him world fame.[134] He suddenly found himself in the center of scientific, philosophical, and religious controversies which he attempted to avoid as well as he could. Among his later works was *The Descent of Man,* which extended to man the theories developed in *The Origin of Species,* and *The Expression of Emotions* in which a clue is sought to that old problem in an analysis of the instincts underlying the various emotions. When Darwin died in 1882, a parliamentary petition requested his burial in Westminster Abbey, where his grave can be found near that of Newton.

Darwin's fame is associated foremost with transformism, which he called the theory of descent, the evolution of species, a theory opposing the conception of the constancy and immutability of species. Actually, the transformism theory can be traced as far as the Greek philosophers Anaximander and Empedocles and their Chinese contemporary, Tson-Tse who, according to Nehru, had written the following in the sixth century B.C.:

All organizations are originated from a single species. This single species has undergone many gradual and continuous changes and then given rise to all organisms of different forms. Such organisms were not differentiated immediately, but on the contrary they acquired their differences through gradual change, generation after generation.

Historians of science have found a number of forerunners of Darwin during and after the seventeenth century and concluded that evolutionist thinking was fairly widespread in the century before Darwin.[136] The weak point of the early systems was their lack of convincing arguments supporting the theory and of a plausible explanation for the mechanism of the transformation of the species. Lamarck (1744–1829) explained the transformation of species by the effect of adaptation, the prolonged use and nonuse of organs, and the transmission of acquired characteristics, but evidence was scarce. The merit of Charles Darwin is not that he introduced the notion of transformism but that he proposed a new causal explanation and substantiated his theory with an overwhelming amount of arguments patiently accumulated for twenty years.

Darwin began with the fact that many spontaneous chance variations occur in plants and animals and are transmitted to their descendants. This fact is well known to breeders of plants and animals, who select varieties with certain characteristics, cross them, and thus obtain new races bearing the sought-for characteristics. Sometimes, breeders merely select those samples that they consider the best, cross them and obtain new, unforeseen variations (this is what Darwin called unconscious selection). So much for the artificial selection by the breeders. In regard to natural selection, Darwin surmised that new species could originate through chance variations and their hereditary transmission could occur in the same way as with new races. But how does nature carry through a process of selection comparable to the directed selection of the breeders? Darwin thought that the main agent must be the struggle for existence within nature, a process similar to the one invoked by Malthus in the field of demography. This would mean that, in a given species of plant or animal, the number of individuals exceeds the limitations set by space and fodder, that there is an incessant struggle for existence and that those individuals will survive who belong to a spontaneous variation that makes them more fit for that struggle, whereas the unfit are eliminated. However, modifications of environment constantly set up challenges to the fitness of living beings.

Among the arguments brought forward by Darwin in favor of transformism were facts such as the homologous structure in individuals of related species, the existence of rudimentary organs (surviving from prior ancestral species), phenomena of reversion, the resurgence of ancestral forms, and numerous facts pertaining to the distribution of animals in the geologic periods and in space. But in order to make his explanatory theory consistent, Darwin had to assume several other hypotheses: that spontaneous variations could give rise to new species (not only to new races), that acquired characteristics could be hereditarily transmitted, that the duration of geological periods had been immensely long, and that the progress of paleontology would provide the missing links connecting the known species with their supposed ancestral forms.

In *The Origin of Species,* Darwin had said nothing about the human species, but his theory was soon extended to the origin of man by Thomas Huxley in England and by Ernst Haeckel in Germany. In his second major book, *The Descent of Man,* Darwin brought forward the hypothesis that "man is descended from a hairy, tailed quadruped, probably arboreal in its habits, and an inhabitant of the Old World." [137] This ancestor of man was as different from the most primitive savages living today as those savages are from civilized man. Darwin tried to reconstruct a picture of that ancestor and to give a purely biological explanation of its evolution toward the present human species. Society, he says, issued from the instinct of parental and filial love, from the instinct of sympathy and mutual help between animals of the same species. Language issued from cries uttered as an accompaniment to certain emotions and from the imitation of cries proffered by other animals. Morals resulted mainly from the above-mentioned instincts, reinforced by man's sensitivity to public opinion and later by reason, instruction, and habit. In *The Descent of Man,* Darwin departs from the almost exclusive role he had ascribed in *The Origin of Species* to the struggle for existence. He speaks of the instinct of mutual help, and declares that, in the evolution of man, the most important factor was sexual selection, that is, the fact that the stronger individuals tend to choose the more attractive females, that these females show a preference for the stronger males, and that these selected individuals have the more numerous offspring.

The story of Darwinism is a typical instance of a theory that emancipates itself from its founder and takes an autonomous and unexpected course of life. *The Origin of Species* had hardly been published when Darwin found himself identified with many contradictory interpretations of his work and became a living legend. [138] It was said that Darwin, a white-bearded old patriarch of natural sciences and of broken health, living in isolation and seclusion, had achieved the most momentous intellectual revolution since the time of Copernicus. [139] He was said to have been the first to enunciate the theory of evolution (former supporters of this theory, including his grandfather Erasmus Darwin, were called precursors if not simply ignored). Moreover, forgetting that Darwin had proposed the theory of evolution as a hypothesis, it was now assumed that he had proved it and raised it to the level of indisputable scientific truth. The notion of the struggle for existence, far from being just an explanatory hypothesis, was now considered the mainstay of Darwinism. It was overlooked that Darwin had proposed several other mechanisms (one of which was sexual selection). The struggle for life, now understood in a more Hobbesian sense as a "war of everyone against everyone," was proclaimed a universal law discovered and demonstrated by Darwin, an "iron law" governing the living world and mankind and providing a yardstick for ethics. There were, however, a few scientists who tried to acertain in an objective way the real meaning of Darwin's thoughts, to assess them scientifically, and to discard the misinterpretations of his enthusiastic supporters as well as those of his blind opponents. [140]

The historical importance of a theory is not restricted to what was originally in the mind of its author. It is also consists of the extensions, adjunctions, interpretations, and distortions to which it is submitted, and the reactions that result from the impact of the theory and of its distortions.

The proper field of the Darwinian theory was natural history, and it was offered by its author as a hypothesis tending to substantiate the theory of transformism. In that regard, its effects were manifold. It provided a strong impulse to the natural sciences. The search for the missing links in the reconstruction of the transformations of species furthered the progress of paleontology, and the embryological arguments in favor of transformism were the starting point of new studies in comparative embryology. Above all, the publication of *The Origin of Species* changed the general outlook of naturalists; the theory of fixism lost practically all of its supporters, and transformism, now called the Theory of Evolution, was adopted by the vast majority of scientists. But whether this means that the particular hypotheses formulated by Darwin to explain the mechanism of evolution were confirmed is one of the most controversial questions in modern science. In spite of the widespread acceptance of the Darwinian theory, doubts are still being expressed in regard to the true role played by the struggle for existence, [141] [142] and to its effect on evolution, as to whether chance variations can result in new species (not only new races), and as to the existence of most of the missing links.[143] Gertrude Himmelfarb quotes statements of several prominent contemporary naturalists who claim that the common acceptance of Darwinism is not the result of any satisfactory evidence, but stems from the fear in the human mind of any gap in our knowledge and from the fact that scientists prefer an unsatisfactory explanation to no explanation at all.[144]

Had it remained restricted to its original field, Darwinism would never have attained the fame it did reach. But its principles were soon extended to other sciences. Biologists called "intra-selection" the supposed struggle between parts of the organism during its development. Psychologists assumed that instincts and mental faculties also originated in a process of natural selection. The evolution of human societies, the family, languages, moral institutions, or religions, were reconstructed in similar ways, and no branch of science remained free from such speculation.[145]

Darwin had been cautious not to encroach upon the field of philosophy, but his followers decided that a philosophical system could be deduced from his ideas, and particularly a new concept of evolution and progress.

The Enlightenment had understood the idea of progress as a continuous process, which mankind had followed under the guidance of reason, a process aiming at the good and the happiness of mankind (including its disinherited members). Romantics had speculated about a hidden process underlying nature, of unconscious irrational forces, which, however, worked toward a rational aim. Now, Darwinism pointed to the occurrence of biological progress among living species and of social, and even moral, progress within mankind as a result of the automatic and mechanic effect of chance happenings and of a blind, universal struggle. This idea was seized by atheists who used it as a weapon against the religious belief in the creation and against religion itself. But while certain circles identifying with biblical fundamentalism pursued the fight against Darwinism, most theologians soon reconciled the idea of evolution with religion. The American botanist Asa Gray (1810–1888), Darwin's first advocate in America, had been the proponent of the "theistic wing" of evolutionary thought from the beginning. [146]

In the United States, Darwinism exerted a strong influence on philosophy and a new mode of thinking arose that no longer considered things as permanent entities but rather from the universal viewpoint of evolution. [147] Instrumentalism, pragmatism, and utilitarianism are favorite expressions of that philosophical attitude.

In Germany, philosophical Darwinism took a different form under the influence of Ernst Haeckel, a biologist who had gained praise by his excellent research on infusoria, medusae, and sponges. Haeckel proclaimed himself the prophet of Darwinism and claimed to substantiate it with a new proof, the "fundamental biogenetic law,"[148] In its embryonic stages, he said, any living being goes through the transformations that its ancestors went through during the entire evolution ("ontogeny recapitulates phylogeny"). However, he later recognized that this law was not constant, since the series of metamorphoses could be abridged or even altered. But Haeckel incorporated Darwinian transformism into a vast philosophical system called monism. Nature, he said, is the theater of a universal process of evolution, from molecule to celestial bodies. There is no difference between organic and inorganic nature, life is a physical phenomenon characterized by a peculiar kind of vibration in matter. All the living species in nature originated from matter through the intervention of one elementary living being, the "monere," a unicellular being without a nucleus. Haeckel claimed to have seen the monere through the microscope. The entire process of transformism, starting with the monere, embraces the three kingdoms of the "protistes," plants, and animals. Haeckel reconstructed the whole genealogic tree of man in twenty-two degrees, of which the monere was the first and man the twenty-second; all others were hypothetical beings. The twenty-first, that is, the closest ancestor of man, was supposed to be a "pithecanthrope," related to the apes. Man had appeared in Lemuria, now a submerged continent between India and Africa; there had been twelve species and thirty-six races of men. Haeckel taught that cells, and even molecules, are endowed with elementary consciousness, and he proposed the creation of a new religion based on the worship of the cosmos. Haeckel never understood that his system was but a late resurgence of philosophy of nature. He considered it to be absolutely scientific, and it is difficult today to imagine the fantastic success that his theories enjoyed during several decades, especially in Germany where they were often identified with Darwinism. It was mostly under that cloak of Haeckel that young men of Freud's generation first became acquainted with Darwinism, and his prestige remained so high that, when young Rorschach hesitated in 1904 between the vocations of art or natural science, it was a logical step for him to write to Haeckel and ask his counsel.

The most important influence of Darwinism was felt through *Social Darwinism,* that is, the indiscriminate application of the concepts of "struggle for life," "survival of the fittest," and "elimination of the unfit" to the facts and problems of human societies. It was the naturalist Thomas Huxley, one of Darwin's first disciples, who summarized that philosophy in a famous speech made in 1888, relating to England's contemporary situation:

> From the point of view of the moralist, the animal world is on about the same level as a gladiators' show. The creatures are fairly well treated, and set to fight —whereby the strongest, the swiftest and the cunningest live to fight another day. The spectator has no need to turn his thumbs down, as no quarter is given (. . .) In the cycle of phenomena presented by the life of man, the animal, no more moral end is discernible than in that presented by the life of the wolf and the deer (. . .) So among primitive men, the weakest and stupidest went to the wall, while the toughest and shrewdest, those who were best fitted to cope with their circumstances, but not the best in any other sense, survived. Life was a continuous free fight and, beyond the limited and temporary relations of the family, the Hobbesian war of each against all was the normal state of existence (. . .) But the effort of ethical man to work toward a moral end by no means abolished, perhaps has hardly modified, the deep-seated organic impulses which impel the natural man to follow his non-moral code (. . .).[149]

If Darwin's teaching could be thus interpreted by a naturalist, one can easily imagine how it became distorted in the writings of sociologists and political authors who had learned of it only by hearsay. In the name of that fantasy Darwinism, this alleged universal law was used as a rationalization to justify the extermination of primitive populations by the white man. Marxists used it as an argument in favor of class struggle and revolution. The criminologists Ferri and Garofalo of the Italian Positive School used the concept of the "elimination of the unfit" as an argument for the preservation of capital punishment. Atkinson extended the notion of universal struggle to the realm of the family and described the murder of the old father by the adult sons as being the rule among primitive men.[150] Militarists throughout the world turned it into a scientific argument for the necessity of war and for maintaining armies. The pseudo-Darwinian philosophy that persuaded the European elite that war is a biological necessity and an inescapable law has been held responsible for the unleashing of World War I.[151] A long series of politicians proclaimed the same principle, culminating with Hitler who repeatedly invoked Darwin.[152] In short, as stated by Kropotkin, "There is no infamy in civilized society, or in the relations of the Whites toward the so-called lower races, or of the strong toward the weak, which would not have found its excuse in this formula."[153] This line of thought, which could be traced from Hobbes' principle of "man is a wolf to man" to Malthus and from Darwin to Kipling's literary description of "the law of the jungle," gave its specific coloring to the Western world particularly in the last decades of the nineteenth and the beginning of the twentieth centuries.

The impact of any doctrine consists also in its distortions and in the contradictions that arise against both the doctrine and its distortions. From the very beginning there was strong opposition to the ideology derived from Darwin. During his imprisonment at Clairvaux (1883–1886), the Russian anarchist Kropotkin saw the necessity of reassessing Darwin's formula on the basis of data that he found in the works of the Russian zoologists Kessler and Syevertsoff. He elaborated his theory of mutual aid as the basic law of living beings.[154] This theory seems to have gained some ground, also, characteristically, with contemporary British naturalists.[155] Other naturalists have long pointed out that even if the so-called struggle for life was applicable to the animal world, this was still no reason to apply it to human society, which has its specific laws and structure.[156] The English economist Norman Angell warned before World War I against the fallacy of that alleged law that was leading the nations of Europe into catastrophe.[157]

The principle of evolution itself met with contradictions. The French biologist René Quinton proclaimed the "principle of constancy." He said that, if the sea had been the birthplace of all living things, including man, these had in turn retained through all phases of evolution the *milieu intérieur,* which, from the physical and chemical points of view, is very similar to the composition of sea water.[158] Rémy de Gourmont applied this principle to intellectual life and denied that there had been any real progress in the development of man's intelligence. Inventors and artists of prehistoric times, he said, possessed as much genius as any modern inventors or artists. The highest level of human intelligence had remained the same throughout all phases of cultural evolution.[159]

The law of the "survival of the fittest" and of the "elimination of the unfit" is of particular interest to dynamic psychiatry. Actually, few men had been less fit for a life of harsh competition than Darwin himself, whose early ambition had been to become a country clergyman and to devote his spare time to his hobby of natural history. His poor health would have barred him from any university career. He would not have been able to carry out his work had it not been for his personal fortune and the care of a devoted wife. He avoided personal participation in the controversies aroused by his theories and left this to his supporters.

Alfred Adler systematically reversed the principle of the "elimination of the unfit." He showed that organic inferiorities often gave an impulse for biological compensation. He then extended this principle to the psychological realm as well, making "compensation" a basic concept of his system. Thus inferiority, far from being a cause of failure, would appear on the contrary to be the best stimulant for social struggle and victory.

Like so many of his contemporaries, Freud was an enthusiastic reader of Darwin, and the influence of Darwinism on psychoanalysis is manifold.[160] First, Freud followed Darwin in the shaping of a psychology based on the biological concept of the instincts. A psychology of that kind had already been formulated by Gall and his followers and by a few psychiatrists such as J. C. Santlus.[161] But Freud's theory of the instincts is obviously derived from Darwin. It is worthy of note that Freud started with the exclusive consideration of the libido and later came to the assumption of a separate aggressive and destructive instinct, whereas Darwin had followed the opposite path. In *The Origin of Species* he had centered his theory around the fact of the struggle for existence, whereas in *The Descent of Man* he supplemented it by assigning the primary role in the origin and development of man to sexual attraction. Second, Freud followed Darwin in his genetic outlook on the manifestations of life. Darwin elicited facts of localized arrests of development and of "reversion," that which Freud later called fixation and regression. Third, Freud seems to have transposed to psychology and anthropology Haeckel's "law of recapitulation"; the principle that "ontogeny recapitulates phylogeny" finds its equivalent in Freud's assumption that man's individual development goes through the same phases as the evolution of the human species, and that the Oedipus complex is the individual's revival of the murder of the old father by his sons. Finally, Darwin's influence can be recognized in Freud's elaboration of a biological theory on the origin of human society and of morals, taking as a starting point the consideration of an early, hypothetical ancestor of man who lived in small groups or hordes. Another indirect influence of Darwin on Freud can also be traced. Paul Rée explained the elaboration of moral conscience as issuing from a kind of legalized Darwinian struggle for life, such as is reported to have existed among ancient Icelanders.[162] They proclaimed that man has no right to that which he cannot defend, so that, if someone wanted another person's property, he could challenge the owner to a duel. If the owner refused, or if he was killed in the fight, his property legally passed on to his challenger. But there came a time when the law no longer tolerated that primitive custom, and the frustrated aggressive and acquisitive drive of man became the root of remorse, hence of conscience. This theory was developed by Nietzsche in his *Genealogy of Morals*, which was the prototype of the notions later expounded by Freud in *Civilization and Its Discontent.*[163]

KARL MARX (1818–1883)

We have seen how Darwinism, which had been originally a system of hypotheses enunciated in support of the Theory of Evolution, was transformed by Darwin's followers into Social Darwinism, a philosophy that gave a seemingly scientific rationalization to the spirit of ruthless competition that animated the industrial, commercial, political, and military world during the last decades of the nineteenth century. In contrast to Social Darwinism, Marxism was a philosophical system from the start; but it soon also became a philosophy of history, an economic theory, a political doctrine, and even a way of life. Its author was Karl Marx, who collaborated with his friend Friedrich Engels (1820–1895).

Both Marxism and Darwinism share the notion of the progress of mankind, but their doctrines diverge in their views of the nature of the underlying process. Darwinism ascribes progress (in the evolution of species as well as in that of mankind) to the mechanical and deterministic effect of biological phenomena; Marxism ascribes it to a "dialectical" process, which, however, must be aided by man's conscious effort.

Another feature shared by Marxism and Darwinism alike is the idea that justice and morality are not absolute, permanent principles as had been taught by traditional philosophies and by the Enlightenment, but that they are relative. For Darwin they are the outcome of social evolution, for Marx they are intelligible in terms of "historical materialism" and the history of class struggle.

As a philosophical system, Marxism's main source was Hegel, directly as well as through certain of his disciples. Hegel's philosophy provided Marx with the "dialectic method," that is, a method for analyzing seemingly contradictory concepts and for discovering the common principle that would unite them in a higher synthesis, progressing thus from notion to notion toward the absolute. But whereas Hegel had used his dialectical method for the construction of a powerful system of philosophical idealism, Marx applied it to a materialistic philosophy.

Marx also took from Hegel the concept of "alienation," that man is "alienated" (estranged) from himself. "Alienation" means that man has externalized a part of himself, which he then perceives as an external truth. There were extensive discussions about alienation among Hegel's followers. One of them, Ludwig Feuerbach, claimed that man is "alienated from himself" because he created a God in his own image, thus projecting the best part of his spirit outside himself and adoring it as though it were a superior being. By putting an end to this "alienation," man would reconstruct the synthesis of his own being. Marx modified and enlarged the concept of alienation. Not only are religion and abstract philosophies an alienation, but there is also a political, social, and economic alienation. Man is alienated from himself, Marx contends, because of the division of society into classes, the ruling class oppressing and exploiting the ruled classes. Therefore, he said, a classless, socialist society would bring about the disappearance of alienation and all its manifestations.

Marx claimed that up to that time, philosophy had tried to *explain* the world, whereas the true problem consisted in *changing* it. His philosophy is therefore inseparable from action, that is, practically, from revolutionary action. (In fact, Marx and Engels were not content with directing revolutionary organizations, but participated in various revolutionary movements in Germany.)

As does Hegel, Marx says that the human species undergoes a dialectical process of evolution, but he views that process in a substantially different way. Marx's philosophy of history is based on the idea that history can be interpreted by class struggle, and class struggle can itself be understood by the notion of an ideological superstructure superimposed upon a social substructure.[164] The discovery of means of production determined changes in the social structure, that is in the division of classes and the relationship of these classes to each other. The ruling classes oppress the inferior ones; to that end, they impose their political systems and organizations. But the ruling class also creates an "ideology," which includes religions, morals, and philosophy, and which is at the same time a reflection of the social structure and a means of oppressing the inferior classes. By means of that ideology, the ruling class establishes a body of laws and the judicial apparatus required to maintain its domination over the inferior classes.

When applying their ideology, men of the ruling classes are often unaware of what they are doing. In Friedrich Engel's words, "The reflection of economical relations under the form of legal principles . . . occurs without the awareness of those who are acting; the lawyer believes to act in accordance with *a priori* propositions, whereas they are only economical reflections."[165] Therefore, one practical rule of Marxist analysis is: "Behind that which people *say*, behind that which they *think* of themselves, to discover what they *are* by analyzing what they *do*."[166] The work of Marx contains many analyses of what he calls "mystifications," that is those processes by which people deceive both themselves and the others to their own advantage.

The ideological superstructure determined by the social substructure must necessarily follow its changes. However, there may be delays, discrepancies, and resistance to those changes. This is particularly true when the structure of class relationship has been modified in such a way that the upper class is declining while the inferior class is in a position to overthrow it. In such cases, people of the inferior class may be unaware of the situation, and men of the upper class may consciously resist the change or elaborate new ideologies in order to deceive the lower class. According to Marx, war is a "mystification" of the lower classes by the ruling ones who hope to thus divert an impending revolution.

As a political doctrine, classical Marxism, as expressed in Marx's and Engel's *Communist Manifesto* (1848) and in further works, does not believe in the possibility of a gradual and peaceful shifting of power from one class to another. The structure of class relationship may become gradually modified up to a critical point at which revolutionary activity must interfere and bring about the inevitable change. Revolutionary intervention first implies a "dialectic analysis" of the economic and social situation in order to assess its inner contradictions and the direction toward which it is aiming. At this point, the first phase of revolutionary activity consists in bringing awareness to the lower classes or at least to its elite, and the last step is the revolutionary activity proper. A further contention of Marxism is that under given circumstances it may be necessary to provoke the "revolutionary situation" in order to precipitate the crisis.

It is not necessary for our purposes to develop further these considerations. With regard to dynamic psychiatry, what has been said should suffice to enlighten certain features of Freud's and Adler's dynamic psychologies. In Adler's case, the relationship to Marx is quite obvious and direct since, although he was not a Communist or an orthodox Marxist, he was a supporter of socialism. To a certain degree, Adler considers a neurosis as a reflection of social relationships as internalized by the individual. The influence of the socialist August Bebel is apparent in Adler's concept of the relations between man and woman.

Curious parallels have been pointed out between some of Freud's basic ideas and those of Marx.[167] Marx and Freud each had rabbis among his ancestors; each belonged to a family within that circle of Jewry that had come under the influence of the Enlightenment; in the work of each theory is indissolubly linked to practice (in the form of revolutionary activity for Marx, of psychotherapy for Freud). Each man considered religion as an "illusion." In Marx's view, religion is a consoling dream to the frustrated proletariat created by the ruling class in order to exploit the proletariat and perpetuate its oppression. "Religion is the opium of the people." In Freud's view, religion is an illusion determined by wishful thinking, as stated in *The Future of an Illusion*. Although there is no evidence that Freud read either the works of Marx or of his followers, similarities can be found in their ways of thinking. If we transposed certain Marxist concepts from the social and political fields to that of psychology and therapy, we would obtain the following parallels:

MARX	FREUD
Emphasis on the economic aspect of man	Emphasis on the sexual part of man (libido theory).
A society's culture is a superstructure built on a substructure of class relationships and economic factors.	Conscious life is a superstructure built on the substructure of unconscious and conflicting forces.
The ruling class creates an ideology to further its class interest, and the individual, under the influence of that ideology, unconsciously believes himself to be acting and thinking freely.	The individual believes himself to think and act freely, whereas his conscious thoughts and actions are determined by unconscious complexes (rationalization).
The inferior classes are the victims of "mystifications," by which the ruling classes also deceive themselves (for example, war).	This would be at the same time a "rationalization" and a "defense-mechanism."
Man is "alienated" from himself because of the division of society into social classes, which bring forth class struggle.	The neurotic individual is alienated from himself because of his inner conflicts.
In order to bring about the revolution, it is necessary to perform a "dialectic analysis", to bring awareness, and to provoke a "revolutionary situation."	In order to cure the patient, the therapist must perform a "dynamic" analysis, bring the individual to awareness ("Where Id was must Ego be"), and provoke a transference neurosis to resolve it.
The goal is the establishment of a classless society where man will no longer be alienated from himself.	The goal is to have a healed person, conflictless and fully aware of himself.

These similarities should not be pushed too far. However, there is no doubt that a common pattern of thought existed that Marx applied to economic and social facts and Freud to the psychology of the individual.

Changes in Nineteenth-Century Psychiatry

There was a duality during the nineteenth century between the first dynamic psychiatry, which issued from Mesmer and Puységur, and official psychiatry. Despite certain reciprocal influences, each had its separate development and underwent changes that we will briefly summarize.

Official psychiatry was the name given by magnetists to the psychiatry that was recognized by the state, taught in medical schools, and expounded in their textbooks. During 1850 to 1860 a gradual shift occurred from mental hospital psychiatry (*Anstaltspsychiatrie*) to university psychiatry.[168] During the first half of the century mental hospitals had been the hearths of psychiatric progress where original theories were developed and moral treatment applied to mental patients. Around the middle of the century, psychiatry came under the strong influence of positivism and scientism, and the organicist viewpoint prevailed while romantic psychiatry rapidly declined. Men such as Reil, Ideler, Neumann, and Heinroth were now forgotten or ignored, and moral treatment was impeded almost everywhere.

At this turning point stands the name of one great pioneer, Wilhelm Griesinger (1817-1869), the representative psychiatrist of the mid-century. In 1845 he published a textbook on psychiatry, after which he spent several years in Egypt as director of the public health service and physician to the khedive.[169] After his return to Europe, he became in 1860 the first director of the newly founded university mental hospital of Zurich, the Burghölzli. In 1867 he published a considerably enlarged second edition of his textbook on psychiatry, which became the standard textbook of that science for an entire generation. Griesinger is often considered as the man who won the victory of the *Somatiker* over the *Psychiker*. It is true that he proclaimed that "mental diseases are brain diseases" and that he expected the secret of mental illness to be elucidated through the progress of brain anatomo-pathology. He also introduced the physiological concept of the reflexes into the theory of mental diseases. Nevertheless, Griesinger was all but an exclusive *Somatiker*. He applied to psychiatry the dynamic associationistic concepts of Herbart, and he retained many of the principles of the *Psychiker*. Recent studies have shown to what an unexpected extent Griesinger was a representative of dynamic psychiatry.[170] He proclaimed that the greatest and most important part of the psychic processes were unconscious. He took over and developed the *Psychiker's* concept of the pathogenetic role of emotions and thus explained the psychogenesis of fixed ideas. "Almost all fixed ideas are essentially expressions of a frustration or gratification of one's own emotional interest" so that, in certain cases, the therapy can only be based on ascertaining what are the underlying psychic states. Griesinger also developed an entire ego-psychology. Distortions of the ego can result from nonassimilated clusters of representations, which then may face the ego as though they were a stranger and come in conflict with it. Griesinger thus stands at the crossroad of most of the psychiatric trends of the nineteenth century—brain anatomo-pathology, and neuro-psychiatry, clinical psychiatry, and dynamic psychiatry. Moreover, he was a good organizer of mental hospitals. He is also regarded as the founder of university psychiatry, and after him the great leaders in psychiatry were of necessity university professors. Finally, he inaugurated the predominance of German psychiatry over French psychiatry. Until 1860,

French psychiatry was so much in the foreground that most of the case histories given in Griesinger's textbook itself were borrowed from French authors.

Griesinger's followers, men such as Westphal, Meynert, and Wernicke took over and developed his organic approach to mental illness, but they seem to have had a blind spot in regard to the dynamic psychological part of his teaching. A new synthesis of organic and dynamic psychiatry was to be achieved only later by Griesinger's remote successor at the Burghölzli, Eugen Bleuler.

At the same time, there was also an official psychiatry of neuroses, which was mostly practiced by neurologists (seeing that patients were reluctant to go to mental hospital psychiatrists). This branch of psychiatry also underwent certain important changes in the course of the nineteenth-century, the most important of which was in the neuroses themselves. Devilish possession had by now disappeared, although sporadic cases could still be observed (as seen in Chapter 1 with the case of Gottliebin Dittus and the Pastor Blumhardt), and two neuroses typical of the eighteenth century had rapidly declined. The *vapeurs* of society women disappeared with the downfall of the aristocracy, and hypochondriasis, which had been the fashionable male neurosis, gradually became old-fashioned. But a new disease entity took its place. It first appeared under the name of "wear and tear syndrome." As pointed out by Ilza Veith,[171] the English physician James Johnson described it in 1831 as a disease peculiar to the English as opposed to their French neighbors, and ascribed it to the physical and mental overexertion and the manifold tensions resulting from contemporary life in England under the impact of the Industrial Revolution.[172] Johnson emphasized the role played by overwork, lack of outdoor exercise, and the murky smoke hanging over the cities. He saw no remedy for it except annual relaxation and travel abroad.

In 1869, a somewhat similar disease, neurasthenia, was described in the United States by George M. Beard.[173] The basic symptom of neurasthenia, he said, was physical and mental exhaustion manifested in the impossibility of performing physical and mental work. The patient complains of headaches, neuralgias, a morbid hypersensitivity to weather, noise, light, the presence of other people, and any kind of sensory or mental stimuli, sleeplessness, loss of appetite, dysphagia, disturbances of the secretions, and tremors of the muscles. Neurasthenia, though, was compatible with a long life. One of Beard's patients, an active seventy-year-old "man of business," had suffered from it every day for the past fifty-five years. Beard first ascribed neurasthenia to a dephosphorization of the nervous system. As a therapy, he recommended an abundant use of physical and chemical "tonics" of the nervous system, including muscular exercise, "general electrization," phosphorus, strychnine, and arsenic. Beard later revised his description. He now viewed neurasthenia as an essentially American neurosis.[174] Its causes lay in the climate (extremes of heat and cold, humidity and dryness, electricity in the air) and above all in the peculiar way of life of North America, a young and rapidly growing nation with religious liberty ("liberty as a cause of nervousness") in the process of an intensive economic development. This way of life entailed an increased amount of work, forethought, and punctuality, an increase in the speed of life (railways, the telegraph), and also the repression of emotion ("an exhausting process"). Beard foresaw that neurasthenia would reach the old continent if Europe ever became Americanized. In later publications, Beard reinterpreted neurasthenia in terms of the balance of nervous energy proper to individuals. There are people with very small resources, he said, and there are "millionaires of nerve force." Some have a small amount of reserve force, others a large amount. "Men, like batteries, need a reserve force, and men, like batteries, need to be measured by the amount of the reserve, and not by what they are compelled to expend in ordinary daily life." Beard liked to express these ideas with financial comparisons. "The man with a small income is really rich as long as there is no overdraft on the account, so the nervous man may really be well and in fair working order as long as he does not draw on his limited store of nerve-force." On the other hand, "a millionaire may draw very heavily on his funds and yet keep a large surplus." What matters, therefore, is not to expend more force than one can afford to. A neurasthenic is a person who is overdrawing his account and, if he persists, he goes into "nervous bankruptcy." It is noteworthy that both the notion of the budget of nervous forces and the financial comparisons were to be found again in a more systematized way in Janet's writings. In Beard's description, neurasthenia was a disease proper to men. Women benefited from what Beard called an "unusual social position" so that, in his own words, "the phenomenal beauty of the American girl of the highest type" was the counterpart of the social factors that made neurasthenia prevalent among men. In a posthumous work, he put an increased emphasis on the sexual etiology of neurasthenia.[175]

Beard was one of the first if not the first physician to seek a dynamic psychological explanation of alcoholism. The nineteenth century saw an extreme growth and spread of alcoholism, and clinicians everywhere described and classified the various conditions resulting from the intake of alcohol. Pathologists described the lesions, but no one seems to have investigated the problem of why men aware of the dangers of alcohol resorted to drinking. Beard suggested that men began to drink when there was a discrepancy between the effort they had to furnish and the amount of nervous force that they felt within themselves.[176] Interestingly enough, a similar theory of the psychogenesis of alcoholism was later to be proposed by Janet.

Beard's ideas met with great success. Not only was neurasthenia a disease of professional men and hard workers, but it was the neurosis of modern life itself. Sanitariums for its treatment were erected in America and in Europe. However, in the measure in which neurasthenia became a more widespread diagnosis its origin was ascribed more to constitutional factors and to factors other than hard work, for instance to sexual disturbances and masturbation.

Beard's clinical studies of neurasthenia were more successful than the therapies he proposed against the illness. It was given to another American physician, Silas Weir Mitchell (1829–1914), to devise a standard method for its cure.[177] Weir Mitchell, who had become known as one of America's foremost neurologists, had Philadelphia's most fashionable practice.[178] His method[179] was based on rest, isolation, and on a feeding cure. The patient was isolated in a sanitarium, lay in bed, was given a rich diet, and submitted to at least one hour's daily massage. In order to compensate for the effects of prolonged rest and rich diet, massage and electricity were considered indispensable parts of the treatment program. This treatment could last for months and sometimes for years, and became fashionable among the well-to-do. It was given the nickname "method of Dr. Diet and Dr. Quiet." Weir Mitchell apparently did not suspect that a good part of the therapeutic success of that method could be ascribed to the strong psychological rapport, which was established between the patient and the masseur.

By the end of the nineteenth century, two conditions were universally considered to be the main neuroses: hysteria and neurasthenia, the former being mainly a neurosis of women, the latter predominantly a neurosis of men. Hysteria and neurasthenia were often described side by side and contrasted with each other. However, this concept was criticized and efforts were made to delineate other specific types of neurosis.

Even before Beard's description of neurasthenia, Benedict Augustin Morel (1809–1873) had described a new neurosis under the name of *délire émotif* (emotional delusions).[180] He gave remarkable case histories of that supposedly new condition, which he considered to be a disease of the vegetative system. After Morel, "emotional delusion" was given the name "phobia," and there was a competition toward the isolation and description of new subforms of phobia: agoraphobia, claustrophobia, topophobia, and the like. The nosologic situation of these phobias was controversial, and they were often incorporated as subforms of neurasthenia.

In 1873, Krishaber described 38 observations of a new type of neurosis, which he called cerebro-cardiac neuropathia.[181] His patients were suddenly seized with fits of anxiety, beating of the heart, and dizziness. They also suffered from sleeplessness and nightmares. These feelings of anxiety were not related to any definite object of fear, as was the case with phobias, and this neurosis was obviously identical with what was later called anxiety neurosis.

With the advance of the century, the field of neurosis seems to have become increasingly complex. Aside from the two great neuroses, hysteria and neurasthenia, there were now a multitude of neurotic cases that were difficult to classify. With the development of industry and the multiplication of industrial accidents on one side, and the development of insurance companies on the other, traumatic neuroses arose that authors classified either under the heading *hysteria* or under *neurasthenia*. More and more, "official medicine" was on the search for new theories and new therapeutic methods for these neuroses.

Such was the situation around 1880, and explains, at least to a certain extent, the sudden revival of interest in hypnosis. It was hoped that hypnosis would provide a new solution to the problems of neuroses. But as we will see, this hope remained unfulfilled, and it was given to Janet and Freud to find new ways of approaching that old problem.

Conclusions

The history of dynamic psychiatry becomes fully intelligible only after considering its sociological, economic, political, cultural, and medical backgrounds.

At the end of the eighteenth century, the populations of Europe were divided into rigid social classes, the two main classes being those of aristocrats and commoners. This explains why animal magnetism assumed different characteristics with Mesmer and with Puységur. When treating the distinguished ladies of his aristocratic clientele, Mesmer elicited crises, which were in fact abreactions of their fashionable neurosis, the *vapeurs*. When Puységur treated his peasants, he provoked magnetic sleep, a phenomenon expressing a relationship of authority and subordination between the aristocratic master and his peasant-servant, a relationship that was not exempt, however, from a peculiar feature of bargaining. Mesmer's *baquet*, a would-be physical apparatus, appealed to the contemporary aristocracy's taste for amateur physics. Puységur's magnetized tree fitted into the peasant folklore and its belief in sacred trees. The overthrow of the aristocracy and the subsequent rise of the bourgeoisie resulted in the propagation of a more authoritarian way of individual and collective psychotherapy, the hypnotic suggestion.

The birth of dynamic psychiatry can also be understood as a manifestation of the victory of the cultural movement of the Enlightenment over the spirit of the Baroque in the latter's stronghold, Austria. The vicissitudes of dynamic psychiatry during the nineteenth century may be regarded as manifestations of the struggle between the Enlightenment (which stressed the cult of reason and of society), and Romanticism (which emphasized the cult of the irrational and of the individual). Romantic philosophy and psychiatry exerted a particularly great influence on dynamic psychiatry. After the mid-century political and cultural crisis,

Romanticism was defeated and gave way to positivism, which was a late offshoot of the philosophy of Enlightenment; hence a temporary decline of dynamic psychiatry.

Meanwhile, the Industrial Revolution, the growth of the proletariat, and the growth of nationalism furthered the advent of two new doctrines: Darwinism (and its distortion of social Darwinism) and Marxism. These two new ideologies were also reflected in dynamic psychiatry. All these changes also found an expression in the form of neuroses, of which new types developed: neurasthenia and phobias, bringing with them the need for new methods of psychotherapy.

Through the combined action of all these factors, a new type of dynamic psychiatry superseding the first one finally emerged. The circumstances that preceded and accompanied its birth need closer examination and will be dealt with in the following chapter.

Notes

1. Louis-Antoine de Bougainville, *Voyage autour du monde* (2nd ed.; Paris: Saillant et Nyon, 1772). See particularly II, 44–47, 86–88.

2. Denis Diderot, *Supplément au voyage de Bougainville* (1772), in *Oeuvres,* éd. Pléïade (Paris: Gallimard, 1957), pp. 993–1032.

3. Henri Carré, *La Noblesse en France et l'opinion publique au XVIIIe siècle* (Paris: Champion, 1920).

4. Alexandre Bertrand, *Lettres sur la physique* (Paris: Bossange, 1825), pp. 422–432.

5. Joseph Raulin, *Traité des affections vaporeuses du sexe, avec l'exposition de leurs symptômes, de leurs différentes causes, et la méthode de les guérir* (2nd ed.; Paris: Hérissant, 1759).

6. Pierre Pomme, *Traité des affections vaporeuses des deux sexes, ou maladies nerveuses vulgairement appelées maux de nerfs* (Paris: Desaint et Saillant, 1760).

7. Paul Sébillot, *Le Folk-Lore de France* (Paris: Guilmoto, 1906), III, 367–442.

8. Aubin Gauthier, *Traité pratique du magnétisme et du somnambulisme* (Paris: Baillière, 1845), pp. 154–162.

9. Gustave Flaubert, *Bouvard et Pécuchet* (1881), in *Oeuvres complètes,* II, éd. Pléïade (Paris: Gallimard, 1952), 888–891.

10. Viscount du Boisdulier, Letter of May 22, 1963.

11. Virey, "Magnétisme animal," *Dictionnaire des Sciences Médicales,* XXIX (Paris: Panckoucke, 1818), 495, 547.

12. Wilhelm Mühlmann, *Chiliasmus und Nativismus* (Berlin: Reimer, 1961), pp. 215–217.

13. Madame Roland, *Oeuvres de J. M. Ph. Roland, femme de l'ex-Ministre de l'Intérieur,* I (Paris: Bideault, an VIII), pp. 148–150.

14. *Exposé des différentes cures opérées depuis le 25 d'août 1785 . . jusqu'au 12 du mois de juin 1786 . . .* (2nd ed.; Strasbourg: Librairie Académique, 1787).

15. *Suite des cures faites par différents magnétiseurs, Membres de la Société Harmonique des Amis-Réunis de Strasbourg* (Strasbourg: Lorenz et Schouler, 1788), Vol. II.

16. T. S. Ashton, *The Industrial Revolution, 1760–1830* (New York: Oxford University Press, 1948). Paul Mantoux, *La Révolution industrielle au XVIIIe siècle* (1906) (revised ed.; Paris: Génin, 1959).

17. Walter Prescott Webb, *The Great Frontier* (Boston: Houghton Mifflin, 1952).

18. Georges Weill, *L'Europe du XIXe siècle et l'idée de la nationalité* (Paris: Albin-Michel, 1938).

19. Boswell mentions that Johnson spent two months in Paris in the year 1775 and that he spoke nothing but Latin during his entire stay. See James Boswell, *The Life of Samuel Johnson* (1791). Great Books of the Western World (Chicago: Encyclopedia Britannica, Inc., 1922), XLIV, 272.

20. Ernst Mach, *Popular Lectures* (Chicago: Chicago Open Court, 1897), pp. 309–345.

21. Condorcet, *Esquisse d'un tableau historique des progrès de l'esprit humain* (Gênes: Yves Gravier, 1798), pp. 209, 337.

22. F. Baldensperger, *Etudes d'histoire littéraire* (Paris: Hachette, 1907), pp. 46–53 (a summary description of the successive ideal types of man in Europe since the Renaissance).

23. Jacob Burckhardt, *Die Cultur der Renaissance in Italien, ein Versuch* (Basel: Schweighauser, 1860).

24. The ideal type of the Renaissance man was described in the famous book *Il Libro del Cortegiano* by Baldassare Castiglione (Venice: Aldo Romano, 1528). Eng. trans., *The Book of the Courtier* (New York: Scribner's Sons, 1903).

25. Baltasar Gracián, *Oráculo manual y arte de prudencia* (Huesca: Juan Nogués, 1647). Eng. trans., *The Art of Worldly Wisdom* (London and New York: Macmillan and Co., 1892).

26. Henry Sigerist, *Grosse Ärzte: eine Geschichte der Heilkunde in Lebensbildern* (5th ed.; Munich: Lehmanns Verlag, 1965), pp. 115–122.

27. Ernst Troeltsch, "Die Aufklärung," (1897). Reprinted in *Gesammelte Schriften* (Tübingen: Mohr, 1925), IV, 338–374.

28. Immanuel Kant, *Beantwortung der Frage: Was ist Aufklärung?* (1784), in *Werke*, (Berlin: Buchenau-Cassirer, 1913), IV, 167–176.

29. W. E. H. Lecky, *History of the Rise and Influence of the Spirit of Rationalism in Europe*, 2 vols. (London: Longmans, Green, 1865). Ernst Cassirer, *Die Philosophie der Aufklärung* (Tübingen: J. C. B. Mohr, 1932). Eng. trans., *The Philosophy of Enlightenment* (Princeton: Princeton University Press, 1951). Daniel Mornet, *La pensée française au XVIIIe siècle* (Paris: Colin, 1932). Baron Cay von Brockdorff, *Die englische Aufklärungsphilosophie* (Munich: Reinhardt, 1924). E. Ermattinger, *Deutsche Kultur in Zeitalter der Aufklärung* (Potsdam, 1935). Hans M. Wolff, *Die Weltanschauung der deutschen Aufklärung* (Bern: Francke, 1949).

30. This is particularly well illustrated by the life of Moses Mendelssohn. See Bertha Badt-Strauss, *Moses Mendelssohn, der Mensch und das Werk* (Berlin: Welt-Verlag, 1929).

31. Immanuel Kant, *Die Religion innerhalb der Grenzen der blossen Vernunft* (1793), in *Immanuel Kants Werke*, Ernst Cassirer, ed. (Berlin: Bruno Cassirer, 1914), VI, 139–353.

32. Gustav Roskoff, *Geschichte des Teufels* (Leipzig: F. A. Brockhaus, 1869), II.

33. E. H. Ackerknecht, "Medizin und Aufklärung," *Schweizerische medizinische Wochenschrift*, LXXXIX (1959), 20.

34. Immanuel Kant, *Von der Macht des Gemüths, durch den blossen Vorsatz seiner krankhaften Gefühle Meister zu sein*, in *Immanuel Kants Werke*, Ernst Cassirer, ed. (Berlin: Bruno Cassirer, 1916), VII, 411–431.

35. A literary instance of the treatment that a mental patient received in that kind of family setting was shown by Goethe, in *Wilhelm Meisters Lehrjahre*, Book IV, Chap. 16.

36. Gaston Bachelard, *La Formation de l'esprit scientifique. Contribution à une psychanalyse de la connaissance objective* (Paris: Vrin, 1947).

37. John Hampton, *Nicolas Antoine Boulanger et la science de son temps* (Geneva: Droz, 1955).

38. Abbé Terrasson, *Séthos. Histoire ou vie des monumens anecdotes de l'ancienne Egypte. Traduite d'un manuscrit grec*, 3 vols. (Paris: Jacques Guérin, 1731).

39. Antoine Court de Gébelin, *Le Monde primitif, analysé et comparé avec le monde moderne*, 9 vols. (Paris, 1773–1782).

40. Rudolf Haym, *Die romantische Schule. Ein Beitrag zur Geschichte des deutschen Geistes* (Berlin: Rudolf Gaertner, 1870). Ricarda Huch, *Die Romantik. Blütezeit der Romantik* (Leipzig: Haessel, 1920). Ricarda Huch, *Die Romantik. Ausbreitung, Blütezeit und Verfall* (Tübingen/Stuttgart: Hermann Leins, 1951). Richard Benz, *Die deutsche Romantik. Geschichte einer geistigen Bewegung* (Leipzig: Reclam, 1937). Paul Kluckhohn, *Das Ideengut der deutschen Romantik*. a. edition (Halle: Max Niemeyer, 1942).

41. Henri Brunschwig, *La Crise de l'état prussien à la fin du XVIIIe siècle et la genèse de la mentalité romantique* (Paris: Presses Universitaires de France, 1947).

42. Friedrich Schlegel, quoted by Ricarda Huch, in *Die Romantik. Ausbreitung, Blütezeit und Verfall* (Stuttgart: Leins, 1951), p. 257.

43. Novalis, *Neue Fragmente* N. 146, in *Werke und Briefe* (Munich: Winkler-Verlag, n.d.), pp. 452–453.

44. Schleiermacher, *Monologen* (1800), in *Kritische Ausgabe,* Friedrich Michael Schiele, ed. (Leipzig: Dürr, 1902).

45. Max Scheler, *Vom Umsturz der Werte* (4th ed.; Francke, 1951), p. 126.

46. Friedrich Schlegel, *Lucinde* (Berlin: Fröhlich, 1799).

47. Novalis, quoted by Ricarda Huch, *Die Romantik. Blütezeit der Romantik* (Leipzig: Haessel, 1920), p. 258.

48. Fritz Ernst, *Die romantische Ironie* (Zurich: Schulthess, 1915).

49. Friedrich Wilhelm von Schelling, see notably *Ideen zu einer Philosophie der Natur* (Leipzig, 1797); *Von der Weltseele* (Hamburg, 1798); *Werke* (Leipzig: Fritz Eckard, 1907), Vol. I.

50. Friedrich Hufeland, *Ueber Sympathie* (Weimar: Verlag des Landes-Industrie-Comptoirs, 1811).

51. K. E. Rothschuh, *Geschichte der Physiologie* (Berlin: Springer, 1953), pp. 112–118.

52. August Winkelmann, *Einleitung in die dynamische Physiologie* (Göttingen: Dieterich, 1802).

53. J. W. Goethe, *Versuch, die Metamorphosen der Pflanzen zu erklären* (Gotha: C. W. Ettinger, 1790).

54. See Agnes Arber, "Goethe's Botany: The Metamorphosis of Plants" (1790), and "Tobler's Ode to Nature" (1782), *Chronica Botanica*, X (1946), 63–126.

55. Adolf Meyer-Abich, *Biologie der Goethezeit* (Stuttgart: Hippocrates-Verlag, 1949).

56. F. Giese, *Der romantische Charakter*, Bd. I. *Die Entwicklung des Androgynenproblems in der Frühromantik* (Langensalza, 1919). Ernst Benz, *Adam. Der Mythus vom Urmenschen* (Munich-Planegg: Otto-Wilhelm-Barth Verlag, 1955).

57. Philip Lersch, *Der Traum in der deutschen Romantik* (Munich: M. Hueber, 1923). Albert Beguin, *L'Ame romantique et le rêve. Essai sur le romantisme allemand et la poésie française,* 2 vols. (Marseilles: Cahiers du Sud, 1937).

58. W. Leibbrand, "Schellings Bedeutung für die moderne Medizin," *Atti del XIVo Congresso Internazionale di Storia della Medicina* (Rome, 1954), II.

59. Ernest Jones, *The Life and Work of Sigmund Freud* (New York: Basic Books, 1955), II, 318.

60. G. H. von Schubert, *Ahndungen einer allgemeinen Geschichte des Lebens* (Leipzig: Reclam, 1820) and *Ansichten von der Nachtseite der Naturwissenschaft* (Dresden and Leipzig: Weigel, 1808).

61. Hans Kern, *Die Seelenkunde der Romantik* (Berlin-Lichterfelde: Widukind-Verlag, 1937).

62. G. H. von Schubert, *Die Symbolik des Traumes*. Neue, verbesserte und vermehrte Auflage (Leipzig: Brockhaus, 1837). (First ed., 1814.)

63. Two of his works are particularly important: Ignaz Troxler, *Blicke in das Wesen des Menschen* (Aarau: Sauerländer, 1812). *Naturlehre des menschlichen Erkennens oder Metaphysik* (Aarau: Sauerländer, 1828).

64. Carl Gustav Carus, *Psyche, zur Entwicklungsgeschichte der Seele* (Pforzheim: Flammer and Hoffmann, 1846).

65. Paul Janet, *Principes de métaphysique et de psychologie* (Paris: Delagrave, 1897), pp. 189–390, contends that Schopenhauer's belated fame resulted, not from a conspiracy

of silence (as Schopenhauer believed), but from the fact that his philosophy, which was incompatible with the *Zeitgeist* of the period between the 1820's and the 1840's, could be better understood after the disillusion of 1848.

66. Arthur Schopenhauer, *Die Welt als Wille und Vorstellung* (1819). The following quotations are taken from Book IV, ed. Frauenstädt (Leipzig: Brockhaus, 1873), II, 584–591, 607–643.

67. Arthur Schopenhauer, *Die Welt als Wille und Vorstellung*, Book III, *op. cit.*, II, 456–460.

68. Ernst Cassirer, *The Myth of the State* (New Haven: Yale University Press, 1946), pp. 31–32.

69. Max Scheler, *Mensch und Geschichte* (Zurich: Verlag der Neuen Schweizer Rundschau, 1929).

70. Thomas Mann, *Freud und die Zukunft* (Vienna: Bormann-Fischer, 1936). Eng. trans. in *Essays of Three Decades* (New York: Knopf, 1947), pp. 411–428.

71. Luis S. Granjel, "Schopenhauer y Freud," *Actas Luso-Españolas de Neurología y Psiquiatría*, IX, (1950), 120–134.

72. Eduard von Hartmann, *Philosophie des Unbewussten* (Berlin: Duncker, 1869).

73. Werner Leibbrand, *Romantische Medizin* (Hamburg and Leipzig: H. Goverts, 1937).

74. Novalis, "Fragmente über Ethisches, Philosophisches und Wissenschaftlisches," *Sämmtliche Werke*, herausg. Carl Meissner (1898), III, 164, 169, 170.

75. H. F. Ellenberger, "La Notion de maladie créatrice," *Dialogue*, III (1964), 25–41.

76. Ernst Freiherr von Feuchtersleben, *Zur Diätetik der Seele* (1838) (23rd ed.; Vienna: Gerold, 1861), p. 144.

77. The best available sources are Theodor Kirchhoff, *Deutsche Irrenärzte*, 2 vols. (Berlin, 1924), and A. Wettley, *Der Wahnsinn: Geschichte der abendländischen Psychopathologie* (Munich: K. A. Freiburg, 1961).

78. Ernest Harms, "Modern Psychotherapy–150 Years Ago," *Journal of Mental Science*, CIII (1957), 804–809.

79. Johann Christian Reil, *Rhapsodien über die Anwendung der psychischen Cur-Methoden auf Geisteszerrüttungen* (Halle: Curt, 1803).

80. Ernest Harms, "Johann Christian Reil," *American Journal of Psychiatry*, CXVI (1960), 1037–1039.

81. J. C. H. Heinroth, *Lehrbuch der Störungen des Seelenlebens oder der Seelenstörungen und ihrer Behandlung*, 2 vols. (Leipzig: F. C. W. Vogel, 1818).

82. Ernest Harms, "An Attempt to Formulate a System of Psychotherapy in 1818," *American Journal of Psychotherapy*, XIII (1959), 269–282.

83. Karl Wilhelm Ideler, *Grundriss der Seelenheilkunde*, 2 vols. (Berlin: Verlag von T. C. F. Enslin, 1835).

84. *"Jeder Gemütstrieb ist einer unbegrenzten Entwicklung fähig."*

85. *". . . und mit Abscheu und Widerwille aus demselben in das Gebiet der Phantasie sich flüchtet."* (II, 365.)

86. Heinrich Neumann, *Lehrbuch der Psychiatrie* (Erlangen: F. Enke, 1859).

87. *"Also, der Trieb, wenn er nicht befriedigt werden kann, wird Angst"* (p. 43).

88. Most of these psychiatrists were Germans. However, the Belgian psychiatrist Guislain, who expounded original ideas about the role of anxiety in the genesis of mental illness, belongs to the same group. See J. Guislain, *Traité sur les phrénopathies, ou doctrine nouvelle des maladies mentales* (Brussels: Etablissement Encyclopédique, 1833). *Traité sur l'aliénation mentale* (Amsterdam, 1826). *Leçons orales sur les phréno-pathies*, 2 vols. (Ghent, 1852).

89. Johannes Kuntze, *Gustav Theodor Fechner (Dr. Mises). Ein deutsches Gelehrten-leben* (Leipzig: Breitkopf & Härtel, 1892). Wilhelm Wundt, *Gustav Theodor Fechner. Rede zur Feier seines hundertjährigen Geburtstages* (Leipzig: W. Engelmann, 1901). Kurd Lasswitz, *Gustav Theodor Fechner* (Stuttgart: Fromanns Verlag, 1902).

90. Dr. Mises, *Vergleichende Anatomie der Engel. Eine Skizze* (Leipzig: Baumgartner, 1825).

91. G. T. Fechner, *Das Büchlein vom Leben nach dem Tode* (Dresden: Grimmer, 1836).

92. An English translation of Fechner's account of his illness can be found in Gustav Theodor Fechner, *Religion of a Scientist* (selections from Gustav Theodor Fechner, ed. and trans. by Walter Lowrie (New York: Pantheon Books, 1946), pp. 36–42.

93. G. T. Fechner, *Über das höchste Gut* (Leipzig: Breitkopf & Härtel, 1846).

94. G. T. Fechner, "*Über das Lustprinzip des Handelns*," *Fichtes-Zeitschrift für Philosophie und philosophische Kritik,* XIX (1848), 1–30, 163–194.

95. Dr. Mises, *Rätselbüchlein* (Leipzig: G. Wigard, 1850).

96. G. T. Fechner, *Nanna, oder über das Seelenleben der Pflanzen* (Leipzig: Voss, 1848). (Nanna was the name of the goddess of vegetation of the old Germans.)

97. G. T. Fechner, *Zend-Avesta, oder Über die Dinge des Himmels und des Jenseits,* 2 vols. (Leipzig: Voss, 1851).

98. G. T. Fechner, *Elemente der Psychophysik,* 2 vols. (Leipzig: Breitkopf & Härtel, 1860).

99. G. T. Fechner, *Einige Ideen zur Schöpfungs—und Entwicklungsgeschichte der Organismen* (Leipzig: Breitkopf & Härtel, 1873).

100. G. T. Fechner, *Vorschule der Aesthetik,* 2 vols. (Leipzig: Breitkopf & Härtel, 1873).

101. G. T. Fechner, *Die Tagesansicht gegenüber der Nachtansicht* (Leipzig: Breitkopf & Härtel, 1900).

102. Imre Hermann, *Gustav Theodor Fechner: Imago* (1925), II, 371–421. Maria Dorer, *Historische Grundlagen der Psychoanalyse* (Leipzig: F. Meiner, 1932). Siegfried Bernfeld, "Freud's Earliest Theories and the School of Helmholtz," *Psychoanalytic Quarterly,* XIII (1944), 341–362. Rainer Spehlmann, *Sigmund Freuds neurologische Schriften* (Berlin: Springer, 1953). H. F. Ellenberger, "Fechner and Freud," *Bulletin of the Menninger Clinic,* XX (1956), 201–214.

103. A short biography of Bachofen, written by Karl Meuli, can be found in *Johann Jakob Bachofens Gesammelte Werke, herausgegeben von Karl Meuli* (Basel: Benno Schwabe, 1948), III, 1011–1128.

104. Johann Jakob Bachofen, *Das Mutterrecht. Eine Untersuchung über die Gynaekokratie der alten Welt nach ihrer religiösen und rechtlichen Natur* (Stuttgart: Kreis & Hoffman, 1861). Reedition in *Johann Jakob Bachofens gesammelte Werke, herausgegeben von Karl Meuli* (Basel: Benno Schwabe, 1948), II, III.

105. Lafitau, *Moeurs des sauvages amériquains, comparées aux moeurs des premiers temps* (Paris: Saugrain, 1724), I, 69–89.

106. Abbé Desfontaines, *Le nouveau Gulliver, ou Voyages de Jean Gulliver, fils du capitaine Lemuel Gulliver,* 2 vols. (Paris: Clouzier, 1730).

107. Bachofen's interpretation of the Oedipus myth is to be found in *Das Mutterrecht.* Reedited in *Gesammelte Werke,* Karl Meuli, ed. (Basel: B. Schwabe, 1948), II, 439–448.

108. See Charles Andler, *Nietzsche, sa vie et sa pensée,* II, *La jeunesse de Nietzsche* (Paris: Bossard, 1921), 258–266. Karl Albrecht Bernoulli, *Nietzsche und die Schweiz* (Frauenfeld, Huber & Co., 1922). A. Baeumler, *Bachofen und Nietzsche* (Zurich: Verlag der Neuen Schweizer Rundschau, 1929).

109. Friedrich Nietzsche, *Die Geburt der Tragödie aus dem Geiste der Musik* (Leipzig: Fritzsch, 1872).

110. Lewis Morgan, *Ancient Society, or Researches in the Lines of Human Progress from Savagery through Barbarism to Civilization* (New York: Macmillan, 1877).

111. Friedrich Engels, *Der Ursprung der Familie, des Privateigenthums und des Staats* (Höttingen-Zürich: Volksbuchhandlung, 1884).

112. Mathias and Mathilde Vaerting, *Neubegründung der Psychologie von Mann und Weib,* 2 vols. (Karlsruhe im Braunschweig: Hofbuchdruckerei, 1921–1923). English adaptation by Eden and Cedar Paul, *The Dominant Sex. A Study in the Sociology of Sex Differentiation* (London: Allan and Unwin Ltd., 1923).

113. August Bebel, *Die Frau und der Sozialismus* (Stuttgart: Dietz, 1879).

114. See particularly Ludwig Klages, *Vom kosmogonischen Eros* (Iéna: E. Diederichs, 1922). *Der Geist als Widersacher der Seele* (Leipzig: J. A. Barth, 1929).

115. Edgar Salin, "Bachofen als Mythologe der Romantik," in *Schmollers Jahrbuch* (1926), Vol. V.

116. Adrien Turel, *Bachofen–Freud. Zur Emanzipation des Mannes vom Reich der Mütter* (Bern: Hans Huber, 1939).

117. A. Baeumler, *Bachofen und Nietzsche* (Zurich: Verlag der Neuen Schweizer Rundschau, 1929).

118. Walter Prescott Webb, *The Great Frontier* (Boston: Houghton Mifflin, 1952).

119. Alexis de Tocqueville, *De la Démocratie en Amérique* (Brussels: Méline, Gans & Cie., 1840), III, 283–284.

120. Quoted by Karl Meuli in *Nachwort. Bachofens gesammelte Werke* (Basel: B. Schwabe, 1948), III, 1011–1128.

121. François Fejto, ed., *1848 dans le monde. Le printemps des peuples*, 2 vols. (Paris: Editions de Minuit, 1948).

122. Emile Littré, "Des tables tournantes et des esprits frappeurs," *Revue des Deux Mondes* (1856). Reprinted in *Médecine et Médecins* (2nd ed.; Paris: Didier, 1872).

123. Comte de Saint-Simon, *Lettres d'un habitant de Genève à ses contemporains* (1803). Reprint (Paris: Alcan, 1925).

124. Johann Christian Reil, *Rhapsodien* (Halle: Curt, 1803), pp. 42–43.

125. Heinrich Deiters, "Wilhelm von Humboldt als Gründer der Universität Berlin," in *Forschen und Wirken. Festschrift zur 150-Feier der Humboldt Universität zu Berlin* (Berlin: VEB Deutscher Verlag der Wissenschaften, 1960), I, 15–39.

126. Friedrich Nietzsche, *Die fröhliche Wissenschaft* (1882), in *Nietzsches Werke*, Taschen-Ausgabe (Leipzig: C. G. Naumann, 1906), VI, 255.

127. Charles Richet, *Le Savant* (Paris: Hachette, 1923).

128. Bakunin quoted in, *The Political Philosophy of Bakunin: Scientific Anarchism*, G. P. Maximoff, ed. (Glencoe: The Free Press, 1953), pp. 77–81.

129. Ernest Renan, "Dialogues et fragments philosophiques" (1876), in *Oeuvres Complètes* (Paris: Calmann-Lévy, n.d.), I, 614–619.

130. Alfred Sauvy, *Théorie générale de la population* (Paris: Presses Universitaires de France, 1954), II, 75.

131. René Leriche, "Règles générales de la chirurgie de la douleur," *Anesthésie et Analgésie*, II (1936), 218–240.

132. Charles Darwin, *Life and Letters*, Francis Darwin, ed., 3 vols. (London: Appleton, 1887). *The Autobiography of Charles Darwin*, new ed., Nora Barlow (New York: Harcourt, Brace, 1959). Walter von Wyss, *Charles Darwin, ein Forscherleben* (Zurich: Artemis-Verlag, 1959). Gertrude Himmelfarb, *Darwin and the Darwinian Revolution* (London: Chatto & Windus, 1959).

133. "On the Tendency of Species to Form Varieties, and on the Perpetuation of Varieties and Species by Natural Means of Selection," by Charles Darwin, Esq., and Alfred Wallace, Esq. Communicated by Sir Charles Lyell and J. D. Hooker, Esq.. *Journal of the Proceedings of the Linnean Society. Zoology*, III, No. 9 (1858), 45–62.

134. Charles Darwin, *The Origin of Species by Means of Natural Selection, or the Preservation of Favoured Races in the Struggle for Life* (London: John Murray, 1859).

135. Jawaharlal Nehru, *Glimpses of World History* (New York: John Day Co., 1942), pp. 525–526.

136. Heinrich Schmidt, *Geschichte der Entwicklungslehre* (Leipzig: A. Kröner, 1918). John C. Green, *The Death of Adam* (Ames: The Iowa State University Press, 1959). Gerhard Wichler, *Charles Darwin, der Forscher und der Mensch* (Munich: Reinhardt, 1959). Bentley Glass, *Forerunners of Darwin* (Baltimore: Johns Hopkins, 1959).

137. Charles Darwin, *The Descent of Man, and Selection in Regard to Sex* (London: John Murray, 1871), II, 389.

138. A common story has it that the 1,250 copies of the first edition of *The Origin of Species* were sold on the first day of its sale. According to Gertrude Himmelfarb (*Darwin and the Darwinian Revolution*, p. 395), the term "sold out" actually means that the whole issue was fully subscribed by the dealers.

139. Darwin was compared to Copernicus by Emil du Bois-Reymond: *Darwin und Kopernikus* (January 25, 1883, Friedrichs-Sitzung der Akademie der Wissenschaften); in: *Reden* (Leipzig: Von Veit, 1912), II, 243–248; and by Thomas Huxley, *Lectures and Lay Sermons* (New York: E. P. Dutton, 1926).

140. For instance A. de Quatrefages, *Les Emules de Darwin*, 2 vols. (Paris: Alcan. 1894).

141. The zoologist Adolf Portmann, *Natur und Leben im Sozialleben* (Basel: F. Reinhardt, 1946), gives a devastating criticism of the concept of "struggle for life" in natural science.

142. E. Rabaud, "L'Interdépendance générale des organismes," *Revue Philosophique*, LIX, No. 2 (1934), 171–209 (says that the basic law of the living world is interdependence; the role of competition is subordinate and of restricted importance).

143. Evan V. Shute, *Flaws in the Theory of Evolution* (London, Ontario: Temside Press, 1961).

144. Gertrude Himmelfarb, *Darwin and the Darwinian Revolution*, pp. 366–367.

145. Karl Du Prel seriously applied Darwinism to astronomy and described the "elimination" of "unfit" celestial bodies from the solar system such as the meteors, asteroids, and certain comets. (Quoted by Oscar Hertwig, *Zur Abwehr des ethischen, des sozialen, des politischen Darwinismus* [Jena: Gustav Fischer, 1918].)

146. A. Hunter-Dupree, *Asa Gray* (Cambridge: Harvard University Press, 1959).

147. John Dewey, *The Influence of Darwin on Philosophy, and Other Essays in Contemporary Thought* (New York: H. Holt, 1910).

148. Ernst Haeckel, *Anthropogenie, oder Entwicklungsgeschichte des Menschen* (Leipzig: W. Engelmann, 1874), and other works.

149. Thomas H. Huxley, *The Struggle for Existence in Human Societies* (1888). Reprinted in *Evolution and Ethics and Other Essays* (New York: D. Appleton & Co., 1914), pp. 195–236.

150. J. J. Atkinson, *Primal Law*. Published as a second part to Andrew Lang, *Social Origins* (London: Longmans, Green and Co., 1903), pp. 209–294.

151. Gottfried Benn, *Das moderne Ich* (Berlin: Erich Reiss, 1920).

152. See among others Henry Picker, ed., *Hitlers Tischgespräche, 1941–1942* (Bonn: Athenaeum-Verlag, 1951), p. 227.

153. Prince Piotr A. Kropotkin, *Memoirs of a Revolutionist* (Boston: Houghton Mifflin, 1899), p. 498.

154. Prince Piotr Kropotkin, series of eight articles in the *Nineteenth Century*, (1890–1896). Later in book form, *Mutual Aid as a Factor in Evolution* (New York: McClure, Phillips and Co., 1902).

155. See Ashley Montague, *On Being Human* (New York: Schuman, Ltd., 1950).

156. Oscar Hertwig, *Das Werden der Organismen. Eine Widerlegung von Darwins Zufallstheorie* (Jena: Gustav Fischer, 1916). *Zur Abwehr des ethischen, des sozialen, des politischen Darwinismus* (Jena: Gustav Fischer, 1918). Adolf Portmann, *Natur und Kultur im Sozialleben* (Basel: Reinhardt, 1946).

157. Norman Angell, *The Great Illusion, a Study of the Relation of Military Power in Nations to Their Economic and Social Advantage* (London: W. Heinemann, 1910).

158. René Quinton, *L'Eau de mer, milieu organique* (Paris, Masson, 1904).

159. Rémy de Gourmont, "Le Principe de constance intellectuelle," in *Promenades Philosophiques*, 2nd series (Paris: Mercure de France, 1908), pp. 5–96.

160. See among others Walter von Wyss, *Charles Darwin, ein Forscherleben* (Zurich and Stuttgart: Artemis-Verlag, 1958).

161. J. C. Santlus, *Zur Psychologie der menschlichen Triebe* (Neuwied and Leipzig: Heuser, 1864).

162. Paul Ree, *Die Entstehung des Gewissens* (Berlin: Karl Duncker, 1885).

163. Friedrich Nietzsche, *Zur Genealogie der Moral;* in *Nietzsches Werke*, Taschenausgabe, VIII (Leipzig: C. G. Naumann, 1906).

164. The economic and social interpretation of history exists of course in its own right independently of Marxism. Examples are the works of the American historian Charles Austin Beard, *An Economic Interpretation of the Constitution of the United*

States (New York: Macmillan, Inc., 1913). *Economic Origins of Jeffersonian Democracy* (New York: MacMillan, Inc., 1915). *The Economic Basis of Politics* (New York: Knopf, Inc., 1945).

165. Friedrich Engels, Letter to Conrad Schmidt, October 27, 1890. Karl Marx, Friedrich Engels, *Ausgewählte Briefe* (Berlin: Dietz, 1953), p. 508.

166. Henri Lefebvre, *Pour connaître la pensée de Karl Marx* (Paris: Bordas, 1947), pp. 42–43.

167. See above all Max Eastman, *Marx and Lenin: The Science of Revolution* (New York: Albert and Charles Boni, 1927), Chap. 8.

168. This point has been emphasized by Karl Jaspers, *Allgemeine Psychopathologie* (Berlin: Springer, 1913).

169. Wilhelm Griesinger, *Pathologie und Therapie der psychischen Krankheiten* (Stuttgart: Adolph Krabbe, 1845), p. 60.

170. Mark D. Altschule, *Roots of Modern Psychiatry. Essays in the History of Psychiatry* (New York: Grune & Stratton, 1957). Roland Kuhn, "Griesingers Auffassung der psychischen Krankheiten und seine Bedeutung für die weitere Entwicklung der Psychiatrie," *Bibliotheca psychiatrica et neurologica*, C (1957), 41–67.

171. Ilza Veith, "The Wear and Tear Syndrome," *Modern Medicine* (December 1961), pp. 97–107.

172. James Johnson, *Change of Air or the Pursuit of Health* (London: S. Highly, T. & G. Underwood, 1831).

173. George M. Beard, "Neurasthenia, or Nervous Exhaustion," *Boston Medical and Surgical Journal*, III (1869), 217–221.

174. George M. Beard, *A Practical Treatise on Nervous Exhaustion (Neurasthenia), Its Symptoms, Nature, Sequence, Treatment* (New York: W. Wood, 1880). *American Nervousness, Its Causes and Consequences* (New York: Putnam's Sons, 1881).

175. George Beard, *Sexual Neurasthenia (Nervous Exhaustion)*, A. D. Rockwell, ed. (New York: E. B. Treat, 1884).

176. George Beard, "Neurasthenia (Nervous Exhaustion) as a Cause of Inebriety," *Quarterly Journal of Inebriety* (September 1879).

177. Anna Robeson Burr, *Weir Mitchell, His Life and Letters* (New York: Duffield, 1929).

178. S. Weir Mitchell, *Wear and Tear, or Hints for the Overworked* (Philadelphia, 1871).

179. S. Weir Mitchell, *Fat and Blood, or How to Make Them* (Philadelphia, 1877).

180. B. A. Morel, "Du Délire émotif. Névrose du système nerveux ganglionnaire viscéral," *Archives Générales de Médecine*, 6th series, VII (1866), 385–402, 530–551, 700–707.

181. M. Krishaber, *De la névropathie cérébro-cardiaque* (Paris: Masson, 1873).

5

On the Threshold of a New Dynamic Psychiatry

THE PERIOD FROM 1880 to 1900 was crucial in two respects. It was then that the first dynamic psychiatry was at long last recognized by "official medicine" and that it acquired a great diffusion; it was also the period of the dawn of a new dynamic psychiatry. The history of those two processes cannot be separated from the new social, political, and cultural context.

The World in 1880

The general face of the world had changed radically in the course of the century, through the French Revolution and the Napoleonic wars; the rise of new national states; the rapid progress of science, industry, and commerce; and the exploration of the remaining unknown regions of the world. The feeling prevailed that human culture was reaching a peak. However, in retrospect, that world was in many regards very different from ours, and it requires a real effort to visualize it as it was.

Above all, there prevailed a feeling of deep-rooted security. In spite of local and limited wars, workers' strikes, socialist agitation, and the anarchists' criminal attempts, the world seemed unshakable. The same was true in economic matters, despite periodical crises. There were no problems of devaluation or of variations in the rates of exchange between the national currencies. Since financial transactions were effected with gold coins, money seemed to be something constant, reliable, and of universal and lasting value. In spite of national rivalries, in that era of "armed peace," boundaries could almost be forgotten at times; anyone could leave his residence at any time and, provided he could afford it, travel to any part of the world without a passport, visa, or any other formality (with the sole exception of Russia and Turkey). This firm and stable basis of life was also reflected in the architecture: Bank buildings and hotels were built with walls as strong as those of a fortress, private villas were often surrounded by stone walls. Life seemed so secure that many people lost interest in social and political problems and lived from day to day.

There was a strong emphasis on male domination. It was a world shaped by man for man, in which woman occupied the second place. Political rights for women did not exist. The separation and dissimilarity of the sexes was sharper than today. The army was an exclusively male organization—a women's auxiliary service was unheard of. Office employees, including secretaries, were all males. The universities admitted no female students (the first ones appeared in the early 1890's). There were many gentlemen's clubs, and even in mixed social gatherings men would go to the smoking room while the ladies went to the drawing room, once dinner was over. Male virtues (ambition, aggressiveness, toughness) were extolled in literature. Virile manners included the wearing of a beard, moustache, or whiskers, walking with a stick or a cane, the practice of athletics, horseback-riding and fencing, rather than other sports that are more widespread today. Another virile custom, the duel, existed among officers, in German student associations, and in certain aristocratic and "high life" circles.[1] However, women had their salons, their committees, their journals, and trains had special compartments for ladies. Women who wore slacks, wore their hair short, or smoked, were hardly to be found. Man's authority over his children and also over his wife was unquestioned. Education was authoritarian; the despotic father was a common figure and was particularly conspicuous only when he became extremely cruel. Conflicts between generations, particularly between fathers and sons, were more frequent than today. But authoritarianism was a feature of the times and reigned everywhere, not only in the family. The military, magistrates, and judges enjoyed great prestige. Laws were more repressive, delinquent youth sternly punished, and corporal punishment was considered indispensable. All this must be considered with regard to the genesis of Freud's Oedipus complex.

Some classes were more strictly divided than they are today. The aristocracy, although deprived of factual authority, enjoyed much prestige, especially in the majority of countries that had a royal or an imperial court. (In Europe, only France and Switzerland were republics.) But everywhere, the leading class was the high bourgeoisie. The largest part of the wealth and political power was in its hands, and it controlled industry and finance. Below the bourgeoisie were the working classes. To be sure, the conditions of laborers had much improved since the beginning of the century but, despite the progress made, laborers were much poorer than they are now and were also less protected by social laws. The working hours were long; many laborers felt exploited, and demonstrations during strikes or on the first of May often took place in a "loaded" atmosphere. Child labor had been prohibited, but women's work and sweatshops were no myth. The material conditions of the peasantry had also largely improved, but not enough to prevent a constant stream of farmers from emigrating to the towns and cities. The impoverishment or disappearance of folklore was noticeable everywhere. The lowest step of the social ladder was occupied by the so-called *Lumpenproletariat,* that is, people living in slums in the utmost misery. Inextricable social problems were linked with the existence of these classes. Another feature of that period was the existence of a large number of domestics. Practically every bourgeois family had at least one servant, and wealthy and aristocratic families often had a dozen or more. Their material conditions were mostly mediocre. The relationship between masters and servants was no longer a patriarchal one, as it had been a century earlier, but mostly an authoritarian and unsentimental one.

The white man's domination, celebrated in Kipling's work, was unquestioned and proclaimed as a necessity for the welfare of the colonial peoples. When attention was drawn to the rapid disappearance of primitive populations in various parts of the world, it was often explained as a sad but necessary consequence of progress or the struggle for life. The objectors were rebuffed by phrases involving the civilizing mission of Europeans and the "white man's burden."

Another characteristic feature was the great amount of leisure enjoyed by certain classes. Not only did women of the aristocratic and bourgeois society not work, but there were also many men of leisure among the aristocrats, the wealthy, and men of private means. There was also a special world of artists, writers, journalists, and people of the theater, who spent much of their time in cafés and other public places. In that period when neither radio, nor television, nor the cinema existed, the theater had an enormous importance. Great actors enjoyed immense popularity comparable to that of today's most famous film stars. A publicity industry as it exists today was hardly known at the time, so that every man had to make his own publicity either through journalistic acquaintances, salon gossip, or by making himself conspicuous in some other way. Hence the theatrical way of life, poses, verbal violence, public quarrels and reconciliations of prominent figures. Marcel Proust's work has captured the spirit of that time in his descriptions of those men and women of leisure, their carriage drives, their idle talk. It has often been asked why hysteria was so frequent in the 1880's and so rapidly declined after 1900. One plausible explanation is that it was in accord with the theatrical and affected way of life of that period.

In a world of leisure, love was naturally a prime concern of men and women. No wonder that the spirit of that time was permeated with refined eroticism. Those people who were "in love with love" gave to their amorous intrigues the peculiarly formal or theatrical character of their period, as seen in their literature and theater (for instance in the work of Arthur Schnitzler). This same atmosphere bred sudden fads such as the craze for Wagner's music, for Schopenhauer's and Von Hartmann's philosophies of the unconscious, later for Nietzsche's writings, for the Symbolists, the Neo-Romantics, and others. Only in that particular perspective can the origin of the new dynamic psychiatry be understood.

The Political Background

The birth of the new dynamic psychiatry must also be viewed within its setting in the political background of the period. The world was now divided between powers, national sovereign states, which were in harsh competition with each other and linked by a complex network of treaties and shifting alliances.

The dominant power was the British Empire, although it was more and more closely followed by the United States. The British Navy controlled the seven seas, the Union Jack was flying over vast colonies and territories scattered over the globe, British currency was the soundest, and London was the world's greatest commercial and financial center. Queen Victoria, who in 1876 had also been crowned Empress of India, was the incorporation of England's might and of its traditions of dignity and respectability.

To present-day generations, the Victorian spirit represents ugly architectural style, cumbersome furniture, heavy draperies, pompous ceremonies, solemn phraseology, old-fashioned prejudices, and ridiculous prudishness. But to its contemporaries, the word "Victorian" was rather suggestive of "victory," and in fact England was constantly victorious over land and sea. What their present-day descendants term hypocrisy was to Victorian ancestors rather self-discipline and dignity. The Victorian spirit was actually the outcome of a cultural change that had taken place during the fifty years preceding the coronation of Queen Victoria in 1837.[2] It had started as a reaction against the dissolute life of eighteenth-century English society and against the deadly danger that had imperiled England during the French Revolution and the reign of Napoleon. A movement of religious zeal was initiated by William Wilberforce, an influential member of Parliament who was also instrumental in abolishing the slave trade. The movement for religious and moral reform parallelled a series of movements for social and educational reforms of all kinds.[3] It was also felt that England, having to govern a large empire, also had the task of educating generations of efficient and honest civil servants. Contrary to present-day assumptions, sexual matters were treated frankly in medical and anthropological literature. They also were discreetly hinted at in literature. Far from being old-fashioned, England was at the peak of its strength and produced many heroic personalities, empire-builders, explorers, and philanthropists, as well as many remarkable women, such as Florence Nightingale. One need only look at portraits of Victorian personalities and see their expressions of quiet and concentrated energy. Longfellow's verse "Life is real! Life is earnest!" seemed to be their motto. They did not resent the fact that England, being so powerful, had many enemies. Britain also exerted a great attraction upon foreigners, who zealously imitated British manners. But the Victorian spirit, which had started before Queen Victoria and prevailed during most of the nineteenth centuury, was already in sharp decline in 1880.

On the Continent, the leading power was now Germany, which, after having been for several centuries a "nation without a state," had finally achieved its unity. However, this had not come about under the democratic Parliament of Frankfort in 1848, but in 1871 under Prussia's leadership with its Iron Chancellor, Bismarck. During its stateless nationhood, Germany had vacillated between two poles of attraction, Austria and Prussia. The former had been eliminated by Prussia's victory over Austria in 1866, and German unification had finally been reached as a result of Germany's victory over France in the Franco-Prussian War of 1870–1871. In Europe the Germans had hitherto been considered as a nation of romantics, musicians, philosophers, poets, and selfless scientists; now, after they had come to a full political awareness, they often gave the impression of being an aggressive people who only respected force. The German population increased enormously in spite of the ceaseless massive emigration to America. There was an extraordinary industrial and commercial expansion, and Germany built a gigantic and well-trained army. By now, however, the other European nations shared among themselves the best of the overseas territories, and Germany, who entered the colonial competition only in the 1890's, had to be content, grudgingly, with the leftovers. Then, remembering that Germany had owned a powerful navy in the Middle Ages, Emperor William II decided to build a new one, to Britain's great annoyance. Germany's resentment was increased by the fear of French revenge and Russia's ambitions. As time went by, the Germans became obsessed with the fear of "encirclement" by the combined forces of France, England, and Russia. German leadership remained almost unchallenged in the fields of science and culture, with the exception of the fine arts in which the French prevailed. German had become the foremost scientific language of the Western world, to the extent that the lack of its knowledge could be a severe handicap to scientists in many fields (including psychology and psychiatry).

Germany's victory over France in the war of 1870–1871 had disastrous consequences for Europe. In the eyes of many Germans, the annexation of Alsace was only a reconquering of old German territory "stolen" by Louis XIV (which, however, did not justify their simultaneous annexation of a large part of French-speaking Lorraine, which had strategic importance). But, under Napoleon III, France had proclaimed the right to self-determination of peoples, a principle that the French had applied when taking over the provinces of Savoy and Nice in 1860. Since the population of Alsace and Lorraine had clearly manifested their desire to be French, their annexation by Germany was regarded by the French as a political anachronism as well as a crime, and they remained irreconcilable. A collective feeling of inferiority permeated France following its defeat by Germany and its inferior position toward the British Empire. But it found partial compensation through the acquisition of a new colonial empire, through brilliant financial prosperity, and through its cultural and scientific achievements that challenged those of Germany. In contrast to the stern, disciplined, authoritarian Germans, the French claimed to personify spontaneous creativeness and intellectual freedom. A peculiar feature of France was the extraordinary concentration of the intellectual life of the entire country in its capital. Art, music, literature, and science flourished in Paris, the *Ville Lumière,* which the French considered the capital of the civilized world. Though the French language was gradually losing its former preponderance, it was still widely used and remained the official language of international diplomacy. In the eyes of many Frenchmen, their country was the champion of the "spirit," facing the heavy German "cult of the force." But France's population did not increase as did that of other countries, which contributed to the stereotyped image of France as a "declining nation," a feeling widely held in Germany.

In central Europe, the Austro-Hungarian monarchy occupied a vast area between Germany on the north, Switzerland and Italy on the west, Russia on the east, and the new Balkan nations and Turkey on the south. Austro-Hungary was not a unified national state such as France or Germany, but was described as "a mosaic of nations and debris of nations" mixed in the most complex way. Present-day opinion often views the Austro-Hungarian monarchy as ridiculously old-fashioned with its Imperial Court and its aristocracy that still held on to traditions from the Baroque. It is accused of having "oppressed" some of its nations, and sometimes, on the contrary, of having granted them too much freedom. Actually, as well expressed by Somary, far from being a political anachronism, Austro-Hungary was well ahead of other countries in having established what would today be called a "supranational state," which those who strive today for Europe's unification study with wonder.[4] After the Emperor had relinquished his absolute power in 1859, and following a few years of crises, the Empire was given a constitution based on the *Ausgleich* ("compromise") of 1867. The Empire was divided into two states having strictly equal rights, both subject to the same sovereign who was Emperor of Austria and "apostolic King" of Hungary. Each of these states comprised one dominating nation and several national minorities. The two states were united, not only through their loyalty to their sovereign, the Hapsburg Emperor, but by an "Imperial and Royal" (*K.u.K.*) government, which was responsible for certain matters such as war and diplomacy. The internal matters were the responsibility in Austria of the "Imperial-Royal" (*K.K.*) government and administration, and in Hungary of the "Royal" (*Kngl.*) government and administration. The relationships between the central administration and the national minorities within each one of the two states were ruled by complex regulations. Most of the national minorities were turbulent and demanding, and it was a constant concern of the government of the states to grant them as many rights as it deemed necessary or admissable without disrupting the cohesion of the Empire. The unity of that vast political structure was secured, not only through its loyalty to Emperor Franz-Josef, but also by an efficient civil service and by the army. The Austro-Hungarian monarchy was considered by some as a castle in the air that would collapse at the slightest touch, and by others as a miracle of political wisdom and an indispensable element of European equilibrium. Many Austrians and Hungarians considered their country as being the outpost of civilization. Thorny problems resulted from the proximity of Turkey. Because of the Sultan's despotic court with its harem and eunuchs, and the periodic massacres of Armenians and other Christian minorities, Turkey was not considered a civilized country. But the decomposition of the Turkish Empire, called Europe's sick man, had given rise to newly independent countries whose turbulence and aggressiveness were a threat to peace. But the dual monarchy felt threatened by Russia, whose government, while oppressing the Slavic minorities within its own territory, claimed to be their protector and encouraged their rebellion outside.

The Austro-Hungarian monarchy embraced a large and diversified country with the entire gamut of landscapes, from seaside to mountains, wide plains, lakes and forests, and three beautiful historical cities, Vienna, Budapest, and Prague. The capital of the Empire and the seat of a glorious and ancient court, Vienna was one of the most famed cities in the world. In spite of the multilingual character of the monarchy, German was its main language, being spoken at the court and having cultural prestige. Vienna was the seat of many public offices, an important diplomatic center, a place of great culture concentration where the level of education was extremely high. Numerous artists, musicians, poets, writers, and playwrights, as well as scientists of the highest distinction lived there. Because of the constant flow of people belonging to the various minorities of the Empire, life in Vienna was most picturesque. But many of its inhabitants led a rather provincial kind of life. The Viennese population, very different from the cold, stern, and disciplined Germans, was cordial, easygoing, good-humored, and fond of jokes. They spoke German with a specific accent and used particular terms and idioms that constituted the so-called "Viennese dialect." A typical feature of Viennese life was the cafés, which at that time were still frequented only by men. Many of these cafés had a distinct clientele of a given social class, occupation, and political outlook.

In Eastern Europe, Russia was a rapidly expanding empire, and after the emancipation of over twenty-two million serfs by Czar Alexander II in 1861, it had also become the scene of a rapid industrial and commercial expansion. The autocratic government had granted a number of liberties to the people. The arts were flourishing. Russia had produced some of the world's greatest writers and distinguished scientists in various disciplines, including psychiatry. Two other features deserve special mention. First is the fact that, whereas in the rest of Europe the higher classes looked down upon the peasantry, there was among the Russian intelligentsia a widespread belief that the people were the source of all culture. Under the motto "the return to the people," many intellectuals and artists tried to renew their inspiration at that yet untouched source. Actually, the Russian peasantry still enjoyed their rich folklore and popular arts, and was endowed with an innate sense of beauty. A second feature was that Russia was the chosen ground for "nihilism," a trend that could be defined as a fascination with the idea of destruction. Remote sources of nihilism can be traced back to the wide-scale genocide perpetrated by the Mongols, who from the thirteenth to the fifteenth centuries, swarmed over half of Asia and central Russia, massacred countless millions of human beings, reduced whole countries to deserts, and destroyed flourishing towns to the last resident. In Russia mass slaughter became in turn a political method in the hands of Czar Ivan the Terrible. But an apocalyptic mentality spread among the people and resulted in mass self-destruction. Thus, in the mid-seventeenth century, the *Raskolniki* ("old believers") destroyed their farms and burned themselves to death rather than accept certain modifications in Church books. The *Raskolniki* inspired a number of sects in which self-destructive tendencies were conspicuous (such as the Skoptzy or "self-castrates" and the Khlisty or "self-flagellants"). It was also among *Raskolniki* communities that the political nihilists originated, particularly the notorious Nechayev, whose *Revolutionary Catechism* is a textbook in the science of the destruction of society by violent means.[5] Russia's political history of the nineteenth century was dominated by the activities of revolutionary groups more or less influenced by nihilistic trends, and nihilism was a general concern of thinkers and writers. One may wonder whether it was by sheer chance that the concept of the death instinct was expressed by two Russian scientists around the end of the nineteenth century: the psychiatrist Tokarsky[6] and the physiologist Metchnikoff.[7] To other Europeans, the Russian trends of the "return to the people" and of nihilism appeared as disquieting features of the Russian soul, which did not concern them directly.

Most Europeans still considered their country as the leading part of the world and Russia and America as being on the borderline. The picture of the United States in European eyes, however, had changed greatly since the time of the American Revolution. The French, who had at first looked upon the new republic as being a revival of ancient Greek or Roman democracy, now viewed it as a political experiment on a mass scale. DeTocqueville, a representative of the declining French aristocracy, studied the development of the American democracy with passionate interest, and foresaw the model of European governments of the future.

A romantic view of America as being the land of noble Indians and carefree cowboys was also popular in Europe, and no doubt contributed in furthering the mass-scale emigration of German youth to the United States. America also soon became praised for its ingenious scientists, and in the 1880's Edison became a popular figure in Europe. Europeans began to look with wonder at the unprecedented American economic and industrial development, and shortly before the end of the century, in 1898, the Spanish-American War brought the sudden revelation that the United States had taken its place among the leading world powers. American cultural achievements were less known in Europe. However, as we shall see in the following chapter, the psychiatric work of George Beard, and S. Weir Mitchell, the philosophy of Josiah Royce, the psychology of William James and James Mark Baldwin exerted a great influence on the dynamic psychiatry of Pierre Janet.

Culture, Science, and University

Two basic facts are characteristic of that period: the predominance of classical culture in education, and the predominance of the university as a center of science.

The meaning of Greco-Latin culture had changed since the Renaissance and the Baroque eras. Latin was no longer the great universal language for science, culture, church, or government. It had lost its last stronghold when Magyar was proclaimed Hungary's official language in place of Latin in the 1840's. Yet Latin had not quite disappeared as a scientific language: a Latin dissertation remained compulsory for the *doctorat ès-lettres* in France until 1900. In addition to the main dissertation in French, Bergson, Durkheim, Pierre Janet, and others, still had to write a Latin thesis. It was believed that nothing was more important than the imparting of a thorough knowledge of Latin in the secondary schools through the method of analysis and synthesis. The young student first had to memorize the declensions, conjugations, and grammatical rules, as well as the vocabulary, and then went on to compose sentences, translate from and into Latin, write compositions first in prose and then in verse, while paying much attention to his style so that it would be as close as possible to that of the great Roman classics. After six or eight years of such study, he would have a perfect command of Latin, but this was used only for writing, hardly ever for speaking. Some people scoffed at the "wasted hours spent at learning a dead language, which would be of no use in life," but, seen in the perspective of that period, it fitted perfectly into the rationale of what was expected from a liberal education. As the philologist Wilamowitz-Moellendorf said, it was an *exercitio intellectualis* comparable to the spiritual exercises of the Jesuits.[8] It was a method of acquiring an ever-increasing capacity for mental concentration and mental synthesis, which might also be compared with the study of mathematics. Men who underwent such training became capable of constructing a vast synthesis of their own. This is how we can understand that Janet, Freud, or Jung were well prepared for the construction of an immensely systematized building of knowledge. Another advantage of this classical education and culture was that it provided the student with the key to ancient Greco-Roman culture and to everything that had been written in Latin in the course of twenty-five centuries. Janet who read Bacon's works in Latin. Freud who read old books on witchcraft in the original texts, and Jung, who read the medieval alchemists in their difficult Latin, were no exceptions among men educated at that time. The teaching of Latin was given precedence over that of foreign languages, because learning Latin meant acquiring a knowledge of the roots of one's own national culture, whereas learning a foreign language was acquiring unconsciously the pattern of thought of an alien culture. A Frenchman, an Englishman, or a German who underwent a classical education was thus more French, English, German than their present-day descendants, but they were at the same time more European because they all shared the knowledge of the common basis of their respective cultures. They also shared a common treasure from their knowledge of the classics. They were able to recognize many quotations and allusions from Greek and Latin authors, which few would be able to do today. For instance, there was nothing extraordinary in putting in an epigraph to a scientific book a verse of Virgil, as Freud did to his *Interpretation of Dreams*. Not only Rousseau or Puységur, but also contemporaries, such as Frazer or Myers, did so. These men expected the reader to understand the quotation, to locate it in the context of the poem, and to grasp the meaning.

In addition to the study of ancient Greco-Roman culture, much time was given to the study of national and foreign classics. In France a working knowledge of German was considered indispensable for any intellectual. In Germany the knowledge of French was considered essential, and familiarity with Goethe and Shakespeare a matter of course. Another basic element of culture was philosophy. In France the final year of the lyceum was devoted to its study; in Germany and Austria, those aspiring to a doctorate had to take a compulsory course in philosophy.

The main center of science and culture was the university. Every cultured man had gone to a university, and a scientific career was necessarily linked with a university career. Exceptions such as Bachofen and Darwin were very rare (both men enjoyed the advantage of a substantial personal fortune). It was not so much the aim of the university to graduate specialists, but rather to develop men of general culture who specialized in one branch of science. It emphasized the value of unbiased research. "Pure" research often had more status than "applied" research, especially if that applied research was being performed outside of the university. Within the university, professors enjoyed a wide autonomy and there was a general respect for the learned professions, at least in continental Europe.

A university career was usually long and arduous. It was exceedingly rare that a scholar should be appointed a titular university professor while he was still young. The twenty-five-year-old Nietzsche, who was appointed in 1869, was a conspicuous exception. Not only was there fierce competition, but material conditions in the lower university degrees were precarious. The time had disappeared when young scholars could wait for university openings while tutoring the children of wealthy families, a task that Fichte, Hegel, and others had so much disliked. In Germany and central Europe, the prevailing system was that of the *Privatdozent,* which consisted in lecturing at the university with the sole remuneration being the fees paid by the students who attended the lectures. Even at its best, this could never enrich the lecturer. Thus, the young scientist could spend the best years of his life in tedious and wearisome waiting for the longed-for appointment as *Extraordinarius,* which at least brought with it some financial security. As for the appointment as *Ordinarius,* or titular professor, which was the crowning of a successful university career, there were "many called but few chosen." Still more, it was not sufficient to be talented or to be a hard worker, one also had to conform to certain rules. Though it was necessary to be ambitious, it was no less necessary to avoid being what Germans call the *Streber* and the French the *arriviste.* Albert Fuchs tells how his father, whose life had been devoted to his university career in Vienna, carefully taught him to distinguish between those two things. Efforts toward securing a superior title in the university hierarchy belonged to the legitimately ambitious, but it was considered *Streberei* to seek to obtain a title of nobility or a decoration.[9] Fuchs admits that the difference between legitimate ambitions and *Streberei* was at times rather nebulous.

In his memoirs, Max Dessoir made a sketch of the rules leading to success at the university in Germany around 1885.[10] The surest way was to attach oneself to a leading university personality. Another way was to write papers that would be noticed by specialists and through which one could get in touch with leading personalities. However, it was wise to avoid writing too much and becoming a "Narcissus of the inkpot." The fastest way was to do active research in one of the acknowledged prevalent trends, which also meant that it was dangerous to remove oneself too far from the beaten track. One should also avoid being too versatile, and try rather to dominate one narrow field. It was good for one's name to be synonymous with a certain book, a certain invention, or a certain theory. But it was undesirable and dangerous to be better known by the public at large than in university circles, as had been the case with Haeckel who had started a brilliant university career but whose popular writings about science and philosophy had evoked ferocious attacks upon him by his colleagues.

It is obvious from the literature of that time that a university career was fraught with many handicaps and that it took little to destroy it. The anatomo-pathologist Lubarsch tells how his career was nearly ruined through a faux-pas of his. Working as an assistant at the Rostock Pathological Institute, he asked one morning "who was the idiot who had put an anatomic piece into a given chemical solution," to which the second assistant replied that it had been done on the order of Herr Professor. The next day, Lubarsch received a letter from Professor Thierfelder, who, on account of the insult directed against him, immediately dismissed Lubarsch from the Institute. Lubarsch adds that in some scientific fields such as anatomy, physiology, bacteriology, and chemistry, the young scientist was utterly dependent on the material and on the working opportunity provided by an institute. Thus, to be forced to leave the institute could amount to having one's career ruined. It was also dangerous suddenly to change the direction of one's work or to shift into another field. Thus Bachofen, who had embarked on a promising career as a historian of law, saw this career shattered when he published his work on ancient tombs. The same happened to Nietzsche, whose brilliant career as a philologist was threatened when he published his *Origin of Tragedy,* and definitely ended when he published his subsequent philosophical works. The possession of a large fortune was also a double-edged sword; it could make the years of the *Privatdozent* tolerable, but it complicated matters when the scientist later became his own Maecenas. Difficulties arose, for instance, for the physiologist Czermak, who erected a large auditorium in Leipzig, at his own expense, especially designed for experimental demonstrations. Obersteiner, professor of anatomy and pathology of the nervous system, taught without remuneration at Vienna University for thirty-seven years. He founded an institute at his own expense, and later donated to the university all his material, his collections, and his library of 60,000 volumes. But he experienced much resistance and hostility on the part of the university's administration and of certain of his colleagues. Those who did not have the advantage of owning a large fortune not infrequently died in poverty in spite of their fame. Benedikt relates that when the illustrious pathologist Rokitansky died, his widow was left with a meager pension, which was later supplemented only because of Benedikt's personal intervention.[12] The same applied to clinical medicine. Although a physician could rely on his clientele, this could never replace the scientific resources provided by a hospital or other official institution.

The interrelationships of university scholars were marked by intensive rivalries, paradoxically allied to a stiff *Korpsgeist* or traditional professional solidarity. On account of the *Korpsgeist,* universities sometimes retained old professors on their staff whose teaching had become quite obsolete or who were eccentric or incapable. A tragic example was the case of the Vienna University Obstetrics Hospital in the years 1844 to 1850. Hundreds of mothers lost their lives there because of endemic puerperal fever, whereas the other obstetrical hospital attached to the university, which served as the midwives' training school, showed no such mortality records. The chief assistant, Dr. Semmelweiss, tirelessly pointed to the source of the evil and denounced the incapacity of his chief, Professor Johann Klein, against whom no action was ever taken, and the university collegium, which consisted of honest and responsible persons, did not interfere on account of the *Korpsgeist.* When the professor finally left, Semmelweiss was not given the appointment because he had broken an ethical rule in denouncing his chief.[13] This story, which provoked so much indignation at the time, had a recent counterpart in the story of Professor Ferdinand Sauerbruch (1875–1951), a brilliant surgeon whose conceit about his capabilities had become pathological. In his later years one patient after another died on the operating table without anyone daring to intervene.[14]

It was inevitable that a system that entailed such hardships and competition would also breed much envy, jealousy, and hatred between the rivals. But these feelings had to be repressed in order to conform to the official standards of behavior. Hence the manifestation of resentment so aptly analyzed by Nietzsche and Scheler. The French writer Léon Daudet has described, under the name of *invidia,* the kind of professional resentment that arose among writers, but his description would be equally applicable to university scholars of his period.[15] Rarely did the *invidia* degenerate into an open conflict between professors in the same university. One of the few examples is the dispute between the Viennese professors Hyrtl and Brücke. These two renowned scholars lived at the Anatomy Institute, Brücke on the ground floor and Hyrtl on the upper floor. Hyrtl enjoyed the reputation of being one of the greatest anatomists of his time; he was extremely wealthy but equally stingy, and eccentric, and heartily disliked by all his colleagues. A stern, rigid, and disciplined Prussian, Brücke hated Vienna and was hated in turn by many of his students for his excessive severity. His conflict with Hyrtl began on the day when he announced that he would give a course of "higher anatomy" (*höhere Anatomie*). This way of designating histology struck Hyrtl as a personal insult. He took to using noisy tools when he knew that Brücke had company in the apartment below. Brücke retaliated by placing the dogs, on whom he conducted hunger experiments, under Hyrtl's windows, expecting to disturb him with their howling. To his amazement, however, Brücke found that the animals failed to lose weight as expected, until one day he discovered that Hyrtl secretly fed the poor beasts with meat that he threw down to them from his windows.[16] But ususally, within the same university, professors who disliked each other maintained a facade of correctness, if not of courtesy, and never spoke ill of each other in public. But, from one university to another, they felt less obligation for self-restraint and would vehemently attack one another, either verbally (one example is the vitriolic speech Virchow delivered in Munich against Haeckel in 1877), or in the form of venomous pamphlets. When Nietzsche published his *Birth of Tragedy*, the philologist Von Wilamowitz-Moel lendorf severely critized it in writing.[17] Nietzsche's friend, the philologist Erwin Rohde,[18] replied with a virulent pamphlet beginning with the famous sentence "When a head and a book collide and it sounds hollow, does it necessarily stem from the book?"[19] New ideas and discoveries were sometimes accepted immediately with enthusiasm (such as Roentgen's discovery of the X rays), but not infrequently they aroused stormy controversies. When Pasteur invented his preventive treatment for rabies, he was the object of such violent attacks on the part of the internist Peter that he fell into a depression and had to take some months' vacation.[20] In Germany, when Ehrlich discovered the treatment for syphilis with arseno-benzols, he was mercilessly attacked for several years afterward. Certain topics such as hypnotism were constantly brought back to light and dropped again because of such attacks. When Krafft-Ebing, then professor in Graz, started working with hypnosis, he was furiously attacked by Benedikt, who said that he would submit him to a "psychological analysis," that is, have his personality analyzed and reconstructed by synthesis.[21] Whatever the explanation, there is no doubt that there was much more verbal violence in the scientific world then than there is today, and this should be taken into account in judging the current controversies against Freud, Adler, and Jung.

However, it must be said in all fairness that distrust of new ideas and discoveries was justified more than once. It would be simple to list alleged discoveries that turned out to be erroneous. How often did archeologists claim to have deciphered the Etruscan language, physicists to have discovered new rays, physicians a cure for cancer, or historians of literature to have identified the true author of Shakesperean drama. Sometimes and erroneous discovery would induce other researchers into the same illusions, thus bringing false confirmation that was to be refuted by a more critical inquiry. This happened to the physicist Blondlot in Nancy, who believed that he had discovered a new kind of rays, N rays, which were eventually shown to be the result of an illusion.[22] Another collective illusion, which was more long-lived, was the alleged discovery of the canals of the planet Mars by the Italian astronomer Schiaparelli in 1879. Several astronomers all over the world started believing that they saw these canals and other similar ones in increasing numbers; maps of Mars were published showing up to eight hundred such canals. The conclusion was then drawn that Mars was inhabited by intelligent beings.[23] However, nobody was ever able to obtain a photograph of the canals. In this case the illusion was more tenacious because of the emotional connotation relating to the problem of the existence of intelligent beings in other worlds. One should not overlook that official science also had to resist persistent attacks on the part of several pseudosciences such as phrenology, homeopathy, and astrology, which enjoyed popularity among large sections of the public and of the intellectual world.

The intensity of competition between scientists also explains the extraordinary bitterness of priority contestations. Certain scientists of gentle character would become enraged if someone published as a new discovery something that they had already published. In the eighteenth century, there had been a controversy between Leibniz and Newton about the discovery of the infinitesimal calculus that embittered Newton's last years. In that case, it concerned one of the greatest discoveries in the history of science. But all through the nineteenth century, controversies raged over the priority of matters, which, in retrospect, seem petty or ridiculous. Seldom was a question of priority concluded in the generous way in which Darwin and Wallace settled their dispute in 1858 under the auspices of the Linnean Society. It was not very frequent either to see a discovery actually stolen from its discoverer, although several instances have been reported. Auguste Forel insists that he had discovered the nucleus of the origin of the rabbit's auditory nerve in 1884 and sent a paper about this discovery to Professor Bechtereff in Petersbourg, who informed him that he had himself just made the same discovery, and who published it sometime later in the *Neurologisches Zentralblatt*. Forel never doubted that Bechtereff had stolen his discovery.[24] In most of these controversies, however, the disputes were about the priority of the discovery. The rule had been established that priority was given to the first one to publish the discovery; the official date of publication was considered decisive. As a result, disputes arose about the length of time authors had to wait between the date of sending in the manuscript and the date of its printed appearance in the journals. Forel claimed to have discovered the unity of the nervous cell in 1886 and sent his work to the *Archiv für Psychiatrie,* which published it only in January 1887. The same discovery was made simultaneously by His, who had sent his paper to another journal, which published it in October 1886, with the result that he was given priority. After them, Ramon y Cajal, Kölliker, and finally Waldeyer published the same discovery, but the latter, having coined the term "neuron," was generally credited with that discovery.[25] Rumors were circulated that certain authors did not hesitate to alter the date of publication of their books or pamphlets in order to secure priority.

Scientific controversies were also embittered by nationalistic passions. From the beginning of the century, there had been growing rivalries between German science, French science, and English science, each country trying to push its own scientists into the foreground. The Franco-Prussian war of 1870–1871 further inflamed the passions. Disputes arose between scientists of both countries, sometimes in a dignified form as between Renan and David Strauss, sometimes in a more hostile manner as between Fustel de Coulanges and Mommsen. At times there were exchanges of insults. After their military defeat, the French upheld Pasteur with his epoch-making discoveries for the benefit of mankind as a symbol of French superiority in the realm of the spirit. Germany opposed Koch to Pasteur. At the International Congress for

Hygiene in Geneva in 1882, Pasteur read a paper in defense of his discoveries against Koch's arguments. He happened to quote a *recueil allemand* (German collection) of papers about hygiene. Koch, who was among the assembly, understood Pasteur to say *orgueil allemand* (German conceit), arose, interrupting Pasteur with vehement protestations, to the surprise of the audience who could not understand what Koch was protesting.[26] There is no doubt that science had lost much of the international character it still had in the eighteenth century. Attempts to create a new international science met with increasing difficulties because of the expansion of science in the meantime and the increasing number of scientists. In the past, a scholar was able to concentrate for years on one important volume, which would be the synthesis of the work and thought of a lifetime. With the development of the scientific movement came the era of academies and learned societies that met regularly at which scientists announced summarily any new discovery as soon as they had made it. It was also the era of the numerous congresses, at which scientists hastily announced discoveries that were still in the making and results they expected to find. It is not generally realized that scientific congresses are a relatively new thing. There had been annual national meetings of professional scientific associations, and also meetings of scientists delegated by their respective governments for the discussion of certain problems, but the large congresses that we take for granted were quite new in the 1880's.[27] The first international congresses were small gatherings. As an example, the first International Congress of Psychology in 1886 had one hundred sixty registered participants; the second, in Paris in 1889, two hundred ten; the third, in London in 1892, three hundred; the fourth, in Munich in 1896, five hundred three. The official languages were French, German, English, and sometimes Italian. Scientists from all countries were expected to be able to understand one another without interpreters, (there being of course no simultaneous translation, a procedure that did not even exist in the science fiction of that time).

The history of science, as it is usually taught, extolls the victors and ignores the many who were vanquished in that fierce struggle. Some of the latter were men of the most brilliant qualities, if not of genius. We will cite but one example, that of Moritz Benedikt (1835–1920) whose *Memoirs* tell a disconsolate account of a life of scientific and professional frustration in Vienna.[28] At first glance it would seem that Benedikt had had a successful career: a pioneer in neurology, electrology, criminology, and psychiatry, he taught at Vienna University, had a wealthy private clientele, published numerous papers, and traveled widely in foreign countries where he was hailed as one of the heads of Austrian medicine. He had won the admiration and friendship of Charcot, who gave his name to a rare disease (the Benedikt Syndrome, which Benedikt had actually been the first to describe). However, Benedikt's *Memoirs* are those of a frustrated man who literally chokes with resentment. He tells how his discoveries had, one after the other, been appropriated and developed by other scientists who then gleaned the credit that was due to him; how he was never appointed to the professorship that he felt was his by right, and how his merits were never acknowledged by his countrymen. He describes the hostility of the Austrians toward any kind of greatness and recalls their ingratitude toward great artists, musicians such as Mozart, Haydn, Schubert, the poet Grillparzer, and others. It is unquestionably true that Benedikt's contribution to dynamic psychiatry was of great value, as we will see later.

It would be a great contribution to the secret history of science to analyze in detail those factors that bring fame to some scientists, oblivion to others. As an example, a comparison could be made between Champollion (1790–1832), who is hailed as a genius for having deciphered the Egyptian hieroglyphics, and Grotefend (1775–1853) who, although he deciphered the ancient Persian cuneiform script, is almost forgotten today.[29] There is no evidence to assume that there was more merit in deciphering the one rather than the other. How then can the difference of attitude toward them be explained? In the first place, Champollion benefitted from a century-old myth surrounding ancient Egypt. The hieroglyphics (sacred writing) were supposed to contain the mysteries of a prodigious and forgotten wisdom of unfathomable antiquity. On the other hand, ancient Persia had been so thoroughly destroyed by the Islamic and Mongolian conquerors that little of it had survived. Only later, with Fechner's book *Zend-Avesta* and Nietzsche's *Zarathustra,* did it become a little more fashionable. Second, the cuneiform characters were more abstract and less decorative than the highly artistic Egyptian hieroglyphics. Third, Champollion's discovery had a political background: Napoleon's Egyptian expedition (itself a most romantic episode of history) had been frustrated by the English, and the Anglo-French strife was being pursued in the scientific field. While British scholars were on the track, the deciphering of the hieroglyphics was first achieved by a Frenchman, which meant a revenge for France. Grotefend's discovery, however, occurred at a time of unreceptiveness in Germany. Fourth, the life of Champollion himself is filled with adventurous and romantic episodes. While still a child, he experienced the thrill of the Egyptian expedition. At the age of twelve, he made a solemn vow that he would decipher the hieroglyphics. He then met an Egyptian monk who taught him the Coptic language, which he soon mastered and knew as well as his mother tongue by the time he was sixteen. His first paper on the Coptic language received an enthusiastic reception at the Institut de France. When he made his decisive discovery, he ran to his brother, shouting: "*Je tiens l'affaire!*" (I got it!), upon which he fainted and had to rest for five days. His discovery was celebrated as a national triumph by the French in the face of violent British protestations. Grotefend's life, on the contrary, was that of a cobbler's son who had painstakingly become a teacher in a small classical college and who could climb no higher on the academic ladder. His discovery met with incredulity, suspicion, and hostility on the part of the orientalists, who found it inadmissible that so great and important a discovery should have been made outside of university circles. With much effort, Grotefend was able to publish part of his discovery, and spent the rest of his life struggling desperately to win the recognition that was given him only posthumously. Many parallels could be drawn in other sciences to the fates of Champollion and Grotefend. Truly, in the scientific world, perhaps more than anywhere else, did Kipling's verse apply: "Triumph and disaster. . . these two impostors."

The Prophet of a New Era: Nietzsche

Around 1880 the Western world lay under the influence of positivism, scientism, and evolutionism. The predominating trends were, besides the remnants of the old Enlightenment philosophy, Social Darwinism, Marxism, and the newer materialistic and mechanistic philosophies. Among the leading thinkers were the utilitarianists and social philosophers Herbert Spencer, John Stuart Mill, and Hippolyte Taine. In literature, naturalism aimed at reproducing as exactly as possible the picture of life and facts as Balzac had done and as was then being done by Flaubert, Maupassant, and Zola. Romanticism seemed a thing of the past.

However, around 1885, a new cultural turn, a marked change in intellectual orientation could be felt throughout Europe. It affected many aspects of culture, and the birth of the newer dynamic psychiatry can be understood only in its context. Friedrich Nietzsche stands out among the leaders of this new movement. Nietzsche (1844–1900), was the son of a Protestant minister, who died when Nietzsche was very young. Nietzsche's first vocation was Greco-Latin philology. An exceptionally brilliant student, he was appointed professor of classical philology at the University of Basle in 1869 at the age of twenty-five—a legendary feat. In 1872 he surprised and disappointed his colleagues with his book *The Birth of Tragedy*. Illness forced him to resign from his post in 1879. He had already started to write a series of books in which he proclaimed in a brilliant aphoristic style and a prophetic tone the necessity of overthrowing the accepted values of contemporary society, the principle of the will to power, and the more obscure teaching of the superman and the eternal return. In 1889 he was struck with general paresis and spent his remaining years in total mental alienation until his death in 1900.

Nietzsche represents to a high degree what the Germans call a problematic nature, that is, a personality that is difficult to assess and gives rise to conflicting opinions. His entire development followed a pattern of successive crises. After the dramatic loss of his Christian faith in early youth, came his enthusiasm for Schopenhauer and Wagner, his shift from philology to philosophy, and then the abrupt break of his friendship with Wagner. These experiences combined with a succession of severe physical and neurotic sufferings, from which he emerged each time with new philosophic conceptions, the last of which was his celebrated book *Thus Spake Zarathustra*. It is difficult to ascertain to what extent Nietzsche's last works express a further evolution in his thinking or its distortion through mental illness.

Three facts contributed to confer a particular importance in the contemporary European world on Nietzsche: his legend, his style, and his ideas. The legend around him had started in his lifetime: that of a man severing himself from society, living in solitude in the Swiss mountains like Zarathustra in his cave, and throwing an anathema on contemporary society. [30] Then came his mental illness that some purported to be fate's vengeance against a human who pretended to rise above his fellow beings. After his death, Nietzsche's legend was furthered mainly through the Nietzsche Archives, whose true purpose seems to have been to propagate that legend in accordance with the wishes of his sister and a small group of followers who did not hesitate to publish falsified versions of his posthumous works. [31] Nietzsche's legend, in turn, was to be exploited by various ideologies, including Nazism.

The influence of Nietzsche's work is perhaps due as much to its style as to its content The *Birth of Tragedy* is his only book of which the outline is consistently clear. The following works were successions of sparkling aphorisms. *Thus Spake Zarathustra,* the story of a prophet and of his utterances, a book filled with allegories and myths, exerted an extraordinary fascination upon European youth between 1890 and 1910.

Nietzsche's ideas are particularly difficult to appraise, because of their lack of systematization and innumerable contradictions. No wonder they have given rise to so many conflicting interpretations. Contemporaries were impressed by their polemic character and by Nietzsche's vehement attacks against the current ideologies, the social order, established religion, and conventional morality. He denied the existence of causality, natural laws, and the possibility of man reaching any truth, a conclusion expressed in one of his aphorisms: "Nothing is true, everything is allowed!" In that perspective, Nietzsche's thought has been understood as a radical system of philosophical and moral nihilism. [32] Most interpreters of Nietzsche, however, consider the negative aspect of his thought as being a preliminary to a philosophical reconstruction of man, society, and ethics.

In his positive aspects Nietzsche is as important for his psychological as for his philosophical concepts. The novelty of the former was belatedly recognized chiefly through the work of Ludwig Klages,[33] Karl Jaspers, [34] and Alwin Mittasch.[35] Klages goes so far as to call Nietzsche the true founder of modern psychology. Thomas Mann considered Nietzsche to be "the greatest critic and psychologist of morals known to the history of the human mind."[36] Even his ideas on crime and punishment have been shown to be of great originality and interest from the point of view of modern criminology.[37]

Alwin Mittasch has depicted the connection between Nietzsche's psychological ideas and contemporary discoveries on physical energy. Nietzsche transposed into psychology Robert Mayer's principle of conservation and transformation of energy. In the same way that physical energy can remain potential or be actualized, Nietzsche visualized how "a quantum of dammed up (psychic) energy" could wait until it could be utilized, and how sometimes a slight precipitating cause could release a powerful discharge of psychic energy. Mental energy could also be voluntarily accumulated with a view toward later utilization on a higher level. It could also be transferred from one instinct to another. This led Nietzsche to consider the human mind as a system of drives, and eventually the emotion as a "complex of unconscious representation and states of the will."

Ludwig Klages has characterized Nietzsche as an eminent representative of a trend that was prevalent in the 1880's, the "uncovering" or "unmasking" psychology, which Dostoevsky and Ibsen developed in other directions. It was Nietzsche's concern to unveil how man is a self-deceiving being, who also is constantly deceiving his fellow men. "With all that which a person allows to appear, one may ask: what is it meant to *hide*? What should it divert the eyes from? What prejudice should it conceive? How far goes the subtlety of this dissimulation? How far does he deceive himself in this action?"[38] Since man lies to himself even more than to others, the psychologist should draw conclusions from what people really mean, rather than from what they say or do. For instance, the Gospel's saying, "He that humbleth himself shall be exalted" should be translated into, "He that humbleth himself *wishes* to be exalted."[39] Furthermore, what man believes to be his own true feelings and convictions are often but the remainders of convictions, or simply assertions, of his parents and ancestors. We thus live from the folly as well as the wisdom of our ancestors. Nietzsche is inexhaustible in his attempts to show how every possible kind of feeling, opinion, attitude, conduct, and virtue, is rooted in self-deception or an unconscious lie. Thus, "everyone is the farthest to himself," the unconscious is the essential part of the individual, consciousness being only a kind of ciphered formula of the unconscious, "a more or less fantastic commentary on an unconscious, perhaps unknowable, but felt text."[40]

Nietzsche conceived the unconscious as an area of confused thoughts, emotions, and instincts, at the same time as an area of reenactment of past stages of the individual and of the species. The obscurity, disorder, and incoherence of our representations in dreams recall the condition of the human mind in its earliest stages. The hallucinations of dreams also remind us of those collective hallucinations that seized whole communities of primitive men. "Thus, in sleep and dream, we repeat once more the task

(*Pensum*) performed by early mankind."[41] Dream is a reenactment of fragments of our own past and of the past of mankind. The same holds true for outbreaks of uncontrolled passion and mental illness.[42]

Klages and Jaspers have both shown the great interest of Nietzsche's theories of the instincts, their interplay, their conflicts, and metamorphoses. In his first works he tells of the need for pleasure and struggle, of the sexual and herd instincts, and even of the instinct for knowledge and truth. Gradually he gave prevalence to one basic instinct, the will for power. Above all, Nietzsche describes the vicissitudes of the instincts, their illusory compensations and vicarious discharges, their sublimations, inhibitions, turning against oneself, not forgetting the eventuality of their conscious and voluntary control.

The concept of sublimation, which was not new, was applied by Nietzsche both to the sexual and the aggressive instincts.[43] He considered sublimation a result of inhibition or of an intellectual process, and a very widespread manifestation. "Good actions are sublimated evil ones."[44] Even in their most sublimated forms, instincts retain their importance: "The degree and quality of a person's sexuality finds its way into the topmost reaches of his spirit."[45]

Under the name of inhibition (*Hemmung*), Nietzsche describes what is called today repression, and applies it to perception and memory. "Oblivion is not a mere force of inertia . . . On the contrary, it is an active, and in the strictest sense, a positive capacity for inhibition."[46] "I have done it, says my memory. I cannot have done it, says my pride and remains inexorable. Finally, the memory gives way."[47]

As for the turning against oneself, it furnishes the key to several of Nietzsche's basic concepts: resentment, moral conscience, and the origin of civilization.

The word "resentment," which comprehended all sorts of feelings of rancor, spite, envy, grudge, jealousy, and hatred, was given a new meaning by Nietzsche. When such feelings are inhibited and therefore become unconscious to the subject, they manifest themselves in disguised forms, notably as false morality.[48] Christian morality, Nietzsche proclaimed, was a refined form of resentment; it was a morality of slaves who were unable to overtly rebel against their oppressors and therefore took to this devious way of rebelling, thereby feeling superior while humiliating their enemies. The Christian command, "Love thine enemy," Nietzsche says, is a subtle way of driving one's enemies to exasperation, hence a most cruel vengeance. Nietzsche's concept of resentment was to be taken over, modified and developed by Max Scheler[49] and Marañon.[50]

Nietzsche's theory of the origin of moral conscience was inspired by his friend Paul Rée, who contended that conscience originated in the impossibility of discharging man's aggressive instincts, which man met at a given period of history.[51] In his *Genealogy of Morals*, Nietzsche, like Rée, figured primitive man as a "wild beast," a "beast of prey," "the magnificent roving blond beast, craving booty and victory."[52] But with the founding of human society, the instincts of the wild, free man, could no longer be discharged outwardly and thus had to be turned inwardly. This was the origin of guilt feelings, which in turn were the first roots of moral conscience in mankind. In the individual, this process is enforced by the action of moral commands and inhibitions of all kinds. "The content of our conscience consists of all that which, in our childhood, was demanded from us, without explanation and regularly, from persons we respected or feared . . . Faith in authority is the source of conscience; it is not the voice of God in man's breast, but the voice of several men in man."[53] Moreover the individual bears within himself all kinds of opinions and feelings stemming from his parents and ancestors, but which he believes to be his own. "In the son becomes conviction what in the father was still a lie."[54] Not only fathers, but mothers also determine the conduct of the individual. "Every person carries within a picture of woman which he acquired from his mother. From this picture, he will be determined to respect or despise women or be indifferent toward them."[55]

Nietzsche explains the origin of civilization in a way identical with that of the origin of conscience: from a renunciation of the gratification of our instincts. We recognize here the old theory of Diderot and his followers. Civilization is equated with the illness and suffering of mankind, because it is "The consequence of a forcible separation from the animal past, . . . a declaration of war against the old instincts, which, up to then, constituted his strength, his pleasure, and his awesomeness."[56]

A conspicuous feature of Nietzsche's psychology is the importance he ascribes not only to aggressive but also to self-destructive instincts. Among the manifestations of the latter, according to Nietzsche is the thirst for knowledge. In Nietzsche's words, science is "a principle inimical to life and destructive. The will for truth could be a disguised wish for death."[57] Science is an affirmation of a world other than ours, and therefore the negation of our world, which is the world of life.

Among Nietzsche's properly philosophical ideas, two deserve special attention: that of the superman and the eternal return. The concept of the superman has given rise to a wide range of interpretation. It has nothing in common with the picture of a "superman" as an extraordinarily strong and vigorous individual endowed with mysterious powers. The superman was not a new concept, but what Nietzsche exactly meant by it is still a controversial matter.[58] One possible interpretation derives from Nietzsche's contention that "man is something that must be overcome", the first message given by Zarathustra in his predications.[59] Man has to conquer himself, but how and for what purpose? It could be that man is suffering from being caught between his false morality and his deep-seated animal aggressive instincts. In order to resolve this conflict, man must cast off all established values, and experience within himself the upsurge of all violent and repressed instincts; thus, the thoughts of a man thirsty for vengeance ought to revel in such feelings ad nauseam, until he feels ready to forgive, bless, and honor his enemy.[60] Having thus reappraised all his values, man now establishes his own scale of values and his own morality and lives in accordance with them.[61] This man, the superman, is now strong, even hard, but kind to the weak, and follows the highest possible moral rule, that of the eternal return. The latter has also given rise to many diverging interpretations. It should not be understood in the sense of "cyclic palingenesis" proclaimed by certain ancient philosophers who thought that, in view of the physical constitution of the universe, the same events will necessarily repeat themselves at given intervals ad infinitum. As W. D. Williams said, Nietzsche's idea is the following:

> We come back again and again not to a life precisely like this one but to *this very life* . . . Nietzsche's view is that *all* life, the highest and the lowest, the noble and the petty, the good and the evil, is eternal, whether we will or no . . . We may see in the idea an extreme expression of the consciousness of our ultimate responsibility as human beings from which there is no escape. We must answer for every moment of our lives by reenacting it in eternity.[63]

This is also what Nietzsche expressed in the concise formula, "This life—thine eternal life." Nietzsche linked the concepts of the superman and the eternal return. The superman conforms his life to the principle of the eternal return, thus living *sub specie aeternitatis*: hence the awesome majesty of each human act.

Nietzsche once said that every philosophical system is nothing but a disguised confession. "Man can stretch himself as he may with his knowledge and appear to himself as objective as he may; in the last analysis he gives nothing but his own biography."[64] This is true for Nietzsche more perhaps than anyone else. Lou Andreas-Salomé was the first to understand the close relationship between Nietzsche's physical and nervous sufferings and the productivity of his mind.[65] According to Andreas-Salomé, Nietzsche went through a series of cycles that were marked by phases of illness, recovery accompanied with the gain of new philosophical insights, and a period of euphoria that preceded the next relapse into illness. This may also account for his unflinching conviction that he was bringing a new message to mankind and was the prophet of a new era, and may also account for the truly fantastic success that Nietzsche's ideas enjoyed in Europe in the 1890's. An entire generation was permeated with Nietzschean thinking —whatever interpretation was given to it—in the same way as the former generation had been under the spell of Darwinism. It is also impossible to overestimate Nietzsche's influence on dynamic psychiatry. More so even than Bachofen, Nietzsche may be considered the common source of Freud, Adler, and Jung.

For those acquainted with both Nietzsche and Freud, the similarity of their thought is so obvious that there can be no question about the former's influence over the latter. Freud speaks of Nietzsche as a philosopher "whose guesses and intuitions often agree in the most astonishing way with the laborious findings of psychoanalysis," adding that for a long time he avoided reading Nietzsche on that very account, in order to keep his mind free from external influences.[66] It should be recalled, however, that at the time of Freud's early maturity it was not necessary to have studied Nietzsche to be permeated with his thought, seeing how much he was quoted, reviewed, and discussed in every circle and in every journal or newspaper.

Psychoanalysis evidently belongs to that "unmasking" trend, that search for hidden unconscious motivations characteristic of the 1880's and 1890's. In Freud as in Nietzsche, words and deeds are viewed as manifestations of unconscious motivations, mainly of instincts and conflicts of instincts. For both men the unconscious is the realm of the wild, brutish instincts that cannot find permissible outlets, derive from earlier stages of the individual and of mankind, and find expression in passion, dreams, and mental illness. Even the term "id" (*das Es*) originates from Nietzsche.[67] The dynamic concept of mind, with the notions of mental energy, quanta of latent or inhibited energy, or release of energy or transfer from one drive to another, is also to be found in Nietzsche. Before Freud, Nietzsche conceived the mind as a system of drives that can collide or be fused into each other. In contrast to Freud, however, Nietzsche did not give prevalence to the sexual drive (whose importance he duly acknowledged), but to aggressive and self-destructive drives. Nietzsche well understood those processes that have been called defense mechanisms by Freud, particularly sublimation (a term that appears at least a dozen times in Nietzsche's works), repression (under the name inhibition), and the turning of instincts toward oneself. The concepts of the imago of father and mother is also implicit in Nietzsche. The description of resentment, false conscience, and false morality anticipated Freud's descriptions of neurotic guilt and of the superego. Freud's *Civilization and Its Discontent* also shows a noteworthy parallelism with Nietzsche's *Genealogy of Morals*. Both give a new expression to Diderot's old assumption that modern man is afflicted with a peculiar illness bound up with civilization, because civilization demands of man that he renounce the gratification of his instincts. Scattered throughout Nietzsche's works are countless ideas or phrases whose parallels are to be found in Freud. Nietzsche taught that no one will complain or accuse himself without a secret desire for vengeance, thus "Every complaint (*Klagen*) is accusation (*Anklagen*)."[68] The same idea with the same play on words is to be found in Freud's celebrated paper *Mourning and Melancholia*: "Their 'complaints' are actually 'plaints' in the older sense of the word."[69]

Should the interpretation of the superman hinted at by Lou Andreas-Salomé be the right one, it would contain the seed of Freud's concept of psychoanalytic treatment. The superman, who has overcome the conflict between his conventional morality and his instinctual urges, has become free in his innermost, he has erected his own scale of values and his own autonomous morality. If he is "good," it is for no other reason than that he has decided to be so. He has overcome himself in somewhat the same way as the neurotic after a successful psychoanalysis.

Although the influence of Nietzsche on psychoanalysis had not been very thoroughly investigated as yet,[70] Crookshank has made a detailed study of Nietzsche and Adler.[71] Extensive parallels can be drawn. For Nietzsche as for Adler, man is an incompleted being who must achieve his own completion himself. Nietzsche's principle "man is something which must be overcome" finds its equivalent in Adler's principle "to be human means to be stimulated by a feeling of inferiority which aims at being overcome." Nietzsche's later concept that the one basic drive in man is the will to power is reflected in Adler's teaching of man's basic striving toward superiority. In that regard Nietzsche's works are an inexhaustible mine of instances showing how the will to power manifests itself under countless disguised forms, including even asceticism and voluntary subjection to other men (in modern language, moral masochism). The main divergence between Adler and Nietzsche is that the former equates man's overcoming of himself with his acceptance of the "community feeling," whereas Nietzsche, a radical individualist, speaks with contempt of the "herd instinct." However, Nietzsche's idea that "the error about life is necessary to life" and that self-deceit is necessary to the individual, anticipates Adler's concept of the "guiding fiction" in the neurotic.

Unlike Freud, Jung has always openly proclaimed the enormous stimulation he received from Nietzsche. Jung's theories are filled with concepts that can be traced, in more or less modified form, to Nietzsche. Such are Jung's reflections on the problem of evil, on the superior instincts in man, on the unconscious, the dream, the archetypes, the shadow, the persona, the old wise man, and many other concepts. Jung also gave an interpretation of Nietzsche's personality. *Zarathustra,* he said, was a secondary personality of Nietzsche, which had formed and slowly developed in his unconscious until it suddenly erupted, bringing with it an enormous amount of archetypical material. Jung's courses on *Zarathustra* are contained in ten unpublished typewritten volumes, which constitute the most thorough exegesis that has ever been attempted on Nietzsche's celebrated work.[72]

Neo-Romanticism and Fin de Siècle

As already stated, a rapid and marked change of intellectual orientation occurred throughout Europe around 1885. This movement was a reaction against positivism and naturalism and, and to a certain extent, a return to romanticism, which is why it was given the name of Neo-Romanticism.[73] It did not supersede the positivist and naturalist trends but went side by side with them for the remainder of the century. It affected philosophy, literature, the arts, music, and the general way of life, and exerted an unmistakable influence upon the deep-reaching changes that took place at that time in dynamic psychiatry.

In its restricted sense, the term Neo-Romanticism designates a number of German poets, including Stefan Georg, Gerhard Hauptmann, Hugo Von Hofmannsthal, and Rainer Maria Rilke. In its extended sense, it includes a much wider range of poets, artists, musicians, and thinkers who belonged to a variety of local and temporary groups. Such were the pre-Raphaelites in England, the symbolists in France, and the *Jugendstil* movement in Germany. It culminated in the "decadence" and the *fin de siècle* spirit.

In spite of its name, this movement was far from simply a return to Romanticism. In certain regards it could be called a distorted imitation, almost a caricature, of Romanticism. The relationship with nature first of all, could not possibly be the same. Owing to large-scale industrialization, urbanization, and new scientific discoveries, life in the course of the nineteenth century had become increasingly artificial. No wonder one does not find in Neo-Romanticism that immediate, poignant feeling of intimate contact with nature that was at the root of Romanticism. Even where there was no direct search for the artificial and where it came closest to nature, Neo-Romanticists visualized it stylized, as seen through the eyes of artists and esthetes. Whereas Romanticism had viewed everything in the process of growth and evolution, Neo-Romanticism was inclined to view it in the process of decay. Whereas Romanticism had had the peculiar ability for empathy with almost all periods of history, Neo-Romanticism showed a predilection for the periods of decadence. Nor could Neo-Romanticism find a direct contact with the soul of the population, as German Romantics had done. With the decline of peasantry, the folklore, which had been a rich source of inspiration for the Romantics, was disappearing in the nineteenth century, and Neo-Romantics had to be content with a more or less vague search for myth. Romanticism had emphasized the unique and irreplaceable value of the individual, seeing him at the same time in the context of interpersonal contacts in friendship, love, small groups, and the community. Neo-Romanticism stressed the worship of the individual to the point where it isolates him from others, so that narcissism is one of its common features. Never, in the history of literature, did poets celebrate Narcissus and narcissistic heroes to such an extent. It has been shown that the Narcissus figure was a general symbol and incarnation of the spirit of that time.[74] However, the Neo-Romantics were no less concerned than their predecessors with the irrational, the occult, and the exploration of the hidden depths of the human mind. As the Romantics had turned to Mesmer and animal magnetism, the Neo-Romantics were now enthusiastic toward hypnotism, and demanded new evidence about the unconscious.

In his memoirs, Jules Romains has pointed out the extraordinary contrast between the symbolist movement in France and the general march of civilization in the contemporary world:

> The world was on an ascending march and was overflowing with vitality. Everywhere, political freedom and social justice were in progress. Man's material condition did not cease to improve, not for a privileged few, but for the greatest number. Science and modern technique had hardly shown more than their beneficial aspects, and seemed to promise nothing but a continuous improvement of the earthly sojourn . . . In a world becoming filled with giant enterprises, factories, machines, unfolding immense power, and where one of the main problems is to become aware of it all, to incorporate all that in the life of the spirit, to master all this turmoil in order to draw from it the harmony of a new civilization, the pure symbolist, in his ivory tower, tells legends to himself, sometimes pleasant, sometimes bookish or childish. . . . [He considered his time as a decadence, a Byzantine rottenness] . . . which is certainly the most phenomenal misinterpretation ever committed by literature. There was a kind of collective schizophrenia, the meaning of which was probably not negligible.[75]

What Jules Romains says of the symbolist movement in France could, of course, be said in exactly the same way of other similar movements throughout Europe, that is, of all those that proclaimed the decadence of modern civilization and belonged to the Neo-Romantic trend.

A historian of literature, A. E. Carter, describes this tendency in a similar way:

> Nearly all authors of the time thought their age decadent. This was not the whim of a few eccentrics, but the settled opinion of pathologists, philosophers and critics . . . Seen from the ruins of the present, the 19th century looks almost unbelievably massive, an accumulation of steam, cast iron and self-confidence, rather like one of its international expositions. It was the century which absorbed continents and conquered the world . . . Why such an age, which lived a vigorous life vigorously, should have spent so much time in sullen musing on its own "decadence," real or imagined, is a strange problem to which no simple answer can be given.[76]

As shown by Carter, the word "decadence" had changed its meaning and by the end of the nineteenth century, had acquired a peculiar connotation of rich and alluring corruptness. Men of that time compared their era to that of the decline of Rome (or rather to a legendary and fanciful picture of imperial Rome), to a no less legendary picture of Byzantine decadence, and to the frivolous debauchery of the court of Louis XV. Everywhere one found expressions of the idea that the world had grown old, supported by pseudoscientific theories, particularly that of degeneration. Hence the success of Max Nordau's book *Degeneration,* which contained a radical condemnation of contemporary cultural movements of that time.[77]

The notions of decadence and degeneration, under all imaginable forms and disguises, pervaded the thinking of that time. In the 1850's, Morel had formulated a psychiatric theory in which almost all mental chronic disturbances were united under the name of "mental degeneration." Morel's theory met with great success, and in the 1880's it dominated French psychiatry with Magnan. There came a point where almost all diagnostic certificates in French mental hospitals began with the words *dégénérescence mentale, avec . . .* ("mental degeneracy, with . . ."), upon which the main symptoms were listed. In the early 1880's, Lombroso told of the "born criminal," who supposedly resulted from a regression to an ancestral type of man. Morel's and Magnan's medical theories were popularized by the novels of Zola and other naturalist writers. But it also spread in a more subtle way through Neo-Romantic groups. The Count de Gobineau contended that human races were unequal and that all existing civilizations had been founded by superior races, which, through the process of inter-marriage with inferior races, had been absorbed by the latter, so that mankind was doomed to a final state of mongrelization in which it will have lost all its creative ability.[78] More often, however, thinkers were content to describe the alleged decadence of one specific race or nation. In France and Italy, and also in Spain after its defeat of 1898 in the Spanish-American War, the idea of the inferiority of the Latin peoples was fairly widespread and was often associated with an obsession of the superiority of the Anglo-Saxons.[79] Nevertheless, the British Houston Stewart Chamberlain asserted the superiority of the Germans and the need for them to protect themselves by racial selection.[80] Another version of the decadence concept was the idea of "aristocratic decay": as a consequence of the universal spread of democracy, superior individuals and families would be swallowed up by the masses. Finally, there was Nietzsche's contention that the human species as a whole was in decline, because civilization is incompatible with the nature of man. Hence also the then current nostalgia for primitive life, primitive populations, and primitive art.

This general trend culminated in the *fin de siècle* spirit. This expression seems to have appeared in Paris in 1886 and was made fashionable by Paul Bourget in 1887 through his novel *Mensonges*. By 1891, it had become a "literary calamity," which occurred at every moment during conversations and could be read a dozen times in every page of the newspapers.[81] Just as the epoch of Romanticism had experienced the *mal du siècle,* the period before the end of the century was now impregnated with the *fin de siècle* mood. There was, firstly, a general feeling of pessimism allegedly founded upon the philosophical doctrines of Von Hartmann and of Schopenhauer. It is difficult for us today to imagine the fascination that Schopenhauer's philosophy exerted upon the intellectual elite of that time. Malwida von Meysenbug, a friend of Wagner and Nietzsche, tells in her *Memoirs* how the discovery of Schopenhauer's work was a kind of religious conversion for her.[82] Philosophical problems that had preoccupied her for years were suddenly clarified. She found a new interpretation of Christian faith, together with peace of mind and a new meaning of life. But more often, Schopenhauer's and Von Hartmann's pessimism was expressed in less dignified forms, and inspired gloomy and morbid essays, plays, and novels.

A second feature of the *fin de siècle* was the cult of the *Anti-Physis,* that is, of everything that is the opposite of nature. Whereas, in the eighteenth century, the prevailing myth was that of the "noble savage," of the vigorous, primitive man living in his forest and fighting for his freedom, there was now an inverted myth of a "corrupt civilized man," weakened and sophisticated amidst the luxuries of the great city.[83] In direct contrast with the Romantics' communion with nature, the man of the *fin de siècle* feels at home in the monstrous, sprawling cities, the *villes tentaculaires* of the poet Verhaeren, and revels in the corrupt and perverted luxuries that they offer. All this was allied with the cult of estheticism, of refined elegance in clothing and furnishings, and of the search for the rare that led to every possible kind of eccentricity. Seldom in the history of culture were there as many eccentrics as in that period.

A further characteristic of the *fin de siècle* spirit was its vague mysticism. In the most favorable cases, it led some literary men to a more or less sensational religious conversion (as it had also happened with several Romantics), but it led others to join spiritistic or occult sects of one kind or other. It frequently heightened the interest in the phenomena of hypnosis, somnambulism, dual personality, and mental illness. A new literary device, the inner monologue, was adopted, purporting to be an exact reproduction of the individual's stream of consciousness. The French writer Edouard Dujardin,[84] and the Austrian Arthur Schnitzler,[85] began writing novels in which there was no action, only description of the alleged unrolling of the character's thread of thoughts during a given period of time.

Another major characteristic of the *fin de siècle* spirit was its cult of eroticism. The so-called Victorian spirit, which had reigned mostly in England until the middle decades of the century, had declined everywhere, and little of it remained in continental Europe. On the contrary, books, journals, and newspapers were filled with erotic preoccupations, though with slightly more restraint and more subtlety of expression than today. The abundance of obscene literature was such that Jules Claretie, in a review of the year 1880, wrote the epitaph "Here rests the pornographic year 1880."[86] Eroticism dominated literature from the very top in the refined works of men such as Anatole France and Arthur Schnitzler down to the trashiest publications for the uneducated. An abundant medical or pseudo medical literature on perversions was readily available and found a large audience. Sexual perversions were also described, in a more or less veiled form, in many novels of that time. It was actually then that some sexual perversions were given the names under which they are still technically referred to today: sadism, masochism, fetishism, and the scientific description often followed the literary one. Mario Praz has shown the role played by vampirism in the nineteenth century, and that the character of the "male vampire" (destructive seducer or wolf) was gradually replaced by the character of the "female vampire" (the *femme fatale*) by the end of the century.[87] Another conspicuous theme was the cult of the prostitute: artists such as Toulouse-Lautrec and Klimt painted these women with a certain fondness; writers such as De Maupassant, Wedekind, Wildgans, and Popper-Lynkeus glorified them.

The *fin de siècle* spirit prevailed particularly in two cities: Paris and Vienna. Historians of thought emphasize that the generation that was twenty to thirty years old in France in 1890 was one of the most gifted France had ever known. There was a flowering of genius and talent in the philosophical, scientific, artistic, and literary realms, and a flurry of new contradictory ideas. Representatives of the older generations were often apprehensive of that spiritual anarchy; they did not suspect that the *fin de siècle* was a temporary mood and that original forms of thought were in the making. Writers such as Paul Morand, looking back in retrospect at that period, are prone to view it as a frivolous one that produced nothing but trivialities, and insist on the morbid eroticism that permeated life.[88] André Billy, however, claims that that eroticism, which he does not deny, was of a high quality and part of the then current search for happiness.[89] He thinks that the *fin de siècle* period suffered above all from an over-abundance of cultural riches.

Vienna was the other great center of the *fin de siècle* atmosphere. In Austria, the idea of decadence that prevailed over Europe took on special meaning because it was being applied to the monarchy and the empire, of which many predicted the forthcoming downfall and disintegration. As in Paris, Vienna's young generation was extraordinarily talented and brilliant. The circle "Young Vienna" counted among its members poets such as Hermann Bahr, Richard Beer-Hofmann, Hugo von Hofmannsthal, Richard Schaukal, and Arthur Schnitzler. Here, too, the main evil was probably the over-abundance of ideas and cultural riches.

The deep-reaching affinity between the new, incipient dynamic psychiatry and the spirit of the times is revealed by the similarity between patients described by the psychiatrists and by the novelists and playwrights. It has already been pointed out that many of Pinel's case histories seem to be borrowed from Balzac's novels. In the same way, Janet's patients show remarkable similarities with some of Zola's characters. (Janet's Irène, for instance, with Pauline, the heroine of Zola's novel *La Joie de Vivre*). However, Hofmannsthal's Elektra resembles Breuer's celebrated Anna O. much more than Euripide's Elektra, and Freud's Dora seems to belong to one of Schnitzler's short stories. No wonder, since writers and psychiatrists had grown up in the same generation and lived in the same atmosphere, and since it was from the same refined and highly eroticized *fin de siècle* milieu that the ones drew their literary characters, the others their patients.

Psychiatry and Psychotherapy

As we have seen in the preceding chapter, two main psychiatric trends prevailed in the first decades of the nineteenth century: that of the *Somatiker,* and that of the *Psychiker* (as they were called in Germany). The first attributed mental diseases to physical causes and to brain conditions, the second emphasized the emotional causes of such diseases. As we have also seen, the latter tendency declined around 1840, and a combination of both trends was attempted by Griesinger. After him, however, the organicist tendency dominated the entire field of psychiatry. Throughout Europe, two main principles apparently presided over the treatment of mental patients. First, a humanitarian principle issued from Pinel and his contemporaries: mental patients must be treated as humanely as possible. The second was the principle that "mental diseases are brain diseases"; therefore, the best thing a psychiatrist could do for his patients was to study brain anatomy and pathology, with the hope that this investigation would eventually lead to the discovery of specific treatments for mental diseases. This attitude resulted in many mental hospitals becoming centers for the study of brain anatomy and pathology. Occasionally a physician was appointed medical director of a mental hospital, his only qualification being that he was a good student of brain anatomy. Several outstanding discoveries in that field were thus actually made in small remote mental hospitals.

With his slogan that "mental diseases are brain diseases," Griesinger declared war against the survivors of the old romantic psychiatry. At that time, Rokitansky and Virchow were laying the foundations of cellular anatomo-pathology, which appeared to be the one firm basis of all medicine. Thereupon Meynert, Wernicke, and their followers tried to found psychiatry on this same basis. Theodor Meynert (1833–1892) and Carl Wernicke (1848–1905), two keen students of brain anatomy and skilled clinicians, attempted to build an over-all system of organic and mechanistic psychiatry. But they often supplemented their objective findings with hypotheses on the anatomical and physiologic substratum of psychic activity, and by the end of the nineteenth century many psychiatrists used to formulate psycho-pathological disturbances in terms borrowed from brain anatomy: this was called *Hirnmythologie* (brain mythology).

The credit for overcoming that tendency goes to Emil Kraepelin (1856–1926) with his multiple approach to psychiatry—neurology and brain anatomy, experimental psychology with the application of new elaborated test methods, and the thorough investigation of the patient's life history. Kraepelin has become the whipping boy of many present-day psychiatrists who claim that his only concern for his patients was to place diagnostic labels on them, after which nothing more was done to help them. In fact, however, he took the greatest care that every one of his patients should receive the best treatment available in his time, and he was an extremely humane person.[90] One of his major achievements was the construction of a rational nosology and classification of mental illness, with the conception of "dementia praecox" and "manic-depressive illness." Around 1900, Kraepelin was being praised as the man who had introduced clarity into the chapter of mental diseases, and his system gradually found acceptance everywhere.

Meanwhile, the work of men such as Heinroth, Ideler, Neumann, and the other *Psychiker,* which had perhaps never been completely forgotten, experienced a revival in the 1880's. Two men deserve special mention in this connection: Forel and Bleuler.

Auguste Forel (1848–1931) was an extraordinarily vigorous personality whose life is fairly well known thanks to his autobiography[91] and to a biography by Annemarie Wettley.[92] His life is a typical example of a young boy suffering from feelings of inferiority, finding compensation, and becoming one of the foremost scientists of his generation. The compensation that he found in his childhood was the study of ants, of which he became probably the world's greatest specialist. Forel's wish was to study the natural sciences, but he chose medicine for practical reasons and soon distinguished himself by his discoveries in the field of brain anatomy, which led him to the post of professor of psychiatry at the University of Zurich, a function that included the supervision of the Burghölzli mental hospital. He brought about a much-needed reform in this institution, with such success that the Burghölzli achieved world renown. Forel initially belonged to the school of the organicists, but his attitude gradually changed. He wondered why psychiatrists were unable to cure alcoholics, whereas some laymen succeeded in doing so. He asked one of these laymen, the cobbler Bosshardt, what his secret was, and was told: "No wonder, Herr Professor, I am an abstainer while you are not."[93] This reply impressed Forel so much that he himself signed a pledge of abstinence, and from then on he was able to treat alcoholics successfully. This was Forel's first step toward the realization that the secret of successful therapy resided in the personal attitude of the psychotherapist. His second step in this direction was his discovery of hypnosis. Having heard of Bernheim's work, he forthwith traveled to Nancy and remained there long enough to acquire the technique of hypnotic treatment, which he then brought back to Zurich. Forel soon became one of the leading specialists of that method. He organized an out-patient service in which hypnotic treatment was also successfully applied to patients afflicted with rheumatism and various physical ailments. Among Forel's students were Eugen Bleuler (1857–1939), who became Switzerland's most prominent psychiatrist, and Adolf Meyer (1866–1950), who became the foremost psychiatrist in the United States.

Eugen Bleuler[94] is universally known for his theory and description of "schizophrenia" (a term he coined to replace the term "dementia praecox," the original meaning of which was no longer understood).[95] It is hardly possible to understand Bleuler's work without taking into account the background of social and political struggles in the canton of Zurich in the nineteenth century. Eugen Bleuler was born in 1857 in Zollikon, then a farming village and now a suburb of Zurich. His ancestors were farmers, but his father was a merchant and the administrator of the local school as well. Bleuler's father, grandfather, and all the members of his family still had a vivid recollection of the times when the farming population of the canton was under the domination of the Zurich City authorities, which narrowly restricted the farmers' access to certain trades, professions, and above all to higher education. The farming population was class-conscious, sometimes in an aggressive or revolutionary fashion, sometimes in a more progressive way. They organized reading circles and other cultural activities. The Bleuler family had taken part in the political struggle which, in 1831, finally led to the winning of equal rights for farmers and to the founding of the University of Zurich in 1833, which was destined to further the intellectual development of the young farming generation. Many foreign professors were called to occupy the posts that could not be filled by the Swiss citizens.

The first professors who came to teach psychiatry in Zurich were Germans: Griesinger, Gudden, and Hitzig. They were also the first directors of the Burghölzli mental hospital. Complaints arose that these men busied themselves more with their microscopes than with their patients and that they were unable to make themselves understood by the patients because they spoke only High German and were not familiar with the local dialect. During the years he spent in secondary school, Bleuler often heard such complaints from people in his own environment. He decided to become a psychiatrist who would understand mental patients and make himself understood to them.

As soon as he had obtained his diploma, Bleuler became a resident in the Waldau mental hospital near Bern, where he showed an unusual devotion toward his patients. He then left to study with Charcot and Magnan in Paris, traveled to London and Munich, and then joined the staff of the Burghölzli Mental Hospital, which was at that time under the direction of Forel. In 1886, Bleuler was appointed medical director of the Rheinau mental hospital, a large asylum inhabited by old demented patients that was considered to be one of Switzerland's most backward institutions. Bleuler undertook the task of rehabilitating this hospital and cared for his patients with unusual selflessness. A bachelor, he lived in the hospital and spent all his time with his patients, from early morning till late at night, taking part in their physical treatment, organizing work therapy, and achieving a close emotional contact with each one of his patients. He thus attained a unique understanding of mental patients and the most intimate details of their psychological life. From this experience he drew the substance of his future book on schizophrenia and his textbook on psychiatry.

In 1898, Bleuler was chosen to succeed Forel as head of the Burghölzli Mental Hospital. His duties included teaching, which provided him with the possibility of transmitting the results of his Rheinau experience to his students, and these lectures became the core of his celebrated book on schizophrenia, which he published belatedly in 1911.[96] Meanwhile, he had continued his investigations with the help of his staff which, after 1900, included C. G. Jung.

As Bleuler's doctrine on schizophrenia has often been misunderstood, it is perhaps not amiss to recall its main features here. Its starting point was Bleuler's own effort to understand a category of people who had never been understood before, that is the schizophrenics. During the twelve years that he spent at Rheinau, continuously living with a great number of such patients, he not only talked with them in their own dialect but made every possible effort to understand the meaning of their supposedly "senseless" utterings and their delusions. Bleuler was thus able to establish an "emotional contact" (*affektiver Rapport*) with each one of his patients. This clinical approach was supplemented later at the Burghölzli Mental Hospital with an investigation by means of the word-association test under the direction of Jung, and still later with the help of Freud's psychoanalytic concepts.

On the basis of his clinical research, Bleuler developed a new theory of schizophrenia. In contradistinction with the purely *organicist* theories that were prevalent in his time, Bleuler professed a theory that would be called organo-dynamic today. He assumed that schizophrenia derived from an unknown cause (perhaps from the action of toxic substances on the brain) and in which heredity played an important part. In the chaos of the manifold symptoms of schizophrenia, he distinguished primary or physiogenic symptoms caused directly by the unknown organic processus, and secondary or psychogenic symptoms deriving from the primary symptoms. This distinction was probably inspired by Janet's concept of psychasthenia. Just as Janet distinguished a basic disturbance in psychasthenia, that is, the lowering of psychological tension, so did Bleuler in much the same way conceive the primary symptoms of schizophrenia to be a loosening of the tension of associations, in a manner more or less similar to what happens in dreams or in daydreams. He thought that all the rich varieties of the secondary symptoms derived from these basic symptoms, notably the *Spaltungen* or splits between the various psychic functions, for instance between effectivity and intellect, and between effectivity and will. The autism, that is the loss of contact with reality, was in Bleuler's original concept a consequence of the dissociation (only later did Bleuler's students see in it the basic symptom of schizophrenia). A curious comparison could at this point be made between Bleuler's concept of schizophrenia and Schlegel's philosophical theory[97] that man is severed from communication with God, nature, and the universe because he is split within himself between reason, will, and fantasy, and that it is the task of philosophy to reestablish harmony within man. It is doubtful, however, that these ideas of Schlegel's influenced Bleuler's theory of schizophrenia, in spite of the similarities of thought.

From the nosological point of view, Bleuler's concept of schizophrenia is wider than that of Kraepelin's *dementia praecox*, since Bleuler includes in schizophrenia various acute conditions that were previously considered disease entities of their own. This was more than a diagnostic subtlety. Bleuler contended that if patients with these acute conditions received proper intensive care they had good chances of recovery, whereas if they were neglected or improperly treated, many of them would evolve toward chronic schizophrenia.

Bleuler's concept of schizophrenia was not only a new theory but, as emphasized by Minkowski, it had in itself a therapeutic implication.[98] Bleuler introduced the optimistic notion that schizophrenia would be stopped or regressed at any stage of its evolution and, at a time when physiological and pharmacological treatment methods did not exist, he used a number of devices, which, according to the testimony of all those who have worked at the Burghölzli Mental Hospital at that time, sometimes produced miraculous effects. He would, for instance, resort to the early discharge of apparently severely ill patients, or to a sudden and unexpected transfer to another ward, or assign a responsibility to the patient. He also organized a system of work therapy and arranged the leisure time of his patients as well as the functioning of a human community in the mental hospital. Bleuler was not the only psychiatrist who, in the years 1890 to 1900, strove to introduce psychological understanding and treatment of mental patients, but he was probably the one whose efforts in this direction were most successful. He pioneered in the path that was later followed in the United States by Adolf Meyer.[99] In Germany, similar experiments were conducted in many mental hospitals and gradually brought about improvements that often astounded foreign visitors. In 1906, Stewart Paton emphasized the optimism of German psychiatrists and praised the psychiatric institutes at Erlangen, Würzburg, and Munich as model mental hospitals.[100] He also noted the establishing of out-patient services and the resulting improvement in the general mental health of the population. These efforts culminated in Hermann Simon's *aktivere Therapie* (more active therapy), a method that he worked out a few years before World War I.[101] It was an elaborate system of work therapy in which each patient was assigned a particular task with a given amount of work to accomplish, and which was designed to bring forth the maximum improvement in him, with the result that agitation completely disappeared from the mental hospital; this at a time when physiological and pharmacological treatments were unknown. Work therapy had also been organized in private institutions by Möbius, Grohmann, and others, for the treatment of neurotics.[102]

Another feature of the years 1880 to 1900 was the gradual elaboration of the notion of a dynamic psychiatry. The word "dynamic" came to be commonly used in psychiatry, although with a variety of meanings that often entailed some confusion. Philosophers and physiologists had used it with meanings that were often unclear, so that the dictionary of the French Society of Philosophy warned against its use. "The word dynamic," it says, "is seductive through its scientific aspect, but it is nonetheless (especially as an adjective) one of the most current false coins in the philosophical language of students and pseudo-philosophical writers."[103] Let us now examine the various meanings that the term acquired in neuropsychiatry.

1. Leibniz is generally credited with having coined the word "dynamic" in contradistinction to the words "static" and "cinematic." He used it in mechanics. The term was taken over and applied to psychology by Herbart, who distinguished the static and dynamic states of consciousness, and later to sociology by Auguste Comte, who distinguished between a static and a dynamic sociology. In physiology, the word had been used as early as 1802, and German magnetizers commonly spoke of "dynamic-psychic" forces.[104] However, it was mainly Fechner who gave the impulse to the concept of psychic energy and, as we shall later see, during the second half of the nineteenth century there were theories of nervous energy and mental energy modeled more or less on the physical theory of energy.

2. French physiologists, however, had used the word "dynamic" to express the notion of "functional" as opposed to "organic." Macario wrote an often-quoted study on "dynamic paralyses," by which he meant paralysis without lesions of the nervous system. Later, Charcot taught the distinctions between "organic" and "dynamic" paralysis, the latter group including those paralyses resulting from hysteria, hypnosis, and psychic traumatism.

3. A third meaning was introduced by Brown-Séquard with his theory of "dynamic actions" in the nervous system.[106] A stimulation of one part of the nervous system, he said, could bring forth effects in one of its other parts, either as "dynamogenesis" (a stimulation of functioning), or as "inhibition" (a lessening of functioning). Psychiatrists began to apply these concepts to the phenomena of mental disturbances, especially to neurosis, supplemented sometimes by other concepts taken over from brain physiology such as that of "facilitation."[107]

4. Meanwhile, the term "dynamic" had been applied to the motor power of images, a concept probably dating to the philosopher Malebranche and his successors. According to De Morsier, this concept was transferred from philosophy to psychiatry by Esquirol who had attended the lectures of the

philosopher Laromiguière from 1811 to 1813.[108] This concept was taken over by Bernheim, who centered his theory of suggestion around it. Under the name "law of the ideodynamism," he expounded his contention that "any suggested and accepted idea tends to turn into acts."[109]

In 1897, Aimé sketched a theory of dynamic psychology based on the teachings of Brown-Séquard and of the Nancy School.[110] He distinguished three classes of nervous disturbances: purely organic ones, purely dynamic ones (without known lesion), and intermediate conditions (which today would be called organo-dynamic). He taught that ideas and emotions are "dynamic nervous facts," that is, expressions of dynamogenic or inhibitory phenomena in certain nervous structures. A true diagnosis aims at making an evaluation of the respective parts of organic and dynamic factors in illness. There are two classes of dynamic treatments: those based on inhibition, and those based on dynamogenesis. Among the latter are suggestion proper, hypnotic suggestion, "materialized suggestion" (now called placebo therapy), and finally, methods of training. The author attributes a particularly important role to dynamic therapy in the treatment, or at least alleviation, of many physical diseases.

5. Finally, the word "dynamic" acquired yet another meaning related to the concept of evolution and regression. It would seem that the first one to apply these notions to psychiatry (without as yet using the term "dynamic") was Moreau (de Tours), who taught that mental illness is a world of its own, basically different from our world and comparable to the world of dreams, even though its elements are all taken from the real world.[111] The basic fact underlying this world of delusion and hallucination is not the stimulation of any brain function, but, on the contrary, a modification bringing about a diminution of intellectual functions and a disproportionate development of vestigial psychic activities. Janet always insisted that his own dynamic theory had been inspired by what he called Moreau de Tours' "fundamental law of mental illness."[112] Henry Ey repeatedly underlines the originality of Moreau's ideas.[113] A similar concept was later introduced in neurology by Hughlings Jackson, who first applied it to the study of aphasia and epilepsy.[114] Jackson took into consideration the evolution of the nervous system. In the human nervous system, certain centers have appeared at a more recent phase of human evolution than others. The more recent the centers, the more vulnerable they are, and when one of them is damaged, the activity of the older centers increases. Hence the distinction made in nervous lesions of negative symptoms (caused directly by the lesion) and positive symptoms (resulting from the reactivation of the functions of the more ancient centers). Actually, the term "dynamic," as Jackson used it, combined several of the previous meanings of that word. It designated the physiological aspect in contrast to the anatomic, the functional in contrast to the organic, the regressive in contrast to the status quo, and it expressed at the same time the energetic aspect, even including

at times the connotation of conflict and resistance. Jackson's conception, as it is well known today, had a great influence not only on neurologists such as Head and Goldstein, but also on psychiatrists: probably on Freud, and certainly on Adolf Meyer, who studied under Jackson in London in 1891.

Sexual Psychology and Pathology, 1880–1900

One of the characteristics of the 1880's and 1890's was the rapid progress of investigations into sexual psychology and psychopathology. Although this period is not too distant, it is very difficult for us to get an exact picture of it. The usual stereotype represents it as an era of sexual ignorance, repression, and hypocrisy, which "tabooed" sexual subjects. A closer examination shows, however, that in the 1880's, "Victorian hypocrisy" was mostly a thing of the past, although it still persisted in some "genteel" bourgeois circles. The stereotype image we have of that period may result from our misunderstanding of the fact that its social code made people refer to sexual matters in a more discreet way than is the case today, and that certain matters, like homosexuality, were ignored and banned. Sexual repression, a supposedly characteristic feature of that period, was often merely the expression of two facts: the lack of diffusion of contraceptives, and the fear of venereal disease. Gonorrhea entailed several months of painful treatment, and syphilis, as a rule, remained with the patient for the duration of his life, often threatening to end it in general paresis. Syphilis was the cause of innumerable tragedies, which literature reflected in works such as Ibsen's *Ghosts,* Brieux' *Les Avariés,* and Anton Wildgans' poems. But literature was unable to express the full horror of individual fates that occurred in reality. Young Nietzsche, who, at the age of twenty, stopped over for one night in Cologne, in February 1865, and was taken unawares to a house of prostitution, contracted syphilis, and was never treated. The illness went insidiously on its course, and led to general paresis and the ultimate catastrophe of 1889.[115] Venereal disease was all the more dangerous because of the great spread of prostitution, and because prostitutes were almost invariably contaminated, and therefore potential sources of infection. We can hardly imagine today how monstrous syphilis appeared to people of that time, made worse by the fact that it was likely to be transmitted to the next generation in the form of "hereditary syphilis," which, in turn, had become a nightmarish myth and to which many physicians attributed all diseases of unknown origin. Thus, when Freud considered hereditary syphilis as one of the main causes of neuroses, he simply reflected an opinion that was common to medical circles of that time.

Another feature of that period was the struggle for the recognition of women's rights. The feminist movement went back to Mary Wolstonecraft and to some French revolutionaries of the end of the eighteenth century, but it had developed slowly. In the period 1880 to 1900, however, the struggle was taken up again with renewed vigor, even though most contemporaries viewed it as idealistic and hopeless. Nevertheless, it resulted in ideological discussions about the natural equality or nonequality of the sexes, and the psychology of women. Several opinions were represented.

The common opinion maintained that man was naturally superior to woman, not only in physical strength, but in character, will power, intelligence, and creativity. In 1901, the German psychiatrist Moebius published a treatise, *On the Physiological Imbecility of Woman,* according to which, woman is physically and mentally intermediate between the child and man.[116] She has a more animal nature than man, she displays a total lack of criticism and of self-control, but this is fortunate, because, in Moebius' words, "if woman were not bodily and mentally weak, she would be extremely dangerous." There was no lack of men, and even of women, who supported this view. Even at the beginning of the twentieth century, the inferiority of woman was generally taken for granted, and the only problem discussed in that connection was that of the reason for her inferiority. The opposite theme, that of the natural superiority of woman, was claimed by a few passionate feminists, and no one could have guessed that there would also be men to advocate it later on.[117]

The thesis of the natural equality of the sexes was claimed by most feminists, who replied to the argument of the lesser creativity of woman, that this intellectual inferiority was the result of centuries of male oppression. Bachofen's writings were used as an argument in such discussions, notably by the socialist Bebel, who demanded exactly the same rights and duties for women as for men, and equal education for both sexes.

A third thesis was that of a qualitative difference rather than one of superiority and inferiority, which held that the sexes were psychologically complementary to each other. This theory was sometimes associated with that of the fundamental bisexuality of human beings. It was the old Romantic myth of the Androgyne, which came back to light under a psychological cloak. Michelet had already said that "man and woman are two incomplete and relative beings, since they are but the two halves of the same whole."[118] This theory was now being revived under various forms.

It is noteworthy that each of the three great pioneers, Freud, Adler, and Jung, later adopted one of these three theories. Freud seems to have taken the natural inferiority of woman for granted, since, in one of his early writings, he assumed that the stronger sexual repression in woman is the cause of her intellectual inferiority. Later, he came to speak of the natural masochism of woman. Adler, on the other hand, was a staunch defender of the theory of the natural equality of the sexes. As for Jung, it is obvious that his theory of the Anima in man and the Animus in woman is related to the third contention.

During the last two decades of the nineteenth century, many ideas sprang up around these discussions, and many of them found their way later into the theories of the newer dynamic psychiatrists. One favorite idea maintained that man, instead of seeing woman as she really is, projects onto her images that could be classified into three categories: (1) the imaginary ideal; (2) images drawn from his own past; and (3) what could be called archetypal images. E. T. A. Hoffmann, Achim von Arnim, and other Romantics had already depicted at length the imaginary and illusory character of the beloved's image as seen by the lover, and had written of the destructive consequences of such delusions. The conflict between the illusory and the real woman was later to be used by Spitteler as the theme of his novel *Imago,* a novel greatly admired by Freud and Jung, whose title furnished psychoanalysis with one of the favorite terms of its vocabulary.[119] Another theme was that of the lasting influence of the first love, whether forgotten or not. In *The Disciples in Sais,* Novalis had already told the story of a young man who wanders from place to place, searching for the object of his vision, arriving finally at the temple of Isis, this object is revealed to him and he recognizes in her his childhood sweetheart.[120] The theme of this novel anticipates that of Wilhelm Jensen's *Gradiva,* which Freud admired so much and honored with a commentary.[121] For others such as Nietzsche the ideal guiding figure was thought to be that of the mother. Karl Neisser contended that, if a woman is to be loved by a man, she will have to resemble his female ancestors, those women who have in the past aroused the love of his forefathers.[122] What Neisser explained in one hundred pages of psychological language was expressed by Verlaine in his beautiful sonnet "My Familiar Dream," and this concept is not very far removed from Jung's concept of the Anima. A third favorite theme was that man projects onto woman one of several ready-made pictures that he carries within him: the picture of the mere sexual object, of the *femme fatale,* of the muse, the virgin-mother, those figures belonging to what Jung later called archetypes. Some of those archetypes were the object of much discussion at the time.

One of those archetypal figures (or *Frauenphantome* as they were called in German-speaking countries) was that of the woman as a mere sexual object, an image that could be traced from Luther to Schopenhauer, and was being revived at that time in the writings of Laura Marholm: the goal of woman is to gratify man's desires, this being the only meaning of her life.[123] This idea was to be developed and pushed to its extreme by Weininger in his celebrated book *Sex and Character.*[124] He contended that woman possessed neither intelligence, nor character, nor any relationship to the world of ideas or to God. She is an individual, but not a person, that the essence of her being is sex, that she is a born prostitute, and that, on becoming older, she schemes to make young women follow the same path. Weininger's book was enormously successful and was greatly admired by several prominent writers of that time.

Another "phantom" or archetype was the muse, or what the French called the *femme inspiratrice,* who often played a great role in the lives and work of writers and thinkers.[125] Biographies of an author would be divided into periods according to the women who had inspired him successively. There was a variety of *inspiratrices,* ranging from the *aventurière* seeking love affairs with famous men, to the idealist seeking platonic friendships with thinkers of whom they could be in turn disciples, spiritual collaborators, or protectresses. One celebrated *femme inspiratrice* was Malwida von Meysenbug, a woman from a German aristocratic family, who fled to England because of her democratic convictions, lived in France and Italy, and played a great role in the lives of Alexander Herzen and Richard Wagner.[126] Her *Memoirs* describes an impressive gallery of famous men: patriots and revolutionaries, composers, novelists and playwrights, philosophers and scholars.[127] She was instrumental in introducing Nietzsche to another, younger *femme inspiratrice,* Lou Andreas-Salomé. The latter was to play an important role in the lives of a succession of great men, from Nietzsche to Rilke, and was to end her career as a psychoanalyst.

The *femme fatale* was also a popular "phantom." She is the woman who destroys the genius of a man, or even leads him to his death. Sometimes she is all the more dangerous because she appears in the disguise of the inspiring muse, like Rebecca in Ibsen's drama *Rosmersholm.* Not very different from her, but of a somewhat more ambiguous character, is the type of woman that Jung named the *Anima-Figur* in whom he sees an example in Ayesha of Rider Haggard's novel *She,* the woman who is fascinating to man and who could easily destroy him, but whose spells can be overcome, as seen in the story of Ulysses and the magician Circe.

Another archetypal figure, that of the Virgin-Mother, was defined by Ria Claassen as the woman who helps man to "sublimate and spiritualize" his lower instincts.[128] Such was the role of the Holy Mother's image in the spiritual life of Catholic monks, and the image of Beatrice for Dante.

A curious literary product of these preoccupations about women is found in Villiers de L'Isle-Adam's novel *L'Eve Future,* in which we can find several of these female archetypes.[129] There is the vamp Evelyn, who seduces an honest family man and leads him to ruin and suicide. There is Alicia, the beautiful but stupid and vulgar woman. There is a make-believe woman, made up by Thomas Edison to be the exact physical resemblance of Alicia, but whose inner void is to be filled with the spirit of a deceased woman, Hadaly, who will be the *femme inspiratrice* of the novel's hero. It is indicative of the spirit of that period that the author also resorted to the themes of dual personality and spiritism when writing this typical master-piece of 1886 science fiction.

While all these psychological discussions about the sexes were taking place, biologists were seeking new approaches to the same problems in their laboratories. Decisive progress had been made around 1830 when Baer in Germany and other scientists after him had discovered or clarified the phenomena of ovulation. Michelet, in France, emphasized the importance of these discoveries for the understanding of the psychology of woman and vulgarized them in a somewhat romantic tone.[130] Later, in the 1880's, when physiologists were beginning to lay the foundations of endocrinology, the seventy-two-year-old physiologist Brown-Séquard on June 1, 1889, read a paper at the Société de Biologie in Paris on the effects produced on man by subcutaneous injections of a product extracted from guinea pigs' and dogs' testicles.[131] He related that he had given a series of eight injections of that product to an old man with the result of an extraordinary physiological and psychological rejuvenation. The subject was Brown-Séquard himself, and the listeners who knew him could not but recognize the fact that he looked twenty years younger. It had been known for centuries, from the example of the castrates, that male sexual glands contained a product that had a powerful action upon the male organism and furthered aggressiveness among others. A proof was now given of the "dynamogenetic" action of that glandular secretion and was to be confirmed later by the discovery of the male hormone itself. Brown-Séquard emphasized the parallelism between the physiological phenomenon and the psychological effects. This may well have been the starting point for Freud's theory of the libido, which he first conceived as a psycho-biological phenomenon on the substratum of an unknown chemical substance.

The psychological approach to the study of sexual facts was no less fruitful, but here two remarks are necessary. First, it is a frequent occurrence in the history of science that certain facts are common knowledge to scientists in one discipline and are completely overlooked in others. Certain facts could be well known to gynecologists and unknown to neurologists, well known to educators and unknown to physicians. The other fact is the great persistence of certain errors once they have taken root. Thus, during the eighteenth and nineteenth centuries there were current, false ideas about the alleged dangers of masturbation, such as the belief that it could be the cause of severe medulla and other brain diseases or hebephrenia. At the end of the nineteenth century, such contentions began to be questioned, but they still reigned in popular literature and in part of the scientific literature. It was commonly believed that masturbation was one of the main causes of neurasthenia, and this idea is even to be found in Freud's earlier writings.

While physicians generally considered child sexuality as a rare abnormality, it had been taken for granted for a long time by priests and educators. Father Debreyne, a moral theologian who was also a physician, insisted in his books upon the great frequence of infantile masturbation, of sexual play between young children, and of the seduction of very young children by wet nurses and servants.[132] Bishop Dupanloup of Orleans, an eminent educator, repeatedly emphasized in his work the extreme frequency of sex play among children, and stated that most children acquired "bad habits" between the ages of one to two years.[133] Similar ideas were brilliantly expounded by Michelet in some of the works that he wrote for popular education. In *Our Sons* he warned parents against the dangers of what would be called today child sexuality and the Oedipus complex.[134] He cites with approval the ancient Jewish writings that recommend that the father keep a certain distance from his daughter, and the Catholic moralists who recommend the same behavior on the part of mothers toward their sons. Michelet says that modern science confirms the wisdom of such commands, and shows that the boy is a man almost at his birth: "If he lacks the power, he has the instincts and dreams of vague sensuality." Infants in the cradle can already be amorous, he says, and therefore the mother should be careful in that regard. Almost always the infant is jealous of its siblings and of its father. Michelet perceptively describes how the small child simulates sleep in order better to watch with acute attention the conversations and intimacies between its parents. If the mother makes a habit of taking the child to bed with her, a "magnetic" tie is established between them, which may result in grave dangers for the child in the future. Michelet also warns against incestuous attachments between siblings at an early age and says that he has observed at least five or six esteemed and well-known families where such attachments have yielded bitter fruits. As so many of his contemporaries, Michelet also warns of the possible seduction of young children by servants, and against the dangers of a marked preference of the mother for one of her children. Michelet's works were widely read and from his example, as well as from many of his contemporaries, it is obvious that in his mind the "angelic purity of the small child" was by no means a common belief.[135]

The medical and psychiatric study of sexual deviations also made decisive progress after 1880, but this study was no novelty.[136] For centuries it had been dealt with by moral theologians, for instance, in the seventeenth century in the *De Sancto Matrimonii Sacramento* by Sánchez, an enormous work, of which abridged versions were known to many parish priests.[137] In the eighteenth century a work by Alfonso de Liguori gained an even wider audience.[138] From the theological viewpoint of sin, Liguori distinguished between acts committed according to nature such as rape, adultery, and incest, and those committed contrary to nature such as sodomy and bestiality. A further distinction was made between "consummated acts" and "nonconsummated acts" (the latter including an entire gamut ranging from impure thoughts and obscene words to physical contact without actual consummation). This classification was expanded by Father Debreyne, who, being also a physician, developed the psychological aspect of the problem and should be considered one of the pioneers of sexual pathology.

Rémy de Gourmont said that sexual pathology originated from two main sources: the works of Catholic moral theologians and those of pornographic writers. But the time had come when writers began to treat sexual matters in an objective and nonpornographic way. Jean-Jacques Rousseau (1712–1778) claimed to give in his *Confessions* a complete and sincere account of the most intimate experiences of his life, including his sexual experiences concerning masturbation, sexual inhibition, exhibitionism, and moral masochism. One generation later, Restif de la Bretonne (1734–1806) described his fetishism in several of his novels, particularly in *Monsieur Nicolas*. The Marquis de Sade (1740–1814), who belonged to a French aristocratic family, was a psychopath of dissolute mores but of brilliant intelligence, who, as a result of several offenses, spent fourteen years of his life in prison and thirteen years in mental hospitals.[139] He used his forced leisure to write novels which had been considered boring for a long time. Recently it has been believed that Sade was a profound genius and a great pioneer in sexual pathology. It should be remembered, however, that he had spent his childhood and youth with his uncle, the learned and wealthy Bishop de Sade. If the young Sade read treatises of moral theology in his uncle's large library, he could have drawn from them a good part of his supposedly original concepts of sexual pathology. Among more recent writers, Leopold Sacher-Masoch (1836–1895), described his own abnormal sexual tendencies in several novels, principally in *Venus in Furs.*[140] The hero of that novel craves humiliation on the part of the woman he loves and is morbidly attracted by her furs.

Meanwhile, a Russian physician, Kaan, published a treatise in Látin, *Psychopathia Sexualis,* in 1844, describing succinctly the modifications of the *nisus sexualis* (sexual instinct).[141] A German psychiatrist, Jakob Christoph Santlus, founded a system of psychology and psychopathology on a theory of the instincts.[142] The basic tendency to being (*Seinstrieb*) was divided by Santlus into the animal and the spiritual parts of man, hence two fundamental drives: the sexual and the spiritual. These two drives develop, but there are interactions between them that include many deviations of which a variety is described by Santlus. Among others, he emphasizes the connection between religious delusions and the sexual drives. In France, Pierre Moreau (de Tours) wrote a classical treatise on sexual deviations.[143] In 1870, under the name of "contrary sexual feeling," Westphal inaugurated the objective psychiatric study of male homosexuality.[144]

But the honor of being the founder of modern scientific sexual pathology goes to the Austrian clinician, Richard von Krafft-Ebing (1840–1902), already known as a prominent forensic psychiatrist. In 1886 he published his *Psychopathia Sexualis*, based on many case histories of sexually abnormal individuals. The book was an enormous success and was constantly reedited, as Krafft-Ebing modified the contents of the book and his classifications of sexual abnormalities from one edition to the other. He coined the terms "sadism" and "masochism"; the first in memory of the

Marquis de Sade, to designate that deviation in which sexual pleasure is associated with physical cruelty inflicted upon the partner, and the term "masochism" in memory of Sacher-Masoch, to designate an association of sexual pleasure with the idea or the fact of being humiliated and mistreated by a woman.[145] Contrary to a frequent assumption, Krafft-Ebing did not speak of physical pain in that connection; on the contrary, he said that masochists loathe the idea of flagellation. He considered the latter to be a quite different condition not necessarily connected with sexual pathology. Krafft-Ebing's first classification of sexual pathology distinguished four classes of sexual abnormalities: (1) Absence of sexual drive. (2) Pathological increase of sex drive. (3) Abnormal period of emergence of the sex drive (either too early or too late in life). (4) Perversions: sadism, necrophilia, and "contrary sexual feeling."[146] In the subsequent editions of *Psychopathia Sexualis* he modified his classification several times and finally came to distinguish two main groups: the first according to the goal (sadism, masochism, fetishism, and exhibitionism), the second according to the object (homosexuality, pedophilia, zoophilia, gerontophilia, and autoerotism). Krafft-Ebing gave a tremendous impulse to the study of sexual pathology, and after 1880 studies on the subject appeared in increasing numbers, particularly in Germany. In 1899 Magnus Hirschfeld founded the first specialized periodical in that field, the *Jahrbuch für sexuelle Zwischenstufen*, and he was the first to make a radical distinction between homosexuality and transvestism. Among other studies were those by Iwan Bloch, Löwenfeld, Marcuse, Moll, and those of German anthropologists on comparative sexual psychopathology. In France, Lasègue had already presented the first psychiatric study of exhibitionism in 1877.[147] Alfred Binet coined the word "fetishism" in an extensive study devoted to that deviation.[148] One of Charcot's pupils, Chambard, mentioned erotogenic zones, for the first time in 1881, a term taken over by Krafft-Ebing that later found its way into psychoanalysis.[149] In England, Havelock Ellis became known mainly for his great compilation on *The Studies on the Psychology of Sex.*

These studies by Krafft-Ebing and others provoked a deep interest that soon reached a wide public, which, as we have seen, was already provided with a great number of novels on the subject of sex. Contrary to the present-day legend that would have us believe that those were days of sexual obscurantism, on the Continent there were no barriers to the publication, distribution of, and access to such writings. It was also the time when popular books on sexual matters began to appear everywhere. In Germany for instance, a book by Bölsche, *Love Life in Nature,* describing in detail the manifold varieties of the processes of reproduction throughout the animal kingdom, became a best seller.[150] It is true that criticism was growing against this overflow of sexual literature, but the real meaning of this criticism is misunderstood today. Moritz Benedikt relates that when Krafft-Ebing's *Psychopathia Sexualis* was published, he had to dissuade the committee of the British Medico-Psychological Association from canceling Krafft-Ebing's honorary membership in the Association.[151] The complaint against Krafft-Ebing was not in publishing his book, but that he had not prevented it from being sold indiscriminately. Benedikt noticed that "today, the students of higher schools for girls were more knowledgeable on the theme of sexual perversions than we were as young physicians." Benedikt adds that Mantegazza, an Italian professor, published a book on sexual matters that also became a best seller and was translated into several languages, and justified himself by saying that, because of his modest remuneration as a professor, he had to find other sources of income. Obviously, the dividing line between scientific vulgarization and pornography was difficult to determine from the very beginning. Another objection that Moritz Benedikt and others made to the new "sexologists" was that they had created a kind of "romanticization" of the sexual perversion. Whereas in the past sexual deviants were regarded as being similar to outlaws, they were now often pictured as undergoing unheard-of sufferings. Also in that regard, the delineation was not always easy between the writings of professional psychiatrists and those of sexual deviants defending their cause.

A much-discussed question at that time was whether sexual deviations were inborn or acquired. Here also can be seen the difference in outlook of people according to their field of activity. For the educators, the problem was simple: they saw homosexuality as an almost natural result of certain unfavorable conditions among adolescents and young men. The same applied to the army, the navy, and the prisons. Krafft-Ebing, who as a forensic expert, had to examine the most severe cases of sexual abnormalities brought before the courts, and who had been influenced by the degeneration theory of Morel and Magnan, was inclined to attribute most severe sexual perversions to a constitutional origin. This opinion was shared at first by many psychiatrists; however, the notion that psychological causes can be the origin of sexual perversion gained ground. The origin of many perversions was traced to a particular event in childhood. Rousseau had already described how a spanking he had received from a young woman, at the age of eight, had been the starting point of his sexual deviation. Binet, without denying the role of predisposition, noted in the history of his fetishists an occurrence that had given the perversion its characteristic form. In 1894, Féré told of two women who, in early childhood, had been the object of sexual caresses by domestics, without any immediate effect, but later in life, under circumstantial stress, a sexual deviation appeared.[152] Féré believed that the same could happen in cases of sexual seduction in infants. In 1901, Moll emphasized the danger of corporal punishment for young children, warning that it could become the cause of sexual stimulation in the teacher, in the schoolmates who witness the punishment, and particularly in the punished child on whom it can have a lasting effect.[153]

The occurrence of sexual deviation originating in certain interpersonal situations in early youth was taught by Theodor Meynert.[154] His clinical experience, he said, had led him to find that homosexuality was always of acquired origin. As an example, he related the story of a man who was attracted to his own sex, and whose mother had become a widow early in her life and invited young boys of her son's age to keep him company, being unable, however, to help his perceiving her own erotic feelings toward them. By merely following her example, he thus found himself becoming attracted toward his own sex. Meynert also tells the story of a necrophile whose deviation originated in his having been working in a morgue where he received his first sexual stimulation from the sight of naked female corpses.

The idea became prevalent that sexual disturbances could result from unconscious psychological causes whose origins were to be found in childhood. Dallemagne told of transient sexual arousals at the age of five or six, producing associations that in turn formed in later years the unconscious substratum of our feelings and acts.[155] Ribot, in 1886, gave a classification of sexual disturbances based on their origin: (1) anatomical and physiological causes; (2) sociological causes (closed communities of men); (3) unconscious psychological causes of the type described by Dallemagne, expressing the action of an unconscious subpersonality that directs the conscious personality, and (4) conscious psychological causes (the imagination working on an erotic theme, much as it might do on an artistic or scientific theme).[156]

The assumption of a psychogenesis of sexual perversions naturally led to attempts to treat them by psychotherapy. Such was the case with a patient of Charcot and Magnan, who, at the age of six, had watched soldiers masturbating, and who from that time on had been stimulated only by the sight of men, showing no interest in women.[157] The treatment consisted in substituting the picture of a naked woman for that of a man, and after some months the patient became able to have satisfactory relations with a woman. Twenty years later, Magnan published the follow-up to that story: the patient had become convinced that his "obsession" was not invincible and after a great effort in view of creating new, heterosexual associations, he was able to marry and had never relapsed into his former habits at the time of that publication.[158]

During the period 1880 to 1900, a growing interest was taken in the disguised manifestations of the sexual instinct, which had previously been made the object of investigations by Ideler, Neumann, Santlus, and others. The role of the sexual instinct in hysteria had been taken for granted by almost all physicians up to Briquet, who, as we have seen above, expressly denied it in his textbook written in 1859. After Briquet, opinions on this subject were divided. Here occurred one of those curious splits that sometimes happen in the history of science: whereas most neurologists tended to follow Briquet's and Charcot's view, gynecologists still believed in the sexual psychogenesis of hysteria. We have described in Chapter 3 how the American gynecologist, A. F. A. King, after adopting Binet's theory of the dual personality of hysterical patients, contended that these two personalities are the "reproductive ego" and the "self-preservative ego."[159] If a woman decides to say "no" to the demands of reproductory functions, hysteria is liable to occur, unless the woman's need for activity is totally absorbed in the struggle for existence. Among neurologists, however, one did not accept Briquet's theory: Moritz Benedikt contended in 1864 that hysteria depended on functional (not physical) sexual disorders.[160] In 1868 he substantiated this theory with clinical observations on the relationship of hysteria and disorders of the libido (as he called it), published four cases of male hysteria that he blamed on mistreatment in childhood, and proclaimed the necessity for psychotherapy.[161] In 1891 and the following years, he described what he called the second life, the existence and importance of a secret life in many persons, particularly in women, and the pathogenic role of a secret, which he said almost always concerns some aspect of the sexual life of the patient.[162] He gave examples of severe hysterical conditions rapidly cured by the confession of such pathogenic secrets and the subsequent disappearance of the patient's problems.

In regard to the other then current neurosis, neurasthenia, most specialists still believed that masturbation was one of its most frequent causes, but the belief began to grow that there were other sexual causes, especially coitus interruptus. Alexander Peyer, a Zurich physician, quoted a dozen authors who shared this opinion with him.[163] Peyer also contended that there was also a special form of asthma caused by a variety of disturbances in sexual life and especially by coitus interruptus.[164]

Another frequent topic for discussion was the various reactions assumed when sexual instincts were ungratified, aside from psychosis or classical neurosis. The Austrian criminologist Hans Gross gave special attention to that problem, because he assumed that frustrated sexual instinct could in given circumstances become the starting point of crimes, and that it was therefore necessary for the investigator of justice to know the various masks of hidden sexuality.[165] One of them, he said, is false piety; another one is boredom, that is, an inner void, which, no matter how busy life may be, is never filled. A third one he described as "morbid vanity," and a fourth one, resentment. A much discussed question was whether sexual abstinence could be harmful. Most authors believed that it was. Krafft-Ebing, however, was one of those who thought that sexual abstinence could harm only predisposed individuals, in whom its effects could range from slight agitation or sleeplessness to hallucinations.[166]

No less discussed were the normal or superior metamorphoses of the sexual instinct. Curiously enough, Gall, although the initiator of a psychology based on the study of instincts, objected to that idea and exclaimed: "Who would dare derive from a condition of the organs of generation, poetry, music and the graphic arts?"[167] Ostwald in his biography of great scientists, pointed out that their love lives had been of little importance and had exerted no influence on their discoveries.[168] But Metchnikov, followed by the majority of authors, believed in the importance of sexuality in the creativeness of geniuses, and had gathered many documents on that problem.[169]

Many went even further and attributed a sexual origin to the feeling for beauty. Espinas presented a theory of esthetic feeling originating in the competition between males for winning females in the form of brilliant plumage, song, and dances, and in the effort of the female to make herself attractive to the male.[170] Nietzsche said that "every kind of beauty incites to reproduction, this being its specific effect from the lowest sensuality to the highest spirituality."[171] Steinthal held that in the course of man's ascent from the animal world, a part of his sexual instinct became transformed into the sense of beauty.[172] Moebius taught that everything that we find beautiful in nature stems from the sexual instinct, and that the esthetic feeling itself shows a direct connection with it.[173] Santayana taught that the sexual impulse irradiates into religion, philanthropy, love for nature, and animals, and the sense of beauty.[174] Naumann stressed that "the primitive and all-powerful source of esthetic activity as well as enjoyment is sexual life."[175] Yrjö Hirn more moderately saw sexual instinct as one of four basic factors of the origin of art, and considered eroticism a means of selection in evolution and as an emotional stimulant.[176] Rémy de Gourmont contended that neither men nor women are beautiful in themselves, woman even less so than man; if the female body has become the incarnation of beauty, it is through a sexual illusion of man.[177] In short, this concept of the sexual origin of the feeling of beauty was the most prevalent, and fitted well into the general picture of that time.

Also in that period investigations began into the stages of evolution of the sexual instinct, both in the history of the human species and in the development of the individual. In 1894 Dessoir gave an account of the evolution of the sexual instinct in young people. There is, he says, a phase of nondifferentiation, followed by a phase of differentiation leading either normally to heterosexuality or abnormally to homosexuality. Disturbances in that differentiation process can lead to sexual abnormalities, but sexual feeling can also remain at such an "embryonic" stage that the individual remains sexually indiscriminating and may be attracted by any warm living body, even that of an animal. It is important to distinguish between actual homosexuals and individuals who have remained at a stage of nondifferentiation, and who can be attracted by both sexes. Albert Moll in his book

Inquiry into Libido Sexualis continued Dessoir's idea of a phase of sexual nondifferentiation before puberty, preceding the phase of differentiation.[179] Incidentally, the word "libido" had been used many times before by those physicians who more or less loosely mixed Latin words into their terminology. To them, it simply meant sexual desire. It had been used occasionally by Meynert,[180] more frequently by Benedikt,[181] and by Krafft-Ebing,[182] and quite currently by lesser-known authors such as Effertz,[183] and Eulenburg.[184] It seems that it was Moll who gave it the wider meaning of sexual instinct in its evolutionary sense, and Freud refers to Moll in that connection.

In 1886, the French philosopher Arréat suggested that just as the sexual act is but a moment in the sexual instinct itself, sexual instinct could be a part of a more general instinct.[185] In the married couple there is a wider circle of conjugal love around the nucleus of pure sexuality that is impregnated, however, with sexual feeling. In the love of parents toward their children, there is more than just parental love; the father is jealous of his daughter, more often even than the mother of her son. The reverse is already seen in the child, in the sensuous avidity with which the infant sucks his mother's breast and young children kiss their parents. Arréat tells of a six or seven-year-old girl who rolled herself in her father's dirty clothes, saying "it smells of Daddy." He also quotes Perez and many others of the role of sex in the emotional feelings of young siblings. In common acts of politeness (especially of a man toward a young woman) and of "pure friendship," there is always a sexual undertone. The contribution of sexual instinct to social feelings is considerable, he says. In that frame of reference, sexual abnormalities could be considered in Lombroso's sense as an arrested development.

From the foregoing it can be seen that by the year 1900 sexual psychology and psychopathology had already been in full development for twenty years, and had made numerous contributions that tended to be synthesized in the new science of sexology.

The Study of Dreams

Because of the importance that the theory and interpretation of dreams were destined to acquire in dynamic psychology, it is appropriate to inquire about their development during the decisive period between 1880–1900. At that time there was actually a great amount of research being done on dreams. However, to understand its meaning, we must go back a few decades.

We remember that Romanticism placed an enormous emphasis on dreams, that almost all the Romantics either had a complete theory or scattered ideas about them, and most of those authors insisted on the creative process of dreams. Ennemoser[186] said "the essence of dream is a potential life of a genius." Troxler[187] went so far as to say that dreaming was a more fundamental process than waking life, by which he apparently meant that the process of dreaming under the conscious state was a continuous one, of which we become aware only when dreaming in sleep. The Romantic conception of dreams culminated with Von Schubert whose ideas were summarily reviewed in Chapter 4.

After the decline of Romanticism, the era of positivism brought the notion that dreams were a meaningless by-product of automatic and uncoordinated brain activity occurring during sleep. It was, however, during that period that the work of three great pioneers of dream investigation appeared—that of Scherner, Maury, and Hervey de Saint-Denis. Their work was basic to the further elaboration of dream theory from 1880 to 1900 and still later in the dream theories of Freud and Jung.

Meanwhile, students of dreams gradually established a set of techniques for the investigation of dreams based on observation, experimentation, and the mastery of dreams. It was found that observation could be conducted either while falling asleep, when being awakened during sleep, or when spontaneously waking up. It is important to remain still after waking in order to recall one's dream, which should then be written down immediately on a prepared sheet of paper lying nearby. Hervey de Saint-Denis supplemented the writing down of his dreams with the drawing of them. Students of dreams noticed that they could easily train themselves to the point of being able to remember their dreams fairly well. The method of experimentally producing dreams was inaugurated by Maury and that of the mastering of one's dreams by Hervey de Saint-Denis.

Scherner's book *The Life of the Dream* appeared in 1861 as the only one of a proposed series of eight discoveries in the realm of the soul.[188] Scherner's work has never been popular. Some readers disliked the romantic tone with which he speaks of the soul in the introduction, which manifests itself in dreams "like a lover to his beloved." Other readers were discouraged by the dryness of the main text and what they felt was an exaggerated tendency toward classification. When we add that the book is extremely condensed and that it has become very scarce, one can understand why it is so rarely read today. Scherner begins his investigation with what would be today called a phenomenology of dreams. Light in dreams, he says, is the expression of clear thinking and of sharpness of will; chiaroscuro, the expression of imprecise feelings. He also describes the stages of dreaming in falling asleep, full sleep, and awakening. With regard to the dream's inner organization, he distinguishes between the decentralization (which would be today called dissolution or regression), and the positive manifestations of the dream fantasy. His main idea is that psychic activity in dreams is directly expressed in a language of symbols, hence the possibility of interpreting them. Scherner proposed a system of dream interpretation based on a plausible theory, which resulted from prolonged objective observations.

Some symbols are determined by spiritual stimulation, others by bodily stimulation. Religious feelings are expressed in the form of revelation brought by a respected master, intellectual feelings in the form of discussion between equals, feelings of diminished vitality are seen in the vision of a sick individual, and so on. A great part of Scherner's book is devoted to an analysis of the symbols elicited from bodily sensations. Certain symbols correspond to each one of the organs and are not arbitrary but revealed by experience. Scherner studied the correlation between the dreams and the dreamer's physical diseases or functional modifications at the time of awakening. He found, for instance, that dreams of flying were related to an increased functioning of the lungs; dreams of heavy traffic through streets would sometimes express heart or circulatory conditions. According to Scherner, there is one basic dream symbol: the image of a house, which is the expression of the human body, parts of the house representing parts of the body. Scherner relates the story of a lady who went to bed with a violent headache and who dreamed that she was in a room in which the ceiling was covered with cobwebs swarming with large and disgusting spiders. A dozen pages in Scherner's book are devoted to symbols related to the sex organs. As male symbols he mentions high towers, pipes, clarinets, knives and pointed weapons, running horses, and fluttering birds being chased; among female sex symbols Scherner mentions a narrow courtyard and a staircase that one must climb up.

After Scherner, several authors, either with or without reference to him, found the same symbols relating to the same parts of the body.[189] In his explanation of sexual symbols Freud refers to Scherner; however, Freud's symbols are more abstract units of meaning and are independent from physiological conditions. But Scherner's work had other, unexpected developments. Friedrich Theodor Vischer showed the parallelism of the Schernerian symbolism with the architectural symbolism of temples in ancient Egypt and in India, which seem to have been conceived as a symbolic representation of the human body. Recently, much speculation of that kind has been given to the Temple of Luxor.[190] Scherner's idea was also the starting point of a new concept of esthetics, first expressed by Robert Vischer, and developed by Friedrich Theodor Vischer.[191] We have the tendency to project (*hineinversetzen*) our bodily feelings onto things, as revealed by certain idioms (for instance, "a dwarfed tree") in the waking state as well as in dreams. Artistic empathy (*Einfühlung*) rests on an obscure drive to unite with other beings (in modern language one would say to project our body image into other beings or representations).

Maury's classical book *Sleep and Dreams* appeared in the same year as Scherner's, but in contrast to the latter it was reedited many times.[192] Maury experimented on himself with two methods of dream investigation. First, he trained himself to write down his dreams as soon as he awoke, and devoted considerable attention to writing down all the circumstances that might have led to each one of them. He was struck by the great sensitivity of his own dreams to any change in diet or in atmospheric conditions. He also believed that he observed that the hypnagogic illusions of hallucinations were furnishing the "embryogenesis" of the night's dream. His other method was experimentation with sensory stimulation. Maury's assistant would give him perfume to breathe during his sleep, and Maury dreamed that he was in Cairo, in the shop of a perfume merchant. His assistant would make a noise with metallic vibrations and Maury dreamed of hearing the alarm bell and that a revolution had broken out.

Maury understood that sensory stimulation did not account for the greatest part of the dreams. His prolonged observation and noting of his dreams led him to reduce the part of fantasy and creativeness in dreams. He noticed that many things that he believed to have imagined in his dreams were but forgotten memories, sometimes going back to early childhood. Maury also believed that the speed of dreams greatly exceeded that of thought in the waking state.

Maury's work inaugurated the study of experimental stimulation of dreams. John Mourly Vold, of Norway, performed experiments upon himself and his students in which the limbs were tied, and found that this induced dreams of movement (the dreamer saw either himself or someone else moving).[193] Incidentally, this later became the theoretical basis of Hermann Rorschach's concept of "kinesthetic responses" in his inkblot test. Sante de Sanctis' criticism of Maury's experiments was that his expectation to have certain dreams sufficed to create in the dreamer dreams fit to confirm the theory of the dreamer-experimenter, a criticism that also applied to all those who experimented with dreams.[194]

The third great pioneer of dream psychology was the Marquis Hervey de Saint-Denis (1823–1892), who taught Chinese language and literature at the Collège de France. His book *Dreams and the Means to Direct Them*, published anonymously in 1867, is one of the most extensive and thorough studies ever devoted to the author's own dreams.[195] It is also one of the most-quoted but least-read books on dream literature because it is exceedingly rare. Freud stated that he had never been able to find a copy of it. The scarcity of the book is the more regrettable because it contains the findings of a lifetime of dream investigation by a man who opened new paths that few men were able to follow.

In the first part, Hervey de Saint-Denis tells how, as a thirteen-year-old boy, the idea occurred to him to draw a curious dream he had had the night before. He was pleased with the result and started an album in which he drew all his dreams. He noticed that he became increasingly able to remember them, so that after six months he rarely forgot any of his dreams. But he became so absorbed in this occupation that he could think of nothing else and had headaches, so that he was obliged to stop for a while. He took it up again and continued noting and drawing his dreams for the next twenty years. He said that he never missed a single dream during all that time and thus obtained twenty-two notebooks containing the dreams of nineteen hundred and forty-six nights. Hervey describes the successive stages of the training he went through in order to master his dreams. The first step was taken when, a few months after the beginning, he became aware that he was dreaming. The second step was achieved when he became able to wake himself at will in order to note interesting dreams. The third step was acquiring the ability to concentrate at will on any part of the dream that he wished to explore more deeply. The fourth and last step was the voluntary directing of at least a part of his dreams, although he had to recognize that there were certain limitations. To give but one example, Hervey wished to dream about his own death, and directed his dream to take him to the top of a tower from which he threw himself, but at this point he found himself dreaming that he was among the crowd of spectators watching a man who had thrown himself from the top of a tower.

The second part of Hervey's book is devoted to a critical survey of previous dream theories, to which Hervey adds a great amount of material drawn from his own experience. The first question is: from where do dream images come? Here, Hervey confirms Maury's observation that memory's part is far greater than we imagine. Like Maury, he cites examples of dream pictures that seemed quite new to him, but which he was able to identify later by chance as forgotten memories, dream images being mostly the reproduction of *clichés-souvenirs* (which could be translated as "snapshot-memories"). To the question, "Why are dreams sometimes confused or absurd?" Hervey answers that the perception may have been quick and unclear, so that the reproduction in the dream is itself unclear and blurred. Sometimes dreams are obscure because there are two or more *clichés-souvenirs* superimposed on one another. Finally, there is sometimes an "abstraction," that is a certain quality is abstracted from one object and attributed to another. Thus what Hervey calls abstraction and superimposition is what is today called displacement and condensation. Conversation between several persons, another occurrence in dreams, represents, according to Hervey, a conflict within the dreamer.

Image-memories, however, do not account for the entire material of dreams, Hervey says. Creative fantasy also plays its part. Although he once relates the story of a chess problem solved in a dream, Hervey emphasizes the imaginative dream performances. Several of his dreams are actually of high poetic quality and beauty. In one of them Hervey looks into a magic mirror, sees himself as a youth growing older until he becomes an ugly old man, and awakens in fright. Another one (pp. 322–323) curiously anticipates an episode in H. G. Wells *Invisible Man*. Still more remarkable are those dreams that would be called archetypal in Jungian terminology, and that would actually seem, to the present-day reader, to be borrowed from one of Jung's writings.

Hervey also contributed to the experimental study of dreams. Whereas

Maury had been content to experiment with simple sensory stimulation and the response to them, Hervey imagined a technique of *solidarité remémorative,* that is, something similar to dream-conditioning. During a two-week stay in a picturesque part of the French countryside, he put a drop of a certain perfume on his handkerchief every day, and ceased to do so on his return to Paris. Several months later, he asked his assistant to put some drops of that same perfume on his pillow during his sleep. Actually, twelve days later he dreamed of Vivarais, the region where he had spent his holiday and, when waking up, realized that the perfume had been put on his pillow that night. He then devised more complicated experiments. In a ball where he danced with two ladies, he had paid the musicians so that they would always play a given tune when he danced with each lady in turn. Sometime later, he had the tunes played to him from a music box, during his sleep, and found that each one of the two waltzes brought the dream image of the lady with whom he had danced that particular tune.

It is to Hervey's credit that he drew attention to the plasticity of the dream process. But the technique that he devised for mastering and consciously directing his own dreams was so difficult that he found few imitators. One of these few was the Dutch psychiatrist and poet, Frederik van Eeden, who began in 1896 to study his dreams with a technique similar to Hervey's. Like Hervey, to whom he refers, Van Eeden says that as a first step he became conscious of his dreams and later acquired the ability to direct them at will. He first condensed his observations into a novel, *The Bride of Dreams.*[196] He had been reluctant to publish his findings as his own, because of their unusual character. However, he reported on them in a paper read at a meeting of the Society for Psychical Research, and he distinguished several classes of dreams, among them demon-dreams, in which he had to deal with demon personalities, that is non-human, acting and speaking, independent beings.[197] He also had lucid dreams, in which he directed himself to meet dead people with whom he had been acquainted. He also claimed to have been able in a lucid dream to transmit a subliminal message to a medium. Hervey's experiments may have inspired George du Maurier's novel *Peter Ibbetson,* a best seller of the 1890's, in which two lovers, who are separated, manage to meet every night in their dreams and together explore the world of their childhood, of their ancestors, and of past centuries.[198] Robert Louis Stevenson's dream life, which we have mentioned in Chapter 3, could be called semiconsciously directed.[199] He reports having used the help of his "little people" or "brownies" as collaborators for the writing of his novels. It is strange to see how, after Hervey de Saint-Denis, the plastic power of dreams—conscious or unconscious—has been neglected by students of dreams, with few exceptions.[200]

The work of the three pioneers, Scherner, Maury, and Hervey de Saint-Denis, dominated the subsequent dream investigation during the last third of the nineteenth century. A considerable amount of research was devoted to dreams, during that period, by authors who are, for the most part forgotten today and who have scarcely been mentioned by historians, with the exception of Binswanger.[201] Strümpell, a professor at Leipzig University, wondered why the world is so different in dreams from what it is in waking life, and gave this answer: when we awaken, we are unable to place the dream into our past or our present, and this is also why men have had a tendency to seek its meaning in the future.[202] To the question "Why does the dreamer believe that his dream is real?" he answers that the dreaming soul constructs a "dream space" in which images and memories are projected that give the impression of true perception at the moment when the distinction between the objective and subjective and the sense of causality disappears. To the problem "Why is the dream so easily forgotten?" Strümpell points to the weakness, looseness, and incoherence of most dream images, and says that the true question should be "Why do we remember so much of it?" He also pointed to the role of speech images in dreams.

Volkelt's book *Dream-Phantasy* criticizes previous students of dreams because they gave too much importance to the negative processes in dreams and not enough (with the sole exception of Scherner) to the positive element, dream-phantasy.[203] They also gave too much importance, he believed, to the role of associations, and not enough to the fact shown by Scherner that dream-phantasy translates bodily impressions directly into symbols. Volkelt brings several personal instances of dreams in which Scherner's symbols are confirmed. Far from admitting, as most Romantics did, that in dreaming the soul escapes from the ties of the body, Volkelt says that, on the contrary, it falls into a more immediate dependency upon the body. The perception of one's body as a whole occurs in a very different way in dreams from that which it does during the waking state. Volkelt here tackles the problem of the modification of the body image in dreams.

In the same year, 1875, Friedrich Theodor Vischer's study on dreams appeared which presents a searching analysis of the process by which the dreamer surrenders himself to his images, thus creating the possibility of seeing himself mirrored in these images.[204] Scherner's ideas are developed from the point of view of their application to the theory of esthetics.

In 1876, Hildebrandt's study on dreams and their utilization in life appeared.[205] He distinguishes four possibilities in that regard. First, the beauty of some dreams can be a comfort to the dreamer. Second, the dream gives a magnified image to the dreamer of his moral tendencies. The Scriptural words "Whosoever is angry against his brother is a murderer" are confirmed in dreams in which the dreamer commits an immoral act that distresses him when he awakes. On closer examination, he may find that the dream was the materialization of some incipient immoral thought. Hildebrandt concludes that a perfectly moral man would never dream anything impure. Third, the dream can give clear insight into certain things that in waking life had been obscurely perceived, for instance, that someone wants to harm the dreamer. Fourth, there are those dreams that announce an illness, such as have been reported since Aristotle, and those dreams that inform us about physiological conditions of the body such as those described by Scherner.

Incidentally, Hildebrandt's discussion of the dreamer's moral responsibility for his dreams was later taken over by Josef Popper, who, in a curious essay, describes how, whether awake or asleep, it is the same person who has the same thoughts and feelings, and therefore, if there is something hidden or unchaste in a person, his dreams will appear senseless or even nonsensical.[206] We recognize here the notion that was to become the cornerstone of Freud's theory on dreams.

Binz, in 1878, pointed out the role of chemical and toxicological causes in the genesis of dreams.[207] Certain chemical substances give specific dreams, such as the dream brought forth by opium, atropine, alcohol, hashish, and ether. According to Binz, students of the dream have over-emphasized the psychological side and have largely ignored the physiological factors causing dreams.

Robert introduced a new point of view.[208] Nature, he believes, does nothing unnecessarily. If dreaming exists, it must have a necessary function. What could this be? Robert assumes that it is an elimination process that occurs in the brain and whose reflection we perceive as the dream. Therefore, it is not that man can dream, but that he must dream, in order to eliminate the images that burden his mind; such as the case when there is an overflow of perceptions from outside, or of fantasy images. Such is particularly the case for unclear perceptions or ideas that have not been completely thought out. The elimination occurs through a process that Robert calls the dream-work (*Traumarbeit*), through which they are either incorporated into the memory or forgotten. The eliminated images are perceived by us as dream-images; they are "chips from the workshop of the mind." An important consequence of this is that "a person from whom one would take the capacity for dreaming would sooner or later become mentally deranged," and the kind of the mental derangement would be determined by the type of preoccupation that was not eliminated in dreams. He gives the example of two merchants, each of whom receives a letter at his office but which each neglects to read. The first merchant is in great business difficulties from which the second has just recovered. Therefore they are in different moods and this will be reflected in their dreams. But should these merchants not be able to unload their minds in dreams, the first would develop delusions of persecution, the second, delusions of grandeur.

Yves Delage, a French biologist, devoted many years to the study of dreams. He gave a first sketch of his theory in 1891.[209] He started his investigation from an original perspective: what are the things of which we do *not* dream? He found that things that occupy the mind heavily during the day do not appear in dreams, nor do the important events in life. Lovers, for instance, do not dream of each other before marriage, during the honeymoon, or for some time afterward; only later, when they have become used to each other, do they dream about each other. To the question "what do we actually dream?" he answered that the great majority of dream images come from unfinished acts or thoughts or from elusive perceptions, mostly of the day before. (Delage does not seem to have known of Robert.) This does not exclude the fact that dreams can be elicited by an actual sensory stimulation, such as described by Maury. Delage's psychology is an energetic-dynamic one, along the lines of Herbart's. Our impressions, he says, are "accumulators of energy," in other words each one has its own charge of energy, and depending on the charge of energy, they repel or inhibit each other. Although in our dreams recent unfinished thoughts or images dominate, impressions that are complete can break through, if they have a very strong charge of energy; this is precisely what happens in nightmares. But there is also an independent activity in dreaming, which proceeds in decreasing order from daydream to half-dream, and from partially directed dream to ordinary dream. But the dream does not only consist of recent unmodified images. In that connection, Delage mentions two processes that had already been described by Maury and Hervey de Saint-Denis. One is the fusion of representations into one image and the other the attribution of a neutral act to another subject (in modern terms, condensation and displacement). Furthermore, not only recent memories but old ones may occur in dreaming. One finds that old memories are brought back through associations with recent memories, and chains of associations may sometimes be reconstructed (as Maury did with chains of verbal associations). Delage believed that such chains of associations must exist within the dreams.

From this brief review it can be seen that investigators of dreams from 1860 to 1899 had already discovered almost all the notions that were to be synthesized by Freud and by Jung, and many others who have not yet received sufficient attention. In Freud's theories can be recognized the influences of Maury, Scherner. Strümpell, Volkelt, and Delage. As for Jung, his theory of dreams reminds us more of Von Schubert and the Romantics, and shows at times striking analogies with Hervey de Saint-Denis.

The Exploration of the Unconscious

In the last decades of the nineteenth century, the philosophical concept of the unconscious, as taught by Schopenhauer and Von Hartmann, was extremely popular, and most contemporary philosophers admitted the existence of an unconscious mental life. Psychologists were seeking scientific evidences, and in that regard, decisive contributions were made in the years 1880 to 1900. Here, too, we have to go back in order to see the problem in its proper context. The assumption that a part of psychic life escapes man's conscious knowledge had been held for many centuries. In the seventeenth and eighteenth centuries, it attracted more attention; in the nineteenth, as one of the most highly debated problems, it became finally one of the cornerstones of modern dynamic psychiatry. The traditional speculative approach, which was also that of the Romantics, was now supplemented by two other approaches, the experimental and the clinical.[210]

The speculative approach was that of the pantheistic philosophers and the mystics of India and Greece, the Vedanta, Plotinus, Dionysius Areopagita, many mystics of the Middle Ages, Boehme, Schelling, and the philosophers of nature, Schopenhauer, C. G. Carus, and Von Hartmann. It should be noted, however, that in the course of time, the arguments brought forth by these philosophers were more and more of a psychological nature. The speculative approach was also used by certain philosopher-psychologists. It was Leibniz who proposed the first theory of the unconscious mind supported by purely psychological arguments.[211] He pointed to the small perceptions, that is, those that are under the threshold of perception even though they play a great part in our mental life. Herbart took the concept of small perceptions and the threshold from Leibniz, but introduced a dynamic viewpoint.[212] Herbart thought of the threshold as a surface where an everchanging multitude of perceptions and representations constantly fight against one another. The stronger ones push the weaker ones down under the threshold, the repressed representations strive to reemerge, and for that reason often associate themselves with other representations. Under the threshold, the obscure representations constitute a kind of chorus that accompanies the drama being played on the conscious stage. Lying below the threshold is also the apperception mass, a compact organized bundle of unconscious representations. Whether a new perception will be retained or not depends on whether it fits into the apperception mass and can be readily assimilated by it. Herbart gave mathematical formulations of the relationships of forces between perceptions. Although his theory of the unconscious was a largely speculative one, it exerted a great influence on German psychology throughout the nineteenth century, extending up to Griesinger and to Freud's psychoanalytic concept. A biological, speculative approach was used by Hering, who contended that memory is a general function of organized matter and that besides the individual's memory there is also a memory of the species of which the instinct is one manifestation. Similar ideas were expressed in England by the novelist Samuel Butler, and were later developed by Richard Semon, Hans Driesch, and Eugen Bleuler.

The experimental approach to the study of the unconscious was introduced by Fechner with his psychophysics.[213] In order to check his metaphysical hypothesis about the relationship of mind and body, about 1850 he began a long series of experiments on the mathematical relationship of the intensity of stimulations and the intensity of perceptions. While computing the intensity of perceptions, he gave negative values to those below the threshold of perception. However, he found that the difference between the waking state and the sleeping state was not mainly a difference in the intensity of a certain mental function. It was as if the same mental activities were displayed alternately on different theater scenes or stages (a remark that was to be the starting point of Freud's topographical concept of the mind). While Fechner and his successors tried to measure unconscious perceptions, Helmholtz discovered the phenomenon of "unconscious inference": we perceive the objects not as they impress our sensory organs, but "as they should be."[214] Perception is a kind of instantaneous and unconscious reconstruction of what our past experience taught us about the object. It not only adds to sensation, it also abstracts from it, retaining only that which is utilizable for our knowledge of objects, from the sensory data.

A new experimental approach was devised by Chevreul,[215] who was able to show that the movements of the divining rod and the pendulum resulted from unconscious muscular movements of the subject caused by unconscious thoughts. Chevreul extended his research to the movements of the "turning tables": it is not the "spirits," he said, who are moving the tables, but the unconscious muscular movements of the participants; the alleged messages of the "spirits" are the expression of unconscious thoughts of the medium.[216] Chevreul's concept of unconscious thoughts being expressed through unconscious movements was later applied to the phenomena of "Cumberlandism" (that is, mind-reading) and automatic writing. Another experimental approach was conceived by Galton when he devised the word-association test. He found that answers were not given haphazardly but had some relevance to the thoughts, feelings, and memories of the individual.[217] This aspect of the word-association test, however, was overlooked by Galton's followers, and it was C. G. Jung who first used that test as a detector of unconscious representation. Finally Narziss Ach, who, in a series of perfected laboratory investigations, directly tackled the problem of unconscious activity in thinking and in will, showed experimentally the role of unconscious determining tendencies in the execution of conscious acts of will and thought.[218]

Another approach was given by the new parapsychological research, which had its origins in England. In the 1870's, a movement arose at Cambridge University to explore the depth of the unknown mind and particularly the facts of clairvoyance, foreknowledge of the future, and purported communications with the deceased. After a long period of informal association, the Society for Psychical Research was founded in 1882 by a physicist, William Barrett; a clergyman, Reverend Stainton Moses; a philosopher, Henry Sidgwick; and a young classical scholar, Frederick

Myers, who was to play the major role in the first twenty years of the Society.[219] The basis of Myers' thinking was the philosophical question: "Is the Universe friendly?" A satisfactory answer to this, he thought, could be given only after answering a preliminary question, "Does man's life have any continuity beyond the grave?" in order to secure further development and fulfillment. The problem of survival after death was thus set in the foreground of parapsychological research. In this context many other problems arose, and Myers believed that a thorough analysis had to be made of the problems of hypnosis and dual personality, as well as the current parapsychological phenomena, before the question of the communication with deceased spirits could be properly approached. He began a critical examination into the entire literature dealing with these topics. The results of this inquiry, in addition to the results of his own parapsychological research and that of his colleagues, were compiled in an encyclopedic work that was published posthumously in 1903.[220] Myers was thus not only a parapsychologist, but also one of the great systematizers of the notion of the unconscious mind. In Myers' view, the "subliminal self" (as he called it) has inferior and superior functions. The inferior functions are shown in those processes of dissociation, described by psychopathologists, and the superior functions are revealed in certain works of genius, which could be understood as the "subliminal uprush" of rich storehouses of information, sentiment, and reflection that lie beneath the consciousness of the creative thinker. Myers believed that through the superior functions, the human mind can also occasionally be in communication with the spirits of the deceased. A third function of the unconscious Myers called mythopoetic function, that is the unconscious tendency to weave fantasies. It is unfortunate that Myers did not follow the implication of this very fruitful notion to its full extent.

The clinical approach to the exploration of the unconscious had largely been utilized during the entire nineteenth century, since a great part of the work of the magnetists and hypnotists was basically a clinical investigation of the unconscious, although it was largely done in an unsystematic way and often without criticism or sufficient distinction between experimental concepts and theory.

In France the interest in such research was renewed after Charles Richet's publication in 1875.[221] In the early 1880's, when Charcot and Bernheim initiated the clinical study of hypnosis, a continuous flow of research and publications began to emerge. The state of the problem of the unconscious, as it was in the late 1880's, was sketched by Héricourt in a survey published in 1889, stating that the unconscious activity of the mind is a scientific truth established beyond any doubt, and he gave credit to Chevreul for having experimentally proved this.[222] As everyday manifestations of the unconscious life, Héricourt mentions habits and instinct, forgotten memories, occurring spontaneously in the mind, problems being solved during sleep, unconscious movements that have psychological content and meaning, and unaccountable feelings of sympathy and antipathy. Even in daily life, our conscious mind remains under the direction of the unconscious. We receive suggestions from the environment not only in hypnotic experiments, but in the waking state, and transform them into thoughts and feelings that we believe to be our own. Other proofs of the activity of the unconscious are found in hysteria, mediumism, and automatic writing. The relationship of the conscious and unconscious mind can be of three types: (1) Normally, there should be peaceful collaboration, the unconscious being content to be a silent auxiliary. (2) But a kind of estrangement may occur and the unconscious then organizes itself in the form of a "second personality"; this is what occurs temporarily in hypnosis and permanently in such patients as Felida. (3) Finally, an open rebellion of the unconscious against the conscious mind can take place with a more or less prolonged struggle and a variety of results such as impulses, phobias, and obsessions may occur. Insanity is manifested when the conscious mind has yielded to the unconscious.

Between 1889 and 1900, great strides were made in the clinical exploration of the unconscious. Janet published his *Automatisme Psychologique* in 1889, the impact of which, as we shall see in the following chapter, was considerable and dominated the exploration of the unconscious for some time to come. Janet pursued his investigations in that line for several years. Meanwhile, Breuer and Freud published their "preliminary paper" of 1893, and their *Studies in Hysteria* in 1895, to which we will return in Chapter 7. At the same time, Flournoy independently conducted in Geneva a research of great originality.

Theodore Flournoy (1854–1920), a physician, philosopher, and psychologist, and a disciple of Wundt's, was appointed as professor of psychology at the University of Geneva in 1891. He had learned the techniques of experimental psychology and undertook to apply them to problems of parapsychology. He took as his maxims what he called the *principle of Hamlet*: "Everything is possible," and the *principle of Laplace*: "The weight of evidence must be in proportion to the strangeness of the fact." He carried on a lengthy study of the mediums of Geneva. In December 1894, Flournoy was invited to a sitting at which a medium, Catherine Muller, was revealing her capacities. He was intrigued to hear the medium tell of certain events that had occurred long ago in his own family, and wondered how she could know of them. But Flournoy did not hasten to draw any conclusion. He conducted a lengthy inquiry into the origin and background of the medium, and found that, long ago, there had been some temporary connection between the medium's parents and his own, so that she could have heard about these events and forgotten them. Flournoy became a regular attendant at the sittings with the subject, and from that time on her mediumism underwent a remarkable change.[223] She now fell into a full somnambulistic state and manifested changes in personality in which she supposedly reenacted scenes from her previous lives. This was the beginning of a five-year investigation. Catherine Muller, the medium, better known under the pseudonym of Helen Smith, was a tall and handsome woman thirty years of age, who worked as a saleslady in a department store. She was a fervent believer in spiritism, and never accepted any money for her mediumistic work. Her utterances were considered by her circle of admirers as being revelations from another world, whereas the skeptics considered her a fraud. Flournoy asserted that it was neither one nor the other, and that a natural explanation could be given. He began by analyzing the three cycles of the medium. In the first cycle, she reenacted her supposed previous life as a fifteenth-century Indian princess. In the second cycle, she reenacted scenes of the life of Marie Antoinette, of whom she also claimed to be a reincarnation. In the Martian cycle, she pretended to be familiar with the planet Mars, its landscapes, inhabitants, and language, which she could speak and write. Flournoy was able to identify a great deal of this material as coming from books she had read as a child. In a *History of India,* he found the main details that had given birth to the Hindu cycle. The result of Flournoy's five-year investigation was published in a book *From India to the Planet Mars,* in which he showed that the revelations of the medium were "romances of the subliminal imagination" based on forgotten memories and expressing wish fulfillments, and that Helen Smith's guiding spirit, Leopold, was an unconscious subpersonality of the medium.[224] Each one of the cycles, Flournoy added, was built upon a "reversion" of the personality to a different age: the Marie Antoinette cycle to the age of sixteen, the Hindu cycle to the age of twelve, and the Martian romance to early childhood. Flournoy concluded, "Just as teratology illustrates embryology, which in turn explains teratology, and as both of these unite in throwing light on anatomy, similarly, one may hope that the study of the facts of mediumship may some day help to furnish us with some just and fruitful view of normal psychogenesis." One aspect of the investigation that seems insufficient today is that of the rapport (in present-day language, transference) between the medium and the investigator. The attachment of Helen Smith to Flournoy is intimated more than once in the book. According to Claparède, Flournoy had understood its psychosexual nature very well, but discretion prevented him from enlarging upon it, since he knew that the book would be read by the medium and her circle of acquaintances.[225]

The publication of the book had unexpected repercussions. Whereas Flournoy had shown that the "Martian" language was constructed on the grammatical pattern of the French language, a linguist, Victor Henry, contended that a great part of the vocabulary was composed of distorted Hungarian words.[226] (Hungarian was the mother tongue of the medium's father.) Helen Smith thereupon broke with Flournoy and with her spiritist friends. A wealthy American woman gave her a fortune large enough to enable her to devote herself entirely to her mediumistic activity. This was a fatal blow to the mental health of the medium. She left her position, thus severing her last tie with reality, and lived in almost complete isolation, entering into somnambulism in order to paint religious paintings.[227] After her death, these paintings were exhibited in Geneva and Paris.[228]

This was the best known of Flournoy's investigations into the realm of the unconscious, and it shows the direction that he followed. His first concern was to avoid unnecessary hypotheses involving parapsychological processes. He could trace many of these phenomena back to unconscious forgotten memories (for which he coined the word "cryptomnesia"). In the same manner, he demonstrated the psychological, though unconscious, origin of certain spiritistic messages.[229] Another main concern of Flournoy was the investigation of the various functions of the unconscious, with the first one being the creative activity. He describes a young mother who from time to time dictated philosophical fragments that were far above the scope of her interests and knowledge.[230] Second, the unconscious has protective functions. Flournoy mentions cases where the unconscious provides warning, comfort, or means of recovering from a blunder one has committed. A third function is compensation, and it was particularly noticeable in the case of Helen Smith, a well-educated and ambitious young woman who felt frustrated in her social and financial conditions and to whom romances of subliminal phantasy brought vicarious wish-fulfillment. Finally, the ludic, or play function, of the unconscious is manifested in these romances of subliminal imagination. According to Flournoy this is essential to the understanding of the psychology of the medium. Most mediums do not wish to deceive, they just wish to play, like little girls with their dolls, but sometimes fantasy life gains control.

At the end of the nineteenth century, the problem of the unconscious had been approached from several points of view. To summarize, we can say that by the year 1900 four different aspects of the activity of the unconscious had been demonstrated: the conservative, dissolutive, creative, and mythopoetic.

1. The *conservative* functions were recognized as being the recording of a great number of memories, even of unconscious perceptions, that have been stored away and of which the conscious individual knows nothing at all. There were case histories of patients who during a fever spoke a language that they had learned as young children and completely forgotten.[231] Hypnotism provided abundant instances of "hypermnesia," and we have seen that shrewd students of dreams such as Maury and Hervey de Saint-Denis were able to identify seemingly new dream images as forgotten memories. The continuing action of forgotten perceptions and memories was illustrated by Korsakoff, who told of an amnestic patient who manifested his fear of electric machines although each time he seemed to have com-

pletely forgotten his previous electric treatments.[232] Flournoy insisted upon the persisting action of cryptomnesia and how it could explain supposed facts of clairvoyance or telepathy. A classical discussion at the end of the nineteenth century among psychologists and philosophers was whether the individual retains an unconscious record of the totality of the memories of his entire life.

2. The *dissolutive* functions of the unconscious were understood to include two sets of phenomena. One is made up of those psychic phenomena that at one time were conscious but have become automatic (such as is the case with habits). The other is made up of dissociated parts of the personality that may still lead a parasitic existence and interfere with normal processes. The classical instance was posthypnotic suggestion. There were also the facts investigated by Charcot, Binet, Janet, Delboeuf, and Myers. Around 1895, "the assumption that disturbing tendencies were forced into the unconscious was a matter of course."[233] These phenomena were the starting point of the research of both Janet and Freud.

3. The *creative* function of the unconscious had been emphasized long ago by the Romantics, then in a more psychological way by Galton, and later by Flournoy and Myers.[234]

4. The *mythopoetic* function (a term apparently coined by Myers) is a "middle region" of the subliminal self where a strange fabrication of inner romances perpetually goes on.[235] Its great explorer was Flournoy with his research on Helen Smith and other mediums. In this conception the unconscious seems to be continually concerned with creating fictions and myths, which sometimes remain unconscious or appear only in dreams. Sometimes they take the form of daydreams that evolve spontaneously in the background of the subject's mind (a fact hinted at by Charcot). Sometimes, these fictions are acted out in the form of somnambulism, hypnosis, possession, medium's trance, mythomania, or certain delusions. Sometimes the mythopoetic functions express themselves organically, and this suggests one of the possible concepts of hysteria. It is surprising, however, to see that the notion of the mythopoetic function of the unconscious, which seemed so promising, was not more fully investigated.

The Great Year

The last fifteen years of the nineteenth century cannot be well understood without the notion of the *fin de siècle* that permeated the life and thought of that era. But as the century drew to an end, the preoccupation of *fin de siècle* was being replaced by that of the Great Year, which was to close the century and open the way to a new unknown era. The year 1900 acquired the value of a symbol, meaning at once the end of a century and the birth of a new one. Astronomers, of course, pointed out that the year 1900 would be a year like any other, but the popular feeling persisted with the symbolic meaning which the Etruscans or the Aztecs had given to the change of centuries and to the Great Year. It was at least the golden opportunity for philosophers, teachers, scientists, and writers to draw the balance of the nineteenth century and make their predictions for the twentieth.

Alfred Wallace in his *Wonderful Century* tried to evaluate the successes and failures of the nineteenth century.[236] The positive aspects included a catalog of discoveries in all fields of science, from physics and astronomy to natural science including the theory of natural selection, and of the application of these sciences to the modes of traveling, the conveyance of thought, labor-saving machines, and so on. On the negative side, Wallace grouped vaccination (a delusion) and its penal enforcement (a crime), the shameful neglect of phrenology, which, he predicted, would "assuredly attain general acceptance in the 20th century," and also hypnotism and psychical research. Above all, the three great plagues of the nineteenth century had been the "demon of greed," the "plundering of the earth," and the "vampire of war." The first had brought with it an enormous increase in the total mass of misery in the world, the second was an injury done to posterity, and the third had made the world into "the gambling table of the six great Powers," not to speak of the extermination of the native populations. As viewed from that aspect, the prospects for the twentieth century seemed rather gloomy.

Most of the new prophets saw the future from the viewpoint of their own interests. An author of well-known books on popular science, Büchner, foretold that the twentieth century would accomplish all that the nineteenth had left undone, and would bring about the synthesis of science and life.[237] Ellen Key, a Swedish woman who had distinguished herself as a fighter for the rights of women, announced that the twentieth century would become aware of the rights of and be concerned with the welfare of children; it would be "the century of the child."[238] A socialist, Hertzka, described the future world in a novel as a socialist paradise provided with all kinds of technical improvements, including airplane trips.[239] Haeckel prophesied the disappearance of the old religions based on superstitious beliefs, and the appearance of a new religion, the Monistic Church, based on science but performing esthetic rites in imitation of ancient religious ceremonies.[240] In the new temples there would be neither crosses nor statues of saints, but beautiful palm trees and aquariums with medusae, corals, and seastars. The altar would be replaced by a celestial globe showing the movements of the stars and planets.

The Marxists did not fail to make prognoses on the basis of their dialectic analysis. Friedrich Engels wrote that a Damocles sword of war was hanging over the heads of mankind and that on the first day of that war, all the treaties and alliances would be broken. It would be a war of races, with the Germans on one side, the Latin and Slavic peoples on the other. There would be fifteen to twenty million fighters, and the only reason why this war had not yet broken out was the total unpredictability of its outcome.[241]

H. G. Wells attempted rational predictions based on a careful analysis of the social, political, and scientific trends of the end of the nineteenth century.[242] He foresaw a tremendous development of science and technology, and of traffic; the death of the railways, which would be replaced by motorized traffic (air traffic he considered impractical); an enormous expansion of cities; the emergence of a new middle class composed mostly of technicians; the disappearance of the peasant class and of social parasites, that is of both the idle rich and the unproductive poor; the disappearance of "secondary languages," leaving only English and French; new types of wars that would be "a monstrous thrust and pressure of people against people"; and the disrespect of the rights of civilian populations. But in the midst of these turmoils, the emergence of a group of "kinetic men" would bring about a new philosophy and a new morality.

Perhaps the most widely read of all these predictions were the "twentieth-century novels" of the French writer Albert Robida, who illustrated them with fanciful drawings of people in 1895 fashions, in the midst of fantastic machines and gigantic buildings in "modern style."[243] He, too, foresaw a fabulous development of science and technology, and that all manifestations of life would be dependent on electricity. Weather would be controlled by the meteorologic institute; deserts would be irrigated and all unused land reclaimed and populated. Everywhere, the cities would spread; the population of Paris would rise to eleven million inhabitants. There would be a ceaseless traffic from one place to another through pneumatic tunnels and by airplane. It would be possible to have instantaneous communication with people all over the world through the "tele," that is, a telephone combined with a kind of mirror in which one could see the person with whom one was talking. People would no longer write to each other but would send records. Books would be replaced for the most part by "phonobooks." It would be an era of linguistic and cultural confusion in which the old classics would be read only in condensed form. Housewives would no longer cook; a supervised food institute would dispatch meals through pneumatic tubes. Science would make it possible to hear voices from the past, to revive extinct animal species, to produce artificially a living human being under artificial experimental conditions. Woman would everywhere be the equal of man. A new business feudality would emerge and it would be a life of terrible harshness for millions of workers. Life would be feverish, harassing, and under constant over stimulation. There would be new art forms and new sports such as submarine hunting. Privacy would disappear because science would provide unlimited means for spying. There would be terrifying wars, no longer for outmoded ideals, but for the conquest of commercial markets. Individual courage would now seem pointless in such wars where poisonous gases and microbes were used. There would, however, remain a few havens of peace. Brittany, for instance, would be transformed into a reservation in which the Bretons would live exactly in the style of the nineteenth century, whereas Italy would be transformed into a gigantic attraction park for tourists.

At least one psychiatrist tried his hand at that game. Concluding a book about the great collective psychoses from the sixteenth to the nineteenth centuries, Regnard tried to sketch what would be the mass psychosis of the twentieth century.[244] Taking into consideration the decline of family, aristocracy, and religion, the unleashing of uncontrolled social competition, the spreading of revolutionary ideologies, and the pernicious action of alcoholism, he foretold that the mass psychosis of the twentieth century would probably be "the folly of slaughter, the madness of blood and destruction."

In psychology and psychiatry, as elsewhere, few people seemed to doubt that the future would bring great progress and perhaps big surprises. In 1892, Janet contended that in the twentieth century "all patients, from the simple rheumatic to the general paretic, will have their psychology minutely investigated in all their details," an assumption that looked paradoxical at that time.[245] Bergson declared in 1901: "To explore the unconscious, to work in the subterranean of the mind with especially adequate methods, this will be the main task of psychology in the opening century. I do not doubt that fine discoveries will follow, as important perhaps as have been in the preceding centuries those of physical and natural sciences."[246]

Meanwhile, a new term had become fashionable, the word "psycho-therapy," used at first by some of Bernheim's disciples.[247] It was rapidly adopted by writers and by the public, and guesses were made about the psychotherapy of the future.[248] Van Eeden recognized that hypnosis and suggestion worked only with patients of the lower classes; "it is inadmissible that a therapy be fit only for hospital patients," he added.[249] One had to find a psychotherapy for educated people; it would be a non-authoritarian method, which would keep personal liberty intact, explain to the patient what is going on in his mind, and guarantee "that all the methods employed act only through his own psyche."

Thus many people in 1900 were expecting the rise of a new dynamic psychiatry, but few, apparently, realized that it had already been born.

Notes

1. According to André Billy, *L'Epoque 1900: 1885–1905* (Paris: Tallandier, 1951). Between the years 1895–1905, there were at least 150 political, journalistic, and literary duels in Paris, of which two resulted in death.

2. Muriel Jaeger, *Before Victoria* (London: Chatto and Windus, 1956).

3. Strathearn Gordon and T. G. B. Cocks, *A People's Conscience* (London: Constable & Co., 1952).

4. Felix Somary, *Erinnerungen aus meinem Leben* (Zurich: Manasse-Verlag, 1959).
5. Robert Payne, *Zero. The Story of Terrorism* (New York: The John Day Co., 1950).
6. A. Tokarski, *Voprosy Filosofiy i Psikhologiy* (Moscow, No. 40, 1897), p. 93.
7. Elie Metchnikoff, *Etudes sur la nature humaine. Essai de philosophie optimiste* (3rd ed.; Paris: Masson, 1905), pp. 343–373.
8. Ulrich von Wilamowitz-Moellendorf, *Erinnerungen, 1848–1914* (Leipzig: Koehler, 1928), p. 70.
9. Albert Fuchs, *Geistige Strömungen in Oesterreich* (Vienna: Globus-Verlag, 1949), p. viii.
10. Max Dessoir, *Buch der Erinnerungen* (Stuttgart: Enke, 1946), p. 217.
11. Otto Lubarsch, *Ein bewegtes Gelehrtenleben. Erinnerungen und Erlebnisse Kämpfe und Gedanken* (Berlin: Springer, 1931), p. 107.
12. Moritz Benedikt, *Aus meinem Leben. Erinnerungen und Erörterungen* (Vienna: Carl Konegen, 1906), p. 66.
13. Moritz Benedikt, *Aus meinem Leben, Erinnerungen und Erörterungen* (Vienna: Carl Konegen, 1906), pp. 76–77.
14. Jürgen Thorwald, *Die Entlassung* (Munich-Zurich: Droemersche Verlagsanstalt, 1960). Eng. trans., *The Dismissal* (New York: Pantheon Books, 1962).
15. Léon Daudet, "L'Invidia littéraire," in *Le Roman et les nouveaux écrivains* (Paris: Le Divan, 1925), pp. 106–111.
16. Dora Stockert-Meynert, *Theodor Meynert und seine Zeit* (Vienna and Leipzig: Österreichischer Bundesverlag, 1930), p. 52. Moritz Benedikt, *Aus meinem Leben*, p. 58.
17. Ulrich von Wilamowitz-Moellendorf, *Zukunftsphilologie!* 2 vols. (Berlin: Bornträger, 1872–1873).
18. Erwin Rohde, *Afterphilologie* (Leipzig: Fritzsch, 1872).
19. "Wenn ein Kopf und ein Buch zusammenstossen, und es klingt hohl, ist denn das allemal im Buche?"
20. René Vallery-Radot, *La Vie de Pasteur* (Paris: Hachette, 1900).
21. Moritz Benedikt, *Hypnotismus und Suggestion* (Leipzig and Vienna: Breitenstein, 1894).
22. Henri Piéron, "Grandeur et décadence des Rayons N. Histoire d'une croyance," *L'Année Psychologique*, XIII (1907), 143–169.
23. Percival Lowell, *Mars and Its Canals* (New York: Macmillan, 1906).
24. Auguste Forel, *Mémoires* (Neuchâtel: La Baconnière, 1941), p. 125. In the English translation, Auguste Forel, *Out of My Life and Work* (London: Allen & Unwin, 1937), p. 157, the relevant paragraph has been edited in such a way that the incident becomes incomprehensible. In a biographic notice on Forel, Hans Steck does not hesitate to write that Bechtereff had stolen Forel's discovery. *Schweizer Archiv für Neurologie und Psychiatrie*, LXV (1950) (I), 421–425.
25. Auguste Forel, *Mémoires* (Neuchâtel: La Baconnière, 1941), pp. 131–133.
26. Pasteur Vallery-Radot, *Pasteur inconnu* (Paris: Flammarion, 1954), pp. 101–102.
27. Werner Leibbrandt, "Der Kongress," *Medizinische Klinik*, LVI (1961), 901–904.
28. Moritz Benedikt, *Aus meinem Leben. Erinnerungen und Erörterungen* (Vienna: Carl Konegen, 1906).
29. See Cyrus H. Gordon, *Forgotten Scripts: How They Were Deciphered and Their Impact on Contemporary Culture* (New York: Basic Books, 1968).
30. Geneviève Bianquis, *Nietzsche devant ses contemporains. Textes recueillis et choisis* (Monaco: Editions du Rocher, n.d.), has shown that Nietzsche was by far not so solitary as legend would have had it and that he had, on the contrary, extremely devoted friends.
31. Erich F. Podach, *Friedrich Nietzsche's Werke des Zusammenbruchs* (Heidelberg: Wolfgang Rothe, 1961).
32. Hans M. Wolff, *Friedrich Nietzsche. Der Weg zum Nichts* (Bern: Francke, Sammlung Dalp, 1956).
33. Ludwig Klages, *Die psychologischen Errungenschaften Nietzsches* (Leipzig, A. Barthes, 1926).

34. Karl Jaspers, *Nietzsche. Einführung in das Verständnis seines Philosophierens* (Berlin: De Gruyter, 1936), pp. 105–146.

35. Alwin Mittasch, *Friedrich Nietzsche als Naturphilosoph* (Stuttgart: Alfred Kröner, 1952).

36. Thomas Mann, *Nietzsche's Philosophy in the Light of Contemporary Events* (Washington: Library of Congress, 1947).

37. Kurt Heinze, *Verbrechen und Strafe bei Friedrich Nietzsche. Versuch einer Deutung and Zusammenschau seiner Gedanken zum Strafrecht* (Berlin: DeGruyter, 1939).

38. Friedrich Nietzsche, *Morgenröthe*, in *Nietzsches Werke*, V, No. 523, Taschen-Ausgabe (Leipzig: Nauman, 1906), 338.

39. Friedrich Nietzsche, *Menschliches, Allzumenschliches*, I, No. 87, *op. cit.*, III, 91.

40. Friedrich Nietzsche, *Morgenröthe*, *op. cit.*, V, No. 119, 123.

41. Friedrich Nietzsche, *Menschliches, Allzumenschliches*, I, No. 12, *op. cit.*, III, 27.

42. Friedrich Nietzsche, *Morgenröthe*, No. 312, *op. cit.*, VI, 253–254.

43. Walter Kaufmann, *Nietzsche—Philosopher—Psychologist—Antichrist* (Princeton: University Press, 1950).

44. Friedrich Nietzsche, *Menschliches Allzumenschliches*, I, No. 107, *op. cit.*, III, 110.

45. Friedrich Nietzsche, *Jenseits von Gut und Böse*, IV, No. 75, *op. cit.*, VIII, 95

46. Friedrich Nietzsche, *Zur Genealogie der Moral*, II, No. 1, *op. cit.*, VIII, 343.

47. Friedrich Nietzsche, *Jenseits von Gut and Böse*, IV, No. 68, *op. cit.*, VIII, 94.

48. This is explained mainly in Nietzsche's *Genealogy of Morals*, *op. cit.*

49. Max Scheler, "Ueber Ressentiment und moralisches Werturteil," *Zeitschrift für Pathopsychologie*, I (1911–1912), pp. 269–368.

50. Gregorio Marañon, "Theorie des Ressentiments," *Merkur*, VI, 241–249. *Tiberius. A Study in Resentment* (London: Hollis & Carter, 1956).

51. Paul Rée, *Der Ursprung der Moralischen Empfindungen* (Chemnitz: Ernst Schmeitzner, 1875).

52. Friedrich Nietzsche, *Zur Genealogie der Moral*, I, No. 11, *op. cit.*, VIII, 322.

53. Friedrich Nietzsche, *Der Wanderer und sein Schatten*, No. 52, *op. cit.*, IV, 230–231.

54. Friedrich Nietzsche, *Der Antichrist*, No. 55, *op. cit.*, X, 438.

55. Friedrich Nietzsche, *Menschliches, Allzumenschliches*, I, No. 380, *op. cit.*, III, 301.

56. Friedrich Nietzsche, *Zur Genealogie der Moral*, II, No. 16, *op. cit.*, VIII, 380–381.

57. Friedrich Nietzsche, *Die fröhliche Wissenschaft*, No. 344, *op. cit.*, VI, 301.

58. Ernst Benz, ed., *Der Uebermensch* (Zurich: Rhein-Verlag, 1961). Julius Wolff, "Zur Genealogie des Nietzsche'schen Uebermenschen," *Veröffentlichungen der Deutschen Akademischen Vereinigung zu Buenos Aires*, Vol. I, No. 2.

59. Fritz Ernst, *Die romantische Ironie* (Zurich: Schulthess, 1915), p. 125, has shown that this celebrated phrase was already contained in Friedrich Schlegel's *Athenäum*.

60. Friedrich Nietzsche, *Die fröhlische Wissenschaft*, No. 49, *op. cit.*, VI, 111–112.

61. This is the interpretation suggested by Lou Andreas-Salomé, *Friedrich Nietzsche in seinen Werken* (Vienna: Carl Konegen, 1894), p. 205.

63. W. D. Williams, *Nietzsche and the French* (Oxford: Basil Blackwell, 1952), p. 100.

64. Friedrich Nietzsche, *Menschliches, Allzumenschliches*, I, No. 513, *op. cit.*, III, 369.

65. Lou Andreas-Salomé, *Friedrich Nietzsche in seinen Werken* (Vienna: Carl Konegen, 1894).

66. Sigmund Freud, *Selbstdarstellung* (1925), *Gesammelte Werke*, XI, 119–182. Standard Edition, XX, 60.

67. Friedrich Nietzsche, *Zarathustra*, I, "Von den Verächtern des Leibes," *op. cit.*, VII, 46–48.

68. Friedrich Nietzsche, "Alles Klagen ist Anklagen," in *Der Wanderer und sein Schatten,* II, No. 78, *op. cit.,* IV, 45.

69. Sigmund Freud, "Ihre Klagen sind Anklagen," in *Trauer und Melancholia, Internationale Zeitschrift für ärztliche Psychotherapie* (1916–1917), IV, 288–301.

70. A few remarks were given by Charles Baudouin, "Nietzsche as a Forerunner of Psychoanalysis," in *Contemporary Studies* (London: Allen and Unwin, 1924), pp. 40–43.

71. F. G. Crookshank, *Individual Psychology and Nietzsche.* Individual Psychology Pamphlets, No. 10 (London: C. W. Daniel Co., 1933).

72. A. J. Leahy, "Nietzsche interprété par Jung," *Etudes nietzschéennes,* I, No. 1, (Aix-en-Provence: Societé Française d'Etudes Nietzschéennes, 1948), 36–43.

73. Ika Thomese, *Romantik und Neu-Romantik* (Den Haag: Martinus Nijhoff, 1923). Eudo C. Mason, *Rilke, Europe and the English-speaking World* (Cambridge, England: Cambridge University Press, 1961), pp. 67–80.

74. Heinz Mitlacher, "Die Entwicklung des Narziss-Begriffs," *Romanisch-germanische Monatsschrift,* XXI (1933), 373–383.

75. Jules Romains, *Souvenirs et confidences d'un écrivain* (Paris: Fayard, 1958), pp. 15–16.

76. A. E. Carter, *The Idea of Decadence in French Literature, 1830–1900* (Toronto: University of Toronto Press, 1958), pp. 144–151.

77. Max Nordau, *Entartung* (Berlin: C. Dunker, 1892).

78. Count Arthur de Gobineau, *Essai sur l'inégalité des races humaines,* 4 vols. (Paris: Firmin-Didot, 1853–1855).

79. The best known expression of that feeling is to be found in the book of the French writer Edmond Demolins, *A quoi tient la supériorité des Anglo-Saxons?* (Paris: Firmin-Didot, 1897).

80. Houston Stewart Chamberlain, *Die Grundlagen des neunzehnten Jahrhunderts* (Munich: F. Bruckmann, 1899).

81. Keith G. Millward, *L'Oeuvre de Pierre Loti et l'esprit "fin de siècle"* (Paris: Nizet, 1955), pp. 11–36.

82. Malwida von Meysenbug, *Memoiren einer Idealistin* (Berlin: Auerbach, n.d.), III, 223–234.

83. This antithesis has been well described by A. E. Carter, *The Idea of Decadence in French Literature, op. cit.*

84. Edouard Dujardin, *Les Lauriers sont coupés* (Paris: Revue Indépendante, 1888).

85. Arthur Schnitzler, *Leutnant Gustl* (Berlin: S. Fischer, 1901).

86. "Gi-gît 1880—l'année pornographique." Jules Claretie, *La Vie à Paris* (1880) (Paris: Victor Havard, 1881), p. 507.

87. Mario Praz, *The Romantic Agony.* Translated from the Italian (London: Oxford University Press, 1933).

88. Paul Morand, *1900* (Paris: Les Editions de France, 1931).

89. André Billy, *L'Epoque 1900—1885–1900* (Paris: Tallandier, 1953).

90. His first book was a plea against the death penalty. Emil Kraepelin, *Die Abschaffung des Strafmasses* (Stuttgart: F. Enke, 1880).

91. August Forel, *Rückblick auf mein Leben* (Zurich: Europa-Verlag, 1935). The French edition is often more complete: *Mémoires* (Neuchâtel: La Baconnière, 1941).

92. Annemarie Wettley, *August Forel, ein Arztleben im Zwiespalt seiner Zeit* (Salzburg: O. Müller, 1953).

93. August Forel, *Rückblick auf mein Leben* (Zurich: Europa-Verlag, 1935), pp. 126–127.

94. No biography of Eugen Bleuler has been published as yet. The following have been consulted: Manfred Bleuler, "Eugen Bleuler, die Begründung der Schizophrenie-Lehre," in *Gestalter unserer Zeit,* IV (Erforscher des Lebens, Oldenburg: Gerhard Stalling, n.d.), 110–117. Jacob Wyrsch, "Eugen Bleuler und sein Werk," *Schweizerische Rundschau,* XXXIX (1939–1940), 625–627. Manfred Bleuler, "Geschichte des Burghölzli und der psychiatrischen Universitäsklinik," in *Zürcher Spitalgeschichte* (Regierungsrat des Kantons Zürich, 1951), pp. 317–425.

95. In 1852, Morel had coined the term *démence précoce* to label patients who fell into severe mental impairment soon after the outbreak of the illness. (B. A. Morel, *Etudes cliniques,* I [1852], 37–38). It was believed that all mental diseases would sooner or later terminate in severe mental impairment (called *démence,* although it lacked the present-day connotation of intellectual deterioration). Thus, the term *démence précoce* actually meant "rapid mental impairment." Later, it came to be misunderstood as meaning "dementia at an early age."

96. Eugen Bleuler, *Dementia Praecox, oder Gruppe der Schizophrenien,* in Aschaffenburg, *Handbuch der Psychiatrie,* spezieller Teil, 4. Abt., I (Vienna: F. Deuticke, 1911).

97. Friedrich Schlegel, "Philosophie des Lebens" (1827), in *Schriften und Fragmente,* Ernst Behler, ed. (Stuttgart: Kröner, 1956), pp. 245–249.

98. Eugène Minkowski, *La Schizophrénie* (Paris: Payot, 1927), pp. 249–265.

99. Adolf Meyer's paper, "Fundamental Concepts in Dementia Praecox," *British Medical Journal,* II (1906), 757–760, and *Journal of Nervous and Mental Disease,* XXXIV (1907), 331–336, was a milestone in the history of psychiatry.

100. Stewart Paton, "The Care of the Insane and the Study of Psychiatry in Germany," *Journal of Nervous and Mental Disease,* XXXIII (1906), 225–233.

101. Hermann Simon, *Krankenbehandlung in der Irrenanstalt* (Berlin and Leipzig: De Gruyter, 1929).

102. A. Grohmann, *Technisches und Psychologisches in der Beschäftigung von Nervenkranken* (Stuttgart: Enke, 1899).

103. André Lalande, ed., *Vocabulaire technique et critique de la philosophie* (fifth ed.; Paris: Presses Universitaires de France, 1947), p. 246.

104. A. Winkelmann, *Einleitung in die Dynamische Physiologie* (Göttingen: Dieterich, 1802).

105. Maurice Martin Antonin Macario, "Mémoire sur les paralysies dynamiques ou nerveuses," *Gazette médicale de Paris* (1857–1858).

106. Charles-Edouard Brown-Sequard, "Inhibitions et dynamogénie," *Académie des Sciences* (1885).

107. Sigmund Exner, *Entwurf zu einer physiologischen Erklärung der psychischen Erscheinungen* (Leipzig and Vienna: Deuticke, n.d.), II, 69–82.

108. Georges De Morsier, "Le mécanisme des hallucinations," *Annales Médico-Psychologiques,* LXXXVIII (1930), (II), 365–389. "Les Hallucinations," *Revue d'Oto-Neuro-Ophthalmologie,* XVI (1938), 244–248.

109. *"Toute idée suggérée et acceptée tend à se faire acte."*

110. Henri Aimé, *Etude clinique du dynamisme psychique* (Paris: Doin, 1897).

111. Jacques-Joseph Moreau (de Tours), *Du Hachisch et de l'aliénation mentale* (Paris: Fortin, 1845).

112. Pierre Janet, *Névroses et idées fixes* (Paris: Alcan, 1898), I, 469.

113. Henri Ey et Hubert Mignot, "La psychopathologie de J. Moreau (de Tours)," *Annales Médico-Psychologiques* (1947), (II), 225–241.

114. John Hughlings Jackson, "The Factors of Insanity," *Medical Press and Circular* (1874). Reprinted in *Selected Writings* (London: Hodder & Stoughton, 1932), I, 411–421. See also A. Stengel, "The Origin and the Status of Dynamic Psychiatry." *British Journal of Medical Psychology.* XXVII, Pt. 41 (1954), 193–200.

115. Hellmut Walther Brann, *Nietzsche und die Frauen* (Leipzig: Felix Meiner, 1931), pp. 139–140, 207–208. This incident has been transposed by Thomas Mann in his novel *Doktor Faustus* (Stockholm: Bermann-Fischer, 1947), Chaps. 16 and 17.

116. Moebius, *Über den physiologischen Schwachsinn des Weibes* (Halle: C. Marhold, 1901).

117. Lester Ward; quoted by Samuel Chugerman, *Lester F. Ward, The American Aristotle* (Durham: Duke University Press, 1939), pp. 378–395. Ashley Montague, *The Natural Superiority of Women* (London: Macmillan, 1953).

118. Jules Michelet, *La Femme,* in *Oeuvres Complètes* (Paris: Flammarion, 1860), Vol. XXXIV, p. 605.

119. Carl Spitteler, *Imago* (Jena: E. Diederichs, 1906).

120. Novalis, *Die Lehrlinge zu Sais* (1802), in *Schriften*, Minor, ed. (Jena: Diederichs, 1907), Vol. IV.

121. Wilhelm Jensen, *Gradiva, Ein pompejanisches Phantasiestück* (Dresden and Leipzig: Carl Reissner, 1903).

122. Karl Neisser, *Die Entstehung der Liebe* (Vienna: Carl Konegen, 1897).

123. Laura Marholm, *Zur Psychologie der Frau*, 2 vols. (Berlin: C. Duncker, 1897, 1903).

124. Otto Weininger, *Geschlecht und Charakter* (Vienna: Wilhelm Braunmüller, 1903).

125. Hugues Rebell, *Les Inspiratrices* (Paris: Dujarric, 1902). Edouard Schuré, *Femmes inspiratrices et poètes annonciateurs* (Paris: Perrin, 1908).

126. Emil Reicke, *Malwida von Meysenbug* (Berlin and Leipzig: Schuster & Loeffler, 1911).

127. Malwida von Meysenbug, *Memoiren einer Idealistin*, 3 vols. (Berlin: Auerbach, n.d.). *Das Lebensabend einer Idealistin* (Berlin and Leipzig: Schuster & Loeffler, n.d.).

128. Ria Claassen, "Das Frauenphantom des Mannes," *Zürcher Diskussionen, Flugblätter aus dem Gesamtgebiet des modernen Lebens*, Vol. I, No. 4 (1897–1898).

129. Auguste Villiers de l'Isle-Adam, *L'Eve future* (1886), in *Oeuvres Complètes* (Paris: Mercure de France, 1922), Vol. I.

130. Jules Michelet, *La Femme* (1860), in *Oeuvres Complètes* (Paris: Flammarion, 1895), Vol. XXXIV, pp. 13–17.

131. Brown-Séquard, "Des Effets produits chez l'homme par des injections souscutanées d'un liquide retiré des testicules frais de cobayes et de chiens," *Comptes-Rendus hebdomadaires des séances et Mémoires de la Société de Biologie*. 9th series, I (1889), 415–419.

132. P. J. C. Debreyne, *Essais sur la théologie morale considérée dans ses rapports avec la physiologie et la médecine* (Paris: Poussielgue-Rusand, 1844). *Moechialogie. Traité sur les péchés contre le sixième et le neuvième commandements du Décalogue* (2nd ed.; Paris: Poussielgue-Rusand, 1846).

133. Bishop Dupanloup, *De l'éducation*, 3 vols. (Paris: Douniol, 1866). (See I, 86, III, 444–460).

134. Jules Michelet, *Nos Fils* (1869), in *Oeuvres Complètes* (Paris: Flammarion, 1895), XXXI, 283–588.

135. The frequency of masturbation among infants, and its substitute, thumbsucking, were also known to contemporary sexologists. See Hermann Rohleder, *Vorlesungen über Sexualtrieb und Sexualleben des Menschen* (Berlin: Fischer, 1941). Albert Fuchs, "Zwei Fälle von sexueller Paradoxien, "*Jahrbuch für Psychiatrie und Neurologie,* XXIII (1903), 206–213.

136. The history of sexual pathology has been treated in the following: Maurice Heine, *Confessions et observations psychosexuelles tirées de la littérature médicale* (Paris: Crès, 1936). Annemarie Wettley, *Von der "Psychopathia Sexualis" zur Sexualwissenschaft* (Stuttgart: Enke, 1959).

137. Thomas Sanchez, *De Sancto Matrimonii Sacramento*, 3 vols. (Antwerp, 1607).

138. Alphonse de Liguori, in *Oeuvres* (Paris: Vivès, 1877), IX, 217–223.

139. Gilbert Lely, *Vie du marquis de Sade*, 2 vols. (Paris: Gallimard, 1957).

140. Leopold Ritter von Sacher-Masoch, *Venus in Pelz* (Dresden: Dohrn, 1901). Eng. trans., *Venus in Furs* (Paris: C. Carrington, 1902).

141. Henricus Kaan, *Psychopathia sexualis* (Lipsiae: Voss, 1844).

142. Dr. Santlus, *Zur Psychologie der menschlichen Triebe* (Neuwied and Leipzig: Heuser, 1864).

143. Pierre Moreau (de Tours), *Des aberrations du sens génésique* (Paris: Asselin, 1880).

144. C. Westphal, "Die Conträre Sexualempfindung," *Archiv für Psychiatrie,* II (1870), 73–100.

145. Richard von Krafft-Ebing, "Beiträge zur Kenntnis des Masochismus," *Arbeiten aus dem Gesammtgebiet der Psychiatrie und Neuropathologie* (Leipzig: Barth, 1897–1899), IV, 127–131.

146. Richard von Krafft-Ebing, Über gewisse Anomalien des Geschlechtstriebes," *Archiv für Psychiatrie und Nervenkrankheiten,* VII (1876–1877), 291–312.

147. Ernest-Charles Lasegue, "Les exhibitionnistes," *Union médicale* (May 1877.) Quoted by R. Krafft-Ebing, *Psychopathia Sexualis* (Stuttgart: Enke, 1893), p. 380.

148. Alfred Binet, "Le fétichisme dans l'amour," *Revue Philosophique,* XII (1887) (II), 143–167.

149. Ernest Chambard, *Du Somnambulisme en général,* Thèse Med. (Paris: 1881), No. 78 (Paris: Parent, 1881), pp. 55, 65.

150. Wilhelm Bölsche, *Das Liebesleben in der Natur,* 3 vols. (Jena: Diederichs, 1898–1902).

151. Moritz Benedikt, *Aus meinem Leben. Erinnerungen und Erörterungen* (Vienna: Carl Konegen, 1906), p. 163.

152. Charles Féré, "Contributions à l'histoire du choc moral chez les enfants," *Bulletin de la Societé de Médecine mentale de Belgique,* LXXIV (1894), pp. 333–340.

153. Albert Moll, "Über eine wenig beachtete Gefahr der Prügelstrafe bei Kindern," *Zeitschrift für Psychologie und Pathologie,* III (1901), 215–219.

154. Theodor Meynert, *Klinische Vorlesungen über Psychiatrie auf wissenschaftlichen Grundlagen* (Vienna: Braunmüller, 1889–1890), p. 185.

155. J. Dallemagne, *Dégénérés et déséquilibrés* (Brussels: H. Lamertin, 1894), pp. 525–527.

156. Théodule Ribot, *La Psychologie des sentiments* (Paris: Alcan, 1896), pp. 253–255, p. 527.

157. Charcot and Magnan, "Inversion du sens génital," *Archives de Neurologie,* III (1882), 53–60; IV, 296–322.

158. Valentin Magnan, "Inversion sexuelle et pathologie mentale," *Bulletin de l'Académie de Médicine,* LXX (1913), 226–229.

159. A. F. A. King, "Hysteria," *American Journal of Obstetrics,* XXIV (1891), 513–532.

160. Moritz Benedikt, "Beobachtung über Hysterie." Reprint from *Zeitschrift für practische Heilkunde* (1864).

161. Moritz Benedikt, *Elektrotherapie* (Vienna: Tendler & Co., 1868), pp. 413–445.

162. Moritz Benedikt, "Second Life. Das Seelenbinnenleben des gesunden und kranken Menschen," *Wiener Klinik,* XX (1894), 127–138.

163. Alexander Peyer, *Der unvollständige Beischlaf (Congressus Interruptus), (Onanismus Conjugalis) und seine Folgen beim männlichen Geschlecht* (Stuttgart: Enke, 1890).

164. A. Peyer, *Asthma und Geschlechtskrankheiten (Asthma sexuale),* Berline Klinik, Sammlung klinischer Vorträge, No. 9 (Berlin: Fischer, 1889).

165. Hans Gross, *Criminalpsychologie* (Graz: Langsehner and Lubensky, 1898).

166. Richard von Krafft-Ebing, "Uber Neurosen und Psychosen durch sexuelle Abstinenz," *Jahrbuch für Psychiatrie,* VIII (1889), 1–6.

167. J. F. Gall, *Sur les fonctions du cerveau et sur celles de chacune de ses parties* (Paris: Baillière, 1925), III.

168. Wilhelm Ostwald, *Grosse Männer* (Leipzig: Akademische Verlags gesellschaft, 1909).

169. Elie Metchnikov, *Souvenirs. Recueil d'articles autobiographiques* (Moscow: editions en langue étrangère, 1959), p. 261.

170. Alfred Espinas, *Des Sociétés animales* (Paris: Baillière, 1877).

171. Friedrich Nietzsche, *Götzendämmerung,* X, 22.

172. H. Steinthal, *Einleitung in die Psychologie und Sprachwissenschaft,* 2, Aufl. I (Berlin: Dümmler, 1881), 351–353.

173. P. J. Moebius, *Ueber Schopenhauer* (Leipzig: J. A. Barth, 1899), pp. 204–205.

174. George Santayana, *The Sense of Beauty* (New York: C. Scribner's Sons, 1896), pp. 57–60.

175. Gustav Naumann, *Geschlecht und Kunst* (Leipzig: Haessel, 1899).

176. Yrjö Hirn, *Origins of Art* (London: Macmillan Co., 1900).

177. Rémy de Gourmont, "La Dissociation des idées," reprinted in *La Culture des*

idées (Paris: Mercure de France, 1900), pp. 98–100.

178. Max Dessoir, "Zur Psychologie der Vita Sexualis," *Allgemeine Zeitschrift für Psychiatrie*, L (1894), 941–975.

179. Albert Moll, *Untersuchungen über die Libido Sexualis* (Berlin: Kornfeld, 1898).

180. Theodor Meynert, *Klinische Vorlesungen über Psychiatrie aus wissenschaftlichen Grundlagen* (Vienna: Braunmüller, 1889–1890), p. 195.

181. Moritz Benedikt, *Elektrotherapie* (Vienna: Tendler, 1868). The word "libido" occurs nine times between pages 448 and 454.

182. Richard von Krafft-Ebing, "Ueber Neurosen und Psychosen durch sexuelle Abstinenz," *Jahrbuch für Psychiatrie*, Vol. VIII (1889). The word "libido" occurs three times between pages 1 and 6.

183. Otto Effertz, *Ueber Neurasthenie* (New York, 1894).

184. Albert Eulenburg, *Sexuale Neuropathie, genitale Neurosen und Neuropsychosen der Männer und Frauen* (Leipzig: Vogel, 1895).

185. Lucien Arreat, "Sexualité et altruisme," *Revue philosophique*, XXII (1886) (II), 620–632.

186. Joseph Ennemoser, "Das Wesen des Traumes ist ein potentielles Geniusleben," *Der Magnetismus in Verhältnisse zur Natur und Religion* (Stuttgart and Tübingen: Cotta, 1842), pp. 335–336.

187. Ignaz Troxler, *Blicke in das Wesen des Menschen* (Aarau: Sauerländer, 1812).

188. Karl Albert Scherner, *Das Leben des Traums* (Berlin: Heinrich Schindler, 1861).

189. "Cardiac dreams" with symbols similar to those of Scherner can be found for instance in F. J. Soesman, "Rêves organo-génésiques," *Annales médico-psychologiques*, LXXXVI (1928) (II), 64–67. Jean Piaget, *La Formation du symbole chez l'enfant* (Neuchâtel: Delachaux et Niestlé, 1959), p. 213. Marcel Déat, "L'Interprétation du rythme du coeur dans certains rêves," *Journal de Psychologie*, XVIII (1921), 555–557.

190. R. A. Schwaller de Lubicz, *Le Temple de l'homme. Apet du Sud à Louqsor*, 3 vols. Paris: Caractères, 1958).

191. Robert Vischer, *Über das optische Formgefühl* (Leipzig: Credner, 1873).

192. Alfred Maury, *Le Sommeil et les rêves* (Paris: Didier, 1861. Edition revue et augmentée, 1878).

193. John Mourly Vold, "Einige Experimente über Gesichtsbilder in Traume." *Dritter Internationaler Congress für Psychologie in München 1896* (Munich: J. F. Lehmann, 1897). *Uber den Traum. Experimental-psychologische Untersuchungen*, O. Klemm ed. (Leipzig: Barth), 2 vols., 1910–1912, p. 338.

194. Sante De Sanctis, *Die Träume, Medizin-psychologische Untersuchung*, German trans. from the Italian (Halle: Marhold, 1901).

195. Marie-Jean-Léon Hervey de Saint-Denis, *Les Rêves et les moyens de les diriger* (Paris: Amyot, 1867).

196. Frederik van Eeden, *De Nachtbruid* (1909), Eng. trans.; *The Bride of Dreams* (New York and London: Mitchell Kennerley, 1913).

197. Frederik van Eeden, "A Study of Dreams," *Proceedings of the Society for Psychical Research*, LXVII, No. 26 (1913), 413–461.

198. George Du Maurier, *Peter Ibbetson* (New York: Harper, 1891).

199. Robert Louis Stevenson, *A Chapter on Dreams*, in *Across the Plains* (London: Chatto and Windus, 1898), Chap. 8.

200. George Dumas, "Comment on gouverne les rêves," *Revue de Paris*, XVI (1909), 344–367.

201. Ludwig Binswanger, *Wandlungen in der Auffassung und Deutung des Traumes, von den Griechen bis zur Gegenwart* (Berlin: Springer-Verlag, 1928).

202. L. Strümpell, *Die Natur und Entstehung der Träume* (Leipzig: Von Veit & Co., 1874).

203. Johannes Volkelt, *Die Traum-Phantasie* (Stuttgart: Meyer & Zeller, 1875).

204. Friedrich Theodor Vischer, *Der Traum* (1875). Reprinted in *Altes und Neues* (Stuttgart: Adolf Bonz, 1882), I, 187–232.

205. F. W. Hildebrandt, *Der Traum und seine Verwertung für's Leben. Eine psycho-*

logische Studie (Leipzig: Reinboth, n.d.).

206. Lynkeus (pseudonym of Joseph Popper), *Phantasien eines Realisten* (Dresden: Reissner, 1899), II, 149–163.

207. C. Binz, *Über den Traum. Nach einem 1876 gehaltenen öffentlichen Vortrag* (Bonn: Adolph Marcus, 1878).

208. W. Robert, *Der Traum als Naturnothwendigkeit erklärt*, 2 Aufl. (Hamburg: Hermann Seippel, 1886), pp. 13–17.

209. Yves Delage, "Essai sur la théorie du rêve," *Revue Scientifique*, XLVIII, No. 2 (1891), 40–48. This paper was later expanded in book form, *Le Rêve, étude psychologique, philosophique et littéraire* (Paris: Presses Universitaires de France, 1919).

210. The history of the theories of the unconscious has been treated many times. See among others: James Miller, *Unconsciousness* (New York: John Wiley, 1942). Donald Brinkmann, *Probleme des Unbewussten* (Zurich: Rascher, 1943). Edward L. Margetts, "The Concept of the Unconscious in the History of Medical Psychology," *Psychiatric Quarterly*, XXVII (1953), 115. H. Ellenberger, "The Unconscious before Freud," *Bulletin of the Menninger Clinic*, XXI (1957), 3–15. Lancelot Law Whyte, *The Unconscious before Freud* (New York: Basic Books, 1960).

211. G. W. von Leibniz, *Nouveaux essais sur l'entendement humain* (1704), *Monadologie* (1714).

212. J. F. Herbart, *Psychologie als Wissenschaft, neugegründet auf Erfahrung, Metaphysik und Mathematik* (1824), in *Sämtliche Werek* (Leipzig: Voss, 1850), Vols. V and VI.

213. G. T. Fechner, *Elemente der Psychophysik*, 2 vols. (Leipzig: Breitkopf & Härtel, 1860).

214. Hermann von Helmholtz, *Handbuch der physiologischen Optik*, III (1859), 3 Aufl. (Hamburg: L. Voss, 1910), 3–7.

215. Michel-Eugène Chevreul, "Lettre à M. Ampère," *Revue des Deux Mondes*, 2nd series (1833) (II), 258–266.

216. Michel-Eugène Chevreul, *De la Baguette divinatoire, du pendule explorateur, des tables tournantes, au point de vue de l'histoire, de la critique et de la méthode expérimentale* (Paris: Mallet-Bachelier, 1854).

217. Francis Galton, "Antechamber of Consciousness," reprinted in *Inquiries into Human Faculty* (London: Dent, 1907), pp. 146–149.

218. Narziss Ach, *Über die Willenstätigkeit und das Denken* (Göttingen: Vandenhoek und Ruprecht, 1905).

219. Gardner Murphy, "The Life and Work of Frederick W. H. Myers," *Tomorrow*, II (Winter 1954), 33–39.

220. Frederick W. H. Myers, *Human Personality and Its Survival of Bodily Death*, 2 vols. (London: Longmans, Green & Co., 1903).

221. Charles Richet, "Du Somnambulisme provoqué," *Journal de l'Anatomie et de la Physiologie normales et pathologiques de l'homme et des animaux*, II (1875), 348–377.

222. Jules Héricourt, "L'Activité inconsciente de l'esprit," *Revue scientifique*, 3rd series, XXVI (1889), II, 257–268.

223. Edouard Claparède, "Théodore Flournoy. Sa vie et son oeuvre," *Archives de Psychologie*, XVIII (1923), 1–125.

224. Théodore Flournoy, *Des Indes à la Planète Mars. Etude sur un cas de somnambulisme avec glossolalie* (Paris and Geneva: Atar, 1900). *From India to the Planet Mars. A study of a case of somnambulism with glossolalia* (New York and London: Harper, 1900).

225. Edouard Claparède, "Théodore Flournoy. Sa vie et son oeuvre," *Archives de Psychologie*, XVIII (1923), 1–125.

226. Victor Henry, *Le Langage martien. Etude analytique de la genèse d'une langue dans un cas de glossolalie somnambulique* (Paris: Maisonneuve, 1901).

227. H. Cuendet, *Les Tableaux d'Hélène Smith peints à l'état de sommeil* (Geneva: Atar, 1908).

228. A detailed follow-up of the medium has been given by Wladimir Deonna, *De la planète Mars en Terre Sainte* (Paris: De Boccard, 1932).

229. Theodore Flournoy, "Genèse de quelques prétendus messages spirites," *Annales des Sciences psychiques,* IX (1899), 199–216.

230. *Congrès International de Psychologie* (Munich: 1896), pp. 417–420.

231. Henry Freeborn, "Temporary Reminiscence of a Long-Forgotten Language During the Delirium of Broncho-Pneumonia," *Lancet,* LXXX (1902) (I), 1685–1686.

232. Sergiei Korsakoff, "Etude médico-psychologique sur une forme de maladies de la mémoire," *Revue Philosophique,* XXVIII (1889) (II), 501–530.

233. Gardner Murphy, *Historical Introduction to Modern Psychology* (New York: Harcourt Brace, 1949), p. 204.

234. Francis Galton, "Antechamber of Consciousness," reprinted in *Inquiries into Human Faculty* (London: Dent, 1907), pp. 146–149.

235. Gardner Murphy and Robert O. Ballou, *William James on Psychical Research* (London: Chatto & Windus, 1961), p. 221.

236. Alfred Russel Wallace, *The Wonderful Century. Its Successes and Failures* (London: Sonnenschein, 1898).

237. Ludwig Büchner, *Am Sterbelager des Jahrhunderts. Blicke eines freien Denkers aus der Zeit in die Zeit* (Giessen: Emil Roth, 1898).

238. Ellen Key, *The Century of the Child* (1899). Eng. trans. revised by the author (London and New York: G. P. Putnam's Sons, 1909).

239. Theodor Hertzka, *Entrückt in die Zukunft. Sozialpolitischer Roman* (Berlin: F. Dümmler, 1895).

240. Ernst Haeckel, *Die Welträthsel* (Bonn: Emil Strauss, 1899).

241. Friedrich Engels, "Einleitung zu 'Der Bürgerkrieg in Frankreich' von Karl Marx Ausgabe 1891," in *Karl Marx—Friedrich Engels Werke* (Berlin: Dietz, 1962), XVII, 616.

242. H. G. Wells, *Anticipations of the Reaction of Mechanical and Scientific Progress upon Life and Thought* (New York and London: Harper Bros., 1902).

243. Albert Robida, *Voyage de fiançailles au XXe siècle* (Paris: Conquet, 1892). *Le Vingtième Siècle. La vie électrique* (Paris: Librairie Illustrée, 1895). *Le Vingtième Siècle. Texte et dessins* (Paris: Montgrédien, n.d.).

244. Paul Regnard, *Les Maladies épidémiques de l'esprit* (Paris: Plon, 1887), pp. 423–429.

245. Pierre Janet, "L'Anesthesie hystérique," *Archives de Neurologie,* XXIII (1892), 323–352.

246. Henri Bergson, "Le Rêve," *Bulletin de l'Institut psychologique international,* I (1900–1901), 97–122.

247. Frederick Van Eeden, in his autobiography *Happy Humanity* (New York: Doubleday, Page & Co., 1912), claims to have introduced the term; adding, however, that Hack Tuke already used the word "psycho-therapeutics."

248. Maurice Barrès, *Trois stations de psychothérapie* (Paris: Perrin, 1891).

249. Frederick van Eeden, "The Theory of Psycho-Therapeutics," *The Medical Magazine,* I (1895), 230–257.

FRANZ ANTON MESMER (1734–1815), the initiator of animal magnetism, was the first of the great pioneers of dynamic psychiatry. *(From the picture collection of the Institute for History of Medicine, Vienna.)*

AMAND-MARIE-JACQUES DE
CHASTENET, Marquis de Puysé-
gur (1751–1825), the true
founder of animal magnetism, is
shown here in his uniform of
General of the French Artillery.
(*Bibliothèque Nationale, Paris,
Cabinet des Estampes.*)

This print shows the "magnetized" elm of Buzancy, during the performance of
cures. Leaning on Puységur, Victor Race is falling into magnetic sleep. (*From
A.M.S. de Puységur: Mémoires pour servir à l'histoire et à l'établissement du
Magnétisme Animal, 3rd ed. [1820].*)

JUSTINUS KERNER (1786–1862), romantic physician and poet; Kerner's house in Weinsberg, Germany, was a meetingplace for philosophers, writers, and other influential people. *(Engraving by Anton Duttenhofer.)*

The "magnetic" condition of Friederike Hauffe is described in *The Seeress of Prevorst*, a monograph which brought fame both to the "seeress" and to Kerner. *(From the Bibliothèque Nationale, Paris, collection Laruelle.)*

GUSTAV THEODOR FECHNER (1801–1887) was a physicist, philosopher of nature, and founder of experimental psychology. Fechner was greatly admired by Freud, who drew from him several of the basic concepts of his metapsychology. *(Photograph by Georg Brokesch, Leipzig.)*

JOHANN JAKOB BACHOFEN (1815–1887), the founder of the theory of matriarchy, exerted an intensive though indirect influence on the dynamic psychiatry of Freud, Adler, and Jung. (*From the picture collection of the Library of the University of Basel.*)

JEAN-MARTIN CHARCOT (1825–1893); Before reaching a belated fame, Charcot, a rather shy and aloof man, struggled through many years of hard and obscure toil. (*Courtesy Professor Paul Castaigne, Paris.*)

Charcot's autograph; Charcot had been called to Russia as a consultant for a highly placed personage. He wrote vivid accounts of his journey to his family, illustrating his letters with water color drawings. (*From the Bibliothèque Nationale, Paris, Cabinet des Estampes.*) (The water colors do not appear on this reproduction.)

"A Clinical Lecture at the Salpêtrière." A. Brouillet's painting shows Charcot at the height of his fame, demonstrating a case of "grande hystérie" to an elite audience of physicians and writers; behind him is his favorite disciple, Babinski. The painter has involuntarily shown Charcot's fatal error: his verbal explanations and the picture on the wall suggest to the patient the crisis which she is beginning to enact; two nurses are ready to sustain her when she falls on the stretcher, where she will display her full-fledged crisis. *(From* Le Salon de 1887, *Paris, facing page 62.)*

JOSEF BREUER (1842–1925) was an eminent Viennese physician who also distinguished himself in physiological research; the half-legendary story of Breuer's patient "Anna O" became one of the starting-points of psychoanalysis. *(From the picture collection of the Institute for History of Medicine in Vienna.)*

BERTHA PAPPENHEIM (1860–1936) was Breuer's mysterious patient, "Anna O." The photograph was taken in Konstanz, Germany, in 1882 at a time when, according to Jones' version, she was supposed to be severely ill in a sanitarium near Vienna. *(Reproduced from the original photograph, by permission of Ner-Tamid-Verlag and Congregation Solel.)*

THÉODORE FLOURNOY (1854–1920), one of the great pioneers of the exploration of the unconscious, was a close friend of William James. The photograph shows James sitting with his host in Flournoy's garden in Geneva in May, 1905. *(Courtesy Mrs. Ariane Flournoy.)*

MORITZ BENEDIKT (1835–1920) possessed a most versatile mind and was an all-too-forgotten pioneer of dynamic psychiatry. The picture shows him as an old man, ruined by postwar inflation and forgotten by the new generation, experimenting here with the divining rod. *(From the picture collection of the Institute for the History of Medicine, Vienna.)*

RICHARD VON KRAFFT-EBING (1840–1903), the celebrated Austrian psychiatrist, forensic expert, and founder of modern sexual psychopathology, took great trouble to answer personally the many unknown deviants who wrote him about their distressing problems. *(From the picture collection of the Institute for History of Medicine, Vienna.)*

CHARLES RICHET (1850–1935); A brilliant physiologist, recipient of the Nobel Prize, Richet also pioneered in the scientific study of hypnotism. Max Dessoir, who visited him in 1894, wrote in his memoirs: "His personality could be compared with that of G. Th. Fechner, for it was a strange mixture of scientific rigor and poetic indulgence." *(Courtesy Mr. Alfred Richet.)*

AMBROISE LIÉBEAULT (1823–1904)   HIPPOLYTE BERNHEIM (1840–1919)

AUGUSTE FOREL (1848–1931)   PAUL DUBOIS (1848–1918)

Four foremost psychotherapists of the period between 1880 and 1910. (*The pictures of Liébeault, Bernheim, and Forel come from the collection of the Institute for History of Medicine in Zurich. The picture of Dubois comes from the collection of the Institute for History of Medicine in Bern.*)

EUGEN BLEULER (1857–1939); One of the pioneers of a psychological approach to psychosis in the early 1890's, Bleuler was noted as much for his boundless devotion to his patients as for his scientific achievements. *(Courtesy Professor Manfred Bleuler.)*

Like Bleuler, ADOLF MEYER (1866–1950) was a disciple of Forel at the Burghölzli and, like him, he promoted a new psychological approach to the study and treatment of psychoses. *(From the picture collection of the Institute for History of Medicine in Zurich.)*

6

Pierre Janet and Psychological Analysis

CHRONOLOGICALLY SPEAKING, Pierre Janet was the first to found a new system of dynamic psychiatry aimed at replacing those of the nineteenth century, and because of this, his work is also the link between the first dynamic psychiatry and the newer systems. None of the new pioneers had a better knowledge of the first dynamic psychiatry or drew more (or, at any rate, more consciously) from it. His work was also one of the main sources for Freud, Adler, and Jung who, unlike Janet, derived more or less directly from Romanticism whereas Janet pursued his own development. In the contrast between Janet on the one side, Freud, Adler, and Jung on the other, one can see a later manifestation of the contrast between the spirit of the Enlightenment and that of Romanticism.

The Setting of Pierre Janet's Life

Pierre Janet was born in Paris in 1859 and died there in 1947. Apart from seven years spent teaching in the provinces and several trips abroad, he lived his entire life in Paris and was thoroughly Parisian in manners and customs.

At Janet's birth in 1859, the reign of Napoleon III was at its zenith; a few years later, however, Napoleon III became involved in the disastrous Mexican war; the régime declined, and was eventually swept away by defeat in the Franco-German war of 1870. At the age of eleven, Pierre Janet endured with his family the siege of Paris with the hunger and bombardments that went with it. Strasbourg, his mother's birthplace, was occupied and annexed by the Germans. The years of his adolescence and youth were those of France's swift recovery and great economic and intellectual prosperity and of the constitution of the French colonial empire. In 1886 when Janet published his first scientific papers, France was experiencing the fever of the *Boulangism* movement that aroused, temporarily, a patriotic exaltation and the wish to reannex Alsace and Lorraine. Janet's first major works were published during the relatively peaceful period of 1889 to 1905. Increasing tensions were felt in Europe from 1905 to 1914, manifested by a series of crises, the seriousness of which increased until, in 1914, World War I broke out. Janet was sixty years old when the war ended with the Allies' victory and the Treaty of Versailles. France, exhausted by the war, had lost its status as a great world power and underwent an intellectual and moral crisis. Janet started reconsidering his theories in 1925 and built a new system which remained almost unnoticed in the midst of the political and moral confusion. When Hitler seized power in Germany in 1933, Janet was seventy-three. He retired two years later, but remained productive. At the outbreak of World War II he had reached eighty years of age. He then experienced the German invasion and occupation of France, and by the time of the liberation of Paris in 1944, he was an old man of eighty-four. He seemed to be a "man of another age" when he died in 1947 at the age of eighty-seven.

Janet came from the upper middle class, from a family that had produced many scholars, lawyers, and engineers. He belonged to professional circles and was acquainted with the foremost French *savants* of his time. He was an agnostic and a liberal, but never took part in politics. From 1907 to his death he lived in the Rue de Varennes in an exclusively aristocratic and diplomatic environment. However, most of the patients whom he treated and who provided the material for his psychiatric work belonged to the poorer classes.

Thus, Janet may be depicted as a representative of the French upper middle class, whose life, covering the entire period of the Third Republic, was spent almost entirely in Paris.

The Family Background[1]

Pierre Janet's great-grandfather, Pierre-Etienne Janet (1746–1830), was the prosperous founder and owner of a bookstore that he had established on the Rue Saint-Jacques in Paris.[2] He had cultivated a taste for literature and the theater in his six sons. One of these sons was Pierre-Honoré Janet, who also became a bookseller, specializing in music. He died prematurely in 1832, leaving two sons and a daughter, Jules, Paul, and Félicité. The younger son, Paul (1823–1899), became the well-known philosopher and the pride of the family. The older son, Jules (1813–1894) began a commercial career, although according to family records he was encouraged by Paul to switch to the study of law. However, even though Jules is referred to as an *avocat,* in certain documents, it seems that he never actually practiced law but earned his living as a legal editor. He married twice. His first wife, a cousin, was Adelaïde-Antoinette Janet, to whom he was married on September 5, 1832. In 1850 she bore him a daughter, Berthe. Not long afterward she died, and several years later, while he was visiting his brother Paul, who was then a university professor in Strasbourg, Jules became acquainted with Fanny Hummel, a young neighbor of Paul's. They were married on April 10, 1858, and had three children, Pierre, Marguerite, and Jules.

Little is known about the Hummel family. Fanny Hummel's father, Francois-Jacques Hummel, was a building contractor in Strasbourg. He had five children of whom Fanny, born September 4, 1836, was the eldest. The Hummels were devout Catholics and Fanny, Pierre Janet's mother, was very attached to her faith all of her life. Her sister Marie, born May 2, 1838, became a nun in the order of the *Assomption* and spent her life in convents of that order, first in France, later in England. (Janet's daughter, Madame Hélène Pichon-Janet, recalled a childhood visit to her aunt in London where her father had taken her.) The Hummels belonged to the group of Alsatians who were intense French patriots and for whom the annexation of Alsace and Lorraine by Germany was considered a family tragedy.[4] In many of these families, some members remained in Alsace while others went to live in France. Family tradition tells of one of Fanny's brothers escaping into France and joining the French army, where he became an officer (thus being suspicious from the German viewpoint) and of how he once returned for a clandestine visit to Strasbourg in civilian clothes, accompanied by his young nephew Pierre.

Little is known about the personality of Pierre Janet's father. According to family tradition, he was a very kind man, although shy, seclusive, and "psychasthenic." Details about him are scarce and not easy to interpret. Pierre Janet once mentioned an incident remembered from his childhood. He was in his father's study, going to and fro and kicking the door, while his father kept placidly looking on without saying a word. Finally, young Pierre became tired of his game and left the room. Did this mean that his father was so passive that he was unable to show a reaction, or, on the contrary, was he a very wise man who triumphed over his child's bad temper by his display of patience?

Pierre Janet's mother is said to have been a very wise, sensitive, and warm person. Pierre was profoundly attached to her and always spoke of her with the deepest affection. He was the oldest child of a young mother (who was twenty-one at his birth), whereas the father was forty-five, one generation older. Pierre Janet's stepsister and his mother's younger siblings belonged chronologically to an intermediate generation.

Jules and Fanny had three children, Pierre, Jules, and Marguerite. Marguerite, who married a man named Vuitel, remained a devout Catholic like her mother. Jules (born December 22, 1861) became a physician and a well-known specialist in urology. He was greatly interested in psychology, and during his years of internship collaborated with his brother in hypnotic experiments. His medical dissertation, devoted to neurotic disturbances of urination, is a fine contribution to what today is called psychosomatic medicine, as was true of a later study he made on anuria. Pierre and Jules remained close to their respective families throughout their lives.[5]

The one person in the family who exerted a major influence on Pierre Janet was his uncle Paul. Not only did he help Pierre in his career, but he seems to have been the model the young man strove to imitate. Remarkable parallels can be drawn in the lives of these men. Both were timid, seclusive boys who underwent a period of adolescent depression, and who, after overcoming it, engaged in a successful career. Both went to the Lycée Louis-le-Grand, entered the Ecole Normale Supérieure, became Agrégés de Philosophie, taught philosophy in a lyceum, and then became university professors and members of the Institut de France. Paul Janet was also the author of textbooks of philosophy, which were classics in France for two or three generations, and he also wrote numerous studies on the history of philosophy. The philosopher's son, whose name was also Paul Janet, became a well-known electrical engineer who founded the Electrotechnical Institute in Grenoble and later the Ecole Supérieure d'Electricité in Paris. He, too, was philosophically oriented and wrote studies on the philosophy of science and on the psychology of scientific discoveries.[6] Through his numerous relatives, Pierre Janet had various other connections in the world of the university, engineering, and public administration.

Events in Pierre Janet's Life

Pierre Janet was born in Paris on May 30, 1859, at 46 rue Madame, a little street near the Jardin du Luxembourg. Soon afterward, his parents moved to Bourg-la-Reine where they had bought a house. Bourg-la-Reine, now a suburb of Paris, was at that time still a small township. The house was an old one, which, in contrast to the other houses in the area, had been built in the Renaissance style, with slanted slate roofs and pink walls. According to family tradition, the house was the last remnant of a residence given by the gallant King Henry IV to his celebrated mistress Gabrielle d' Estrées. To this day, the street actually bears the name "Impasse Gabrielle d'Estrées." Pierre Janet always kept a fond image of that house and its garden.

He went to school at the Collège Sainte-Barbe-des-Champs in the neighboring town of Fontenay-aux-Roses. He is said to have been a very shy boy who found contact with his schoolmates difficult. A few years later, he went to the Collège Sainte-Barbe in Paris, which was the main school. The Collège Sainte-Barbe is one of the oldest and most highly reputed schools in France. Few schools can boast of having produced such an impressive list of great men as St. Ignatius of Loyola, St. Francis Xavier, and Calvin, and numerous prominent scientists, writers, politicians, and military men. The scholastic level was high, as might be expected from such a time-honored institution. When Janet was eleven, at the outbreak of the Franco-Prussian war of 1870, his parents had the unfortunate idea of leaving Bourg-la-Reine to settle temporarily in Paris, thinking that they would be safer there. As a result, the Janet family suffered the siege of Paris with its consequences. As soon as the fighting was over, the children were sent to the mother's family in Strasbourg. Consequently, young Pierre witnessed the pain and anguish suffered by those Alsatians, who, like his mother's family, were ardent French patriots, and saw Alsace torn away from France and annexed by Germany.[7]

At the age of fifteen, Pierre went through a period of depression, which interrupted his studies for several months and which was at the same time a religious crisis. He was able, however, to overcome the depression and to find a new equilibrium. From that time on Janet became a brilliant student and decided to devote himself to philosophy.

After successfully passing his *baccalauréat* examination on July 10, 1878, and completing one year of a special preparatory class at the Lycée Louis-le-Grand, Janet succeeded in the rigorous competition for admission to the Ecole Normale Supérieure. This is a well-known preparatory school where an elite group of students live for three years and are trained intensively toward professorships in French lyceums. It also produces many university professors. The Ecole Normale Supérieure provides students with an education of the highest quality, but also leaves a great deal of freedom and spare time to the students in order to allow them to develop their own independent thinking. Notwithstanding the affection of cynicism and controversialism—the so-called Normalian spirit which is often the form taken by such independent thinking—the milieu is nevertheless highly propitious for the establishment of lasting friendships between men who are destined to be the intellectual leaders of their generation.[8] When Janet was admitted to the competitive examinations of 1879 there were, among the successful candidates, several who were to become well-known scholars, particularly Durkheim (the future sociologist) and Goblot (the logician). Very little is known about the three years that Janet spent at that school,[9] although it is known that he obtained his *Licence ès Lettres* on August 3, 1880, and that Director Ernest Bersot,[10] a philosopher and a moralist, died the same year, on February 1, and was replaced by the historian Fustel de Coulanges. Janet spent part of his spare time studying science and obtained the degree of *baccalauréat restreint* in science on April 7, 1881.[11] On September 7, 1882, he attained second place in the stiff competitive examinations of the *Agrégation de Philosophie* (only eight candidates were received, among whom was Durkheim who came in seventh). During Janet's stay at the Ecole Normale Supérieure in 1881, the International Electrical Exposition was organized in Paris, bringing the revelation of a new world of the future in which life would be dominated by science, technology, and electricity. Another sensational event in 1882 was Charcot's paper read at the Académie des Sciences, bringing about an official rehabilitation of hypnosis, which suddenly acquired scientific status. Charcot was greatly discussed at that time and, according to Parodi, Janet was already visualizing his future as a physician able to discuss Charcot's theories.[12] Among the students who were admitted the year before Janet were Bergson and Jaurès. The latter was to acquire fame as a great French socialist leader; the former was to become the most celebrated French philosopher of his generation. Bergson and Janet were to remain in close intellectual contact for the duration of their lives.

After placing second at the *Agrégation de Philosophie* on September 7, 1882, Janet immediately embarked upon his professional career. At that time the Normalians were exempted from military service, the ten years of teaching to which they had pledged themselves were considered sufficient service.[13]

The twenty-two-year-old professor was appointed by a Ministry decision of September 23, 1882, to teach philosophy at the Lyceum of Châteauroux, in the rural province of Berry, where he assumed his task on October 4, 1882. Curiously enough he left the Lyceum on February 22, 1883, having been appointed to the Lyceum in Le Havre.[14] It was rather unusual for a professor to transfer from one lyceum to another in the middle of a scholastic year; the only plausible explanation is that as a result of a sudden vacancy at Le Havre, a professor was urgently needed there. Le Havre was considered to be a far superior position than Châteauroux. Shortly before his departure from Châteauroux on February 10, 1882, Janet gave a lecture on *The Foundation of the Right of Property*.[15] It is interesting to see, in this first-known publication by Pierre Janet, the logical outline, the firmness of thought, and the clarity of style that he was to display in all of his subsequent writings. Private property, he wrote, has not always existed; it is neither a metaphysical nor a natural necessity, but has been invented by man on account of its utility. It should be perfected, and the goal should be to reconcile interest and justice.

Pierre Janet spent the following six and one-half years (from February 1883 to July 1889) in Le Havre, a maritime, industrial, and commercial city that counted 105,000 inhabitants at that time. It was administered by a progressive mayor, Jules Siegfried, who belonged to an Alsatian Protestant family that had left Alsace after the German annexation. Siegfried was an active and energetic administrator, much concerned with the welfare of the city. A perusal of two local weekly periodicals of the day, *Le Passe-Temps du Havre* and *Le Carillon* shows that the Victorian spirit (which allegedly predominated Europe at that time) certainly had no stronghold in Le Havre, two weekly papers being filled with gibes at the puritanical mayor who was trying to control prostitution and vice in the city. Another aspect of the city's life was the political fervor—waves of nationalistic and anti-German feelings swept over Le Havre from time to time. With regard to entertainment and social activity, there were, in addition to frequent performances by theatrical groups from Paris, spectacular stage performances by hypnotists. In May 1883, for instance, the weeklies reported a professor who had had the unfortunate idea of trying to expose the tricks used by Donato and who was forced to leave the scene under the sneers of the audience. Cases of women falling in love with musicians, or sending anonymous letters, were ascribed to "hysteria," which in turn was considered to be the result of sexual nongratification in women. Such hysterical women were sarcastically advised in these newspapers to see Charcot. It is not known to what extent Janet was interested in that feverish life or whether he took part at all in the social life of the city. To him, a great advantage of living in Le Havre was that communication with Paris was rapid and easy so that he was able to visit his family fairly often. During his stays in Paris, he also used to see patients with his brother Jules who was a medical student and who was also deeply interested in neuroses and in hypnotism. It was also during those years that Pierre Janet lost his mother (who died on March 3, 1885, at the age of forty-nine).

We do not know much about Janet's professorial activities. No doubt he gave a carefully prepared and original course in philosophy, as can be seen from the textbook that he later published. It is the custom in French schools that the concluding ceremony of the scholastic year is devoted to the *distribution des prix* (the awarding of prizes to the most successful students), which is preceded by a speech given by one of the younger members of the teaching staff, who chooses his own theme. Thus on August 5, 1884, Pierre Janet came to give an address entitled *On the Teaching of Philosophy,* under the chairmanship of Mayor Jules Siegfried.[16] We take for granted, Janet said, that philosophy is being taught in every French lyceum; but we forget the struggles fought by our predecessors in order to establish the right to teach an independent philosophy in our schools. Now that we enjoy so many civilian and political liberties, the teaching of philosophy has become still more important, since the true aim of philosophy is to teach man to beware of his own preconceived opinions and to respect the opinions of his fellowmen. Two years later, in 1886, Janet published an edition of one of Malebranche's works with an introduction and notes for use in secondary schools.[17]

In Le Havre Janet shared a house with a friend. It was surrounded by a garden, in which he could enjoy his hobby of gardening. For some time the other occupant of the house was the mathematician Gaston Milhaud, a colleague and, like Janet, a bachelor. It is known that Janet devoted the greatest part of his spare time to voluntary work at the Le Havre hospital and to the psychiatric research that he was pursuing on his own.

In an autobiographical note, Janet described his arrival in Le Havre as a young professor eager to find a suitable topic for his thesis for the *doctorat ès-lettres.*[18] He was considering a thesis on hallucinations in connection with the mechanism of perception and turned to Dr. Gibert, a well-known physician in Le Havre, who had no suitable patient to suggest but who had told Janet of a remarkable subject, Léonie, who could be hypnotized from a distance. Léonie, at Dr. Gibert's request, was called to Le Havre and submitted to Janet's experiments for a period lasting several years, at various intervals. Janet's first experiments with Léonie took place from September 24 to October 14, 1885. He was able to prove to himself that it was easy to hypnotize Léonie, not only directly but also from a distance, and to give her "mental" suggestions that she would carry out exactly. He wrote a paper about his first experiments, which was read by Paul Janet on behalf of his nephew at the *Société de psychologie physiologique* in Paris on November 30, 1885, under the chairmanship of Charcot.[19] It is not known whether Pierre Janet was present at that session. However, the paper created a sensation, as can be seen from the discussion that followed the reading as was reported by one of the participants, Dr. Ochorowicz.[20] Janet had been careful to state his observations without drawing any conclusions, but, as a result of that communication, a number of distinguished visitors came to Le Havre, eager to see Léonie. From Paris came Charles Richet, Julian Ochorowicz, and Marillier; and from England came a delegation from the Society for Psychical Research with Frederick Myers, his brother A. Myers, and Sidgwick. Janet's uncle Paul and brother Jules also joined the group. Preliminary experiments started on April 13, and the main experiments took place from April 21 to 24, 1886. The result seemed to confirm the existence of the phenomenon of suggestion from a distance. These experiments, however, were apparently kept from the public at that time, when there was such a craze for stage hypnotism in Le Havre.[21] Nonetheless, these experiments were highly regarded in the scientific world, and Janet became acquainted with Charcot, Richet, Myers, and others. But to Janet's "astonishment and regret," many people quoted him from hearsay instead of writing to him for exact information. He felt that not enough precautions had been taken to avoid indirect suggestion and that the reports published were not accurate enough. He also acquired a lasting suspicion of parapsychological research, and decided to restrict himself, at least temporarily, to the systematic investigation of the elementary phenomena of hypnosis and suggestion.

Meanwhile, Janet had already begun regular clinical work at the hospital in Le Havre where Doctor Powilewicz had placed a little ward at his disposal where he could examine hysterical women. It is reported that Janet jokingly called this room *Salle Saint-Charcot* (at that time, wards in many French hospitals were named after saints). The great advantage of working in Le Havre, Janet felt, was that the patients there were fresh and unsophisticated and, unlike the inmates of the Salpêtrière, had not been examined hundreds of times by physicians and students. But Janet was soon to make an unexpected discovery: Léonie had already been magnetized in the past. Her present performances were the repetition of magnetic exercises she had performed previously and which Janet now found described in the writings of the magnetizers of the past generation. Everything taught by Charcot and Bernheim as amazing novelties had already been known to these obscure men. It was a world of forgotten knowledge that Janet rediscovered and, going back into the past from generation to generation, he found that even the earliest magnetizers, Puységur and Bertrand, had already known most of what the moderns believed they discovered. Janet began collecting the works of these old pioneers and later used this knowledge for the historical part of *Les Médications Psychologiques.*

On the basis of his experience with Léonie and with the delegation that had come to examine her in Le Havre, Janet imposed three methodological rules upon himself: first, always to examine his patients by himself, without witnesses; second, to take an exact record of everything the patients said or did (this he called the fountain-pen method); and third, to scrutinize the entire life history of the patients and their past treatments. Such principles may seem obvious today, but in those times they were a novelty. The first results of those investigations were published serially in the *Revue Philosophique* from 1886 to 1889 and were the basis for Janet's main thesis, *L'Automatisme Psychologique.*

The *doctorat ès-lettres* required the elaboration of a main thesis in French and a lesser one in Latin on a different subject. For his Latin dissertation, Janet chose as a topic *Bacon and the Alchemists.*[22] Francis Bacon's personality, that of one who was at the same time a pupil of the old alchemists (thus heir to an obsolete knowledge) as well as a pioneer of the new experimental science, seemed to fascinate Janet. One might assume that he found a reflection of his own problem. He, too, was the heir to a century-old tradition of philosophical psychology of which his uncle Paul was one of the late representatives, and at the same time he felt himself called to participate in the founding of a new experimental psychology to which Ribot was pointing and to which his main thesis, *L'Automatisme Psychologique,* was a first step.

A picture of 1889 shows the thirty-year-old Janet seated at the foot of his favorite tree in his garden in Le Havre, toward the end of his stay in that city. He was shortly to leave for Paris to face the trial of the *soutenance de thèse,* after which he was to begin a new scientific career. His face shows an expression of calm energy and concentrated thought, which is found on most pictures taken of him during these years.

The ceremony of the presentation of the thesis took place at the Sorbonne on June 21, 1889, under the chairmanship of Dean Himly.[23] The jury was composed of professors Boutroux, Marion, Séailles, Waddington, and Paul Janet.[24] Many objections and arguments were brought against the thesis, but Janet impressed the jury with his sharp mind and the subtleties of his arguments and his eloquence. The jury congratulated him and acknowledged the fact that he had remained firmly on philosophical ground and had carefully refrained from encroaching onto the medical field.

Janet, who was already well known in philosophical and psychological circles for his publications during the previous three-and-one-half years, now acquired the reputation of a master. He moved to Paris where he had been appointed to a new post. The ceremony of the presentation of his thesis took place during the great Universal Exposition of 1889 in Paris. Scientists from all over the world were meeting in the *Ville-Lumière* at congresses that were held at the rate of three or more at a time without interruption. Among many other events, the International Congress for Experimental and Therapeutic Hypnotism took place from August 8 to 12.[25] Janet was one of the committee members together with Liébeault, Bernheim, Déjerine, and Forel, and had ample opportunity to become acquainted with celebrities of the psychological and psychiatric world. Among the 300 participants of the congress were Dessoir, Myers, William James, Lombroso, and a Viennese neurologist named Sigmund Freud.

Janet knew from the beginning that he would be unable to pursue his psychopathological research if he did not acquire the M.D. degree, and he decided to take up his medical studies while continuing his profession and his own research. The years from 1889 to 1893 saw him intensely absorbed in his work, having to meet his teaching commitments at the Lycée Louis-le-Grand during the scholastic year 1889 to 1890 and from then on at the Collège Rollin. The only trace of his activities during that time is the address he gave at the distribution of prizes on July 30, 1892, in which he talked thus to the finishing students: "What did you learn during your ten years of secondary school? Some knowledge and basic science—certainly, and also the habit of intellectual work acquired through such exercises as translation and composition. But there is more: the aim of secondary education is to help one understand others as well as social problems; to acquire an attitude of reasonable doubt and tolerance toward the opinions of others."[26]

Janet began his medical studies in November 1889.[27] At that time medical studies took only four years, including one preparatory year of physics, chemistry, and natural science, and usually required a fifth year for the concluding examinations and the thesis. Janet was, however, exempted from the first year. Having furthermore the good fortune of being freed from many obligations through the benevolence of his teachers, he spent from 1890 on much time in Charcot's wards at the Salpêtrière, examining patients. There are also records of his clinical stages at the hospitals Laennec and St.-Antoine. At the latter, he observed the case of a fourteen-year-old girl who was admitted with apparently neurotic symptoms and who soon died. A post-mortem showed that she had a hydatic cyst on the brain. Janet published a paper about that case and wondered how a brain lesion of such importance could have produced so few clinical symptoms.[28] The patient, he added, belonged to a family strongly tainted by neuropathic heredity, which could perhaps account for the fact that the cyst had been located in the brain rather than in another organ. Janet passed his terminal examinations on May 31, 1893, and presented his medical thesis on July 29 of the same year. Charcot was chairman and Charles Richet one of the three other members of the jury. He was graduated with high honors.

Meanwhile, in 1890, Janet had again taken up his clinical research, investigating at the Salpêtrière the patients Madame D, Marcelle, Isabelle, and Achille, who played an important role in the elaboration of his theories. On the basis of his findings, he built his theory of hysteria that he expounded first in various journals and then in his MD thesis in 1893. His reputation had already crossed the English Channel, and at the International Congress of Experimental Psychology in London in July 1892 he read a paper on his research on the relation of amnesia to unconscious fixed ideas.[29]

For a long time Charcot had been keenly interested in psychology. He founded the *Société de Psychologie Physiologique* with Charles Richet. Desiring to incorporate experimental psychology into the great research unit he had built at the Salpêtrière, he opened a laboratory for this purpose, which he entrusted to Pierre Janet. Since Charcot needed Janet in that regard and Janet needed Charcot for the rich clinical material to be found at the Salpêtrière, this promised to be the beginning of a long and rewarding collaboration. But on August 17, 1893, merely three weeks after Janet had obtained his M.D. degree with Charcot as one of his examiners, came the news of the master's sudden and unexpected death.

During the period from 1893 to 1902 Janet worked with relative freedom at the Salpêtrière. Charcot's successor, the neurologist Professor Fulgence Raymond, was personally not interested in neuroses but maintained the psychological laboratory at the Salpêtrière and gave his approval to Janet's research. Inasmuch as they concerned patients of the Salpêtrière, most of Janet's articles were for several years published under the joint signatures of Raymond and Janet. It was also a period of intensive work in other areas. Janet still taught philosophy at the Collège Rollin until 1897 and during the scholastic year 1897–1898 at the Lycée Condorcet. He was then appointed, first as *chargé de cours* (1898–1899) in experimental psychology at the Sorbonne, then as *maître de conférences* (1898–1902). During that same period, he was asked by Ribot to replace him temporarily at the Collège de France from December 1895 to August 1897.[30] In 1894, Janet published the textbook of philosophy on which he had been working for twelve years and of which we will speak later.

Janet's private life had also undergone changes. In 1894 he married Marguerite Duchesne, the daughter of an auctioneer in Le Havre, who had come to live in Paris after her father's death. The young couple took an apartment in the Rue de Bellechasse and moved, in 1889, to the Rue Barbet-de-Jouy near the Quartier Latin. They had three children: Hélène (who was to marry the psychoanalyst Edouard Pichon), Fanny (who became a French teacher), and Michel (who had a brief career as an engineer and died prematurely). Janet led the usual academic life, that is, he taught for nine months in Paris, taking three months' vacation in which he wrote or prepared his lectures for the following academic year. He usually spent his vacation at Fontainebleau, where he would go for long botanical walks through the forest. His father died on October 22, 1894, at the age of eighty-two.

During those years Janet's interest covered a wide field, as shown by his book reviews on topics ranging from brain histology to experimental psychology and criminology. The focus of his clinical research shifted from the clinical investigation of hysteria to that of neurasthenia. Janet's research was at once extensive, in that he saw many patients at the out-patient clinic and in the wards, and intensive, in that he chose a small number of patients whom he submitted to careful and prolonged studies lasting for years. Among the latter was a woman whom he names "Madeleine" admitted to the Salpêtrière with a religious delusional ecstasy and stigmata in February 1896. She was to occupy an almost central place in his studies for several years. In addition he had a practice of his own and private patients in a sanatorium in Vanves. His reputation as a foremost specialist in neuroses was by then well established and he received many foreign visitors. In 1896 he read a paper on "somnambulic influence" at the International Congress of Psychology in Munich, which was a new elaboration of the old concept of the rapport.

For many years Janet had been thinking of founding a new psychological society to replace the *Société de Psychologie Physiologique*, which had not long survived Charcot's death. In 1900 an *Institut Psychologique International* was founded in Paris with the financial help of a number of donors, among whom was Serge Yourievitch, an attaché of the Russian Imperial Embassy. It was under the sponsorship of an international committee among whose members were William James, Frederick Myers, Lombroso, Théodore Flournoy, and Théodule Ribot.[31] The aims of that institute do not seem to have been well defined; it was intended to have a psychopathological clinic, laboratories, a library, and to publish a bulletin. Most of these ambitious projects could not be realized, but at least a new psychological society was founded with forty charter members, which held its monthly meetings in the precincts of the institute and used its bulletin to publish proceedings. Among its active members were Pierre Janet and a younger colleague of his, Dr. Georges Dumas, who was appointed secretary of the new society. The history of that *Institut Psycho-logique* has never been written; it would be interesting to know why it did not develop further but disappeared a few years later.

In 1902, Théodule Ribot left his post as titular professor of experimental psychology at the Collège de France. There were two candidates for his post, Pierre Janet and Alfred Binet. At the assembly of the professors on January 19, 1902, Janet's candidacy was defended by Bergson and Binet's by the physiologist Marey.[32] Marey enumerated the many experiments conducted by Binet in various fields of psychology and emphasized his skill in experimental psychology. Bergson stressed the methodical and concentrated way in which Janet conducted his research and experiments, and the extreme importance of his discoveries in the field of the subconscious mind. The decision rested in the hands of the Minister of Education who decided in Janet's favor on February 17, 1902. Janet had already replaced Ribot from December 1895 to August 1897 and from November 1900 onward. From that time on, the Collège de France became the center of his activities. His lectures there were mostly attended by foreign visitors, by nonspecialists, and by very few students. It is the rule at the Collège de France that the professors lecture once a week and that they choose a new topic for each academic year, announcing this topic in advance. Between 1902 and 1912, Janet taught about the normal and the morbid emotions, consciousness, hysteria and psychasthenia, psychotherapy, the psychology of tendencies, perception, and social tendencies. Part of the material was incorporated into his books, particularly in *Les Obsessions et la Psychasthénie* and in *Les Médications Psychologiques*. In 1904, Janet founded the *Journal de Psychologie* with his friend Georges Dumas, in which he published most of his articles from then on. In 1907 he moved to a large and beautiful apartment in which he was to live until his death. It was located at 44 rue de Varenne in the so-called Faubourg Saint-Germain, the aristocratic neighborhood of Marcel Proust's novels. The apartment comprised seven large rooms, a splendid hall, and a balcony where Janet grew flowers and cacti.

Meanwhile, Raymond of the Salpêtrière had died in 1910 and had been replaced by Déjerine, who was hostile to Janet and his work. On the other hand, men such as Babinski, who had retained only the neurological part of Charcot's teaching, were very suspicious of Janet, whom they accused of perpetuating Charcot's errors. It is not clear what kind of intrigues were devised to remove Janet from his laboratory and Charcot's former wards. However, within the Salpêtrière there were wards administered by other physicians, among them Dr. Nageotte, a neurologist whose almost exclusive interest was brain histology. He taught this subject at the Collège de France. Nageotte placed a room in his ward at Janet's disposal, where he could keep a small number of patients and visit them regularly. These precarious conditions did not enable Janet to give clinical teaching, so that he was forced to turn down applications from students.[33]

However, Janet's fame continued to spread abroad. On September 24, 1904, he lectured on psychopathology at the International Congress during the great Universal Exposition at St. Louis, Missouri, under the chairmanship of Dr. Edward Cowles and with Dr. Adolf Meyer as secretary of the section.[34] According to family accounts, Janet was enthusiastic about the United States and the splendid reception he was given in St. Louis, Boston, Chicago, and elsewhere. He visited the Rocky Mountains and Niagara Falls. In June 1906, he was one of the delegates of the Collège de France who traveled to London to participate in the festivities organized by London University. In October and November of the same year, he was invited by Harvard University for a second time to the United States where he gave a series of fifteen lectures on hysteria.[35] He also took part in various international congresses in Rome (1905), Amsterdam (1907), and Geneva (1909).

In August 1913 the International Congress of Medicine took place in London. In the psychiatric section, a session had been organized to discuss Freud's psychoanalysis. Janet was to read a criticism of it and Jung was to defend it. Janet's main criticism concerned two points: first, he claimed priority in having discovered the cathartic cure of neuroses brought forth by the clarification of traumatic origins, and he believed that psychoanalysis was simply a development of that fundamental concept. Second, he sharply criticized Freud's method of symbolic interpretation of dreams and his theory of the sexual origin of neurosis. He considered psychoanalysis a "metaphysical" system.[36] We shall return at a later point to that memorable session of August 8, 1913, with Jung's report on psychoanalysis and the discussion that ensued. In that circumstance, Janet seems to have departed from his usually conciliatory attitude in scientific discussions. Customarily he always took the utmost care to enumerate his sources and give his predecessors their due, even in minute details. However, he expected the same courtesy from others, and was therefore no doubt hurt and irritated at seeing Freud develop what he considered were originally his own ideas with hardly a mention of obligation. Janet regretted having shown his irritation, but remained convinced for the rest of his life that Freud had done him an injustice. Yet when Freud was fiercely attacked at a meeting of the *Société de Psychothérapie* on June 16, 1914, Janet defended him, an act that took courage considering the growing anti-German feeling in France. His intervention was published in the *Revue de Psychothérapie* in 1915, when the war was already raging.[37]

From 1910 onward, Janet developed his teaching toward a more perfected system of the "hierarchic functions of the mind." His study on alcoholism in 1915 also revealed a preoccupation with social and national problems. In the flood of jingoism, which submerged France as well as Germany during World War I, only a few scientists remained immune to that mental contagion. In all of Janet's writings of those years one cannot find the slightest trace of chauvinism, despite—or perhaps because of—his mother being Alsatian and some of his Alsatian relatives probably serving in the German army, while some members of the Janet family were in the French army.

The publication of *Les Médications Psychologiques,* into which Janet had put many years' toil, was postponed until 1919. A thorough and systematic treatise on psychology comprising more than 1,100 pages, it was, however, in organization and style not in keeping with the postwar outlook and feeling. The spirit of the times had changed. Of all of Janet's works, this was the last to be translated into English.

But Janet had started to develop his system in new directions. In 1921 and 1922 he gave a course on the evolution of moral and religious conduct. An American who attended the course, the Reverend W. M. Horton of New York, published a digest of it in the *American Journal of Psychology.*[38] Janet, who had for twenty-five years been fascinated by the case of Madeleine, made this a starting point around which he organized a great deal of psychological research that was expounded in his book *De l'Angoisse à l'extase.* Scientific communications between France and other countries were gradually reorganized, and in May 1920 Janet gave three lectures at the University of London in May 1921 he was invited to attend the ceremonies of the Centennial of Bloomingdale Hospital near New York, where he gave a lecture on May 26. In May 1922 he attended the ceremonies marking the centennial of the independence of Brazil as a delegate of the Institut de France and of the Collège de France. He also took part in the International Congress of Psychology in Oxford (July 27 to August 2, 1923). In 1925 he was delegated by the French government as an exchange professor to Mexico and was given a grand reception at the University of Mexico City, where he gave fifteen lectures in French.[39] He also gave two in Puebla and one in Guadalajara. On his return voyage to France, he again visited the United States with stopovers in Princeton, New Jersey; Philadelphia; and Columbia University in New York.

From 1925 on, Janet further developed his new system of the Psychology of Conduct. His courses at the Collège de France from 1925 to 1930 were published in a version that did not pass under his revision. In the following years he began writing down his courses, and later used them for the preparation of his last books. But in spite of the enormous amount of work devoted to this new system and to the originality of his new theories, it seems that not many people in France were able to follow Janet in that new path. Apparently his name had been too long identified with the concept of psychological automatism and psychasthenia.

His fame, however, was still great abroad. In September 1932 he was invited to give a series of lectures in Buenos Aires and traveled through the country as far as the Iguassu Falls.[40] In 1933 he again gave a series of twenty lectures in Rio de Janeiro. In April 1937 he also went to Vienna and visited Wagner von Jauregg. Freud, though, refused to see him.[41]

In February 1935 Janet retired from the Collège de France but kept his private practice. He now turned his curiosity to new realms of psychology (such as graphology) and to new types of patients. He examined paranoic cases at the Hôpital Henri-Rousselle and was led to modify and complete his theory of delusions of persecution.[42] He also examined delinquent and criminal women at the prison Petite-Roquette.[43] It is regrettable, however, that he never wrote anything about his criminological research. Between 1935 and 1937 he published his last three books, and in 1938 he wrote a condensed outline of his entire psychological system in the form of a contribution to the official French Encyclopedia.[44] He was invited in September 1936 to take part in the ceremonies of the tercentenary of Harvard University, where he also lectured.

Janet celebrated his eightieth birthday in 1939. A *festschrift* in his honor was compiled by his son-in-law, Edouard Pichon, containing papers written by relatives. His brother Jules wrote reminiscenses of the Léonie case and about the experiments in Le Havre.[45] On June 22, 1939, the centennial of Théodule Ribot was celebrated at the Sorbonne, and the organizers decided to combine the celebration for Janet with that of his master Ribot. Janet passed his thesis *L'Automatisme Psychologique* exactly fifty years and one day earlier. There were addresses in Janet's honor by Piaget, Minkowski, and others, after Janet himself had read an address in memory of Ribot.[46]

But the year was not over when World War II broke out. At the beginning of the invasion of France, Janet and his wife left Paris and spent some time at Lédignan, in the south of France, with their friends Professor and Mrs. Georges Dumas, but then chose to return to Paris. Besides the general tribulations of the French people, Janet suffered the loss of his closest relatives and friends. He had already lost his son-in-law Edouard Pichon in January 1940; his sister Marguerite and his brother Jules died in 1942, his wife in October 1943, shortly before their fiftieth wedding anniversary, his son Michel in January 1944; his sister-in-law in 1945; as well as many dear old friends.

After the death of his wife, Janet continued to live in his large apartment on the Rue de Varenne with his daughter Fanny. In 1942 Dr. Jean Delay, who had been one of his students, was appointed professor of psychiatry and head of the University Psychiatric Clinic Sainte-Anne in Paris. He invited Janet to come to see a few patients each week.[47] Janet was seized with a renewed interest in psychiatry and during the scholastic year

1942–1943, at the age of eighty-three, he regularly attended Professor Delay's lectures, never missing one, to the astonished admiration of the students who were also attending the course. They were not a little surprised to see the passionate interest of the grand old man. He was also asked to give several lectures to the students. Keenly observant, Janet witnessed the achievements of a new psychiatry, vastly different from that which he had learned at the Salpêtrière. He was also delighted to see how some of his own ideas had taken a new shape. Narco-analysis was the fulfillment of his old prediction that a new kind of hypnosis would be induced by chemical substances, and he noticed the similarity of the narco-hypnotic treatment of psychic traumata with his old experiments with his first patients in Le Havre.[48] He was keenly interested in electric shock therapy and in seeing a depressed patient, who had been undergoing psychoanalysis for almost a year without success, cured after the third electric shock.[49]

In August 1946 Janet was invited to Zurich and received at the Burghölzli Mental Hospital by Professor Manfred Bleuler, the son of Eugen Bleuler with whom he had been well acquainted. Janet gave talks at the Burghölzli Mental Hospital and at the Swiss Society of Applied Psychology.

He was still working on a book on the psychology of belief in 1947, but that work remained unfinished. He died during the night of February 23–24, 1947, at the age of eighty-seven. The funeral ceremony took place on February 27 at Sainte Clotilde Church in Paris, and he was buried in the family grave in the cemetery of Bourg-la-Reine beside his mother, father, wife, brother, and sister-in-law. His tomb bears this simple inscription: PIERRE JANET + 1859–1947.

The Personality of Pierre Janet

It is not easy to make an exact appraisal of the personality of Pierre Janet. He always drew a sharp line of distinction between his public and private lives, and shunned all publicity. He never, for instance, granted any interviews to journalists.[50] Even when talking freely with intimate friends, he did not easily reveal his own feelings.

Pierre Janet was a man of rather short stature, lean in his youth but thickset in later years, with brown hair, dark eyes, thick black eyebrows, and a well-kept beard. Many people remember him as a very active and lively man, vivacious, sharp-witted, and a brilliant conversationalist. Others describe him as a quiet man who listened with an expression of concentrated attention, but who would also become absorbed in his meditation, was often absent-minded, and had a tendency to depression. It would seem that these two facets reflected the personalities of his active and vivacious mother on the one hand and of his "psychasthenic" father on the other. Both facets are also reflected in the photographs that exist of Pierre Janet.

Those photographs for which he sat usually show him in an attitude of quiet attention. Some snapshots taken unexpectedly show him engaged in vivacious conversation. His handwriting was clear and legible. As most scholars of his time, he had an active correspondence with colleagues. He never dictated his letters but wrote them himself, and later typed his own manuscripts.

Janet twice wrote short autobiographical notices, the first for Carl Murchison's *History of Psychology in Autobiography*.[51] In the second, written one year before his death and more complete than the first, he explains his psychological vocation as a kind of compromise between his definite inclination for natural science and the strong religious feelings of his childhood and adolescence.[52] He always repressed mystical tendencies and dreamed, like Leibniz, of achieving a reconciliation of science and religion in the form of a perfected philosophy that could satisfy reason as well as faith. "I have not discovered that marvel," he wrote, "but I remained a philosopher." Turning his efforts toward psychology, Janet built an extremely vast and comprehensive system in which almost every possible aspect of that science found its place. There is a remarkable continuity between his first philosophical writings and those that death prevented him from completing. There were, of course, many changes, but these assumed rather the character of new developments that rarely superseded his previous theories. The same continuity can also be noted in the unfolding of his life. As a child, Janet was said to have been shy and secluded. Then came the crisis of his seventeenth year with his depression and religious preoccupations, after which he became a brilliant student and the hard worker he remained throughout his entire life. Unfortunately, we have few testimonies regarding the seven years that he spent in Le Havre, but his publications of that time show him not only as a scholar but also as an extremely skillful clinician and psychotherapist. These brilliant qualities must have developed further in Paris after he had broadened his clinical experience at the Salpêtrière. Max Dessoir, who visited Janet in Paris in 1894, spoke of him thus: "He was a reputed scholar and a sought-after specialist of nervous diseases . . . He was a vivacious, black-haired man who spoke French in the Parisian manner and who liked to talk about his experiences."[53] Dessoir adds that although Janet had made successful experiments with telepathy and suggestion at a distance, he had remained skeptical about these matters. "His criticism contained an acid which would dissolve the platinum of facts. But he always remained courteous in his manners." At this point, a hypothesis might be proposed: In 1893 Marcel Prévost published a novel, *The Autumn of a Woman,* describing several neurotic persons as well as a certain Dr. Daumier of the Salpêtrière who gives extremely skillful psychotherapeutic treatments with methods reminiscent of Janet's.[54] One cannot help thinking that Dr. Daumier, as described in his mannerisms and speech, was a portrait of Janet himself.

During his entire Paris career Janet was not only a busy physician and hard-working scholar but was also engaged in an extensive social life, giving fine receptions in his apartment. He had close friends among his colleagues, at home and abroad, two of the latter being Morton Prince and James Mark Baldwin. According to all testimonies, Janet was a man of refined courtesy, with, however, a penchant for paradox, so that people not well acquainted with him were sometimes in doubt as to whether or not he spoke in earnest. Thus at times he gave the impression of playing with ideas rather than appearing to seek a serious exchange of thought.

In his later years it seems that the psychasthenic features, which had never been completely lacking in Janet, became more conspicuous. He may well have been more affected than he wished to reveal by the hostility of his colleagues at the Salpêtrière and by the relative isolation that ensued. Perhaps the hard worker had gone beyond the limit of his strength. Janet is depicted as having had increasingly frequent depressive moods and as having also become more and more impractical and absent-minded. According to his family, his judgment about the people he met in everyday life was often superficial, unless they became his patients. These traits became more pronounced during the last years of his life in the midst of gloomy world events and personal losses. Janet was also reported to cling obstinately to old habits and notions. However, when he came to accept new ideas, he showed a renewed freshness of mind. Madame Pichon-Janet reports that, once he was convinced that he should go beyond his old favorite authors such as Victor Hugo, he became enthusiastic about Marcel Proust and Paul Valéry, to the point of quoting frequently from the former and learning by heart *Le cimetière marin.*

Janet was a man of regular habits, thrifty and orderly, and was a fervent collector. His main collection was that of his patients' case histories, minutely recorded in his own handwriting. They eventually numbered more than five thousand and occupied an entire room in his apartment. Another room was taken up with his extensive library, which contained a unique collection of the works of the old magnetizers and hypnotists, and also a large number of books presented to him by the authors. He kept a card catalog of all his books. A third collection was his sizeable herbarium, containing plants collected and classified throughout his entire life.

Pierre Janet belonged to that generation of scientists who considered it their duty to give much of their time and activity to official academic organizations and to the acknowledged scientific societies and journals. He thus was an active member of the *Société de Neurologie,* the *Société Médico-Psychologique,* and particularly the *Société de Psychologie,* and fulfilled various functions at the *Académie des Sciences Morales et Politiques.* According to all accounts, Janet was always punctilious in his dealings with colleagues. At the *Société de Psychologie,* he did not speak frequently, but regularly attended meetings, listened attentively to speakers, and sometimes took notes. If he did discuss the papers, he would "translate" their contents, so to speak, into the language of his own theories.

We have found no descriptions of Janet's teaching of philosophy at the lyceums, but it is likely that he carried it out in much the same way as he lectured later at the Collège de France and elsewhere. The universal consensus is that he was an admirable lecturer. Whatever the subject matter, his audience was captivated from the start. Reverend Walter Horton of New York, who attended Janet's lectures in the winter of 1921–1922, writes of the listeners:

> . . . they crammed his dingy lecture-room to its capacity at the first session, and all the winter long they cheerfully endured the discomfort of backless benches and bad ventilation without once flagging in their interest. The popularity of the course was due in some measure, to be sure, to the scintillations of Janet's Voltairean wit—which no dull reproduction could ever hope to preserve undimmed—but chiefly, I believe, to the intrinsic importance of the subject and the originality of the views presented. I am confident that I was not the only foreign auditor who felt that these lectures alone had repaid him for his trip to France.[55]

Janet's manner of speech was clear and lively, and his style somewhat between the written and the oral style. His way of lecturing is illustrated in the publication of the stenographic records of his lectures from 1926 to 1929, as these were not revised by him prior to publication and sometimes even contain slips of the tongue such as "Arnold Meyer" instead of "Adolf Meyer" or some of those little jokes that a teacher sometimes tells in a course but will not retain in his published papers. He would say, for instance, that "love is a hypothesis transformed into a fixed idea."[56] Sometimes, when discussing a matter that was close to his heart, Janet spoke more vivaciously and made movements with his hands to underline his thoughts. An eyewitness says that at the International Congress of Psychology in Paris in 1937 Janet had been asked to speak slowly for the interpreter's sake, but forgot this request after a few minutes and started talking with animation. The interpreter in his booth, who could not see Janet, was seized with the same animation and made the same gestures as Janet "as if in a kind of telepathy."

In Janet's relationship with his patients, two features stand out. The first is his perspicacity. He was extremely keen in discerning what was authentic in the patient and what was feigned. He repeatedly insisted upon the fact that in the behavior of many patients an element of play was involved (that is, the same "ludic function" that Flournoy had shown at work in his mediums), as well as the need for being admired. This was particularly true, he said, in regard to sexual perversions. In a meeting of the *Société de Psychologie* in 1908,[57] Janet expressed doubts about the sincerity of many sexual deviants, and in his foreword to the French translation of Krafft-Ebing's *Psychopathia Sexualis,*[58] Janet did not hesitate to say that a great part of abnormal sexual behavior is nothing but acting and play. He went so far as to question the sincerity of many severe psychotics: "Most frequently, psychotics are acting. Don't believe one-fourth of what they say. They try to impress you with their grandeur or their guilt, in which they themselves believe only half-heartedly or not at all."[59]

Another of Janet's features was his skill as a psychotherapist, "his prodigious ingeniousness," as the editors of *Hommage à Janet* put it.[60] Although examples of it can be found in the *Médications Psychologiques,* they do not exhaust the subject, and one should read many of his short papers to learn of the almost unlimited variety of his psychotherapeutic devices. But there seems to be no record of a cure with Janet written by one of his former patients, although one of them, Raymond Roussel whom Janet had treated for several years for megalomanic ideas and who later became known as a surrealist writer, copied in one of his books without any commentary what Janet had written about his illness.[61] Very few students could learn psychotherapy from Janet (who, as already mentioned, had been deprived of the material possibility of giving any consistent clinical teaching following the intrigues at the Salpêtrière). Dr. Ernest Harms, who visited Janet at the Salpêtrière, wrote the following:

When I went to Paris to study Janet's techniques, I was directed to familiarize myself with the inmates and their living quarters. Coming from Kraepelin and Zurich, I was startled by the set-up. I found housed together many persecutionist patients who fired one another emotionally with fantastic tales. When I asked Janet what his therapeutic approach here was, I received the strange reply: "I believe those people, until it is proven to me that what they say is untrue." I had just faced a young man who avoided stepping into any shadow because, in shadows, roamed Napoleon, who wanted to draft him into the army. Beside him was a woman of past 70 who feared persecution from the Mayor of Paris, who wanted to make love to her. I found it difficult to see any truth in such fixed ideas. Janet noticed my perplexity at his oracular words. He came over to me. "You see, these people are persecuted by something, and you must investigate carefully to get to the root." What he wanted to make me see was that one ought not discard persecutional fantasies as ridiculous, or view them only symptomatically; one ought to take them seriously and analyze them, until the causal conditions were revealed. I have never forgotten Janet's wise words about persecution, nor the many others which were a major element in his relations with his students. They represented a Socratic art which I have never experienced from any other prominent teacher of psychiatry. In Janet's case it was inseparable from his concept of psychiatry.[62]

One small incident shows Janet's consideration for his hospital patients and how he protected them from indiscretions and inopportune curiosity: During one of Madeleine's stays at the Salpêtrière, the President of the Republic paid a visit to the hospital. The intern—who was none other than

Jean Charcot, son of the great neurologist—called her to demonstrate her to the President. "Immediately," wrote Madeleine to her sister in a letter of June 26, 1898, "Doctor Janet, who knows my reluctance, stepped forward and motioned to Mr. Charcot to say nothing."[63] Some people thought that Janet went too far to disguise the identity of patients whose case histories he published. When he died, his five thousand or more patient files were burnt according to his will. One cannot help regret the loss of this extraordinarily rich and well-classified material and particularly of the files of patients such as Léonie and Madeleine, but at the same time one feels compelled to respect this act of reverence for professional secrecy.

About Janet's family life, a few notes have been written by Madame Hélène Pichon-Janet. Her parents were both rather reserved in the expression of their feelings, she said, but they never left each other and were inseparable, Madame Janet accompanied her husband in all his travels and was indispensable to him in his social life and in practical matters. She adds that he was an affectionate and tender father. For example, although he was extremely absorbed in his work, he always found a moment to read to his children after lunch.

As is the case with many scientists, Janet started out with manifold interests in his youth, but gradually restricted his field of interest in order to concentrate on his life work. At the time he studied at the Ecole Normale Supérieure, the teaching of Greek and Latin was excellent and the philosophy students were thoroughly conversant with Cicero and Virgil, as well as with the French classics. Janet seems to have somewhat lost the living contact with the classics, although he could occasionally demonstrate his ability in the Latin language. According to family tradition on his first meeting with J. M. Baldwin, neither of them could speak the language of the other and so they resorted to a conversation in Latin, which the difference in pronunciation made rather laborious. Janet had learned German at school, but (possibly due to the influence of his patriotic mother) he seemed to have developed an inhibition for that language. The lack of a fluent knowledge of German was a severe handicap for him. As to English, he learned it later and came to master it, though always speaking it with a pronounced French accent.

Perhaps because of lack of time, Janet did not read much besides psychological and psychiatric literature. Nor was he particularly interested in music, art, or architecture. But nothing would be further from the truth than to picture Janet as an absent-minded old scholar or bookworm. Deepseated in his soul was the love of nature. The herbarium, which he collected for so many years, was only one aspect of his love of flowers. Beginning with his childhood, when he kept a little garden of his own, he liked to grow plants of all kinds. Each species of flowers, he said, had its own individuality, which he described in poetic terms. Janet had done some horseback riding with one of his uncles Hummel. Later, he learned to ride a bicycle, at that time a new invention. But his preference was for walking. Even in his old age he liked to wander through the streets of Paris. He rested from his work during the year in hiking and botanizing in the Fontainebleau woods. The highlights of his life were his journeys to the Rocky Mountains and to Yellowstone Park, and to the Brazilian primeval forests and the Iguassu Falls.

Before becoming a psychologist and psychiatrist, Janet had long been a philosopher. His textbooks on philosophy reveal his opinion about many matters. He shows himself preoccupied with social justice and the future emancipation of colonies. He says that the idea of private property is a notion that should be perfected, that the death penalty is a leftover from barbarism, and that it would be good for mankind to have an international artificial language.[64] Although he took great care never to mingle philosophical concepts with psychological theories, there is one metaphysical idea that occurs repeatedly in his writings as a kind of leitmotiv: the idea that the past of mankind as a whole has been preserved in its entirety in some manner.[65] He went so far as to predict that the time would come when man would be able to travel through the past in the same way as he now travels through the air. "Everything that has existed," he said, "still exists and endures in a place which we do not understand, to which we cannot go." He also said that should the "paleoscope" ever be invented, man would learn extraordinary things about which we do not have the slightest inkling today.

In the background of all his philosophical ideas lay not only the influence of the "spiritualist philosophy" of his uncle Paul Janet, but the suppressed religious feelings of his childhood. Although he was commonly designated as an atheist, Janet was actually an agnostic who probably never completely relinquished his ties with religion. His wife, who had been brought up in a convent, seems to have gone further than him in her dissociation from religion and to have been openly opposed to the Catholic Church. Madame Hélène Pichon-Janet told the author of her father's insistence that the three children attend the Protestant religious instruction in one of the Protestant churches in Paris. It was apparently his idea that his children might wish to turn to religion later in life, and that in that eventuality he would not deprive them of elementary religious teaching. At the death of Madame Janet, he insisted that she have a Catholic burial, as he himself was given some years later. The more one studies Janet's works, the more one gets the feeling that his Socratic smile concealed a wisdom that he took to the grave.

Janet's Contemporaries

No creative mind ever works alone. The greatest pioneers have not only masters and disciples, but also fellow-travelers, men of the same generation who may be friendly, hostile, or indifferent, but who follow a parallel course of evolution and whose ideas are bound to influence one another.

If we take a bird's-eye view of Pierre Janet's generation, that is of the men who were born in the same year or within one or two years from that year, we find, in France, an impressive list of great thinkers. To Pierre Janet's generation belong among others the philosophers Henri Bergson (1859–1941), Emile Meyerson (1859–1933), Edmond Goblot (1858–1935), and Maurice Blondel (1861–1949); the sociologists Émile Durkheim (1858–1917) and Lucien Lévy-Bruhl (1857–1939); the socialist leader Jean Jaurès (1859–1914); the mathematician and philosopher Gaston Milhaud (1858–1918); and the psychologist Alfred Binet (1857–1911).

A rapid glance at Bergson's biography shows a certain parallelism between his life and that of Janet.[66] Both were born in Paris in 1859. Both studied in a lyceum in Paris (Bergson at the Lycée Condorcet, Janet at the Collège Sainte-Barbe). Both were accepted at the Ecole Normale Supérieure, Bergson in 1878, Janet in 1879. Both taught philosophy first in a provincial lyceum (Bergson spent one year in Angers and five years in Clermont-Ferrand, Janet, one-half year in Châteauroux and six-and-one-half years in Le Havre). For both men, these years spent in the provinces were a period of maturation and intensive work. Both experimented with hypnotism. Bergson's first paper, in 1886, was devoted to the subject of unconscious simulation in hypnosis, and Janet's first paper in the same year was about his experiments with Léonie.[67] Both papers revealed their authors' skepticism about parapsychological interpretations. Both men also edited the work of a philosopher, and both presented their theses at the Sorbonne in 1889.[68] Each man sought to find a starting point for psychology in the most elementary psychological phenomena; Bergson in his *Essay on the Immediate Data of Consciousness* and Janet in his *Psychological Automatism* approached the same problem, though in a different way. Both were appointed to teach philosophy in a Paris lyceum; Bergson coming somewhat earlier in the Collège Rollin where Janet became his immediate successor. Both also taught at the Sorbonne and later at the Collège de France, where Bergson had been appointed earlier than Janet and defended Janet's candidacy at the assembly of professors. For many years afterward they were colleagues at the Collège de France, later also at the Académie des Sciences Morales et Politiques, and they also met socially. Finally, it is also remarkable that both men revealed their deep-seated preoccupation with religion late in life.

Bergson's influence on Janet's work was extremely important, as Janet duly acknowledged. Bergson's notion of the "attention to life" (*attention à la vie*) shows much similarity to Janet's *fonction du réel,* and what Bergson said about the spearhead of life as the avant-garde of evolution also shows much similarity with Janet's concept of "psychological tension." Janet also acknowledged that when he began presenting psychological facts as conducts, it was most probably through the influence of Bergson's first books.[69] But Janet's influence on Bergson was of no lesser importance. In *Matter and Memory*, Bergson refers to Janet's research on the dissociations of personality, and he also borrowed the term *fonction fabulatrice*, from Janet, a concept that is perhaps not very different from what Frederick Myers had called the mythopoetic function of the unconscious.

No less complex were the reciprocal influences between Janet and Binet. Alfred Binet was two years older than Janet, having been born in 1857 in Nice.[70] He first studied at the Nice lyceum, then in Paris at the Lycée Louis-le-Grand where Babinski was his schoolmate. His first interest lay in law, later in biology, and then in psychology. He then became acquainted with Ribot and Charcot, who allowed him to examine patients on his wards. One of his first pieces of research was on the "psychic life of micro-organisms."[71] Like Janet and Bergson, Binet was also interested in the problem of the most elementary form of psychological life, and he approached the problem by examining living creatures that he considered to be on the lowest degree of the life scale, that is, the infusoria, and he believed to have evidenced in them manifestations of sensory activity, intelligence, and even rudiments of mutual help. His first book, published in 1886, was the *Psychology of Reasoning*, in which he chose hypnotism as a method of approach, and concluded that there is a permanent and, automatic process of unconscious reasoning at the bottom of man's psychic activity.[72] For several years he devoted himself to investigations of hypnosis, hysteria, and dual personality. Binet's investigations ran parallel to those of Janet, so that either the one or the other was ahead in his research at given times. When Janet published his *L'Automatisme Psychologique*, Binet wrote a detailed review for the *Revue Philosophique* in which he acknowledged that Janet had anticipated certain results that he had expected to find in his own research, thus making it unnecessary for him to continue.[73] Like Janet, Binet was also interested in the history of animal magnetism and wrote a book on that subject in collaboration with Féré.[74] However, he lacked the penetrating knowledge that Janet had of the subject. In following years, Janet and Binet must have met fairly frequently. They each referred to the work of the other, and both worked for some time at the laboratory of experimental psychology at the Sorbonne. But it seems that for some reason an estrangement took place between them. In 1893, Binet founded *L'Année Psychologique,* a well-known yearbook of psychology that he used to publish his numerous articles but that never carried any contribution by Janet. Binet suffered serious setbacks in his career. When he applied for a professorship at the Collège de France, he lost out to Janet, and when he applied for a professorship at the Sorbonne, Georges Dumas was given preference. This caused Binet gradually to withdraw from contact with his colleagues. His laboratory at the Sorbonne was located in a remote attic to which few people could find the way, and, owing to his extreme shyness, he never attended any congresses. But he was a hard worker who pioneered in many fields of psychology. In his *Experimental Study of Intelligence,* he published a detailed investigation of the intellectual functions of his two daughters, Armande and Marguerite, conducted with the help of psychological tests, and showed that they represented two psychological types—precisely those that, some years later, C. G. Jung was to call the introvert and the extrovert.[75] It was Binet who established the first scale for measuring the intelligence of schoolchildren, the Binet and Simon test, in 1905; he was a pioneer in child psychology and experimental pedagogy; and in sexual psychology. He described fetishism, which term he coined. Binet also wrote gloomy theatrical plays under a pseudonym, either alone or in collaboration. He was an indefatigable writer who unfortunately scattered his activities in many fields and never succeeded in creating the final work in which he would have concentrated the result of his life's work. When he died prematurely in 1911, he had apparently lost all contact with Janet, with whom his work had been so closely related for a long time.

Other parallels could be drawn between Janet and Durkheim, Lévy-Bruhl, and others among his contemporaries. It would be an impossible undertaking to try to ascertain the mutual influences these men had on one another. Seen from a distance, they appear like statues standing in majestic isolation; seen at close range, it becomes apparent that they were engaged in more or less intermittent dialogues.

Janet's Work: I—Philosophy

One cannot fully understand Pierre Janet's psychological system without taking into account its philosophical substructure. Janet had studied philosophy at the Lycée Louis-le-Grand, and then at the Ecole Normale Supérieure, where that discipline was taught by the moralist Bersot, the logician Rabier, the academic philosopher Ollé-Laprune, and the neo-Kantian Boutroux. No doubt Janet was also familiar with the works of his uncle Paul Janet. As he says in his autobiography, Janet had shown deep religious feelings in his youth and underwent a religious crisis at the age of seventeen. He had dreamed of building a philosophy that would achieve a reconciliation of science and religion. "I have not found that marvel," he admitted in his old age, adding that his endeavors to build a new psychology had been a substitute for the dream of his youth. There is reason to believe, however, that Janet did more than merely dream, for some time, but actually sought for that philosophical system. The only way to gain some clarity in this question is to examine Janet's philosophical writings, i.e. his textbooks of philosophy.

In his first textbook, published in 1894, Janet makes a sharp distinction between scientific and moral philosophy.[76] The first part starts with a definition of science: men have defended themselves against natural forces, have mastered them, and have then tried to modify the world. Science was born out of man's urge to conquer the world, which implied understanding it, first by means of acquiring knowledge of it, hence the need for an appropriate method based on analysis and synthesis. Janet then gives a classification of sciences and a survey of the main ones: mathematics, natural sciences, moral sciences (which include psychology and sociology), and history. Next comes a chapter on the great scientific hyphotheses; it includes a criticism of the Darwinian theory and of the exaggerated cult of progress, saying that it is dangerous to expect too much of progress because it leads to contempt for the present and destruction of the past. The second part of the book, devoted to moral philosophy, includes an analysis of such problems as freedom, responsibility, conscience, and justice, and finally the existence of God and religion. The book, which had started with a Baconian outlook, ends with a quotation from Epictetus: "I am a rational being and I have to praise God; that is my calling and I follow it." It is clear that Janet devoted considerable care and thought to that book. It contains almost verbatim the lecture he gave in 1882 at the age of twenty-two in Châteauroux on the concept of property. Each philosophical term receives a clear definition. For each problem, the main theories are expounded in an objective way. It would seem that, under the guise of a textbook for schools, Janet had given a sketch of his own philosophy. Two years later, in 1896, the second edition was fully recast. It contained the same matter, but now ranged according to the syllabus of the official teaching of philosophy in the lyceums, as were the following and often augmented editions.

It is not clear at what point Janet's main interest shifted from philosophy to psychology, as it had previously shifted from religion to philosophy. His later attitude toward philosophy may be inferred from what he wrote in his introduction to his edition of Malebranche: Science is possible only through the inspiration of some general ideas that furnish a method and means of explanation. These general ideas are invented by philosophers, who, in order to conceive them, need a metaphysical or mystical scaffolding.[77] In that regard, it is interesting to see what Janet took from philosophy when he turned to psychology. His concern was to use a strictly scientific method, to approach psychological phenomena in a scientific spirit of which he said curiosity and independence were the basis, to the exclusion of the principle of authority and tradition. Janet defined the scientific method as a combination of analysis and synthesis. Analysis means to break down a whole into its elements, provided that the latter are the true constituent elements. An anatomist, for instance, does not cut the body into four or one hundred parts, but separates the muscles, nerves, blood vessels, and other parts of the body. Janet visualized scientific psychology in the same manner: it must begin with psychological analysis, that is, identification and separate study of elementary psychological functions, a phase that would be followed later by psychological synthesis, that is, the reconstruction of the whole on the basis of the separate parts.

Janet's Work: II—Psychological Automatism

Quite a number of philosophers before Janet had attempted to reconstruct the human psyche by means of analysis and synthesis. Most of them had used sensation as the basic element and starting point. Condillac had imagined the philosophical myth of a statue that would be endowed with one sense after another, and with this starting point he described the hypothetical development of the statue's mind; the only drawback was that it was a purely fictitious construction. When Janet embarked on a similar undertaking, he remained on the solid foundation of experimental psychology. His main thesis, *Psychological Automatism*, bears the revealing subtitle: "Experimental-Psychological Essay on the Inferior Forms of Human Activity." Thus, Janet does not start, as did Condillac, from "pure sensation," but from "activity," or rather he never dissociates consciousness from activity.

Psychological Automatism contains the fruit of the research performed by Janet in Le Havre from 1882 to 1888. The articles he published serially in the *Revue Philosophique* during that time enable us to follow the development of that research. After the first experiments with hypnosis at a distance on Léonie that Janet found unconvincing, he examined Lucie, a young woman of nineteen, who was seized with fits of terror without apparent motivation. By means of automatic writing, Janet found both the cause and the meaning of the terror fits. When she was seven, two men hiding behind a curtain had made a practical joke of frightening her. A second personality within Lucie, Adrienne, was reliving this initial episode when she had her fits of terror. Janet described how he made use of the rapport in order to relieve the patient of her symptoms, and how the second personality eventually disappeared.[78] Lucie had a relapse eight months later, which, however, receded rapidly with the help of a therapy combining hypnosis and automatic writing. Janet described the phenomenon of the rapport in a more precise way, and particularly its characteristic feature of electivity, that is, the permanent state of suggestibility toward one person only, Janet, to the exclusion of all others.[79]

New experiments with Léonie brought Janet to a number of discoveries of particular interest.[80] He showed that, under hypnosis, two very different sets of psychological manifestations can be elicited: on one side are the "roles" played by the subject in order to please the hypnotist, on the other side is the unknown personality, which can manifest itself spontaneously, particularly as a return to childhood. In hypnosis, Léonie referred to herself by her childhood surname of Nichette. But behind that hypnotic personality, a third hidden one may exist and emerge in turn as the hypnotization of the second personality. The remarkable fact was that this third personality was a reviviscence after twenty years of an old hypnotic personality that the magnetizers had elicited in Léonie in the past. It had never manifested itself in the meantime, but now appeared exactly as it had been in the past. Janet found that a similar case had already been published by Bertrand in 1823.

L'Automatisme psychologique was dedicated to the doctors Gibert and Powilewicz who had provided Janet with the patients: fourteen hysterical women, five hysterical men, and eight psychotics and epileptics. Most of the research, however, was based on the investigation of four women: Rose, Lucie, Marie, and above all the celebrated Léonie. Janet strove to remain on the solid ground of objective facts, and for that reason refrained from speaking of parapsychological experiments with Léonie. He also had to be careful about and abstained from reporting on the therapeutic implications of his research, first because the Faculté des Lettres was sensitive on this point, and second in order not to arouse the suspicion of the physicians.

The term "psychological automatism" was not new. It had been used among others by Despine, who defined it as "very complex and intelligent acts reaching a goal which is perfectly specific and adjusted to circumstances; acts exactly similar to those which the ego commands in other occasions through the same apparatus."[81] However, for Despine, psychological automatism is the product of a living machine devoid of consciousness, whereas for Janet it is a psychological phenomenon in its own right, always entailing a rudimentary consciousness.

Janet classified the manifestations of psychological automatism into two groups: total automatism, a process extending to the subject as a whole, and partial automatism, which implies that a part of the personality is split off from the awareness of the personality and follows an autonomous, subconscious development.[82] The most rudimentary form of total automatism, he said, is catalepsy. The state of consciousness of a cataleptic could be compared to that of an individual who begins to recover from a syncope: there is some consciousness without consciousness of the ego. Janet's investigations on catalepsy revealed three findings: (1) That these states of consciousness tend to continue without modification unless there is some stimulation from outside; (2) That there is no consciousness without some form of motility; (3) That any emotion that is elicited during that state tends to determine a movement adequate to that feeling, provided that the feeling is not contrary to the personality of the subject.

A less rudimentary state than catalepsy is artificial somnambulism, that is, the hypnotic state of which Janet gives three criteria: (1) amnesia upon awakening; (2) memory of previous hypnotic states during hypnosis; and (3) memory of the waking state during hypnotic states. But things are more complex, and here Janet gives an account of his experiments with Léonie and her three conditions: Léonie I, Léonie II, and Léonie III (alias Léonore), and of the relationships of these three existences to one another. Janet believed that he had found definite correlations between the various conditions of amnesia and memory on one hand and the various conditions of amnesia and memory on other hand, and he interprets the phenomenon of posthypnotic amnesia by a changed condition in sensitivity.

More complex than the hypnotic state is that which Janet calls successive existences (thus avoiding the expression alternating personalities). Janet analyzes how each of these personalities feels about the others: sometimes the other ones are not perceived as such, but there is a sense of something strange or peculiar in oneself; sometimes they are perceived with a feeling of hostility or contempt. Sometimes the other personality is more childish and adopts the nickname of its childhood.

Janet begins the study of Partial Automatism with its simplest forms, partial catalepsy and the distractions, that is peculiar states of absent-mindedness. In the latter, while the subject's attention is kept absorbed with something else, the physician whispers a question to which the subject will answer unaware. Janet showed that by means of distractions, suggestions or even hallucinations can be impressed upon the subject, which produces curious mixtures and interferences between conscious and subconscious manifestations. Closely related to the distractions is the phenomenon of automatic writing, widely practiced by the spiritists since 1850. Placing a pencil in the hand of an individual, and keeping his attention elsewhere, one can see him starting to write things of which he is not aware, and elicit in that way large fragments of subconscious material. Another manifestation of partial automatism is posthypnotic suggestion, a controversial problem for which Janet proposed the following explanation: the subconscious mind, which has been brought to the fore during hypnosis and has now receded, persists and will see to the punctual execution of orders given by the hypnotist during hypnosis. The difficult problem of the simultaneous existences is interpreted by Janet's general theory of the *désagrégations psychologiques,* a concept not very different from that of psychological dissolution, first propounded by Moreau (de Tours) and later by Hughlings Jackson.

The remainder of the book is devoted to the description and interpretation of various forms of Partial Psychological Automatism: the divining rod, spiritism and mediumism, obsessive impulses, fixed ideas and hallucinations of psychotic patients, and finally what he calls possession, that is, the attitudes, acts, and feelings of the individual being controlled by a subconscious idea, unknown to him, as was the case with "Lucie." She would say with gestures of terror, "I am afraid and I don't know why." Janet explains, "It is because the unconscious has its dream; it sees men behind the curtains, and puts the body in the attitude of terror." When Léonie says, "I cry and I don't know why," one may also assume that a subconscious idea is acting behind things. "One should go through the entire field of mental diseases and a part of physical diseases to show the mental and bodily disturbances resulting from the banishment of a thought from personal consciousness," Janet concludes.

Psychological Automatism, of which parts had been known through the publication of excerpts in the *Revue Philosophique,* was hailed from the start as a classic of the psychological sciences. It clarified many controversial matters while raising new questions. Its main features can be summarized as follows: (1) Seeing that he worked with fresh patients, Janet escaped the objection that the symptoms investigated were the product of the hothouse culture of the Salpêtrière and its mental contagion. One patient, however, Léonie, had already been experimented on by old magnetizers, and by investigating her life history, Janet was led to discover the forgotten world of one century of research by magnetizers and hypnotists.[83] (2) In his psychological analysis Janet departed from the frame of reference of classical psychology, with its sharp distinction between intellect, affectivity, and will. Janet contended that even at the lowest levels of psychic life there was no sensation or feeling without movement, and he agreed with Fouillée that it is the natural tendency of an idea to develop into an act. (3) Janet utilized the dynamic approach in terms of psychic force and weakness. In severe cases of hysteria he told of psychological misery (*misère psychologique*). (4) Janet emphasized the notion of the "field of consciousness" and its narrowing in hysterical patients as a result of their psychological weakness. (5) At the lowest degree of mental life, Janet found the two levels of feeling *per se,* and feeling in relation to the conscious ego. This caused him to formulate the concept of function of synthesis (the embryo of his future concept of the hierarchy of psychic functions and of psychological tension). (6) Turning to the century-old concept of the rapport, Janet conceived it as a particular form of *anaesthesia,* that is, a distortion in the perception of the world, in other words as a peculiar mode of perception of the world centered around the person of the hypnotist. (7) Janet contended that certain hysterical symptoms can be related to the existence of split parts of personality (subconscious fixed ideas) endowed with an autonomous life and development. He showed their origin in traumatic events of the past and the possibility of a cure of hysterical symptoms through the discovery and subsequent dissolution of these subconscious psychological systems. In that regard, the story of the illness and psychological cure of Marie deserves special mention:

This young person was brought from the country to the hospital of Le Havre at the age of 19 because she was considered insane, and the hope of seeing her cured had almost been given up. The facts were that she had periods of convulsive attacks with delirium which lasted for days. After a period of observation, it became clear that the sickness consisted of periodical manifestations which occurred regularly at the time of her menstruations, and of less severe manifestations which were more prolonged and occurred at irregular times during the intervals.

Let us begin with the first ones. At the time preceding her menstruations, Marie's character changed; she became gloomy and violent, which was not in her habits, and suffered pains, nervous spasms, and shivering in her entire body. However, things went on almost regularly during the first day, but hardly 20 hours after the beginning, the menstruation stopped suddenly and a great tremor seized the whole body; then, a sharp pain ascended slowly from the abdomen to the throat, and a great hysterical crisis ensued. The attacks, although they were very violent, never lasted for a long time, and never had resembled epileptoid tremors; instead, there was a very long and severe delirium. At times, she would utter cries of terror, ceaselessly speaking of blood and fire, fleeing in order to escape the flames; at other times she would play as a child, speak to her mother, climb on the stove or on the furniture, and create havoc in the ward. This delirium and the violent bodily contortions alternated with short periods of rest during 48 hours. The attack ended with vomiting blood several times, after which everything came back approximately to normal. After one or two days of rest, Marie would quiet herself and remembered nothing of the episode. During the intervals of those intense monthly manifestations, she maintained limited contractures at the arms or the intercostal muscles or various, changing anaesthesias, and above all a complete and permanent blindness of the left eye (. . .) Furthermore, she occasionally had smaller crises without the great delirium, but which were characterized predominantly by attitudes of terror. This sickness, which was so obviously linked to the menstrual periods, seemed to be uniquely a physical one, and of little interest for the psychologist. Therefore, at the beginning, I dealt very little with this person. At most, I performed on her a few hypnotic experiments and a few studies on her anaesthesia, but I avoided anything which could have disturbed her at the time when her major manifestations were approaching. She remained for seven months at the hospital, during which the various medications and hydrotherapy had not brought forth the least modification. Moreover, therapeutic suggestions, notably suggestions concerning her menstruation, had nothing but bad effects and increased the delirium.

Around the end of the eighth month she complained about her sad lot and said, with a kind of despair, that she was well aware that her symptoms would continue to recur. "Look here," I told her out of curiosity, "explain to me now what happens when you are going to be sick."—"But, you know it . . . everything stops, I have a big shivering, and I don't know what happens next." I wanted to get precise information about the way her periods had been inaugurated and had been interrupted. She did not give a clear answer, and seemed to have forgotten most of the events about which I asked her. It then occurred to me to put her into a deep somnambulic condition, a state where (as we have seen) it is possible to bring back seemingly forgotten memories, and thus I was able to find out the exact memory of an incident which had hitherto been only very incompletely known.

At the age of 13, she had had her first menstruation, but, as a result of a childish idea or of something she had heard and misunderstood, she imagined that there was some shame in it, and she tried a means of stopping the flow as soon as possible. About 20 hours after the beginning, she went out secretly and plunged herself into a big bucket of cold water. The success was complete; the menstruation was suddenly stopped, and in spite of a violent shivering, she was able to come back home. She was sick for a rather long time and had several days of delirium. However, everything settled down, and the menstruation did not appear again until five years later. When it reappeared it brought back the disturbances I observed. Now, if one compares the sudden stopping, the shivering, the pains she describes today in waking state, with what she describes in a somnambulic condition—which, incidentally, was confirmed from other sources—one comes to this conclusion: Every month, the scene of the cold bath repeats itself, brings forth the same stopping of the menstruation and a delirium which is, it is true, much more severe than previously, until a supplementary hemorrhage takes place through the stomach. But, in her normal state of consciousness, she knows nothing about all this, not even that the shivering is brought forth by the hallucination of cold. It is therefore probable that this scene takes place below consciousness, and from it the other disturbances erupt.

This assumption—true or false—being made, and after consulting Dr. Powilewicz, I tried to take away from somnambulic consciousness this fixed and absurd idea that the menstruation was stopped by a cold bath. At first, I could not manage to do it; the fixed idea persisted; and the menstruation, which was due for two days later, occurred as usual. But, since I now had more time at my disposal, I tried again: I was able to succeed only thanks to a singular means. It was necessary to bring her back, through suggestion, to the age of thirteen, put her back into the initial circumstances of the delirium, convince her that the menstruation had lasted for three days and was not interrupted through any regrettable incident. Now, once this was done, the following menstruation came at the due point, and lasted for three days, without any pain, convulsion or delirium.

After noticing this result, the other symptoms were to be investigated. I omit the details of the psychological exploration, which was at times difficult. The attacks of terror were the repetition of an emotion which this young girl had felt when seeing, at the age of 16, an old woman killing herself by falling down stairs; blood, of which she always spoke during her crises, was memory from this scene; in regard to the picture of the fire, it was probably an association of ideas, because it was not linked with anything precise. Through the same procedure as before, through bringing the subject back by suggestion to the moment of the accident, I succeeded, not without difficulty, to show her that the old woman had only stumbled but had not killed herself: the attacks of terror did not recur.

Finally, I wanted to study the blindness of the left eye; but Marie was opposed to it and said that she was like that from birth. It was easy to check by means of somnambulism that she was mistaken; if one transforms her into a five year-old child, by the well-known methods, she takes back the sensitivity she had at that age and one observes that she sees well with both eyes. Therefore, it was at the age of six years that the blindness had started. On what occasion? Marie maintains, in waking state, that she does not know. During somnambulism, I make her play the chief scenes of her life at that time, and I see that the blindness starts at a certain point on the occasion of a trifling incident. She had been compelled, in spite of her cries, to sleep with a child of the same age who had impetigo on the entire left side of her face. Some time later, Marie developed an almost identical impetigo, in the same place. Then plagues appeared again several times at about the same time of year and were finally cured; but no one noticed that, henceforward, she had an anaesthesia of the left side of her face and was blind in the left eye! Since that time the anaesthesia had persisted or at least—in order not to go beyond that which can be observed—whatever be the period into which I set her back through suggestion, this anaesthesia remains constant although her various other anaesthesias would disappear completely at times. Same attempt as previously at cure. I put her back with the child who had so horrified her; I make her believe that the child is very nice and does not have impetigo (she is half-convinced. After two re-enactments of this scene I get the best of it); she caresses without fear the imaginary child. The sensitivity of the left eye reappears without difficulty, and when I wake her up, Marie sees clearly with the left eye.

It is now five months since these experiments were performed. Marie has never shown the slightest signs of hysteria, she is doing well and above all is becoming stronger. Her physical aspect has changed thoroughly. I do not attach to this cure more importance than it deserves, and do not know how long it will last, but I found this story interesting as showing the importance of fixed subconscious ideas and the role they play in certain physical illnesses, as well as in emotional illnesses.[84]

Janet's Work: III—Psychological Analysis

As soon as he started his medical studies in Paris at the end of 1899, Janet took up his psychological investigations at the Salpêtrière, where he had the patients of the wards of Charcot, Falret, and Séglas at his disposal.

One of the first patients on whom he demonstrated his method of psychological analysis and synthesis was Marcelle, a young woman of twenty.[85] She had been admitted to the ward of Dr. Falret on account of severe mental disturbances that had started at the age of fourteen and had gradually worsened. She showed a peculiar difficulty in moving her legs although she was not paralyzed, and also had severe disturbances of memory and thought. How could such a patient be approached from the point of view of experimental psychology? Janet warned that any kind of psychological measurement of functions would be fruitless. "An experimental approach," he said, "consists above all in knowing one's patient well—in his life, his schooling, his character, and his ideas—and to be convinced that one never knows him enough. . . . Then one must put that person in simple and specific circumstances and note accurately what he will do and say." The observation must be directed first toward the behavior of the patient, beginning with his actions and words, then scrutinizing each specific function. The most conspicuous symptom in Marcelle was her difficulty in movement. It appeared that automatic habitual movements were easy, whereas movements implying a voluntary decision were hampered. The stream of thought was often interrupted by what the patient called clouds during which her mind was invaded by all kinds of confused ideas and hallucinations. Memory proved good for all events that had occurred before the age of fifteen, vague for the events extending from fifteen to nineteen, and there was complete amnesia for all that had happened from that time onward. The patient was absolutely unable to picture the future and felt estranged from her own personality.

Janet now undertook to range the symptoms according to their depth (*profondeur*). On the most superficial level were the clouds, which he compared to the effects of posthypnotic suggestions. He wondered whether their content might not be a partial reflection of the popular novels she had read with passion for several years. On an intermediate level were the impulses that Janet ascribed to the action of subconscious fixed ideas issuing from certain traumatic memories. Deep-seated was the morbid ground, depending on heredity, severe past physical illnesses, and early traumatic events.

Psychological analysis had to be followed by psychological synthesis, that is, a reconstruction of the development of the illness. First there had been hereditary constitution, then a severe typhoid fever at the age of fourteen, which had struck a fatal blow by robbing the patient of the capacity for adjustment. This resulted in a vicious circle; being unable to adjust to new situations, Marcelle retreated into her daydreams, which made her more maladjusted, and so on. Another trauma came a year later. Her father, who had been a paraplegic for the past two years, died. An unfortunate love affair was the last blow, bringing suicidal ideas. At this point the patient lost her memory of recent events.

What could be done for this patient? At first, Janet tried vainly to develop the function of synthesis by means of elementary reading exercises. Then he tried using suggestion to combat the fixed ideas, but one symptom was hardly dispelled when it was replaced by another, while the patient's resistance during hypnosis was increased. Attempts with automatic writing resulted in classical hysterical crises. However, Janet soon noticed that these various attempts were not fruitless. To be sure, hypnosis and automatic writing unleashed crises, but afterward the mind was clearer. The crises became increasingly severe, and the fixed ideas that emerged were of increasingly ancient origin. All those ideas that the patient had developed in the course of her life appeared one after the other, in reverted order. "By removing the superficial layer of the delusions. I favored the appearance of old and tenacious fixed ideas which dwelt still at the bottom of her mind. The latter disappeared in turn, thus bringing forth a great improvement." Among other points discussed in that case history was the statement emphasized by Janet that "in the human mind, nothing ever gets lost," and "subconscious fixed ideas are both the result of mental weakness and a source of further and worse mental weakness."

Though Janet was careful to choose only fresh patients at the Salpêtrière in order to avoid the ill effects of mental contagion that was rampant there, he made an exception in the case of an almost legendary patient, Madame D., around whom Charcot had developed his concept of dynamic amnesia. In a town in western France, the thirty-four-year-old married seamstress was found on August 28, 1891, in a state of utmost anxiety. An unknown man, she said, had just called her by her name and told her that her husband was dead. The news was untrue and the incident was never clarified, but for three days, the patient remained in hysterical lethargy and delirium. On August 31, she manifested a retrograde amnesia extending over six weeks. She remembered her entire life up to July 14, 1891. During the previous six weeks there had been some events in her life such as the prize distribution ceremony at her children's school, and a trip she had made to Royan, but she did not remember any of it. She also had a complete anterograde amnesia. She forgot from one minute to the next as do patients afflicted with Korsakov disease. Thus, she was bitten by a presumably rabid dog, burned with a cautery, brought to the Pasteur Institute in Paris by her husband, but could remember nothing of this. Before leaving Paris, her husband brought her to Charcot at the Salpêtrière, where she was admitted. It was observed that she spoke at night in her dreams and told of seemingly forgotten incidents. This prompted Charcot to have her hypnotized by one of his assistants. In one of Charcot's memorable clinical lectures, on December 22, 1891, Madame D. was shown to the audience before being hypnotized. Charcot asker her about her husband's death, Royan, the dog bite, the Eiffel Tower, the Pasteur Institute, and the Salpêtrière. She could remember nothing of that. After this first interrogation, the patient was taken away, hypnotized, and brought back to the auditorium. This time, when Charcot asked the same questions, she was able to answer all of them.[86] The patient was entrusted to Janet for psychotherapy. He noticed that, in spite of the continuous amnesia, recent memories must have been somehow retained, otherwise the patient could not have become so well adjusted to hospital life. Janet then undertook to explore those subconscious memories. In addition to the manifestation of forgotten memories in dreams and in hypnotic state, he was able to elicit them by means of automatic writing and distractions, and by a new procedure, automatic talking, consisting of letting the patient talk aloud at random instead of writing automatically.[87] But why had the patient been unable to remember those latent memories? Janet assumed that it was because of the psychic trauma, and so undertook the dissolution of the fixed ideas. Under hypnosis, he cautiously evoked the figure of the man who had frightened her, and suggested to the patient a modification of the man's picture. He then brought her to reenact the scene, in which the unknown man was now replaced by Janet himself asking her if he could be a guest in her house. Memories crowded back into consciousness, but the patient now had severe headaches and suicidal impulses, which eventually disappeared. The hypnotic treatment was supplemented by a specially devised program of intellectual training. Here, too, Janet emphasized the twofold aspect of the fixed ideas as being both result and cause of mental weakness.[88] In the last volume of Charcot's *Clinics of Diseases of the Nervous System,* Madame D.'s story was included with a note acknowledging the favorable result of Janet's treatment.[89]

Another of Janet's first patients in Paris was Justine, a forty-year-old married woman who came to the outpatient service of Dr. Séglas at the Salpêtrière in October 1890. For several years she had a morbid fear of cholera and would shout repeatedly, "Cholera . . . it's taking me!" which would signal a hysterical crisis. As a child she already had a morbid fear of death, probably because she sometimes helped her mother who was a nurse and who had to watch dying patients. She also once saw the corpses of two patients who had died of cholera. Janet treated Justine as an out-patient for three years and achieved one of his most celebrated cures with her.[90] Here too, psychological analysis could not be separated from the therapeutic process.

Janet began by analyzing the content of the hysterical crises. It was useless trying to talk to Justine during her crisis. She did not seem to hear. Janet therefore entered the private drama of her crisis as a second actor. When the patient cried, "Cholera! He will take me!" Janet answered, "Yes, he holds you by the right leg!" and the patient withdrew that leg. Janet then asked, "Where is he, your cholera?" to which she would reply, "Here! See him, he's bluish, and he stinks!" Janet could then begin a dialogue with her and was able to carry it on throughout the crisis and gradually transform the crisis into an ordinary hypnotic state. Later he could easily elicit hypnosis directly and obtain a full description of her subjective experience during the crisis. She saw two corpses standing nearby, one of whom stood closer to her, an ugly naked old man of greenish shade with a stench of putrefaction. Simultaneously she heard bells tolling and shouts of "Cholera, cholera!" Once the crisis was over, Justine seemed to have forgotten everything but the idea of cholera, which remained constant in her mind. Janet elaborated on how hypnosis could be used in such a case. Commands given to the hypnotized patient were of limited usefulness. The breaking down of the hallucinatory picture was more effective but it was a slow procedure and also had limitations. The most effective method proved to be substitution, that is, suggestions of a gradual transformation of the hallucinatory picture. The naked corpse was provided with clothes and identified with a Chinese general whom Justine had been greatly impressed to see at the Universal Exposition. The Chinese general started to walk and act so that instead of being terrifying his picture became comical. The hysterical attack changed in that it now consisted of a few cries followed by fits of laughter. Then the cries disappeared, and the visions of cholera persisted only when she dreamed, until Janet expelled them in turn by suggesting innocuous dreams. This result had required about one year of treatment. But the fixed idea of cholera persisted both on the conscious and the subconscious level. Sometimes Justine was observed whispering the word "cholera" while her mind was taken up with some other activity. Attempts with automatic writing produced nothing but endless repetitions of the word "cholera, cholera. . . ." Janet now directed his attack against the word itself, and suggested that *Cho-le-ra* was the name of the Chinese general. The syllable *cho* was associated with other terminations until the day arrived when the word "cholera" lost its evil connotations.

But the patient was not yet cured. After the disappearance of the main fixed idea, secondary fixed ideas began to develop. Janet classified them into three groups: (1) The *derivative fixed ideas* resulting from association with the main one (for example, morbid fear of coffins and cemeteries). (2) The *stratified fixed ideas*: One is surprised, after having removed a fixed idea, to see another one emerge that has no connection with the first, or any relation to circumstances surrounding it. It is then a more ancient idea, previous to the one just treated, which reappears. When this one is removed in turn, one discovers a third, even older one, so that treatment of the principal fixed ideas from which the patient has suffered during his life must be applied in reverse order. (3) The *accidental fixed ideas* that are absolutely new and provoked by any incident in daily life are easy to erase, however, provided they are treated immediately. The fact that they can occur so easily proves that the patient is in a state of high perceptivity, which in turn creates the need for further treatment. Suggestive treatment cannot be applied here. Rather, the solution of the problem lies in developing the capacity of attention and mental synthesis in the patient. To that end, Janet devised a program of elementary school exercises for Justine, beginning with easy arithmetic operations or a few lines of writing, for which he secured the cooperation of her very understanding husband. After one year of training, that is, by the end of the third year, the patient was in an apparently normal condition, but Janet still cautioned against talking of full recovery.

In the synthetic reconstruction of Justine's illness, Janet considered heredity and the life history of the patient. In the latter, he discussed the reciprocal action of physical illnesses and psychic trauma. At the age of six or seven, Justine had a severe disease of unknown nature, perhaps meningitis. Later she had typhoid fever (Janet stresses that in many patients typhoid fever or influenza often occur prior to a severe neurosis). As a child, Justine had suffered several frights and emotional shocks, culminating in the episode of the corpses of the patients who had died from cholera. Reconstructing the genealogy of the patient over three or four generations, Janet found that there had been, in the older generations, morbid impulses and obsessions, and alcoholics, in the younger generations, epileptics and imbeciles, exactly as in those pedigrees on the basis of which Morel based his theory of mental degeneration. However, Janet did not believe in the fatal character of degeneration; he contended that diseases of families can recede just as can diseases of individuals. The main point, he said, was to understand that the disease extends beyond the individual, this being also the reason why, in a case of that kind, one should never expect complete recovery. Warning against another illusion, he stressed that "the easier the cure seems to be, the sicker the mind actually is," because a high suggestibility is the mark of great weakness of the mind, which leads the patient to a need for somnambulism, a need that can become a kind of addiction, which Janet deemed as dangerous as morphinism. Such patients not only crave to be hypnotized but have a permanent need to confess to the psychiatrist whose picture they keep constantly in their subconscious mind, and to be scolded and directed by him. Justine had frequent visions of Janet and heard his voice. In a hallucinatory state she asked him for advice, and he answered with good counsel which, interestingly enough, was more than a mere repetition of what he had actually said, but proved to be of a novel and wise nature. The therapeutic problem, Janet concluded, consists first of assuming direction of the patient's mind, and second of reducing that direction to the necessary minimum, particularly by spacing the sessions with the patient. At first he saw Justine several times a week, then once a week, and, in the third year, once a month. For how long would such treatment have to go on? Janet answers by quoting the story of Morel who had magnetized a psychotic patient at his mental hospital and cured her. The patient was discharged but came to see him at regular intervals. However, when Morel died, she relapsed abruptly and had to be committed permanently. "Let us hope that this accident will not happen too soon to our patients," Janet concluded.

Another of Janet's celebrated cures was that of Achilles. This man of thirty-three was brought to the Salpêtrière at the end of 1890 with manifestations of demoniacal possession. He came from a superstitious environment and his father was said to have met the Devil once at the foot of a tree. Achilles was in a state of furious agitation, repeatedly striking himself, proffering blasphemies, and speaking at times with the voice of the devil, which alternated with his own. Charcot asked Janet to treat this patient. The history of the illness did not greatly clarify matters. About six months before the patient had gone on a short business trip for a few days, and upon his return his wife noticed that he was preoccupied, gloomy, and taciturn. The doctors who examined him could find nothing wrong with him. Suddenly, the man had a terrific fit of laughter, which lasted for two hours, and claimed that he saw hell, Satan, and demons. Then, after tying his legs, he threw himself into a pond, from which he was fished out, and said that this had been a test to make sure whether or not he was possessed. Achilles remained in that condition of devilish possession for several months and Janet noticed that he bore the old classical stigmata of devilish possession. But Achilles refused to speak, and it proved impossible to hypnotize him.

Janet then took advantage of the patient's distractions, put a pencil in his hand, and whispered questions at him from behind. As the hand started to write answers, Janet whispered, "Who are you?" The writing answered, "the Devil," and Janet replied, "Then we can talk together," and required as a proof of the Devil's identity that he should raise the patient's arm against the patient's will, which the Devil did. As a further proof, he asked the Devil to put the patient in a hypnotic condition even against the latter's will, which was also done. Once hypnotized, the patient himself began to answer and told his own story. During his business trip six months before, he had been unfaithful to his wife. He had tried to forget the incident but found then that he was unable to speak. He began to dream of the Devil a great deal, whereupon he suddenly found himself possessed.

As Janet explained, the patient's delusions were more than the mere development of his dreams: "It is the combination, i.e. the reaction of two groups of thoughts which divide this poor mind; it is the mutual interaction of the dream he has and the resistance of the normal person." This is also why suggestion would be insufficient treatment. "One has to search for the basic fact which is at the origin of the delusion. . . . The illness of our patient does not lie in the thought of the demon. That thought is secondary and is rather the interpretation furnished by his superstitious ideas. The true illness is remorse." Janet assured the hypnotized patient of his wife's forgiveness. The delusion disappeared outwardly, but persisted in the dreams, from which it had to be expelled in turn. When publishing this observation in December 1894 Janet said that the patient had so far remained cured for three years, and he drew the conclusion, "Man, all too proud, figures that he is the master of his movements, his words, his ideas and himself.[91] It is perhaps of ourselves that we have the least command. There are crowds of things which operate within ourselves without our will." He added that humans have a propensity to comfort themselves against dull reality by telling themselves fine stories. In some people these stories take the upper hand, to the point where they assume more importance than reality.[92]

Another classical, somewhat later case was that of Irène who was brought to the Salpêtrière at the age of twenty-three with severe hysterical disturbances, somnambulic crises, hallucinations, and amnesia.[93] The illness had started after her mother's death two years before. Irène was the only child of an alcoholic worker and a neurotic mother. She was very intelligent, dutiful, and a hard worker, but anxious and extremely shy. At twenty, she had to take care of her mother who had a severe case of tuberculosis, while at the same time being burdened with having to earn a livelihood for the entire family. During the last two months of her mother's life, Irène had nursed her day and night, without even going to bed. On her mother's death in July 1900, Irène's behavior changed completely. She laughed in the cemetery, did not go into mourning; and began going to the theater. She knew that her mother was dead, but spoke of it as a historical incident that did not concern her. A severe amnesia extended over the three or four months that had preceded her mother's death, and she also had a fairly high degree of amnesia for the events that had followed. From time to time, however, she had hallucinations in which she saw the picture of her mother and heard her voice that sometimes ordered her to commit suicide. Above all, she had somnambulic attacks in which she reenacted her mother's death. This would go on for hours, and Janet said that it was an "admirable dramatic spectacle" and that no actress could have performed these gloomy scenes with such perfection. Irène then spoke for some time with her dead mother and upon her command stretched out on the railway tracks, showing her terror in an impressive way when the train arrived to crush her. She also reenacted other traumatic experiences, such as that of witnessing a man shooting himself with a revolver. Irène had spent three months in isolation at the hospital and had been treated with hydrotherapy and electricity without any result. When Janet tried to hypnotize her, he met with a very strong resistance. Memories returned only with a great deal of effort and stimulation on the part of the therapist. Moreover, the recapture of lost memories was accompanied by severe headaches, as had been the case with Madame D., and recovered memories would easily relapse into amnesia. The main therapeutic agent was the stimulation of memory: "From the moment when Irène became able to think of her mother at will, she ceased to think of her involuntarily; afterward, neither amnesia nor hypermnesia remained; hysterical crises, hallucinations, sudden terrors of subconscious origin disappeared completely."

Janet noticed that in Irène's case the therapeutic process had been the reverse of that of Madame D., in whom the dissolution of the fixed idea had brought forth the disappearance of amnesia. Janet concluded that in such hysterical cases "the illness consists in two things simultaneously: (1) The patient's inability to consciously and voluntarily evoke certain memories; (2) the automatic, irresistible and inopportune revival of these same memories. We thus have to deal with a psychological system which escapes the control of consciousness and develops independently." In the case of Irène as in the others, the hypnotic and suggestive treatment had to be supplemented by a treatment of mental stimulation and re-education.

Gradually, Janet extended the notion of subconscious fixed ideas beyond the field of classical hysteria, for instance, to occurrences of stubborn sleeplessness, recalling that Noizet and the old magnetizers had emphasized the role of will and suggestion in sleep. Janet pointed out that one form of sleeplessness is caused by subconscious fixed ideas, of which he gave the following illustration: A woman of thirty-seven who had lost a child suffered from severe typhoid fever four months later, in the wake of which she manifested an obsessive preoccupation with her dead child for one or two months.[94] When this obsession disappeared, her insomnia started and had now lasted for three years. Soporific medication brought headaches and mental confusion but no sleep. The patient was admitted to the Salpêtrière and watched during the night. At no time was she found asleep. When Janet started to hypnotize her, she first fell asleep for two or three minutes and then woke in terror. Thus, it was established that she could fall asleep but not continue to sleep. Janet succeeded in establishing rapport with her during her few minutes of spontaneous sleep, and, speaking to her gently, he could keep her asleep for as long as two hours. During that time she was able to talk to him and told him that she was constantly faced with the fixed idea of her child's death and burial, which was sometimes replaced by the idea of her father's death. The fixed idea had thus first been an obsessive conscious idea and had then become subconscious, causing the insomnia. Here also, the treatment consisted in the dissociation of the fixed idea, but after the disappearance of the symptoms, the patient remained in need of Janet's persistent direction.

In a study of eight patients suffering from spasms of the trunk muscles, Janet found that each of them had suffered from psychic trauma or emotional shocks.[95] The contracture persists because the emotion persists, he said. It is a kind of "congealed emotion" of which the patient is unaware. Suggestive treatment, he continued, is not enough. One has to treat the subconscious fixed idea and supplement the psychological treatment with massage, the results of which, according to Janet, depend greatly on the personal influence exerted by the masseur upon the patient.

Janet's work features numerous other detailed stories of diseases cured through the identification and dissolution of the "subconscious fixed ideas," beginning with the story of Lucie (1886), Marie (1889), and Marcelle (1891), from which research Janet was to draw the conclusion that "psychological analysis can also have a therapeutic value."[96]

We will now briefly summarize the main findings of Janet's "psychological analysis."

1. There was the discovery of the "subconscious fixed ideas" and of their pathogenic role. Their cause was usually a traumatic or frightening

event that had become subconscious and had been replaced by symptoms. This process was connected, Janet thought, with a narrowing of the field of consciousness.

2. Janet found intermediate levels of subconscious ideas between clear consciousness and the constitutional make-up of patients studied. Furthermore, there appeared even greater complexity in that around primary fixed ideas emerged secondary fixed ideas, through association or substitution. Sometimes there might even be a whole array of subconscious fixed ideas, each one originating at a given point of the patient's life..

3. Subconscious fixed ideas, according to Janet, are at the same time cause and effect of mental weakness, and in that regard constitute a pathological vicious circle. They undergo slow changes. Sometimes they spontaneously develop and increase, sometimes they become modified within the subconscious mind.

4. It is not always easy to identify these subconscious fixed ideas. Sometimes the content of the crisis is revealing (such as in Irène's somnambulic reenactments of her mother's death). More frequently, hysterical crises are disguised reenactments of the subconscious fixed idea. Janet sometimes mentioned the symbolic character of the symptoms (for instance in Marie's case). The subconscious fixed idea has to be sought for by objective means of investigation. Sometimes (as with Madame D.) an inquiry into the patient's dreams would give some clues, but Janet's main approach was through hypnosis, whereby the patient would yield his forgotten memories with more or less resistance. Hypnosis could often be supplemented by automatic writing or the use of distraction. Janet also occasionally used the method of automatic talking (as in the case of Madame D.) or that of crystal gazing. [97]

5. Subconscious fixed ideas are a characteristic feature of hysteria, in contrast to obsessive neuroses where they are conscious. However, Janet soon discovered the existence of subconscious fixed ideas in conditions such as severe sleeplessness and muscular spasms. His study on ambulatory automatism, published jointly with Raymond, seems to have been the first study in which the various acts accomplished during the fugues were explained as the coordinated effects of a variety of subconscious fixed ideas. [98]

6. The therapy must be aimed at the subconscious fixed idea, but Janet emphasized from the beginning that bringing the subconscious ideas into consciousness was not sufficient to cure the patient. It could merely change such an idea into a conscious fixed obsession. Fixed ideas must be destroyed by means of dissociation or transformation. Obviously, since the fixed idea is itself a part of the whole illness, its removal has to be supplemented by a synthesizing treatment in the form of reeducation or other forms of mental training. Electricity and massage, Janet thought, work to a large extent as disguised forms of psychotherapy. [99]

7. Janet stressed the role of the rapport in the therapeutic process. In *Psychological Automatism* he had already discussed the rapport from the viewpoint of the elective narrowing of the field of consciousness around the person of the hypnotist. Janet paid due acknowledgment to the work of the old magnetizers who had described and investigated the rapport and had shown how it extended beyond the time of the hypnotic session (Janet's "somnambulic influence"). In his paper of 1891 about Marcelle, Janet gave rules for the handling of the "influence" for the benefit of the patient. In the first period, the rapport was to be established; in the second period, one had to prevent its undue development and restrict it by spacing the therapeutic sessions. In August 1896, at the International Congress of Psychology in Munich, Janet read a paper on "Somnambulic influence and the need for direction."[100] He noted that the interval between two hypnotic sessions could be divided into two periods. In the first the patient felt relieved, happier, and more efficient, and did not think much about the hypnotizer. In the second the patient became depressed and felt the need for hypnosis, and constantly thought of the hypnotist. The feeling toward the hypnotist varied: passionate love, superstitious terror, veneration, or jealousy. Some patients accepted that influence, others rebelled against it. But even when the influence was not so clearly conscious, it existed beneath the surface and could be evidenced, for instance, in the patient's dreams, in crystal gazing, and in automatic writing. Janet soon noticed that an analogous phenomenon existed in nonhysterical patients. But whereas, with hysterics, it took the form of a need to be hypnotized, it developed in obsessive or depressed patients as a "need for being directed." Such manifestations of psychological dependency, Janet thought, would be a good starting point for the study of the psychology of social feelings and interrelationships between people in general. He developed these ideas in greater detail in further publications.[101]

When he spoke of psychological analysis, Janet never claimed it to be his own method. He apparently used this term in the same general sense that mathematicians do when speaking of algebraic analysis and chemists of chemical analysis. Nevertheless, it would seem that the words "psychological analysis" at times became, identified with Janet's exploration of subconscious processes.[102]

Janet's Work: IV—The Exploration of Neuroses

Janet began his clinical research on hysterical patients and from there shifted to other neurotics, having at his disposal numerous out-patients of the Salpêtrière and later also his private clients. He endeavored to bring some order into that field and elaborated a synthetic theory of neurosis, which he expounded in two lengthy books: *Neurosis and Fixed Ideas,*[103] and *Obsessions and Psychasthenia.*[104] The essential features of that conception were summarized later in a short book, *Neuroses.*[105]

Janet never separated his theoretical work from clinical observation and, in that regard, whatever the changes in the theory of neuroses, Janet's case histories keep their value in regard to the description of symptoms. That clinical material was classified and integrated into a synthesis characterized by the distinction of two basic neuroses: *hysteria* and *psychasthenia*. Janet discarded the word "neurasthenia," which implied a neurophysiological theory for which there was no evidence, and coined the term "psychasthenia" for a group of neuroses in which he incorporated the obsessions, phobias, and various other neurotic manifestations.

Janet's research on hysteria was published in a series of papers from 1886 to 1893 and compiled in his medical dissertation (1893),[106] which was followed two years later by a contribution on the psychotherapy of hysteria.[107] Later he made certain revisions, as can be seen in the book *Les Névroses. (Neuroses)*. The essence of Janet's concept of hysteria is the distinction between two levels of symptoms: the "accidents" (accidental or contingent symptoms), and "stigmata" (permanent, basic symptoms). The "accidents" depend on the existence of subconscious fixed ideas. The "stigmata," which Janet also calls negative symptoms, are the expression of one basic disturbance that Janet calls "the narrowing of the field of consciousness."

In 1893, Janet made a survey and revision of the various theories of hysteria that had been propounded up to that time.[108] He rejected both the purely neurological theory and the theory according to which hysterical symptoms were "faked." Following Briquet and Charcot, Janet considered hysteria as a psychogenic disease (though developing on the basis of an abnormal physiological make-up). The theory of "morbid representations," defended by Moebius and Strümpell, was accepted by Janet insofar as it concerned the pathogenesis of hysterical "accidents." He agreed with Binet's theory of hysteria as a form of dual personality; he said that in hysterical persons, there actually is a subconscious existence that overtly manifests itself during the attacks and in hypnosis, and which is the invisible cause of "accidents." However, a full account of the nature of hysteria must involve a more basic feature, the "narrowing of the field of consciousness." To quote Janet, "The hysterical personality cannot perceive all the phenomena; it definitively sacrifices some of them. It is a kind of autotomia, and the abandoned phenomena develop independently without the subject being aware of them."[109] The "narrowing of consciousness," in turn, is conditioned by the patient's lack of psychological strength.

Janet's descriptions and investigations of hysteria bear no mention of metalloscopy and "transfer" phenomena, in which certain of Charcot's students were keenly interested. Obviously, Janet never believed in them, but he abstained from contradicting them.

Janet also gathered a great amount of material on psychasthenia, which he systematized into a vast theoretical framework. Here, too, he distinguished two levels of symptoms. On the more superficial level were the various types of psychasthenic crises, fits of anxiety, and all kinds of conspicuous manifestations related to fixed ideas. But in contrast to hysteria, those fixed ideas were conscious in the form of obsessions and phobias. On the lower level were the psychasthenic "stigmata," which Janet related to a basic disturbance of the "function of reality." "The most difficult mental operation, since it is the one which disappears first and most frequently, is the *fonction du réel,*" says Janet. He equated it to what Bergson had called the "attention to present life," but gave a more detailed analysis of it.[110]

The most conspicuous manifestation of the function of reality is the ability to act upon exterior objects and to change reality. Its difficulty increases when it has to deal with the social environment, with the more complex activities of one's profession, with adjusting to new situations, and when it has to bear the stamp of our freedom and personality, that is, when the action must be coordinated both with the requirements of the outer world and with the whole of our personality. The function of reality implies attention, which is the act of perceiving outside reality as well as our own ideas and thoughts. These two operations, voluntary action and attention, are combined into a synthetic operation, *présentification,* that is, the formation in the mind of the present moment. The natural tendency of the mind is to roam through the past and the future; it requires a certain effort to keep one's attention in the present, and still more to concentrate it on present action. "The real present for us is an act of a certain complexity which we grasp as one single state of consciousness in spite of this complexity, and in spite of its real duration which can be of greater or lesser extent. . . . Presentification consists of making present a state of mind and a group of phenomena."[111] The operations of the mind at a lower level are called disinterested activity by Janet (habitual actions, indifferent and automatic actions). At a still lower level are the functions of imagination (representative memory, fantasy, abstract reasoning, daydreaming). There are finally two inferior levels, that of the emotional reactions and that of useless muscular movements.

One can see how Janet's concepts had developed: In *L'Automatisme Psychologique* he distinguished only two levels: the function of synthesis and the automatic function. Later, he conceived a system of the hierarchy of functions with five levels, at the top of which is the function of reality whose highest point is the *présentification* (that is, the capacity for grasping reality to the maximum) and having at its lowest level the motor discharges. This new conception makes it possible to ascribe to each operation of the mind a "coefficient of reality," which provides the key to the understanding of the symptoms of psychasthenia. "If one considers the order of frequency and rapidity in which psychological functions disappear in the patient, one sees that the higher the coefficient of reality, the more rapidly they recede, but the lower the coefficient, the longer they persist."

Janet now came to think that it was not sufficient to think of mental energy in terms of its quantity, but that one must also take into account the individual's "psychological tension," that is, his ability to raise that energy to a certain level in the hierarchy of functions. Psychological tension, as defined by Janet in 1903, consists in the combination of two facts: (1) the act of concentrating and unifying psychological phenomena in a new mental synthesis; (2) the number of psychological phenomena that are synthesized in this way.[112] The degree of psychological tension of an individual is manifested by the highest level that he reaches in the hierarchy of mental functions. In *Les Obsessions et la psychasthénie* Janet thus sketched that dynamic theory that he was to develop considerably in the following years.

Janet's concept of neuroses belongs neither to the purely organicist nor to the purely psychogenic theories. In hysteria as well as in psychasthenia, he distinguished a psychogenetic process deriving from life events and fixed ideas and an organic substratum, that is, a neurotic predisposition. He ascribed the latter to those hereditary and constitutional factors, which, at the end of the nineteenth century, in France were lumped together under the improper term of "mental degeneration," a term inherited from Morel that had lost all meaning but was still being used in a routine way.

The duality between the role of psychogenesis in the shaping of symptoms and the role of organic factors in causing the disease itself was well illustrated in a paper of 1906: A male patient was admitted to the Salpêtrière with delusions of persecutions that had started long ago and could be partially explained by certain life events. However, subsequent examination showed that the patient was afflicted with general paresis; in his paretic delusions "he had fallen to the side toward which he was leaning."[113]

Janet's Work: V—The Dynamic Theory

Janet's distinction of two main neuroses, hysteria and psychasthenia, was taken over by C. G. Jung, who made them the prototypes of the extroverted and introverted personalities (the latter being also linked with Bleuler's theory of schizophrenia). Meanwhile, at any rate in France, the neurological school that had succeeded Charcot questioned the very existence of a hysterical neurosis, and hysterical patients gradually disappeared from French hospitals. The concept of psychasthenia was also criticized: was it really a nosological entity?

Janet went over his research on neuroses and developed a dynamic theory of which he had given the first outline in *Les Obsessions et la Psychasthénie* (1903). These newer developments are to be found in *Les Médications Psychologiques* (1919), and still later in *La Force et la Faiblesse Psychologiques* (1930). In time it became an elaborate construction, which we will try to summarize here as briefly as its complexity will allow.

In Janet's time, many authors assumed the existence of a hypothetical nervous or mental energy whose insufficiency would result in neurasthenic disturbances. But they were puzzled by some facts, such as an individual who looked completely exhausted but could suddenly, under certain stimulations, find the strength necessary to accomplish difficult actions. Janet overcame these seeming contradictions by elaborating a system in which psychological energy is characterized by two parameters: force and tension.

Psychological force is the quantity of elementary psychic energy, that is, the capacity to accomplish numerous, prolonged, and rapid psychological acts. It exists in two forms: latent and manifest. To mobilize energy means to have it pass from the latent to the manifest form.

Psychological tension is an individual's capacity to utilize his psychic energy at a more or less high level in the hierarchy of tendencies as described by Janet. The greater the number of operations synthesized, the more novel the synthesis, and thus the higher the corresponding psychological tension.[114]

Comparisons have been made with physical phenomena. The relation of psychological force and tension has been compared to that of heat expressed in terms of calories and in terms of temperature, and to that of electricity in terms of current and voltage.

These relations of psychological force and tension are manifested by various phenomena. Agitations occur when the quantity of force is maintained whereas psychological tension is lowered. Psycholeptic crises and other discharges are the effects of a sudden lowering of psychological tension. Drainage occurs when psychological energy of a certain level is utilized on a higher level. There ought to be an equilibrium between force and tension. This equilibrium is often difficult to maintain, hence the oscillations, which, according to Janet, play an important role in mental pathology.

With the help of these concepts of psychological force, psychological tension, and their interrelationships, Janet was able to construct a new theoretical model relative to neurotic conditions and to psychotherapy.

"It is probable that we will some day be able to establish the balance-sheet of the budget of the spirit much as one does today in business. The psychiatrist will then be able to effectively utilize weak resources while avoiding unnecessary expenditures and directing the effort exactly where needed; better still, he will teach his patients to increase their income, to enrich their minds."[115] This is the principle that Janet developed in the 1,100 page volume of his *Médications Psychologiques*. His system has been further elaborated and codified by his Swiss disciple Leonhard Schwartz.[116] The following material is based on both Janet's principles and Schwartz's elaborations.[117]

When dealing with any neurotic patient, the first concern should be to make an evaluation of his psychological force and tension. This implies that careful attention must be given to the patient's description of his way of life and of his relationships within his social environment. This systematic inquiry will enable the physician to disentangle the respective parts of the two basic syndromes of the neurosis: the asthenic and the hypotonic syndromes, which are almost always mingled with each other.

The *asthenic syndrome*, defined as insufficiency of psychological force, is manifested above all by a lassitude, which increases after effort and diminishes after rest.

There is a great variety of asthenic conditions. Janet distinguished three main groups.[118] In mild asthenias the patients are dissatisfied with themselves, unable fully to enjoy happiness or pleasure, and become easily anxious or depressed. Knowing that they tire easily, they avoid efforts, initiative, and social relationships, and are considered selfish or dull. They restrict their interests, feelings, and actions as much as possible to the point of leading an ascetic life (neurotic asceticism). They are suspicious of others, unstable, and slow in adjusting to new situations; they try to be secretive but cannot easily keep a secret, and are often great liars. As a consequence of their asthenia, they give much effort and attention to things that others would consider unnecessary.

The intermediate group of asthenias, which Janet also calls social asthenias, includes patients who suffer from the feeling of void (*sentiment du vide*): things or persons or their own personality seem to them to be empty—even repulsive if the asthenia is worse. They do not like people, nor do they feel liked by others, hence their feeling of isolation. They often seek out a person to whom they could submit; part of their activity is devoted to finding means of avoiding effort. Many alcoholics belong in this category.

The third group comprises those patients whose asthenia is so severe that they are unable to remain in a steady occupation. Here belong severe schizophrenic conditions—which at that time were still called dementia praecox. Janet used to say that *la démence précoce est une démence sociale* (dementia praecox is a social dementia).

The "hypotonic syndrome," defined by an insufficiency of psychological tension, is characterized by two orders of symptoms: primary symptoms resulting from the incapacity to perform acts of psychological synthesis at a certain psychological level, and secondary symptoms (or derivations) expressing a waste of nervous force that cannot be utilized at the desired level. The basic subjective symptom is a feeling of inadequacy (*sentiment d'incomplétude*) expressing the fact that, owing to his inability to perform completed acts at a certain level, the individual has to work on an inferior level of activity. The secondary symptoms consist of a wide gamut of those agitations to which Janet had given minute descriptions in *Obsessions et Psychasthénies* in 1903: motor agitations, tics, gesticulation, garrulousness, anxiety, obsession, mental ruminations, and also asthma, heart palpitations, and migraines. Characterististically, tiredness here is increased by rest and often diminishes with exertion. Also, this type of patient spontaneously seeks stimulation, because stimulation not only mobilizes latent forces but also raises these forces to a higher level of psychological tension.

It is obvious, then, that these two syndromes demand different kinds of treatment, which may sometimes even be diametrically opposed.

The treatment of the asthenic syndrome must consider that the asthenic individual is psychologically poor. The treatment can be summarized in three points: (1) to increase the income, (2) to diminish expenditure, and (3) to liquidate debts.

First, to increase the income. We do not know the exact nature of psychological forces. Janet never doubted that they are of a physiological nature, and he seems to have believed that the day would come when they could be measured. He considered that these forces were, to a great extent, connected with the condition of brain and organs and also related to the various tendencies. Each tendency has a certain charge of psychic energy that differs from one individual to another. These forces can obviously be reconstituted and stored in some way. "I don't know where these reserves are, but I do know that they exist," said Janet. One of the main sources of this reconstitution is sleep; hence the importance for the therapist to teach his patient the best way of preparing himself for sleep. The same could be said about the various techniques of rest and relaxation, the distribution of pauses during the day, of rest days during the month, and of vacations during the year. Another source of forces resides in nourishment, not in the sense of Weir Mitchell's method of overfeeding, but rather in the sense of a qualitative diet utilizing the action of vitamins and other yet insufficiently known dietetic agents.

Stimulants are usually not helpful here because they tend to mobilize reserves that are often insufficient, and waste them. However, it seems that some kinds of stimulation are actually energy-increasing. They include certain endocrinic products and physiotherapeutic methods that exert a stimulating action upon the skin.[119]

Second, to diminish the expenditure is what Janet called psychological economy (*économies psychologiques*). Here, too, one should recall that psychological forces are to a certain extent identical with physiological forces. Therefore, one has to look for all possible leakages of physiological force, sometimes connected with chronic infections, diseases of the digestive tract, and eye strain. There are also superfluous or excessively energy-consuming activities. But, as emphasized by Leonhard Schwartz, the two weak spots are usually found in the patient's relationship with his social environment and his professional work.

The physician will first inquire about the various people with whom the patient comes in contact and about his relationship with each of them, in order to ascertain to what degree they give him strength or deprive him of it. Most dangerous are the energy-eaters (or "leeches"), that is, those people who, through their perpetual ill temper, quarrels, jealousy, and authoritarianism, exhaust their fellow men. Their action is sometimes sufficiently noxious that the psychiatrist might feel authorized to carry out an operation of "social surgery," as Janet said, that is, to space or separate individuals, or even to part them permanently. Asthenic women, for example, should not have children. Or if they do, for a time they should have them cared for in an institution or at a vacation camp. In milder cases it would be sufficient to give a family certain rules or advice in regard to the handling of the situation and treatment of the patient. It is fair to add here that the neurotic patient himself is often an energy-eater to his environment and that he is greatly in need of counsel about his attitudes toward the people around him. The most important goal is to arrive, in one way or another, at the resolution of the conflicts.[120]

It would also be of the utmost importance to give the patient advice in regard to his professional work. This is a point that Dr. Leonhard Schwartz elaborated because of his knowledge of psychotechniques and the psychology of professional work. Schwartz had inquired in detail into the demands placed upon the worker by various professions with regard to psychological force and tension. It is regrettable that he never published more than a preliminary outline of his findings.[121] Many neurotics, he said, can be greatly helped merely by changing their occupation, or perhaps the timing or duration of their work. The human element, the relationship with superiors, fellow-workers, and subordinates must also be considered. The Janetian concepts thus should have a great relevance with regard to industrial hygiene and industrial psychology.

Third, to liquidate debts. When the patient, thanks to the aforementioned treatments, has regained a certain amount of strength, the liquidation of psychological debts can then be undertaken. In certain cases one will consider what Janet called the moratorium: following physical or emotional overwork, an individual may appear normal for a certain time and then suddenly collapse. This happens when he has lived for some time at the expense of his latent reserves and has depleted them. The psychiatrist who sees an individual in that latent period should be able to diagnose real exhaustion under the mask of apparent health, and give treatment as he would to an asthenic.

Here belong also the subconscious fixed ideas, or traumatic reminiscences, with which Janet had been so concerned in the past. Later he came to consider them as one particular form of a more general phenomenon, that of non-liquidated acts. Any event, any conflict, any illness, even any phase of life should be liquidated at a certain point, otherwise pathogenetic traces may subsist and cause a continuous invisible loss of mental energy. With the psychiatrist the patient should make a survey of his entire life history, discuss with him the interpretation of certain facts, and also the desirability of performing certain acts of renunciation and liquidation. Janet insisted on the great importance of acts of termination. It is striking to see, when looking over the life histories of neurotic and mental patients, the number and the importance of inadequately terminated, nonliquidated situations, among which mental disease itself can be ranged.[122]

The treatment of the hypotonic syndrome includes two groups of therapeutic devices, the proportion of which will vary from one case to another. The first group is related to the derivations; the second aims at the heightening of psychological tension.

First, it is necessary *to resorb the derivations.* It would be possible to diminish the derivations to a certain extent by weakening the patient's energy, as happens naturally in a fever. According to Janet, bromides and sedatives work in a similar way, thus giving only a kind of pyrrhic victory.

A far better method consists of channeling agitations by transferring them into useful or tolerable activities. This is similar to the strategy of a clever mother who assigns specific games and occupations to her children so that, instead of quarreling and disrupting the peace of the household, each will be absorbed in his own task. This principle also lies at the basis of the method of systematized work therapy elaborated in Germany by Hermann Simon.[123] By determining the exact type of work that for each patient would bring a resorption of his agitation, Simon succeeded in having all noise and agitation disappear from his mental hospital at a time when physiological treatment methods did not exist and there were almost no sedatives. In regard to hypotonic neurotics, a psychiatrist could commit no greater error than to treat them with rest, which is advisable for asthenic patients. Depending on the individuals' strength and the degree of their agitations, they should be engaged in active occupations: hiking, sports, hunting, or manual work. The problem becomes more difficult when the derivations have taken a character of autonomous organization, as is the case with obsessive compulsive syndromes. In such cases the aforementioned prescriptions must be combined with other devices aimed at obtaining the dissociation of these autonomous activities.

Second, it is necessary *to heighten psychological tension.* By raising psychological tension to a sufficiently high level, the primary hypotonic symptoms disappear, as well as the secondary symptoms resulting from the derivations. In Janetian terms, the surplus of psychological energy is now drained, that is, utilized at a higher level.

A first means of heightening psychological tension is stimulation, a procedure that the patient has a natural tendency to seek out. Stimulation is a complex phenomenon combining the mobilization of latent forces with a heightening of these forces to a higher level of psychological tension. Janet has described in detail the various kinds of stimulants, both the chemical type (alcohol, coffee, and strychnine) and the psychological type (stimulating emotions, travels, changes in life, love affairs), which patients spontaneously seek out. But stimulation is no more than a displacement or transformation of energy, and is therefore a temporary and uneconomical method.

A much better procedure, though a longer and more difficult one, is training, whose underlying principle is that by performing a complete and achieved action, a heightening of psychological tension is obtained. This method, as applied and perfected by Schwartz, consists of four steps:

1. To ascertain the level at which a patient is able to accomplish a complete action.
2. To have him execute and complete a task of that kind, first slowly and minutely, then more rapidly but always perfectly, until the task presents no further difficulty.
3. To shift the patient to another type of work, more difficult, and of a somewhat higher level.
4. To find various other psychological investments.

This is indeed exactly the principle of all varieties of education and re-education worthy of that name.

Janet and Schwartz have pointed out that disturbances exactly similar to those of the hypotonic syndrome can appear in individuals who are compelled to work on a level of psychological tension lower that their own, for instance in immigrants having to work in an occupation inferior to their previous profession, and of course still more in unemployed workers.

The Janetian theory of mental energy goes far beyond the interpretation of the above-mentioned neurotic conditions. There are infinite transitions between the normal individuals, the neurotics, and the psychotics. Janet never elaborated a typology based on his concepts of dynamic energy, but it would be easy to establish one by putting together various observations scattered throughout his work.

Janet sometimes mentions the psychological millionaires, that is, those endowed with a great amount of psychological force combined with a high level of psychological tension,. Such people are able to perform a great number of highly synthesized acts. One might think of Napoleon on the battlefield combining a large number of known and assumed data about the strength and the movements of the enemy and having to guess, weigh, and make decisions rapidly over a prolonged period of time.

Another type frequently referred to by Janet are those individuals who are prone to a sudden lowering of psychological tension. The epileptic crisis is nothing but a sudden collapse of psychological tension in the form of a discharge of energy, the individual sinking to a low level from which he slowly rises. Less spectacular are the psycholeptic crises of the psychasthenics.[124] There is a sudden blurring of action and perception and a loss of the feeling of reality, and its termination can be either sudden or gradual. Janet assumed that in certain individuals the oscillations of psychological tension had a cyclic pattern; these patients could live for a certain length of time in a state of perfect equilibrium, then, due either to exhaustion or to the effect of external events, their psychological tension could decrease and stay at a lower level for a given period, and this would give certain patients the aspect of suffering from a manic-depressive illness.

The type of individual whose psychological tension is permanently below the desirable level though he has sufficient psychological force is also frequently referred to by Janet. Not only does this make-up account for a great number of psychasthenics in the classical forms of obsession, phobias and the like, but it also enables an understanding of a variety of psychopathological disturbances. The need for stimulation may bring such individuals to resort to artificial ways of raising their psychological tension. This is in Janet's view the main psychogenesis of alcoholism and it also accounts for many cases of drug addiction, sexual perversion, and certain forms of criminality.[125] The relationship between kleptomania and mental depression was well illustrated in the case of a patient who had accidentally learned to relieve her depression through the stimulation provided by shoplifting.[126]

The individual who has a very small amount of psychological energy, at a low level, would be the reverse of the psychological millionaire. Such men are sometimes able to attain a certain adjustment in life, adopting a humble and restricted way of life. Their occupation may be poorly paid but quiet and secure. They have few acquaintances, no wife, no mistress. Janet wrote, "People consider them selfish and cowardly; perhaps they are merely wise individuals."[127]

On a still lower level are certain schizophrenics about whom Janet speaks in terms of asthenic dementia.

Though always acknowledging the importance of hereditary, congenital, and organic factors, Janet ascribes a large place to the autonomous dynamism of psychic energy. Provided that the psychiatrist understands and knows how to utilize the laws of that psychological dynamism, he is entitled to expect substantial psychotherapeutic results. In that regard, the main law of psychological dynamism could be formulated as follows: "The completed and terminated act heightens the psychological tension of the individual, while an incomplete and unachieved act lowers it." Janet makes comparisons with financial investments: A sound investment brings benefits; a succession of good investments brings increasing gains and an increase in fortune. A bad investment brings a loss; a succession of bad investments ends with debts and ruin.[128] This is exactly what happens spontaneously with numerous individuals. Leaving aside all intermediate forms, let us consider the two extreme cases. On one side would be the person who, thanks to an uninterrupted succession of well-completed and terminated acts, becomes able to increase his psychological tension. Janet particularly refers to the case of shy persons who may make efforts to learn social conducts so that they eventually overcome their shyness and become able to enjoy social triumphs.

Diametrically opposed is the case of the individual who leaves his actions incomplete and unachieved, each time lowering his psychological tension and leaving him each time less capable of adjusting; he thus falls into a vicious circle whose logical termination is an asthenic-hypotonic syndrome, of which hebephrenic schizophrenia is the extreme expression. This conception is strikingly close to Adolf Meyer's theory of schizophrenia as being the outcome of a long series of inadequate reactions and habit deterioration.

The Janetian concept might also shed light upon the much-discussed mechanism of work-therapy. It is clear that in Janet's mind there were two different kinds of work-therapy. The first one works through the channeling of the derivations. It is that type of therapy that one finds recommended in certain popular books written for neurotics and which advise that nervous individuals get busy and take up as many hobbies and occupations as possible.[129] In psychiatry this is also the principle that Hermann Simon developed to its fullest extent with his method of more active therapy of mental diseases.

The second, quite different method, is that of training, that is, giving the patient a manual or intellectual task that requires him to operate at a fairly high level of his ability, teaching him to do it slowly, completely, and perfectly, and then gradually raising the level. This was the principle of classical education and also of professional schools, but it can be used with mental patients in teaching them a new skill, a new trade, or a new language. The results of that method may not be as immediately obvious as those of Hermann Simon, but they are more rewarding in the long run.

One may wonder what is the place of hypnosis within that frame of reference. Janet never gave up this method and used it with hysterical patients. From his new dynamic point of view, hypnosis was a means of regulating mental energy in patients in whom an unequal distribution had occurred.[130]

The old concept of the therapeutic rapport, which Janet had studied in 1886 under its aspect of electivity and in 1896 under the more general aspects of somnambulic influence and need for direction, was now also enlarged and became the act of adoption. In the relationship between the patient and the director, as Janet said, there sooner or later appeared, sometimes quite suddenly, a remarkable change. The patient would show a specific behavior toward the therapist, which he had toward no one else. He would assert that the therapist was an exceptional being and that he, the patient, had at last found someone who could understand him and take him seriously. This meant in reality that the patient was now able to tell of his own feelings and to speak seriously about himself. The unreal picture he had of the director was a mixture of all kinds of previous more or less similar inclinations toward other persons, now synthesized in a particular way. These opinions and attitudes of the patient, expressed in the act of adoption, and his raised self-esteem, enabled him to perform acts that he had been unable to achieve heretofore, and would also enable the therapist to help the patient out of many of his difficulties.

One could say more about Janet's dynamic psychotherapy; however, what has been said above should suffice to show that it is a flexible and inclusive method that can be adjusted to any disease and any patient. More than a specific psychotherapy, it is a general system of psychotherapeutic economics.

Janet's Work: VI—The Great Synthesis

To Janet, psychological analysis was always the first phase of a method whose second phase was to be psychological synthesis. In *Psychological Automatism* he made the distinction of the conscious and the subconscious mind with a function of synthesis performed by the conscious mind. In *Obsessions and Psychasthenia* he presented a more complex hierarchy of the mind with five levels, the concept of psychological tension, and the interpretation of psychasthenia as being a lowering of psychological tension along those levels. From 1909 on, in his lectures at the Collège de France, Janet began to create a greater and more complete synthesis whose first sketch appeared in 1926 in the first volume of *From Anguish to Ecstasy.*[131] Janet once declared that psychologists at the end of the nineteenth century had written too many monographs on limited topics, to the point of creating great confusion. There was now a need for comprehensive systems that would enable psychologists to order, classify, and interpret facts and provoke discussion that would later lead to the superseding of those systems.

Janet undertook the construction of a vast conceptual model that was based not only on adult psychology and psychopathology but also on data furnished by child psychology, ethnology, and animal psychology. Within that frame of reference there is hardly one phenomenon of the mind that cannot be illumined in some way. Perception, memory, belief, and personality are given new interpretations, as are abnormal manifestations such as hallucinations and delusions.

In that perfected system, Janet retains his former concepts of psychological energy and tension but he now concentrates on the psychological analysis of the tendencies (a concept that he prefers to that of instinct;

tendencies are more flexible and can combine with each other). Each tendency is endowed with a certain load of latent energy that differs from one individual to another. Each tendency, once activated by proper stimulation, can be brought more or less close to its complete achievement. Each tendency is ranged on one level in the hierarchy of tendencies, and this gives the key to the understanding of many psychopathological conditions. In that new frame of reference, a subconscious act is now defined as "an act which has kept an inferior form amidst acts of a higher level"; in other words, an act on any level can become subconscious when the individual is consciously performing acts of a higher level.[132]

Janet's great psychological synthesis is a monument of such amplitude that it would require a volume of at least 400 to 500 pages to expound its elements. Janet never realized that volume.[133] The author who came nearest to writing it was Leonhard Schwartz, whose posthumous book remained unfinished (it lacked, among other things, the chapters on Janet's concepts of hallucinations and delusions).[134]

In the following, we will try to give an extremely succinct view of Janet's great synthesis. Let it be recalled that, in his work, this requires about twenty books and several dozens of articles.

We will now give a brief summary of each one of these tendencies. The nine tendencies are divided into three groups:

I.   *The Lower Tendencies*
  1. Reflexive tendencies
  2. Perceptive-suspensive tendencies
  3. Sociopersonal tendencies
  4. Elementary intellectual tendencies

II. *The Middle Tendencies*
  5. Immediate actions and assertive beliefs
  6. Reflexive actions and beliefs

III. *The Higher Tendencies*
  7. Rational-ergetic tendencies
  8. Experimental tendencies
  9. Progressive tendencies

We will now give a brief summary of each one of these tendencies.

I.1. REFLEXIVE TENDENCIES: These are explosive acts that are unleashed only when a stimulus has attained a certain degree, have an organized form, and are adjusted to some exterior object or situation. Sometimes they consist of movements of repulsion, drawing toward, excretion, or incorporation. Sometimes they are more complex acts, chains of reflexes, kinetic melodies. Here there are no psychological regulations as in emotions, and once started, the movement must follow its course until its end. Psycho-pathology shows us instances of such reflexive tendencies in the behavior of certain cases of severe idiocy. An epileptic attack is a transient regression to that level.

I.2. PERCEPTIVE-SUSPENSIVE TENDENCIES: These are tendencies whose full activation requires a stimulation in two steps: the first stimulation stirs the tendency and is followed by a period of suspense (waiting period), after which a second stimulation is necessary to bring the act to its completion. Sometimes the tendency is more complex and includes a sequence of actions. In contrast to the merely explosive tendencies, the perceptive-suspensive tendencies, once unleashed by an external stimulus, aim at modifying some-thing in the exterior world (such is the action of the wild beast upon its prey) and thus imply a certain degree of adjustment. Perceptive-suspensive tendencies are the starting point of all forms of action that imply phases of waiting or searching. They are the basis of the act of per-ception and of the notion of objects. Perception is midway between the first and second stimulations. An object, basically, is a perceptive scheme (for instance, the perception of an armchair is a perceptive scheme of the move-ments involved in the act of sitting down in it). Among the various objects, one has a privileged condition: One's body, because of its lack of exteriority and because of our conservative conduct toward it.

A psychopathological illustration of that level is Janet's story of the bicycle racer who starts his race in a competitive spirit (sociopersonal tend-ency) but under the effect of growing exhaustion becomes indifferent to the spectators, the landscape, and toward the idea of winning. His field of per-ception is narrowed within the form of the intermediate stage of the per-ceptive-suspensive tendency. The next step in regression would be falling asleep and riding in a purely reflexive way.[135]

I.3. SOCIOPERSONAL TENDENCIES: A differentiation has occurred between two groups of conducts, those toward the *socius* and those toward our own body. However, there are interactions and reciprocal influences between these two lines of conduct.

The individual adjusts his own acts to the acts of the *socius*. As a result, such acts are always in variable proportions combined acts or, as Janet says, *actes doubles*. Among these acts are imitation, collaboration, and command and obey. In regard to imitation, Janet adopts Durkheim's definition: The perception of the act of another man seems to control the execution of the act of the imitator, but imitation is a "double act" implying an action not only of the imitator, but also of the imitated one. Spontaneous imitation is perfected by the conscious imitation which children learn in the process of playing. In collaboration, two *socii* share in a common action aiming at a common result and giving to both the feeling of triumph. The act of com-manding and obeying can be considered as a special kind of collaboration where members of a group accept the act of the chief as a part of the total act and the other roles are distributed among the participants. But how do the *socii* arrive at that distribution of roles? Through acts of *valorisation sociale* (competitive value-setting), ascribing to one's self a certain value and bringing others to accept it. Among various other acts on the same level Janet analyzes pity, rivalry, struggle, gift and theft, hiding and showing, sexual conduct, and so on.

But the individual does not only adjust his own acts to the acts of the *socius*, he makes the same adjustment toward himself. In other words, he acts toward himself in the same way as he acts toward others. Here is the starting point of what Janet calls the act of secrecy, a conduct to which he ascribes the utmost importance, since its last term is inner thought.[136] Being alone means not being observed and not having to maintain duties of respect and consideration (*égards*); it means a simplification of conduct, a lesser expenditure of energy.

On the same level, from the viewpoint of social psychology, belong the ceremonies. In his studies on the *intichiuma* of the Australians, Durkheim emphasized the role of mutual stimulation provided by the participants.

According to Janet, this is also the level on which belong the four basic emotions. The greatest number of feelings that constitute a person's emotional life depend upon the combination of certain social conducts with four basic emotions—effort, fatigue, sadness, and joy. These four basic feelings correspond to mechanisms of regulation of actions. As a comparison, there are not only functions of respiration and circulation of blood, but also regulatory mechanisms which, depending on the need or circumstance, increase or diminish respiration and circulation. In the same way there are psychological regulations that either increase or diminish the energy necessary to activate a tendency. After having learned to react to the acts of his *socii*, man applies the same conducts to himself, thus learning to react to his own actions. In some conditions these regulations are lacking, and the patient experiences a feeling of emptiness or *sentiment du vide*. The two elementary emotions, effort and fatigue, are compared by Janet to the action of the accelerator and the brakes on a car. The obsessive neurotics are people who always make exaggerated and unnecessary efforts, whereas laziness is a propensity toward insufficient effort. In the same theory, sadness is the fear of action and a reaction to perpetual failure, whereas joy is a surplus of energy left after a successfully terminated action (the reaction of triumph). Janet compares sadness to a change into reverse gear in driving. In that case, joy would be compared with a surplus gas expenditure after a slamming on of the brakes. Actually, however, Janet's theory of emotions is infinitely more complex. In his book on love and hate, for instance, Janet gives a thorough analysis comprehending many nuances and implications of these two feelings.[137]

From the viewpoint of psychopathology, Janet was greatly interested in all forms of social conduct below the level of speech, such as those that occur among idiots. On the other hand, regression to the level of sociopersonal tendencies gave him the clue to many psychopathological manifestations on higher levels. The disturbances in *valorisations sociales* are manifested in two different ways among the timid and the authoritarians. It is also a lack in *valorisation sociale* that brings about the reaction of failure. Delusions of persecution originate through the process of social and intentional objectivation. Another type of delusion of persecution, the delusion of reference (as in patients who believe they are constantly being watched and that others read their thoughts), is ascribed by Janet to deficiencies in the patient's ability to perform the "act of secrecy."

I.4. ELEMENTARY INTELLECTUAL TENDENCIES: This level became one of Janet's favorite subjects, to which he devoted two of his last books.[138] It is the level of intelligence before language and the beginnings of language, memory, symbolic thought, production, and explanation.

The most elementary act of intelligence, according to Janet, consists in the confrontation and combination of two conducts toward two different objects. As an illustration, Janet analyzed the conduct of the apple basket. It consists of two actions that belong neither to the basket nor to the apples: filling the basket and emptying it. In the same manner, Janet analyzed the meaning of the elementary tool, of the portrait or statue, of the chest of drawers, of the door, and of the street and the public place. In each one of these subtle analyses Janet showed how there is a combination of two actions in which two objects are involved.

It is also the level of the beginning of language, which is also an *acte double,* that is, a combination of speaking and being spoken to.[139] Janet thought that language originated in a transformation of acts of commanding and obeying. Vocal acts such as a war cry replaced the necessity of gesturing a command for the chief. A similar theory would explain the beginnings of memory. Memory is a transformation of action such as that which can be communicated even to the absent (for example, a sentry, upon arrival of the enemy, will give the alarm, and this is incipient language; in the absence of the enemy, he will give a report to the chief, and this is incipient memory). Thus, "memory is the order given to the absent ones, before becoming the order given by the absent."

Another elementary intellectual conduct also explains the origin of production: the potter, in his mind, combines two representations, that of the act to which the object will serve, and that of the act which he is performing. He shifts ceaselessly from one vantage point to the other, inventing actions that combine the two views. Close to the origin of production is the origin of explanation, the becoming aware of other acts of production.

On this level there are also psychopathological implications. Certain idiots and imbeciles who are on the prelanguage level are able to perform certain acts of rudimentary intelligence. Regressions to that level may occur in certain states of mental confusion and oneirism.

II.5. IMMEDIATE ACTIONS AND ASSERTIVE BELIEFS: Once it was born, language developed enormously, extending to every human act. Each motor act was now paralleled by an act of speech. This development had momentous consequences. Language was dissociated from action and man utilized it to speak to himself as well as to the *socii*. Human conduct began to be dissociated into bodily conduct and verbal conduct. As Janet put it, at this stage "the whole conduct of man becomes the analysis of the relationships between bodily conduct and speech." Bodily conduct, the only one that can immediately and directly change the world, is the only efficient one, but it is slow, heavy, and exhausting. Verbal conduct is easy, quick, and inexpensive, but it cannot immediately change the world. Janet thought that this great difference between the two conducts became the starting point of the concept of the separation of body and mind.

At the beginning the spoken word was just the beginning of an action. But speech now emancipated itself from bodily conduct; man began to play with language, and this is what Janet calls inconsistent language.[140] Inconsistent language may be observed in children three to six years of age who often speak together without paying attention to what the other is saying, as described by Piaget. It is also seen, Janet adds, in the collective monologues of certain imbeciles, and even at times among normal adults. A reaction against inconsistent language was manifested in two ways. First, by means of the *affirmation*, which Janet equates with a promise and considers as the origin of belief. Second, by the act of *will*, which is a way of forging a close link between language and act.

Finally, language was applied by man to speak to himself in the form of inner language. This was the origin of thought. Janet devoted a whole course of lectures to the origin of inner thought.[141] One of the main features of this stage is what Janet calls assertive belief, that is, that belief is adequate to feelings rather than to facts, and therefore often contradictory or absurd. At this stage man believes what he wishes or fears. It is the kind of belief that is usual in children, in the feeble-minded, or in the process of suggestion, and occasionally among many normal persons. Man's representation of the world takes the form of what Janet calls the world of assertive belief: just as perceptive conduct created objects, affirmative conduct now creates *beings*; beings are nothing but objects to which the name and the belief add persistence and stability.

Memory at this stage undergoes a process similar to that of language; inconsistent memory is emancipated from memory congruent with acts. Inconsistent memory ignores an accurate localization in time and is the starting point of legends and myths.

At this point the individual develops in the form of the personage, characterized by attitudes and roles. The personage is an individual who acts according to the picture that he has made of himself and that he presents to other men. Hence his suggestibility and plasticity; he also ascribes roles to others.

From the psychopathological point of view, this is the level not only of inconsistent language and memory, but of suggestibility (which is a kind of inconsistent belief) and of confabulation. Janet sharply distinguishes between confabulation and mythomania. In the latter the individual is conscious that he is lying, but the level of assertive belief is below the level of the more complex conduct of lying.

II.6. REFLECTIVE ACTIONS AND BELIEFS: Reflection, according to Janet, issues from discussion between an individual and several *socii*. This collective conduct was internalized in the form of an inner discussion in which several phases can be distinguished. First comes doubt, which is a suspension of affirmation, then deliberation, which is a struggle between tendencies and arguments, and then a conclusion in an act of decision. The struggle of these tendencies is called deliberation when it terminates with either a will or with a belief. Reflective actions and beliefs are not yet on the logical level. Nevertheless, they imply a coherent knowledge of an external object and of oneself.

Man's representation of the world at this stage takes the shape of the world of reflective belief (which Janet also calls *le réel réfléchi*, the reflective real) where there are not just beings, but bodies and spirits. At this point Janet brings a new concept of the real, more complex than the one he proposed in 1903. This is the part of Janet's teaching that has the closest connections with his theories of hallucinations and delusions. Conscious reality, Janet says, is a complex structure with the interplay of three levels of reality: the *réel complet* (the complete real), the *presque réel* (the almost real), and the *demi-réel* (the semi-real).

The complete real is the fruit of a belief bound to the possibility of an immediate action or intangible permanence. It comprises bodies and spirits. A body is a persistent reality about which one affirms with reflection that it has a place, a form, perceptive qualities—that it is distinct and devoid of intentionality. A spirit is the invisible reality that is distinct from the individual who speaks and distinct from other spirits, and is endowed with intentionality. These two distinct realities (body and spirit) can be united in man in general and in oneself in particular.

The almost real is bound with the conduct of expectation and reporting to oneself, and it corresponds somewhat to what Janet had previously called presentification. It includes the notion of the present instant, of the action that we are performing and have immediately in mind, and the reporting to oneself, and takes in the world of consciousness, which is the regulation of our present actions.

The semi-real comprises the fringes of reality, which are, in order of decreasing proximity: the perception of the near future, of the recent past, of the ideal, of the remote future, of the imaginary, and finally the abstract idea.

In the normal state there must be an adequation between reality and the feeling we have of it. In mental disease inadequations occur, either in the form of *surréalisation* (overrealization), that is, as when an event of the distant past is endowed with a feeling of belief that sets it in the present, or underrealization, that is, the inability to feel the objects of the present as being really perceptible, as when the patient's report no longer corresponds to the ideas that his *socii* have about the same events or objects. In these concepts Janet found a key to the understanding of delusions that he developed in several elaborate papers.

On the same level belong consistent memory, acts of conscious will, and a further development of the individual in the form of the reflective self (*moi réfléchi,* ego). Compared with the *personnage,* the conscious ego implies a temporal organization of personality and an integrated biography.

This level is of particular importance from the psychopathological point of view. Regression to that level, or disturbances in the process of reflective belief, are evidenced in those individuals who complain of a loss of the feeling of reality and develop an anxious search for the real. This is also the level to which belong disturbances of will such as abulia and, as already mentioned, mythomania. Individuals who do not go beyond the level of reflective action and belief show such characteristics as passion, egoism, laziness, and lying.

III.7. Rational-ergetic tendencies: The rational-ergetic level is the first of the higher tendencies. A new function is added here, namely the tendency to work. Work does not exist among animals, "the labour of an ox is not real work"; work hardly exists among primitive people. It disappears in certain categories of civilized individuals such as criminals and prostitutes, as well as in many neurotics and psychotics.

Work implies a particular distribution of force. Force is drawn not only from inferior tendencies but from a special reserve. This means that an individual on that level carries out decisions and promises even if he derives no satisfaction from it. Kant expressed this in philosophical language with his concept of the "categorical imperative." Janet adds that "The value of the person can be measured by his capacity to accomplish chores" (*corvées*).[142] Duty is one among the many chores that the superior man is able to impose upon himself. Here also belong voluntary action, initiative, perserverance, and patience, that is, the capacity to endure waiting, boredom, and fatigue. Here also belongs the concept of truth. Truth implies individual belief in a permanent reality extending beyond the field of man's present knowledge. Here also belong, according to Janet, the rules of logic. Before there were abstract concepts, there were rules of conduct that man imposed upon himself. Here, further, belongs the act of teaching, a procedure which, in its full extent, pervades the whole of culture. On this level the individuality develops further, from the ego to the person. The difference between the ego and the person is that the person implies a coherence of acts and a unity of life.

Although the rational-ergetic tendencies belong to the superior levels, they are not completely devoid of psychopathological implications. A person remaining on that level runs the risk of becoming impractical and an *esprit faux*, a dogmatic and pedantic individual whose judgment is based on theoretical systems and rigid principles rather than experience.

III.8. EXPERIMENTAL TENDENCIES: In contrast with the rational-ergetic level, experimental conduct takes experience into account and submits to facts. This conduct is therefore the starting point of science. The feeling of the absolute is replaced by the concept of the possible. Nature is now conceived of as a system of natural laws. Man feels a need to "check an apparatus as well as what is said" and to criticize a system according to its practical success. These tendencies also include what moralists call virtuous conduct in which there is humility, firmness of character, and acceptance of objective truth.

III.9. PROGRESSIVE TENDENCIES: What Janet calls "progressive tendencies" is the highest development of individual and original conduct. On this level man achieves his own unique individuality, but he also recognizes the fullest individuality of each one of his fellow men, establishing with them a relationship of spiritual intimacy. The search for individuality extends also to events, notably to historical ones. Janet arrives here at one of his favorite speculations, which he expresses in veiled terms: "We grow in time like plants in space." This means that the evolution of man, even of man as a biological entity, is open toward the future. In that regard, Janet seems to agree with certain thoughts expressed by Bergson in his *Creative Evolution*.[143] "Evolution," he concludes, "is not finished, and human action has been and will be a source of marvel."

Janet's Work: VII—Psychology of Religion

Janet never lost the deep preoccupation with religion that had marked his youth, and in the course of his clinical work he met several cases of particular interest from the viewpoint of religious psychology and psychopathology. He subsequently elaborated a complete psychological theory of religion, which he expounded in his lectures of 1921–1922. Janet never wrote the book he had planned on that subject, but we are acquainted with his theories from a condensed version published by one auditor, the Reverend Walter Horton, and from hints given by Janet in several of his later publications.[144]

It may be appropriate briefly to describe some of Janet's clinical cases. One was the celebrated story of Achilles, the man who, in 1891, had been admitted to the Salpêtrière with demoniac possession and whom Janet succeeded in curing through the unraveling of the patient's subconscious fixed ideas. Another case was that of Meb, a young lady of twenty-six, who came to the Salpêtrière because of hysterical hallucinations with mystical and erotic themes.[145] The patient claimed to have had hallucinations from the age of eight to twelve. She received visitations from angels, one of whom she called Sainte Philomène. At the age of seventeen, following emotional trauma, the hallucinations started again. The patient's mother and aunt were fervent spiritists. One of the manifestations occurring in the house were the *apports*: shining pebbles were found on the staircase, birds' feathers fell on the table during meals; on her bedroom table Meb found little pieces of glass shaped in the form of a cross; and the entire family believed that these objects had been put there by spirits. Under hypnosis, the patient told Janet that she remembered having disposed the cross during the night in a somnambulic state. She had also placed the stones on the staircase, believing to have seen it done by Sainte Philomène. She also recalled that, during the day, she had fallen into a kind of trance or somnambulic state in which she believed herself to be Sainte Philomène. She reenacted the scene as it had happened: she had climbed onto a table and stuck the feathers onto the ceiling with flour and water paste, and they had subsequently become unstuck and had fallen onto the table during the meal. She, too, was exorcised by Janet in the same way as Achilles had been.

The third, and by far the most interesting, patient was Madeleine, a woman about whom very much has been written, by Janet as well as by Catholic theologians. The forty-two-year-old woman, who had been admitted to the Salpêtrière in February 1896, was placed under Janet's care from May 10, 1896, to December 2, 1901, and again from January 2, 1903, to March 5, 1904. After her discharge and until her death in 1918 she wrote to Janet almost daily, so that he was able to follow her for twenty-five years. Madeleine's life had been extraordinary from the beginning.[146] She was born in 1853 in a traditionally Catholic part of western France. From early childhood she had been most devout. When she was eighteen, she left for England as a governess, but returned after a few months and upset her family by telling them that she wanted to live a life of absolute poverty and anonymity. She maintained communication with her family through her sister. She spent much time caring for the poor, nursing a woman who had cancer, and had served a prison sentence for refusing to reveal her true name to officials. Actually, Madeleine had been admitted to the Salpêtrière because of a peculiar and painful contracture of the leg muscles, which permitted her to walk only on tiptoe. These motor disturbances had been attributed to hysteria. Janet suspected syringomyelia or some other lesion of the medulla, but the final diagnosis was never made. Madeleine also had peculiar mystical delusions. She believed that she had divine revelations and that she was capable of levitation.

During her stay in the Salle Claude Bernard (where Janet kept his few patients) it was observed that Madeleine at times had peculiar bleeding skin lesions on the backs of her hands, on the feet, and one on the left side of the thorax. These five spots were bleeding all at once, at irregular intervals, several times a year, and corresponded to the stigmata of the Passion such as were also reported in Saint Francis of Assisi and several other saints. During all the time she was followed up by Janet, Madeleine was subjected to a twofold direction: she had a religious director and she had Janet as her psychotherapist whom she always called *mon Père*

("Father"). It is obvious from Madeleine's letters and from Catholic publications that Janet always treated her with the deepest respect for her personality, but as a psychologist he approached her case in a strictly objective way. Janet observed great oscillations within Madeleine's condition and distinguished five abnormal states, which he called the states of consolation, ecstasy, temptation, dryness, and torture, as well as the state of equilibrium, which was temporary at the beginning but became predominant in the last years of her life. These various conditions have been described at length by Janet in the first volume of his book *From Anguish to Ecstasy*. It is to a large extent from these observations that Janet developed his theory of emotions and part of his concepts of religious psychology.

The publication of Janet's book in 1926 aroused controversy in certain Catholic circles. Janet became the object of vehement attacks and was branded as an atheist. On the other hand, a Catholic theologian, Father Bruno de Jésus-Marie, wrote an account of Madeleine's case that supplements Janet's publications in a very interesting way. From his point of view, Madeleine was undoubtedly neurotic, but she was also a fine and remarkable person whose mysticism was a mixture of psychopathology and genuine religious feelings.

Janet's psychology of religion has to be seen within the frame of reference of his concepts of psychic energy and the hierarchy of the tendencies. The moral-religious conduct, Janet says, is originally a function of government, that is, the function of controlling the budget of mental forces. The instinct of economy is the root of all morality. Man applies it primarily to the economy of his mental resources, and secondarily applies these principles to the economy of his financial resources. Financial economy is but an outgrowth of the original control of the budget of the mind. Moral conduct is basically the individual's control over all his functions for the sake of conservation of mental energy. But on the sociopersonal level he goes a step forward, since there occurs a reciprocal consideration of the mental energy of the individual and the *socii* in the process of imitation. Mental energy is handled in a different way by the imitators and the leader. For the imitator, imitation is a less costly action. For the leader, giving the example is a costly action for which he is more than repaid by the feeling of satisfaction that he derives from being imitated. Thus, imitation is energy-conserving both for the imitated leader and his imitators. On the level of elementary intelligent tendencies, social specialization increases. The leader tends not only to continue to perform his functions but to increase them, and he insists upon being obeyed.

On the assertive level, rites and myth are created. Rites are complicated conducts in which the least details are rigidly fixed, which men compel one another to observe, and for which no reason, either logical or moral, can be given. Myths, Janet says, are not so primitive as rites and are usually attached to them as an afterthought, to explain them. The function of the rite is the stimulation of mental reserves, the toning-up of the emotional content of consciousness. At their highest pitch, collective rites bring forth a kind of collective intoxication. It is not surprising that in many primitive religions orgiastic rites were performed in which alcoholic intoxication played a prominent part. Even mourning ceremonies aim at heightening the energy of the participants, as pointed out by Durkheim.

The reflective level is, according to Janet, the one in which the god idea arises. Janet says that there is no real religion where there are no gods. The characteristic of a god (or spirit) is to be anthropomorphic, invisible, powerful, and to have a special function that no ordinary human being could perform. These functions vary with the needs of the worshipper. The god's characteristics are correlated with the conduct of the believer, who honors the god as he would flatter men. He humbles himself as before a chief; he prays for favors and gives thanks for past favors. In return, the believer expects an answer from the god. The god answers through the believer, or at any rate through the priest, whose function it is "to make the god answer."

To explain how these beliefs and practices have arisen, Janet resorts to the analysis of the phenomenon of thought. Thought is an interiorized language and, as mentioned previously, with this internalization originated the idea of a double, or spirit, existing invisibly behind the visible actions of the individual. This was also the origin of animism. "Animism springs up spontaneously the moment you first learn the necessity of distinguishing between the man who talks and acts as if he were your friend, and the invisible, inaudible enemy who lurks behind him." The idea of god-spirits also grew from the conduct with respect to the absent ones, a special category of the absent being the dead. But why did the god-spirits come to play such an important part? Janet answers that all religions have alliances (covenants) with a god, either out of fear, or for the sake of moral strengthening, or because man craves direction and love. Man searches for an ideal, invisible, all-powerful, and all-comprehending director and friend, that is, a god. Here is revealed the function of religion, which is "making the god speak" and, according to Janet, "we are not to suppose that religion ever could have persisted if the gods had never spoken."

The gods can be made to speak in various ways. One is prayer, which is interior conversation. The believer asks something from the god, and something inside himself then gives the answer and comfort in the god's name. Here is a part of automatism, which may be observed as if under a magnifying glass in pathological states. Meb, for instance, invoked Sainte Philomène, whose role she would herself play when in a somnambulic state, granting her own requests. Madeleine also alternately plays the role of the humble supplicant and of Christ answering her and comforting her. Janet assumes that the same occurs in prayers, although the believer is unaware of it. Somewhat more complex is the Tromba cult in Madagascar, where the entire tribe prays to the spirits, following which some among the crowd are possessed by the spirits and thus reveal their answer to the community. However, it also occurs that the expected answer is not forth-coming, as in occurrences of *acedia* (a condition that was frequent in monasteries in the Middle Ages); *acedia* could be explained as a gradual impoverishment of mental energy. The reverse of *acedia* is "conversion," which involves a recovery of faith and a new sense of mental power and stability, following a certain process of recovery of mental energy and of certain stimulations.

This is also where the phenomena of fanaticism and proselytism enter. Fanaticism can be made explicit by pointing out the difference between a philosophical and a religious discussion. In a philosophical discussion there is acceptance of a possible defeat, respect for the adversary, and intellectual honesty. In a religious discussion there is a lack of scientific resignation, scorn for the adversary, and a lack of intellectual honesty, for example, in the form of incorrect quotations from the adversary's writings. Proselytizing zeal is another characteristic mark of every real religion. Depending on the times, converts may be frightened into the fold or seduced into it by the promise of benefits. Among arguments in religious discussion, a prominent one is the occurrence of miracles that Janet defines as "events following some religious act and bearing the official religious stamp." The highest degree of proselytism is religious persecution, which Janet explains as a desire for mastery, for intellectual unity, and for relief from mental depression.

The phenomenon of demoniac possession is considered by Janet as being the reverse of prayer. As in prayer, it is a double conduct in which the subject plays two roles, but, whereas in prayer the second personality is good (a god or saint), in possession it is evil (a devil or demon). In prayer, the believer remains master of the inward drama—the divinity's speech can be stopped at will—while in possession, the second role gets beyond control and the first role disappears.

In regard to ecstasy, which mystics regard as being the authentic form of communion with the divine, Janet refers to his observations on Madeleine. During ecstasy, movements are reduced to a minimum, the ecstatic wishes to be left alone, his psychological tonus mounts, and a wave of calm, passive, beatitudinous joy sweeps over him. He feels illuminated and has an emphatic conviction that whatever happens to be in his mind is true and immensely important. In some ways, it resembles somnambulism, but differs from it in that the memory of the experience is preserved and the effects of it often last throughout life. It is an experience that religion treasures but also mistrusts, for the ecstatic is prone to have private revelations, apart from the church dogma.

The question "Do the gods exist?" is approached by Janet from the point of view of the psychological analysis of belief. The gods are neither "things" nor "facts," but in Janet's terminology "beings," that is, religious entities. Facts are on the level of experimental verification, but religious entities are on the assertive and reflective levels. Belief in a fact of science and belief in a religious reality are two entirely different matters. In the former, belief comes step-by-step through hypothesis and experimentation. Religious belief comes all at once, and no amount of experience can discredit it. It can also go all at once, and the loss of belief is often accompanied by nervous collapse. Scientific or philosophical truths never engage our loyalties as does religious belief, for which one may die as one does for one's country.

The influence of religion, Janet says, has been immeasurable. It is religion that has created morality in the modern sense. Compared with the usual commands of the leader, moral commands have dignity (categorical quality), an imperative quality (that is, they must be also obeyed in secret), and obedience to them gives a feeling of pride. The reason for that difference, Janet says, is that duties are the commandments not of the chief or leader, but of the gods. Thus morality has a religious stamp and is an outgrowth of religion. Because of religious morality man has become an ego, that is, he has learned to subordinate and organize his desires. Logic, Janet adds, which is intellectual morality, also bears the imprint of religious influence.

The rational-ergetic and the experimental levels have introduced influences making for the destruction of religion. According to Janet, four important types of conduct appear for the first time at the ergetic or the experimental level: work, education, philosophy, and science. All are directly or indirectly the fruit of religion, but all tend to exercise a destructive influence upon religion. Religion is challenged by philosophy and most of all by science, so that the problem arises as to what will happen to mankind should religion be destroyed. Because of the enormous role religion has played and still plays in the life of mankind, the problem is to find a substitute for religion. Religion in recent years has been breaking up into its constituent moments, as made explicit in the three phases of prayer: interrogation (the search for the god), answer of the god, and satisfaction at the answer. The interrogatory moment has been taken over by philosophy, which, however, will never be able to replace religion. The responsive moment has been taken over by spiritism, a movement to which Janet devoted much attention.[147] Spiritism, being the attempt to converse through "mediums" with disembodied spirits, is a very ancient phenomenon, but modern spiritism, which developed around 1850, is different from all that went before because it is analytic and performed in an atmosphere of scientific curiosity. Thus spiritism involuntarily furnished valuable contributions to scientific psychology (such as the work of Flournoy), but for most of its adherents, spiritism became a kind of popular metaphysics, a cheap and unsatisfactory substitute for religion. As for the "moment of satisfaction" in religion, it has been taken over by Romanticism, a term that Janet uses here in an extended sense as the religion of sentiment. Its fundamental proposition is that wherever you find joy, strength, and satisfaction, there you have the immediate evidence of the Divine. The classic example would be William James' *The Varieties of Religious Experience*. However, as Boutroux remarked in his introduction to the French edition of that work, "there is no evidence that enthusiasm and joy always go with the truth."

Searching for more satisfactory substitutes for religion, Janet thought of two of them, one that he thought was "destined to do perhaps more than all others to put religion out of style" was scientific psychotherapy, which aims to treat scientifically those states of mind for which religion is the sovereign but imperfect popular remedy. A second substitute would be the worship of progress. Janet does not take this word in the sense of material or mechanical progress and seems to think of even more than intellectual and social progress. His central maxim is that of Guyau, a philosopher he much admired, "To be confident in ourselves and in the world."

This is an extremely schematic summary of Reverend Horton's account of Janet's lectures of 1921–1922. The book that Janet had planned to write on the psychology of religion never materialized. One reason for this may be that, during the rest of his life, his thoughts about religion developed along somewhat new lines. An inference can be drawn from an article published by Janet in 1937.[148] In the meantime, Bergson's book *The Two Sources of Moral and Religion* had been published, as well as other studies on mysticism. Janet now no longer seemed to consider mysticism as being a merely assertive kind of belief. He now tended to consider mystics as a group of progressive thinkers who tried to go beyond the types of belief that the science and logic of their time offered to them. Mystics have opened up new avenues to mankind: "Many notions which are current today have started in the works of the mystics as mere aspirations towards a more perfect knowledge." They were the first to consider truth as "a virtue acquired through ascetic practices and deserved through moral conduct." The mystics have also inaugurated a new kind of logic that considered human feelings, particularly that of love, as having a demonstrative value. In the same connection, Janet points out how the concept of individuality is penetrating even physics, the concept of value into society, and how history in the nineteenth century was pervaded by the two principles of "historical truth" and of "progress," that is, two concepts that are absolutely foreign to positive sciences. It is as if history assumes that the past of mankind is a permanent space that someday should be accessible to man's direct investigation. Here again Janet concludes with his favorite Promethean thought that the evolution of mankind is not terminated and will eventually take an undreamed-of course.

Janet's Sources

The first and most immediate source of any creative thinker is his own personality. Though Janet carefully avoided speaking of himself, he did give a few hints that throw some light on certain aspects of his work. In *Psychological Automatism*, Janet incidentally mentions that he belongs to the motor type.

> When I am awake, I can think only by talking out loud, or writing, and my thought is always a half-arrested gesture. By night, on the contrary, I keep, as I have often noticed, the most absolute immobility. I am merely a spectator and no longer an actor; images and sounds forming tableaux and scenes pass before me. I see myself acting, or hear myself talking, though rarely,—and I always keep, at the same time, a vague feeling of my immobility and powerlessness. Precisely because of this great difference between my dreams and my thought in the waking state I find it difficult to remember my dreams.[149]

Elsewhere in the same book Janet makes a curious digression about the phenomenon of falling in love, which he considers to be a kind of illness that would not occur in a perfectly healthy or balanced person.[150] In these two places, Janet gives a clue that could explain the general direction of his thinking. He obviously belongs to the active, non-emotional type of individual. All those who knew him emphasized his prodigious activity, as well as his equanimity. It is not surprising that Janet was led to elaborate a psychological theory centered around the notion of activity and in which emotions were considered a somewhat troublesome disturbance of action, or at best regulations of action. No wonder that Jean Delay called Janet "the psychologist of efficiency."

Two other features in Janet's personality are also noteworthy. The first is the episode of depression that he underwent at the age of fifteen, and the tendency to psychasthenia, which was not much visible in his mature years but came to the fore later in his life. One may assume that his fine analyses of psychasthenia were to a certain extent derived from self-observation. The second feature is the religious crisis that he underwent at age seventeen and which no doubt was also a decisive event in his life. It is doubtful that he would have so attentively followed the case of Madeleine for twenty-five years, had it not been for his continuous preoccupation with the lost faith of his youth.

In Janet's family, his uncle Paul was among the main sources of Janet's thought. Paul Janet was a representative of the spiritualist school in philosophy, a school whose credo can be summarized in three points: belief in human liberty based on the direct testimony of consciousness—a morality based on the principle of absolute good—and belief in absolute duty, which relates human liberty to absolute good, as a means to its end. Paul Janet expounded his philosophy in many books whose principal merit, according to Fouillée, was the great number of secondary questions, examples, and arguments treated by him and not to be found elsewhere.[151] Though Pierre

Janet, under the influence of the positivist spirit prevailing at that time, distanced himself from the spiritualist outlook professed by his uncle, and shifted from philosophical to scientific psychology, the lasting influence of Paul Janet's thought can be recognized in his nephew's work. What Paul Janet expounded in detail under the name of "moral" was incorporated by Pierre Janet in his hierarchy of tendencies under the name of "rational-ergetic," "experimental," and "progressive" conducts. A more personal influence on Janet was that of J. M. Guyau, the author of *The Irreligion of the Future*, which had greatly influenced young French intellectuals of Janet's generation.[152] Guyau's *weltanschauung* was that of a deeply religious man affiliated with no established religion, and who could neither adopt a religious creed nor atheism.

It is not known which philosophers were the particular object of Janet's studies at the Ecole Normale Supérieure and during his teaching years. He seems to have had a fairly good knowledge of the history of philosophy in general.[153] Among the philosophers he most often quoted were Francis Bacon (the subject of his Latin thesis), Malebranche, Condillac, the school of the Ideologists, and particularly Maine de Biran. The latter is both a direct and an indirect source of Janet's psychology. In the eighteenth century, a prevalent theory was that sensation was the primary substance from which the entire life of the mind developed. Around 1750, philosophers became interested in occurrences of blind persons who became able to see after surgical operations. They began speculating about the role of vision and of each of the other types of sensory perception in mental life. Thereupon, Condillac (1715–1780) published his once-famous *Traité des Sensations* (1754), in which he imagined the myth of a statue whose physical make-up would be that of a human being, but which would be devoid of psychic life and would then be endowed with one sense after the other. Condillac speculated on how the statue would become animated, passing from sensations to images, ideas, thoughts, judgments, and the elaboration of science. Maine de Biran (1766–1824) elaborated a new theoretical construction of the human mind in which the basic fact is effort.[154] Consciousness is the apperception of the effort. Descartes' principle "I think, therefore I am" is replaced by "I will, therefore I am." Voluntary effort creates consciousness and uplifts the mind from sensation to perception and to higher operations of the mind, and furnishes the notions of force, causality, unity, identity, and liberty. Beneath that properly human life of conscious effort there is an animal life that is the realm of habit, elementary emotions, and instincts, a life that continues below consciousness and is manifested in sleep and somnambulism. Later in his life, Maine de Biran came to assert that above the properly human life of voluntary effort there was a third spiritual and religious life.

Maine de Biran's influence on Janet's psychology was both direct—seeing that he had read his works—and indirect, on account of the great influence exerted by Maine de Biran on the French *aliénistes* of the middle of the nineteenth century. Henri Delacroix has well shown how the theoretical concepts of Baillarger and Moreau de Tours derived from Maine de Biran's teaching.[155] In his theory of hallucinations, Baillarger contended that hallucinations and delusions occur when memory and imagination emancipate themselves from the conscious personality. The same idea is more systematically expressed in Moreau de Tours' theory of the *désagrégation* (which would today be called regression). "Hallucination and delusion occur through a gradual weakening of free will, of the power through which we bind and coordinate our ideas." For that reason, Moreau de Tours considered the dream as the key to the knowledge of mental illness. Janet constantly referred to what he called "Moreau de Tours' basic law of psychic life."

Among psychologists, Janet's master was undoubtedly Théodule Ribot, for whom he had the deepest personal respect and affection. Whereas experimental psychology at that time developed in Germany under the influence of Wundt as the science of the measurement of psychological factors, the French school with Taine and Ribot preferred the psychopathological approach. Ribot had borrowed from Claude Bernard the idea that disease is an experience instituted by nature. He applied this idea in the field of psychology. In order to study the normal functions of memory, will, and personality, Ribot investigated the diseases of those functions, and devoted a monograph to each one. However, not being a physician, Ribot had to rely on the descriptions given by a psychiatrist, whereas Janet took his medical degree in order to perform direct clinical studies. Ribot also introduced in France Jackson's principle of evolution and dissolution and of the positive and negative symptoms in nervous illness. Ribot applied this principle to the psychopathology of memory (that in senile amnesia, the more recent memories disappear before the earlier ones, has been called "Ribot's law"), and to will (in diseases of the will, Ribot said, voluntary activities disappear before automatic ones, and this is the origin of Janet's theory of psychasthenia).

From the clinical point of view, Janet is usually regarded as a disciple of Charcot. It is often overlooked that, before coming to the Salpêtrière in 1899, Janet already had six or seven years' experience in clinical work with neuroses and mental diseases in Le Havre with Doctor Gibert and Doctor Powilewicz, so that he came to the Salpêtrière, not as a student, but rather as an experienced collaborator. He learned to deal with psychotics, mostly on the wards of Doctor Séglas and Doctor Falret at the Salpêtrière.

Another fundamental source of Janet's work was the first dynamic psychiatry. We recall that while in Le Havre he discovered the work of Doctor Perrier and the small group of magnetizers in Caen, and that he subsequently explored the entire world of the forgotten knowledge investigated by men such as Puységur, Deleuze, Bertrand, Noizet, Teste, Gauthier, Charpignon, the two Despines, Du Potet, and a long series of pioneers whose merits and discoveries Janet never failed to mention.

Janet's theories of psychological energy have much in common with ideas that had been expressed by George Beard and S. Weir Mitchell, and particularly by William James. William James' paper *The Energies of Man* treats the problems of our energy-budget, of the rate of energizing, and of the various ways of mobilizing energy.[156] William James mentions effort, prayer, and religious conversion among dynamogenic factors. Janet's favorite notion of psychological tension is foreshadowed here.

Janet's later theories of the hierarchy of tendencies, his enlarged behaviorism, were also undoubtedly largely inspired by the work of Josiah Royce and James Mark Baldwin. Josiah Royce contended that "the distinction between the Self and the not-Self had a predominantly *social origin*." Our empirical self-consciousness, he added, depends upon a series of contrast-effects, whose psychological origin resides in social life. The Self of the child grows and forms itself through imitation. "In origin, then, the empirical Ego is secondary to our social experiences. In literal social life, the Ego is always known as in contrast to the Alter." The child, Royce says, idealizes (that is, internalizes) his social relationships, so that the contrast between Ego and Alter "can be refined into the conscious contrast between present and past self, between my higher and lower self, or between my conscience and my impulses. My reflective life, as it empirically occurs in me from moment to moment, is a sort of abstract and epitome of my whole social life."[157] Royce also drew the psychopathological implications of these theories.[158] The social self has its maladies, can be depressed, exalted, or deluded. Delusions of suspicion, persecution, and grandeur are pathological variations of the social aspect of self-consciousness, which under normal states would mean to be a person aware of social position, dignity, place in the world, and character.

J. M. Baldwin's theories are similar to those of Royce, but with more accent on the genetic aspect of this development. Baldwin distinguishes three stages in the genesis of the Ego and the Other.[159] First, there is a projective stage in which the infant "projects," in other words senses, other personalities before it has a sense of its own. After the seventh month comes the subjective stage in which imitation enables the child to "pass from my experience of what you are to an interpretation of what I am." Then comes the "ejective" stage, in which the child reverses the process; this means going "from the fuller sense of what I am, back to a fuller knowledge of what you are." This also means that the Ego and the Alter are born together. "My sense of myself grows by imitation of you, and my sense of you grows in terms of my sense of myself. Both *Ego* and *Alter* are thus essentially social; each is a *Socius* and each is an imitative creation."

Janet never concealed the fact that many of the ideas he developed so extensively in his great synthesis were inspired by Royce and Baldwin. Even the term *"socius,"* which he liked so much, was taken over from Baldwin.

The influence of German psychology on Janet's work is not easy to ascertain. Though Janet did not read German psychologists directly in the text, he knew of them through Ribot and other sources. The influence of Herbart's psychology is particularly open to question. One of Janet's favorite concepts, "the narrowness of the field of consciousness," seems to have been unknown to French psychologists before him, but can be definitely traced back to Herbart. In Herbart's theory, repression and narrowness of field of consciousness were two aspects of the same phenomenon. Since the field of consciousness is too narrow, a limited number of representations can come to the fore simultaneously, hence a struggle between the stronger and the weaker representations and the repression of the weaker by the stronger.[160]

It becomes impossible to trace Janet's sources among his contemporaries. As already mentioned in regard to Bergson, Durkheim, and Binet, it is more a matter of reciprocal influences, which often came about through conversation and personal contact rather than through writing.

Another problem is presented by the similarities that can be found in Janet's theories in comparison with theories of certain of his foreign contemporaries. W. Drabovitch has pointed out the "convergence of doctrines" between Janet and Pavlov.[161] Both proclaimed the importance of force or energy in psychic activity, though Pavlov expressed it in physiological terms and Janet, in psychological terms. According to Drabovitch, Janet's concepts of psychological tension, of the "drainage," of suggestion, of hypnosis are parallel to Pavlov's concepts. Pavlov occasionally commented on Janet's theories.[162]

Similarities between the theories of Janet and McDougall have been pointed out by Kerris.[163] Both describe the process of the development and construction of personality on the basis of the tendencies. McDougall, however, does not give such an elaborated picture or scale of the hierarchy of tendencies. He shows more the rivalry and struggle between the tendencies and emphasizes the integrative process of the nervous system. On the other hand, Janet keeps closer to the clinical experience.

Analogies between the later theories of Janet and the teachings of George Herbert Mead are particularly striking. Mead's system is also a social behaviorism, which takes as its starting point the individual's social activity and the cooperation of several individuals around a social object.[164] Consciousness, according to Mead, is an interiorization of the action of the others, and reasoning is the symbolic interiorization of discussion between several individuals.[165] Mead also considers emotion as the response of the human organism to our own attitudes. He views perception as an intermediary stage evolving from impulsion to manipulation (Janet's "suspensive perceptive" conduct). Mead distinguishes in the conscious personality the *I*, the *Me*, and the *Self*, which correspond fairly well to Janet's *individu, personnage,* and *moi.* The me, the same as Janet's "personnage," is a collection of internalized roles. Other similarities could be quoted and inevitably bring up the question: did Mead influence Janet or did Janet influence Mead? The problem is rendered particularly difficult through the fact that Mead's works were published posthumously in 1934 and later, although in his lifetime they had appeared fragmentarily in articles scattered in journals not easily accessible in Europe. On the other hand, Janet's first important publication of his later system appeared in 1926 in his book *From Anguish to Ecstasy,* although he too had already taught these theories for fifteen years in his lectures at the Collège de France. There is no evidence that Janet and Mead had been personally acquainted. A possible explanation might be that they each developed separately the same concepts that they had found in the works of Josiah Royce and James Mark Baldwin.

The Influence of Janet

Janet stands at the threshold of all modern dynamic psychiatry. His ideas have become so widely known that their true origin is often unrecognized and attributed to others. Few people realize, for instance, that the word "subconscious" was coined by Janet.

Bleuler's conception of schizophrenia as consisting of primary symptoms with a lowering of the tension of the association and secondary symptoms derived from the primary ones was to a large extent a transposition of Janet's concept of psychasthenia with its lowering of psychological tension. Bleuler himself said that the word "autism" essentially designates from the positive angle that which Janet called the "loss of the sense of the real" from the negative angle.[166]

C. G. Jung repeatedly referred to Janet (whose lectures he had attended in Paris during the winter semester 1902–1903). The influence of *Psychological Automatism* can be seen from Jung's way of considering the human mind as comprising a number of subpersonalities (Janet's "simultaneous psychological existences"). What Jung called "complex" was originally nothing but the equivalent of Janet's "subconscious fixed idea."

Janet's work also exerted a great influence on Adler's individual psychology. Adler acknowledged that his work on the feeling of inferiority constituted a development of Janet's observation on the *sentiment d'incomplétude.*[167]

The influence of Janet on Freud is a controversial problem which will be treated in a further chapter. We shall now be content to give a few glimpses of it. In their preliminary report (1893) and in their *Studies on Hysteria* (1895), Breuer and Freud referred to Janet's work. Janet's case histories of Lucie (1886), and Marie (1889), Marcelle (1891), Mme. D (1892), Achilles (1893), and several shorter ones published between 1886 and 1893 contained examples of hysterical patients being cured by bringing subconscious fixed ideas back to consciousness and by working them through. The close affinity of Freud's concept of transference with Janet's concept of somnambulic influence and need for direction has been noted by Jones in one of his earlier writings.[168]

In *Formulation of the Double Principle of Psychic Life*, Freud, in defining his principle of reality, refers to Janet's function of the real. Janet's function of synthesis, which he later enlarged in his psychology of tendencies and in his theory of the construction of personality, anticipated the shift of Freud's psychoanalysis from a psychology of the unconscious to an ego-psychology.

Janet's influence has also been considerable upon French psychiatry and its three main contemporary leaders, Henri Baruk, Henri Ey, and Jean Delay. At Janet's centennial, Henri Baruk hailed him as the man who had given clinical basis to the development of modern psychophysiology and proclaimed that in the future Janet's work would lead to the development of new discoveries in neurophysiology.[169] Henry Ey's organodynamic psychology and his theory of the structure of states of consciousness are to a large extent developments of Janet's thought.[170] Jean Delay believes that modern discoveries in neurophysiology give support to Janet's concept of psychological tension. The functions of vigilance as well as Janet's *présentification* have a substratum in certain parts of the diencephalon. Psychopharmacology, Delay adds, brought a confirmation of certain of Janet's ideas, and Delay for this reason has classified the psychotropic drugs as "psycholeptic," "psychoanaleptic," and "psychodysleptic," a classification based on Janetian concepts.[171]

Pierre Janet is a remarkable example of the way in which fame and oblivion are unequally distributed among scientists. Around 1900 his contemporaries had the impression that he would soon be the founder of a great school. However, in spite of the constant development of his work, it is as if he slowly slipped aside from the general current. Many psychiatrists and psychologists, as well as the cultured public, still saw him as only the author of *Psychological Automatism* and the clinician who had given accurate descriptions of obsessive neurosis. Comparatively few seemed to notice that he was creating a synthesis of immense scope and dimensions.

It is tempting, at this point, to speculate about the reasons why Janet was favored by Lesmosyne, the goddess of oblivion, rather than by Mnemosyne, the goddess of memory. Explanations may be found in Janet's enemies, in Janet himself, and in fluctuations in the spirit of the times.

In the course of his career Janet met at least three times with strong resistances or implacable enmities. The first time was following Charcot's death; we have already told elsewhere of the strong reaction that then arose against Charcot's teaching on hysteria and hypnotism. Although Janet had carefully abstained from following the reckless speculations about metallotherapy and transfer, nonetheless he became identified with Charcot's teachings simply because at the Salpêtrière he was the only one who persisted in utilizing hypnosis and in believing that hysteria was more than a fake. The reaction against Charcot went so far as to promote a rigidly organicist, antipsychological spirit among French neurologists. Men such as Babinski and Déjerine were openly hostile toward Janet and finally managed to check his influence at the Salpêtrière. Janet was no less attacked by the Nancy School against which he maintained the distinction between hypnotism and suggestion. A second wave of attacks against Janet, unleashed by a number of Catholic theologians and laymen, followed the publication of his work *From Anguish to Ecstasy*. However, the fiercest attacks came from the psychoanalysts. Though Freud had summarily acknowledged Janet's previous research in 1893 and 1895, he became increasingly critical of him. Janet's report on psychoanalysis at the London Congress in 1913, at which he claimed priority for the discovery of subconscious fixed ideas and cathartic therapy, was the signal for violent attacks against Janet by certain psychoanalysts. Ernest Jones publicly and expressly accused him of dishonesty, asserting that Freud's discoveries owed nothing to Janet.[172] In 1945, the French psychoanalyst Madeleine Cavé, in defiance of chronology, accused Janet of hurried plagiarism upon the publication of Breuer and Freud's paper of 1893.[173] Janet, she said, had published in 1889 the case of Marie without understanding how and why the patient had been cured, but that, after the publication of Breuer's and Freud's paper of 1893, he did understand and hastened to apply this therapy and to publish other cases, referring to Breuer and Freud as being his imitators. The eighty-six-year-old man was perhaps unaware of this attack and did not reply to it, but it certainly contributed to the maintaining of a hostile attitude toward him among the younger psychoanalytic generation.

Other reasons for Janet's lack of fame could be found in his personality. He always maintained an unrelenting independence; he had actually no master, not even Charcot or Ribot. Nor did he ever belong to a group or team. He had no disciples and no school; any kind of proselytism was absolutely alien to him. In order to have students, Janet needed either a post at the Sorbonne where he would have taught psychology, or a ward of his own at the Salpêtrière, which would have enabled him to give clinical teaching to medical students. However, he had none of those, and his teaching activity was restricted to the Collège de France, a place of higher learning independent of any university and therefore frequented mainly by specialists, foreign visitors, and the educated public rather than by students. A small number of his auditors became enthusiastic over Janet's teaching and tried to propagate it. Among them were the Reverend Horton, who published a condensed version of Janet's lectures on the psychology of religion, Dr. Benjamin Subercaseaux of Chile[174] who expounded Janet's theory of the hierarchy of tendencies in Spanish, and Dr. Leonhard Schwartz of Basle, whose posthumously published book on Janet's psychology unfortunately remained unfinished.[175]

The third reason for which Janet's fame did not develop as one might have expected can be sought for in the *Zeitgeist*. Janet's lectures on psychotherapy were given in 1909, and in 1910 he was starting with the psychology of tendencies. But it took him several years to write the *Médications Psychologiques*, the publication of which had to be postponed on account of the war. When it did appear in 1919, the public had the impression that Janet's concepts had not changed for ten years, and few realized that by that time his interests had taken a new turn. On the other hand, the postwar period was one of general upheaval and iconoclasm, in the field of ideas as well as in that of politics and mores, and as more time passed the greater became the gap between Janet and the preoccupations of the young psychiatrists.

It would seem almost as if some mysterious fate had decreed the erasing of Janet's memory. When he died on February 24, 1947, no newspapers were appearing in Paris as a result of a printers' strike; his death remained, therefore, almost unnoticed. When the newspapers again appeared on March 18, it was mentioned in two lines amid a great backlog of information of all kinds.[176] The movie theaters did announce his death, but since no films had ever been taken of him, they had to be content with projecting Janet's picture onto the screen. The only known record of his voice seems to have disappeared. In 1956, Freud's centennial was celebrated at the Salpêtrière and a memorial was erected to him in remembrance of his visit to Charcot's clinic in 1885–1886. But no one thought of erecting at the Salpêtrière a memorial to Janet at his centennial in 1959, although it was there that he had made his celebrated studies of Madame D, Marcelle, Justine, Achilles, Irène, the famous Madeleine, and so many others. In 1960, when a volume was published for the celebration of the foundation of the Collège Sainte Barbe, a list of the illustrious men who had studied there did not contain Janet's name. Still worse, Janet's works have never been reprinted; they are becoming increasingly scarce or unobtainable.[177]

Thus, Janet's work can be compared to a vast city buried beneath ashes, like Pompeii. The fate of any buried city is uncertain. It may remain buried forever. It may remain concealed while being plundered by marauders. But it may also perhaps be unearthed some day and brought back to life.

And so, while the veil of Lesmosyne was falling upon Janet, the veil of Mnemosyne was lifted to illuminate his great rival, Sigmund Freud.

Notes

1. The author is particularly grateful to Madame Hélène Pichon-Janet and Mademoiselle Fanny Janet who provided him with much information about their father's life and the history of the Janet family.
2. These details are borrowed from a biography of Pierre Janet's uncle by Georges Picot, *Paul Janet. Notice historique* (Paris: Hachette, 1903).
3. Particulars about names and dates of the Janet family have been provided by the Archives du Département de la Seine.
4. Philippe Dollinger, director of the Strasbourg Archives, kindly provided the author with photocopies concerning the Hummel family from the town registry.
5. Jules Janet, *Les Troubles psychopathiques de la miction. Essai de psycho-physiologie normale et pathologique.* Thèse méd., 1889–1890, No. 216 (Paris: Lefrançois, 1890).
6. Paul Janet, *Notes et souvenirs* (Paris: Gauthier-Villars, 1933).
7. These details are borrowed from the article by Mme. Hélène Pichon-Janet, "Pierre Janet–Quelques notes sur sa vie," *L'Evolution Psychiatrique* (1950), No. 3, pp. 345–364.
8. Jules Lemaître, "L'Esprit normalien," *Le Centenaire de l'Ecole Normale Supérieure, 1795–1895* (Paris: Hachette, 1895), pp. 566–571.
9. Professor Martin of the École Normale Supérieure, who was kind enough to take the author to the school's archives and to locate Pierre Janet's file, found only two documents in it: Janet's application of February 1, 1879, and his father's written authorization.
10. Bersot was also the author of a book, *Mesmer et le magnétisme animal* (Paris: Hachette, 1852), which had just been reedited in 1879 in an enlarged edition and which may have drawn the attention of young Pierre Janet to the history of animal magnetism.
11. These details have been taken from Pierre Janet's file at the archives of the Faculté de Médecine of Paris.
12. Dominique Parodi, Obituary of Pierre Janet, *Association Amicale de secours des anciens élèves de l'École Normale Supérieure* (1948), pp. 27–30.
13. Compulsory military service of one year was later imposed on the Normalians by a new law of 1888. See André Lalande, "L'Instruction militaire à l'école," *Le Centenaire de l'École Normale Supérieure*, pp. 544–551.
14. The author is obliged for these details to J. Dupré, Proviseur of the Lycée Jean Giraudoux in Châteauroux.
15. *Le Fondement du droit de propriété. Conférence de M. Pierre Janet.* Ligue Française de l'enseignement, cercle de Châteauroux (Châteauroux; Imprimerie Gablin, 1883). A copy, perhaps the only one extant, exists at the Bibliothèque Nationale in Paris.
16. The author is indebted to Mr. Alekan, Proviseur of the Lycée du Havre, for a copy of that address, which was published in the "palmarès" of the Lycée du Havre in 1884.
17. Nicolas Malebranche, *De la Recherche de la vérité*, edited by Pierre Janet (Paris: Alcan, 1886), Book II.
18. Pierre Janet, "Psychological autobiography," in Carl Murchison, *A History of Psychology in Autobiography* (Worcester, Mass.: Clark University Press, 1930), I, 123–133.
19. Pierre Janet, "Note sur quelques phénomènes de somnambulisme," *Bulletins de la Société de psychologie physiologique*, I (1885), 24–32.

20. J. Ochorowicz, *De la Suggestion mentale* (Paris: Doin, 1887), p. 118.

21. No mention of these experiments is to be found in *Le Passe-Temps du Havre* and *Le Carillon*. Mr. A. Lecrocq, the Chief Archivist of Le Havre, who was kind enough to go through the daily newspapers of Le Havre for that critical period and the following weeks, told the author he found no mention of these experiments.

22. Pierre Janet, *Baco Verulamius alchemicis philosophis quid debuerit* (Angers: Imprimerie Burdin, 1889).

23. These details are borrowed from an address by Edmond Faral at the commemorative session at the Sorbonne on June 22, 1939. See *Le Centenaire de Théodule Ribot et Jubilé de la psychologie scientifique française* (Agen: Imprimerie moderne, 1939).

24. Paul Janet's objections and criticisms of *L'Automatisme psychologique* are contained in his *Principes de métaphysique et de psychologie* (Paris: Delagrave, 1897), II, 556–572.

25. *Premier Congrès international de l'hypnotisme expérimental et thérapeutique.* Comptes-rendus publiés par Edgar Bérillon (Paris: Doin, 1890).

26. *Discours de M. Pierre Janet à la distribution des prix du Collège Rollin* (July 30, 1892) (Paris: Chaix, 1892).

27. The author is greatly indebted to Dr. Hahn, Chief Librarian and Archivist of the Faculté de Médecine in Paris, for providing him with a photocopy of Pierre Janet's entire file.

28. Pierre Janet, "Kyste parasitaire du cerveau," *Archives Générales de Médecine,* 7th series, XXVIII (1891) (II), 464–472.

29. Pierre Janet, "Etude sur quelques cas d'amnésie antérograde dans la maladie de la désagrégation psychologique," *International Congress of Experimental Psychology,* Second Session, London, 1892) (London: William and Norgate, 1892), pp. 26–30.

30. It has not been possible thus far to find a list of the topics on which Janet lectured at the Sorbonne and the Collège de France in those years.

31. "Réunion constitutive de l'Institut Psychique," *Bulletin de l'Institut Psychique International,* I (1900), 13–21.

32. These details have been borrowed from Pierre Janet's file in the archives of the Collège de France.

33. Such was the case of Ernest Jones as told by himself in his autobiography, *Free Associations* (London: Hogarth Press, 1959), p. 175.

34. "The Relationships of Abnormal Psychology," *International Congress of Art and Science, Universal Exposition, St. Louis, 1904,* V, Howard J. Rogers ed. (Boston, 1906), 737–753.

35. These lectures were published in a volume entitled *The Major Symptoms of Hysteria* (London: Macmillan Co., 1907).

36. In Janet's mind this term was no doubt a reference to Auguste Comte's idea that man's interpretation of Nature went through three stages: a "religious" one, where natural phenomena were explained through the intervention of gods or spirits, a "metaphysical" one, where fictitious abstract concepts were resorted to, and a "scientific" one, where only experimental data are taken into account for the formulation of general laws.

37. Pierre Janet, "Valeur de la psycho-analyse de Freud," *Revue de Psychothérapie et de Psychologie Appliquée,* XXIX (1915), 82–83.

38. Walter M. Horton, "The Origin and Psychological Function of Religion According to Pierre Janet," *American Journal of Psychology,* XXXV (1924), 16–52.

39. See Ezequiel A. Chavez, *Le Docteur Pierre Janet et son oeuvre. Discours prononcé dans le grand auditoire de l'Université Nationale de Mexico, le 14 août 1925.* Publicaciones de la Secretaría de Educación Pública (Mexico, D. F.: Editorial Cultura, 1925).

40. Janet gave his impressions on Argentina in the *Journal des Nations Américaines: Argentine,* Nouvelle Série, I, No. 7 (June 18, 1933).

41. Freud commented on this incident in a letter to Marie Bonaparte, the original text of which can be found in the German edition of Jones' *Das Leben und Werk von Sigmund Freud* (Bern: Huber, 1962), III, 254.

42. E. Minkowski, "A propos des dernières publications de Pierre Janet," *Bulletin de Psychologie*, XIV (November 1960), 121–127.

43. As stated by Janet in "Perspectives d'application de la psychologie à l'industrie," *Premier cycle d'étude de psychologie industrielle. Fascicule No. 1, Psychologie et Travail* (Paris: Cégos, 1943), pp. 3–8.

44. Pierre Janet, "La Psychologie de la conduite," *Encyclopédie Française*, VIII, La vie mentale (1938), 8° 08–11 to 8° 08–16.

45. *Mélanges offerts à Monsieur Pierre Janet par sa famille, ses amis et ses disciples à l'occasion de ses quatre-vingts ans* (Paris: d'Artrey, 1939).

46. *Centenaire de Théodule Ribot. Jubilé de la psychologie française* (Agen: Imprimerie Moderne, 1939).

47. These details have been kindly provided by Professor Jean Delay.

48. Pierre Janet, *Les Médications psychologiques* (Paris: Alcan, 1919), I, 280.

49. Janet is credited with having said that if we could find a means of provoking epileptic attacks at will, they could be applied successfully to the treatment of certain patients. The author has not been able to find this as definitely formulated in his works, but the idea is implicit in *Les Médications psychologiques* (Paris: Alcan, 1919), II, 124.

50. The only interview given by Janet, to our knowledge, was published by Frédéric Lefèvre, dated March 17, 1928. It was reprinted in Frédéric Lefèvre. *Une heure avec . . . ;* 6th series (Paris: Flammarion, 1933), pp. 48–57. It is not an interview proper but an account of a discussion between Janet and a certain Marcel Jousse at which the journalist had been present.

51. Carl Murchison, *A History of Psychology in Autobiography* (Worcester, Mass.: Clark University Press, 1930), I, 123–133.

52. Pierre Janet, "Autobiographie psychologique," *Les Etudes philosophiques*, Nouvelle série, No. 2 (April–June 1946), pp. 81–87.

53. Max Dessoir, *Buch der Erinnerungen* (Stuttgart: Enke, 1946), p. 122.

54. Marcel Prévost, *L'Automne d'une femme* (Paris: Calmann-Lévy, 1893). Mme. Hélène Pichon-Janet, in reply to the author's inquiry, told him that her father had actually been casually acquainted with Marcel Prévost.

55. Walter M. Horton, "The origin and psychological function of religion according to Pierre Janet," *American Journal of Psychology*, XXXV (1924), 16–52.

56. Pierre Janet, *L'Evolution psychologique de la personnalité* (Paris: Chahine, 1929), p. 332: "*L'amour n'est autre chose qu'une hypothèse transformée en idée fixe.*"

57. *Journal de Psychologie*, V (1908), 516–526.

58. Richard Krafft-Ebing, *Psychopathia Sexualis*, trad. fr. (Paris: Payot, 1931), préface, pp. 4–8.

59. Pierre Janet, *L'Evolution psychologique de la personnalité* (Paris: Chahine, 1929), p. 328.

60. *L'Evolution psychiatrique* (1950), No. 3, p. 344.

61. Raymond Roussel, *Comment j'ai écrit certains de mes livres* (Paris: Lemerre, 1935), pp. 27, 175–183.

62. Ernest Harms, "Pierre M. F. Janet," *American Journal of Psychiatry*, CXV (1959), 1036–1037.

63. Fr. Bruno de Jésus-Marie, "A propos de la 'Madeleine' de Pierre Janet," *Etudes Carmélitaines*, XVI, No. 1 (1931), 20–61.

64. At an international congress in Amsterdam in 1907, seven of the participants signed an address in favor of the use of Esperanto in international congresses. One of those seven was Pierre Janet, *Compte-Rendu des Travaux du 1er Congrès International de Psychiatrie et de Neurologie, tenu à Amsterdam en 1907* (Amsterdam: J. H. de Bussy, 1908), p. 908.

65. Pierre Janet, "La Tension psychologique, ses degrés, ses oscillations," *British Journal of Psychology, Medical Section*, I (1920–1921), 164. "Les souvenirs irréels," *Archives de Psychologie*, XIX (1925), 17. *L'Evolution de la mémoire et la notion du temps* (Paris: Maloine, 1928), p. 491. *L'Evolution psychologique de la personnalité* (Paris: Chahine, 1929), p. 579. *Les Débuts de l'intelligence* (Paris: Flammarion, 1935), pp. 166–168. "La Psychologie de la croyance et le mysticisme," *Revue de Métaphysique*

et de Morale, XLIII (1936), 399. "L'Acte de la destruction," *Revue Générale des Sciences,* LI (1940–1941), 145–148.

66. Jean Guitton, *La Vocation de Bergson* (Paris: Gallimard, 1960).
67. Henri Bergson, "De la simulation inconsciente dans l'état d'hypnotisme," *Revue Philosophique,* XXII (1886) (II), 525–531.
68. Bergson published a commented edition of excepts of Lucretius' *De Natura Rerum* (1883), and Janet a commented edition of Book II of Malebranche's *Recherche de la vérité* (1886).
69. *Revue de Métaphysique et de Morale,* XLIII (1936), 531.
70. François-Louis Bertrand, *Alfred Binet et son oeuvre* (Paris: Alcan, 1930).
71. Alfred Binet, "La Vie psychique des micro-organismes," *Revue Philosophique,* XXIV (1887) (II), 449–489, 582–611.
72. Alfred Binet, *La Psychologie du raisonnement* (Paris: Alcan, 1886).
73. Alfred Binet, *Revue Philosophique,* XXIX (1890) (I), 186–200.
74. Charles Féré et Alfred Binet, *Le Magnétisme Animal* (Paris: Alcan, 1887).
75. Alfred Binet, *L'Etude expérimentale de l'intelligence* (Paris: Schleicher, 1903).
76. Pierre Janet, *Manuel du baccalauréat de l'enseignement secondaire classique Philosophie* (Paris: Nony, 1894).
77. Malebranche, *De la Recherche de la vérité,* Pierre Janet, ed. (Paris: Alcan, 1886) (II), 22.
78. Pierre Janet, "Les Actes inconscients et le dédoublement de la personnalité pendant le somnambulisme provoqué," *Revue Philosophique,* XXII (1886) (II), 577–592.
79. Pierre Janet, "L'Anesthésie systématisée et la dissociation des phénomènes psychologiques," *Revue Philosophique,* XXIII (1887) (II), 449–472.
80. Pierre Janet, "Les Actes inconscients et la mémoire pendant le somnambulisme," *Revue Philosophique,* XXV (1888) (I), 238–279.
81. Prosper Despine, *Psychologie Naturelle* (Paris: Savy, 1868) (I), 490–491.
82. Pierre Janet always contended that he was the originator of the word *subconscious.* (The author has not found any instance of that word being used before him.) He had coined it apparently in order to show that he used a psychological approach quite distinct from the metaphysical concept of the unconscious of Von Hartmann, which was so fashionable at that time.
83. Janet was well aware of the plasticity of hysterical phenomena and mentions that three hysterical patients, who had had crises of very different types, were put in the same ward, after which their symptoms merged into the same type of crisis. A new type of hysteria was thus in the making of that ward, which one might have studied as a natural one had one not known its origin. (*L'Automatisme psychologique* [Paris: Alcan, 1889], p. 449.)
84. Pierre Janet, *L'Automatisme Psychologique* (Paris: Alcan, 1889), pp. 436–440. This was the second case of cathartic cure published by Janet, the first being that of Lucie, published in 1886.
85. Pierre Janet, "Etude sur un cas d'aboulie et d'idées fixes," *Revue Philosophique,* XXXI (1891) (I), 258–287, 382–407.
86. J. M. Charcot, "Sur un cas d'amnésie rétro-antérograde probablement d'origine hystérique," *Revue de Médecine,* XII (1892), 81–96. (With follow-up by A. Souques, same journal, same year, and volume, 267–400, 867–881.)
87. Pierre Janet, "Etude sur un cas d'amnésie antérograde dans la maladie de la désagrégation psychologique," *International Congress of Experimental Psychology,* London, 1892. (London: Williams & Norgate, 1892), pp. 26–30.
88. Pierre Janet, "L'amnésie continue," *Revue Générale des Sciences,* IV (1893), 167–179.
89. J. M. Charcot, *Clinique des maladies du système nerveux,* Georges Guinon, ed. (Paris: Progrès Médical et Alcan, 1893), II, 266–288.
90. Pierre Janet, "Histoire d'une idée fixe," *Revue Philosophique,* XXXVII (1894) (I), 121–168.
91. Pierre Janet, "Un Cas de possession et l'exorcisme moderne," *Bulletin de l'Univer-*

sité de Lyon, VIII (1894), 41–57. Janet had already summarized the story of that patient in his medical thesis *Contribution à l'étude des accidents mentaux chez les hystériques* (Paris: Rueff, 1893), pp. 252–257.

92. In his foreword to *Névroses et idées fixes,* Janet mentions that Achilles was still in good health seven years after the cure.

93. Pierre Janet, "L'Amnésie et la dissociation des souvenirs," *Journal de Psychologie,* I (1904), 28–37.

94. Pierre Janet, "L'Insomnie par idée fixe subconsciente," *Presse Médicale,* V (1897) (II), 41–44.

95. Pierre Janet, "Note sur quelques spasmes des muscles du tronc chez les hystériques," *La France Médicale et Paris médical,* XLII (1895), 769–776.

96. Janet's psychological analysis had from the beginning therapeutic implications, but as long as he had not started his medical studies Janet could not emphasize that aspect of his work.

97. Pierre Janet: "Sur la divination par les miroirs et les hallucinations subconscientes," *Bulletin de l'Université de Lyon,* XI (July 1897), 261–274.

98. Raymond and Janet, "Les délires ambulatoires ou les fugues," *Gazette des Hôpitaux,* LXVIII (1895), 754–762.

99. In his paper "L'Anesthésie hystérique," *Archives de Neurologie,* XXIV (1892), 29–55, Janet mentioned the phenomenon of "imaginary electrization," which he observed in 1887 at the hospital of Le Havre. While giving electric treatment to a patient afflicted with hysterical paralysis, he marvelled how favorably the patient reacted to the contact of the electrode, until he suddenly noticed that the plug was not connected.

100. "L'Influence somnambulique et le besoin de direction," *III. Internationaler Congress für Psychologie, vom 4. bis 7. August 1896* (Munich: J. F. Lehmann, 1897), pp. 143–145.

101. Pierre Janet, "L'Influence somnambulique et le besoin de direction," *Revue Philosophique,* XLIII (1897) (I), 113–143. *Névroses et idées fixes* (Paris: Alcan, 1903), II, 423–480.

102. As in a review of Janets medical thesis in *Mind,* New Series, II (1893), 403.

103. Pierre Janet, *Névroses et idées fixes,* 2 vols. (Paris: Alcan, 1898).

104. Pierre Janet, *Les Obsessions et la psychasthénie,* 2 vols. (Paris: Alcan, 1903).

105. Pierre Janet, *Les Névroses* (Paris: Flammarion, 1909).

106. Pierre Janet, *Contribution à l'étude des accidents mentaux chez les hystériques* (Paris: Rueff et Cie, 1893).

107. Pierre Janet, "Traitement psychologique de L'hystérie," *Traité de Thérapeutique Appliquée* (Dir. Albert Robin). Fascicule XV, IIe. partie (Paris: Rueff, 1898), pp. 140–216.

108. Pierre Janet, "Quelques définitions récentes de l'hystérie," *Archives de Neurologie,* XXV (1893), 417–438; XXVI, 1–29.

109. Pierre Janet, "Quelques définitions récentes de l'hystérie," *Archives de Neurologie,* XXV (1893), 417–438; XXVI, 1–29.

110. Henri Bergson, *Matière et mémoire* (Paris: Alcan, 1896), p. 119.

111. Pierre Janet, *Les Obsessions et la psychasthénie* (Paris: Alcan, 1903), I, 491.

112. Pierre Janet, *Les Obsessions et la psychasthénie* (Paris: Alcan, 1903), I, 505.

113. Pierre Janet, "Un Cas de délire systématisé dans la paralysie générale," *Journal de Psychologie,* III (1906), 329–331. A somewhat similar study was made by S. Ferenczi and S. Hollos, *Zur Psychoanalyse der paralytischen Geistesstörung* (Vienna: Internationaler Psychoanalytischer Verlag, 1922). Eng. trans., *Psychoanalysis and the Psychic Disorders of General Paralysis,* Nervous and Mental Disease Monograph Series, No. 42 (1925).

114. It is hardly necessary to point out that "psychological tension" in Janet's sense had nothing in common with what is called "tension" in the colloquial sense of anxiety or irritation, which, in Janet's terminology, would, on the contrary, be *low* states of "psychological tension."

115. Pierre Janet, *Les Médications psychologiques* (Paris: Alcan, 1919), III, 469–470.

116. Leonhard Schwartz, *Neurasthenie: Entstehung. Erklärung und Behandlung der nervösen Zustände* (Basel: Benno Schwabe, 1951).

117. It is difficult to distinguish to what extent Schwartz elaborated on Janet's principles. As Schwartz told the author, he had kept in constant correspondence with Janet and had discussed these problems with him.

118. They are described extensively in a multigraphed course, Pierre Janet, *Psychologie Expérimentale. Compte-Rendu du cours de M. Janet,* Collège de France (Paris: Chahine, 1926), pp. 223–317.

119. Pierre Janet, *La Force et la faiblesse psychologiques* (Paris: Maloine, 1930), pp. 127–128.

120. Incidentally, Ernst Kretschmer, in his *Psychotherapeutische Studien* (Stuttgart: Thieme, 1949), p. 198, contended that "the clarification and the entire and total liquidation of the present conflicts is the alpha and omega of any therapeutic of neurosis."

121. Leonhard Schwartz, "Berufstätigkeit und Nervosität," *Schweizerische Zeitschrift für Hygiene,* No. 4 (1929).

122. A personal note is appropriate here: a very intelligent patient, after recovering from an acute schizophrenic episode, related to the author the story of his illness and added, "Doctor, you should never discharge a patient without explaining his illness to him." To be sure, when a patient is discharged from a mental hospital, the resident will "terminate" his case history, but all too often it will not occur to anyone to help the patient make an "act of termination" in regard to the illness he has gone through.

123. Hermann Simon, *Aktivere Krankenbehandlung in der Irrenanstalt* (Berlin and Leipzig: De Gruyter, 1929).

124. Pierre Janet, "The Psycholeptic Crises," *Boston Medical and Surgical Journal,* CLII (1905), 93–100.

125. Pierre Janet, "L'Alcoolisme et la dépression mentale," *Revue Internationale de Sociologie,* XXIII (1915), 476–485.

126. Pierre Janet, "La Kleptomanie et la dépression mentale," *Journal de Psychologie,* VIII (1911), 97–103.

127. Pierre Janet, *Les Médications psychologiques* (Paris: Alcan, 1919), II, 97–98.

128. Pierre Janet, *Les Médications psychologiques* (Paris: Alcan, 1919), III, 249–297, and *La Force et la faiblesse psychologiques,* 179–180.

129. See, for instance, M. B. Ray, *How Never to Be Tired* (Indianapolis and New York: Bobbs Merrill Co., 1938). The advice given in that book would be quite advisable for hypotonic neurotics but disastrous for the asthenics.

130. Pierre Janet, *Les Médications psychologiques* (Paris: Alcan, 1919), III, 414–417.

131. Pierre Janet, *De l'Angoisse à l'extase* (Paris: Alcan, 1926), I, 210–234.

132. Pierre Janet, *Les Débuts de l'intelligence* (Paris: Flammarion, 1935), pp. 44–45.

133. The best all-over account given by Janet was his contribution "La psychologie de la conduite," in the *Encyclopédie Française,* VIII (1938), 8° 08–11 to 8° 08–16.

134. Leonhard Schwartz, *Die dynamische Psychologie von Pierre Janet* (Basle: B. Schwabe, 1951). See also, I. Meyerson, "Janet et la théorie des tendances," *Journal de Psychologie,* XL (1947), 5–19.

135. Pierre Janet, *De l'Angoisse à l'extase* (Paris: Alcan, 1926), II (1928), 262.

136. Pierre Janet, *La Pensée intérieure et ses troubles* (Paris: Maloine, 1927).

137. Pierre Janet, *L'Amour et la haine* (Paris: Maloine, 1937).

138. Pierre Janet, *Les Débuts de l'intelligence* (Paris: Flammarion, 1935). *L'Intelligence avant le langage* (Paris: Flammarion, 1936).

139. Janet apparently did not suspect that this theory of language had already been set forth by Heymann Steinthal, *Einleitung in die Psychologie der Sprachwissenschaft,* 2. Aufl. (Berlin: Dümmler, 1881), pp. 372–374.

140. Pierre Janet, "Le Langage inconsistant," *Theoria,* III (1937), 57–71.

141. Pierre Janet, *La Pensée intérieure et ses troubles* (Paris: Maloine, 1927).

142. Pierre Janet, *De l'Angoisse à l'extase* (Paris: Alcan, 1926), I, 229.

143. Henri Bergson, *L'Evolution créatice* (Paris: Alcan, 1907). Similar thoughts have been expressed by Gardner Murphy, *Human Potentialities* (New York: Basic Books, 1958).

144. Walter M. Horton, "The Origin and Psychological Function of Religion According to Pierre Janet," *American Journal of Psychology*, XXXV (1924), 16–52.

145. Pierre Janet, "Un Cas du phénomène des Apports," *Bulletin de l'Institut Psychologique International*, I (1900–1901), 329–335. See also Janet's preface to J. Grasset, *Le Spiritisme devant la science* (Montpellier and Paris, 1904), pp. VII–XXIX.

146. Janet took great pains to disguise factual details of name and place in Madeleine's life when talking of her. The biographical details given here are borrowed from the probably more accurate account of her life given by Bruno de Jésus-Marie, "A propos de la Madeleine de Pierre Janet," *Etudes Carmélitaines*, XVI, No. 1 (1931), 20–61.

147. Pierre Janet, "Le Spiritisme contemporain," *Revue Philosophique*, XXXIII (1892) (I), 413–442.

148. Pierre Janet, "La Psychologie de la croyance et le mysticisme," *Revue de Métaphysique et de Morale*, XLIII (1936), 327–358, 507–532; XLIV (1937), 369–410.

149. Pierre Janet, *L'Automatisme psychologique* (Paris: Alcan, 1889), pp. 118–119.

150. Pierre Janet, *L'Automatisme psychologique* (Paris: Alcan, 1889), pp. 466–467.

151. Alfred Fouillée, *Critique des systèmes de morale contemporaine*, 4th ed. (Paris: Alcan, 1883), pp. 281–317.

152. Jean-Marie Guyau, *L'Irréligion de l'avenir. Etude Sociologique* (Paris: Alcan, 1887).

153. In the *Manuel du Baccalauréat* by Pierre Janet, Henri Piéron, and Charles Lalo, the chapter on History of Philosophy (pp. 329–367) is by Pierre Janet (Paris: Vuibert, 1925).

154. See Paul Janet, *Les Maîtres de la pensée moderne* (Paris: Calmann Lévy, 1888), pp. 363–403; André Cresson, *Maine de Biran, sa vie, son oeuvre* (Paris: Presses Universitaires de France, 1950); and the special issue of the *Bulletin de la Société Française de Philosophie*, Vol. XXIV (1924), devoted to Maine de Biran.

155. Henri Delacroix, "Maine de Biran et l'École médico-psychologique," *Bulletin de la Société Française de Philosophie*, XXIV (1924), 51–63.

156. William James, "The Energies of Man," *The American Magazine* (1907). Reprinted in *Memories and Studies* (New York and London: Longmans Green & Co., 1911), pp. 229–264.

157. Josiah Royce, *The World and the Individual* (New York: Macmillan, 1901), pp. 245–266.

158. Josiah Royce, *Studies of Good and Evil* (New York: Appleton, 1898), pp. 169–197.

159. James Mark Baldwin, *Mental Development in the Child and the Race, Methods and Processes* (New York: Macmillan, 1895), pp. 334–338.

160. This part of Herbart's theories may have been known to Janet, through an article by Straszewski, "Herbart, sa vie et sa philosophie," *Revue Philosophique*, VII (1879) (I), pp. 504–526, 645–673.

161. W. Drabovitch, *Fragilité de la liberté et séduction des dictatures. Essai de psychologie sociale* (Paris: Mercure de France, 1934).

162. Ivan Pavlov, "Lettre ouverte à Janet, Les sentiments d'emprise et la phase ultraparadoxale," *Journal de Psychologie*, XXX (1933), 849–854.

163. Felicitas Kerris, *Integration and Desintegration der Persönlichkeit bei Janet und McDougall*, Phil. Diss. (Bonn-Würzburg: Richard Mayr, 1938).

164. See C. W. Morris, in his introduction to G. H. Mead, *Mind, Self and Society* (Chicago: University of Chicago Press, 1934).

165. David Victoroff, *G. H. Mead, sociologue et philosophe* (Paris: Presses Universitaires de France, 1953), pp. 62–63, Victoroff argues that Mead's and Janet's theories of reflected thought are identical and expressed in almost the same terms.

166. Eugen Bleuler, *Dementia Praecox oder Gruppe der Schizophrenien* (1911) in Aschaffenburg, *Handbuch der Psychiatrie*, Spezieller Teil, 4. Abt., 1. Hälfte, p. 52.

167. Alfred Adler, *Ueber den nervösen Charakter* (Wiesbaden: J. F. Bergmann, 1912), p. 3.

168. Ernest Jones, "The Action of Suggestion in Psychotherapy," *Journal of Abnormal Psychology,* V (1911), 217–254.

169. *Revue Philosophique,* CL (1960), 283–288.

170. Henri Ey, "La Psychopathologie de Pierre Janet et la conception dynamique de la psychiatrie," *Mélanges offerts à Monsieur Pierre Janet. . . .* (Paris: d'Artrey, 1939), pp. 87–100.

171. Jean Delay, "Pierre Janet et la tension psychologique," *Psychologie Française,* V (1960), 93–110.

172. Ernest Jones, "Professor Janet on Psychoanalysis: A Rejoinder," *Journal of Abnormal Psychology,* IX (1914–1915), 400–410.

173. Madeleine Cavé, *L'Oeuvre paradoxale de Freud. Essai sur le théorie des névroses* (Paris: Presses Universitaires de France, 1945).

174. Benjamin Subercaseaux, *Apuntes de Psicología Comparada* (Santiago de Chile: Bardi, 1927).

175. Leonhard Schwartz, *Die Neurosen und die dynamische Psychologie von Pierre Janet* (Basel: Benno Schwabe, 1950).

176. *Le Monde,* March 18, 1947.

177. One of Janet's former publishers, with whom the author raised the question, declared emphatically: "No, sir, Janet's works will *never* be reprinted."

7

Sigmund Freud and Psychoanalysis

WITH SIGMUND FREUD, a new feature is seen in the history of dynamic psychiatry. Whereas men such as Pierre Janet kept closely within the bounds of the traditional scientific organizations, of the university, of established learned societies, wrote in journals open to any psychological or medical viewpoint, and never attempted to found a school, Freud openly broke with official medicine. With Freud begins the era of the newer dynamic schools, with their official doctrine, their rigid organization, their specialized journals, their closed membership, and the prolonged initiation imposed upon their members. The founding of this new type of dynamic psychiatry was linked with a cultural revolution comparable in scope to that unleashed by Darwin.

The Life Frame of Sigmund Freud

Sigmund Freud was born in Freiberg, Moravia, in 1856 and died in London in 1939. Except for his first four years and his last one, he spent his entire life in Vienna.

In 1856 the Austrian Empire was still feeling the shock of the revolution of 1848, which had been suppressed by the army, and the twenty-six-year-old Emperor Francis-Joseph I was trying to restrain the military and implement his personal power.[1] The Crimean War had left Austria the dominant power in central Europe. In 1857, the young Emperor decided to make Vienna the modern capital of a great empire. The old city walls were demolished to leave room for the "Ring," a large avenue encircling the city, on both sides of which splendid palaces and buildings were to be erected in the following decades. During these founding years, the Empire enjoyed an unprecedented industrial and economic development, although it also suffered political upsets. In 1859, Austria was defeated in Italy by the Piedmontese and the French, and lost Lombardy. In 1866, Austria, at war with Prussia, suffered a swift and crushing defeat at Sadowa and lost Venetia. The Austrian Empire had to abandon its ambitions regarding Germany and Italy and begin to look upon the Balkan Peninsula for political and economic expansion, where it met the growing rivalry of Russia. In 1867, the Austrian Empire became the Austrian-Hungarian Dual Monarchy. In 1875, the neighboring provinces of Bosnia and Herzegovina rebelled against the Turks, which brought forth a Russian-Turkish War (1877–1878). This conflict was settled by the Congress of Berlin, which put these two provinces under the protection and administration of Austria-Hungary. In 1890, the suburbs of Vienna were incorporated into the capital, which now had more than a million inhabitants and had become one of the world's most beautiful cities.

The assassination of King Alexander of Serbia and his wife in 1903 inaugurated a period of open hostility on the part of Serbia against Austria-Hungary. In 1908 came the revolution of the Young Turks, and Bosnia and Herzegovina were annexed by Austria-Hungary. Ethnic conflicts and problems of official administrative languages became increasingly complex within the Dual Monarchy. Public opinion was concerned with the Balkan Wars, which raged during 1912 and 1913.

In June 1914 the assassination in Sarajevo, of Archduke Francis-Ferdinand, heir to the throne, and his wife unleashed World War I, and subsequently the defeat and the collapse of Austria-Hungary, in November 1918. The little Austrian Republic that emerged from its ruins was shaken by social and political convulsions. In 1926 the economic and political situation improved temporarily in Austria, but soon afterward came the riots of 1927, the socialist insurrection, the assassination of Chancellor Dollfuss, and, finally, the Nazi occupation of Vienna in February 1938. Freud was saved through the intervention of influential friends. He left for England, and died in London on September 23, 1939, at the age of eighty-three, three weeks after the onset of World War II.

Sigmund Freud's life is an example of gradual social ascension from the lower middle class to the high bourgeoisie. After the difficult years of the Privat Dozent, he became one of the best-known physicians in Vienna, with the envied title of Extraordinary Professor. The patients on whom he made his neurological studies belonged to the lower strata of the population, but his private practice, on which he based his psychoanalysis, was made up of patients from the higher social circles. In his early fifties he found himself the chief of a movement whose influence gradually spread over the cultural life of the civilized world, so that in his late sixties he had attained world fame. When he died an exile in England, he was celebrated as a symbol of the struggle of freedom against the fascist oppression.

Family Background

Much of the family background of Sigmund Freud is still unknown or unclear. The little we know must be understood within the larger frame of reference of the conditions of the Jews in Austria-Hungary in the nineteenth century. Before the Emancipation, the Jews of Austria and Hungary belonged to several groups living under widely different political, social, and economic conditions.

In Vienna there were the so-called tolerated families.[3] Although the Jews had been banned from Vienna in 1421, and again in 1670, in the second half of the eighteenth century a "third community" was reconstituted around several wealthy, influential families. In *Vormärz* (the period from 1790 to 1848) their number increased, and in spite of restrictive regulations they achieved a great role in the economic life, and controlled, notably, the textile and grain trades.

Another Jewish group in Vienna, the so-called Turkish-Israelite community, consisted of Sephardic Jews who had come from Constantinople and Salonika, and who for a long time enjoyed the protection of the Sultan.[4] They spoke a Spanish-Jewish dialect, and pronounced Hebrew in a different manner from the German-speaking Jews. Supposedly, they were envied by the other Jews, and rumor had it that certain of the latter tried to join the Spanish-Jewish community but were disdainfully rejected.

There were also the ghetto Jews of certain towns. The mode of living of the Jews of Pressburg has been well described by Sigmund Mayer, a rich merchant who was born and educated there.[5] Pressburg, a town of 40,000 inhabitants at that time, had 5,000 Jews, all of them living on one long, narrow street enclosed at each end by a gate that was locked by the police every evening. One side of that street belonged to the town, the other to the estate of Count Palffy, a Hungarian magnate, and the tenants of the latter side suffered less despotic restrictions. However, nobody on either side had the right to buy a house or property. Each side consisted of shops and dwellings where the people lived under crowded conditions. Some of the Jews were craftsmen, but most of them were shopkeepers A few had large enterprises, particularly in the textile business. Since the Jews were the only merchants in the town, the ghetto streets were overcrowded all day long with customers. The Jews lived under great pressure, owing to the competition, and worked feverishly from early morning to late evening for six days a week. The rest of their time was absorbed by religion. They went to the Synagogue for prayers twice a day, and celebrated the Sabbath and the Jewish holidays in a strictly orthodox manner. The children attended school at the Synagogue, where most of the teaching consisted of reading the Sacred Books in Hebrew, without understanding the meaning, an ordeal for most of them. Family life was rigorously patriarchal, the man was the undisputed authority in the home. Discipline was strict, but the parents did their utmost to secure a better future for their children. Under such confining conditions, where everybody knew what the other was doing, there developed a special mentality of harsh instinctual repression, unavoidable honesty, quick wit in a sarcastic vein (as seen in those writers such as Heinrich Heine and Ludwig Börne, who grew up in a ghetto). The main feature was fear, fear of their parents, their teachers, their husbands, the rabbis, God, and above all the Gentiles. "In Pressburg, no Jew would have dared to give back a blow received from a Christian, and even we children would not have dared to fight back against Christian children who had attacked us," wrote Sigmund Mayer. Finally, within the ghetto there was a certain social structure consisting of the successful and unsuccessful, the rich and the poor, and an aristocracy of a few wealthy families, such as the Gomperz, the Todesco, the Ullmann, the Pappenheim, who kept up a large network of business and social connections.

Other Jewish groups were scattered in places where they lived under very different conditions. There was an active and prosperous Jewish community in the little town of Kittsee, between Vienna and Pressburg, at the foot of the castle of Count Batthyaniy. They were grain traders who had their warehouses and their homes there, enjoyed relative freedom, and were actively engaged in trade with Vienna and Budapest.

The bulk of the Jewish population of Austria lived in small towns and villages in Galicia, in such close relationship with the Polish peasants that they often addressed each other with the familiar *Du* (thou). The mentality of these Jews was different from that of the ghetto Jews. Among them were ambulant merchants. The poor ones went on foot with their merchandise on their backs, the others had horse-drawn carts. There were also many dealers and craftsmen, innkeepers, and petty farmers. The life of those Jewish communities of Galicia at the end of the eighteenth century has been pictured in a lively way in the memoirs of Ber of Bolechow (1723–1805), a Jewish merchant who was keenly interested in the cultural life of his community.[6] He described their trade, rules of business, commercial dealings, coinage and currency, credit and prices, the close relationship of some of them with foreign commercial centers, their distant journeys on horseback, their knowledge of languages, and their friendly relations with the Gentiles. Ber also described the autonomy of these Jewish communities under the administration of the *Kahal,* whose functions covered legal questions, economic activities, and charitable institutions, and who also collected the taxes for which he was responsible. The *Kahal* had his own administration and kept a police force. Besides the *Kahal* were the rabbi, religious chief, and the *Dayan* (judge). One striking feature in Ber's description is the intensity of the cultural life. Apart from the general respect for learning and the reverence for wise rabbis, there were lively controversies between Orthodox Jews and the followers of Hassidism, and of the Haskalah. Ber speaks with irony of his Talmudic education and of the *pilpul,* that is, a keen discussion of learned men about obscure points of the Talmud, each one rivaling the others in subtle arguments, hair-splitting distinctions, and audacious assertions obtained from ingenious combinations of the text. Among these Galician Jews, the revival of the Hebrew language and literature had occurred in the first half of the eighteenth century. Therefore, there is nothing surprising in the fact that Jacob Freud (Sigmund's father), who came from Tysmienica, could write Hebrew fluently.

In Moravia, Jews were not permitted to settle on a permanent basis. Moravian Jews were mostly immigrants from Galicia with a residency permit limited to six months, which had to be renewed after this period. Furthermore, they could live only in special inns, the so-called *städtische Bestandhäuser,* owned by the town and leased to innkeepers. Permission to stay in private quarters could be granted upon the payment of a special tax. These drastic conditions did not prevent many Jews in Moravia from conducting commercial activities, which were encouraged by local authorities as long as they were profitable to the community.

Such was the condition of the Jews before the Emancipation. The unsuccessful revolution of 1848 was followed by a short but harsh reaction, which also affected the Jews, but in 1852 a period of liberal policy began. In 1867 the Jews were officially granted equal political rights, which in practice they had already enjoyed for one decade. There was a great influx of Jews from all parts of the monarchy to Vienna, and also from the neighboring parts of the Russian Empire to Austria-Hungary.

The Emancipation and the abolition of the ghettos completely changed the life of the Jews. Not only did many of them migrate from the country to the towns, and from the provinces to Vienna, but most of them underwent a radical modification in their way of life. A large fraction of the Jews, especially in the towns, strove toward "assimilation" by adopting the customs, manners, clothes, and way of life of the surrounding population, and those Jews who spoke Yiddish (a fourteenth-century German dialect interspersed with Hebrew words) adopted the use of standard, modern German. Many of these "assimilated" Jews kept their religion in the form of the so-called liberal Judaism; others who had little or no religious feeling remained traditionally attached to their communities. Certain Jews went further and discarded their allegiance to the religion of their ancestors, which no longer meant anything to them, and since it was obligatory to be classified in a religion, they registered as Catholics or Protestants. A few communities of Orthodox Jews rigorously maintained their beliefs, rites, and customs. Reading certain descriptions of ghetto life, such as those of Sigmund Mayer[7] or H. Steinthal,[8] one senses a curious undertone of nostalgia for that time when religious life and moral discipline were so strict.

It is clear that such a widespread social, political, economic, and cultural revolution entailed difficult problems for the families or the individuals concerned. The situation somewhat resembled that of the European immigrants in the United States in the process of shifting from one culture to another. For many young men the Emancipation was a tremendous experience which opened a world of unsuspected possibilities to them. Josef Breuer said of his father, Leopold Breuer:

He belonged to that generation of Jews which was the first to step from the spiritual ghetto to the air of the Western world. . . . One cannot evaluate highly enough the spiritual energy which was displayed by that generation. To exchange the jargon for the correct German, the narrowness of the ghetto for the educated mores of the Western world, to gain access to the literature, poetry and philosophy of the German nation. . . . [9]

On the other hand, numerous conflicts arose between Orthodox parents and their estranged children, who could not realize the harsh conditions under which their parents had lived. Freud relates that when he was ten or twelve years old, his father told him how once in his youth, as he was walking in the street, a Gentile passed by and threw young Jacob's cap in the mud saying: "Jew, get off the sidewalk!" Sigmund asked his father what he did then, and Jacob replied: "I went to the road and picked it up."[10] The young boy was indignant about what he felt was cowardice in his father. An anecdote of that kind illustrates the gulf between the young generation and its elders, and may help to explain the genesis of the concept of the Oedipus complex.

As a further consequence of the Emancipation, the Jews had to submit to the same civil registration as other citizens. Many adopted new names, surnames, and fictitious dates of birth; they were registered in the Jewish community with a Hebrew first name, and in the community register with another first name, so that they had a kind of dual identity. In Austria the civil registration was often conducted in a haphazard way. On marriage or death certificates, the civil register relied for birth dates on the information given verbally by the people, and it could also happen that on an official document the place of birth had been confused with a former place of residence. For such reasons historians must be careful in the utilization of Austrian official documents of that time, especially those relating to Jewish people.

The trend toward assimilation was facilitated by the fact that, for two or three decades, anti-Semitism was almost completely unknown in Austria. In Vienna the Jewish population increased steadily, and from a few hundreds at the beginning of the nineteenth century, their members attained 72,000 in 1880, 118,000 in 1890, and 147,000 in 1900.[11] There were many Jewish lawyers, doctors, and scientists. Among the Jewish professors of the Viennese Faculty of Medicine, Max Grünwald mentions the oculist Mauthner, the physiologist Fleischl von Marxow, the anatomist Zuckerkandl, the dermatologists Kaposi and Zeissl, the laryngologists Stoerk and Johann Schnitzler, the hydrologist Winternitz, the pediatrician Kassowitz, the otologist Politzer, the experimental pathologist Stricker, and the neurologist Moritz Benedikt.[12] There also were Josef Breuer, the two Nobel prize winners, Fried and Barany, and many others. It would seem that the first signs of anti-Semitism appeared after the

1873 Stock Exchange panic, and that it increased slowly in the 1880's
and 1890's, although certain prominent Jews who lived in Vienna at
that time assert that they perceived nothing, or very little of it.[13] However,
even during these two or three decades during which anti-Semitism was
practically nonexistent in Vienna, many Jews remained hypersensitive to
anything that seemed to imply the slightest antagonism. Josef Breuer
criticized that attitude in a paper that he wrote in 1894 in answer to an
inquiry made by the *Kadimah,* a Jewish student association:

> Our epidermis has almost become too sensitive, and I would wish that we
> Jews had a firm consciousness of our own value, quiet and half indifferent to
> the judgement of the others, rather than this wavering, easily insulted, hyper-
> sensitive *point d'honneur.* Be that as it may, that *point d'honneur* is certainly
> a product of the "Assimilation."[14]

Among the Jews living in Vienna in the second half of the century, a
discerning eye could recognize various features in regard to the family
background. Depending on whether they originated from the Viennese
"tolerated" families, from the "Spanish-Turkish" community, from other
privileged communities, from the ghetto, or from some Galician township,
their general outlook on life was bound to be very different. It is not
irrelevant to note that Josef Breuer's father had been emancipated in his
young years from a closely knit, rigid community, that Bertha Pappenheim's grandfather was a prominent man in the Pressburg ghetto, that
Adler's father came from the prosperous Jewish community of Kittsee,
that Moreno originated from a Spanish-Jewish family, and that Freud's
ancestors had lived in Galicia and Russia.

The foregoing will help us to understand the problem of Freud's family
background in its full complexity. Factual and reliable data on Freud's
ancestors, even about his parents, are scarce. Like many of their contemporaries, they were very discreet in what they divulged of their past.
Almost everything about the life and personality of Jacob Freud is
obscure. Only recently have painstaking researches made by Dr. Renée
Gicklhorn and Dr. J. Sajner brought some light.[15]
The oldest document we possess about the history of Freud's family is
a letter dated July 24, 1844, written by a Jewish merchant, Abraham
Siskind Hoffman, who lived in the little town of Klogsdorf, near Freiberg,
in Moravia. He informed the authorities that "as an old man of 69" he
has taken as a business partner his grandson Jacob Kelemen (Kallamon)
Freud, from Tysmienica, in Galicia. Abraham Hoffman reminds the
authorities that he buys woolen cloth in Freiberg and surroundings, has it
dyed and dressed, sends it to Galicia, and brings regional products from

Galicia to Freiberg. He adds that he has procured for himself and his grandson a traveling passport from the government of Lemberg, valid until May 1848. He requests from the authorities the permission for both of them to reside in Freiberg for the same period.

After approval of the Clothmakers' Guild, Abraham Hoffman's application was granted. Jacob Freud's age is given as twenty-nine at that time. We know from other acts that he was the son of Salomon Freud, a merchant, and of Pepi Hoffman, from Tysmienica. His wife, Saly Kanner, remained in Tysmienica with his two children. Both Abraham Hoffman and Jacob Freud belonged to the group of *Wanderjuden* (traveling Jews) who constantly moved between Galicia and Freiberg. All of them were kinsmen from Tysmienica, Stanislau, and Lemberg. We know from the city register of Freiberg, and from Jacob Freud's passport, that in the following years he spent six months in Klogsdorf or Freiberg and traveled the rest of the year to Galicia, Budapest, Dresden, and Vienna.

In February 1848, the city of Freiberg decided to impose a tax on the group of eight Galician Jewish merchants. This entailed an inquiry into each one's business. The Clothmakers' Guild declared that Abraham Hoffman and Jacob Freud were known as honest businessmen, and that their presence was of great advantage to the population. This happened shortly before the revolution of 1848, which gave the Jews freedom of residence. Documentary evidence points to the fact that Jacob Freud's business reached its peak in 1852. In the same year his second wife Rebecca came to reside in Freiberg with the two sons of his first wife, Emanuel, aged twenty-one, and Filip, aged sixteen. Emanuel was married and had a child. Rebecca Freud died some time between 1852 and 1855. Jacob Freud married for the third time on July 29, 1855, in Vienna, Amalia Nathanson.[16]

It is not known when Jacob took over his grandfather's business. We do not know either for what reason he left it to his son Emanuel in 1858. In 1859 he requested a certificate of morals and good conduct from the authorities, and shortly afterward he left Freiberg. This, incidentally, was during the year when all legal restrictions for the Jews were officially abolished in Austria.

Aside from these few documentary data, we know very little about Jacob Freud, and even his birth date is uncertain.[17] We know nothing of his childhood, his youth, his first wife and first marriage, nor where he lived until 1844, nor about his second wife, nor when and how he met his third wife, what he did in Leipzig in 1859, and finally how he earned his living in Vienna, and what was his financial situation.

Jacob Freud's occupation in Vienna is generally listed as "wool merchant," but even that matter is uncertain. Renée Gicklhorn states that she was unable to find a mention of him in the Vienna Trade Register (*Gewerberegister*), or in the Trade Tax Register (*Gewerbesteuerkataster*), which would rule out the possibility of his having practised any trade in Vienna.[18] According to Jones, Jacob Freud was always in a precarious financial situation and received money from his wife's family.[19] However, as Siegfried Bernfeld remarks:

> . . . Jacob Freud had, in fact, somehow managed to keep the family reasonably well-fed and clad and living in a spacious apartment. None of the children had to interrupt his education, and even some of the luxuries were provided. There was money for books, for theatre tickets, for a piano, for music lessons, for an oil painting of Sigmund at the age of nine, and of all the children several years later, for the modern and improved petroleum lamp—the first of its kind in Vienna—and even for summer vacations at a resort in Moravia.[20]

Renée Gicklhorn adds that according to archive data, Jacob Freud always paid the full tuition for his son at the gymnasium, although the boy could easily have obtained an exemption since he always was the first in his class. (However, this would have entailed an inquiry into the financial state of the family.)

Even more obscure are the personalities of Jacob Freud's brothers, particularly of Sigmund's uncle Josef and the latter's conflicts with the law.

Jacob's third wife, Amalia Nathanson, according to the marriage certificate, was "from Brody" (which does not necessarily mean that she was born there), was nineteen years old (so the date of her birth would be 1836), and her father Jacob Nathanson was a "trade agent" (*Handelsagent*) in Vienna. A part of her childhood was spent in Odessa, southern Russia, from where her parents moved to Vienna at an unknown date. Testimonies about her concord on three points: her beauty, her authoritarian personality, and her boundless admiration for her firstborn Sigmund. She died in 1931 at the age of ninety-five.

Jones pointed out the unusual setup of the Freud family, with the two stepbrothers Emanuel and Filip being about the same age as Sigmund's mother, and Sigmund being only slightly older than his nephew John.[21] Of his younger siblings only one, Anna, was born in Freiberg; the five others, Rosa, Marie, Adolfine, Paula, and Alexander, were born in Vienna. The seven children of Jacob and Amalia Freud were born in the space of ten years.

Obviously the Freud family followed the trend of a great many Jews in Vienna toward assimilation. Whatever may have been the mother tongue of Jacob Freud and Amalia Nathanson, it seems that they spoke only standard German in their home, and that they soon adopted the way of life of the Viennese middle class. As to religion, they did not belong to the Orthodox group, but since religious instruction was compulsory, Sigmund received it from Jewish teachers.

Though he was not raised in the Orthodox Jewish fashion and was unable to read Hebrew, Freud kept an attachment for Judaism that seems to have developed under the impact of growing anti-Semitism and was reflected later in his fascination for the figure of Moses. Freud's personality had been strongly shaped by the traditions of his Jewish community.[22] He kept the patriarchal ideology, with its belief in the domination of man and subordination of woman, its devotion to the extended family, and its severe puritanical mores. Also he always had a deep respect for his masters, as shown in the way he named some of his children after them. Another typical feature was his prompt and sarcastic wit, and his predilection for Jewish anecdotes.

Freud had in common with some Austrian Jews his extreme sensitivity to any (true or supposed) form of anti-Semitism, as well as his discretion in talking of his family and of himself, revealing nothing although appearing to say much. He attributed to his Jewish origin his capacity for not letting himself be influenced by the opinions of the majority; to that, he could have added his readiness to believe that he was rejected.

Events in Sigmund Freud's Life

The difficulty in writing about Freud stems from the profusion of the literature about him, and from the fact that a legend had grown around him, which makes the task of an objective biographer exceedingly laborious and unrewarding. Behind this mountain of factual and legendary material are wide gaps in our knowledge of his life and personality. Moreover, many of the known sources are not available, particularly those contained in the Freud archives deposited in the Library of Congress in Washington. The available sources may be roughly divided into four groups:

1. Besides an autobiographical sketch, Freud mentions many details of his life throughout his work, particularly in the *Interpretation of Dreams.*[23] A comparatively small portion of his wide correspondence has been published, such as part of his letters to Fliess,[24] to Pfister,[25] to Abraham,[26] to Lou Andreas-Salomé,[27] and a choice of other letters.[28] Of his nine hundred letters to his fiancée, only a few have been published, but many others were utilized by Jones.

2. Memories of Freud have been published by his son Jean Martin, and by numerous disciples, colleagues, visitors, and interviewers.[29] Most of these publications are related to the later years of Freud's life.

3. An accurate investigation of Freud's life, based on archive material, has been inaugurated by Siegfried Bernfeld, with his articles on Freud's childhood,[30] medical studies,[31] first research,[32] cocaine studies,[33] and his first year of medical practice.[34] Of basic value are the documentary researches by Josef and Renée Gicklhorn on Freud's academic career,[35] supplemented by Renée Gicklhorn's clarification of certain episodes in Freud's life and her book on the so-called "Wagner-Jauregg Process."[36] Other docu-

ments have been brought by K. R. Eissler.[37] The objective study of Freud's sources has been inaugurated by Maria Dorer,[38] and an inquiry into the development of Freud's concepts on the basis of source material has been undertaken by Ola Andersson.[39]

4. Biographical sketches on Freud were published by Wittels,[40] Puner,[41] and Sachs.[42] The main, and as it were official, biography by Ernest Jones[43] is invaluable, because this author had access to much material which was, and will probably remain for a long time, unavailable to other researchers. It is, however, not free from inaccuracies. On the whole, we are far from having the thorough and exact knowledge of Freud's life which is generally supposed to exist. But even a complete reconstruction of Freud's life and of the development of his work would not suffice to give an accurate picture, because these must be viewed against the background of contemporary events, and the originality of his work cannot be measured without knowledge of preexisting and contemporary ideas.

It would be redundant to write a new biography of Freud. Our concern will be to give a chronological vista, attempting to separate the certain from the uncertain, the historical data from the legend, and to place Freud's personal achievements in their historical context.

Sigmund Freud was born in Freiberg (in Czech, Přibor), Moravia.[44] In Jacob Freud's family Bible, his birth was recorded under his Jewish name of Schlomo, as having occurred on Tuesday, Rosch Hodesch Iyar 5616 of the Jewish calendar, that is, on May 6, 1856.[45] In 1931, when the town council decided to place a commemorative plaque on the house where he was born, it was allegedly found in the town register that the real birth date was March 6, 1856. Jones assumed that it was a slip of the clerk's pen. In fact, Renée Gicklhorn and Doctor Sajner have shown that the birth date was undisputably May 6, 1856.[46]

The first three years of Freud's life were spent in Freiberg. It was, at that time, a little town of about 5,000 inhabitants, in a picturesque landscape of meadows and woods, away from the railroad tracks. The German-speaking Jews were a minority among the Czechs. The house where Freud was born belonged to the family of the locksmith Zajić and bore the number 117 in Freiberg. There were two rooms downstairs for the workshop, and two rooms upstairs, one for the landlord's family and one for Jacob and Amalia's family. Emanuel Freud and his family lived in another house and had Monica Zajić at their service as a maid, who had to look after the children of both Freud families, and she was probably the "nanny" of Freud's earliest memories. The allegation that Jacob Freud possessed a weaving mill belongs to the legend, as well as the story that he left Freiberg on account of the raging anti-Semitism.

No less fragmentary is our knowledge of the year in Leipzig that followed, and the journey from there to Vienna, where Jacob Freud settled around February 1860.

Almost nothing, either, is known about Freud's early childhood in Vienna. The only certain point is that Jacob Freud changed his residence several times between 1860 and 1865, and after that lived in the Pfeffergasse, in the predominantly Jewish quarter of Leopoldstadt.[47] Nor is it known whether Sigmund received his first schooling at home from his father, or whether he went to one of the elementary Jewish schools in the neighborhood.

Sigmund Freud went to secondary school from 1866 to 1873. That school, the first Leopoldstädter Communal Gymnasium, commonly called *Sperl-gymnasium* or *Sperlaeum*, had high educational standards. Among the teachers were the naturalist Alois Pokorny, the historian Annaka, and the future politician Victor von Kraus. The research of the Bernfelds and of Renée Gicklhorn has brought forth precise information about the curriculum of that school and Freud's achievements. Freud's assertion that throughout his schooling he had constantly led his class has been confirmed by the school archives. Freud also reports that when he was fifteen, his class decided to revolt in a body against an ignorant and unpopular teacher, and that he was chosen by common acclaim to act as spokesman for the group.[48] No mention of that incident has been found in the school's well-preserved archives, but another episode has emerged through the research of R. Gicklhorn.[49] In June 1869 (Freud was thirteen) the teaching staff was upset to learn that several pupils had visited places of doubtful repute. Inquiries were made, and a meeting of the principal and the teachers of the school was called to institute disciplinary action against the culprits. Sigmund Freud was not among these, and his name is merely mentioned as one of those who told what he had heard on the matter.

Not much is known about young Sigmund's life at home during these years. We may somewhat visualize it through a description of Jacob Freud's household written by Judith Bernays-Heller who stayed for one year with her grandparents in 1892 and 1893.[50] At that time Jacob Freud was no longer working, and Judith wondered "who really supported this establishment." He divided his time between reading the Talmud and many other Hebrew and German books, sitting in a coffee house, and walking in the parks. He lived somewhat aloof from the other members of the family and took no real part in the talk during meals. Grandmother Amalia, in contrast, is depicted as tyrannical, selfish, and subject to emotional outbursts. At this time Sigmund had left home for quite some time, but all the details that we have point out the fact that as long as he was there, he enjoyed a privileged position.

Freud's biographers have been puzzled by his knowledge of Spanish, a language not usually learned in Austria at that time. A Spanish-Jewish dialect was the language of the not numerous Sephardic community. Could the prestige of that community have enticed young Sigmund to learn their language? On the other hand, it has been found that Freud learned Spanish with a schoolmate named Eduard Silberstein. The two adolescents had founded between them a kind of "Spanish Academy" of two members, with a "mythology" of their own. Later Silberstein studied law and settled in

Romania. They exchanged letters for a period of ten years, and Freud's letters to Silberstein were recently discovered. When they are published they will no doubt provide valuable information about Freud's life between the ages of sixteen and twenty-six.[51]

Sigmund left the Gymnasium in the middle of 1873. It was a year of dramatic events in Vienna. An International Exhibition had hardly been opened when a cholera epidemic broke out and the visitors from outside Vienna fled in panic, whereupon the stock market crashed, causing bankruptcies, suicides, and a deep economic depression. Whether, and to what extent, this affected the business of Jacob Freud is not known. In any case it did not seem to have deterred Sigmund from his studies. According to his own account, he was influenced in his choice of a vocation when he went to a lecture by the zoologist Carl Brühl, who read a poem, *Nature*, ascribed to Goethe.[52] For many young men at that time, the study of medicine was a means of satisfying their interest in the natural sciences. August Forel and Adolf Meyer also came to the study of medicine in this way.

At that time, medical studies in Austria lasted a minimum of ten semesters (five years). The academic year was divided into a winter semester lasting from October to March, and a summer semester lasting from April to July. The student could begin his studies in either semester. In the medical school, as in the university in general, academic freedom reigned. This term meant that a student was absolutely free to work, or not to work; that there were no controls on attendance, no tests or assignments, and no examinations except the final ones. A student could choose any courses for which he registered and paid fees. However, there were a number of compulsory courses. Few students restricted themselves to the obligatory courses, most of them also registered for medical courses in line with their personal interests or future specialization. Frequently, a student took one or two courses in another faculty, especially if the course was given by an outstanding professor. Most students did not misuse "academic freedom"; they knew they would have to pass exacting final examinations. Medical students had to pass the three *rigorosa*, the first two at given points during the five years, and the third at the end; however, they had the right to postpone the first two *rigorosa* until the end. Many students did additional work, particularly during the university vacations, engaged as *famuli* in hospitals or laboratories, that is, doing menial work, in order to be gradually allowed to do more important jobs, even paid ones, if they showed zeal and capability. Many students also gave a part of their free time to the "Students' Corporations" (fraternities).

Freud began his medical studies in the winter term of 1873, and received his medical degree on March 31, 1881. The fact that his medical studies lasted eight years puzzled Freud's biographers, the more so because his family is said to have been poor. Siegfried Bernfeld published a list of the courses taken by Freud during his medical studies on the basis of an inquiry conducted in the archives of the University of Vienna.[53] During the first three semesters,

Freud followed the courses taken by the other students, with a few additional ones. Starting in the fourth semester, he engaged in an intensive study of the natural sciences, particularly zoology. At the end of his fifth semester, he began regular work in the laboratory of the professor of comparative anatomy, Carl Claus. This lasted for two semesters, with two sojourns at the Marine Zoological Station in Trieste, and it was crowned with the publication of his first scientific paper. Freud seems to have been disappointed by Claus, and after his two semesters with him he moved from his laboratory to that of Brücke, who taught physiology and "higher anatomy" (as he called histology). Freud adopted Ernst Brücke (1819–1892) as his venerated teacher, and found in his laboratory a congenial place where he was to work for the following six years. Benedikt has given, in his memoirs, a curious picture of that rigid, authoritarian Prussian, who never felt comfortable in Vienna, and who impressed the Viennese as a foreigner, with his red hair, stiff face, and Mephistophelean smile.[54] The scientific level of his teaching was far too high for his students, and he never deigned to teach at their level. Most dreaded of all examiners, he asked only one question, and if the candidate did not know the answer, he was never asked a second one. Brücke waited in impassive silence until the allotted fifteen minutes were through. "It shows what enormous respect he infused into the students, that they never rioted against him," Benedikt adds. The story of his long and fierce enmity with the anatomist Hyrtl became legendary in the scientific world of Vienna.[55] Brücke had been a pupil of Johannes von Müller, the great German physiologist and zoologist, who marked the shift from philosophy of nature to the new mechanistic-organistic trend inspired by positivism.[56] This means that together with Helmholtz, Dubois-Reymond, Carl Ludwig, and a few others, Brücke rejected any kind of vitalism or finalism in science, but strove to reduce psychological processes to physiological laws, and physiological processes to physical and chemical laws.[57] Brücke's interest covered many fields; he wrote about the scientific principles of fine arts, the physiological basis of German poetry, and invented *Pasigraphia,* a universal writing purportedly applicable to all the languages of the world.

In Brücke's Institute, Freud became acquainted with his two senior assistants, the physiologist Sigmund Exner and the highly gifted Fleischl von Marxow, and also with Dr. Josef Breuer, who was pursuing some research there. Freud found Breuer a stimulating colleague, a fatherly friend who helped him in later years with substantial loans of money and who also whetted his curiosity with the story of the extraordinary illness and cure of a young hysterical woman·who was to become famous under the pseudonym of Anna O.

Josef Breuer (1842–1925) was born in Vienna, where his father Leopold was a teacher of religion in the Jewish community.[58] In a short autobiographical note Breuer says that he lost his mother at an early age, and that he spent his childhood and youth "without misery and without luxury."[59] He

bestowed the highest praise on his father, a devoted educator, always ready
to help the members of the community (obviously his father was the model
whom Breuer strove to imitate throughout his life). Leopold Breuer composed a textbook of religion, which was used in the Jewish schools in Vienna
for many years.[60] Josef Breuer, however, departed from orthodox Judaism[61]
and adopted the views of the so-called liberal Judaism. He studied medicine,
but followed courses in many other sciences as well. His keen interest in and
great talent for the experimental sciences were manifested by two outstanding
pieces of research, one on the mechanism of the self-regulation of respiration,
and the other on the mechanism of the perception of bodily movements and
positions through the ear labyrinth. According to his biographers, he had begun
a brilliant scientific career, but resigned his position of Privat Dozent and
refused the title of Extraordinary Professor. One explanation is that he was
so thoroughly devoted to his patients that he did not want to sacrifice them
to a scientific career; another one that he resigned his post as Privat Dozent
following intrigues of colleagues. He was certainly not of a belligerent nature.
All those who have known him agree in saying that he was "the most
unassuming man one can imagine." An admirable clinician, he combined
scientific acumen with humaneness. He treated two groups of patients gratuitously: his colleagues and their families on one side and the destitute on the
other, and many of these expressed their gratitude toward him in touching
ways.[62] As one of the most sought-after physicians in Vienna, he had a large
income and could afford a high standard of living, including regular journeys
to Italy. An exceptionally cultured man, he was a connoisseur of music,
painting, and literature, and was an inspiring conversationalist. He was
personally acquainted with the composer Hugo Wolf, the writer Schnitzler,
the philosopher Brentano, and he carried on a correspondence with the
poetess Maria Ebner-Eschenbach.[63] According to certain witnesses he was
selfless to a fault, and overly trusting.[64] The physiologist De Kleyn, who visited
him in his old age, admired him for "his perfect mental vigour, his familiarity
with the most recent medical publications, the unerring judgment of the near-
octogenerian," and also tells of his "extreme simplicity and personal warmth,"
as well as of his critical faculty which "remained remarkably acute, though
benevolent, to the end."[65] He had so many devoted friends and admirers
in Vienna that when Sigmund Exner organized a subscription in honor of
Breuer's seventieth birthday in 1912, the best-known personalities of Vienna
contributed to it. Thus was founded the *Breuer-Stiftung*, a foundation whose
aim was to give awards for meritorious scientific research, or invite prominent
scientists to give lectures in Vienna.[66]

Freud had not yet completed his medical studies when he had to fulfill one
year of military service (1879–1880). His main achievement during that
time was his translation of one volume of John Stuart Mill's *Collected Works*.[67]
He realized that he had to concentrate upon obtaining his medical degree. In
The Interpretation of Dreams he says that he was getting the reputation of a

perennial student. Though still working in Brücke's laboratory, he passed his two first *rigorosa* in June 1880, and his third *rigorosum* on March 30, 1881, so that he received his medical degree on March 31, 1881. Thereupon he received a temporary post of "demonstrator" (a kind of teaching assistant) in Brücke's laboratory, with a small salary, and pursued his histological research there. He also worked for two semesters in Professor Ludwig's chemistry laboratory, but it was obviously not his specialty.

At this point a remarkable change occurred in Freud's life. Until now he seemed to have decided upon a scientific career. Now, in June 1882, he suddenly left Brücke's laboratory where he had worked for six years—maintaining a good relationship with him—and turned to a career of practicing physician, visibly without great enthusiasm.

In those days there were three paths to a medical career. The first entailed five years of concentrated work with emphasis on the clinical, and working as a *famulus* in hospitals during vacations, after which one could put a sign on one's door and wait for the patients to come. The second was to supplement one's regular studies with two or three voluntary internship years, to acquire more experience or to specialize. The third and hardest way was, after completion of one's studies, to compete for successive ranks in the academic career in one of the branches of theoretical or clinical medicine. It took from two to five years to become Privat Dozent, and five or ten years more of hard competition to become an Extraordinary Professor. Only very few were able to attain the rank of ordinary Professor, a position of substantial advantages and high social status. Freud, in 1882, seemed to turn to the second solution, namely that of specialized medical practice, but he did not give up his interest in brain-histological work, where he perhaps already saw the means of a future scientific career. Two explanations have been given for this change: Freud himself explained that Brücke pointed out the lack of prospects in his institute, since his two assistants, Exner and Fleischl, had ten years' seniority, which meant that Freud would have to be content for a very long time with an inferior and poorly paid position. Siegfried Bernfeld and Jones suggested that the true reason was to be found in Freud's new plans of marriage and founding a family.

Freud had met Martha Bernays, fallen in love, and become engaged to her in June 1882. According to Jones she belonged to a well-known Jewish family of Hamburg.[68] Her father, a merchant, had come to Vienna several years before and had died in 1879. Those who knew her described her as being very attractive, and endowed with a firm character. In those two regards she resembled Freud's mother. Both women also lived very long (Martha Bernays was born on July 26, 1861, and died on November 2, 1951, at the age of ninety.) Following the custom of the time, a marriage was expected to take place only after a proper financial situation had been established. Long engagements, entailing separation and assiduous corresponding, were

frequent. The ties between the Freud and the Bernays families were reinforced by the marriage of Martha's brother Eli to Sigmund's sister Anna.

At this turning point of his life, Freud's situation was far from easy. He
began three years of hospital residency at a low salary, and found himself
four years behind those who had chosen clinical medicine initially. His prospects were bright, but set in a remote future time. The only way to shorten
that slow and arduous career would have been to make a brilliant discovery
that would bring him rapid fame (the secret hope of many young physicians).

The old Viennese General Hospital, with its four or five thousand patients,
was one of the most famous teaching centers of the world, where almost
every head of a department was a medical celebrity. There was great emula-
tion among the medical staff and a keen competition for the much-coveted and
poorly paid positions.[69] Sigmund Freud began by working two months in
the Surgical Department, then worked with the grade of Aspirant under the
great internist Nothnagel from October 1882 to April 1883. On May 1, 1883,
he was appointed as Sekundararzt in the Psychiatric Department, headed
by the illustrious Theodor Meynert. Freud had already engaged in histological
research on the medulla oblongata in Meynert's laboratory, where he remained
and worked from 1883 to 1886, and it appeared as if he now had found a new
master.

Theodor Meynert was a prominent figure in Vienna, but he also had what
the Germans call a problematic nature.[70] Bernard Sachs, who worked in
his laboratory during the same period as Freud, describes him as "striking
enough in appearance—a huge head poised on a short body—dishevelled
locks that had an annoying habit of falling down over the forehead and had
to be pushed back every so often."[71] Meynert was considered the greatest
brain anatomist in Europe, along with Flechsig. Unfortunately he gradually
lapsed into "brain mythology," the then current trend to describe psychological
and psychopathological phenomena in terms of real or hypothetical brain
structures. August Forel tells in his memoirs how disappointed he was when
he came to work with Meynert only to realize that many of the brain tracts
allegedly discovered by him were but the creations of his imagination.[72]
Meynert was known as a good clinician, but a rather tedious lecturer, and he
had little contact with his students. He was also a poet,[73] a connoisseur of
music and art, and his social circle comprised the intellectual elite of Vienna,
even though he was a difficult personality and had violent enmities.[74]

After spending five months in Meynert's department, in September 1883,
Freud moved to the fourth Medical Division headed by doctor Scholtz, where
he acquired excellent clinical experience with neurological patients.

Meanwhile an article written by Doctor Aschenbrandt, in December 1883,
pointed out the interest of cocaïne, the alkaloid of coca.[75] Freud experimented
on himself and others with the supposedly harmless substance, which he found
to be effective against fatigue and neurasthenic symptoms. In July 1884
Freud published a paper in which he praised the virtues of the new drug with

eloquence.[76] He asserted that cocaine could be used as a stimulant, as an aphrodisiac, against stomach disorders, cachexia, asthma, and for the removal of the painful symptoms that accompany the withdrawal of morphine in addicts. He actually applied it in that way in treating his friend Fleischl, who, following severe neuralgia, had become a morphine addict. However, this treatment resulted in Fleischl becoming a severe cocaine addict.

While talking about cocaine with his colleagues Leopold Königstein (a Privat Dozent six years his senior) and Carl Koller (one year younger than himself), Freud mentioned that cocaine caused a numbness of the tongue. Koller was currently searching for a product that would produce anesthesia of the eye. While Freud left on a vacation to visit his fiancée in Wandsbek (a suburb of Hamburg) in August 1884, Koller went to Stricker's laboratory and experimented with cocaine on the eyes of animals, and he rapidly discovered its anesthetic properties. As was often the custom among scientists eager to secure the priority of a discovery, he kept silent and hastened to send a preliminary report to be read by a friend, Doctor Brettauer, at the Ophthalmological Congress in Heidelberg on September 15.[77] The paper aroused a sensation. Königstein hurried to perform experiments of the same kind and to apply the discovery to human surgery. He and Koller presented the discovery to the Society of Physicians on October 17, 1884. When Freud returned from Wandsbek, he found that Koller was the lucky winner who had acquired sudden fame, and it was all the more frustrating to him since it was he who had given Koller the hint that led to the discovery. But Freud did not give up his study of cocaine.[78] He experimented with its effect on muscular force and continued to advocate the medical use of the new drug. It was not long before Albrecht Erlenmeyer published a paper warning against the danger of cocaine addiction, and this was to be the beginning of a storm against Freud.[79]

Meanwhile, on January 21, 1885, Freud had applied for the post of Privat Dozent in Neuropathology, and in March he applied for a traveling grant of six months from the University of Vienna. Freud worked in the Ophthalmology Department from March to the end of May, and in the Dermatology Department in June. His paper on the roots and connections of the acoustic nerve also appeared in June and was well received. In the same month he passed the oral examination for Privat Dozent and gave the trial lecture.[80] He was appointed on July 18, and then he learned that as a result of the intervention of Brücke and Meynert, he had been elected as the recipient of the traveling grant over two other candidates, which he decided to spend studying in Paris with Charcot.

On August 1, 1885, Freud left the Viennese General Hospital, where he had spent the previous three years. He then took a six weeks' vacation at Wandsbek near his fiancée, and on October 11 left for Paris. Apparently he considered this sojourn in Paris as the great opportunity of his life.[81]

For a serious, unworldly young scientist such as Freud it must have been an overwhelming experience to be thrown suddenly into the feverish milieu of the French capital. With keen interest he observed the daily life of Paris, visited the museums and the Cathedral of Notre Dame, and attended plays in which great actors performed. But he could not at first help feeling lost at the Salpêtrière. In spite of Benedikt's letter of introduction, Freud was, to Charcot, just another one of the many visitors who came to the Salpêtrière. He began doing research in the pathology laboratory with the Russian neurologist Darkschewitch, and apparently was disappointed in the working conditions. Freud then offered his services to Charcot as a translator of some of his work into German. The great man invited Freud to some of his fashionable receptions. From the beginning Freud had been under the spell of Charcot, who impressed him not only by the boldness of his conceptions of hypnosis, hysteria, and traumatic neuroses but also by the immense prestige and sumptuous life of the Prince of Science. Apparently, Freud did not realize that Charcot was surrounded by fierce enemies, and he did not stay long enough to sense (as did Delboeuf who was there at the same time) the amount of suggestion that was fed to many of Charcot's hysterical patients.

Freud liked to say that he had been Charcot's student in Paris during 1885 and 1886. This sometimes led people to believe that he had stayed there for a long time. Actually, Jones states, on the basis of Freud's letters to his fiancée, that Freud saw Charcot for the first time on October 20, 1885, and took leave of him on February 23, 1886, and from these four months must be subtracted one week of the Christmas holiday, which Freud spent with his fiancée in Germany, and "a couple of weeks" of Charcot's illness. We may assume that Freud's meeting with Charcot was more in the nature of an existential encounter than of normal relationship between master and disciple. Freud left Paris on February 28, 1886, with the impression of having met a great man, one with whom he would keep in touch for the translation of his books, and who had provided him with a world of new ideas.

After spending the month of March in Berlin studying pediatrics with Baginsky, Freud returned to Vienna on April 4, 1886. He took an apartment in the Rathausstrasse and opened his practice at the end of April 1886. It was a busy period in his life, with preparations for his marriage and his preoccupation with his scientific work. He wrote a report on his traveling grant activities for the assembly of professors,[83] and in May he read papers on hypnotism before the Physiological Club and the Psychiatric Society.[84] In the same month a second paper by Erlenmeyer appeared that warned of the dangers of cocaine and mentioned Freud's name critically.[85] Freud had few paying patients and filled his forced leasure by translating a volume of Charcot's lectures that appeared with a foreword by Freud, bearing the date July 18, 1886.[86]

From August 11 to September 9, Freud completed a period of military service with the rank of batallion physician in a German-speaking regiment that performed maneuvers in Olmütz. It is curious to compare Freud's letter to Breuer,[87] expressing his complaints about military life and his contempt for it, with the report written by Freud's superiors after completion of that period of service.[88] On September 30, 1886, Sigmund Freud's marriage to Martha Bernays took place in Wandsbek, and they spent the rest of the month on their honeymoon, on the shores of the neighboring Baltic Sea.

Upon their return to Vienna, Freud moved his practice to a new apartment in the Kaiserliches Stiftungshaus, a large apartment house built at the instigation of Emperor Francis Joseph I on the site of the Ring Theater that had burned down on December 8, 1881, with a loss of about 400 lives. He was not yet able to start his Privat Dozent teaching, but began working at the Kassowitz Institute, a private children's hospital, where he had been appointed to the neurological department and could gather rich material for clinical studies.[89]

Freud had returned from Paris enthusiastic about what he had learned at the Salpêtrière and eager to make it known in Vienna. The paper that he read at the Viennese Society of Physicians caused him disappointment, and this incident has given rise to a tenacious legend. Since it is impossible for us to discuss the numerous episodes of Freud's life in the limited frame of this book, we will single out this particular one as an example.

The standard account of that event reads as follows: Freud presented a paper on male hysteria before the Society of Physicians on October 15, 1886. This paper was received with incredulity and hostility. Freud was challenged to present a case of male hysteria to the Society, and though he met this challenge on November 26 of the same year, the reception was cool, and this was the starting point of Freud's life-long feud with the Viennese medical world.

When checking the story, four points must be clarified: (1) What kind of scientific body was the Society of Physicians? (2) What did the concept of male hysteria mean at that time? (3) What actually occurred during the meeting? (4) How can the events of the meeting be explained?

The Imperial Society of Physicians (*Kaiserliche Gesellschaft der Ärzte in Wien*) was one of the most reputed medical societies in Europe. [90] Its origin dated back to a group of physicians, who, around 1800, had begun to meet once a week to discuss problems of medicine and public hygiene. After various vicissitudes, the Society received official recognition and its present status in 1837. The Society had kept its original special concern with problems of public health, but also dealt with all branches of medicine and strove to maintain the highest possible scientific standard in each branch. Many important discoveries were first announced before the Society. In 1858, Czermak demonstrated the laryngoscope discovered by Türck. On May 15, 1850, Semmelweiss explained his discovery that puerperal infection in the maternity section of a hospital was carried there from the anatomy rooms. In 1879 Nitze and Leiter demonstrated their cystoscope; and in October 1884, two years prior to Freud's paper, Königstein and Koller announced their use of cocaine in eye surgery. Another feature of the Society was that any physician could present papers, provided that he offered something original. But though the speakers never departed from their dignified and courteous manner, contributions were exposed to sharp criticism. The surgeon Breitner described in his autobiography how, during the discussion of one of his papers, Wagner-Jauregg "crushed him against the wall like a fly."[91] The sessions took place every Friday evening in the building of the Academy of Sciences, in a rather formal way. The discussions were recorded by a secretary (*Schriftführer*) and summarized in the fortnightly bulletin of the Society. Sessions were attended by medical journalists who sent accounts to their respective periodicals.

What actually occurred at the meeting of October 15, 1886, is unintelligible if one does not define what the term "male hysteria" meant at that time, and to do so we must go back a few decades. In the past decade there had been an enormous increase in railway traffic, railway accidents, and insurance claims. A new chapter of pathology had opened, pioneered by British physicians, who described railway spine and railway brain, and distinguished nervous shock from traumatic shock. In England, Doctor Page contended that many cases of railway spine did not result from nervous lesions but from functional disturbances, which he called hysterical; he found in these patients hemianesthesia and other symptoms generally considered stigmata of hysteria.[92] Dr. Page's assertions created lively discussions around two points: first, the comparative frequency of organic and dynamic (in modern language functional) lesions, and second, whether these nonorganic nervous conditions were identical to hysteria. These points were of considerable practical importance to the patients, to the insurance companies, and to the medical experts who had to assess the claims. Dr. Page's viewpoint was widely held in England, and was accepted in the United States by Walton,[93] Putnam, and others.[94] In Germany two leading neurologists, Thomsen and Oppenheim, objected that hemianesthesia was no proof of hysteria (because, as they showed, it could be found in many other conditions), and that in their own cases of railway spine they found that the hemianesthesia was much more severe than in hysterical patients, that the depression was deeper, and that there was little response to therapy.[95] Nonorganic cases of railway spine were described by them as a specific traumatic neurosis distinct from hysteria. In France, Charcot denied the existence of Thomsen's and Oppenheim's traumatic neurosis; he admitted that nonorganic cases of railway spine had certain symptomatic peculiarities (as stated by the Germans), but he insisted that they belonged to hysteria. As proof, Charcot said that under hypnosis he had produced paralyses that were symptomatically identical with traumatic paralyses. Since many accident victims were men, the diagnosis male hysteria, formerly restricted to men with classical hysterical symptoms, was now extended to men with functional, posttraumatic disorders. Thus the frequency of male hysteria increased in France, at least as a diagnostic label, and there were now two kinds of male hysteria in Paris: the classical one (in which heredity was considered the main etiological factor), and the posttraumatic (in which heredity played a lesser role, if any). In Vienna the existence of classical male hysteria was no longer questioned, but the leading neurologists did not accept Charcot's identification of traumatic paralysis in men with male hysteria.

Thus, to understand the discussion that followed Freud's paper, two facts must be remembered: that the term "male hysteria" applied to two different conditions, namely classical male hysteria, whose existence was accepted by everyone, and Charcot's traumatic male hysteria, which was the object of heated discussions among neurologists; and that the discussion of traumatic male hysteria was itself part of a wider controversy pertaining to the consequences of railway accidents and other trauma.

The best way to reconstruct what happened at the meeting of October 5, 1886, is to rely on reports published immediately afterward. We do not possess the text of Freud's paper, but it was probably similar to the report he sent to the *Professoren-Collegium*.[96] A brief survey of the discussion that followed Freud's presentation was recorded in the next issue of the bulletin of the Society of Physicians, and more detailed proceedings were given in five medical journals.[97] [98] [99] [100] [101] [102]

Freud's paper was preceded by the clinical demonstration of a case of lupus of the larynx and palate, by a laryngologist, Dr. Grossmann. Then Freud told the Society how he had spent a few months in Paris with Charcot, and explained the latter's concept of hysteria. Charcot, he explained, distinguished between a *grande hystérie* (with a specific type of convulsions, hemianesthesia, and various other stigmata) and *petite hystérie*. Charcot, he added, had the merit to show that hysterical patients were not malingerers, that hysteria did not issue from disturbances of the genital organs, and that male hysteria was more frequent than was generally assumed. Freud then related a case of male hysteria he had seen while in Charcot's service. It was a young man who had suffered an accident at work and had then contracted paralysis in one arm and an entire range of stigmata as well. On the basis of such cases Charcot was inclined to equate most cases of railway spine and railway brain with male hysteria.

The discussion was opened by Professor Rosenthal, a neurologist. Male hysteria, he said, was no rarity. He had described two such cases sixteen years earlier.

Professor Meynert stated that he had repeatedly observed cases of epileptic seizures and disturbances of consciousness after trauma, and that it would be interesting to check whether these cases always presented the symptoms depicted by Freud.

Professor Bamberger, the chairman, acknowledged Charcot's merits, but saw nothing new in Freud's interesting paper. He questioned Charcot's distinction of *grande* and *petite hystérie* because some of the most severe cases of hysteria did not belong to *grande hystérie*. As for male hysteria, it was a well-known condition, but on the basis of his own observations Bamberger disagreed with the equating of railway spine with genuine male hysteria, in spite of certain similarities in the clinical picture.

Professor Leidesdorf mentioned that he had often examined patients who, following a railway accident or similar trauma, had developed organic symptoms that had nothing in common with hysteria. He did not deny that there were cases where the shock had been followed by hysteria, but he warned against concluding that the hysteria was a consequence of the trauma, because the true extent of the lesions could not yet be evaluated at that stage.

Freud's paper was followed by one presented by Professor Latschenberger, on the presence of gall pigment in tissues and liquids in severe diseases in animals. Professor Bamberger objected sharply to Professor Latschenberger's assertions. (Obviously coolness was the tone of the Society, and in that regard Latschenberger was not treated any better than Freud, in spite of his professor's title).

In the legendary accounts of that meeting it would seem as though tremendous discoveries, which had not yet reached Vienna, had been revealed to Freud in Paris (such as the existence of male hysteria), and that, while acting as Charcot's missionary to the Viennese "pundits," he was shamefully scorned and rejected. Actually, things were quite otherwise. Freud had returned from Paris with an idealized picture of Charcot. Much of what he attributed to Charcot were the views of previous authors, and male hysteria was a well-known condition of which case histories had been published in Vienna long since by Benedikt,[103] Rosenthal, and others.[104] Charcot was popular in Vienna; Benedikt visited him every year. Meynert[105] was on friendly terms with him, and Leidesdorf spoke highly of him.[106] But the German-speaking medical world was disquieted by the new turn taken by Charcot's research since 1882. It is characteristic that the *Neurologisches Centralblatt* published a detailed review of Freud's translation of Charcot's lectures, in which the highest praise was bestowed on Freud as a translator, but a sharp though polite criticism was expressed about Charcot's new teaching.[107]

From the proceedings it is obvious that no one denied the existence of classical male hysteria. Of the four discussants two, Rosenthal and Bamberger, expressly stated that male hysteria was well known, and Leidesdorf spoke of it as a current notion. Meynert necessarily shared the same opinion since a case of classical male hysteria from his wards had been published just a month before under his auspices, not because male hysteria was unusual, but as a result of a rare hysterical symptom that the case presented.[108] It is clear that the crux of the discussion was Charcot's equation of traumatic neurosis with male hysteria.

It thus appears that the Viennese neurologists took issue with three points in Freud's paper. First, Freud had not conformed with the Society's tradition that the speaker bring something new and original. (This is the meaning of Bamberger's remark: "All this is very interesting, but I see nothing new in it.") Freud would probably have been received better if instead of relating one of Charcot's case histories he had brought one of his own. Second, Freud intervened upon the sole authority of Charcot in a controversy of which he did not seem to have seized the complexity and the practical implications. Actually, the cautious attitude of the Viennese neurologists in regard to the diagnosis of hysterical disturbances was to the advantage of their patients. (This is the meaning of Leidesdorf's remark). Third, it might have been irritating to these neurologists that Freud attributed to Charcot the discovery that hysteria was neither malingering nor the result of disturbances of the genital organs, two points that had been known in Vienna for a long time, so that Freud seemed to treat them as ignorants and to be talking down to them.

One may wonder how it happened that Freud did not realize he was offending these men who had been well disposed toward him.[109] One reason was that Freud, who had always been subject to prompt and strong enthusiasms, was now under the spell of Charcot. Another reason was Freud's craving for the great discovery that would bring him fame. He was still aching with the disappointment caused by the cocaine episode, and he apparently thought that the revelation he had received at the Salpêtrière could be the starting point for further discoveries. Thus the cool reception given to his paper was all the more painful to him.

There is no documentary evidence that Freud was challenged to show the Society a case of male hysteria. Be that as it may, Freud himself felt obligated to do so. He was able to find a case one week after the meeting, had the ophthalmologic examination performed by Dr. Königstein on October 24, and the demonstration took place on November 26. Freud began his paper by stating that he was meeting Professor Meynert's challenge to demonstrate to the Society a case of male hysteria with the stigmata described by Charcot.[110] The patient was a twenty-nine-year-old worker, who at the age of eight had been run over in the street, suffered the loss of an eardrum, and was afflicted with convulsions of an unclear nature during the two years that followed the accident. Now, after a nervous shock experienced three years previously, he had developed hysterical symptoms. He showed a severe hemianesthesia and other hysterical stigmata, such as described by Charcot. In fact it was an ambiguous case that could be diagnosed either as revived traumatic hysteria (because of the old accident), or as classical male hysteria (because of the nervous shock), and it could hardly contribute to elucidate the point that had been criticized during the meeting of October 15. This time there was no discussion, perhaps on account of the heavy schedule. Freud stated later in his autobiography that this paper had been applauded, but apparently it did not dissipate the impression created by the previous meeting.

Contrary to the legend, Freud did not break his ties with the Society after that meeting. His candidacy was submitted by seven prominent members of the Society on February 16, 1887, and he was elected on March 18, 1887. He never ceased to be a member of the Society until he left Vienna.[111]

The session of October 15, 1886, was recalled three months later by Arthur Schnitzler in a review of Freud's translation of Charcot's book.[112] Schnitzler tells of the "fantasy of the ingenious physician" (die Phantasie des geistreichen Arztes), that is, Charcot, and how his concept of traumatic male hysteria was received with reserve.[113] This had been borne out "when doctor Freud recently spoke on the topic before the Imperial-Royal Society of physicians in Vienna, and a lively discussion developed." The controversy on traumatic neurosis versus male hysteria continued to rage in Europe for a few years, until, around 1900, the medical world lost interest in hysteria, ceased to believe in the existence of Charcot's stigmata, and the disease itself became much less frequent.[114]

In the ten years that followed Freud struggled to raise his family, build up his practice, achieve neurological work, and create a new psychology. Freud started out, in 1886, with the usual handicap of the young doctor who has debts and no fortune. Private patients were slow in coming, and he had difficulty in finding cases for his demonstrations as a Privat Dozent. A few facts show that he must have been under some criticism during this period. He was accused of having unleashed upon mankind that "third scourge," cocaine addiction (the others being alcoholism and morphinism). In a last paper on cocaine, of July 1887, Freud tried to justify himself: cocaine, he said, was dangerous only to those addicted to morphine, but wonderful results could be obtained from treating morphinists with cocaine during the withdrawal stage.[115] And he added: "It is perhaps not superfluous to note that this is not personal experience, but advice given to someone else." A medical journal having published a short review by Freud of a book by Weir Mitchell, brought soon afterward a more extensive review of the same book by another reviewer.[116] Freud had broken with Meynert, and an acrimonious quarrel broke out between them in 1889. In a paper on traumatic neuroses, Meynert criticized Charcot's theories on traumatic paralyses and added in a footnote that Freud's opinions were more dogmatic than scientific and contradicted Charcot's teaching.[117] To this Freud replied with a vehement attack on Meynert, whom he accused of being prejudiced. Such episodes illustrate the atmosphere of isolation and distrust in which Freud began his career.

But Freud also had assets. His old friend Josef Breuer, who enjoyed one of the wealthiest clienteles in Vienna, sent him patients. Moreover, Freud had been placed in charge, after his return from Paris, of the neurological department of the Kassowitz Institute.[118] An assiduous worker, Freud gradually created for himself his social position and his reputation as a specialist.

According to all testimonies, his marriage with Martha was a happy one. Six children were born to them: Mathilde on October 16, 1887, Jean-Martin on December 7, 1889, Oliver on February 19, 1891, Ernst on April 6, 1892, Sofie on April 12, 1893, and Anna on December 3, 1895.[119] The household also comprised Freud's sister-in-law, Minna Bernays, and two or three servants. In the summer of 1891 the family moved to the apartment at Berggasse 19, which Freud was to leave only in 1938.

Freud's apartment was located in a residential quarter, close to the *Innere Stadt* or old town, in the almost immediate vicinity of the University, the museums, the opera house, the Burgtheater, the great government buildings, and last, but not least, the Imperial Court. The latter included the Imperial Palace (*Hofburg*), its gardens, art galleries, library, crown jewels (*Schatzkammer*), and the Spanish Imperial Riding School. The family thus lived and grew up near the pulsating heart of the great Empire. It was a frequent occurrence to see the Emperor passing through the neighborhood in his stagecoach. In many regards life was very different from what it is now. Professionals received their clients at their place of residence, so that they found it easy to interrupt their work to see their family. Children had glimpses of their father's occupation, which enjoyed enormous prestige in their eyes. It was not unusual to work from early morning to late at night, six days a week, but professionals and well-to-do people took three months of summer vacation, which they spent either in the country or traveling with Baedeker in hand.

Freud's scientific evolution during those ten years is shown by the fact that in 1886 he was mainly a neurologist who completely accepted Charcot's theories of neurosis, whereas by 1896 he was no longer interested in neurology, and after having given up Charcot's and Bernheim's ideas, had slowly come to elaborate his own system.

The first step was his growing interest in Bernheim, whose textbook he translated, and then, in July 1889, he went to Nancy to visit him and Liébeault, whereupon he attended the International Congress of Psychology in Paris.[120]

In 1891 Freud's book on cerebral palsy in children appeared in collaboration with Oscar Rie, as did his critical study of the theory of aphasia, and in 1892 Freud published the translation of another of Bernheim's books.[121] In a series of two lectures he gave on April 27 and May 4, 1892, at the Wiener Medizinischer Klub, the concept of suggestion

THE DISCOVERY OF THE UNCONSCIOUS

that he expounded was almost exactly that of Bernheim.[122] But Freud also translated a further volume of Charcot's lectures, which he provided with footnotes, some of them explaining Charcot's ideas, others stating his own concept of hysteria or contradicting Meynert.[123]

In 1893 a biographical sketch of Freud appeared in *Das geistige Wien*, a sort of *Who's Who* of Viennese celebrities.[124] Freud published several articles on hysteria, notably his "Preliminary Communication" with Josef Breuer entitled "Psychic Mechanisms of Hysterical Phenomena." Charcot's concept of the mechanism of traumatic neurosis was extended to hysteria in general, and a psychotherapeutic method proposed, based on the concept of catharsis and abreaction. In 1894, in his paper "Defense Neuro-Psychosis," Freud had gone on from hysteria to phobias, obsessions, and even hallucinations. Freud pressed Breuer for the completion of *Studies on Hysteria*, and it was published in 1895. It was a well-organized book. After a short foreword stating that they did not use as many case histories as they would wish, because of professional secrecy, the "Preliminary Communication" of 1893 was reprinted, followed by the case of the patient Anna O., given as a prototype of a cathartic cure. Then came four of Freud's case histories, the first of which was Emmy von N., Freud's first cathartic treatment. The book was concluded by a chapter on the concept of hysteria by Breuer, and another by Freud on its psychotherapy. We will return later to the effect produced by this book and the contemporary papers of Freud. By that time Freud's professional and financial position had improved to the point where he could afford periodical travels in Italy and the collecting of art objects. In the following year he felt that his theory and therapeutic method was sufficiently original to be given a new and specific name: psychoanalysis. But the birth of this new science was to come through a very unusual process that had by then already begun.

Over a period of about six years (1894 to 1899) four events are inextricably intermingled in Freud's life: his intimate relationship with Wilhelm Fliess, his neurotic disturbances, his self-analysis, and his elaboration of the basic principles of psychoanalysis. We will first summarize the known facts, then propose an interpretation. The two main sources are Freud's *Interpretation of Dreams*, which analyzes several dozen of Freud's dreams of that period, and the published part of his correspondence with Fliess. (The complete publication of these letters will possibly modify somewhat our picture of that period.)

Freud had become acquainted in 1887 with Wilhelm Fliess, an ear and nose specialist of Berlin. Fliess was the author of theories whose three main points were the correspondence between the nose mucosa and the genital organs, the bisexuality of human beings, and the existence in each individual of a double periodicity, a feminine one with a cycle of twenty-eight days, and a masculine one with a cycle of twenty-three days.[125]

Freud's first letter to Fliess of November 24, 1887, concerns the diagnosis of a patient. A friendship developed, marked in June 1892 by the adoption of the familiar mode of address *Du* (thou). It soon acquired a more emotional character. To Freud, Fliess was a scientific correspondent, a physician who treated his nose condition, and a confidant who also stimulated him and in whose judgment he placed boundless trust.

At the beginning of 1894 Freud suffered from heart symptoms. On Fliess's advice he stopped smoking, and in spite of much distress kept to his decision. At this time an episode occurred as described by Max Schur.[126] Freud was treating a woman, Emma, for hysteria, and he called Fliess to determine whether there was a connection between her symptoms and a possible nose condition. Fliess operated on Emma's nose and returned to Berlin. The patient, however, suffered from severe postoperative complications, and another specialist found that Fliess had accidentally left a long piece of iodoform gauze in the cavity. Weeks later the patient had a hemorrhage of such severity that her condition remained critical for quite some time. According to Schur, Freud expressed, in letters hitherto unpublished, his full confidence in Fliess who remained for him the healer "into whose hands one confidently entrusts one's life." These events came at a time when Freud was entirely absorbed by his cogitation on a new psychology. In June 1895 he wrote to Fliess that he had resumed smoking after an interruption of fourteen months. He could bear it no longer. It was during the night of July 23 to 24, 1895, that Freud had his celebrated dream of Irma's injection, the first dream of which he made a complete analysis with his new technique of associations. It was to become the prototype of a dream analysis, not only in Freud's *Traumdeutung*, but in the eyes of all psychoanalysts. Max Schur has shown that the basic elements of that dream were present in the story of the patient Emma, and that it can be interpreted as the dreamer's attempt to justify Fliess. Freud had the feeling that he had solved the mystery of dreams and found a key to their interpretation, a key that he could now utilize in the investigation and treatment of his patients.

In the period from July 1895 to the death of his father on October 23, 1896, Freud published, together with Breuer, the *Studies in Hysteria*, broke off his relationship with Breuer, and wrote a *Project for a Scientific Psychology* which he, however, soon abandoned so that it remained unpublished. Freud's sufferings increased. During an excursion in the mountains he lost his breath and was obliged to turn back. Once again he gave up smoking, but soon resumed it. Feelings that he had made great discoveries were followed by tormenting doubts. Jacob Freud, who had been severely ill for several months, died on October 23, 1896. During the night following the funeral, Sigmund dreamed that he was in some premises where he read a poster: "One is requested to shut the eyes."[127] There was a connotation of self-reproach in the dream. Freud now realized how much his father had meant to him. Most likely he had guilt feelings about the hostility he had long felt toward him. From that time on, Freud's self-analysis, which seemed to have proceeded intermittently until then, became systematic and absorbed him increasingly, particularly the analysis of his dreams. Edith Buxbaum[128] in an article, and Didier Anzieu in a book,[129] have tried to reconstruct Freud's self-analysis by placing the dreams in chronological order and in juxtaposition with the Fliess correspondence.

For about one year after his father's death, Freud's inner sufferings became worse, as shown by his letters to Fliess. He brooded day and night over the psychological apparatus and the root of neuroses. He paid increased attention to the fantasies covering certain memories. He felt on the verge of discovering great secrets, or to have discovered them, but soon fell back, the prey of doubts. He told of his neurosis, his little hysteria. He claimed to be indifferent to the intrigues that may have occurred at the University. On August 14, 1897, he told Fliess that "the main patient who keeps me busy is myself," and that his analysis was more arduous than any other.

On September 21, 1897, Freud wrote Fliess a startling confidence. The stories of early seduction by the father, as told by all of his hysterical patients, were mere fantasies, so that his entire theory of hysteria was shaken. The lack of therapeutic success, the improbability that so many seductions by the father could pass unnoticed, the impossibility of distinguishing in the unconscious a memory from a fiction, were the main reasons that now led him to give up the hope of elucidating the mystery of neurosis. Gone were the expectations of a great discovery that would bring fame and wealth. However, the tone of this letter was optimistic. There remained to Freud his method of interpreting dreams and his incipient metapsychology (his system of psychic apparatus). From this moment on, his self-analysis underwent a fruitful phase. Childhood memories rushed forth. The ugly, old "nanny," who told him about God and hell, he now saw as being at the root of his earliest sexual experience, whereas the libido toward his mother had been aroused at the age of 2½ years. Relationships with his one-year-old nephew furnished the pattern for the neurotic side of his subsequent friendships. He remembered his jealousy toward his little brother and subsequent guilt feelings after his death. Searching for memories about his nanny, he discovered an example of what he later called screen memory. He assumed that the little boy's amorous feelings for his mother and jealousy of his father were general phenomena. He invoked the names of Oedipus and Hamlet. He gave increasing importance to resistance, now considered as the persistence of infantile characteristics. He reformulated his idea about the origin of hysteria and obsessions. In this process, self-analysis and the analysis of his patients were narrowly intermingled, and Freud told Fliess: "I cannot give you any idea of the intellectual beauty of the work."

In November 1897, Freud wrote that his self-analysis was stagnating again. More childhood memories slowly emerged. Freud was preoccupied with problems pertaining to former sexual zones, particularly the anal memories and fantasies. He compared dreams, fantasies, neurotic symptoms, witticisms, and artistic creations. He felt an improvement in his neurosis, emancipated himself from the influence of Brücke and Charcot, and identified himself with Goethe. His letters to Fliess became less frequent, shorter, and manifested a shift from dependency to competition. At the beginning of 1898 he began to write a book on dreams. That work was interrupted by the summer vacation, and in the autumn by a new period of depression and inhibition, but was resumed and completed by September 1899.

The publication of *The Interpretation of Dreams* marked the end of Freud's neurosis, but he never ceased his self-analysis, and from that time on devoted a moment to it daily. He emerged from this experience with a deep-reaching interior transformation. He outgrew his dependency on Fliess, and their close friendship ended at the beginning of 1902. Freud was able to overcome a mysterious inhibition that had prevented him from visiting Rome, and in September 1901 he spent twelve days in that city of his dreams. He finally took steps to further his nomination as a professor, and now felt ready to gather around him a small circle of adherents.

The strange malady that Sigmund Freud underwent between 1894 and 1900, together with his self-analysis, have given rise to various interpretations. Some of his adversaries contend that he was a severely ill man, and psychoanalysis was the expression of a neurosis. His followers, such as Jones, claim that his self-analysis was a heroic feat without precedence, which was never to be performed again, by which the abysses of the unconscious were revealed to mankind for the first time. It is our hypothesis that Freud's self-analysis was one aspect of a complex process (the others being his relationship with Fliess, his neurosis, and the elaboration of psychoanalysis), and that this process was an example of what may be called a creative illness.

This compels us to define creative illness and give its main features.[130] It occurs in various settings and is to be found among shamans, among the mystics of various religions, in certain philosophers and creative writers. One example already mentioned in this book is that of Fechner,[131] and we shall describe in a later chapter the creative illness of C. G. Jung.[132] A creative illness succeeds a period of intense preoccupation with an idea and search for a certain truth. It is a polymorphous condition that can take the shape of depression, neurosis, psychosomatic ailments, or even psychosis. Whatever the symptoms, they are felt as painful, if not agonizing, by the subject, with alternating periods of alleviation and worsening. Throughout the illness the subject never loses the thread of his dominating preoccupation. It is often compatible with normal, professional activity and family life. But even if he keeps to his social activities, he is almost entirely absorbed with himself. He suffers from feelings of utter isolation, even when he has a mentor who guides him through the ordeal (like the shaman apprentice with his master). The termination is often rapid and marked by a phase of exhilaration. The subject emerges from his ordeal with a permanent transformation in his personality and the conviction that he has discovered a great truth or a new spiritual world.

In Freud's case all these features are to be found. Ever since his visit to Charcot in 1885 and 1886, he had been preoccupied with the problem of the origin of neurosis, a problem that at some point became a dominating concern. From 1894 onward Freud's sufferings as described in his letters to Fliess would undoubtedly be classified as neurotic, and at times as psychosomatic. But to the difference of neurosis, the concentration upon a fixed idea had not merely an obsessive, but also a creative character. Intellectual speculation, self-analysis, and work with his patients occurred in a kind of desperate search for an elusive truth. Repeatedly he felt that he was on the verge of discovering a great secret or to be now in its possession, only to be again seized with doubts. The characteristic feeling of utter isolation is one of the leitmotivs in his letters to Fliess. There is no evidence that Freud was really isolated, and still less that he was ill-treated by his colleagues during those years. His three lectures before the Doktorenkollegium were well received in spite of the strangeness of the theories. Another, on dreams, before the B'nai B'rith, Freud says, was given an enthusiastic reception. Even more, one can speak of genuine respect and tolerance toward Freud on the part of his colleagues. On May 2, 1896, when Freud gave a lecture before the Society of Psychiatry and Neurology, expounding his theory of early seduction as the cause of hysteria, Krafft-Ebing, who was chairman, simply remarked that it sounded like a scientific fairy tale, and nonetheless proposed Freud's nomination to the title of Extraordinarius the following year.[133] As for the audience, who would blame it for its skepticism when Freud himself, a few months later, discovered that he had been mistaken? A frequent feature in neurosis is the abundance of pejorative judgments; such were those emitted by Freud in these letters in regard to his colleagues. As early as August 1888, he said that his colleagues had to moderate him in his attacks on Meynert. His book on aphasia is an attack on various colleagues, and particularly on "the high-enthroned idol" Meynert. Even the good Breuer was treated with contempt. In these letters also appears a strong intolerance of any kind of criticism. Strümpell's review of the *Studies in Hysteria*, which acknowledges the merits of the book, though with certain reservations, Freud qualified as "base" (*niederträchtig*).[134] When C. S. Freund published an article on psychic paralyses,[135] Freud called it "almost a plagiarism,"[136] although the article expressed a theory quite different from that of Freud, whom the author even mentions in that regard. Freud was sensitive in matters of priority and was anxious not to be forestalled, for instance by Moebius or Janet. His attitude toward his colleagues appeared in these letters as one of distrust or as provoking them.[137]

Freud's relationship with Fliess, which has puzzled so many psychoanalysts, can be easily understood when placed in the context of creative illness. The person has the feeling of blazing a trail in an unknown world in complete isolation. He desperately needs a guide to help him in that ordeal. Freud had left behind those fatherly figures: Brücke, Meynert, Breuer, and Charcot, and he now resorted to a friendship with a man of the same generation as his own. In his adolescent years Freud had had a close friendship with a schoolmate, Eduard Silberstein, with whom he spent most of his free time. The two friends learned Spanish, to use as a kind of secret language, took Spanish names, founded a Castilian Academy, and continued to correspond for about ten years. On a somewhat similar model, Freud and Fliess engaged in a narrow friendship. They exchanged ideas, and particularly new insights and discoveries still kept secret from the rest of the world. However, a perusal of Freud's letters to Fliess shows that the initial relationship of two equal friends was gradually replaced by another of intellectual subordination of Freud to Fliess, until Freud eventually regained his former position of an equal. This shows that during the crucial period of Freud's creative illness, Fliess had involuntarily and unconsciously taken the role of the shaman master before the shaman apprentice, and of spiritual director to the mystic.

Typical for creative illness is the spontaneous and rapid recovery accompanied by a feeling of elation. We recall how Fechner went through a slightly hypomanic phase during which he thought that he could decipher all the enigmas in the world. A somewhat similar feeling is expressed in the sentence: "Whosoever has eyes to see and ears to hear convinces himself that mortals can keep no secret hidden. He whose lips are silent prattles with his fingertips, and self-betrayal gushes forth through all the pores of his skin."[138] All the years of suffering had vanished, but there remained the impression of having passed through a long period of terrible isolation in a hostile world. Typical for the end of creative illness is the gradual shift of interest from the interior to the exterior world. Whereas in his letters he had told Fliess that he was indifferent to his nomination and even visualized a complete break with the University, Freud now intervened actively at the Ministry to further his interests.

How the personality of a scientist can be affected by his discovery is shown, for instance, in the case of Robert Bunsen, as depicted by Von Uexküll.[139] When Bunsen discovered spectral analysis, his vision of the world changed, and so did his personality; from then on "he bore himself as a king travelling incognito." Paul Valéry has shown how the personality of a creative writer can also be reshaped after the image of his work.[140] In regard to the creative illness the resulting transformation of personality is even deeper. It is as if the individual had followed the call of Saint Augustine,

"Seek not abroad, turn back into thyself, for in the inner man dwells the truth."[141] For that reason, too, the transformation of personality is indissolubly united with the conviction of having discovered a grandiose truth that must be proclaimed to mankind. In Freud's case it was the discovery of the psychoanalytic method and of a new theory of the mind, and its first evidence lay in his book *The Interpretation of Dreams,* (*Traumdeutung*).

Freud always considered *The Interpretation of Dreams* his capital work, and it is certainly an extraordinary book. While much was published every year about dreams, the topic of their interpretation had not been renewed since Scherner in 1855. Second, the book brought not only an original theory of dreams, but the foundation of a new psychology. And third, the book was, to an unprecedented degree, bound to the life and personality of its author. Hervey de Saint-Denis and others had filled up entire books with their own dreams and explanations thereof, but none had analyzed dreams that were had during a creative illness.

Today *The Interpretation of Dreams* is a classic, and we are so familiar with it that it is difficult for us to visualize the impression it made in 1900. The current version today is that Freud was at that time an obscure neurologist who was "ostracized" by his colleagues, and that the book that brought so many innovations was scorned or received with deathly silence. An objective scrutiny of the facts gives a different picture. During those years of creative illness Freud's reputation had slowly grown in Vienna and abroad. At the International Psychological Congress in Munich in August 1896, Freud's name was mentioned as one of the foremost authorities on hysteria.[142] Van Renterghem in 1897 listed Freud among the leading representatives of the Nancy School.[143] As mentioned previously, a biographic sketch on Freud appeared in 1901 in a kind of *Who's Who* of medical celebrities.[144] Moreover, in Lyons a gynecologist, Dr. César Tournier, as early as 1895 became deeply interested in Freud's ideas on infantile sexuality.[145] The assertion that Freud was ostracized in Vienna is unfounded. He never ceased to be a member of the Imperial-Royal Society of Physicians,[146] and at least in 1899–1900 was an assessor of the Association for Psychiatry and Neurology,[147] (the same group where his lecture on hysteria had been received with disbelief in 1896). An official certificate of October 4, 1897, stated that "Freud lives in obviously very good circumstances, has three servants, and enjoys a not very extensive but lucrative practice," and it is clear that his position had improved even more in the meantime.[148]

In spite of its fame, *The Interpretation of Dreams* is one of the least understood works of Freud today, for several reasons. First, because the text has undergone many changes, additions, and subtractions from one edition to another, so that the edition now available is rather different in shape and content from the original. Second, the book was difficult to translate, and many nuances of the original escape in the best translation.[149] The only way to gain a real knowledge of its content is to read the original German edition, which, unfortunately, is very scarce. Third, *The Interpretation of Dreams* is filled with allusions to events and customs that were familiar to the contemporary reader, but are nearly incomprehensible today without a commentary.[150] It literally swarms with humorous details about life in the *fin de siècle* Vienna.

Furthermore, the book could be called an autobiography in disguise. Freud mentions his birth and the prediction of an old peasant woman made at the time, the rough education he received from an old nurse, the peculiar mixture of friendship and hostility between him and his nephew John, one year older than he, the emigration of his half-brothers to England, a childhood nightmare in which he saw his mother and bird-beaked figures, his position as first in the class at school, the "conspiracy against the unpopular teacher," the first inklings he had of anti-Semitism in schoolmates, and many other details. Freud also mentions political events: the liberal government in 1866 in which there were two Jewish Ministers, the Spanish-American War of 1898, the anarchist criminal attempts in Paris. Freud tells of his previous works, his disappointment in the cocaine affair, his feeling of exhilaration when he set foot in Paris in 1885, and of his friend Fliess. He hints at his discoveries about screen memories, childhood sexuality, and the Oedipus complex. He carefully conceals everything pertaining to his own love life, but he tells about his children and gives examples of their dreams. He does not hide his atheistic feelings, nor his disbelief in immortality.

On the other hand, Freud made use of the stratagem resorted to by Dante when he cast the people he disliked into hell. Such was Uncle Josef, the black sheep of the family, whom Freud claimed "never, of course, to have loved"; such was the old nanny who treated him harshly as an infant, and the stupid gymnasium teacher against whom there was a rebellion. The all too severe Brücke was pictured in a dream as compelling Freud to dissect his own leg and pelvis. Meynert was said to have been treated for chloroform addiction in a private mental hospital. Mention was made of Meynert's bitter struggle against Freud, and that shortly before his death Meynert confessed to Freud that he was afflicted with male hysteria, which he had carefully concealed all his life.[151] Most striking are the reminiscences concerning Freud's father: when Sigmund was six years old, Jacob gave him and his sister a picture book to tear into pieces, "which was hardly justifiable from a pedagogical point of view." After little Sigmund had urinated in his parents' bedroom, his father told him that he would never amount to anything. There was also the incident of the Christian who had insulted Jacob, and of Jacob's cowardly behavior. In one dream he was shown as having been inebriated and under arrest. There were also the painful symptoms that grieved Jacob and the family in the last days before his death. There is not much on the positive side, and this makes one wonder whether Freud had not more deep-reaching reasons for this attitude toward his father than just the early childhood rivalry for his mother.

One peculiar feature of the book is an element of deliberate but well concealed provocation. At that time the word *Traumdeutung* was used to designate the popular interpretation of dreams by fortune tellers; thus the philosopher Gomperz[152] had published a pamphlet, *Traumdeutung und Zauberei* (Dream Interpretation and Magic). To contemporary scientists the title *Traumdeutung* held something intriguing and shocking.[153] Freud placed at the beginning of his book a motto borrowed from Virgil's *Aeneid*:

Flectere si nequeo Superos, Acheronta movebo!
(If Heaven I cannot bend, then Hell I will arouse!)[154]

These were Juno's words when Jupiter refused to prevent Aeneas from becoming king of Latium; she then summoned out of Hell the Furia Allecto, who with a band of enraged women attacked the Trojans. This motto can be interpreted as an allusion to the fate of repressed drives, but also as referring to Freud's failure to obtain academic recognition and his revolutionizing the science of the mind. Freud, in a letter to Fliess, on February 9, 1898, writes that he is enjoying in thought all the "headshaking" over the "indiscretions and impudences" the book contains.[155]

These unusual features of the *Traumdeutung*, the provoking title and motto, the high literary quality, its intimate connection with Freud's life and personality, its humorous allusions to the Viennese life in those days, all this contributed to the effect the book had on the readers. Some were critical of what appeared to them as a lack of scientific rigor, but for certain others it was a revelation that shook them and set their lives on a new course. The German psychiatrist Blüher[156] tells in his autobiography how he had little interest in Freud's work until a friend lent him *The Interpretation of Dreams* which he could not put down until he had finished it and which gave a decisive orientation to his career. It is through similar experiences that Stekel, Adler, and Ferenczi became disciples of Freud. As to the assertion that the book was met with silence or annihilating criticism, it has been refuted by Ilse Bry and Alfred Rifkin.[157]

An obscure point in Freud's life is why his nomination as Extraordinary Professor came so belatedly. The traditional story tells of anti-Semitism, of the scandal caused by Freud's sexual theories, and of the pettiness of his colleagues who resented his superiority. Freud's final nomination, the legend adds, was obtained when one of his rich patients bribed the Minister of Education into nominating him, with a gift of a painting by Böcklin to the art gallery he patronized. An objective study of the facts was made possible when Joseph and Renée Gicklhorn found a series of forty documents pertaining to Freud's university career in the archives of the University of Vienna and in the Austrian State Archive.[158] Two other documents were added subsequently by K. R. Eissler.[159] It is a confirmed fact that in January 1897, Professors Nothnagel and Krafft-Ebing asked the assembly of professors to propose Freud for the position of Extraordinary Professor. In its meeting of February 13, 1897, the assembly charged a committee of six professors to make a report on the matter. On June 12, 1897, after hearing a favorable report read by Krafft-Ebing, the assembly proposed to the Ministry the nomination of Freud as Extraordinary Professor. However, it was only on February 27, 1902, that the Minister of Public Education, Freiherr W. von Hartel, proposed the nomination, which was signed by Emperor Francis Joseph on March 5, 1902. What happened during that interval of five years is not sufficiently explained by the available documents. In a letter to Fliess dated March 11, 1902, Freud tells how, when coming back from Rome, he realized that he had to act himself if he ever wanted to receive the long-postponed nomination, how in the Ministry it was intimated to him by Sigmund Exner that "influences" were working against him, and that he had better look for "counter-influences," how he found these in a former patient, Frau Elise Gomperz, and how he asked Nothnagel and Krafft-Ebing to renew the request in his favor. Finally, as a result of the intervention of another former patient, the Baroness von Ferstel, the extraordinary professorship was granted.

It is certain that Nothnagel's and Krafft-Ebing's renewed request of December 5, 1901, was followed by Freud's nomination, but this still does not explain the reason why the first request of the assembly of professors remained buried for more than four years. To that, the Gicklhorns have given the following explanation. On May 28, 1898, by a secret decree (*Geheimerlass*) the Ministry of Education decided to reduce the number of nominations for the title of Extraordinary Professor, stipulating that those nominated should be able to replace the Titular Professor, and also that one had to consider those Privat Dozents who already had an extensive teaching practice. According to the Gicklhorns, Freud did not comply with these conditions: he had the title of Privat Dozent in neurology, but not (as was the case with Wagner-Jauregg) in psychiatry. Further, he had given more attention to his lucrative practice than to his function of Privat Dozent. These conclusions by the Gicklhorns have been disputed point by point by K. R. Eissler.[160] It is certain that candidates who had been proposed at the same time as Freud and after him received their nominations before him. To be sure, there had been repeated changes in the Ministry, and the new Minister, Wilhelm von Hartel, an extraordinarily active man, who was responsible for the entire Austrian school system as well as for religious and cultural affairs, could not be expected to keep informed of each individual candidature.[161] But he was subjected to all kinds of political pressures; many professorial nominations were obtained because of political influences rather than the merits of the candidates. For that reason Von Hartel was the object of vehement attacks by Karl Kraus.[162] Von Hartel was also attacked by anti-Semites because he had been instrumental in awarding a literary prize to Arthur Schnitzler and because he had publicly condemned anti-Semitism before the Austrian Parliament. That Freud was not nominated earlier cannot, therefore, be ascribed to anti-Semitism. As to the legend that the nomination of Freud was obtained by Frau Ferstel in exchange for a painting by Böcklin (*Die Burgruine*), Renée Gicklhorn has shown that this painting remained in the possession of its owners, the Thorsch family, until 1948, and that the Modern Gallery had already acquired another of Böcklin's pictures.[163] K. R. Eissler rejoined that the Modern Gallery had in fact received a painting from Baroness Marie von Ferstel in 1902, by the artist Emil Orlik: "Church in Auscha."[164] In view of the small value of the painting, this would rather confirm the improbability of the story of Freud's nomination being obtained through bribery.[165] Possibly this gift was no more than a token of gratitude of the Baroness to the Minister. It may be concluded that the major reason for the delay in Freud's nomination was the bureaucratic *vis inertiae*, and that priority was always given to recommended candidates, while Freud had been too absorbed in his self-analysis to see to his interests.

Thus in 1902 Freud saw this one of his ambitions fulfilled. The title of Extraordinary Professor was an acknowledgment of his scientific work and also permitted him to expect higher fees. There then came for Freud a period of intense productivity. In the autumn of 1902 he gathered together a small group of interested people, who met at his home each Wednesday evening to discuss problems of psychoanalysis. They called themselves The Wednesday Psychological Society. The first followers were Kahane, Reitler, Adler, and Stekel. This was the onset of the psychoanalytic movement, which was to expand until it reached worldwide dimensions.

From that time on, Freud's life story is largely that of the psychoanalytic movement. In 1904, Freud published *The Psychopathology of Everyday Life* in book form. In spite of an unpleasant polemic with Fliess, he found increasing recognition in various quarters; in September he began to correspond with Eugen Bleuler. In 1905, three of his best-known works appeared: *Three Essays on Sexuality, Jokes and the Unconscious,* and the story of the patient Dora. The perspective of those who saw psychoanalysis from without changed. Whereas around 1900 Freud was seen as an explorer of the unconscious and interpreter of dreams, he now appeared as the proponent of a sexual theory. The traditional story is that these new theories aroused a storm of indignation and abuse; but here too an objective examination reveals a different picture. Bry and Rifkin, on the basis of reviews of Freud's works of that time, conclude that "knowledge and appreciation of Freud's work spread widely and rapidly," that "for the time during which Freud is supposed to have been ignored, a great many signs of recognition and extraordinary respect could be added to the few illustrations given in his paper."[166] Freud had become a celebrity and a much sought after therapist. In 1906, on the occasion of his fiftieth birthday, Freud received a medallion embossed with his portrait from his disciples. With the exception of a polemic from Fliess, whose former friendship had turned into hatred, Freud received signs of acknowledgment and devotion from everywhere.

In March 1907, C. G. Jung and Ludwig Binswanger came to visit Freud, and on their return to Zurich they founded a small psychoanalytic group. In 1908 the movement acquired an international character and the first International Congress of Psychoanalysis met in Salzburg, and in 1909, the first psychoanalytic periodical was founded. Freud was invited to give lectures at Clark University in Worcester, Massachusetts, and made the American journey with Jung and Ferenczi. This highlight in Freud's life was, as he put it, "the end of isolation."

This brings us to examine the meaning of that isolation about which Freud complained so much. In his autobiography he tells of "ten years or more of isolation" without specifying in which year it started or ended. This alleged isolation was certainly not in relation to his immediate circle: he had a happy family life, and Jones speaks of his "astonishingly wide" circle of acquaintances.[167] There is little evidence of envy and meanness on the part of colleagues. Wherever animosity succeeded friendship (as in the cases of Meynert, Breuer, Fliess), it is difficult to evaluate who was at fault. So far as is known, none of Freud's articles were ever refused by a journal, nor were any of his books rejected by a publisher. Contrary to the usual assertion, his publications did not meet with the icy silence or the disparaging criticism that are said to have existed. Actually the reception was mostly favorable, though at times accompanied by a mixture of surprise and puzzlement. It was seldom a direct rejection, and in that regard others fared no better than he. It might be that the feeling of utmost and bitter isolation, which is a characteristic feature of creative neurosis, persisted in Freud and was reinforced because during those years he had markedly isolated himself from the Viennese medical world.

During the year 1910 a peak came in Freud's life and in the history of psychoanalysis. The Wednesday Psychoanalytic Society, which in 1908 had become the Viennese Psychoanalytic Society, could no longer meet in Freud's apartment, with its increased membership. At the second International Congress, in Nuremberg, the International Psychoanalytic Association was founded, as well as a second psychoanalytic periodical. Freud published *A Childhood Memory of Leonardo da Vinci*. But the very fact that psychoanalysis was proclaimed a "movement" (and not just a new branch of science) inevitably provoked opposition in psychiatric circles, and crises within the initial group, and an antipsychoanalytic feeling rapidly arose in psychiatric circles.[168] In June 1911, Alfred Adler left Freud and founded a dissident society. In October 1912, Stekel left, but for some time the defections were largely compensated by progressions. The great crisis came in September 1913, when Freud and Jung broke their relationship and the Swiss group was disorganized. In that year, Freud published another of his major works, *Totem and Taboo.*

At the end of July 1914, World War I broke out. Freud, whose two sons Jean-Martin and Ernst were mobilized in the Austrian Army, followed the general trend of patriotic enthusiasm. His practice was seriously diminished. He wrote down his considerations on war and death, and his last lectures at the University were published under the title *Introductory Lectures in Psychoanalysis.* Concern about war neuroses revived interest in psychoanalysis, and a congress to that effect was organized in Budapest in September 1918. But soon after came the defeat, the disintegration of Austria-Hungary, and the years of economic ruin and famine. Freud was officially nominated Ordinary Professor in January 1920, and in the following month took part in the so-called Wagner-Jauregg Process.

Gradually, international ties were renewed. Freud's practice again grew with patients coming from foreign countries. He expounded his revised theories in *Beyond the Pleasure Principle,* and in *Mass Psychology and Ego Analysis.*

The year 1923 was a critical and ominous one.[169] In February, Freud noticed a leukoplakia on his palate and jaw. In April he consulted a specialist who performed an operation and found that it was cancerous. This was the first in a series of thirty operations that he was to undergo until his death. At that time Freud had just lost his daughter Sophie; and his grandson Heinerle Halberstadt, to whom he was particularly attached and who was staying with them, died on June 19, 1923. This caused Freud the greatest grief of his life. On October 4 and 11 of that year Freud underwent a major operation in which his upper jaw and palate were partly removed and replaced by a prosthesis. During that year he wrote *The Ego and the Id.* From then on, until his death sixteen years later, Freud lived in the aura of world fame, but his life also consisted of a long series of sufferings borne with stoical courage. The psychoanalytic movement spread swiftly; in 1925, Freud wrote *Inhibition, Symptom and Anxiety* and an autobiographic sketch. In 1926 his pamphlet on *Lay Analysis* was a strong plea in favor of the practice of psychoanalysis by laymen. Psychoanalysis became immensely popular in England, and still more in the United States, to Freud's surprise and sometimes disquiet.

In 1927, Freud published *The Future of an Illusion,* one of the sharpest criticisms of religion ever published, and in 1929, *Civilization and Its Discontents* appeared. In August 1930, he was awarded the Goethe Prize and in October 1931, a ceremony was held in the town of his birth, Freiberg, now called Przibor. In 1932, Freud revised part of his ideas written in the form of lectures before an imaginary audience, the *New Introductory Lectures in Psychoanalysis*. In 1933, Hitler seized power, and the future looked gloomy for Europe. In 1934, Freud's books were burned in Berlin, and in 1936, the entire stock of the International Psychoanalytic Publishing House was confiscated in Leipzig. In that year, on the occasion of Freud's eightieth birthday, an address was read by Thomas Mann.[170] In the following month, there was a recurrence of Freud's cancer.

Freud's friends and disciples tried to persuade him to emigrate, but he refused. On March 12, 1938, the Nazis entered Vienna, and Freud finally resigned himself to emigration, but the Nazis made this difficult. Freud's escape was obtained through arduous negotiations, on the part of Princess Marie Bonaparte and other influential and devoted friends. He had already been provided with a refuge in London by his son Ernst, and he left Vienna on June 4, 1938. In passing through Paris he was greeted at the railway station by the American Ambassador Bullitt.

Freud was received in London with great honor. In spite of his age and his intolerable sufferings, his mind remained alert. After some hesitation, he published *Moses and Monotheism*, perhaps his most controversial writing. He received visits and homage of many fervent admirers, and was made a Fellow of the Royal Medical Society; the delegation brought the act of nomination to his home by unique exception. Since his first operation in April 1923, Freud had undergone another thirty-two operations, as well as X-ray and radium treatments. There were scars in his mouth, and for years he had to wear a complicated prosthesis. There were times when he could not speak, could hardly swallow, and heard with difficulty. Freud showed neither impatience nor irritation, nor did he ever give way to self-pity. He refused all analgesics in order to keep a fully alert mind. Sigmund Freud died in London at his son's Hampstead home, on September 23, 1939, at the age of eighty-three. He was cremated at Golders Green Crematorium. There was no religious ceremony, but tributes were paid by Dr. Ernest Jones in the name of the International Psychoanalytic Association, by Dr. P. Neumann in the name of the Committee of Austrians in England, and by another prominent refugee, the writer Stefan Zweig.[171]

The Personality of Sigmund Freud

Freud belongs to those few men who saw their life and personality placed in the limelight and themselves exposed as an object to the curiosity of mankind. He tried to protect himself behind a screen of secrecy, but legends grew all the more around him, and he has been subjected to many contradictory judgments.

One reason for this may be that his personality underwent substantial changes during his life. Accounts of his childhood depict him as the first-born son of a young mother, who lavished love and reassurance upon him. Most probably she was the one who inspired him with that ambition that was to grow ever stronger throughout his life. In the reminiscences of his sister Anna, Sigmund appears as the privileged oldest boy and a young family tyrant, who forbade her to read Balzac and Dumas, who was the only one to have a room and an oil lamp to himself.[172] He objected to the disturbance of piano practice, causing the piano to be sold and his sisters to be deprived of the musical training usual in Vienna. At school he was a brilliant pupil, always at the head of his class. This is confirmed by the school archives, which also reveal that in a school scandal he was not among the misdemeanants, but one of those who cooperated with the authorities by giving information.[173] As a medical student, Sigmund still appeared ambitious and hardworking, but his protracted studies and extracurricular courses seem to suggest a certain lack of practical sense.

From his twenty-seventh to his thirtieth year, his correspondence with his fiancée still reflected ambition and hard work; Freud showed himself a man of strong likes and dislikes, a fervent and devoted lover, although at times possessive and jealous.

We do not know much about Freud's relationship with Martha after their marriage. Disciples and visitors merely speak of her as a good housewife and mother, although not too closely acquainted with her husbands' scientific work. She is reported to have said: "Psychoanalysis stops at the door of the children's room," and an intimation in a letter to Fliess, of February 8, 1897, seems to support this. Laforgue relates that while walking in the Viennese woods with her, she cryptically remarked that "nature provided that the trees do not grow into the sky."[174] His son, Jean-Martin, describes Freud as a good educator and kind father, who had time for his family on Sundays and during summer vacations.[175] He also tells of Freud's rigid adherence to the conventions of professional life, and his reluctance to accept such innovations as the bicycle, the telephone, and the typewriter.

The first available document that gives a substantial description of Freud's character is a report about his qualifications as a medical officer, written after a period of military service in the Austrian Army, from August 11 to September 9, 1886. We will give a translation of its essential parts.[176]

REPORT ON QUALIFICATIONS

Name:	Dr. Sigmund Freud
Rank:	K. K. Oberarzt, nominated June 13, 1882
Military promotion:	From August 11 to September 9, 1886, during the principal exercise, Batallion Head Physician, and during the concentration of the Regiment from August 31 to September 6, Regimental Chief Physician.
Knowledge of languages:	German perfect in word and writing, French and English good, Italian and Spanish fairly good.

Professional aptitudes and knowledge of the sanitary service:	Very skilful in his profession, knows the sanitary prescriptions and the sanitary service exactly.
Does he enjoy the confidence of the military and civilians?	Enjoys great confidence among military and civilians.
Qualities of mind and character:	Honest, firm character, cheerful.
Zeal, orderliness, and reliability in service:	Very zealous in performing duty, is orderly and very reliable in service.
Is he in possession of the prescribed uniform and bandage material?	Possesses prescribed uniform and bandage material.
Conduct in service:	
1. *Before the enemy:*	Not served.
2. *Toward superiors:*	Obedient and open, moreover modest.
3. *Toward equals:*	Friendly.
4. *Toward subordinates:*	Benevolent and exerting a good influence.
5. *Toward patients:*	Very solicitous of their well-being, humane.
Conduct outside of duty:	Very decent and modest, pleasant manners.
Condition of health, fitness for war service:	Delicate, but completely healthy, fit for war service.
Qualifications for promotions:	In the rank order.

This evaluation confirms other statements that depict Freud as a man of solid character and a strong sense of duty. Noteworthy is the word "cheerful" (*heiter*), which has not always been associated with the traditional picture of his character.[177]

The letters to Fliess, written during the following period in Freud's life, reveal his ambition, his wish to perform a work of great magnitude, his passionate friendship toward Fliess, much complaining about depressive ailments, his critical judgment of many people, and his feeling of being isolated in a hostile world.

From 1900 on, Freud's personality appears in a new light. His self-analysis had transformed the unsure young practitioner into a self-assured founder of a new doctrine and school, convinced that he had made a great discovery, which he saw as his mission to give to the world. Unfortunately, we lack contemporary descriptions of Freud during that period. Most accounts of him were written much later, after 1923.

In that period Freud's personality was transformed through his world fame and the physical sufferings caused by an unrelenting illness. His letters, as well as testimonies of his disciples, show him as a good husband, father, son, friend, and physician, kind at heart, tactful in the writing of letters and the choice of gifts, devoid of any kind of pose or theatricalism,

as a master able to conduct a movement in the midst of difficult circumstances, and as a man facing his physical sufferings and the knowledge of his
impending death with the utmost courage. He thus appeared to those close
to him as a rare personification of a wise man and a hero.

A few examples of the impression Freud made on those who interviewed
him are as follows:

The first known interview of Freud was given during his American journey to a Boston journalist who pictured him as follows:

> One sees at a glance that he is a man of great refinement, of intellect, and of a
> many-sided education. His sharp, yet kind, clear eyes suggest at once the doctor.
> His high forehead, with the large bumps of the observation, and his beautiful,
> energetic hands are very striking.[178]

There is a long gap between that interview and the next ones, which
fall into the period following 1923, that is, when Freud's personality had
undergone a transformation caused by his world fame and the cancer
that made his life a martyrdom. It was during this period that he had the
most visitors and that most was written about him.

Recouly, a French journalist, found that Freud's apartment resembled
a museum, and that Freud himself was like an old rabbi:

> We see an extremely accentuated Jewish type, the air of an old rabbi just
> arrived from Palestine, the thin and emaciated face of a man who has passed
> days and nights discussing with his initiated followers on the subtleties of the
> Law, in whom one feels a very intense brain life and the power of playing with
> ideas as an Oriental plays with the amber beads of his chaplet. When he speaks
> of his doctrine, of his disciples, he does so with a mixture of pride and detach-
> ment. However, it is pride that dominates.[179]

Max Eastman, in 1926, was taken aback by the outrageous prejudice
Freud displayed against the United States and the shockingly overt way he
expressed it before American visitors.[180]

André Breton reported that "the greatest psychologist of this time lives
in a house of mediocre appearance, in a lost quarter of Vienna."[181] He did
not find the maid who opened the door pretty. When he finally came to
Freud's office, Breton says, "I found myself in the presence of a small,
unassuming old man who received in his shabby office, like a physician
for the poor."

The playwright Lenormand found Freud's office "like that of any university professor."[182] Freud showed him the works of Shakespeare and of
the Greek tragedians on his shelves and said: "Here are my masters." He
maintained that the essential themes of his theories were based on the
intuition of the poets.

Schultz, a German psychiatrist, saw Freud as a man of a little more than middle height, slightly bent, strongly built, with the typical manner of a professor, strikingly reminiscent of Paul Ehrlich.[183] He had a short, full beard, wore glasses, and had a penetrating look. He combined an objective, intellectual attitude with a sprightly spirit and a typical Austrian amiability and expressed himself in classically stylistic language. Schultz called Freud an extraordinarily gifted man with a harmony of personality. "You do not really believe that you are able to cure?" Freud asked him. Schultz replied: "In no way, but one can, as a gardener does, remove impediments to personal growth." "Then we will understand each other," Freud answered.

Viktor von Weizsäcker described Freud as a "learned man of the world, of bourgeois high culture."[184] In his office there was a long row of antique statuettes in bronze and terra cotta, satyrs and goddesses and other curios. "He showed no trace of academic pedantry, and his conversation glided easily from serious and difficult themes to light and gracious chatting. The eminent man was always present." It was obvious that Freud was suffering physically, but it was not oppressive to those around him.

Emil Ludwig told of visiting Freud in the fall of 1927 and of finding his interpretation of the lives of Goethe, Napoleon, and Leonardo da Vinci to be fantastic.[185]

An interview was extorted from Freud by a French journalist, Odette Pannetier, who had made herself a reputation for literary hoaxes.[186] Knowing that the eighty-year-old, physically suffering Freud had closed his door to journalists, she pretended to be a patient with a phobia about dogs, and brought Freud a letter of recommendation from a French psychiatrist. The interview, as she reported it, far from making Freud look ridiculous, showed him as a likeable, good-humored old man who did not seem to have taken her phobia too seriously. He asked to see her husband, explained the costs and difficulties of treatment; "I extended an envelope. His manner seemed friendly rather than professional. But he took the envelope."

Accounts given by persons who have been analyzed by Freud mostly date from the later years of his activity. Roy Grinker pictures Freud as a sage and a fountain of wisdom.[187] Hilda Doolittle described the inspiration she drew from her analysis with him in highly poetic terms. Joseph Wortis, who underwent a four months' didactic analysis with Freud in 1934, kept a diary of his sessions and recast it in book form.[189] His report shows much of the technique used by Freud, and that Freud related his opinion on all possible topics: money, socialism, old age, American women, the Jewish question, and so on; he also made biting comments on certain colleagues.

To conclude, we will mention the interviews that Bruno Goetz had with Freud in 1904 and 1905, and which he reported from memory almost half a century later.[190] In those years Goetz was a poor and hungry student in Vienna suffering from violent facial neuralgia. One of his professors advised him to consult Dr. Freud, to whom he had shown some of Goetz' poems. Goetz was impressed by the way Freud looked attentively at him with his "marvellously kind, warm, heavy-hearted, knowing eyes." Freud told him he found his poems very fine, but: "You hide yourself behind your words instead of letting yourself be borne by them." Freud also asked why the sea recurred in his verses and whether it was a symbol or a reality to him. Goetz then poured forth his life to him, telling him that his father had been a sea captain, how he had spent his childhood with sailors, and many other details. Freud told him that he did not need an analysis and prescribed a medication for his neuralgia. Freud inquired into Goetz' financial situation and thus learned that he had eaten a steak for the last time four weeks prior to their meeting. And apologizing for playing the part of a father, Freud handed him an envelope with "a small honorarium for the pleasure you gave me with your verses and the story of your youth." The envelope contained 200 crowns. One month later Goetz, whose neuralgia by that time had disappeared, paid a second visit to Freud, who warned him against his enthusiasm for the *Bhagavad-Gita* and disclosed his ideas about poetry to him. Several months later, before returning to Munich, Goetz went to take leave of Freud, who criticized some of his articles he had read in the meantime, and added: "It is good that we do not see each other for a while and do not speak together," and asked Goetz not to write to him.

Freud was a man of middle stature (some found him short), slender in his youth, more rotund as the years passed. His eyes were brown, his hair dark brown, his well-groomed beard was longer in his younger years than later. He was a hard worker and remained so, even during the worst period of his illness. His only sport was hiking during the summer vacations. He became a heavy cigar smoker to the point of endangering his life, but attempts to give up smoking caused him so much discomfort that he relapsed every time. From the accounts we have of Freud, two very different pictures can be drawn. Some persons were impressed by what they called Freud's coldness, and C. G. Jung even stated that Freud's main characteristic was bitterness, "every word being loaded with it . . . his attitude was the bitterness of the person who is entirely misunderstood, and his manners always seemed to say: 'If they do not understand, they must be stamped into hell.' "[191] Freud no doubt belonged among those who "cannot suffer fools gladly." He also could go far in bearing grudges and in his resentment against those he believed, rightly or wrongly, to have offended him.[192] Many others depicted him as an extremely kind and civil man, full of wit and humor and altogether charming. It is as if both his mother's cool aloofness and his father's easygoing nature were united in him.

One basic feature of Freud was his tremendous energy; he combined his boundless capacity for work with an intense concentration on one goal. Physical courage was allied with moral courage, which culminated in his stoic attitude during the last sixteen years of his life. His conviction of the truth of his theories was so complete that he did not admit contradiction. This was called intolerance by his opponents and passion for truth by his followers.

Freud lived, morally, socially, and professionally, according to the highest standards of a man of his time and status. A man of scrupulous honesty and professional dignity, he contemptuously rejected any suggestions of lending his name to commercial ends. He was extremely punctilious, kept his appointments exactly, and set all his activities to a timetable, to the hour, the day, the week, and the year. He was equally punctilious about his appearance. In retrospect, some of these traits have been considered obsessive-compulsive, but they are normal if seen in the context of the times.[193] Considerable dignity and decorum were expected of professional men of his standing. To call Freud un-Viennese shows a confusion between the stereotype of a Viennese operetta and the historical reality.[194]

The difficulty in understanding the complex personality of Freud has led many to seek a basic notion that would make him intelligible. Interpretations have been given of Freud as a Jew, as a Viennese professional man of his time, as a Romantic, as a man of letters, as a neurotic, and as a genius.

Freud[195] wrote in 1930 that he was completely estranged from the religion of his ancestors (as well as from any other), and that he could not espouse the Jewish nationalistic idea, but he never denied belonging to his people, that he felt his singularity as a Jew and did not wish it to be otherwise, and that if one wondered what was still Jewish in him, he would answer: "Not very much, but probably the main thing."[196] His Jewish feeling seems to have followed the same curve as that of many of his Austrian contemporaries. Anti-Semitism was almost nonexistent in Austria at the time of his birth. There was some in certain student associations during his youth. In the last two decades of the nineteenth century, anti-Semitism increased, but it could hardly impair the career of a professional man. In proportion to the increased anti-Semitism, particularly after World War I, the feeling of Jewish identity was revived, and many Jews who had been inclined to reject their Jewish identity came to emphasize it. Probably the best interpretation of Freud's personality as a Jew was given by Hyman:

Here is the boy, growing up in a middle class Jewish family with a fable of descent from famous scholars, and a legendary family history going back to the destruction of the Temple. He was his mother's first-born and darling, his father's spoiled "scholar" and pride, the pet of his teachers. We know that he will be a little radical as a young man, but will settle down, and that he will become a good husband and a loving and indulgent father, a passionate card player, a great talker among his cronies. He is ambivalent about his Jewishness, like a hundred semi-intellectuals we know. He dislikes Christianity without any corresponding new faith, his friends are almost entirely Jewish, he is fascinated by Jewish rituals but mocks it all as superstition, he toys with conversion, but is never serious, he has a burning ambition for success and fame, and a corresponding contempt for ambitionless *Goyim*, he is incredulous that any Gentile author (in this case George Eliot) could write about Jews and know things "we speak of only among ourselves," he suffers from *"schnorrer"* fantasies (Freud's own term) about inheriting undeserved wealth, he identifies himself with Jewish heroism in history and legend ("I have often felt as if I had inherited all the passion of our ancestors when they defended their Temple"). We can be sure that this fellow will end up in B'nai B'rith, and he does. If we had been told that this Dr. Freud made a good living as a general practitioner, provided a first-class education for his children, and was never heard of outside the neighbourhood, we would not have been surprised.[197]

No doubt there were many among Freud's Jewish contemporaries whose lives and careers followed a similar pattern (without, however, gaining world fame). A comparison of Freud and Breuer may be instructive: Breuer, who had been the victim of intrigues and who had missed the opportunity of a brilliant academic career, never attributed any of his setbacks to anti-Semitism, and declared that he was perfectly content with the life he had; whereas Freud repeatedly referred to the hostile attitude of anti-Semitic colleagues and officials. Speaking of his father, Breuer emphasized how wonderful it had been for a man of his generation to be free from the ghetto and able to enter the wider world; Freud's only reference to his father's youth was the story of the affront he suffered from a Gentile. Breuer devoted half of his autobiography to a eulogy of his father, in contrast to Freud who had no compunction against expressing hostile feelings toward his father. Breuer criticized the hypersensitivity of the Jew to the slightest anti-Semitic touch, and ascribed it to imperfect assimilation; from the beginning Freud felt he belonged to a persecuted minority and attributed his creativeness partly to the fact that he had been compelled to think differently from the majority. Benedikt, in his autobiography, gave a long list of complaints about many of his contemporaries, but never accused them of anti-Semitism. Thus, to be a Jew in Vienna could lead one to adopt different attitudes toward Judaism and the Gentile world, and it was no obstacle to feeling thoroughly Viennese at the same time.

Freud could also be understood if seen as a typical representative of the Viennese professional world of the end of the nineteenth century. It was not unusual in Vienna, an ethnic and social melting pot, that a gifted man from the lower middle class could climb the social ladder and reach, by middle life, a fairly high social and financial status, provided that he had gone to secondary school and a university. One example was Josef Breuer, son of a modest teacher, who became one of the most well-to-do physicians in Vienna and who could certainly have gone farther if he had wanted to. The man, of course, had to be gifted, a hard worker, and ambitious—and Freud was all of these. For a medical man, this meant facing a period of poorly paid hospital jobs, Privat Dozent teaching, intense competition, and years of plodding through little-rewarded scientific work. Freud was one of those who successfully underwent these trials. From his thirty-fifth year on he was able to live the life of a wealthy Viennese bourgeois, who had a large apartment with several servants in one of the best residential quarters in Vienna, took three months of summer vacation in Austria and abroad, read the *Neue Freie Presse,* and strictly conformed to the obligations of his profession. Freud also possessed to a high degree the manners of the Viennese high bourgeoisie of his time, the refined and many-sided culture, the exquisite urbanity, the good-natured humor, and the art of conversation. *The Interpretation of Dreams, The Psychopathology of Everyday Life,* and *Jokes and Their Relation to the Unconscious,* are filled with allusions to Viennese life and contemporary local events. Freud was Viennese to his fingertips (including the characteristic affectation of hating Vienna).

Freud also shared the values of his class. David Riesmann, in trying to reconstruct Freud's *weltanschauung* from his writings, emphasized his notions of work and play.[198] Freud viewed the world of work as the real world, and even extended this into the unconscious in the form of the "dream work" and the "work of mourning," as opposed to the world of pleasure, which is the world of the child, the immature, the neurotic, the woman, and the aristocrat. Criteria of mental health, according to Freud, were the capacities to work and to enjoy pleasure. In this formula, Freud expressed the ideal of the industrious Viennese bourgeois who conformed to the exacting requirements of his position, but claimed his share of the pleasures of the city. Freud viewed society as being naturally and necessarily authoritarian and the family as paternalistic. As he had respected his masters, so he expected his disciples to respect him. To be sure, Freud did not conform in every detail to a certain type of upper-class Viennese. He was not a frequenter of the theater or opera, nor did he have affairs with actresses. But puritanical behavior and monogamy, such as Freud's, were not as exceptional as the legend would have it. Those who called Freud un-Viennese have misunderstood the character of both Freud and Vienna.

Freud's personality could also be seen as that of a Romantic. Wittels has said that though Freud was a contemporary of Bismarkian Germany, he ideally belonged to the Germany of Goethe.[199] In his style of life there was much of Romanticism. His letters to his fiancée show the exaltation one meets, for instance, in the letters of Herzen to his beloved. Freud's passionate relationship with Fliess, which is so foreign to our present-day standards, was similar to those found among young Romanticists. It is as though Freud identified himself with the Byronic figure of the lonely hero struggling against a host of enemies and difficulties. Weekly gatherings of friends in *Cénacles* were a habit with Romantic poets, students, and young scientists. By 1900, however, scientists gathered in meetings of official societies. Freud's Wednesday evening group would have been more in context among Neo-Romantic poets, or a century earlier among Romantic scientists. The formation of a secret group of six chosen disciples who pledged their allegiance to the defense of psychoanalysis, each of them receiving a ring from Freud, was an eminently Romantic idea. That Freud should suddenly harbor feelings of Austrian patriotism, after a long period of political indifference, when the war broke out, is reminiscent of the patriotic fervor of the young German Romanticists in 1806. Finally, much in psychoanalysis can be understood as a revival of the concepts of the philosophy of nature and Romantic medicine.

Wittels found the key to Freud's personality in his identification with Goethe, recalling that Freud's vocational choice was made after hearing Goethe's poem *On Nature*.[199] Both Goethe's idea of beauty and interest in art and archeology, as well as his concept of science with its search for archetypal patterns, can be found in Freud. Freud's literary style is modeled after Goethe's; the influence of Goethe can even be found in Freud's predilection for certain words, such as "international" (in the sense of supranational).

Freud can also be understood as a man of letters. He possessed the attributes of a great writer to a supreme degree. First he had linguistic and verbal gifts, the love of his native language, a richness of vocabulary, the *Sprachgefühl* (feeling for the language) that infallibly led him to choose the appropriate word.[200] Even his early articles on histology are written in magnificent style. As Wittels wrote:

> For his readers who are not professionally interested, often what he says is not so important as the fascinating manner in which he says it. The translations of his writings cannot reproduce the thoroughly German spirit which Freud's works breathe forth. The magic of the language cannot be carried over. If one wishes actually to comprehend Freud's psychoanalysis from the bottom up, one must read his books in their own language . . .

Second, he had that gift of intellectual curiosity that impels a writer to observe his fellow men, to try to penetrate their lives, their loves, their intimate attitudes. (This burning curiosity has been well described by Flaubert and Dostoevsky.) Third, Freud loved writing and had a propensity for writing letters, diaries, essays, and books: *Nulla dies sine linea*. For a man of letters, to write down one's thoughts and impressions is more important than to check their exactness. This is the principle of Börne's method, that is, to write down one's immediate impressions of everything, seeking sincerity above all; this is also the way Popper-Lynkeus wrote his essays. Freud's essays on Michelangelo and Leonardo da Vinci could be considered as essays written in the Börne manner. Fourth, Freud possessed one of the rarest qualities in a great writer, which Paul Bourget called credibility. Mediocre writers will make a true story seem manufactured, while a great writer can make the most implausible story seem true. A Hebraic historian, commenting on *Moses and Monotheism,* gave a long list of inaccuracies and impossibilities contained in it, but added that by his great talent Freud had made a plausible story of this network of impossibilities.[201] Freud repeatedly referred to the fact that the great poets and writers had preceded psychologists in the exploration of the human mind. He often quoted the Greek tragedians, Shakespeare, Goethe, Schiller, Heine, and many other writers. No doubt Freud could have been one of the world's foremost writers, but instead of using his deep, intuitive knowledge of the human soul for the creation of literary works, he attempted to formulate and systematize it.

There have been interpretations of Freud's personality in the form of those "pathographies" made famous by Moebius and developed later by psychoanalysts.[202] Maylan explained Freud's work and personality through his father complex.[203] Natenberg collected, from Freud's writings and available biographical material, all evidence of neurosis, and fitted it together into a portrait of a deeply disturbed individual with a delusional system.[204] In Erich Fromm's pathography, Freud is perceived as a fanatic for truth, who, aided by various neurotic traits, was imbued with the conviction that it was his mission to lead an intellectual revolution to transform the world by means of the psychoanalytic movement.[205] Percival Bailey portrays Freud as a kind of eccentric and clumsy genius who invoked anti-Semitism and the hostility of his colleagues as an excuse for his failures, and who went astray construing fantastic theories.[206] Maryse Choisy sees at the root of his personality and his work the weakness of his libido: "Is not then Freud's theory a rationalization of his own sexual inhibition?"[207] According to Alexander, Freud suffered from an unsolved conflict between having to remain in the opposition and his craving to be fully recognized.[208]

A variety of other traits have been pointed out in Freud and stamped as neurotic. Freud is said to have been credulous in certain matters (he believed, for instance, the war propaganda of the central empires), to have committed errors of judgment in regard to certain persons, to have kept unjustified grudges against others, as well as prejudices against the American civilization, to have been intolerant, to have committed indiscretions when speaking of some of his patients, to have shown inordinate concern over matters of priority while pretending not to care for it, to have attributed to himself the origin of many extant concepts, and to have been a tobacco addict.[209] Even his puritanical behavior and his strict monogamy have been deemed abnormal: the poetress Anna de Noailles, after paying him a visit, was shocked that a man who had written so much about sexuality should never have been unfaithful to his wife.[210] Marthe Robert excused his puritanical way of life because, she said, by the time he had acquired his knowledge of sexuality, he was too old to change.[211] Actually in all this there is nothing to justify a diagnosis of neurosis. One far more difficult problem is how Freud's oversensitiveness and subjective feeling of isolation could have led him to the conviction that he was rejected and ostracized, a conviction that all available documents show to have been unfounded.[212]

To our knowledge, K. R. Eissler is the only author who attempted a systematic study of Freud as a genius.[213] In a previous book on Goethe, Eissler defines men of genius as ". . . persons who are capable of re-creating the human cosmos, or part of it, in a way that is understandable to mankind, and contains a new, hitherto unperceived aspect of reality." Genius is the result of an extraordinary combination of factors and circumstances. At the root lies an innate, biological factor: in Goethe it was the intensity and quality of the dream function, which was at the service of creation; in Freud, a perfect mastery of the language. But the emergence of genius requires also a whole set of environmental factors. Being the beloved first-born of a young mother, who herself was the second wife of an older man by the name of Jacob, Freud was predestined to an early identification with the biblical character of Joseph, the interpreter of dreams who came to surpass his father and brothers. The young Sigmund had invested his libido in his scientific work and ambitions; his encounter with Martha Bernays brought him to turn a part of his libido toward Martha and the outside world; but the four years of his engagement entailed a severe frustration, hence a higher degree of sublimation. For Martha's sake, Freud gave up his dreams of scientific ambition, turning to clinical work, and it is this renunciation that enabled him to make discoveries in the field of neuroses. The daily correspondence with Martha sharpened his ability for psychological observation and introspection. Eissler thinks that this four-year engagement period was instrumental in causing a restructuring of Freud's personality, which in turn made his self-analysis possible, and subsequently the gradual emergence of a new vision of the world, that is, of psychoanalysis.

However, the time has not yet come when one may acquire a truly satisfying appraisal of Freud's personality. Data are still insufficient (our knowledge of his childhood is as meager as was our knowledge of his self-analysis before the publication of the Fliess correspondence). It is not inconceivable that, as time passes, it will become more and more difficult to understand him. Freud belonged to a group of men of the same mold, including Kraepelin, Forel, and Bleuler, who had gone through long training in intellectual and emotional discipline; they were men of high culture, puritanical mores, boundless energy, and strong convictions, which they vigorously asserted. Despite all personal or doctrinal divergencies, these men were able to understand each other immediately, whereas their ascetic-idealistic type is becoming increasingly foreign to a hedonistic-utilitarian generation.

Freud's Contemporaries

Freud's personality, like that of any man, cannot be fully understood if isolated from the context of his contemporaries, their parallelisms, divergencies, and interrelationships. From among these men, we will choose Wagner von Jauregg, who, while following the traditional path, made outstanding discoveries in psychiatry, and Arthur Schnitzler, who began as a neuropathologist and became one of the great Austrian writers.

Julius Wagner von Jauregg, the son of a civil servant, was born on March 7, 1857, one year later than Freud.[215] According to his autobiography, he chose medicine without having a special vocation for it, and registered at the Vienna Medical School in October 1874 (one year after Freud).[216] Unlike Freud, he finished his medical studies in the minimum time, although he too did extra work in laboratories from the third year on. His great master was the professor of experimental pathology, Salomon Stricker. As did Freud's, his first scientific publication appeared in the *Proceedings of the Imperial-Royal Academy of Sciences*, when he was a fourth year student. He graduated as M.D. on July 14, 1880, and remained in Stricker's laboratory, where he met Freud, and they came to address each other by the familiar *Du*. Realizing that there was no future for him with Stricker, Wagner-Jauregg turned to clinical medicine, toyed for some time with the idea of emigrating to Egypt, studied with Bamberger and Leidesdorf, and was even, at one time, interested in research on the anesthetic properties of cocaine. In 1885 he became Privat Dozent in Neuropathology, after his master Leidesdorf had overcome the strong opposition of Meynert. Three years later, Wagner-Jauregg's privat-dozentship was extended to psychiatry. This step, which Freud had not taken, gave Wagner-Jauregg the possibility for a later appointment as Titular Professor. In 1889, he was appointed Extraordinary Professor of Psychiatry in Graz, and in 1893 (while Freud and Breuer had just published their Preliminary Communication), he was appointed Titular Professor of Psychiatry in Vienna.

Wagner-Jauregg's psychiatric work was marked by three major accomplishments. First, in view of the fact that cretinism is correlated with a deficiency of iodine and could be avoided by the regular intake of iodized salt, he fought for the widescale application of this prophylactic measure, which resulted in the almost total disappearance of cretinism in certain parts of Europe. Second was his discovery of the cure of general paresis (a condition heretofore considered incurable) by malaria therapy. This discovery was the outcome of systematic experiments conducted for many years. The third great achievement was his proposing and having carried out a reform of Austrian law in regard to mental patients. Wagner-Jauregg was awarded many honors, culminating, in 1927, with the Nobel Prize. He was the first psychiatrist to receive it.

Wagner-Jauregg was an active mountain climber and horseman, and had received a many-sided education. He wrote in a clear and concise style, avoiding comparisons and literary imagery. His teaching was considered good, but not eloquent. His manner toward his students was said to be both authoritarian and benevolent. Besides his teaching, research, hospital responsibilities, and private practice, he was active in many scientific societies and academic functions.

The personality orientations of Freud and Wagner-Jauregg were so different that the two could hardly be expected to understand each other. Wagner-Jauregg fully recognized the value of Freud's neurological work, and possibly his early studies in neurosis, but he could not accept as scientifically valid Freud's further developments, such as the interpretation of dreams and the libido theory. Much has been said of Wagner-Jauregg's hostility toward Freud, though in his autobiography Wagner-Jauregg maintained that he never expressed any animosity toward Freud, apart from a few words in jest at private gatherings. However, one of his pupils, Emil Raimann, became a sharp adversary of Freud, and Freud seemed to blame Wagner-Jauregg for these attacks. Wagner-Jauregg said that Freud, being an intolerant man, could not understand that anyone else could allow their pupils to have opinions of their own, but at Freud's request, Wagner-Jauregg asked Raimann to cease criticizing Freud, which Raimann did. When Freud finally received the title of Ordinary Professor in 1920, it was Wagner-Jauregg who wrote the report recommending his nomination. Freudians have pointed out that, at the end of this report, Wagner-Jauregg made a slip of the pen, recommending Freud's appointment as "Extraordinary" Professor, and then striking the prefix "Extra." One may draw the conclusion that Wagner-Jauregg was reluctant, but supported Freud's candidature out of professional solidarity.

Many contradictory statements have arisen around the so-called Wagner-Jauregg Process of 1920, an event to which we shall return.[217] Even if Freud's expert report on Wagner-Jauregg's process was moderate in terms, it is clear that he, in turn, was reluctant. The reluctance appeared more openly during discussions, and Wagner-Jauregg resented it, as we learn from his autobiography. When these two men had grown old and world-famous, however, they exchanged congratulations on their eightieth birthdays, in an almost royal manner. As K. R. Eissler said:

Given their enormous difference in personality and temperament, one could have expected the development of a personal enmity between Freud and Wagner. The friendship which had been contracted in their young years, however, outlasted all vicissitudes of life. The mutual respect and friendly esteem was not destroyed by the scientific differences, and this is a truly exemplary episode in the biography of the two researchers.[218]

Parallels between Sigmund Freud and Arthur Schnitzler have repeatedly been drawn. In a letter to Schnitzler on the occasion of his sixtieth birthday, Freud wrote: "I shall make you a confession . . . I think I have avoided you from a kind of fear of finding my own double (*Doppelgänger-Scheu*).[219] Like Freud, Schnitzler belonged to a Jewish family that had severed its ties with the religion of its ancestors. He was born in Vienna on May 15, 1862 (which makes him six years younger than Freud). His father, a noted laryngologist and professor at the Vienna University, was the editor of a medical journal, and had actresses and opera singers among his clients. Arthur studied medicine in Vienna from 1879 to 1885, and thus graduated three years after Freud. Like Freud, he spent three years at the Viennese General Hospital, was Meynert's pupil, and was interested in the current discussions on hysteria and hypnosis. His first paper concerned six patients he had cured of hysterical aphonia in one or two hypnotic sessions each. He preferred to call it functional aphonia because he had some doubts about the diagnosis and concepts of hysteria.[220]

Following in the footsteps of his father, Schnitzler launched himself in a career in medical journalism. He reported in the *Wiener Medizinische Presse* about the meetings of the Imperial-Royal Society of Physicians, and this is how he came to give an account of the meeting of October 15, 1886, in which Freud talked about male hysteria.[221] In a subsequent article, recalling that lively discussion, Schnitzler expressed his fears that as a consequence many cases of supposed male hysteria would be presented in future meetings; but overeagerness, he said, was certainly more beneficial to science than a negative attitude.[222] Schnitzler also wrote many reviews of medical books in the *Internationale Klinische Rundschau*, with a preference for those dealing with hysteria, neurosis, and hypnosis. Commenting on Freud's translations of Charcot's and Bernheim's books, he praised his ability as a translator, but questioned some of the content. In his review of Bernheim's book on suggestion, Schnitzler spoke of the "posing" and "role acting" of the hypnotized individual, drawing on his own experience.[223] Similarly, Schnitzler gave due credit to Liébeault, but deplored the "ingenious fantasies" (*geistvolle Phantastereien*) in which he had indulged. On October 14, 1895, when Freud read that celebrated paper at the Doctorencollegium in which he proposed his classification of four basic neuroses, with a specific sexual origin for each, it was Schnitzler who wrote the most exhaustive and objective review.[224]

Meanwhile, Schnitzler's time and interest were being increasingly absorbed by literature and the theater, and his practice gradually shrank. Stormy love affairs with actresses caused him to suffer, but provided him with the material for his plays. Around 1890 he gathered together a group of gifted young Austrian poets and playwrights, who called themselves Young Vienna.[225] Schnitzler's literary fame began with *Anatol*, the story of a Viennese playboy of the time.[226] One episode of his play deals with hypnosis: Max congratulates Anatol on the manner in which he hypnotizes his young mistress, and has her play various roles. He suggests that, through hypnosis, Anatol find out whether she is faithful to him. Anatol hypnotizes Cora, who tells him she is twenty-one years old, and not nineteen as she had let him believe, and that she loves him. Anatol is afraid to question her further and wakes her. Max concludes: "One thing is clear to me, that we men also tell lies under hypnosis."

One of Schnitzler's next plays, *Paracelsus*, also revolves around hypnosis.[227] In sixteenth-century Basle, Paracelsus is rejected by the authorities as a charlatan, but he attracts the masses and performs miraculous cures. He hypnotizes Justina, the wife of a rich citizen, claiming that he can make her dream anything she wants. Justina then makes startling revelations. No one knows how much of it is true. The point at which she awakens from the hypnotic state is not made clear. The moral of the play is the relativity and the uncertainty, not only of hypnosis, but of mental life itself. Paracelsus contends that if a man could see his past years pictured, he could hardly recognize them, "because memory deceives almost as much as hope," that we are always acting a part even in deeper matters, and that "whosoever knows it is wise." Schnitzler's *Paracelsus* thus gives a very different picture of hypnosis and mental life than do Breuer's and Freud's studies in hysteria. Breuer and Freud seemed to take the revelations of their hypnotized subjects at face value, and built their theories on that basis, while Schnitzler had always emphasized the element of fabrication and role acting in hypnosis and hysteria.

Similarities between Schnitzler and Freud should not be overemphasized. If Freud introduced the method of free association in psychotherapy, Schnitzler was one of the first to write a novel entirely in the "stream of consciousness" style.[228] Common to both Schnitzler and Freud was their interest in dreams. Schnitzler is said to have recorded his own dreams, and he made an extensive use of the dream motif in his works. In his novels, people have dreams in which recent events, past memories, and current preoccupations are distorted and intermingled in manifold variations. But there is nothing of "Freudian symbols," and in spite of their artistic beauty and richness, these dreams provide little material for psychoanalytic interpretations. The same independence from Freud's psychoanalysis is shown in Schnitzler's novel *Frau Beate,* a story of incest between a youth and his widowed mother.[229] Here, no reference was made to an Oedipus complex or to childhood situations; an extraordinary combination of circumstances made the outcome seem almost inevitable.

World War I caused many men to reflect on the tragedy in which they were taking part. Freud concluded his *Thoughts for the Times on War and Death* by stating that aggressive instincts were stronger than contemporary civilized man had believed, and he saw the handling and channelizing of aggressiveness as the main problem.[230] Schnitzler contested the role of hatred: neither soldiers, nor officers, nor diplomats, nor statesmen really hated the enemy.[231] Hatred is artificially introduced into public opinion by the press. The true causes of war are the malevolence of a few individuals who have a vested interest in warfare, the stupidity of a few men in power who resort to war to solve the problems that could be solved in another way, and above all the incapacity of the masses to visualize the true picture of war. Finally, a war ideology is imposed upon the people with pseudophilosophical and pseudoscientific allegations, and false political imperatives, using an emotionally charged vocabulary. The prevention of war, Schnitzler said, entailed the eradication of all possibility of profiteering, a permanent Parliament of Nations to solve the problems usually leading to war, the unmasking of war ideology, and the silencing of warmongers.

After World War I the new Austrian generation despised Schnitzler as a prototype of "the corrupt spirit of the decaying Monarchy" and of "the frivolous life of the Viennese leasure class." In 1927 he published a booklet, *The Spirit in Work and the Spirit in Action,* a curious attempt at typology of such varieties of men as the poet, the philosopher, the priest, the journalist, the hero, the organizer, the dictator, and so on.[232] Another collection of thoughts and fragments would have required only a little organization to form an outline of a philosophy.[233] Schnitzler revealed himself as much less skeptical than one would have thought from his earlier literary work. He took a stand against the theory of universal determinism. He viewed freedom of will not only as the basis of morality, but as the basis of esthetics; his belief in the existence of God is expressed, though in veiled terms.

Both Freud and Schnitzler were afflicted with physical suffering toward the ends of their lives, Freud with his cancer, and Schnitzler with otosclerosis. In those painful last years Schnitzler wrote the novel that is generally considered his masterpiece, *Flight into Darkness*: the subjective state of a man's schizophrenic mind is described in such a way that the development of his illness to the point of murdering his physician-brother is made intelligible.[234]

Freud saw similarities between his thinking and that of Schnitzler, but Schnitzler, despite all his admiration for Freud's writings, emphasized his disagreement with the main tenets of psychoanalysis.[235] Both men actually explored, in their own ways, the same realm, but came to different conclusions. It is easy to imagine what kind of depth psychology Schnitzler could have devised: he would have emphasized role playing and the deceitful element in hypnosis and hysteria, the unreliability of memory, the mythopoetic function of the unconscious, the thematic rather than the symbolic element in dreams, and the self-deceptive rather than the aggressive component in the origin of war. He would also have written philosophical essays in a less pessimistic vein than Freud. One is free to speculate about the literary possibilities had Freud left medicine to develop his great talent as a writer. Emmy von N., Elisabeth von R., and young Dora would have become heroines in short stories à la Schnitzler. The obsessions of the Wolf-Man would have been made a nightmarish novel in Hoffmann's fashion, and a story about Leonardo da Vinci would have overshadowed Merezhkovsky's historical fiction. A novel by Freud about the cruel old father and the horde would have brought to perfection that literary genre of prehistoric novels that the brothers Rosny had made popular in France, although Freud would have conceived it more in the style of Hesse's *Rainmaker*.[236] The story of Moses would have made a novel comparable to the biblical novels of Sholem Asch and Thomas Mann. It would then have remained for Schnitzler's disciples to analyze such writings and reconstruct the psychological system implicit in them. Freud, however, obviated this possibility, since he chose psychology, with the aim of annexing to science a system of that psychological intuition and knowledge possessed by great writers.

Freud's Work—I—From Microscopic Anatomy to Theoretical Neurology

So many accounts of Freud's work have been given that we will not attempt here more than a brief survey, with special regard to its sources, relation to contemporary science, and particularly to its line of evolution.

The first historians of psychoanalysis divided Freud's scientific career into a prepsychoanalytic and a psychoanalytic period. They considered Freud as a neurologist who left his first vocation to found a new psychology. It was later recognized that a knowledge of the first period is necessary for a full understanding of the origin of psychoanalysis. An even closer examination of the facts reveals a definite line of evolution throughout the prepsychoanalytic period.

When the nineteen-year-old student Sigmund Freud began to do research in Professor Claus' Institute of Comparative Anatomy, he was engaging in a career of a particularly exacting nature. Work with a microscope was a school of scientific asceticism and self-denial. Agassiz has well described the long and arduous training of the eyes, the hand, and the intellect that is necessary before one can work efficiently with the microscope or the telescope:

> I think that people are not generally aware of the difficulty of microscopic observation, or of the amount of painful preparation required merely to fit the organs of sight and touch for the work . . . It seems an easy matter for a man to sit down and look at objects through a glass which enlarges everything to

his vision; but there are subjects of microscopic research so obscure that the student must observe a special diet before undertaking his investigation, in order that even the beating of his arteries may not disturb the steadiness of his gaze, and the condition of the nervous system be so calm that his whole figure will remain for hours in rigid obedience to his fixed and concentrated gaze.[237]

It often requires years of training before the young scientist is able to make his first discovery, and as Agassiz pointed out, the life work of a scientist may be summed up in one sentence.[238] But even those adept at this method were not immune against self-deception: Haeckel described and illustrated imaginary configurations that confirmed his theories and caused him to be accused of fraud, Meynert described illusory tracts in the brain substance, and several generations of astronomers saw and mapped the "canals" on Mars.

The young student was usually given a small piece of research to do, as much to test his capabilities as for the results. Freud's first investigation was on the gonadic structure of the eel. Jones has told how Freud dissected about four hundred eels but could not come to any decisive conclusion. Nevertheless Claus was satisfied with Freud's work and presented his paper at the Academy of Sciences, yet Freud was dissatisfied.[239] (Apparently the ambitious young man had not yet understood the philosophy of microscopic research.)

During the six years spent in Brücke's laboratory, Freud did research of high quality on limited subjects. At that time brain anatomy was a newly opened field, where any diligent researcher could make discoveries. To that end there were three approaches: the first was routine investigation of new cases with current techniques; the second, the perfecting of a new technique (such as a microtome or coloring agent) to give new possibilities for studies; and the third, conceptualization (an approach taken by those who presented the neurone theory). Freud tried all these approaches in turn. He started with a limited investigation on certain cells in the spinal chord in a species of fish, the Petromyzon.[240] Here too the master was more satisfied than the pupil with the results. A noteworthy feature is the high quality of the style in which this technical paper is written. Freud then turned his investigations to the lesser known regions of the nervous system. Such was his work on *corpus restiforme*, and on the nucleus of the acoustic nerve. This was the type of work through which men such as August Forel and Constantin von Monakow were making themselves known to the neurological world. In regard to the second approach, Freud introduced a method of coloration with gold chloride, which, however, did not produce uniform results, and so was not widely adopted.[241] From the conceptual point of view, Freud wrote a paper "On the Structure of Elements of the Nervous System," which some historians consider an anticipation of the neurone theory.[242]

During his three years of residency at the Viennese General Hospital, Freud for the first time came in contact with patients, and his research changed accordingly. It was the period of his attempts with cocaine, during which he also experimented with the anatomoclinical method, that is, checking clinical diagnoses against the findings of autopsies. Freud showed skill in this art and published three of the cases he diagnosed in 1884.[243] [244] [245]

In the following period, after Freud left the Viennese General Hospital and Meynert's laboratory, he turned to purely clinical neurology. At that time the neurologist depended heavily on the hospital or institution for patients. Freud was put in charge of neurology at the Kassowicz Institute, where he examined so many children with cerebral palsy that he became a specialist in that condition. In 1891 he was able to publish, with Oskar Rie, a study of thirty-five cases of hemiplegia in cerebral palsy.[246] This study points out the existence of two extreme types, the one of acute onset of paralysis, and the other a gradual onset with chorea, and all possible intermediate combinations of symptoms. This shows an instance of what Freud later called complementary series.

In 1891, Freud published a book on aphasia dedicated to Josef Breuer.[247] This book was long overlooked by psychoanalysts; later it was praised as a milestone in the history of the study of aphasia and a herald of later psychoanalytic concepts. Actually it is easier to ascertain its significance in the evolution of Freud's work than in the history of aphasia. At that time there was a flood of literature on aphasia. Today these writings are not easily accessible; much in them is written in the style of the contemporary brain mythology. The prevalent theories of aphasia, such as those of Wernicke and Lichtheim, were based on the assumption that sensory images were stored in certain centers of the brain, and that lesions in these areas were the cause of aphasia. In the early 1880's, Heymann Steinthal[248] proposed what today would be called a dynamic theory of aphasia, but being a linguist he was ignored by neuropathologists.[249] Historians of aphasia[250] point out that from the time of Bastian to that of Déjerine there occurred a gradual recognition of the dynamic factors in aphasia. In this monograph, Freud foreshadowed the concepts of Déjerine; he was probably the first on the continent to refer to the work of Hughlings Jackson, and he introduced and defined the term "agnosia." Freud apparently did not consider this work a major contribution to the problem of aphasia; it was a theoretical discussion without new clinical observations or new pathological findings. The traditional story that Freud's book on aphasia met with no success at all and was never quoted by further authors is, to say the least, an exaggeration.[251]

In 1892 Freud's pupil Rosenthal published in his medical dissertation fifty-three observations on cases of diplegic forms of cerebral palsy, which he had seen in Freud's service.[252] In 1893, Freud expounded his conception of cerebral diplegia in children.[253] An anonymous book review argued that Freud had described the pathological anatomy of this condition, not from his own observations, but from a compilation of the findings of other authors, which made Freud's physiopathological interpretations unconvincing, because the connection suggested by Freud between certain groups of symptoms and certain etiological factors was not sufficiently substantiated by the facts.[254] On the other hand, Freud's study was given the highest praise by Pierre Marie, and Freud wrote a paper in French on the same topic for the *Revue Neurologique*.[255]

Freud's reputation as a specialist in cerebral palsy was now so well established that Nothnagel asked him to write a monograph on the topic, which appeared belatedly in 1897.[256] This work received great appreciation in France from Brissaud and Raymond.[257] In Belgium, Freud's theory of cerebral palsy and its classification of subforms was criticized by Van Gehuchten, who found that it was an artificial conception lacking any anatomo-pathological basis.[258] These facts are of interest because they show that, in his neurological period, too, Freud received both praise and criticism, contrary to the assumption that he received nothing but praise as long as he was a neurologist, and nothing but abuse as soon as he turned to the study of neuroses. From the beginning it was Freud's tendency to make bold generalizations that gave rise to criticism.

We thus see that during the twenty years of his prepsychoanalytic period, Freud had followed a long line of evolution, going from microscopic anatomy to anatomo-clinical neurology, and from there to purely clinical neurology, and even to the kind of nonclinical theoretical neurology, manifested in his book on aphasia. This last trend was to reach its acme with Freud's *Project for a Scientific Psychology*, to which we now turn.

Freud's Work—II—The Search for a Psychological Model

There are two ways of building a psychological theory. The first is to gather facts and find common factors from which to deduce laws and generalizations. The second is to build a theoretical model and see how the facts fit it, in order to recast the model if necessary. Following a trend common in his time, Freud's preference went to the latter. Among those who attempted to correlate psychological functions with the structure of the brain, Meynert distinguished himself, but unfortunately often slipped over into brain mythology. Others, inspired by Fechner's psychophysics, postulated the existence of nervous energy on the model of physical energy, and tried to express mental phenomena in terms of that hypothetical nervous energy. Still bolder attempts were made to interpret mental phenomena in terms of both brain anatomy and nervous energy.

Freud devoted a great deal of time and care to the elaboration of a theoretical model of that kind. His correspondence with Fliess has preserved the 1895 draft known as the *Project for a Scientific Psychology*.[259]

Students of psychoanalysis agree on two facts: first, that this model was highly artificial, and second, that it can help us to understand the origin of certain psychoanalytic concepts.

The main idea of the *Project* is the correlation of psychological processes with the distribution and circulation of quantities of energy throughout certain material elements, that is, hypothetical brain structures.

The energy called quantity by Freud is equated to sums of excitation originating either from the outer world through the sensory organs, or from the inner world, that is, the body. Quantity is ruled by two principles, inertia, which is the tendency to the full discharge of the energy, and constancy, which is the tendency to keep constant the sum of excitation.

Freud's material elements were the neurones, of which he postulated three types. The phi neurones receive quantities of excitation from the outer world, but do not retain the current, because they are regulated by the principle of inertia. The psi neurones receive quantities of excitation either from the body or from the phi neurones, but because they are ruled by the principle of constancy, they retain traces of any stimulation received; they therefore constitute the substratum of memory. The omega neurones receive quantities of stimulation from the body and from the phi neurones, and have the peculiarity of transforming quantity into quality, because of a period of movement. These neurones constitute the substratum of perception. The pleasure-unpleasure principle is explained in the sense that unpleasure is a heightening and pleasure a discharge of the level of quantity.

The ego is an organization of neurones endowed with a constant reserve of quantity, and able to inhibit incoming excitation. This provides a criterion of reality; reality testing is equated to an inhibition by the ego.

Freud distinguished a primary and a secondary process. In the primary, a quantity of excitation stimulated memory images in the Psi neurones and then reverted to the Omega neurones, evoking hallucination; in this process, energy was tonic and bound, and hallucinations were checked through inhibition by the ego.

These are some of the basic principles of the 1895 *Project*; they were developed into an extraordinarily complex system; within this framework almost any psychological function and several psychopathological manifestations were given an explanation.

To make the *Project* intelligible it must be placed in its context, that is, in the long line of evolution, which had started with Herbart. Throughout the nineteenth century, brain anatomy and physiology were constructed on a scientific and experimental basis, but there was also a parallel line of speculative brain anatomophysiology, which in the latter part of the century was called *Hirnmythologie* (brain mythology). Curiously enough, it was sometimes the same men who pioneered scientific anatomophysiology of the brain who also indulged in brain mythology, although they conceived of themselves as "positivists" and scorned the philosophy of nature. Freud's *Project* is but a late offspring of this speculative sequence. Its initial dynamic-speculative philosophy may be traced back to Herbart, and the greatest part of its energetics to Fechner.[260] The principle of inertia and the principle of constancy are very similar to what Fechner called absolute stability and approximate stability. Fechner had already connected the pleasure-unpleasure principle with the idea of approach and retreat from approximate stability, and he also equated quality of perception with the periodicity of a stable movement. These Fechnerian principles were later complemented by Heinrich Sachs with his alleged law of the constant quantity of psychic energy: "The sum of the tensions of all present molecular waves is, within certain time limits, in the same individual approximately constant."[261] The three main other sources of the *Project* are Brücke, Meynert, and Exner. This has been well shown in a study by Peter Amacher.[262]

Brücke was one of those who reduced psychology to neurology, and explained the entire functioning of the nervous system as a combination of reflexes.[263] Stimulation of the same organs determined quantities of excitation, which were transmitted throughout the nervous system, transferred from cell to cell, and often accumulated in certain centers until they could be discharged in the form of movements. Brücke, as well as Meynert and Exner, described mental processes indifferently in physical and psychological terms.

Meynert also described psychological processes in terms of quantities of excitation and of reflex neurology, though more elaborately than Brücke.[264] He took from Herbart and from the English empiricists the doctrine of associationism, but he reduced it to a reflex neurology similar to that of Brücke, and to his own concepts of the structure and functioning of the brain. He distinguished two kinds of reflex responses, those determined at birth, which followed subcortical pathways, and those that were acquired, which followed cortical pathways. There were association bundles between cortical centers, and when an inflow of excitation arrived simultaneously at two centers, a cortical pathway was opened and a phenomenon of induction took place, the physical concomitant of an association and an elementary logical function. Such experiences, beginning on the first day of life, developed a system of cortical pathways (that is of associations) which constituted the primary ego, that is the nucleus of individuality. Later, a secondary ego was constituted, whose function was to control the primary ego, and which was the substructure of ordered thought processes. As a clinician, Meynert described *amentia,* a mental condition with incoherent hallucinations and delusions, which reproduced a state of infantile confusion when there was no ego control. Meynert equated the cortical activity during dreaming with the cortical activity that produced amentia.

Exner, the third of Freud's neurological teachers, published his *Entwurf* in 1894, which may be considered a synthesis of Brücke's and Meynert's systems.[265] In the meantime, though, the neurone theory had appeared, and Exner discussed how quantities of excitation could be transferred at the junctions between neurones, where he believed that summations of excitations took place. Exner also assumed that junctions could be changed during the life of the individual, though the simultaneous excitation of two cells. Exner called the processes *Bahnung* (channeling), by which the simultaneous excitation of two cortical cells would open a nerve pathway between themselves and would transfer excitation from one to the other, when either of them was subsequently engaged by excitation. He described emotion centers, particularly the pain, or unpleasure, center. Under the name of instincts, he described associations between ideas and emotion centers. He extensively developed his neurological psychology, giving explanations of perception, judgment, memory, thinking, and other mental processes.

Freud's *Project* of 1895 may be understood as a logical development of the theories of his predecessors, particularly of his masters Brücke, Meynert, and Exner. It is the outcome and legacy of a century of brain mythology. This is probably why Freud abandoned this *Project* as soon as he had completed it. But many of the ideas formulated in the *Project* were to reappear under various new forms in Freud's subsequent psychoanalytic theories.

Freud's Work—III—The Theory of Neuroses

The circumstances that brought Freud to devise a new theory of neuroses belong both to the zeitgeist and to specific personal experiences. In shifting from neuro-anatomy to anatomo-clinical neurology, and from there to a dynamic concept of neuroses, Freud followed a contemporary pattern also illustrated by Charcot, Forel, and later by Adolf Meyer. Neuropathology (in that time quite distinct from psychiatry) was beginning to be a fashionable medical specialization. Two personal experiences oriented Freud along this path: his visit to Charcot, and the story of Breuer's patient Anna O.

Freud saw the starting point of psychoanalysis in Breuer's experience with Anna O. To this day, the most elementary account of psychoanalysis begins with the story of that young lady "whose numerous hysterical symptoms disappeared one by one, as Breuer was able to make her evoke the specific circumstances that had led to their appearance." The veil of legend surrounding this story has only partially been lifted by objective research.

Ernest Jones has revealed the real name of the patient: Bertha Pappenheim (1860–1936). Her life is known through a brief biographical notice published after her death,[266] and a short biography by Dora Edinger.[267] Bertha Pappenheim belonged to a distinguished old Jewish family. Her grandfather, Wolf Pappenheim, was a prominent personality of the Pressburg ghetto, and her father, Siegmund Pappenheim, was a well-to-do merchant in Vienna. Little is known of her childhood and youth. She had received a refined education, spoke English perfectly, and read French and Italian. According to her own account, she led the usual life of a young lady of high Viennese society, doing a great deal of needlework, and outdoor activities, including horseback riding. In the biographical notices of 1936, nothing was said of a nervous illness in her youth. It was reported that after her father's death, she and her mother left Vienna to settle in Frankfurt on the Main, where Bertha gradually became concerned with social work. In the late 1880's she began to display remarkable philanthropic activity. For about twelve years she was the director of a Jewish orphanage in Frankfurt. She traveled in the Balkan countries, the Near East, and Russia, to inquire into prostitution and white slavery. In 1904 she founded the *Jüdischer Frauenbund* (League of Jewish Women), and in 1907 she founded a teaching institution affiliated with that organization. Among her numerous writings are short stories, theatrical pieces on social themes, travel accounts, studies on the condition of Jewish women and on the criminality of Jews. In her late years she reedited ancient Jewish religious works into modernized form, and a history of her ancestors with extensive genealogical tables. Toward the end of her life, she was depicted as a deeply religious, strict. and authoritarian person, utterly selfless and devoted to her task, who had retained from her Viennese education a lively sense of humor, a taste for good food, and the love of beauty, and who possessed an impressive collection of embroideries, china, and glassware. She died in March 1936, early enough to escape the fate of a martyr, but late enough to foresee the impending extermination of her people and the destruction of her life work. After the Nazi domination, she was remembered as an almost legendary figure, to the extent that the government of Western Germany honored her memory in 1954, by issuing a postage stamp with her picture.

There is a wide gap between the descriptions of the Jewish philanthropist and pioneer social worker Bertha Pappenheim, and of Breuer's hysterical patient Anna O. Nothing in Bertha Pappenheim's biography would let us guess that she was Anna O., and nothing in Anna O.'s story, either, would let us guess that she was to become known as Bertha Pappenheim. If Jones had not revealed the identity of the two figures, it is likely that no one would have ever discovered it.[268] As for the story of Anna O., there are two versions, the one given by Breuer in 1895,[269] and the other by Jones in 1953.[270]

According to Breuer, Fräulein Anna O. was an attractive, intelligent young lady, endowed with a strong will and much imagination. She was kind and charitable, but afflicted with a certain emotional instability. She was brought up in a strongly puritanical family, and there was a marked contrast between the refined education she received and the monotonous home life she led. This caused her to escape into daydreams, which she called her private theater. Her illness, as told by Breuer, goes through four periods:

> From July 1880 to December 1880, she cared for her severely ill father and manifested signs of physical weakness. This, Breuer called the period of latent incubation.
>
> From December 1880 to April 1881, there was a period of manifest psychosis. A great variety of symptoms appeared within a short time: paralyses, contractions, ocular disturbances, linguistic disorganization; she spoke a kind of agrammatical jargon; her personality was split into one normal, conscious, sad person, and one morbid, uncouth, agitated person, who sometimes had hallucinations of black snakes. During that period, Breuer visited her frequently; under hypnosis, she told him her latest daydreams, whereupon she felt relieved. That is what she called her talking cure.
>
> From April to December 1881, her symptoms became markedly worse. The death of her father on April 5 was a severe shock. She recognized no one, except Breuer, who had to feed her for some time, and she spoke nothing but English. She was transferred to a private sanitarium near Vienna, where Breuer visited her every three or four days. Her symptoms now appeared in a regular cycle, and were relieved by Breuer's hypnotic sessions. Instead of telling him her daydreams, she told him her recent hallucinations.
>
> From December 1881 to June 1882 recovery came slowly. The two personalities were now sharply distinct, and Breuer could make her shift from one to the other by showing her an orange. The main feature was that the sick personality lived 365 days earlier than the healthy one. Thanks to the diary her mother had kept, Breuer was able to check that the events she hallucinated had occurred, day by day, exactly one year earlier. Once, under hypnosis, she told Breuer how her difficulty in swallowing water had started after she had seen a dog drinking from her glass. Having told Breuer this, the symptom disappeared. Here started a new kind of treatment: She told Breuer, in reverse chronological order, each appearance of a given symptom with exact dates, until she reached the original manifestation and initial event, and then the symptom disappeared. Breuer eradicated every symptom in this tedious way. Finally, the last symptom was traced back to an incident that occurred while she was nursing her sick father; she had had a hallucination of a black snake, had been upset, and had muttered a prayer in English, the only one that came to her mind. As soon as Anna had recovered that memory, the paralysis left her arm, and she was able to speak German. Anna had decided and announced in advance that she would be cured by the end of June 1882, in time for her summer vacation. Then, according to Breuer, she left Vienna for a trip, but it took her some time to recover her full equilibrium.

The current accounts of Anna O.'s illness do not emphasize the unusual features of this story. First, was the coexistence of one personality living in the present and one living 365 days earlier. Second, the fact that each of the symptoms allegedly appeared immediately after the traumatic event, without any period of incubation. Third, that the symptoms could be made to disappear. However, it is absolutely not so (as the current accounts would have it) that "it sufficed to recall the circumstances under which the symptoms had appeared the first time." Anna had to recall each instance when the symptom had appeared, whatever the number, in the exact reverse chronological order. These features make Anna O.'s story a unique case of which no other instance is known, either before or after her.

In a seminar given in Zurich in 1925, Jung revealed that Freud had told him that the patient had actually not been cured.[271] In 1953 Jones published a version of the story that differs notably from that given by Breuer. According to it, Freud had told Jones that at the time of the alleged termination of the disease, the patient was far from cured, and was in the throes of hysterical childbirth after a phantom pregnancy, that Breuer had hypnotized her and then left the house in a cold sweat, whereupon he left for Venice to spend a second honeymoon, which resulted in the conception of a daughter, Dora. The patient Anna O. was admitted to an institution in Gross Enzersdorf, where she remained ill for several years. Jones' version indicates that Breuer had been fooled by the patient, and that the supposed "prototype of a cathartic cure" was not a cure at all.

Comparing Bertha Pappenheim's biography with the two versions of the story of Anna O., one notes that, in the former, Bertha left Vienna for Frankfurt in 1881, whereas Anna remained in the Viennese sanitarium until June 1882 according to Breuer, and much longer according to Jones.[272] A still stranger fact is that the photograph of Bertha (the original of which the author has seen) bears the date 1882 embossed by the photographer and shows a healthy-looking, sporting woman in a riding habit, in sharp contrast to Breuer's portrait of a home-bound young lady who had no outlet for her physical and mental energies.

In regard to Breuer's version, it must be remembered that at that time psychiatrists went to great length and took great trouble to disguise the identity of their patients when they published their histories, altering the names, places, professions, and sometimes the dates.[273] Breuer's case history is obviously a reconstruction from memory, written thirteen or fourteen years later, as he himself said, "from incomplete notes," and published half-heartedly, to please Freud.

As for Jones' version, it is fraught with impossibilities. First, Breuer's last child Dora was born on March 11, 1882 (as evidenced by the *Heimat-Rolle* in Vienna), and thus could not possibly have been conceived after the supposed terminal incident of June 1882.[274] Second, there was never a sanitarium in Gross Enzersdorf; Mr Schramm, who wrote a history of the locality, told the author that it must have been confused with Inzersdorf, where there was a fashionable sanitarium. Upon inquiry, the author learned that it had been closed, whereupon its medical archives were transferred to the Vienna Psychiatric Hospital. No case history, however, of Bertha Pappenheim could be found there.[275] Jones' version, published more than seventy years after the event, is based on hearsay, and should be considered with caution.[276]

Returning to Breuer's story of Anna O., it is clear that it radically differs from other cases of hysteria at that time, but is analogous to the great exemplary cases of magnetic illness in the first half of the nineteenth century, like those of Katharina Emmerich, Friedericke Hauffe, or Estelle L'Hardy.[277] Anna O.'s hallucinations about what had happened to her, day after day, exactly one year previously, could be compared to Katharina's nightly visions that coincided exactly with the Church calendar. Anna O.'s recollections of every occurrence of each of her symptoms, with the exact dates, will remind one of the prodigious mnemonic feats of the Seeress of Prevorst. Breuer and his patient played a close game, as Despine and Estelle had done in the past, though Breuer was less successful than Despine. To the older magnetizers, Anna O.'s story would not have seemed as extraordinary as it did to Breuer. It was one of those cases, so frequent in the 1820's, yet so scarce in the 1880's, in which the patient dictated to the physician the therapeutic devices he had to use, prophesied the course of the illness, and announced its terminal date. But in 1880, when authoritarian use of hypnosis had supplanted the former bargaining therapy, a story such as that of Anna O. could no longer be understood. Juan Dalma[278] has shown the connection between Anna O.'s cure and the widespread interest in catharsis that followed the publication, in 1880, of a book on the Aristotelian concept of catharsis by Jacob Bernays[279] (the uncle of Freud's future wife). For a time catharsis was one of the most discussed subjects among scholars and was the current topic of conversation in Viennese salons.[280] No wonder a young lady of high society adopted it as a device for a self-directed cure, but it is ironic that Anna O.'s unsuccessful treatment should have become, for posterity, the prototype of a cathartic cure.

The second personal experience that oriented Freud toward his new theory of neuroses was his visit to Charcot, where he saw the latter's demonstrations of traumatic paralyses, and their reproduction under hypnosis. The common opinion today is that these experiments with hysterical patients had no scientific value, because with such suggestible and mythomaniac subjects anyone could have demonstrated anything. Nevertheless, together with Anna O.'s story, they were the incentive for the creation of Freud's psychoanalysis.

The development of Freud's new theory of neuroses, from 1886 to 1896, may be followed through his publications and his letters to Fliess.[281]

In 1886 and 1887, Freud was filled with respect for Charcot, showed himself as his zealous disciple, and presented the master's theories such as he understood them. In 1888 a medical encyclopedia published an unsigned article on hysteria, almost certainly written by Freud.[282] The author mentioned Charcot's theory, although he merely questioned the cerebral localization of hysteria and mentioned Breuer's therapeutic method.

In July 1889 Freud, who had just translated one of Bernheim's textbooks, went to visit him and Liébeault in Nancy, and thereupon went to the International Congress of Psychology in Paris. It is likely that he saw Janet there, although there is no record of their meeting. Whether Freud already knew Janet or not, he could not have failed to become acquainted with *Psychological Automatism*, with its story of Marie and her cathartic cure. At about the same time Freud tried a similar therapeutic method with his patient, Emmy von N.[283] As usual in such cases, Freud altered many facts to protect his patient, whose true identity was later discovered by Ola Andersson.[284] Freud's account gives the impression that the treatment took place in one period before he went to Paris, but Andersson's findings indicate that the treatment actually occurred in two periods, before and after Freud's journey. Leibbrand assumes that interest in Anna O.'s case was revived by the publication of Janet's book; this would explain why Freud waited from 1882 to 1889 to apply the same method.[285] In fact, the chronology of the case of Emmy von N. is so obscure[286] that no conclusion can be drawn from the extant data.[287] This story shows Freud's first attempt to work with Breuer's method, differing from that method by having the patient recall under hypnosis only the initial traumatic event and that once the event had been recalled, the doctor had to suggest that the symptom disappear. This procedure was thus identical with that inaugurated by Janet in 1886.

In 1892 and 1893, Freud seemed to oscillate between the Nancy School, his old allegiance to Charcot, and the adoption of Breuer's cathartic method. In a lecture given on April 27, 1892, to the Viennese Medical Club, Freud openly espoused Bernheim's concept of hypnosis, recommended its application, and advised physicians to go to Nancy to learn it.[288] In 1893, Freud published the story of a woman who was prevented from breast feeding her child because of various hysterical symptoms; two sessions of hypnotic suggestions sufficed to remove all the symptoms, and the same happened after the birth of another child a year later.[289] There was no question here of catharsis. It was a cure in Bernheim's style. On May 24, 1893, before the Viennese Medical Club, Freud gave a lecture on hysterical paralyses,[290] which he wrote in French for Charcot's *Archives de Neurologie*.[291] Here he referred constantly to Charcot, giving only a slight modification of his theory (instead of dynamic lesion of motor brain centers, he assumed that the representation of the arm was dissociated from other representations). Referring to Janet, Freud emphasized that hysterical paralyses do not correspond to the distribution of nerves, as if hysteria knew nothing of anatomy. But four months earlier, on January 11, 1893, Freud had already disclosed to the same audience the new theory of hysteria on which he was working with Breuer.[292] This was the basis for the "Preliminary Communication" that many consider the first stone in the construction of psychoanalysis.

The authors extended Charcot's concept of traumatic hysteria to hysteria in general. Hysterical symptoms, they said, are related, sometimes clearly, sometimes in symbolic disguise, to a determined psychic trauma. This trauma may have occurred during a state of slight auto-hypnosis, or its painful character caused it to be excluded from consciousness. In both cases it was not followed by sufficient reaction (for instance cries, or acts of vengeance), and it disappeared from consciousness. Under hypnosis, however, the memory of the trauma is as vivid as was the actual event. Psychotherapy cures the hysterical symptoms (though not the hysterical predisposition) by bringing the trauma to consciousness and discharging it through affect, words, or corrective association. This theory may be considered a combination of Benedikt's concept of the pathogenic secret and Janet's therapy of bringing "subconscious fixed ideas" back into consciousness. In regard to Janet, the authors recalled in a footnote his case of a hysterical young woman who had been cured "through the application of a procedure analogous to our own." Another footnote said that "the closest approach to our theoretic and therapeutic statements we did find in the occasionally published remarks of Benedikt, with which we will deal in another place." [There was, however, no further reference to Benedikt.][293]

The Breuer-Freud paper aroused much interest and was favorably reviewed in several neurological journals.[294]

In the same year Freud wrote a eulogy of Charcot, crediting him with a theory of hysteria that in fact belonged to his predecessors, and added a respectful criticism.[295] He wondered what Charcot would have found if he had taken the discharge of strong emotion during hysterical attacks as his starting point. He could have looked for trauma in the patient's life history, of which the latter was not aware. This would have explained these emotions. Strangely enough, this was not very far from Charcot's theory of the *grande hystérie*, as could be found in the thesis of his disciple Richer.[296]

In 1894 something definitely new emerged in Freud's writing, the concept of defense (*Abwehr*).[297] This term came from Meynert, who distinguished two basic attitudes of the organism, attack and defense, which were reflected in the themes of delusional ideas. Freud gave the word "defense" the meaning of "forgetting" painful memories or ideas, and emphasized four points. Not the trauma in itself is pathogenic, but its representation or idea; the defense is directed against sexual ideas; the defense is a common feature in neuroses and was found in one case of psychosis; the degeneration theory is denied.

In 1895, Freud published a contribution on anxiety neurosis, that is, on patients who suffered constantly from diffuse anxiety and had acute attacks of anguish, without knowing the cause.[298] This neurosis had already been described by Hecker[299] as a subform of neurasthenia, by Krishaber[300] as a specific entity, and by Kowalewsky[301] as a toxication of the organism following consecutive stimulation and exhaustion of certain brain centers. The assumption that sexual frustration caused anxiety symptoms was then already fairly widespread, and Freud's innovation was the linking of a specific form of anxiety neurosis with an etiological theory of sexual frustration.

The year 1895 also saw the publication of Breuer's and Freud's *Studies in Hysteria*.[302] The "Preliminary Communication" was reprinted. Then came a reconstruction by Breuer of the case of Anna O., given as a prototype of a cathartic cure, and four of Freud's case histories, the first of which was Emmy von N. (Freud's first cathartic treatment of 1889), followed by the stories of Lucie R., Katharina, and Elisabeth von R. (all three during the latter part of 1892). The book closed with a chapter on the theory of hysteria by Breuer, and another by Freud on its psychotherapy. Freud now openly stated his divergences with Breuer; he saw only one possible origin of hysteria: through the *Abwehr*. In the story of Elisabeth von R. he described the new method of "free association," which had been suggested to him by the patient herself. Freud's four case histories are strongly reminiscent of those of Benedikt. Janet's influence was still apparent in Freud's use of the terms "psychological analysis" and "psychological misery."

At the beginning of 1896, Freud sketched his new classification of neuroses.[303] He still invoked the great name of Charcot, but emphasized his divergence from Janet. Thus, Freud no longer spoke of psychological analysis, but called his own method psychoanalysis. Neuroses were divided into actual neuroses, whose source was in the present sexual life of the patient, and psychoneuroses, whose sources were in his past sexual life. Actual neuroses were subdivided into neurasthenia, whose specific origin was masturbation, and anxiety neurosis, whose specific origin was frustrated sexual stimulation, particularly in the form of coitus interruptus. Psychoneuroses were subdivided into hysteria and obsessions. The specific cause of hysteria was sexual abuse by an adult, passively suffered in childhood. Such trauma often made little apparent impression, and may have seemed to be forgotten until puberty, when a slight cause revived the earlier impression, and acted as an actual trauma. The specific etiology of obsessive neuroses was the same as that of hysteria, with the difference that the child's role was more active, that he felt pleasure. Obsessive ideas were merely self-reproach in modified form. In this way Freud explained the prevalence of hysteria in women and of obsessions in men.

In the same year Freud's paper "On the Etiology of Hysteria" marked a point of achievement in the theory of hysteria on which he had worked for ten years.[304] The cornerstone of his theory remained Breuer's assumption that hysteria is determined by traumatic experiences whose memory unconsciously reappears in a symbolic way in the symptoms of the illness,[305] and which can be cured by recalling the memory into consciousness.[306] Building on this, Freud now states that things are considerably more complex.

The trauma must have both determining quality (a logical connection between cause and effect), and traumatic power (it must be able to cause an intense reaction). The difficulty was that in the search for trauma, one often found events either unrelated to the symptoms, or harmless. The difficulty could be explained with Breuer's idea that the trauma occurred during a hypnoid state, but Freud rejected this theory and assumed that the themes recorded by the patient were only links in a series, and that behind them were more formal, elemental trauma. Actually, Freud said, as chains of memories were revealed, they diverged and converged in nodal points, finally arriving at events of a sexual nature in puberty. Here, a new difficulty arose, because these pubertal events were often of a rather trivial character, hardly justifying their giving rise to hysteria. Then Freud assumed that the pubertal events were only precipitating causes that revived unconscious memories of much earlier trauma in childhood, which were always of a sexual nature. In eighteen fully analyzed cases, Freud said that he had found that the patient had been the victim of a seduction by an adult of his immediate environment, often followed by a sexual experience with children of the same age. These experiences, Freud added, had at the moment left no apparent impression; the traumatic effect was revived by trivial events in puberty, though the childhood experience remained lost to memory.

Freud proclaimed this theory as a great discovery, which he compared to that of "the source of the Nile in neuro-pathology". In contrast with the "Preliminary Communication" of 1893, he now contended to be able to cure not only the symptoms of hysteria, but hysteria itself. Actually, only a year passed before Freud, as seen in a letter to Fliess, had to admit that he had been misled by his patients' fantasies.[307] This was a decisive turning point in psychoanalysis: Freud found that in the unconscious it is impossible to distinguish fantasies from memories, and from that time on he was not so much concerned with the reconstruction of events from the past through the uncovering of suppressed memories, than with the exploration of fantasies.

The sources of Freud's new theory of hysteria are manifold. First were Breuer's theory of hysteria deduced from the misunderstood case of Anna O., Charcot's and Richer's concepts of the *grande hystérie,* and

Charcot's experiments with his Salpêtrière patients. Second was Janet, who had explained, particularly in the case of Marcelle in 1891, that in the exploration and treatment of hysterical patients one had to retrace a chain of unconscious fixed ideas. Third was Herbart's associationistic psychology. Lindner's textbook, which Freud had used at the Gymnasium, explained how chains of associations could diverge and converge in nodal points. Fourth was Benedikt's emphasis on the extreme importance of fantasy life in the normal and the neurotic, and the frequency of early sexual trauma in hysteria. Fifth was a current interest in childhood sexuality (in that regard Freud quoted a paper of Stekel). In 1894, Dallemagne had contended that many sexual deviations in adolescence resulted from childhood sexual experiences, which had been revived in puberty. What belonged to Freud was the particular emphasis on the role of defense (*Abwehr*), and the confidence with which he synthesized these elements into a general theory of hysteria.

In view of its great importance, we will show here a graphic representation of that model. (The diagram is the author's, not Freud's, but follows his thought as accurately as possible.)

Freud's Work—IV—Depth Psychology

It might have seemed, in 1896, that Freud had now reached his goal of building a new theory of neuroses, explaining every detail of their symptoms and origins. This theory was seen by some, such as Krafft-Ebing, with benevolent scepticism, by others such as Löwenfeld with interest, but in the literature of that time no expression of hostility is to be found. For Freud, however, this was just the starting point for the creation of what came to be called depth psychology.[308] Depth psychology claimed to furnish a key to the exploration of the unconscious mind, and through this a renewed knowledge of the conscious mind, with wider application to the understanding of literature, art, religion, and culture.

The first dynamic psychiatry had been, in the main, the systematization of observations made on hypnotized patients. With Freud's method of free association, a new approach was introduced. The patient relaxed on a couch, and was told the basic rule, to tell whatever came to his mind, no matter how futile, absurd, embarrassing, or even offensive it seemed. In trying to do so, the patient felt moments of inhibition and other inner difficulties, which Freud termed "resistance." As the sessions went on from day to day, the patient began to manifest irrational feelings of love or hostility toward the therapist; Freud called them "transference."

Actually, both "resistance" and "transference" had been known to magnetizers and hypnotists. The hypnotists knew that their subjects often showed resistance to falling into a hypnotic sleep, and that once hypnotized, they resisted certain commands, or they would perform suggested acts in a distorted or incomplete way. Forel had described how, when recalling forgotten events, under hypnosis, the procedure became increasingly difficult the closer he came to the critical points that were painful to the patient.[309] As to transference, it was a reincarnation of what had been known for a century as rapport and which Janet had recently brought back into focus as somnambulic influence.[310] Freud's innovation lay not in introducing the notions of resistance and transference, but in the idea of analyzing them as a basic tool of therapy.

Depth psychology can be understood as the combined findings from Freud's self-analysis and the analysis of his patients. In his mind the findings confirmed each other and confirmed much of the theory of neurosis and the model of the mind he had previously formulated.

The main aspects of depth psychology were Freud's dream theory and his theory of parapraxes, the first two generalizations of the pattern he had worked out for hysteria. These theories were elaborated simultaneously and presented in two of his best-known books: *The Interpretation of Dreams*, in 1900, and *The Psychopathology of Everyday Life* in 1904.

Freud's theory of dreams has been told so often that it has become common knowledge. Viewed in the line of development of psychoanalysis, it follows almost the same pattern as his theory of hysteria in 1896. This becomes obvious if the dream theory is also represented graphically, and the graphs of the two compared.

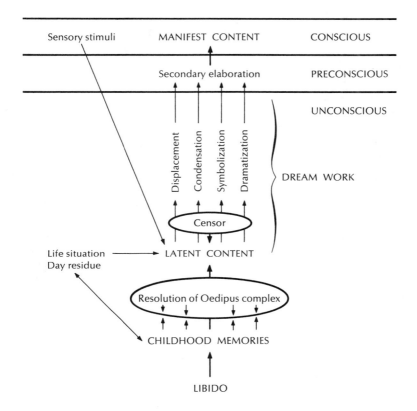

At the top of the graph we have the manifest content, that is, the dream itself, insofar as we are able to remember it. Experimental psychologists tried to connect this manifest content with the actual sensory or motor stimulations occurring during sleep. Freud considered their roles as minor. He viewed as the main point the relationship between the manifest content and the latent content, a relationship similar to that which he had found in his patients between the hysterical symptom and the pathogenic memories. To detect them and distinguish one from the other he used the same method, that is, free association. Between the hysterical symptom and the pathogenic memory extended a network of diverging and converging associations. In the same way, between the manifest content and the latent content, Freud described the dream work with its mechanism of displacement and condensation, in which the process of symbolization also occurred. As the hysterical symptom expressed the trauma in symbolic form, in the dream the latent content also tends to express itself in dream symbols. Why does the dream work transform the latent into the manifest? Because just as there is a dynamic conflict between the trauma and the hysterical symptom, there is a dynamic factor, the censor striving to keep down the latent content in the unconscious. The censor does not permit latent content to find expression in the dream unless it is modified by means of displacement, condensation, and symbolization.

But Freud's theory of the dream, as well as his hysteria theory, was an edifice having two stories. The upper story was the dream itself with its latent and manifest contents. In the latent content, Freud finds as one constant element the *day residue,* that is, some more or less insignificant event of the day preceding the dream. And just as he connected a pubertal trauma with an early forgotten sexual experience, Freud also found a connection between the day residue and childhood memories. Among the many trivial events of the day, the dream chooses the one that shows some relationship to a childhood memory, and as Freud puts it, the dream stands with one foot in the present and one foot in childhood. Thus one is led from the latent content still farther back to a childhood memory expressing an unfulfilled wish of that remote time. Here Freud introduced the notion he had found in his self-analysis and in his patients, the *Oedipus complex*: the little boy wants to possess his mother, wishes to get rid of his father, but is frightened of this threatening rival and of castration as a punishment for his incestuous feelings toward the mother. Such is, Freud says, the terrible secret that every man keeps in the recesses of his heart, repressed and forgotten, and which appears in a veiled form in a dream every night.

To complete the picture, we should add the secondary elaboration, that is, the changes occurring in the manifest content when the dreamer is awakening. We should compare it to the editing done by certain journals to articles sent by authors; the article may acquire a more organized and pleasant form, while the author may find that much of what he actually meant has been lost or distorted.

Freud considered as his major discovery that the dream is a fulfillment of a wish, or, to put it more accurately, the vicarious fulfillment of a repressed, unacceptable sexual wish, and this is why the censor must intervene, to keep it down or to allow its appearance only in disguised form. Freud also defined the dream as the guardian of sleep: feelings that might awaken the dreamer are disguised in such a way that they do not disturb him. Should this mechanism fail, the dreamer has a nightmare and awakens. The dream is also, Freud says, a process of regression that manifests itself simultaneously in three fashions: as topical regression from the conscious to the unconscious, as temporal regression from the present time to childhood, and as form regression from the level of language to that of pictorial and symbolic representations.

The sources of Freud's dream theory are numerous. To begin with, Freud was a good dreamer, who remembered his dreams and had years earlier kept a record of them for some time. The dream of Irma's injection (June 24, 1896) furnished him with a prototype of dream analysis and the notion that the essence of dreams is wish fulfillment. Like those great dream students of the past, Scherner, Maury, and Hervey de Saint-Denis, Freud used much intimate experience reflected in his dreams to nourish his book. To be sure, Hervey de Saint-Denis revealed more of his amorous life, but Freud more of his childhood, his family, and his ambitions.

The second source was Freud's inquiry into the vast dream literature of the nineteenth century.[311] His complaints to Fliess about the futility of that literature should not be taken too literally, since he drew heavily on it. However, he was unable to find a copy of Hervey de Saint-Denis' book, and he apparently knew Scherner's work only through accounts given by Volkelt, so that he underestimated Scherner's originality.[312] It was Scherner who maintained that dreams can be interpreted scientifically according to rules inherent to their nature, and that certain dream symbols have general value. Among others were sexual symbols, which were much the same as those later described by Freud.[313] The mechanism of displacement and condensation had been described under other names by many authors. The term "dream work" (*Traumarbeit*) was used by Robert. Much of Freud's theory can be found in Maury, Strümpell, Volkelt, and particularly Delage. Delage propounded a concept of dynamic energy, implying that the representations loaded with psychic energy repress or inhibit each other, or can fuse together, that there are in dreams chains of associations that can sometimes be partially reconstructed, and that old memories can be called forth from dreams through association with recent images.

Freud's originality resides in four innovations. The first is his model of the dream with its distinction of manifest and latent content and its specific pattern of being lived simultaneously in the present and the remote past. The second is Freud's contention that the manifest content is a distortion of the latent content, resulting from repression by the censor. To be sure Popper-Lynkeus had recently expressed the idea that the absurdity and senselessness of dreams derived from something unchaste and hidden in the dreamer.[314] But Freud certainly did not draw his theory from him.[315]

Freud's third innovation was the application of the free association as a method for the analysis of dreams, and the fourth was the introduction of systematic dream interpretation as a tool of psychotherapy.

Curiously enough, Freud attributed to Liébeault the idea that the dream is the guardian of sleep, whereas nothing of the kind can be found in Liébeault's works.[316] In later editions, Freud gave further examples of dreams and enlarged the section devoted to dream symbols, partly under the influence of Abraham, Ferenczi, Rank, and Stekel. Freud also incorporated the findings of Silberer about dramatization in hypnagogic dreams. He treated specific types of dreams in more detail, such as those of passing examinations, of being without clothes, or of the death of loved ones.

After the theory of hysteria and the theory of dreams, Freud's third great contribution to depth psychology was his "Psychology of Everyday

Life," which was also worked out by him during and from his self-analysis. It was published serially in a psychiatric journal, from 1898 to 1903,[317] and the greatest part of it appeared in book form in 1904.[318]

In the first contribution of 1898, Freud dealt with the situation of the person who suddenly forgets a name, cannot recall it in spite of his efforts, and would recognize it at once if he heard it. Making efforts to find the forgotten name only brings other words to mind. Freud found that these other words do not come at random, that they form chains of associations that diverge and converge in nodal points, and that these associations pertain to repressed material. Forgetting is thus the outcome of a conflict between the conscious and the unconscious, rather than merely the result of the weakening of the representation.

In 1899 Freud's paper on "Screen Memories" (*Deckerinnerungen*) appeared. Among our oldest memories, some are seemingly insignificant though remarkably vivid. Freud distinguished two kinds of screen memories. In the simpler type the preserved memory is but a part of a more significant whole, which has been repressed. For instance, a man had a memory dating from his fourth year: the picture of a table with a basin full of ice; this was linked to an upsetting event, the death of his grandmother, and only this fragmentary picture had not been submerged by repression. In the more complex type the memory, as it appears to the individual, is a construction in which a certain event of early childhood has been combined with a repressed event of adolescence. The earlier memory is not necessarily untrue, but it is a harmless substitute for the memory of a later, unacceptable, representation. As an example, Freud told of an analysis of the screen memory of a supposed patient, which Siegfried Bernfeld has convincingly shown to be a slightly modified autobiographical account.

The narrator tells how, when he was three years old, his family was obliged to move from a happy life in the country to a harder life in the city. He remembered playing, at the age of two and a half, in a meadow full of dandelions, with a boy and a girl cousin of his own age. He and the boy cousin snatched from the girl the bunch of dandelions picked by her, and she was given a piece of black bread by a peasant woman as a consolation. The boys too received pieces of the delicious bread. This memory occurred to the narrator after he had, at the age of seventeen, visited his town of birth and become enamored of a girl of fifteen in a yellow dress. When he was twenty, the narrator visited a well-to-do uncle and again met the girl cousin of the early memory; the two young people failed to fall in love and marry as their elders wished them to, a plan that would have ensured the narrator's economic security. The meaning of the screen memory was thus to offer an innocent childish "defloration" as a substitute for the adolescent wish; and of the yearning to taste the bread of economic security. From this example one sees that the relationship between the more recent event of youth and the early childhood memory is similar to the relationship between the "day residue" and the childhood events in Freud's dream theory.[319]

The bulk of the *Psychopathology of Everyday Life* consists of further articles on slips of the tongue, of the pen, and other acts that have been grouped under the name of parapraxes. Although the source of these studies resides primarily in Freud's self-analysis and the observations made on his patients, the field was not quite new. Schopenhauer and Von Hartmann had already pointed out such facts as manifestations of the unconscious.[320] Goethe, who used to dictate his work, once analyzed the errors made by his secretaries.[321] He found that some errors were his own, some were due to the secretary's unfamiliarity with difficult or foreign words, but others came from the emotional state of the secretary, who, for instance, thought he heard the name of the person he loved and wrote it in the place of what had actually been said. In Freud's time psychology had begun to investigate the problem. In 1895 Meringer and Mayer had published a study on the slips of the tongue, but they were more concerned with pronunciation than with meanings.[322] Several other sources were closer to Freud's approach: one was the studies of Hanns Gross, the celebrated criminalist of Graz and founder of judicial psychology.[323] In the 1880's Gross systematically searched the testimony of witnesses and accused persons for meaningful slips of the tongue and kindred manifestations, and published relevant observations in his articles and textbooks. Gross told of a man who substituted for a genuine witness in order to give false testimony, first verbally and then in writing, and who betrayed himself at the very last moment by inadvertently signing his real name under his false testimony. Gross found that false witnesses invariably betrayed themselves, even if by only one word, and also by their attitude, mien, or gestures. There also was a humorous novel by Theodor Vischer in which he created and made popular the term "the malice of objects" (*Tücke des Objekts*) to describe the misadventures that continually happened to some people, as if some little demon controlled the objects, hiding or substituting them.[324]

The notion of parapraxes, if not their theory, was well known to some of Freud's contemporaries. Karl Kraus, in his journal *Die Fackel*, used to collect amusing misprints that showed that the typographer had guessed and involuntarily betrayed the true thought of the writer. Some writers currently used parapraxes as a device that was so obvious that it was not necessary to explain it to the reader.

In his *Journey to the Center of the Earth*,[325] Jules Verne depicted an old German professor trying to decypher a cryptogram with the help of his nephew, who is secretly in love with the professor's daughter Gräuben. The young man believes to have found the key, and to his amazement it gives him these words: "I am in love with Gräuben." In *Twenty Thousand Leagues under the Sea*[326] the same author tells how Professor Arronax seeks for giant pearls at the bottom of the sea. He omits to inform his companions that the place is infested by sharks, but when he tells them about a giant oyster, he says it contains "no less than one hundred and fifty sharks." Seeing his companions' surprise he promptly exclaims, "Did I say sharks? I mean one-hundred-and-fifty pearls! Sharks would have no meaning."

The *Psychopathology of Everyday Life* was well received, frequently reedited, enlarged, and translated into many languages, and psychoanalysts began publishing their own collections of parapraxes.[327]

Freud's fourth great contribution to depth psychology was his book *Jokes and Their Relation to the Unconscious,* a topic on which he had started to work in 1897.[328] Many theories had arisen about the psychology of jokes, the comic, and of humor. Freud had been stimulated by Theodor Lipps' book *Komik und Humor,* but his true starting point was his observation of certain similarities between the mechanisms of jokes and of dreams.[329]

Freud distinguished in jokes a certain technique and a certain tendency (in other words, an element of form and one of content). He found techniques of condensation, displacement, expression of an idea by the contrary, and so on, similar to those of the dream work. In regard to the tendencies, Freud distinguished harmless jokes, whose pleasure came only from the technique, and the tendentious, whose mainsprings were either aggressiveness or obscenity, or both. Obscene jokes imply the presence of at least three persons, the joker, the subject, and a spectator. They mentally express the desire to strip or seduce. Jokes are enjoyed both because of the tendencies and the techniques. The tendentious jokes also help us to tolerate repressed needs by allowing a socially acceptable way of giving vent to them. The two main differences Freud found between dreams and jokes were that dreams express wish fulfillment and jokes satisfy the pleasure of play; dreams are a regression from the level of language to thinking in pictures, but in jokes the regression is from logical language to play language (the ludic function of language in which young children find so much pleasure).

Freud's book on jokes is one of the least read of his works. It is full of amusing but untranslatable puns and implies the reader's knowledge of the German classics such as Heine and Lichtenberg. Its "Jewish stories" were funnier to readers of that time than to readers of today. It is the work of a man who immensely enjoyed topical anecdotes and wit, but much of it would need a commentary today. To a greater degree than *The Interpretation of Dreams* this book reflects contemporary Viennese life. With this work Freud erected a little memorial to the spirit of the Vienna of the Dual Monarchy.[330]

We have so far summarized depth psychology's assumptions regarding hysteria, dreams, parapraxes, and jokes; now we will try to define the two common models that lie under these assumptions. The one is simple, the other more complex.

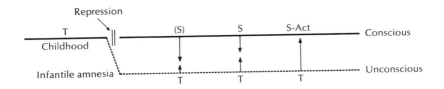

The simple model can be expressed graphically by two lines running parallel, the upper is the level of consciousness and apparent manifestations, the lower is the level of unconsciousness and the hidden manifestations that are the cause of the conscious manifestations. Psychological life is displayed simultaneously on these two levels, which can be very different from each other and can conflict. This model was originally worked out by Breuer and Freud in their *Studies in Hysteria.* On the upper line we put the hysterical symptoms, and on the lower the unconscious motivations that Breuer and Freud, following Charcot and Janet, found to be unconscious representations (or in the language of that time traumatic reminiscences). Suppose the symptom S is on the upper line, and the traumatic reminiscence T is on the lower, the association between S and T is threefold. There is a hermeneutic relationship, the symptom is like the cipher in a known language that helps one to decipher the text in an unknown language. There is a relationship of effect to cause, and thirdly there is a therapeutic relationship. S can be removed by exerting a certain maneuver on T, such as bringing it into awareness and abreacting it. The clinical interpretation, the scientific understanding, and the therapeutic removal of the symptom thus almost coincide.

This is a development of what Janet and Breuer had found. Freud's innovation was his dynamic concept of the relationship of S and T. T has a tendency to express itself in consciousness, but T is checked and held in the unconscious by means of an active force called *repression.* This inner conflict absorbs psychological energy that can be freed when the patient is cured of his symptom.

The success of repression is variable. If repression is extremely strong, the traumatic reminiscences can remain latent and S disappears, at least temporarily. If repression is extremely weak, T emerges directly to the surface and expresses itself in undisguised form; here S and T are so similar that there is no need of deciphering. We have to deal with a symptomatic action. In the intermediate cases, when repression is unable to keep T entirely in the unconscious, there is a kind of balance or compromise between both forces in the form of a symptom. S expresses T in disguised form and needs to be deciphered.

The same model applies to the psychology of dreams, with the difference that instead of symptom S we have the manifest content, instead of the trauma T we have the latent content, and between them the forces of repression are called censor and result in the mechanisms of displacement and condensation. Here, too, we find three types of dreams. The first are irretrievably lost as soon as the dreamer awakens, comparable to those latent symptoms where repression is so powerful that nothing appears at the surface. The opposite type are those lucid, infantile dreams comparable to the symptomatic acts; the repression is so weak that the latent content is shown undisguised in the manifest content. Most dreams are of the intermediate type, a compromise between the unconscious forces striving to express themselves in consciousness, and the forces of repression.

The same schema also applies to parapraxes. In the case of symptomatic forgetting, for instance, we have as S the loss of memory, instead of T the disturbing latent representation, and between them the force of repression. Here also we see the three types, as distinguished by Dalbiez.[331] The first are the inhibited acts where there is complete and successful repression, as in forgetting something important that one has known well. The opposite are the symptomatic acts performed under the influence of an unconscious impulse, where the individual does not know why he acts as he does. Between the two is a group of disturbed acts where repression is incomplete. Most slips of the tongue and slips of the pen belong in this group.

In regard to jokes a similar model can be applied, provided that the play on words itself is given instead of S and the underlying thought instead of T, and the technique of witticism is given instead of repression.

Thus far we have described the simpler model of depth psychology, but there is also a more complex model that comprises an upper and a lower floor. In hysteria we find on the upper floor the symptoms connected by chains of memory to some traumatic reminiscence of puberty, and from there to the childhood memory on the lower floor. In the dream the upper floor shows the manifest content connected through the dream work and the censor to the latent content. The latter is related to the lower floor, the seat of repressed childhood wishes. In the *Psychopathology of Everyday Life* an equally complex model applies to those screen memories where an event of adolescence, between the present memory and the childhood event, gives the clue. Finally, the two-story model applies to those jokes in which preliminary pleasure is offered by the "technique" (comparable to the dream work), but on the lower level a malicious or sexual pleasure finds its gratification.

But this is not all, since depth psychology offers the kernel of a third, still more complex model. As in the adult mind Freud found the influence of the forgotten world of childhood, so he visualized a deeper layer, common to mankind, to which belong many of the universal sexual symbols found in dreams. It was not long before Freud was to deduce, from the universal character of the Oedipus complex, the concept of the murder of the primordial father by his sons.

All these concepts of depth psychology may appear theoretical and abstract, but they become a living reality when illustrated with a clinical case. Such is the classical story of Dora, who was treated by Freud in 1900, although he published her history only in 1905.[332] This history is remarkable for its literary value and the skill with which the author maintains the reader in suspense throughout. At the start Freud takes great pains to explain that there is nothing wrong in discussing sexual matters under a scientific viewpoint (this precaution seems strange when one considers the flood of sexual-pathological literature that continued to submerge Europe since Krafft-Ebing). The story of Dora may also be viewed as belonging to the contemporary uncovering literature. In truly Ibsenian fashion we are at first confronted with a seemingly harmless situation, but as the story unfolds we are led to discover complex relationships, and weighty secrets are disclosed.

Dora, a young lady of eighteen, afflicted with a few classical symptoms of *petite hystérie*, lives with her father, a well-to-do industrialist, her mother, who is totally absorbed in her household duties, and an older brother. As in many families, the daughter is attached to the father, and the son to the mother. Dora's parents have a close friendship with Mr. and Mrs. K. with whom they often spend their vacations, and Dora gives her affectionate care to their two small children.

A first inquiry already shows a turbid situation. Dora's father, who is frequently ill, is nursed by Mrs. K., and Dora resents this. Mr. K. overwhelms Dora with presents and flowers, to her annoyance. Indignantly, Dora reveals to her mother that Mr. K. has been making propositions to her, which her father refuses to believe. Mr. K. denies everything and retorts that he learned from his wife that Dora has been reading the semi-pornographic writings of Mantegazza[333] Gradually Dora makes increasingly surprising confessions to her analyst. She is fully aware of her father's and Mrs. K.'s adulterous relationship. Four years earlier, Mr. K. had kissed her and she had been strongly repelled by him. She feels herself delivered up to Mr. K. by her father in exchange for Mr. K.'s consent to her father's affair with Mrs. K. On the other hand, it becomes obvious that Dora abets her father's actions. Thereupon one also learns of a governess who had enlightened her upon sexual matters, had explained to her the nature of her father's relationship with Mrs. K., and, being herself in love with Dora's father, she lavished her care upon the young person. But when Dora realized this she caused her parents to discharge the governess. Conversely it becomes clear that if Dora is so strongly attached to the K.'s small children it is because she is deeply in love with Mr. K., in spite of her assertions to the contrary. Nonetheless, Dora is much attached to her father, and it appears that the secret aim of her hysterical neurosis is to touch the heart of her father and detach him from Mrs. K.

But this is not all. By means of veiled intimations Dora gives to understand that she is aware that her father is sexually impotent and that therefore his relationships with Mrs. K. must necessarily be of an abnormal nature. Indeed, it seems that Dora is far better informed on sexual matters than it appeared at first. It is there that the analyst finds the key to an understanding of Dora's hysterical cough. But Dora is not only in love with her father and with Mr. K.; she also had a romantic attachment to Mrs. K. In former years Dora used to share a room with her and still speaks of her "adorable white body," and it was Mrs. K. who, even before the governess, had taught her sexual matters and lent her the books by Mantegazza. But from the moment when Dora understood that Mrs. K. cared for her only because she loved her father, she rejected her exactly as she did the governess later.

At this point psychoanalysis shows itself able to go farther than anything that "uncovering literature" would have attained. Freud wants to demonstrate how dream interpretation will further a treatment in filling in memory gaps and by furnishing an explanation of the symptoms. The two dreams of Dora and their interpretation are far too complex to summarize here. Let it merely be said that the first dream expressed her wish for her father to help her to ward off the temptation of Mr. K., that it reveals her old incestuous love for her father, that she had indulged in childhood masturbation, that she knew that her father had gotten syphilis and had transmitted it to her mother, and that she had overheard sexual intimacies between her parents. The second dream leads the reader still farther into the realms of Dora's secret sexual wishes and of the symbolism of a kind of "sexual geography."

This short account cannot convey the full complexity of Dora's story with the intricacies of the interpersonal relationships and their reflection as neurotic symptoms. So we see how Dora's mother regularly becomes ill on the eve of her husband's return, whereas Dora is ailing as long as Mr. K. is away and recovers when he comes back. We also learn how people borrow, as it were, each other's neurotic symptoms, how in other instances somatic symptoms are the expression of hidden or unconscious feelings, how a denial can be the equivalent of a confession, and how accusations against others may represent self-accusations. The hermeneutic and therapeutic importance of transference is also brought to light.

Present-day psychoanalysts would consider Dora's three-month treatment far too brief and the technique employed no longer adequate in many regards. But aside from its intrinsic interest, the Dora case shows exactly the stage reached by depth psychology in the early 1900's. Freud himself had proclaimed that the unconscious makes no distinction between facts and fantasies. Some readers found that this distinction was not sharp enough in the Dora case and remained unconvinced. It is in this light that the early controversies around psychoanalysis must be viewed.

Freud's Work—V—The Libido Theory

In 1905 Freud published his *Three Essays on Sexual Theory*.[334] This concise pamphlet gives the impression of being a digest of a more extensive book, rather than an original work in itself. Here, too, later editions have been considerably augmented, and to understand the original theory one should read it in the 1905 edition.

The first essay classifies sexual deviations according to object and to aim. In the former group is inversion (homosexuality), in whose etiology Freud pointed out the basic bisexuality of human beings, and the lack of sharp delineation between perversion and the normal varieties of sexuality. In the sexuality of neurotics, Freud saw three features: the forceful repression of a strong sexual drive, a sexuality of a perverse quality (neurosis is the negative of perversion), and its infantile characteristics (as yet ununified, partial drives localized in erogenous zones).

The second essay deals with infantile sexuality. "Why has this phenomenon been almost unknown?" asked Freud. Not only because of conventional ideas about the innocence of the child, but because a peculiar amnesia, similar to that caused by repression in neurotics, blots out the memory of the first six or eight years of life. "This amnesia serves for each individual as a prehistory." The "latency period," which follows, results not only from cultural but from organic conditions, and enables the sublimation of sexual instincts for the benefit of society. Freud then described the successive phases of the development of infantile sexuality. First there is an auto-erotic phase, in which any part of the body can be an erogenous zone, but its usual site is the mouth, with gratification in the form of sucking. After this "oral phase," the anus becomes the main erogenous zone, and the retention of feces provides gratification. This zone is replaced in the third phase by the genitals, hence the frequency of infantile masturbation. During these phases the child is "polymorph perverse," which means that the potentialities for all perversions are present, and under specific circumstances may be developed in many adults. Freud also gave a list of sources of sexual stimulation (including rhythmic movements, muscular activity, strong emotions, and intensive intellectual work), and he pointed out the constitutional element in the individual varieties of sexuality. In later editions Freud added to this second essay details of infantile sexual theories, and the effects of the "primal scene" (the observation by the child of parental sexual intercourse).

The third essay is entitled "The Transformations in Puberty." Following the biological upheaval of puberty, there is a shift from auto-eroticism to sexual objects, from partial drives to their unification under the primacy of the genital zone, and from individual pleasure to the service of procreation. At this stage, sexual pleasure, such as it existed in the child, survives in the form of "preliminary pleasure," an incentive to fuller gratification. Freud compared this mechanism to that of those jokes where the technique provides preliminary pleasure, and stimulates deeper gratification through release of aggressive or erotic feelings. There follows the psychosexual differentiation of men and women. Libido, Freud said, is fundamentally masculine in nature, whether it occurs in men or women, and whatever its object; but at the same time Freud adopted from Fliess the fundamental bisexuality of human beings. Freud then described the development of psychosexuality in men, in whom it is simple, and in women, where it is more complex, hence woman's greater predisposition to hysteria. The remainder of the essay is devoted to the problem of finding a love object. The very first object of infantile sexuality is one's own body and the mother's breast; after weaning, sexuality becomes auto-erotic and only later does sexuality have to be redirected to an object. The first object, the mother, in kissing and fondling the infant, awakens his infantile sexuality, which leads to the Oedipus situation—a point that was to be considerably developed in later psychoanalytic literature. Freud pointed out the importance of this early education for the future love choice and the destiny of the individual. In his recapitulation, Freud emphasized the role of the constitutional element, in which he also refers to the frequency of hereditary syphilis in neurotics.

In spite of their brevity, the *Three Essays* contain a synthesis of considerable width and scope, upon which Freud himself, and generations of psychoanalysts, were to expand. We shall not dwell upon these developments that have been explained in detail by so many authors. We shall only try to place Freud's theories into the context of contemporary sexual pathology.

Freud's sexual theories revolve around several themes. First, the concept of libido, that is of the sexual instinct with its embryology, successive phases of evolution, and metamorphoses. Second, an emphasis on the vicissitudes of the love object choice, particularly on the Oedipus complex. Third, based on the preceding, an interpretation of certain character types (notably the oral and the anal types), of neuroses and sexual deviations. Fourth, a system of sexual symbolism. And finally, an inquiry into early events of sexual life, early sexual fantasies, and their roles in subsequent emotional life.

When the *Three Essays* appeared in 1905, the zeitgeist was of extreme interest in sexual problems, and it is difficult to distinguish the limit between Freud's sources and the parallel developments that were taking place around him.[335] Contemporary sexual mores at that time had retained little, if anything, of the attitudes symbolized by the word "Victorianism." August Forel, in his memoirs, gives a lively description of the laxity of sexual mores in Vienna, adding that it was not any better in Paris.[336] Zilboorg mentions that "leagues of free love" were thriving all over the Czarist Empire among students and adolescents, and that this was "a phenomenon of a sociological nature" by no means limited to Russia. Problems of venereal diseases, contraception, and sexual enlightenment of children were discussed freely everywhere. All possible facets of sexual life appeared "with glaring frankness" (in Zilboorg's terms) in the works of Maupassant, Schnitzler, Wedekind, and many others; they also were discussed in a somewhat vehement fashion in journals such as Karl Kraus' *Die Fackel*. Schopenhauer had already given metaphysics of Sexus a central place in his philosophy; now, Weininger had brought forth a doctrine of sexual mysticism in a book that was enormously successful.[338] Further similar systems were to be developed by Rozanov and Winthuis.[339] Above all, the new science of sexual pathology, which had grown slowly during the nineteenth century, had received its decisive impetus thirty years earlier with the publication of Krafft-Ebing's *Psychopathia Sexualis*. Since 1886, the flow of literature on that subject had grown steadily and had become difficult to survey. In 1899 Magnus Hirschfeld had started the publication of a yearbook, part of which tried to cover the then current bibliography.[340] Whereas the first volume had 282 pages, the fourth (in 1902) counted 980 pages, the fifth (in 1903) had 1,368 pages, the sixth (in 1904) 744 pages, and that of 1905, 1,084 pages. No wonder that there is not much in Freud's *Three Essays* that cannot be found among the facts, theories, and speculations contained in that flood of literature.

The sources of the libido theory are multiple. Let it be recalled that the terms *auto-erotism, erogenous zones,* and *libido,* were already in use.[341] The first models of a unified concept of the sexual instinct had been drawn by philosophers, beginning with Plato. Both Plato and Freud taught the original bisexuality of the human being and the sublimation of the sexual instinct. Georgiades points out that Freud considered libido as masculine, while Plato valued homosexual love above heterosexual, and considered the sublimation of a homosexual love as the origin of all higher feelings.[342] Deep-reaching analogies between Freud's libido theory and Schopenhauer's philosophy have been mentioned previously,[343] as well as Arréat's widened concept of the sexual instinct.[344] Biologists followed in the footsteps of the philosophers. Gley, in 1884, suggested that the original anatomical bisexuality could leave physiological traces in the human, and that these in turn could be the starting point of homosexuality.[345] In turn, similar theories were developed by clinicians. Dessoir[346] in 1894, and Moll[347] in 1898, described two stages of evolution of the sexual instinct, an undifferentiated stage followed by a differentiated one; some individuals, they said, remain at least partly in the undifferentiated stage, hence the occurrence of homosexuality or other perversions. Two works in 1903 proposed a theory based on the concept of the fundamental bisexuality of man. One was Weininger's celebrated *Sex and Character* already referred to; the other was—in a less philosophical but more clinical approach—Herman's book, *Libido and Mania*.[348] All sexual deviations, Herman says, originate from the combined effect of human bisexuality and disturbances in the stages of evolution of the *libido* (in the sense given to that term by Moll). Sexual abnormities are classified in three groups: first, the various forms of "asexualism" (sexual infantilism, auto-erotism, and the like). Second, those derived from "bisexualism." Third, those that belong to "suprasexualism" (mostly the abnormal, senile sexuality). The bulk of sexual deviations belong to the second group in which Herman classifies in pairs (uranism-lesbianism, sadism-masochism, and so on). Whether the undifferentiated libido will be directed toward a man or a woman greatly depends upon chance: Meynert is referred to in that regard.[349] Herman's *Libido and Mania* was certainly known to Freud, since he mentioned it in his *Three Essays*.

Notions of infantile sexuality and early phases of sexual development were not quite new. The idea that the infant's pleasure at the mother's breast found later expressions in esthetic pleasure was already seen by Erasmus Darwin.[350] The pioneer investigator of oral eroticism in children was the Hungarian pediatrician Lindner, who described many varieties of thumb sucking, simple and combined, and assumed that these were expressions of infantile erotic gratification.[351] This paper had drawn some attention from Krafft-Ebing and others, who assumed that certain nursing women also obtained erotic gratification from breast feeding.

Freud's concept of anal eroticism seems to be more original, although some of its aspects had been anticipated. Charles Fourier, the utopian French socialist, ranged the drive to play with mud and dirt as a transient childhood phase among the basic human instincts.[352] Fourier proposed to socialize that drive: children in this phase would be organized into "little gangs" of dung collectors, to their own delight and the benefit of society. On a more speculative level, a representative of Romantic medicine, K. R. Hoffmann, had developed a theory that to excrete was not just a bodily function, but was a "basic drive of life" (*Grundtrieb des Lebens*), which could occasionally turn itself against the individual.[353] A correlation between Freud's theory of anal eroticism and the zeitgeist may also be pointed out. It is a human tendency to neglect things that are too obvious, and to pay attention to them when they disappear. Thus the folklore of European peasants remained unknown to scientists or was despised by them, until it began to decline, and only then did folklorists arise to record it. In a similar way, for centuries mankind had taken the sight and smell of excrements for granted, but when, at the end of the nineteenth century, plumbing became general, when men began to live in a dulcified and deodorized world, attention was drawn to this matter. The new preoccupation was illustrated by a 600-page compilation by Krauss and Ihm, giving a general survey of the roles of excrement in various populations of the world, with a laudatory foreword written by Freud in which he speaks of coprophilic manifestations in children, their repression, and their connection with the sexual instinct.[354]

What Freud said of the phallic phase of libido reflected a general concern of his time. Educators, pediatricians, and sexual pathologists all knew of the frequency of masturbation among infants and young children, and were concerned about the possibilities of the seduction of children by servants and other adults.[355] The existence of childhood sexuality was no doubt ignored by many, or considered a rare and abnormal occurrence, but there were those who knew better. Special mention should be made of the popular books by Michelet: *Our Sons*, and *Woman*; the latter was known to Freud, since he quoted it in another connection.[356]

The term and concept of sublimation were well known, and Freud never claimed to have introduced them. They are mentioned as a current idea in a novel published in 1785, and later used by Novalis, Schopenhauer, and particularly by Nietzsche.[357]

Freud systematized the idea that the sexual instinct underwent its first phases of development in infancy, followed by a latency period, that its apparent beginning at puberty was really a revival and reorganization. Similar facts had been observed and described first by Dallemagne, and then by Ribot, but these authors considered such development an exception.[358]

The idea of the sexual instinct being directed toward the subject itself instead of toward an exterior object was fairly widespread. The concept of narcissistic love, having been abundantly developed by poets and writers, had reached psychiatrists.[359] Havelock Ellis had described various forms of "autoerotism," and Naecke introduced the term "narcissism."

The great importance of the images of the mother and father for the future love life of the individual had also been anticipated, and Nietzsche was not the only one who had believed that "every man bears in himself the image of his mother, and on the quality of that image will depend his future attitude to women." In a celebrated novel, Laclos had his arch-seducer Valmont explain that one cannot seduce an innocent and honest young lady until one has destroyed in her her respect for her mother.[360] Jules Laforgue explained that it was his loss of respect for his mother that caused Hamlet to treat Ophelia so roughly.[361] Freud's innovation was the introduction and systematization of this concept of the father and mother *imago* into psychiatry.

That an erotic bond can arise between infant and mother was well known by many educators. Stendhal had told of his early incestuous love for his mother.[362] Michelet had popularized this notion. Freud now asserted that, within limits, this bond was natural and normal, and added the ideas of the child's death wishes toward his father, and of his fear of punishment and castration by the father. The full concept of the Oedipus complex, as Freud was later to systematize it, included these three components: an incestuous wish toward the mother, a wish to kill the father, and the image of a cruel, castrating father.

Actually, the mythological model of that complex is not so much to be found in the Oedipus drama as it is in the myth of Saturn and Jupiter. Saturn was threatened with death by his father Uranus, the first god of the world, but was saved by his mother. Saturn then castrated his father. Later, Saturn ate his own children except for the youngest, Jupiter, who was saved by his mother. Jupiter then supplanted his father. The same myth has been found in India and among the Hittites.³⁶³ To Dumézil, a historian of religions, this myth is simply a reflection of conditions that once existed. ³⁶⁴ In ancient dynasties of India, political and sexual powers were identified with each other, and the king was a great tyrannical male, fearful of being dethroned and robbed of his virility by his sons. On the other hand, philosophers of India explained the process of rebirth by attributing feelings to the reincarnate similar to those of the Oedipus complex. Vasubandhu described it in the following way:

> The intermediate being . . . possesses the divine eye. It sees the place of its birth, however far. It sees its father and mother united. Its spirit is disturbed by the effect of complacency and hostility. If it is a male, it is seized by the desire of a male toward his mother; if it is female, it is seized by the desire of the female toward the father; on the other hand it hates the father or the mother, which it regards as either a male or a female rival. As it is said in the Prajnapti: 'then occurs in the Gandharva either a thought of lust or a thought of hatred.' The Spirit being so troubled by these two erroneous thoughts that, by amorous wish, it attaches itself to the place where the two organs are joined, fancying that it is itself which becomes united . . . the intermediate being thus enjoying the pleasure of installing itself in the matrix.³⁶⁵

One of the aspects of psychoanalysis that became most popular pertains to sexual symbols (the "Freudian symbols"). In this field, Freud's many predecessors can be placed into four groups:

1. Anthropologists made collections of the traditional obscene symbols found in priapic poetry, and of "Kryptadia" from all countries. Freud thus was asked to give psychoanalytic comments for a collection of that kind by the folklorist Oppenheim.³⁶⁶
2. The interest in dream symbols also drew attention to those with a sexual meaning. According to Laignel-Lavastine and Vinchon, a dream book of the Renaissance, that of Pierus, describes dreams of serpents, trees, flowers, gardens, teeth, columns, and grottoes, having meanings similar to those of Freudian symbolism.³⁶⁷ The first objective study of dream symbolism was by Scherner, and we recall that the symbols found by him as being sexual were identical to those described thirty-nine years later in Freud's *Interpretation of Dreams*.³⁶⁸
3. Wide investigations of sexual symbolism in cults, myths, and religions had been carried out throughout the nineteenth century. The pioneer of these studies, Jacques-Antoine Dulaure, contended that early civilizations who worshiped the sun incorporated its regenerative forces into the image of the phallus.³⁶⁹ He described at length the cult of the phallus and its symbolism, with innumerable examples from ancient civilizations. This book had enormous success, and popularized the idea that a universal cult

of the phallus had existed. Many amateur archeologists became infatuated with the search for symbolic relics of that cult. To give only one example: in Flaubert's novel, *Bouvard et Pécuchet*, the two heroes of the story, in their preoccupation with "Celtic archeology," take for granted that the "tumulus" symbolizes the female organ and the "pierre levée" the male; that the towers, pyramids, church candles, milestones, and trees were phallic symbols. They opened a Department of Phalluses in their private museum. Meanwhile, a serious scholar, Adalbert Kuhn, interpreted ritual fire kindling as symbolic of human generation.[370] In the middle of the Victorian era in England, George Cox explained the sexual symbolism of ancient religions: the rod, the tree, the shepherd's staff, the scepter, the serpent, the bull, were male symbols; and the ark, the ship, the cup (including the Holy Grail), the well, the basket, the lamp, the lotus, were female symbols. Since "the thoughts aroused by the recognition of the difference between men and women are among the most mysterious stirrings of the human heart," Cox admitted that "a philosophy which professed to reconcile the natural impulses of the worshippers with a sense of right and duty would carry with it a strange and almost irresistible fascination." In Germany, Nagele interpreted the cult of the serpent in antiquity as a phallic cult.[372] In Italy, Gubernatis developed a systematic theory of the universal sexual symbolism taken from botany[373] and zoology.[374]

4. Clinical experience had furnished many data on sexual symbolism. Romantic psychiatry dwelt on the role of sexual impulses and frustrations in psychoses.[375] Neumann, later Santlus, and to a lesser extent Griesinger, described the disguised manifestations of the sexual instinct in their patients. The awareness that many forms of pathological mysticism resulted from repressed sexuality was current knowledge among novelists, psychiatrists, and religious writers.[376] The criminologist Hanns Gross also made a systematic inquiry into the disguised forms of frustrated sexuality and their role in criminality.

Another field of Freud's inquiry was the varieties and vicissitudes of sexual fantasies and their subsequent role in emotional life. Freud contended that the observation by young children of their parents' sexual intercourse, that is, of what he called the primal scene, had a deep-reaching disturbing influence on the child, especially when interpreted as a sadistic act. Freud also attributed a great deal of importance to the theories young children imagine in order to answer their own questions about how babies come into the world, and their parents' sexual relations. Freud mentioned it as a further argument in favor of the contemporary trend to give children sexual enlightenment. Another fantasy was the Family Romance occurring in certain children who imagine their real parents to be of much higher social status than their actual parents. This topic was considerably developed by Otto Rank.[377] Here again we find a psychoanalytic reflection of a contemporary, popular theme. In that period, when most European countries had a king or emperor, many mental patients claimed to be descendants of sovereign families, or even to be the legitimate monarch. Krafft-Ebing described a variety of these delusions under the name of *Originäre Paranoia* (this term has often been misunderstood as "delusion about one's family origin"; actually, it meant a form of paranoia whose "origin" could be traced to the age of beginning memory). In France, one celebrated patient, Hersilie Rouy, was, following her claims of royal birth, committed to a mental hospital, but released with a substantial compensation because of a technical error in the committal order. She published two "autobiographies": in one she dissembled a great part of her delusional ideas, in the other she expressed them fully.[378] Freud's originality was in showing that the Family Romance does not only exist under extreme paranoid forms, but is frequent among children in its embryonic form, and also has some relevance to folklore and mythology.

Current accounts of Freud's life state that the publication of his sexual theories aroused anger because of their unheard-of novelty in a "Victorian" society. Documentary evidence shows that this does not correspond to fact. Freud's *Three Essays* appeared in the midst of a flood of contemporary literature on sexology and were favorably received.[379] Freud's main originality was to synthesize ideas and concepts, the majority of which lay scattered or partially organized, and to apply them directly to psychotherapy. A clinical illustration was the case of little Hans, which was for the libido theory what the Dora case had been for depth psychology.

The story has less literary quality than the Dora case and makes for lengthier reading. It was told by the father of little Hans and commented upon by Freud.

Hans was the first-born of a psychoanalyst who was one of Freud's closest disciples. His mother lavished tender care upon him. She often took him in her bed, and even, as it appears later, she often took him with her when she went to the toilet. At the age of three, Hans was much interested in his "widdler." Having asked his mother whether she had one she said: "Yes." When he was 3½ his mother discovered that he masturbated and threatened him with castration. At about the same time his little sister was born. Hans was told that the stork had brought her, but he was impressed by the doctor's bag and the basins full of water and blood in his mother's room. He became preoccupied with whether other people and animals had a "widdler" and seemed particularly interested by the large size of those of horses. He came to the conclusion that the presence of that organ distinguished animate from inanimate beings; however, he noticed that his little sister did not have one, and he said that it would grow. Even before the age of four, Hans was of a "polygamous" disposition; he fell in love with a series of girls from 7 to 11 years of age, but he also put his arms tenderly around a five-year-old boy cousin.

At the age of 4¾ years, Hans (as it was found later) saw a horse, which was drawing a heavily loaded carriage, fall to the ground. Shortly afterwards he became increasingly anxious, clung much more to his mother, and then expressed fear of going into the street lest a horse bite him. Freud advised the father to tell Hans that he feared horses because he was so much interested in their "widdlers," and to gradually start giving him some sexual enlightenment.

This was the beginning of a four-month-long process (January to May, 1908). The boy's sayings, dreams, spontaneous plays, were recorded by his father and communicated to Freud. The phobia extended to giraffes, elephants, and pelicans, after a visit to the Schönbrunn zoo. One morning Hans told of the fantasy of two giraffes in his room, a big one and a crumpled one; the big one cried because Hans took the crumpled one. This was interpreted by the father as a transposition of a little family scene: Hans was in the habit of coming into his parents' room early in the morning, his father would say his mother should not take him in her bed, and she would say it did not matter if she took him for a short while, which she did. The big giraffe was interpreted as being his father's big penis, the crumpled one his mother's genital organs.

On March 30, 1908, his father took Hans on a short visit to Freud's office. Freud explained to the boy that he feared his father because he loved his mother so much. This visit was followed by a substantial improvement, but the phobia soon expanded to new topics, namely large, rough horses drawing heavily loaded carts, furniture vans, and the like; Hans told of horses falling down and kicking with their feet. Then he took a disgust for yellow ladies' pants and was preoccupied with excrement, with bathtubs, with loaded carts and boxes, and so on. One morning Hans fantasied that while he was in his bath, the plumber unscrewed the bathtub and stuck him in the stomach with a borer. The father's interpretation was: being in his mother's bed, his father pushed him out with his big penis. A later interpretation was in the sense of a generation fantasy: the father put him in his mother's womb with his big penis. Hans' aversion for baths was connected with his wish that his mother take away her hand while bathing his little sister, so that the child would drown. The fantasy of the falling horse was interpreted as being the wish (and at the same time the fear) that his father would fall down and die, and also as a fantasy of his mother in the process of childbirth. In fact, it was found that Hans had not believed the stork story and had understood much about his mother's pregnancy.

At the root of Hans' phobia thus appeared his wish to possess his mother, and that his father and little sister be dead; his castration complex; the influence of early, infantile sexual theories; and his resentment against his parents for having told him the untrue story about the stork.

On April 25, 1908, Hans, who had just reached the age of five, was answering some of his father's questions. In a climate of confidence and acceptance, he admitted that he would like to see him dead and marry his mother. This was the culminating point of the therapeutic process, and from that time on, the remnants of the phobia gradually receded: the Oedipus complex had been overcome.[380]

The story of little Hans was not accepted as easily as had been Freud's prior publications, but the meaning of that scepticism had been misunderstood. It is not so much that it was found immoral, but rather that some readers found that the child had been erotically precocious to an unusual extent before his phobia; they also wondered whether the phobia itself had not developed as a consequence of the father's inquisitive attitude and suggestive questions. Testimonial psychology, which was in 1909 a new and fashionable branch of psychology, brought numerous examples of children giving false testimonies, which proved to be the response to unconscious suggestion (children having an uncanny ability to sense what adults expect them to testify). Psychoanalysts hailed the story of little Hans as the first confirmation of Freud's theory of infantile sexuality obtained by direct observation on a child. It was also the first example of child analysis (which, however, was to develop later along different lines), and was also the first control analysis on record.

Rev. Oskar Pfister[381] commented upon the changes that had occurred in psychoanalysis. Originally, Freud attributed neurotic symptoms to the repression of painful memories, mostly of a sexual nature (the term "sexuality" being taken in its usual sense); healing was achieved through abreaction. In 1913, psychoanalysis told of the repression of fantasies as well as of memories, and of neurotic symptoms originating in the Oedipus complex; healing occurred through the analysis of transference and resistance: the concept of sexuality was now extended to include, under the name of "psychosexuality," all categories comprised under the word *Liebe* (love). This would absolve psychoanalysis of the accusation of pansexualism. However, certain critics felt that the concept of psychosexuality made the theory of libido and especially that of sublimation even more difficult to grasp.

Freud's Work—VI—From Metapsychology to Ego Psychoanalysis

By 1913 it would have seemed that the psychoanalytic theory had achieved its completion. However, and to the surprise of Freud's followers, a great metamorphosis was still to occur. This time the newer teaching was not contained in a single book (such as *Interpretation of Dreams* and the *Three Essays*), but in a series of articles and brief monographs spaced over a period of ten years.

In 1914, Freud proposed, in the *Introduction to Narcissism,* his new views as a hypothesis which he was willing to retract or alter, should facts contradict it.[382] Until then the notions of the conflict between conscious and unconscious, and the dualism of libido and ego drives, had been fundamental in psychoanalysis. In the *Three Essays* Freud had already spoken of an early stage of auto–erotism preceding the cathexis of the libido on the first object, the mother. In the meantime Jung had explained that schizophrenia resulted from an "introversion of libido," and Adler had emphasized the importance of self-esteem. Havelock Ellis in England, and Naecke in Germany, had described narcissism as a specific form of sexual deviation in which the individual is in love with himself. Freud's theory of narcissism seems to have been designed to meet all these.

This theory entailed a new systematization of the drive theory. Freud's former distinction of (nonsexual) ego drives and (sexual) libido was modified by the new concept of ego-libido, so that there were now two kinds of ego drives, libidinal and nonlibidinal. Freud kept the concept of an early stage of auto-erotism, but said that as the ego begins to be differentiated, the heretofore diffuse libido focused thereon, and this was primary narcissism. In the following stage, a portion of primary narcissism is retained, and the libido is largely cathected on the mother and subsequently on other objects. The object-libido may retract and be reinvested in the ego, what Freud later called "secondary narcissism."

A residue of primary narcissism will be found through analysis of normal individuals, and even more in neurotics, homosexuals, and others. Retraction of the object-libido explains such conditions as delusions of grandeur, hypochondriasis, schizophrenia, and paraphrenia.

Normally, amorous feeling proceeds directly from object-libido and this is anaclitic love. If the entire libido is cathected in another person, and not enough retained for the ego, it is infatuation. Love of the narcissistic type happens when primary narcissism has been unduly prolonged: the individual then sees in the object only what he himself is, has been, and would like to be.

This theory of narcissism was to be the prelude to a complete restructuring of the framework of psychoanalytic theory. In 1915, Freud announced that he was working on a book entitled *Introduction to Metapsychology,* consisting of twelve essays, but of these only five were ever published. Freud felt the need of rebuilding a conceptual framework that would be sufficiently comprehensive to encompass all the facts and aspects of psychoanalysis. He defined *metapsychology* as a system that would describe psychological facts from the topographical, the dynamic, and the economic points of view. The topographical (referring to a well-known quotation from Fechner) meant the distinction of the unconscious, the preconscious, and the conscious. The dynamic referred to psychic forces in conflict with each other. The economic meant the regulation of mental forces through the pleasure-unpleasure principle.

In *Drives and Their Vicissitudes,* Freud defined the drives as "psychical representatives of endo-somatic, continuously flowing sources of stimulation," in contrast with the sensory stimuli that originate in specific external excitation.[383] Freud then defined the general features of the drives, their force, their aim, their source, and their vicissitudes: reversal into the opposite, turning against the subject, repression, and sublimation. Freud also mentioned the process of introjection (the infant introjects pleasure and projects unpleasure). Finally, Freud touched on the genesis of love and hate, contending that though they form a pair of opposites, hatred has its root in an earlier stage of psychic life than love. The last point, which contradicted the original libido theory, was the forerunner of further changes.

The paper on repression surprised those analysts who considered repression the one explanatory concept of pathogenesis.[384] Repression (now placed third among the vicissitudes of drives) was divided into primary repression, in which the mental representations of instincts have never been allowed into consciousness, and later repression, in which conscious representations are dragged into the unconsciousness through their association with one of the primal repressed ideas. When emotionally charged ideas are repressed, the fate of the idea and of the emotion may be different; repressed ideas organize themselves into fantasies, and emotions are transformed into anxiety.

In the third metapsychology paper Freud emphasized that the unconscious contains more than repressed material, and restated the main features of the unconscious mind (previously called the primary process).[385] The unconscious has no relationship to reality, it does not know the principles of contradiction or time; unconscious energy is unbound. Freud also stressed the importance of unconscious fantasies, and that unconscious representations must go through a stage of verbalization at the preconscious level before becoming conscious.

In a fourth essay Freud restated some aspects of the dream theory from the viewpoint of metapsychology.[386] In the fifth, *Mourning and Melancholia,* he gave an interpretation of melancholic depression in terms of the new metapsychology, by comparing it with the normal mourning reaction that follows the death of a loved person.[387] The mourning work consists of a slow, gradual dissolution of the emotional ties with the lost object, and the incorporation of its idealized picture into the subject. In melancholia, it is as if the patient had unconsciously lost an object for which he had ambivalent feelings of love and hatred. As a consequence of its incorporation "the shadow of the object has fallen upon the ego," hence the melancholic self-hatred and suicidal tendencies.

In 1920 Freud greatly surprised his followers once again with the publication of his book *Beyond the Pleasure Principle*, which seemed to give metapsychology its final shape.[388] If its title evoked Nietzsche, its content was definitely inspired by Fechner. One of the three elements of metapsychology, the economic aspect, had until now been equated by Freud with the pleasure-unpleasure principle, a concept borrowed from Fechner. Before Fechner, the principle of pleasure had been commonly understood as simply seeking pleasure and avoiding unpleasure. Fechner had related it to the principle of stability, and Freud, following Fechner, had related unpleasure to the increase of tension, and pleasure to the decrease of tension to an optimum level. Thus the basic rule of life was the regulation of the quantum of stimulation through the mechanism of the pleasure-unpleasure principle. Freud, however, had already recognized that the pleasure-unpleasure principle was limited, first through the principle of reality, which had to be taken into account throughout human development, and second, because originally pleasurable drives, once repressed, lost that quality. Now, he contended that these limitations went "beyond the pleasure principle." Another, more ancient principle, the "compulsion to repetition," he now saw as the sole possible explanation of certain clinical facts. In the repetitive dreams of traumatic neuroses, in hysterical attacks, in certain forms of child play, we see unpleasant events repeated. Transference during analysis is revealed as the unconscious revival of childhood situations. In neurosis, as in normal life, certain individuals find themselves repeatedly in the self-same situations, leading to a belief in predestination. Freud differentiated between the pleasure-unpleasure principle that is beneficial to the organism, and the demonic character of the compulsion to repetition, and this led him to an excursion into philosophy.

After various considerations on the *Reizschutz* (the tendency of the organism to protect itself from overstimulation), he proposed a new definition of the drives. Drives do not have a progressive character, they do not tend to further the development of the individual and the species. Their aim is conservative, they tend to reestablish prior conditions. In truly Fechnerian style, Freud goes so far as to say that the evolution of organisms is the reflection of the evolutionary history of the earth and its relationship to the sun. Freud now suggested, as a hypothesis, a new dual classification of the instincts: *Eros* (grouping together all forms of libidinal instincts), and the *death instinct* (which Freud's followers were soon to call *Thanatos*). In that dual system Freud seemed to postulate that the death instinct was the more fundamental. Like Schopenhauer, Freud now proclaimed that "the goal of life is death," that the preservation instinct itself is one aspect of the death instinct because it protects against accidental, externally caused death, in order to preserve the individual for death from internal causes. Eros is now far more than sexual instinct, it exists in each living cell and drives the living substance to constitute larger beings, it is a postponement of death by flight forward. The death instinct is the tendency toward dissolution of living substance and return to a state of inanimate matter. The two instincts are inseparable, and life is a compromise between Eros and the death instinct until the latter prevails. Freud expressed the hope that the progress of biology would make a formulation of these speculations possible in scientific terms. Meanwhile he had to reformulate a great part of his clinical conceptions. For many years he had proclaimed the primacy of libido, and in 1908, he had rejected Adler's idea of an autonomous aggressive drive. In his first metapsychology paper in 1915, however, he had attributed the origin of hatred to nonlibidinal ego instincts, placing its origin prior to that of love. Now with his new theories, he had to admit that there was a primary masochism that was not simply sadism turned inward, and in his further writings he ascribed more and more importance to the role of aggressive and destructive instincts. He seemed to put as much emphasis on these as he had formerly placed on the libido.

The theories contained in *Beyond the Pleasure Principle* were not all as new as they appeared to some of Freud's followers. Freud was returning to the tendency for speculation he had gratified in 1895 by writing his *Project for a Scientific Psychology*, as well as to Fechner, who had inspired his former speculative works. At the beginning of *Beyond the Pleasure Principle* Freud connected the principle of pleasure-unpleasure and Fechner's principle of constancy.[389] As Freud remarked: "The principle of constancy is but one particular case of Fechner's more general 'principle of the tendency to stability.' " Fechner distinguished three forms of stability: absolute stability (implying a permanent immobility of the parts of a whole), full stability (the parts of the whole are animated by movements so regular that each part of the whole returns to the same place at regular intervals), and "approximate stability" (a more or less imperfect tendency to return to the same place at regular intervals, as in the movements of the heart and other rhythmic psychological activities). It would seem that this systematization of Fechner inspired a similar framework for Freud's ideas. To the pleasure-unpleasure principle he added the death instinct (a return to Fechner's full stability) and the repetition compulsion, as intermediate between approximate and absolute stability.

The notion of repetition compulsion was, from the clinical point of view, the most original contribution contained in *Beyond the Pleasure Principle*, though it had been expressed by other authors. Tarde had already described the propensity of a criminal to relive his crime in imagination, to return to the scene of his crime, and to repeat his crime, as a particular example of a more general tendency to repeat, consciously or not, acts and situations from one's own history.[390]

Freud's concept of the death instinct also had many precursors. Von Schubert among the Romantics had expressed it clearly, mainly as a wish, in the latter part of life, to die.[391] Closer to Freud's idea, Novalis proclaimed that "life is for the sake of death," and that "the characteristic of illness is the instinct of self-destruction."[392] Opposite to the death instinct Novalis placed the instinct of organization, whose highest expression was human language, culture, and philosophy. At the end of the nineteenth century, the Russian psychiatrist Tokarsky wrote a philosophical essay on death, in which, in the manner of the ancient Stoics, he dissociated the various feelings and images that are associated with the idea of death, until there remained nothing frightening in it.[393] He quoted a centenarian, who said that at a certain age there came a need to die as natural as the need to sleep. Another Russian, Metchnikoff, maintained that there was such a thing as an instinct to die.[394] He added further observations, surmising that the wish to die must be a particularly pleasant feeling, but that few people experience it, either because they die early, or because of the diseases of old age. These two Russians, however, viewed the death instinct simply as a wish to die, whereas the idea of destructive and self-destructive instincts was much more widespread throughout the nineteenth century. It followed a tradition going back to Hobbes and popularized by Darwin and the social Darwinians, by Lombroso, and by Nietzsche. Fechner had written a curious little essay in which he advanced the idea that destruction was a more fundamental principle than creation.[395] In the beginning was destruction; then destruction began to destroy itself, and this was creation. Even among psychoanalysts, the concept of a death instinct had been occasionally expressed. Sabina Spielrein had written on "Destruction as the cause of becoming."[396] Rank's theory that every man longs to return to the mother's womb was considered by Moxon as an anticipation of Freud's concept of the death instinct.[397]

The classical pairs of opposites were *Eros-Neikos* (Love-Strife), and *Bios-Thanatos* (Life-Death), but not *Eros-Thanatos,* although an Austrian writer, Schaukal, had published a series of five short stories of a rather gloomy quality under that title.[398] Freud first brought forth his concepts as hypotheses, but in later writings he showed that he firmly believed in them. In every psychological process he saw the presence of the two processes, Eros as a tendency to form larger units, and the death instinct Thanatos as the reverse tendency; this latter concept was very close to Spencer's definition of evolution and dissolution. Freud once more was compelled to reinterpret his theories of the various clinical conditions; melancholia, for instance, he now viewed as disintrication of the libido and the death instinct.

Freud's concept of the death instinct met resistance, even among the most faithful psychoanalysts. Brun, in Switzerland, objected that there was no biological support for the notion of a death instinct; death, he said, was the *finis* (termination), but not the *telos* (final aim) of life. Those psychoanalysts such as Karl Menninger, who utilize the notion of life and death instincts, do so from an empirical and clinical rather than a biological point of view.[399] Actually, as shown by Mechler, Freud's concept of the death instinct can be best understood against the background of the preoccupation with death shared by a number of his eminent contemporaries: biologists, psychologists, and existential philosophers.[400]

While the notions in *Beyond the Pleasure Principle* were received with mixed feelings by psychoanalysts, those presented three years later in *The Ego and the Id* enjoyed great success, though they meant extensive modifications in psychoanalytic theory.[401] For many years psychoanalysis had been considered a depth psychology, primarily focused on the unconscious mind and its influence upon conscious life. Freud had distinguished three layers of the mind: the conscious, preconscious, and unconscious. Neuroses were manifestations of conflicts between the conscious and the unconscious, the former being implicitly equated with the ego. Freud now felt that his conceptual framework had become inadequate; he considered mental life as produced by the interaction of three psychic agencies

(*Instanzen*), the ego, the id, and the superego. The ego was defined as "the coordinated organization of mental processes in a person." There was a conscious and an unconscious part in the ego. To the conscious ego belonged perception and motor control, and to the unconscious ego, the dream censor and the process of repression. Language was an ego function; unconscious contents became preconscious through the medium of words.

The id was not very different from what Freud had originally described as the unconscious, the seat of both the repressed material and the drives, to which had been added the unconscious fantasies and unconscious feelings, notably guilt feelings. The word "unconscious" was now an adjective, used to qualify not only the id, but parts of the ego and superego. The term "id" (*das Es*) could be traced to Nietzsche, but Freud admitted borrowing it from *The Book of the Id*, by George Groddeck,[402] an admirer of psychoanalysis.[402]

The most novel part of *The Ego and the Id* is that devoted to the third agency, the superego, though Freud had already touched on some of its aspects under the name of ego ideal. The superego is the watchful, judging, punishing agency in the individual, the source of social and religious feelings in mankind. Its origin was in the individual's former ego configurations, which had been superseded, and above all in the introjection of the father figure as a part of the resolution of the Oedipus complex.

The construction of the superego in an individual is thus dependent on the manner in which the Oedipus complex has been resolved. On the other hand, the superego receives its energy from the id, hence its frequently cruel, sadistic quality. This new concept explained the role of neurotic guilt feelings in obsessions, melancholia, hysteria, and in criminality. The ideas of self-punishment and criminality because of guilt feelings were later to be expanded and emphasized in psychoanalysis and criminology. Freud concluded that the "Id is quite amoral, the Ego strives to be moral, and the Superego can be hyper-moral and cruel as only the Id can be."

As a consequence of these new theories, the ego was now in the limelight of psychoanalysis, especially as the site of anxiety: reality anxiety, that is, fear caused by reality, drive anxiety from pressures from the id and guilt anxiety resulting from the pressures of the superego. Freud concluded with a description of the pitiful state of the ego, suffering under the pressures of its three masters. It was clear that the main concern of psychotherapy would now be to relieve the ego by reducing these pressures and helping it acquire some strength.

To many of Freud's contemporaries, the theory of the human psychological structure consisting of these three entities, the ego, the id, and the superego, seemed perplexing, even though there was nothing revolutionary in it. As already mentioned, the notion of the id can be traced to the Romantics, and the essence of the superego unmistakably originated with Nietzsche, especially in *The Genealogy of Morals*. To define the ego as the coordinating organization of the mental processes in a person was reminiscent of Janet's function of synthesis, and ego strength was not very different from Janet's psychological tension. The ego was an old philosophical concept in new psychological dress. Nacht's definition of the ego as "the entity through which the individual becomes conscious of his own existence and of the existence of the external world" is almost identical with that which Fichte had given in philosophical terms.[403]

In 1936 Freud published *Inhibition, Symptom and Anxiety*, a book that some analysts have found the most difficult among his works. Inhibition was redefined as a limitation of the functions of the ego; anxiety as a painful emotional condition accompanied by processes of discharge (both of which are perceived by the individual). Anxiety was no longer a symptom, but a condition necessary for the formation of symptoms. As already stated in *The Ego and the Id*, the ego is the only site of anxiety; anxiety can occur in two circumstances: either when the ego's protective barriers are overrun, or as a warning signal against danger from the drives— to which the ego reacts with various forms of "defense" (*Abwehr*). Repression is now but one of the defenses; the others being reaction formation, isolation, and undoing. Repression is characteristic of hysteria, the other three of obsessive-compulsive neuroses. In this new theory, repression is no longer the cause of anxiety; on the contrary, anxiety gives rise to repression and other defenses.

Inhibition, Symptom and Anxiety marked a new phase in the transformation of Freud's theories, from metapsychology to ego psychology. It would seem that this booklet was, at least partly, a refutation of Rank's theory that all anxiety arises from the trauma of birth. With the increased importance Freud ascribed to the ego, he came closer to the concepts of Janet (for instance, the idea of the isolation mechanism in compulsive neuroses), and of Adler (reaction formation as a form of compensation). There are also noteworthy similarities between Freud's new theories of anxiety and those expressed in 1859 by Heinrich Neumann.[404]

As a consequence of these new theories, the focus of Freudian therapy shifted from the analysis of the instinctual forces to that of the ego, from the repressed to the repressing. Analysis of defenses would necessarily uncover anxiety, and the task of the analyst was now to dispel the excess of anxiety and to strengthen the ego, so that it could face reality and control the pressure of drives and the superego.

A further step toward ego psychoanalysis was taken by Anna Freud with her book *The Ego and the Mechanisms of Defense*, describing a variety of defense mechanisms from the theoretical and practical viewpoint.[405] Freud himself had redefined the ego as a system of functions (facing reality, controlling drives, and integrating the three "agencies" of personality), a system working with its own, desexualized energy. In his last works he emphasized the biological aspects of the ego, suggested that it possessed inherited characteristics, and indicated self-preservation as one of its main functions.[406]

The final step toward modern ego psychoanalysis was marked by Heinz Hartmann's celebrated monograph of 1939, which emphasized the autonomy of the ego and its function of adaptation. This writing was to inspire a generation of psychoanalysts, but Freud by that time had accomplished his work.[407]

Freud's Work—VII—The Psychoanalytic Technique

Freud's creation of a new psychotherapeutic method was a long process that underwent a succession of metamorphoses from his earliest attempts to the end of his life, and which was to be continued by his disciples after his death.

It is not certain how Freud treated his first neurotic patients. He may have used that unsystematized, intuitive approach, traditional with those physicians who understood their patients' problems and helped them by giving support and direction. He most probably benefited from the teachings of Moritz Benedikt about the importance of the second life (daydreams, suppressed wishes, and ambitions) and of the pathogenic secret, and it is known that he applied Bernheim's technique of hypnotic suggestion.

The first picture of a properly Freudian psychotherapy appeared in 1895, in Freud's contribution to the *Studies in Hysteria*. At this stage it was an adaptation of Breuer's cathartic treatment, and almost identical to Janet's procedure. Probably inspired by Weir Mitchell's cure was the adjuvant use of physical relaxation (which was to become the psychoanalytic couch). In view of the difficulty he had in hypnotizing his own patients, and remembering that Bernheim was able, in the state of post-hypnotic amnesia, to have the subject recall what had happened under hypnosis, Freud told his patients to close their eyes and concentrate. While he pressed a hand on the patients' forehead, he would then assure them that the forgotten memory would return. At times it did so directly, at others it did so through chains of associations. Freud, too, noticed the intensification of neurotic symptoms when he came close to the pathogenic nucleus.

In the same contribution the concepts of "resistance" and "transference" are first defined. Freud noticed a slowing down or stoppage of the free association in some cases;' he termed this phenomenon resistance and attempted to analyze it.[408] He considered resistance as the result either of inner causes (from the material itself), or external causes related in some way to the therapist. Sometimes the patient felt neglected by the doctor, and a simple explanation would suffice to restore the flow. Sometimes the patient was afraid of becoming too dependent on the doctor. Sometimes also, the patient transferred painful memories to the doctor; the latter's task was to make the patient aware of the resistance and find its origin in the life history.

Five years later, in 1900, *The Interpretation of Dreams* made a practical method for the interpretation of dreams available to psychotherapy.

An account of Freud's psychoanalytic method, written in 1904 at the request of Loewenfeld, shows the modifications it had undergone in the previous ten years.[409] The patient still reclined on a couch, but the doctor now sat on a chair behind his range of vision. The patient no longer closed his eyes, nor did Freud place his hand on the patient's forehead. The method of free association was now dominated by a basic rule: the patient should say anything that came to his mind, no matter how absurd, immoral, or painful it seemed. Freud explained how he analyzed resistance with the gaps and distortions in the material obtained. A new comprehensive technique of interpretation utilized as material, not only the free associations and resistance, but the patient's parapraxes, symptomatic acts, and dreams as well. Freud now rejected the use of hypnosis and contended that the psychoanalytic technique was much easier than the reader could surmise from its written description.

One year later, in 1905, Freud showed in the Dora case how dream interpretation could be used for psychotherapy. Transference was redefined as an unconscious revival of life events, in which the therapist is viewed as if he had been one of the participants. Transference, the greatest obstacle to the cure, was now considered the most powerful therapeutic tool, if skillfully handled by the doctor.

In 1910, Freud drew attention toward counter-transference, that is, the irrational feelings of the therapist toward the patient.[410] In his pamphlet on "Wild Analysis" Freud departed from the opinion he held in 1904, by saying that it was very difficult to learn psychoanalysis and that in view of the danger of "wild analysis," an organization should be set up to teach analysis and qualify analysts.[411]

In 1912, Freud stated that it was not necessary to interpret all the dreams of a patient; many did not require complete interpretation, and often no interpretation was needed.[412] In a further paper Freud distinguished positive and negative transference, adding that there were mixed (ambivalent) forms, and that transference was a general phenomenon in human life.[413] In a third paper he introduced the principle of free-floating attention: the analyst, far from concentrating too intensively on the utterances of the patient, should trust his "unconscious memory"; he should not take abundant notes, but content himself with noting the dates, important facts, and texts of dreams.[414] He should not speculate about the causes and structure of the case until he was well advanced: "Go on without definite intention," Freud advised. The analyst should follow the model of the surgeon in regard to emotional coldness toward the patient; his concern should be to act as a mirror, reflecting for the patient what he shows to the analyst, and the analyst should therefore be opaque to the patient. Neither should the analyst demand intellectual tasks of the patient (such as the thinking over of a certain period of his life), nor should he seek to channel the patient's sublimation process. Freud proclaimed that it was necessary for a psychoanalyst to have undergone a training analysis. In 1914 Freud explained that in the transference situation all the symptoms have replaced their previous meaning by a new one within the framework of a transference neurosis, which can be cured.[415] Transference neurosis is an artificial illness, an intermediate realm between illness and real life, a transition from neurosis to health. Thus not only the patient's utterances but also his behavior are analyzed, and once all is interpreted to the patient, he is expected to apply this new insight. In the presence of a woman patient manifesting transference love, Freud added in 1915, the role of the analyst is to show her that the alleged love is a form of resistance.[416]

In 1919 Freud warned analysts against taking false routes.[417] He disavowed Ferenczi's innovation and precept of the active role of the analyst, and also rose up against the idea of the analyst giving emotional gratification to the patient; the analysis should be conducted in an atmosphere of abstinence. Neither did Freud admit that a psychoanalysis should be supplemented by psychosynthesis, nor that it should deal with religion or philosophy and undertake to educate the patient. Nevertheless Freud was preoccupied with future application of psychoanalysis to the underprivileged; in that event he considered that psychoanalysis would have to be supplemented by hypnosis.

In *Beyond the Pleasure Principle* Freud reinterpreted the meaning of transference as being the manifestation of the compulsion to repetition. The concept of the death instinct and the new theories that were soon to follow entailed deep-reaching modifications in the psychoanalytic techniques, and further ones were introduced by the promoters of ego psychoanalysis. The focus of the analytic work was now no longer the direct investigation of the unconscious, but the exploration of the ego's defenses. The unconscious drives were felt as threats by the ego, which experienced anxiety, and protected itself through a system of defenses. The task of the analyst was the cautious uncovering of these defenses and the working through of at least a part of the underlying anxiety (Freud now admitted that anxiety could not be completely removed). The therapist analyzed these defenses, whether they were anachronic or inappropriate, and their relationship to the neurotic symptoms. He taught the patient to use more appropriate defenses, permitting a better adjustment.

In Freud's last publications, an almost pessimistic tone could be perceived. He conjectured that the future would attribute far greater importance to psychoanalysis as a science of the unconscious than as a therapeutic method. In *Analysis Terminable and Interminable* Freud admitted that certain psychoanalytic treatments have to be resumed after a number of years, while others must be pursued, though intermittently, the whole life long.[418] The therapeutic prospects are limited by biological factors, by the constitutional strength of the drives, by the weakness of the ego, and particularly by the death instinct. Least accessible to psychoanalysis are the woman's wish for a penis and the man's feminine attitude toward his own sex. In the posthumous *Outline of Psychoanalysis* Freud added to these negative factors psychic inertia, a kind of viscosity of the libido, and a weak capacity for sublimation.[419] He visualized the final outcome of the treatment as depending upon the balance between the forces that the analyst and the patient are able to mobilize to their advantage, and the sum of the negative forces working against them.

The best way to assess the novelty and originality of Freud's psychoanalytic methods is to contrast them with the preexisting ones, from which he started.

Freud was not the first therapist who spent considerable time with his patients, allowed them to speak in an atmosphere of benevolence, listened to all their complaints, recorded their whole life history, and took in account the emotional causes of disease. All this had been done by Janet, by Bleuler, and many others before them, and was preliminary to the use of a particular method. But psychoanalysis can be primarily understood as being a modification of the previously extant techniques of hypnotism.

The hypnotist, sitting in a chair, faced his subject seated in another chair and instructed him how to attain the hypnotic sleep; the patient showed more or less resistance, but yielded in favorable cases. These sessions were repeated, often daily, until the patient learned to fall rapidly into hypnotic sleep. The hypnotic cure could then take weeks or months. Unknown capacities and forgotten memories were uncovered in hypnotic sleep, new roles were played by the subject, and the hypnotist was able to induce regression to earlier periods in the patient's life. But the patient often opposed a resistance to the hypnotizer's interventions. In the course of the hypnotic treatment a singular rapport was established between the subject and the hypnotist. The strong erotic element of rapport, as well as the possibility of infantile dependency in the patient, making the termination of hypnotic treatment a delicate exercise, were emphasized by many authors.

In psychoanalytic technique the patient reclines on a couch, and the therapist sits on a chair behind him, seeing but unseen. The analyst explains the basic rule, which is to tell anything that comes to mind. This rule is, of course, difficult to follow, and the patient has to overcome resistances, which in the best of cases would never completely disappear. After a few weeks, however, the patient learns to overcome his resistance, and even to take pleasure in talking at random. A gradual loosening of associations occurs, and instead of following one train of thought, the subject jumps from one idea to another. As the analysis proceeds, more and more memories of even more remote childhood events appear interspersed with memories of dreams and fantasies, and the patient begins to have a strangely distorted picture of the analyst. The analyst offers interpretations, which the patient accepts or not. Whereas with hypnosis resistance is merely considered a nuisance, in psychoanalysis it becomes a relevant phenomenon to be analyzed. What the hypnotist calls rapport, the analyst terms transference, and considers it to be a revival of early attitudes toward parents, requiring analysis. It is the slow development and subsequent resolution of the transference neurosis that are considered the main tools of the psychoanalytic technique.

The contrast can be summarized as in the following table:

HYPNOSIS	PSYCHOANALYSIS
Setting: Patient sitting. Subject facing hypnotist.	*Setting:* Patient lying down. Analyst sitting behind patient, seeing but unseen.
Preliminary instructions: How to become hypnotized.	*Preliminary instructions:* Psychoanalytic basic rule.
First week: Subject learns to become hypnotized.	*First week:* Patient overcomes aversion to the basic rule.
Following weeks or months: Emergence of unknown capacities, new roles, latent memories.	*Following weeks, months, or years:* Loosening of association process, fragmentary memories and fantasies, distorted picture of the analyst.
Hypnotic age regression.	Psychoanalytic regression to pre-Oedipal stages.
Hypnotic suggestions (formerly "bargaining", used by magnetizers).	Interpretations offered to subject, who is free to accept them or not.
Resistance as troublesome element.	Resistance, and analysis of resistance.
Rapport often utilized as therapeutic tool	Transference utilized and analized as therapeutic tool.
Risk of hypnotic dependancy makes termination of treatment difficult.	Treatment terminated through resolution of transference neurosis.

Certain features of psychoanalytic technique can be understood in the context of what neuropathologists wrote at the end of the nineteenth century about the "diabolical cleverness" of hysterics in deceiving the therapist and involving him in their games. It is as if each rule of Freudian technique was devised to defeat the cunning of these patients. The specific setting (the psychoanalyst seeing without being seen) deprives the patient of an audience and of the satisfaction of watching the therapist's reactions.

The basic rule, together with the analyst's neutral attitude, prevents the patient from distorting words of the analyst, and places the latter in the position of a sensible parent who ignores the silly utterances of a little child. The rule that all appointments must be paid, whether kept or not, and in advance, prevents the patient from punishing the therapist by absenteeism and nonpayment. The analysis of transference as it occurs defeats the hysteric's concealed but always present aim: the seduction of the therapist. For the same reason, full liberty is given to verbalization, but any kind of acting-out is prohibited, and no contact with the therapist is allowed outside the hours of treatment. Because of the hysteric's tendency to defeat the therapist by any means, even at the cost of remaining sick, a cure is never promised, and the patient is told that the healing depends on his or her own efforts.

Psychoanalytic techniques may thus be considered a transformation of the old techniques of the hypnotists, especially devised to defeat the underlying maliciousness of hysterics and their constant endeavor to fool the hypnotist. However, it appears that the ever-present resistance of psychoanalyzed subjects had inherited this hysterical feature.

Psychoanalysis also incorporated the principles of other, previously known, psychotherapeutic techniques. Relief from painful, pathogenic secrets through confession no doubt plays a role in certain psychoanalytic cures. The exploration of the inner life of frustrated wishes and ambitions, and of fantasies, as taught by Benedikt, is an integral part of psychoanalysis. Relief from symptoms through becoming aware of unconscious influences was not unknown. In a letter to his friend Chanut, Descartes told of his propensity to fall in love with cock-eyed women.[420] In thinking about it he remembered that as a child he loved a young lady who had that defect. After he had recognized and understood the connection, his predilection disappeared. In this letter we find the theory of complex (determination of a conscious act through an unconscious or half-conscious memory), and the notion of its therapy through bringing it to awareness and interpretation. [421] The therapeutic utilization of transference neurosis is comparable to the conjuring up of a latent possession in exorcism, or to Mesmer's techniques of bringing forth crises in order to control them gradually.[422] The concept of transference itself was but the late metamorphosis of the rapport, whose long evolution has been described in former chapters, as well as its therapeutic utilization by Janet.[423]

Certain writers or philosophers resorted to spontaneous thinking, as a help toward the creative work. The Romantic poet and physicist, Johann Wilhelm Ritter, used to jot down any thoughts that occurred to him, sometimes in incomplete and unclear form, but from the midst of that tangle brilliant aphorisms and suggestions for scientific experiments could emerge.[424] A somewhat different technique was that of Ludwig Börne. In an essay entitled *The Art of Becoming an Original Writer in Three Days*, Börne recommended shutting oneself away for three days with a supply of paper, to write, "without falsehood and without hypocrisy," about every topic that comes to mind.[425] Börne's idea was that men are stifled by the burden of conventional ideas, and that they do not dare to think for themselves. His aim was to free the mind from adulterated thinking. "Sincerity is the source of any kind of genius," Börne pro-claimed.[426] In another essay, Börne said "what is dangerous is the *repressed* word, what has been despised avenges itself, but what has been spoken out is not in vain."[427] Börne's work was held in great esteem by members of Freud's generation, and by Freud himself.

Other techniques of spontaneity utilized psychic automatism. From the beginning of magnetism, it was known that in a hypnotic trance a subject could be brought to draw, paint, write, and so on, of which he would remember nothing in the waking state. Later, automatic writing (an activity in which the subject was conscious that he was writing, but not of what he was writing) was introduced into psychopathology by Charles Richet and used as a psychotherapeutic device by Janet. Crystal gazing also became the object of systematic studies: an individual looked into any reflecting surface and began to see clouds that formed themselves into visual projections of unconscious thoughts. Automatic drawing also became fashionable in the 1880's, and we have seen that Janet utilized automatic talking with his patient, Madame D., in 1892. This was the nearest approach to Freud's technique of free association.

Freud had his patients' free associations met by the analysts free-floating attention, and here also he had a predecessor. In his autobiography, Galton said that at one time in his life he was interested in mesmerism and magnetized about eighty people, in the process of which he made an unexpected observation:

> I had been assured that success was the effect of strength of will on the part of the magnetizer, so at first I exerted all the will-power I possessed, which was fatiguing; I then, by way of experiment, intermitted a little, looking all the time in the same way as before, and found myself equally successful. So I intermitted more and more, and at last succeeded in letting my mind ramble freely while I maintained the same owl-like demeanor. This acted just as well.[428]

All these technical devices, and perhaps many others, can be recognized within Freud's therapeutic procedure. But this does not account for its truly unique characteristics, that is, to have originated in Freud's self-analysis. Freud's analysis was an application of the self-treatment he imagined for his creative neurosis to other persons. This does not preclude the fact that he may have previously applied some of its devices (for instance, free associating), and that he simultaneously analyzed his patients and himself. Psychoanalysis essentially differs from other psychotherapeutic methods in that the patient repeats the experience of Freud's own creative illness, though in attenuated form and under qualified guidance. To undergo a successful psychoanalysis thus amounts to a journey through the unconscious, a journey from which a man necessarily emerges with a modified personality. But this in turn leads to a dilemma. Psychoanalysts proclaim that their method is superior to any other kind of therapy, being the only one able to restructure personality. On the other hand, an increasing number of limitations, contra-indications, dangers, have been pointed out by Freud and his successors. Could it be that psychoanalysis, as a therapy, will come to be replaced by other less laborious and more effective therapies, whereas a few privileged men will afford it as a unique experience apt to change their outlook upon the world, their fellowmen, and themselves?

Freud's Work—VIII—Philosophy of Religion, Culture, and Literature

Soon after he had conceived his psychoanalytic theory, Freud expanded his reflection upon the fields of religion, sociology, cultural history, art, and literature. The works he wrote on these topics have given rise to conflicting opinions. Certain critics were inclined to understand them as essays in the Börne manner, that is, as thoughts jotted down to clarify one's thinking by discarding all merely conventional ideas and putting down all one sincerely feels about a topic. But there have been Freudians and non-Freudians alike who considered them a legitimate extension of psychoanalytic research upon the realms of philosophy, culture, sociology, and the theory of art and literature.

Although Freud claimed to be scornful of philosophy, he definitely expressed philosophical ideas, in the sense of a materialistic, atheistic ideology. His philosophy was an extreme form of positivism, which considered religion dangerous and metaphysics superfluous. In 1907, Freud compared obsessive compulsive symptoms of neurotics with religious rituals and creeds, and concluded that religion was a universal obsessional neurosis, and obsession an individualized religion.[429] Twenty years later, in *The Future of an Illusion*, Freud defined religion as an illusion inspired by infantile belief in the omnipotence of thought, a universal neurosis, a kind of narcotic that hampers the free exercise of intelligence, and something man will have to give up.[430] Religiously minded psychoanalysts objected that Freud had overstepped the boundaries of psychoanalysis and was expressing his personal philosophical opinion; but Freud no doubt believed that psychoanalysis could unmask religion as it could any neurotic symptom.

With *Totem and Taboo* Freud undertook to retrace the origin, not only of religion, but of human culture, and to find a link between the individual Oedipus complex and the prehistory of mankind.[431] Reading the works of Tylor, Lang, Frazer, and other ethnologists, Freud noted that in primitive populations as well as in neurotics there was the same abhorrence of incest, the same irrational character in primitive taboo and in neurotic phobias, the same omnipotence of thought in magic procedures and in neurotic fantasies. Freud proposed a comprehensive theory furnishing a common basis to explain neurotic symptoms, social and cultural manifestations in primitive peoples, and the origin of civilization. The common nucleus is demonstrated in the story of the murder of the primeval father, an extension of the notion of the Oedipus complex. Every little boy, Freud said, has to overcome his secret wish to kill his father and marry his mother. If he is able successfully to overcome this trial, the child incorporates the image of his father in himself, his superego is built, and he will be ready for a normal maturity and adult life; if he fails he is bound to be neurotic. Such is every man's fate, but that individual fate is the reflection of one decisive event that occurred in the prehistory of mankind. Ages ago, men lived in hordes under the despotism of a cruel old father, who kept all the females for himself and exiled his growing sons. The banished sons lived in a community united by homosexual feelings and behaviour. Eventually, the sons killed and ate the father, gratifying their hatred, but this was the beginning of totemism. They revered that animal as a benevolent ancestor (as the father ought to have been), but at regular intervals they killed and devoured it. After killing the father, they did not dare to take his women, as an effect of delayed obedience; moreover, the new organization would have been threatened if the males had quarreled over the females. Such was the origin of the first two commands of mankind, the patricide prohibition and the incest prohibition, the beginning of human culture, morals and religion, and at the same time the prototype of the Oedipus complex.

The idea of primitive mankind living in hordes under the leadership of a tyrannical male was a hypothetical assumption of Darwin's. J. J. Atkinson enlarged Darwin's description: as a result of the father exiling his rival sons, there were two groups living in close proximity; one was the "cyclopean family" comprising the male head, captured females, his own adult female offspring, and a troop of infants of both sexes, the other a band of exiled sons "living most probably in a state of polyandry," and in "peaceful union."[432] When a troop of males felt itself stronger than the father, it attacked and killed him, and the strongest young male succeeded him. This fighting might have perpetuated itself, but Atkinson supposed that at some time one wife was able to persuade the patriarch to keep one of his sons, so that he might succeed him, on the condition of not touching the older man's wives, and this was the beginning of the incest prohibition. Freud was also inspired by William Robertson Smith's theory of the origin of Semitic cults: in the time when men lived in small clans under the belief and rule of totemism, they used to sacrifice a totemic animal at regular intervals and eat it at a ceremonial banquet.[433]

It is likely that C. G. Jung's *Metamorphoses and Symbols of Libido* focused Freud's interest on cultural history, but there was also a keen interest in the subject of totemism among his contemporary ethnologists. Numerous theories, many of them forgotten today, sprang up everywhere.[434] Durkheim contended that totemism had been the common root of all the religions of mankind. Frazer enounced three successive theories, the third being expounded in his book, *Totem and Exogamy*, which was one of

Freud's main sources. In 1912, Wundt attempted a reconstruction of the successive stages gone through by mankind, one of which being totemism.

Actually, it is not impossible that the inspiration for *Totem and Taboo* came less from an unfathomable prehistory than from contemporary events. In those years Turkey, an anachronistic empire and neighbor of Austria, was ruled by the "Red Sultan", Abdul Hamid II. This despot had the power of life and death over his subjects, kept hundreds of wives in a harem guarded by eunuchs, and from time to time massacred entire populations of his empire. In 1908 "the sons banded together against the cruel old man," the Young Turks rebelled and overthrew the Sultan, in order to start a national community where civilization and the arts could flourish. These events were watched with the keenest interest in Austria, more than anywhere else. Whatever ethnologists may think of the murder of the primal father, the story retains its value as a philosophical myth, corresponding to Hobbes' myth of the origin of society.[435] The original condition of mankind, according to Hobbes, was "the war of everyone against everyone"; then a number of men united and delegated their rights to a sovereign, and this power was to be used by him for the common good and as he thought expedient. Such was the origin of absolute monarchy, which for many centuries was the most common form of government, for better or for worse. As Hobbes gave a philosophical myth of the origin of absolute monarchy, Freud gave one of its dissolution.

In *Group Psychology and the Ego*, in 1921, Freud proposed the rudiments of a sociology that rejected the concept of an autonomous social instinct, and was based on the libido theory.[436] Freud discussed the theories of Le Bon, MacDougall, and Trotter. Le Bon's theory of crowds, he said, did not explain the secret of the leader's power, which resides in "Eros, that binds everything together in the world." Libido binds the individual to the leader and induces him to give up his individuality. Besides the transient, unorganized crowds, there are also "durable and artificial crowds," such as the Church and the Army, in which the tie of the individual to the leader is one of love, strengthened by the illusion that the leader loves him. Individuals identify themselves with the leader, and are bound together through their common identification. All of these manifestations of libido, furthermore, cover something more fundamental: the aggressive drives. When a group collapses, aggressiveness is released in the form of outbursts of violence, or the loss of security produces anxiety that takes the form of panic. What actually binds individuals together are the elementary feelings of envy and aggressiveness. When a popular singer attracts a swarm of young women, their common admiration for him is the only thing that keeps them from pulling each other's hair. "Social feeling thus resides in the turning of a previously hostile feeling into a positive attachment in the nature of identification . . . all the individuals would like to be equal but also to be ruled by one person"—an assumption not very far from Hobbes' theory of the origin of society. Freud concluded by pointing out the similarity between these groups of equals with their leader, and the primal horde.

Group Psychology and the Ego obviously was inspired by the collapse of the Hapsburg Empire at the end of 1918, with the panic and distress that followed. But it also inserted itself into the context of a previous trend of "mass psychology," whose origin and history are not generally known. As shown by Dupréel, there had been in Western Europe after the insurrection of the Commune in Paris in 1871 a "wave of anti-democratic pessimism," which was kept alive by the socialist agitation, the strikes, and the bloody riots so frequent at that time.[437] The philosopher Taine turned his activity toward writing a history of the French Revolution, in which special attention was devoted to the riots and collective murders, with an analysis of their social and psychological causes. Taine's findings were developed and systematized by Tarde in France and Sighele in Italy.

Tarde postulated a basic interpsychological process, which he called imitation.[438] Imitation can be conscious or unconscious, it'applies to individuals as well as groups. According to Tarde, the father is the first lord, priest, and model for his son; the son's imitation of the father is the primal phenomenon that lies at the root of society. This imitation does not dwell upon force or cunning, but upon prestige, a phenomenon that Tarde, at first, compared with hypnotism. Later he explained that prestige derives neither from intelligence nor strength of will, but from "an un-analyzable physical action" that "could possibly be related through some invisible link to sexuality."[439] Tarde emphasized the role of the unconscious in mass psychology. He described crowds united by love and others by hatred. As to Sighele, he stressed that no mass phenomena could be understood without an analysis of their historical and social context and also of the specific composition of the given crowds.[440]

These teachings of Tarde, Taine, and Sighele were adopted, over-simplified, and popularized by Le Bon in his *Psychology of Crowds.*[441] Any man within a crowd, Le Bon said, loses his individuality and acquires a parcel of the "crowd soul"; the "crowd soul" is intellectually inferior and shows a kind of intrinsic malignity. This can only be explained through a kind of hypnotic regression to a prehistoric mental stage of mankind. Le Bon applied these concepts of the crowd soul to the psychology of social groups and the vicissitudes of history. This book enjoyed enormous success. Le Bon's theory was considered as indisputable scientific truth by many. One may wonder that Freud took it as starting point for his own theory. As shown by Reiwald, Freud's theories, while contradicting Le Bon, show noteworthy similarities with those of Tarde.[442] What Tarde had called imitation, Freud called identification, and in many regards Freud's ideas appeared to be those of Tarde transposed in psychoanalytic concepts.

In 1930, in *Civilization and Its Discontents,* Freud presented additional views on the origins of civilization.[443] A number of men discovered that if they put limits on the gratification of their instinctual drives, they were able to build a strong, united community. This situation, however, inevitably led to an insolvable conflict between the urges of the individual and the demands of society. The latter increased in the course of civilization's progress, deepening the conflict, and Freud wondered if the demands of contemporary, civilized society did not exceed the individual man's power of repressing his instincts, thus creating a neurosis of civilization. The problem discussed in this essay at times recalls Hobbes, but can be distinctly traced to Nietzsche's *Genealogy of Morals*, and through him to Diderot's *Supplement to the Travel of Bougainville*.[444]

In the same essay, Freud proposed a new hypothesis about the taming of fire. Whenever primitive man came upon fire, he would extinguish it by urination. Owing to the phallic shape of the flames, he experienced an erotic feeling of a homosexual contest. The first man to renounce this erotic pleasure was able to put fire to practical use. "This great cultural conquest was thus the reward for instinctual renunciation." The woman was constituted keeper of the hearth because she was anatomically incapable of extinguishing fire as a man does. In another place Freud suggested that woman was the inventor of clothing because she wanted to hide her shameful lack of a penis; pubic hair inspired the invention of weaving.[445]

Whereas he found religion noxious and philosophy useless, Freud deemed art beneficial to man. But what is the essence of art? Freud defined it as "a combination of the principle of pleasure and the principle of reality" (much as Nietzsche had considered it a fusion of the Dionysian and the Apollonian principles).[446] As an infant, the individual lives entirely according to the principle of pleasure, but the latter gradually recedes in favor of the principle of reality, which will dominate throughout his adult life. The artist maintains the pleasure principle more than others do, but compromises with the reality principle by creating works of art that will gratify the pleasure principle in other men. In a further paper, referring more to the poet than to the artist, Freud emphasized the role of fantasy: predominant in the child, it gradually recedes, but the creative writer is able to retain and convert it into literary work through certain devices, mainly by providing the preliminary pleasure in elements of form.[447] Another of Freud's contributions to esthetics is his analysis of the uncanny, the particular feeling of creeping horror that pervades the works of a writer such as E. T. A. Hoffmann.[448] It sometimes appears in the inexplicable recurrence of events, which, in themselves, may be harmless; sometimes in the belief of a double, or the dread of ghosts or other malevolent beings. A feeling of the uncanny, Freud believed, arises in situations where deeply repressed material or animistic attitudes of childhood are stimulated.

The only piece of art criticism left by Freud was his article on the Moses of Michelangelo, which at first appeared anonymously.[449] Binswanger noted that the method used by Freud in this study belongs to the psychology of expression, which is also one of the first stages in psychoanalytic methodology.[450] As to literary criticism, Freud devoted an eighty-one page monograph to a short novel, *Gradiva,* by Wilhelm Jensen.[451] Freud showed that a psychoanalytic interpretation could be given to the delusions and dreams of the hero of that story, but he did not pursue his interpretations into the personality of the author.

Under the name of "pathographies," Moebius had published a series of monographs purporting to elucidate a writer's thought through an assessment of his heredity, constitution, and life history. It was not long before Freud's disciples wrote similar monographs based on psychoanalytic concepts. Freud himself gave the classical model of these studies with his essay, *A Childhood Memory of Leonardo da Vinci.*

Leonardo da Vinci is generally considered a universal genius who was misunderstood by his contemporaries. In his personality, Freud emphasized three features. First, that his thirst for knowledge led him to neglect his outstanding gifts, and to turn his interest more and more to scientific investigation; second, that being a slow worker, he left numerous sketches, but most of his works remained unfinished; third, his "cool repudiation of sexuality" that caused a presumption of his homosexuality. Freud traced the common root of these three features to Leonardo's infantile sexuality. An illegitimate child, he spent the first three or four years of his life with his forsaken mother until his father, by then married, adopted him. A mother, in such circumstances, is prone to turn her libido onto her infant, thus determining an incestuous attachment in him, in which psychoanalysis sees a possible root of later homosexuality. Actually, no objective records of Leonardo's early childhood are extant, but the artist recorded one early childhood memory: when as an infant he was lying in his cradle, a bird (called *nibbio* in Italian) flew to him, opened his mouth and inserted its tail. This fantasy could have the meaning of a passive kind of sexual perversion, or be a reminiscence of sucking at his mother's breast. The German text utilized by Freud translated *nibbio* as "vulture," and Freud commented that in ancient Egypt, a vulture was the hieroglyph for mother, that the vulture-headed goddess *Mut* (reminiscent of the German *Mutter,* mother) had an androgynous structure and a male organ; that furthermore, in the Middle Ages, the vulture species was considered entirely female, to be impregnated by the wind. All this, said Freud, is reminiscent of infantile sexual theories. Leonardo's infantile sexual curiosity was unusually stimulated because of his family situation, and became the root of his later, insatiable curiosity. His unconscious fixation to the image of his mother can be discerned, according to Freud, in his art masterpieces. Freud assumed that the vulture incident was a symbolic memory of the passionate kisses he received from his mother; that the smile of the Mona Lisa evoked a reminiscence of his mother's enigmatic smile in Da Vinci, so that it appeared in the Gioconda and several other paintings. In the painting of the Madonna and Child with St. Anne, Anne looks as young as Mary, and both are smiling. Freud saw a synthesis here, of Leonardo's childhood, divided between his true mother and his stepmother. Finally, the artist's rebellion against his father was another determinant in Leonardo's scientific research and non-Christian belief.[452]

Freud's essay on Leonardo da Vinci gave rise to conflicting opinions. Rev. Oskar Pfister believed one could detect a vulture as a picture riddle in Leonardo's Madonna and Child with St. Anne. Meyer Schapiro compiled criticisms made by art historians.[453] The word *nibbio*, erroneously translated as "vulture," actually meant a kite. The fantasy of the kite inserting its tail in the infant's mouth was (as shown by parallels in folklore) an omen of inspiration. Previous artists had painted St. Anne and Mary together, looking the same age; the motif of the smiling face belonged to the School of Verrocchio, Leonardo's master. There is no evidence that Leonardo spent his first years alone with his mother; there are reasons, in fact, to assume that he was taken by his father at birth. Some of these arguments have been questioned by K. R. Eissler.[454] Freud's essay on Leonardo da Vinci has been generally admired for its beautiful style and its indefinable charm; it has been compared to the enigmatic smile of the Gioconda. Possibly some of Freud's interpretations of Leonardo applied to what his self-analysis had revealed to him of his own infancy.

One may classify among the pathographies the study of Freud devoted to the case of a German magistrate, Daniel Paul Schreber.[455] A man of unusually high intelligence and ability, Schreber spent ten years in mental institutions on account of a severe mental illness. After his discharge, he published in 1903 a long narrative of his delusions, with the text of the legal reports written about him by the experts. In spite of its great phenomenological interest, this book was a somewhat narrow basis for a pathography; it lacked data about Schreber's family, his childhood, and his life history before his commitment. The illness itself was not exposed in its chronological evolution, but only in the shape it had reached after long years of evolution.[456] Furthermore, the editors had cut out from Schreber's *Memoirs* those parts that would have been the most important from the psychoanalytic point of view. There remained, nonetheless, an inextricable amount of delusional ideas of all kinds. Schreber told how he conversed with the sun, the trees, the birds (which were fragments of deceased persons' souls), how God spoke to him in a dignified German language, how nearly all the organs of his body had been altered, how the end of the world was coming, how God had elected him to save mankind, and so on. Among all these delusions, Freud singled out two particular ones that he held as fundamental: first, Schreber contended that he was in the process of being changed from man to woman, second, he complained of having suffered homosexual assaults on the part of his first physician, the neurologist Flechsig. Freud assumed that repressed homosexuality was the cause of Schreber's paranoid illness. Schreber's homosexual love object had been his father, then Flechsig, later God, or the sun. Freud explained that in repressed homosexuality the sentence "I love him" could be denied in different ways, each one giving rise to a variety of delusions (persecution, erotomania, delusions of jealousy, of grandeur). Fundamental in delusions of persecution was the mechanism of *projection*. The denied sentence "I love him" was replaced by, "I do not love him," "I hate him" . . . "because he hates and persecutes me."

Freud's theory of the homosexual origin of paranoia was adopted by many psychoanalysts, while others felt that it was valid for only a certain form of this illness. Some critics pointed out that Schreber's deviation was transsexuality, rather than homosexuality, and that his mental illness was schizophrenia and not paranoia. They added that even if it was proved that there had been repressed homosexuality, this would not explain the causation of the illness, but only its symptomatic picture. Macalpine and Hunter proposed another psychoanalytic interpretation of the Schreber case: a deep regression to an early stage of undifferentiated libido would bring about the reactivation of infantile procreation fantasies.[457]

Freud also analyzed the case of Christoph Haizmann, a painter of the seventeenth century, who allegedly signed two pacts with the Devil, one signed with ink, and one with his own blood, but succeeded to redeem himself and get back the two pacts from the Devil.[458] On the basis of available documents (including paintings by him and fragments of his diary), Freud concluded that Haizmann, like Schreber, was the prey of a powerful father complex. The Devil was a projection of his hostility against his father, and here too there was a conflict about homosexuality and castration anxiety. Macalpine and Hunter reinterpreted the Haizmann story as they had done for the Schreber case, in the light of the notions of sex confusion and procreation fantasies.[459] Vandendriessche found new documents about Haizmann, but they did not substantially change our knowledge of the case.[460] No critics, as yet, seem to have wondered whether a part of the delusions of Schreber and Haizmann could not be ascribed to exaggeration or mythomania.

A psychoanalytic appraisal of Dostoevski was given by Freud as a foreword to the publication of hitherto unknown drafts of *The Brothers Karamazov*.[461] Freud said that Dostoevski was able to render an unforgettable narrative of a patricide because he himself suffered from a devastating father complex. During these paroxysmal fits where he looked as if he were dead, Dostoevski identified himself with his father such as he wished him to be (that is, dead), and at the same time it was a punishment for that wish. Dostoevski's passion for gambling originated in his self-destructive tendencies, linked with his father complex. "Destiny itself is finally nothing but a late projection of the father," Freud concluded.

Moses and Monotheism, which appeared serially in *Imago* in 1937 and 1938, is neither a pathography, nor a scholarly book, nor a novel.[462]

While admitting that much of it was hypothetical, Freud believed it plausible enough to justify its publication. In summary:

> Freud started with the contention that Moses was not a Hebrew, but an Egyptian of high rank and status. The Egyptian King Akhenaton proclaimed a monotheistic religion, but after his death a counter-revolution fomented by priests reestablished the pagan cults. Having refused to lay aside monotheism, Moses was rejected by the Egyptians and chose the Hebrews as his people. With the help of his followers, the Levites, Moses imparted monotheism to the Jews and led them out of Egypt, to the Sinai Peninsula, where they united with the Midianites, a tribe that worshipped a local petty god named Jahweh. A rebellion arose against Moses and he was killed by his people. About sixty years later, however, the two populations were reunited by a new chief, also named Moses (the two being later confused and considered as one), who formed a compromise of monotheism and Jahweh worship. This dual structure of Hebrew nation and religion contained the germs of the later political secessions and political vicissitudes. The memory of the first Moses was revived in the teachings of subsequent prophets, and the wish for the return of the murdered Moses resulted in the belief of the return of the Messiah. The story of Jesus Christ was a reenactment of the story of the first Moses.

Moses and Monotheism bewildered many of Freud's disciples and provoked indignant protests from Jewish circles. Historians of religion pointed out its errors and impossibilities. It was also recalled that innumerable legends had grown around Moses, from centuries before .Christ to that time. The idea that Moses was an Egyptian had been advanced many times, by Eduard Meyer, among others, whose works were well known to Freud.[463] Much of what Freud advanced could also be traced to Schiller[464] and to Karl Abraham.[465] According to David Bakan, Freud's aim was to ward off anti-Semitism by separating the Mosaic characteristics (the burden of the historical superego) from the image of the Jew, and this only a Jew was able to do.[466] Thus Freud would play the role of "a new Moses who comes down with a new Law dedicated to personal psychological liberty." Another interpretation, as plausible as any, would be that Freud identified himself with the first Moses and his own faithful followers with the Levites, that he viewed his departure from Vienna as the flight of Moses from Egypt, and contemporary psychoanalysis as a mixture of his own doctrine with "impure" pseudoanalytic teachings. (Actually he was concerned by the turn taken by the movement and feared its distortions in the Anglo-Saxon world.) He foresaw prolonged inner strife between the two elements in psychoanalysis, but there would also come prophets to restore it to its original purity.

In spite of his rejection of philosophy and his lack of interest in politics, Freud could not help expressing opinions about many problems of general

interest. A brief mention must be made, at least, of his opinion about war
and peace, and about parapsychological phenomena.

In a letter to Einstein, in September 1932, Freud expressed the feeling
that the greatest obstacle to the creation of a central organization to
secure peace lies in the existence of aggressive and destructive instincts in
man.[467] The death instinct can be turned inward or outward. Not infrequently it is turned outward to preserve the individual. Confronting these
instincts are the various forms of libido that can be used to counteract
destructive instincts to a certain extent; however, Eros and the death instinct
are always alloyed with each other. Another would be the formation of a
superior class of independent and fearless intellectuals, able to guide the
masses into the path of reason.

For a long time Freud remained sceptical in regard to parapsychological
phenomena, but in 1911 he became a member of the Society for Psychical
Research.[468] In September 1913, he told Lou Andréas-Salome[469] of
strange cases of thought transmission that had come to his knowledge, but
he did not publish them, along with other similar cases, until much later.[470]
Freud contended that the psychoanalytic transference situation opened a
new approach toward the exploration of telepathic and kindred phenomena.
His attitude toward parapsychology remained a cautious one, as shown
by the interview he granted to Tabori in 1935.[471] Freud compared discussions about so-called occult phenomena with an argument about the composition of the interior of the earth. We know nothing for certain, but infer
that it is composed of heavy metals at very high temperature. A theory
that it is composed of water saturated with carbonic acid does not appear
logical, but would deserve some discussion. However, should anybody come
up with a theory that the inside of the earth is made of marmalade, this
would not be worthy of any scientific attention.

A note jotted down by Freud in 1938, perhaps his last thought, has the
enigmatic simplicity of a Delphic oracle: "Mysticism—the obscure self-
perception of the realm outside the Ego, the Id."[472]

Freud's Sources

The sources of Freud's psychoanalysis are multiple and still incompletely known. A man of great scientific and literary culture who stood
at the crossroads of the main cultural currents of his time, an omnivorous
reader, able to grasp quickly the interest of new ideas in order to adopt them
and give them original form, Freud was the author of a powerful synthesis in
which it is an almost hopeless task to discern what came from outside
and what was his personal contribution. In fact, many of Freud's theories
were known before him or belonged to contemporary trends. Freud drew
from his masters, his colleagues, his rivals, his associates, his patients, and
his disciples. "A good writer," Nietzsche said, "has not only his own mind,
but the minds of his friends as well."[473] A great part of the present book
was devoted to authors and systems of thought, which, according to the

point of view, could be called sources or precursors of Freud. In the following we shall try to give a succinct list of these sources, insofar as they are known today.

The first and main source of any creative thinker lies in his own personality. Freud possessed that kind of asceticism that makes the scientific researcher, and a superior command of his native language, which (together with the keen interest for the secret life of people and the psychological intuition) produces a great writer. He was also the good dreamer who could illustrate *The Interpretation of Dreams* with his oneiric productions. Above all it is (as we believe) from his creative illness that the main tenets of psychoanalysis originated: the notions of child sexuality, of the libido with its successive stages, fixations, and transformation in anxiety, of the Oedipus situation, the family romance, the theory of dreams, parapraxes, and screen memories, the concept of symptoms as vicarious realization of wishes, the notion that fantasies play a major role in neuroses and in poetical creation, and that these early fantasies, as well as genuine early sexual experiences, play a major role in the destiny of the individual.[474]

Freud's immediate masters, Brücke, Meynert, and Exner, were the promoters of a positivist, strictly scientific approach to the study of neurophysiology and neuropsychiatry. However, as we have seen, these men indulged in the contemporary trend of brain mythology. They produced vast speculative constructions, which, apparently unknown to them, were nothing but the late resurgence of the philosophy of nature. Here was the source of Freud's "Model of the Mind" of 1895, whose influence can be followed in his later metapsychological constructions. Maria Dorer has emphasized the influence of Meynert on Freud's theories.[475] Meynert's basic assumption was that the phylogenetically older parts of the brain were the center of involuntary movements and were controlled by the cortex, which appeared at a more recent stage of evolution, and was the site of the ego-building function. Meynert distinguished a primary ego issuing from the immediate functioning of the cortical centers, and a secondary ego resulting from the activity of the association bundles. Meynert thought that when the activity of more recent centers was disturbed, the activity of the phylogenetically older ones gained more importance. In this way he explained the origin of the ideas of grandeur and persecution. He considered these delusions as a psychological manifestation of two basic instincts, attack and defense, which the illness had brought to the fore. Freud's concept of regression was built on a similar pattern. We have seen that Meynert and Freud disagreed about hypnosis; Meynert was one of those who strongly questioned its efficacy and objected to its use on the grounds of its erotic nature; Freud did not accept these arguments, but he later asserted similar ideas of his own. Freud also adopted ideas previously taught by Meynert, about the psychogenesis of sexual perversion, and particularly of homosexuality.[476]

Among Freud's immediate masters were also Moritz Benedikt and Josef Breuer. The influence of Breuer was of such a nature that he was sometimes considered the cofounder of psychoanalysis. We have seen how the misunderstood case, and failed cure, of Anna O. inspired Freud to search for a theory and treatment of neuroses. It would seem that Breuer also inspired Freud with some of his brain mythology. Benedikt's role in the origin of psychoanalysis has been generally overlooked, though a footnote in Breuer and Freud's *Preliminary Communication* ought to have attracted attention.[477] We have seen how Benedikt[478] taught the importance of the secret life, daydreams, fantasies, suppressed wishes and ambitions, the importance of the sexual element in hysteria and other neuroses, and how he achieved brilliant psychotherapeutic cures by relieving the patients from their pathogenic secrets.[479]

Maria Dorer has shown that one of the main sources of psychoanalysis was the psychology of Herbart, which was predominant in Austria at the time of Freud's youth.[480] Herbart taught the dynamic concept of a fluctuating threshold between the conscious and the unconscious, of conflicts between representations that struggle with each other to gain access to the conscious and are repressed by stronger ones but strive to return, or else produce an indirect effect in consciousness, and the notion of chains of associations that cross each other at nodal points, but also of "free emerging associations," the idea that mental processes as a whole are ruled by a striving for equilibrium. All this is to be found in psychoanalysis, though sometimes in modified form. Whether Freud read Herbart is not known, but it is sure that he had been introduced to Herbart's psychology while at the Sperläum, through Lindner's textbook.[481] The psychology of Griesinger and Meynert was also Herbartian to a great extent. Freud also refers to Griesinger's idea that in certain hallucinatory psychoses the patient denies the event that has called forth the mental illness.[482]

A more obscure problem is that of the possible influence of Romantic psychiatry upon Freud.[483] We have seen that Reil taught that many mental diseases had a psychogenic cause and could be cured by psychotherapy. Ideler considered the passions as the main cause of psychoses (especially frustrated sexual love). He told of the flight into illness, contended that the origin of delusions can be traced back to childhood, and was a believer in the psychotherapy of psychoses. Heinroth emphasized the noxious effect of guilt feelings, and utilized a differentiated psychotherapy. Neumann pointed out the relationship between anxiety and frustrated drives; he explained the hidden sexual meaning of the various types of delusions and psychotic behavior. It is open to question to what extent these authors had been forgotten in central Europe by the end of the nineteenth century. Probably during that century there always flowed an undercurrent of Romantic psychiatry, which was to be revived in the 1890's. Much of what, in retrospect, looks to us as startling novelties in the theories of psychosis of men such as Bleuler, Freud, and Jung, appeared to their contemporaries as a return to old-fashioned psychiatric conceptions.

The origin of psychoanalysis cannot be understood without taking into account several scientific trends of the last decades of the nineteenth century. Three of them have been described in previous chapters. One was the new science of sexual pathology that was given its decisive impetus by Krafft-Ebing.[484] The second was the psychological study of dreams,[485] and the third the exploration of the unconscious.[486]

Another important source of Freudian thinking, the "unmasking trend," deserves to be mentioned here with more detail, because it has been generally overlooked. It is the systematic search for deception and self-deception and the uncovering of underlying truth (currently known in France as *démystification*). This trend seems to have started with the French moralists of the seventeenth century. La Rochefoucauld in his *Maxims,* unmasked virtuous attitudes and acts as disguised manifestations of *amour-propre* (in today's language narcissism). Schopenhauer described love as a mystification of the individual through the Genius of the Species, meaning that the qualities ascribed to the beloved are illusions, issuing from the unconscious will of the species. Karl Marx stated that the opinions of an individual, unknown to him, are conditioned by social class, which is determined by economic factors. War and religion are "mystifications," in which the ruling classes deceive the lower classes and themselves. Nietzsche, who was an admirer of both the French moralists and of Schopenhauer, was another exponent of the unmasking trend. He untiringly pursued the manifestations of the will to power under its many disguises, and those of resentment under the guise of idealism and love of mankind. He emphasized man's need for "fictions." In contemporary literature, "unmasking" became an overdone theme. In Ibsen's plays, for instance, some of the characters live in complete unawareness of the ugly reality behind the facades of their lives, until it is slowly or brutally revealed. The destruction of their illusions then brings a catastrophe as in *Rosmersholm,* and *The Wild Duck.* In *Ghosts* (1881), Ibsen dramatized the idea that many of our free and voluntary actions are but the reenactment of actions performed by our parents—"we live in a world of ghosts." Ibsen's concept of ghosts was quoted several times by Freud in *The Interpretation of Dreams* and can be recognized in his concept of transference. The essayist Max Nordau wrote books denouncing the "conventional lies of civilization." The economist Vilfredo Pareto emphasized the importance of self-deception in social and economic phenomena.[487] Hanns Gross, the founder of judicial psychology, conducted inquiries in parapraxes and in the manifestations of concealed or repressed sexual feelings.[488]

Another major source of psychoanalysis was the previous dynamic psychiatry, from which it drew much more than is generally believed. It will suffice to refer to its five characteristic features.[489] First, hypnosis, the main approach, was practiced for some time by Freud, and psychoanalytic technique came about through gradual modification of hypnosis.[490] Second, the first dynamic psychiatry devoted particular interest to certain clinical pictures, particularly to hysteria, and it was on hysterical patients that Freud made his most decisive investigations. Third, the first dynamic psychiatry devised two models of the human mind; one based on the coexistence of conscious and unconscious psyches, and the other in the form of a cluster of sub-personalities. Freud began with a model of the first type, and then adopted the cluster type model of the ego, id, and superego. Fourth, the first dynamic psychiatry based its theories of the pathogenesis of nervous illness on the concepts of an undetermined fluid, of mental energy, and of the autonomous activity of split fragments of personality. There is a recognizable link between these concepts and those of libido and unconscious complexes. Finally, the essential psychothera-peutic tool of the magnetizers and the hypnotists was rapport, and we have seen that psychoanalytic transference was one among the various meta-morphoses of rapport.

In the 1880's the first dynamic psychiatry had finally been given an official stamp of approval by Charcot, of whom Freud proudly claimed to have been the disciple, and by Bernheim, whom Freud visited in Nancy. It is not easy to evaluate Charcot's influence on Freud. As previously men-tioned, this influence seems to have been mostly of a personal nature, in the fashion of an existential encounter. Freud had an idealized picture of the French master and did not stay at the Salpêtrière long enough to realize that Charcot's demonstrations with hypnotized hysterics lacked any scientific value. Freud exaggerated the importance that Charcot ascribed to dissimilar heredity (degeneration in the medical jargon of the time) in the etiology of hysteria; and he apparently did not read Richer's book where it is shown that hysterical attacks were reenactments of psychic trauma that were mostly of sexual nature (an idea that Freud was to later develop as his own). All this shows once more that the influence of a master often exerts itself less in his factual teachings than in the distorted perceptions of the disciples' minds. This is also true of the influence of the Nancy school upon Freud, who thus ascribed to Liébeault the idea that "the dream is the guardian of sleep," a statement in direct opposition to Liébeault's theory of sleep. The phenomenon of patients giving rational explanations for obeying posthypnotic suggestions was well known; Freud did not have to go to Nancy to learn it from Bernheim. Bernheim's procedure of making his subjects recover the memory of what had happened under hypnosis did not have the significance attributed to it by Freud, because in Bernheim's demonstration this occurred immediately after a short and light hypnotic state. It is to Freud's credit that this gave him the idea of having his patients recover long-forgotten memories in a waking state. This is another example of a discovery through a misinterpretation of the facts.

The influence of Janet on Freud is a controversial problem that has never been objectively studied. In his early writings, Freud acknowledged Janet's priority in regard to the discovery of the role of "subconscious fixed ideas" (in Janet's terms) in the etiology of hysterical symptoms, and of their subsequent cure through "catharsis" (in Breuer and Freud's words). When Breuer and Freud published their *Preliminary Communication* in 1893, Janet's priority was of seven years, and he had published six or seven relevant case histories.[491] To those contemporaries acquainted with both French and German psychiatric literature, Janet's priority and the similarity of his and Breuer and Freud's procedure were indisputable. Janet also anticipated Freud in showing, from the beginning, that the mere recovery of the traumatic memory did not suffice and that the "psychological system" (the "complex") had to be "dissociated" ("worked through," in Freudian terms). Janet's influence on Freud is obvious in the *Studies in Hysteria*, even in its terminology; Freud used Janet's words "psychological misery" and "psychological analysis." In 1896 Freud called his system "psychoanalysis" to distinguish it from Janet's "psychological analysis," and he began to emphasize the differences between his ideas and those of Janet. In so doing, Freud gave a distorted picture of Janet's concepts by asserting that Janet's theory of hysteria was based on the concept of "degeneration." Janet actually taught that hysteria resulted from the interaction in differing proportions of constitutional factors and psychic traumata, and this is exactly what Freud later called a "complementary series." Freud emphasized the role of repression in the pathogenesis of hysterical symptoms, but overlooked the "narrowing of the field of consciousness" in Janet's theory. Janet contended that "Freud calls 'repression' what I called 'narrowing of the field of consciousness,' "[492] and it is noteworthy that the two can be traced back to Herbart,[493] for whom they were two aspects of the same phenomenon. Freud also criticized Janet's concept of hysteria resulting from a weakness of the "function of synthesis." A similar concept, however, was later adopted by psychoanalysis under the name of "ego weakness." Janet's shifting from the study of "subconscious" phenomena to that of "psychological tension" anticipated the shifting of psychoanalysis from "depth psychology" to "ego psychology." Janet's "function of reality" was transposed into psychoanalysis under the name of "reality principle." In regard to the psychoanalytic technique, there is a certain analogy between the "automatic talking" used by Janet in the case of Madame D. and Freud's method of free association.[494] A more remarkable similarity is that between psychoanalytic transference and Janet's systematic use of those varieties of rapport between therapist and patient that he called "somnambulic influence" and "need for direction,"[495] a similarity that has been recognized by Jones.[496] Indeed, it is difficult to study the initial periods of Janet's psychological analysis and of Freud's psychoanalysis without coming to the conclusion, expressed by Régis and Hesnard, "The methods and concepts of Freud were modeled after those of Janet, of whom he seems to have inspired himself constantly"—until the paths of the two diverged.⁴⁹⁷

Freud always acknowledged the great writers as his masters: the Greek Tragedians, Shakespeare, Goethe, and Schiller. No doubt he received much inspiration from them, but the influence of writers of lesser magnitude on his thought should not be forgotten, particularly that of Heine, Börne,⁴⁹⁸ and Lichtenberg.⁴⁹⁹ Psychoanalysis shows a definite analogy with certain contemporary literary trends, such as the Young Vienna circle, neo-Romanticism, and, as already mentioned, Ibsen's way of unmasking conventional lies and unawareness.

The philosophical sources of Freud are many, but in spite of many investigations, they are not yet well known.⁵⁰⁰ Although Freud repeatedly expressed contempt for philosophy, and never accepted the idea of making a philosophy of psychoanalysis, he had a distinct philosophical background that was revealed in his weltanschauung as well as in the way he psychologized certain philosophical concepts.

Freud was exposed from his youth to the kind of philosophical thinking prevalent in Europe after 1850, which claimed to reject any sort of metaphysics and to study the world only from a scientific point of view. In fact, this rejection of philosophy is tantamount to a specific philosophy: Scientism, the doctrine according to which knowledge of the world could be acquired only through science. But since science has its limits, a large part of reality (perhaps the greatest part) is unknowable. Logically, positivism should imply agnosticism, since the existence of God cannot be proved or disproved by science. However, Freud, like many other contemporary scientists, was a resolute atheist. This mixture of positivism, scientism, and atheism is revealed in Freud's *Future of an Illusion*.

Curiously enough, this extreme positivist thinking led to a resurgence of the philosophy of nature in a disguised form during the second half of the nineteenth century. The tenants of positivism, in their zeal to clear science of any vestige of metaphysics, expelled the soul from psychology, vitalism from biology, and finality from evolution. Neurophysiologists asserted that they could explain mental processes in terms of—extant or hypothetical— brain structures (this was the brain mythology already referred to), or even exclusively in terms of physical and chemical processes. These physiologists ignored Bichat's dictum that "Physiology is no more the physics of animals than astronomy is the physiology of the stars."⁵⁰¹ The principles of conservation and transformation of energy were transposed into physiology and psychology as the basis of speculative constructions that could be called Energetics Mythology. Darwin's hypothesis that the evolution of the species is directed by the hereditary transmission of chance modifications through the struggle of life and the elimination of the unit became a scientific dogma. It remained for Haeckel to transform Darwinism into a pseudo-religion under the name of Monism. Freud was immersed in that kind of philosophical thinking. We have seen how Meynert's brain mythology, Brücke's energetics mythology, and Exner's combination of both, led Freud to build his *Outline of a Scientific Psychology* of 1895.

Darwin's influence on Freud has been treated in a previous chapter.[502] Let it be recalled that Darwin introduced a psychology centered around the instincts, with special reference to aggressive and love instincts. Among Darwin's proofs of the theory of evolution were phenomena of "reversion," which Freud, in the psychological field, termed "regression." Darwin also sketched a biological theory of the origin of society and morals. Freud took from him the picture of primitive men as brutish beings living in bands under the tyranny of an old man (the cruel old Father of *Totem and Taboo*). Lombroso, too, shared the idea that prehistoric man was a brutish and murderous being. Lombroso believed that the "born criminal" was a resurgence of that primitive man, and Freud's picture of the unconscious of the civilized man was not very different from Lombroso's picture of the primitive man. To the Darwinian doctrine Haeckel added his so-called fundamental biogenetic law,[503] which Freud seems to have taken for granted. We have also seen how Karl Marx' patterns of thought could be recognized in certain aspects of psychoanalysis.[504]

The only philosopher whose lectures Freud attended was the promoter of a quite different philosophy, Franz Brentano. Brentano came from an illustrious family that included the poet Clemens Brentano, and was a brother of the noted economist Lujo Brentano. He became a Dominican priest and professor of philosophy at Würzburg, but as he could not accept the dogma of the infallibility of the Pope, he left the Church and came to Vienna to teach philosophy as a Privat Dozent (a unique example of a reversal of the usual university career). Brentano taught a new psychology based on the concept of intentionality, which he had revived from medieval scholastic philosophy. Rudolf Steiner, who was one of his auditors, said that Brentano was a perfect logician to whom every concept had to be perfectly clear and have its definite place in a dialectic argumentation, but he sometimes gave the impression that his thinking was a world in itself, outside reality. Brentano was a brilliant speaker, and the distinguished ladies of Vienna swarmed to his lectures. Among his auditors were men of such varied interest as Edmund Husserl, Thomas Masaryk, Franz Kafka, Rudolf Steiner, and Sigmund Freud. Brentano was a noted figure in Viennese social life. Dora Stockert-Meynert described him as resembling a Byzantine Christ, soft spoken, punctuating his eloquence with gestures of inimitable grace, "the figure of a prophet with the spirit of a man of the world."[505] Brentano was endowed with a prodigious linguistic gift, and in addition to his fame as an erudite and original philosopher, he was known for his extemporization of elaborate plays on words. He imagined a new kind of riddle he called *dal-dal-dal* that became the rage in Viennese salons, was imitated, and many of which he published anonymously. Freud mentioned them in a footnote in *Jokes and the Unconscious*; it is the sole mention of Brentano in his writings. Any evidence that Freud might have been influenced by Brentano could be produced only by carefully studying the writings of Freud and finding there ideas specific to Brentano. James Ralph Barclay did so and concluded that several of Freud's concepts could be traced to Brentano.[506] The notion of intentionality appears in Freud in the modified form of a psychic energy channeled toward instinctual goals and wish-fulfillment. Brentano's "intentional existence" became Freud's "cathexis." To Freud, as to Brentano, perception was not a passive process but an activity endowed with psychic energy. The evolution of primary process to secondary process, as described by Freud, is also traceable to Brentano.

The influence of Romantic philosophy upon Freud cannot be traced directly either, though it is unmistakably there. We have told in a previous chapter of the similarities between Romantic thinking, Goethe, and Von Schubert, on one hand, and some of Freud's concepts on the other.[507] The main influence, however, exerted on Freud by the philosophy of nature stemmed from its two epigones, Bachofen and Fechner.[508] A close parallel can be drawn between Bachofen's stages of evolution of human society and the Freudian stages of libido. Freud, however, never mentions Bachofen. In regard to Fechner, it should be recalled that Freud repeatedly quoted him and took from him the topographical concept of the mind, the concept of mental energy, the principle of pleasure-unpleasure, of constancy, of repetition, and possibly the idea of the predominance of the destructive instinct over Eros. Thus the main concepts of Freud's metapsychology derive from Fechner.

However, the closest approach to psychoanalysis is to be found in the philosophers of the unconscious, Carus, von Hartmann, and particularly Schopenhauer and Nietzsche. For those familiar with the latter two philosophers, there cannot be the slightest doubt that Freud's thought echoed theirs. Thomas Mann[509] said that psychoanalytic concepts were Schopenhauer's ideas "translated from metaphysics into psychology." F. W. Foerster[510] went so far as to say that no one should deal with psychoanalysis before having thoroughly studied Schopenhauer. Such a study would show psychoanalysts that they are even more right than they themselves believe. The same is even more true of Nietzsche, whose ideas pervade psychoanalysis, and whose influence is obvious, even in Freud's literary style. This has not escaped the attention of some psycho-analysts. Wittels, for instance, spoke of "Nietzsche's division into Dionysian and Apollonian, which is almost completely identical with that of the primary and the secondary function."[511] Freud in his celebrated paper on the "Criminals From a Sense of Guilt" noted that Nietzsche had described the same individuals under the name of "the pale criminals."[512] Typically Nietzschean are the concept of the self-deception of consciousness by the unconscious and by emotional thinking, the vicissitudes of instincts (their combinations, conflicts, displacements, sublimations, regressions, and turnings against oneself), the energy load of representations, the self-destructive drives in man, the origin of conscience and morals through the turning inward of aggressive drives, resentment and neurotic guilt feelings, the origin of civilization in the repression of instincts, not to speak of the atttacks against contemporary mores and religion.[513]

The enumeration of Freud's sources should also take into account his patients and his disciples. Examples have been given in the preceding chapters of this book, illustrating the role played by patients in the history of dynamic psychiatry. Freud, too, learned much from several of his patients. It was one of them, Elisabeth von R., who suggested to him the procedure of free association. How many other suggestions he received from other patients is not known. But one man, at least, played an important role as an exemplary patient from whom Freud learned very much (like Janet from Madeleine). This patient became famous under the name of the Wolf-Man. A summary follows:

The twenty-three-year-old man arrived in Vienna at the beginning of 1910 and started an analytic treatment with Freud. The son of a wealthy Russian landowner, he was intelligent, lucid, kind-hearted, but afflicted with abulia to an extraordinary degree, which made him unable to accomplish anything in life. Actually, this case must have appeared less strange in Russia than in the rest of Europe; it was exactly the picture of that condition which in Russian is called *oblomovshtchina*,[514] a condition that was not exceptional in the sons of wealthy landowners, who led a thoroughly passive, idle life. The patient was called the Wolf-Man on account of a terrifying dream of wolves he had at the age of 3½. Because of his unusually passive attitude in the analytic situation, as in the rest of his life, there was no progress during four years, until Freud set a term to the treatment and declared it would be terminated in June 1914. This decision brought a rapid improvement and the patient was able to return to Russia. His case was of enormous interest to Freud because of the amount of material that emerged, some of which confirmed Freud's own theories while contradicting those of Adler and Jung. But some was also quite new and sounded almost incredible to him. Freud published, in 1918, an abstract of the case, enlarged in a further edition, but never the whole case history.[515] When the Wolf-Man fled to Vienna after losing his fortune in the Bolshevik revolution, Freud analyzed him gratuitously for a few months and organized a subcription, so that the man could live in Vienna with his wife, and later receive supplementary psychoanalytic treatment from Mrs. Ruth Mack Brunswick.[516] The Wolf-Man became a well-known figure in psychoanalytic circles, and a kind of expert in psychoanalytic problems. No doubt he played a significant role in Freud's evolution to "metapsychology," and he also helped him to understand the phenomenon of counter-transference.

Another problem in need of clarification is the influence of Freud's disciples upon the thinking of their master. It is certain that Freud drew many ideas from Stekel, Adler, Ferenczi, Abraham, Rank, Silberer, Pfister, Jung, and others. Individual psychologists stress the fact that in 1908 Adler proposed the concept of a primary aggressive drive, which Freud denied but adopted under another form in 1920; he also took over from Adler the concepts of confluence of drives (which originated from Nietzsche). Jung introduced into psychoanalysis the terms "complex" and "imago," emphasized the idea of the little boy's identification with his father, stimulated Freud's interest in the study of myths, and also forwarded the institution of compulsory training analysis for the future psychoanalyst. Actually, it is practically impossible to discern the part that disciples play in the shaping of a master's ideas. Not only do disciples bring new advances, but their particular interests, their questions, and the challenge brought by their contradiction of the master's opinions, all stand beyond the reach of any complete appreciation.

It is quite possible that further, to this date undetected, sources of Freud will be discovered. An attempt in that direction was made by David Bakan, who claimed to have traced the connection between Freud and the Cabalistic tradition.[517] Every Jew, Bakan said, whether he learns Hebrew or not, will inevitably absorb something of the Jewish mystical tradition, and this was even more so for a Jew of Galician extraction such as Freud, whose parents and ancestors had been long steeped in the currents of Hasidism. In the rather stormy history of Jewish mysticism, Freudian psychoanalysis would thus appear as one among its many vicissitudes. The Cabalistic thinking is pervaded by a sense of mystery and power, aims at extracting hidden meanings from the Scriptures, and teaches a kind of metaphysics of sex. According to Bakan, the reigning anti-Semitism caused Freud to hide his Jewish identity, so that he presented a derivation of Jewish mysticism in a veiled manner in his writings. An objective scrutiny of the facts shows, however, that Bakan considerably exaggerated the intensity of anti-Semitism in Vienna in Freud's youth and mature years, and many of his interpretations of Freud's works are debatable. To be sure, some of the analogies he draws between psychoanalytic concepts (notably those of sexuality) and cabalistic teachings are striking, but the matter is more complex than this. There is no evidence that Freud ever had cognizance of Jewish mystical writings. On the other hand, cabalistic metaphysics of sex is but one episode of a trend of sexual mysticism whose history is not well known. It is a wide field, of which we find major and minor representatives before and contemporary to Freud.

Let us remember that Schopenhauer's philosophy was, to a large extent, a brand of sexual mysticism among several others. Two later representatives of that trend were acquainted with Freud—Wilhelm Fliess and Otto Weininger. Wilhelm Fliess combined sexual mysticism with a mysticism of numbers. As we have seen, Fliess contended to have found a correlation between the nasal mucosa and the genital organs, and that he had discovered the fundamental bisexuality of humans.[518] In both men and women there were both male and female physiological components, in each there was a law of periodicity based on the cipher twenty-eight for the female component, and twenty-three for the male. By using the two numbers in various combinations, Fliess was able to compute, in retrospect, the occurrence of any biological event. During those years, Freud and Fliess were enthusiastic about each other's theories. Fliess later completed and perfected his own. There was an acrimonious dispute between Fliess and Weininger about the priority of the fundamental bisexual theory; a strange illusion in both of them, since the theory was far from new. It was characteristic of the times that Fliess was criticized for his nasal-genital theory and his numerology, but not for his pansexualism.[519] As to Otto Weininger, his celebrated book, *Sex and Character,* was the outline of a metaphysical system centered around the concept of the fundamental bisexuality of the living being.[520] In the light of that basic principle, Weininger attempted to find answers to unsolved philosophical problems. The sexual mysticism that pervaded the intellectual atmosphere in Vienna at the end of the nineteenth and the beginning of the twentieth century even expanded over the new science of sexual pathology. We have seen that certain authors romanticized sexual perversions, insisting on the unheard-of emotional sufferings of sexual deviants.[521] Nothing is more remote from the truth than the usual assumption that Freud was the first to introduce novel sexual theories at a time when anything sexual was "taboo". It is noteworthy that other systems of sexual mysticism developed contemporary to Freud, but quite independently from him. In Russia, Vassili Rozanov, the promoter of sexual transcendentalism, taught the holiness of sex, which he identified with God.[522] To summarize:

The sexual act, he said, is the center of existence and the moment when man becomes a god. Sex is the metaphysical source of the mind, the soul, and religion. Ancient oriental religious and primitive Hebraism he called Sun religions, because they were earthly and worldly, exhalted procreation and fertility, the continuity of the family, and the perpetuation of the species. Ancient Egyptian civilization was "a sort of phallic lyricism." Christianity, that teaches asceticism, chastity and virginity, is a religion of death. Life is the home; the home must be warm, nice, and round like a womb. Homosexuals created the Greek civilization and were the greatest geniuses. Prostitution is "the most social phenomenon, to a certain extent the prototype of sociality; . . . the first States were born of the instincts of women toward prostitution." Rozanov interpreted writers through their intimate lives (their "under-clothing," as he said); his extensive sexual symbolism led him to see the phallus everywhere in nature.[523]

Another much-discussed system of sexual mysticism was that of Winthuis.

The Catholic missionary Joseph Winthuis,[524] who worked among the Gunantuna tribe in New Guinea, startled ethnologic circles with a book, *The Two-Sexed Being.*[525] He said that the Gunantuna language contained a great number of words and idioms with a double meaning, that these people also had a sign language, every gesture of which had a sexual meaning, and a language of pictorial symbols based on two fundamental lines: straight (the phallus) and curved (the vagina). Having recorded thirty seemingly inoffensive songs of the Gunantuna, Winthuis found that twenty-nine of them had a hidden meaning so crude that he felt obliged to translate them in Latin rather than German. Winthuis concluded that the primitive mind is pervaded with sexuality. He then evolved a theory of primitive religion as a worship of a bisexual god, a theory that he gradually extended to all primitive populations, to prehistoric peoples, and to the history of religion as a whole.[526] The essence of that religion was the belief in and worship of a bisexual god. Sexuality in that religion is sacred, because the sexual act is a repetition of the primordial event by which the bisexual god created the world, and is thus a perpetuation of the divine act of creation in the name of God, and by his order. Violent polemics arose around those theories, which Winthuis defended with almost fanatical conviction.

One may wonder about the similarities and possible connection between cabalistic mysticism, Schopenhauer's metaphysics of Sexus, Fliess' and Weininger's systems, Rozanov's sexual transcendentalism, and Winthuis' alleged discovery of a universal worship of a bisexual god. Unfortunately, sexual mysticism is one of the least-explored trends in the history of ideas, and it would be premature to attempt to evaluate the role it played in the cultural atmosphere in which Freud's psychoanalysis grew.

In this incomplete enumeration of Freud's sources, we may see that they belong to three distinct periods of unequal length. In the first period Freud drew directly or indirectly from his masters and the numerous authors he read. In the second and relatively short, period of his self-analysis, Freud learned primarily from himself. In the third period, which extended from 1902 to his death, Freud learned mostly from a few privileged patients and from his disciples.

The Influence of Freud

An objective appraisal of the influence of Freud is inordinately difficult. The story is too recent, distorted by legend, and all the facts have not yet come to light.

The consensus is that Freud exerted a powerful influence, not only on psychology and psychiatry, but on all the fields of culture and that it has gone so far as to change our way of life and our concept of man. A more intricate question pertains to the divergencies that arise as soon as one tries to assess the extent that that influence was beneficial or not. On one side are those who include Freud among the liberators of the human spirit, and who even think that the future of mankind depends on whether it will accept or discard the teachings of psychoanalysis.[527] On the other side are those who claim that the effect of psychoanalysis has been disastrous. La Piere, for instance, claims that Freudianism ruined the ethics of individualism, self-discipline, and responsibility that prevailed among the Western world.[528]

Any attempt to give an objective answer to these two questions—namely of the extent and nature of the influence of psychoanalysis—has to face three great difficulties.

First: as in the case of Darwin, the historical importance of a theory is not restricted to what it originally was in the mind of its author, but also of the extensions, adjunctions, interpretations, and distortions of that theory.[529] Thus, an evaluation of Freud's influence should begin with a historical account of the Freudian school and the various trends that issued from it: the orthodox Freudians, the more original successors (for instance, the promoters of ego psychoanalysis), the deviant schools proper, with their own schisms and deviant branches, and those other schools (Adler and Jung), which were founded on radically different basic principles, though as a response to psychoanalysis. And, last but not least, one should take into account the distorted pseudo-Freudian concepts that have been widely vulgarized through the newspapers, magazines, and popular literature.

Second: a still greater difficulty arises from the fact that from the beginning, psychoanalysis has grown in an atmosphere of legend, with the result that an objective appraisal will not be possible before the true historical facts are completely separated from the legend. It would be invaluable to know the starting point of the Freudian legend and the factors that brought it to its present development. Unfortunately the scientific study of legends, of their thematic structure, their growth, and their causes, is one of the least-known provinces of science[530] and to this date nothing has been written in regard to Freud that could be compared to Etiemble's study of the legend that grew around the poet Rimbaud.[531] A rapid glance at the Freudian legend reveals two main features. The first is the theme of the solitary hero struggling against a host of enemies, suffering "the slings and arrows of outrageous fortune" but triumphing in the end. The legend considerably exaggerates the extent and role of anti-Semitism, of the hostility of the academic world, and of alleged Victorian prejudices. The second feature of the Freudian legend is the blotting out of the greatest part of the scientific and cultural context in which psychoanalysis developed, hence the theme of the absolute originality of the achievements, in which the hero is credited with the achievements of his predecessors, associates, disciples, rivals, and contemporaries.

The legend discarded, we are permitted to see the facts in a different light. Freud is shown as having an average career of the contemporary academic man in central Europe, a career whose beginnings were only slightly hampered by anti-Semitism, and with no more setbacks than many others. He lived in a time when scientific polemics had a more vehement tone than today, and he never suffered the degree of hostility as did men such as Pasteur and Ehrlich.[532] The current legend, on the other hand, attributes to Freud much of what belongs, notably, to Herbart, Fechner, Nietzsche, Meynert, Benedikt, and Janet, and overlooks the work of previous explorers of the unconscious, dreams, and sexual pathology. Much of what is credited to Freud was diffuse current lore, and his role was to crystallize these ideas and give them an original shape.

We now come to the third great difficulty in appraising the extent and nature of the influence exerted by psychoanalysis. Many authors have attempted to make an inventory of the impact of Freud's ideas upon normal and abnormal psychology, sociology, anthropology, criminology, art, the theater, and movies, as well as philosophy, religion, education, and mores. We shall not attempt to reiterate these inquiries, nor even to summarize them, but must point out a fact that has been sometimes overlooked: psychoanalysis itself was from the beginning linked to other preexisting or contemporary trends of a more general nature. Around 1895 the profession of neuropsychiatrist had become fashionable, there was an active search for new psychotherapeutic methods, and men such as Bleuler and Moebius were trying to "re-psychologize" psychiatry—Freud's first publications appeared as manifestations of this new course. In the same period there was an intensive development of sexual psychopathology—Freud's libido theory was one among many novelties in that field. We have already mentioned the affinities between early psychoanalysis and the literary works of Ibsen, Schnitzler, the Young-Vienna group, and the neo-Romanticists, and to these must be added the avant-garde movements that arose later, namely the Futurists, Dadaists, and Surrealists.[533] Freud's open proclamation of atheism was in tune with the attitude of many contemporary scientists and brought him the favor of Haeckel's *Monisten Bund*.[534] His system was judged materialistic enough to be adopted by Soviet Russian psychologists before it was superseded by Pavlovian psychiatry.[535] World War I gave rise to a "decline of the West" trend of which Freud's *Reflections on War and Death* were but one of many manifestations.[536] The disasters of World War I and the impending catastrophe of World War II compelled thinkers to search for ways of saving the world.[537] The task of psychotherapy was now to give the individual a means of tolerating tensions and anxiety, hence the shift of psychoanalysis from depth psychology to ego psychoanalysis.[538]

However, this was not all, because in the meantime the progress of technology had inaugurated the affluent society. To a system based on hard work and intense competition that social Darwinism had given its ideology succeeded a system based on mass consumption with a hedonistic-utilitarian philosophy. This is the society that enthusiastically adopted Freudian psychoanalysis, often in its more distorted form. The facts brought by La Piere in his book, *The Freudian Ethic*, may be accurate, but it is not right to make Freud responsible for them, no more than to make Darwin responsible for the way the militarists, colonialists, and other predatory groups and finally Hitler and the Nazis, availed themselves of pseudo-Darwinist theories. It thus happened to Freud as it had happened to Darwin and to others before them, that they seemed to launch an overwhelming cultural revolution when actually it was the revolution rooted in socioeconomic changes that carried them. Coming back to Freud, it will certainly be a long time before one will be able to discern what can be attributed to the direct impact of his teaching, and to what extent the diffuse social, economic, and cultural trends prevailed themselves of Freudian, or pseudo-Freudian, concepts toward their own end.

We are perhaps prepared, now, to give an answer to that difficult question: What does certainly belong to Freud and constitutes the inmost originality of his work? We may distinguish three great contributions: the psychoanalytic theory, the psychoanalytic method, and the psychoanalytic organization.

Whatever the number of its sources and the intricacies of its context, the psychoanalytic theory is universally recognized as a powerful and original synthesis that has been the incentive to numerous researchers and findings in the field of normal and abnormal psychology. However, the problem of its scientific status is not yet clarified. In that regard, the situation of psychoanalysis is strikingly similar to that of animal magnetism in 1818, when the physician Virey wondered why discoveries made in the field of physics at the time of Mesmer were now taken for granted whereas the validity of Mesmer's doctrine was still the object of emotionally charged discussions.[539] Conversely, discoveries made in Freud's time in the field of endocrinology, bacteriology, and the like, are unequivocally integrated into science, whereas the validity of psychoanalytic concepts is still questioned by many experimental psychologists and epistemologists.[540] This paradox has brought many Freudians to view psychoanalysis as a discipline that stands outside the field of experimental science and more akin to history, philosophy, linguistics,[541] or as a variety of hermeneutics.[542]

Even more than the conceptual framework of psychoanalysis, the psychoanalytic method is Freud's creation and constitutes the inmost originality of his work. Freud was the inventor of a new mode of dealing with the unconscious, that is, the psychoanalytic situation with the basic rule, free associating, and the analysis of resistances and transference. This is Freud's incontestable innovation.

But Freud's most striking novelty was probably the founding of a "school" according to a pattern that had no parallel in modern times but is a revival of the old philosophical schools of Greco-Roman antiquity, such as we described them in a former chapter.[543] Almost from the beginning Freud made psychoanalysis a movement, with its own organization and publishing house, its strict rules of membership, and its official doctrine, namely the psychoanalytic theory. The similarity between the psychoanalytic and the Greco-Roman philosophical schools was reinforced after the imposition of an initiation in the form of the training analysis. Not only does the training analysis demand a heavy financial sacrifice, but also a surrender of privacy and of the whole self. By this means a follower is integrated into the Society more indissolubly than ever was a Pythagorian, Stoic, or Epicurean in his own organization. Freud's example in that regard was to be followed by Jung and a few other dynamic psychiatric movements. We are thus led to view Freud's most striking achievement in the revival of the Greco-Roman type of philosophical schools, and this is no doubt a noteworthy event in the history of modern culture.

Notes

1. We follow here the chronology given by Alfred Kasamas, *Österreichische Chronik* (Vienna: Hollinak, 1948).

2. Gerson Wolf, *Die Juden*, in *Die Völker Oesterreich-Ungarns. Ethnographische und culturhistorische Schilderung* (Vienna u.Teschen: Karl Prochaska, 1883), Vol. VII.

3. Hans Tietze, *Die Juden Wiens. Geschichte—Wirtschaft—Kultur* (Leipzig and Vienna: E. P. Tal, 1933).

4. Adolf Zemlinsky, *Geschichte der Türkisch-Israelitischen Gemeinde zu Wien* (Vienna: M. Papo, 1888).

5. Sigmund Mayer, *Ein Jüdischer Kaufmann, 1831 bis 1911. Lebenserinnerungen von Sigmund Mayer* (Leipzig: Duncker and Humblot, 1911).

6. M. Vishnitzer, trans. and ed., *The Memoirs of Ber of Bolechow (1723–1805)* (London: Oxford University Press, 1922).

7. Sigmund Mayer, *Ein Jüdischer Kaufmann, 1831 bis 1911. Lebenserinnerungen von Sigmund Mayer* (Leipzig: Duncker and Humblot, 1911).

8. Heymann Steinthal, *Ueber Juden und Judentum. Vorträge und Aufsätze*, G. Karpeles, ed. (Berlin: M. Poppelauer, 1906).

9. Joseph Breuer, *Curriculum Vitae* in Hans Meyer, *Dr. Joseph Breuer, 1842–1925, Nachruf, 23. Juni 1925* (n.d), pp. 9–24.

10. Sigmund Freud, *Traumdeutung* (Leipzig and Vienna: Deuticke, 1900), p. 135.

11. Hans Tietze, *Die Juden Wiens. Geschichte—Wirtschaft—Kultur* (Leipzig and Vienna: E. P. Tal, 1933), p. 231.

12. Max Gruenwald, *Vienna* (Philadelphia: Jewish Publication Society of America, 1936), pp. 518–523.

13. Such were, for instance, Stefan Zweig, *Die Welt von Gestern* (1944) (Stockholm: Fischer, 1958); and Otto Lubarsch, *Ein bewegtes Gelehrtenleben* (Berlin: J. Springer, 1931).

14. Letter to the president of the *Kadimah*, signed *Joseph Breuer, stirpe Judaeus, natione Germanus.* (Josef Breuer, Jew by origin, German by nation.) The author is

much obliged to Mrs. Käthe Breuer, who showed him this letter and gave him authorization to quote from it.

15. Renée Gicklhorn, F. Kalivoda, J. Sajner, "Nové archíví nálezy o dêtství Sigmunda Freuda v Príbore," *Ceskoslovenská Psychiatria,* LXIII (1967), 131–136. R. Gicklhorn and J. Sajner, "The Freiberg Period of the Freud Family," *Journal of the History of Medicine,* XXIV (1969), pp. 37–43.

16. A photocopy of the marriage certificate of Freud's parents is reproduced in the article of Willy Aron, "Notes on Sigmund Freud's Ancestry and Jewish Contacts," *Yivo Annual of Jewish Social Sciences,* XI (1956–1957), 286–295.

17. The chronology of Jacob Freud's life is uncertain. He is said to have been twenty-nine in 1844 and to have been married at seventeen. This would put his birthday in 1815 and his first marriage in 1832. But Emanuel is said to have been twenty-one in 1852, which puts his birth date in 1831. In that case his father would have been sixteen at the time of his birth.

18. Renée Gicklhorn, "Eine Episode aus Freuds Mittelschulzeit," *Unsere Heimat,* XXXVI (1965), 18–24 (see footnote on p. 23).

19. Ernest Jones, *The Life and Work of Sigmund Freud* (New York: Basic Books, 1953), I, 2, 17, 60.

20. Siegfried Bernfeld, "Sigmund Freud, M.D., 1882–1885," *International Journal of Psychoanalysis,* XXXII (1951), 204–217 (excerpt from p. 207).

21. Ernest Jones, *The Life and Work of Sigmund Freud* (New York: Basic Books, 1953), I, 9–11.

22. Ernest Simon, *Sigmund Freud, the Jew,* Leo Baeck Institute Year Book, II (1957), 270–305.

23. Sigmund Freud, "Selbstdarstellung," In L. R. Grote, *Die Medizin der Gegenwart in Selbstdarstellung* (Leipzig: Meiner, 1925), IV, 1–52. (With a postscript in the 2nd ed., 1935.) Eng. trans., Standard Edition, XX, 7–74. All references to the Standard Edition of Freud's writings are given according to James Strachey, trans. *The Standard Edition of the Complete Psychological Works of Sigmund Freud* (London: Hogarth Press, 1953).

24. Sigmund Freud-Wilhelm Fliess, *Aus den Anfängen der Psychoanalyse; Briefe an Wilhelm Fliess, Abhandlungen und Notizen aus den Jahren 1887–1902* (London: Imago. 1954). Eng. trans., Sigmund Freud, *The Origins of Psychoanalysis* (New York: Basic Books, 1954).

25. Sigmund Freud–Ernst Pfister, *Briefe (1909–1937)* (Frankfurt a.M.: S. Fischer, 1963).

26. Sigmund Freud–Karl Abraham, *Briefe (1907–1926)* (Frankfurt a.M.: S. Fischer, 1965).

27. Sigmund Freud–Lou Andreas-Salome, *Briefwechsel* (Frankfurt a.M.: S. Fischer, 1966).

28. Sigmund Freud, *Briefe (1873–1939)* (Frankfurt a.M.: S. Fischer, 1960).

29. Martin Freud, *Glory Reflected* (London: Angus L. Robertson, 1957).

30. Siegfried and Suzanne Bernfeld, "Freud's Early Childhood," *Bulletin of the Menninger Clinic,* VIII (1944), 107–114.

31. Siegfried Bernfeld, "Sigmund Freud, M.D.," *International Journal of Psychoanalysis,* XXXII (1951), 204–217.

32. Siegfried Bernfeld, "Freud's Scientific Beginnings," *American Imago,* VI (1949), 165–196.

33. Siegfried Bernfeld, "Freud's Studies on Cocaine, 1884–1887," *Journal of the American Psychoanalytic Association,* I (1953), 581–613.

34. Siegfried and Suzanne Bernfeld, "Freud's First Year in Practice, 1886–1887," *Bulletin of the Menninger Clinic,* XVI (1952), 37–49.

35. Josef and Renée Gicklhorn, *Sigmund Freud's akademische Laufbahn im Lichte der Dokumente* (Vienna: Urban & Schwarzenberg, 1960).

36. Renée Gicklhorn, *Der Wagner-Jauregg "Prozess"* (unpublished).

37. K. R. Eissler, *Sigmund Freud und die Wiener Universität* (Bern and Stuttgart: Hans Huber, 1966).

38. Maria Dorer, *Historische Grundlagen der Psychoanalyse* (Leipzig: F. Meiner, 1932).

39. Ola Andersson, *Studies in the Prehistory of Psychoanalysis* (Stockholm: Svenska Bokförlaget, 1962).

40. Fritz Wittels, *Sigmund Freud. Der Mann, die Lehre, die Schule* (Leipzig: E. P. Tal, 1924).

41. Helen Walker Puner, *Freud: His Life and His Mind* (New York: Howell and Soskin, 1947).

42. Hanns Sachs, *Freud, Master and Friend* (Cambridge: Harvard University Press, 1945).

43. Ernest Jones, *The Life and Work of Sigmund Freud*, 3 vols. (New York: Basic Books, 1953, 1955, 1957).

44. The reason why his first name was later changed into Sigmund is not known.

45. Willy Aron, "Notes on Sigmund Freud's Ancestry and Jewish Contacts," *Yivo Annual of Jewish Social Sciences*, II (1956–1957), 286–295.

46. The word *May* was written with the old spelling *May* instead of *Mai*, so that it was easy to confuse with *März* (March).

47. Renée Gicklhorn informs the author that, according to town directories, Jacob Freud lived in 1860 at Weissgärberstrasse 114, in 1864 at Pillersdorfgasse 5, in 1865 at Pfeffergasse 1, in 1872 at Pfeffergasse 5. It is not known at what date he later moved to Kaiser Josefstrasse.

48. Sigmund Freud, *Die Traumdeutung* (1900), p. 146. Standard Edition, IV, 211–212.

49. Renée Gicklhorn, "Eine Episode aus S. Freuds Mittelschulzeit," *Unsere Heimat*, XXXVI (1965), 18–24.

50. Judith Bernays-Heller, "Freud's Mother and Father," *Commentary*, XXI (1956), 418–421.

51. Heinz Stanescu, "Unbekannte Briefe des jungen Sigmund Freud an einen Rumänischen Freund," *Neue Literatur. Zeitschrift des Schriftstellerverbandes der RVD*, XVI, No. 3 (June 1965), 123–129.

52. This celebrated poem, an imitation of an Orphic Hymn, was included in Goethe's complete works and believed to be an unpublished work of his youth. Subsequant research, however, has shown that its true author was Georg Christoph Tobler (1757–1812), a young Swiss poet who had sent it to Goethe. See Rudolph Pestalozzi, "Sigmund Freuds Berufswahl," *Neue Zürcher Zeitung*, Fernausgabe 179 (July 1, 1956).

53. Siegfried Bernfeld, "Sigmund Freud, M.D.," *International Journal of Psychoanalysis*, XXXII (1951), 204–217 (the complete list of the courses for which Freud registered is on pp. 216–217).

54. Moritz Benedikt, *Aus meinem Leben. Erinnerungen und Erörterungen* (Vienna: Carl Konegen, 1906), pp. 60–62.

55. See Chap. 5, p. 266.

56. There never was such a thing as a "school of Helmholtz" in the sense purported by Siegfried Bernfeld. It is unfortunate that this false conception has been uncritically accepted by so many historians.

57. K. E. Rotschuh, *Geschichte der Physiologie* (Berlin: Springer-Verlag, 1953), pp. 139–141.

58. Erna Lesky, *Die Wiener medizinische Schule im 19. Jahrhundert* (Graz: Verlag Böhlau, 1965), pp. 535–537.

59. *Dr. Josef Breuer, 1842–1925. Curriculum Vitae und Nachruf*, von Hofrat. Prof. Dr. Hans Meyer am 23. Juni 1925.

60. Leopold Breuer, *Leitfaden beim Religionsunterrichte der Israelitischen Jugend*, 2. umgearbeitete Auflage (Vienna: Klopfsen und Eurich, 1855).

61. From the letter to the *Kadimah* (1894) (with kind authorization of Mrs. Käthe Breuer).

62. These details have been provided by Mrs. Käthe Breuer.

63. A copy of this correspondence is in the possession of Mrs. Käthe Breuer, who kindly authorized the author to read it.

64. Rudolf Steiner, *Mein Lebensgang* (Dornach: Philos. Anthropos. Verlag, 1925), pp. 134–135.

65. A. de Kleyn, "Josef Breuer (1842–1925)," *Acta Otolaryngologica*, X (1926), 167–171.

66. See Chapter 10, p. 809. The author is grateful to Mrs. Käthe Breuer, who showed him the documents of the *Breuer-Stiftung*, and to Josef Breuer's grandson, George Bryant, of Vancouver, for further information.

67. John Stuart Mill, *Gesammelte Werke*, "Autorisierte Uebersetzung unter Redaktion von Prof. Dr. Theodor Gompertz," XII. Uebersetzung von Siegmund (*sic*) Freud (Leipzig: Fües's Verlag, 1880).

68. Ernest Jones, *The Life and Work of Sigmund Freud* (New York: Basic Books, 1953), Vol. I, Chap. 7.

69. No documentary inquiry has been conducted as yet in the Viennese General Hospital's archives. We are following Jones' account, which was based on Freud's letters to his fiancée.

70. Erna Lesky, *Die Wiener Medizinische Schule im 19. Jahrhundert* (Graz and Cologne: Verlag Hermann Böhlaus Nachf, 1965), pp. 373–379.

71. Bernard Sachs, *Barnay Sachs (1858–1944)* (New York: privately printed, 1949), p. 55.

72. August Forel, *Rückblick auf mein Leben* (Zurich: Europa-Verlag, 1935), p. 64.

73. Theodor Meynert, *Gedichte* (Vienna and Leipzig: Braumüller, 1905).

74. Dora Stockert-Meynert, *Theodor Meynert und seine Zeit* (Vienna and Leipzig: Oesterreichischer Bundesverlag, 1930).

75. Theodor Aschenbrandt, "Die physiologische Wirkung und Bedeutung des Cocain insbesondere auf den menschlichen Organismus," *Deutsche medizinische Wochenschrift*, IX (1883), 730–732.

76. Sigmund Freud, "Ueber Coca," *Centralblatt für die gesamte Therapie*, II (1884), 289–314.

77. Carl Koller, "Vorläufige Mitteilung über locale Anästhesierung am Auge," *Klinische Monatsblätter für Augenheilkunde*, XXII (1884), 60–63.

78. Sigmund Freud, "Beitrag zur Kenntnis der Cocawirkung," *Wiener medizinische Wochenschrift*, XXXV (1885), 129–133.

79. Albrecht Erlenmeyer, "Ueber die Wirkung des Cocain bei Morphiumentziehung," *Centralblatt für Nervenheilkunde*, VIII (1885), 289–299.

80. Sigmund Freud, "Ueber den Ursprung des Nervus acusticus," *Monatsschrift für Ohrenheilkunde*, Neue Folge, XX (1886), 245–251, 277–282.

81. In the *Interpretation of Dreams*, Freud says that Paris was, for many years, the aim of one of his dreams, and that the bliss he felt when setting foot on the pavement of Paris was for him the warranty that other dreams would be fulfilled in turn. *Traumdeutung* (1900), p. 133. Standard Edition, IV, 195.

82. Ernest Jones, *The Life and Work of Sigmund Freud* (New York: Basic Books, 1953), I, 186–189.

83. This document has been published in the book by Josef and Renée Gicklhorn, *Sigmund Freuds akademische Laufbahn im Lichte der Documente* (Vienna-Innsbruck: Urban & Schwarzenberg, 1960), pp. 82–89.

84. Ernest Jones, *The Life and Work of Sigmund Freud* (New York: Basic Books, 1953), I, 229.

85. Albrecht Erlenmeyer, "Ueber Cocainsucht," *Deutsche Medizinalzeitung*, VII (1886), 672–675.

86. Jean-Martin Charcot, *Neue Vorlesungen über die Krankheiten des Nervensystems insbesondere der Hysterie*. Uebers. von Sigmund Freud (Leipzig and Vienna: Toeplitz und Deuticke, 1886).

87. Ernest Jones, *The Life and Work of Sigmund Freud* (New York: Basic Books, 1953), I, 193–195.

88. See Chap. 7, pp. 458–459.

89. Renée Gicklhorn, "Das erste öffentliche Kinder-Kranken-Institut in Wien," *Unsere Heimat*, XXX (1959), 146–157.

90. Erna Lesky, *Die Wiener medizinische Schule im 19. Jahrhundert* (Graz: Böhlau, 1965), passim. Erich Menninger-Lerchenthal, "Jubiläum der Gesellschaft der Aerzte in Wien," *Oesterreichische Aerztezeitung* (1964).

91. Burghard Breitner, *Hand an zwei Pflügen* (Innsbruck: Inn-Verlag, n.d.), pp. 222–224.

92. Herbert Page, *Injuries of the Spine and Spinal Chord without Apparent Mechanical Lesions, and Nervous Shock* (London: Churchill, 1882).

93. G. L. Walton, "Case of Typical Hysterical Hemianesthesia in a Man Following Injury," *Archives of Medicine*, X (1883), 88–95. "Case of Hysterical Hemianaesthesia, Convulsions and Motor Paralysis Brought on by a Fall," *Boston Medical and Surgical Journal*, CXI (1884), 558–559.

94. James J. Putnam, "Recent Investigations into the Pathology of So-called Concussion of the Spine," *Boston Medical and Surgical Journal*, CIX (1883), 217–220.

95. R. Thomsen and H. Oppenheim, "Ueber das Vorkommen und die Bedeutung der Sensorischen Anästhesie bei Erkrankungen des Zentralen Nervensystems," *Archiv für Psychiatrie*, XV (1884), 559–583; 633–680; 656–667.

96. Josef and Renée Gicklhorn, *Sigmund Freud's akademische Laufbahn*, pp. 82–89.

97. *Anzeiger der K. K. Gesellschaft der Aerzte in Wien* (1886), No. 25, pp. 149–152.

98. *Allgemeine Wiener Medizinische Zeitung*, XXXI (1886), 505–507.

99. *Wiener Medizinische Wochenschrift*, XXXVI (1886), 1445–1447.

100. *Münchner Medizinische Wochenschrift*, XXXIII (1886), 768.

101. *Wiener Medizinische Presse*, XXVII (1886), 1407–1409. (Detailed account by Arthur Schnitzler.)

102. *Wiener Medizinische Blätter*, IX (1886), 1292–1293.

103. Moritz Benedikt, *Elektrotherapie* (Vienna: Tendler & Comp., 1868), pp. 413–445.

104. Moriz Rosenthal, *Klinik der Nervenkrankrankheiten* (1870). 2. Aufl. (Stuttgart: Enke, 1875), pp. 466–467.

105. Dora Stockert-Meynert, *Theodor Meynert und seine Zeit* (Vienna and Leipzig: Oesterreichischer Bundesverlag, 1930) (giving a copy of a very flattering letter from Charcot to Meynert and telling about a visit by Meynert to Charcot in 1892).

106. Paul Richer, *Etudes cliniques sur l'hystéro-épilepsie ou grande hystérie* (Paris: Delahaye et Lecrosnier, 1881), p. 258.

107. Laquer, in *Neurologisches Centralblatt*, VI (1887), 429–432.

108. A. V. Luzenberger (Assistent an der Psychiatrischen Klinik des Hofrathes Professor Meynert in Wien), "Ueber einen Fall von Dyschromatopsie bei einem hysterischen Manne," *Wiener Medizinische Blätter*, IX (September 16, 1886), 1113–1126.

109. Bamberger had been one of the four members of the jury that had granted Freud the stipend to go to Paris. Freud had worked for three years in Meynert's laboratory. In the previous year he had replaced a physician in Leidesdorf's sanatorium for three weeks.

110. Sigmund Freud, "Beiträge zur Kasuistik der Hysterie. I. Beobachtung einer hochgradigen Hemianaesthesie bei einem hysterischen Manne," *Wiener Medizinische Wochenschrift*, XXXVI (1886), 1633–1638. Standard Edition, I, 25–31.

111. This has been shown on the basis of inquiries in the Society's Archives by K. Sablik, "Sigmund Freud und die Gesellschaft der Aerzte in Wien," *Wiener klinische Wochenschrift*, LXXX (1968), 107–110.

112. Arthur Schnitzler, "Review of Charcot's Lectures on the Diseases of the Nervous System, Translated by Sigmund Freud," *Internationale Klinische Rundschau*, I (1887), 19–20.

113. The adjective *geistreich*, literally meaning "full of wit," could at times have an ironic connotation when used to qualify a man of science. It implied that the same might have more imagination than critical sense.

114. See Georges Gilles de la Tourette, *Traîté clinique et thérapeutique de l'hystérie d'après l'enseignement de la Salpêtrière* (Paris: Plon, 1901), pp. 76–88.

115. Sigmund Freud, "Bemerkungen über Cocainsucht und Cocainfurcht," *Wiener Medizinische Wochenschrift*, XXXVII (1887), 929–932.

116. *Wiener Medizinische Wochenschrift*, XXXVII (1887), 138, 200–201.

117. Theodor Meynert, "Beitrag zum Verständnis der traumatischen Neurose," *Wiener Klinische Wochenschrift* (1889), pp. 489–502.
118. Renée Gicklhorn, "Das erste öffentliche Kinder-Kranken-Institut in Wien," *Unsere Heimat*, XXX (1959), 146–157.
119. We follow the dates and spelling of names provided by the *Heimat-Rolle* in Vienna.
120. Hippolyte Bernheim, *Die Suggestion und ihre Heilwirkung*, Uebersetzung von Sigmund Freud (Leipzig and Vienna: Deuticke, 1889).
121. Hippolyte Bernheim, *Neue Studien über Hypnotismus, Suggestion und Psychotherapie*, Uebersetzung von Sigmund Freud (Vienna and Leipzig: Deuticke, 1892).
122. Sigmund Freud, "Ueber Hypnose und Suggestion," Originalbericht. *Internationale Klinische Rundschau*, VI (1892), 814–818.
123. This translation exists in two forms. The text is identical; the only difference is in the titles and the dates, which are: *Poliklinische Vorträge* von Prof. J. M. Charcot übersetzt von Sigmund Freud. Mit zahlreichen Holzschnitten im Text (Leipzig and Vienna: Deuticke, 1892). *Poliklinische Vorträge* von Prof. J. M. Charcot übersetzt von Sigmund Freud. I Band. Schuljahr 1887/88. Mit 99 Holzschnitten (Leipzig and Vienna: Deuticke, 1894).
124. Ludwig Eisenberg, "Das geistige Wien. Künstler- und Schriftstellerlexikon," II, *Medicinisch-naturwissenchaftlicher Theil* (Vienna: Daberkow, 1893), 132–133.
125. See Chap. 8, p. 545.
126. Max Schur, "Some additional 'Day Residues' of 'The Specimen Dream of Psychoanalysis,'" in Rudolf M. Loewenstein *et al.*, *Psychoanalysis, a General Psychology. Essays in Honor of Heinz Hartmann* (New York: International Universities Press, 1966), pp. 45–85.
127. This is how he tells it to Fliess shortly afterward. In *The Interpretation of Dreams*, however, the notice is worded: "You are requested to shut the eyes or one eye."
128. Edith Buxbaum, "Freud's Dream Interpretation in the Light of His Letters to Fliess," *Bulletin of the Menninger Clinic*, XV (1951), 197–212.
129. Didier Anzieu, *L'Auto-Analyse. Son Rôle dans la découverte de la psychanalyse par Freud. Sa Fonction en psychanalyse* (Paris: Presses Universitaires de France, 1959).
130. H. F. Ellenberger, "La Maladie Créatrice," *Dialogue, Canadian Philosophical Review*, III (1964), 25–41.
131. See Chap. 4, pp. 215–216.
132. See Chap. 9, pp. 670–673.
133. Sigmund Freud, *Aus den Anfängen der Psychoanalyse*, p. 178. *The Origins of Psychoanalysis*, p. 167.
134. Sigmund Freud, *Aus den Anfängen der Psychoanalyse*, p. 167. *The Origins of Psychoanalysis*, p. 156.
135. C. S. Freund, "Ueber psychische Lähmungen," *Neurologisches Centralblatt*, XIV (1895), 938–946.
136. Sigmund Freud, *Aus den Anfängen der Psychoanalyse*, p. 145. *The Origins of Psychoanalysis*, p. 135. Actually there is nothing in C. S. Freund's article that would justify such an accusation.
137. This is shown by certain expressions, such as *"meinen Kollegen zum Trotz"* (in defiance of my colleagues) in a letter of May 30, 1896; or when he boasts of having been "rude" (*frech*) to them.
138. Sigmund Freud, "Bruchstück einer Hysterie-Analyse," *Monatsschrift für Neurologie und Psychiatrie*, XVIII (1906), 436. (Let it be recalled that this paper was written in 1901 and published five years later.) Standard Edition, VII, 130–243.
139. J. von Uexkuell, *Niegeschaute Welten* (Berlin: S. Fischer, 1936), pp. 133–145.
140. Paul Valéry, *Autres Rhumbs*, in *Oeuvres*, Ed. Pléiade (Paris: Gallimard, 1960) II, 673.
141. "Noli foras ire, in teipsum redi; in interiore homine habitat veritas." *De vera religione*, Chap. 39, par. 72.
142. *III. Internationaler Kongress für Psychologie in München vom 4.–7. August, 1896* (Munich: J. F. Lehmann, 1897), p. 369.

143. A. W. Van Renterghem, *Liébeault en zijne School* (Amsterdam: Van Rossen, 1898), p. 133.

144. Julius Leopold Pagel, *Biographisches Lexikon hervorragender Aerzte des neunzehnten Jahrhunderts* (Berlin: Urban, 1901), p. 545.

145. C. Tournier, "Essai de classification étiologique des névroses," *Archives d'Anthropologie Criminelle,* XV (1900), 28–39. Throughout his life Tournier gathered an immense amount of material but published very little.

146. See Chap. 7, p. 442.

147. *Jahrbuch für Psychiatrie und Neurologie,* XX (1901), 391.

148. Joseph and Renée Gicklhorn, *Sigmund Freuds Akademische Laufbahn* (1960), p. 99.

149. This has been well demonstrated by Erik H. Erikson, "The Dream Specimen of Psychoanalysis," *Journal of the American Psychoanalytic Association,* II (1954), 5–56.

150. To give an example, Freud tells of going twice a day to a house to give an injection to a patient, and of spitting on the stairs, to the annoyance of the concierge, but says it was her fault since she did not provide a spittoon. (*Traumdeutung,* p. 165.) This detail seems rather uncouth to the modern reader, but in that time, when spitting was customary and acceptable, and spittoons were provided almost as generously as ashtrays are today, there was nothing unusual in this behavior.

151. The story does not sound altogether convincing. Meynert did not deny the existence of male hysteria, as shown by the publication of Luzenberger's article (see Chap. 7, p. 440). Hysteria is the disease, par excellence, which one does not conceal. Inquiries the author made among Austrian connoisseurs of the history of medicine revealed their skepticism about Meynert's alleged "male hysteria." Even supposing that Meynert had been able to conceal that he suffered from male hysteria, is it likely that, after several years of polemics with Freud, he would call him to his death bed to make such a confession?

152. Theodor Gomperz, *Traumdeutung und Zauberei, ein Blick auf das Wesen des Aberglaubens* (Vienna: Carl Gerold's Sohn, 1866).

153. There were several available synonyms, *Traumauslegung, Interpretation der Träume, Deutung des Traumes,* and so on. *Traumdeutung* reminded one of *Sterndeutung* (astrology).

154. Virgil, *Aeneis,* VII, v. 312, trans. H. Rushton-Fairclough, Loeb Classical Library, Virgil, revised ed. (1954), II, 25.

155. Sigmund Freud, *Aus den Anfängen der Psychoanalyse,* p. 260. (In the authorized English translation, *The Origins of Psychoanalysis,* p. 244, the terms used by Freud have been played down.)

156. Hans Blüher, *Werke und Tage. Geschichte eines Denkers* (Munich: Paul List, 1953), p. 253.

157. Ilse Bry and Alfred H. Rifkin, "Freud and the History of Ideas: Primary Sources, 1886–1910," *Science and Psychoanalysis,* V (1962), 6–36. See also Chap. 10, pp. 783–784.

158. Joseph and Renée Gicklhorn, *Sigmund Freuds akademische Laufbahn im Lichte der Dokumente* (Vienna: Urban and Schwarzenberg, 1960).

159. K. R. Eissler, "Zwei bisher übersehene Dokumente zur akademischen Laufbahn Sigmund Freuds," *Wiener klinische Wochenschrift,* LXXVIII (1966), 16–19.

160. K. R. Eissler, *Sigmund Freud und die Wiener Universität* (Bern: Verlag Hans Huber, 1966).

161. A. Engelbrecht, "Wilhelm Ritter von Hartel," *Jahresbericht über die Fortschritte der klassischen Altertumswissenschaft,* CXLI (1908), 75–107.

162. Karl Kraus, "Die Fakultät in Liquidation," *Die Fackel,* V (October 17, 1903), No. 144, pp. 4–8.

163. Renée Gicklhorn, "Eine mysteriöse Bildaffäre," *Wiener Geschichtblätter,* XIII (1958), 14–17.

164. K. R. Eissler, "Kritische Bemerkungen zu Renée Gicklhorns Beitrag 'Eine mysteriöse Bildaffäre,'" *Wiener Geschichtsblätter,* XIII (1958), 55–60.

165. Thanks to the kindness of Frau Prof. Ebenstein, Director of the Oesterreichische Galerie, the author was able to see the Orlik painting in the stacks of the Museum. It is an oil, measuring 55 by 37 cm., valued at about $100.

166. Ilse Bry and Alfred H. Rifkin, "Freud and the History of Ideas: Primary Sources, 1886–1910," *Science and Psychoanalysis*, V (1962), 6–36.

167. Ernest Jones, *The Life and Work of Sigmund Freud* (New York: Basic Books, 1953), I, 332.

168. See Chap. 10, pp. 802–803.

169. We follow here Ernest Jones, *The Life and Work of Sigmund Freud* (New York: Basic Books, 1957), III, 89.

170. Thomas Mann, *Freud und die Zukunft* (Vienna: Bermann-Fischer Verlag, 1936). Eng. trans., in *Essays of Three Decades* (New York: Alfred Knopf, 1947), pp. 411–428.

171. Stefan Zweig, "Worte am Sarge Sigmund Freuds," *Erbe und Zukunft*, II (1947), pp. 101–102.

172. Anna Freud Bernays, "My Brother, Sigmund Freud," *American Mercury*, LI (1940), 335–342.

173. Renée Gicklhorn, "Eine Episode aus Sigmund Freuds Mittelschulzeit," *Unsere Heimat*, XXXVI (1965), 18–24.

174. René Laforgue, "Ein Bild von Freud," *Zeitschrift für Psychotherapie und Medizinische Psychologie*, IV (1954), 210–217.

175. Martin Freud, *Glory Reflected. Sigmund Freud. Man and Father* (London: Angus and Robertson, 1957).

176. This document has been found in the Archive of the Austrian Ministry of War by Frau Professor Renée Gicklhorn, who most generously provided the author with a photocopy of it and authorized him to use it for the present book.

177. The author showed this document to an elderly friend in Vienna who is familiar with archive research and who, in his youth, served in the Austrian-Hungarian army. After a careful reading, he handed it back to him with a smile and said: "It proves that Freud was on good terms with the officer who wrote the report."

178. Adelbert Albrecht, "Prof. Sigmund Freud. The Eminent Vienna Psycho-Therapeutist Now in America," *Boston Evening Transcript* (September 11, 1909), p. 3.

179. Raymond Recouly, "A Visit to Freud," *Outlook*, New York, CXXXV (September 5, 1923), 27–29.

180. Max Eastman, *Heroes I Have Known. Twelve Who Lived Great Lives* (New York: Simon and Schuster, 1942), pp. 261–273.

181. André Breton, *Les Pas perdus* (Paris: Gallimard, 1924), pp. 116–117.

182. H. R. Lenormand, *Les Confessions d'un auteur dramatique*, 2 vols. (Paris: Albin Michel, 1949), I, 270–271.

183. J. H. Schultz, *Psychotherapie, Leben und Werk grosser Aerzte* (Stuttgart: Hippokrates-Verlag, 1952).

184. V. von Weizsäcker, *Erinnerungen eines Arztes. Natur und Geist* (Göttingen: Vandenhoeck & Ruprecht, 1954), pp. 173–174.

185. Emil Ludwig, *Der entzauberte Freud* (Zurich: Carl Posen Verlag, 1946), pp. 177–180.

186. Odette Pannetier, "Visite au Professeur Freud. Je me fais psychanalyser," *Candide*, XIII, No. 645 (July 23, 1936). Eng. trans., "Appointment in Vienna," *The Living Age*, New York, CCCLI (October 1936), 138–144.

187. Roy R. Grinker, "Reminiscences of a Personal Contact with Freud," *American Journal of Orthopsychiatry*, X (1940), 850–854.

188. Hilda Doolittle, "Writings on the Wall," *Life and Letters To-day*, XLV (1945), 67–98, 137–154; XLVI, 72–89, 136–151; XLVIII, 33–45.

189. Joseph Wortis, *Fragments of an Analysis with Freud* (New York: Simon and Schuster, 1954).

190. Bruno Goetz, "Erinnerungen an Sigmund Freud," *Neue Schweizer Rundschau*, XX (May 1952), 3–11.

191. C. G. Jung, *Notes on the Seminar in Analytical Psychology Conducted by C. G. Jung* (Zurich, March 23–July 6, 1925).

192. One example was in 1936, when he refused to see Janet in Vienna, believing (quite incorrectly) that Janet had insulted him in 1913. Another was his comment when he heard of Adler's death. (See Chap. 8, pp. 647–648.)

193. Ernest Jones, in *The Life and Work of Sigmund Freud* (New York: Basic Books, 1953), I, 335–336, spoke of "travelling phobia," because Freud went to the station one hour before the train was due to leave. Actually, this was the practical thing to do in a time when seats could not be reserved.

194. Those Viennese who really disliked Vienna emigrated; those who loved it pretended to hate it, but stayed. "The Viennese is a man unhappy with himself, who hates the Viennese but cannot live without the Viennese," said Hermann Bahr, *Wien* (Stuttgart: Krabbe, 1906), p. 9. Martin Freud, *Glory Reflected* (London: Angus and Robertson, 1957), p. 48, expresses strong doubts about his father's supposed dislike of Vienna.

195. Sigmund Freud, Foreword to the Hebrew translation of *Totem and Taboo, Gesammelte Schriften,* XII (1934), 385. Standard Edition, XIII, 15.

196. Freud never showed any sympathy for the Zionist movement, nor did he have personal contact with Theodor Herzl although both lived. in Vienna and had many acquaintances in common. Freud's name does not appear in the 1800 printed pages of Herzl's diary; Theodor Herzl, *Tagebücher,* 3 vols. (Berlin: Jüdischer Verlag, 1922–1923).

197. Stanley Edgar Hyman, "Freud and Boas: Secular Rabbis?" *Commentary,* Vol. XVII (1954).

198. David Riesman, *Individualism Reconsidered and Other Essays* (New York: The Free Press, 1954), pp. 305–408.

199. Fritz Wittels, *Freud and His Time* (New York: Grosset and Dunlap, 1931), pp. 3–46.

200. Among various studies on Freud as a writer, see particularly that of Walter Muschg, "Freud als Schriftsteller," *Die Psychoanalytische Bewegung,* II (1930), 467–509.

201. Ludwig Koehler, *Neue Zürcher Zeitung,* No. 667 (April 16, 1939).

202. P. J. Moebius, *Augewählte Werke,* Vol. V, *Nietzsche* (Leipzig: Barth, 1904).

203. Charles E. Maylan, *Freuds tragischer Komplex. Eine Analyse der Psychoanalyse* (Munich: Ernst Reinhardt, 1929).

204. Maurice Natenberg, *The Case History of Sigmund Freud. A Psycho-biography* (Chicago: Regent House, 1955).

205. Erich Fromm, *Sigmund Freud's Mission. An Analysis of his Personality and Influence* (New York: Grove Press, 1963).

206. Percival Bailey, *Sigmund the Unserene. A Tragedy in Three Acts* (Springfield, Ill.: Charles C Thomas, 1965).

207. Maryse Choisy, *Sigmund Freud: A New Appraisal* (New York: Philosophical Library, 1963), p. 48.

208. Franz Alexander, "The Neurosis of Freud," *Saturday Review of Literature* (November 2, 1957), pp. 18–19.

209. Robert Merton, "Resistance to the Systematic Study of Multiple Discoveries in Science," *Archives Européennes de Sociologie,* IV (1963), 237–282.

210. Maryse Choisy, *Sigmund Freud. A New Appraisal* (New York: Philosophical Library, 1963), pp. 48–49.

211. Marthe Robert, *La Revolution psychanalytique* (Paris: Payot, 1964), I, 93–94.

212. One example among many is Freud's belief that *The Interpretation of Dreams* met only silence or destructive criticism, when, in fact, it had a fairly large number of positive or enthusiastic reviews. See also Chap. 10, pp. 783–784.

213. K. R. Eissler, *Freud: Versuch einer Persönlichkeitsanalyse.* (Typescript.) The author is most grateful to Dr. K. R. Eissler for having lent him this study and authorized him to quote it here.

214. K. R. Eissler, *Goethe: A Psychoanalytic Study, 1775–1786,* 2 vols. (Detroit: Wayne State University Press, 1963).

215. E. Menninger-Lerchenthal, "Julius Wagner-Jauregg," *Die Furche* (April 20, 1957).

216. Julius Wagner von Jauregg, *Lebenserinnerungen,* L. Schönbauer and M. Jentsch eds. (Vienna: Springer-Verlag, 1950).

217. See Chap. 10, pp. 837–839.

218. K. R. Eissler, "Julius Wagner-Jaureggs Gutachten über Sigmund Freud und

seine Studien zur Psychoanalyse," *Wiener Klinische Wochenschrift*, LXX (1958), 401–407.

219. Henry Schnitzler, "Freuds Briefe an Arthur Schnitzler," *Die Neue Rundschau*, LXVI (1955).

220. Arthur Schnitzler, "Ueber funktionelle Aphonie und deren Behandlung durch Hypnose und Suggestion," *Internationale Klinische Rundschau*, III (1889), 405–408.

221. *Wiener Medizinische Presse*, XXVII (1886), 1407–1409.

222. *Internationale Klinische Rundschau*, I (1887), 19–20.

223. *Internationale Klinische Rundschau*, III (1889), 891–893.

224. Arthur Schnitzler, *Wiener Klinische Rundschau*, IX (1895), 662–663, 679–680, 696–697.

225. See Olga Schnitzler, *Spiegelbild der Freundschaft* (Salzburg: Residenz Verlag, 1962).

226. Arthur Schnitzler, "Anatol" (1889), in *Gesammelte Werke. I. Abt. Die Theaterstücke* (Berlin: S. Fischer, 1912), I, 9–107.

227. Arthur Schnitzler, "Paracelsus" (1892) in *Gesammelte Werke. I. Abt. Die Theaterstücke* (Berlin: S. Fischer, 1912), II, 957.

228. Arthur Schnitzler, *Leutnant Gustl* (Berlin: S. Fischer, 1901).

229. Arthur Schnitzler, *Frau Beate und ihr Sohn* (Novella) (Berlin: S. Fischer, 1913).

230. Sigmund Freud, "Zeitgemässes über Krieg und Tod," *Imago*, IV (1915), 1–21. Standard Edition, XIV, 275–300.

231. Arthur Schnitzler, *Ueber Krieg und Frieden* (Stockholm: Bermann-Fischer Verlag, 1939).

232. Arthur Schnitzler, *Der Geist im Wort und der Geist in der Tat* (Berlin: S. Fischer, 1927).

233. Arthur Schnitzler, *Buch der Sprüche und Bedenken. Aphorismen und Fragmente* (Vienna: Phaidon-Verlag, 1927).

234. Arthur Schnitzler, *Flucht in die Finsternis* (Berlin: S. Fischer, 1931).

235. Ernest Jones, *The Life and Work of Sigmund Freud* (New York: Basic Books, 1957), III, 84.

236. Hermann Hesse, *Der Regenmacher* in *Das Glasperlenspiel* (Zurich: Fretz and Wasmuth, 1943), II, 261–328.

237. Louis Agassiz, *Methods of Study in Natural History* (14th ed.; Boston: Houghton, Mifflin and Company, 1882), pp. 296–298.

238. Agassiz said, "I have shown that there is a correspondence between the succession of Fishes in geological times and the different stages of their growth in the egg—this is all." As to Karl Ernst von Baer, his life work is condensed in this sentence: "All animals arise from eggs, and those eggs are identical in the beginning."

239. Sigmund Freud, "Beobachtungen über Gestaltung und feineren Bau der als Hoden beschriebenen Lappenorgane des Aals," *Sitzungsberichte der Kaiserlichen Akademie der Wissenschaften*, LXXV, I, Abt. (1877), 417–431.

240. "Ueber den Ursprung der hinteren Nervenwurzeln im hinteren Rückenmark Ammocoetes (Petromyzon Planeri)," *Sitzungsberichte der Mathematisch-Naturwissenschaftlichen Classe der Kaiserlichen Akademie der Wissenschaften*, LXXV, III, Abtheilung (1877), 15–27.

241. Sigmund Freud, "Eine neue Methode zum Studium des Faserverlaufes im Centralnerven-system," *Archiv für Anatomie und Physiologie, Anatomische Abt.* (1884), pp. 453–460.

242. Sigmund Freud, "Die Struktur der Elemente des Nervensystems," *Jahrbücher für Psychiatrie*, V (1884), 221—229.

243. Sigmund Freud, "Ein Fall von Hirnblutung mit indirekten basalen Herdsymptomen bei Skorbut," *Wiener Medizinische Wochenschrift*, XXXIV (1884), 244–246, 276–279.

244. Sigmund Freud, "Ein Fall von Muskelatrophie mit ausgebreiteten Sensibilitätsstörungen (Syringomyelie)," *Wiener Medizinische Wochenschrift*, XXXVI (1886), 168–172.

245. Sigmund Freud, "Akute multiple Neuritis der Spinalen- und Hirnnerven," *Wiener Medizinische Wochenschrift*, XXXVI (1886), 168–172.

246. Sigmund Freud and Oscar Rie, *Klinische Studie über die halbseitige Cerebellähmung der Kinder* (Vienna: Deuticke, 1891).

247. Sigmund Freud, *Zur Auffassung der Aphasien. Eine kritische Studie* (Leipzig and Vienna: Deuticke, 1891).

248. H. Steinthal, *Einleitung in die Psychologie der Sprachwissenschaft*, 2. Auflage (Berlin: Dümmler, 1881).

249. "The importance of the Steinthal theory was pointed out by Henri Delacroix, "Linguistique et psychologie," *Journal de Psychologie*, XX (1923), 798–825. *Le Langage et la pensée* (Paris: Alcan, 1924), pp. 493–494. See also Otto Marx, "Aphasia Studies and Language Theory in the 19th Century," *Bulletin of the History of Medicine*, XL (1966), 328–349.

250. André Ombredane, *L'Aphasie et l'élaboration de la pensée explicite* (Paris: Presses Universitaires de France, 1951), pp. 107–109.

251. Jones says that no copy of Freud's aphasia book is extant in English libraries, and that it was not mentioned by Head. The author checked with two libraries in London, those of the British Museum and the Wellcome Historical Museum, and found that both possessed a copy of the original German edition. Freud's new concept of agnosia is acknowledged by Henri Head, *Aphasia and Kindred Disorders of Speech* (Cambridge: Cambridge University Press, 1926), I, 105. Freud's book was quoted, among writings of other authors, by Henri Bergson in *Matière et Mémoire* (Paris: Alcan, 1896), p. 131.

252. Emil Rosenthal, *Contribution à l'etude des diplégies cerébrales de l'enfance*. Thèse Méd. Lyon, No. 761 (1892–1893).

253. Sigmund Freud, *Zur Kenntniss der cerebralen Diplegien des Kinderalters* (Leipzig and Vienna: Deuticke, 1893).

254. *Internationale Klinische Rundschau*, VII (1893), 1209.

255. Sigmund Freud, "Les Diplégies cérébrales infantiles," *Revue Neurologique*, I (1893), 177–183.

256. Sigmund Freud, "Die infantile Cerebellähmung," in Hermann Nothnagel, *Spezielle Pathologie und Therapie*, IX. Band, II. Theil, II. Abt. (Vienna: Alfred Hölder, 1897).

257. Quoted by Van Gehuchten in the following article.

258. Van Gehuchten, "Contribution à l'étude du faisceau pyramidal," *Journal de Neurologie et d'Hypnologie*, I (1897), 336–345.

259. First published as *Entwurf einer Psychologie*, in Sigmund Freud, *Aus den Anfängen der Psychoanalyse* (London: Imago Publishing Co., 1950), pp. 371–466. Sigmund Freud, *The Origins of Psychoanalysis*, 347–445.

260. See H. F. Ellenberger, "Fechner and Freud," *Bulletin of the Menninger Clinic*, XX (1956), 201–214.

261. Heinrich Sachs, *Vorträge über Bau und Thätigkeit des Grosshirns und die Lehre von der Aphasie und Seelenblindheit für Aerzte und Studierende* (Breslau: Preuss and Jünger, 1893), p. 110.

262. Peter Amacher, *Freud's Neurological Education and Its Influence on Psychoanalytic Theory*, published as IV, No. 4, of *Psychological Issues* (New York: International Universities Press, 1965).

263. E. Brücke, *Vorlesungen über Physiologie*, 2 vols. (Vienna: Braumüller, 1876).

264. Theodore Meynert, *Klinische Vorlesungen über Psychiatrie* (Vienna: Braumüller, 1890).

265. Sigmund Exner, *Entwurf zu einer physiologischen Erklärung der psychischen Erscheinungen* (Vienna: Deuticke, 1894).

266. *Blätter des Jüdischen Frauenbundes*, Vol. XII, No. 7–8 (July–August 1936), special issue devoted to Bertha Pappenheim.

267. Dora Edinger, *Bertha Pappenheim, Leben und Schriften* (Frankfurt-am-Main: Ner-Tamid-Verlag, 1963). Eng. trans., *Bertha Pappenheim, Freud's Anna O.* (Highland Park, Ill.: Congregation Solel, 1968).

268. The identity of Bertha Pappenheim and Anna O. is stated by Dora Edinger in

her biography, and has been confirmed to the author in personal communication from members of both the Breuer and the Pappenheim families.

269. Joseph Breuer and Sigmund Freud, *Studien über Hysterie* (Leipzig and Vienna: Deuticke, 1895), pp. 15–37. Standard Edition, II, 21–47.

270. Ernest Jones, *The Life and Work of Sigmund Freud* (New York: Basic Books, 1953), I, 223–225.

271. *Notes on the Seminar in Analytical Psychology Conducted by Dr. C. G. Jung*, Zurich, March 23–July 6, 1925. Arranged by Members of the Class. (Typewritten), Zurich, 1926.

272. Mrs. Dora Edinger informed the author that according to a document *(Meldezettel)* recently found in the Frankfurt City Archive, Bertha Pappenheim and her mother moved to that city in November 1888. It has not been possible to find out where they lived between 1882 and 1888.

273. The date given by Breuer for the death of Anna O.'s father is, however, identical with that of the death of Siegmund Pappenheim, as stated in the *Heimat-Rolle* in Vienna.

274. Jones adds that Dora Breuer committed suicide in New York in 1942; actually, according to information received from the Jewish community in Vienna, she committed suicide in Vienna, to escape being murdered by the Nazis.

275. For assistance in the author's inquiries he is indebted to Mr. Schramm, of Gross Enzersdorf, to Mr. Karl Neumayer, Mayor of Inzersdorf, and to Dr. W. Podhajsky, Director of the Viennese Psychiatric Hospital (Psychiatrisches Krankenhaus der Stadt Wien).

276. *Mea culpa!* In previous publications the author related Anna O.'s story according to Jones' version, having failed to apply the rule: Check everything!

277. See Chap. 2, pp. 72–81; Chap. 3, pp. 129–131.

278. Juan Dalma, "La Catarsis en Aristoteles, Bernays y Freud," *Revista de Psiquiatría y Psicología Medical*, VI (1963), 253–269; "Reminiscencias Culturales Clásicas en Algunas Corrientes de Psicología Moderna," *Revista de la Facultad de Medicina de Tucumán*, V (1964), 301–332.

279. Jacob Bernays, *Zwei Abhandlungen über die Aristotelische Theorie des Drama* (Berlin: Wilhelm Hertz, 1880).

280. Wilhelm Wetz, *Shakespeare vom Standpunkte der vergleichenden Literaturgeschichte* (Hamburg: Haendcke, Lehmkübe, 1897), I, 30. Wetz complained that following the treatise by Bernays there had been such a craze for the subject of catharsis that comparatively few people remained interested in the history of drama.

281. See Ola Andersson, *Studies in the Prehistory of Psychoanalysis* (Stockholm: Norstedts, 1962).

282. Albert Villaret, "Article Hysterie," *Handwörterbuch der gesamten Medicin* (Stuttgart, 1888), I, 886–892.

283. Joseph Breuer and Sigmund Freud, *Studien über Hysterie* (Leipzig and Vienna: Deuticke, 1895), pp. 37–89. Standard Edition, II, 48–105.

284. Ola Andersson, "A Supplement to Freud's Case History of Frau Emmy v. N." (unpublished paper).

285. Werner Leibbrand, "Sigmund Freud," *Neue Deutsche Biographie* (Berlin: Duncker and Humblot, 1961), V, 407–409.

286. "The Chronology of the Case of Frau Emmy von N.," Appendix to the English translation of Breuer and Freud, *Studies in Hysteria*, in Sigmund Freud, *Complete Works*. Standard Edition, II, 307–309.

287. In Freud's case history of Frau Emmy von N. there is only one precise chronological reference: the patient was frightened after having read on May 8, 1889, in the *Frankfurter Zeitung* a story of ill treatment having been inflicted upon an apprentice. The archive department of that newspaper informed the author, upon his request, that no such article could be found in the *Frankfurter Zeitung* throughout the month of May 1889. This would confirm the assumption expressed by the editors of the standard edition that Freud modified not only the names and places, but also the chronology of that case history.

288. This lecture was reviewed in *Internationale Klinische Rundschau*, VI (1892),

814–818, 853–856.

289. Sigmund Freud, "Ein Fall von hypnotischer Heilung nebst Bemerkungen über die Entstehung hysterischer Symptome durch den Gegenwillen," *Zeitschrift für Hypnotismus*, I (1893), 102–107, 123–129. Standard edition, I, 117–128.

290. Reviewed by Dr. Em. Mandl, *Internationale Klinische Rundschau*, VII (1893), 107–110.

291. Sigmund Freud, "Quelques considérations pour une étude comparative des paralysies motrices et hystériques," *Archives de Neurologie*, XXVI (1893), 29–43. Standard Edition, I, 160–172.

292. Reviewed by Dr. Em. Mandl, *Internationale Klinische Rundschau*, VII (1893), 868–869.

293. Josef Breuer and Sigmund Freud, "Ueber den psychischen Mechanismus hysterischer Phänomene (Vorläufige Mitteilung)," *Neurologisches Centralblatt*, XII (1893), 4–10, 43–47. Standard Edition, II, 3–17.

294. See Chap. 10, p. 768.

295. Sigmund Freud, "Charcot," *Wiener Medizinische Wochenschrift*, XLIII (1893), 1513–1520. Standard Edition, III, 11–23.

296. Paul Richer, *Etudes cliniques sur l'hystéro-épilepsie ou Grande Hystérie* (Paris: Delahaye and Lecrosnier, 1881), pp. 103, 116, 122.

297. Sigmund Freud, "Die Abwehr-Neuro-Psychosen," *Neurologisches Centralblatt*, XIII (1894), 362–364, 402–409. Standard Edition, III, 45–61.

298. Sigmund Freud, "Ueber die Berechtigung, von der Neurasthenie einen bestimmten Symptomcomplex als 'Angstneurose' abzutrennen," *Neurologisches Centralblatt*, XIV (1895), 50–66. Standard Edition, III, 90–115.

299. Ewald Hecker, "Ueber larvierte und abortive Angstzustände bei Neurasthenie," *Centralblatt für Nervenheilkunde*, XVI (1893), 565–572.

300. Maurice Krishaber, *De la névropathie cérébro-cardiaque* (Paris: Masson, 1873).

301. P. J. Kowalewsky, "Die Lehre vom Wesen der Neurasthenie," *Centralblatt für Nervenheilkunde*, XIII (1890), 241–244, 294–319.

302. Joseph Breuer and Sigmund Freud, *Studien über Hysterie* (Leipzig and Vienna: Deuticke, 1895). Standard Edition, Vol. II.

303. Sigmund Freud, "L'Heredité et l'étiologie des névroses," *Revue Neurologique*, IV (1896), 161–168. "Weitere Bemerkungen über die Abwehr-Neuropsychosen," *Neurologisches Centralblatt*, XV (1896), 434–448. Standard Edition, III, 143–156, 162–185.

304. Sigmund Freud, "Zur Etiologie der Hysterie," *Wiener Klinische Rundschau*, X (1896), 379–381, 395–397, 413–415, 432–433, 450–452. Standard Edition, III, 191–221.

305. This was already implicit in Charcot's theory of the *Grande hystérie* as developed by Paul Richer, *Etudes cliniques sur l'hystéroépilepsie ou grande hystérie* (Paris: Delahaye et Lecrosnier, 1881).

306. This was Janet's therapeutic procedure, see Chap. 6, pp. 372–374.

307. Sigmund Freud, *Aus den Anfängen der Psychoanalyse* (London: Imago, 1950), 229–232. (Letter to Fliess of September 21, 1897.) *Origins of Psychoanalysis*, pp. 215–218.

308. Eugen Bleuler is commonly credited with having coined the term *Tiefenpsychologie* (depth psychology), which was popular at the time when psychoanalysis was equated with the psychology of the unconscious.

309. See Chap. 3, pp. 125–126.

310. See Chap. 3, pp. 152–155.

311. See Chap. 5, pp. 303–311.

312. Freud's contention (*Traumdeutung*, p. 58, Standard Edition, IV, 83) that Scherner's book is written in such a bombastic style that it is repulsive to the reader, is true only of the foreword, not of the bulk of the book, whose style is concise and matter-of-fact, though not lively.

313. Karl Albert Scherner, *Das Leben des Traumes* (1861), p. 203.

314. Lynkeus (pseudonym of Josef Popper), *Phantasien eines Realisten* (Dresden: Carl Reissner, 1899), II, 149–163.

315. Incidentally, Philo of Alexandria had already written: "The very visions seen in their sleep are, of necessity, clearer and purer in the case of those who deem the morally beautiful eligible for its own sake, even as their doings by day are bound to be more worthy of appreciation." Philo, *On Dreams*, trans. by F. H. Colson and G. H. Whitaker, Loeb Classical Library, Philo, V, 453.

316. Dr. André Cuvelier of Nancy, who has made a special study of Liébeault's work, informs the author that the idea that "the dream is the guardian of sleep" is in direct opposition to Liébeault's doctrine. (To Liébeault, the fixation on the idea of rest is the guardian of sleep, and the dream a perturbing element.) It would seem that Freud, when referring to Liébeault, confused him with another as yet unidentified author.

317. Sigmund Freud, "Zum psychischen Mechanismus der Vergesslichkeit," *Monatsschrift für Psychiatrie und Neurologie*, IV (1898), 436–443. "Ueber Deckerinnerungen," VI (1899), 215–230. "Zur Psychopathologie des Alltaglebens (Vergessen, Versprechen, Vergreifen) nebst Bemerkungen über eine Wurzel des Aberglaubens," X (1901), 1–32, 95–143.

318. Sigmund Freud, *Zur Psychopathologie des Alltagslebens* (Berlin: Karger, 1904). Standard Edition, Vol. VI.

319. Siegfried Bernfeld, "An Unknown Autobiographical Fragment by Freud," *American Imago*, IV (1946), 3–19.

320. Schopenhauer had noticed that people making an involuntary error in making change most often do so to their own advantage.

321. Wolfgang von Goethe, *Hör-, Schreib- und Druckfehler*, in *Goethes Werke* (Stuttgart and Tübingen: J. G. Cotta, 1833), XLV, 158–164.

322. Rudolf Meringer and Carl Mayer, *Versprechen und Verlesen* (Berlin: Behrs Verlag, 1895).

323. Hanns Gross, *Handbuch für Untersuchungsrichter*, 2te. Vermehrte Aufl. (Graz: Leuschner and Lubensky, 1894), pp. 90, 93.

324. Friedrich Theodor Vischer, *Auch Einer. Eine Reisebekanntschaft* (Berlin: Machler, 1879).

325. Jules Verne, *Voyage au centre de la terre* (Paris: Hetzel, 1864).

326. Jules Verne, *Vingt Mille Lieues sous les mers* (Paris: Hetzel, 1869).

327. For instance, Herbert Silberer, *Der Zufall und die Koboldstreiche des Unbewussten* (Bern: Bircher, 1921).

328. Sigmund Freud, *Der Witz und seine Beziehungen zum Unbewussten* (Leipzig and Vienna: Deuticke, 1905).

329. Theodor Lipps, *Komik und Humor* (Hamburg: L. Voss, 1898).

330. Incidentally, this is one more evidence against the legend that Freud "hated Vienna his whole life long." (See Chap. 7, p. 465.)

331. Roland Dalbiez, *La Méthode psychanalytique et la doctrine freudienne* (Paris: Desclée de Brouwer, 1936), I, 7–37.

332. Sigmund Freud, "Bruchstück einer Hysterie-Analyse," *Monatsschrift für Psychologie und Neurologie*, XVIII (1905), 285–310. Standard Edition, VII, 7–122.

333. See Chap. 5, p. 299.

334. Sigmund Freud, *Drei Abhandlungen zur Sexualtheorie* (Leipzig and Vienna: Deuticke, 1905). Standard Edition, VII, pp. 130–243.

335. See Chap. 5, pp. 291–303.

336. August Forel, *Rückblick auf mein Leben* (Zurich: Europa-Verlag, 1935), pp. 64–65.

337. Gregory Zilboorg, *Sigmund Freud. His Exploration of the Mind* (New York: Charles Scribner's Sons, 1951), pp. 73–75.

338. See Chap. 5, p. 293; Chap. 10, pp. 788–789.

339. See Chap. 7, pp. 545–546.

340. *Jahrbuch für sexuelle Zwischenstufen unter besonderer Berücksichtigung der Homosexualität*, I (Leipzig: Max Spohr, 1899).

341. See Chap. 5, p. 298, 303.

342. Patrice Georgiades, *De Freud à Platon* (Paris: Fasquelle, 1934).

343. See Chap. 4, pp. 208–209.

344. See Chap. 5, p. 303.

345. E. Gley, "Les Aberrations de l'instinct sexuel," *Revue Philosophique*, XVII (1884) (I), 66–92.

346. Max Dessoir, "Zur Psychologie der Vita sexualis," *Allgemeine Zeitschrift für Psychiatrie*, L (1894), 941–975.

347. Albert Moll, *Untersuchungen über die Libido sexualis* (Berlin: H. Kornfeld, 1898), Vol. I.

348. G. Herman, *"Genesis." Das Gesetz der Zeugung*, Vol. V, *Libido und Manie* (Leipzig: Strauch, 1903).

349. See Chap. 5, p. 300.

350. Erasmus Darwin, *Zoonomia; or, the Laws of Organic Life*, I (London: J. Johnson, 1801), 200–201.

351. S. Lindner, "Das Saugen an den Fingern, Lippen etc. bei den Kindern (Ludeln)," *Jahrbuch für Kinderheilkunde und Physische Erziehung*, Neue Folge, XIV (1879), 68–89.

352. Charles Fourier, *Pages choisies*, Charles Gide, ed. (Paris: Recueil Sirey, 1932), pp. 174–182. See also Maxime Leroy, *Histoire des idées sociales en France* (Paris: Gallimard, 1950), pp. 246–292.

353. K. R. Hoffmann, *Die Bedeutung der Excretion im thierischen Organismus* (1823). Quoted by Friedrich von Müller, *Spekulation und Mystik in der Heilkunde. Ein Ueberblick über die leitenden Ideen der Medizin im letzten Jahrhundert* (Munich: Lindauer, 1914).

354. Friedrich S. Krauss and H. Ihm, *Der Unrat in Sitte, Brauch, Glauben und Gewohnheitsrecht der Völker von John Gregory Bourke* (Leipzig: Ethnologischer Verlag, 1913).

355. See Chap. 5, pp. 295–296.

356. Sigmund Freud, *Der Witz und seine Beziehung zum Unbewussten* (1905), p. 47. Standard Edition, VIII, 59–60.

357. Heinrich Jung-Stilling, *Theobald oder die Schwärmer, eine wahre Geschichte* (Frankfurt and Leipzig, 1785).

358. See Chap. 5, p. 300.

359. See Chap. 5, p. 279.

360. Choderlos de Laclos, *Les Liaisons dangereuses* (1782), éd. Pléiade (Paris: Gallimard, 1959), p. 263.

361. Jules Laforgue, "Hamlet, ou les suites de la pitié filiale," *La Vogue*, III (1886), reprinted in *Oeuvres Complètes* (Paris: Mercure de France, 1901), II, 17–72.

362. Stendhal, *Vie de Henry Brulard* (1836) (Paris: Union Générale d'Edition, 1964), Chap. 3, pp. 57–67.

363. Hans Gustav Guterbock, *Kumarbi, Mythen vom churritischen Kronos* (Zurich: Europa-Verlag, 1946).

364. Georges Dumezil, "Religion et mythologie préhistoriques des Indo-Européens," in *Histoire générale des religions*, Maxime Gorce and Raoul Mortier, eds. (Paris: Quillet, 1948), I, 448–450.

365. Vasubandhu, *L'Abhidharmakosa de Vasubandhu*, trans. and annotated by Louis de La Vallee Poussin (Paris: Geuthner, 1923–1926), II, 50–51. A similar belief is to be found in *The Tibetan Book of the Dead*.

366. Sigmund Freud, "Träume im Folklore," in Sigmund Freud and D. E. Oppenheim, *Dreams in Folklore* (New York: International Universities Press, 1958), pp. 69–111.

367. Laignel-Lavastine et Vinchon, *Les Maladies de l'esprit et leurs médecins du XVIe au XIXe siècle* (Paris: Maloine, 1930), pp. 101–118.

368. See Chap. 5, pp. 304–305.

369. Jacques-Antoine Dulaure, *Histoire abrégée des différents cultes* (2nd ed.; Paris Guillaume, 1825), Vol. I, *Des Cultes qui ont précédé et amené l'idolâtrie;* Vol. II, *Des Divinités génératrices chez les anciens et chez les modernes*.

370. Adalbert Kuhn, *Die Herabkunft des Feuers und des Göttertranks* (Berlin: Dümmler, 1859).

371. George W. Cox, *The Mythology of the Aryan Nations* (London: Longmans Green and Co., 1870), II, 112–130.

372. Anton Nagele, "Der Schlangen-Cultus," *Zeitschrift für Völkerpsychologie und Sprachwissenschaft*, Lazarus und Steinthal (1887), XVII, 264–289.

373. Angelo de Gubernatis, 2 vols. *La Mythologie des plantes ou les légendes du règne végétal* (Paris: C. Reinwald, 1878).

374. Angelo de Gubernatis, *Zoological Mythology or the Legends of Animals*, 2 vols. (London: Trübner & Co., 1872).

375. See Chap. 4, pp. 212–215.

376. The philosopher Léon Brunschvicg pointed out later that the mystical interpretations to the Song of Solomon given by grave churchmen were the exact reverse of Freudian commentaries on mystical writers, "both with the same air of infallibility." Léon Brunschvicg, "A propos de l'analogie," in *Mélanges offerts à Monsieur Pierre Janet* (Paris: d'Artrey, 1939), 31–38.

377. Otto Rank, *Der Mythus von der Geburt des Helden; Versuch einer psychologischen Mythendeutung* (Leipzig und Vienna: Deuticke, 1909).

378. An account of that patient, about whom so much was published, is to be found in Paul Sérieux and Joseph Capgras, *Les Folies raisonnantes; le délire d'interprétation* (Paris: Alcan, 1909), pp. 386–387.

379. See Chap. 10, p. 792.

380. Sigmund Freud, "Analyse der Phobie eines 5-jährigen Knaben," *Jahrbuch für psychoanalytische und psychopathologische Forschungen*, I (1909), 1–109. Standard Edition, X, 5–147.

381. Oskar Pfister, *Die psychanalytische Methode* (Leipzig and Berlin: Klinkhardt, 1913), pp. 59–60.

382. Sigmund Freud, "Zur Einführung des Narzissmus," *Jahrbuch für psychoanalytische und psychopathologische Forschungen*, VI (1914), 1–24. Standard Edition, XIV, 73–102.

383. Sigmund Freud, "Triebe und Triebschicksale," *Internationale Zeitschrift für Psychoanalyse*, III (1915), 84–100. Standard Edition, XIV, 117–140.

384. Sigmund Freud, "Die Verdrängung," *Internationale Zeitschrift für Psychoanalyse*, III (1915), 129–138. Standard Edition, XIV, 146–158.

385. Sigmund Freud, "Das Unbewusste," *Internationale Zeitschrift für Psychoanalyse*, III (1915), 189–203, 257–269. Standard Edition, XIV, 166–204.

386. Sigmund Freud, "Metapsychologische Ergänzung zur Traumlehre," *Internationale Zeitschrift für Psychoanalyse*, IV (1916–1917), 277–287. Standard Edition, XIV, 222–235.

387. Sigmund Freud, "Trauer und Melancholie," *Internationale Zeitschrift für Psychoanalyse*, IV (1916–1917), 288–301. Standard Edition, XIV, 243–258.

388. Sigmund Freud, *Jenseits des Lustprinzips* (Vienna: Internationaler Psychoanalytischer Verlag, 1920). Standard Edition, XIV, 7–64.

389. Freud's principle of pleasure-unpleasure and its economic function is "essentially identical" with Fechner's concept, according to Ludwig Binswanger, *Erinnerungen an Sigmund Freud* (Bern: Francke, 1956).

390. Gabriel Tarde, *Philosophie pénale* (Lyon: Storck, 1890).

391. See Chap. 4, pp. 205–206.

392. Novalis, *Fragmente über Ethisches, Philosophisches und Wissenschaftliches*, in *Sämmtliche Werke*, herausg. Carl Meissner, III (1898), 292, 168, 219.

393. A. Tokarsky, '*Voprosi Filosofii i Psychologii*, VIII, Moskva (1897), 931–978. The author is grateful to Professor Schipkowensky, of Sofia, who was kind enough to read that booklet and send him a summary of it.

394. Elie Metchnikoff, *Etudes sur la nature humaine. Essai de philosophie optimiste* (3rd ed.; Paris: Masson, 1905), 343–373.

395. G. T. Fechner, "Vier Paradoxa," in *Kleine Schriften von Dr. Mises* (Leipzig: Breitkopf and Härtel, 1875).

396. Sabina Spielrein, "Die Destruktion als Ursache des Werdens," *Jahrbuch für psychoanalytische und psychopathologische Forschungen*, IV (1912), 464–503.

397. Cavendish Moxon, "Freud's Death Instinct and Rank's Libido Theory," *Psycho-*

analytic Review, XIII (1926), 294–303.

398. Richard Schaukal, *Eros Thanatos, Novellen* (Vienna and Leipzig: Wiener Verlag, 1906).

399. Karl Menninger, *Man Against Himself* (New York: Harcourt and Brace, 1938).

400. Achim Mechler, "Der Tod als Thema der neueren medizinischen Literatur," *Jahrbuch für Psychologie und Psychotherapie*, III, No. 4 (1955), 371–382.

401. Sigmund Freud, *Das Ich und das Es* (Vienna: Internationaler Psychoanalytischer Verlag, 1923). Standard Edition, XIX, 12–66.

402. Georg Groddeck, *Das Buch vom Es; psychoanalytische Briefe an eine Freundin* (Vienna: Internationale Psychoanalytischer Verlag, 1923). Eng. trans., *The Book of the Id* (New York: Nervous and Mental Disease Publishing Co., 1928.)

403. Sacha Nacht. Quoted from memory. To the author's request, Dr. Nacht answered that he remembered having given this definition but could not find the reference either.

404. Sigmund Freud, *Hemmung, Symptom und Angst* (Vienna: Internationaler Psychoanalytischer Verlag, 1926). Standard Edition, XX, 87–172.

405. Anna Freud, *Das Ich und die Abwehrmechanismen* (Vienna: Internationaler Psychoanalytischer Verlag, 1936). Eng. trans. by Anna Freud, *The Ego and the Mechanisms of Defence* (New York: International Universities Press, 1946).

406. Heinz Hartmann, "The Development of the Ego Concept in Freud's Work," *International Journal of Psychoanalysis*, XXXVII (1956), 425–438.

407. Heinz Hartmann, "Ich-Psychologie und Anpassungsproblem," *Internationale Zeitschrift für Psychoanalyse*, XXIV (1939), 62–135.

408. The slowing down or arrest of associations could have been explained in many ways. To attribute it to inner resistance of the patient, and to attribute the resistance, in turn to repression, was Freud's two-fold hypothesis, as pointed out by Rudolf Allers, *The Successful Error: A Critical Study of Freudian Psychoanalysis* (New York: Sheed and Ward, 1940), Chap. 1.

409. Sigmund Freud, "Die Freudsche psychoanalytische Methode," in Loewenfeld, *Die psychischen Zwangserscheinungen* (Wiesbaden: Bergmann, 1904), pp. 545–551. Eng. trans., *Freud's Psychoanalytic Method*. Standard Edition, VII, 249–254.

410. Sigmund Freud, "Die zukünftigen Chancen der psychoanalytischen Therapie," *Centralblatt für Psychoanalyse*, I (1910), 1–9. Standard Edition, XI, 141–152.

411. Sigmund Freud, "Ueber 'wilde' Psychoanalyse," *Centralblatt für Psychoanalyse*, I (1910), 91–95. Standard Edition, XI, 221–227.

412. Sigmund Freud, "Die Handhabung der Traumdeutung in der Psychoanalyse," *Centralblatt für Psychoanalyse*, II (1911), 109–113. Standard Edition, XII, 91–96.

413. Sigmund Freud, "Zur Dynamik der Uebertragung," *Centralblatt für Psychoanalyse*, II (1912), 167–173. Standard Edition, XII, 99–108.

414. Sigmund Freud, "Ratschläge für den Arzt bei der psychoanalytischen Behandlung," *Centralblatt für Psychoanalyse*, II (1912), 483–489. Standard Edition, XII, 111–120.

415. Sigmund Freud, "Erinnern, Wiederholen und Durcharbeiten," *Internationale Zeitschrift für Psychoanalyse*, II (1914), 485–491). Standard Edition, XII, 147–156.

416. Sigmund Freud, "Bemerkungen über die Uebertragungsliebe," *Internationale Zeitschrift für Psychoanalyse*, III (1915), 1–11. Standard Edition, XII, 159–171.

417. Sigmund Freud, "Wege der psychoanalytischen Therapie," *Internationale Zeitschrift für Psychoanalyse*, V (1919), 61–68. Standard Edition, XVII, 159–168.

418. Sigmund Freud, "Die endliche und die unendliche Analyse," *Internationale Zeitschrift für Psychoanalyse*, XXIII (1937), 209–240. Standard Edition, XXIII, 216–253.

419. Sigmund Freud, "Abriss der Psychoanalyse," *Internationale Zeitschrift für Psychoanalyse*, XXV (1940), 7–67. Standard Edition, XXIII, 144–207.

420. René Descartes, Letter of June 6, 1647, in *Oeuvres et Lettres* (Paris: Pléiade, 1958), pp. 1272–1278.

421. One of Descartes' editors says that somewhat similar stories were told by Stendhal and Baudelaire. Samuel De Sacy, *Descartes par lui-même* (Paris: Editions du Seuil, 1956), p. 119.

422. See Chap. 2, p. 63.

423. See Chap. 3, pp. 152–155; Chap. 6, p. 374.

424. R. Haym, *Die romantische Schule* (Berlin: R. Gaertner, 1870), p. 617.

425. Ludwig Börne, *Gesammelte Schriften* (Milwaukee: Bickler & Co., 1858), II, 116–117.

426. *Aufrichtigkeit ist die Quelle aller Genialität.* This has become a proverbial expression in German.

427. Ludwig Börne, *Lichtstrahlen aus seinen Werken* (Leipzig: Brockhaus, 1870), p. 150.

428. Francis Galton, *Memories of My Life* (2nd ed.; London: Methuen, 1908), p. 80.

429. Sigmund Freud, "Zwangshandlungen und Religionsübung," *Zeitschrift für Religionspsychologie,* I (1907), 4–12. Standard Edition, IX, 117–127.

430. Sigmund Freud, *Die Zukunft einer Illusion* (Vienna: Internationaler Psychoanalytischer Verlag, 1927). Standard Edition, XXI, 5–56.

431. Sigmund Freud, "Totem und Tabu, Ueber einige Uebereinstimmungen im Seelenleben der Wilden und der Neurotiker," *Imago,* I (1912), 17–33, 213–227, 301–333; II (1913), 1–21, 357–409. Standard Edition, XIII, 1–161.

432. James Jasper Atkinson, *Primal Law,* published as a second part to Andrew Lang, *Social Origins* (London: Longmans Green and Co., 1903), pp. 209–294.

433. William Robertson Smith, *Lectures on the Religion of the Semites,* 1st Series, *The Fundamental Institutions* (London: A. Black, 1894).

434. A detailed account and criticism of these theories was given by Arnold Van Gennep, *L'Etat actuel du problème totémique* (Paris: Leroux, 1920).

435. Thomas Hobbes, *Leviathan* (1651), in Great Books of the Western World, XXIII, Part II, Chap. 17, 99–101.

436. Sigmund Freud, *Massenpsychologie und Ich-Analyse* (Vienna: Internationaler Psychoanalytischer Verlag, 1921). Standard Edition, XVIII, 69–143.

437. E. Dupréel, "Y a-t-il une foule diffuse?" *Centre International de Synthèse; 4e semaine internationale: la Foule,* Georges Bohn, ed. (Paris: Alcan, 1934), pp. 109–130.

438. Gabriel Tarde, *Les Lois de l'imitation* (Paris: Alcan, 1890).

439. Gabriel Tarde, "Les crimes des foules," *Actes du IIIe Congrès d'Anthropologie criminelle,* Bruxelles, août 1892 (Brussels: Hayez, 1894), pp. 73–90.

440. Scipio Sighele, *La foule criminelle. Essai de psychologie collective,* French translation (Paris: Alcan, 1892).

441. Gustave Le Bon, *Psychologie des foules* (Paris: Alcan, 1895). Eng. trans. *The Psychology of Peoples* (New York: Macmillan, 1898).

442. Paul Reiwald, *Vom Geist der Massen* (Zurich: Pan-Verlag, 1946), pp. 131–142.

443. Sigmund Freud, *Das Unbehagen in der Kultur* (Vienna: Internationaler Psychoanalytischer Verlag, 1930). Standard Edition, XXI, 64–145.

444. See Chapter 4, pp. 183–184; Chapter 5, p. 277.

445. Sigmund Freud, *Neue Folge der Vorlesungen zur Einführung in die Psychoanalyse* (Vienna: Internationaler Psychoanalytischer Verlag, 1933). Standard Edition, XXII, 132.

446. Sigmund Freud, "Formulierungen über die zwei Prinzipien des psychischen Geschehens," *Jahrbuch für psychoanalytische und psychopathologische Forschungen,* III (1911), 1–8. Standard Edition, XII, 218–226.

447. Sigmund Freud, "Der Dichter und das Phantasieren," *Neue Revue,* I (1908), 716–724. Standard Edition, IX, 143–153.

448. Sigmund Freud, "Das Unheimliche," *Imago,* V–VI (1919), 297–324. Standard Edition, XVII, 219–252.

449. Anon. (Sigmund Freud), "Der Moses des Michelangelo," *Imago,* III (1914), 15–36. Standard Edition, XIII, 211–236.

450. Ludwig Binswanger, "Erfahren, Verstehen, Deuten," in *Ausgewählte Vorträge und Aufsätze,* II (Bern: Francke, 1955), 40–66.

451. Wilhelm Jensen, *Gradiva; ein pompeianisches Phantasiestück* (Dresden and Leipzig: Reissner, 1903).

452. Sigmund Freud, *Eine Kindheitserinnerung des Leonardo da Vinci* (Leipzig and Vienna: Deuticke, 1910). Standard Edition, XI, 63–137.

453. Meyer Schapiro, "Leonardo and Freud: An Art Historical Study," *Journal of the History of Ideas*, VII (1956), 147–178.

454. K. R. Eissler, *Leonardo da Vinci: Psychoanalytic Notes on the Enigma* (London: Hogarth, 1962).

455. Sigmund Freud, "Psychoanalytische Bemerkungen über einen autobiographisch beschriebenen Fall von Paranoia (Dementia Paranoides)," *Jahrbuch für psychoanalytische und psychopathologische Forschungen*, Vol. III (1911). Standard Edition, XII, 9–82.

456. Some data pertaining to Schreber's familial and personal background, as well as fragments of hospital case histories, have been supplied by Franz Baumeyer, "The Schreber Case," *International Journal of Psychoanalysis*, XXXVII (1956), 61–74.

457. Ida Macalpine and Richard A. Hunter, "The Schreber Case," *Psychoanalytic Quarterly*, XXII (1953), 328–371.

458. Sigmund Freud, "Eine Teufelsneurose im siebzehnten Jahrhundert," *Imago*, IX (1923), 1–34. Standard Edition, XIX, 72–105.

459. Ida Macalpine and Richard A. Hunter, *Schizophrenia 1677: A Psychiatric Study of an Illustrated Autobiographical Record of Demoniacal Possession* (London: Dawson and Sons, 1956).

460. Gaston Vandendriessche, *The Parapraxis in the Haizmann Case of Sigmund Freud* (Louvain: Publications Universitaires, 1965).

461. Sigmund Freud, "Dostojewski und die Vatertötung," in F. M. Dostoievski, *Die Urgestalt der Brüder Karamazoff. Dostojewskis Quellen, Entwürfe und Fragmente. Erläutert von W. Komarowitsch* (Munich: Piper, 1928), pp. xiii–xxxvi. Standard Edition, XXI, 177–194.

462. Sigmund Freud, *Der Mann Moses und die monotheistische Religion* (Amsterdam: Albert de Lange, 1939). Standard Edition, XXIII, 7–137.

463. Eduard Meyer, *Geschichte des Altertums*, I Band, II Hälfte, 5. Aufl. (Stuttgart, 1926), p. 679.

464. Friedrich Schiller, *Die Sendung Moses*, in *Sämtliche Werke* (Stuttgart and Tübingen: Cotta, 1836), X, 468–500.

465. Karl Abraham, "Amenhotep IV (Ichnaton)" *Imago*, I (1912), 334–360.

466. David Bakan, *Sigmund Freud and the Jewish Mystical Tradition* (Princeton: Van Nostrand Co., 1958).

467. The correspondence between Einstein and Freud can be found in *Einstein on Peace*, Otto Nathan and Heinz Norden, eds. (New York: Simon & Schuster, 1960).

468. Emilio Servadio, "Freud's Occult Fascinations," *Tomorrow*, VI (Winter 1958), 9–16.

469. Lou Andreas-Salome, *In der Schule bei Freud* (Zurich: Max Niehans, 1958), pp. 191–193. Eng. trans., *The Freud Journal* (London: Hogarth Press, 1965).

470. Sigmund Freud, "Psychoanalyse und Telepathie," *Gesammelte Werke* (1941), XVII, 27–44. "Traum und Telepathie," *Imago* (1922), VIII, 1–22. Standard Edition, XVIII, 177–193, 197–220; XXII, 31–56. *Neue Folge der Vorlesungen zur Einführung in die Psychoanalyse* (Vienna: Internationaler Psychoanalytischer Verlag, 1933), Chap. 30.

471. Cornelius Tabori, *My Occult Diary* (London: Rider & Co., 1951), pp. 213–219.

472. Sigmund Freud, *Gesammelte Werke* (London: Imago, 1941), XVII, p. 152. Standard Edition, XXIII, 300.

473. Friedrich Nietzsche, *Menschliches, Allzumenschliches*, I, No. 180. In: *Friedrich Nietzsches Werke*, Taschen-Ausgabe (Leipzig: Naumann, 1906), III, 181.

474. See Chap. 7, pp. 444–450.

475. Maria Dorer, *Historische Grundlagen der Psychoanalyse* (Leipzig: Felix Meiner, 1932), pp. 128–143.

476. See Chap. 5, p. 300.

477. The author is grateful to Frau Professor Erna Lesky, Director of the University Institute for the History of Medicine in Vienna, who drew his attention to the work of Moritz Benedikt and to his influence upon dynamic psychiatry.

478. See Chap. 5, p. 301.

479. Moritz Benedikt, "Aus der Pariser Kongresszeit. Erinnerungen und Betrachtungen," *Internationale klinische Rundschau*, III (1889), 1611–1614, 1657–1659.

480. Maria Dorer, *Historische Grundlagen der Psychoanalyse*, pp. 71–106.
481. Gustav Adolf Lindner, *Lehrbuch der empirischen Psychologie nach genetischer Methode* (Graz: Wiesner, 1858).
482. Sigmund Freud, "Formulierung über die zwei Prinzipien des psychischen Geschehens," *Jahrbuch für psychoanalytische und psychopathologische Forschungen* (1911), III, 1–8. Standard Edition, XII, 218–226.
483. See Chap. 4, pp. 210–215.
484. See Chap. 5, pp. 291–303.
485. See Chap. 5, pp. 303–311.
486. See Chap. 5, pp. 311–318.
487. Vilfredo Pareto, *Le Mythe vertuiste et la littérature immorale* (Paris: Rivière, 1911). See also G. H. Bousquet, *Vilfredo Pareto, sa vie et son oeuvre* (Paris: Payot, 1928), p. 144.
488. See Chap. 5, p. 301; Chap. 7, p. 495.
489. See Chap. 3, p. 111.
490. See Chap. 7, pp. 521–522.
491. See Chap. 6, pp. 360–372.
492. *XVIIth International Congress of Medicine*, London, 1913, Sec. XII, Part I, pp. 13–64.
493. See Chap. 6, p. 415.
494. See Chap. 6, pp. 366–367.
495. See Chap. 6, p. 374.
496. Ernest Jones, "The Action of Suggestion in Psychotherapy," *Journal of Abnormal Psychology*, V (1911), 217–254.
497. Emmanuel Régis and Angelo Hesnard, *La Psychoanalyse des névroses et des psychoses* (2nd ed.; Paris: Alcan, 1922), p. 352.
498. See Chap. 7, pp. 523–524.
499. E. Krapf, "Lichtenberg und Freud," *Acta Psychotherapeutica, Psychosomatica et Orthopaedagogica*, I (1954), 241–255.
500. John A. Sours, "Freud and the Philosophers," *Bulletin of the History of Medicine*, XXXV (1961), 326–345.
501. Xavier Bichat, *Recherches physiologiques sur la vie et la mort* (Paris: Brosson, Gabon et Cie, 1796), p. 84.
502. See Chap. 4, pp. 236–237.
503. See Chap. 4, pp. 233–234.
504. See Chap. 4, pp. 239–240.
505. Dora Stockert-Meynert, *Theodor Meynert und seine Zeit* (Vienna and Leipzig: Oesterreichischer Bundesverlag, 1930), pp. 149–156.
506. James Ralph Barclay, *Franz Brentano and Sigmund Freud: An Unexplored Influence Relationship* (Idaho State College, October 17, 1961). (Multigraphed.)
507. See Chap. 4, pp. 204–206.
508. See Chap. 4, pp. 215–223.
509. See Chap. 4, p. 209.
510. Friedrich Wilhelm Foerster, *Erlebte Weltgeschichte, 1869–1953. Memoiren* (Nuremberg: Glock und Lutz, 1953), p. 98.
511. Fritz Wittels, *Freud and His Time* (New York: Grosset and Dunlap, 1931).
512. Sigmund Freud, "Die Verbrecher aus Schuldbewusstsein," *Imago*, IV (1916), 334–336. Standard Edition, XIV, 332–333.
513. See Chapter 5, pp. 276–278. See also C. Dimitrov and A. Jablenski, "Nietzsche und Freud," *Zeitschrift für Psychosomatische Medizin und Psychoanalyse*, XIII (1967), 282–298.
514. This word was coined after the name of the hero of a novel by Ivan Gontcharov, *Oblomov* (1859).
515. Sigmund Freud, "Aus der Geschichte einer infantilen Neurose," *Sammlung kleiner Schriften zur Neurosenlehre*, IV (1918), 578–717; V (1922), 1–140. Standard Edition, XVII, 7–122.
516. Ruth Mack Brunswick, "A Supplement to Freud's 'History of an Infantile

Neurosis,' " *International Journal of Psychoanalysis,* IX (1928), 439–476.

517. David Bakan, *Sigmund Freud and the Jewish Mystical Tradition* (Princeton: D. Van Nostrand Co., 1958).

518. Wilhelm Fliess, *Die Beziehungen zwischen Nase und weiblichen Geschlechtsorganen in ihrer biologischen Bedeutung dargestellt* (Leipzig and Vienna: Deuticke, 1897). In this book Freud is frequently quoted, notably on pp. 12, 99, 192, 197–198, 218.

519. There were, for instance, the sarcastic attacks by Moritz Benedikt, "Die Nasen-Messiade von Fliess," *Wiener Medizinische Wochenschrift* (1901), LI, pp. 361–365.

520. See Chapter 5, p. 293; and Chapter 10, pp. 788–789.

521. See Chapter 5, p. 299.

522. Renato Poggioli, *Rozanov* (New York: Hillary House, 1962). V. V. Rozanov, *Solitaria,* with an abridged account of the author's life by E. Gollerbach. Trans. by S. S. Koteliansky (London: Wishart & Co., 1927).

523. V. V. Rozanov, *Izbrannoe. Vstupilelnaya Statya i Redaktsiya Iu,* P. Ivaska (New York: Izdatelstvo Imeni Chekhova, 1956).

524. Carl Laufer, "Dr. Joseph Winthuis zum Gedächtnis," *Anthropos,* LI (1956), 1080–1082.

525. J. Winthuis, *Das Zweigeschlechterwesen bei den Zentralaustraliern und anderen Völkern* (Leipzig: Hirschfeld, 1928).

526. J. Winthuis, *Einführung in die Vorstellungswelt primitiver Völker. Neue Wege der Ethnologie* (Leipzig: Hirschfeld, 1931). *Mythos und Kultgeheimnisse* (Stuttgart: Strecker and Schröder, 1935). *Mythos und Religionswissenschaft* (Moosburg: Selbstverlag des Verfassers, 1936).

527. K. R. Eissler, *Medical Orthodoxy and the Future of Psychoanalysis* (New York: International Universities Press, 1965).

528. Richard LaPiere, *The Freudian Ethic* (New York: Duell, Sloane and Pierce, 1959).

529. See Chapter 4, pp. 231–233.

530. One of the first pioneers of that study was the French ethnologist Arnold van Gennep. His book, *La Formation des légendes* (Paris: Flammarion, 1929), is now obsolete, but had the merit of indicating the way.

531. René Etiemble, *Le Mythe de Rimbaud* (Paris: Gallimard, 1961).

532. See Chap. 5, pp. 266–267.

533. See Chap. 10, pp. 804, 827, 834–836.

534. See Chap. 10, pp. 810–815.

535. See Chap. 10, p. 847, 852.

536. See Chap. 10, pp. 830–831.

537. See Chap. 10, p. 855.

538. See Chap. 7, pp. 516–517; Chap. 10, p. 860.

539. See Chap. 4, p. 246, n. 11.

540. See, for instance, *Critical Essays on Psychoanalysis,* Stanley Rachman, ed. (New York: Macmillan, 1963).

541. Jacques Lacan, *Ecrits* (Paris: Editions du Seuil, 1966).

542. Ludwig Binswanger, "Erfahren, Verstehen, Deuten," 1926, reprinted in *Ausgewählte Vorträge und Aufsätze* (Bern: Francke, 1955), II, 67–80. Paul Ricoeur, *De l'Interprétation. Essai sur Freud* (Paris: Editions du Seuil, 1965).

543. See Chap. 1, pp. 41–42.

8

Alfred Adler and Individual Psychology

CONTRARY TO COMMON ASSUMPTION, neither Adler nor Jung is a "psychoanalytic deviant," and their systems are not merely distortions of psychoanalysis. Both had their own ideas before meeting Freud, collaborated with him while keeping their independence, and, after leaving him, developed systems that were basically different from psychoanalysis, and also basically different from each other.

The fundamental difference between Adler's individual psychology and Freud's psychoanalysis can be summarized as follows: Freud's aim is to incorporate into scientific psychology those hidden realms of the human psyche that had been grasped intuitively by the Greek tragedians, Shakespeare, Goethe, and other great writers. Adler is concerned with the field of *Menschenkenntnis*, that is, the concrete, practical knowledge of man. The interest of individual psychology is that it is the first recorded, unified, complete system of *Menschenkenntnis*, a system vast enough to encompass also the realm of neuroses, psychoses, and criminal behavior. For that reason, when studying Adler, the reader must temporarily put aside all that he learned about psychoanalysis and adjust to a quite different way of thinking.

The Life Frame of Alfred Adler

Alfred Adler was born in a suburb of Vienna in 1870 and died in Aberdeen, Scotland, in 1937. He spent the greatest part of his life in Vienna. The events of his life, like those of Freud, must be viewed against the background of the vicissitudes of Austrian history, but being fourteen years younger than Freud, Adler experienced those changes in a somewhat different manner. His childhood and youth were spent during the most prosperous years of the Dual Monarchy. When World War I broke out, the forty-four-year-old Adler was still young enough to be mobilized as a military doctor and was able to acquire a direct knowledge of war neuroses. The catastrophe of 1918 also affected the forty-eight-year-old Adler differently than the sixty-two-year-old Freud. Thus the advent of the new political regime offered him the possibility of materializing his projects and founding his institutions. The years 1920 to 1932 were, in spite of political upheavals, the years of Adler's greatest achievements. But he did not wait for Hitler to come to power, and emigrated to the United States in 1932. Black clouds were gathering over Europe when he suddenly died in 1937, two and one-half years before the catastrophe he had foreseen.

Both Freud and Adler were the sons of Jewish merchants of the lower middle class with the difference that Adler's father dealt in grain and Freud's in wool. Both were raised in the suburbs of Vienna, were thoroughly Viennese, and became the founders of new schools and acquired world fame. However, they achieved their success in different ways. Freud's was a university career, with the customary vicissitudes of the time. He lived in a residential part of the town and had a choice clientele. Adler's university career was checked from the beginning. He began as a general practitioner in a nonresidential quarter, and struggled for the creation of social medicine. After his association with Freud, the group he founded had, more than psychoanalysis, the feature of a political movement. His patients belonged mostly to the lower or middle class, and social problems always remained the focus of his interest.

Thus we see Alfred Adler's career as an example of the social ascension of a man who remained emotionally attached to the lower class of the population in whose midst he had spent his childhood. The disintegration of the Austrian-Hungarian Empire favored the transformation of his teaching from its marginal position to that of a socio-ethical movement of worldwide scope.

Family Background

Behind the superficial analogies between Freud and Adler there were deep-reaching differences. We have seen that during the second half of the nineteenth century the attitude and mentality of the Austrian Jews largely depended upon the group to which their parents or grandparents belonged before the emancipation.[1] Freud's parents carried with them the resentment accumulated by the Jews of Galicia and south Russia throughout the centuries. Adler's parents came from the comparatively privileged community of Kittsee, in the province of Burgenland.

Burgenland is a picturesque countryside with lakes surrounded by reeds, with fields, groves, vineyards, castles on hilltops, little villages of old-world charm. It is noted for the great variety of its birds; nearly every village rooftop had its stork's nest. Burgenland is proud of its historical past and of its great men, among whom are the composers Haydn and Liszt. Throughout the centuries, Burgenland was a kind of buffer state between

Austria and Hungary. It actually belonged to Hungary, but the Hungarian magnates who possessed a great part of the land were friendly with Austria (this was an exception among the Hungarian nobility). At that time the population of Burgenland was about 300,000. The majority were German-speaking, but there were also Hungarians, Croatian immigrants, Gypsies, and prosperous Jewish communities. The Jews of Burgenland enjoyed a more liberal status than most of the other Jews of the empire. Many of them were traders, and as such, they served as intermediaries between the ghetto Jews of Pressburg and the commercial centers of Vienna.

The difference in background may explain certain characteristic features in the Jews who had their origin in Burgenland. Above all they did not have the feeling of belonging to a persecuted minority. Moritz Benedikt, who came from the *kille* (Jewish community) of Eisenstadt, and who in his autobiography complained of having been the victim of countless injustices, never complained of having suffered because of anti-Semitism. The same holds for Alfred Adler, in whose writings the term anti-Semitism is never even mentioned. Men of that background could keep their religion (as did Benedikt, who remained a member of the Synagogue), but when they lost their faith, the Jewish tradition no longer held any meaning for them. Not being sentimentally attached, they could easily shift to Protestantism or Catholicism without having the feeling of betraying their ancestors or being disloyal to their fellow Jews. Thus Alfred Adler later became a Protestant, while two of his brothers (Max and Richard) converted to Catholicism, and the oldest brother (Sigmund) left the Jewish community as *konfessionslos* (without a declared religious adherence).

We do not know much about Alfred Adler's upbringing. In a short autobiographical account,[2] he relates that he was his father's favorite child but for a long time felt rejected by his mother, that he once hurt another boy, that at an early age he suffered from rickets and fits of breathlessness, that he was impressed by the death of a younger brother, and narrowly escaped dying from a severe case of pneumonia. These were the two events that inspired him in his future vocation as a physician. From other childhood memories recorded by Phyllis Bottome, we may infer that Jewish rites were performed at home and that he went to the Synagogue[3] with his parents. Once, at the age of five, during prayers at the Synagogue, he pulled at a piece of vestment sticking out of a cupboard, causing the whole cupboard to fall with a crash. One Passover night at home, he crept downstairs to substitute leavened bread for the unleavened, and watched the rest of the night from a cupboard to see whether the angel would notice the difference if it came. Should these two early memories be true, one could, according to Adler's own method, infer a negative attitude toward the Jewish religion.

This difference in the Jewish background of Adler and Freud may also explain why, in contrast to Freudian psychoanalysis, Adler's individual psychology contains nothing that could plausibly be attributed to the Jewish tradition.

Our knowledge of Alfred Adler's genealogy and family is fragmentary. Data contained in the usual biographies are often erroneous. The only systematic inquiry conducted to this date is that of Dr. Hans Beckh-Widmanstetter, which we are following here.[4]

Alfred Adler's grandfather, Simon Adler, was a master furrier (*Kürschnermeister*) in Kittsee. Nothing is known of him, except that his wife's name was Katharina Lampl, and that he was no longer living in 1862 when his son David married. Nor is it known how many children he had, aside from David (Alfred's uncle) and Leopold (Alfred's father). David was thirty-one years old when he married in Vienna, on June 29, 1862. He worked as a tailor in the Jewish suburb of Leopoldstadt.

Leopold Adler (whose Jewish name was Leb Nathan) was born in Kittsee on January 26, 1835. Nothing is known of the first thirty years of his life. When he married in Vienna, on June 17, 1866, the marriage certificate gives his address as the same as his father-in-law's in Penzing; this indicates that for at least some time he lived in the latter's house, and probably worked in his business firm.

Alfred Adler's ancestors on his mother's side came from the little town of Trebitsch, in Moravia. It is not known how long they had lived there, but when they migrated to Penzing, in 1858 or 1859, they had at least five children: Ignaz (born before 1839), Moriz (born in April 1843), Pauline (Alfred's mother, born in January 1845), Salomon (born in July 1849), and Albert (born in 1858). Two other children were born in Penzing: Ludwig (in December 1859) and Julius (in December 1861). Adler's grandfather Hermann Beer had founded the firm Hermann Beer and Sons, dealing in oats, wheat, and bran. This was a prosperous trade at the time, but with the development of railway transportation it was doomed to decline. Later, the firm was taken over by his son Salomon.

Two years after settling in Penzing, on October 10, 1861, Hermann Beer bought a house at Poststrasse 22. It is likely that Alfred Adler sojourned there several times during his childhood. This house still stands and is now on Linzerstrasse 20, near the corner of Nobilegasse. In spite of modernizations of the new buildings that surround it, its main structure has not changed. On the ground floor there is a shop, and on the first floor is the dwelling to which one has access from the courtyard in the back that is reached through the carriage gateway. The courtyard is large enough to accommodate a dozen cars. On the left is the workshop of an automobile mechanic, and the stables have been converted into garages. A wide stone staircase leads up to the apartment on the first floor, where the Beer family lived for many years.

Hermann Beer and his wife Elisabeth (also called Libussa) Pinsker had at least seven children, who in turn had large families, so that Alfred

Adler had numerous relatives on his mother's side. One of his uncles, Julius Beer, was only eight years older than he.

We know very little about the life, occupation, and economic situation of Leopold Adler. During 1866 to 1877 he lived in the neighboring villages of Penzing and Rudolfsheim, changing his address several times and his occupation is recorded as "merchant." For unknown reasons he then moved to Leopoldstadt, the Jewish suburb on the northeast of Vienna, where he lived from 1877 to 1881, but here too he changed his address every year. Then, for two years, he lived in Hernals (at that time outside Vienna) where he rented a house at Hauptstrasse 25 with attached business premises at No. 23. These two houses were dependencies of the *Grossmeierei* (a kind of wholesale dairy farm) that belonged to Count Palffy, one of the Hungarian magnates of Burgenland. It is very likely that Leopold Adler acted as middleman for the sale of the Count's produce.

Hermann Beer died on February 5, 1881, and his wife, on January 15, 1882. Their property was divided among the seven living children, but Pauline sold her part to one of her brothers, and very shortly thereafter, on July 27, 1883, she and Leopold bought a property at Währing, which at that time was still a sparsely populated area outside the city limits of Vienna[5] with one-story houses and gardens. This property, located at Hauptstrasse 57–59 (today Währingerstrasse 129–131) is still standing. It was a typical commercial house of that time; it comprised business premises, a dwelling on the first floor, with two large and two smaller rooms, as well as a kitchen, and stables below.[6] This house nearly faced the cemetery in which were the tombs of Beethoven and Schubert (today the Schubert Park). According to Phyllis Bottome, the family not only kept horses, but cows, goats, chickens, and rabbits as well, but it would be an exaggeration to depict young Alfred as growing up in a sort of miniature Garden of Eden, as has sometimes been done. This property, which belonged equally to Leopold and Pauline, remained in their hands from July 1883 to July 1891. But Leopold was not successful, and according to family tradition the Adlers were increasingly harassed by financial difficulties. This is confirmed by the fact that in time the property became heavily mortgaged and was finally sold in 1891, at a loss.

The family then returned to Leopoldstadt, where it lived under considerable material strain, until Sigmund, the eldest brother, became a successful businessman and was able to reestablish all his relatives in comfortable living conditions.

Since Alfred Adler always insisted as much as Freud upon the importance of family constellation in the shaping of the personality, it would be appropriate to know how it was in his own case. But here too our knowledge is incomplete. Very little is known of the personality of his father, Leopold Adler, and the data we have about him come from impressions of people who knew him as an old man. Phyllis Bottome writes that he had a carefree and happy personality, was humorous and tremendously proud, that he was a handsome man who took great care of his personal appearance, brushed his clothes meticulously himself, cleaned his boots so that they shone like glass, and appeared invariably as if dressed for a party.[7] His grandson Walter Fried, who lived with him for several years when he was a child, says:

> He was a man of very stately appearance, always elegant and neat, and who was in the habit of living well. I had extraordinary respect for him, though he always was especially good to me. I still see him as he stroked my head and gave me new copper coins of which I was inordinately proud.[8]

Another grandson, Ferdinand Ray, says that

> Grandfather Leopold Adler was a rather elegant, good-looking gentleman who held himself erect and was particular with his dressing. . . . In the last few years of his life he had his meal in the *Rathauskeller* at lunch, always with a glass of wine, then a ham sandwich at 5 P.M. and to bed at 6 P.M.[9]

It seems that the relationship of Alfred with his father was a good one. According to Phyllis Bottome, Alfred was Leopold's favorite son, and he constantly gave him encouragement (we know that encouragement was to become one of the leitmotivs of Adler's educational system). The same author also says that Leopold often repeated to Alfred: "Never believe what anyone tells you," which probably meant that one should judge people according to their conduct rather than their words (this too was to become a basic axiom of individual psychology).

Pauline Adler certainly did not enjoy good health as her husband, who died at the age of nearly eighty-seven years. According to all testimonies, when she died at sixty-one, she was worn out by illness and overwork. Phyllis Bottome depicts her as "nervous and gloomy," without any sense of humor. According to family tradition she sacrificed herself too much for certain members of the family. One of her grandsons describes her as being "a gentle and fine woman, who ran the business, and with husband, children, household and dog, had her hands full." She and Alfred failed to understand each other, and it is said that she played the part in his life that he later called the *Gegenspieler* (counterfoil), that is, the person against whom one measures and exercises one's strength.

Whereas Freud primarily stressed the importance of the child's relationship with its parents, and secondarily with its siblings, Alfred Adler attributed more importance to the position of the child in the line of siblings than to his relationship with his parents, and this leads us to examine the nature of the sibling constellation in his case.

Alfred was the second in a family of six children, not counting two who died in early infancy.[10] His relationship with his eldest brother Sigmund is of particular interest.

Sigmund Adler (his Jewish name was Simon) was born on August 11, 1868, in Rudolfsheim. All testimonies confirm that he was a most intelligent and gifted person, so that in Phyllis Bottome's words, "Alfred Adler felt himself put in the shade of a model eldest brother, a true 'first born,' who always seemed to Alfred to be soaring far beyond him in a sphere which Alfred—for all his efforts—could never attain. Even at the end of his life, Alfred had not wholly got over this feeling." Sigmund's successful career was the more remarkable because life had been hard for him. He had to leave school before obtaining his Matura because of his family's impoverishment, and went to work, first in his father's business and later on his own. For some time he was a sales agent for Hungarian grain mills, but later he established himself in real estate. Thus, in time he became a very successful businessman and acquired a fortune which he later lost, however, in the postwar inflation. One of his sons relates that because he was a Hungarian citizen, he served in the Hungarian army for one year, that he married in 1900, had three sons, and in view of the political situation, eventually emigrated to the United States, where he remained until his death.[11] Another of his sons describes him as follows:

> Sigmund was truly a self-made man, had a big library, and was proud of his friends (better middle class, doctors, lawyers, and so on). . . . We children through him (and mother) learned to appreciate the higher things in life, good music, good books, travelling, and so on. He was a good chess player, and we children learned the game from him, but here too he was almost always too busy to play.
>
> As to his relation with Alfred, he respected him highly, both as a medical doctor as well as a psychologist, and relied quite often on Alfred's judgment when one of us was sick. Later on, when Alfred's fame spread, he spoke of Alfred with admiration and great respect always.[12]

According to all testimonies, Sigmund Adler was a straightforward man, selfless to a rare degree, who supported not only his own family, but also his father Leopold in his old age as well as many other of his relatives.

Alfred's rivalry with his successful brother Sigmund seems to have played a major role in his life. Like all boys, they fought with each other, and according to family tradition, they eventually became of equal strength. It has also been said that if Alfred left his general practice to specialize in neuropsychiatry, it was because he followed the example of his brother, who had shifted from being a sales agent to the more lucrative business of real estate. Whatever might have been, they were always good friends, and it was through Sigmund that Alfred found and bought his beautiful country house at Salmannsdorf. Both brothers emigrated to America and died similarly, Alfred of a stroke in a street of Aberdeen in 1937 and Sigmund in a street in New York twenty years later, on February 25, 1957, at the age of eighty-nine.[13]

After Sigmund and Alfred came the third child Hermine, a daughter, born in Rudolfsheim on October 24, 1871. Phyllis Bottome says she was Alfred's favorite sister, who also greatly admired him. Her son writes about her:

> Hermine, my mother, played the piano very well and was a very good sight reader of music. She had a nice singing voice, but untrained. She used to play with Alfred, who was playing the piano too, music for four hands. They had a great affinity and all her children, when they got married, brought their partners for approval to Alfred.[14]

After Hermine there came a little brother, Rudolf, who was born in Penzing on May 12, 1873, and died of diphtheria on January 31, 1874.[15] As we shall see, the birth and premature death of the little brother were significant events in Alfred's childhood.

The next child, Irma, was born in Penzing on November 23, 1874. Her life was to end tragically in an extermination camp in Poland in 1941. She married the printer Franz Fried and had a son, Walter.

After Irma came Max, who was born in Leopoldstadt on March 17, 1877.[16] In spite of the family's difficult situation, he was able to complete his secondary school at the Sperläum, where he received his Matura in September 1896. Thereupon he studied history and the German language and literature for nine semesters at the University of Vienna. His dissertation[17] was approved in October 1903, and he received his doctorate in philosophy on June 23, 1904.[18] Max Adler seems to have worked mainly as a journalist, writing on philosophical, economic, and political topics. He lived for many years in Dresden, but later went to Rome, where he died on November 5, 1968, at the age of ninety-one. According to Phyllis Bottome, "he was highly envious and jealous of the popular Alfred, nor did he ever recover from this state of mind. Adler was fond of him but never succeeded in winning his affection." These details must be borne in mind when referring to the picture Alfred Adler gave of the personality of the second child in a large family: always under pressure, trying hard to compete with the older brother, and himself narrowly followed by a competitive younger brother.

The last child, Richard, was born in Währing on October 21, 1884. During his childhood the economic situation of the family was at its worst, and it seems that his education was sacrificed. On the other hand, he seems to have been the favorite child of his mother. He had a great admiration for Alfred, who also helped him in all possible ways. As a piano teacher, he claimed to apply the principles of individual psychology to the teaching of music. For some time he stayed in Alfred's country home in Salmannsdorf.

During, World War II he worked at cultivating Alfred's large garden in Döbling, which still belonged to the family.[19] He was able to escape the notice of the Nazis and to survive along with his wife Justine. He died in January 1954, leaving no children.

The difference between the social and family backgrounds of Alfred Adler and Sigmund Freud is not without relevance in regard to the difference in their respective psychological systems. The Jewish tradition had a very strong impact on Jews whose families had come from Galicia, even if they had lost their religious faith. Though Freiberg was for him the lost paradise of early childhood, Freud was an Austrian citizen with the full rights of an Austrian. But he grew up in Leopoldstadt, a densely populated suburb of Vienna where the poorer Jews from the eastern part of the empire had settled, and where there were slums with numerous children and beggars, so that Freud always considered himself a member of a minority group. Since Freud had always remained under the watchful eyes of his parents and teachers, he was led to emphasize his childhood relationships with his parents more than with his siblings and peer group. Moreover, Freud was the firstborn and cherished child of his mother and felt antagonistic to his father, which made the Oedipus situation seem natural to him.

In Adler's case, the situation was quite different. The Jewish tradition was not as important to Jews originating from the privileged communities of Burgenland. Because he was born in Vienna, Burgenland did not have the quality of a lost paradise for Adler; on the contrary, it was even a drawback in his life. It meant that he was not registered as an Austrian, but as a Hungarian, thus making him the subject of a country whose language he did not speak and depriving him of many privileges granted only to Austrians in Vienna. (He belatedly acquired Austrian citizenship in 1911.) In contrast to Freud, Adler spent most of his childhood in the outskirts (*Vororte*) of Vienna,[20] in places such as Rudolfsheim, Penzing, Hernals, and Währing, which had at least partly kept their rural character. They were not so densely populated; one feature of these "outskirts" was the existance of large pieces of land that had been bought up by speculators and left in a state of abandon until prices rose enough for them to make a substantial profit. These places were commonly called the *Gstätten*; street urchins used to go there to amuse themselves. Thus Adler spent most of his childhood in the "outskirts" of the town, playing or fighting with non-Jewish boys many of whom belonged to the lower classes. Obviously, parental supervision for Adler was not as strict as for Freud. All accounts of Adler's life tell of his escapades and fights with street boys. This necessarily led him to emphasize, more than did Freud, the role of the peer group and siblings in the shaping of personality. The family constellation, too, was quite different with these two men. Adler was the second-born who felt rejected by the mother but protected by the father, so having experienced the opposite situation from Freud's he could never accept the idea of the

Oedipus complex. It is noteworthy that Adler, though he was a Jew and a foreigner in his own country, never felt as if he belonged to a minority; he saw himself as participating in the popular life of the city, and his intimate knowledge of the Viennese idiom made it possible for him to give public speeches as a man of the people. One can understand, therefore, how the concept of community feeling was to become the central point in his teaching.

Events in Alfred Adler's Life

Whereas the difficulty in writing about Freud consists in the super-abundance of biographic material, for Adler, as for Janet, exactly the opposite is true. We have very few short autobiographical notes of Adler, in addition to those recorded by Phyllis Bottome. There have been, as yet, four biographies of Adler: One by Manes Sperber,[21] another by Hertha Ogler,[22] the third by Phyllis Bottome,[23] and a fourth by Carl Furtmüller, known only by its English translation.[24] Phyllis Bottome also gave details on Adler in a book of psychological essays and in the second volume of her autobiography.[25] Whatever the merit of these publications, the information they contain is based mainly on memories and hearsay, and is marred by numerous inaccuracies. From Adler's abundant correspondence, hardly more than a half dozen letters have been published.[26] There had been no Adler archive to collect documents and testimonies about Adler, and there are no films of him or recordings of his voice. A systematic inquiry based on archival material has been recently conducted by Dr. H. Beckh-Widman-stetter of Vienna, but only a small part of the material gathered by him has appeared as yet. His short narrative of Adler's childhood and youth is still to be published.[27] The following sketch of Alfred Adler's life is based mainly on Dr. H. Beckh-Widmanstetter's research, supplemented by verbal and written information supplied by members of his family.[28]

Alfred Adler was born in Rudolfsheim on February 7, 1870. The house where he was born was on the Hauptstrasse at the corner of Zollernsperg-gasse. At that time it was a large house divided into fifteen small apartments, and the house that has replaced it is at Number 208 Mariahilferstrasse.[29] The house was facing a large market place (Central-Markt Platz). Nearby was a large space of open land (*Gstätte*) (now the Gustav Jäger Park with the Technical Museum), where the children of the neighborhood would play. During the first seven years of Alfred Adler's childhood, the family lived at various addresses in Rudolfsheim and the neighboring Penzing. In those years young Alfred often escaped to play with street boys and went so far as to pinch the flowers in the gardens of the Imperial castle of Schön-brunn, which was not far from Penzing. Though Alfred thought that he went to the public school in Penzing, neither his nor his brother Sigmund's names were found in the archives of that school. Possibly he went to a private school whose archives have not been preserved. One important event of that period was the birth of Alfred's little brother, Rudolf, and his death a few days before Alfred's fourth birthday. If his early memories are to be believed, this event, combined with a severe childhood illness some time later, inspired him with the early wish to become a physician.

When Adler was seven years old, the family had to move to the Jewish suburb of Leopoldstadt, where they lived for four years. It is characteristic that none of Adler's biographers mentioned that he ever lived in Leopold-stadt. Probably he had unpleasant memories of those years, and did not wish to discuss them. During that time, in 1879 (thus, when he was aged nine), Alfred was sent to the Communales Real-und Obergymnasium in the Sperlgasse, better known as the Sperlgymnasium, or Sperläum, the same one to which young Sigmund Freud had been sent fourteen years earlier at the same age. In the meantime, however, school regulations had been changed, setting the age of ten as a minimum for entry. Dr. Beckh-Widmanstetter found that in the *Klassenbuch* (class register) Alfred Adler's date of birth, 1870, had been corrected by an unknown hand and changed to 1869. We know from the school archives that young Alfred failed this first year and had to repeat it.

In the middle of 1881, the family left Leopoldstadt and moved to Hernals, where Alfred went to the Hernalser Gymnasium in the street bearing the same name. He continued to attend that school when the family moved, once again, to the neighboring *Vorort* of Währing, until he was eighteen years old and received his Matura. Unfortunately the archives of that school were destroyed during the Allied occupation of Vienna after World War II. Thus it is impossible to know what kind of pupil Alfred Adler was. It is certain that he received an excellent education, studying Latin, Greek, and German classics taught at that time.

Almost nothing is known about Alfred's adolescence outside of school. According to his biographers he had a passion for music, song, and the theater, and was quite a good actor himself.

As soon as he completed secondary school, he registered at the Faculty of Medicine in Vienna, in the winter semester of 1888 to 1889. Dr. Hans Beckh-Widmanstetter found the complete record of Adler's academic achievements in the archive of the Medical School, of which we extract the following details. Adler completed his medical studies in the average length of time, followed only the obligatory courses necessary to pass the examinations, and passed his three Rigorosa with the note *genügend* (sufficient), which was the lowest for passing. Since at that time psychiatry was not an obligatory course, Adler did not receive any psychiatric teaching; nor did he hear the lectures of the Privat Dozent Sigmund Freud on hysteria. However, in his fifth semester he followed Krafft-Ebing's course on "the most important diseases of the nervous system."

Alfred Adler's University records show that his fifth, sixth, and seventh semesters were particularly strenuous. During these three semesters he took among others a ten-hour weekly course of surgery, and a ten-hour weekly course of medicine, the latter with the internist Nothnagel (whose teaching also included lectures on organic nervous diseases). After his seventh semester, Adler passed his first Rigorosum on March 24, 1892, and then went for the first six months of his one year of obligatory military service in the first and fourth Tyroler-Kaiserjäger-Regiment from April 1, 1892, to October 1, 1892.

The following semesters were also strenuous. In his ninth semester, he took, among others, a course in the pathology of the nervous system with Salomon Stricker. In the tenth semester he took only a ten-hour weekly course of surgery. Thereupon he passed his second Rigorosum on May 22, 1894, and waited almost one and one-half years before presenting himself to the third Rigorosum.

It is likely that he devoted this time to perfecting himself in clinical medicine. In those days even a young doctor who did not wish to pursue an academic career or become a specialist would usually spend two or three years either in the General Hospital or in the Poliklinik, to acquire clinical experience. In the archives of the General Hospital, Beckh-Widmanstetter found that no appointment was held there by Alfred Adler. In view of the fact that paid positions were reserved for Austrian citizens, and being that Adler was a Hungarian, he could have done only voluntary, unpaid work there. We do find his name, however, on the list of those young doctors who worked at the Poliklinik in 1895 and 1896. The Viennese Poliklinik, a benevolent institution, was founded in 1871, mainly under the initiative of Moritz Benedikt, to provide free medical care to people of the working class at a time when there was no social security. The doctors who worked there were not paid. For young physicians it was an opportunity to acquire clinical experience and perhaps also to find prospective clients. Alfred Adler worked in 1895 in the Department of Ophthalmology of the Poliklinik, with Professor von Reuss. It is likely that he met Moritz Benedikt, who gave electric treatment to patients of that department.

During that period he passed his third Rigorosum on November 12, 1895, and received his medical degree on November 22, 1895. In 1896 he again worked at the Poliklinik, but this cannot have been very long, since he was called away from April 1, 1896, to September 30, 1896, to complete his second semester of obligatory military service in the Eighteenth Military Hospital of Pressburg, in a Hungarian unit, under his Magyar name of Aladár Adler.

It has been asserted that Adler took other postgraduate studies, namely in pathology, but it has not been possible to find any documentary evidence.[30] If he ever worked at the General Hospital, it must have been on a voluntary basis, because no evidence was left of this.

The years 1896 to 1902 of Adler's life are not completely documented. Accounts given in his biographies are short, often contradictory, and based on hearsay. It has not been possible as yet to find when he opened his practice. According to Carl Furtmüller, Adler had taken a deep interest in socialism in his student days, had attended socialist political meetings, without, however, taking an active part, and met in these groups his future wife, Raissa Timofeyevna Epstein, who had come to Vienna as a student, since women were not allowed to study in Russian universities at that time. Actually, documentary evidence shows that she studied three semesters at the University of Zurich in 1895 and 1896[31] but never registered at the University of Vienna, although she came to live in that city in 1897.[32]

On December 23, 1897, Alfred Adler married Raissa Epstein. According to records of the Jewish community in Vienna, she had been born in Moscow on November 9, 1873, the daughter of a Jewish merchant. The marriage was celebrated in the Jewish community in Smolensk. After their marriage, they settled in the apartment of Adler's parents at Eisengasse 22 (today Wilhelm-Exnerstrasse), while his parents moved to another place.

In 1898 two events are significant: the birth of Adler's oldest child, a daughter, Valentine Dina, who was born on August 5, 1898, and the publication of Adler's first writing, the *Health Book for the Tailoring Trade*.[33]

In 1899 Adler set up his practice in the Czerningasse at No. 7. It seems likely that as a young practitioner he would have found it difficult to practice in the Eisengasse, which was in the vicinity of the quarter where many distinguished specialists had their practices. He had better opportunities in that popular street, not far from the Prater.

From 1899 to 1902, we have no documentary data, except of the birth of his daughter Alexandra, on September 24, 1901. From August 12, 1902, to September 15, 1902, Adler spent thirty-five days of military service with the Eighteenth Infantry Regiment of the Honved, the Hungarian reserve army. This regiment was composed mainly of German-speaking soldiers and was stationed in the Burgenland town of Oedenburg.[34]

In that same year Adler began his collaboration with Heinrich Grün, the editor of a new medical journal, the *Aerztliche Standeszeitung*. It is not known what kind of an agreement there was between the two men, but a perusal of that journal shows that Heinrich Grün obviously considered Adler his principal contributor.

It is in that crucial year 1902 that Adler became acquainted with Freud. The usual story is that the *Neue Freie Presse* had published a derogatory review of Freud's *Interpretation of Dreams*, whereupon Adler wrote a letter of protest, which was also published by that paper. This brought Adler to the attention of Freud, who thanked him with a postcard, inviting him to visit him. In point of fact the *Neue Freie Presse* never published a review of *The Interpretation of Dreams*, nor any article against Freud, and it is not known under what circumstances the two men met.[35]

In 1904 Alfred Adler converted to the Protestant faith. According to

Phyllis Bottome, he resented the fact that the Jewish religion was only for one ethnic group and preferred to "share a common deity with the universal faith of man."[36] He was baptized on October 17, 1904, together with his daughters Valentine and Alexandra, but without Raissa, in the Protestant Church of the Dorotheergasse[37]

From 1902 to 1911, Adler belonged to the psychoanalytic circle of which he had been one of the first four members and that slowly grew around Freud. Until 1904 he pursued his collaboration with Heinrich Grün's journal. But from 1905 on he wrote various psychoanalytically oriented contributions for medical and pedagogical journals. His activities in Freud's Wednesday evening meetings are known to us from the minutes of the Viennese Psychoanalytic Society, which summarized the talks he gave there and his interventions in the discussions. It seems that he was the most active member of the circle and that Freud held him in high esteem during those first years.[38] In 1907 his book, *Studies of Organ Inferiority*, appeared, which was considered a physiological complement to the psycho-analytic theory and was well thought of by Freud. At the first international psychoanalytic meeting in Salzburg, on April 26, 1908, Adler read a paper on "Sadism in Life and Neurosis." He was the chairman and one of the main contributors to the Society's discussion of children's suicide in April 1910, which was subsequently published. In October 1910, after the Society had moved into its new premises, Adler was elected as its president and Stekel as its vice-president.

Meanwhile changes were occurring in Adler's life. His family had grown, with the birth of Kurt on February 25, 1905, and Cornelia (Nelly) on October 18, 1909. He moved from the Czerningasse to a more residential part of the town, taking a large apartment at Dominikanerbastei 10.[39] He now specialized as Nervenarzt although it seems that for some time thereafter he was still often called as a consultant in matters of general medicine. In 1911 he acquired Austrian citizenship.[40]

At the same time it became more and more apparent that Adler's own views on neuroses diverged from those of Freud. Adler's contributions could no longer be viewed as complements to psychoanalysis, since they contradicted Freud's basic assumptions. Nevertheless, when the question arose of organizing the Viennese Psychoanalytic Society, Freud recom-mended Adler for president, and for the newly founded *Centralblatt*, that Adler and Stekel became the joint editors. But soon afterward the diverg-encies between his and Freud's views became so acute that it was deemed necessary to devote several sessions to their clarification. On January 4, 1911, and February 1, 1911, Adler read two papers, one on "Problems of Psychoanalysis" and the other on the "Masculine Protest." On February 8 and February 22, animated discussions, to say the least, took place, and Stekel was the only one to maintain that there was no contradiction between Freud's and Adler's views. But at the end of the February session, Adler and Stekel resigned their posts of president and vice-president of the Society. After vainly attempting a reconciliation, Adler left the Society together with his friend Furtmüller and a few others.

With the six members who had resigned with him and some others, Adler founded a new group, the *Society for Free Psychoanalysis*, which soon after was named the *Society for Individual Psychology*.

It seems that during these lengthy discussions with the psychoanalytic group, Adler had become more conscious of the originality of his thoughts. Just at that time Hans Vaihinger's celebrated book, *The Philosophy of the As If*, appeared which greatly impressed Adler, and provided him with a new conceptual framework for his own system.

Whereas Freud gathered his disciples around him in his apartment and later on the premises of a medical association, Adler preferred to meet with his followers in some of the Viennese cafés. A few of his adversaries considered this as undignified, even if their discussions were more serious than the usual talk that took place in the Viennese coffeehouses. During that time Adler was reshaping his system and organizing his own school. In 1912 he published his second book, *The Nervous Character*, and inaugurated the publication of a series of monographs. In 1913 and 1914 he published numerous papers on neuroses and kindred topics. Then he and Carl Furtmüller founded the *Zeitschrift für Individual-Psychologie* (*Journal for Individual Psychology*). A collective volume, *Heilen und Bilden* (*Healing and Education*), contained several of his older papers, together with new ones from him and his followers, arranged so as to constitute a textbook of individual psychology. Adler now had clients, not only from the lower and middle classes, but from the upper class as well. Among his patients was the Russian revolutionist Yoffe, a friend of Trotzky's. (Trotzky lived in Vienna from 1907 to July 1914; his wife was a friend of Raissa Adler.) [41]

Adler, as we have seen, had applied in July 1912 for the title of Privat Dozent at the university. The reply was given only on January 1915. It is not known why the delay was so unusually long. The report about his candidature was written by Wagner-Jauregg (who, incidentally, had presided at Adler's third Rigorosum and at the ceremony when he received his medical degree).

In this report the section devoted to Adler's academic achievements is surprisingly short: "According to him, he was active during the four years following his medical degree in the Vienna General Hospital and in the *Poliklinik* in the field of Psychiatry, Internal Medicine and Ophthalmology, in which institutes and in which position is not said." This somewhat flippant way of putting it suggests that Wagner-Jauregg was not quite convinced of the reality of Adler's statements. Thereupon Wagner-Jauregg holds that Adler's two books and his numerous articles stand out against the scientific works of all the other candidates without exception, by one important feature: All the other candidates had brought forward works on their research in histology, anatomy or experimental physiology

of the nervous system, or clinical investigations on the symptoms and etiology
of nervous diseases, whereas in the works of Alfred Adler there is nothing of the
kind. He gives only "explanations of a purely speculative nature." Adler, who
belonged to the psychoanalytic school, has remained faithful to its method, if
not of its teaching. It is the first time that a follower of that school applies to the
post of Privat Dozent and for that reason it is very important that the *Professorenkollegium* should take position.

Wagner-Jauregg considers Adler's theory of organ inferiority "interesting and
reasonable" (*ansprechend und vernünftig*), namely that such a condition entails functional increase and maybe neurosis, but finds Adler's conception of the
organ much too general, since it includes whole systems, which does not allow
for accuracy.

As for *The Nervous Character*, Wagner-Jauregg criticizes Adler's wide
definition of neurosis and his purely psychogenetic concept of its etiology. In
regard to his concepts of the "fictitious aim" and "masculine protest," Adler
gives case histories that are explained by the theories they should prove. Wagner-
Jauregg will not take the psychoanalytic method seriously and criticizes other
theories, some of which he finds "as grotesque as with Freud."

Can Adler's works be called scientific? asks Wagner-Jauregg. Adler's main
tool is intuition and his convictions his sole proof. Adler's works are "ingenious"
(*geistreich*), but for a scientist it is dangerous to be only ingenious. Imagination
should be checked by criticism. This leads to the question, "Is it desirable to
teach at the Medical School what Adler has to teach?" And it is to be assumed
that he will never teach anything else. "Therefore my answer must be a
definite *no*," concludes Wagner-Jauregg.[42]

Following this report, the Professorenkollegium rejected Adler's candidature unanimously by twenty-five voices out of twenty-five.

Reading Wagner-Jauregg's report, one cannot help but think that his
criticism of Adler was above all meant for Freud, who is mentioned several
times. For Adler it was a severe disappointment. It has been said that his
socialist opinions were the cause of that setback, but this is improbable.
Incidentally, Adler's pamphlet on the tailor trade and his early publications
on social medicine are nowhere mentioned in Wagner-Jauregg's report.

Meanwhile World War I had broken out. In the midst of the world
tragedy Adler had his own private worries. His wife had gone for a vacation
to Russia with their four children, and when he sent her a telegram urging
her to return to Vienna, she did not realize how serious the situation was,
postponed her return, and was caught. It took several months of arduous
negotiations to have her released from Russia and returned to Vienna via
Sweden and Germany. Adler, who was forty-four years old, had not been
mobilized, since he was exempt from further military service in December
1912. But by 1916 the military situation had grown worse in Austria-
Hungary and regulations were revised so that many men were mobilized
who otherwise would have been exempt. Thus Adler was sent as an army
physician to the neuropsychiatric section of the military hospital of Semmer-

ing. In his autobiography, Stekel mentions that he worked in the same section of this hospital where Adler had preceded him and had done excellent work, that his examinations were thorough, his case histories faultless, and that he was a model physician.[43] Thereupon Adler was transferred to the neuropsychiatric section of the Garrison Hospital No. 15 in Cracow. This transfer of an army physician, who had no army grade, to a garrison hospital in a university town was rather unusual, and it has been suggested that it could have been possible only through very high channels.[44] The only event that is known of his stay in Cracow is the mention of a lecture on war neuroses delivered before a meeting of army physicians in November 1916.[45]

It is not known exactly how long Adler worked there. It is known that in November 1917, Adler was transferred to the military hospital of Grinzing and for some time was responsible for the care of typhus patients. The presence of Adler in Switzerland before the end of the war is known by a postcard; it has been assumed that he went there to accompany a convoy of wounded or sick prisoners.

Austria-Hungary's defeat brought a long period of utmost distress in Vienna. There was famine, lack of fuel, darkened streets, epidemics, and insufficient medication. Most people were financially ruined, fortunes and savings were lost by rich and poor alike, and families were disorganized because thousands of men were retained as prisoners in other countries without being able to correspond. Revolutionary propaganda was rampant among the returning soldiers and workers. Juvenile delinquency was growing from day to day. It also was a depressing thought for the Viennese, who had been at the center of a powerful empire to be now the hypertrophic center of of a small resourceless republic.

During that state of general misery and depression, Adler's socialist opinions again came to the fore although in an original and renewed fashion. This was shown in three publications that appeared in 1918 and 1919.

Three months before Austria's collapse, in July 1918, the Swiss journal *Internationale Rundschau* published a short note with the title: "A Psychiatrist on War Psychoses" and the signature A. A., which almost certainly stood for Alfred Adler.

> The author points out the paradox of the common people going to war with such a show of enthusiasm to endure so many sufferings for a cause that was not their own. The answer is that they acted in that way in order to escape the distressing feeling of their helplessness.[46]

In December 1918 the same journal published an article entitled "Bolshevism and Psychology," this time with Adler's full signature.

> "We have lost our domination over other peoples, and we see without envy and ill will the Czecks, the South Slavs, the Hungarians, the Poles, the Ruthenians gaining in strength and awakening to a new independent life . . . We

were never more miserable than when we were at the peak of our power . . . We are closer to that truth than the victors." The author adds that the Socialists had until now been the only ones to claim that peaceful life in common was the highest aim for society. Now the Bolsheviks have seized the power and are proclaiming that they will use it for the good of mankind. The Communist idealogy seems identical to that of Socialism but there is an essential difference, namely that the power of the former is based and maintained by violence. Violence provokes counterviolence: "Already others are preparing to expand their offensive against Bolshevism under a flood of moralistic slogans towards the conquest and subjection of Europe."[47]

His third piece of writing was a pamphlet, *The Other Side*, in which he briefly sketched the events of the five preceding years with an attempt to extract the lesson.

Before the war the whole population was intoxicated by militaristic drill and propaganda so that when the war did come the people allowed themselves to be led blindly, under increased poisoning of the mind. The expected uprisings did not occur, but more and more men tried to escape battle duty and there were conflicts between military physicians and those commissions whose function it was to send men back to the front. Attemps at mass desertion during the Russian offensive were severely checked by the military police. The only means left at disposal was secret passive resistance, and when the collapse came the people rejoiced at having won their freedom, realizing that its true enemy, the ruling class, was defeated. Now was the time for the ruling men, the profiteers, the sadistic judges and physicians, the journalists, the writers, and even certain scientists to account for their actions. But what about the mass enthusiasm at the beginning of the war and the numerous volunteers? Many of the latter went to war because they were dissatisfied with their position or their family life. These were often the ones who were the most rapidly disenchanted. But the people should not be held responsible for their attitude at the beginning, because they had no means of assessing the situation, having been thoroughly deceived by their leaders. Here too Adler gives his explanation that since there was no way out, the only possible salvation was to fight under the banner of the oppressor. Incidentally, this is what several years later psychoanalysts were to call the "identification with the enemy."[48]

After Austria's defeat and the ensuing social upheaval, the Social-Democrats had come to power in Vienna. Despite the economic distress, they undertook a program of welfare institutions: construction of low-cost housing for workers, medical dispensaries, and educational reform were made a major part of their program. The new Minister of Education, Otto Glöckel, a former teacher, forwarded the application of a new educational system based on democratic principles and the respect of the individual needs of the children.[49] Audacious new methods were applied in a number of experimental schools, so that for a dozen years Vienna was a kind of Mecca for modern pedagogues.[50] This situation gave Adler a golden opportunity to proceed to the materialization of his own ideas. In 1920 he started the founding and the gradual development of those institutions (consultations for teachers, medico-pedagogical consultations, kindergartens, and experimental schools), which will be described in more detail.[51]

In his second article in the *Internationale Rundschau*, Adler mentioned his former friends now in power (an obvious reference to Trotsky and Yoffe). But he refused to let himself become involved in militant political activity. According to Furtmüller, he only went to a Communist meeting once. Although he still wrote occasional contributions for the *Arbeiter Zeitung* he had long ceased to be a member of the Social Democratic party—to the irritation of some his former associates—and he proclaimed that the most pressing need of mankind was the reform and spreading of education under the viewpoints of individual psychology. In 1920, Adler organized his first consultations for teachers. They would meet with him or his associates to discuss problems pertaining to the difficult children they had in their classes.

From this point on, Adler's life became more and more identified with the development and the history of individual psychology.

The publication of the *Zeitschrift für Individualpsychologie*, which had been stopped during the war, was resumed in 1923 under the name of *Internationale Zeitschrift für Individualpsychologie* (*International Journal of Individual Psychology*), and it now contained reports from various Adlerian groups throughout Europe and North America. In the same year Adler gave lectures in England and read a paper at the International Congress of Psychology in Oxford. In 1924 he was appointed a professor at the Pedagogical Institute of the City of Vienna, and his courses were attended by many teachers. In 1926 a large textbook of 864 pages appeared, in which, under the editorship of Erwin Wexberg, every possible aspect of individual psychology was expounded.[52]

The year 1926 was one of great activity, in which Adler published many papers and inaugurated the publication of a collection of monographs written by some of his followers.[53] An increasing amount of his time was devoted to lecture tours, which now extended to the United States. He also explained his ideas in interviews given to journalists from time to time.[54]

The social and economic situation in Austria improved markedly, and Adler regained a measure of prosperity. On September 9, 1927, he bought a country house in Salmannsdorf, a village at the extreme northwest part of the city. It was a large house with a beautiful garden and orchard, and a magnificent view of the Viennese woods. Adler often went there to spend Sundays and holidays during the summer and receive his friends who came in great numbers. On October 19 to 23 of that year, he participated in the Wittenberg Symposium, held at Wittenberg College, Springfield, Ohio, together with a host of eminent American and European psychologists. In the same year Adler's third major book *Menschenkenntnis* (*Understanding Human Nature*) appeared which gave a clear picture of the most recent shape taken by his teaching.

Gradually, Adler came to spend a larger portion of his time in the United States. He would pass the summer with his family in Vienna, where he pursued his already established activities, and then return to America for the rest of the year, usually after giving lectures in other European countries. In 1929 he was appointed Medical Director at the Mariahilfe Ambulatorium, in Vienna, which was an outpatient clinic for the treatment of neuroses. He also was lecturer in University Extension courses at Columbia University, New York, in the spring session of 1929 and the winter session of 1930 to 1931.

Following a decision of the City Council of Vienna of July 11, 1930, Alfred Adler received the title, Citizen of Vienna, "in acknowledgment of the great merits that he acquired in science and on the occasion of his sixtieth birthday."[55] A ceremony was held, under the direction of the Mayor, Karl Seitz.[56] Phyllis Bottome reports that the Mayor greeted Adler as a deserving pupil of Freud's, a blunder that Adler deeply resented. According to the same biographer, another painful incident occurred that year in New York: without his knowledge an admirer proposed him for titular professorship at Columbia University, which the university authorities deemed premature. Adler heard of the incident, was incensed, and resigned his post. In 1932 he began teaching at Long Island Medical College. At this time he had other worries, because some of his leftist followers persistently maintained that individual psychology was an emanation of Marxism.

In 1934 the Social Democratic party was suppressed in Austria. The Nazi menace became increasingly ominous. Adler had foreseen the catastrophe that was soon to break over Europe, and he thought that the future of individual psychology depended upon its implantation in North America. The *Journal for Individual Psychology* was founded, the first of its kind in the English language. Adler settled in the United States, and was felled by a severe illness. When it was believed that he was on his deathbed, his wife came from Vienna with his daughter Alexandra to nurse him. He recovered, however, from that illness and from that time on the family made America its home.

After long negotiations the Salmannsdorf house was sold on February 24, 1937.[57] A program of lectures and conferences had been scheduled for Adler in England from May 24, 1937, to August 2, 1937. However, he was deeply anxious about his eldest daughter, Valentine, who had disappeared in Russia. On the way to England he gave a lecture in The Hague, Holland, for the Child Study Association. On the same evening his friend, Dr. Joost Meerloo, received a telephone call from him that he had pain, most probably angina pectoris. Dr. Meerloo came with a cardiologist. The pain had disappeared, however, the cardiologist recommended a thorough cardiologic examination, and a period of rest.[58] But Adler left the following day for England. On the fourth day of his lecture tour, he collapsed in Aberdeen, on Union Street, on the morning of Friday, May 28, 1937, and died in the police ambulance on the way to the hospital. At the invitation of Aberdeen University a memorial service was held in King's College Chapel on June 1, in the presence of some members of his family, along with representatives from the Town Council, universities, and scientific societies. His remains were taken to Edinburgh, where they were cremated at Warriston Crematorium. A religious service was conducted and a funeral oration delivered in German by Dr. Ronge, of the Dutch Individual Psychological Group.[59]

The Personality of Alfred Adler

It is difficult to make an appraisal of Alfred Adler's true personality, in view of the contradictory statements given by his contemporaries and the changes that his personality went through during the course of his life.

Our oldest data show a sickly child, inhibited by his brighter older brother, and later a not particularly brilliant student. Still later, we see him as an ardent socialist and a skillful young practitioner interested in social medicine. Descriptions of Adler during his associations with Freud depict him as an active but oversensitive and querulous person. Dr. Alphonse Maeder, who met him in Nuremberg in March 1910, writes the following:

> After I had read my report, Adler came to me and holding each button of my waistcoat, one after the other, started to explain his ideas to me. He wanted to win me for his theories . . . There was something unpleasant in his manners . . . He was rather peculiar, not handsome, and had nothing winning in him.[60]

It would seem that war events brought forth a remarkable metamorphosis in him, which Jones characterized as follows:

> My own impression of Adler was that of a morose and cantankerous person whose behavior oscillated between contentiousness and sulkiness. He was evidently very ambitious and constantly quarreling with the others over points of priority in his ideas. When I met him many years later, however, I observed that success had brought him a certain benignity of which there had been little sign in his early years.[61]

More and more he had become the apostle of an ideal, which for him was the only salvation of the world, and for whose propagation he fatally overworked himself.

Individual psychologists have often tried to understand Adler by means of his own method, that is, by interpreting his early memories and analyzing his setting in the family constellation.

> One of my earliest recollections is of sitting on a bench, bandaged up on account of rickets, with my healthy elder brother sitting opposite me. He could run, jump, and move about quite effortlessly, while for me movement of any sort was a strain and an effort. Everyone went to great pains to help me, and my mother and father did all that was in their power to do. At the time of this recollection I must have been about two years old. [62]

These first memories are indeed characteristic. The rickets represent that experience of organ inferiority, which he later was temporarily to place at the center of his psychological system. The picture of the helpless, immobilized child is an illustration of man's striving toward movement, a basic element of Adler's teaching. The intense rivalry with his older brother appears in the first formulation of the concept of the position in the line of siblings. The picture of the child surrounded by others trying to help him is an early version of his description of the life-style of the neurotic.

Another early memory was the birth and death of a younger brother who distracted a part of the attention which he, as a sickly child, had been receiving from his mother. The early realization of the fact of death was reinforced a year later when he nearly succumbed to pneumonia. This resulted in the decision to become a physician, that is, to challenge death.

A school incident of his eighth or tenth year has become a classic story. Alfred was a complete failure in mathematics. One day the teacher set a problem that no one in the class could solve. Young Alfred felt he had the right solution and found the courage to go to the blackboard to give it, to the great surprise of everyone present. From that day on he felt that he could be as good as anyone in mathematics and excelled at the subject. (In Phyllis Bottome's version of the story the teacher himself could not find the solution, and after his exploit Alfred became a "mathematical prodigy!")

As to the family constellation, we have already noted that Alfred's relationship to his parents was the reverse of Freud's "Oedipus situation." His mother was the rival against whom he exercised his strength, a situation not without analogy to his later rivalry with his wife. And was not his position of a second boy between a very brilliant older brother and a competitive younger one revived later when he found himself between Sigmund Freud and Carl Gustav Jung?

Alfred Adler was a short, sturdy man, who could not be called handsome. He had a large, round head, a massive forehead, and a wide mouth. He wore no beard but grew a large black mustache, which he trimmed in later years. His eyes have been greatly admired because of their varying expressions, sometimes veiled and withdrawn, sometimes piercing. He was a man of strong emotions, great activity, and a quick mind. He generally mastered his emotions, but could be hypersensitive. The rejection of his application for Privat Dozent was a lifelong wound, as later was the Columbia University incident, and the blunder of the Mayor of Vienna.

As already mentioned, Adler had received a classical education, which included the study of Greek, Latin, and German authors, and he had also read much, but he disdained any unnecessary display of erudition. His favorite authors were, among the classics, Homer, Shakespeare, Goethe, Schiller, Heine; the Austrian poets Grillparzer and Nestroy; and among the moderns Dostoevski and other Russian novelists.[63] He was particularly fond of Vischer's novel, *Auch Einer*, whose delightful humor was much like his own.

His favorite sports were swimming, hiking, and mountain climbing in his youth, but he had to give them up later in his life because of his heart condition. He was nearly sixty when he learned to drive an automobile, but could never become a really good driver. Adler had a great talent for music, song, and acting. He sang remarkably well. During his adolescent and young adult years he often went to concerts and plays. Later, in his lonely years in New York, his only pastime was the frequenting of movie theaters.

Adler was not a brilliant conversationalist, but was at his best in familiar talk interspersed with the telling of jokes of which he was very fond. On the other hand, it is generally agreed that he was a splendid lecturer with a gift for prompt and witty repartee. As a writer he lacked both style and organization, nor was he a good linguist. Although he was fluent in his native German (including the so-called Viennese dialect), he had difficulty in learning foreign languages. He could never learn French and could speak only a few words of Hungarian, Russian, and other continental languages. However, he was able to learn English late in his life and spoke and wrote it fairly well, although with a pronounced foreign accent.

To some of his visitors, Adler's way of living was a cause for surprise. Unlike Freud, he had no art collection; he lived the life of a petty bourgeois. One of his former neighbors, a very old man whom the author interviewed in August 1963, told him the following:

> There was nothing conspicuous about him. He was modest and made no particular impression. You would have taken him for a tailor. Though he had a country house, he did not look as if he had a large income. His wife was a normal, decent housewife. There was only one maid in the house. Although he traveled much and received many visitors, I had never realized that he was a famous man until the day came when a great ceremony was organized in his honor.

Dr. Eugène Minkowski, who visited him in Vienna, found him unsophisticated and charming.[64] "He did not at all play the great Master."

Phyllis Bottome tells in her autobiography of her disappointment at her first encounter with Adler in the summer of 1927:

> I had expected a Socratic genius, who would plunge us all into the depths of psychology. I found a very kindly and considerate guest who talked about nothing in particular and to everyone in general.[65]

Those who have known Adler agree that he possessed the gift of *Menschenkenntnis* (intuitive practical understanding of man) to a supreme degree. This was particularly noticeable in his clinical work. In the presence of a new patient, about whom he knew nothing, he would look at him a moment, ask a few questions, and then get a complete picture of the subject's difficulties, clinical disturbances, and life problems. After hearing a report of the case history of a new patient, he would guess what the behavior of the patient would be and what he would say when he would be introduced to the psychologists' assembly. He came to be able to almost instantaneously guess any person's position in the sibling constellation. Adler was also reputed for his gift of rapidly establishing contact with any person, including rebellious children, psychotics, and criminals. He felt a genuine interest for all human beings and compassion for their sufferings, but, like Janet, he would immediately detect the part of play-acting and mendacity on the part of his patients.

Adler possessed the same foresight in regard to political events. As we have seen, as early as 1918 he predicted that the Bolsheviks' use of violence would unleash a counterviolence that would attempt to conquer Europe. This was long before Hitler had founded his party and attempted his first putsch, and as the years went by he clearly predicted the catastrophe of the Nazi invasion and World War II.

In sharp contrast with his psychological acumen was his lack of practical qualities, which often proved disastrous for his movement. In the early years it was a serious mistake to have held so many informal gatherings in the Viennese coffeehouses and to have invited so many neurotic patients to these gatherings. He had earned a reputation for being superficial.[66] With the passing of the years, this lack of practical sense became more apparent. Many difficulties arose from his horror of compromise, which was often viewed by others as a lack of flexibility and diplomatic sense. When Adler emigrated to the United States, practical difficulties reached their peak. He found himself, at the age of sixty, alone, in a new country and unfamiliar with the language and customs. Phyllis Bottome believed that a good secretary would have prolonged his life by ten years, but his choice of secretarial help was unfortunate, so that articles sent to him would become lost, and important letters remained unanswered.[67]

The story of Alfred Adler's love for Raissa Epstein and their marriage has been told by Phyllis Bottome.[68] Raissa Epstein had received a liberal education. At that time many women students went to the universities of central Europe, and some of them married fellow students or professors. One could list the French, German, and Austrian scholars who married Russian students in that way. It would be interesting to discover what influence these Russian wives exerted upon their husband's thought and life's work. In Adler's case the influence seems to have been considerable. Raissa Epstein was an ardent socialist, and Furtmüller says that she and Adler both frequented socialist meetings together before she became his wife. Raissa was extremely independent and strong-willed, and after the initial period of boundless happiness, difficulties arose. As Phyllis Bottome says, "Fighting for the emancipation of women, and living with a woman who has emancipated herself, are two wholly different things."[69] There were many points of contention between them. Adler belonged to the Austrian lower middle class, in which a woman above all was expected to be a housewife and conform to accepted standards of decorum, whereas Raissa came from the intelligentsia, where such standards were considered secondary. Another source of contention was that Raissa, who always remained a convinced radical, could not understand why Alfred had given preference to his individual psychology. And in 1914 their sympathies went to their respective countries of origin, which were at war with each other.

Phyllis Bottome has pointed out that these marital difficulties influenced much of what Adler described in his book, *The Nervous Character*, expecially his concept of "masculine protest." Alfred Adler's last years were spent peacefully in the reestablished home in America, where Raissa had joined him during his severe illness of 1934.

Alfred Adler's philosophical interests underwent some modifications in the course of his life. In his youth he was deeply attracted by Marxism, and for a time he was a member of the Social Democratic party. He retained a great interest in politics and never sought to hide his political opinions. But gradually he came to grant priority to problems of education and of the message of individual psychology.

It is not exactly known when he lost his ties with the Jewish religion. A skeptical attitude toward religion itself could be inferred from his remarks about certain neurotics who escape their life task by taking refuge in religion. However, no definite antireligious tenets are to be found in his writings. It is noteworthy that when he left the Synagogue in 1904, he joined the Protestant Church. According to Phyllis Bottome, he resented the fact that the Jewish religion limited itself to one ethnic group, and he wished to belong to a universal one. He also found it worthwhile to have discussions with a Protestant minister, Reverend Jahn, on the topic of religion and individual psychology, in which Adler acknowledged that both had much in common in the ideals they pursued, though one remained in the field of science and the other in that of faith.[70]

Adler's weltanschauung can be aptly confronted with that of Freud.[71]

Freud, who was a pessimist somewhat after the fashion of Schopenhauer, viewed the neurotic as the victim of a grandiose and tragic self-deception of mankind. Adler, an optimist who leaned toward the ideas of Leibniz, saw the neurotic as a pitiful individual who made use of transparent tricks in order to escape his life duties. He came to believe that the drive toward self-perfection was the essence of man. The difference between Adler and Freud can be seen in the organization of their respective movements. Whereas the Psychoanalytic Society was organized to the last detail, in a pyramidal way with the central committee at the top and a secret "ring" around Freud, Adler's Individual Psychology Society was loosely consti- tuted. Sessions were attended by numerous patients because Adler expected each one of them to join the movement and become his flag-bearer (*Bannerträger*). With an almost messianic attitude, Adler expected his movement to conquer and transform the world through education, teaching, and psychotherapy.

Alfred Adler's Contemporaries

The evolution of any thinker or scientist can be understood only if it is viewed within the network of his personal and scientific relationship with a number of his contemporaries. As we have done with Janet and Freud, we will try to give a glimpse into that complexity by singling out Adler's relationships with one of his contemporaries, Wilhelm Stekel.[72] His life is mostly known from the English version of his autobiography.

Wilhelm Stekel spent his childhood and youth in Czernowitz in the province of Bukovina. He belonged to a family of German-speaking Orthodox Jews. After completing his secondary studies, he went to Vienna to study medicine and immediately after began the general practice of medicine while continuing to learn and study. He wrote with ease and regularity, contributed to newspapers, and also sent articles to medical journals. His paper about early sexual experiences in children, with three clinical cases, attracted the attention of Freud who quoted it.[73] Stekel wrote an enthusiastic review of Freud's *Interpretation of Dreams* in the *Neues Wiener Tagblatt* of January 29 and 30, 1902. From that time on he became an ardent follower of Freud and, according to Stekel, it was he who suggested to Freud the Wednesday evening meetings in his home. He participated in all the events of the early history of psychoanalysis. In 1908 his book *Conditions of Nervous Anxiety and Their Treatment* appeared with a fore- word by Freud.[74] In 1911 his textbook on dreams appeared,[75] and in 1912 his study on the dreams of poets appeared.[76] His literary output seemed inexhaustible. Gradually his ideas began to diverge from Freud's. For instance, he viewed anxiety as the reaction of the life instinct against the death instinct; he insisted upon the importance of aggressive drives, and explained the epileptic attack as criminal drives turned against oneself. He also contended that neurosis often issued from the repression of religion or morals.

When Adler and his small group separated from Freud, Stekel remained faithful to him for some time, but was attacked by the other members of the group, so that he in turn left the psychoanalytic society. Stekel remained a prolific writer in other fields. Not only did he compose music and songs for children, but wrote theatrical plays both in prose and verse, as well as collections of humorous stories, either under his own name or under the pseudonym of Serenus. Some of the characters in his plays and humorous stories seem more real than the case histories of his psychoanalytic publications.

During World War I, Stekel worked as a military physician and had to treat many cases of shell shock. However, he found time to write often for newspapers and medical journals. After the war he gathered pupils around him. He continued to call himself a psychoanalyst and to refer to Freud as his great master, but his cures were much briefer and comprised an element of reeducation. His literary activity continued unabated.

As the years continued, his school gained in importance. He traveled and lectured in foreign countries. His literary production took on the form of large monographs filled with numerous case histories. When the Nazis invaded Austria, he escaped at the last minute to Switzerland and went from there to England where he settled. Stekel committed suicide during the darkest period of World War II.

Both Adler and Stekel were the sons of Jewish merchants and both considered that their childhoods had been unhappy. Both played with street boys and were very gifted in music, song, and play-acting. Both achieved their medical studies in Vienna and became general practitioners. Both were attracted to Freud at the same time, were among the first four members of the Wednesday evening group, of which they became the most active participants for a number of years. Each published his first monograph at about the same time, Adler in 1907 and Stekel in 1908. They described what they called Organ Jargon (Adler) and Organ Language (Stekel), a novelty for which each later claimed priority. When the psychoanalytic movement was organized, they respectively became president and vice-president of the Viennese Society and co-editors of the *Zentralblatt*. Both Adler and Stekel then left the psychoanalytic society and went their own ways. During World War I they worked in turn in the same military hospital and later both acquired a house in Salmannsdorf.[77] It is not known why after such a long friendship they were on such bad terms that they did not even exchange words nor did they greet each other in the street. Fate decreed that both men had to leave their country and end their days in the British Isles.

At the beginning Stekel was so much of a psychoanalyst that some of his ideas on dream symbolism and on the meaning of neurotic symptoms were accepted by Freud. From the start Adler remained much more independent of Freud's basic ideas. As the years went by many of Adler's ideas were quietly taken over by Stekel, whose teaching became a mixture of Freudian and Adlerian concepts, together with his own.

In his book on organ inferiority in 1907, Adler tells of the symbolic meaning of physical symptoms, which he terms "organ jargon." In 1908 Stekel's *Conditions of Anxiety* contained an impressive collection of case histories in which the various symptoms are explained as a language of organs symbolically expressing unconscious feelings. In 1908 Adler upheld, contrary to Freud's opinion, the existence and importance of primary aggressive drives; Stekel went even further by maintaining that the criminal instinct played an important role in neurosis,[78] melancholia, epilepsy, and in the choice of a profession.[79] When Adler developed his concept of "masculine protest," Stekel followed with his description of the "war of the sexes," and what Adler termed "psychic hermaphroditism," Stekel called "sexual bipolarity."

Where Freud speaks of repression, both Adler and Stekel contend that in fact the neurotic does not want to see what is allegedly repressed. Stekel's emphasis on the actor in every neurotic is not far removed from what Adler says about the life style of a patient. What Stekel called the neurotic's concept of his great mission corresponds to Adler's desire to be like God. When Freud declared that perversion is the negative of neurosis, Stekel and Adler disagreed: for them perversion was but another form of neurosis.

In the early 1920's the Adlerian element in Stekel's work became even more apparent. In his pamphlet on telepathic dreams, Stekel writes, "Dreams always seek to explore the future, they show us our attitudes toward life and the ways and aims of life."[80] In his *Letters to a Mother*,[81] he tells of the meaning of the first memories and that education should never make use of force against the child because it provokes a similar counter-tendency in the child.[82] In another place Stekel discussed the "Life goals" (*Lebensziele*): the child sets himself an unattainable goal and the growing individual renounces them gradually.[83] The neurotic has been unable to do so, and the condition is the result of that broken ambition. The central problem of self-education is the "courage to one's-self" (*Mut zu sich selbst*). These are Adler's ideas expressed almost in his own words.

The similarities between Stekel and Adler should not cause us to overlook the great difference between the two men and their work. Stekel was one of Freud's disciples, who even after he left him claimed to have remained a psychoanalyst. Actually he kept the clinical and empirical element of psychoanalysis, leaving aside the theoretical system. Adler's case is quite different. He came to Freud with some original ideas already formed and slowly developed them throughout the period he worked with Freud. And when Adler left Freud he developed a conceptual framework, which was basically different from psychoanalysis.

Stekel's teaching shows the aspect psychoanalysis might have taken if it had been a purely empirical, practical method without the solid foundation of a theoretical substructure. At the same time, Stekel's brand of "deviant" psychoanalysis shows exactly what individual psychology is not; in other words, it shows what it could have become if Adler had not radically broken his ties with psychoanalysis and had not constructed a conceptual framework of his own.

Adler's Work—I—Social Medicine

Before he participated in Freud's group, Adler had conceived and expressed original ideas in the field of social medicine. His subsequent elaboration of individual psychology cannot be properly understood without taking into account the concepts he formulated in his prepsychoanalytic period.

In 1898, Dr. G. Golebiewski of Berlin, a specialist of occupational diseases, accepted to publish as the fifth of a series of monographs on the subject the work of a hitherto-unknown author, Alfred Adler, with the title *Health Book for the Tailor Trade*.[84] This booklet of thirty-one pages has become so scarce, that even among individual psychologists doubts have been expressed as to its very existence.[85] In the foreword the author explains that he wants to show the relationship of economic situation and disease in a given trade, and the resulting prejudice to public health. This will give evidence that disease can be a product of society, which adds to the causes of disease commonly accepted by medical men.

In the first part of the monograph, Adler sketches a picture of the social and economic conditions of the tailor trade in Austria and Germany, with the changes it had undergone during the previous decades. Once, tailors worked independently for individual customers and were united and protected by their Guilds. Now, the advent of manufactured ready-made clothing determines a decline in the condition of the small tailor. In the factories the workers enjoy better conditions because of state control and it is easier for them to unite for the defense of their common interests. The factory has the advantage of using all kinds of large machines and of working for a wide market, both at home and abroad.

In contrast to the working conditions in the large factory, the author gives a rather gloomy picture of the plight of the small tailor-master and his employees. Technical progress, which is such an advantage for the clothing manufacturers, is far less beneficial for him: he uses only the sewing machine, he works only for a small local market, and is much more exposed to economic fluctuations. The worst calamity is the uneven distribution of work throughout the year: there are five or six months of intensive overwork, during which the tailor labors sixteen, or eighteen hours, a day, if not more, assisted by his wife and children. And during the remaining part of the year there is almost no work at all, forcing him to lower the wages of his assistants or to dismiss them. Astonishingly in spite of the low salary conditions there are not less than 200,000 small tailors in Germany and about as many again in Austria-Hungary. The small tailor has not only to put up with the competition of the clothes factories, but also with that of the *Sitzgeselle* who does piece work at home and readily consents to make complete suits for individual customers. The living conditions of the small tailor are miserable in every regard. His lodging and working space, which are one and the same and are situated in the cheapest and unhealthiest part of the town, are damp, dark, airless, and overcrowded, which favors contagion of infectious diseases. In case of epidemics this can be dangerous for the customers as well. Material worries undermine his health and he is insufficiently protected by labor laws.

The second part of the monograph is devoted to the description of the diseases common among the small tailors. Pulmonary diseases take the lead. No wonder since they work in a stooped sitting position, breathing in the dust of the cloth. Pulmonary tuberculosis is twice as frequent among them than in the average of the other trades. Another result of the stooping position are circulatory disturbances such as varicose veins and hemorroids, as well as frequent stomach and intestinal diseases by which more that 30 per cent of the tailors are afflicted. The peculiar stooped sitting position determines deformations such as scoliosis, cyphosis, rheumatism, and arthritis of the right arm, callousities of the ankles, and so on. The tailor frequently suffers from cramps in his hands or arms. Skin diseases are frequent; scabies is to be found among 25 per cent of the tailors. Because of neddle pricks, they often suffer from abscesses on fingers, and owing to the pressure of scissors the luxation of the right thumb is frequent. Their habit of putting threads into their mouths causes gum infections and various mouth and stomach ailments. Their type of close work determines shortsightedness and cramps of the eye muscles. They are the victims of slow poisoning through toxic dyes and of infectious diseases transmitted to them by means of old clothes brought for repair. The incidence of work accidents is not particularly high, though more than one would commonly assume. According to statistics, disease frequency among tailors is higher than in any other trade and the average life expectancy is the lowest of all trades.

Analyzing the causes of this high morbidity, Adler underlines undernourishment, poor lodging conditions, overwork, the absence of social protection of the workers, and the fact that many tailors choose their trade because they are physically inapt for any other, resulting in a "selection of the unfit."

In the third part of the monograph the author suggests a program to put an end to this situation. First of all new labor legislation must be enacted. Existing regulations must be enforced (such as the sick fund), accident insurance, which was only compulsory in workshops with twenty workers or more, should become generalized, inspectors should control working conditions everywhere and not only in factories, old-age and unemployment insurance should be made obligatory, a maximum number of working hours should be imposed by law, working premises should be obligatorily separate from the lodgings of the workers, and piece work should be prohibited. Another part of the program makes provision for the building of adequate lodging and eating houses for the workers.

The red thread that runs through the monograph is the denunciation of contemporary academic medicine, which ignores the very existence of social diseases. As in the past, when it was found that contagious diseases could be controlled only with the introduction of public hygiene, occupational diseases such as those of the tailor will be successfully controlled only by means of a new social medicine of which present-day medicine is unaware.

The circumstances in which Alfred Adler wrote this monograph are unknown to us. As sources of information, he refers to various writings on trade and occupational diseases and to commercial and health statistics. What Adler says about the superiority of the large factory over the small workshop seems to reflect the then much-discussed theory of Schulze-Gaevernitz, who contended that the conditions of the working class could not be improved as long as there was no powerful and expanding heavy industry.[86] Adler's description of the tailor trade suggests that he had more than just a theoretical knowledge of it, possibly through his uncle David, the tailor. Apparently Adler was an ardent socialist and was obviously steering toward a synthesis of socialism and medicine.

Four years elapsed between Adler's monograph and his next known writing. According to family tradition, during this time Adler contributed articles under various pseudonyms to the *Arbeiter-Zeitung*, the Viennese Social Democratic newspaper. It has not been possible as yet to identify these articles.

On July 15, 1902, a new medical journal, the *Aerztliche Standeszeitung*, was launched by a certain Dr. Heinrich Grün. It was to appear twice a month with a circulation of 10,000 copies. The first issue was sent gratuitously to every physician in Austria. The lower part of the first three pages were devoted to an article by Alfred Adler (which obviously was meant as a manifesto) entitled "The Penetration of Social Forces into Medicine."[87]

Medicine has always been open to the influence of all possible philosophical, scientific, and even pseudo-scientific trends. The etiology of many diseases has been clarified with the help of physics, chemistry, and ethnology, . . . But of all sciences the one which contributed most to the progress of medicine has been optics: the microscope has enabled Virchow to give a new scientific basis to pathology with his "cell theory," it has made possible the foundation of bacteriology, which in turn has led to the control of contagious diseases through public health measures. Meanwhile, the state has already come to recognize that medicine was a public concern since a healthy population was needed to provide the country with good soldiers and workers, and alleviate the public funds of its burden of destitute sick. Up to now the solution had been that physicians gave cheap care to the poor. Now the rise of the working classes obliged a reconsideration of the problem in terms of sick fund insurance and similar institutions. Thus the medical profession had reached the point where it had to face the issue of social medicine and take a stand. Medical men have been less aware of this need than administrators and technicians, who now are used to solving problems of medical import without referring to the physicians. Will the medical profession continue to let itself be taken in tow by officials, or will it take its place at the head of the movement? Will it finally shift from its policy of limited endeavors to one that would favor conscious, succcessful disease prevention?

In the issue of October 15, 1902, an article appeared under the pseudonym of Aladdin, which was almost certainly written by Adler (we recall that his Hungarian name was Aladár).[88] Its author said that the most urgent problem of present-day medicine was to make good medical care available to the poor. Any such demand in that direction previously received the answer: "We have no money" from the authorities. To do away with this annoyance Adler felt that an intitution was needed that would be recognized by the state and would possess scientific authority: a teaching post with a seminar for social medicine where problems of social hygiene would be explored with a view to finding their solution.

In September and October 1903 an article written by Adler, entitled "Town and Country," took issue with the common assumption that life in the villages and countryside was markedly better than in the towns.[89] Quite the contrary was true. The progress of hygiene had increased much greater in the towns, which with their growing population and number of electors received more attention from the public authorities. Nevertheless, Adler felt that this neglect of rural hygiene would eventually be detrimental to the towns as well.

In November 1903, an article by Adler entitled "Government Aid or Self-Help?" once again deplored the discrepancy between the scientific and the social aspects of medicine.[90] Adler felt that medical science was progressing rapidly and could advance even more so if it were not constantly slowed down by the authorities. In view of the paramount importance of research, he felt that there should be suitable, permanent, and well-paid positions open to researchers and teachers in the various fields of medicine (including social medicine).

In July and August 1904 a long article appeared: "The Physician as Educator," in which he revealed a new facet of his thought.

The social role of the physician is not exhausted as described in the previous articles and should be supplemented by his function as an educator. This educational role is shown in the fight against alcoholism, infections, venereal diseases, tuberculosis, child mortality, and in regard to school hygiene, but it must be more: the physician should be able to give advice on the education of children. In the presence of weak and sickly children it is not enough to prescribe their diet, exercises and other physical measures. Such children easily lose their best support, i.e. confidence in their own strength. The first concern of the physician should be to give them back their self-confidence and courage by a proper utilization of exercise, games, and sports.

These assertions of Adler's are followed by an epitome of education of the child. Education should begin with the education of the child's parents even before the birth of the child. The most powerful means of education is love, provided it is evenly distributed among all the children and not given in excess. Among common errors in education, one of the worst is to pamper children, which deprives them of self-confidence and courage, but it is dangerous to apply severe punishment, such as blows, shutting in and constant scolding. A brief sending away from the family table, a few admonishing words, a stern look should suffice. One should be very wary of entrusting a child to servants. Adler then discusses certain types of difficult children such as the stubborn child, the young liar, the coward, the masturbator, and the anxious child. The best prevention of mendacity is the development of courage, the most dangerous of all defects being cowardice: "If need be I would venture to make of the most cruel boy a competent butcher, hunter, insect collector, or surgeon. But the coward will always remain of lower cultural value." Adler concludes with the assertion: "Self-confidence of the child and his personal courage are his highest good."[91]

This article of Adler's showed that in 1904 he had already elaborated a complete theory of education, and we find in it an early statement of some of his favorite ideas: the role of organ inferiority, the picture of the pampered child, and the therapeutic value of self-confidence and courage.

Adler referred to the contemporary child psychologists, Preyer and Karl Grooss, and also for the first time to Freud as the man who had shown the extreme importance of the young child's first impressions and the existence of child sexuality.

In September to October 1904, Adler expounded his own ideas in an article entitled "Hygiene of Sexual Life," while reviewing a book by Max Gruber of the same title.

Adler opposes the views of Max Gruber in regard to a topic that was much discussed at that time. Adler contends that sexual abstinence can cause inconveniences for emotional health, with some rare exceptions. In regard to sexual excesses, Adler thinks Max Gruber has exaggerated their noxious effects, and that there is no evidence that they can cause neurasthenia. Adler also says that the alleged dangers of birth control have been much overstated. (We may note that Adler's opinion contradicts that of Freud in that regard). As for homosexuality, Adler agrees with the author that it is not a congenital abnormality, and that it should be punished only if it brings prejudice to another party and to protect minors. Adler sees the dangers of masturbation in another perspective than the author. They do not exist so much in regard to physical health as they do in regard to harmonious emotional development[92]

Although the publication of the *Aerztliche Standeszeitung* continued for several years, this was to be Adler's final contribution. To be sure, when he joined Freud's small group, he had definite ideas on social medicine, education, the role of organ inferiorities, and educational errors in the genesis of emotional disturbances. For the following several years Adler was to develop his ideas in a new direction within the frame of the psychoanalytic movement.

Alfred Adler's Work—II—Theory of Organ Inferiority

Adler assiduously participated in Freud's Wednesday evenings, where he contributed to the discussions and read his own papers.[93] Thus in the discussion of a paper on Nietzsche's *Genealogy of Morals,* Adler expressed his keen admiration for Nietzsche's psychological insights; in 1909 he credited Karl Marx with important psychological discoveries. In April

1910 he presided over a symposium on suicide of schoolchildren; it soon appeared with a foreword by Adler and a concluding comment by Freud.

Among Adler's numerous published articles of that time, two lean strongly toward psychoanalysis. Both appeared in 1905, one, in the style of Freud's *Psychopathology of Everyday Life*, tries to elucidate the meaning of obsessions with numbers in three patients.[94] The other, on sexual problems in education, discusses problems of child sexuality in a similar manner to the *Three Essays*.[95]

Adler's main achievement during his psychoanalytic period was a short book of ninety-two pages on organ inferiority.[96] This notion was by no means new. Clinicians spoke of *locus minoris resistentiae*, that is the organ of lesser resistance, which risked being the area of complications during a general infection. Adler referred to his predecessors in that regard, but his originality was in developing a systematic theory of organ inferiority.

Adler begins with the fact that there are many conditions of which we know the symptoms but not the causes. Among known causes are general ones (such as infections or toxications), or local ones (which originate in the malfunctioning of an organ). But for many other diseases, we find no satisfactory explanation, and Adler thinks that the theory of organ inferiority may account for many such cases.

The inferiority of an organ can be manifested in several ways. In most cases microscopic abnormalities cannot be easily detected, but sometimes they may be detected by outer signs such as the so-called degeneration stigmata or the existence of a nevus in the vicinity of the affected organ. Since the organ inferiority originates in a deficiency in the fetal development, it extends itself over an entire embryonic segment. Second, it can be a matter of functional inferiority, for instance, an insufficiency in the secretion of the organ, or sometimes merely reflex abnormalities (a reflex can be increased, diminished, or absent). Third, an organ inferiority can be surmised from the patient's case history: a lack of proper functioning of the given organ during childhood (as an example, Adler tells of patients suffering from early intestinal disturbances, who much later became diabetics). Frequent illnesses of a given organ are another indication of its inferiority.

An organ inferiority can thus be absolute or relative. It may take a favorable course by means of compensation. Compensation can occur at various levels: within the organ itself, through another organ, or through the nervous centers. In the latter the organ inferiority results in a general compensatory process. Compensation occurs as a result of the concentration of the patient's attention upon the functioning of the inferior organ. This amounts to a training that leads to a satisfactory or even superior level of adjustment of the inferior organ.

Without denying that certain specific diseases can be hereditary, Adler seems to assign a greater role to the heredity of organ inferiorities. As a result, in certain families the same organ inferiority is manifested in various forms. In one member it is a severe disease of a given organ, in another it can be a mere functional disturbance, in a third a proneness to transient diseases of that organ, and in yet another in a superiority through compensation. Adler quotes instances of musicians whose relatives or who themselves were afflicted with ear diseases, painters in whose families there were eye diseases or who themselves were afflicted with eye disorders.

According to Adler, the part played by chance in the localization of illnesses is less than is commonly believed. Thus an eight-year-old boy received a minor blow in the eye when a classmate who was playing with a pen accidently hit him with it; two months later he got a coal smut in the same eye; three months later the same accident with the pen occurred in the same manner to the same eye. Did these three accidents occur by sheer chance? Adler learned that the patient's maternal grandfather suffered from diabetic iritis, the mother from strabism, the younger brother from strabism as well as hypermetropy and lowered sharpness of vision. His mother's brother also had strabism and frequent conjunctivitis. The young patient himself showed a total lack of conjunctival reflexes in both eyes. This lack of reflexes, entailing a lack of protection, would explain the succession of accidents.

Adler's theory of organ inferiority and the compensatory process seems to be independent from psychoanalysis and more complementary than opposite to it. Freud had always maintained that neurosis developed on the basis of a predisposition. Adler was endeavoring to offer a plausible theory of the substratum of neurosis. Two places in the book point to the link with psychoanalysis. Compensation, according to Adler, issues from concentration of the patient's attention on the inferior organ as well as on the adjacent bodily surface, and should the latter be an erogenous zone, it will necessarily result in its overstimulation and the inception of a neurotic process. A second link with psychoanalysis is found in Adler's contention that there is "no organ inferiority without sexual inferiority," especially in the case of multiple organ inferiorities.

Adler's theory of organ inferiority was well accepted by the psychoanalytic group. Freud himself seemed to consider it a valuable addition to the knowledge of neurosis.

As early as 1908, Adler took issue with Freud's basic concept of the libido as being the main dynamic source of psychic life. Adler contended that there is an aggressive drive that cannot be explained as the result of frustrated libido and that it plays a no less important part than the libido in normal life as well as neurosis.[97]

In 1910, Adler sketched a theory of psychological hermaphroditism.[98] Experience, he says, has shown him the striking frequency of secondary sexual characteristics of the opposite sex among neurotic patients. This brings a patient to a subjective feeling of inferiority and to a striving toward compensation in the form of masculine protest. In the case of a young boy, he will equate masculinity with aggression and femininity with passivity. Exhibitionism and fetishism can be traced to masculine protest. This same masculine protest will also lead him to try to surpass his father, and secondarily direct his wishful representations toward his mother. This is how Adler explains the Oedipus theme (*Oedipusmotiv*).

Alfred Adler's Work—III—Theory of Neurosis

After his separation from Freud in 1911, Adler reformulated his theory of neurosis. Much of this reformulation was a return to his earlier concepts of social pathogenesis and of the role of organ inferiority. Though rejecting a great deal of Freud's theories, Adler above all maintained the notion of the importance of early childhood situations, which he combined with his own ideas on aggressive drives and psychological hermaphroditism. Vaihinger's *Philosophy of the As If* appeared just at the right time to furnish a new conceptual framework.

Adler's book *The Nervous Character* appeared in 1912 with the motto from Seneca: *Omnia ex opinione suspensa sunt* ("All things depend upon opinion"), an allusion to Vaihinger's concept of "fictions."[99] The book was divided into two parts, a theoretical and a practical one, but the division is not as clear as is indicated, and it is not always easy to grasp the full meaning of Adler's thought.

The basic concept is that of "individuality," a term expressing both the uniqueness and the indivisibility of the human being. This is best illustrated in the foreword by a quotation of Virchow: "The individual represents a unified whole of which all parts cooperate towards a common goal." As a consequence each isolated psychological feature of the individual reflects his whole personality.

The individual is also viewed in the temporal dimension. At any point in time, any symptom shows marks of the past, present, and future. Psychic life is future-directed and teleologic, that is tending toward a goal. The goal is not set once and for all, but can be modified.

This is where Adler utilizes Vaihinger's concept of "fiction." Things proceed *as if* an ideal norm was set to human activity, and this ideal norm Adler called absolute truth, or absolute logic of social life, which is the same as perfect conformity with social and even cosmic demands. Adler calls abnormity the degree of an individual's deviation from that fictitious norm. Neuroses are conceived as varieties of such a deviation.

The origin of neuroses is sought by Adler in the feelings arising from organ inferiorities, and here he refers to his book of 1907. Aside from purely physiological compensation, organ inferiority sets in motion a complex psychological process of self-assertion, which becomes a permanent factor of psychic development. As sketched in the book on organ inferiority, this psychological process implies a constant observation and training of the supposedly inferior organ function. But to these phenomena, which he had already described, Adler now adds the notion that feelings of inferiority can also be brought forth by purely social factors, such as early competition between siblings and the position of the child in the sibling row. Even when there is organ inferiority, the psychological reaction becomes the main element.

Whatever the varieties of neurosis, there is a training process common to all of them, which results from the increased attention bestowed by the patient upon himself and his relationships with others, a lowering of the threshold of excitability, and a sharpening of his powers to foresee certain events. All this is subjectively viewed by the patient as a striving toward superiority and fear of being outmatched. Furthermore, the neurotic resorts to auxiliary means, such as a leading image to live up to, and a neurotic technique of life. With time these various means become an end in themselves.

The neurotic lives in a fictitious world that is structured around pairs of opposing concepts. The main one of these is the opposition between the deep-seated feeling of inferiority and the subject's exalted personality feeling. This opposition is equated with the concepts of "high" and "low," "masculine" and "feminine," "triumph" and "defeat." The opposition high-low plays a great role in the fantasies, the dreams, the figures of speech of normal people, and acquires an increased importance for the neurotic who equates the idea of superiority with high and that of inferiority with low. The same is true in regard to triumph and defeat, and for the neurotic individual, the slightest success or setback acquires tremendous importance. The opposition of "masculine-feminine" is treated at length in *The Nervous Character*. Adler seems to ascribe less importance than he previously did to biological marks of intersexuality. What really matters is the persisting subjective impression in the patient. Because society assumes that woman is inferior to man, masculine protest is likely to develop in man as well as in woman. In woman, masculine protest is an almost normal reaction to the role that is imposed on her in a man's world. In man, it is the result of doubts about his sexual role or fear of not being able to live up to it, and at the same time it reinforces his prejudices against woman. On this basis Adler describes various forms of neuroses in man and in woman, and here, too, his ideas widely diverge from those of Freud: far from viewing the libido as the root of neuroses and sexual deviations, Adler emphasizes the symbolic character of sexual behavior.

Unlike Freud, Adler stresses the social factor in the origin of neurosis and its social defects. Certain neurotics, for instance, take refuge from society by restricting their social field of activity to the family circle, and sometimes even prefer their parental family to their own.

The progress of neurosis is compared by Adler to the evolution of fictions, as depicted by Vaihinger. Certain scientists proposed a theory in the form of a fictitious model, in whose reality they did not believe. The fictitious model was then mistakenly taken for a hypothesis, and the hypothesis transformed into dogma. In the same way the neurotic toys with fantasies, and later comes to believe them. This is what Adler calls substantiation. A dangerous situation arises whenever the substantiated fiction has to face reality. This general pattern of evolution with its phases of fiction, substantiation, and critical confrontation of reality, exists regardless of the variety of neuroses. Adler does away with the classical distinctions of neuroses (hysteria, phobia, and obsessions), which had been retained by Freud. He goes so far as to include sexual deviations in the field of neuroses.

The Nervous Character is lacking in style and composition, but the book is rich in ideas and clinical facts. A great variety of authors are quoted: physicians, pediatricians, and university psychiatrists such as Kraepelin, and Wernicke, and among representatives of newer schools, Janet, Bleuler, Freud, and many psychoanalysts. Among philosophers Nietzsche and Vaihinger are the most frequently referred to, and among writers Goethe, Schiller, Shakespeare, Tolstoy, Dostoevsky, Gogol, and Ibsen.

Alfred Adler's Work—IV—Individual Psychology

After World War I, Alfred Adler reconsidered and reformulated his psychological system. The notion of community feeling (*Gemeinschaftsge-fühl*), which had been implicit in his previous theory of neurosis, was now designated by that term and brought into the foreground. The new system was expounded in 1927 in the clearest and most systematic of his books, *Understanding Human Nature*.[100] We will now sketch a general survey of Adler's individual psychology, taking this book as a basis and supplementing it at times with other writings of that period.

Adlerian psychology belongs neither to the traditional academic psychology nor to experimental psychology, and it radically differs from Freudian psychoanalysis. It is unfair to Adler to evaluate his system with the yardstick of academic, experimental, or Freudian psychology. The term *Menschenkenntnis* designates the particular psychological trend to which Adler's Individual Psychology belongs. This kind of pragmatic psychology, sometimes called concrete psychology, does not pretend to go into matters very deeply, but to provide principles and methods that enable one to acquire a practical knowledge of oneself and of others. This was also what Kant attempted in his *Anthropology from the Pragmatic Point of View*.[101] Incidentally, in his foreword to this book, Kant twice uses the term *Kenntnis des Menschen* (knowledge of Man) and once the word *Menschenkenntniss*, which was to be used by Adler almost as a synonym to individual psychology. Henri Lefebvre has shown that a system for the practical knowledge of man in general and daily life could be deduced from Marxism.[102] Another system of pragmatic psychology could even more easily be extracted from Nietzsche's works.[103]

Adler's *Menschenkenntnis*, however, is much more systematized and encompassing than those of Kant, Marx, or Nietzsche. The starting point of Adler's system can be expressed by the sentence: "Everything occurs in mental life *as if* . . . certain basic axioms were true." Which are these axioms?

First, the *principle of unity*: a human being is one and indivisible both in regard to the mind-body relationship and to the various activities and functions of the mind. Adler's individual psychology thus differs from Freud's emphasis on man's basic ambivalence and conflicts between the conscious and the unconscious, the ego, the id, and the superego.

Second, the *principle of dynamism;* life cannot be conceived without movement. But whereas Freud places the emphasis more on the cause, Adler emphasizes the aim and intentionality of psychic processes (what he calls the *Zielstrebigkeit*, the "striving toward a goal"): "No man can think, feel, will, nor even dream, without everything being defined, conditioned, limited, directed by a goal which floats before him." Such intentionalism necessarily implies the freedom to choose. Man is free insofar that he can choose a goal or change it for another, but as soon as this is done he is determined insofar that he obeys his self-imposed law.

Alexander Neuer considered the concept that man constantly finds himself in situations of inferiority, and it is up to him whether he will overcome it or not as basic in individual psychology.[104] To overcome it, insight is not enough; he must act and for that he needs courage. (As in the anecdote of the child who was a failure in mathematics until the day when he was the only pupil in his class to see the solution to a problem he had the courage to go to the blackboard and demonstrate.) Thus an act of courage will also enable a man to change his life style after he has consciously changed his life goal. According to Neuer, Adler calls courage (*Mut*) that kind of higher psychic energy or *thymos*, which the ancient Greeks considered the essence of the soul. To impart *thymos* to a child would be the basic concern of the educator, as well as that of the psychotherapist, regardless whether his patient is a child or an adult.

Third, the *principle of cosmic influence:* an individual cannot be conceived isolated from the cosmos that influences him in a thousand ways. But apart from these universal influences, each individual perceives the cosmos in his own specific way. *Community feeling* is a reflection of the general interdependence of the cosmos, which lives within us, from which we cannot abstract ourselves completely, and endows us with the faculty to feel into, that is to empathize with other beings. Above all, it is the spontaneous acceptance to live in conformity to the natural and legitimate demands of the human community.

It is perhaps not superfluous to eliminate a few misunderstandings. Community feeling has nothing to do with the mere ability to mix with others and is much more than loyalty to a group or a cause. It should also not be confused with the abdication of an individual's personality to the hands of a community. The Adlerian notion of community includes the structure of familial and social ties, creative activities (it is the community that creates logic, language, proverbs, and folklore), and an ethical function (justice is an emanation of the community). Thus, community feeling is the individual's perception of these principles that rule the relationships of men with each other.

Community feeling is more or less developed according to individuals: sometimes it is restricted to the family or the group of origin, but it can extend to the nation, to mankind as a whole, and beyond it to animals, plants, inanimate beings, and the universe.

Fourth, *the principle of spontaneous structuration of the parts in a whole*: all the components of the mind spontaneously organize and equilibrate themselves according to the individual self-set goal. Sensations, perceptions, images, memories, fantasies, dreams—everything converges toward the line of direction of the individual. Similarly, with mankind as a whole, we see this spontaneous structuration appear in the form of division of labor. For the individual as well as for mankind, this spontaneous structuration is a manifestation of the principle of the adjustment to one's own law.

A fifth basic axiom is the *principle of action and reaction between the individual and his environment*. On one side the individual must adjust and constantly readjust to his environment. When he is in a position of inferiority, he spontaneously seeks to overcome it, directly or indirectly. This is true for the individual as well as for the species. Like Marx, Adler views man's ability to modify his environment as his distinguishing feature. But here, as in the mechanics of fluids, every action brings a reaction, and this is particularly true for the individual within his social group: "Nobody can stand out from the midst of the community and extend his power over others without immediately awakening forces which will tend to check his expansion."

As a consequence, Adler's psychology is essentially a dynamics of interpersonal relationships. It never considers the individual in an isolated and static situation, but sees him in the light of his actions and of the reactions of his environment.

A sixth axiom is what Adler called *the law of absolute truth*, a fictitious norm set for the conduct of the individual that consists of an optimal balance between the requirements of the community and those of the individual, in other words, between community feeling and legitimate self-assertion. The individual who conforms to that ideal stands in absolute truth, meaning that he conforms to the logic of life in society and, as it were, to the rule of the game. The occurrence of unhappiness, failure, neuroses, psychoses, perversions, and criminality gives a measure of the degree of deviation from this basic rule.

From these premises it is possible to deduce a dialectic that would define the relationships of mankind with nature, of social groups within mankind, of the individual with the community, of the individual within small groups, and of individuals with each other.

The dialectic of the *relationship of the human species and nature* is barely hinted at by Adler. Because man is the weakest among the higher animal species, he developed a psychic organ with the faculty of foreseeing, and he imagined the division of labor. In this way he was able to overcompensate his natural inferiority and conquer nature. Adler could have discussed the problem of the damage caused to nature by man and its disastrous aftereffects on man, but he did not pursue his dialectic in this direction.

The dialectic of the *relationships of social groups with each other* had been abundantly treated by Marx and Engels with their theory of the class struggle. Adler could easily have enlarged this topic, but for some reason he seems to have avoided doing so. However, he remarked upon the feeling of envy as being a natural consequence of social inequality, as opposed to pathological envy resulting from aggressive drives. There is, however, one point common to sociology and biology to which Adler devotes much attention, that is the respective roles of man and woman. The physiological differentiation does not account for the discrepancy in regard to their psychological and sociological roles. All of our public and private institutions rest upon the prejudice of the superiority of the male. Following Bachofen and Bebel, Adler assumes that this attitude of superiority of man over woman was historically a reaction against an ancient period of matriarchy. This attitude is perpetuated and reenforced in the boy as well as in the girl by education and subtle and often unconscious suggestion. That is one of the main roots of neurosis and of the phenomenon of masculine protest, which Adler so thoroughly described in *The Nervous Character.*

The dialectics of the interrelations of human groups was approached by Adler in other publications. We remember how in 1918 and 1919 he tried to elucidate the phenomenon of war and explained it by the criminally irresponsible attitude of those in power and the helplessness of the people when they became aware of the deception.[105] War can be thus considered as one of the forms of mass psychosis provoked by a few men in search of power in their own selfish interests.[106] Adler, however, did not consider the striving for personal power as a primary drive, but as the result of a false guiding ideal that could be replaced by that of community feeling, hence the paramount importance of education in the prevention of war.[107]

This dialectics of the *interrelation of the individual and the community* occupies a large part of Adler's *Menschenkenntnis* and of his other writings. The balance between community feeling and the drive toward self expansion can be disturbed very early. How does Adler explain the origin of imbalance when it occurs? He sees it in the feeling of inferiority, which can be acquired at the earliest age.

At this point a linguistic remark is appropriate. The term "feeling of inferiority," as used by Adler, actually has two different meanings. One is related to a natural inferiority, such as that of the size of a child when compared to that of an adult, or a factual inferiority resulting from disease. But individual psychologists mostly use the term in the sense of a value judgment, which is implicit in the German word—*Minderwertigkeitsgefühl*—which includes the radicals *minder*, "lesser," and *Wert*, "value." It thus means a judgment of "lesser value" pronounced by an individual upon himself. This semantic misunderstanding has been pointed out by Häberlin.[108] But in 1926 Alexander Neuer had distinguished "positions of inferiority," which are numerous and manifold, and "feelings of inferiority," which are the result of the "positions of inferiority" insofar as they are not overcome with courage.[109] This same point was also treated by Brachfeld in detail.[110] Later Adler himself was to make the distinction between the natural feeling of inferiority and the subjective complex of inferiority.[111]

Adler distinguishes several causes of the inferiority feeling. There are the organ inferiorities, as depicted in his monograph of 1907, but Adler now emphasized the importance of the individual's reaction to his organ inferiority rather than the inferiority itself. Another frequent source are the educational errors, such as demanding too much of the child, overemphasizing his weakness, making him a plaything of one's mood, giving him to understand that he is a burden, ridiculing him, and lying to him. There are also social causes, such as those that may be produced by economic and social inferiority among the children of the poor.

Whatever its cause, a feeling of inferiority can develop along two different lines, which are already discernible in the young child. Both set themselves a goal of superiority, but follow a different route to achieve it.

In the first case the individual will directly seek superiority over others. His guiding line will be oriented toward this goal, as well as his psychological functions and his character. He will display ambition, arrogance, jealousy, and hatred. Nietzsche's will to power is one among other manifestations of the superiority complex, and as Nietzsche had already shown, these aggressive feelings can wear many masks.

In the second case the individual will try to reach his goal of superiority by indirect means and will retreat behind barricades such as weakness, shyness, anxiety, or a restricted family or social circle, and this position permits him to exert his tyranny and domination over at least a few other persons. Here, too, there are innumerable varieties of behavior patterns.

Adler believed that as a rule an individual will choose the first direct line, and will only resort to the second when he has met with failure. This may happen sooner or later, often very early in childhood. In all cases, however, the discrepancy between the self-set goal of superiority and his power to reach it will lead the individual to defeat. For a long time he will try to avert it by making use of distance.[112] The subject will suddenly retreat when he should be nearing his goal, he will stop shortly before reaching it, adopt a wavering attitude, or he will cunningly construct artificial obstacles that will impede success. Whenever the clever use of distance does not suffice, the subject will have to confront his dream with stark reality, and in order to avoid a catastrophe, he resorts to what Adler calls the *arrangement*. This can be a depression, anxiety, phobia, amnesia, or any kind of neurosis; sometimes it takes the form of a physical disease or a psychosis. The aim of the *arrangement* is to conceal to the environment and to the subject himself the imminent defeat of his unachievable ambitions.

In the light of these concepts, the many kinds of neurosis, depression, perversion, addiction, criminality, and even psychosis are but varieties of disturbances in the relationship of the individual with the community.

The interrelations of individuals within a small group are another concern of individual psychology. This could be applied to any natural or artificial group situation. Professor Biäsch, in Zurich, currently applies Adlerian principles in his investigations in industrial and business psychology. Actually Adler gave his attention mainly to the psychology within the family group.

In the life of a child the strongest influence comes from the mother; she is the one who imparts (or should impart) the seeds of the community feeling; the father's role is to teach self-reliance and courage. The Oedipus situation, which Freud contends to be a normal and universal stage of human life, is considered by Adler the result of faulty education in a spoiled child. Relationships with the parents are not limited to those of love and hate as depicted by Freud, but either can play the role of *Gegenspieler* (the "played against," the partner against whom the child measures his strength). This role can also be played by one of the siblings, especially the oldest one.

According to Adler, each one of the children in a family is born and grows up with a specific perspective according to its position in relation to the other siblings. From the onset the position of the oldest brother is better than that of the younger ones. He is made to feel that he is the stronger, the wiser, the most responsible. That is why he values the concept of authority and tradition, and is conservative in his views. The youngest brother, on the other hand, is always in danger of remaining the spoiled and cowardly family baby. Whereas the oldest will take his father's profession, the youngest may easily become an artist, or then, as the result of overcompensation, he will develop tremendous ambition and strive to be the savior of the entire family. The second child in a family is under perpetual pressure from both sides, striving to outmatch his older brother and fearing to be overtaken by the younger one. As for the only child, he is even more exposed to be spoiled and pampered than the youngest one. His parents' preoccupation with his health may cause him to become anxious and timorous. Such patterns are subject to modifications according to the distance between the siblings and according to the proportion of boys and girls and their respective position in the family. If the oldest brother is closely followed by a sister, there comes a time when he will fear being outdistanced by the girl who will mature more rapidly than he. Among many other possible situations are those of the only girl in a family of boys, and of the only boy among a constellation of girls (a particularly unfavorable situation according to Adler).

The *interrelations of two individuals* has also been touched upon by Adler. There is normal obedience, guided by community feeling; there is disobedience due to a lack of community feeling or the will to power; there is a blind obedience that is particularly noxious when met within delinquent groups. Adler considers hypnosis a specific kind of interpersonal relationship that is equally degrading for the subject and the hypnotizer. Suggestion, according to Adler, is a way of reacting to a certain exogenous stimulation; some individuals are ready to overevaluate the opinion of others and underevaluate their own, other men are prone to consider only their own opinion as right and indistinctly reject those of others. Implied, but nowhere clearly described in Adler's works, is the immediate interpersonal relationship that is spontaneously established between two men who meet for the first time.

One of the great difficulties in interpersonal relationships is the lack of understanding. Most men have little insight in regard to themselves and others, and worse, experience will not help them because they will evaluate it in the light of their already distorted perspective. Moreover, they do not like to be enlightened about themselves. But Adler is convinced that if knowledge of man were more general, social relationships would be facilitated, because then people could not deceive each other so easily. Hence the need of a technique for practical psychological diagnosis.

Adler's technique begins with the axiomatic principle that most individuals are striving toward a hidden goal, of which they are unaware. The knowledge of that goal would provide the key to the understanding of a man's personality, and conversely, the nature of that goal can be deduced from the critical examination of an individual's behavior. Because the hidden goal determines both the guiding line and the perspective (or world picture) of the individual, we possess a number of clues pointing toward the secret goal. The individual psychologist will proceed somewhat like the astronomer who wants to determine the trajectory of a new star. He determines a number of successive positions and from there onward reconstructs the line and direction followed by the star. Thus the individual psychologist will start with two points as remote from each other as possible; one could be a childhood memory and the other a recent occurrence that enlightens the individual's social behavior. Of course, the psychologist will also take intermediary points, and the more there are the more exact will be the reconstruction of the line. Among the data utilized by the individual psychologist are the first memories, the child's spontaneous play activities, the child's and adolescent's successive wishes for his future profession, and his dreams.

According to Adler the first memories have a great diagnostic value, whether or not they are historically true. They reflect the life goal and life style of the individual, provided they are examined in connection with other psychological indications.

Adler feels that dreams show something of the life style of the individual, particularly that aspect of himself that he wants to hide from his fellow men (because the censorship of the social control is temporarily removed). They also have a prospective function: they express a tentative solution to the dreamer's present problems, or rather a flight from a true rational solution, and are therefore a self-deception.[113]

This kind of investigation of present attitudes, first memories, childhood activities, adolescent wishes, and dreams, simultaneously uncovers the individual's perspective, that is his specific, selective perception of the world, and his style of life. Every individual utilizes his particular tactics to reach his goal, and this is what Adler calls the style of life (*Lebensstil*). One will resort to arrogance, the other to feigned modesty, a third will arouse pity in others and so on, but mostly it is a complex combination of devices. In diagnosing a life style the actions and behavior of an individual are far more revealing than his words. Thus it is possible to simply and rapidly diagnose the secret goal pursued by those with whom we deal and to see how they attempt to influence us. One can thus see through their mask, and avert their attacks. In children it is easy to discover the secret of their character difficulties and the obstacles to their education.

To fully assess a character, one must consider other facts. Every individual's picture of the world largely depends upon whether he is a visual, auditive, or motor type. The latter needs more movement. Adler also came to attribute much importance to the degree of mental and physical energy of the individual, independently from his courage. We thus see that for the full evaluation of a man's personality it is necessary to find out about his organ insufficiencies, his early interpersonal relationships and family situation, whether he is a sensory or a motor type, his natural physical and mental energy, his free choices, and his courage.

The course and development of human life is viewed by Adler in the light of the above concepts. The individuality of man is manifested very early. According to Adler it is possible to evaluate the degree of community feeling in an infant after a few months of age, and in the second year it can be deduced from the way in which the child expresses itself in words. As the child grows, his way of playing becomes characteristic. Adler agrees with Groos that play is a spontaneous preparation of the child for the future, but he adds that it is also an expression of his creative activity, or his community feeling, and his will to power. Early childhood is also the period when man learns from his environment in many subtle ways, along with the commonly accepted ideas about the respective roles of men and women in society, and also finds his identity. Adler considered the child's successive wishes about his future profession to be important, and he thought that the absence of any such wish could be the sign of a serious underlying disturbance. The adult age is the period when the individual must fulfill his three life tasks: love and family, profession, and relationships with the community. The way in which the individual fulfills these three life tasks gives the measure of his adjustment. New problems brought about by the later process of aging have to be viewed in that perspective.

The book *Menschenkenntnis* also contains a typology, and a chapter that ancient authors would have called a treatise on the passions. Though emphasizing that every human being is unique, Adler gives a rule-of-thumb classification wherein he distinguishes two broad categories: the aggressive and the nonaggressive nature. Among the aggressive he places not only those who show overt but also disguised aggression. This characterology is closely related to Adler's description of the passions, which he divides into separating and uniting.

Adler's conception of psychosis, deviations, and criminality is contained in various other writings of the same period.

Adler's theory of melancholia was published in 1920.[114] In a depressive episode Adler sees nothing but the exacerbation of the patient's characteristic way of handling life situations. The depressed patient, Adler says, is a man who has always been afflicted with a deep-seated feeling of inferiority. But the characteristic feature is his personal way of coping with this inferiority feeling. From early childhood he shows a lack of drive and activity, avoiding difficulties, decisions, and responsibilities. He is distrustful and critical of others, and sees the world as basically hostile, life as a tremendously difficult enterprise, his fellow men as cold and rejecting. On the other hand, the subject has always nourished a secret idea of his own superiority and the wish to obtain the greatest possible advantages from others. In order to attain his secret goal, the subject adopts well-defined tactics: to make himself as small and inconspicuous as possible, and to restrict himself to a narrow circle of persons whom he can dominate, mostly through complaints, tears, and sadness. Melancholia always appears under the impact of a vital crisis, such as a situation of enforced difficulty requiring an uncompromising decision; or because the patient's environment became more critical and escaped his control; or perhaps the patient was becoming critical of himself. At this point melancholia occurs and a vicious circle arises from the fact that sleeplessness, insufficient food intake, and similar factors impair the patient's physiological equilibrium and consequently enforce his fiction. The outcome of the disease depends, Adler says, on whether the patient's tactic triumphs or not. In the former case the disease recedes as soon as the patient has reached his secret goal. But if he fails, he resorts to his *ultima ratio*, suicide, which is at once the only honorable issue from a hopeless situation, and an act of vengeance against the environment.

Paranoia, according to Adler, is the development of another early specific way of handling life situations.[115] When an individual has already shown a lack of community feeling as a child, has always been dissatisfied with life and critical and hostile toward others, he sets himself a secret goal of high ambition, and strives to reach it with activities of a belligerent nature. For some time he progresses in that direction, but there comes a point where he is obliged to come to a halt at some distance from the expected goal. In order to justify himself in the eyes of others and his own, he now resorts to two devices: he creates ficticious obstacles and henceforth exhausts his energies in his struggle to overcome them, and he displaces the battle to another field.

Schizophrenia, Adler thinks, affects individuals who manifest a fear of life quite early. The onset of the disease comes when they must face their life tasks. The disease itself is the manifestation of extreme discouragement.

As to alcoholism, a variety of causes have been pointed out by Adler and his disciples. Organ inferiority may play a role.[116] The intake of alcohol can be a way of soothing feelings of inferiority, a manifestation of masculine protest, or a way of enhancing a hostile attitude toward the other men. Inebriety is a means of cutting oneself out of the community. Alcoholic addiction is a way of escaping from life duties and responsibilities.[117]

Generally speaking, Adler considers sexual perversions as the expression of increased psychological distance between man and woman, of a rebellion of the subject against his normal sexual role, and of a deprecatory attitude and hostility toward a sexual partner.[118]

Homosexuality was the subject of Adler's seventy-five-page study published in 1917[119] and of a larger monograph in 1930.[120] Adler rejects the physical constitution theory of homosexuality. He admits that certain homosexuals may exhibit a few secondary sexual characteristics of the opposite sex, but this happens to many individuals who are perfectly normal. There is no biological determinism, and everything depends on the subjective manner in which the patient assumes his somatic identity, and what use he makes of it. The mainspring is found in the fear of and hostility toward the other sex, because psychological distance is less with the persons of the same sex than those of the opposite one. The child who has not been adequately prepared to assume his social role avoids persons of the other sex and compensates by overemphasizing his relationships with persons of his own sex. From then on, whenever he faces situations in which he must deal with members of the opposite sex, he reacts by discouragement and flight. In his later monograph on homosexuality, Adler underlined the importance of the element of training: usually it is far from easy to become a pervert, and a homosexual, through self-deception, easily convinces himself that as far back as he can remember he has always been attracted to children of the same sex.

Among the great pioneers of dynamic psychiatry, Janet and Adler are the only ones who had personal clinical experience with criminals, and Adler was the only one who wrote something on the subject from his direct experience.[121] At the root of criminality as well as with neurosis, psychosis, and sexual deviation, Adler finds a lack of social interest. But the criminal differs insofar as he does not content himself with receiving help from others and being a burden to them, but acts as if the whole world were against him. The delinquent child can be detected because he gets his own way by hurting others. Adler distinguishes three types of criminals: first those who were pampered children, always used to receiving and never giving, and who have kept their pattern; then there are the neglected children who actually have experienced a hostile world; and lastly there is a lesser group comprising the ugly children. But whatever the original situation, criminals show the same intensive striving toward superiority. Adler considers the criminal as being essentially and always a coward. The criminal never gives a fair fight; he commits his offenses only when he is in a position of advantage. (He will steal from an inattentive or defenseless victim, kill when his victim cannot defend himself, and so on.) His feeling of superiority is strengthened by the fact that, before getting caught, he usually has committed several offenses without being discovered. Adjuvant factors of criminality are a low intelligence level and a lack of training for a profession. According to Phyllis Bottome, Adler found that burglars were easier to cure than other criminals because they are of a higher intelligence level than the average criminal and because, being "experts," it will be easier for them to find an honorable trade and adjust to it.

Unlike Freud, Adler did not greatly infringe upon the fields of art, literature, ethnology, and cultural history. An article casually written for the Viennese Social Democratic newspaper shows how individual psychology can be applied to the interpretation of a historical event, namely, the French Revolution of 1789.

The rapid economic development of France with the urbanization, growth of an industrial proletariat, exploitation of the peasants, had brought the country into chaos. The exclusion of the most capable men from many public functions irritated them. Voltaire and Rousseau gave expression to feelings of the masses and helped to create a "revolutionary line." A critical point came when the first attempts to introduce urgently needed reforms were checked by the government. This set into motion the revolutionary tide and paved the way to its great leaders.

Marat, who was poor, hungry, persecuted by the police, proclaimed the revolt of the poor against the rich. He offered himself as a victim, the more so because his health was ruined. Not being eloquent, his tactic was to write inflamed letters and newspaper articles, and to receive many visitors who would listen to his ideas. He was disinterested and sincere, but failed to notice that the bulk of his adherents was composed of criminals.

Danton, an inordinately ambitious man, had given an early indication of his life style when, being a schoolboy, he escaped in order to watch the King's coronation. During the Revolution, he knew how to sense forthcoming developments, and always be on the spot on important occasions. He was courageous, resolute, and a brilliant orator. His tactics was to keep good relationships with the rich and powerful while seemingly serving the people, and to utilize the people for the sake of his own egoist interests.

Robespierre had been a "model pupil," always at the head of his class. His predominant passion was self-conceit. To a hungry people he preached the abstract ideal of "Virtue" and the cult of the Supreme Being (whom he conceived at his own image). His tactics was to keep himself as much as possible in the background, to slowly and methodically prepare crushing attacks upon his enemies, to maneuver them so that they would destroy each other. But he lacked in flexibility, and when he came to his last enemy he suddenly collapsed.[122]

One may wonder how far these analyses derive from individual psychology, or from Adler's personal acquaintance with the Russian revolutionists.

Alfred Adler's Work—V—Psychotherapy and Education

It is not exactly known when Adler began to study and to practice psychotherapy. Probably he learned something of it from Moritz Benedikt at the *Poliklinik*. In the last decade of the nineteenth century it became fashionable to be a Nervenarzt, that is to treat those numerous patients whose ailments belong neither in organic neurology nor hospital psychiatry. Since there was no organized teaching in this new branch of medicine, those who practiced it had empirically to elaborate their own method, which was likely never to be transmitted. It seems that during his years as a medical practitioner, Adler had an ever increasing number of nervous patients, and it is open to question to what extent he treated them according to his own methods or to the methods he learned from Benedikt, and later from Freud and the psychoanalytic group. It is clear from Adler's writings that during his association with Freud he was actively engaged in the treatment of neurosis. *The Nervous Character* is obviously the work of a man who has had several years of psychotherapeutic experience and who has had fully mastered his technique.

Unfortunately Adler, unlike Freud, never gave a detailed account of his psychotherapeutic technique. References to his technique are scattered throughout his writings and those of his disciples.[123]

One main difference between Adler and Freud was that Freud devised a psychotherapeutic technique only for the individual adult; his daughter Anna first adapted it to child analysis; Pfister and Aichhorn, to therapeutic education; and still others to group therapy. Adler set up a variety of therapeutic methods intended for the adult, the child, and for therapeutic education.

The differences between the methods of Freud and Adler are immediately apparent. With Adler there is no question of the patient lying on a couch and the physician sitting behind him, seeing the patient without being seen himself. The Adlerian therapist and his patient sit face to face and Adler insisted that their two chairs be similar in respect to height, shape, and size. Sessions are less frequent and the treatment much shorter than in Freudian analysis. Usually the one-hour interviews take place three times a week at the beginning, their frequency being reduced gradually to twice, and then to once a week. The rigid rules characteristic of Freudian psychoanalysis are often taken lightly by Adlerians. The therapist will not hesitate to talk with members of the family or friends of the patient in the latter's presence (with his agreement), if he deems it necessary. Individual psychologists never noticed any difference between the outcome of free and paid-for therapies, nor do they believe that a missed appointment should necessarily be paid for, regardless of the cause.

Individual psychotherapy comprises three stages of unequal length. During the first stage the main objective is for the therapist to understand the patient and his problems. Depending upon the experience and the psychological acumen of the therapist, this will take from one day to two weeks or more. Adler was known for the swiftness of his diagnosis. The patient relates his life story and talks about his difficulties, the therapist inquiries about first memories, early childhood situations, dreams, and other characteristic personality features that enable him to reconstruct the life goal and life style of his patient. One of Adler's favorite questions was: "Supposing that you would not have this ailment, what would you do?" The patient's answer indicated what he actually wanted to avoid.

In the second stage the therapist has to make the patient gradually aware of his fictitious life goal and life style. There is, of course, no question of saying this directly to the patient. It has to be gradually achieved while discussing the patient's failure in life or neurotic behavior. The patient is also shown how his life style and goal were in contradiction with the reality of life and the law of social interest.

Once the patient has acquired and accepted a clear, objective image of himself, one has reached the third stage, in which it is up to the patient to decide whether he wants to change his life goal and style. In that case the patient has to be helped in his endeavors to readjust himself to the newly discovered reality, and this can last a few more months. However, the total length of an individual psychology therapy rarely extends over more than one year and whereas Freud considered as criteria for a successful therapy when the patient recovered the ability to enjoy and to work, Adler took as criteria the ability to fulfill the three main tasks of life: occupation, love and family, community. The phenomena of resistance and transference, which are so basic in Freudian psychoanalysis, tend to be considered by Adlerians as artifacts. Adler equated resistance with a form of masculine protest, which had to be immediately pointed out to the patient as undesirable. Transference was considered by Adler as a neurotic wish that had to be eradicated.

In contrast to Freud, Adler never published full case histories comparable to the story of the wolf-man or little Hans. But we possess two fairly long fragments of case histories. They are known as the case of Miss R.[124] and the case of Mrs. A.[125] although they are not case histories in the proper sense. The first one is a short life history written by the patient herself, and the second is a short account written by the physician about the patient. Each was read to Adler (who did not know the patients), and he commented upon the story, sentence by sentence. The idea was to show how any clinical document can be interpreted in order to reconstruct the subject's life goal and life style.

Adler's technique of child psychotherapy differed in many respects from the technique he used with adults. It varied according to the child, the child's age, and his problems. Adler never treated a child without having interviews with his parents, and at least part of the therapeutic sessions was given in the presence of one of the parents or a qualified person.

Adler's method of psychotherapy for the individual patient covers only one aspect of his total activity as a psychotherapist. The other aspect is shown in the organizations for therapeutic education that he conceived and organized in Vienna.[126]

In 1920 Adler felt that the main effort in therapeutic education should be directed toward teachers rather than toward families and he organized consultations for teachers. They would meet with Adler or his associates at regular intervals to discuss problems pertaining to the difficult children they had in their classes. Teachers were brought to understand these problems in the light of individual psychology. The need for consultations where the parents could also participate soon became apparent and were held free of charge, twice a week, in one of the classrooms. The teacher prepared a file on the child prior to the consultation and Adler, or his substitute, always first spoke with the mother, then with the child, and last with the teacher. Several other teachers were always present, and Adler had at least one of his associates with him at all times who recorded the interview. Adler emphasized the value of having several teachers and educators present, not only so that other teachers and psychologists could learn his methods, but also to impart the feeling to the child that he was in the care of a group that was genuinely interested in his welfare. This was an early example of what was later to be called multiple therapy. Adler did not resort to psychological tests. One of his principles was to treat the child in the home in view of teaching the child to adjust to difficult surroundings. It was only in extreme cases that children were referred to an institution. Some of the children were sent to a *Hort*, a kind of part-time shelter where the child did his homework and played after school.

Adler never tried to impose his services and waited to be invited before starting work in a new school. According to Madelaine Ganz, he was already conducting work in twenty-six schools by 1929. Vienna became the first city in the world where all schoolchildren could enjoy free educational therapy when it was needed.

Experience had taught Adler that the earlier educational therapy was started, the more effective it was. And this led him to the creation of kindergarten classes conducted according to the principles of individual psychology. The aim was to make the very young child independent and adjustable. Madelaine Ganz, who visited one of them in 1932, noticed that the children seemed less disciplined than in the Montessori kindergarten. They were free to pursue their activities either in small groups or alone. The only rule imposed upon the child was that it had to conduct any chosen task to the end. Community feeling was encouraged not only by a lesson in rhythmic gymnastics, but also by one hour set aside for conversation presided over by the teacher. The children would bring a snack at ten o'clock around a common table, and they would spontaneously come to exchange and share their food.

Another educational achievement was the experimental school that was opened in September 1931 after ten years of preliminary work and negotiations with school authorities. The school was operated by three of Adler's most experienced followers: Oskar Spiel, Birnbaum, and Scharmer. Their task was not easy because the school board had stipulated that the school program and general regulations be exactly the same as in the other *Hauptschulen* in Vienna. The school was in one of the poorer quarters of Vienna with classes of thirty and forty children. At that time the Great Depression had set in, and many of the parents were unemployed so that pupils were often undernourished. Madelaine Ganz speaks of her admiration for the dedication of these educators and their remarkable achievements in spite of numerous obstacles. The classes were divided into work groups of from five to seven pupils each, with a president who kept in touch with the first and the second head pupils. Community spirit for the entire class was maintained through a "conversation group" in which the whole class participated once a week, and they also shared other experiences. Mutual aid was systematically encouraged. For example, a child who was good at mathematics would be seated next to one who was not, so that he could assist him. The teachers gave individual interviews to those pupils who showed a need for them, and there was a monthly meeting of parents and teachers (this was by no means a matter of course at that time).

These organizations were abolished when the Social Democratic party relinquished its last stronghold, "red Vienna," in 1934. But Adler's ideas remained alive, and his inspiration is discernible in creations that were no longer his own but those of his disciples. Dr. Joshua Bierer, who was personally trained and taught by Adler and emigrated to England, proclaimed that any psychiatry that wishes to be called social must include the total community. This was the underlying idea when Bierer[127] founded the first self-governed Social Therapeutic Club for acute and chronic in-patients in Runwell Hospital (1938–1939), the first clubs for discharged patients and out-patients in East Ham and Southend in 1939, and the Social Psychotherapy Centre (today called Day Hospital) in 1946.[128] Group therapy and community psychiatry are clearly the legitimate offspring of Alfred Adler's thought and work.

Alfred Adler's Work—VI—Later Developments

With his book *Understanding Human Nature* in 1927, Adler had given the most systematized exposé of his doctrine. In the following years, particularly after 1933, he introduced certain modifications. Some pertained to new psychological concepts and others to an increased emphasis on the philosophical side of his ideas. These changes are noticeable in his book *The Meaning of Life*[129] and in various of his later articles.[130]

In these later writings Adler attributed an increased importance to the creative power and to the degree of activity of the individual. He now considered the creative power as an essential factor in the construction of the life plan or life style. The latter, therefore, cannot be considered any longer as a mere reflection of the early childhood situations. The same power is to be found in the shaping of a neurosis by the neurotic. Another important innovation in Adler's later teachings is the concept of "degree of activity" in problem children: the difference in degree of activity determines differences in the later psychopathological outcome in the adult, and correspondingly, different measures of education. A third innovation is the increased emphasis on the striving for superiority, which he now considers essential and normal. The striving for superiority is no longer seen as antagonistic to community feeling. The latter is a normative ideal that gives direction to the striving for superiority. Adler no longer considers inferiority feelings as primary (with the striving for superiority as its compensation). On the contrary, he now understands feelings of inferiority as being secondary to the striving for superiority. The opposite of community feeling is now "private intelligence."

In his description of neurosis and delinquency Adler now uses new terms. The neurotic and the delinquent who follow their private intelligence instead of the logic of community life devote their activity to the useless side of life. In all those who depart from the community ideal a restriction of field necessarily occurs: The homosexual, for instance, cuts himself off from the opposite sex, that is, half of mankind. In the habitual criminal the restriction is far more pronounced. The difference between the neurotic and the criminal is that the former has not lost his community feeling, but his answer to the demands of the community is "yes, but," whereas the criminal's answer is, "no." In another of his late papers Adler deals with the problem of death: the mentally healthy person will not let the thought of death detract from the active adaptation to the problems of life; the neurotic will arrange various kinds of obsessive death wishes or fears of death according to his life style.[131]

Adler seems to have hesitated between several systems of typology and proposed others, which, however, are not mutually exclusive. Previously he distinguished four kinds of individuals: those who conformed to the logic of community feeling, the directly aggressive, the indirectly aggressive, and those who retreated into addiction or psychosis. Later he emphasized the importance of the motor and sensory types: the motor type with his need for activity, the visual type, and the auditive type. Adler even speaks of the "gustative" type, in which he places certain alcoholics. In *The Meaning of Life* Adler distinguishes three types of men: those dominated by the intellect (to them belong obsessive compulsive neurotics and most psychotics); those dominated by the affectivity (to them belong the bulk of the neurotics and the alcoholics); those dominated by the activity (to these belong criminals and those who commit suicide). However, Adler does not attribute too much importance to these typologies, and in his later writings he emphasizes the uniqueness of the individual, as the Romantics had done before him and the Existentialists were to do after him.

It seems that Adler did not change greatly in his technique of treatment. In regard to diagnosis, Adler believed that anyone could develop the ability of guessing, by making a diagnosis at first sight and counterchecking, thus training himself. In the process of unveiling the patient's neurotic fictions, one should try to lead him into a "trap" (incidentally this is the old dialectic method applied by Socrates in his discussions with the sophists).[132]

As the year went by, Adler's system took on an increasingly philosophical turn. The feeling of inferiority, far from being a neurotic symptom, became now the most essential feature of man. In *The Meaning of Life* Adler enounced his much-quoted sentence: "To be a man means to suffer from an inferiority feeling which constantly drives him to overcome it."[133] Adler also emphasized man's tendency to shift from a state of inferiority to one of superiority. It is the same process that drives the entire living nature from the first living cell to mankind and to the present world, a striving to challenge and conquer death itself. One will note the similarities of this concept with those of Leibniz and Bergson.

The attitude of Adler, which had been hostile or at least indifferent to religion, also showed a marked evolution. This was manifested by his encounter and discussion with Pastor Jahn in 1932.

Dr. Ernst Jahn, a Lutheran pastor at Stieglitz, near Berlin, had been keenly interested in the new psychotherapeutic schools and the contribution they could offer to the traditional religious "cure of souls" (*Seelsorge*).[134] He had written a book on psychoanalysis;[135] had been in correspondence with Jung, Pfister, and Künkel; and then wrote a comprehensive criticism of individual psychology.[136] When Adler came to Berlin in 1932 the two men became personally acquainted and decided to jointly write a book, confronting cure of souls and individual psychology. This book was published in 1933, but almost immediately seized by the Nazis and destroyed.[137]

In Adler's view man is essentially bound to the earth; religion is a manifestation of community feeling; cure of souls is an anticipation of psychotherapy, God is the materialization of the idea of perfection and the highest of all thinkable ideas; man is neither good nor wicked, it depends upon the evolution of his community feeling; the evil is an error in life style; grace consists of realizing and correcting one's erroneous life style "within the limits of immanence" (that is with human help only). To Reverend Jahn, man is in concrete relationship not only to the earth but to God; God is a supracosmic, living reality; the evil is not only an error but is sin that deserves the wrath of God; but sin is forgiven through grace, which is a gift of God; for all these reasons cure of souls, which reconciles man with God, can never be equated to psychotherapy. Jahn, however, acknowledges the merits of psychotherapy, particularly of individual psychology. He notes that Adler rediscovered one of Luther's essential assertions, that egocentric love is the basic attitude of man (though Adler deems this self-love an error in the life style, and religion a sin against God).

Throughout this controversy, Adler and Reverend Jahn showed great respect for each other. In answer to the author's inquiry, Reverend Jahn told him that he found Adler an unassuming man, a great empiricist, and an experienced psychologist imbued with a high idealism and convinced of the truth of his observations. Perhaps he was a positivist, but he honestly searched for a confrontation with Christianity. Reverend Jahn concludes with these words: "Today I am convinced that Adler was not an atheist."

Adler's Sources

The primary source of any creative man is his own personality. If we refer to the distinction of the visual, auditive, and motor types, Adler was well endowed, since he belonged to all three: he had a great need for movement and activity, he was a good musician and lover of music, and his quick sense of observation enabled him to make a rapid diagnosis. His theory of organ inferiority was not only drawn from clinical research; he had personally experienced this state in his early childhood when illness impeded his need for movement. He also personally experienced the situation of being the second child between and older and a younger brother, one of those sibling situations he was to describe, and the psychological description of the oldest and the youngest child was obviously drawn from his own family. If Phyllis Bottome is to be believed, difficulties with his wife were one of the sources of his theory of masculine protest. His personal reaction to World War I and his experiences as a military physician could have inspired in him the concept of community feeling.

One often-overlooked source of any theory of neurosis is the kind of patients with whom a psychotherapist has to deal. Izydor Wasserman explains the difference between Freud's psychoanalysis and Adler's individual psychology by the fact that, according to his computation, most of Freud's patients belonged to the wealthier upper classes (74 per cent) and the bulk of Adler's patients to the middle and lower classes (74 per cent). [138] To this Ansbacher replied that both psychological theories and the choice of patients derived from the personality of Freud and Adler.[139] According to Wasserman, Adler had 26 per cent of upper-class patients, 28 per cent of middle class, and 36 per cent of lower class, which shows a fairly equal division of his patients among the social classes. Another difference was that Freud had shifted from neurology to the neuroses, and Adler from general medicine to the neuroses; which explains Freud's emphasis on a conceptual model borrowed from brain physiology in contrast to Adler's interest in the relationships of mind and body. Moreover, Freud's first studies of neuroses were made on hysterical patients, but around 1900 hysteria ceased to be fashionable, and Adler's observations were made mostly on obsessive-compulsive neurotics.

It is commonly assumed that Adler knew nothing of the neuroses and psychotherapy before his encounter with Freud. In fact, the actual situation was more complex. In his autobiography, Hellpach described how in the year 1899 it had become fashionable to be a "physician of the nerves" (Nervenarzt), as it had been fashionable a generation earlier to be an ophthalmologist.[140] The main difficulty was to find the right place in which to learn that new branch of medicine. Adler probably received some rudiments of it from Krafft-Ebing's lectures. However, it may be assumed that his first master in the study of neuroses was Moritz Benedikt at the Viennese Poliklinik. Benedikt's abhorrence of hypnosis, his uncovering psychotherapy on the conscious level, and his notion of the individual's second life of secret fantasy are reflected in Adler's method and in his theory of the guiding fiction. The role of environmental, and particularly educational, influences in the psychogenesis of neuroses also belongs to Adler's prepsychoanalytic period.

It is not easy to assess the extent of Freud's contribution to Adler's individual psychology. Though maintaining that he never agreed with Freud's concepts of the libido and the Oedipus complex, Adler acknowledged that he was indebted to Freud for several of his basic tenets: the lasting influence of the infant's first interpersonal relationships, the meaningfulness of symptoms and parapraxes, and the possibility of giving an interpretation of dreams. It is sometimes wrongly asserted that Adler rejected the concept of the unconscious. Adler believed that the early childhood situations and events unconsciously determined the adult's style of life; he spoke of the unconscious fictions and life goals. Neither is it true that Adler's orientation is only teleological and Freud's only causal; Adler maintained that early childhood situations were the real (not the fictitious) causes of neurosis, whereas Freud also taught that neurotic symptoms had a purpose.

It is certain that Freud influenced Adler negatively. During the Wednesday evening discussions, Adler seems to have used Freud largely as an antagonist who helped him to find his own path by inspiring him in opposite ways of thought. Some of these oppositions could be summed up as follows:

FREUD	ADLER
Philosophical pessimism	Philosophical optimism
The individual is divided against himself	Essential indivisibility of the individual.
Predominantly causal orientation	Predominantly teleological orientation.
The ego is oppressed by the superego and threatened by civilization	The individual tends to act aggressively toward community.
Defences of the ego. Acting out may occur when the defences are not strong enough	Styles of aggression of the individual against other men. "Barricades" when active aggression has failed.
The infant has a feeling of omnipotence (hallucinatory wish fulfillment)	The child has a feeling of inferiority (relation of midget to giant).
Basic importance of libido, its fixations and regressions.	Much in man's sexual behavior has a symbolic meaning in relation to striving for superiority.
Emphasis on object relations in the form of cathexis of libido and aggressive feeling.	Concept of the "antagonist" (Gegenspieler).
Emphasis on relationship to father and mother, and Oedipus complex.	Emphasis on relationship to siblings and situation in the sibling set.
Woman has a feeling of inferiority because she has no penis ("penis envy").	Man has a feeling of inferiority because his potency is more limited than in woman.
Neurosis is an inescapable effect of civilization and almost inherent to the human condition.	Neurosis is a trick of the individual to escape fulfilling his duties to the community.
After World War I, Freud developed the concept of the death instinct.	After World War I, Adler developed the concept of social interest.
In psychoanalytic therapy the patient lies on a couch.	During Adlerian psychotherapy the patient sits in front of the therapist.

In any group where a master teaches by means of free discussion with his disciples, it is impossible to discern what influences the master exerts on the disciples, the disciples on the master, and the disciples on each other. This was also true for Adler and his group of disciples. One example, the distinction of the factual and the neurotic feeling of inferiority (in other words the inferiority feeling and the inferiority complex), seems to have been suggested by Alexander Neuer. Objections to a theory may be rejected by its author but they find their way into his mind, perhaps in the guise of cryptomnesias. This happened when Freud, after rejecting Adler's concept of an autonomous aggressive drive in 1908, adopted it later in 1920. Similarly, Hans Kunz published a merciless criticism of individual psychology in 1928, arguing that the striving for superiority was not a compensation for inferiority feelings but an autonomous drive; this same idea was introduced by Adler into his later revisions of individual psychology.[141]

As was true in regard to psychoanalysis, the contribution of various philosophers was an essential element of individual psychology. According to Phyllis Bottome Adler had studied Aristotle and greatly admired him.[142] However, Aristotle's influence is not apparent in Adler's work, unless it is in Aristotle's definition of man as a "political animal." Individual psychology shows a closer analogy with the philosophy of stoicism, which proclaimed the unity of the universe and man, the community of mankind, that wisdom consists of conforming to universal laws, and virtue is to make a constant effort to reach that aim (this main virtue is very similar to what Adler called courage).

The philosophy that predominates throughout Adler's thinking is that of the Enlightenment (though not as exclusively as with Janet). Whereas Freud's philosophical outlook is similar to that of Schopenhauer, Adler follows the line of Leibniz and Kant. As does Leibniz, Adler teaches that the human being is an indivisible entity, a monad who reflects the universe. Each part is coordinated with the whole, and man, like the other monads, continuously strives from a lesser toward a greater perfection.

Adler has many affinities with Kant. What Adler calls absolute truth, that is, the rule that a man should perfectly adjust his life and actions to the demands of the community, is not very different from Kant's categorical imperative. In an ironic pamphlet about Swedenborg, Kant says that the great Swedish mystic built a kind of private metaphysical world for himself distinct from the one in which other men live.[143] In his *Anthropology*, Kant notes that "the only feature common to all mental disorders is the loss of common sense (*sensus communis*) and the compensatory development of a unique, private sense (*sensus privatus*) of reasoning."[144] What Kant calls private sense is similar to what Adler was to call private intelligence.[145]

Adler's individual psychology belongs to this type of psychology to which Kant had given a model with his pragmatic anthropology. Kant had explained that to investigate the brain physiological fundament of memory means to speculate on theoretical psychology, whereas to inquire into what favors or impairs memory in order to improve and develop it means to use pragmatic anthropology. Kant also held the opinion that man was able to overcome many emotional and physical ailments through the power of the will, an example of what Adler called courage.[146]

Adler definitely belongs to the philosophy of the Enlightenment with his emphasis that man is a rational and a social being, endowed with free will and the ability to make conscious decisions. However, several of his basic concepts are in harmony with Romantic philosophy: the absolute uniqueness of the individual and of his vision of the world (Adler's perspective), community as an organic and creative whole (an idea far removed from the Enlightenment's concept of the "social contract"). Another Romantic element in individual psychology can be traced back to Bachofen.[147] Bachofen taught that mankind had lived through a previous stage of matriarchy and that the present domination of man over woman had been achieved after a long struggle. Bebel combined this theory with that of Marxism.[148] Woman had been enslaved by man, as the proletarian class had been by the bourgeoisie; socialism would give equal rights to man and woman. Bebel's theory inspired Adler's concept of the "masculine protest" (a compensatory process in woman against her feeling of being an inferior woman) and of the "fear of woman" in neurotic men. Adler surmised that man had overthrown matriarchy and replaced it with his own domination as a compensation against a feeling of inferiority toward woman: man's potency is more limited than that of woman.[149]

Adler developed in an intellectual atmosphere permeated with Darwinism, and particularly with social Darwinism.[150] Social Darwinism emphasized the struggle for life (often conceived as a Hobbesian war of everyone against everyone), the survival of the fittest, and the elimination of the unfit. Adler belongs to those who responded to Darwinism by taking the reverse position. First, he views organic inferiority, not as a cause for defeat and elimination, but as a result of compensation as a stimulant to attain superiority. Second, he sees man's most basic drive, not in the fighting instinct, but in the community feeling.

Adler's passionate interest in social problems and socialism in his youth necessarily brought him into contact with the teachings of Karl Marx. It is not known whether Adler read the writings of Marx, but he could not avoid absorbing a great deal of Marxian doctrine. Though Adler refused to have his movement identified in any way with socialism or communism, the influence of Marxism can be recognized in several basic concepts of individual psychology. First, we recall that Adler's first writing had been a booklet on the tailor's trade, showing that certain diseases are caused not by microbes or poisons but by society. Adler always emphasized the social and environmental factors in the etiology of neurosis. Second, Marx's concept of the "mystifications" is not dissimilar to those kinds of unconscious deceptions and self-deceptions that were to play such a great role in Adler's theory of neurosis.[151] Conversely, the means of unveiling mystifications is markedly similar in Marxism and individual psychology. One rule of Marxian analysis exemplifies this similarity, "Behind that which people *say*, behind that which they *think* of themselves, to discover what they *are* by what they *do*."[152]

As did all men of his generation, Adler felt the powerful influence of Nietzsche.[153] However, the nature of this influence has often been misinterpreted. It is not so that Adler merely "replaced Freud's libido with Nietzsche's will to power" in his system. In Adler's system the will to power is but one form of the striving to superiority, and in his later revision of individual psychology, Adler conceived the striving to superiority itself as derived from the individual's creative power. Many similarities between Adler and Nietzsche have been recorded by Crookshank and many others probably do exist.[154] However, the concept of community feeling is absolutely foreign to Nietzsche.

A philosopher whom Adler frequently refers to is the neo-Kantian Hans Vaihinger and his *Philosophy of the As If*.[155] Legal fictions had been in use for a long time. Bentham showed that fictions existed in other fields.[156] Nietzsche insisted upon the role of psychological and moral fictions, and that they were essential to man. It became fashionable to speak of conventional lies of civilization. Vaihinger's originality was to establish the role of the fictions in science and define the difference between fiction and hypothesis.

> Both are necessary to the progress of science but should not be confused, their nature being entirely different. With hypothesis the scientist endeavors to reach reality; he proposes a hypothesis as logical and possible, and then proceeds to verify it. If it is proved to be true it henceforth becomes scientific knowledge; if it is disproved it is dropped. A fiction does not need to be true nor even to appear probable, it is not submitted to tests of experience, but is a figure of speech which is kept as long as it shows itself useful and is left aside as soon as it no longer works or when it can be replaced by a better one. It is not always easy to define whether a proposition is a fiction or a hypothesis, and a proposition can be the one or the other in turn. For instance, the idea of the atom was a fiction in the time of Democritus because there was no means of checking whether it was true or not, but it became a hypothesis with the advent of modern physics. When ancient Greek astronomers proposed a model of the universe with the earth fixed in the center surrounded by a succession of concentric transparent spheres to each of which were appended the sun, moon, planets, and stars, they had in mind a fiction that served their purpose well, that is, to predict the movements of the heavenly bodies. But during the Middle Ages the fictitious character of the model was forgotten and it became a dogma.

Among modern psychologists the unconscious has been treated either as a hypothesis or as a fiction. Freud implicitly considered it a hypothesis confirmed by his research, whereas Janet called it a *façon de parler* (figure of speech), obviously meaning that he used it as a scientific fiction.

Adler applied the concept of "fiction" in two ways. First, as a general, methodological concept. In contradistinction to psychoanalysis, individual psychology does not claim to be a system of hypotheses to be checked, but a system of fictions. Everything happens as if human activities were ruled by a normative ideal of human adaptation to the community and the cosmos, and as if the varieties of abnormal behavior were deviations from that norm. Second, the term "fiction" is used to make the behavior of the neurotic intelligible. It is as if the neurotic were striving to reach a fictitious goal and lived accordingly.

Whenever a psychiatrist applies a philosophical concept, it is likely that a philosopher will arise and show him that he misunderstood its true meaning. Thus Wandeler objects that Adler's fictitious goal of the neurotic is not a fiction in Vaihinger's sense, that is, a pragmatic tool for exploring reality that is dropped as soon as it ceases to bring results.[157] The failure of the neurotic, far from deterring him from his error, enmeshes him even further. In fact, it is a delusion. According to Wandeler, much of what Adler calls fictions are either delusions of that kind, or on the contrary hypotheses, or even well-established facts (as for example the life plan).

Later than Vaihinger, probably in 1926, Adler happened to make the acquaintance of the holistic philosophy of Jan Christiaan Smuts. He found in it a confirmation of his ideas and a philosophical basis for individual psychology. Smuts was born on an isolated South African farm in 1870.[158] He acquired world fame as a military leader and statesman, but was also keenly interested in natural science and philosophy. In 1924, after the defeat of his party in the elections, he retired to his farm and wrote his book *Holism and Evolution*

Smuts calls *Holos* a universal principle that creates the "wholes." The wholes are active factors in and through matter, life and mind. Smuts views the evolution as a rising series of wholes from the electrons and atoms to the colloids, the plants and animals, minds and personalities. The whole is greater than its parts, it influences its parts, the parts influence the whole, they influence one another and the whole influences its environment. Smuts sees in the universe "an impulse towards wholeness that manifested itself in each individual by a power of development, growth and evolution from within; and, working in its own environment from itself." Lower wholes give birth to higher wholes and become incorporated with them. Each whole is a laboratory in which time is transmuted into eternity. Smuts finds present-day psychology unsatisfactory. There is room, he says, for a new science of personality, which "as the synthetic science of human nature, will form the crown of all the sciences, and, in turn, become the basis of the new Ethic, a new Metaphysic." As a method of approach to this new science he proposes a comparative study of carefully documented biographies that will enable man to formulate the laws of personal evolution.[159]

According to the biographers of both Smuts and Adler, the two men exchanged a correspondence (of which nothing has been published as yet). Possibly Adler identified his individual psychology with that future science of personality sketched by Smuts. The influence of Smuts' holism is noticeable in Adler's *Understanding Human Nature* and his later works.

We shall give now a brief survey of the sources of a few specific concepts: inferiority feeling, striving for superiority, neurotic fictions, character diagnosis, the law of social interest, and the community feeling.

With regard to inferiority feeling, Oliver Brachfeld proposed a long list of authors who anticipated this concept.[160] Adler wrote that "what I call feeling of inferiority is a development of what Janet calls feeling of incompleteness."[161] Two writers are particularly worthy of mention: Stendhal in France and Ralph Waldo Emerson in the United States.

Stendhal was an excellent example of a life directed by an inferiority complex.[162] He suffered greatly from his natural ugliness, ungainliness, and clumsiness, and compensated with arrogance, affecting the manners of a dandy and seeking fashionable company. In his diary he carefully recorded his social encounters and whether he or the other had had the better in a situation. In his novels he liked to describe individuals who overcompensate for a deep-seated feeling of inferiority. Such is Julien Sorel, the hero of *The Red and the Black*.[163] Stendhal's psychological theories often anticipate those of Adler. Stendhal considers admiration as a position of inferiority and a humiliation for the one who gives way to it. In a love affair it is an intolerable situation to be left by the other and that it should be known, because then one appears inferior. In a social gathering the main concern of the participants is not to appear inferior. Stendhal's theory of the comical could easily be incorporated into individual psychology.[164] The feeling of the comical arises with the sudden apperception of one's superiority over another man. The more we must respect someone, the readier we are to laugh at him. The comical is increased by the sight of the discomfiture of the one who is laughed at. But the one who scoffs at his victim is at the mercy of the rest of the company, who will judge the value of his wit. The comical is checked by indignation and compassion (in Adlerian language, the community feeling).

Ralph Waldo Emerson did not define the inferiority feeling as precisely as Stendhal, but the concept is implicit in his work, particularly in the *Essays* and in *The Conduct of Life*.[165] In the essay that bears the title "Self-Confidence," Emerson depicts what Adler was to call courage and encouragement. Scattered throughout his writings are many thoughts and advice that fit admirably into individual psychology.

The idea that the central drive in human nature is the striving for superiority has been expressed often and in many ways. Hobbes taught that the natural condition of man was the war of everyone against everyone. Helvétius held that the mainspring of human action was a wish to be as powerful as possible in order to control others and thus be able to gratify one's passions.[166] For Nietzsche the will to power is primary, and power an end in itself. Adler's idea of the will to power was but one of the possible deviations of the more basic striving toward superiority, and here, too, he had predecessors. A French psychologist, Prosper Despine, described how social life is ruled by the ascendency of individuals over others.[167]

The notion that the striving toward superiority is innate to every man and is the most potent agent in interpersonal relationships has become common knowledge with the progress of animal psychology. It is not known whether Adler was acquainted with Schjeldrup-Ebbe's pioneer study on the "social rank order" among hens.

If two hens meet for the first time a trial of strength takes place through threatening or direct fighting. Both animals decide which one will dominate the other. If several animals are together the hierarchy of superiority between all of them will be established in a fairly short time. At the top is the alpha animal, to whom all must submit, then the beta animal, which submits only to alpha and dominates the rest, with all the intermediates down to the last animal who submits to all others and dominates none. The higher an animal is in that "social rank order," the more privileges he takes for himself, a larger amount of food, a better place in the shelter, a larger number of females. Young animals are dominated by the older, and in their play they gradually establish their own rank order. When they grow up they challenge the older animals and eventually vanquish them. This social hierarchy is silently adhered to, but as soon as there is some competition, be it for food or otherwise, the pecking starts, and it follows the pecking order, which corresponds to the social rank order: the alpha animal pecks all the others and is pecked by none, the beta animal is pecked only by alpha and pecks all the others, until the lowest, which pecks no-one and is pecked by all. However, things may become more complex. There are triangular relationships where alpha dominates a beta who dominates a gamma, who, paradoxically, dominates the alpha. Or sometimes it may happen that an animal that is in a lower place on the scale will challenge one above and so raise its position in the rank order.[168]

These findings of Schjeldrup-Ebbe have been found to apply to a great number of birds and mammals, and from the very beginning David Katz had demonstrated that they may be extended to explain certain facts in human psychology and sociology.[169] These things, which have been strangely overlooked for a long time by scientists, have been perceived by writers. Emerson wrote, for instance:

When a new boy comes into school, when a man travels and encounters strangers every day, or when into any old club a newcomer is domesticated, that happens which befalls when a strange ox is driven into a pen or pasture where cattle are kept; there is at once a trial of strength between the best pair of horns and the newcomer, and it is settled thenceforth which is the leader. So now, there is a measuring of strength, very courteous but decisive, and an acquiescence thenceforwards when these two meet. Each reads his fate in the other's eyes.

Men take each other's measure, when they meet for the first time, and every time they meet. How do they get this rapid knowledge, even before they speak, of each other's power and disposition? One would say that the persuasion of their speech is not in what they say—or that men do not convince by their argument, but by their personality, by who they are, and what they said and did heretofore.[170]

These things have been known to writers for a long time. A classical instance is to be found in Samuel Butler's novel *The Way of All Flesh* in which we see a young married couple arrive at a hotel a few hours after the wedding ceremony. The husband bids his wife to go downstairs and order the dinner. She is tired and reluctant, but he insists, and from that moment the husband's domination is established once and for all.

All of these facts strikingly correspond to some of the basic concepts of individual psychology, but it should not be overlooked that things are more complex. Relationships between two individuals are not only ruled by the comparative strength of their self-assertion, but also by the individuals' life style and guiding fiction, and by the relationships of individuals with groups which surround them or that they gather around them. These notions were developed in France by an author of whom Adler seems never to have heard, Baron Ernest Seillière[171]

Following Nietzsche, Seillière considers the will to power, which he called imperialism, as the central drive of human actions; it may remain healthy and rational or become pathological. In the latter case imperialism is often sustained by mysticism, that is an irrational belief. Seillière distinguishes three varieties of imperialism. There is individual imperialism, which the individual can gratify by overcoming himself or those around him. Then there is collective imperialism, which means that the individual identifies himself with a group of which he becomes the champion. And finally there is human imperialism, that is mankind's domination of nature. Seillière wrote a long set of monographs, notably on Jean-Jacques Rousseau, the Romantics, and the Neo-Romantics, and Nietzsche. Curiously enough, in the volume devoted to Freud and Adler, Seillière failed to notice the striking analogy between his concepts of imperialism and mysticism, and Adler's striving to superiority and guiding fiction.[172] In other volumes Seillière went a step further than Adler. He said that the true nature of interhuman relationships can be more easily ascertained in the field of international life than on the individual level, because interpersonal relationships are more or less kept in check by social control.

The idea that men conduct their lives according to a fictitious idea of themselves and of others has been expressed many times by writers. Characters such as Don Quixote or Tartarin de Tarascon are somewhat overdone illustrations of this theme. In regard to characters of everyday life no writer has shown with more acumen than Flaubert the discrepancy between what men really are and what they believe they are, and how their life fiction misleads them and sometimes (as in the case of Madame Bovary) may cause their downfall. Sometimes the fiction has a protective value, and its brutal unveiling can bring a catastrophe, as in Ibsen's celebrated play, *The Wild Duck*. A French author, Jules de Gaultier, systematized under the name of "bovarysm" (for Madame Bovary in Flaubert's novel) the idea that many individuals create a fictitious image of themselves and do not accord their actions to their true personality but to this false image.[173] More recently this notion has been applied to biographies. For instance, N. B. Fagin tried to show that Edgar Allan Poe fashioned for himself and played the role of a distinguished melancholic and misunderstood genius, a role in which he was highly successful.[174] A somewhat similar interpretation of Thorstein Veblen's personality has been given by Joseph Dorfman.[175]

These facts necessarily lead to the problem of how to ascertain the true character of a man, and here also Adler has been anticipated. Goethe said, "It is in vain that we endeavour to represent the character of a man; if we put together his deeds and achievements, then a picture of his character emerges."[176] The same idea has been more explicitly expressed by F. J. Gall:

> Do you want to spy out the character of a person without running the risk of an error even if that person is informed and on his guard? Then let him speak about his childhood and prime youth, make him relate his schoolboy pranks, his behaviour towards his parents, brothers and sisters and schoolmates, his disloyalties, his competitiveness, the account of his friendships with some children and enmities with others, how he played, and so on. Rarely will he think that it is worthwhile to keep these things secret. He will not realize that he is dealing with a man who knows perfectly that the main character traits are permanent and that only the objects of interest change with age and social position.[177]

It would be difficult to find a closer anticipation of Adler's method of individual psychological diagnosis. It remains for us to examine the sources of Adler's concept of the community and of community feeling. It would be an impossible task to ascertain how far Adler could have been inspired by the Stoicists, the German Romanticists, the Socialists, and many others, but two possible sources at least should be singled out.

It is unlikely that Adler would not have heard of Josef Popper-Lynkeus and of his grandiose scheme for a radical solution of social problems.[178] Popper-Lynkeus proposed the institution of a kind of labor army in which every man and every woman would have to enroll for several years. This would ensure an acceptable minimum of vital, material, and cultural requirements for every member of society. Because man would thus/ be freed of the intolerable burden of material worries, he would be restored to his original dignity. The project of Popper-Lynkeus was inspired by an ideal of the human community that is not without analogy to Adler's community feeling. And Popper-Lynkeus, much like Adler, insisted on the importance of education which will impart to every child as early as possible the true notion of the value and dignity of every human being and of his duties toward mankind.

Another very likely source of Adler's idea of community feeling must have been Kropotkin, and the ideology of those Russian thinkers who held that the true source of national culture resides in the people. The people were the creators of the language, the art, epic and lyric poetry of the country, and the upper classes, by rising over the masses, had impoverished themselves. The true calling for young men and women of the upper class was to go to the people, not in order to teach, but to learn. This idea was foreign to Western European thought, with the possible exception of the German Romantics. These opinions had been professed by certain groups of revolutionists, the *Narodniki* (populists); later it permeated the work of Tolstoy and Dostoevsky. With Maxim Gorki we see this idea taking the form of a philosophical myth exposed in his essay, *The Downfall of Personality*.

> At the beginning was the people, and the people was the source of every material and spiritual value. The people created language, myth, religion, epic poetry and also the images of heroes. With the growth of communities and their struggle against other groups, leaders and priests became a necessity. Individuals were invested with the attributes of the epic heroes. This was the beginning of the ego. At first these privileged individuals were organs of the community, but they emancipated themselves and led an independent life next to the community and, later, above it. Still they participated with the community in so far as they were the incarnation of epic heroes who were an emanation of the people. But a day would come when these men, having acquired a taste for power over others, desired it for its own sake. This was followed by a period of struggles between community and those individuals who tried to rise above the masses. Private property was one of the devices introduced by these men, in order to gain power, and the community declined henceforth. They became stronger and more aggressive as time went by, and in the end came the era of the struggle of everyone against everyone, which resulted in the decline of the individual himself.[179]

Translated into Adlerian terms, we find here the story of the individual who is led by his striving for superiority to rise against the community, to the detriment of his fellow men and of his own personality. Thus Gorki provided the central myth, which is to individual psychology what the myth of the murder of the primeval father is to psychoanalysis.

Adler's Influence

In order to ascertain the influence exerted by Alfred Adler, it must be kept in mind that his individual psychology is not just a deviation of psychoanalysis but radically differs from it. As a psychological theory, it is a system of pragmatic (or concrete) psychology that analyzes human behavior in regard to two opposite drives: community feeling versus a deviated striving for superiority. Neuroses, psychoses, and psychopathy are viewed as varieties of deviation from the law of social interest. It also teaches the uniqueness, self-consistency, and creativeness of the individual and his life style, the concepts of organic inferiorities, feelings of inferiority, compensation, masculine protest, fictitious goal, neurotic training, arrangement, the meaning of early memories, and the influence of the position in the sibling set. As a therapeutic method, individual psychology applies, on the one hand, techniques of rational individual therapy by means of the uncovering of fictitious goals and life style, imparting of courage, and retraining toward community orientation; and on the other hand, a variety of techniques of child guidance, group therapy, and community psychiatry. Individual psychology emphasizes that its main concern does not lie with a few privileged, wealthy patients but with a large cross section of the total population. Because these features are so characteristic, it would seem that individual psychology could not be confused with the other dynamic schools, nor its influence with the influence of the other schools. Yet the paradox is that it is extremely difficult to trace the influence exerted by Adler's work and thought in the contemporary world.

As to the individual psychological movement itself, its story can be summed up rapidly. It remained somewhat informal for the first years, and even later the structure of the organization remained far less rigid than that of the psychoanalytic association. The Adlerian movement suffered comparatively more than the Freudian association under the National Socialist oppression because it was not so well established outside of Central Europe. It began again after World War II and now has its training centers, periodicals, and international congresses. Nevertheless, it cannot be compared to the psychoanalytic movement in regard to its membership, rigidity of organization, and popularity.

As happens in any movement, there also were members who separated from Adler and founded their own schools, either under the form of a slightly modified individual psychology, such as Hans Künkel, or a new teaching, such as Victor Frankl's existence analysis.

However, paradoxically it is upon psychoanalysis that individual psychology exerted its greatest impact, in spite of the fundamental difference between the two schools. Adler's influence has even affected Freud, certain trends within the movement (the so-called neo-Freudians), and psychoanalysis itself in the form of an almost imperceptible assimilation of individual psychological concepts.

During the years of his association with Freud, a few ideas proposed by Adler were adopted by Freud, either immediately or belatedly. In 1908 Adler contended that there was an autonomous aggressive drive, but Freud denied it; in 1920, however, he came to speak of a primary destructive instinct.[180] In the same paper of 1908 Adler utilized the concepts of "confluence of drives," displacement of drives, turning of a drive against oneself, displacement upon another strong drive, and transformation into its opposites. These concepts (which incidentally originated with Nietzsche) found their way into Freudian thought at various periods.[181] Another vicissitude of the drives is the internalization of external demands, which has been described by Furtmüller and by Adler, which was taken over by Freud in 1921 and expanded later by Anna Freud under the name of identification with the aggressor. The shift of psychoanalysis to ego psychology was to a great extent an adaptation of former Adlerian concepts, so that Adler was hailed by certain psychoanalysts as "a precursor of the later developments of psychoanalysis."

A more remarkable event was the adoption by several psychoanalytic groups of a massive amount of concepts closely similar to those of individual psychology, while keeping psychoanalytic terminology for the most part. Among these neo-psychoanalysts we find Edward Kempf, Harry Stack Sullivan, Karen Horney, Erich Fromm, and Clara Thompson in the United States, and Harald Schultz-Hencke in Germany.

The neo-psychoanalysts do not constitute a school. Each one has his own theory, but all of them reject certain of Freud's basic ideas and replace them by other concepts strikingly similar to those of Adler (without, however, mentioning his name). Most neo-psychoanalysts share the following ideas: They deny the concept of the libido with its stages, and when they keep the Oedipus complex they give another interpretation of it. The role of inborn instinct is played down and emphasis is laid on the role of the environment, particularly of interpersonal relationships. Man is no longer conceived as a naturally anxious and destructive being. Instead of analyzing the conflicts between the id, ego, and superego, current patterns of neurotic behavior are analyzed in the form of neurotic styles. The role attributed to sexuality is strongly reduced. Sexuality is considered as a means of expression for other behavior. Conversely, more importance is given to self-assertive, competitive drives. There is less room for dream and symbol analysis. Therapy, though still called psychoanalytic, largely departs from Freudian standards, insofar as it focuses on the present rather than on the past, on the interpersonal rather than the intrapersonal relations, and it does not consider free association, dream analysis, or the use of the couch as primordial.

Edward J. Kempf was the author of a voluminous textbook of psychiatry on a psychoanalytic basis, abundantly illustrated with reproductions of art masterpieces and photographs of his patients.[182]

Though the author claims to be a psychoanalyst, the word libido appears nowhere. Adler's name is quoted only once in the 762 pages, but his spirit pervades the whole book. Much emphasis is laid on the concepts of organ

inferiority, inferiority feelings, and the varieties of healthy and morbid compensation. Among the defences against inferiority feelings, Kempf describes that
of "avoiding competition," whose extreme form is "general dread of all personal
contact," characteristic of the hebephrenic. Even the peculiar situation of the
second child in a family is mentioned.

The interpersonal theory of psychiatry of Harry Stack Sullivan shows
a close approach to Adlerian views, although there is no mention of Adler
throughout the four volumes of Sullivan's compiled lectures, which were
edited posthumously.

Sullivan defines psychiatry as the study of interpersonal relationships, and goes
further than Adler when he claims that personality does not exist apart from
the individual's relationship with his fellowmen. According to Sullivan, personality
is a pattern of recurrent interpersonal situations. His self system is a stable
organization of interpersonal processes (much like Adler's style of life). Also
like Adler, Sullivan considers the self concept conditioned by reflected appraisals,
that is by reflections of the judgments of his parents and close relations about
him in early childhood. What Sullivan calls personifications are the distorted
images that the individual has of himself and of others, like Adler's fictions.
Adler's concept of perspective with the individual distortions of perception,
memory, and logics, is found in Sullivan's psychology under a different
terminology. What Sullivan calls selective inattention is one aspect of those
distortions of perception that conform to one's style of life. And what Sullivan
calls parataxic mode of thinking are, in Adlerian terminology, individual
distortions of logic. In regard to psychotherapy, Sullivan did not use the couch
for many of his patients, but had them seated in a chair before him; he made
moderate use of free association and dream interpretation; he did not hesitate
to intervene actively (especially with his obsessional and schizoid patients); he
sought primarily to make his patients aware of their parataxic and other distortions. In short, it looks as if Sullivan practiced a kind of Adlerian psychotherapy
while still calling himself a psychoanalyst. The main differences are that Sullivan
gave elaborate descriptions of the individual stages of development, and viewed
society more as a source of emotional illness than Adler did.[183]

No less remarkable similarities to Adler's teachings are found in Karen
Horney's work. After having been an orthodox psychoanalyst for fifteen
years, she broke with Freud's school, and founded her own association.
As early as 1926, Karen Horney had begun to question Freud's concept
of the "penis envy."[184] In 1927 her paper on the "Masculinity Complex
of Women" was strongly reminiscent of Adler's "masculine protest."[185]
A few years later another paper of hers bore the title "The Dread of
Woman," a typically Adlerian term.[186] After her emigration to the United
States in 1932, she was struck by the differences between European and
American patients, differences that she could ascribe only to cultural
factors. The teachings of Karen Horney are contained in four major books.

Karen Horney criticized Freud's overemphasis on biology and his disregard of cultural factors. Thus, she definitely rejected the theory of the libido with its stages of development, and Freud's theory of neurosis. At the root of neurosis Karen Horney saw an effort to ward off anxiety. (Adler would have called it lack of courage). Like Adler, she also departed from the traditional classification of neuroses still adhered to by Freud. She knows of only one general neurosis with several types of developments: the compliant (or submissive), the aggressive type guided by the will to power, and the withdrawing type. These neurotic types of development are traced back to specific childhood situations. As for the Oedipus complex, Karen Horney, exactly like Adler, admits that it sometimes exists but explains it as a type of development of an initially spoiled child. Narcissism she explains not as self-love, as Freud does, but as self-admiration, that is admiration for an idealized picture of oneself. In her later works, Karen Horney came to consider the striving toward self-realization as the main drive of the human being, a drive that she said was impeded by the individual's idealized picture of his person. Here, too, we recognize the importance Adler later attributed to the creative drive and to the role played by the individual's fictitious view of himself.[187]

Erich Fromm's theory as expressed in several of his well-known books is yet another type of neo-psychoanalysis influenced by sociology and by philosophical ideology.

He too criticizes Freud's theory of drives, but from the point of view of the difference between instinct in human beings and in animals. As compared to the animal, the development of the human being takes on a quite different and specific form (amounting, incidentally, to what Jung calls individuation), which had freedom as its end. Neurosis Fromm considers as a misuse or escape from freedom. Fromm no longer accepts traditional neurosis entities. He speaks of various types of neurotic mechanism: the drive to selfless submission to authority, the craving for power (the authoritarian character), the drive to destruction, and the compulsion to automaton conformity. Fromm attributes the causes of these neurotic mechanisms to social and cultural factors, namely to the capitalistic system. On the other hand, he tells of a productive character, which resembles what Adler says about man ruled by social feeling and stands on the useful side of life. Fromm does not deny the existence of the Oedipus complex but explains it as a rebellion of the young boy against the patriarchal, authoritarian order personified by his father. We see that Marxism influenced Fromm even more strongly than Adler. Among the neo-psychoanalysts Fromm is the only one in whom we find a near equivalent of Adler's social feeling.[188]

Neo-psychoanalytic thought is also to be found in such writers as Thomas French, Clara Thompson, Sandor Radó, Theodore Reik, and Abram Kardiner. In Europe the only author who called himself a neo-psychoanalyst was Harald Schultz-Hencke. His ideas have been compiled in several works, and he founded a school of his own in Germany. His teaching is an original mixture of Freudian and Adlerian concepts.

At the root of all neuroses and psychoses he sees one basic disturbance: inhibition (*Hemmung*), which plays the role of lack of courage of individual psychology in his system. Schultz-Hencke distinguishes four basic drives: The captative and retentive drives correspond fairly well to Freud's oral and anal tendencies. The drive to aggression and self-valorization has much in common with Adler's striving to superiority. The fourth one is the sexual drive, which he sees primarily as a need for tenderness; the word libido is never used by Schultz-Hencke. Inhibition can be traced back to the action of the environment upon the infant; this action determines the permanent attitudes that will rule the behavior of the individual throughout life. Schultz-Hencke brings forward a theory of inferiorities of psychic functions and their manifestations in neurotic structures. He uses the terms "compensation" and "over-compensation" as abundantly as Adler. In his system the unconscious has secondary importance; the same can be said for transference in his therapeutic technique.[189]

After having seen the influence individual psychology exerted on the neo-psychoanalysts (who would better be called neo-Adlerians), we must now mention subtler and more diffuse influence it had on the main body of the psychoanalysts. It is difficult to describe because it can be found everywhere in more or less disguised form. Some psychoanalysts are resolutely Freudian in regard to the theories that they consciously profess, but use Adlerian thinking in matters of everyday life. A Swiss psychoanalyst once publicly declared that Adler's thought was nonsense and unworthy of attention; a moment later, referring to a common acquaintance in a private talk, he said: "This man suffers from a grievous inferiority feeling which he compensates with arrogant manners." Officially, Adler is disregarded, but without realizing it, one is a crypto-Adlerian. This is also the reason why a perusal of psychoanalytic periodicals will show a surprising number of articles illustrating a classical Adlerian notion without reference to Adler, or sometimes with a brief mention that the present study is not to be related to his work. However, this attitude toward Adler's work is by no means limited to psychoanalysts, and we find here one of the most paradoxical features in the history of dynamic psychiatry.

Joseph Wilder wrote in 1959: "I realize that most observations and ideas of Alfred Adler have subtly and quietly permeated modern psychological thinking to such a degree that the proper question is not whether one is Adlerian, but how much of an Adlerian one is."[190]

This can be shown easily, for instance, in regard to existential psychiatry.[191] Victor Frankl began as a disciple of Adler and never denied it. In a comparison between Frankl and Adler, Birnbaum claims that the "para-religious" attitude of Frankl with his patients found its model in the "cosmic feeling" of Adler in his later development.[192] The influence of Adler on Binswanger's existential analysis is no less obvious, though Binswanger never quotes Adler. Binswanger's dual mode, plural mode, and singular mode of being-with-others are not very different from Adler's descriptions of community feeling, active striving for superiority, and retreating behind barricades. Binswanger's phenomenological descriptions of the vertical dimension seem to be a development of what Adler wrote on the dialectics of above and below.

When Jean-Paul Sartre sketched his existential psychoanalysis as a part of his philosophical existentialism, there was a unanimous rejoinder from psychoanalysts that this had nothing in common with psychoanalysis.[193] The basic principle of existential psychoanalysis is that man is a totality and therefore expresses himself even in the most insignificant and superficial of his actions. The method consists of deciphering the various modes of behavior of individuals. To that aim one will compare the various empirical tendencies to ascertain the fundamental project, which underlies each one of these modes of behavior. Sartre's existential psychoanalysis rejects the concept of the unconscious mind. It does not seek to find out complexes, but to strive to define the original choice of the individual. This choice is at first a free and conscious decision of the individual and as such it is fully lived by him, although he is not necessarily aware of it. The aim of the therapy is to bring the subject to an awareness of his fundamental project. Modes of behavior scrutinized by this method are not only (as in Freudian analysis) dreams, parapraxias, and neuroses, but are above all conscious thought, successful and adjusted actions, and style. Sartre concludes with this surprising statement: "This psychoanalysis has not yet found its Freud!" How could Sartre be unaware that this method already existed and had Alfred Adler for its author?

Those who were taught psychiatry by Professor Klaesi in Berne could not help but notice the striking analogy of many of his ideas with those of Adler (though he never referred to him). Klaesi's interpretation of the Oedipus complex was identical with Adler's. Klaesi contended that neurosis resulted from a conflict between cratophorous instincts, that is the egoistic domination instincts and aristophorous instincts, that is, social instincts.[194]

The holistic aspect of individual psychology has been developed under the name of self-consistency by Prescott Lecky, an American psychologist who studied under Adler in Vienna during 1927 and 1928.

The prime need of an organism, Lecky says, is to maintain its mental organization as a unified whole. Personality is an organization of values that are felt to be consistent with one another. Behavior expresses the effort to be consistent and unified in organization and action. The individual is a unified system with two sets of problems, one the problem of maintaining inner harmony within himself, and the other the problem of maintaining harmony with the environment, especially the social environment. Perception, memory and forgetting, feeling, thinking, imagination and so on, must be constantly adjusted by the individual in order to maintain his self-consistency. The nucleus of the system is the individual's valuation of himself. Any value that is consistent with this self-valuation is assimilated and conversely, any value that is inconsistent with it meets with resistance. Then it is rejected unless a general reorganization takes place. As a psychotherapist, Lecky said that symptoms are the expressions of attitudes, and he devised an inventory of attitudes. Then he demonstrated to the patient the irrelevance and obsolete character of his present attitudes, thus leading to substitute it better ones. Resistance was not more neurotic perseveration for Lecky, but a natural device for avoiding the effort of reorganization.[195]

The notion that man possesses a basic tendency toward self-perfecting, a notion that Adler particularly emphasized in his late period, has been developed by several authors, particularly by Wilhelm Keller.[196] According to Keller, in man there is a basic striving to self-esteem, and this striving expresses itself in many ways. Although Adler is only mentioned in passing, this book is manifestly an elaboration of his ideas.

Adler's studies on the role of the individual's position in the row of siblings have found original and unexpected developments. Walter Toman has enounced a theory based on the observation of several hundred individuals whose positions in the sibling row were carefully recorded.[197] In his analysis of family constellations, Toman takes into account the number of children, the distribution of boys and girls, the interval between the children, and the occurrences of death among the siblings. The analysis is extended to the family constellation of the parents, children, and spouses. For each one of the numerous possible combinations, Toman gives a short description of the major personality features to be expected.

The family constellation analysis of Martensen-Larsen was conducted from a different approach.[198] Martensen-Larsen, working with alcoholics, conducted a genealogical research that led him to discover that the position in the family constellation extended to the generation of the grandparents and not heredity was the determining factor in the etiology of alcoholism. Later this research was extended to male homosexuality.

In regard to the style of life, we have seen that many authors have written on this subject with or without reference to Adler. But neither Adler nor his disciples seem to have greatly investigated the varieties of interplay of two different styles of life. At least one attempt has been made by Dr. Eric Berne, whose best seller *Games People Play* shows how rewarding it would be to make a systematic and scientific exploration of that little-known field.[199]

The notion of inferiority feeling has been so quickly accepted by the public, that a man such as Paul Häberlin could write a book on that topic, describing the numerous forms, varieties, compensations, and causes of inferiority feelings without even once mentioning the name of Adler.[200] To give one other instance among many, a psychoanalyst published the story of a neurotic whose phobia was reflected in his earliest memory (being frightened by a mouse); as a little boy, he played with a doll.[201] As his feeling of inferiority became worse, he sought compensation by means of grandiose daydreams in which he visualized himself as a superman. This patient was cured by a method that the author calls psychoanalysis.

Numerous other examples could be given of the slow and continuous penetration of Adlerian insights into contemporary psychological thinking. Among them are the concepts of inferiority feelings, style of life, the role of organ inferiority, the application of Vaihinger's as if to the theory of neurosis, the role of the masculine protest and of the dread of woman in the etiology of homosexuality and other sexual deviations. We could give a list of at least a dozen authors who recently rediscovered the symbolic meaning of the earliest memories. Departing from the traditional view that the turmoils of adolescence result from the intensification of the libido, a few psychoanalysts now admit that the adolescent ego is driven by powerful energies that depend neither directly nor exclusively on the libido. Similarities have been pointed out between excerpts of Margaret Mead's book, *Family*, and excerpts of Adler's, *What Life Should Mean to You*.[202] Walter Goldschmidt's theory of the social imperatives shows analogies with Adler's concepts of the community feeling: man is committed to social life, and each individual, as he grows, must subordinate his personal ends to the requirements of society; "society must be organized to balance off the pull of individual self-seeking against the demands of social harmony."[203] Certain features of individual psychological therapy can also be recognized in recent methods such as Ellis' rational therapy and Glasser's reality therapy.

It is likely that the influence of individual psychology will prove most fruitful in criminology and therapeutic education. The utilization of plastic surgery in the treatment of a limited group of ugly offenders is an application of one of Adler's ideas.[204] A correctional technique, creative restitution, although developed independently from individual psychology, is related to Adlerian theory, as shown by Ernst Papanek.[205] Father Noël Mailloux, the well-known Montreal psychologist, contends that the usual psychoanalytic theories of juvenile delinquency (lack or distortion of the superego, unresolved Oedipus complex, and identification with a criminal model) are not confirmed by experience.[206] He is led to explain juvenile delinquency as resulting from a specific process of dissocialization, that is, a distortion of a normal process of socialization. Socialization, Father Mailloux says, follows its own line of evolution parallel to that of sexuality, with its own vicissitudes and critical points, and an initial conflict comparable to the Oedipus conflict (though by no means identical with it). Faulty, overcritical attitudes of the parents bring the child to see himself as a kind of pariah, ostracized by family and community. Since he believes he is evil, the child feels himself doomed to commit evil actions. This behavior in turn provokes the reprobation of those around him. He then considers himself a victim of hatred and will strive to avenge himself, hence to commit more severe offenses and seek a refuge in the gang. The treatment of juvenile delinquents implies an encounter with therapeutic educators and a collective treatment in the frame of a delinquent group. We may notice how easily these theories and methods can be formulated in individual psychological terms: because the morally belittled child finds himself in a position of inferiority he adheres to a life style that fits into his depreciated self-image, hence a punishing reaction of the environment (pressure engenders counter pressure); the treatment aims at reawakening and restoring the distorted community feeling.

Any attempt to assess the influence of Adler's work brings about a paradox. The impact of individual psychology upon contemporary psychology stands beyond any doubt. Hans Hoff, declared that Adler inaugurated modern psychosomatic medicine, was the forerunner of social psychology and the social approach to mental hygiene, a founder of group psychotherapy, that his conception of the creative self being in its goal-directedness, responsible for the life style makes him the father of ego psychology.[207] To this he could have added that Adler was the founder of the first unified system of concrete psychology on record.

However, there is the puzzling phenomenon of a collective denial of Adler's work and the systematic attribution of anything coined by him to other authors. We have numerous instances of psychoanalysts picking up some of Adler's most original findings and asserting that they were implicitly contained in Freud's writings, or neglected aspects of Freud's thinking, and should Adler be mentioned it is with the proviso that in spite of apparent similarities with Adler's ideas, these are basically different. The same attitude is found among non-Freudian psychologists, sometimes with an even sharper rejection of Adler. Typical is their tone of righteous indignation in denying the influence of Adler. Even those psychologists who admit that they happened to meet Adler personally and to have read something of his work, energetically maintain that their ideas do not have anything to do with those of Adler.

It would not be easy to find another author from which so much has been borrowed from all sides without acknowledgment than Alfred Adler. His teaching has become, to use a French idiom, an "open quarry" (*une carrière publique*), that is, a place where anyone and all may come and draw anything without compunction. An author will meticulously quote the source of any sentence he takes from elsewhere, but it does not occur to him to do the same whenever the source is individual psychology; it is as if nothing original could ever come from Adler. This attitude even extends to the public at large. It is ironic that *The Times* of London in its obituary of Freud wrote: "Some of his terms have become part of everyday language, the inferiority complex, for example."[208] Twenty-two years later, when Jung died, the *New York Times* published this head-line: "Dr. Karl Jung is dead . . . coined Introvert, Extrovert and Inferiority Complex."[209]

To this perplexing question of the discrepancy between greatness of achievement, massive rejection of person and work, and wide-scale, quiet plagiarism, several answers could be brought.

First of all, one has to agree on which criteria a man may be called a genius or denied that quality. Conflicting theories have been proposed about the essence of genius. According to Lange-Eichbaum the problem is a psycho-sociological one, that is, to define what features must be present in a work so that it will be called that of a genius.[201] The association of a somewhat psychotic content with a perfect form would offer the maximum chance of being labeled "work of genius." (By "psychotic" the author actually means strange, paradoxical, bewildering.) If things be so, then Adler's thought is too rational, his style too imperfect to allow him to be called a genius.

An opposite theory is that of Bernard Grasset, who contends that genius is the capacity to create a new obviousness.[211] This means that genius is the ability to discover and to formulate something that was always there, that no one had noticed. As soon as genius formulates it, that thing seems so obvious that it is quickly assimilated to common knowledge and one forgets that it has been newly discovered. (In a somewhat similar way, it is reported that Franz Schubert once heard washerwomen singing his own *Lieder*: when he asked them where they had learned them, they answered that these were old folksongs that had always been sung in the country.) Bernard Grasset's theory might be applied to Adler and the quick assimilation of his concepts, notably that of inferiority feeling.

A third theory contends that genius is a microsociological phenomenon and a voluntary construction. No isolated man could ever acquire the distinction of being called a genius. It is imperative that he should be surrounded by a group of followers who not only proclaim his teachings but create a reputation (if not a positive legend) for their master. Their success depends largely upon organization and method. In that regard Freud was much more favored than Adler; he had a larger, better-organized following. Adler had fewer disciples, was never a good organizer, nor was he interested in keeping records of his life and work. Freud's followers propagated for him the positive image of the archetypal genius: work of unheard-of novelty accomplished in spite of universal rejection, terrible hardships, and persecution. As for Adler, a few of his disciples called him the Confucius of the West and a savior of mankind, but did not succeed in producing a convincing positive image nor to prevent a negative image to prevail: a petty bourgeois, envious disciple of a great master, betrayed him, taught a caricature of psychoanalysis, a psychology for schoolteachers, and a tedious psychological appendix to socialist doctrine.

The problem is now: why did this negative image happen to prevail? A possible explanation could be found in victimology, that newly founded branch of criminology that analyzes the personality of potential victims of crimes.[212] The same psychological factors found in those personalities may also be found in those who are persistently victims of bad luck or failure. In the personality of Adler we recognize the features of one particular type of potential victim, the so-called Abel syndrome. This is the case of the man whose superiority in a certain field is likely to attract envy, but who is not able or willing to defend himself. This is a widespread occurrence that can be met every walk of life. In a study of Jean-Jacques Rousseau, Cocteau explained the persistent misfortunes and persecutions that befell the great writer as follows: "When certain men received a slap in the face, it will be told everywhere that they gave it, when certain others give a slap it will be told that they received it"[213] (meaning that Rousseau belonged to the latter group). Without going as far, how many times does it not occur in a social group that a man who enjoys a certain prestige can say any banality and still draw the attention of the audience, whereas another may say the most judicious and witty thing and pass unnoticed (or else what he said will be quietly picked up and retold elsewhere with great success)?

How far this applies to Adler may be ascertained by comparing his personality to that of Freud.

FREUD	ADLER
Handsome, imposing, with a well-groomed beard.	Not particularly handsome, unassuming, with a small moustache, and pince-nez.
Lived in the best residential quarter, had an art collection, and kept several servants.	Lived in a more bourgeois residential area, in an ordinarily furnished apartment, with only one servant.
Acquired University titles.	Was refused a University title.
Gave academic lectures and had his circle of enthusiastic disciples.	Gave courses mainly to school teachers, and held informal meetings in cafés.
Was a master of German prose and a superior writer who knew how to use striking images.	Works written in ordinary style and poorly organized, with no striking images.
Founder of depth psychology, a science bent on discovering the mysteries of the soul.	Promotor of a rational, common sense psychology with immediate practical application.

The comparison could be pursued further and more parallels found elsewhere in the history of science, for instance, that of Champollion and Grotefend.[214] Freud's life, as embellished by the legend, shows romantic features; Freud's way of life was that of an aristocrat of the mind who had identified himself with Charcot and Goethe; Adler lived as a petty bourgeois who had identified his cause with that of the people. When Freud heard of Adler's death, he wrote to Arnold Zweig: "For a Jew boy out of a Viennese suburb to die in Aberdeen is an unheard-of career in itself and a proof of how far he had got on."[215] Could Freud have forgotten that he himself had been "a Jew boy out of a Viennese suburb"?

There is still another possible explanation to the paradox. The success of a man largely depends upon whether he is the spokesman of contemporary cultural and social trends. If Schopenhauer met no success for three decades and enjoyed a belated fame, it is not because of a conspiracy of silence, but because his philosophy was incompatible with the zeitgeist of the period between the 1820's and the 1840's but could be better understood by the new generation after 1848.[216]

Contemporary trends themselves are often the revival of previous movements. In the opposition of individual psychology and psychoanalysis we see a revival of the old opposition of Enlightenment versus Romanticism. We have seen in a previous chapter how the vicissitudes of dynamic psychiatry during the nineteenth century may be regarded as manifestations of the struggle between the Enlightenment and Romanticism, with Janet and to a lesser degree Adler as late epigones of Enlightenment, Freud and even more Jung as late epigones of Romanticism.[217] Going back further still, we find that the Hellenistic and the Roman worlds were divided between the philosophies of Stoicism and Epicurism, and we noted that Stoicism shows features that can be found today in the Adlerian and existentialist schools, whereas the philosophy of Epicurus has been aptly compared by De Saussure to Freud's psychoanalysis.[218] And finally since time immemorial there have been two approaches to healing: one by use of rational means and the other by mobilizing irrational forces. Thus the parallel between Adler and Freud is merely one of the many illustrations of a fundamental law of the history of culture, namely, the swinging back and forth between two basic attitudes of the human mind.

Notes

1. See Chap. 7, p. 424.

2. Alfred Adler, "Something About Myself," *Childhood and Character*, VII (April 1930), 6–8.

3. Phyllis Bottome, *Alfred Adler, Apostle of Freedom* (London: Faber and Faber, 1939), pp. 34–35.

4. The data concerning Alfred Adler's ancestors and family has been provided by the painstaking inquiries of Dr. Hans Beckh-Widmanstetter in the archives of the Jewish Community and other official archival sources in Vienna. The author is greatly obliged to Dr. Hans Beckh-Widmanstetter for his assistance in his research.

5. These data have been obtained through the inquiries of Dr. H. Beckh-Widmanstetter in the cadastral register and other archives in Vienna.

6. H. A. Beckh-Widmanstetter, "Alfred Adler und Währing," *Unser Währing*, I (1966), 38–42 (with two pictures of the house).

7. Phyllis Bottome, *Alfred Adler, Apostle of Freedom* (London: Faber and Faber, 1939), pp. 28–30.

8. Letter of Walter Fried, of Vienna.

9. Letter of Ferdinand Ray, of Bentley, Australia.

10. According to family tradition, before Sigmund there came a first-born child, Albert, who died at an early age. There is no record of his existence in the archives of the Jewish Community of Vienna, or in the Heimat-Rolle.

11. Letter of Dr. Ernst T. Adler, of Berlin.

12. Excerpt from a letter of Kurt F. Adler, of Kew Gardens, New York.

13. This detail has been provided by Kurt F. Adler.

14. From a letter of Ferdinand Ray.

15. These data have been provided by the Archives of the Jewish Community in Vienna.

16. This brother of Alfred Adler should not be confused with the noted economist, Max Adler.

17. The title of his dissertation was: *Die Anfänge der merkantilistischen Gewerbepolitik in Oesterreich* ("The Beginning of the Mercantilistic Trade Policy in Austria").

18. These data have been found by Dr. H. Beckh-Widmanstetter in the Archives of the University of Vienna.

19. From a letter of Frau Justine Adler, of Vienna.

20. Dr. Beckh-Widmanstetter draws the author's attention to the fact that the Viennese made a sharp distinction between the "interior city" (*innere Stadt*), which was the old, historical city surrounded by walls that were demolished in 1856, the "suburbs" (*Vorstädte*) of urban character and protected by a fortified barrier, and the "outskirts" (*Vororte*), places of predominantly rural character, which were incorporated in the *Stadt* in 1890. It made a great difference if a child was raised in a *Vorort* or a *Vorstadt*.

21. Manes Sperber, *Alfred Adler, der Mensch und seine Lehre* (Munich: Bergmann, 1926).

22. Hertha Ogler, *Alfred Adler, the Man and His Work* (London: The C. W. Daniel Co., 1939).

23. Phyllis Bottome, *Alfred Adler, Apostle of Freedom* (London: Faber and Faber, 1939).

24. Carl Furtmueller, "Alfred Adler, a Biographical Essay," in Heinz and Rowena Ansbacher, *Superiority and Social Interest* (Evanston: Northwestern University Press, 1964), pp. 330–376.

25. Phyllis Bottome, "Some Aspects of Adler's Life and Work," in *Not in Our Stars* (London: Faber and Faber, n.d.), pp. 147–155; and *The Goal* (New York: Vanguard Press, 1962).

26. See Alfred Adler, "Two letters to a Patient," *Journal of Individual Psychology*, XXII (1966), 112–116.

27. Hans Beckh-Widmanstetter, *Kindheit und Jugend Alfred Adlers bis zum Kontakt mit Sigmund Freud 1902.* Typescript, unpublished.

28. The author is greatly indebted to Dr. Beckh-Widmanstetter, who helped him in his investigations and most generously put at the author's disposal his own findings.

29. This detail and most of the following have been provided by Dr. Beckh-Widmanstetter on the basis of archival inquiry.

30. Dr. Beckh-Widmanstetter assumes that Adler worked for some time at the Department of Experimental Pathology of Professor Salomon Stricker, who disposed of several positions for young assistants and with whom Wagner-Jauregg and Freud had worked previously.

31. According to information provided by the archives of the University of Zurich, Raissa Epstein was registered there from May 17, 1895, to October 2, 1896, and took courses in zoology, botany, and microscopy.

32. Information provided by the archives of the University of Vienna.

33. See pp. 599–601.

34. In 1919, after the dislocation of the Austrian-Hungarian Monarchy, the Burgenland, being a German-speaking province of Hungary, was attributed to Austria, but the southern part remained Hungary's, with the town of Oedenburg, now Sopron.

35. In spite of time-consuming research, no trace had been found in any Viennese

newspaper of a derogatory article against Freud, followed by a rejoinder by Adler. The *Neue Freie Presse,* which was Freud's daily newspaper, published book reviews or notices written by Freud on several occasions.

36. Phyllis Bottome, *Alfred Adler, Apostle of Freedom* (London: Faber and Faber, 1939), p. 65.

37. These data have been provided by the Heimat-Rolle.

38. Ernest Jones, *The Life and Work of Sigmund Freud,* II, 130–131.

39. According to family tradition, the Adlers moved to Dominikanerbastei in October or November 1908. According to the Heimat-Rolle, they still lived at Czerningasse in 1910.

40. Information provided by Dr. Beckh-Widmanstetter.

41. Léon Trotzky, *Ma Vie,* Maurice Parijanine, trans. (Paris: Gallimard, 1953), pp. 230–231, 285. I. Deutscher, *The Prophet Armed, Trotzky: 1879–1921* (London: Oxford University Press, 1954), p. 193.

42. This document has been discovered in the archives of the Viennese Medical School and published by Hans Beckh-Widmanstetter, "Zur Geschichte der Individualpsychologie," *Unsere Heimat,* XXXVI (1965), 182–188.

43. Wilhelm Stekel, *The Autobiography of Wilhelm Stekel: The Life History of a Pioneer Psychoanalyst,* Emil A. Gutheil, ed. Introduction by Hilda Stekel (New York: Liveright Publishing Corporation, 1950), p. 158

44. Dr. Beckh-Widmanstetter points out that Adler had among his patients the wife of a general who belonged to the highest military circles.

45. Alfred Adler, "Die neuen Gesichtspunkte in der Frage der Kriegsneurose," *Medizinische Klinik,* XIV (1918), 66–70.

46. A. A., "Ein Psychiater über die Kriegspsychose," *Internationale Rundschau,* IV (1918), 362.

47. Alfred Adler, "Bolschevismus und Seelenkunde," *Internationale Rundschau,* IV (1918), 597–600.

48. Alfred Adler, *Die andere Seite: eine massenpsychologische Studie über die Schuld des Volkes* (Vienna: Leopold Heidrich, 1919).

49. His ideas about the school reform were summarized in a booklet. Otto Glöckel, *Drillschule, Lernschule, Arbeitsschule* (Vienna: Verlag der Organisation Wien der sozial-demokratischen Partei, 1928).

' 50. See Robert Dottrens, *The New Education in Austria,* Paul L. Dengler, ed. (New York: John Day, 1930).

51. See pp. 621–622.

52. Erwin Wexberg, *Handbuch der Individual-Psychologie* (Munich: Bergmann, 1926).

53. Alfred Adler, L. Seif, O. Kaus, eds., *Individuum und Gemeinschaft: Schriften für Individualpsychologie* (Munich: Bergmann, n.d.).

54. Interviews published in the *New York Times,* September 20, 1925, Sec. 9, p. 12; the *New York World,* December 26, 1926, Sec. E, p. 3; and particularly "A Doctor Remakes Education," *Graphic Survey,* LVIII (September 1, 1927), 490–495 ff.

55. The title conferred upon Adler was not Honorary Citizen of Vienna, as erroneously reported by Phyllis Bottome, but Citizen of Vienna. This was an honorary title in itself, and had nothing to do with political or other rights.

56. Information provided by the archive department of the City of Vienna. It has not been possible to find the text of the Mayor's address, which apparently was not officially recorded.

57. The data about the purchase and the sale of the Salmannsdorf house has been kindly provided by its present owner, Manfred Reiffenstein.

58. Personal communication from Dr. Joost Meerloo.

59. These data have been kindly provided by Marcus K. Milne, City Librarian in Aberdeen, and C. S. Minto, City Librarian of Edinburgh.

60. Dr. Alphonse Maeder, personal communication.

61. Ernest Jones, *The Life and Work of Sigmund Freud* (New York, Basic Books, 1955), II, 130.

62. Phyllis Bottome, *Alfred Adler, Apostle of Freedom* (London: Faber and Faber, 1939), p. 30.

63. Personal information from Dr. Alexandra Adler.

64. Dr. Eugène Minkowski, personal communication.

65. Phyllis Bottome, *The Goal* (New York: Vanguard Press, 1962), p. 138.

66. A witness during these heroic days assured the author that it was Karl Novotny who drew Adler's attention to the danger of making the Viennese coffeehouses the center of the individual psychology movement.

67. Phyllis Bottome, *Alfred Adler, Apostle of Freedom* (London: Faber and Faber, 1939), p. 266.

68. *Ibid.*, pp. 50–57, 129–130.

69. *Ibid.*, p. 57.

70. See pp. 624–625.

71. These considerations have been largely inspired by a conversation with Professor Viktor Frankl, of Vienna.

72. Wilhelm Stekel, *The Autobiography of Wilhelm Stekel: The Life History of a Pioneer Psychoanalyst*, Emil Gutheil, ed., Introduction by Mrs. Hilda Stekel (New York: Liveright Publishing Co., 1950).

73. Dr. Wilhelm Stekel, "Über Coitus im Kindesalter, eine Hygienische Studie," *Wiener Medizinische Blätter*, XVIII (1895), 247–249.

74. Wilhelm Stekel, *Nervöse Angstzustände und ihre Behandlung*, Vorwort von Prof. Dr. Siegmund Freud (Berlin and Vienna: Urban and Schwarzenberg, 1908).

75. Wilhelm Stekel, *Die Sprache des Traumes* (Munich: Bergmann, 1911).

76. Wilhelm Stekel, *Die Traüme der Dichter* (Munich: Bergmann, 1912).

77. Adler's house was at Am Dreimarkstein 16, Stekel's house (called Lindenhof) was at Am Dreimarkstein 2, at the corner of the Salmannsdorfstrasse.

78. See Emil Gutheil, "Stekel's Contributions to the Problem of Criminality," *Journal of Criminal Psychopathology*, Vol. II (1940-1941).

79. Wilhelm Stekel, "Berufswahl und Kriminalität," *Archiv für Kriminal-Anthropologie und Kriminalistik*, XLI (1911), 268–280.

80. Wilhelm Stekel, *Der telepathische Traum. Meine Erfahrungen über die Phänomene des Hellsehens im Wachen und im Traume* (Berlin: Johannes Baum, 1920).

81. Wilhelm Stekel, *Briefe an eine Mutter* (Zurich and Leipzig: Wendepunkt-Verlag, 1927, Vol. I.

82. Stekel's formula, *Zwang erzeugt Gegenzwang* (force engenders counterforce) is almost identical with Adler's phrase *Druck erzeugt Gegendruck* (pressure engenders counter-pressure).

83. Wilhelm Stekel, *Das Liebe Ich. Grundriss einer neuen Diätetik der Seele*, 3. Aufl. (Berlin: Otto Salle, 1927).

84. Alfred Adler, *Gesundheitsbuch für das Schneidergewerbe*, No. 5 of the series: *Wegweiser der Gewerbehygiene*, G. Golebiewski, ed. (Berlin: Carl Heymanns, 1898).

85. No copy of this booklet seems extant in Austria, Switzerland, France, or North America. After long research a copy has been found in the public library of Mönchengladbach in Germany, to which the author is very much indebted for its loan.

86. Gerhart von Schulze-Gaevernitz, *Der Grossbetrieb, ein wirtschaftlicher und socialer Fortschritt. Eine Studie auf dem Gebiete der Baumwollindustrie* (Leipzig: Duncker and Humboldt, 1892).

87. Alfred Adler, "Das Eindringen sozialer Triebkräfte in die Medizin," *Aertzliche Standeszeitung*, I, No. 1 (1902), 1–3.

88. Aladdin, "Eine Lehrkanzel für Soziale Medizin," *Aerztliche Standeszeitung*, I, No. 7 (1902), pp. 1–2.

89. Alfred Adler, "Stadt und Land," *Aerztliche Standeszeitung*, II, No. 18 (1903), 1–3; No. 19, 1–2; No. 20, 1–2.

90. Alfred Adler, "Staatshilfe oder Selbsthilfe," *Aerztliche Standeszeitung*, II, No. 21 (1903), 1–3; No. 22, 1–2.

91. Alfred Adler, "Der Arzt als Erzieher," *Aerztliche Standeszeitung*, III, No. 13 (1904), 4–6; No. 14, 3–4; No. 15, 4–5.

92. Alfred Adler, "Hygiene des Geschlechtslebens," *Aerztliche Standeszeitung*, III, No. 18 (1904), 1–2; No. 19, 1–3.

93. See the *Minutes of the Vienna Psychoanalytic Society. I: 1906–1908*, Herman Nunberg, Ernst Federn, eds., M. Nunberg, trans. (New York: International Universities Press, 1962).

94. Alfred Adler, "Drei Psycho-Analysen von Zahleneinfällen und obsedierenden Zahlen," *Psychiatrische-Neurologische Wochenschrift*, VII (1905), 263–266.

95. Alfred Adler, "Das Sexuelle Problem in der Erziehung," *Die Neue Gesellschaft*, VIII (1905), 360–362.

96. Alfred Adler, *Studie über Minderwertigkeit von Organen* (Vienna: Urban und Schwarzenberg, 1907). Eng. trans., *Study of Organ Inferiority and Its Psychical Compensation* (New York: Nervous and Mental Disease Publishing Co., 1917).

97. Alfred Adler, "Der Aggressionstrieb im Leben und in der Neurose," *Fortschritte der Medizin*, XXVI (1908), 577–584.

98. Alfred Adler, "Der Psychische Hermaphroditismus im Leben und in der Neurose," *Fortschritte der Medizin*, XXVIII (1910), 486–493.

99. Alfred Adler, *Ueber den Nervösen Charakter: Grundzüge einer vergleichenden Individual-Psychologie und Psychotherapie* (Wiesbaden: Bergmann, 1912). Eng. trans., *The Neurotic Constitution* (New York: Moffat, Yard, 1917).

100. Alfred Adler, *Menschenkenntnis* (Leipzig: Hirzel, 1927). Eng. trans. *Understanding Human Nature* (New York: Greenberg, 1927.)

101. Immanuel Kant, *Anthropologie in Pragmatischer Hinsicht* (1798), in *Kants Werke* (Berlin: Georg. Reimer, 1971), VII, 117–333.

102. Henri Lefebvre, *Critique de la vie quotidienne*, Introduction (Paris: Bernard Grasset, 1947).

103. This has been shown notably by Ludwig Klages, *Die psychologischen Errungenschaften Nietzsches* (Leipzig: A. Barthes, 1926). See Chap. 5, pp. 272–278.

104. Alexander Neuer, *Mut und Entmutigung. Die Prinzipien der Psychologie Alfred Adlers* (Munich: Bergmann, 1926), p. 12.

105. See Chap. 8, p. 558.

106. Alfred Adler, "Zur Massenpsychologie," *Internationale Zeitschrift für Individualpsychologie*, XII (1934), 133–141.

107. Alfred Adler, "Psychologie der Macht," in Franz Kobler, *Gewalt und Gewaltlosigkeit. Handbuch des aktiven Pazifismus* (Zurich: Rotapfel-Verlag, 1928), pp. 41–46.

108. Paul Häberlin, *Minderwertigkeitsgefühle* (Zurich: Schweizer Spiegel Verlag, 1936).

109. Alexander Neuer, *Mut und Entmutigung. Die Prinzipien der Psychologie Alfred Adlers* (Munich: Bergmann, 1926), pp. 13–14.

110. F. Oliver Brachfeld, *Les sentiments d'infériorité* (Geneva: Mont-Blanc, 1945).

111. Alfred Adler, "Der Komplexzwang als Teil der Persönlickheit und Neurose," *Internationale Zeitschrift für Individualpsychologie*, XIII (1935), 1–6.

112. Alfred Adler, "Das Problem der Distanz; über einen Grundcharakter der Neurose und Psychose," *Zeitschrift für Individual-Psychologie*, I (1914), 8–6.

113. Alfred Adler, "On the Interpretation of Dreams," *International Journal of Individual Psychology*, II, No. 1 (1936), 3–16.

114. Alfred Adler, *Praxis und Theorie der Individualpsychologie* (Vienna: Bergmann, 1920), pp. 171–182. Eng. trans., *The Practice and Theory of Individual Psychology* (London: Routledge and Kegan Paul, 1925).

115. Adler's theory of paranoia is given in the same article as that of melancholia. See also Georges Verdeaux, *La Paranoia de compensation* (Paris: Le François, 1943).

116. Vera Strasser-Eppelbaum, *Zur Psychologie des Alkoholismus. Ergebnisse experimenteller und individualpsychologischer Untersuchungen* (Munich: Reinhardt, 1914).

117. P. Nussbaum, "Alkoholismus als individualpsychologisches Problem," in Stavros Zurukzoglu, *Die Alkoholfrage in der Schweiz* (Basel: B. Schwabe, 1935), pp. 603–618.

118. Adler expounded his concepts of normal and abnormal sexual life in several articles of a medical encyclopedia: A. Bethe, ed., *Handbuch der normalen und pathologischen Physiologie*, XIV, No. 1 (Berlin: Springer-Verlag, 1926).

119. Alfred Adler, *Das Problem der Homosexualität* (Munich: Reinhardt, 1917).

120. Alfred Adler, *Das Problem der Homosexualität, Erotisches Training und erotischer Rückzug* (Leipzig: S. Hirzel, Verlag, 1930).

121. Alfred Adler, "The Individual Criminal and His Cure," *National Committee on Prisons and Prison Labour* (New York: Annual Meeting, 1930). See also Phyllis Bottome, *Alfred Adler, Apostle of Freedom* (London: Faber and Faber, 1939), pp. 228–235.

122. Alfred Adler, "Danton, Marat, Robespierre. Eine Charakterstudie," *Arbeiter-Zeitung*, No. 352 (December 25, 1923), pp. 17–18.

123. We are mainly following the systematization written by Dr. Alexandra Adler, "Individualpsychologie (Alfred Adler)," in *Handbuch der Neurosenlehre und Psychotherapie*, Frankl, Gebsattel, and Schultz, eds. (Munich: Urban and Schwarzenberg, 1959), III, 221–268.

124. Alfred Adler, "Die Technik der Individualpsychologie," *Die Kunst eine Lebens—und Krankengeschichte zu lesen* (Munich: Bergmann, 1928), Vol. I. Eng. trans., *The Case of Miss R.; The Interpretation of a Life Story* (New York: Greenberg, 1929).

125. Alfred Adler, "The Case of Mrs. A.," *Individual Psychology Pamphlets*, Vol. I (1931).

126. Adler himself wrote very little about these organizations. To our knowledge the most complete description we have of them was written by Madelaine Ganz, *La Psychologie d'Alfred Adler et le développement de l'enfant* (Neuchâtel: Delachaux et Niestlé, n.d.). Eng. trans., *The Psychology of Alfred Adler and the Development of the Child* (London: Routledge and Kegan Paul, 1953).

127. Information kindly provided by Dr. Joshua Bierer.

128. Dr. D. Ewen Cameron also opened a day hospital in Montreal in 1946, although on somewhat different principles.

129. Alfred Adler, *Der Sinn des Lebens* (Vienna: Passer, 1933). Eng. trans., *Social Interest: A Challenge to Mankind* (London: Faber and Faber, 1938).

130. Most of these later writings have been collected in the volume edited by Heinz and Rowena Ansbacher, *Superiority and Social Interest* (Evanston: Northwestern University, 1964).

131. Alfred Adler, "Das Todesproblem in der Neurose," *Internationale Zeitschrift für Individualpsychologie*, XIV (1936), 1–6.

132. Alfred Adler, "Case Interpretation," *Individual Psychology Bulletin*, II (1941), 1–9. Reprinted in H. and R. Ansbacher, eds. *Superiority and Social Interest*, pp. 143–158.

133. *"Menschsein heisst, ein Minderwertigkeitsgefühl zu besitzen, das ständig nach seiner Überwindung drängt"* (*Der Sinn des Lebens*, p. 48).

134. The author is most grateful to Reverend Ernst Jahn, who kindly lent him his own copies of his books (they seem to be the only extant copies and have never been reprinted), and sent him much information about Alfred Adler and several contemporaries.

135. Ernst Jahn, *Wesen und Grenzen der Psychanalyse* (Schwerin i.M.: Bahn, 1927).

136. Ernst Jahn, *Machtwille und Minderwertigkeitsgefühl* (Berlin: Martin Warneck, 1931).

137. Ernst Jahn and Alfred Adler, *Religion und Individualpsychologie. Eine prinzipielle Auseinandersetzung über Menschenführung* (Vienna and Leipzig: Passer, 1933). See also the new preface by Ernst Jahn in Heinz and Rowena Ansbacher, *Superiority and Social Interest* (Evanston: Northwestern University Press, 1964), pp. 272–274.

138. Izydor Wasserman, "Letter to the Editor," *American Journal of Psychotherapy*, XII (1958), 623–627. "Ist eine Differenzielle Psychotherapie möglich?" *Zeitschrift für Psychotherapie und Medizinische Psychologie*, IX (1959), 187–193.

139. Heinz Ansbacher, "The Significance of the Socio-Economic Status of the Patients of Freud and of Adler," *American Journal of Psychotherapy*, XIII (1959), 376–382.

140. Willy Hellpach, *Wirken und Wirren. Lebenserinnerungen. Eine Rechenschaft*

über Wert und Glück, Schuld und Sturz meiner Generation, I (Hamburg: Christian Wegner, 1948), 413.

141. Hans Kunz, "Zur grundsätzlichen Kritik der Individualpsychologie Adlers," *Zeitschrift für die gesamte Neurologie und Psychiatrie*, CXVI (1928), 700–766.

142. Phyllis Bottome, *Alfred Adler. Apostle of Freedom* (London: Faber and Faber, 1939), p. 17.

143. Immanuel Kant, "Träume eines Geistessehers, in *Immanuel Kants Werke*, Ernst Cassirer, ed. (Berlin: Bruno Cassirer, 1912), II, 329–390.

144. Immanuel Kant, "Anthropologie in pragmatischer Hinsicht," in *Immanuel Kants Werke*, Ernst Cassirer, ed. (Berlin: Bruno Cassirer, 1922), VIII, 3–228.

145. This has been pointed out by Heinz Ansbacher, "Sensus Privatus versus Sensus Communis," *Journal of Individual Psychology*, XXI (1965), 48–50.

146. See Chap. 4, p. 197.

147. See Chap. 4, p. 223.

148. August Bebel, *Die Frau und der Sozialismus* (Stuttgart: Dietz, 1879).

149. Sofie Lazarsfeld, *Wie die Frau den Mann erlebt* (Leipzig and Vienna: Verlag für Sexualwissenschaft, 1931), 79–82.

150. See Chap. 4, pp. 234–235.

151. Henri Lefebvre, *La Conscience mystifiée* (Paris: Nouvelle Revue Française, 1936).

152. Henri Lefebvre, *Pour connaître la pensée de Karl Marx* (Paris: Bordas, 1947), pp. 42–43.

153. See Chap. 4, pp. 271–278.

154. F. G. Crookshank, *Individual Psychology and Nietzsche, Individual Psychology Pamphlets*, No. 10 (London: C. W. Daniel Co., 1933).

155. Hans Vaihinger, *Die Philosophie des Als Ob. System der theoretischen, praktischen und religiösen Fiktionen der Menschheit auf Grund eines idealistischen Positivismus* (Berlin: Reuther and Reichard, 1911). There are several enlarged later editions.

156. Bentham's definition of fictions is given in his paper, *Logical Arrangements, or Instruments of Invention and Discovery*, in *The Works of Jeremy Bentham*, John Bowring, ed. (Edinburgh: William Tait, 1843), III, 286.

157. Joseph Wandeler, *Die Individualpsychologie Alfred Adlers in ihrer Beziehung zur Philosophie des Als Ob Hans Vaihingers*. Ph.D. Diss. Freiburg, Schweiz, 1932 (Lachen: Buchdruckerei Gutenberg, 1932).

158. Sarah Gertrude Millin, *General Smuts*, 2 vols. (London: Faber and Faber, 1936).

159. Jan Christian Smuts, *Holism and Evolution* (London and New York: Macmillan, 1926).

160. F. Oliver Brachfeld, *Les Sentiments d'infériorité* (Geneva: Mont-Blanc, 1945).

161. Alfred Adler, *Über den Nervösen Charakter* (Wiesbaden: Bergmann, 1912), p. 3. Engl. trans., *The Neurotic Constitution* (New York: Moffat, Yard, 1917).

162. This has been well demonstrated by Georges Blin, *Stendhal et les problèmes de la personnalité* (Paris: Corti, 1958), I, 169–217.

163. Stendhal expressly mentioned Julien Sorel's "continuous feeling of his inferiority": *Le Rouge et le noir*, Chap. 40. See Stendhal, *Romans et Nouvelles* (Paris: Pléiade, 1952), I, 507.

164. Stendhal, *Du Rire. Mélanges d'art et de littérature* (Paris: Calmann-Lévy, 1924), pp. 1–30.

165. Ralph Waldo Emerson, *The Complete Works. Centenary Edition* (Boston and New York: Houghton, Mifflin and Co., 1903–1912), Vols. II–III, VI.

166. Helvétius, *De l'Esprit* (Paris: Durand, 1758).

167. Prosper Despine, *Psychologie naturelle. Etude sur les facultés intellectuelles et morales dans leur état normal et dans leurs manifestations anormales chez les aliénés et chez les criminels* (Paris: Savy, 1868), I, 291–292.

168. Thorleif Schjeldrup-Ebbe, "Beiträge zur Sozialpsychologie des Haushuhns," *Zeitschrift für Psychologie und Physiologie der Sinnesorgane*, LXXXVIII (1922), 225–253.

169. David Katz, "Tierpsychologie und Soziologie des Menschen," *Zeitschrift für Psychologie und Physiologie der Sinnesorgane*, LXXXVIII (1922), 253–264.

Psychologie und Physiologie der Sinnesorgane, LXXXVIII (1922), 253–264.

170. Ralph Waldo Emerson, *The Conduct of Life, Centenary Edition* (Boston and New York: Houghton, Mifflin and Co., 1903–1912), VI, 59, 190.

171. See Louis Esteve, *Une Nouvelle Psychologie de l'impérialisme* (Paris: Alcan, 1913).

172. Ernest Seilliere, *Le Néoromantisme en Allemagne. I. Psychanalyse freudienne ou psychologie impérialiste* (Paris: Alcan, 1928).

173. Jules de Gaultier, *Le Bovarysme* (Paris: Mercure de France, n.d.).

174. N. Bryllion Fagin, *The Histrionic Mr. Poe* (Baltimore: Johns Hopkins Press, 1949).

175. Joseph Dorfman, *Thorstein Veblen and His America* (New York: Viking Press, 1934), pp. 313–319.

176. Johann Wolfgang von Goethe, *Zur Farbenlehre* (1810), in *Sämtliche Werke* (Stuttgart: Cotta, 1833), LII, xi.

177. Franz Joseph Gall, *Sur les Fonctions du cerveau et sur celles de ses parties* (Paris: Baillière, 1825), III, 181–182.

178. Josef Popper-Lynkeus, *Die allgemeine Nährpflicht als Lösung der Socialen Frage* (Dresden: Carl Reissner, 1912).

179. Maxime Gorki, "Razrushenye Lichnosti," in *Ocherki Filosofiy Kollektivizma*, I, 351–403 (St. Petersburg, 1909). German trans., *Die Zerstörung der Persönlichkeit*, in *Aufsätze* (Dresden: Kaemmerer, 1922), pp. 17–86.

180. Alfred Adler, "Der Aggressionstrieb im Leben und in der Neurose," *Fortschritte der Medizin,* XXVI (1928), 577–584.

181. Heinz and Rowena Ansbach, *The Individual Psychology of Alfred Adler* (New York: Basic Books, 1956), pp. 31, 32, 37, 39, 458, 459.

182. Edward J. Kempf, *Psychopathology* (St. Louis: C. V. Mosby Co., 1920).

183. Harry Stack Sullivan, *Conceptions of Modern Psychiatry* (Washington: William Alanson White Psychiatric Foundation, 1947). *The Interpersonal Theory of Psychiatry* (New York: Norton, 1953). *The Psychiatric Interview* (New York, Norton, 1954). *Clinical Studies in Psychiatry* (New York: Norton, 1956).

184. Karen Horney, "Flucht aus der Weiblichkeit," *Internationale Zeitschrift für Psychoanalyse,* XII (1926), 360–374.

185. Karen Horney, "Der Männlichkeitskomplex der Frau," *Archiv für Frauenkunde,* XIII (1927), 141–154.

186. Karen Horney, "Die Angst vor der Frau," *Internationale Zeitschrift für Psychoanalyse,* XVIII (1932), 5–18.

187. Karen Horney, *The Neurotic Personality of Our Time* (New York: W. W. Norton, 1937). *New Ways in Psychoanalysis* (New York: W. W. Norton, 1939). *Our Inner Conflicts: A Constructive Theory of Neurosis* (New York: W. W. Norton, 1945). *Neurosis and Human Growth: The Struggle towards Self-Realization* (New York: W. W. Norton, 1950).

188. Erich Fromm, *Escape from Freedom* (New York: Farrar, Strauss & Giroux, Inc., 1941). *Man for Himself* (New York: Reinhart, 1947). *The Sane Society* (New York: Reinhart, 1955).

189. His two main works are *Der gehemmte Mensch* (Berlin: Springer-Verlag, 1940), and *Lehrbuch der analytischen Psychotherapie* (Berlin: Springer-Verlag, 1950).

190. Joseph Wilder, "Introduction," to Kurt A. Adler and Danica Deutsch, eds., *Essays in Individual Psychology* (New York: Grove Press, 1959), p. XV.

191. This has been repeatedly pointed out. See, for instance, Ernest L. Johnson, "Existential Trends toward Individual Psychology," *Journal of Individual Psychology,* XXII (1966), 33–42.

192. Ferdinand Birnbaum, "Victor E. Frankls Existentialpsychologie individualpsychologisch gesehen," *Internationale Zeitschrift für Individualpsychologie,* XVI (1947), 145–152.

193. J. P. Sartre, *L'Etre et le néant. Essai d'Ontologie Phénoménologique* (Paris: Gallimard, 1943), pp. 643–663. Eng. trans., *Being and Nothingness* (New York: Philosophical Library, 1956), pp. 557–575.

194. Jakob Klaesi, *Vom seelischen Kranksein. Vorbeugung und Heilen* (Bern: Paul Haupt, 1937).

195. Prescott Lecky, *Self-Consistency. A theory of personality* (New York: Highland Press, 1945).

196. Wilhelm Keller, *Das Selbstwertstreben: Wesen. Formen und Schicksale* (Munich: Reinhardt, 1963).

197. Walter Toman, *Family Constellation* (New York: Springer Publishing Co., 1961). Enlarged German edition, *Familienkonstellationen. Ihr Einfluss auf Menschen und seine Handlungen* (Munich: C. H. Beck, 1965).

198. The standard analysis technique for his research is described in O. Martensen-Larsen, "Family Constellation Analysis and Male Alcoholism," *Acta Psychiatrica Scandinavica*, Supp. Vol. CVI (1956), 241–247.

199. Eric Berne, *Games People Play* (New York: Grove Press, 1964).

200. Paul Häberlin, *Minderwertigkeitsgefühle* (Zurich: Schweizer Spiegel-Verlag, 1936).

201. Gustav Hans Graber, "Untermensch-Uebermensch, Ein Problem zur Psychologie der Ueberkompensation," *Acta Psychotherapeutica*, IV (1956), 217–224.

202. Margaret Mead and K. Heyman, *Family* (New York: Macmillan, 165). See Danica Deutsch, "Alfred Adler and Margaret Mead, a Juxtaposition," *Journal of Individual Psychology*, XXII (1966), 228–233.

203. Walter Goldschmidt, *Man's Way* (New York: Holt, Rinehart and Winston, 1959), p. 220.

204. Alfred Adler, Introduction to Maxwell Maltz, *New Faces, New Futures* (New York: Richard K. Smith, 1936), p. vii.

205. Albert Eglash and Ernst Papanek, "Creative Restitution: A Correctional Technique and a Theory," *Journal of Individual Psychology*, XV (1959), 226–232.

206. Noël Mailloux, O.P., "Genèse et signification de la conduite antisociale," *Revue Canadienne de Criminologie*, IV (1962), 103–111.

207. Hans Hoff, "Opening address to the Eighth International Congress of Individual Psychology, Vienna, August 28, 1960," *Journal of Individual Psychology*, XVII (1961), 212.

208. *The Times* (London), September 25, 1939, p. 10.

209. *New York Times*, June 7, 1961.

210. G. Lange-Eichbaum, *Genie, Irrsinn und Ruhm* (Munich: Reinhardt, 1927).

211. Bernard Grasset, *Remarques sur l'action* (Paris: Gallimard, 1928).

212. See about victimology, Hans von Hentig, *The Criminal and His Victim* (New Haven: Yale University Press, 1948). Hans von Hentig, *Das Verbrechen* (Berlin: Springer, 1962), II, 364–515. H. F. Ellenberger, "Psychological Relationships between Criminal and Victim," *Archives of Criminal Psychodynamics*, I, No. 2 (1955), 257–290.

213. Jean Cocteau, "Rousseau," in *Oeuvres complètes* (Paris: Marguerat, 1950), IX, 365–373.

214. See Chap. 5, pp. 270–271.

215. Ernest Jones, *The Life and Work of Sigmund Freud* (New York: Basic Books, 1955), III, 208.

216. See Chap. 4, pp. 248–249, n. 65.

217. See Chap. 4, p. 199.

218. See Chap. 1, p. 42.

JULES JANET, his father.

FANNY, née HUMMEL, his mother.

The three siblings,
PIERRE, MARGUERITE, JULES.

PIERRE JANET at the age of 17.

PIERRE JANET (1859–1947) sits at the foot of his favorite tree in his garden in Le Havre. He was on the point of moving to Paris to take his *doctorat-ès-lettres* and to begin his medical studies and his research at the Salpêtrière. *(Courtesy Mrs. Hélène Pichon-Janet.)*

PIERRE JANET at the height of his fame: a noted professor, sought–after psychotherapist, and man of the world. *(Courtesy Mrs. Hélène Pichon-Janet.)*

In 1912 a group of friends and admirers of Josef Breuer organized a subscription in his honor and established the Breuer Foundation to promote scientific research and teaching. This is a microfilm reproduction of one page from the original document. *(Courtesy Mr. George Bryant, Vancouver.)*

28. October 1886.   Nr. 25.

Anzeiger
der
k. k. Gesellschaft der Aerzte in Wien.

Inhalt: Protokoll der Sitzung vom 15. October 1886. — Summarischer Bericht der Sitzung vom 22. October 1886. — Programm der Sitzung am 29. October 1886.

Protokoll der Sitzung vom 15. October 1886.

Vorsitzender: Herr Hofr. Prof. v. Bamberger.
Schriftführer: Herr Doc. Dr. Bergmeister.

Herr Dr. Grossmann stellt einen Fall von Lupus des Larynx vor.

Herr Doc. Dr. Freud hält seinen angekündigten Vortrag: Ueber männliche Hysterie.

Herr Prof. Rosenthal bemerkt, dass die Hysteria virilis in ihrem Symptomenbilde mit der in der Neuzeit besser gezeichneten vulgären Hysterie übereinstimme. Die männliche Hysterie wird bereits von Romberg erwähnt. Sie fand sich unter 1000 von Briquet gesammelten Fällen von Hysterie fünfzigmal; der Mann wäre demnach zwanzigmal weniger zur Hysterie disponirt als das Weib. Redner erwähnt ferner, dass er bereits im Jahre 1870 in seinem Handbuche der Nervenkrankheiten einen Fall von Knabenhysterie beschrieb (mit Streckkrämpfen, Aphonie und Rülpsen, Lähmung des M. transversus und spastischen Bewegungen des Oesophagus). Bei einem anderen 18jährigen Manne waren auch Gemüthsbewegungen, Gliederzittern, Zuckungen und Anästhesie an der Vorderseite der Unterextremitäten erweislich. Am Oberkörper allenthalben normale Sensibilität. Aehnliche Formen wurden wiederholt beobachtet. Auch der Traumatismus von Charcot wirke nur als psychischer Shok, die örtliche Verletzung sei meist eine geringfügige.

Noch gestattet sich Redner zur Charakteristik der wenig gewürdigten hysterischen Convulsionen einiges beizufügen. Bei initialen, sich langsamer entwickelnden hysterischen Krämpfen konnte R. beobachten, wie letztere von den Gesichts-, Hals-, Kiefer- und Nackenmuskeln sich über die oberen und unteren Gliedmassen verbreiteten. Bei einem anderen Cyklus folgten auf

The first page of the October 28, 1886, issue of the *Bulletin of the Imperial Royal Society of Physicians in Vienna* gives an account of the discussion which followed Freud's paper on male hysteria. *(From the collection of the Institute for the History of Medicine, Vienna.)*

SIGMUND FREUD in 1891, age thirty–five. *(From Volume I of* The Life and Work of Sigmund Freud *by Ernest Jones* [New York: Basic Books, 1953].)

Despite his absorbing professional pursuits, Freud found time to walk in the streets of Vienna, where little escaped his searching eye. *(Courtesy Dr. Emil Oberholzer.)*

ALFRED ADLER (1870–1938); This chalk drawing by Horowicz emphasizes the peculiar mixture of attentive observation and reflective thought in Alfred Adler. *(Courtesy of Mrs. Cornelia N. Michel.)*

Alfred Adler is seen here with two of his brothers. On the left is the older one, Sigmund, a successful businessman who long inspired in Alfred feelings of inferiority and rivalry. On the right is the youngest, Richard, the artist of the family, who greatly admired Alfred. *(Courtesy Mr. Kurt Adler, Kew Gardens, N.Y., Dr. Alexandra Adler, New York, and Mrs. Justine Adler, Vienna.)*

C. G. JUNG THE ELDER (1794–1864), an almost legendary personality, was the model with whom his grandson more or less consciously identified himself. *(From the picture collection of the Library of the University of Basel.)*

CARL GUSTAV JUNG (1875–1961); Jung's pragmatism was reflected in his therapy, which first sought to bring his patient to the awareness of his real-life situation. *(Courtesy Mr. Franz Jung.)*

One of Carl Gustav Jung's fascinating traits was his ability to shift instantaneously from matter-of-fact considerations to the loftiest abstract speculations. *(Courtesy Mr. Franz Jung.)*

REV. OSKAR PFISTER, Protestant minister in Zurich, pioneered in the application of psychoanalysis to education and to the religious "cure of souls." *(Courtesy Rev. Oskar Pfister.)*

DR. ALPHONSE MAEDER, after his association with Freud and Jung, devised an original method of brief therapy. *(Courtesy Dr. Alphonse Maeder.)*

HERMANN RORSCHACH (1884-1922) is pictured here on Christmas Day, 1917, when he was beginning to devise his inkblot test. *(Courtesy Mrs. Olga Rorschach.)*

LUDWIG BINSWANGER (1881-1966), the founder of existential analysis and an early adherent of psychoanalysis, never severed his personal ties with Freud. *(Courtesy Dr. Wolfgang Binswanger.)*

9

Carl Gustav Jung and Analytical Psychology

CARL GUSTAV JUNG, no more than Alfred Adler, is a deviant from Freud's psychoanalysis, and his analytic psychology should not be measured with the yardstick of Freudian psychoanalysis any more than psychoanalysis should be measured with the yardstick of analytic psychology. Both should be understood in terms of their own philosophy.

The fundamental differences between Jung's and Freud's systems can be summed up as follows:

First, the philosophical foundation is quite another. Jung's analytic psychology, like Freud's psychoanalysis, is a late offshoot of Romanticism, but psychoanalysis is also the heir of positivism, scientism, and Darwinism, whereas analytic psychology rejects that heritage and returns to the unaltered sources of psychiatric Romanticism and philosophy of nature.

Second, whereas Freud's aim is to explore that part of the human mind that was known intuitively by the great writers, Jung claims to have approached objectively and annexed to science a realm of the human soul intermediate between religion and psychology.

The Life Frame of Carl Gustav Jung

Carl Gustav Jung was born in a little village of Thurgovia, Switzerland, in 1875, and died in Küsnacht, on the shores of Lake Zurich, in 1961. He spent his entire life in his native Switzerland, aside from a number of journeys to France, England, Italy, North America, Africa, and India. When he was born, Freud was nineteen years old, Janet sixteen, and Adler five. Jung was thus the youngest of the great pioneers of the new dynamic psychiatry, and he also survived them all. And since he lived in neutral Switzerland, he did not suffer the vicissitudes that afflicted the lives of Freud and Adler.

The first half of Jung's life, from 1875 to 1914, that is, the years of his youth, his psychiatric career, his association with Freud and their subse-

657

quent separation, evolved during the period of European "armed peace." After World War I he founded his school and expounded his ideas in numerous books. During World War II and afterward he loosened his ties with his school and expressed his thoughts in an increasingly personal way. His patients were at first institutionalized psychotics from the lower social strata, and later they were mostly neurotics from the upper classes.

The life of Carl Gustav Jung can be viewed as an example of social ascension. Born into an impoverished middle-class family, he was an impecunious student, began his career as a mental hospital doctor and university psychiatrist, and then became a psychotherapist of world renown and the founder and head of a school. Toward the end of his life he personified the almost legendary figure of the "old wise man of Küsnacht," whom people from all parts of the world came to visit.

Family Background

It is impossible to understand the personality and work of Carl Gustav Jung without considering his Swiss background and his family.

Switzerland is a multinational state, as was Austria-Hungary, with the difference being that in Switzerland there are only three major ethnic groups and languages, and that political unity had been achieved before the rise of fierce nationalism. Those problems for which the Austrian-Hungarian monarchy desperately sought a solution had already been solved in Switzerland through federalism. Although the three main ethnic groups speak the languages of the neighboring countries—Germany, France, Italy—the Swiss national identity is very strong because Switzerland's political institutions differ considerably from those of the other European countries.

For the Swiss, federalism and democracy are almost synonymous terms. Every Swiss exercises his political rights on three levels: community, canton, and federation. Each community enjoys a large autonomy, and all male citizens are constantly and actively engaged in community affairs. Each Swiss belongs to a community of origin, and this privilege is transmitted to his descendants, regardless of their actual place of residence. A foreigner applying for Swiss citizenship must first seek acceptance by a given community, whereupon he becomes a citizen of the canton and consequently of the Swiss Federation. Self-rule in Switzerland developed within the community and the canton to the extreme limit compatible with national unity. Nothing would seem more abhorrent, more undemocratic to a Swiss than the idea of imposing a common language·on the entire country. German, French, and Italian are considered the three national languages, and each one becomes the official language in that part of the country where it is spoken. Moreover, in German-speaking Switzerland a variety of dialects are used as spoken languages, in contrast to *Schriftdeutsch* (written German), the official administrative and academic language.

Another feature that differentiates Switzerland from other countries is the organization of the army. Each Swiss male, as long as he is in active service, keeps his military uniform and arms at home, remains under the orders of the section chief of his community, and has his equipment inspected regularly. In contrast to the other European armies, which impose a period of one, two, or more years of military service, the young recruits undergo a few weeks of intensive military instruction and drill. Thereupon they return each year for a short training period. Those who wish to become officers are subject to similar periodical training. Thus each Swiss male is simultaneously a soldier or officer and a civilian. The permanent military staff is kept to a minimum.

The Swiss is strongly integrated in the life of his community, canton, and country. He is deeply concerned with local politics and military life, and he is often deeply interested in the genealogies and the history of his family, and (in truly democratic fashion) not only the aristocrats but almost all families have their coat of arms. One result of the system of community of origin is that it is very easy for a Swiss to reconstruct his genealogy by means of the community registers.

This accounts for the general stability of the Swiss population and its adherence to tradition, for its respect for local usage and dialects, and hence also for the great differences that exist between localities. Switzerland arrived at this situation after a long and difficult historical evolution, including much civil warfare. The vicissitudes of history caused Switzerland gradually to become a federative state composed of twenty-two cantons, three of which are divided into half-cantons, thus forming twenty-five autonomous political units. During the second half of the nineteenth century, Switzerland became a kind of experimental laboratory for democratic institutions. Although Switzerland is one of the last countries not to accept the feminine vote, it enjoys the benefit of institutions that are unknown elsewhere, such as the citizens' right of initiative and the referendum.[1]

Switzerland is commonly identified today with the picture of a country that enjoyed a prolonged period of peace throughout the turmoil of European history. Actually, when Carl Gustav Jung was born in 1875, his parents and grandparents could certainly not have held this opinion. His grandparents had lived their youth during that period when Switzerland was enmeshed in the French Revolution and in the Napoleonic wars. Then, between 1815 and 1830, the country had suffered from a great deal of civil strife, notably when the farmers' parties in several cantons attempted to abolish the privileges of the city patriciate. In the canton of Basel it came to armed warfare between country and city, which ended in 1833 with the separation of the canton into two political units: Basel-City and Basel-Land. In 1838 Switzerland mobilized and was on the brink of a war with France. In 1845 the seven Catholic cantons constituted a separate league, the *Sonderbund*, causing a civil war that ended with the victory of the Federation and the reunification of Switzerland in 1847. In 1857 Switzerland mobilized again, this time against Prussia, but the conflict was settled by means of negotiation. There had also been much strife in religious matters.

The personality of Carl Gustav Jung reflected to a high degree not only the characteristics of Swiss mentality, but also the spirit of his home town, Basel, his ancestors, and his family. Basel is not only a city but an almost unique example of a self-contained political unit, with its government, its assemblies, its ministerial departments, and its administration. An international industrial and commercial center located at the crossroads of Switzerland, France, and Germany, Basel was at that time small enough so that its citizens could know each other. In 1875, the year of Jung's birth, Basel had 50,000 inhabitants. Since the Renaissance, Basel had remained one of the hearths of European culture. In his childhood Jung, when walking in the streets, could see the eminent historian-philosopher Jacob Burckhardt, or old Bachofen; he heard talk about Nietzsche everywhere, whom so many people had known; and he was infallibly identified as "the grandson of the famous Carl Gustav Jung."

His grandfather, Carl Gustav Jung (1794–1864),[2] was a legendary figure in Basel.[3] The son of a German physician, he had studied medicine in Heidelberg and had been acquainted with the Romantic poets and had written poems and student songs himself.[4] He had been converted to Protestantism by the celebrated Schleiermacher. A group of university professors organized a religious and patriotic feast at the Wartburg, in Saxony, on October 17, 1817, with the government's permission. Although they carefully abstained from any political manifestations, the authorities took advantage of a futile incident in order to intervene and subsequently crush the student organizations throughout Germany. Carl Gustav Jung, one among many other young men, was thrown into jail without judgment. After his release, thirteen months later, he found his career broken and emigrated to France. In Paris he met Alexander von Humboldt who, knowing the University of Basel was searching for an energetic young man to reorganize its medical school, recommended him, and so Carl Gustav Jung the elder became a Swiss citizen and one of the foremost personalities of Basel. According to all accounts of the time he was a man of irresistible charm and won the hearts of all those with whom he came in contact. However, one of his sons depicted him as a despotic father, though he would at times participate in the amusements and pranks of his children.[5] After the death of his first wife, with whom he had three children, he went to the Mayor of Basel asking for his daughter in marriage. The Mayor refused his request, whereupon Carl Gustav Jung directly went to a tavern and asked the waitress there whether she would consent to marry him. She immediately accepted, and the marriage was concluded to the consternation of the whole town. She died three years later, having given him two children. He decided to marry again, and this time the Mayor consented to give him his daughter,

Sophie Frey. In all he had thirteen children, several of whom caused him great sorrow during the latter period of his life. In 1857 he founded a home for retarded children to which he came to devote the greater part of his time.

Carl Gustav Jung the elder enjoyed an uncommonly successful career, was one of the most sought-after physicians in Basel, was elected rector of the University, became Grand Master of the Swiss Freemasons, and wrote scientific treatises as well as theatrical plays under several pseudonyms. According to rumor, he was an illegitimate son of Goethe. No doubt there was a certain physical resemblance between the two men. Carl Gustav Jung the elder never referred to this topic, but it is perhaps noteworthy that in a page of his diary he passed a severe judgment upon Goethe's lack of moral sense in two of his plays, and that in an anatomic treatise on supernumerary bones he did not refer to Goethe's classical study on the intermaxillary bone.[6] This story of an alleged tie with Goethe contributed to make the old Carl Gustav Jung a legendary figure during his lifetime. Such was the fascinating man whom the psychiatrist Carl Gustav Jung had never known, but whose name he had been given, and whose image undoubtedly exerted a great influence on his destiny.[7]

Carl Gustav Jung's maternal grandparents were no less remarkable than the paternal ones. Samuel Preiswerk (1799–1871), a distinguished theologian and Hebraist, suffered many vicissitudes in his life, until he became *antistes* of the Basel Church, that is president of the company of pastors. He left the reputation of a pious and learned man who composed numerous poems and church hymns and wrote a Hebrew grammar. He was convinced that Palestine should be given back to the Jews and actively defended that idea, so that today he is considered a precursor of Zionism. He married twice: from his first wife he had only one child, and from the second Augusta Faber, thirteen. According to family tradition, he had visions and conversed with the world of the spirits, and in his study a special chair was reserved for the spirit of his first wife, who visited him every week to the great sorrow of his second wife. It is also said when he wrote his sermons he would have his daughter Emilie sit behind him so that the spirits could not read over his shoulder. His second wife (C. G. Jung's grandmother) was said to possess the gift of second sight, and several members of her family to have parapsychological abilities.[8]

Both of C. G. Jung's parents were the last-born children of large families, and belonged to the "sacrificed generation," as it were, since they were born when their respective fathers had become impoverished. Paul Achilles Jung (1842–1896) was very interested in classical languages and Hebrew, but became a modest country pastor. He married Emilie Preiswerk, the youngest child of his professor of Hebrew. Jung had the impression that their marriage was not a happy one. Let it be added, however, that the author once met an old lady who had been well acquainted with Reverend Paul Jung in her youth. She described him as a quiet, unassuming, kind-hearted man who admirably knew how to preach to peasants and was universally loved and respected by his parishioners. According to another reliable source, Reverend Paul Jung was considered by his colleagues as a somewhat boring man.

After completing his theological studies, Reverend Paul Jung was assigned to the parish of Kesswil on the shores of Lake Constance, and then for three years to that of Laufen, near Schaffhausen. In 1879 he received his final appointment in Klein-Hüningen, a small village that belonged to Basel-City. He became the Protestant chaplain of the Friedmatt Mental Hospital in Basel.[9] We do not know enough about the personality of Reverend Paul Jung to understand the reason for the strong resentment that his son felt toward him during his whole life. He certainly did not accuse him of being tyrannical. It is rather his father's alleged immaturity that he resented, the fact that he was a scholar and had not developed intellectually, but scattered his activity in amiable but futile pursuits. C. G. Jung also believed that his father had religious doubts that he would not admit to himself.

We are even less informed about the personality of Carl Gustav Jung's mother, Emilie Preiswerk. The same aged person who told the author about Jung's childhood and his father described Mrs. Paul Jung as being fat, ugly, authoritarian, and haughty. Her son refers to her as a somewhat difficult character, and as a dual personality. At times, he said, she was highly sensitive to the point of showing parapsychological abilities, and at others she was rather down-to-earth and commonplace.

Reverend and Mrs. Paul Jung had three children. The eldest, Paul, born in August 1873, lived only a few days. Then came Carl Gustav, the future psychiatrist, and after an interval of nine years, Johanna Gertrud, born on July 17, 1884. She never married, does not seem to have had a professional occupation, remained in the shadow of her brother, whom she greatly admired, and died in Zurich on May 30, 1935.

This family setting may explain certain aspects of C. G. Jung's thinking and his divergencies from Freud. Freud had been the beloved first-born son of a beautiful young mother, whereas Jung kept the image of a homely, ambivalent mother. The idea of every little boy being in love with his mother and jealous of his father seemed absurd to him. On the other hand, Jung emphasized not so much the son's hostility toward the father, but the unconscious identification with him and the ancestors on the father's side. No doubt Jung identified himself less with his father than with his brilliant, romantic, and successful grandfather. Jung used to smile when denying the rumors that the latter was the illegitimate son of Goethe. This legend might have been one of the incentives that brought him to personify the figure of the old wise man at the end of his life.

Jung lived his childhood and youth in a country pastor's house. The presbytery (*Pfarrhaus*) has been called "one of the germinal cells of

German culture."[10] In a quiet spacious house with a large garden, the minister accomplished his ecclesiastic duties, practised cure of souls, gave the example of domestic virtues, raised his family, and kept some time for contemplation and study. Many pastors' sons became prominent men, although a few rebelled against their father's religious orthodoxy (if not against religion itself, like Nietzsche). In Jung's case it seems that his religious and philosophical interests were awakened, but because he could not receive an answer that would satisfy him from his father, he turned his inquiry to other problems beyond the scope of traditional religion.

Events in Carl Gustav Jung's Life

Our knowledge of Carl Gustav Jung's life is still imperfect. Biographic accounts are sketchy and reveal wide gaps.[11] A few memories of his childhood and youth were related by his lifelong friend, Alfred Oeri.[12] No documentary study of Jung's life, similar to those of the Bernfelds and the Gicklhorns for Freud, and of Beckh-Widmanstetter for Adler, has been conducted as yet, with the sole exception of Gustav Steiner's study of Jung's activity in his students' association on the basis of the archives of that association.[13] Jung had always declined his friends' suggestion to write the story of his life. At the end of 1957, when Jung was eighty-two, he changed his mind and wrote what has become the first chapters of his autobiography; the remainder he narrated to his secretary who later edited and published it.[14] However, here, too, there are wide gaps, and contradictions between certain of Jung's assertions and the version given by other sources.[15] One may also wonder how the eighty-two-year-old man could remember his earliest memories with such accuracy. A small part of Jung's extensive correspondence has been published, and many of his writings are not available in printed form.[16]

According to Basel civil data, Jung was born on July 26, 1875 in Kesswil, Canton of Thurgovia, on the shores of Lake Constance.[17] Six months later his family moved to Laufen, near Schaffhausen, where they remained for three years. The presbytery was situated in close proximity to the Rhine Falls. It was a most picturesque location, but somewhat frightening for the young child, if we refer to Jung's earliest memories as recorded in his autobiography.

In 1879, when Carl was not quite four years old, the family moved to Klein-Hüningen, which was at that time a small village of peasants and fishermen located on the shores of the Rhine.[18] Today, Klein-Hüningen is an industrialized suburb of Basel (in which it was incorporated in 1908). The original rural population has been replaced by workers recruited from other regions for the chemical plants and the Basel harbor. But in that remote time, Klein-Hüningen was still a patriarchal village, and Carl Gustav went to school with the children of peasant families. The presbytery was a large old house with a garden and stables, which had been the country house of the Iselin family, a rich patrician family whose coat of arms with three roses is still to be seen over one of the doors. There was a discrepancy between the aristocratic style of the house and the means of a country pastor in those times.

We do not know much about Carl Gustav's childhood. Albert Oeri merely relates a few pranks he played on other children. In his autobiography, Jung emphasizes childhood fantasies, dreams, and anxiety. He went to the village school with the children of local farmers, and felt that he was different from them. Jung reports that when he was six years old his father began to teach him Latin. He subsequently acquired a good knowledge of the language, though apparently he could never equal his father's mastery of it.

In the spring of 1886, at the age of eleven, Jung began his secondary studies at the Gymnasium in Basel. According to his autobiography, it was the beginning of a difficult period for him in which he did not easily relate to his schoolmates. He was good in Latin, but poor in mathematics. An episode that occurred involving Jung is curiously similar to one in André Gide's life. A schoolmate had treacherously thrown him to the ground; Carl Gustav fainted for a short while, but simulated a longer period of unconsciousness to frighten the culprit. From then on he lost consciousness whenever he wanted to escape going to school or even doing his homework. For six months he shirked school and went roaming and daydreaming through the countryside. The doctors were puzzled; one of them spoke of epilepsy. Then one day Carl Gustav overheard his father expressing his concern over the future of his son to a visiting friend. The boy suddenly realized that life was a serious matter and that he would have to prepare himself to earn his living. From that day onward he strove to repress his fainting spells and resumed his schoolwork. This episode reveals, not only how a childhood neurosis can start, but also how it can be spontaneously cured in contrast to André Gide whose entire childhood was spoiled by a similar neurosis.[19] We also find foreshadowed here one of the main principles of Jungian psychotherapy, namely, bringing the patient back to reality.

It seems that from then on all went fairly well with Jung's secondary studies. However, Jung tells in his autobiography almost nothing about his studies and his masters, but emphasizes the events of his interior life: dreams, daydreams, fantasies, and intuitions. After having seen an old eighteenth-century carriage, he suddenly felt that he had lived in those days and began to have memories of this previous life. It seemed to him that he had two personalities: that of the nervous and difficult boy as he appeared to his environment, and also, unknown to all, that of a prominent man of the eighteenth century.[20] Moreover, the young Carl Gustav read extensively. He was impressed by Schopenhauer, whose pessimistic philosophy was then at the height of its popularity, and by Goethe in whose

Faust he saw an interpretation of the problem of evil. He also underwent a religious crisis between his fifteenth and eighteenth year, a time which, as clearly indicated in his autobiography, was marked by long, tedious, and sterile discussions with his father. In this manner he came to the attitude toward religion that he later expressed in a favorite statement: "I cannot believe in what I do not know, and what I know I need not believe in.[21]

Carl Gustav Jung passed his final examinations, the Matura, in the spring of 1895.[22] According to Oeri it was lucky for him that the regulations of that time allowed a candidate to pass on the average note, so that he could compensate for his great weakness in mathematics. When the time came to select a vocation, he chose medicine. His father had secured a scholarship at the University of Basel for him. (It should be noted that scholarships at that time were scarce and given only to students of very modest means). His father was already severely ill and was to die a year later. Carl Gustav Jung registered at the Medical School of the Basel University on April 18, 1895, and studied medicine there from the summer semester of 1895 to the winter semester of 1900–1901.[23] His father died on January 28, 1896, when he was a first-year medical student. Jung now lived with his mother and sister, and was from then on the head of the family. They had moved to a little house in the village of Binningen, from which he would walk to the medical school every day. He completed his studies in five years, which was a relatively short time even in those days and this allows us to surmise that he worked very hard.

Nevertheless, he devoted some time to student activities. On May 18, 1895, he was admitted to the Basel section of the Zofingia, a Swiss student society. Gustav Steiner reports that the Basel section had at that time about 120 members, from four faculties (theology, philosophy, law, and medicine), and that there was an average of 80 members at the weekly meetings.[24] Albert Oeri, who belonged to the same society, writes that Jung was not interested in the social balls, nor in the revelries of its members, but mainly in the discussion evenings in which he participated actively, particularly when the topic was on matters of philosophy, psychology, or occultism. Gustav Steiner describes how Jung captivated the minds of his audience. He was passionately interested in such authors as Swedenborg, Mesmer, Jung-Stilling, Justinus Kerner, Lombroso, and above all Schopenhauer. As we shall see later, Jung's speeches and his participation in the discussions were recorded in the Society's archives, and this allows us to trace the origin of several of the basic concepts of analytic psychology to this early period. Gustav Steiner also tells of Jung's ascendency over his student companions, and relates how Jung once boasted to be a descendant of Goethe. "It was not the legend that perplexed me," Steiner adds, "but the fact that he told us about it."

In his autobiography Jung relates that he considers his discovery of Nietzsche's *Zarathustra* as a major event of this period, a book that exerted an extraordinary fascination on him as it did on so many of the young men of his generation. He also tells of a summer's day, while he was working in his room and his mother was knitting nearby in the dining room by the window. They heard a violent noise, like that of an explosion. Jung's mother was frightened; a round walnut table had nearly split in two. Two weeks later another explosion resounded, this time within a cupboard. The blade of a bread knife had "exploded" into four pieces as if it had been cut straight through. Shortly afterward Carl Gustav learned that a fifteen-year-old cousin on his mother's side, Helene Preiswerk, was active in spiritistic experiments and was subject to fits of mediumistic somnambulism. This was the onset of an important episode in Jung's life.

Carl Gustav, who was then twenty-three years old, joined the group that performed experiments with the young medium, Helene Preiswerk.[25] The notes gathered by Jung about these experiments were to be the basis for his subsequent medical dissertation. Meanwhile he devoured whatever he could find that had been written on spiritism and parapsychology, and discussed these matters in the meetings of Zofingia, championing the cause of spiritism, and talking of Zöllner and Crookes as being martyrs of science.

By the end of Jung's medical studies, his interest had shifted toward psychiatry. According to his autobiography, this was the result of a sudden impulse that he felt when reading Krafft-Ebing's *Lehrbuch der Psychiatrie*. But was psychiatry as new to him as he implied? According to the Archive of the Basel University he had taken a course in psychiatry with Professor Wille during the winter semester of 1898 to 1899 and the summer semester of 1900, not to speak of the fact that his grandfather Carl Gustav Jung had been deeply interested in retarded children, and his father had been the chaplain of the Friedmatt Mental Hospital. At that time, in Switzerland, the sole means for becoming a psychiatrist was to join the staff of a university mental hospital as an assistant (resident) and to gradually ascend the degrees of the medical hierarchy. Jung wished to leave Basel, where he felt he was too closely identified with his parents' families, and he applied for a post in the famed Burghölzli Psychiatric Hospital in Zurich.

Meanwhile Jung had passed his final examination, probably in October 1899 and had completed his first period of military service (the so-called Recruits School) as an infantryman in Aarau.[26] He then started his new activity at the Burghölzli on December 11, 1900.[27]

The newly appointed resident who arrived at the Burghölzli was introduced by the doorman into a waiting room, where, a moment later, Professor Eugen Bleuler came to greet him with a few words of welcome. Then, despite the protests of the young physician, the professor would take his suitcase and bring it himself to the resident's room. From this moment on, the young man was to live in a kind of psychiatric monastery. Eugen Bleuler was the personification of work and duty.[28] He was exacting toward himself and toward his staff. He demanded a strenuous amount of work and unlimited devotion to the patients. The residents had to make the first rounds on their wards before the daily staff meeting that took place at 8:30 A.M., where they had to report about their patients. Two or three times a week at 10:00 A.M. there was a meeting called the *Gemeinsame* (a common discussion among the staff about the case histories of new patients), under the direction of Bleuler. Evening rounds had to be made between 5:00 and 7:00 P.M. There were no secretaries, and the residents had to type their case histories themselves, often working until 10:00 or 11:00 P.M. Hospital doors were closed at 10:00 P.M. Junior residents did not have the key and if they wanted to come back after 10:00 P.M., they were obliged to borrow one from an older resident. Bleuler showed the utmost devotion to the patients; he used to make short visits on the wards up to four or six times a day. Dr. Alphonse Maeder who was on the Burghölzli staff in that heroic time reports the following:

> The patient was the focus of interest. The student learned how to talk with him. Burghölzli was in that time a kind of factory where you worked very much and were poorly paid. Everyone from the professor to the young resident was totally absorbed by his work. Abstinence from alcoholic drinks was imposed on everyone. Bleuler was kind to all and never played the role of the chief.[29]

Professor Jakob Wyrsch adds the following:

> Bleuler never blamed a resident. If something had not been done, he would just inquire about the reasons for the omission. There was nothing dictatorial in him. He often came to the residents' room after lunch and took coffee with them. Then he would ask about new developments in medicine or surgery, not to test the knowledge of the residents, but just to keep himself informed.[30]

Jung relates that he spent the first six months there cut off from the outer world and without being able to establish much contact with his colleagues, and that he read the fifty volumes of the *Allgemeine Zeitschrift für Psychiatrie* in his spare time. It is extraordinary that in his autobiography the name of Bleuler is not mentioned once, and that Jung states that when he arrived at the Burghölzli the psychiatrists there were merely interested in describing symptoms and labeling patients, and "the psychology of the mental patient played no role whatsoever." This assertion is unanimously contradicted by all those who worked with Bleuler. In that first year Jung also completed his officer's training course in Basel and received the grade of lieutenant in the Swiss army. His medical dissertation, devoted to the story of his young medium-cousin, appeared in 1902.

He then took a leave of absence to study with Janet in Paris during the winter semester of 1902 to 1903. Curiously enough, this period of his life is also not mentioned in his autobiography. According to informed sources in Jungian circles, he was not a particularly assiduous student and spent much time visiting the points of interest of the French capital.

Upon his return from Paris, Jung resumed his work at the Burghölzli and was married on February 14, 1903, to Emma Rauschenbach, the daughter of a wealthy industrialist of Schaffhausen. Bleuler, who had just introduced the use of psychological tests such as they existed at that time to Burghölzli, asked Jung to experiment with the Word Association Test, research in which he subsequently showed himself very successful.

Those who were acquainted with Jung at that time had the impression that he was starting an unusually brilliant career as a university psychiatrist. The year 1905 was felicitous for him. First, he was appointed First Oberarzt, a title that is equivalent to that of clinical director in an American institution; this means that he came just after Bleuler in the hospital hierarchy. Second, he was appointed head of the outpatient service, in which hypnosis was then gradually being replaced by other forms of psychotherapy. Third, he acquired the envied title of Privat Dozent at the university. He inaugurated his teaching in the winter semester of 1905 to 1906 with a course on psychiatry with demonstrations. This he followed, during the summer semester of 1906, with a course on psychotherapy, also with demonstrations. For several years he was to alternate a course on hysteria during the winter semester and one on psychotherapy in the summer semester.[31]

In 1906 Jung published the first volume of the studies that he had conducted with several collaborators on the Word Association Test. He exchanged his first letters with Freud, and from that time on he was fully dedicated to the cause of psychoanalysis. In November 1906 he published a sharp rejoinder to a mild criticism that Aschaffenburg had made of Freud's theory of hysteria. In February 1907 he went to visit Freud in Vienna. In September 1907 he attended the International Psychiatric Congress in Amsterdam as the spokesman of Freud in the discussion of hysteria. On November 26 of the same year he gave a lecture on psychoanalysis at a meeting of the Medical Society of Zurich, which brought forth a lively discussion in which he was backed by Bleuler.[32] Also that year Jung's *Psychology of Dementia Praecox* appeared, the first monograph devoted to the "depth psychological" investigation of a psychotic patient. Meanwhile the entire staff of the Burghölzli was fascinated with Freud's ideas and sought to elucidate to what extent they could be applied to the understanding of mental illness.

In 1908 Jung had a large and beautiful house built according to his own design in Küsnacht on the shore of the lake near Zurich. He acquired international recognition, and in 1909 he was invited to participate in the ceremonies for the twentieth anniversary of the foundation of Clark University in Worcester, Massachusetts. Freud, as we have seen, was also one of the invited guests, and they both gave lectures in September 1909.

About the same time, Jung left the Burghölzli and moved to his house in Küsnacht, where he was to spend the rest of his life. This turning point in his life has been explained in various ways, but no doubt an acute conflict had developed between him and Bleuler. It was felt that Jung was so involved with psychoanalysis that he neglected his hospital duties, and the two men had frequent clashes of opinion.[33] Jung now devoted himself to his growing private practice, and played an eminent role in the psychoanalytic movement during 1909 to 1913. He was the first president of the International Psychoanalytic Association and the managing editor of the *Jahrbuch*, the first psychoanalytic periodical. Beginning in 1910, during every summer semester Jung gave a course of lectures at the Zurich University entitled "Introduction to Psychoanalysis."

The history of the relationship between Freud and Jung for a long time had been known only through the accounts given by Freud and his disciples. Jung's version of the story was presented by him in 1925 in a seminar for a limited group of students, and in 1962 to a larger audience in his autobiography. Jung never concealed his admiration for Freud and his discoveries. But Freud also represented for him the father figure he had failed to discover in Flournoy and in Janet. Freud was looking for a disciple worthy of succeeding him, and he believed to have found him in Jung. There was thus a period of mutual enthusiasm, which was heightened by the fact that it was not only Jung, but his master Bleuler, who publicly took the defense of Freud. But from the very start there also was a fundamental misunderstanding. Freud wanted disciples who would accept his doctrine without reservation. Bleuler and Jung saw their relationship as a collaboration that left both sides free. At the beginning, the relationship was facilitated by mutual good will. Jung had the same winning and flexible nature as his paternal grandfather; Freud was disposed to be patient and to make certain concessions, although he remained unyielding in regard to his theory of the Oedipus complex and the libido. But these were the ideas that Jung never accepted, and so it was inevitable that Freud would come to reproach Jung for his opportunism, and Jung to reject Freud for his authoritarian dogmatism. The true story of their relationship will probably be known only when their correspondence is published.

Psychoanalysis was not yet the unified doctrine it was later to become. As explained by Maeder, the members of the Zurich psychoanalytic group were not submitted to the strict control of Freud, as were those of Vienna.[34] They felt free to develop their ideas in their own way, so that early divergencies could remain unchecked longer. The first serious ones appeared in 1911 in Jung's *Metamorphosis and Symbols of the Libido*. Then, from December 1911 to February 1912, in Zurich there took place a lively polemic in which Jung intervened as a champion of Freud.[35] In November 1912 Jung was invited to give lectures on psychoanalysis in New York, where he gave his own version of psychoanalysis as being a further development of Freud's basic ideas. Freud became increasingly suspicious of these divergencies. Nevertheless, he entrusted Jung with the mission of defending psychoanalysis against Janet at the International Congress of Medicine held in London in August 1913. But Jung's report on psychoanalysis contained mostly his own views on the subject.[36] When the International Psychoanalytic Association met the following month in Munich, the conflict between Jung and the psychoanalytic group took on a more acute character.[37] In October 1913 Jung resigned from the Psychoanalytic Association and the editorship of the *Jahrbuch*. Jung also resigned his post of Privat Dozent; he gave his last course of lectures in the winter semester of the academic year 1913 to 1914, after which he broke his ties with the Zurich University as he had broken them with Burghölzli in 1909 and with the Psychoanalytic Association in 1913.[38] These events marked the beginning of an intermediate period of six years (from the end of 1913 to 1919), that had long remained the most obscure in Jung's life and whose full meaning has been revealed by his autobiography.

It was known that after his rupture with Freud and his resignation from the Zurich University, Jung devoted himself to his private practice. During World War I he was mobilized intermittently for periods amounting to a few months every year, and from 1914 to 1919 he published very little. In a seminar that took place in 1925, Jung exposed the stages of his confrontation with the unconscious which he undertook during those years.[39] These facts, which had been known only to a small circle of adherents, have now been disclosed to the public through his autobiography. They give us the key to the understanding of Jung's doctrine and the explanation of their origin.

Jung, who had been working at the Burghölzli with severe psychotic patients, had been struck by the frequent occurrence of universal symbols. (which he later called archetypes) in their delusions and hallucinations. This brought him to assume that there existed another realm of the unconscious, besides that of repressed representations, which was the object of Freud's inquiry. Jung had now reached the age, which according to his own theories marks the "turning of life," that is the period between thirty-five and thirty-eight. He undertook a four-day cruise on Lake Zurich with Albert Oeri and three younger friends. Albert Oeri would read aloud to the others the *Nekyia* episode of Homer's Odyssey (the Journey of Ulysses to the Sojourn of the Dead) in Voss' classical German translation.[40] It was a pleasant prelude to the journey through the unconscious that Jung was to accomplish and what he often referred to as his own *Nekyia*. It seems that between 1910 and 1913 Jung made a few attempts to fathom that unknown realm by allowing unconscious material to emerge in dreams and fantasies. Then came the moment when he took the decisive step and launched himself into the solitary and dangerous undertaking.

This new experiment was analogous to Freud's "self-analysis," which was most likely unknown to Jung, although the method was quite different.

Whereas Freud had used free association, Jung resorted to the technique of provoking the upsurge of unconscious imagery and its overflowing into consciousness by two means: first by writing down and drawing his dreams every morning, and second by telling himself stories and forcing himself to prolong them by writing down everything that his unfettered imagination could dictate. It was, according to Jung, on December 12, 1913, that he started these exercises. At first he directed his daydreams by fancying that he was digging into the earth and into underground galleries and caves, where he encountered all kinds of weird figures. On December 18, the archetypes began to manifest themselves more directly. Jung dreamed that he was with a young savage on a desert mountain where they killed the old Germanic hero, Siegfried. Jung interpreted this dream as meaning that he had to kill a secret identification in himself with a heroic figure that had to be overcome.[41] In the subterranean world where his fantasies now led him he met the figure of an old man, Elias with a young blind woman, Salome, and later a wise and learned man, Philemon. By conversing with Philemon, Jung learned that man can teach himself things of which he is not aware.

But the world of archetypes threatened to submerge him, and Jung was aware that this type of exercise was very dangerous. He thus imposed on himself several rules. First, he had to maintain a strong tie with reality. Fortunately for him he had a house, a family, a profession, and a clientele, and he compelled himself scrupulously to fulfill his duties toward all of them.

Second, he had to examine carefully each image from the unconscious and to translate it, insofar as this was possible, into the language of consciousness. Third, he had to ascertain how far the revelations of the unconscious could be translated into actions and incorporated in daily life. As a result of these rules, Jung says, he was able to achieve this descent into Hades and emerge victoriously from a perilous experiment. Jung held that Nietzsche had had a similar experience. His *Zarathustra* was a formidable eruption of archetypical material, but because he was not firmly anchored in reality, living alone without a family and without occupation, Nietzsche was overwhelmed.

One of the most singular episodes of Jung's experiment occurred when one day, while writing under the dictation of the unconscious, he asked himself: "Is this really science what I am doing?" and heard a woman's voice answer him: "It is art!" He denied it, but the voice insisted that it was art and they conversed for a while. He thus perceived that he had in himself an autonomous, feminine subpersonality whom he named his *anima*. The anima spoke with the voice of a lady who at this time had a certain influence on him. Jung was aware that what the anima told him was not true, and he learned after a long confrontation with the anima that her influence could be either beneficial or detrimental; the matter was to establish with her the appropriate relationship.

Another step forward was taken when Jung felt the need to elaborate on these messages from the unconscious. According to his autobiography, on a certain Sunday of 1916 he heard the bell of the main door of the house ring, although no one was to be seen. He then had the impression that a crowd of ghosts was invading the house. Jung exclaimed within himself: "What is the meaning of all this?" and it was as though a chorus answered: "We are the souls of the dead who have returned from Jerusalem without having found what they were seeking." This answer provided the first sentence for his *Septem Sermones ad Mortuos* (Seven Sermons to the Dead), which he wrote in three evenings and published in a private edition, attributing them to Basilides of Alexandria.[42] Subsequently he wrote two other works, probably in the same neo-Gnostic vein, the *Black Book* and the *Red Book*, which have remained unpublished.

Gradually Jung had the impression that he was emerging from a long night, and he made another notable discovery: the process in which he had been engaged had an aim; it led the individual to the discovery of the most intimate elements of his personality, the self.[43] This progression from the unconscious to the conscious and from the ego to the self Jung named the *individuation*. Toward the end of World War I, Jung discovered that a decisive advance in individuation was often marked by the occurrence of a specific quadratic figure in his dreams, more or less similar to the mandalas of India and Tibet. At the beginning of 1919 Jung terminated his experiment, from which he emerged as a new man with a new teaching. He was now to devote the rest of his life to the application and propagation of his discoveries.

We thus see that the intermediate period from 1913 to 1919 was that of a *creative illness*. It had the same features that we have already singled out in Freud's illness. The creative illnesses of both these men succeeded a period of intense preoccupation with the mysteries of the human soul. Both Freud and Jung cut or restricted to the minimum their ties with the university and professional or scientific organizations. Both suffered symptoms of emotional illness: Freud spoke of his "neurasthenia" or his "hysteria"; Jung spent long periods brooding by the lake, or piling stones into little castles. Both men underwent self-imposed psychic exercises, each according to his own method: Freud by free association, endeavoring to recover the lost memories of his early childhood; Jung by forced imagination and the drawing of his dreams. In both men these exercises worked as a self-therapy, although in the beginning they increased their sufferings. These experiments were certainly not without danger. Freud's paradoxical friendship with Fliess can best be understood as a means of maintaining a tie with reality. As for Jung, we do not know what part human relationships might have played during those years, but he deliberately clung to his duties toward his family, profession, and country.

Jung's journey through the unconscious is known to us only from the descriptions he gave of it in his seminars of 1925, and later in his autobiography.

Unfortunately there are no contemporary documents about it comparable to Freud's letters to Fliess, and very few accounts about his professional activity during that period exist. Jung says that during this time he was completely isolated and abandoned by all his friends. This is no doubt exaggerated, since he had kept a few disciples, and a small Jungian group was founded in 1916 in Zurich under the name of Psychologischer Club.[44]

The termination of a creative illness usually occurs rapidly and is followed by a short phase of euphoria, a feeling of exhilaration, and a need for activity. In his seminars Jung sometimes alluded to the feelings of the individual who has overcome extreme introversion and progresses toward extroversion, and to the "sense of relief and freedom" of the man who no longer feels the burden of social conventions.

When the outcome of such an experiment is successful it is manifested in a permanent change in personality. Jung, as Freud, was now able to be the founder and leader of his own school. But in contrast to Freud, Jung also emerged from his creative illness with an increased propensity to intuitions, psychical experiences, and meaningful dreams. It is another characteristic of those who have lived through such a spiritual adventure to attribute a universal value to their own personal experience. Those who have known Jung remember the tone of absolute conviction with which he spoke of the anima, the self, the archetypes, and the collective unconscious. For him they were psychological realities that existed as certainly as did the material world around him.

In the period following World War I Jung emerged from his psychological experience as a man who had undergone a deep-reaching interior metamorphosis. He was now the head of a psychological school and a much sought-after psychotherapist who attracted many patients from England and America. He lived in his beautiful patrician house of Küsnacht with his family, which now included five children: Agathe (born December 26, 1904), Anna (born February 8, 1906), Franz (born November 28, 1908), Marianne (born September 20, 1910), and Emma (born March 18, 1914). His wife was an exceptional woman, an extremely capable mother and housewife, with lively interests, who became his collaborator and applied his psychotherapeutic methods. From his "Journey through the Unconscious" Jung had brought back such an abundance of archetypes and symbols that he could now spend about twenty years elaborating this material, using it in therapy and in whole series of typewritten seminars and printed volumes.

Some of Jung's disciples describe his life during the twenty years that followed as being exclusively devoted to psychotherapy, teaching, and the writing of his books. Jung himself held that his life had been "singularly poor in outward happenings." This is no doubt an oversimplification, since he traveled a great deal and had encounters with outstanding personalities.

In 1919 Jung went to England to lecture on the belief in spirits at the Society for Psychical Research: in his opinion, "spirits" were no more than the projections of the split parts of the unconscious. However, in the following year he again went to England, this time for a longer stay, during which according to his own account, he had a curious experience culminating in a brief vision of a ghost; he subsequently learned that that house was considered to be haunted.[45] In 1920 he also went on a trip to Algiers, Tunis, and to some parts of the Sahara, observing the life and mentality in non-European civilizations with keen interest.

In 1921 one of Jung's best-known works, *The Psychological Types*, appeared.[46] A substantial book of 700 pages, it contains not only his theory of introversion, extroversion, and the typological system, but also a general view of his new theories of the unconscious. Many of his further works are but elaborations of the thoughts he had outlined in this book.

In the early 1920's Jung became acquainted with the reputed sinologist, Richard Wilhelm. In 1923, Jung invited him to give lectures at the Psychological Club in Zurich. But even before Wilhelm published his German translation of the *I Ching*, Jung was passionately interested in that Chinese method of oracles and experimented with it, apparently with some success. But he carefully abstained from commenting on his experiences for many years afterward. In the same years Jung participated in mediumnistic experiments in Zurich with Eugen Bleuler and Von Schrenck-Notzing. They worked with the then famous Austrian medium, Rudi Schneider. Jung, however, refused to draw any conclusions after these experiments and did not even mention them at the time. In 1923 Jung bought a piece of property in Bollingen on the shore at the other end of Lake Zurich, on which he subsequently built a tower, where he was to spend his weekends and holidays.

At this point it seems that in order to increase his knowledge of the unconscious, Jung felt it would be more profitable if he experienced contact with men of primitive societies. Thus, when he went to the United States in 1924 and 1925 he joined a group of American friends and went with them to visit the Pueblo Indians of New Mexico. Jung was impressed by the atmosphere of extreme secrecy that reigned among the Pueblo Indians, and by the unflattering picture of the white given to him by an intelligent Taos man. One year later Jung went to live for several months among an African tribe on Mount Elgon in Tanganyika. Jung, it is said, lived in a little hut just outside the village so that he could watch the daily life and talk to the people without intruding in their lives. He had interesting conversations with some of the men, especially with the medicine man, and kept a diary of his observations.[47]

In the 1930's Jung's fame was growing. In 1930 he was nominated honorary president of the German Society of Psychotherapy. On November 25, 1932, the Zurich City Council decided to grant him the Award for Literature of the City of Zurich, amounting to 8,000 Swiss francs.[48] The ceremony took place in the Zurich Town Hall on December 18.

Jung was lauded because, thanks to him, the "psychology without a soul" of the nineteenth century had been overcome as well as the one-sided conceptions of Freud, because his ideas had exerted a notable influence on literature, and he had himself commented upon literary works.[49]

Jung resumed his interest in mediumnistic experiments during the 1930's. He now felt convinced of the reality of these phenomena, which seemed inexplicable to him. But he carefully abstained from publicly referring to them. He also took great interest in the writings of the alchemists, whom he saw as the precursors of the psychology of the unconscious.

In January 1933 Hitler came to power in Germany. The German Society of Psychotherapy was reorganized according to National Socialistic principles and its president Ernst Kretschmer resigned his post. An International Society was organized with Jung as its president, but this society was a so-called *Dachorganisation*, "roof organization," consisting of the national societies (among which was the German one) and of individual members. As Jung explained later, this had been a subterfuge to enable Jewish psychotherapists expelled from the German society to remain within the organization.

From October 1933 to February 1934, at the Swiss Polytechnical School in Zurich Jung gave a course on the History of Psychology, in which he surveyed the psychological thinking of philosophers since Descartes, with particular emphasis on Fechner, C. G. Carus, and Schopenhauer. But the greater part of the course was devoted to Justinus Kerner and the Seeress of Prevorst. Flournoy was also given recognition for his research on Hélène Smith.

In February 1934 Gustav Bally expressed surprise that Jung should continue his functions within the Society for Psychotherapy and that he had become the chief editor of the *Zentralblatt für Psychotherapie*.[50] Jung replied that Bally was mistaken. It would have been easy for him to give up the entire matter, but he had preferred to help his German colleagues at the risk of being misunderstood.[51] He explained that he had not taken the place of Kretschmer in the former German Society for Psychotherapy, but had been elected president of the newly constituted International Society for Psychotherapy. He protested against the accusation of siding with the Nazis and of anti-Semitism. Bally did not reply, but a few years later he published an appreciation of Jungian psychology of rare impartiality, showing much sympathy for Jung.[52]

In 1935 Jung was appointed as Titular Professor of Psychology at the Swiss Polytechnical School in Zurich. In the same year he founded the Swiss Society for Practical Psychology. In September 1936 he was one of the participants in the tercentenary celebration at Harvard University; he read a paper and was conferred the honorary degree of Doctor of Science.

At the end of 1937 Jung was invited to take part in the celebration of the 25th anniversary of the University of Calcutta, which gave him an opportunity to travel throughout India and Ceylon.[53] However, according to his autobiography, Jung was more concerned with finding his own truth than receiving teachings from the wise men of India. Nevertheless, he experienced a deeply stimulating journey.[54] Jung was also awarded an honorary doctorate at the University of Oxford in 1938, and elected an Honorary Fellow at the Royal Society of Medicine in London on May 15, 1939.

As the international situation was becoming worse, Jung, who had never shown an excessive interest in world politics, became increasingly concerned with them. From interviews he gave to various magazines we see that he tried to analyze the psychology of chiefs of state, and particularly of dictators. On September 28, 1937, he was in Berlin during the historical visit of Mussolini with Hitler and closely observed them for three-quarters of an hour during the parade. From that time on problems of mass psychoses and the dangers threatening the existence of mankind gradually became the focus of Jung's preoccupations.

On October 15, 1943, Jung was granted the title Professor of Medical Psychology with special regard to psychotherapy, by the University of Basel. He gave only two or three lectures and resigned on account of his poor health. He had thus belatedly received from his home city the academic recognition he had missed twenty years before in Zurich.

A new turning point occurred in Jung's life by the end of World War II. His autobiography has shed new light on the hitherto unknown aspects of this further evolution. At the beginning of 1944, Jung reports, he broke his foot and then suffered an infarctus of the heart during which he lost consciousness and felt as if he were dying. He had a cosmic vision, perceiving our planet as from an immense distance, and his personality seemed no more than the sum total of what he had said and done during his life. Then, at the moment when he was going to enter a kind of temple, he saw his physician coming toward him; he had taken on the features of a king of the island of Cos (the homeland of Hippocrates) to bring him back to earth, and Jung had the impression that the life of the physician was in danger while his own was saved (actually the physician died unexpectedly a few weeks later). Jung declared that he first felt a bitter disappointment when he returned to life. Actually something had been changed in him, his thought had taken on a new direction as shown by the works he wrote from that time on. He now was the "old wise man of Küsnacht." For the remainder of his life he was to write books that would startle his disciples (such was his *Answer to Job*), grant interviews to visitors from all over the world, and was given many honors but also suffered many indignities.

At the close of World War II Jung was the object of a campaign instigated by persons who accused him of having exhibited a pro-Hitlerian and anti-Semitic attitude during the period from 1933 to 1940.[55] Jung was accused of having become president of the Nazified German Association of Psychotherapy after the Jewish members had been expelled and Kretschmer had resigned. The accusation of anti-Semitism dwelt on a few quotations from an article in which Jung spoke of a Jewish and an Aryan psychotherapy.[56] To this Jung's friends replied: First, that Jung had never taken the succession of Kretschmer in the German Association, but accepted the presidency of the International Association in order to give what help could be given to the Jewish members.[57] At that time, that is in 1934, people still believed that one could negotiate with the Nazis, and as late as 1936 Jones himself had talks in Basel with Dr. Goering and other representatives of the Nazi movement.[58] Jung's friends replied, second, that the incriminating sentences had not the anti-Semitic meaning that Jung's accusers found in them. Jung held the opinion that there was no universal method in psychotherapy and that the Zen or Yoga, which could be effective in Japan or India, was not necessarily so in Europe; in a similar way, the Swiss who had been deeply rooted for generations in the structures of his specific culture (family, community, canton, and Federation) would need a different kind of psychotherapy than the Jew who had been uprooted and had assimilated the culture of an adopted country.[59] In fact, what Jung said about the lack of a Jewish cultural identity was not very different from what Theodor Herzl and the Zionists had proclaimed. It remains that Jung, like many of his contemporaries, had initially underestimated the pervasiveness of the Nazi evil. Possibly he was influenced by the memories of his grandfather's participation in the German nationalist and democratic movement that was crushed after the Revolution in 1848. Jung may have unconsciously identified the incipient Nazi movement with the patriotic and creative upsurge of the German youth in 1848, and the article he wrote in 1945 shows how he felt about it when he had realized the terrible truth.[60]

Meanwhile Jung and his work were also receiving recognition from many sides. The University of Geneva conferred on him the title of Doctor *honoris causa* on July 26, 1945. A *Journal of Analytical Psychology* was founded in England. In the United States, Paul and Mary Mellon, who had been personally acquainted with Jung, established the Bollingen Foundation, which sponsored the publication of an English translation of Jung's *Complete Works* and other scholarly writings.

On April 24, 1948, the C. G. Jung Institute was opened in Zurich through the initiative of a committee of Swiss, English, and American personalities. This Institute is primarily devoted to the teaching of Jung's theories and methods of analytic psychology. The Institute gives lectures in German and English, and provides for training analysis. It has a well-furnished library containing Jung's unpublished seminars and lectures. It also endeavors to stimulate research inspired by Jungian theories and provides for the publication of the results of this research.

During his entire life Jung had been intensely interested by Gnosticism, and in 1945 he had been stirred by the news that a collection of Gnostic manuscripts had been discovered in the village of Khenoboskion in upper

Egypt. Little could he suspect that he would be presented with one of these manuscripts by an influential friend who had managed to purchase it. Jung was presented with it in November 1953 in Zurich, and it was given the name of *Codex Jung*. Jung provided for the publication of this manuscript by scholars.[61]

Throughout 1955, his eightieth year, Jung was greatly honored and feted. An International Congress of Psychiatry took place in Zurich under the chairmanship of Professor Manfred Bleuler, the son of Eugen Bleuler (under whom Jung had started his psychiatric career at the Burghölzli). Jung was asked to speak of the psychology of schizophrenia, a topic that he had begun investigating as early is 1901. But Jung's eightieth anniversary was also marked by a renewal of the campaign that attempted to stigmatize him for his alleged collaboration with the Nazis. Jung, it was said, had carefully concealed his anti-Semitic feelings and disclosed them at the moment when he believed that Hitler would prevail in Europe. He had allegedly betrayed Freud in 1913 and tried to crush psychoanalysis in 1933.[62] A group of Jewish disciples of Jung published a protest in the *Israelitisches Wochenblatt*.[63] Jung's friends maintained that the accusations against him dwelt on a few sentences that had been taken out of their context, misinterpreted, and sometimes mistranslated, that Jung had openly sided against anti-Semitism, that he had given discreet and efficient help to Jewish refugees in Switzerland, that his name had been put on the "black list" by the Nazis, and that his works were suppressed by the Nazis in Germany and occupied countries. Nevertheless, the campaign against Jung was to follow its course, even after his death.

On his eighty-fifth birthday Jung received the honorary citizenship of the little town of Küsnacht, where in 1908 he had bought the piece of land on which he built his house and where he had lived since June 1909. The mayor handed him the "letter and seal" in a little ceremony, and Jung answered with an address to "mayor and councillors" in his native Basel dialect.[64] To Jung, who was greatly attached to Swiss customs and traditions, this meant a great deal, all the more because this honor is very seldom bestowed in Switzerland. But during the last years of his life solitude grew around him. He had lost his wife on November 27, 1955, and many of his old friends had also died. He became a favorite target for interviewers who eventually prepared entire books of these conversations.[65] After a long period of reluctance he wrote the first three chapters of his autobiography and dictated the rest to his private secretary, Mrs. Aniela Jaffé. He also accepted an invitation to write, along with a few of his disciples, a richly illustrated book, which was to be his last work, *Man and His Symbols*.[66]

Carl Gustav Jung died in his Küsnacht home on June 6, 1961. The funeral ceremony took place in the Protestant church in Küsnacht and was attended by a vast assembly. Reverend Werner Meyer, the pastor of Küsnacht, celebrated him as a prophet who had stayed the overwhelming flow of rationalism and had given man the courage to have a soul again. Two other of Jung's disciples, the theologian Hans Schär and the national economist Eugen Böhler, celebrated the scientific and human merits of their master. The body was cremated and the ashes were deposited in the cemetery of Küsnacht, in the family grave that Jung had designed himself and decorated with Latin inscriptions and the coat of arms of his family, and where already lay the mortal remains of his father, mother, sister, and wife.

The Personality of Carl Gustav Jung

Carl Gustav Jung used to speak of life as being a succession of psychic metamorphoses. His own life was no exception in that regard, and this may explain the contradictory judgments that have been passed about him. In his autobiography he says that from his earliest years he had a rich interior life of which no one was aware, and that he appeared to his parents and teachers as a nervous child. Former schoolmates of Jung told Gustav Steiner that at the Gymnasium Jung was oversensitive and irascible, did not seek the company of his schoolmates, and was distrustful of his teachers.[67] During his student years Steiner was directly acquainted with Jung, and he tells of his vitality, his impetuosity, his eloquence, and his unswerving self-confidence. Jung gave the impression that he felt himself superior to the others, needed companions who would listen to him, and knew how to captivate their minds. He was still oversensitive to the criticism of others, although he was not always tactful himself. No one at that time would have imagined that he could feel himself isolated in the way he reports in his autobiography.

During his Burghölzli period Jung is depicted as an unusually brilliant psychiatrist who exerted a fascination upon the younger members of the staff, even if they sometimes resented his authoritarian and egocentric manners. When Freud came to Zurich on his way to America in 1909, Jung received him as his guest and did not introduce him to the rest of the Burghölzli staff, which considerably antagonized them.[68] Jean-Martin Freud, in his account of Jung's first visit to his father in Vienna, said that Jung did all the talking, speaking only to Freud, and never once attempted to make polite conversation with Mrs. Freud or the children.[69] There are contradictory statements about Jung's attitude during his psychoanalytic period of 1909 to 1913. Above all, we lack information concerning the intermediate years of 1914 to 1919. According to Maeder, Jung was extremely reserved and somewhat distrustful, even toward his most faithful disciples.[70] None of them suspected the interior experience he was then undergoing.

Nearly all the persons who have described Jung's personality refer to the period after 1920, when he had acquired full mastery of his psychological system and his therapeutic method, and was the head of a school. It is that picture that we will henceforth have in mind.

Carl Gustav Jung was a tall, broad-shouldered man with a dominating appearance. He had blue eyes, high cheekbones, a firm jaw, an aquiline nose, and wore a small moustache. All those who met him were struck by an impression of physical and moral strength emanating from him, and by that particular look of stability and firmness of those who are well rooted in their environment. Some people believed to recognize in him a peasant ancestry, although he actually was the descendant of extremely intellectual families. He liked to work with earth, stone, and wood, and took a particular delight in building and constructing. He enjoyed sailing on the Lake of Zurich, and he continued this sport until late in his life.

Jung conveyed the impression of being a practical man firmly anchored in reality, and thus certain visitors were surprised at the absolute conviction with which he spoke of the anima, the self, the archetypes, and other intangibles. However, this strong sense of reality was also manifested in his psychotherapy of which the first phase was to bring the patient back to awareness.

Jung was anything but a bookish scholar. He delighted in human contacts and the little incidents of daily life. When he traveled he not only visited monuments and museums, but took enjoyment in everything he saw. Jean-Martin Freud relates that one day, when his sister Mathilde was in Vienna with Jung and his family and they were all shopping, the Emperor happened to pass.[71] Jung excused himself and ran to join the crowd "as enthusiastic as any boy." Jung was also very sociable. Ernst Kretschmer tells how in the social gatherings following the meetings of the Medical Association for Psychotherapy Jung would take off his jacket and yodel and dance until late at night and generally contribute to the merry atmosphere.[72] He had a keen sense of humor and was known for the varieties of his laughter, which would run the gamut from a low and subtle one to a Homeric guffaw.

Those who had personal contact with Jung, even if it was brief, agree on the brilliance and fascination of his conversation. The most subtle, profound, and sometimes paradoxical views succeeded each other with incomparable speed and ease. In his unpublished seminars some of the unique qualities characterizing his conversations are still to be found, in contrast to the often heavy and laborious style of his books.

Much has been said about Jung's vast erudition. His early interests were in psychology and archaeology. Later, when he began to investigate the symbols, he acquired an extensive knowledge of the history of myths and religions. Among his particular interests were Gnosticism and alchemy, and later the philosophies of India, Tibet, and China. Throughout his life he was greatly interested in ethnology. This variety of interests was reflected in his library. Though he did not collect books for their rarity, he came to possess a unique library of old works on alchemy.

Jung had good linguistic aptitudes. Aside from classical German, and from the Basel dialect that he used in his daily speech, he spoke excellent French. He learned English somewhat later and came to master it fairly well, although he did not succeed in losing his Swiss-German accent. He was proficient in Latin and had a fairly good knowledge of Greek but, unlike his father, he knew no Hebrew. Before he went to east Africa he took lessons in Swahili in Zurich, but he relied mostly on an interpreter in his conversations with the natives.

Many admired the particular talent Jung had of speaking to people in all walks of life; he was equally at ease with simple peasants and with men in the highest positions (no doubt a precious gift for a psychotherapist). Jung also held the opinion that whoever wished to be a good psychiatrist should leave the consultation office and go abroad to visit the prisons and poorhouses, the gaming houses, the brothels and taverns, the distinguished salons, the stock exchange, the socialist meetings, the churches, and the sects. Once he had acquired this experience, he could return to his patients with an increased understanding. Setting aside the part of exaggeration, Jung aptly pointed out the need for the psychotherapist to supplement professional learning with a practical knowledge of life. The saying went in Jungian circles that Jung had been rude and intolerant with certain patients. Contradictory accounts have been given in regard to his attitude toward money; according to reliable sources he demanded 50 Swiss francs an hour for psychotherapy in the early twenties (a very high fee for those days in Switzerland), but there are other reports that many years later people were surprised at the low fees he demanded from his patients. The consensus is that Jung was an unusually skilled psychotherapist who took a different approach with each one of his patients according to their personality and needs.

Jung held the opinion that one cannot be a normal man without accomplishing all one's duties as a citizen. He made a point of participating in all public votes, whether they were of the community, the canton, or the Confederation. A reliable witness said that when Jung was ill, he asked to be transported to the polls. As do many Swiss, Jung took a deep interest in his genealogy, his coat of arms, and the history of his ancestors. He was proud of his service in the Swiss Army and of his rank of captain. He liked to recall events of his military service and to tell about the soldier's hard life in the mountains that he had known during his periods of duty. With his children he liked to play military games of his invention that involved the building, attacking, and defending of stone forts.[73]

We have already told of Jung's wife, who is remembered by all those who knew her as a remarkable woman. Of all the great pioneers of dynamic psychiatry, Jung is the only one whose wife became his disciple, adopted his teachings, and applied his psychotherapeutic method.

Perhaps the most striking feature of Jung's personality was the contrast between his keen perception of reality on one side, and his secret life of meditation, dreams, and parapsychological experiences on the other. He was a most sociable man, but he exemplified in all possible ways Goethe's aphorism: "The highest possible good of the sons of man is personality." He went so far as to say that "society does not exist, there are only individuals." But he also maintained that the individual could not develop unless he enjoyed a certain material stability, hence the value for the sake of mental health of owning a house and a garden.

Jung applied these principles by having a house built for himself in Küsnacht and by participating in the civic and political life of his community. It was a large, splendid house somewhat in the style of a patrician mansion of the eighteenth century, with Latin inscriptions engraved above the main door, including the devise:

> *Vocatus atque non vocatus, Deus aderit*
> (Called or not called, God will be there)

The house was situated in the middle of a beautiful garden. There was a boat house for his sailboats and an observation pavilion giving a magnificent view of the lake (he used it often in summer for psychotherapy). As mentioned above, Jung acquired in 1923 some land in Bollingen, at the other end of the Lake of Zurich, and around 1928 he had a tower built there. As the years went by, he gradually enlarged the original building, adding several rooms, a second tower, and a yard. He would go there to spend his free days, and in that house he could apply another of his favorite principles, namely, that one should live as simply as possible. The Bollingen house had neither a telephone nor an electric light, nor central heating. Water was fetched from the well, and food was cooked on a wood stove that Jung lit himself. There was a room in the house where no one was ever admitted and where he could meditate undisturbed. It is as if the transition from the Küsnacht to the Bollingen house symbolized for Jung the transition from the ego to the self, in other words, the path of individuation.

In his later years Jung became physically weak, but his mind remained alert. He fascinated his visitors with his reflections on the mysteries of the human soul or the future of mankind. He now personified the almost legendary figure of the "old wise man of Küsnacht."

Carl Gustav Jung's Contemporaries

In order to define with more precision the position of analytic psychology among the sciences of the spirit, it might be useful to contrast Jung with three of his contemporaries: the theologian Karl Barth, the philosopher Paul Häberlin, and the anthroposophist Rudolf Steiner.

Denis de Rougemont said that: "Possibly the greatest theologian and the greatest psychologist of our century are two Swiss: Karl Barth (1886–1968) and C. G. Jung."[74] These two men, De Rougemont explained, devoted themselves to the cure of souls and to the edification of a vast system. Both men were the sons of Basel pastors, they were tall and strongly built, were pipesmokers, had a good sense of humor, and neither was "scholarly" in his way of life and his approach to people. Barth also had in common with Jung his pride of being a Swiss citizen and his fondness for military life. In most other respects, however, they differed widely from each other. As a small village pastor, Barth published a commentary on the *Epistle to the Romans*, which revolutionized theological thought. He was called to be professor of theology at German universities. When Hitler came to power, Barth became the great leader of the resistance of the Protestant Church against the Nazis. For that reason he was tried and expelled from Germany. On his return to Switzerland he was appointed Professor of Theology at the Basel University. Barth, who had written countless books and articles, now concentrated upon a vast and all-encompassing treatise of theology, the *Kirchliche Dogmatik*, which has been compared to the *Summa* of Thomas Aquinas for its magnitude and profundity. Barth is unanimously considered the greatest Protestant theologian since Luther and Calvin, and enjoys a universal audience not only among Protestants but among Catholics as well.

If Jung is also widely read among Protestant, Catholic, and Orthodox theologians, it is for quite other reasons. Whereas Barth calls man back to an unconditional obedience to the transcendent God of biblical revelation, Jung deciphers veiled religious values in man, notably in the analysis of symbols and rites. Both Barth and Jung display immense knowledge and scholarship, but whereas the former draws his conclusions from the canonic interpretation of the Bible, the latter shows a predilection for the apocryphal gospels, the Gnostics, and the sacred books of the East. Barth's dogmatics stand resolutely outside psychology; his God is the "entirely other" who speaks to man by the intermediate of his Word and of the Church. Jung, on the contrary, never leaves the realm of psychology. What he calls God is a kind of psychic reality whose source remains mysterious. A synthesis between the thoughts of those two men is hardly conceivable, but at times they happen to share a few ideas, for instance the notion that the essence of man is his complementary relationship to woman and vice versa.[75]

Paul Häberlin (1878–1960), who is usually considered the greatest modern Swiss philosopher, has a few features in common with Jung such as the fact that he too was born in the little town of Kesswil. The son of a teacher, he felt himself destined to the Church ministry, studied theology in Basel, where he had discussions with Jung at the *Zofingia*, and passed his examination in 1900. He then shifted to philosophy, took his Ph.D. in Basel in 1903, and from then on he held teaching posts, devoting himself to the education of problem children. For years he always had two or three difficult children living with his own family. From 1914 to 1922 he was Titular Professor of Philosophy at Berne. His lectures drew a considerable audience and his success was compared to that enjoyed by Bergson at the Collège de France. He occupied this post at the University of Basel from 1922 until his retirement in 1944. Häberlin's writings are remarkable by their extraordinary abundance, the clarity of his style, their didactic qualities, their flawless organization, and their thoroughness that covers every possible detail. His *Philosophical Anthropology* is considered outstanding.[76] Häberlin's work covers the realms of metaphysics, logic, philosophy of nature, religion, esthetics, morals, characterology, psychology of marriage, and education.[77] Some people expressed their surprise that, in spite of his brilliant academic career, the popularity of his lectures, his versatility, and the number of his writings, Häberlin did not enjoy fame comparable to that of Jung. The reason may be that there was no romantic aura around his life and work. Two of Häberlin's writings stand in sharp contrast to the rest of his work: his autobiographical sketch[78] and a little booklet relating his experiences when hunting in the Swiss mountains in which he informally relates his thoughts about life and men.[79] Häberlin considers depression as the effect of an arrogance toward life and a lack of humor, and anxiety as often due to guilt feelings. As for the "anxiety of modern man," he saw in it nothing but a fad comparable to the "Malady of the Century" of the Romantics. Analyzing the varieties of bragging indulged in by hunters, Häberlin extends this notion to the "braggings" of philosophers and psychologists. Häberlin assures that Jung once admitted to him that there actually was such an element in his work, adding that *mundus vult decipi* (the world asks to be deceived).

The contrast between Häberlin and Jung is shown in their respective attitudes toward Freud. Jung's was one of passionate interest and enthusiasm at the beginning, followed by an increasingly critical attitude culminating in a break, after which he rejected almost everything that Freud had taught him. Häberlin's attitude, though one of sharp curiosity, was always critical; however, he could never be called an anti-Freudian. In these two little books Häberlin tells of his encounters with Freud.[80] As much as he respected the man, he was not impressed by his ideas. In the Freudian theory of drives Häberlin merely saw a reflection of Freud's life events. Psychoanalysis is not an all-encompassing psychological theory, Häberlin said, since Freud himself admitted that he could not explain the mystery of artistic and poetic genius. Freud was unable to explain to Häberlin how the drives could be checked by a censor originating in the drives themselves (this was before the introduction of the superego concept). During this conversation Freud contended that religion, philosophy, and science were forms of sublimated sexuality. Häberlin objected that psychology must then also be a form of sublimated sexuality, to which Freud answered evasively: "But it is socially useful." Häberlin took from psychoanalysis all that appeared true to him. The ideas he did not accept he occasionally used as a starting point for his own research, and thus Freud's theory of dreams, which Häberlin rejected, led him to edify a dream theory of his own.[81]

Carl Gustav Jung has often been compared with Rudolf Steiner (1861–1925) the founder of anthroposophy. The teachings of both these men, it has been alleged, are varieties of weltanschauung that stand outside experimental science. The life of Rudolf Steiner is known to us chiefly through his autobiography, which, in contrast to that of Jung, deals mainly with the exterior events of his life, but not much with his innermost spiritual development.[82] The son of a small employee of the Austrian railroads, he manifested early a remarkable gift for mathematics and natural science. He received his secondary and technical education in Vienna, where he heard the lectures of the philosopher Franz Brentano. Unknown to his family, from the age of seven onward he had had parapsychological experiences. He also encountered men who, while living very simply, belonged to a mysterious spiritual world. From the age of twenty-three to twenty-nine he was at the service of a distinguished Austrian family as educator to a difficult child, with whom he obtained remarkable success. He had acquaintances among the intellectual elite in Vienna, for instance with Josef Breuer. Steiner then worked for seven years in the Goethe-Schiller-Archiv, in Weimar, and was entrusted with the edition of the scientific works of Goethe. It was then generally assumed that this part of the great writer's work belonged to an obsolete variety of the philosophy of nature. Steiner maintained, however, that Goethe's approach constituted the basis for a truly scientific approach to the study of nature. It was a time of deep introversion for Steiner. In his autobiography he states that he perceived the world around him as in a dream and that the inner spiritual world was the only reality to him. No doubt it was during these years that Steiner experienced that spiritual adventure that he unfortunately only alluded to in his writings. In 1896, at the age of thirty-five, a deep-reaching psychological metamorphosis occurred in him. He now saw the material world sharply and accurately; his relationships with people became "open." Thereupon he lived for several years in the half-bohemian literary world of Berlin. From 1902 onward he was an influential member of the Theosophic Society but he gradually developed his own ideas in a direction that eventually brought him to found a movement of his own in February 1913, the Anthroposophic Society. In the same year the construction of the great Anthroposophic center was undertaken in Dornach, Switzerland, not far from Basel. It was called the *Goetheanum* in honor of the man whom Steiner held to have reached the highest possible degree of human wisdom. From then on, Steiner's life was identified with the development of the anthroposophic movement and its application to the various fields of human activity.

The word "Anthroposophy" was coined by the Swiss Romantic philosopher Ignaz Troxler (1780–1866) to designate a cognitive method, which, taking as a starting point the spiritual nature of man, investigates the spiritual nature of the world (as sensory organs explore its physical nature and intelligence its abstract laws).[83] Rudolf Steiner contended that every man is able, with the help of a system of psychic training, to become aware of certain latent psychic faculties, by means of which he may acquire a direct knowledge of superior, purely spiritual worlds. His method of psychic training has been compiled in a little book.[84] The prospective disciple should be filled with a deep reverence for truth and live inconspicuously, turning his attention toward the inner life, striving to learn that which can be of use to man and the world rather than to gratify his own curiosity, make a sharp distinction between the essential and the nonessential, and give some time every day to meditation. One basic exercise consists in beholding every being in its temporal dimension, that is, in imagining how it was before and how it will be after. Another is immediately to distinguish sensory perceptions emanating from the animate and the inanimate. When these ways of perceiving have become second nature, the individual is able to sense certain qualities of things that elude others. A further stage confers the faculty to master not only one's feelings and thoughts, but one's sleep and dreams, and to acquire the continuity of consciousness. Eventually the disciple has to endure hard spiritual trials, and Steiner speaks of encounters with mysterious spiritual beings. But in contrast to Jung, Steiner does not consider them mere projections of split-off contents of the unconscious.

Though many people tried to apply Rudolf Steiner's method, it would seem that no one ever reached the point attained by the master. He contended that, as a result of his knowledge of the spiritual world, he was able to state many truths about the structure of man, his ethereal and astral body, reincarnation, and so on. Gradually Steiner's revelations extended across many fields of science, art, and political and economic life. He taught a new architectural style, new principles of painting, declamation, and drama. His new principles in the education of the normal and the abnormal child have aroused wide interest, far beyond the anthroposophical circles.

Similarities between Jung and Steiner were repeatedly pointed out. Both men had parapsychological experiences, both imagined a method of self-training that led them to explore the abysses of the unconscious mind, and both emerged from their respective spiritual journeys with a new personality. No wonder both of them view life as a succession of metamorphoses, the central one being "the turning of life," around the age of thirty-five.[85]

Jung's concept of the shadow and of the projected subpersonalities of man sometimes find their parallel in Steiner. In his commentary of Goethe's *Faust*, Steiner explains that Wagner and Mephisto are different aspects of the personality of Faust.[86] Curiously enough, exactly the same example is often used to illustrate Jungian teaching, which, on this point, is identical with Steiner's. However, in most cases when Jung sees projected contents of the unconscious, Steiner is inclined to see independent spiritual beings.[87]

The essential difference between Jung and Steiner is shown on the use each made of his journey into the unconscious. Both men, as we have seen, underwent what might be called a creative illness toward the middle of their lives (as did Fechner and Freud), and drew the basic concepts of their teaching from that experience. However, Steiner claimed that he had reached a spiritual source of knowledge, which enabled him to make revelations, whereas Jung (and Freud) kept strictly to the practical work offered by their psychotherapeutic practice.

These considerations may help us more accurately to define Jung's position. Jung has been taxed with being a mystic, a metaphysician, a neo-Gnostic, and so on. Jung always maintained that he was not a philosopher but an empirist, who merely described whatever observations he had made in the course of his psychotherapeutic activity. However, the main spring of Jung's concepts is to be found in his *Nekyia*, that is his journey through the unconscious. That experience belongs to the same category as Freud's self-analysis, that is, a creative illness, which was channeled into the foundation of a system of dynamic psychology. Although Jung's conceptual framework differs radically from that of Freud, Jung stands infinitely closer to Freud than to a theologian such as Barth, a philosopher such as Häberlin, or an anthroposophist such as Rudolf Steiner.

C. G. Jung's Work—I—The Notion of Psychological Reality

The germinal cell of Jung's analytic psychology is to be found in his discussions of the Zofingia Students Association and in his experiments with his young medium cousin, Hélène Preiswerk.

It was known from Albert Oeri's reminiscences that Jung often engaged in stimulating discussions with his fellow students. As stated previously, Jung was a member of the Basel section of the Zofingia and an active participant in its weekly meetings. Since an account of the talks and of the main arguments advanced by the discussants was recorded and kept in the Association's archive, Gustav Steiner was able to supplement his personal remembrances with a documentary inquiry and reconstruct the lineaments of Jung's thinking in those formative years.[88] As Steiner points out, "the Zofingia furnished him the invaluable opportunity of shifting from the monologues of his dreams and ponderings to impassionate discussions, and to test the proud rigidity of his ideas by means of intellectual struggles with intelligent companions."

During the first three semesters of his medical studies Jung did not raise his voice in the discussions, not even when a theology student, Altherr, gave a talk about spiritism. In the fourth semester, on November 28, 1896, Jung gave his first talk: "On the Limits of the Exact Sciences." It was a vehement attack against contemporary materialistic science and a plea in favor of the objective study of hypnotism and spiritism. During the discussion Jung emphasized that exact research can be conducted in a metaphysical field. This talk was so successful that the assembly unanimously decided to recommend Jung's talk for publication in the central journal of the association. It is not known why it was not accepted by the editorial committee in Berne. Gustav Steiner points out that the great success of this talk contradicts what Jung wrote in his autobiography, namely, that whenever he told his fellow students about spiritism, they reacted with derision, incredulity, or anxious withdrawal.[89]

In the summer semester of 1897 Jung gave a talk entitled: "A Few Thoughts about Psychology." Jung deplored the current lack of interest in metaphysics. "When the normal man fancies that nothing metaphysical ever occurs in his life, he forgets one metaphysical happening: his death." Death has always been the starting point for transcendent hopes, and these hopes postulate the existence of the soul. The task of a rational psychology is to demonstrate the existence of a soul. The soul can be conceived as an intelligence independent from time and space. Somnambulism was invoked as an argument against the prejudices of materialism. The debate was extraordinarily animated, the number of discussants very large.

In the winter semester of 1897 to 1898 Jung was elected president of the Basel Zofingia. In his opening speech he declared that an educated man should not take an active part in political life. (This was a common attitude held by intellectuals before 1914.)

In January 1899 Jung—to the surprise of the theology students of the group—gave a talk on the theology of Albrecht Ritschl, whom he criticized for his denial of a mystical element in religion. In that year Jung was very active in the discussions. When a medical student gave a talk on the topic of sleep, Jung criticized him for having left aside the phenomenon of dreams, adding that: "In dreams we are our own wish and at the same time various actors."

Jung's last intervention at the Zofingia took place after a talk by a theology student, Lichtenhan, on "Theology and Religion." Jung criticized the idea that God could be experienced. As for himself, Jung said, he never had such an experience. Religious experiences, Jung added, are often accompanied by erotic emotions. Modern psychiatry was inclined to admit the existence of an interior connection between religion and the sexual instinct.[90] The objection to religious experiences occurring in normal men was no evidence against the morbid nature of religious impulses, because all this could originate from one's unconscious. To an argument brought by Paul Häberlin, Jung replied that the concept of a "good God" was self-contradictory. The discussion was fiercer than usual, but Lichtenhan gained the upper hand.

Throughout Steiner's article we notice that Jung already maintained the ambiguous relationship with the theology students that he was to have later with many religious ministers. Namely, they feared his criticism of traditional religion, but approved his attacks against contemporary materialism. Several other points are noteworthy. One is Jung's early preoccupation with the problem of evil, a problem to which he was to devote one of his last works, the *Answer to Job*. Though he was by no means an atheist, Jung attacked several forms of religiosity: traditional religious faith, rationalism (such as he saw in Ritschl's theology), and the interest in "religious experiences" (in William James' style). Remarkable was the tone of Jung's absolute conviction when speaking of the *soul* (a term that had disappeared from psychology) and the way he defined it as immaterial, transcendent, outside of time and space—and yet to be approached scientifically. Among the means of obtaining cognizance of the soul were the study of somnambulism, hypnosis, and spiritistic manifestations. Thus to Jung spiritism was not a matter of occultism, but of unknown psychic phenomena that needed to be investigated with proper scientific methods.

Prior to his entry at the Burghölzli Jung had also made the observations that were to become the object of his dissertation in 1902.[91] There, too, we find several of Jung's most basic ideas in their embryonic state. The observations had been made on a young medium, Helene Preiswerk.

According to Jung's account, the young lady first experimented with turning tables, in July 1899, and at the beginning of August she began to manifest mediumnistic somnambulism. She first incarnated the spirit of her grandfather Samuel Preiswerk, and witnesses admired how accurately she reproduced his pastoral tone, although she had never known him. From then on Jung assiduously frequented the sessions. Helene also personified a number of deceased members of her family and acquaintances, and displayed a remarkable talent for acting. It was surprising how during these sessions she spoke perfect High German instead of her customary Basel dialect. It was not clear to what extent she remembered what she had said during her somnambulic state when the sessions were over, but she always maintained that it was truly the spirits of the dead who spoke through her mouth. She attracted respect and admiration from several relatives and friends who would come to ask her for advice. About one month later she fell into semi-somnambulic states, in which she remained aware of her surroundings but kept a close communication with the spirits. In that condition she said her name was Ivenes, spoke in a quiet, dignified tone, and showed no trace of her usual unstable and giddy character.

In September the young medium was shown Justinus Kerner's book *The Seeress of Prevorst* and her manifestations changed.[92] Following the example of Friedericke Hauffe, she magnetized herself toward the end of the session and talked in an unknown language, which vaguely resembled a mixture of Italian and French.

Ivenes said that she journeyed to the planet Mars, saw its canals and flying machines, and visited the inhabitants of the stars and the spirit world. She was instructed by clear spirits and she herself instructed black spirits. The controlling spirit remained that of her grandfather, Reverend Samuel Preiswerk, with his edifying speeches. Other spirits could be classified into two groups. Some were rather dour and others exuberant. Jung noticed that these characteristics corresponded with the two aspects of the young medium's personality, between which she constantly oscillated. These personifications were gradually replaced by revelations. The medium poured out an extraordinary abundance of details about her own previous lives. She had been the Seeress of Prevorst, and before that a young woman seduced by Goethe—and this allegedly made her Jung's great-grandmother. In the fifteenth century she had been the Countess of Thierfelsenburg, in the thirteenth century she had been Madame de Valours, who had been burned as a witch, and earlier still, a Christian martyr under Nero in Rome. In the course of each of her previous lives she had given birth to children with numerous descendants. In the space of a few weeks she had woven an immense network of fancied genealogies and found herself the ancestor of most people she knew. Any new person she met was immediately integrated into that system. She assured Jung that a female acquaintance of his had been a famous poisoner in Paris in the eighteenth century and had committed all sorts of secret crimes in her present life.

In March 1900 she began to describe the structure of the mystic world with the aid of seven circles: the primary force in the central circle, matter in the second, light and darkness in the third, and so on. Once these revelations were exhausted it seemed that the medium's inspiration declined. Jung said that he left the sessions at this point and that six months later she showed her audience "apports," that is, objects allegedly brought to the sessions by spirits. But here she was caught red-handed and this marked the end of her mediumistic career.

In the discussion of this case Jung defined and classified the various mediumistic phenomena presented by the subject: somnambulism, semi-somnambulism, automatic writing, and hallucinations. He also tried to identify the sources of her mediumistic romances. One of them was Kerner's Seeress of Prevorst, another one the conversations she had heard about Kant's cosmogony. But Jung did not mention the verbal and written traditions about old Basel families. Only in such a setting could a patient have constructed a system of genealogic delusions of such fantastic proportions.

Two features in the medium's story struck Jung. First, her ability, when in a mediumistic state, to accomplish performances that were far superior to those she was capable of in her conscious state. Second, the contrast between the personality of Ivenes, who was serious, poised, and thoughtful, and the medium's unbalanced habitual personality. Jung concluded that Ivenes was none other than the adult personality of the medium that was in the process of elaboration in her unconscious. The patient's psychic growth was impeded by psychological and social obstacles, and the mediumistic career was but a means resorted to by the unconscious to overcome these obstacles. We find here the germ of what was to become Jung's theory of individuation. The medium's romances abounded in stories about overt or secret love affairs and illegitimate births, and Jung thought that her desire for an immense family was the manifestation of a dream of sexual gratification. It seems that only much later did Jung realize that his young cousin had been in love with him and had multiplied her mediumistic revelations in order to please him.

The remainder of the story was divulged by Jung in a seminar given in 1925.[93] Helene Preiswerk left Basel and went to learn dressmaking in Montpellier and Paris. In 1903, Jung visited her in Paris and was surprised to see that she allegedly had forgotten everything relating to the mediumistic sessions. Later she returned to Basel, where she had a dressmaker's shop with one of her sisters, and Jung asserted that she created extremely elegant dresses.[94] Unfortunately, she died prematurely of tuberculosis in 1911.

Jung's dissertation obtained an enthusiastic review from Théodore Flournoy.[95] A curious epilogue was the story of the French painter, Cornillier, who in 1910 discovered that his nineteen-year-old model Reine was a medium, and over a span of two years she had sessions with him during which she made revelations about her previous lives and the lives of deceased persons, and explained to him the complexities of the other world with its laws, morals, and customs, as well as the hierarchy of spirits.[96] The French playwright, Lenormand, understood that the whole process had been brought about by the secret passion of the medium for the painter, and quoted Jung in that regard.[97] This story was the inspiration for his play *L'Amour Magicien.*[98]

When Jung entered the Burghölzli in December 1900, he had quite definite ideas about what psychology should be. He defined it as the scientific study of the human soul, taking manifestations that he called psychological reality as a starting point. He had learned by experience that split-off contents of the unconscious can take the appearance of a human personality, whether they are projected on the outside in the form of hallucinations or take control of the conscious mind as in mediumistic sessions. Following the example of Myers, Janet, Binet, and Flournoy, Jung's interest was directed toward the exploration of these psychological realities.

Carl Gustav Jung's Work—II—The Burghölzli Period

The nine years that Jung spent at the Burghölzli were a period of intensive and concentrated work. After writing his dissertation and a few papers mostly on clinical cases, he concentrated his work on research with the word association test. This test consisted of enunciating to a subject a succession of carefully chosen words; to each of them the subject had to respond with the first word that occurred to him; the reaction time was exactly measured.

Jung once gave a full account of the history of the test.[99] It was invented by Galton, who showed how it could be used to explore the hidden recesses of the mind. It was taken over and perfected by Wundt, who attempted to experimentally establish the laws of the association of ideas. Then Aschaffenburg and Kraepelin introduced the distinction of inner and outer associations;

the former are associations according to meaning, the latter according to forms of speech and sound; they could also be called semantic and verbal associations. Kraepelin showed that fatigue caused a gradual shift toward a greater proportion of verbal associations. Similar effects were observed in fever and alcoholic intoxication. The same authors compared the results of the word association test in the various mental conditions. Then a new path was opened by Ziehen who found that the reaction time was longer when the stimulus word was related to something unpleasant to the subject. Sometimes, by picking out several delayed responses, one could relate them to a common underlying representation that Ziehen called *gefühlsbetonter Vorstellungskomplex* (emotionally charged complex of representations), or simply a complex. Ziehen found that in giving these answers the subject was usually unaware of the connection between his answers and the complex.

At this point Bleuler introduced the test method at the Burghölzli in order to supplement the clinical exploration of patients. Since Bleuler believed that the basic symptom in schizophrenia was the loosening of the tension of associations, it was also logical to check this hypothesis by means of the word association test, and he entrusted Jung with that research. Jung launched himself in wide-scale experimentation with the test together with a few of the other Burghölzli residents. These researches conducted over several years were collected in book form.[100] Jung perfected the technique of the test. Comparing the findings of the test on educated and noneducated people, he found a larger percentage of semantic associations among the noneducated. One of his collaborators found that statistically there were more similarities in tests of persons belonging to the same family, particularly between father and son and mother and daughter.

But Jung's main objective was the detection and analysis of the complexes (in the original meaning given to this term by Ziehen). Jung distinguished among normal, accidental, and permanent complexes. He compared the normal complexes in men and women. In women, erotic complexes were in the foreground with complexes related to family and dwelling, pregnancy, children, and marital situation; in older women he detected complexes showing regrets about former lovers. In men, complexes of ambition, money, and striving to succeed came before erotic complexes. Accidental complexes related to specific events that had happened in the life of the patient. Permanent complexes were of particular interest in patients suffering from hysteria and dementia praecox.

In hysteria Jung found that the associations were submerged by one great tenacious complex related to an old secret wound, but the individual could be cured if one could bring him to conquer and assimilate his complex. In dementia praecox, Jung found one or more fixed complexes no longer to be conquered.

A new approach was now opened to the problem of dementia praecox, supplementing the research in which Bleuler had been engaged during the previous fifteen years. Jung compiled his first findings in a volume: *Psychology of Dementia Praecox.*[101] In this book Jung is still greatly under the influence of Janet and Flournoy. He gives credit to Bleuler, and expresses serious reservations in regard to Freud's theories. The term "complex" was now being used beyond its original scope, so that Jung had to distinguish varieties of complexes: whether they were related to a single event or to a continuous situation, whether they were conscious, partly conscious, or fully unconscious, and whether they were strongly or less strongly emotionally loaded. To demonstrate his method, Jung gives a fairly detailed analysis of one case of a sixty-year-old female patient who had spent almost twenty years at the Burghölzli, and had abundant hallucinations and delusional ideas that seemed all but incoherent. Jung tested her repeatedly with the word association test and let her give free associations for what seemed to be the key words to her delusions. In this way he found himself able to identify a great number of complexes that he classified into three groups: dreams of happiness, complaints of suffering injustices, and sexual complexes. The seemingly incoherent utterances of the patient thus expressed a systematic wish fulfilment to compensate for a life of toil and deprivation. Jung pointed out the analogy of his findings with those of Flournoy in his work with Hélène Smith: her "romances of the subliminal imagination" were a compensation for the mediocrity of her life. Jung himself had the same experiences in his work with the young Basel medium, except that he had found that her subliminal romances were an attempt to force the obstacles that impeded her development. The Burghölzli patient, in contrast, was imprisoned in her delusions.

But why could the complexes be conquered in hysteria and not in dementia praecox? Jung submitted the hypothesis that the complexes of the latter produce a toxin that exerts a noxious action on the brain, thus rendering the disease irreversible. This theory conflicted with Bleuler's own theory of dementia praecox, namely, that the primary cause of the illness was the action of a hypothetical toxin upon the brain and that the complexes did not cause the symptoms but gave them their form. In a joint declaration Bleuler and Jung defined their divergencies in that regard.[102] In the same year Jung enunciated the supposition that the delusional ideas of a psychotic were the expression of his efforts to create a new vision of the world.[103]

Meanwhile Jung had redirected the application of the word association test. In 1905 an elderly gentleman came to him because money had been stolen from him and he suspected his ward, an eighteen-year-old boy. Jung gave the young man a word association test that had been adapted to the case. The young man responded in such a way that Jung was certain he merely had to say "you have stolen" to him to obtain a confession, and this actually happened.[104] There was also the story of a theft of money in a hospital that could have been committed only by one of three nurses. Jung gave them the test and found the culprit, who incidentally was not the nurse who had been suspected most.[105]

For a time Jung believed that he had discovered a new method for detecting criminals, but he soon realized that things were not that simple. Freud pointed out that the subject did not react to the test according to his objective guilt, but according to his subjective guilt feelings and anxieties.[106] After several years of intensive application of the test, Jung ceased to use it altogether. He never disowned it, and its practice was kept at the C. G. Jung Institute for its disciplinary value. But Jung proclaimed that "whosoever wishes to know about the human mind will learn nothing, or almost nothing, from experimental psychology."[107]

C. G. Jung's Work—III—The Psychoanalytic Period

Jung's acquaintance with psychoanalysis dated back to the beginning of his stay at the Burghölzli. In an interview given in 1957[108] Jung stated that as early as 1900[109] Bleuler had requested him to report on Freud's *Interpretation of Dreams* during one of the doctors' discussion evenings.[110] Freud is quoted four times in passing throughout Jung's dissertation of 1902, a few times in his articles written from 1902 to 1905, and in his writings on the word association test Jung refers to Freud as an authority. Jung's interest had first been directed to the split-off contents of the unconscious (Janet's subconscious fixed ideas), then he assimilated these to Ziehen's emotionally loaded representation complexes, and now he encountered them again in Freud's traumatic reminiscences.[111] From then on Jung studied Freud's work with passionate interest. In it he found the confirmation of his own findings with the word association test, but his own findings also acquired a new meaning in the light of Freud's ideas. Jung's writings of that period express enthusiasm for Freud, an aggressive attitude toward the adversaries of psychoanalysis, but also a quiet statement of his divergencies with Freud. In the foreword to *Psychology of Dementia Praecox*, dated July 1906, Jung writes that he does not concur with Freud's ideas on the importance of the infantile sexual trauma, that he does not place sexuality as much in the foreground as Freud does, and that he considers Freud's psychotherapy as "at best a possible one."

Jung's psychoanalytic period extends from 1909 (when he left the Burghölzli), to 1913 (when he left the Psychoanalytic Association). During that period a gradual change occurred in his own concepts: at first he did no more than propose alternatives to certain of Freud's ideas, but soon his divergencies became unacceptable to Freud.

Jung never accepted the concept of the Oedipus complex. In an article published in 1909, entitled "The Meaning of the Father for the Destiny of the Individual," Jung recalls that he had been struck by the way in which the word association test brought similar responses between fathers and sons and mothers and daughters.[112] Both boys and girls, he says, unconsciously conform to family attitudes as if there were a kind of psychic contagion. Once these attitudes are fixed, they will persist throughout life. Jung illustrated with several impressive case histories how these attitudes unconsciously directed the lives of individuals and constitute what is called destiny. In short, Jung attributed to that early assimilation of family attitudes ("identification" in later terminology) all the effects that Freud ascribed to the resolution of the Oedipus complex. In a footnote Jung contended that libido is what the psychiatrists called will and striving.

In the following year Freud published his case history of Little Hans. Shortly afterward, in the same journal, Jung published a paper entitled "Psychic Conflicts in a Child," a story somewhat parallel to that of Little Hans.[113] Just as the phobias of this five-year-old boy had started after the birth of a baby sister, Jung's four-year-old Anna had problems following the birth of a little brother. This event elicited numerous preoccupations and fantasies in the mind of the little girl, not only relative to the origin of children, but also about life after death and before birth. The child had even spontaneously imagined the theory of reincarnation. Her father had decided that it was best to answer all questions as simply and frankly as possible. The enlightenment included an explanation of the role of the father, and Anna was eventually completely reassured. In a later edition of the same paper Jung mentioned that the child had subsequently set aside the "enlightening" explanation and returned to a childish theory.

An early application of psychoanalysis to social psychology was Jung's paper on "Psychology of Rumors": a thirteen-year-old schoolgirl had told her schoolmates of a dream she had had about her teacher. The story aroused a scandal, and the girl had been suspended from school. However, the school board was then ready to readmit her on psychiatric approval. Jung, who was asked to make the report, gives the dream as told by the subject as well as the version of how it was related by eight witnesses. The dream itself contained nothing scandalous, but the witnesses had elaborated a number of scabrous details. Jung concluded that the dream indeed represented the unconscious wishes of the girl and that the witnesses had supplied new versions, as if they had interpreted the dream in a psychoanalytic fashion.[114]

Meanwhile Jung had launched himself in the preparation of a work of great scope. With Freud's encouragement, several psychoanalysts had been engaged in the study of myths, particularly Abraham, Rank, and Silberer, as well as Riklin in Zurich. Jung, who had been interested for a long time in the history of religion, resumed his old studies. As he states in his autobiography, he read the works of Creuzer with particular interest.[115] But he did not only give a psychoanalytic interpretation of myths, he also used his knowledge of myths as a means of understanding his patients' dreams and fantasies. Jung devoted more than four hundred pages to a mythological interpretation of a few daydreams and fantasies of a person he had never met. This work was published in two parts in the *Jahrbuch*, in 1911 and 1912.[116]

In 1906 Flournoy had published a few notes he had received from a young American student, Miss Frank Miller.[117] This young lady was greatly prone to experiences of suggestion and autosuggestion. While daydreaming during a cruise in the Mediterranean, she heard a poem of three stanzas, "Glory to God." During one night when she was on a train she created a hypnagogic poem of ten verses called "The Moth and the Sun." Some time later, after an evening of trouble and anxiety, she fancied a hypnagogic drama centered around the figure of an Aztec or Inca hero, Chiwantopel. While recording these fantasies, Miss Miller tried to trace their source, either to previous events in her life or to her readings. It is on this scanty material that Jung worked to find an interpretation based on mythology and the history of religion.

Jung's work does not make easy reading. In its original German version it abounds with untranslated Latin, Greek, English, and French quotations, and long etymologies copied from dictionaries. The reader is submerged under an avalanche of erudite references to the Bible, the Upanishads and other sacred books; to the Gilgamesh epic and the Odyssey; to poets and philosophers (particularly Goethe and Nietzsche); to archaeologists, linguists, and historians of religion; to Creuzer, Steinthal, and other students of mythology, not to speak of Jung's contemporary psychologists, psychiatrists, and psychoanalysts. Amidst this wealth of material the reader is constantly afraid he will lose the thread, but from time to time he is brought back to Miss Miller. It seems as if the author wished to liberate himself of an excess of material accumulated over the years. Even a hymn composed by his grandfather Samuel Preiswerk is quoted. But there still are few references to the works of ethnologists (aside from Frobenius), and almost nothing from the Gnostics and alchemists.

In spite of the arduous reading, Jung's work aroused much interest. It brought three novelties to the psychoanalytic world. The first was a departure from Freud's original concept of libido: Jung finds it impossible to explain the phenomenon of psychosis by the withdrawal of the libido from the exterior world. This would only be possible if the libido were more than sexual instinct, and for that reason Jung now identifies libido with psychic energy. Second, Jung contends that the libido in its new meaning naturally expresses itself only through symbols. As Jung said later in one of his seminars, the libido always appears in crystallized form, that is, in the form of universal symbols, as we know them from the study of comparative mythology. One sees here the beginnings of what was soon to become Jung's concept of the collective unconscious and the archetypes. Third, among all the myths discussed in this book, one emerges as particularly important: the myth of the hero. Rank had already treated the myth of the birth of the hero. Jung now tells of the hero's battle for deliverance from the mother and of his struggle with a monstrous beast.

The book, in its original German version, terminated with a somewhat ambiguous remark that could apply to Freud's adversaries as well as to Freud himself: "I do not consider it the business of science to compete for the last word, but rather to work toward the augmentation and deepening of knowledge."[118]

In September 1912 Jung gave a series of nine lectures on psychoanalysis in New York. They were compiled and published in 1913.[119] Jung points out that the psychoanalytic theory had changed over the years and that Freud had abandoned his early theory that all neuroses could be traced back to a sexual trauma in childhood. Similarly, Jung purports to develop the psychoanalytic theory even further, and particularly to revise the theory of the libido. First, the equation of the libido with the sexual drive seems to him untenable. Why should the pleasure experienced by the infant in suckling be of a sexual nature rather than the gratification of the nutritive instinct? Freud's concept would imply that hunger is a manifestation of the sexual drive; but one could very well, and without less reason, describe the sexual manifestations proper as developments of the nutritive instinct! Unfortunately Freud used the term "libido" as "sexual desire," but later extended its meaning so far that Claparède remarked that he used it in the sense of "interest." All the difficulties, according to Jung, would be settled by giving the word "libido" the meaning of "psychic energy." It is the energy that manifests itself in the life process and is perceived subjectively as striving and desire. This would introduce a revolution in psychology similar to that produced in physics by Robert Mayer when he proposed the theory of the transformation of energy. This readaptation would, moreover, deprive the adversaries of psychoanalysis of a justified argument, namely, that "libido" is a mystical concept. Taken in this new sense the term "libido" would become an abstract concept (as is the concept of energy in physics), and a pure hypothesis.[120] In the light of these new principles, the evolution of the libido must be understood in a new way. Jung distinguishes three stages: The first is the presexual, that is up to three or five years of age; here the libido, alias psychic energy, is at the service of growth and nutrition. There is no infantile sexuality proper, and Jung strongly criticizes the term "polymorph perverse" ascribed by Freud to the infant. The second stage extends from that time until the beginning of puberty. Freud calls it the "latent period," but Jung, on the contrary, asserts that the germs of the sexual instinct appear during this time, to develop in the third stage when the individual will reach sexual maturity. After reviewing the implication of this revised libido theory in regard to perversions and psychosis, Jung dwells upon the implications in regard to neurosis. He does not accept the principle that the roots of neurosis lie in remote childhood, but rather in present situations. (It is, Jung says, as if the political difficulties of nineteenth-century Germany were attributed to the ancient Roman conquests.) Then how are the "parent complexes" to be explained? Jung holds that the natural evolution of the libido is stopped because of present difficulties that cause a reactivation of past conflicts. Moreover, Jung does not accept Freud's notion of the Oedipus complex. He admits that the little boy or girl is more or less intensively attached to the mother, which may bring a certain rivalry with the father, but the mother is viewed as a protective and nourishing figure, not as the object of incestuous wishes. A true childhood neurosis is more likely to appear when the child starts school, and later neurosis may break out when the individual must face marriage or earning his living. In presence of a neurosis, the true question is: "Which task does the patient wish to avoid?" "Which difficulty in life is he trying to escape?" (We may note at this point that Jung's concept of neurosis is reminiscent of both Janet's and Adler's views.)

In regard to psychotherapy, Jung recalls that the confession of a burdensome secret may have an immensely beneficial effect. This has been known for centuries and is still valid, although the healing process is quite different from that of psychoanalysis. As for the psychoanalytic technique itself, Jung emphasizes the role of dream interpretation, acknowledging Maeder's teleological function of dreams and insisting upon the help brought by comparative mythology. Jung also stresses an idea that at the time was quite new: the psychoanalyst should have undergone analysis himself. Self-analysis he considers an impossibility. He concludes that psychoanalysis will be able to elaborate a phylogenesis of the spirit.

An illustration of these views may be found in a lecture that Jung gave in London in August 1913.[121] There was the story of a neurotic young man who reported the following dream: "I was going up a flight of stairs with my mother and sister. When we reached the top I was told that my sister was soon to have a child." In the orthodox psychoanalytic view, this was a typically incestuous dream. Jung objected: "If I say that the stairs are a symbol for the sexual act, whence do I obtain the right to regard the mother, the sister, and the child as concrete; that is, not as symbolic?" An inquiry into the present situation showed that the young man had guilt feelings because he had finished his studies several months previous and could not bring himself to exercise his profession. In that light the patient's dream was not so much the fulfilment of infantile incestuous wishes as the call to fulfil the duties he had hitherto neglected.

Carl Gustav Jung's Work—IV—The Intermediate Period

At the end of 1913 Jung broke with Freud and soon afterward resigned his post at the Zurich University. In 1921 his *Psychological Types* offered a full-fledged new system of dynamic psychiatry.[122] During the intermediate period (1914–1920) he did not publish much, but achieved three great tasks. Intimately connected with each other were his journey through the unconscious, his preoccupation with psychological types, and his study of Gnosticism.

We have seen that in December 1913 Jung started his *Nekyia*, applying to himself a method of active imagination with analysis of the emerging symbols. He now applied to his own fantasies as they came forth the same elucidation of symbols with the help of comparative mythology that he had practiced with Miss Miller's fantasies. This experiment was the source of several of the most basic concepts of Jung's psychology: the anima, the self, the transcendent function, and the process of individuation. All these were psychic realities that he experienced personally. In an article published in December 1916, Jung outlined his new concepts of the unconscious, stating that there are several ways of coping with the unconscious.[123] One can try to repress it, or to exhaust it through reductive analysis, but these are impossible attempts because the unconscious can never be reduced to inactivity. One can also be submerged by the unconscious as happens with schizophrenics. One can try to identify oneself in a mystic way with the collective psyche. A preferable solution is to undertake a dangerous but rewarding fight against the contents of the unconscious in order to subdue them. This is the symbolic meaning of those myths that tell of a hero's fight against a monster and of the victory that will secure a treasure, an invincible weapon, or a magic talisman. "It is in the achievement of victory over the collective psyche that the true values lies." This sentence, which most probably refers to his own experience, seems to indicate that before the end of 1916 Jung felt that he had already won the main victory in his self-experiment.

Jung's self-experiment enabled him to ascribe a wider meaning to his earlier concepts of the psychological types. He had presented a first brief sketch of his typology at the Munich Psychoanalytic meeting of September 7 and 8, 1913, and published it in Flournoy's journal in December of the same year.[124] In the contrast between the psychological syndromes of hysteria and of schizophrenia he saw the extreme degree of a contrast between two attitudes that also exists in normal individuals, extroversion and introversion. These two attitudes may undergo modifications in the same individual. Each one entails a different vision of the world, and this may also explain the misunderstandings between introverts and extroverts (such as those between Freud and Adler). Now Jung's journey through the unconscious led him to understand that extroversion and introversion were not just two opposite attitudes but two complementary psychological functions. He experienced the gradually increasing state of introversion himself when the perception of the outer world fades while interior visions and fantasies become the main reality, and later he experienced the gradual return from extreme introversion to overt extroversion with its sharpened perception of the world and other men, and its need for activity and enjoyment.

During these years Jung, who was well read in the history of religion, was seized with a great interest in the Gnostics. These heretics, who flourished in the middle of the second century A.D., claimed to replace pure faith by knowledge. They considered their visions to be realities and systematized them into cosmogonic systems. Jung hailed the Gnostics as the precursors of the psychology of the unconscious. Obviously, Jung assumed that these men had drawn their "Gnosis" from the same source from which he drew his knowledge of the unconscious.

If we compare the material utilized in *Metamorphoses and Symbols of Libido* (1911–1912), and *The Psychological Types* (1921) we can measure how much Jung had enlarged his knowledge: besides the Gnostics he now quotes the Fathers of the Church, medieval theologians, classic poems of ancient India, Chinese philosophers, and a number of ethnological works. This variety of sources explains why *The Psychological Types* is a somewhat puzzling book. The reader who opens that volume of seven hundred pages expecting it to start with a clear psychological description of the psychological types is soon disappointed. The clinical description of the types occupies only the last third of the book, after a lengthy survey encompassing the works of theologians, philosophers, psychologists, poets, and historians of science. But one would be mistaken to see in this survey a mere display of erudition. The notion that there is an introverted and an extroverted vision of the world may help us to understand the divergences and conflicts of opinion between certain philosophers or theologians. The quarrels between Tertullian and Origen, Saint Augustine and Pelagius, the partisans and adversaries of the transsubstantiation dogma, the medieval realists and nominalists, and Luther and Zwingli, were rooted in the divergences between a highly introverted and a highly extroverted vision of the world. So was Schiller's distinction between sentimental and naïve poetry. (Actually Schiller described the difference he observed between himself, the sentimental introverted poet, and Goethe, the naïve extroverted poet.) Such was also Nietzsche's distinction between the apollonian and the dionysian attitudes, and the contrast in the characters of Prometheus and Epimetheus in Spitteler's poem, *Olympic Spring*. Wilhelm Ostwald had recently distinguished two types of scientists, the classic and the romantic; Jung equated them with the introvert and the extrovert types.[125]

Most accounts of Jung's psychological types are oversimplified. To grasp Jung's theory in its full complexity, nothing can replace reading the arduous Chapter X of *The Psychological Types*. Jung's contribution in the *festschrift* for Morton Prince would be a good introduction.[126] Introversion and extroversion are attitudes, spontaneous or voluntary, that are present in each individual in varying degrees. Introversion is the attitude of those individuals who derive their motivations chiefly from within themselves, that is, from inner or subjective factors, and extroversion is the attitude of those persons who derive their motivations chiefly from outside, that is from external factors. The same individual can be more or less an introvert or an extrovert or may shift from one attitude to the other in the course of his life. But one of these attitudes may be fixed in individuals and then one speaks of introverted or extroverted types. It is not always easy to classify an individual because there are intermediate types and, as Jung put it, "every individual is an exception to the rule." A high degree of introversion or extroversion tends to arouse a compensatory process from the subdued attitude in the unconscious. This extroversion of the introvert (or vice versa) is a kind of return of the repressed. Introversion and extroversion entail a specific vision of the world. However, an introverted individual may have an extroverted vision of the world and vice versa. For individuals who are strongly introverted or extroverted, it is difficult to understand an individual of the other type, at least intellectually. But because introverts and extroverts are complementary to each other, marriages between them are frequent and often happy.

To the notions of introversion and extroversion Jung added the system of the four fundamental functions of the conscious psyche. They comprise two pairs of opposite functions: the two rational functions of thinking and feeling, and the two irrational functions of sensation and intuition. Thinking is the opposite of feeling, and sensation is the opposite of intuition. (The word "irrational" does not mean that these functions are antirational, but rather are outside the field of rationality.) The four functions exist in every individual, but in each one function predominates that places the opposite function in a position of inferiority. For instance, when thinking is predominant, feeling is in an inferior position. But here too one can see how a kind of return of the repressed occurs. In a strongly intellectual individual it can take the form of outbursts of grotesque sentimentality, and in a highly sentimental individual that of silly intellectual opinions. The matter is, however, even more complex, because there often exists an auxiliary function, next to the principal one.

The notion of introversion and extroversion and of the four functions enabled Jung to establish a system of eight psychological types, of which four are extroverted and four are introverted.

The *thinking-extroverted* type directs his life and that of his dependents according to fixed rules; his thinking is positive, synthetic, dogmatic. The *feeling-extroverted* type keeps to the values he has been taught, respects social conventions, does what is proper, and is very emotional. The *sensation-extroverted* type is pleasure-loving, sociable, and adjusts himself easily to people and circumstances. The *intuition-extroverted* type shows insight in life situations, detects and is attracted by new possibilities, is talented for business, speculation, and politics. Then we have the *thinking-introverted* type who is described at length by Jung who appears to have taken Nietzsche as his model for it: a man who lacks practical sense, he isolates himself after unpleasant experiences with his fellow men, desires to go to the bottom of things, and shows great boldness in his ideas, but is often hindered by hesitations and scruples. The *feeling-introverted* type is an unassuming, quiet, oversensititive individual, difficult to understand by his fellow men; in the case of woman, she exerts a mysterious power over extroverted men. The *sensation-introverted* type is also a quiet person who looks upon the world with a mixture of benevolence and amusement, and is particularly sensitive to the esthetic quality of things. The *intuitive-introverted* type is a daydreamer who ascribes the utmost value to his inner trend of thought and who is easily considered odd or eccentric by the others.

As a mnemotechnic device Ania Teillard[127] imagined the story of the dinner of the psychological types: The perfect hostess (feeling-extroverted) receives the guests with her husband, a quiet gentlemen who is an art collector and expert in ancient paintings (sensation-introvert). The first guest to arrive is a talented lawyer (thinking-extroverted). Then comes a noted businessman (sensation-extroverted) with his wife, a taciturn, somewhat enigmatic musician (feeling-introverted). They are followed by an eminent scholar (thinking-introverted) who came without his wife, a former cook (feeling-extrovert), and a distinguished engineer (intuitive-extroverted). One vainly waits for the last guest, a poet (intuitive-introverted), but the poor fellow has forgotten the invitation.

The sources of Jung's typology are manifold. One was the current psychiatric preoccupation of finding correlations between clinical entities and psychological types. Janet, Bleuler, Kretschmer, and Rorschach utilized this approach at different times.[128] Basic to Jung's conception was his personal, real-life experience of the process of increasing introversion and the return to extroversion in the course of his creative illness. And finally there was Jung's extensive research throughout the history of philosophy, theology, and literature. But other anticipations of Jung's typology could be found, besides those indicated in his historical survey.

The mystical writer Swedenborg (whose works Jung had devoured in his youth) claimed to have visited heaven and hell.[129] He had found two separate heavenly kingdoms and two categories of angels. Celestial angels receive the divine truth directly from the Lord, perceive it inwardly, and immediately recognize it as such. Spiritual angels receive truth indirectly through their intelligence, and examine whether it is such before accepting it. It suffices to read poet instead of angel, and poetic inspiration instead of divine truth, to have Schiller's distinction of naïve and sentimental poets and poetry.[130]

Oliver Brachfeld[131] pointed out the similarity between Jung's types of introversion and extroversion and the two types of intellectual attitudes described by Binet.[132]

For three years Binet conducted investigations on his two young daughters, Armande and Marguerite, by means of numerous psychological tests of his invention. Armande he called a subjectivist and Marguerite an objectivist. Asking each child to write a given number of words at random, Binet found that Armande gave more abstract words and more related to fantasies and ancient memories; Marguerite chose more concrete words and words associated with present objects and recent memories. In Armande there was more spontaneous imagination, whereas Marguerite was able to control the course of her imagination. Armande also described an object less methodically than Marguerite, who stated exactly the situation of the object in space. Spontaneous attention dominated in Armande, active, voluntary attention, in Marguerite. Armande could measure more accurately intervals of time, and Marguerite those of space. Binet concluded that there are two different attitudes and qualities of the mind, which he calls *introspection* and *externospection*. Introspection, as illustrated by Armande, is "the knowledge we have of our inner world, our thoughts, our feelings." Externospection is "the orientation of our knowledge toward the exterior world as opposed to the knowledge of ourselves." Thus Armande better described her states of consciousness but was less accurate in her descriptions of the outside world, and the reverse was true for Marguerite. Binet stressed that sociability and the aptitude to mix with others is not necessarily bound to one or the other attitude. However, the "introspection type" is more gifted for art, poetry, and mysticism, and the "externospection type" is more gifted for science.[133] Binet concluded that these two mental types played a great role in the history of philosophy and this would explain among other things the medieval quarrel between the realists and the nominalists.

Since Binet's book appeared approximately at the time that Jung studied in Paris with Janet, Jung may have read it and then forgot it, and this would be one more example of those cryptomnesias, so frequent in the history of dynamic psychiatry.

Carl Gustav Jung's Work—V—Analytic Psychology

After Jung left the psychonalytic movement, he no longer called himself a psychoanalyst, nor did the Freudians recognize him as such. From the very beginning he had brought forth a number of non-Freudian concepts and now he was free to follow his own ideas and to develop his system, which he called analytic psychology or complex psychology. His new concepts were defined in 1922 in the last chapter of *The Psychological Types*. This is the material that he was to develop for the rest of his life in at least twenty books and numerous articles. In the following we shall endeavor to give a very succinct outline of Jung's analytic psychology. A complete survey of that broad system would itself require a five-hundred-page book, which unfortunately Jung never wrote himself. We must be content with a brief outline of the main points of analytic psychology: psychic energetics, the unconscious and the archetypes, the structure of human psyche, the individuation, the dreams, and Jungian concepts of psychosis and neurosis.

Psychic Energetics

As did many of his contemporaries, Jung developed a system of psychic energetics. His ideas on that subject are to be found in his *Metamorphoses and Symbols of Libido* and in a book on psychic energetics.[134] At the end of the nineteenth century the word "libido" was often used to indicate "sexual desire" or "sexual instinct," Moll gave it the connotation of the stages of evolution of the sexual instinct, and Freud extended its meaning to the sum total of the evolution stages and possible transformations of the sexual instinct. What Freud did for Moll, Jung did for Freud; he extended the meaning further—namely, to psychic energy as a whole. Later Jung ceased to use the word libido altogether and spoke only of psychic energy.

Thus the question of the relationship of psychic energy to physical energy necessarily arises. Like Janet, Jung assumes that such a relationship exists but cannot be demonstrated, and that in contradistinction to physical energy, psychic energy cannot be measured. No equivalents can be established between physical and psychic energy. Otherwise Jung assumes that the ruling principles of physical energy are paralleled in psychic energy, namely, the principles of conservation, transformation, and degradation of energy. But to the difference of physical energy, psychic energy has not only a cause but an aim.

Psychic energy has its source in the instincts and can also be transferred from one instinct to the other (sublimation is but one among other various processes). Throughout these transformations the quantity of energy remains constant; when energy seemingly disappears, it simply means that it has been stored in the unconscious, from whence it can again be mobilized. Though we have no means of measuring psychic energy, it is possible to estimate quantitative differences in energy. There are indicators to make a rough estimate of the amount of energy that charges a complex. Such are the number of constellated words and the intensity of disturbing elements in the word association test.

There are also levels in psychic energy. Jung, following the example of Janet, speaks of higher and lower psychic energy. Even the principle of entropy can be applied to psychology insofar as there exist closed systems of psychological nature. The old schizophrenic patient who has lost contact with the exterior world and remains motionless and mutistic manifests an extreme degradation of psychic energy and an increase of entropy.

Jung assumes that psychic energy is directed either in the form of progression or regression. Progression is a continuous process of adjustment to the demands of the external world. Failure to do so produces phenomena of stagnation or regression, which result in the reactivation of unconscious contents and old interior conflicts. Nevertheless, progression should not be confused with evolution: an individual can remain well adjusted to the demands of the exterior world but lose contact with his interior psychic reality, and in such a case a temporary regression might be useful insofar as it would enable him to adjust to the demands of the unconscious.

In that same perspective, symbols become transformers of energy. When a symbol is assimilated, a certain amount of psychic energy is liberated and can be used on the conscious level. Religious and magic rites, such as those of primitive people before the hunt or warfare, are means of mobilizing energy for definite purposes.[135]

The Collective Unconscious and the Archetypes

For several years Jung was mostly concerned with the personal unconscious, though from the very beginning he did not assign a purely regressive character to the personal unconscious. (We recall the story of the young medium in one of whose unconscious personalities Jung saw the future personality trying to break through.) Then, in his experiments with the word association test, Jung had to deal with complexes, and he found all possible varieties of them from the small groups of unconscious representations to the full-fledged dual personalities. Two features seemed remarkable: the autonomous development of complexes and their tendency to assume the form of a personality (as can be seen in dreams, spiritism, mediumism, possession, and multiple personality).

The next step was the notion of *imago*. Freud had emphasized the importance and lasting influence of the relationships of children with their parents; what mattered was not how the father and mother really were, but how the child saw them subjectively. Jung proposed to call this subjective representation the *imago*, a term inspired by the title of Carl Spitteler's novel.[136] Freud pointed out that the *imago* unconsciously directs the choice of the love-object. Jung wondered about the discrepancies between the real mother and the mother imago. He came to assume that the main fact was the preexistence in man of an unconscious image of woman. The concept of *imago*, which was one of the most popular among psychoanalysts around 1907, gradually lost its importance, though it was never formally denied. In Jung's psychology it was a stage of transition between the notion of complex and that of archetype, the latter being closely bound to the Jungian concept of the collective unconscious.[137]

Jung's concept of the unconscious differs from that of Freud on three main points: (1) It has an autonomous course of development. (2) It is complementary to consciousness. (3) It is the seat of universal primordial images, the *archetypes*. Jung says that one of the first experiences which led him to the idea of archetypes was the case of an old schizophrenic patient of the Burghölzli who abundantly hallucinated, day and night. This patient once declared to the physician in charge, Dr. Honegger, that he saw that the sun had a phallus whose movements produced the wind. The origin of that strange delusion seemed inexplicable, until Jung's eyes fell on a recent book by a historian of religion, Dieterich,[138] about the liturgy of the Mithraic religion, such as revealed by a hitherto-unpublished Greek papyrus. This text contained the mention of the wind originating in a tube hanging from the sun. The possibility that the patient had read that recently discovered text was ruled out. To Jung[139] the only explanation seemed to be that there are universal symbols which may appear in religious myths as well as in psychotic delusions.[140] Coincidences of this kind proved to be not very rare, even if not so striking as the preceding case.

706 THE DISCOVERY OF THE UNCONSCIOUS

Jung's theory of the archetypes has often been misunderstood. A distinction must be made between the "archetypes proper" that normally are latent and unconscious and the "archetypal images" that are the manifestations of the latter to consciousness. Archetypes are not the fruit of individual experience, they are "universal." This universality has been interpreted by Jungians either as issuing from the structure of the human brain or as the expression of a kind of neo-Platonic world-soul. Without denying the possibility of either explanation, Jung, who claimed to be an empiricist, said that he had to recognize the archetypes without knowing their intimate nature. Jung's archetypical images remind us of Von Schubert's idea of a universal language of symbols common to mankind. manifested in dreams as well as in the myths of all peoples. However, in Jung's conception, archetypes are more than that: they are the centers of psychic energy; they have a "numinous," life-like quality; and they are likely to be manifested in critical circumstances, either through an exterior event or because of some inner change.

As an example of an archetypical image released by an exterior event we might quote William James' experience of the San Francisco earthquake of 1906.[141] While lying awake in his bed, one morning early, he recognized immediately what was happening, felt no fear but "pure delight and welcome." In James' words:

> I personified the earthquake as a permanent individual entity . . . it came, moreover, directly to *me*. It stole in behind my back, and once inside the room, had me all to itself, and could manifest itself convincingly. Animus and intent were never more present in any human action, nor did any human activity ever more definitely point back to a living agent as its source and origin.

James found that other persons felt in the earthquake an intention, and called it vicious, bent on destruction, whereas others told of its vague demonic power. Still others thought of the end of the world and the final judgment. For James it rather had the quality of an individual being. William James concluded:

> I realize now better than ever how inevitable were men's earlier mythologic versions of such catastrophes, and how artificial and against the grain of our spontaneous perceiving are the later habits into which science educates us. It was simply impossible for untutored men to take earthquakes into their minds as anything but supernatural warnings or retributions.

This is a wonderful picture of how a man experiences the emergence of an archetypical image. In William James' case the archetype was projected under the impact of an exterior event. More frequently archetypes are manifested in conjunction with events of one's innermost life. Archetypes may appear in dreams; they may also be elicited by the use of forced imagination or spontaneous drawings. There is an almost infinite variety of archetypes. Some seem to be very remote from consciousness, others are more immediate, and must be described in connection with the structure of the human psyche.

The Structure of the Human Psyche

Jung sees the conscious ego as being situated at the junction of two worlds: the exterior or spacial world and the interior or psychic objective world. As Baudouin states: "That the unconscious extends so far beyond consciousness is simply the counterpart of the fact that the exterior world extends so far beyond our visual field."[142] Around our ego gravitate a number of subpersonalities whose relationship to the ego are modified throughout the course of life. Such are the persona, the shadow, the anima or animus, the archetype of the spirit, and the self. Toward the exterior, the individual presents a kind of facade or social mask, the *persona*, a word that in Latin means a theater mask. The persona is the sum total of the conventional attitudes that an individual adopts because he belongs to certain groups: occupation, social class, caste, political party, or nation. Some individuals will identify too strongly with these attitudes so that they lose contact with their true personality. The more severe aspects of the persona are manifested in racial, social, and national prejudice.

The *shadow* is the sum of those personal characteristics that the individual wishes to hide from the others and from himself. But the more the individual tries to hide it from himself, the more the shadow may become active and evil-doing. An example from literature was "The Dark Monk," which accompanied the monk Medardus in E. T. H. Hoffman's novel *The Devil's Elixirs*. This was a literary example of the "shadow" emancipating itself from the control of the conscious personality to commit evil actions behind its back. But the shadow can also be projected; then the individual sees his own dark features reflected in another person whom he may choose as a scapegoat. At times too, owing to the influence of alcohol or some other cause, the shadow can temporarily take hold of an individual, who later might be quite surprised that he was capable of such evil behavior.

The Jungian concept of the shadow should not be confused with the Freudian concept of the repressed; it is related to the phenomenon of *unawareness*, as opposed to unconsciousness.[143] To unawareness belong those aspects of the world and of oneself that an individual does not see, although he could if he honestly wanted to. A man can visualize himself as a good husband and father, who is liked by his subordinates and respected by his fellow citizens; and yet this man ignores the fact that he is a selfish husband, a tyrannical father, that he is hated by his subordinates, and more feared than respected by his fellow men. This negative side of which this man is unaware is precisely what Jung calls the shadow.

Whereas the persona and the shadow are the more exterior aspects of an individual, other subpersonalities are related to the inner psychic reality of the collective unconscious. Such are the archetype of the soul (*anima* or *animus*), the archetype of the spirit (the *old wise man*, the *magna mater*), and the most central of all archetypes, the *self*.

As all archetypes, that of the soul is known by its manifestations when it is projected, namely, as a characteristic personification of the other sex. Thus in man it takes the form of a feminine figure, the *anima*, and in woman that of a masculine figure, the *animus*. We have seen how Jung discovered the anima during his self-analysis; later he found it also in his patients' dreams and fantasies, and thereafter under many forms in religions, myths, and literature.[144]

The archetype of the soul assumes the form of an ideal feminine figure in man, the *anima*, and in woman the form of a masculine one, the *animus*, owing to the complementary nature of man and woman, who both hold in their unconscious an ideal representation of the other. The existence of the anima is manifested in the manner in which a man distorts the representation of the real women in his life: his mother, sisters, friends, love-objects, and spouse. The anima is also personified in dreams, visions, and fantasies, in many myths of all populations, and has been a rich source of inspiration for novelists and poets. Sometimes the anima is projected from the unconscious in a dramatic way such as love at first sight, or incomprehensible infatuation, with disastrous results. But the anima does not only have these negative effects. The individual can handle his relationship with the anima in such a way that it becomes a source of wisdom, inspiration, and creativity for him.

Jung's concept of the anima embraces several ideas that were the subject of lively discussions by the end of the nineteenth century. First was the concept of *narcissistic love*, that is the projection of a more or less unconscious self-love on another person. Second was the concept of the *mother imago*. Nietzsche had already said: "Every man keeps in himself an image of the woman deriving from that of his mother, and according to this image he will be prone to respect or to despise women." A not very different idea was developed by Karl Neisser: For a man to love a woman she must resemble the women in his ancestry.[145] Verlaine's poem "My Familiar Dream," tells of an ideal woman picture, loving and much loved, changing though always the same, and resembling the departed women of his family. Third was the theme of an early love being transferred from one woman to another. A literary example is Thomas Hardy's novel *The Well-Beloved*, where in the course of his life a man successively falls in love with three women, in his youth, in his maturity, and when he begins to grow old.[146] He loves each one in vain, they marry other men, and the first one will be the mother of the second, and the second of the third. In the end he realizes that he has always been in love with the same woman. Fourth, the concept of anima also includes the attraction resulting from the physiological bisexuality of the human being. Because there is in man a feminine and in woman a masculine component, man and woman are attracted also to the complementary personality element they find in each other. It belongs to the nature of the anima that a man can project her image upon the woman with whom he is in love, and he then sees her differently from what she really is. Such a man attributes to his beloved qualities that are quite foreign to her. But that is not all. Jung calls *Anima-Gestalt* (anima figure) a specific type of woman who seems to attract the projection of the anima of men. Jung often referred to Rider Haggard's novel *She.*[147]

A young Englishman of Greek ancestry discovers in central East Africa an unknown city that belongs to a white queen: Ayesha, who only shows herself veiled. This enigmatic, fascinating, diabolic woman is two thousand years old and keeps her youth by magic art. She still mourns the only man she ever loved, namely, the Greek Kallikrates. When she discovers that the present visitor is a descendant of that Kallikrates, she falls in love with him and wishes to render him immortal. For this he must go through a pillar of fire, and when he hesitates she herself passes through it to show how it is done. But this causes her to lose her immortality and she falls into dust. This novel was a best seller at the end of the nineteenth century and is said to have been written under a sudden inspiration, in a kind of trance.[148]

One could make a long list of similar anima figures in literature, from Homer's Circe in the *Odyssey* to Pierre Benoit's Antinéa in his novel *L'Atlantide* (to which Jung also frequently referred).

In woman the archetype of the soul is the *animus*. It has been described less extensively than the anima by Jung and his followers.[149] Whereas the anima usually is only one woman figure, the animus is often a plurality of male figures. In a very young woman it will appear as an infatuation for an older man or a paternal figure; in a mature woman the object could be a sports champion or, in negative cases, a playboy or even a criminal; and with an older woman more likely a physician, an ecclesiastic, or a supposedly misunderstood genius. The projection of the animus into a real man can have effects as disastrous as those of a man's projection of the anima on an "anima figure." More commonly the animus can manifest itself in a woman's distorted perception of her husband or other male figures in her life. It may also give rise to fixed ideas and stubborn, irrational opinions which are the source of irritating discussions. (One often has the impression that much of what Adler called masculine protest is considered by Jung as being manifestations of the animus.) But when a woman finds the true relationship with her animus, it will cease to be a disturbing element, and it will become a source of intellectual poise and balance. But it appears that the animus has not inspired novelists as often as the anima.[150]

The *archetype of the spirit* is next in importance to the archetype of the soul (anima and animus). An individual is usually confronted with it in critical life situations when he must make difficult decisions. It appears in dreams under multiple symbolic forms: wind, ancestral figures, helping animals, divinities, and others. This archetype has a tendency to appear as the figure of the old wise man: such is the medicine man of primitive people, the priests and monks of all religions, or any man of good counsel one has known. As is the case for all archetypes, the old wise man may also appear as an evil-doing figure, such as a wizard. This archetype can be projected onto a real human being, as may happen in the process of psychotherapy. The patient will then visualize his therapist as an omniscient magician. To identify oneself with this archetype would be a dangerous example of what Jung calls psychic inflation. In literature the personification par excellence of the old wise man is found in Nietzsche's *Zarathustra*. According to Jung, Nietzsche identified himself with the figure of Zarathustra, that is, with the archetype of the old wise man. This would explain why Nietzsche developed such delusions of grandeur when he became psychotic.

For a long time Jung seemed to consider the archetype of the old wise man as characteristic of masculine psychology, but he later also encountered it in women. Conversely, the archetype of the *magna mater* (or great mother), that Jung had first considered as typical in woman, can also be encountered in man. Jung seems to view it as a particular form of the archetype of the mother, and as is true for all other archetypes, can take many forms.[151] It can be projected upon one's mother, grandmother, or nanny. It can appear as a female ancestor, a saint, the Holy Virgin, the divine wisdom, the Church, the university (the alma mater), or the mother country. Among the negative aspects of this archetype are those deities that regulate human destinies, the witches, dragons, and so on.

The *self* is the most central of all archetypes. The English word self, that has been given so many conflicting meanings, is hardly able to express what Jung meant by the German word *Selbst* (literally the "itself"). It is at the same time the invisible, unconscious, innermost center of personality, and a psychic totality, as it results from the unification of the conscious and the unconscious. Above all, it should not be confused with the conscious ego. As with the other archetypes, the self is normally unconscious but manifests itself in projected form or through the emergence of archetypical figures in dreams or fantasies. The description of the self cannot be separated from that of the process of individuation.

Individuation

We are thus approaching the most central notion of Jung's psychological system and therapy. Jung calls *individuation* the process that normally leads a human being to the unification of his personality. The term individuation was used by medieval theologians but with another meaning.[152] The individuation is a process extending over the entire course of human life.

Freud had given a new conception of the course of human life: a series of stages of libidinal development culminating with the Oedipus situation, then a phase of latency, followed by a second awakening of the sexual instinct at puberty leading into maturity, and from then a period of no substantial change. Jung's conception is quite different. Jung sees human life as a series of metamorphoses. From the emergence of the infant out of the collective unconscious to the completion of the self there is a lifelong process.

The human being enters life with a nondifferentiated unconscious; he then slowly emerges as a conscious ego. Jung insisted upon the psychological symbiosis in which the young child lives, not only with the mother but with the family as a whole. There are examples of parallel dreams in mother and child and a similarity in the responses of parents and children in the word association test. For that reason children's neuroses should call attention to parental attitudes. As for the Oedipus complex, Jung never considered it a universal and necessary feature in human nature, but a possible symptom of faulty attitudes of the minds of the parents toward the child.

Gradually the individuality of the child emerges from that of the family. Beginning school is an important event and one of the first steps of individuation. Further, the adolescent should leave behind childish features, and the youth, those of adolescence. Jung observed in East Africa how this transition from childhood to adulthood was facilitated by the initiation rites. The young people thus escaped the dangers of protracted adolescence so frequent in the Western world. Adulthood brings new concerns bound to social responsibilities and new problems related to the anima and the animus.

One of the main metamorphoses in human life is the "turning of life" (*Lebenswende*). Between the ages of thirty-two and thirty-eight a profound change is bound to occur in a person; it comes about gradually or suddenly, and is sometimes announced by an impressive dream of archetypical quality. Problems, duties, or needs, which have been neglected during the first half of life, now manifest themselves. Sometimes a man who has always repressed his need for love will fall prey to what the French call *le démon de midi* (the "demon of noon") as illustrated in one of Paul Bourget's best-known novels[153] and discussed from the psychoanalytic point of view by Répond.[154] Sometimes the neurosis issues from long-repressed intellectual or spiritual needs.[155] Such a neurosis must be seen as a warning from the unconscious, and the subject should change his way of life, or he might waste the second half of his life. Just as it is important to leave behind what belongs to childhood and adolescence when reaching maturity, so the individual must leave behind what belongs to the first half of life when he starts on the latter. The second half of life is a period of confrontation with the archetype of the spirit and of the self. Jung contrasted the deplorable pseudo-youth of aging people in Western civilization with the dignity of the elders among the Elgoni in East Africa and the respect they inspired in their fellow tribesmen.

When the individuation is achieved, the ego is no longer the center of the personality but is like a planet revolving around an invisible sun, the self. The individual has acquired equanimity and no longer fears death, and as he had found himself he also has found the true link with other men. Jung does not hesitate to use the nearly obsolete word "wisdom" (for which the more modern term "maturity" is an unsatisfactory substitute), and he declares, "The natural end of life is not senility but wisdom."[156]

Individuation may come to a halt, and the task of the psychotherapist is to help the patient to remove the obstacles that impede the continuous development of personality. We shall return to this point when we discuss Jung's psychotherapy.

A progress in individuation is often manifested to consciousness by the emergence of an archetypical image of the self. Among these images three seem to appear with particular frequency: the *quaternity*, the *mandala*, and the *divine child*. The quaternity can appear as a geometric figure of square or sometimes rectangular shape, or it will have some relation with the number four: four persons, four trees, and so on. Often it is a matter of completing a triadic figure with a fourth term, thus making it into a quaternity. In a series of four hundred dreams published by Jung, this symbol appeared no less than seventy-one times.[157] Jung was not the first one to deal with the symbols of quaternity. In France Fabre d'Olivet had previously written about the same subject in the nineteenth century.[158] However, Jung was certainly the first to relate it so closely to the process of individuation. The mandala is a circular figure ornamented with symbols that is generally divided into four sections. It is well known in India and Tibet, where it was used for centuries by ascetics and mystics to aid in contemplation.[159]

One should not confuse the process of individuation with the more temporary processes of regression and progression. What Jung calls regression is an inward movement, that is, a gradual increase of introversion or movement toward the unconscious. On the contrary, progression is a return from the unconscious to the conscious, a decrease of introversion and an increase of extroversion with the individual taking an ever firmer grip on reality. Whenever individuation comes to a halt, regression followed by progression will give it a new impulse. This is exactly the principle of therapeutic individuation. Through dream analysis, active imagination, or painting or drawing of unconscious fantasies, the patient will be able to regress and start his journey through the unconscious. This kind of journey, which Jung experienced from 1913 to 1918, is also the model of his synthetic-hermeneutic therapy. According to Jung, similar experiences provided the model for the old accounts of travels in the land of the dead. A long tradition, probably originating with the shamans' journeys through the land of the spirits, was expressed in the Gilgamesh epic, Homer's *Odyssey*, Virgil's

Aeneis, and Dante's *Divine Comedy,*[160] and could be followed under new forms in modern times.[161]

One characteristic feature of any journey through the unconscious is the occurrence of what Jung called *enantiodromia.* This term, originating with Heraclitus, means the "return to the opposite." Certain mental processes are turned at a given point into their opposites as if through a kind of self-regulation. This notion has also been symbolically illustrated by poets. In the *Divine Comedy* we see Dante and Virgil reaching the deepest point of hell and then taking their first step upward in a reverse course toward purgatory and heaven. This mysterious phenomenon of the spontaneous reversal of regression was experienced by all those who passed successfully through a creative illness and has become a characteristic feature of Jungian synthetic-hermeneutic therapy.

Carl Gustav Jung's Work—VI—Psychotherapy

Jungian psychotherapy comprises several stages of which each one could constitute a method in its own right. We have separately to consider Jung's therapy of bringing into awareness, the treatment of the pathogenic secret, the reductive-analytic method, the forwarding of individuation, and the reeducation.

According to Jung, the first step in any psychotherapy should be bringing the patient back to reality, and particularly to the awareness of his present situation. Some patients need to be awakened to certain aspects of their problems, others live in a general state of unawareness. Jung liked to recall the story of Tartarin, the hero of Alphonse Daudet's novel, who had believed a joke told to him by a blusterer, namely, that the Swiss Alps had been equipped with tunnels and galleries filled with employees so that all danger of mountain climbing was removed.[162] Tartarin then undertook without a qualm the dangerous climb up the Jungfrau, but was seized with mortal panic when he realized the truth. In the same way, Jung says many people live a provisional life; some of them wake up early, some in the middle of their existence, others very late, or even on their deathbed. At times the individual needs to have his eyes opened to some material danger to which he is blind.[163] More often he must realize the moral implications of what he is doing. As an example of the latter, Jung tells of a neurotic young man who had undergone psychotherapeutic treatment.[164] He was living at the expense of a poor old woman teacher, who was greatly attached to him. The first step in therapy was to make him realize that his way of life was immoral and to have him change it. This preoccupation with the actual situation and reality remains in the foreground throughout all Jungian psychotherapy. As we shall see, even when analyzing the most abstruse symbols in dealing with archetypes, the patient is always confronted with the question of how he is to apply those insights to his practical, present life.

A second stage in Jungian psychotherapy is the handling of pathogenic secrets. We have seen in a previous chapter that the discreet and skillful handling of the pathogenic secret had become an effective therapeutic device in the cure of souls practiced by certain Protestant ministers.[165] We have also seen how the therapy of the pathogenic secret was gradually laicized until it was introduced to psychiatry by Moritz Benedikt. It is an open question whether Jung heard about the therapy of the pathogenic secret or rediscovered it by himself. In his autobiography Jung tells of his first clinical experience with this kind of therapy.

As a young resident at the Burghölzli Jung was given the care of a woman whose depression was so severe that it was assumed to be a case of dementia praecox. His findings with the word association test and the patient's dreams led Jung to suspect a tragic secret, which subsequently the patient told to him. She had been shocked to learn that the man she had wished to marry who had not seemed to be interested in her had actually been in love with her. But there was no possible remedy because she had married someone else and had two children. Then she let her small daughter suck a sponge imbibed with polluted water, and even gave her small boy a glass of the same water to drink. When the little girl died of typhoid fever, her mother became so disturbed that she had to be committed. Jung explained to her how it was her secret that was making her ill, and a fortnight later she could leave the hospital, cured. But Jung decided that he had to keep the matter secret from his colleagues. He had the opportunity to reiterate such cures and concluded that the possibility of a pathogenic secret was to be systematically considered in every case.[166]

It is not superfluous to emphasize that this therapy demands from the therapist absolute respect for the patient's secret. There is no question of sharing the information with colleagues or supervisors, recording it in a case history, and still less of using magnetophones or one-way vision rooms. It is, as it were, the therapy "of the secret by the secret."

Before proceeding further in the therapy, the religious problem must be considered. Jung asserts that among all his patients who were in the second half of life there is not one whose main problem is not related to his attitude toward religion.[167] Needless to say, it is not for the psychotherapist to interfere in these matters, but he can point out to his patient that if he had a religious belief he might be cured of his neurosis simply by seriously resuming the practice of his religion. This is especially true for Catholics; it seems more difficult in the case of Protestants. However, Jung tells how some of his Protestant patients were freed of their neurosis after joining the Oxford Group or some similar movement.

Most patients, however, are not opened to such a simple, radical cure and need a full-fledged psychotherapeutic treatment. A prerequisite is to obtain a detailed account of his life and the history of his illness from the patient. The therapist must then decide whether he will give his patients an analytic-reductive therapy (that is, a therapy based on Freudian or Adlerian principles), or a *synthetic-hermeneutic one.*

There are, Jung says, patients whose main characteristic is a kind of infantile hedonism and craving for instinctual gratification; whereas others are possessed by the drive to power and superiority. The first group should be treated by a psychoanalytically oriented therapy and the second group along Adlerian principles: It would be a blunder, for instance, to treat an unsuccessful man with an infantile need for superiority with the Freudian method, and no less to treat a successful man with a strongly hedonistic psychology with the Adlerian method. The preliminary examination will usually suffice to indicate which of the two therapies is the more appropriate; sometimes Jung gave his more educated patients writings of Freud and Adler to read, and as a rule they soon found out by themselves which one was more congenial to them. The reductive-analytic methods will often bring good results, but often they are not entirely satisfactory, and progress is stopped, or the patient will have dreams of archetypical character. All this points to the need for changing the procedure, that is, to work with the synthetic-hermeneutic method. The latter is prescribed from the start for those patients, mostly in the second half of life, who are concerned with moral, philosophical, or religious problems.

The synthetic-hermeneutic method, commonly known as Jungian therapy, differs in many regards from Freudian psychoanalysis. As in Adlerian therapy, the patient does not lie on a couch but sits on a chair facing the psychotherapist. The one-hour sessions are scheduled twice a week to begin with and then once a week as soon as possible. The patient is asked to carry out specific tasks and is often assigned reading matter. In short, he must actively collaborate with his therapist. The advantages of this method, Jung says, are that the analysand is prevented from falling into infantile regression, he is not alienated from his surroundings, the treatment is less expensive, and the psychotherapist has time to treat more patients. Emphasis is laid on the present life situation and the immediate, concrete utilization of whatever insight the patient may have gained in the therapeutic process. Jung conceives transference quite differently than Freud. Jung considers those conspicuous, positive, or negative developments of transference that take place in psychoanalysis as mere artifacts that unnecessarily prolong the treatment or can ruin it. What Freud calls transference neurosis is for Jung a desperate attempt of the patient to compensate his faulty attitudes toward reality and a result of the therapist's lack of skill. That kind of transference is a degrading bondage for the patient, and it is a danger both to him and to the therapist who runs the risk of being infected with his patient's neurosis. Transference not only consists of erotic feelings but of a mixture of possessive and power drives, and fear.[168] According to Jung, the only acceptable transference should be mild and almost unnoticeable. It should be a process of collaboration of patient and therapist, and a confrontation of their mutual findings. Only in this way can the psychotherapeutic process evolve through the action of what Jung calls the transcendent function.[169]

The transcendent function is the progressive synthesis of conscious and unconscious data leading to the individuation. Conscious and unconscious life seldom run parallel to each other, and it is dangerous for the patient when a gap occurs between the two, because it leads to the formation of strong counterpositions of the unconscious resulting in severe disturbances. The therapist must help the patient to confront the conscious and the unconscious so the desired synthesis can take place. Whenever the contents of the unconscious are too weak or inhibited, the therapist will help the patient to stimulate them and make them emerge; he will then help him to confront them with the conscious ego and the daily life situation.

How does one cause the contents of the unconscious to emerge? It is a matter of specific training which comprises mainly the use of dreams, spontaneous fantasies, and free drawing or paintings. Students of dreams such as Hervey de Saint-Denis knew how to provoke frequent and abundant dreams: one begins by writing them down upon awakening and illustrating them with drawings in black and white or colors.[170] The same method can be applied to spontaneous fantasies in the waking state, or else one can draw or paint without determining the subject beforehand. Clay modeling and automatic writing can also be used.

In Jungian therapy the dream, however, remains the most important approach to the unconscious. Whereas many Freudian psychoanalysts today never analyze their patients' dreams, this would be quite impossible in Jungian therapy. Jung's ideas pertaining to dreams and their therapeutical utilization diverge from Freud's theory on almost every point. Whereas Freud holds that every dream is a vicarious fulfillment of a repressed wish, usually related to infantile sexuality, Jung maintains that the functions of dreams are manifold. They can express fears as well as wishes; they can give a mirror picture of the dreamer's actual situation; there are prospective dreams (as depicted by Adler and Maeder); others are creative, warning, or parapsychological. Jung does not accept Freud's distinction of the manifest and latent content of dreams but asserts that the manifest is the dream itself. The associations, as obtained with the Freudian technique, will lead to the current complexes that could be uncovered as well through associating with any other text. Dream symbols can be understood without the notions of repression and censor. Dreams cannot be interpreted if the interpreter is not well-acquainted with the dreamer's life and actual situation, and if he does not have a good knowledge of symbols, and therefore of mythology and the history of religions. One basic feature of Jung's dream interpretation is his emphasis on dream series: a given dream can only be understood in the context of those that precede or follow it and sometimes of the entire set. Where Freud analyzes dreams with the method of free association, Jung resorts to that of amplification. This means the examination of all possible connotations of a given image, among which many might be related to the patient's past or present experiences, while others will perhaps elucidate the significance of an archetypical dream. Great importance is ascribed to archetypical dreams; they must be studied carefully and in sequence as milestones marking the path of individuation.

A similar method of interpretation can be applied to the other data obtained from the unconscious, especially to spontaneous fantasies, drawings, and paintings. In the appreciation of drawings and paintings, neither the content nor the formal aspect should be overemphasized. (For instance, the patient should never come to think that he is an artist.) The drawing and painting method is not only used to obtain the contents of the unconscious but also to control them. When a patient is obsessed by a certain representation, Jung would have him draw or paint it so as to make it gradually less fearful and eventually to gain full control over it.

We will now briefly sketch the successive stages of the average synthetic-hermeneutic psychotherapy.

Let us first recall that Jung resorts to the analysis of the unconscious only when all other methods have failed and only after he had obtained a thorough anamnesis. The first dream is often very clear and sometimes points out the prognosis of the treatment. In the first stage one deals with the *persona* and above all with the *shadow*. The patient dreams of a repulsive individual who is always different but retains certain features throughout, and also shows certain traits resembling those of the dreamer. Eventually the time comes for the patient to understand that this individual is none other than himself, or rather his shadow, and this enables him to become aware of these aspects of his personality that he has refused to see. Once he is fully aware of his shadow, the individual has to assimilate it. The individual cannot sever himself from his shadow, but Jung certainly does not mean that he should now do openly and consciously what the shadow had him do in a state of unawareness all along. One should, of course, accept the shadow, but at the same time one must render it harmless. To illustrate this procedure, the story of Saint Francis of Assisi and the wolf of Gubbio is often told in Jungian circles.[171] The inhabitants of Gubbio were plagued by a wolf and called Saint Francis to help them. He went to the wolf, not to kill him but to speak to him. The wolf voluntarily followed Saint Francis to the town, where he was given shelter and remained as an innocuous guest for the rest of his life.

In a second stage of the therapeutic process, the problems of the anima and animus are spontaneously manifested. In the case of a man, he begins to have frequent dreams in which a woman appears in various aspects and moods. She can be sweet and charming, strange and fascinating, and sometimes threatening. The subject sees that all these figures have something in common, and eventually he perceives that she is none other than his anima. Therapeutic discussions now focus on the anima problem. The subject must realize that in dealing with women he has always more or less projected his anima upon them. His practical task is now to bring himself to see women such as they are without the interference of anima projection. In the case of a woman patient, the problems of animus are treated in a similar way. Once the problems of the anima and the animus are solved, they are no longer disturbing elements in emotional life and social relationships; in Jung's terms the anima and animus become "psychological functions."

In the third stage of the therapy the archetypes of the old wise man and the magna mater come to the foreground. Here too archetypical images appear in dreams as well as in fantasies and drawings. Dangers are also to be avoided: the patient can project the archetype of the old wise man on his therapist, or he can identify himself with it, which would be psychic inflation.

Thus in Jungian therapy there are three main stages, respectively, concerned with the shadow, the anima and animus, the old wise man, and the magna mater. However, things are often more complex, since a great variety of other archetypes may appear at various stages of therapy and must be handled, each one in its own way. The task of the therapist is both to facilitate the emergence of archetypes and to prevent them from overflowing. Each new archetype must be interpreted and assimilated by the conscious mind, and what the patient has learned must be applied in his practical life. Maeder has emphasized that in some cases healing is accelerated when the archetype of the savior emerges, which might be considered as a variety of the old wise man archetype.[172]

As a rule, the average Jungian therapy lasts three years. Experience has shown that the number and frequency of the sessions can be reduced, but not the total length of the treatment. As already mentioned, progress in the individuation can be marked by the appearance of specific archetypical images, especially the mandala or figures of quaternity, sometimes also the archetype of the divine child. The aim of the treatment is the furthering and completion of the individuation, which means that a person has followed the old precept: Become what thou art, which is sometimes attributed to Nietzsche but is actually a quotation from the Greek poet Pindar.

Jung's synthetic-hermeneutic therapy is certainly not an easy undertaking. At times the subject finds himself overwhelmed with the material emerging from the unconscious, and the confrontation with the archetypes can sometimes prove to be frightening. An incessant effort is necessary to keep a firm hold on reality. That is also the reason why a Jungian self-analysis would be a dangerous undertaking against which one should be warned.

Among the therapeutic methods utilized by Jung we also find reeducation. Whereas Freud declares that the psychoanalyst should not endeavor to reeducate his patient, Jung insists that the patient should be helped from the start and throughout the stages of whatever therapy is used. Any insight gained by the patient must be immediately translated by him into a more rational behavior in everyday life. One essential point in that reeducation is to teach the patient to cease projecting his problems onto the people of his environment, Jung defines neurosis as a "sick system of social relationships," a definition that is well in accord with the concepts of Janet as well as Adler.[173] Because of this projection the neurotic unconsciously manipulates the persons around him (spouse, parents, children and friends) and plays them against each other so that he is soon enmeshed in a web of intrigues of which both he and the others are the victims. The settlement and clarification of these difficulties are one of the final aims of psychotherapy.

One of the main features of Jung's therapy is the great emphasis he sets from the beginning on what is now called countertransference. Jung claims that no one is able to lead someone further than he has gone himself. It is generally recognized that the principle of training analysis was introduced by Jung and that it is one of his lasting contributions to Freudian analysis. But after his training analysis, the therapist should always keep on guard and watch his own unconscious, for instance, by analyzing his dreams.

Carl Gustav Jung's Work—VII—Eastern and Western Wisdom

We have thus far drawn a very sketchy picture of Jung's psychology and psychotherapy. But the scope of his work is considerably wider. From the beginning Jung's reflection extended to the history of mankind, the psychology of nations, contemporary problems, art, and literature. In later years he became increasingly concerned with a confrontation of traditional teachings and sacred books of the East and the West, with the principle of "synchronicity," and with religious problems.

We have seen during 1914 to 1920 how Jung was deeply interested in Gnosticism. He hailed the Gnostics as people who did not just believe but knew, and learned from their exploration of the unconscious. Like Jung, they were preoccupied with the problem of evil. Later, in 1937, Jung interpreted, according to his theory of the archetypes, the visions of Zosimos of Panopolis, a Gnostic of the third century A.D., who also marked the transition between Gnosticism and alchemy.[174]

Alchemy had always been a puzzle for the historians of culture. Ever since Greek and Roman antiquity and up to the eighteenth century, a great number of learned men had devoted their lives to the practice of pseudo-chemical operations implying the metamorphoses of substances according to definite rules. Marcellin Berthelot, a historian of science, considered alchemy a "semi-rational, semi-mystical science" based on false interpretations of objective facts.[175] Silberer seems to have been the first to see a sequence of symbolic operations in alchemy which could be psychologically deciphered. In an alchemical treatise of the eighteenth century, Silberer found the symbolic representation of the murder of the father, of infantile sexual theories, and others.[176] Jung, in turn, sees a projection of the process of individuation in the series of operations performed by alchemists. Just as Jung's patients materialized their dreams and fantasies in the form of drawings and paintings, the alchemists materialized their own processes of individuation in the form of pseudochemical operations. It is also the reason, Jung adds, why accounts of visions are often to be found in the writings of alchemists. As the years passed, Jung's interest in alchemy increased and he devoted a considerable amount of time and effort to the deciphering and psychological interpretation of the symbols in old alchemical treatises.[177]

Jung's interest also turned to astrology and astrological symbols. He did not believe in a causal influence of stars upon the individual's destiny, but as we shall see he did not reject the possibility of relationships in the form of synchronicity.

During World War II there was a renewed interest in Switzerland in the celebrated mystical physician and philosopher, Paracelsus. Jung considered him a pioneer of the psychology of the unconscious and of psychotherapy, but apparently Jung was more interested in his personality than in his abstruse writings. "Nothing has a more powerful influence upon children than the life their parents have not lived," Jung noted. He also found in him a good instance of the "turning of life": Paracelsus' philosophy was transformed after the thirty-eighth year of his life.[178]

Jung's early interest in the history of religions brought him to the study of the sacred books of the East. One of these, the *Tibetan Book of the Dead*, was translated into English in 1927.[179] Jung took a special interest in that work and wrote an introduction for the German translation.

> *The Tibetan Book of the Dead* is a description of what the soul will experience between the moment of death and that of the next reincarnation, and it also tells the soul how it can reach final illumination and thus escape reincarnation. The journey through the Bardo Thödol, that is the abode of the dead, is divided into three periods. In a first, short one the soul is in a sleep or trance, unaware of death. Then comes the awakening with the first visions. At this point the enlightened soul can pass directly into a paradise realm, but if the soul misses this moment it will continue to have visions and hallucinations; namely, the delusion of having a body of flesh and blood. It will believe to see other human beings as well as all kinds of gods and fantastic creatures. But the soul should always remain aware that all these things are but the productions of its own mind. These visions ceaselessly change but gradually exhaust themselves as the soul recedes step by step to ever lower levels of consciousness. When the soul reaches the third stage, it perceives males and females in union. If about to be born as a male, the soul will feel as being itself a male and will be animated with intense hatred against the father and jealousy and attraction toward the mother, and will go between them and thus be reincarnated; and if it is to be born as a female the feelings are reversed and it will hate the mother and love the father.[180]

Jung marveled at the psychological knowledge of the unknown authors of the *Tibetan Book of the Dead* and their understanding of the phenomenon of projection. He was struck by the fact that the journey through the Bardo Thödol appeared to be like the course of individuation in reverse.

In 1929 Jung published a psychological commentary as an introduction to the German translation by his friend, the sinologist Richard Wilhelm, of an old Chinese book, *The Secret of the Golden Flower*.[181] In this book Jung saw the equivalent of his description of the self and an analogy between the Chinese symbols and those that spontaneously appeared in his patients, as well as analogies between these symbols and those of certain Christian mystics and of the alchemists.

Richard Wilhelm translated another old Chinese book into German, the *I Ching*, or "Book of Mutations." This book describes a method for obtaining oracles with the help of little sticks or a coin; such an oracle is said to have a personal relevance for the man who uses it and for the moment he uses it. Richard Wilhelm had learned the practice of that oracle with a Chinese master. Jung was interested in the symbolic character of the magic formulas and above all in the principle of the *I Ching*: the latter is based on the assumption that whatever happens in a given moment is necessarily endowed with the specific quality of that moment.[182] This was one of the starting points of Jung's concept of synchronicity.

In regard to Zen Buddhism, Jung pointed out a few parallels with certain experiences of Western mystics, though the method is vastly different from anything that has been conceived in the Western world.[183] As much as Jung warned against underestimating the wisdom of such teachings, he discouraged Westerners from practicing these methods.

Jung also devoted much interest to yoga and repeatedly invited the German Indianists, J. W. Hauer and Heinrich Zimmer, to give seminars about it in Zurich during 1931 to 1933.[184] Though remaining averse to the practice of yoga by Western people, Jung felt that much could be gained from a comparison of yoga with certain Western teachings. The rich symbolism of Tantric yoga brought much comparative material to the study of the symbols of the collective unconscious. Viewed as training systems, certain varieties of yoga could find parallels in the exercises of Ignatius of Loyola, with Schultz's autogenic training, and with Freud's and Jung's methods of dynamic psychotherapy.

In several commentaries on Eastern teachings, and notably in his study on the *I Ching*, Jung announces a new concept that he was to develop only in 1952 under the name of *synchronicity*.[185] He describes it as a principle of a causal connection and was struck by the importance of this principle in Chinese thought. But there also was something of it in Leibniz' concept of "pre-established harmony," in certain remarks of Schopenhauer, and in the fairly common occurrence of the so-called law of series. Jung's attention was drawn to occurrences of "meaningful coincidences." An illustration was the story of a woman patient whose analysis was not progressing because of her hyper-rational animus. She had dreamed that a golden beetle was presented to her, and Jung was discussing the dream with her when a live beetle hit the windowpane. Jung picked it up and gave it to her. She was so impressed that her wall of rationality was thrown over. Jung brought together these phenomena with the experimental data offered by Rhine about extrasensory perception. Whereas Rhine had pointed out the role of the emotional factor in the occurrences of extrasensory perception, Jung found that an archetypal element was implied in his "meaningful coincidences." Finally, Jung came to wonder whether modern physics, by taking its distances from the principle of rigorous causal determinism, did not take a step nearer to the principle of synchronicity.

From all the philosophers that Jung had read in his youth, Nietzsche kept his particular attention throughout the years. Jung considered Nietzsche a man who slowly developed an unconscious dual personality that emerged suddenly, causing a kind of volcanic eruption and bringing to light an enormous amount of archetypical material. This would explain why Zarathustra exerts such a fascination on so many readers. From the spring of 1934 to the winter of 1939 Jung devoted one seminar each semester to *Zarathustra*. The collection of these seminars held at his Institute comprises ten typewritten volumes and certainly constitutes the most thorough commentary that has ever been given on Nietzsche's masterpiece.[186]

Part of Jung's multiple interests went to contemporary art and literature, although not much of it is to be found in his published works. When an exhibition of paintings by Picasso was organized in Zurich, Jung examined them in their chronological sequence and found a characteristic psychological evolution.[187] Picasso's blue period marked the beginning of a *Nekyia*, that is, a "journey through the land of the dead," with a series of "regressions" (in the sense of Jungian psychology), and he wondered what would be the outcome of the painter's spiritual adventure.

Strangely enough, when Jung was asked to write an introduction for the third edition of the German translation of Joyce's *Ulysses*, he failed to recognize that this work was a modern counterpart to the *Odyssey*, even including its *Nekyia*. Jung was puzzled by the apparent nonsense of the book. It seemed to be some sort of interminable "tapeworm," and he felt that the novel could be read as easily backward as forward. These comments were published in a journal[188] and irritated Joyce.[189] It is unfortunate for Jung that this article was the sole piece of literary criticism he ever published. He often referred in his seminars to English, French, or German novels in which he found unexpected illustrations of his theories.

In Jung's articles, and particularly in his seminars, one could find the scattered elements of a philosophy of history centered around the idea that mankind has been undergoing a slow process of collective individuation. Jung considered psychic epidemics to be the effect of reviving an archetype on a mass scale. Jung saw in Hitlerism the resurgence of the archetype of Wotan, the old Germanic god of storm, battle, prophetic inspiration, and secret sciences.[190] He distinguished two types of dictators: the "chieftain" type (such as Mussolini and Stalin) and the "seer" type (such as Hitler). The latter type is able to perceive obscure forces in the unconscious of his followers and lead them as a Messiah.[191] In a little book devoted to "flying saucers," Jung said that, whether these manifestations have a physical reality or not, they are "psychic realities" to those who believe in their existence; they are archetypical symbols of a mediation between two incommensurable worlds; they are a myth originating in the fear of a collective destruction of mankind.[192] The greatest danger threatening mankind, according to Jung, was the substitution of a mass mentality for a true democratic mentality based on educating and perfecting the individual.

Those who visited Jung during the latter part of his life remember his conversation as a unique mixture of lofty psychological concepts and practical wisdom. He emphasized the meaning of awareness, not only as a therapeutic device but as an ethic principle. "Unawareness is the greatest sin" was one of his maxims.[193] Many neuroses, Jung said, originate in unawareness, many others in flight from one's life tasks. Such is the case of the young child who shirks going to school, of the delayed adolescent, the perennial student, the man who does not fulfill his duties as a citizen, the older person who wants to live as a youth. Marriage is a factor of emotional health insofar as husband and wife do not project their respective anima and animus on each other. One function of marriage is to forward the individuation of both spouses. A further factor of emotional stability is the individual's social integration: everyone should possess his own house and garden, be an active member of his community, live in the continuity of his family tradition and his culture, obey the commands of his religion if he believes in one. Though the path of individuation may differ from East to West, it tends toward the same goal: the more an individual has "become what he is," the more he is a truly social man.

Carl Gustav Jung's Work—VIII—The Psychology of Religion

From the time of his religious crisis in adolescence, Jung never ceased to be deeply concerned with religion, even if, in his earlier writings, we find interspersed here and there skeptical remarks in regard to established religion. It seems that his attitude changed as a result of his "Journey through the Unconscious" in the period from 1913 to 1918. He came to ascribe a "numinous" character to the archetypes, and to speak of the "natural function of religion."

As it so often happens in the history of dynamic psychiatry, it was a contemporary publication which instigated a new direction in the development of Jung's ideas. Rudolf Otto's book *The Idea of the Holy* appeared in 1917 and was hailed as a substantial contribution to the psychology of religion.[194] Trying to identify a fundamental experience common to all religions, Otto described the "numinous" as a well-defined, complex, and rigorously specific experience. The "numinous" immediately inspires a "feeling of createdness," that is, a feeling not just of dependency but of the creature's nothingness in the face of its Creator. The presence of the Creator is experienced as a *mysterium tremendum*, that is, with a feeling of awe and shuddering before an unapproachable Being that is a living energy and "totally other." But, in contrast to the *tremendum*, the "numinous" is simultaneously experienced as a *Fascinans*, that is, as something that attracts and fills with blissful exaltation. The numinous is also felt as a confrontation with an unsurpassable value, to which absolute respect and obedience are due out of a feeling of an inner obligation.

Jung took over the term numinous but extended its meaning. Otto saw in the numinous an exceptional experience lived by prophets, mystics, and founders of religions. Jung confers a "numinous quality" upon the experience of the archetype, but this also means that only certain features of the total experience of the numinous (as described by Otto) accompany the manifestation of the archetype. Jung placed the archetypes at the origin of those religious experiences from which are derived the religious rites and dogmas. According to Jung, much of that elementary religious experience is not channeled into established religions.

This explains one of Jung's favorite assertions: man is naturally religious. The "religious function" in man is as powerful, Jung says, as the instinct of sex or aggression. This is also why certain individuals are freed of their neurosis simply by a return to the practice of the religion in which they believe, and why, Jung adds, the mental health of aging persons is better among those who have religious faith. Incidentally, the neopsychoanalyst, Schultz-Hencke, apparently quite independent of Jung, asserted that he encountered religious feelings and attitudes among nonbelievers.[195]

Jung went even further and contended that "among all my patients who are in the second half of life there is not one whose principal problem is not a religious one." It is not quite sure, though, what breadth Jung gave to the word religion. Thus, among the people whom Jung calls "religious" some are believers whether they practice their religion or not, others are religiously minded people without knowing it, and lastly there are those who on the conscious level are antireligious but who under certain circumstances are the subject of an archetypical religious experience.

Sometimes religious archetypes burst out in the form of "immediate religious experience" which changes the life of an individual and therefore may affect the course of history. Such was Saul's vision on the way to Damascus which caused him to become a Christian and the great apostle Saint Paul. Another hardly less impressive immediate religious experience was that of the Swiss mystic Nicholas von der Flüe.[196] A rich and honored citizen, he left his family and worldly interests to become a hermit in Stans. His advice was often sought by the population. Once he had a vision of the Holy Trinity that was so frightening and awe-inspiring that his physical appearance was changed and he himself appeared frightening. For a long time he meditated upon that vision, painting it in different forms, until he could assimilate it. At this point, in 1481, the Swiss cantons were on the verge of civil war, but the Confederation was saved through the timely intervention of Brother Nicholas von der Flüe at the Diet of Stans.

However, it should be remembered that the emergence of such archetypes is not only a frightening experience but a dangerous one. The same archetypes whose crystallized forms are at the origin of religious experience in the normal individual can also be manifested in the religious delusions of schizophrenics.

Among the archetypes the most closely related to religion is that of self. Jung at times seems to consider this archetype as an intermediary link to the religious experience of God, to the point even of calling it the archetype of God. Nevertheless, Jung always proclaimed that he was an empiricist: that man is "naturally religious" does not necessarily prove the truth of religion, nor does the existence of the archetype of God prove the existence of God.

Jung's noncommittal attitude was felt by some to be ambiguous. This feeling increased when Jung published *Aion* in 1951.[197] In *Aion* he seems to identify Christ with the archetype of the self and to imply that mankind as a whole is undergoing a process of collective individuation; Christ was manifested at a predetermined moment, that is, when the point of spring entered the zodiacal sign of the Fishes. In 1952 appeared Jung's most controversial book, *Answer to Job*.[198] Here he returns to the problem which had preoccupied him in his youth, namely, evil. Like thousands before him, Jung pondered on the question of how a perfectly good and almighty God could have permitted evil, particularly the sufferings of the innocent and the just. Could it be that God is both good and evil? Jung critically examines the answers given in the *Book of Job*. He is revolted by God's conduct who caused Adam to fall into a trap in the Garden of Eden, demanded of Abraham the sacrifice of his son, and allowed Satan to torment Job. Because Job has a higher conception of justice than God himself, God meets the challenge by the incarnation of His son. The sacrifice of Christ thus appears as a reparation by God of an injustice he committed toward man. God perfected himself by means of His union with Divine Wisdom, the "Sophia," the feminine counterpart of the Holy Spirit which reappears under the image of the Virgin Mary. For that reason Jung considers that the proclamation in 1950 of the dogma of the Assumption is "the most important religious event since the Reformation."

Jung's *Answer to Job* scandalized some of his disciples and unleashed animated controversies. Some gave it a psychological interpretation, assuming that Jung meant merely to describe the evolution of the image man created for himself about God. Others thought that Jung had wrought speculations about the metamorphoses of God in a neo-Gnostic fashion. The book might also be understood as a cry of existential anguish from a man desperately seeking for the solution of the greatest of all philosophical riddles, the problem of evil.

Asked whether he did or did not believe in the existence of God, Jung never gave a direct answer. At times he cryptically referred to the "Old Man," as if he meant a collective human being with whom every individual is connected through the collective unconscious and the archetypes.[199] Eventually he came to take a more direct stand: he saw the hand of God in those strange, unexpected, but meaningful events which are forced upon each individual during his lifetime. In one of the last interviews he granted to a journalist, he stated that God was at the same time the voice of conscience speaking within us and the inexplicable fateful events: "All of what I have learned had led me step by step to an unshakable conviction of the existence of God. . . . I do not take His existence on belief—I *know* that He exists."[200]

An even greater discretion was observed by Jung in regard to the problem of life after death. His opinions on this were divulged only in his autobiography. Jung said that it was as difficult for a thinker to disclose the intimate paths of his cogitations as it was for a respectable woman to speak about her erotic life. How many thinkers had their unpublished manuscripts burned before their death or, as Bergson, forbade their posthumous publication. Jung, of course, does not pretend to give a definite answer; however, he is sure that the quest for a solution is characteristic of the normal individual. But how is one to find one's way in such an intricate matter? Jung considers various hypotheses. The idea of a world of blissful spirits devoid of all suffering seems improbable to him because of the fundamental unity of the universe; there must be much anguish and suffering in the other world; it must be a "grandiose and terrible" world, but there too, as on earth, there must be some kind of evolution. Jung does not find many arguments in favor of reincarnation. Nevertheless, our individual life must be but a link in a more extended chain, perhaps in relation to the lives of our ancestors. It may be that the life we live on earth is meant to be the answer to questions asked by them or to accomplish an assignment set from without. Or perhaps a life might be no more than the incarnation of an archetype (in other words, a temporary projection of a permanent self). Jung deems it probable that communication exists between the living and the dead. An opinion once enunciated by Fechner and defended with interesting arguments by Frederik van Eeden[201] is that, when in certain dreams a deceased person appears to us and gives us the feeling of absolute reality, this corresponds to an actual apparition of that person. But, when analyzing dreams of this kind which he had had in the course of his life, Jung notes a common feature to them all: far from ever revealing or teaching us anything, the dead need us and ask us questions. Since they live outside time and space they must resort to the help of those who still participate in spatio-temporal life. But all this can be no more than supposition. The main problem is to see whether one takes into account the infinite.[202] Whoever has reached this stage and achieved his individuation is delivered from the fear of death; even less will he be affected by many earthly concerns.

Carl Gustav Jung's Sources

Jung's most immediate sources were his own personality, his family, his ethnic background. He was a practical man, well adjusted to material reality, but also he displayed an acute psychic perceptiveness. This contrast is expressed in his teaching and his therapy. His Swiss background had given him that practical bent that incited him, first, to bring his patients back to awareness and, then, to help them readjust themselves as much as possible to their social and traditional setting. On the other hand, Jung's rare gift for psychological intuition and his aptitude for parapsychological experiences explain that other side of his teaching and therapy: the exploration of the collective unconscious and the world of archetypes.

Being the son of a Protestant minister and having several relatives in the clergy, Jung was familiar with religious problems, and the religious crisis of his adolescence marked him for the rest of his life. He owed to his background a certain familiarity with the thought of Protestant theologians (we have already mentioned Albrecht Ritschl and Rudolf Otto), and probably with the principle of "cure of souls." Interest in medicine, classical languages, and history of religion were again part of the family tradition. There also was the humanistic tradition of Basel, the home city of scholars who combined erudition with imagination (such as Bachofen, with whom Jung has more than one point in common).

As all the intellectuals of his generation, Jung was familiar with Greek and Latin classics, so that, when he undertook his journey of the unconscious, it was natural that he should compare it to the travels of Ulysses and Aeneas through the Land of the Dead. It was also natural that he knew Goethe, and, like Freud, quoted from *Faust* on almost any occasion. We have seen already how Schiller was one of the main sources of Jung's *Psychological Types*.

Jung received his psychiatric training at a time when psychiatry was undergoing fundamental changes. His masters were Bleuler, Janet, Binet, and Flournoy. Bleuler's main concern was to understand the patient and to establish an affective rapport with him; he was foremost among those who during those years were attempting to "re-psychologize" psychiatry.[203] As to Pierre Janet, with whom Jung studied for a semester in Paris, his influence on Jung was considerable. From him Jung learned about "psychological automatism," dual personality, psychological strength and weakness, the "function of synthesis," the *abaissement du niveau mental*, and "subconscious fixed ideas" (which Jung later identified with Ziehen's "complexes" and Freud's "traumatic reminiscences"). Jung learned Janet's distinction of the two basic neuroses: hysteria and psychasthenia (to which he substituted the distinction of extroverted hysteria and introverted schizophrenia). Jung refers to Binet's book on the alterations of personality, and, although he does not quote Binet's book on the two types of intelligence,[204] it is hardly possible that he should not have known it and been inspired by it in his description of the introverted and extroverted types. Jung gave due credit to the help and inspiration he had received from Théodore Flournoy. Jung could not have understood his young Basel medium so well, had it not been for Flournoy's research on Hélène Smith. It was also from Flournoy that Jung took his interest in the phenomenon of cryptomnesia.

From psychoanalysis Jung accepted with enthusiasm Freud's new method of exploring the unconscious through free association, Freud's contention that dreams could be interpreted and thus utilized for psychotherapy, and Freud's emphasis on the lasting influence of childhood and early relationships with parental figures. To be sure, Jung later substituted his own methods and ideas to these three great innovations of Freud, but it was from the latter that he had received the decisive impulse. On the other hand, Jung never accepted Freud's ideas about the role of sexuality in neurosis, sexual symbolism, and the Oedipus complex.

Jung repeatedly acknowledged the importance of Adler; he admitted that the drive for superiority can be found at the root of certain neuroses, and that Adler's theory of dreams could give clues to the interpretation of certain dreams, also that neurotics tend to manipulate their environment, and like Adler, Jung seated his patient on a chair facing his own. What Jung taught about the individual's "social age" and his social duties has much in common with Adler's concept of the "three great life-tasks"; and Jung made "therapeutic reeducation" a part of his own psychotherapy.

Jung accepted Alphonse Maeder's theories on the teleological function of dreams; he incorporated them in his system, giving Maeder due credit for them.[205] Herbert Silberer had also come to the conclusion that certain dream pictures are symbolic self-representations of the dreamer, and he was the first psychoanalyst to be concerned with the symbolic meaning of alchemy.[206]

Jung's "Journey into the Unconscious" was the great mainspring from which originated his system. We know from his autobiography that Jung acquired from this self-experiment his first notions of anima, the self, and individuation, with its symbols. The collective unconscious and the archetypes that had been known to him from his work with patients and from literature he now experienced personally. The methods he had applied in his self-experiment, namely active imagination, amplification of dreams, and drawing and painting from the unconscious, he now systematized as a therapeutic method for his patients.

Jung's extended readings covered the works of philosophers, theologians, mystics, orientalists, ethnologists, novelists, and poets. Perhaps the most important of his sources are to be found in Romantic philosophy and in the Philosophy of Nature. According to Leibbrand Jung's system cannot be conceived without Schelling's philosophy.[207] Rose Mehlich found parallels between Fichte's concepts of the soul and some of Jung's basic assertions.[208] Other parallels can be drawn between Jung's psychology and the philosophy of G. H. von Schubert,[209] and what the latter explained in philosophical terms E. T. H. Hoffmann utilized as a philosophical background for his novel.[210] Like Von Schubert, Hoffmann depicted the coexistence in each individual of an individual soul (the ego) and of another psychic principle related to the activity of the World Soul (the self). The individual may at times become conscious of the World Soul; these moments are called "cosmic moments" by Von Schubert and "exalted states" (*erhöhte Zustände*) by Hoffmann. Such are certain dreams, visions, somnambulic crises, and psychotic hallucinations.

It is customary to designate these great philosophers of the unconscious— Carl Gustav Carus, Arthur Schopenhauer, and Eduard von Hartmann—as Jung's predecessors. It would, however, be fitting to call attention to another Romantic philosopher, Ignaz Paul Vital Troxler, who has recently been rediscovered after a century of oblivion.[211] Troxler saw the course of human life as a series of psychic metamorphoses. The center of the personality is not the ego in the ordinary sense but what Troxler calls the *Gemüt* or the *Ich selbst*, that is, exactly what Jung calls the self. Troxler sees it as a goal to reach in this life and a starting point for life after death and for communication with God. Dream life is a revelation of the essence of man to man himself and is a means of progression. Jung's concept of individuation is also to be found in Schleiermacher.[212] Schleiermacher emphasized the absolute uniqueness of the individual, the idea that every individual is called to bring into being his primordial self-image, and that true freedom is the accomplishment of that self-realization.

Among the other Romantics, Friedrich Creuzer deserves special mention;[213] Jung himself recalls that he had devoured his works with passionate interest.[214] In Creuzer's works Jung found a rich mine of myths and symbols with their interpretations, and also a specific conception of myths and symbols. They are neither historical nor literary material, but specific realities intermediate between abstraction and life. There is in the human mind a twofold symbolic function; primitive people translate certain experiences and knowledge into myths, and endowed persons are able to grasp their meaning and interpret them.

It is not known whether Jung was acquainted with those romantic psychiatrists—like Reil, Heinroth, Ideler, and Neumann—who emphasized the psychogenesis of mental illness, the symbolic meaning of certain symptoms, and the possibility of the psychotherapy of psychosis.[215] But, certainly, he was well acquainted with Justinus Kerner and the story of his famous "seeress," Friedericke Hauffe, who in certain regards served as model to Helene Preiswerk's mediumistic activities.[216]

Though Jung hardly ever quotes Bachofen it is unlikely that he was not acquainted with his work. Bachofen was among those few who, like Creuzer, taught how to decipher the meaning of symbols.[217] He taught that matriarchy had been overthrown and supplanted by patriarchy and how its memory expresses itself in symbolic form. Translated into psychological terms this would give Jung's picture of the masculine individual with his repressed feminine soul and his anima symbols. As for Nietzsche, Jung quoted him freely, and possibly borrowed the concepts of the shadow and the Old Wise Man from him.

It is open to question to what extent the mystics and occultists contributed to Jung's thinking or were merely objects of study for him. Those Romantic philosophers who were Jung's more direct sources had themselves a long series of predecessors, from the Gnostics and alchemists to Paracelsus, Boehme, Swedenborg, Saint-Martin, Von Baader, and Fabre d'Olivet. Some of these men were hailed by Jung as the pioneers of the psychology of the unconscious.

Jung seems to have been influenced by the work of the German ethnologist Adolf Bastian, an erudite, well-traveled, and prolific writer who developed a theory of "elementary thoughts."[218] Bastian contended that the theory of diffusion did not suffice to explain the occurrence of the same rites, myths, and thoughts all over the world, and that this could be explained only by a theory of the universal structure of the human mind. These ideas brought a noted Italian psychiatrist, Tanzi, to draw a parallel between the hallucinations and delusions of his paranoid patients and the rites and beliefs of many primitive peoples.[219] Another German ethnologist, Leo Frobenius, developed a theory that mankind had gone through three successive visions of the world: the oldest was the animalistic in which men worshiped animals. With the beginning of agriculture came a new vision of the world centered around the problem of death and the cult of the dead. Then came the "epoch of the Sun-God," dominated by the cult of the Sun. Men believed that the souls of the dead follow the Sun in the underworld, and this belief gave birth to innumerable stories of mythical heroes who were swallowed by a monster and journeyed through its interior before emerging and starting a new life.[220] Jung recognized this basic myth in the subconscious fantasies of Miss Miller, and for some time he and his pupils found it in patients of the Burghölzli.[221] One may wonder to what extent this myth inspired certain features of Jung's own "Journey through the Unconscious." Albrecht Dieterich's work *Mother Earth*[222] seems to have partially inspired Jung's concepts of the *Magna Mater* and her symbolism.

It is difficult to ascertain what in Asiatic literature served as a source or stimulus for Jung's thinking. The effect of conversations with men like Richard Wilhelm or Heinrich Zimmer was probably more decisive than the widest readings.

We already mentioned the stimulation which Jung received from novels such as Spitteler's *Imago*, Alphonse Daudet's *Tartarin sur les Alpes*, Rider Haggard's *She*, and Pierre Benoît's *L'Atlantide*. Another novelist, Léon Daudet, enunciated ideas which show noteworthy parallels to Jung's psychological theories.[223]

Léon Daudet contends that man's main drive is his tendency to realize himself against noxious hereditary influences and to thus acquire inner freedom. Human personality, Daudet says, consists of two entities, the ego and the self (the *moi* and the *soi*) and the life drama of each man is in the struggle between these two. The ego does not consist only of the conscious personality with its perceptions, memories, moods, and vague aspirations, but also of an unconscious personality with a "generation instinct," psychic automatisms, and scattered remnants of hereditary influences. The self, on the other hand, is the essence of human personality, a true, original, and new being. Creative impulses, major decisions, acts of reason and of faith issue from the self.

When the ego predominates the personality loses its unity and gives way to a number of struggling "personages" that are none other than the vestiges of our ancestors. Sometimes the personality can be wrecked by the sudden emergence of one or several "ancestors" who take possession of the individual, either through the influence of an exterior circumstance or spontaneously through a kind of self-fertilization. At first the individual may experience it as a helpful influence but in the long run it becomes detrimental to him. Such an "ancestor-dominated" individual Daudet calls an *hérédo*; he is restless, impulsive, and moody. The man who is dominated by the self, is poised, well-balanced, and shows insight and moral courage. It is the true possession of the self that enables a man to be a hero or a creative genius. Thus the main goal in human life is to overcome the ego with the uncontrolled ancestral impulses, and to discover and actualize one's self. This should be the object of a new science which Daudet calls "metapsychology."

Many people live their lives in ignorance of their self, discovering it very late or only at the moment of death. There are propitious times in life for the emergence of the self; namely, between the ages of seven years and puberty, then for a passing moment around the twentieth year, and particularly between the ages of thirty-five and forty, when the individual is set before the choice of remaining an *hérédo* for the rest of his life or attaining his self. Daudet considers that longevity depends on the "methodical tonification" of the self. The success of a marriage relationship is bound to how far the two spouses have each attained their self. The self is the eminently sociable part of the personality, whereas ego-domination is the source of disturbances in human relationships.

Daudet calls "imagination" a function of the self by means of which a man becomes aware of his "heredisms," so that he can discard the noxious ones and retain as models the images from wise ancestors only. Mental disease, he adds, is the effect of cataclysms by which certain ancestors take possession of an individual. Thus, "man lives and dies by his images," and Daudet concludes that his "metapsychology" would favor unforeseen applications.

When reading *L'Hérédo* and its sequence, *The World of Images*,[224] one has the feeling of reading the epitome of a full-fledged system of dynamic psychiatry that merely lacks substantiation in psychotherapeutic work. To what extent it inspired Jung is not known, but he certainly read it, since he referred to *L'Hérédo* on at least one occasion.[225]

The Influence of Carl Gustav Jung

Jung's influence has been exerted through his personality, his doctrine, his disciples, his former patients, and his school. At first it was limited to psychiatry and psychotherapy, but after 1920 it extended itself to the circles of religion and the history of culture. Later he also attracted the attention of sociologists, economists, and students of political science.

Jung's name was first made known through his work with the word association test, an already existing method of which he made the first projective test.[226] It became part of the daily routine in Swiss mental hospitals, and also served as an incentive for the Rorschach test and others. Although Jung's attempts to use the test for criminological purposes failed, research in that direction was taken up by other scientists and culminated with the invention of the lie-detector.

Next came Jung's studies on schizophrenia, which was in line with Bleuler's efforts to understand these patients and establish a rapport with them. We have seen how Jung first found "complexes" and then "archetypes" at the root of schizophrenic symptoms. Jung did a great deal to further the psychotherapy of schizophrenia, and he anticipated the research of contemporary existential analysts in their attempts to understand and make intelligible the subjective experience of schizophrenics. A number of Jungian and non-Jungian psychiatrists pointed out the similarity of universal myths and subjective schizophrenic experiences.[227]

C. G. Jung's contributions to psychoanalysis have been duly recognized by Freudians.[228] He introduced the terms "complex" and "imago," and he was the promotor of training analysis. According to Jung, it was he who called Freud's attention to Schreber's *Memoirs*. Jung's criticism of Freud's interpretation of the Schreber case caused Freud to revise his libido theory and introduce the concept of narcissism. Jung's preoccupation with myths and his *Metamorphoses and Symbols of Libido* stimulated Freud to write his *Totem and Taboo*. Child analysts adopted Jung's techniques of therapy through drawing and painting. Recently a number of analysts have discreetly enunciated ideas offering certain resemblances to Jung's teachings. Erikson, for instance, describes the development of the individual in eight stages, the first five of which are analogous to Freud's stages of libidinal development, and the three other ones seem to have been inspired by Jung's concept of individuation.[229]

Jung's method of active imagination inspired Desoille's daydream therapy.[230] Desoille has the patient lie on a couch imagining that he is lifted into the air and further and further up into the sky, telling the therapist all the images that presented themselves to him, thus enabling the therapist to explore his unconscious.

Numerous therapists adopted Jung's method of painting from the unconscious under various forms; psychoanalysts also used it in the psychotherapy of children and psychotics. One of Jung's disciples, Hans Trüb, thought that the one healing factor in psychotherapy was the encounter between the therapist and patient.[231] In developing this theory he parted from Jung, with whom he remained in faithful antagonism, as Trüb described it. Jungian treatment of mental illness has been systematized by H. K. Fierz.[232] Jung touched upon psychosomatic medicine around 1909 and a Jungian approach has been developed by C. A. Meier.[233] A variety of group therapy based on Jung's principles has been introduced by Hans Illing[234]

It should also be mentioned that Alcoholics Anonymous indirectly owes its origin to Jung.

> That little-known story has been clarified by the recent publication of an exchange of letters between one of the cofounders of A.A. and Jung.[235] Around 1931 an American alcoholic patient, Roland H., came to C. G. Jung who gave him psychotherapy for perhaps one year, but he relapsed shortly afterward. He returned to Jung who frankly told him that there was no more hope for him in any further medical or psychiatric treatment. Roland H. asked whether there was any other hope and Jung replied that there might be provided he could become the subject of a spiritual or religious experience, which might remotivate him entirely. Roland H. joined the Oxford Group where he found a conversion experience, was delivered from his compulsion to drink, and devoted himself to helping other alcoholics. One of them, Eddy, followed his example, joined the Oxford Group, and was freed from his drinking compulsion. In November 1934 Eddy visited his friend Bill, whose case was considered hopeless, and told him of his experience. Bill subsequently had a religious experience and a vision of a society of alcoholics transmitting their experience from one to the other. Eddy and Bill then founded the Society of Alcoholics Anonymous whose subsequent development is known.[236]

Jung's typology with its distinction of extroversion and introversion and the four psychological functions has been criticized by students of characterology. Nevertheless, Eysenck adopted the dichotomy extroversion-introversion as one of his dimensions of personality.[237] A Swiss marriage counselor, Plattner, contends that most individuals tend to choose as their partner a person who belongs to the type and function opposite to their own; for instance, a rational extroverted will choose an affective introverted, hence the existence of certain marriage types, each with its own difficulties and possibilities of conflict.[238] The historian Toynbee found that the world's great religions could be classified in terms of Jung's psychological types.[239] Generally speaking, Jung's concepts of extroversion and introversion enjoyed such popularity that they are now used in colloquial language (although not always according to their original meaning). Jung's original concept is sometimes to be recognized under another terminology. Such is David Riesman's distinction between inner-directed and other-directed people.[240]

The intensive preoccupation with symbols, myths, and archetypes is a main feature of Jung's psychology. At first it was a matter of applying depth psychology to the study of myths. In a second period Jung used myths to understand psychological phenomena, applying his method of amplification, a method that requires a thorough knowledge on the part of the therapist of mythology and of the manifold possible meanings of symbols. For instance, to a Freudian analyst the snake is just a phallic symbol; to a Jungian it might be this, but it also can have ten other meanings. In a third period, comparative studies of the same myths were undertaken by mythologists on one side and Jungian psychologists on the other. A prototype of such comparative studies is given by the book published jointly by Karl Kerényi, a Hungarian student of mythology living in Zurich, and C. G. Jung.[241] The myth of the divine child and the divine maiden is analyzed by both Kerényi and Jung in terms of their particular disciplines. Other comparative studies have been presented at the Eranos yearly conferences in Ascona and subsequently published in the *Eranos Yearbooks*.

Jung's concept of the collective unconscious has been applied to the psychology of philosophical insights and scientific discoveries. Such was Jung's interpretation of the discovery of the law of conservation of energy by Robert Mayer. The physicist Pauli gave a somewhat similar interpretation of Kepler's discoveries.[242] Referring to Anaximander's idea of the primordial stuff of a boundless universe without beginning or end, F. M. Cornford remarks that such an idea could not have resulted from observation or from a scientific hypothesis.[243] Therefore the idea emerged "from a level of the unconscious mind so deep that we do not recognize it as a part of ourselves," that is, from Jung's collective unconscious. This would explain the similarity of Anaximander's concept with the primitive image of the Polynesian mana. Indeed, Cornford assumes that "the development of philosophy and science centrally consists in the differentiation, under the action of conscious intellectual criticism, of these primordial images which had, by a different process, previously given birth to every form of religious representation." In that perspective, philosophy, science, and mythology derive through different channels from the collective unconscious.

Jung's concepts of the natural function of religion and the existence of religious archetypes in man provoked lively discussion in religious circles. Several theologians thought that they had found in Jung an ally against atheism, others blamed his psychologism. They said that while Freud was openly atheistic, considering religion an illusion and the result of wishful thinking, Jung saw in religion the projection of religious archetypes about which one does not know to which transcendent reality they correspond. The theologian Frischknecht of Basel designates Jung's system as a "kind and understanding" variety of atheism.[244] Another theologian, Hans Schär, in Berne, contends that no one concerned with religion today could dispense with studying Jung's work.[245] On the basis of Jung's concepts, Hans Schär produced his seven-hundred-page treatise of the psychology of religion.[246]

Another theologian, Rochedieu, developing Jung's idea that man is naturally religious, contends that, unknown to most therapists, transference is in part a religious manifestation.[247] Another well-known theologian, Paul

Tillich, states that Jung's doctrine of archetypes is of great help to Protestant theology, especially in regard to the theory of religious symbols.[248] Jung's ideas also aroused much interest among Catholic theologians.[249] At least three of them wrote a comprehensive study: Father White,[250] Father Hostie,[251] and Father Goldbrunner.[252] Among Russian-Orthodox theologians, Reverend Evdokimov utilized Jung's concepts of the archetypes and of the anima and the animus, in a philosophical anthropological study of woman.[253]

In his textbook of collective psychology, Reiwald devoted a chapter to Jung, emphasizing the great importance of his concepts for the understanding of mass psychoses.[254] Jung stressed the "psychic inflation" of the individual in a crowd. Whereas Freud saw the mass identifying itself with the leader, Jung (like Janet) underlined that the leader also depends on the mass. Jung explains mass psychoses as being the sudden resurgence among a collectivity of latent archetypes.

Among Jung's closest disciples was the Swiss economist Eugen Böhler,[255] who drew the attention of business circles to the psychology of Jung and attempted in numerous publications to apply Jung's concepts of economic science,[256] especially that of myths in relation to mass psychology.[257]

Economic life, according to Böhler, is not so much dominated by national purposes than by collective impulses originating in fantasy and myth. Or more precisely, whereas producing is the outcome of a rational process, consuming depends on irrational impulse similar to the erotic impulse. Fantasy is the true incentive to economic progress: the progress of science and technique had resulted in an enormous increase of the part assigned to fantasy in human life. Literature, art, newspapers, movie theaters, radio, television, are "dream factories" and so are the modern hotels and the tourist business: "Modern economy is as much a dream factory as Hollywood." It is based for a small part on real needs, for the greatest part on fantasy and myth. Hence the central role in modern economics of the advertising business. Science itself is now surrounded with a mythical halo. While gratifying human imagination science also creates new needs among the consumers as well as the means to satisfy these artificially created needs. Fashion means for woman "Dionysian release from rationality" and the enhancement of her personality. And it is its very unpredictability that confers on it the mystery of an oracle that must be fathomed. The Stock Exchange itself has a mythical function; it is not the "brain," but rather the "heart" of economic life, compensating for the pressures endured by *homo economicus* in his relentless striving toward rational organization, order, and thriftiness, and the exactingness of bookkeeping, computing, and the setting up of balance sheets. The Stock Exchange is the only window through which daydreams can enter the life of such a man. At the same time the beliefs, expectations, and desires of numerous men are projected and converge on the Stock Exchange. Far from ruling economic life, the Stock Exchange is itself at the mercy of the tides of collective fantasies; depressions come about when there is a sudden loss of economic myth. Böhler extended his criticism to other economic myths, past or present, such as free trade, the Grossraum, and others.

The application of Jungian concepts to political philosophy was inaugurated in 1931 by Schindler with his study on constitutional law and social structure.[258] In 1954 Hans Fehr applied the concept of archetypes to the philosophy of law.[259] Then Hans Marti proposed a Jungian interpretation of the Swiss Constitution.[260] The most consistent attempts in that direction, however, were those of Erich Fechner in 1956[261] and Max Imboden in 1959.[262]

In a critical survey of all possible theories pertaining to the origin of the notion of law (biological, economical, political, sociological, philosophical, theological theories), Erich Fechner comes to propound a psychological theory based on the Jungian concepts of archetypes. Social instinct, according to Erich Fechner, cannot account for the origin of a legal community and of the State. The commandment "Thou shalt not kill" or the institution of monogamy, for instance, must have been unconscious representations long before they became legal institutions and therefore must have been primordial images, or archetypes.

Max Imboden asserts that the structure of the State is a reflection of psychic reality. The three classical forms of State: monarchy, aristocracy, and democracy, correspond to different development levels of collective consciousness. Monarchy (or autocracy) is the State in which one individual assumes the ego potential and actualizes the unconscious contents of all others. The dominator and the dominated are strongly tied to each other by a phenomenon of transference, which impedes the development of individuals. Aristocracy, which is domination by a group of chosen men, allows for a certain amount of growth in the dominated individuals. But it implies a complex network of relationships between the elite and the masses. There is a variety of such systems depending on whether the tie is more an unconscious transference or a conscious mandate. Democracy should be the State form of citizens when all or the majority among them have reached a sufficient degree of individuation, so that they are clearly aware of their mutual relationship, and become able to create an authentic community. Referring to Montesquieu's theory of the three powers (legislative, executive, and judiciary), Imboden points out certain analogies with the dogma of the Trinity, and he thinks that it actually issued from that dogma, thanks to an increase in collective awareness at the beginning of modern times.

It is the fate of all innovators that the development of their work is unpredictable, because it does not depend so much on its intrinsic value as on material factors, historical circumstances, and the fluctuations of the collective mind.

There is a basic similarity between the system of Freud and Jung, each one deriving from a "creative illness" channeled into a psychotherapeutic method. Both offer the possibility of a journey into the unconscious, in the form of a training or therapeutic analysis. But it is a very different journey.

Those who undertake a Freudian analysis will soon develop an intensive transference neurosis, have Freudian dreams, and discover their Oedipus complex, child sexuality, and castration anxiety. Those who undertake a Jungian analysis will have Jungian dreams, confront their shadow, their anima, their archetypes, and pursue their individuation. A Freudian psychoanalyst who would undergo a Jungian analysis would feel as disoriented as Mephisto in the second part of *Faust*, when he comes to the Classical Walpurgis Night and discovers with amazement that "there is another Hell with its own laws." (Actually the contrast between the Freudian and the Jungian unconscious could aptly be illustrated by the contrast between the Walpurgis Night of the Blocksberg, with its demons and witches, and the Classical Walpurgis Night, with its mythological figures.)

This is also why many people react to Freud and Jung more according to their personal tendencies than to an objective scrutiny of facts. Some persons feel that Freud stands on the solid ground of scientific facts, whereas Jung is lost in a hazy mysticism. Others think that Freud deprives the human soul of its aura of mystery,[263] and that Jung saves its spiritual values. Did not Freud himself (they will say) choose for the epigraph of his *Interpretation of Dreams* Virgil's verse:

Flectere si nequeo Superos, Acheronta movebo
(If I cannot move those of Heaven, I shall rally those of Hell)

In contrast to this, Jung's motto could be another verse of Virgil:[264]

Carmina vel coelo possunt deducere lunam
(Songs can the very moon draw down from heaven)

Thus, the same people who see in Freud the sorcerer who reduced man to his devilish instincts, are likely to visualize Jung as the wizard who was able to sway the moon.

It is to be expected that with the passing of time Jung's work will undergo certain transformations. One reason for this is of general nature: it is the fate of any ideology that each successive generation tends to see it in a new perspective. In Jung's case there is something more. His work is essentially known today through the books, articles, and contributions published during his lifetime and gathered in his *Collected Works*. When the collection of his typewritten seminars is made available in printed form, Jung's personality and work will be shown in a new perspective and it will be even more so when his letters are published. It is not impossible that even his *Red Book* and *Black Book*, perhaps even his diaries, will appear some day and show him in yet another, unsuspected light. Not only a man's life, but also his image and posthumous influence can undergo an unforseeable succession of metamorphoses.

Notes

1. For an account of the Swiss democratic system, see André Siegfried, *La Suisse, démocratie-témoin, édition revue et augmentée* (Neuchatel: La Baconnière, 1956).

2. We give the most probable date for his birth. Certain documents give it as 1793, others 1795, but the majority place it in 1794.

3. Eduard His, *Basler Gelehrte des 19. Jahrhunderts* (Basel: Benno Schwabe, 1941), pp. 69–76.

4. H. Haupt, *Ein vergessener Dichter aus der Frühzeit der Burschenschaft, Karl Gustav Jung (1794–1864)* (n.p., n.d.).

5. Ernst Jung, ed., *Aus den Tagebüchern meines Vaters.* (n.p., n.d.).

6. C. G. Jung, *Animadversiones quaedam de ossibus generatim et in specie de ossibus raphogeminantibus, quae vulgo ossa suturarum dicuntur* (Basileae, 1827).

7. According to the Community Registry in Basle, the psychiatrist's first name was spelled "Karl," but he always used the older spelling "Carl" that had been that of his grandfather.

8. These details are borrowed from a study by Aniela Jaffé on Jung's family, compiled from family documents. C. G. Jung, *Erinnerungen, Träume, Gedanken* (Zurich: Rascher Verlag, 1962), pp. 399–407.

9. Professor P. Kielholz, director of the Friedmatt Mental Hospital, informed the author that the name of Reverend Paul Jung is found in the Annual Reports of that institution for the first time in 1888, and that he held the office of chaplain until his death in 1896. Annual reports of that period expressed high appreciation of his character and services to the patients.

10. Pierre Berteaux, *La Vie quotidienne en Allemagne au temps de Guillaume II* (Paris: Hachette, 1962), p. 27.

11. The book by E. A. Bennet, *C. G. Jung* (London: Barris & Rockliff, 1961), is based mainly on interviews given by Jung in his old age.

12. Albert Oeri, "Ein paar Jugenderinnerungen," in *Die kulturelle Bedeutung der komplexen Psychologie* (Berlin: Springer, 1935), pp. 524–528.

13. Gustav Steiner, "Erinnerungen an Carl Gustav Jung. Zur Entstehung der Autobiographie," *Basler Stadtbuch* (1965), pp. 117–163.

14. The main parts of the autobiography appeared serially in the weekly, *Die Weltwoche* (Zurich) from August 31, 1962, to February 1, 1963, and then in book form, C. G. Jung, *Erinnerungen, Träume, Gedanken,* Aniela Jaffé (Zurich: Rascher, 1962). The English translation, *Memories, Dreams, Reflections* (New York: Pantheon Books, 1963), is somewhat incomplete.

15. To give only one instance: Albert Oeri says that Jung had decided at a very young age to become a physician; in his autobiography Jung relates that the decision was taken abruptly, under the impact of two dreams, shortly before registering at the university.

16. An edition of the correspondence of C. G. Jung is currently being prepared under the direction of Dr. Gerhard Adler.

17. All data pertaining to the names, dates, and places of birth of the members of the Jung family have been supplied by the Registry Office of the City of Basel.

18. Justin Gehrig, *Aus Kleinhünigens vergangenen Tagen* (Basel, 1941).

19. Jean Delay, *La Jeunesse d'André Gide* (Paris: Gallimard, 1956), I, 193–199.

20. Though Jung never named the personage, this second personality was most probably that of Goethe as a reflection of the grandfathers' legend.

21. *Ich kann nicht glauben an was ich nicht kenne, und an was ich kenne brauche ich nicht zu glauben.*

22. Data furnished by Dr. Hans Gutzwiller, rector of the Humanistisches Gymnasium in Basel.

23. Information supplied by the State Archive of the Canton of Basel-City.

24. Gustav Steiner, "Erinnerungen an Carl Gustav Jung. Zur Entstehung der Autobiographie," *Basler Stadtbuch* (1965), pp. 117–163.

25. The identity of the young medium is no longer a secret. She was the eleventh child of Rudolph Preiswerk, who was C. G. Jung's maternal uncle. Further details may be found in the book by Ernst Schopf-Preiswerk, *Die Basler Familie Preiswerk* (Basel: Friedrich Reinhardt, n.d.), p. 122.

26. Details of C. G. Jung's periods of military service were kindly provided by his son, Franz Jung.

27. We owe this information to Professor Manfred Bleuler, Director of the Burghölzli Mental Hospital, Zurich.

28. See Chap. 5, pp. 286–288.

29. Dr. Alphonse Maeder, personal communication.

30. Professor Jakob Wyrsch, personal communication.

31. Professor Erwin Ackerknecht was instrumental in obtaining for the author from the archives of the Zurich University the list of the lectures given by Jung as a Privat Dozent.

32. C. G. Jung, "Ueber die Bedeutung der Lehre Freuds für Neurologie und Psychiatrie," *Korrespondenz-Blatt fur Schweizer Aerzte,* XXXVIII (1908), 218–222.

33. Dr. Alphonse Maeder assures the author he witnessed incidents during which Jung would publicly ridicule Bleuler.

34. Dr. Alphonse Maeder, personal communication.

35. See Chap. 10, pp. 810–814.

36. See Chap. 10, p. 818.

37. See Shap. 10, pp. 819–820.

38. According to Dr. Alphonse Maeder, Jung resigned because the Zurich University refused to grant him the title of Professor.

39. *Notes on the Seminar in Analytical Psychology Conducted by C. G. Jung* (Zurich: March 23–July 6, 1925). Arranged by members of the class. (Typescript.)

40. C. G. Jung, *Erinnerungen, Träume, Gedanken* (Zurich: Rascher Verlag, 1962), pp. 103–104. This episode has been left out of the English translation of Jung's autobiography.

41. Incidentally, the author learned from Dr. Alphonse Maeder that the Viennese psychoanalysts who did not like Jung had nicknamed him "The Blond Siegfried."

42. C. G. Jung's *Septem Sermones ad Mortuos* have been reprinted in the original German edition of his autobiography, pp. 389–398.

43. The term "self" incompletely conveys the meaning of the word *Selbst,* which will be defined later.

44. Dr. Alphonse Maeder informs the author that he remained close to Jung and was his disciple during all this period and until 1928.

45. Fanny Moser, ed., *Spuk: Irrglaube oder Wahrglaube?* (Baden bei Zurich:Gyr, 1950), pp. 250–261.

46. C. G. Jung, *Psychologische Typen* (Zurich: Rascher, 1921). Eng. trans., *Psychological Types* (New York: Harcourt, Brace, 1923).

47. The author asked Jung once why he did not publish his observations on the Elgoni, and Jung answered that being a psychologist he did not want to encroach upon the field of the anthropologist. A short account of this and others of Jung's travels may be found in his autobiography.

48. Information provided by Dr. Paul Guyer, archivist of the city of Zurich.

49. *Neue Zürcher Zeitung,* November 26, 1932, No. 2202, and November 27, 1932, No. 2210.

50. Gustav Bally, "Deutschstammige Psychotherapie," *Neue Zürcher Zeitung,* February 27, 1934, No. 343.

51. C. G. Jung, "Zeitgenössisches," *Neue Zürcher Zeitung,* March 13, 1934, No. 437; March 14, 1934, No. 443. "Ein Nachtrag," *Neue Zürcher Zeitung,* March 15, 1934, No. 457.

52. Gustav Bally, "C. G. Jung," *Neue Zürcher Zeitung,* December 23, 1942, No. 2118, Blatt 2.

53. According to information sent by the Registrar of the University of Calcutta, Jung was awarded an honorary degree of Doctor of Laws on January 7, 1938, but could not attend the ceremony because of illness.

54. Jung published his impressions of India in two articles: "The Dreamlike World of India," and "What India Can Teach Us" in the journal *Asia,* XXXIX (1939), 5–8 and 97–98.

55. The campaign originated in Swiss socialist circles, with Theodor Schwarz and Alex von Muralt; it then extended to certain Jewish periodicals, and was renewed a few years later by a small group of psychoanalysts.

56. The incriminating sentences are to be found in an article by C. G. Jung, "Zur gegenwärtigen Lage der Psychotherapie," *Zentralblatt für Psychotherapie,* VII (1934), 1–16.

57. If Jung really had taken over Kretschmer's post in the German Association, as Jones erroneously contends, it is obvious that Kretschmer would have mentioned the fact in his autobiography. However, Kretschmer does not say anything of the kind and he gives a very sympathetic picture of Jung. See Ernst Kretschmer, *Gestalten und Gedanken* (Stuttgart: Thieme, 1963), pp. 133–136.

58. Ernest Jones, *The Life and Work of Sigmund Freud* (New York: Basic Books, 1957), III, 187.

59. See the article of Ernest Harms, "Carl Gustav Jung—Defender of Freud and the Jews," *Psychiatric Quarterly,* XX (1946), 198–230.

60. C. G. Jung, "Nach der Katastrophe," *Neue Schweizer Rundschau,* XIII (1945), 67–88.

61. M. Malinine, H. Puech, G. Quispel, eds., *Evangelium Veritatis.* Studien aus dem C. G. Jung Institute, VI (Zurich: Rascher, 1957).

62. Ludwig Marcuse, "Der Fall C. G. Jung," *Der Zeitgeist,* No. 36 (1955), pp. 13–15. (Monthly supplement of the journal *Der Aufbau,* New York.)

63. *Israelitisches Wochenblatt,* March 2, 1956, pp. 39–40.

64. Details of the ceremony may be found in the *Zürichsee Zeitung,* July 28, 1960.

65. Such are the books by E. A. Bennet, *C. G. Jung* (London: Barrie and Rockliff, 1961). Richard I. Evans, *Conversations with Carl Jung and Reactions from Ernest Jones* (Princeton: Van Nostrand Co., 1964).

66. Carl Jung, M. L., von Franz, Joseph L. Henderson, Jolande Jacobi, Aniela Jaffé, *Man and His Symbols* (London: Aldus Books, 1964).

67. Gustav Steiner, "Erinnerungen an Carl Gustav Jung," *Basler Standtbuch* (1965), pp. 117–163.

68. Personal communication from Dr. Alphonse Maeder who was on the Burghölzli staff at that time.

69. Martin Freud, *Sigmund Freud, Man and Father* (New York: Vanguard, 1958), pp. 108–109.

70. Personal communication.

71. Martin Freud, *Sigmund Freud, Man and Father* (New York: Vanguard, 1958), pp. 108–109.

72. Ernst Kretschmer, *Gestalten und Gedanken* (Stuttgart: Thieme, 1963), p. 135.

73. Personal information from Franz Jung.

74. Denis de Rougemont, "Le Suisse moyen et quelques autres," *Revue de Paris,* LXXII (1965), 52–64.

75. Karl Barth, *Die kirchliche Dogmatik* (Zollikon: Evangelischer Verlag, 1951), Vol. III/4, Part I, par. 54, I.

76. Paul Häberlin, *Der Mensch, eine Philosophische Anthropologie* (Zurich: Schweizer Spiegel-Verlag, 1941).

77. Among his books on education two are particularly noted, *Wege und Irrwege der Erziehung* (Basel: Kober, 1918). *Eltern und Kinder, Psychologische Bemerkungen zum Konflikt der Generationen* (Basley: Kober, 1922).

78. Paul Häberlin, *Statt einer Autobiographie* (Frauenfeld: Huber, 1959). (Frauenfeld: Huber, 1956).

79. Paul Häberlin, *Aus meinem Hüttenbuch. Erlebnisse and Gedanken eines Gems-jägers* (Frauenfeld: Huber, 1956).

80. Paul Häberlin, *Aus meinem Hüttenbuch* (Frauenfeld: Huber, 1956), p. 54. *Statt einer Autobiographie* (Frauenfeld: Huber, 1959), pp. 52–55.

81. Paul Häberlin, "Zur Lehre vom Traum," *Schweizer Archiv für Neurologie und Psychiatrie*, LXVII (1951), 19–46. Reprinted in *Zwischen Philosophie und Medizin* (Zurich: Schweizer-Spiegel-Verlag, 1965), pp. 96–136.

82. Rudolf Steiner, *Mein Lebensgang* (Dornach: Philosophisch–Anthroposophischer Verlag, 1925).

83. See Chap. 4, pp. 206–207.

84. Rudolf Steiner, *Wie erlangt man Erkenntnisse der höheren Welten?* (Berlin: Philosophisch–Anthroposophischer Verlag, 1922).

85. Rudolf Steiner's concepts of the "turning of life" are scattered throughout his works. His ideas on this point have been summarized by Friedrich Husemann, *Das Bild des Menschen als Grundlage der Heilkunst* (Stuttgart: Verlag Freies Geistesleben, 1956), II, 136.

86. Rudolf Steiner, *Geisteswissenschaftliche Erläuterungen zu Goethes Faust* (Dornach: Philosophisch–Anthroposophischer Verlag, 1931), I, 76.

87. Rudolf Steiner, *Anthroposophie und Psychoanalyse* (Dornach: November 10, 1917), Vol. I. Reprinted in *Anthroposophie*, Stuttgart, Vols. III, IV (April–September, 1935).

88. Gustav Steiner, "Erinnerungen an Carl Gustav Jung," *Basler Stadtbuch* (1965), pp. 117–163.

89. C. G. Jung, *Erinnerungen, Träume, Gedanken* (Zurich: Rascher Verlag, 1962), p. 106. *Memories, Dreams, Reflections*, p. 99.

90. Incidentally, this idea was commonplace at that time.

91. C. G. Jung, *Zur Psychologie und Pathologie sogenannter occulter Phenomäne. Eine Psychiatrische Studie* (Leipzig: Oswald Mutze, 1902). Eng. trans., *On the Psychology and Pathology of So-Called Occult Phenomenon*, in C. G. Jung *Collected Works* (New York: Pantheon Books, 1957), I, 3–88.

92. See Chap. 2, pp. 79–81.

93. *Notes on the Seminar in Analytical Psychology, Conducted by Dr. C. G. Jung, Zurich, March 23-July 6, 1925*, arranged by members of the Class, 1926.

94. A lady who managed a dressmaker's shop in Basel for a long time patronized by a distinguished clientele assured the author that Jung's cousin "worked well but created dresses that lacked originality, copied from fashion magazines." Was this professional rivalry, or is it that psychiatrists are not always the best judges in matters of fashion?

95. *Archives de Psychologie*, II (1903), 85–86.

96. P. E. Cornillier, *La Survivance de l'âme et son évolution après la mort. Comptes-rendus d'expériences* (Paris: Alcan, 1920).

97. H. R. Lenormand, *Les Confessions d'un auteur dramatique* (Paris: Albin Michel, 1953), II, 134–140.

98. H. R. Lenormand, *L'Amour magicien* (1926), in *Théâtre complet* (Paris: Crès, 1930), VI, 1–113.

99. C. G. Jung, "Die Psychopathologische Bedeutung des Assoziationsexperimentes," *Archiv für Kriminal-Anthropologie und Kriminalistik*, XXII (1906), 145–162.

100. C. G. Jung, *Diagnostische Assoziationsstudien* (Leipzig: J. A. Barth, 1906, 1909). Eng. trans., *Studies in Word Association* (New York: Moffat Yard, 1919), 2 vols.

101. C. G. Jung, *Ueber die Psychologie der Dementia Praecox* (Halle: C. Marhold, 1907). Eng. trans., *The Psychology of Dementia Praecox*, Nervous and Mental Disease Monograph Series No. 3 (1909). *Collected Works* (New York: Pantheon Books, 1959), III, 3–151.

102. Eugen Bleuler und C. G. Jung, "Komplexe und Krankheitsursachen bei Dementia Praecox," *Zentralblatt für Nervenheilkunde und Psychiatrie*, XXXI, No. 19 (1908), 220–227.

103. C. G. Jung, *Der Inhalt der Psychose* (Vienna and Leipzig: Deuticke, 1908), *Collected Works*, III, 153–178.

104. C. G. Jung, "Zur psychologischen Tatbestandsdiagnostik," *Centralblatt für Nervenheilkunde und Psychiatrie,* XXVIII (1905), 813–815.

105. C. G. Jung, "Le Nuove Vedute della Psicologia Criminale," *Rivista di Psicologia Applicata,* IV (1908), 287–304.

106. Sigmund Freud, "Tatbestandsdiagnostik und Psychoanalyse," *Archiv für Kriminal-Anthropologie und Kriminalistik* (1906), XXXVI, 1–10.

107. C. G. Jung, *Das Unbewusste im normalen und kranken Seelenleben* (Zurich: Rascher, 1926). Eng. trans. in *Two Essays on Analytical Psychology* (London: Baillière, 1929), pp. 1–121.

108. Richard I. Evans, *Conversations with Carl Jung* (Princeton: Van Nostrand Co., 1964).

109. Since Jung entered the Burghölzli on December 11, 1900, it is more probable that Bleuler assigned him this task in 1901.

110. It was the custom at the Burghölzli about once a month to hold a doctors' meeting called a *Referierabend,* that is, an evening devoted to a report and discussion on a recent psychiatric work of general interest. One member of the staff was assigned the report, after which each one of the others asked questions or made remarks, and Bleuler would make concluding comments.

111. It is therefore erroneous when certain authors contend that the word association test was "an application of psychoanalysis to the test method." The test itself and the notion of "complex" preceded the foundation of psychoanalysis.

112. C. G. Jung, "Die Bedeutung des Vaters für das Schicksal des Einzelnen," *Jahrbuch für Psychoanalytische und Psychopathologische Forschungen,* I (1909), 155–173. Eng. trans. in *Collected Papers on Analytical Psychology* (London: Baillière, (1916), pp. 156–175.

113. C. G. Jung, "Ueber Konflikte der kindlichen Séele," *Jahrbuch für Psychoanalytische und Psychopathologische Forschungen,* II (1910), 33–58.

114. C. G. Jung, "Ein Beitrag zur Psychologie des Gerüchtes," *Centralblatt für Psychoanalyse,* I (1911), 81–90.

115. Friedrich Creuzer, *Symbolik und Mythologie der alten Völker, besonders der Griechen,* 4 vols. (Leipzig: Leske, 1810–1812).

116. C. G. Jung, "Wandlungen und Symbole der Libido. Beiträge zur Entwicklungsgeschichte des Denkens," *Jahrbuch für Psychoanalytische und Psychopathologische Forschungen,* III, No. I (1911), 120–227); IV (1912), 162–464. Published in book form (Leipzig and Vienna: Deuticke, 1912). Eng. trans., *Psychology of the Unconscious* (New York: Moffat Yard, 1916). New edition with the title *Symbols of Transformation* in *Collected Works* (New York: Pantheon Books, 1956), Vol. V.

117. Miss Frank Miller, "Quelques faits d'imagination créatrice subconsciente," *Archives de Psychologie,* V (1906), 36–51.

118. It must be emphasized that the book underwent so many modifications in subsequent editions that the last one (and the English translation) amount to an almost new book.

119. C. G. Jung, "Versuch einer Darstellung der Psychoanalytischen Theorie," *Jahrbuch für Psychoanalytische und Psychopathologische Forschungen,* V (1913), 307–441. Eng. trans., *The Theory of Psychoanalysis,* Nervous and Mental Disease Monograph Series No. 19 (1915). *Collected Works* (New York: Pantheon Books, IV, 1961), 83–226.

120. In Vaihinger's terminology it would not be a hypothesis, but a fiction. (See Chap. 7, p. 630.)

121. C. G. Jung, "Psycho-Analysis," *Transactions of the Psycho-Medical Society,* Vol. IV, Part II (1913).

122. C. G. Jung, *Psychologische Typen* (Zurich: Rascher, 1921). Eng. trans., *Psychological Types* (New York: Harcourt Brace, 1923).

123. C. G. Jung, "La Structure de l'inconscient," *Archives de Psychologie,* XVI (1916), 152–179. Eng. trans., *Collected Works* (New York: Pantheon Books, VII, 1953), 263–262.

124. C. G. Jung, "Contribution à l'étude des types psychologiques," *Archives de*

Psychologie, XIII (1913). 289–299. Eng. trans., *Collected Papers on Analytical Psychology* (London: Baillière. Tindall and Cox, 1916), pp. 287–298.

125. Wilhelm Ostwald, *Grosse Männer* (Leipzig: Akademische Verlagsgesellschaft, 1909).

126. C. G. Jung, *Psychological Types in Problems of Personality: Studies Presented to Dr. Morton Prince* (New York: Harcourt, Brace and Co., 1925), pp. 289–302.

127. Ania Teillard, *L'âme et l'écriture* (Paris: Stock, 1948), pp. 89—94).

128. See Chap. 10, pp. 840–841.

129. Emanuel Swedenborg, *Heaven and Hell.* Eng. trans. (London: Dent, Everyman's Library, 1909), pp. 11–13.

130. Friedrich Schiller, "Ueber naive und sentimentalische Dichtung" (1795–1796) in, *Sämtliche Schriften* (Stuttgart: Cotta, 1871), X, 425–523.

131. Oliver Brachfeld, "Gelenkte Tagträume als Hilfsmittel der Psychotherapie," *Zeitschrift für Psychotherapie,* IV (1954), 79–93.

132. Alfred Binet, *L'Etude expérimentale de l'intelligence* (Paris: Schleicher, 1903).

133. Actually it is reported that Armande became a painter.

134. C. G. Jung, *Uber die Energetik der Seele* (Zurich: Rascher, 1928). Later expanded under the title *Ueber Psychische Energetik und das Wesen der Träume* (Zurich: Rascher, 1948). Eng. trans. in *Collected Works* (New York: Pantheon Books, 1960), VIII, 3–66.

135. This had already been taught by Janet. (See Chap. 6, pp. 396–397.)

136. See Chap. 10, pp. 794–795.

137. The translation "racial unconscious" is improper and should be discarded.

138. Albrecht Dieterich, *Eine Mithrasliturgie erläutert* (Leipzig: Teubner, 1903), pp. 7, 62.

139. C. G. Jung, *Wandlungen und Symbole der Libido,* p. 91.

140. Actually, the symbol of the phallic sun *(Sonnenphallus)* had been mentioned by Friedrich Creuzer in *Symbolik und Mythologie der alten Völker* (3rd ed., Leipzig: Leske, 1841), III, 335, a work with which Jung was well acquainted, and Dieterich stated that a similar conception was popular in many countries.

141. William James, "On Some Mental Effects of the Earthquake" (1906), reprinted in *Memories and Studies* (London: Longmans Green and Co., 1911), pp. 209–226.

142. Charles Baudouin, "Position de C. G. Jung," *Schweizerische Zeitschrift für Psychologie,* IV (1945), 263–275.

143. The German language distinguishes *die Unbewusstheit* (unawareness) and *das Unbewusste* (the unconscious).

144. C. G. Jung, *Erinnerungen, Träume, Gedanken* (Zurich: Rascher Verlag, 1962), pp. 188–191. Eng. trans., *Memories, Dreams, Reflections* (New York: Pantheon, 1963), 185–189.

145. Karl Neisser, *Die Entstehung der Liebe* (Vienna: Karl Koneggen, 1897).

146. Thomas Hardy, *The Well-Beloved, A Sketch of a Temperament* (London: McIlvaine & Co., 1897).

147. H. Rider Haggard, *She. A History of Adventure* (London: Longman's, Green Co., 1886).

148. Morton Cohen, *Rider Haggard, His Life and Works* (London: Hutchinson, 1960), pp. 102–114.

149. Emma Jung, "Ein Beitrag zum Problem des Animus," in C. G. Jung, *Wirklichkeit der Seele* (Zurich: Rascher, 1934), pp. 296–354.

150. Jungian circles refer to literary descriptions of the animus in Mary Hay, *The Evil Vineyard;* Ronald Frazier, *The Flying Draper;* H. G. Wells, *Christina Alberta's Father.*

151. C. G. Jung, "Die psychologischen Aspekte des Mutterarchetypus," *Eranos-Jahrbuch,* VI (1938), 403-443. Eng. trans., *Collected Works* (New York: Pantheon Books, 1959), IX, 75–110.

152. Johannes Assenmacher, *Die Geschichte des Individuationsprinzips in der Scholastik* (Leipzig: Meiner, 1926).

153. Paul Bourget, *Le Démon de midi* (Paris: Plon, 1914).

154. André Repond, "Le Démon de midi," *L'Evolution Psychiatrique* (1939), No. 3, pp. 87–100.

155. See, for instance, the description of Velchaninov's neurosis of the middle of life, in Dostoevski's novel *The Eternal Husband,* and that of Claude Lothaire in Edmond Jaloux's novel *Les Profondeurs de la mer.*

156. This is one of Jung's sayings that circulated among his disciples, but it does not seem to appear in any of his writings.

157. C. G. Jung, *Psychology and Religion,* The Terry Lectures (New Haven: Yale University Press, 1937).

158. Fabre D'Olivet, *Les Vers dorés de Pythagore* (Paris: Treuttel & Würtz, 1813). See Léon Cellier, *Fabre d'Olivet—La Vraie Maçonnerie et la céleste culture* (Paris, 1952), pp. 75–144.

159. Giuseppe Tucci, *Teoria e practica del Mandala con particolare riguardo alla moderna psicologia del profondo* (Rome: Astrolabio, 1949). Anagarika Govinda, *Mandala. Des heilige Kreis* (Zurich: Origo-Verlag, 1960).

160. August Rüegg, *Die Jenseitsvorstellungen vor Dante und die übrigen literarischen Voraussetzungen der Divina Commedia* (Einsiedeln: Benziger, 1944).

161. Jules Verne's *Journey to the Centre of the Earth* could be interpreted in all its details as a journey through the unconscious with the discovery of deeper and deeper archetypes, until the encounter of a fireball (symbol of the spirit) sets about the *enantiodromia,* that is the reversal of regression and the return to the common world.

162. Alphonse Daudet, *Tartarin sur les Alpes* (Paris: Calmann-Lévy, 1885).

163. An example could be found in the autobiographic novel of Gertrud Isolani, *Stadt ohne Männer* (Zurich: Falken-Verlag, 1945). A young Jewish woman finds herself in the concentration camp of Gurs in the first weeks following the French defeat. She and her companions are only concerned with everyday and sometimes frivolous matters, until her eyes are opened by a Catholic nun who tells her of the immensity of the catastrophe that is threatening them.

164. C. G. Jung, *Analytische Psychologie und Erziehung* (Heidelberg: Kampmann, 1926). Eng. trans., *Collected Works* (New York: Pantheon Books, 1954), XVII, pp. 65–132.

165. See Chap. I, p. 43–46.

166. C. G. Jung, *Erinnerungen, Träume, Gedanken* (Zurich: Rascher Verlag, 1962), pp. 121–124. *Memories, Dreams, Reflections,* pp. 115–117.

167. C. G. Jung, *Die Beziehungen der Psychotherapie zur Seelsorge* (Zurich: Rascher, 1932). Eng. trans., *Collected Works* (New York: Pantheon Books, 1958), XI, pp. 327–347.

168. Incidentally this is exactly what Janet had said in 1896 in his paper: *L'Influence somnambulique et le besoin de direction.* See Chap. 6, p. 374.

169. C. G. Jung, "Die transzendente Funktion," in *Geist und Werk* (Zurich: Rhein-Verlag, 1958), pp. 3–33. Eng. trans., *Collected Works* (New York: Pantheon Books, 1960), VIII, pp. 67–91.

170. See Chap. 5, pp. 306–308.

171. It has not been possible as yet to find out whether this comparison issued from Jung himself or from one of his disciples.

172. Alphonse Maeder, *La Personne du médecin, un agent psychothérapeutique* (Neuchatel: Delachaux et Niestlé, 1953), pp. 111–134.

173. C. G. Jung, "Was ist Psychotherapie," *Schweizerische Aerztezeitung für Standesfragen* (1935), XVI, 335–339. Eng. trans., *Collected Works* (New York: Pantheon Books, 1954), XVI, pp. 21–28.

174. C. G. Jung, "Einige Bemerkungen zu den Visionen des Zosimos," *Eranos-Jahrbuch,* V (1937), 15–54.

175. M. Berthelot, *Les Origines de l'alchimie* (Paris: Steinheil, 1885).

176. Herbert Silberer, *Probleme der Mystik und ihrer Symbolik* (Vienna: H. Heller, 1914).

177. C. G. Jung, "Die Erlösungsvorstellungen in der Alchemie," *Eranos-Jahrbuch,* IV (1936), 13–111. *Psychologie und Alchemie* (Zurich: Rascher, 1944). *Die Psychologie der Uebertragung* (Zurich: Rascher, 1946). *Symbolik des Geistes* (Zurich: Rascher, 1948). *Gestaltungen des Unbewussten* (Zurich: Rascher, 1950). *Mysterìum Conjunctionis,* 2 vols. (Zurich: 1955–1956). Eng. trans., *Complete Works* (New York: Pantheon Books), 1962.

178. C. G. Jung, *Paracelsica* (Zurich: Rascher, 1942).

179. W. Y. Evans-Wentz, *The Tibetan Book of the Dead, or the After Death Experiences on the Bardo Plain, according to Lama Kazi Tawa Sandup's English rendering* (London: Oxford University Press, 1927).

180. *Das Tibetanische Totenbuch,* Louise Göpfert-March, trans., with a psychological commentary by C. G. Jung (Zurich: Rascher, 1935).

181. Richard Wilhelm, *Das Geheimnis der goldenen Blüte,* with a commentary by C. G. Jung (Munich: Dorn, 1929).

182. Jung wrote a foreword for the English translation of Richard Wilhelm's German version: *The I Ching, or Book of Changes. Carry F. Baynes, trans.* (New York: Pantheon Books, 1950).

183. Jung wrote an introduction to the book by T. D. Suzuki, *Die grosse Befreiung* (Leipzig: Curt Weller, 1939), pp. 7–37.

184. J. W. Hauer, *The Kundalini Yoga,* Bericht über das Seminar im psychologischen Klub, Zurich, 3–8. October 1932 (Zurich, 1933). Typescript.

185. C. G. Jung, "Synchronizität als ein Princip akausaler Zuzammenhänge," in C. G. Jung and W. Pauli, *Naturerklärung und Psyche* (Zurich: Rascher, 1952), pp. 1–107. Eng. trans., *Collected Works* (New York: Pantheon Books, 1960), VIII, 417–519.

186. C. G. Jung, *Psychological Analysis of Nietzsche's Zarathustra.* Notes on the seminar given by Dr. C. G. Jung, Zurich, 10 vols., 1934–1939, plus an index compiled by Mary Briner. (Typescript.)

187. C. G. Jung, "Picasso," *Neue Zürcher Zeitung,* November 3, 1932, No. 2107, Reprinted in *Wirklichkeit der Seele* (Zurich: Rascher, 1934), pp. 170–179.

188. C. G. Jung, "Ulysses. Ein Monolog," *Europäische Revue,* VIII (II) (1932), 547–568. Eng. trans., "Ulysses: A Monologue," *Nimbus,* II, No. 1 (June–August, 1953), 7–20.

189. Richard Ellmann, *James Joyce* (London: Oxford University Press, 1959), pp. 641, 693.

190. C. G. Jung, "Wotan," *Neue Schweizer Rundschau* (1935–1936), III, 657–669. Eng. trans., "Wotan," *Essays on Contemporary Events* (London: Kegan Paul, 1947), pp. 1–16.

191. C. G. Jung, "Psychology of Dictatorship," *The Observer,* October 18, 1936, p. 15. "Diagnosing the Dictators," *Hearst's International Journal Cosmopolitan,* CVI (January 1939), 22–23, 116–120.

192. C. G. Jung, *Ein moderner Mythus. Von Dingen, die am Himmel gesehen werden* (Zurich: Rascher, 1958). Eng. trans., *Flying Saucers: A Modern Myth of Things Seen in the Skies* (New York: Harcourt Brace, 1959).

193. *Unbewusstheit ist die grösste Sünde.*

194. Rudolf Otto, *Das Heilige* (Breslau: Trewendt und Granier, 1917).

195. Harald Schultz-Hencke, "Das religiöse Erleben des Atheisten," *Psyche,* IV (1950–1951), 417–435.

196. C. G. Jung, "Bruder Klaus," *Neue Schweizer Rundschau,* I (1933), 223–229. Eng. trans., "Brother Klaus," *Psychology and Religion: West and East,* Collected Works (New York: Pantheon Books, 1958, IX, 316–323.

197. C. G. Jung, *Aion. Untersuchungen zur Symbolgeschichte* (Zurich: Rascher, 1951). Eng. trans., *Aion. Researches into the Phenomenology of the Self. Collected Works* (New York: Pantheon Books, 1959), Vol. IX, Part. II.

198. C. G. Jung, *Antwort auf Hiob* (Zurich: Rascher, 1952). Eng. trans., "Answer to Job," *Psychology and Religion: West and East, Collected Works* (New York: Pantheon Books, 1959), XI, 355–470.

199. H. G. Wells, conversation with Jung reported in a letter to the *Neue Zürcher Zeitung,* November 18, 1928, No. 2116, Blatt 9.

200. Interviews with Frederic Sands, *Daily Mail* (London), April 29, 1955.

201. Frederik van Eeden, "A Study of Dreams," *Proceedings of the Society for Psychical Research,* LXVII, No. 26 (1913), 413–461.

202. *Bist Du auf Unendliches bezogen?* This sentence literally means: Are you in relation with the infinite?

203. See Chap. 5, pp. 286–288.

204. See Chap. 6, pp. 355–356; pp. 702–703.

205. Alphonse Maeder, "Uber die Funktion des Traumes," *Jahrbuch für psychoanalytische und psychopathologische Forschungen,* IV (1912), 692–707. "Ueber das Traumproblem," V (1913), 647–686.

206. Herbert Silberer, "Zur Symbolbildung," *Jahrbuch für psychoanalytische und psychopathologische Forschungen,* IV (1912), 607.

207. W. Leibbrand, "Schellings Bedeutung für die moderne Medizin," *Atti del XIVe Congresso Internazionale di Storia della Medicina,* Vol. II (Rome, 1954).

208. Rose Mehlich, *I. H. Fichtes Seelenlehre und ihre Beziehung zur Gegenwart* (Zurich: Rascher, 1935).

209. See Chap. 4, pp. 205–206.

210. This has been well explained by Paul Sucher, *Les Sources du merveilleux chez E. T. H. Hoffmann* (Paris: Alcan, 1912), pp. 132–133.

211. See Chap. 4, pp. 206–207.

212. See Chap. 4, p. 201.

213. Friedrich Creuzer, *Symbolik und Mythologie der alten Völker, besonders der Griechen* (Leipzig and Darmstadt: Leske, 1910), Vol. I; Leipzig and Darmstadt: Heyer & Leske, 1911–1912), Vols. II, III, IV.

214. C. G. Jung, *Erinnerungen, Traüme, Gedanken* (Zurich: Rascher Verlag, 1962), p. 166.

215. See Chap. 4, pp. 211–215.

216. See Chap. 2, pp. 79–81.

217. See Chap. 4, pp. 218–223.

218. Adolf Bastian, *Ethnische Elementargedanken in der Lehre vom Menschen* (Berlin, 1895).

219. Eugenio Tanzi, "Il Folk-Lore nella Patologia Mentale," *Rivista di Filosofia Scientifica,* IX (1890), 385–419.

220. Leo Frobenius, *Das Zeitalter des Sonnengottes* (Berlin: George Reiner, 1904)

221. Jan Nelken, "Analytische Beobachtungen über Phantasien eines Schizophrenen," *Jahrbuch für psychoanalytische und psychopathologische Forschungen,* IV (1912), 504–562.

222. Albrecht Dieterich, *Mutter Erde. Ein Versuch über Volksreligion* (Leipzig, 1905).

223. Léon Daudet, *L'Hérédo, essai sur le drame intérieur* (Paris: Nouvelle Librairie Nationale, 1917).

224. Léon Daudet, *Le Monde des images. Suite de "L'Hérédo"* (Paris: Nouvelle Librairie Nationale, 1919).

225. C. G. Jung, *The Interpretation of Visions* (unpublished seminars) (Winter 1934), XI, 25.

226. See Bruno Klopfer *et al.,* "C. G. Jung and Projective Techniques," Special issue of the *Journal of Projective Techniques,* XIX, No. 3 (1955), 225–270.

227. See for instance John Weir Perry, *The Self in Psychotic Processes, Its Symbolization in Schizophrenia* (University of California Press, 1953). John Custance, *Weisheit und Wahn* (Zurich: Rascher, 1954). John Staehelin, "Mythos und Psychose," *Schweizer Archiv für Neurologie und Psychiatrie,* LXVIII, 1951, 408–414.

228. Sheldon T. Selesnick, "C. G. Jung's Contributions to Psychoanalysis," *American Journal of Psychiatry,* CXX (1963), 350–356.

229. Erik Erikson, *Childhood and Society* (New York: W. W. Norton, 1950), pp. 219–234.

230. Robert Desoille, *Exploration de l'affectivité subconsciente par la méthode du rêve éveillé* (Paris: d'Artrey, 1938).

231. Hans Trüb, *Heilung aus der Begegnung* (Stuttgart: Klett, 1951).

232.. H. K. Fierz, *Klinik und Analytische Psychologie* (Zurich: Rascher, 1963).

233. C. A. Meier, "Psychosomatik in Jungscher Sicht," *Psyche*, XV (1962), 625–638.

234. Hans A. Illing, *International Journal of Group Therapy*, VII (1957), 392–397. "C. G. Jung on the Present Trends in Group Psychotherapy," *Human Relations*, X (1957), 77–83.

235. Bill W.–Carl Jung Letters. *A. A. Grapevine. The International Monthly Journal of Alcoholics Anonymous,* XIX, No. 8 (January 1963), 2–7. (The author is grateful to Mrs. Paula Carpenter, who sent him a copy of this issue.)

236. See, "Bill's Story," in *Alcoholics Anonymous* (New York: Works Publishing, 1939, 10–26.

237. H. J. Eysenck, *Dimensions of Personality* (London: Routledge & Kegan Paul, 1947), pp. 10–14.

238. P. Plattner, *Glücklichere Ehen* (Berne: Hans Huber, 1950).

239. Arnold J. Toynbee, *A Study of History* (London: Oxford University Press, 1954), VII, 722–736 (1954), X, 225–226.

240. David Riesman, *The Lonely Crowd* (New Haven: Yale University Press, 1950).

241. C. G. Jung and Karl Kerenyi, *Eine Einführung in das Wesen der Mythologie* (Zurich: Rascher, 1941).

242. W. Pauli, "Der Einfluss archetypischer Vorstellungen auf die Bildung naturwissenschaftlicher Theorien bei Kepler," in C. G. Jung and W. Pauli, *Naturerklärung und Psyche* (Zurich: Rascher, 1952).

243. F. M. Cornford, *The Unwritten Philosophy* (Cambridge: Cambridge University Press, 1950), pp. 10–13.

244. Max Frischknecht, "Die Religion in der Psychologie C. G. Jungs," *Religiöse Gegenwartsfragen*, Heft 12 (Berne: Haupt, 1945).

245. Hans Schär, *Religion und Seele in der Psychologie C. G. Jungs* (Zurich: Rascher, 1946).

246. Hans Schär, *Erlösungsvorstellungen und ihre psychologischen Aspekte* (Zurich, Rascher, 1950).

247. Edmond Rochedieu, ' Le Transfert et le sentiment religieux," *Acta Psychotherapeutica, Psychosomatica et Orthopaedagogica*, III, supplement (1956), 592–595.

248. Paul Tillich, in *Carl Gustav Jung, 1875–1961, A Memorial Meeting*, The Analytical Psychology Club of New York (1962), pp. 28–32.

249. Here a personal memory is apropos: On a journey to England after World War II the author happened to visit a Benedictine monastery; as soon as the abbott heard that a Swiss psychiatrist was present he called him and asked with vivid interest about C. G. Jung.

250. Victor White, *God and the Unconscious*, with a foreword by C. G. Jung (London: Harville Press, 1952).

251. Father Hostie, *C. G. Jung und die Religion* (Freiburg: Karl Alber, 1957).

252. Josef Goldbrunner, *Individuation. Die Tiefenpsychologie von Carl Gustav Jung* (Krailling vor Munich: Erich Wewel, 1949).

253. Paul Evdokimov, *La Femme et le salut du monde, Etude d'anthropologie chrétienne* (Tournai: Casterman, 1958).

254. Paul Reiwald, *Vom Geist der Massen. Handbuch der Massenpsychologie* (Zurich: Pan-Verlag, 1946), pp. 213–236.

255. Eugen Böhler, "Die Grundgedanken der Psychologie von C. G. Jung," *Industrielle Organisation*, XXIX (1960), 182–191.

256. A good summary of Böhler's ideas is given by Karl Schmid, "Uber die wichtigsten psychologischen Ideen Eugen Böhler's," in *Kultur und Wirtschaft. Festschrift zum 70, Geburtstag von Eugen Böhler* (Zurich: Polygraphischer Verlag, n.d.), pp. 79–86.

257. Eugen Böhler, "Der Mythus in der Wirtschaft," *Industrielle Organisation*, XXXI (1962), 129–136.

258. Dietrich Schindler, *Verfassungsrecht und Soziale Struktur* (Zurich: Schulthess, 1931).

259. Hans Fehr, 'Primitives und germanisches Recht. Zur Lehre vom Archetypus," *Archiv für Rechts–und Sozialphilosophie,* Vol. XLI (1954–1955).

260. Hans Marti, *Urbild und Verfassung* (Bern, 1958).

261. Erich Fechner, *Rechtsphilosophie. Soziologie und Metaphysik des Rechts* (Tubingen: J. C. B. Mohr, 1956).

262. Max Imboden, *Die Staatsformen. Versuch einer psychologischen Deutung staatsrechtlicher Dogmen* (Basel and Stuttgart: Helving & Lichtenhahn, 1959).

263. These feelings are well expressed in a letter from Carl Burckardt to Hofmannsthal. See Hugo von Hofmannsthal–Carl Burckhardt, *Briefwechsel* (Frankfurt-am-Main: S. Fischer, 1957), pp. 161–163.

264. Virgil, *Eclogue VIII.* Great Books of the Western World, No. 13, p. 27.

10

The Dawn and Rise of the New Dynamic Psychiatry

ONE OF THE DIFFICULTIES in writing history is that we are always prone to describe past events in terms of the meaning they have acquired in our time. But men of the past viewed contemporary events in their own perspective. They paid much attention to facts that today are forgotten or considered insignificant, they engaged in vehement controversies about matters that are hardly intelligible today, while many events that seem crucial to us attracted little notice when they occurred. Historians must both depict events in their perspective of the past and focus on those we now consider to be crucial.

This is why, after describing the social, political, cultural, and medical background of the new dynamic psychiatry and attempting to summarize the doctrines of its four great representatives, Janet, Freud, Adler, and Jung, it remains for us to sketch the complex interrelationship of these great systems with one another and with minor ones, as well as with the general background of contemporary events. We will take as our starting point Charcot's memorable paper on hypnosis in February 1882, which opened the new era, and terminate at the end of World War II because after that date we lack sufficient perspective for a synthetic view.

Rivalry of the Salpêtrière and Nancy Schools: 1882–1893

The eleven years between 1882 and 1893 saw the resurrection of animal magnetism in a modified form under the name of hypnosis and suggestion. Scientific sanction was given to these practices by two academic centers: the one around Charcot at the Salpêtrière, and the other around Bernheim in Nancy. The work of these two schools, and their rivalries, dominated the scene. This period may be divided into three subperiods.

Birth and Growth of the Salpêtrière and Nancy Schools: 1882–1885

On February 13, 1882, the celebrated neurologist Jean-Martin Charcot climbed to the tribune at the Academy of Sciences in Paris to read a paper "On the Various Nervous States Determined by Hypnotization in Hysterics." [1] This paper purported to give a rigorously objective picture of the hypnotic states in purely neurological terms. In its full-fledged picture, as can be observed in hysterical women, Charcot said:

> Hypnotism comprises three conditions that can succeed each other in any combination, or exist independently of each other. In the *cataleptic state,* the patient holds his limbs in whatever position they have been placed, tendon reflexes are abolished or very weak; there are long respiratory pauses, and various automatic impulses may be provoked. In the *lethargic state,* muscles are flaccid, respiration is deep and rapid, tendon reflexes are remarkably exaggerated, and the patient shows "neuromuscular hyperexcitability," that is, an aptitude of the muscles to contract strongly if the tendon, muscle, or corresponding nerve is touched. In the third, *somnambulic state,* tendon reflexes are normal, there is no neuromuscular excitability, although certain slight stimulation causes a state of rigidity in the limb; there is usually an "exaltation of certain little-known varieties of cutaneous sensitivity, muscular sense and of certain special senses," and it is usually easy to bring about, on demand, the most complicated automatic acts. One may bring a patient from the cataleptic to the lethargic into the somnambulic state by gentle friction on the vertex. Pressure on the eyeballs brings the patient from somnambulism to lethargy.

In retrospect it would seem that this paper of Charcot meant a sudden revolution. "It was a *tour de force,*" according to Janet, "to bring the Academy of Sciences to recognize hypnotism, which during the past century it had thrice condemned under the name of magnetism." [2] Actually, medical men of that time were not very historically minded. It is doubtful whether many members of the Academy of Sciences had read the works of the former magnetists, and whether any of them (including Charcot himself) had an inkling that something old was being revived. These men shared an illusion, which has by no means disappeared today, that everything they brought forth was new.

It is an exaggeration to say that at that time hypnotism was considered to be nothing but quackery. A growing number of physicians worked with it, either alone or in small societies, although the topic was considered obscure and controversial. However, it is doubtful whether Charcot's authority would have sufficed to bring forth a revival of hypnotism if the ground had not been prepared in an unexpected way, namely, by stage hypnotizers. [3] Hansen (in Germany and Austria) and Donato (in Belgium, France, Switzerland, and Italy) went from town to town organizing theatrical hypnotic performances, attracting large crowds and often leaving trails of psychic epidemics. Many neurologists and psychiatrists watched these performances, and some concluded that "there must be something in it." The physiologist Charles Richet was one of the first who dared to experiment in this apparently new field and publish the results in a scientific journal. [4] This probably stimulated Charcot to take up his own experiments, and as he progressed with his investigations, other men were encouraged to use hypnosis.

Prior to Charcot's paper, the neurologist Heidenhain of Breslau had been impressed by Hansen's performances, had adopted the method, and published a book on hypnosis in 1880. [5] In Austria, Moritz Benedikt had tried it for some time, and his example was followed by Josef Breuer. Hypnosis also had supporters in Belgium, and in Nancy so much was told about Liébeault's cures that the Medical Society of that town devoted one meeting in 1882 to experiments with hypnotism. Bernheim paid Liébeault a visit, was favorably impressed, and decided to adopt and perfect the method. [6] The attention of the public had also been drawn to hypnotism, and it had become a current topic in the newspapers. [7]

From that time on, whether because Charcot had given his sanction to it or otherwise, "the gates were open" (in Janet's words), and the public was submerged with a flood of publications on hypnosis. It was not long before wide divergences appeared among the authors. In 1883 Bernheim read a paper at the Medical Society in Nancy, defining hypnosis as "merely a sleep, produced by suggestion, with therapeutic implications." This was tantamount to a declaration of war against Charcot's doctrine, because for Charcot hypnosis was a physiological condition very different from sleep, a condition that could occur only in individuals predisposed to hysteria, and could not be used for therapeutic purposes.

In the following year, 1884, the "war" between the two schools moved onto new ground. A lawyer from Nancy, Liégeois, had experimented with hypnotized individuals by suggesting that they commit crimes for which he supplied harmless weapons.[8] He induced the subjects to commit pseudo-murders. However, the Salpêtrière School objected to the conclusions drawn by Liégeois, and Bernheim's pamphlet about suggestion was received in Paris with criticism.[9]

In 1885, when the attention of everyone was on hypnosis and hysteria, Charcot gave his lectures on traumatic paralyses as well as clinical demonstrations of how he reproduced analogous paralyses by hypnosis in predisposed individuals. Charcot and many of his auditors considered that these demonstrations provided scientific proof of the psychogenesis of traumatic paralyses. We have seen that these experiments of Charcot had wider implications.[10] Believing that the mechanism of these traumatic paralyses was indentical with that of hysterical paralyses, Charcot now included traumatic paralyses in the field of hysteria. This new terminology aroused marked opposition, especially in Germany, and it revived the controversies about the relative incidence of organic and functional etiology in traumatic paralyses. The opposition to Charcot's new concepts of hysteria generally grew among neurologists.

It is at this point, at the end of 1885, that Sigmund Freud received a grant that enabled him to spend four months in Paris. We find here a typical example of those events that are crucial in retrospect but seemed insignificant at the time. This will appear more clearly if we contrast this event against the background of life in Paris and the Salpêtrière during those four months.

A perusal of the Paris newspapers from October 1885 to February 1886 indicates that it was a period of turmoil all over the world. Much was reported about Anglo-Russian rivalry in central Asia, Franco-English rivalry in Africa, and Spanish-German rivalry in the South Sea Islands; the English were invading Burma; in London there was a scandal caused by the revelation by the *Pall Mall Gazette* about the prostitution of minors. The Italians were invading Eritrea; the French were fighting in Indochina; the French Canadians in Montreal were agitated about the execution of the leader of an Indian rebellion, Louis Riel. Civil war raged in Peru; United States troops were displacing Mormons in Salt Lake City; there was socialist agitation, strikes, and bloody riots in various towns in France, Belgium, and the United States. War had broken out between Bulgaria and Serbia, bringing the rivalry between Russia and Austria-Hungary to a dangerous peak. The Statue of Liberty had just been erected in New York. In France, General Boulanger, the idol of the nationalists, was appointed Minister of War in January 1886, which encouraged those who were seeking revenge for the defeat of 1870 to 1871. There were many protests about the flood of pornographic literature and theatricals, and a scandal about competitive examinations in the Paris hospitals, where certain candidates were said to have been informed of the questions beforehand by one of the examiners. Public opinion was enthusiastic about the first spectacular treatment of rabies by Pasteur, and people who had been bitten by mad dogs rushed to Paris from all over Europe. The main interest of the public, however, seemed to be in the new plays such as Daudet's *Sapho,* in an incognito visit to Paris of the eccentric King of Bavaria, Ludwig II, and in the exhibition of a group of Australian aborigines in a zoological park. We learn from the diary of the brothers Goncourt that Charcot had moved, a year before, into the splendid palace he had built for himself in the Faubourg Saint-Germain, and according to gossip his daughter Jeanne was in love with Alphonse Daudet's son, Léon, whose reluctance aroused Charcot's displeasure. Medical journals faithfully reported on the lectures given by Charcot, who was then at the height of his fame.

No doubt the visit of a young Austrian neurologist at the time when so many distinguished men made a pilgrimage to the Salpêtrière, the "Mecca of neurology," appeared as an incident of minor importance. And yet, in retrospect, we find here one of the historical links between the older and the newer dynamic psychiatry.

Sigmund Freud, who had just won his title of Privat Dozent at the University of Vienna, was the author of several appreciated papers on neuroanatomy, but had suffered disappointments in his cocaine research. He arrived in Paris in October 1885, after visiting his fiancée in Wandsbek, near Hamburg. According to Jones, Freud saw Charcot for the first time on October 20, 1885, and took leave of him on February 23, 1886. During this short period we must include the duration of Charcot's illness and of Freud's Christmas vacation in Wandsbek, but the remaining period of his contact with Charcot sufficed to make an indelible impression on Freud. No doubt, Freud was not one of those who, like Delboeuf, went to the Salpêtrière to watch with critical eyes the way Charcot experimented with his hysterical subjects. Freud was fascinated by the personality of the great man. What Freud saw in Charcot was not only the world fame of the great neurologist, the artistic gifts, the eloquence, and the manner of the man of the world, but also his way of seeing people and things without preconceived ideas. But the time was too short for Freud to acquire a real knowledge of Charcot's work. Freud was impressed by Charcot's experiments on hysterical paralyses, which had taken place not long before, and the idea that an unconscious representation could be the cause of motor disturbances. [11] But Freud built himself a somewhat inaccurate and idealized picture of Charcot's work. Thus, as can be clearly seen from the obituary he later wrote, Freud credited Charcot with what really was Briquet's contribution on hysteria.[12] He exaggerated the importance ascribed by Charcot to dissimilar heredity ("degeneration" in the medical jargon of the time); and he did not seem to have known of Richer's description of the *grande hystérie* in which the hysterical attack was described as being often a reenactment of a psychic, often sexual, trauma.[13] Had he read it, Freud would not have been so surprised when he heard Charcot mentioning the role of sexuality in neurotic disturbances as a matter of course. We may draw the conclusion that Freud's relationship to Charcot was not really that of a disciple to a master; it was more in the guise of an existential "encounter." Charcot provided Freud with a model for identification and with the germinal idea of the unconscious psychic dynamism.

There is some question of whether Freud met Janet during his visit to the Salpêtrière. Freud protested against the rumor that he had followed Janet's teaching at the Salpêtrière, adding that "during my stay at the Salpêtrière, the name of Janet was not even pronounced." [14] It is certain that Janet at that time lived in Le Havre, where in February 1883, he had been appointed Professor of Philosophy at the Lyceum.[15] But he sometimes went to Paris for a vacation and then visited the Salpêtrière.[16] On November 30, while Freud was in Paris, a paper of Pierre Janet about his first experiments with Léonie was read by his uncle Paul Janet at a meeting of the *Société de Psychologie Physiologique*, under the chairmanship of Charcot. [17] This paper aroused much interest and lively discussion, and it is unlikely that the name of Janet would not have been pronounced at the Salpêtrière on that occasion.[18] But there is no evidence to show whether or not Freud and Janet met or heard of each other at that time.

Among the people Freud saw in Paris was Léon Daudet (son of the writer Alphonse Daudet), whom he met at least once in Charcot's house. [19] Though still a medical student, the gifted young man was a social lion, and a brilliant future was predicted for him, either in politics, literature, or medicine. Léon Daudet, who was a keen observer and had a good memory for the people he met, apparently did not notice the Viennese neurologist, because he never mentioned having met him, whereas Freud kept a lasting memory of young Daudet. [20] Who would have thought at that time that the Austrian guest would become world famous and that Léon Daudet would not finish his medical studies, would have a hopeless political career as a leader of the Royalist movement, and in spite of an outstanding literary talent would never quite manage to write a masterpiece? Curious similarities could be found between Freud and Léon Daudet, two men who had been deeply influenced by Charcot's personality. Some of Léon Daudet's novels are about incest and other sexual deviations, morphine addiction, and psychopathic heredity. He also wrote nonfiction about daydreams and human personality, notably on the ego and the Self, and he called his own psychological system a metapsychology. [21] Daudet's conceptions, however, differ notably from those of Freud and show more similarities to those of Jung. [22]

The War of the Schools and the Debut of Pierre Janet: 1886–1889

From 1886 to 1889 the history of dynamic psychiatry was overshadowed by the polemics between the Salpêtrière and the Nancy School. During those years the literature on hypnosis and suggestion increased from year to year.

For the people of the time, 1886 seemed a year of political tension and tragedy. After General Boulanger's triumph, France was the prey of chauvinistic fever that worsened the tension with Germany. In spite of his success with vaccination against rabies, Pasteur was the object of heinous attacks by Peter at the Academy of Medicine, of a campaign in medical journals, and insults of the daily press, so that he broke down and went to Italy to recuperate. On June 13 the young and extravagant King of Bavaria, Ludwig II, who had just been declared psychotic by a medical commission and restricted to his castle of Berg, was found drowned in a lake together with his attending psychiatrist, Professor

Gudden. In the United States there was violent socialist agitation, culminating in the Haymarket case in which four union leaders, victims of a management plot, were sentenced to death and hanged in Chicago on May 1, a date that has since been commemorated every year by socialists throughout the world.

Meanwhile, if Charcot's star was at its zenith, his work was being seriously questioned in competent circles, and his equating of nonorganic traumatic paralyses with male hysteria was generally rejected in German-speaking countries. The cold reception of Freud's paper at the Society of Physicians in Vienna, on October 15, was only one among many other signs of this attitude. [23] In Belgium, Delboeuf explained his doubts about Charcot's experiments. [24] In Clermont-Ferrand a young philosophy professor, Henri Bergson (whose fame still lay far in the future), published a paper on "Unconscious Simulation in the Hypnotic State," which was a discreet warning to the many persons engaged in this field. [25]

Another young philosophy professor, Pierre Janet in Le Havre, after witnessing the experiments performed on Léonie by the Commission, became cautious and decided to refrain from any kind of parapsychological experimentation. He limited himself to fresh patients and proven methods, and in this year of 1886 he published the result of his work with the patient Lucie, which in retrospect is considered as the first cathartic cure on record. [26]

In Nancy, Bernheim published an enlarged edition, in textbook form, of his first pamphlet on suggestion.[27] This book made him the head of a school, and students of hypnotism began to flock to Nancy to visit him and Liébeault. The latter, who had spent his life in obscurity, saw himself suddenly in the limelight; Bernheim proclaimed himself Liébeault's disciple, never missed an opportunity to give him credit, and people marveled that a university professor could have become the disciple of a country doctor. But a still more extraordinary thing was happening in Italy. Enrico Morselli, who was Professor of Psychiatry at the University of Turin and considered a sensitive and distinguished man, attended a stage performance of hypnotism given by Donato, let himself be hypnotized by that coarse and vulgar man, had long talks with him, and thereupon published a book on hypnosis in which thirty pages were devoted to a eulogy of Donato and attacks on those who allegedly plagiarized him. [28]

In England the interest in hypnosis was linked to problems of parapsychology. Myers, who in 1882 had been one of the founders of the Society for Psychical Research, made a careful study of hypnosis and what he called the subliminal self as a preliminary stage in parapsychological studies proper. In 1886 Myers emphasized the analogy of the hypnotic state to genius as well as to hysteria, and foresaw that the pursuit of this research would lead to unforeseeable discoveries in the realm of human nature.[29] In the same year Edmund Gurney and Frederic Myers published *Phantasms of the Living,* which has remained a classic of parapsychology. [30]

In Austria, the main event of 1886 was probably the publication of Krafft-Ebing's *Psychopathia Sexualis.*

> In his foreword, Krafft-Ebing emphasized the "powerful influence of sexual life on individual and social existence, in the areas of feeling, thought, and action." In this connection, he referred to the philosophy of Schopenhauer and Von Hartmann and the assertions of Schiller and Michelet. He quoted Maudsley's theory that sexuality is the basis for the development of social feelings, and added that it gives impetus to the use of physical energy, to the drive for acquisition, to ethics, and to a good part of esthetics and religion. Sexuality is the source of the highest virtues as well as of the vices. "What would be the fine arts without sexual foundation! . . . In all ethics sensuality remains the root." The following chapter is devoted to the physiology of "libido sexualis." The bulk of the book is a description of "general sexual pathology," in which Krafft-Ebing follows the neurological classification used by French authors, distinguishing sexual neuroses of "peripheric," "spinal," and "cerebral" origin. To these he adds a number of unclassified abnormalities. The book closed with two chapters on psychotic and criminal forms of sexual deviations. It contained 45 case histories (of which eleven were Krafft-Ebing's patients).[31]

In Russia, Tarnowsky also published a volume on sexual deviations that met much success.[32] However, it was Krafft-Ebing's work, with its more philosophical scope, perhaps also its striking title, that produced on the field of sexual pathology the same effect as Charcot's paper of 1882 on the field of hypnotism. "The gates were open," and from then on the number of publications on sexual pathology increased from year to year. Although Krafft-Ebing had been careful to write certain parts of his book in Latin, wider circles than just the medical profession showed interest. There is no evidence of criticism caused by the content of the book, but only for not limiting its circulation to the professional world. The first edition with only 110 pages was quickly followed by enlarged editions enriched with many case histories, and a greatly modified classification.

In 1887 the general public's interest was in diplomatic incidents between Germany and France, and political scandals in France. Ceaseless attacks on Pasteur finally brought the intervention of Charcot and Vulpian at the Académie de Médecine, reducing the aggressors to silence. Among the medical events of that year, a few appear to us more important in retrospect than they did to the contemporaries. In 1887 Victor Horsley performed for the first time an operation on a tumor which was compressing the medulla and thus cured his patient. Continental neurologists, however, remained skeptical. In Austria, Wagner-Jauregg, who had noticed the favorable effect of a fever on the mental condition of psychotic patients, started that long series of experiments that was to lead him, many years later, to the discovery of the malaria therapy of general paretics. [33]

In Europe a keen interest was widely manifested in the problems of mental illness, neurosis, and hypnosis. In Zurich, August Forel gave great prestige to the Burghölzli (the Zurich University Mental Hospital). A young German writer, Gehrart Hauptmann, followed Forel's clinical demonstrations with passionate interest and later utilized this knowledge for his literary work. [34] In Holland, Van Renterghem and Van Eeden, on return from Nancy, opened a clinic for hypnotic treatment in Amsterdam on August 15, 1887. In Berlin Albert Moll gave a lecture on hypnotic therapy to a medical audience. [35] It was received, he said, with reluctance, nevertheless a second lecture was better understood. In Stockholm Wetterstrand opened a practice devoted to hypnotic treatment, which was destined for fabulous success. In Paris Bérillon, who had adopted Bernheim's ideas, was authorized to give a series of lectures on the therapeutic application of hypnosis at the Medical School itself, that is, in what was considered Charcot's stronghold. [36]

The year 1888 was believed at the time to be world-shaking. In Germany it was called the fateful year: Emperor William I died in March at the age of ninety-one; but his successor, the liberal-minded Frederick III, who was expected to reverse his father's authoritarian policies, died three months later, to be succeeded by the erratic William II. In France, the Boulangist fever was mounting, and nationalists saw Boulanger as the man to win back Alsace-Lorraine. The French, now thinking of an alliance with Russia, enthusiastically subscribed to Russian loans. European powers were competing harshly for the last remaining colonies; colonization was seen as a civilizing mission by Europeans. When Brazil abolished slavery in 1888, the rest of the world was shocked to learn that it had existed until then.

Such was the general atmosphere in which the knowledge and practice of hypnosis grew and developed. In that year Max Dessoir published a *Bibliography of Modern Hypnotism,* which contained 801 recent titles but did not include articles on hypnotism in popular magazines and newspapers, nor any novels, short stories, or plays based on hypnosis or dual personality. [37] Hypnosis was recruiting new adherents. In Switzerland, August Forel went to Nancy, returned to Zurich enthusiastic about hypnotism, and published a book in which he expressed his belief in the possibility of crime under hypnosis, and also discussed the phenomenon of conscious and unconscious resistance under hypnosis. [38] In Berlin, Preyer gave a series of lectures on hypnosis. In Belgium, Masoin provoked a discussion over hypnosis at the Belgian Academy of Medicine. In France original, independent research in hypnosis was pursued in Paris by Binet and in Le Havre by Janet.

Hypnosis was also the topic of judicial controversies. Since the Nancy school admitted the possibility of crime under hypnosis, and the Salpêtrière denied it, there were valid grounds for battles of words by experts. Such was the famous Chambige trial. [39] In January 1888, in a little town in Algeria, the naked body of Madame Grille was found on a bed in a villa, and near her body was a twenty-two-year-old law student, Henri Chambige, who was shot through the face. The victim's husband preferred to believe that his wife's seduction had taken place under hypnosis. Chambige said there had been a violent passion between Madame Grille and himself, that she had wished to terminate the affair by a double suicide, and that at her request he had killed her and then shot himself. The prosecution maintained that Chambige had hypnotized her or perhaps used some subtle drug to render her unconscious. Chambige denied this, but nevertheless was sentenced to seven years' hard labor.

Everywhere there was also much interest in hysteria. Following Charcot and Strümpell, Moebius in Germany defined hysteria as "morbid changes in the body that are caused by representations."[40]

The year 1889 began by bringing about two sensations. On January 30 the Crown Prince Rudolf, heir to the throne of the Austrian-Hungarian monarchy, was found shot dead in the hunting pavilion of Mayerling in the Viennese woods with his mistress, the young baroness Maria Vetsera. The mystery surrounding that double death has never been cleared. The death was a severe blow to the Emperor Francis Joseph I, and created problems in regard to the succession. Another sensation was the triumphal success of Boulanger in the general elections in France. Enthusiasm for Boulanger had reached a peak, and he was expected to seize power, but at the moment of truth he shrank from the decisive gesture and ran away to Belgium, causing the movement to collapse. Political tension now eased in France, creating a more favorable atmosphere for the Universal Exposition. The French government had organized it to celebrate the centennial of the Revolution, and to show that in spite of her defeat by Germany in 1870–1871, France was still a great power.

A third sensation was the news that Friedrich Nietzsche was seized by acute psychotic disturbances in Turin and had to be committed to a mental institution, where he spent the rest of his life lost in mental darkness. This tragedy helped to draw attention to Nietzsche's work, and for about two decades European youth was inordinately fascinated by him.

The Universal Exhibition attracted enormous crowds to Paris, who were eager to visit the Eiffel Tower, the Moulin Rouge, and other attractions. There was also an uninterrupted sequence of international congresses, sometimes five or six being held simultaneously. Visitors had the impression that intellectual activity had never been so high in France. Among the best sellers of that year were *La Bête Humaine* by Zola, *Thaïs* by Anatole France, *Un Homme Libre* by Barrès, and *Le Disciple* by Paul Bourget (inspired by the Chambige case). Henri Bergson's thesis *The*

Immediate Data of Consciousness earned him status among philosophers. [41] His colleague, Pierre Janet, who had brilliantly defended his own thesis *Psychological Automatism*, also, achieved fame in philosophical and psychological circles. [42] Another talked-about event was Brown-Sequard's paper read on June 1 before the Société de Biologie, on the rejuvenating effects on men of injections of testicular extract. [43] He had used himself as a subject and his colleagues thought that he looked considerably younger. This was one of the earliest-known applications of endocrinology.

Among the congresses that took place during the Exhibition, three are of interest for our purpose, those of physiological psychology, hypnotism, and magnetism. The International Congress on Physiological Psychology took place from August 6 to 10. [44] This title was chosen to indicate that psychology was now a science in its own right and no longer merely a branch of philosophy. Charcot had been designated as president of the Congress, but he excused himself, so that the Congress was opened by one of the vice-presidents, Ribot. There were four sections to the Congress, the first, under the chairmanship of William James, discussed the topic of muscular sensitivity. The second discussed psychological heredity, with Galton as main discussant. The third discussed hallucinations, and particularly their incidence in nonpsychotic individuals, and this offered an opportunity for Frederic Myers and William James to tell of certain parapsychological phenomena. In the fourth section, devoted to hypnotism, three theories were confronted. Bernheim defended the Nancy position, namely, that anyone could be hypnotized, admitting, however, that a certain impressionability was a prerequisite; Janet contended that only hysterics and exhausted individuals could be hypnotized; and Ochorowicz maintained that hypnotizability is an individual condition that can be found both in normal and sick individuals.

The International Congress on Hypnotism took place at the Hôtel-Dieu in Paris from August 8 to 12. [45] It had been widely advertised, and according to the proceedings, it was attended by journalists from 31 newspapers (an unusual feature at that time), including the *Sphinx* of Munich and the *Sun* of New York. Delegates were so numerous that the auditorium was too small to contain them. Among the honorary presidents was Charcot, who had excused himself. Among the participants were Azam, Babinski, Binet, Delboeuf, Dessoir, Sigmund Freud, William James, Ladame, Lombroso, Myers, Colonel de Rochas, Van Eeden, and Van Renterghem, a strange mixture of philosophers, neurologists, psychiatrists, and practitioners of hypnotism. The Congress was opened by Dumontpallier, himself a pioneer of the study of hypnosis, who invoked the memory of a long list of other pioneers and concluded that "hypnotism is an experimental science; its march forward is inevitable." Then Ladame, of Geneva, read a paper attacking Delboeuf, and advocated the forbidding of stage performances of hypnosis. This paper aroused a lively discussion. Van Renterghem and Van Eeden gave a description of the Clinic of Suggestive Psychotherapy they had opened in Amsterdam two years earlier. (This may have been the first time the word "psychotherapy" was used in a congress.)

The following day, August 9, began with Bernheim reporting on the comparative values of the various techniques used to produce hypnosis and to enhance suggestibility, from a therapeutic point of view. He proclaimed: "You are not a hypnotizer when you have hypnotized two or three individuals who hypnotized themselves. You are one when in a hospital service where you have authority over the patients you influence eight or nine subjects out of ten." Bernheim's paper provoked an animated discussion; Pierre Janet declared Bernheim's assertions dangerous because they entailed the elimination of any kind of determinism, and antipsychological because psychology, like physiology, also has its laws. Bernheim replied that there is one basic law: that any brain cell activated by an idea tends to bring the idea into being.

The third day, August 10, was devoted to clinical utilization of hypnotism with case histories. Marcel Briand told the story of one of his female patients who used to cry out at the same hour every night. [46] The suggestion "You shall not cry" did not help. Briand suggested to her husband that he ask her during a crisis what it was about, and he reported that she was seeing herself buried alive. So Dr. Briand had her review, under hypnosis, the whole scene of the burial and told her that he would rescue her in time, and that would be the end of the nightmares. The patient was cured, but Briand preferred to reinforce the effect by repeating the session after five days, and again after a month. Then Bourru and Burot related the case of a forty-five-year-old woman who, following various trials in her life, had become subject to serious hysterical disturbances. [47] She requested hypnosis, feeling certain that it would recreate a pleasant event that had occurred two years earlier. Under hypnosis she relived the happy time, and the symptoms temporarily disappeared. She then recalled her life and the pleasant time in a waking state; from then on the patient became a dual personality, alternating between illness and happiness. From that case history it would appear that the author had achieved limited success, transforming the patient from a permanently ill person into one who was intermittently well; but the paper contains a noteworthy assertion:

> It is not enough to combat the morbid phenomena one by one through suggestion. The phenomena may disappear while the disease persists. This is only a therapeutics of symptoms, nothing but an expedient. A real and lasting improvement was achieved only when careful and logical observation led us to the origin itself of the illness . . . It was the ascertaining of these hallucinatory crises which inspired the idea of bringing the patient back to that period of her life through provoking a change in her personality.

The authors attributed the therapeutic effect of these crises to their being a kind of discharge or explosion.

On August 11, the participants visited the hospital of Villejuif, and August 12, the last day of the Congress, was devoted to a visit to the Salpêtrière. Characteristically enough, the delegates were not shown Charcot's service, but that of August Voisin, a psychiatrist who claimed to be able to hypnotize one out of ten psychotics, improving many of them with that method. At one of the sessions a paper by Liégeois on "Criminal Suggestion" aroused acrimonious discussion, and there was a vehement reply from Delboeuf to Ladame's criticism of him on August 8.

It is a remarkable fact that this Congress was dominated by Bernheim and the Nancy School, and almost no one from the Salpêtrière School participated in the discussions with the exception of Georges Gilles de la Tourette and Pierre Janet.

The International Congress on Magnetism, which took place from October 21 to 26, 1889, under the chairmanship of the Count of Constantin, confirmed that in spite of the recent and widespread popularity of hypnotism, magnetism was not dead. [48] The Congress was attended not only by many of the laymen who practised magnetism in the shadow of official medicine, but also by physicians, and it boasted of enjoying the sympathy of illustrious personalities. Camille Flammarion wrote to excuse his absence, saying that he was "on the planet Mars," that is, completing a geographic study of that planet. The discussants emphasized that their master was Mesmer, that magnetism should not be confused with hypnotism, and that magnetic sleep was not necessarily a part of the magnetic treatment of illness. Acerb comments were made on Charcot's work. The founding of a school of curative magnetism was recommended, where future magnetizers would receive their training.

The year 1889 was a felicitous one for dynamic psychology. Medical journals in Paris were filled with articles by Charcot and reports of his lectures. Obviously he was becoming more cautious about hypnotism, and characteristically he gave a lecture on accidents caused by hypnosis. [49] Recent studies on hypnosis and hysteria by Alfred Binet, as well as Janet's newly published thesis on *Psychological Automatism,* were proof to the public that Charcot's teachings were progressing in new directions. Charcot created a Psychological Laboratory in his wards at the Salpêtrière, to be directed by Pierre Janet, who began his medical studies investigating and treating hysterical patients, while teaching philosophy at the Lycée Louis-le-Grand.

However, we have seen that the Nancy School was steadily gaining ground. Liébeault took advantage of his belated fame to publish a revised edition of his book. [50] Forel, in Zurich, opened an outpatient service where he gave hypnotic treatment. In Berlin, Moll now found receptive audiences and published a book on hypnotism. [51] In Montpellier, Grasset gave a series of lectures on hypnotism and began to devise a theory of his own. But Meynert, in Vienna, emphasized the erotic element in hypnosis and one of his pupils, Anton, published impressive examples of the dangers of the method. [52] Among the partisans of hypnotism was Sigmund Freud who, on his journey to Paris, had made a detour by way of Nancy, to learn from Bernheim and Liébeault.

Dessoir[53] in Germany and Héricourt[54] in France tried to make an inventory of the knowledge acquired on the unconscious mind. Moritz Benedikt published case histories illustrating his observations on the secret life of daydreams and suppressed emotions (especially of the sexual kind) and their role in the pathogenesis of hysteria and neuroses. [55]

Sexual psychopathology was another field that increasingly attracted interest. Physicians not only described and classified varieties of sexual deviations, but also studied the masked effects of sexual disturbances on emotional and physical life. Such were the publications, in Zurich, of Alexander Peyer on the noxious effects of coitus interruptus and particularly its manifestations as "sexual asthma."[56]

The Decline of the Salpêtrière School: 1890–1893

The Congress on Hypnosis had given the first inkling that Charcot's star was on the wane while the Nancy School was in full-fledged development. From 1890 to 1893, that is, up to the time of Charcot's death, the Salpêtrière School lost momentum. Charcot's enemies said that he ignored any work done in hypnosis outside the Salpêtrière; more likely he was alarmed by the ever-increasing flood of publications of dubious value about hypnotism.

The year 1890 seemed to contemporaries to be one of great political and social tensions and of bomb throwing by anarchists, but in the annals of the medical world it remained famous as the year of tuberculin. Robert Koch who had discovered the tuberculosis bacillus and was known for the care with which his experiments were performed, prepared tuberculin from a culture of the bacillus. Early experiments led medical men to believe that tuberculin could have a curative action on tuberculosis. This news provoked an unparalleled sensation among tuberculous patients and their physicians. Doctors rushed to Berlin to get supplies of tuberculin, and their hopeful patients felt a temporary improvement, so that the hastily published reports increased hope even more. It took a few months for the terrible truth to emerge, namely, that patients treated with the new method were dying by the hundreds and thousands. [57]

In the field of psychology the important event was the publication of William James' *Principles of Psychology*. [58] The well-known Harvard psychologist had been working for twelve years on the book, which was the first major work of its kind to appear in the United States, and had an immediate and lasting success on both sides of the Atlantic. This textbook treated not only various aspects of experimental psychology but problems of hypnosis, dual personality, and psychical research as well.

Meanwhile, publications on hypnosis became so numerous that it was impossible to keep up with them. Max Dessoir added a supplement with 382 new titles to the 801 titles of his bibliography of modern hypnotism of 1888. Among these, a good number dealt with the problem of crime under hypnosis. This problem was not merely academic; it caused battles of experts in the courts and impassioned discussion in public and in the newspapers.

One memorable trial of the year 1890 was that of Gabrielle Bompard. [59] In July 1889 the bailiff Gouffé in Paris had been killed. A few months later a young woman, Gabrielle Bompard, came to Paris and denounced herself and her accomplice, Michel Eyraud, as the murderers. She claimed to have been hypnotized by her lover Eyraud into luring Gouffé to an apartment where she put a rope around his neck, then Eyraud strangled and robbed him. Following the denunciation, Eyraud was arrested in Havana and extradited, but he denied having hypnotized Gabrielle. Eyraud was sentenced to death and his accomplice to twenty years' imprisonment. Public opinion was highly inflamed over this case of crime under hypnosis and over the arguments of experts in court. Arguing for the possibility of crime under hypnosis, Liégeois was the spokesman for the Nancy School. Opposing him were the noted experts Brouardel, Motet, and Ballet, who invoked the authority of Charcot in denying such a possibility. Even years later, Bernheim maintained that Gabrielle Bompard had acted under suggestion, adding, however, that she was innately lacking in moral sense. [60]

Other causes tended to discredit the theory of crime under hypnosis. Grasset told of a nineteen-year-old hysterical woman, who, on being found pregnant, claimed to have been hypnotized by a peddler. [61] Experts hypnotized her in turn and thus obtained details on the alleged rape. In spite of his denials, the peddler was arrested. It happened that a full-term baby was born two months before the expected date. The new mother then confessed that her charges against the peddler were not true, and that her hypnotic sessions with the experts were completely simulated.

In 1891, Charcot defended his positions valiantly against the attacks of the Nancy School. His disciple Georges Gilles de la Tourette published his great *Treatise on Hysteria*, a synthesis of Charcot's doctrine and a refutation of his adversaries. [62] Meanwhile, Pierre Janet, the new star at the Salpêtrière, was developing his psychological analysis; he published in that year the story of Marcelle, in which the relationship between the symptoms, the subconscious fixed ideas, and the constitutional background were analyzed in detail. [63]

A ceremony took place in Nancy, on May 25, in honor of Liébeault, who was retiring, with the customary banquet, speeches, and gifts. This provided an opportunity to see how many adherents the Nancy School had gained throughout the world. [64] A Liébeault Prize was founded to reward research in the field of hypnotism.

In Vienna, Moritz Benedikt restated his theory of hysteria, saying its basis consisted of an inborn and acquired vulnerability of the nervous system but its actual cause was either a psychic trauma (in men or in women), or a functional disturbance of the genital system or the sexual life, which a woman will keep secret, even from her nearest relative and her family doctor. [65] Benedikt proclaimed the futility of hypnotic treatment of hysteria and the necessity of psychotherapy on the conscious level. The criminologist Hans Gross, of Graz, published in 1891 his *Handbook of the Criminal Investigator,* which contained keen observations on the deleterious effects of and the various masks taken by frustrated sexual instinct. [66] At that time, Sigmund Freud was still mainly concerned with neurology; he published contributions on cerebral palsy of children and his book on aphasia.

The year 1892 gave the impression of being a particularly violent one, with its numerous criminal attempts by anarchists in Europe and America.

In Paris, Charcot's star was definitely in its decline, and for the first time he suffered a serious setback. Charcot wanted to have Babinski elevated to the rank of professor (most probably he viewed him as his successor); but Bouchard was able to counter Charcot's will, and as a result, Babinski never received the rank of professor and his university career was broken. Charcot was obviously seeking new paths. He had been impressed by seeing some of his patients return from Lourdes free of their symptoms (not only of hysterical paralyses but also of tumors and ulcers), and came to the conclusion that unknown, powerful healing factors existed that the medicine of the future should learn to control. [67] Charcot was also trying to extend the distinction he had made between organic and dynamic paralyses to other fields. A famous patient, known as Madame D., served as a prototype to demonstrate the distinction between organic and dynamic amnesia. [68] That same patient was entrusted to Janet for psychotherapy and became one of his best-known cases of treatment by psychological analysis. [69]

At the Salpêtrière, Janet actively pursued his research quite independent from the neurological staff. His lectures on hysterical amnesia and anesthesia, his article on spiritism in which he gives a dynamic psychological interpretation of mediumnistic phenomena, attracted attention. [70] His psychological analyses of a few chosen patients were establishing a model for later investigation and treatment. Had he published at that time a volume with the case histories of Lucie, Marie, Marcelle, Madame D., and the others he had already treated with success, no one would ever have questioned his priority in regard to the discovery of what was later called cathartic therapy. Janet was also becoming a source of inspiration for other workers, as shown by the medical thesis of Laurent on the pathological variations of the field of consciousness. [71]

Meanwhile, the influence of the Nancy School was spreading throughout Europe. This was obvious at the Second International Congress on Psychology, which took place from August 1 to 4 in London. [72] The first Congress, three years earlier, had been called the Congress on Physiological Psychology, but on the wish of certain members, it was there resolved that the word "physiological" should be changed to "experimental." The president of the second Congress was Sidgwick, and the general secretary F. W. H. Myers. One of the first papers was that of Pierre Janet on "Continuous Amnesia," with three clinical observations. The longest was the story of Madame D. Janet showed how this patient, who was seemingly unable to acquire new memories and immediately forgot things, had a subconsciously preserved memory behind this apparent amnesia. Janet used three means, hypnosis, automatic writing, and automatic talking (a new technique that consisted of having the patient talk at random). He thus was able not only to reach the subconscious fixed ideas and the subconscious dreams, but also to modify them and give back to the patient the greater part of her memories when she resumed her conscious state.

Frederick van Eeden, the young Dutch physician and poet who together with Van Renterghem had opened a clinic of suggestive therapy in Amsterdam, discussed "the Theory of Psychotherapeutics." The term "Psychotherapeutics," introduced by Hack Tuke, was defined as "the cure of the body by means of the psychical functions of the sufferers." Van Eeden now defined "Psycho-Therapy" as "the cure of the body by the mind, aided by the impulse of one mind to another." "Centralization of psychical functions must be the principal maxim of Psycho-Therapy," said Van Eeden, "the centrum being intellect and conscious volition." Psycho-Therapy must guide and instruct, not command, and the best means to that aim is training. The remark "Psycho-Therapy does not heal wholly and lastingly" is ridiculous. Even more than at the First Congress, the Nancy School carried the day. Janet was the only one who intervened to state that there was such a thing as hypnosis.

The demand for a new psychology, wider than just hypnotism and suggestion, was manifested throughout Europe. One further instance was Strümpell's inaugural lecture "On the Origin and Healing of Diseases Through Mental Representations," which was read on November 4, 1892, when he was elected Vice-Rector of the University of Erlangen.

Strümpell recalled that the influence of psychological factors in the etiology of bodily disease had been known from time immemorial, though some persons are more sensitive than others to these influences. If psychological factors can produce disease, they can also cure. Many cures are due less to the medication agents themselves than to the patients' faith in their effectiveness. The fashion today calls for hypnotism and suggestion. Actually hypnosis is effective insofar as the patient believes in its power, and does not realize its true nature. A normal man who knows exactly what hypnosis is will hardly ever be hypnotized, not to speak of the fact that hypnosis is a severe form of artificial hysteria. No healing occurs through hypnosis that could not have been caused by other means. Hypnotism would not have become so widespread if young physicians had received a better psychological education. Strümpell concluded his address by expressing the hope that psychology would become compulsory in medical schools, as was physiology. [73]

The general interest in new forms of psychotherapy was expressed in the novel by Marcel Prévost, *The Autumn of a Woman,* which appeared at the end of 1892, bearing as its date of publication 1893, and as its motto a verse of Alfred de Vigny: *Il rêvera partout à la chaleur du sein.* ("He will dream everywhere of the warmth of the breast").

A young man, Maurice, who had been unusually spoiled by and attached to his mother in his childhood, seeks women with motherly natures. He has a love affair with a frustrated woman who feels that she is getting old, and this love has a tragic quality because of Maurice's immaturity and because his mistress, Madame Surgère, a religious woman, is torn with guilt feelings. On the other hand, her adopted daughter Claire is deeply in love with him and after a superficial flirtation with her, Maurice thinks of her as a future wife when he will be tired of his adventure. Meanwhile, the family has arranged an engagement between Claire and an older man whom she respects but does not love. Claire falls into a deep depression caused by her secret which she dare not reveal to anybody. Her condition worsens and she is actually dying, when someone guesses her secret and obtains it from her, namely, Dr. Daumier, a young neurologist of the Salpêtrière. An unusually skilled psychotherapist, Dr. Daumier handles the whole situation brilliantly and makes each one of the characters aware of the profound cause of his troubles. He shows Maurice what the situation is in reality, and successfully appeals to his sense of responsibility. Maurice ends his affair with Madame Surgère and decides to marry Claire, who, as a result, rapidly recovers. As for Madame Surgère, Dr. Daumier helps her to overcome the shock of breaking with Maurice, and he refers her to her priest, who will reconcile her with religion. As for that serious gentleman to whom Claire had been engaged, Dr. Daumier helps him recognize his true vocation, which is the priesthood. [74]

The interest of this novel is twofold. It is a psychological analysis of several characters: Maurice, who had lacked the authority of a father and had been spoiled by his mother, is an immature, irresponsible youngster, who seeks transient adventures or the love of older, maternal women. Claire's illness begins in the form of an ordinary depression that gradually achieves alarming proportions, and then she has a hemorrhage that brings her close to death. She is rapidly cured when her pathogenic secret is discovered, and a means is found to grant her her wish. (Today her condition would be called a psychosomatic illness.) The other interesting feature of that novel is the picture of the psychotherapist, Dr. Daumier, with his acute sense of perception, his skill in disentangling a situation, and the tact he uses in talking with each one of the characters. For those familiar with the personality and the psychotherapy of Pierre Janet there is hardly a doubt that the writer used him as a model for his character. The psychotherapeutic procedures of this Dr. Daumier also resembled those used by Benedikt in Vienna with the probing for the patient's secret problems while in a conscious state, and then the cure being achieved by helping him to solve these problems.

Thus we can see that in 1892 there was a choice of psychotherapies ranging from hypnotic suggestion and catharsis to the combination of supportive, expressive, and directive therapy. Such was the situation at the beginning of the crucial year 1893.

The year 1893 was another year of political and social tension around the world. A flotilla of the Russian fleet visited Toulon, and was given a triumphant reception by the French population. This was the preliminary to the Franco-Russian Military Alliance. The French felt it as a relief from the threat of Germany's power, the balance of power now being reestablished (Germany, Austria-Hungary, and Italy on one side, France and Russia on the other). The French, meanwhile, were bent upon enlarging their already vast colonial empire. There had never been so much anarchist activity and on December 9 the anarchist Vaillant threw a bomb in the Chambre des Députés. This incident was followed by the celebrated phrase of the president: *"Messieurs, la séance continue."* ("Gentlemen, the meeting will continue.").

Following Pasteur's discovery of a preventive treatment of rabies, the discovery by his disciple Roux of a serum against diphtheria was celebrated in France as a triumph of the French genius.

At the Salpêtrière new tendencies were slowly emerging. Whereas Janet was pursuing his psychological analysis of hysteria, Babinski was seeking precise neurological criteria to define hysterical symptoms and distinguish them from organic symptoms (this was to lead him to the discovery of the cutaneous-plantar reflex, or "Babinski's reflex").

In Vienna the battle for and against hypnosis was raging more than ever. Krafft-Ebing published a series of investigations on hypnosis that met violent criticism by Benedikt, not only in medical assemblies but in the daily press. [75] Sigmund Freud, whose reputation as a neurologist was by then well established, began to make himself known in the field of neuropsychiatry. We have seen that in 1893 Freud still treated patients with Bernheim's method, but also paid his tribute to Charcot with an article on the difference of organic and hysterical paralyses. [76] Freud apparently did not realize the developments that were taking place in Paris; his paper would have been in line with the Salpêtrière doctrine of 1886, but in view of the new direction opened by Babinski, it seemed slightly antiquated in 1893. However, Freud also wrote a joint paper with Breuer: "On the Psychic Mechanism of Hysterical Phenomena," proposing a new theory, a combination of the concepts of Janet and Benedikt. This paper was favorably received. Within one month an objective review appeared in the *Revue Neurologique* and there were also reviews in the German journals. [77] Obersteiner mentioned the paper in his book on hypnosis as being "a very interesting application of hypnotic suggestion."[78] In England, Myers found it a confirmation of his views on the subliminal self.[79] Michell Clarke in *Brain* gave an extensive and sympathetic comment. [80] In Belgium, Dallemagne gave a good summary of the Breuer-Freud theory and expressed a few reservations. [81] Janet wrote, "I am happy to see that the results of my already old findings have been recently confirmed by two German authors, Breuer and Freud." [82] Benedikt who, like Janet, had been mentioned in a footnote, criticized the paper and said that Breuer and Freud must really have been lucky to come upon such an unusually good set of clinical cases.[83]

The sudden death of Charcot, on August 16, 1893, was a shock in France and throughout the scientific world. Charcot, as mentioned elsewhere, was surrounded by a host of enemies eager to exploit every incident against him.[84] He was criticized for his attitude in the Valroff case in which a house servant, Valroff, after attempting to kill the lady of the house and her personal maid, declared that he had acted in a somnambulic state. The accused maintained that he had acted in complete unconsciousness. [85] Charcot's advice was asked. He was noncommittal, giving a description of the somnambulic state, but could not say whether it applied to Valroff's recent condition. Meanwhile the campaign for the general elections began with unusual bitterness. Public opinion was upset by financial scandals. In June, at the Chamber of Deputies, several political men were accused of having been bribed by the English, through the intermediary of the financier Cornelius Hertz. The documents brought as evidence proved to be forged, but Hertz, accused of embezzlement, fled to England. The English refused to surrender him to French authorities, because he was seriously ill. The French sent Charcot with another medical expert to England to report on Hertz's condition. Charcot was criticized for having predicted that the man would die within two weeks (actually, it was Hertz who outlived Charcot). The month of July started with student demonstrations in Paris, and a young man was accidentally killed in a café. This was the signal for violent student riots, which were backed by workers. For a period of four days the Latin Quarter was covered with barricades. The weather was intolerably sultry, making the usual pressures at the Medical School to finish dissertations more intolerable. On July 29, Janet brilliantly defended his medical thesis, under the chairmanship of Charcot. Preparations for the general elections were the occasion for enraged polemics that degenerated, in more than one instance, into acts of violence.

In these troubled circumstances Charcot left Paris shortly before August 15, for a vacation in the district of Morvan, accompanied by two of his favorite disciples, Debove and Strauss. The Russian physician Lyubimov told of going to fetch Charcot at his home and how, unaware of his imminent departure, was struck by Charcot's expression of suffering. [86] Charcot, however, complied with Lyubimov's request, and thus Charcot saw his last patient on the way from his home to the railway station. On the following day it seemed that Charcot was recovering, but in the late evening he felt ill and called his companions. They gave him an injection of morphine and left him to sleep. The next morning, on August 16, they found him dead. [87] Charcot was buried with full national honors. An imposing ceremony was held in the Chapel of the Salpêtrière, with representatives of the government, public administration, scientific bodies, and numerous personalities in attendance. Several medical journals appeared with their covers bordered in black, and newspapers were filled with details—accurate and inaccurate—of Charcot's career and death. It was told that on the morning of his death a delegation of upset hysterical patients went to the director of the hospital and asked if anything had happened to Charcot, because they had dreamed that he was dead. Some obituaries had an ambiguous tone, the *Figaro* of August 17 emphasized Charcot's genius and great scientific achievements, but also exhumed the old accusations of inordinate pride, absorbing egoism, and self-aggrandizement verging on histrionics. Dr. Antoine Emile Blanche, who had died on the same day, was eulogized as a physician of the old school able to write intelligible reports, who was humane, compassionate, and for whom patients were human beings rather than case histories.

Many obituaries of Charcot appeared in medical journals in France and elsewhere. One of the first appeared in the *Wiener Medizinische Wochenschrift* of September 9, 1893, under the signature of Dr. Sigmund Freud. [88] The author, who was proud to recount personal reminiscences, compared Charcot with Adam, who had named the animals in Eden, and with Pinel, who had liberated the insane from their chains; in the same manner Charcot had given names to unknown diseases at the Salpêtrière and had liberated hysterics from the chains of prejudice. To Charcot's neurological work, Freud gave full recognition; to his work on hysteria, Freud credited his pioneering approach to its understanding. As to hypnosis, Freud acknowledged Charcot's serious, if narrow, investigations.

In the eyes of his contemporaries, Freud's obituary of Charcot was just one among many written throughout Europe. In France, after laudatory obituaries by Charcot's pupils, came a perceptive paper by Janet discreetly indicating the weak points in Charcot's methodology. [89] The first book on Charcot, curiously enough, was that by a Russian physician, Lyubimov, who had been acquainted with Charcot for twenty years and recorded information about Charcot that is to be found nowhere else. The general impression was that it would be very difficult to replace Charcot, and that with his death an era in the history of neuropsychiatry had come to an end.

Predominance and Decline of the Nancy School: 1894–1900

With the death of Charcot, the reign of the Salpêtrière seemed over. Charcot had been losing ground to the Nancy School during the last few years, and a reaction against Charcot's ideas also came from within the Salpêtrière. There had been so many dubious elements in the experiments on hysterical patients that a more solid basis for investigations was desired. There were two types of reaction; there were those such as Janet, who were in favor of pursuing psychological studies with objective and critical methods, but the majority of Charcot's pupils rejected the psychological in favor of the neurological method. Charcot's successor, Professor Fulgence Raymond, took a middle course. He strongly leaned to the neurological approach, but encouraged Janet's pursuit of the psychological. The Nancy School now seemed to dominate the scene, and was expanding, but in doing so, its teaching was diluted. Bernheim had started with hypnotic sleep, and subsequently concentrated on "suggestion." The word "suggestion" was becoming increasingly vague in meaning, and was gradually replaced by the new, fashionable term, "psychotherapy."

The Search for New Psychotherapies: 1894–1896

In the year 1894 the political supremacy of Europe was still undisputed, but two events should have served as warnings. Japan, on its own initiative, declared war on China, and after a swift victory made Korea its "protectorate." The Turkish sultan, Abdul Hamid II, chose the Armenians for his latest scapegoats and systematically massacred 80,000 of them. Until then it had been the custom for European countries to intervene by declaring war or threatening to do so as soon as the Turks began a massacre of Christians. But this time, in spite of the indignation among Christian nations, the Red Sultan was not effectively opposed, and this meant another moral defeat for Europe. Anarchist activity, meanwhile, continued in Europe, and the French President Sadi Carnot was assassinated. Czar Alexander III died, and the kind of politics that his successor Nicholas II would follow was a subject of anxiety for the rest of Europe.

In Paris the reaction against Charcot was not long in coming both within and without the Salpêtrière. [90] Nevertheless, Janet, favored by Raymond's attitude of benevolent neutrality, published two of his celebrated case histories, those of Justine and Achilles. [91] But Bernheim now considered himself the great leader of psychotherapy and his influence expanded steadily.

In the German-speaking world, the *Preliminary Communication* by Breuer and Freud had aroused some interest; those who had read Janet, though, could not see much that was new in it. But Freud now insisted upon the differences between his theories and those of Janet, and in 1894 published a paper on the "defense neuroses" in which he took a position against that of Janet.

The events of the year 1895 appeared to those living then as being disastrous for the prestige of the Western world. The massacre of the Armenians continued in spite of protests from Christian powers, and there was a reawakening of anti-Semitism in Europe. The anti-Semitic leader, Karl Lueger, was elected mayor of Vienna, but the Emperor canceled the appointment. There was some agitation during the electoral campaign, although practically no violence against Jewish persons or property occurred. In France, anti-Semitism revolved around the Dreyfus case. Captain Alfred Dreyfus was accused of treason, stripped of his rank, and sentenced to hard labor on Devil's Island. In the same year, two great scientific discoveries were made, that of the X rays by Roentgen, and of cinematography by Lumière. Pasteur, who died on September 28, was buried with national honors as one of the greatest scientists of all times; and the French felt that the history of medicine could now be divided into two periods: before and after Pasteur.

In Paris, Janet published a series of papers illustrating the role of subconscious ideas in the etiology of hysterical symptoms, fugues, and even muscle spasms. [92] But the favor of the educated public went to Gustave Le Bon's *Psychology of Crowds,* which was believed to furnish a new key to the understanding of sociology, history, and political science. [93]

In Vienna, Sigmund Freud, as a student of neuroses, was emerging as the rival of Pierre Janet. This was shown by his papers on psychotherapy of hysteria, anxiety neurosis, by another in French on obsessions and phobias (with his theory of the four types of neuroses and their specific sexual etiology), and above all by his joint publication with Breuer on the *Studies in Hysteria.* [94] This book, as we have seen, contains the account of Breuer's Anna O. and four case histories by Freud. The evolution from the time of the "Preliminary Communication" is noteworthy: of these four patients, only two were treated under hypnosis; the other two were treated by direct handling of their problems in a waking state, much in the manner of Benedikt.

The traditional belief that *Studies in Hysteria* met no success is definitely contradicted by the facts. Umpfenbach wrote that the five case histories were of extreme interest and that the two authors had arrived at the concepts of Janet and Binet. [95] Bleuler gave an objective account of the book and expressed a few reservations (it was not ruled out, he said, that the therapeutic success of the cathartic method was simply the result of suggestion); he regarded the book as one of the most important published during the previous years. [96] According to Jones, the book met uncomprehending and derogatory criticism by Strümpell, but was given an extremely kind review by J. Michell Clarke. Actually, Strümpell and Clarke gave the same praise and the same criticism, though differently phrased. Strümpell said that "both authors have tried to give us, with much adroitness and psychological penetration, a deeper insight into the mental condition of hysterics, and their statements offer much that is interesting and stimulating." [97] He did not doubt the therapeutic success of Breuer and Freud, but he questioned how far one had the right to investigate the most intimate secrets of one's patients, and whether what the patient said under hypnosis really corresponded to the truth, because many hysterics are able to fabricate romances when under hypnosis. The same objections (which Jones finds derogatory when coming from Strümpell) were expressed by Michell Clarke who wrote: "Into the question of the advisability of penetrating so intimately into the most private thoughts and concerns of a patient, I do not enter," and: "It would seem likely that the patients would, in many cases, at least, strongly resent it. The necessity of bearing in mind, in studying hysterical patients, the great readiness with which they respond to suggestion, may be reiterated, as the weak point in the method of investigation may perhaps be found here." [98] The danger, he adds, would be that the patients would "make statements in accordance with the slightest suggestion given to them," even quite unconsciously, by the investigator. In England, too, Myers lauded the book, in which he saw a confirmation of his own views and of the research of Binet and Janet in France. [99] Havelock Ellis made enthusiastic comments, and said that Breuer and Freud had "opened a door," adding: "It seems probable that future advances in the explanation of hysteria must lie in further psychic analysis."[100] The story of Anna O. was utilized by Bressler[101] in a study on Blumhardt's patient and her cure by exorcism;[102] Breuer's and Freud's theory of hysteria, Bressler said, could help us gain a scientific understanding of that case. In Budapest, Ranschburg and Hajos gave a comparative survey of theories of hysteria of Janet and of Breuer and Freud acknowledging the merits of both, although they did not accept Breuer's criticism of Janet's concepts. The most sobering comment came from Krafft-Ebing, who stated that he had tried the Breuer-Freud method on a few hysterical patients and found that bringing the causal trauma to light did not suffice to cure the symptom. [104] Krafft-Ebing also emphasized that the memory of the repressed trauma could emerge into consciousness in a fantastic and distorted fashion. [105]

Studies in Hysteria was also successful in literary circles. The writer Alfred Berger, known for a philosophical essay on Descartes, psychological novels, and also as a literary critic, wrote a review with the title *Surgery of the Soul* in the *Morgenpresse.*[106] He praised the emotional depth, the psychological sagacity, and the goodness of heart manifested in the work of the two authors; he compared their cathartic cures with Orestes' cure in Goethe's play *Iphigenia in Tauris.* Above all, he hailed it as "a piece of ancient writers' psychology." The writers, he said, are as the great Vikings who were in America long before Columbus; now at long last physicians were catching up with them. We also know from Hofmannsthal's correspondence that he was interested in the *Studies in Hysteria* as source material while preparing his play *Elektra.*[107] He wanted his heroine, in contrast to Goethe's, to be a kind of hysterical fury.[108] Hermann Bahr, who had lent his copy of the Breuer-Freud book to Hofmannsthal, utilized their cathartic method for his interpretation of dramatic works.[109]

The year 1896 was marked by another severe blow to Europe's self-esteem. The Italians, who had undertaken the conquest of Ethiopia, suffered a crushing defeat by Emperor Menelik at Adua. But among the events of that year, none perhaps was as terrible as the catastrophe that accompanied the coronation of Czar Nicholas II and the Empress Alexandra, on May 29. During the festivities the crowd panicked, and several thousand men, women, and children were trampled to death. This was followed by protests among the liberals and student riots, all of which had to be repressed. The superstitious saw these events as an ill omen for the reign of the new Czar. The alliance between France and Russia, nevertheless, was taking shape, and when Czar Nicholas visited Paris, he was given a triumphal reception. All this could only increase the tension between the two political blocks in Europe.

Anti-Semitism was becoming an increasing concern in Europe. In France, a group was starting to campaign in favor of Dreyfus, and two opposing camps formed. In Austria, a Jewish journalist and playwright, Theodor Herzl, published his epoch-making book *The Jewish State.*[110] As a journalist in the service of the *Neue Freie Presse,* he witnessed the agitation around the election of Lueger, and the Dreyfus agitation in France. The only alternative he could see to anti-Semitism was the creation of a Jewish national state in Palestine. He was not the first to suggest such a solution, but in his book he proffered complete plans, and he worked toward their realization.

In 1896 the Third International Congress of Psychology took place in Munich from August 4 to 7.[111] The Congress had been prepared with characteristically German *Gründlichkeit,* and gathered about 500 participants, which was considered a very large number. One hundred and seventy-six papers were read in four languages (German, Spanish, English, and Italian). Among the participants were the best-known philosophers, psychiatrists, and psychologists of that time. Many of the papers were of high quality, and a few of them remain of particular interest in retrospect.

Theodor Lipps read an impressive paper on the concept of the unconscious. [112] The unconscious, he said, is "the" question of psychology. The unconscious, the general basis of psychic life, is like a chain of undersea mountains, in which only the peaks emerge, the latter representing the conscious. Our conscious life is, to a great extent, dominated by unconscious representations: "Thus past representations are now active in me, without my awareness of their presence and activity." The unconscious cannot be entirely explained in physiological terms, it is a psychic reality in itself. In a somewhat similar direction was a paper by Georg Hirth on the *Merksysteme,* that is, the lasting associations of perceptions that, below the threshold of consciousness, are actively in conflict with each other. [113] These *Merksysteme* can take possession of an individual without his being aware of it. In the worst cases their tyranny may be such that it brings an individual to his ruin. *Merksysteme* may unite in the form of shadow systems that are at the roots of antipathies, suspicions, perversions, and so on, and are often betrayed by dream systems. "The life path of the hysterical and the melancholic is paved with *shadow systems.*" In the discussion following the conference, the Rector Ufer commented that *Merksysteme* were Herbart's *Vorstellungsmassen,* and Truper said that they were identical with Lazarus' condensations.

In a paper on "The Difference Between Suggestibility and Hysteria," Forel attempted to give an answer to the old question, "What is hysteria?" He defined hysteria as "a pathological complex of symptoms" that can be either constitutional or acquired, or both, though as a rule the constitutional element predominates. This is true, Forel said, even though there was proof, brought "by Charcot, Freud, Breuer, Vogt, and many others before them," that seemingly severe symptoms could be produced by unconscious mental representations and cured by the removal of the latter. Otto Wetterstrand read a paper on his new method of hypnotic treatment and prolonged hypnotic sleep. He rehypnotized patients to keep them in hypnotic sleep for six, eight, or ten days or more, and claimed to be able to cure hysterical patients in this way.

In his paper on "Somnambulic Influence and the Need for Direction," Janet gave a clear description of the specific relationship between therapist and patient. On the basis of his own clinical experience Janet distinguished two types of rapport: somnambulic influence occurring in hysterical patients, and need for direction in psychasthenics. [114]

The papers described here are only a small sampling of those read at this Congress. The number, variety, and originality of the contributions must have given the participants the feeling that psychology was on the verge of a breakthrough.

The General Secretary of the Congress, Von Schrenck-Notzing, in the same year published a study on dual personality.[115] He contended that dual personality was an unconscious revival of forgotten memories. He supported this point of view with a careful review of well-known clinical cases (Azam's Felida, Charcot's Blanche Wittmann, and Janet's various patients) and with recent research by French authors as well as by Breuer and Freud.

The Fin de Siècle Period: 1897–1900

The years 1897 to 1900 were the culmination of the *fin de siècle* spirit in Europe. [116] One of its characteristics, as we have seen, was an extreme interest on the part of the public in psychological and psychopathological problems, and the search for new systems of psychotherapy. Bernheim still considered himself the unchallenged leader of psychological medicine, but the Nancy School became an increasingly hazy concept. In Paris the reaction against Charcot went so far that many deemed psychology unnecessary in the treatment of mental patients. Janet, without denying his previous research on subconscious fixed ideas, gave more attention to minute descriptions of psychasthenia. Few, of course, would know that Flournoy, in Geneva, had engaged on a long-term investigation with the medium Hélène Smith, and who would have guessed that Sigmund Freud, in Vienna, was conducting a self-analysis, together with an investigation of dreams?

The year 1897 gave the impression of being, like the previous ones, heavily fraught with political and social tensions. The population of Crete rebelled against the Turkish rule and was supported by troops from Greece, but the Turks reconquered the island, provoking the intervention of other European powers. The Franco-Russian alliance was strengthened by the visit of the French President Félix Faure to Czar Nicholas II. In Vienna, Karl Lueger, the anti-Semitic leader, was elected for the third time as mayor of Vienna, after the Emperor had twice canceled his appointment, and this time his election was ratified. The first Zionist Congress was held in Basel under the chairmanship of Theodor Herzl. But the event that probably made the most dramatic impression that year was the fire in the Bazar de la Charité, in Paris, on May 4. The organizers and participants of the Bazaar belonged to the elite of French aristocracy. One of the victims of the disaster was the sister of the Empress Elisabeth of Austria. Among the one hundred twenty-five who perished in the fire only five were men (three old men, one twelve-year-old boy, and one physician). It was revealed that the young aristocrats present had kicked their way out, and this disgraceful behavior was the death blow to what remained of respect held for the aristocracy.

Among the numerous publications of that year was Frederic Myers' survey of the relationship between hysterical symptoms and fixed ideas.[117]

Hysterical symptoms, he said, have childish features and "suggest to me irresistibly the fantastic dream-like play of the subliminal self." He added:

> All hysterical symptoms then, I say boldly, are equivalent to *idées fixes*; and a hysterical access is the explosion of an *idée fixe* . . . notions like these, suggested to me largely by Dr. Janet's experiments, find (as seems to me) a strange confirmation in the more recent *Studien über Hysterie* of Drs. Breuer and Freud. These physicians have had to deal, most of all, in Dr. Breuer's case of Anna O. with hysterics of a much higher intellectual caliber than the patients of the Salpêtrière. [Myers compared the mechanism by which hysterical symptoms are produced to that of the creativeness of genius] . . . . Genius consists largely in subliminal uprushes which express symbolically the result of observations and inference of which the subliminal self is not aware.

On the whole, however, all that pertained to hysteria, hypnosis, and suggestion was becoming increasingly suspect, and the word "psychotherapy" was now the accepted term for all methods of healing through the mind. A typical instance of this new attitude is found in Löwenfeld's textbook of psychotherapy.[118] After a historical survey of psychotherapy and general principles of medical psychology, Löwenfeld gives instructions in regard to the patient-physician relationship. Among the chief psychotherapeutic methods, Löwenfeld expounds psychic gymnastics, hypnotic and suggestive treatment, Breuer-Freud's method, emotion therapy, and faith healing.

The year 1898 led Europe to the brink of war. The trigger incident was part of the competition for colonial possession in Africa. The French already possessed a large empire from the Atlantic Ocean to Lake Tchad. An expedition under the command of Colonel Marchand arrived at Fashoda, where it was halted by the English. This aroused much indignation in France, and war between France and England seemed inevitable, but the French finally yielded to English demands (this being an opportunistic concession on account of a possible future war with Germany). A new and serious blow to European narcissism was given by the Spanish-American War. A rebellion against the Spaniards had occurred in Cuba, and the rebels were supported by volunteers from the United States. As the result of an unclarified incident pertaining to the explosion of the American ship *Maine* near Havana, the Americans declared war. The Spanish fleet suffered a crushing defeat, whereupon the Americans occupied Cuba, Puerto Rico, Guam, and the Philippines. In Spain, the defeat initiated what was called *marasmus*. The young generation, later called the 1898 generation, deeply felt the impact of the defeat, but in the long run many of them brought about a renewed intellectual life in their country. The Dreyfus conflict reached its peak in France when the novelist Zola published a libel, *J'Accuse,* and one of the accused, Colonel Henry, caught in forgery, committed suicide. And when the Empress Elisabeth of Austria was assassinated by an anarchist in Geneva, it seemed to many that the hand of fate was at work against the unfortunate Emperor Francis Joseph I.

Also in 1898, Pierre Janet published *Névroses et Idées Fixes,* the first of his large works to appear under the auspices of the psychological laboratory of the Salpêtrière. [119] A great part of it had already been made known in the form of separate articles. Following the French custom of the time, Raymond's patronage was acknowledged by joining his name with the author's, although everything had been written by Janet. *Névroses et Idées Fixes* contains several of Janet's best-known case histories, those of Marcelle, Justine, Marcelline, Madame D., and Achilles, as well as contributions of a more theoretical nature. Following the *Automatisme Psychologique*, and the medical thesis on hysteria, this latest book secured Janet's renown as France's foremost specialist in neuroses. This was the more so because, in the same year, Janet made a substantial contribution on "The Psychological Treatment of Hysteria" for Albert Robin's encyclopedic textbook of therapeutics.

> Janet synthesized there his conceptions about subconscious fixed ideas, their nature, detection, and management, their relation to the symptoms (including the symbolic character of symptoms in certain cases); he emphasized that it was not enough to bring them back to consciousness, that they had to be dissociated in spite of considerable resistance (often in the form of somatic symptoms). Janet also insisted on the capital role of somnambulic influence, and how it had to be utilized for the treatment, though kept down at the minimum compatible with therapeutic effect. Not less essential, Janet said, was to supplement the hypnotic treatment with a program of reeducation. [120]

The Nancy School had mushroomed, and one of its adherents, the Dutchman Van Renterghem, published a survey of the school, first describing the members of the Nancy group, Liébeault and Bernheim, and the adherents of the school in all parts of Europe, such as Poland, Sweden, and Germany. [121] Breuer and Freud represented the Austrian branch.

The physician of 1898, reading in medical journals of university appointments, might have been surprised to notice that the famous Professor August Forel had left his chair of psychiatry at the Zurich University to be replaced by an almost unknown newcomer, Eugen Bleuler, in recognition of the latter's remarkable clinical work during the previous ten years in the Rheinau Mental Hospital. [122]

In the midst of the great output of literature of that year was Albert Moll's *Investigations on Libido Sexualis.*[123] He developed the idea suggested by Dessoir in 1894, that there was an evolution of the sexual instinct, that normally there was a transient undifferentiated stage in young adolescents, and that in some cases a disturbance in development could be the explanation for homosexuality in adults. The word "libido," which had been used by Benedikt, Krafft-Ebing, and others in the sense of sexual desire, was given a new meaning in the sense of the sexual instinct in its phases of evolution. In Vienna, Freud published his paper on the "Psychic Mechanism of Forgetting" and on "Sexuality in the Etiology of Neuroses."

The year 1899 brought about the Boer War. The public had expected that the English would achieve rapid victory, but the English suffered reverses at the beginning and had to send reinforcements. The Boers enjoyed wide sympathy in France and Germany. In France the Dreyfus agitation gradually abated, Dreyfus' sentence was suspended and he was returned from Devil's Island.

The progress of the Nancy School was conspicuous in Holland. The psychotherapeutic clinic of Van Renterghem, situated in a residential quarter of Amsterdam, was solemnly transformed into a Liébeault Institute. It comprised an entry hall, waiting and examination rooms, offices, a library, and twenty-six rooms for patients. In the hall was a plaque inscribed:

Ambrosio Augusto Liébeault
Ex Favereis oriundo (Lotharingia)
Dedicatum

(reminding visitors that Liébeault was born in the village of Favières, in Lorraine). The clinic was decorated with portraits of Liébeault, Bernheim, and Liégeois.

The interest in sexual pathology, which had been very strong since the publication of the first edition of Krafft-Ebing's *Psychopathia sexualis*, was manifested by the foundation of Magnus Hirschfeld's *Jahrbuch*. [124] This publication offered original contributions and a review of current literature on sexual pathology. It also took an active position, advocating a reform of the laws concerning homosexuality. Among the many publications of that year was Féré's book: *Sexual Instinct: Evolution and Dissolution,* in which the author tried to introduce an evolutionary concept in the field of sexual deviations. [125] And on the evidence of the many clinical observations he had made, he emphasized the influence of early sexual experiences on the future sexual development of the individuals.

In that year, Freud published his paper on "Screen Memories," which was commented on favorably in the *Revue Neurologique* and in several psychiatric and psychological journals.

The year 1900 seemed to be one of the bloodiest anyone had yet seen. War raged in South Africa, the English seemed glued there and in spite of local successes seemed unable to achieve any decisive victory. Transvaal's President Kruger traveled in Europe but received only good words and sympathy. In China an insurrection was launched by a secret society, the Boxers. In June, Europeans were besieged in their embassies in Peking and were rescued in August by an international expedition commanded by a

German. There was much talk in Europe of "the yellow peril," and one nightmare was the fear that the Chinese would unite to constitute a powerful army that would submerge and despoil Europe. King Umberto of Italy was assassinated by an anarchist.

However, 1900 seemed to be a productive year in many ways. In Germany, Planck read his first paper on the quanta theory, which was to revolutionize physics. Ellen Key published *The Century of the Child*, in which she proclaimed that the twentieth century would bring the liberation of the child; she advocated revolutionary reforms in education. In art new trends that had grown slowly during the preceding years came to the foreground. "Modern style" triumphed in France, *Jugendstil* in Germany and Austria. In Vienna, Gustav Klimt had been entrusted with the mosaic decoration of the new university building, but the designs raised the indignation of the professors. The news of Nietzsche's death after ten years of dementia reinforced interest in his philosophy throughout Europe. Another German, Edmund Husserl, published a book that attracted little attention outside of a narrow circle of professional philosophers. [126] Who could have guessed that fifty years later it would have become a source of inspiration for a new psychiatric trend, existential analysis?

The new century was expected by many to be the century of psychology. It is perhaps not sheer chance that in 1900 the International Institute of Psychology was founded in Paris with Janet as its animator.[127] In the same year Janet was called to substitute for Ribot in his psychology course at the Collège de France. Janet gave his first series of lectures on "Sleep and Hypnoid States," in which he discussed sleep, dreams, sleep disturbances, and somnambulism.

One of the most talked-about events of 1900 was the great Universal Exhibition in Paris. Even more than in 1889, it was a year of international congresses. The International Congress of Medicine gathered 8,000 participants divided into 23 sections, a very large number of participants for that time. The Neurology section, with Raymond as its chairman, took care to remain on the solid ground of neurology, and did not encroach upon the field of hypnotism.

The Second International Congress of Hypnotism took place from August 12 to 16. [128] The opening address, given by Raymond, illustrates how the ideas on hypnotism had changed at the Salpêtrière since Charcot's death. He said that Charcot had made hypnotism a subject for research with the same methods he applied to neurological diseases, while the Nancy School emphasized the psychological aspects of the same phenomenon. Actually, Raymond continued, both trends had old backgrounds; Pierre Janet had shown that the magnetizers had described the three stages of hypnotism as early as 1840, and the quarrel between the schools was nothing but a revival of the old quarrel between the fluidists and the animists. The one really new fact, Raymond added, was that by now we all believe in psychological determinism, and are striving to discover the laws of the mind. This lecture was followed by a long and detailed survey on the history of hypnotism by Bérillon, beginning with Braid and leading up to his own day.

Oscar Vogt spoke on the value of hypnosis as a tool for psychological investigation. He had worked out a method of having the hypnotized subject concentrate on a certain idea, image, memory, or feeling, which produced increased awareness as if the content and background of the phenomenon under investigation were under a magnifying glass. [129] The participants of the Congress visited the Salpêtrière on August 13, under the guidance of Drs. Cestan, Philippe, and Janet. Journalists who attended probably felt the want of that element of mystery attached to the Salpêtrière in Charcot's time, so they were delighted to spread the news of an extraordinary patient named Madeleine, who bore the stigmata of Christ's passion.

The Fourth International Congress of Psychology took place from August 20 to August 25, with Théodule Ribot as President, Charles Richet as Vice-President, and Pierre Janet as General Secretary. [130] Among the participants were an impressive number of philosophers, psychologists, psychiatrists, and even writers. All possible topics of psychological interest were discussed. The third general session was devoted to the phenomenon of somnambulism. Théodore Flournoy, whose *From India to Planet Mars* had appeared a few months earlier, told of Hélène Smith and her somnambulic utterances; the childishness and ineptitude of what she said showed that these phenomena originate in primitive, infantile layers of the individual's mind. They are a kind of transient emergence of stages of psychological development long left behind. Another feature of somnambulistic performances is the audacity with which the subject tries to impose his drivel as indisputable fact. Here, too, Flournoy saw an infantile characteristic as a reenactment of the candor with which the child lives his fictions and games. All of this should be seen as phenomena of regression.

F. W. H. Myers, in a paper "On the Trance Phenomena of Mrs. Thompson," quoted Pierre Janet, Binet, Breuer, and Freud as authorities on hysteria. Immediately following him, Frederik van Eeden told of his experiments with the same Mrs. Thompson (a clairvoyant medium). While he was in Holland and Mrs. Thompson in England, he called her three times when dreaming, and she was later able to confirm the times and dates. The first two times he had called her Nellie, the third time, by mistake he called her Elsie. Two days later he received a letter from Mrs. Thompson informing him that she had heard him call her Elsie, but that was the name of a spirit of her acquaintance. Van Eeden also said that there is no essential difference between a mediumistic trance and a dream, and that a person could train himself to direct his dreams at will. [131]

Other papers were read by Morton Prince on the multiple personalities of Miss Beauchamp; by Hartenberg on anxiety neurosis, denying Freud's theory of its sexual origin (though in discussion he admitted that it could be so in certain cases); and by Durand (de Gros) on his theory of polypsychism. Following a paper by Jovic, advocating the use of experimental methods in psychology, a young Viennese, Otto Weininger, vivaciously replied that as experimental methods in psychology were being perfected, introspection would reach a degree of refinement impossible to imagine as yet.

There were also papers about clinical cases. Paul Farez, a disciple of Durand (de Gros) distinguished two types of hypnotic treatment, the one where a command given would be sufficient to cure a patient, and the other in which exploration of the unconscious was necessary to find the cause in order to treat it. [132] The cause could be a nightmare or a vivid impression of which the patient had kept no conscious memory. Farez also told the story of a writer who had become the plaything of an actress and complained of gaps in his memory. Under hypnosis he could recall that the actress could hypnotize him and make him do what she wanted and then forget it all. Farez was then able to neutralize the noxious influence of the woman.

Reporting on the Congress the *Figaro* wrote:

> Never have more varied minds disputed more diverse questions. There were there philosophy professors, men of letters, priests, Jesuits, Dominicans, physiologists, magicians, Hindu Brahmins, criminologists, veterinarians, Russian princes, and quite a few women, of whom some had come to discuss spiritism. . . .[133]

Two books that became classics in dynamic psychiatry appeared in 1900: Flournoy's *From India to Planet Mars* and Freud's *Interpretation of Dreams*. (Both actually appeared at the end of 1899, but bore the title date 1900.)

We have already told of Théodore Flournoy's five-year investigation in Geneva of the medium Catherine Muller, who claimed to have the gift of clairvoyance and the ability to reincarnate, in her mediumnistic trances, phases of her previous lives. She had been Queen Simandini in fifteenth-century India, Queen Marie Antoinette at Versailles, and had lived on Mars, whose language she spoke and wrote fluently. [134] Flournoy described these three cycles, calling them romances of subliminal imagination. This book, as entertaining as a novel by Jules Verne or H. G. Wells, is a deep-reaching analysis of some of the subtle processes of the subconscious mind. It brings evidence of subliminal imaging as a creative and continuous activity. Throughout the various subpersonalities of his medium, Flournoy emphasized the fundamental unity of her personality. He also showed the importance of cryptomnesia, the subliminal romances consisting largely of forgotten childhood memories, especially of books. Wish fulfillment was given free reign; dreams of superiority, of being a queen, of giving advice, or information on other worlds, expressed the patient's wishes of grandeur, although mixed with symbolic expressions of humdrum reality. Flournoy traced the regression expressed by each cycle to a specific age. One element that seems underemphasized to the modern reader is the role of rapport or transference, but as pointed out by Claparède, Flournoy was well aware of this phenomenon but treated it discreetly.

Flournoy's book incensed some who believed the medium's utterances were true revelations from other worlds. Others, however, brought sound criticism. Dr. Metzger pointed out the disturbing effect newcomers had exerted during Hélène's séances, hampering the spontaneity of the medium with their clumsy distractions, and influencing her. [135] Comments from Geneva were often less enthusiastic than those from elsewhere. The responsible *Journal de Genève,* in a long review on January 15, gave due credit to the endeavor and psychological acumen of Flournoy. The anonymous critic humorously remarked how strange it was that the very same group of adventurous individuals gathered around Hélène Smith from one incarnation to another were now peaceful bourgeois of Geneva, and that *From India to Planet Mars* really amounted to a novel with a key for the Genevese. The critic even hinted that the medium's smattering of Sanskrit could have originated in a joke played by one of Flournoy's learned friends. He also emphasized the fantastic achievement of the young woman who was able simultaneously to create several characterizations and plots, and read and speak several languages, one of which was of her own creation. He deplored that so much talent was going to waste, and concluded that the medium was, above all, an admirable actress who played her roles with such passion that she bewitched her intimate circle. These allegations were protested against by Flournoy in a letter to the *Journal de Genève*, which appeared in the January 19 issue.

Flournoy's book was widely successful. An English translation appeared in the same year as the French original (Italian and German translations appeared later). According to Claparède it was reviewed in innumerable journals, magazines, and newspapers, and the New York *World* added a colored portrait of Flournoy. [136] It was commented upon in humorous journals such as the London *Punch* of March 14, 1900, and was lampooned by students in end-of-the-year shows. The Casino Theatre, in Geneva, had a play, *En avant, Mars!* ("Forward, Mars!"); Flournoy received letters from all parts of the world. William James wrote: "I think that your volume has probably made the decisive step in converting psychical research into a respectable science." Myers said the book was "a model of fairness throughout" and also considered it as a decisive step forward in the exploration of the subliminal mind, an opinion shared by Morselli, Dessoir, Oesterreich, and others.

The second great book of 1900 was Freud's *Interpretation of Dreams,* with which we have already dealt. [137] Our interest here is only how the book was received upon its publication. Among the many works published each year about dreams, the title *Traumdeutung* attracted attention because so little had been published on the interpreting of dreams since the time of Scherner. Also, the word *Traumdeutung* was reminiscent of *Sterndeutung* (astrology). In spite of this somewhat ambiguous title, Freud's book brought much to the reader, first a historical survey of dream psychology, then an explanation of Freud's own method of dream interpretation, then his theory of the dream, and finally his theory of the mind in general. The book was well written and contained illustrations of the author's own dreams, as well as intriguing details of life in Vienna at the end of the nineteenth century. It gave promise of being the cornerstone for a new science of the mind.

The reception given *The Interpretation of Dreams* has given rise to a tenacious legend. "Seldom has an important book produced no echo whatever," Jones said; and according to Freud, eighteen months after the publication of the book no psychiatric journal had reviewed it. Ilse Bry and Alfred Rifkin have shown that it was, in fact, quite otherwise:

The Interpretation of Dreams was initially reviewed in at least eleven general magazines and subject journals, including seven in the fields of philosophy and theology, psychology, neuropsychiatry, psychic research and criminal anthropology. The reviews are individualized presentations, not just routine notices, and together amount to more than 7,500 words. The interval between publication and review averages' about one year, which was not bad at all. . . . It appears that Freud's books on dreams were widely and promptly reviewed in recognized journals, which included the outstanding ones in their respective fields.

Furthermore, the editors of international annual bibliographies in psychology and philosophy selected Freud's books on dreams for inclusion. In this country the *Psychological Index* listed *The Interpretation of Dreams* within four months of publication. Roughly, by the end of 1901, Freud's publication had been brought to the attention of medical, psychiatric, psychological, and generally educated circles on an international scale.

. . . Some of the reviews are thorough and highly competent, several are written by authors of major research on the subject, all are respectful. Criticism appears after a fair summary of the book's main contents. . . .[138]

To substantiate this statement, Bry and Rifkin gave an excerpt from a review by William Stern, showing how far from "annihilating" it was (to use Jones' word).[139] Stern acknowledges the fact that Freud investigated dreams from a new point of view, and that "many new perspectives are opened," that Freud "had the merit of searching for a new explanation of dreams in the little-known sphere of emotional life," that the book contains "many details of highly stimulative value, fine observations and theoretical outlooks, and above all, an extraordinarily rich material of very accurately recorded dreams." Naecke gave an extremely favorable review of Freud's "excellent book" (*vortreffliches Buch*), in which he says that "the book is psychologically the profoundest that the psychology of dreams has produced so far," and he adds that "the work is cast as a unified whole, and thought through with genius."[140]

Weygandt wrote that "the book offers a well-observed rich material and goes farther in effort toward the analysis of dreams than anyone has hitherto tried." [141] Flournoy gave a most favorable review in which he says that "his book brings us numerous examples (of dream analysis) which are pure masterpieces of sagacious penetration and subtle ingenuity." [142]

In Paris, Henri Bergson quoted it in a lecture on dreams given at the Institut Psychologique on March 26, 1901. [143] Carl Gustav Jung, who was at that time a young resident at the Burghölzli in Zurich, mentioned it in his dissertation in 1902. Emil Raimann wrote in a book on hysteria, "Freud has shown in a quite convincing way that in the dream, the mental life expresses itself, that unconscious wishes and thoughts become the content of dreams in almost unrecognizable disguise." [144] Raimann, however, objected to Freud's sexual theory and suspected that "because Freud's theory is known here in the widest circles," the patients who went to Freud were influenced by it in advance. Raimann emphasized that these objections did not diminish the merit of Freud's teaching. There is no disparaging mention of Freud in the entire book. [145]

The Interpretation of Dreams was also reviewed in a number of newspapers and periodicals destined for a wide public. The book was hardly off the press before it was reviewed in the Viennese journal *Die Zeit* of January 6 and 13, 1900, by no less a personage than its chief editor, Max Burckhardt. [146] It was an extensive and learned, though somewhat glib, review. Actually it was by no means negative; Burckhardt had obviously read the *Traumdeutung* throroughly. He summarized it clearly and accurately, giving many quotations. He thought the author had overemphasized the infantile element, and regretted that he did not explain the dreams of those of the verbal type (those who think in words rather than images), nor the split of personality in dreams. Less than three months after the publication of the *Traumdeutung*, a Berlin magazine, *Die Umschau*, published a review by Dr. C. Oppenheimer, who called it "a highly interesting though strange book." [147] On the same date, a Viennese daily newspaper, the *Fremden-Blatt*, gave an equally positive review of what they called an "extremely ingenious and interesting book," particularly praising Freud's observations on the world of children, which would fill all friends of children with enthusiasm. [148] *The Interpretation of Dreams* was also given a very favorable review in the Viennese socialist newspaper *Arbeiter-Zeitung*[149] and an extensive and enthusiastic one in the *Neues Wiener Tagblatt* [150] by a man who was soon to become one of Freud's first disciples, Wilhelm Stekel. [151]

Psychological Analysis Versus Psychoanalysis: 1901–1914

The entry into the twentieth century was felt by contemporaries as the dawning of a new era. Decadence and the *fin de siècle* atmosphere had become intolerable. The death of Queen Victoria marked the conclusion of outmoded times and the reign of Edward VII was characterized by a combination of "aristocratic grace and modern comfort." This period, the Belle Epoque, seems in retrospect as one of peace, security, and *joie de vivre*, but to contemporaries it was one of "armed peace" with war continually hovering in the near future. This was reflected in works of fiction such as H. G. Wells' *The War in the Air*, and in Colonel Danrit's novels, each of which depicted a terrifying war. There was a general political trend to the left, and many hoped that a triumph of the Socialist parties would secure international peace. An insidious downfall of Europe was manifested in the growth of and defiance shown by non-European powers.

There was a general desire to turn one's back on the nineteenth century and seek new paths. The new sports of motoring and skiing became fashionable. Intellectuals hailed new thinkers: the philosopher Henri Bergson, the economist Vilfredo Pareto, and the political thinker Georges Sorel, who introduced a new antidemocratic ideology. In dynamic psychiatry the same attitude was manifested by the rejection of the first dynamic psychiatry, disinterest in hysteria and hypnosis, and the search for new psychotherapies, such as that of Dubois. Two names, however, seemed to polarize the new dynamic psychiatry: Pierre Janet in Paris, and Sigmund Freud in Vienna.

The Beginning of a New Era: 1901–1905

The year 1901 was marked by an event that was strongly felt by contemporaries, namely, the death of Queen Victoria, the Eternal Queen, and Grandmother of Europe. Her name had been associated with the expansion and world domination of the British Empire, and also with a set of moral and social values, the Victorian Spirit.[152] King Edward VII had been jealously kept away from the Empire's business by his mother, but he had his own political philosophy and had started on a political course of his own. Upon his succession, his first concern was to terminate the Boer War and to establish good relationships with France. Other great events of that year were the imposition of a peace treaty by the European powers on China and the assassination of President McKinley in the United States.

In that year, Joseph Babinski, who had been Charcot's cherished pupil, dealt the death blow to what was left of his master's teaching on hysteria. In a memorable meeting of the Neurological Society in Paris, he read a paper entitled, "Definition of Hysteria," proposing a purely pragmatic definition of hysteria.[153] Hysteria, he said, is the sum total of the symptoms that can be called forth by suggestion and dispelled by countersuggestion (which he called persuasion). Thus certain symptoms such as the alleged hysterical fever, hemorrhages, and so on, were no longer considered as pertaining to hysteria. According to Babinski, there was nothing more to it than a peculiar propensity to respond positively to suggestion. Babinski recommended that the term "hysteria" be replaced with "pithiatism." The majority of French neurologists, who had had their fill of performances by hysterical patients at the Salpêtrière, the Charité, or the Hôtel-Dieu, readily accepted Babinski's ideas. Many did not notice Babinski's admission that certain individuals were predisposed to suggestibility; they merely concluded that hysteria was a nonexistent entity. The number of hysterical patients rapidly and steadily declined; the French tended to attribute the decrease to Babinski's new conceptions, but since the same phenomenon occurred elsewhere in Europe, it is open to question whether social and cultural factors were not at work.

Freud wrote a condensed version of the *Traumdeutung*; this little book, *On Dreams*, appeared early in 1901 as one of a series of medical pamphlets, so that it reached deeper into the medical world than the *Traumdeutung* had.[154] The reviews were even more favorable than those for the *Traumdeutung*. Bry and Rifkin write: "For the essay *On Dreams,* we have found nineteen reviews, all of which appeared in medical and psychiatric journals with a total of some 9,500 words, and an average time interval of eight months."[155] Among these reviews those by Kornfeld,[156] Ziehen,[157] Moebius,[158] Liepmann,[159] Giessler,[160] Kohnstamm,[161] Pick,[162] and Voss[163] should be noted for their objective tenor and the fact that their authors were well-known specialists.

In the same year Freud published the first results of his studies on parapraxes in serial form in a psychiatric journal.[164] These articles were well received. Ziehen, however, contended that what Freud called repression he himself had already described as *Vorstellungshemmung* (inhibition of representation).[165] He concluded that Freud's study "deserved many but critical readers."

Since the publication of Krafft-Ebing's *Psychopathia Sexualis* in 1886, the number of publications on sexual pathology had steadily increased. Sexual pathology now attracted as much attention as Lombroso's theories had during the past two decades. In a treatise on sexual pathology, Rohleder emphasized the frequency of masturbation in the infant, and that "the libido sexualis can manifest itself in the earliest youth, even in the infant age."[166]

The year 1902 was comparatively more peaceful than the preceding ones. The eruption of Mont-Pelée, in Martinique, which swept away the capital of the island was considered by a few contemporaries a sign of God's wrath against the French anticlerical government. The new science of sexual pathology expanded speedily. Among the numerous publications on that field was Albert Moll's warning against corporal punishments, because of the dangers of producing vicarious sexual pleasure in the punisher, the punished, and the unlookers.[167] The ethnologist Heinrich Schurtz proposed the theory that society did not originate in the family (as taken for granted until then) but in men's associations—a theory that was to be taken over by Hans Blüher and others.[168]

In that year Janet was appointed Professor of Experimental psychology at the Collège de France and began lecturing about psychological tension and emotions, while Freud was appointed Extraordinary Professor at the University of Vienna and began to gather his Wednesday evening circle. Current psychiatric literature showed a growing interest in the incipient new dynamic psychiatry. A physician of Warsaw, Theodor Dunin, compared the theories and therapies of hysteria of Janet and Freud, giving his preference to Janet, adding, however, that other treatments could be equally success-ful.[169] In a psychiatric congress at Grenoble, Freud's concepts of anxiety neurosis were the object of lively but objective discussions.[170]

In Zurich, Eugen Bleuler, the new Professor of Psychiatry, after re-organizing the Burghölzli University Mental Hospital, was pursuing his research on dementia praecox and teaching his new concepts of the illness to his interns. A young man, Carl Gustav Jung, who had joined the staff at the end of 1900, published his dissertation *On the Psychopathology of So-Called Occult Phenomena*, whereupon he went to Paris to follow Janet's teaching.[171] This dissertation was very favorably reviewed by Theodore Flournoy, who gave in the same year a follow up of his story of the medium, Hélène Smith.[172] This follow-up contained what almost amounted to a *mea culpa*:

> I deem it not good that a medium be investigated too long by the same investigator, because the latter, in spite of his caution, inevitably ends up by molding the subconscious of his subject, which is so suggestive, and by imprinting more and more persistant distortions that impede any possible expansion of the sphere from which the subject's automatism flows (p. 116).

The year 1903 was marked by tensions throughout the world. In Serbia King Alexander and Queen Draga were assassinated, following a plot organized by a secret society. The new king Peter I opened a new political course. His government was fiercely nationalist, opposed to Austria-Hungary, and supported by Russia. What appeared to be just another palace revolu-tion in a Balkan country actually caused a fearful aggravation of the tensions among European countries. In France the government decreed the expulsion of all religious congregations; the turmoil that followed was such that it was called a war of religion without bloodshed. On the American continent, the United States, which had succeeded in building the Panama Canal where the French had failed, obtained territorial concession of the Canal Zone. At the International Congress on Medicine in Madrid, in April 1903, Pavlov read a report on "Experimental Psychology and Psychopathology of

Animals," which contained his first definitions of conditioned and uncondi-
tioned reflexes.[173]

Among the publications of that year, three had a direct relevance to
dynamic psychiatry. Janet published his two large volumes, *The Obsessions
and Psychasthenia*, a thorough and accurate description of obsessions and
kindred psychasthenic disturbances, with many case histories and an elaboration of his new concepts of psychological force and tension.[174]

The second was Frederic Myers' posthumous work, *Human Personality*.[175] Not only did this book compile an unparalleled collection of source
material on the topics of somnambulism, hypnosis, hysteria, dual personality,
and parapsychological phenomena, but it also contained a complete theory
of the unconscious mind, with its regressive, creative, and mythopoetic
functions.[176]

In the psychological literature of that year, however, nothing could
match the success of Weininger's book, *Sex and Character*.

Weininger purported to create a new metaphysics of sexes: the difference between man and woman is taken as a starting point for the elucidation of numerous
psychological, sociological, moral, and philosophical problems. His basic tenet is
the fundamental bisexuality of the human being. In the first chapters of his book,
Weininger compiles all available anatomical, physiological, and psychological
data on the bisexuality of living beings. He refers to a Danish zoologist, J. J.
Steenstrup, who as early as 1846 proclaimed that sexuality is characteristic not
only of the body as a whole but of every organ and every cell. Weininger considers every man or woman a combination in various proportion of two
"substances," a male one (the *arrhenoplasma*) and a female one (the *thely-
plasma*). Not only does the proportion differ in every cell and organ of each
individual, but it oscillates in the same individual and may change in the course
of his life. The basic law of sexual attraction is that any individual is attracted to
another of complementary proportion (thus a ¾ M. + ¼ F. man would seek
a ¾ F. + ¼ M. woman). Homosexuals are intersexual beings whose love objects
also fulfill this law of complementarity though belonging to the same sex.

According to Weininger, the whole individual is present in every one of his
acts, utterances, feelings, or thoughts, at every moment of his life. This provides
a basis for a science of Characterology. Since bisexuality and the opposition of the
male and the female type are permanent facts, they will be reflected in every
possible sector of psychic life. Weininger sketches a typology of the intermediate
types: the feminine man, the masculine woman (to the latter belong those women
who fight for emancipation; superior women are beings in whom a male element
is predominant). Above all, Weininger describes two opposite ideal types, the
"absolute male" and the "absolute female," not to be confused with the average
man and the average woman. The essential difference between man and woman
is that in woman the sexual sphere extends to the whole personality: "Woman is
nothing but sexuality, man is sexuality plus something else. . . . Woman is *only*
sexual, man is *also* sexual." Man has a few well-localized erogenous zones, in
woman they extend over the whole body. "Woman is continuously, man intermittently sexual. . . . Man has a penis, vagina has the woman. . . . Woman's whole

body is a dependency of her genitals." Man is more objectively conscious of his sexuality, to the difference of woman; he can detach himself from it, either to accept or to reject it.

Another basic difference between the "absolute male" and the "absolute female" lies in their respective level of consciousness. Woman is still on the level of the *henide* (that is, perception and feeling are undifferentiated); in a man perception and feeling are distinct, hence a greater clarity of thought, the ability to express thoughts in words and to attain objectivity. "Man lives consciously, woman unconsciously." The function of the typical male is to bring woman to consciousness. Genius is the ability of higher clarity of thought with a wider consciousness; it thus entails a higher degree of masculinity to which a woman cannot attain. Woman's psychic life and her memory are without continuity; man's memory is continuous. Continuity is the basis of logical thinking, of ethical life, and of personality altogether. Therefore the "abstract female" is alogical, amoral, has no ego, and should be kept out of public affairs.

Weininger distinguishes two opposite ideal types of women: the "absolute prostitute" and the "absolute mother." The mother type exists only for the preservation of the human race; her sole aim is the child, she would become a mother by any man; she is courageous and thrifty. The prostitute type exists only for the sake of sexual intercourse; she is cowardly and lavish. The "prostitute" type perceives and is stimulated by her son's masculinity; and since no woman is entirely of the "mother type," the relationship of mother and infant has always a certain affinity to that of woman and man, as evidenced in the sensuous pleasure of women when feeding at breast. In man, Weininger distinguishes sexuality and eroticism. Love is an illusion created by man's longing. The relation of man and woman is that of subject and object; in Aristotelian terms, woman is the "matter" upon which the male "form" acts. The male and the female principles are unequally distributed, not only among human individuals but among nations: the Chinese, and particularly the Jews, are more "feminine."[177]

The 472 pages of Weininger's book were supplemented with a 133-page appendix, with quotations from Greek, Latin, and German classics, Shakespeare, Dante, ancient and modern philosophers, Fathers of the Church, and contemporary psychiatrists, including Janet, Breuer, Freud, Fliess, Krafft-Ebing and the sexologists, and others. *Sex and Character* was widely reviewed, aroused a storm of controversies, was hailed as a masterpiece, and obtained fabulous success, particularly in German-speaking countries, Italy, Russia, and Denmark. In Sweden it won the enthusiastic admiration of Strindberg. In Vienna it was the talk of the town for months. Its success was enhanced by the fact that the author, who was only twenty-three years old, committed suicide before the year was over.[178]

The concept of the fundamental bisexuality of the human being, together with that of the libido, was the basis of a perfected classification and theory of sexual abnormities expounded by G. Herman in *Libido and Mania*.[179] This little book did not attract much attention at the time but appears to us in retrospect as a forerunner of Freud's *Three Essays*.

Among the literary production of 1903, two other books were destined

to acquire fame later through Freud's commentaries. One was an apologia
by a mentally disturbed magistrate, President Daniel Paul Schreber.[180]
The other was a short novel by Wilhelm Jensen, *Gradiva*.

Norbert Hanold, a young archaeologist, lived only for Greco-Roman antiquity,
and was indifferent to his contemporaries, and especially to women. As a child, he
had been friendly with little Zoe Bertgang, daughter of a zoology professor. He
forgot her, to the point where he did not recognize her, although she lived on the
same street. Once, in Rome, Norbert saw a bas-relief of a young woman lifting her
hemline and walking, her weight on her right foot and the left flexed for the next
step. Hanold fell in love with the relief, and had a cast made of it to hang in his
room. He built a fantasy around the young woman, called her *Gradiva*, the
"walking one" (without noticing that this was a translation of *Bertgang*); and
fancied that she was the daughter of a priest of Pompei who perished in the
catastrophe of A.D. 79. Once he dreamed that he was in Pompei on the day of the
catastrophe, that he saw Gradiva walking under a fall of ashes, then lying down
transformed into stone. This dream inspired a sudden wish to go to Italy, but in
Rome and Naples he was repelled by honeymoon couples from Germany, and
left for Pompei. There, he dreamed that he was under a fall of ashes and saw
Apollo carrying Venus in his arms to a carriage. On the following day, sitting
amidst the ruin at noon, he saw the real Zoe, whom he believed to be Gradiva.
As he had repressed the thought of Zoe and transferred it to the Gradiva of his
fantasy, he now transferred the fantasy onto the real Zoe. The author described
well Norbert's feeling that Zoe was at the same time a stranger and yet familiar.
Zoe gradually understood his delusion and entered into it. On the following day,
he met Zoe's father hunting for lizards, and learned that he was staying at the
Sun Hotel. The following night he dreamed that he saw Gradiva sitting in the
sun catching a lizard, and saying "Keep quiet, the collegue is right—she has
applied the device with success." On the third day, Zoe easily rid him of his
delusion, they became engaged, and decided to honeymoon in Pompei.[181]

To contemporaries, *Gradiva* was just one of these novels in neo-Romantic style that illustrated the current theme of a man's infatuation in a woman's
"phantom."[182] The story of a young man searching for the object of his vision
in real life and finding it in the person of a childhood companion had been
told by Novalis in *The Disciples in Sais*.[183] Norbert's condition would have
been familiar to psychiatrists of the preceding century as an example of
"ecstatic vision": Prichard has described it in 1835 as a transient condition
where a vivid daydream and events of normal life are perfectly blended.[184]
Who could have guessed in 1903 that *Gradiva* was to be rescued from oblivion four years later, thanks to Freud's psychoanalytic commentary? It would
become fashionable for psychoanalysts to have a cast of the Gradiva relief
in their consulting rooms, and those who lived in Paris in 1936 or 1937 may
remember a little art gallery on the rue de Seine under the sign of "Gradiva."
    The year 1904 brought a more severe blow to European prestige than
it had ever known. A great power, Russia, was attacked by a non-European

power, Japan, which had been open to Western civilization for hardly more than half a century. Worse, perhaps, was the fact that no other power protested the treachery of Japan's attack on the Russian fleet without a declaration of war. Having thus gained a strategic advantage from the start, the Japanese steadily beat the Russians. It was insufficient compensation that for the first time a Russian, Pavlov, won the Nobel Prize.

Meanwhile, a universal exhibition was organized in the United States, in St. Louis, Missouri. Following the example of the French exhibitions, it included a Congress of Arts and Sciences. There were numerous sections devoted to the various sciences. In the division of Mental Sciences, Department XV was devoted to psychology and included a section on abnormal psychology, whose secretary was Dr. Adolf Meyer, and the two invited speakers, Pierre Janet and Morton Prince. Pierre Janet went to America for the first time, to read a paper in St. Louis on September 24, 1904, entitled "The Relations of Abnormal Psychology"[185] Following Janet's paper, Morton Prince talked on "Some of the Present Problems of Abnormal Psychology," in the course of which he said that "certain problems in subconscious automatism will always be associated with the names of Breuer and Freud in Germany, Janet and Alfred Binet in France." A list of works of reference on abnormal psychology that had been prepared by Morton Prince included works by Bernheim, Flournoy, Forel, and others, the *Studies in Hysteria* by Breuer and Freud, as well as four books by Janet, three by Binet, and two by Freud.[186]

Janet's fame was by then well established in the United States, and after the Congress he gave lectures in Boston and elsewhere. Among Janet's publications of that year the story of Irène was noteworthy in that hysterical symptoms were traced and explained by traumatic events, exactly as in Janet's earlier case histories of Marie and Justine, but with this difference: Janet now admitted that the memory of the trauma had been somewhat altered (in contradistinction to Freud, who maintained that unconscious memories remained unchanged).

Two French neuropsychiatrists, Camus and Pagniez, outlined a history of psychotherapy, with emphasis on the methods of isolation, suggestion, persuasion, and training.[187] A new star, meanwhile, had appeared in the firmament of psychotherapy. A Swiss physician, Paul Dubois, taught that neurotic disturbances and many physical ailments were the products of imagination and could be cured by the will through self-education.[188] In 1904, Dubois gave lectures at the University of Bern on the psychotherapeutic methods he employed in his practice and sanitarium. According to all accounts, Dubois was a very successful therapist; patients came to him from all over the world, and Professor Déjerine, of the Salpêtrière learned his method from him. The reasons for Dubois' therapeutic success are not apparent from his writings and seemed mysterious to his contemporaries.

In Vienna, Sigmund Freud's *Psychopathology of Daily Life*, now published in book form, was favorably reviewed.[189] When Löwenfeld published a volume on obsessions, he asked Freud to contribute with a survey of his psychoanalytic method.[190]

In Germany, Hellpach emphasized the role of the social class in the etiology of hysteria, but in regard to the psychogenesis he adopted Freud's theories.[191] Emil Raimann (who was later to become a bitter adversary of Freud) reviewed the various theories of hysteria, giving an objective account of the "Breuer-Freud theory," although he was critical of its therapeutic implications.[192]

The year 1905 brought the termination of the Russo-Japanese war. The Russians had suffered defeat after defeat. The Baltic fleet, which reached the Pacific Ocean after navigating halfway around the world, was sunk in a few hours by the Japanese. A Russian army besieged in Port Arthur was compelled to capitulate. President Theodore Roosevelt offered himself as mediator at the peace treaty that was signed in Portsmouth, New Hampshire. Following that national humiliation, a revolution broke out in Russia, but was crushed. The Czar then granted a few reforms and the creation of a representative body, the Duma. Meanwhile the Germans adopted a more aggressive attitude in political affairs and a conflict arose with France over Morocco.

In that year Albert Einstein issued his first publication on the theory of relativity. In Geneva, Claparède published his *Psychology of the Child,* which was considered by many to be a landmark in the history of child psychology and education.[193] In Paris, Alfred Binet, with Théodore Simon, published his method for the measurement of the intelligence of the child.[194] The two authors probably did not foresee to what an extent and with what speed their method would be adopted and applied. Forel's book on the sexual question had an immediate success, was translated into many languages, and was to appear in many revised editions.[195]

The year 1905 was a fruitful one for Sigmund Freud, who published three of his main contributions: The *Three Essays on the Sexual Theory, Jokes and the Unconscious,* and the case history of the patient Dora. The *Three Essays* are often said to have been a "revolutionary novelty" that "aroused a storm of indignation and abuse." These two contentions are, to say the least, exaggerated. During the previous three decades, and particularly since the publication of Krafft-Ebing's *Psychopathia Sexualis,* there had been a flood of literature on sexual psychology and pathology, and there is hardly anything in the *Three Essays* that had not been anticipated in one way or another. An objective survey of contemporary literature, furthermore, indisputably shows that Freud's ideas met with much sympathetic interest. Bry and Rifkin[196] have given excerpts on the favorable reviews written by Eulenburg,[197] Näcke,[198] Rosa Mayreder,[199] Adolf Meyer,[200] and, particularly, by Magnus Hirschfeld.[201] Other examples could be added. In Karl Kraus' journal, *Die Fackel,* Otto Soyka contrasted Freud's

Three Essays with Forel's *Sexual Question.* Soyka wrote sarcastic comments on the latter, but bestowed the highest praise on the content, novelty, and style of Freud's book and equated it with Schopenhauer's *Metaphysics of Love.*[202]

The Flourishing of Psychoanalysis: 1906–1910

Characteristic of this period was the contrast between the slow development of Janet's work in its academic framework and the rapid growth of Freud's psychoanalysis, which had acquired the quality of a movement.

The year 1906 was, again, full of tensions and rumors of war. Conflicts over Morocco and the distribution of colonies again brought the European powers to the brink of war, but the peace was maintained thanks to the Conference of Algeciras, which retained Morocco's sovereignty although under French and Spanish administrative control. The Germans felt they were cheated by these arrangements. San Francisco was destroyed by an earthquake and subsequent fire.[203]

In Geneva Claparède organized a seminar of psychology applied to education, but was compelled to close it as a consequence of an intrigue. A man of wide interests, he had also begun experiments with his students on the psychology of testimony, while Binet, in Paris, conducted research on the testimony of children.

In Paris, Janet faced the growing opposition of Babinski and Déjerine. Babinski, as we have seen, was the leader of a trend that could be called antipsychological. Déjerine was in favor of psychotherapy, but the method he introduced to the Salpêtrière was inspired by Dubois. Janet's reputation was very great in the United States; he was invited to the opening ceremonies for the new buildings of the Harvard Medical School and gave a series of lectures at Harvard from October 15 to the end of November.

Under the guidance of Eugen Bleuler the Burghölzli University Mental Hospital in Zurich had become a very progressive and active center and Bleuler himself published a noted study on paranoia.[204] He had met Freud two years earlier and adopted several of his ideas. He acknowledged that Freud's principles could help in the understanding of the meaning of the delusions of certain psychotic patients.[205] Bleuler had entrusted Carl Gustav Jung with an investigation of "dementia praecox" by means of the word association test. As we have seen this research soon yielded unexpected findings.[206] Jung found that the word association test could be put to use as a detector of complexes. It was the first time that a psychological test was applied for the investigation of the subconscious mind.

As Freud's ideas spread, more criticism was expressed. Aschaffenburg wrote that as long as Freud stood alone with his assertions concerning the role of sexuality in neuroses, one could be content to check his interesting ideas in individual cases; but now that noted authors such as Löwenfeld, Hellpach, Bleuler, and Jung were openly siding with Freud, it was necessary to take a public position. Aschaffenburg did not doubt that there was an element of truth in Freud's assertions about the roles of reminiscences and sexuality in hysteria, but he had reservations about the way Freud explored the minds of his patients, and the enduring quality of his cures. Freud had given no precise indications as to the number of his cases and the proportion of successful treatments. Any psychiatrist, Aschaffenburg said, with any method, devoting as much time as Freud did to a patient, would be successful. Jung soon replied to this criticism in the same journal, saying he had used Freud's method and that he had found confirmation for its use in all respects. [207]

In the United States a Swiss-born psychiatrist, Adolf Meyer, began to teach a new concept of dementia praecox, even more revolutionary than that of Bleuler. [208] Every individual, Meyer said, is capable of reacting to a great variety of situations by a limited number of reaction types. Some of these are wholesome and lead to a satisfying adjustment, others are temporary, substitutive reactions. Still others are harmful and dangerous (rattle fumbling, tantrums, hysterical fits, false lingering attitudes, and the like). In patients who tend to go to confirmed dementia praecox, certain types of inadequate reactions occur with such frequency that this deterioration of habits should be considered the main pathological process, and this would provide a new therapeutic approach.

A novel, *Imago* by the Swiss poet (and future Nobel Prize winner) Carl Spitteler, appeared in 1906 and had an unexpected success among psychoanalysts. [209]

A thirty-four-year-old poet, Viktor, comes back for a short visit to the little town of his birth and youth. Years ago, he had casually met a young woman, Theuda Neukomm; no word of love was exchanged, Theuda never knew of his feelings for her, but Viktor received from this short encounter a "parusia," that is, a kind of spiritual vision or revelation. He made Theuda into an ideal picture and source of inspiration under the name of *Imago*. Now, he learned that Theuda married a certain Director Wyss and had a child. He decided to inflict a symbolic punishment to the "unfaithful" one whom he calls *Pseuda*, in order to reestablish the original picture of *Imago*. Soon after his arrival, Viktor is invited to the meetings of the *Idealia*, a local entertainment and benevolence society. Though he makes blunder after blunder he is invited in the family circle of Director Wyss. The latter asks him to write a poem for the annual feast of *Idealia*. A kind of acted fairy tale is played by disguised members of the group. When the man who was to play the part of the bear is called for an urgent matter Viktor is asked to replace him and he grumbles to the satisfaction of the audience. The highlight comes when Frau Wyss sings a poem to a big "Chrysalis," the veils fall and the "butterfly" gets out: a young orphan girl, the *Idealkind* (ideal child), protected by the *Idealia*, and who now in turn recites a poem to her benefactors. From that moment on, Viktor realizes that he is desperately in love with Theuda, but he commits new blunders. Nevertheless, he is invited by the Wysses to the birthday of their little child. Theuda, in a white gown as a fairy queen, with two wings and a crown on the head, recites a poem; the enraptured Viktor sees her as a goddess. A few days later he throws himself on his knees before her and confesses his love. In order to help him out of this situation, she allows him to come every day and talk to her. Their talks gradually become more impersonal, until she once asks him when he will be leaving town. On a following visit, Theuda is not at home, Viktor is received by her husband kindly, but with unmistakable intimations. On the same evening, Viktor's landlady, Frau Steinbach, a young widow, asks him angrily when he will cease to make a fool of himself. Viktor learns that every word he said to Theuda was repeated by her not only to her husband but to Frau Steinbach. Viktor feels as if he were "drowning in shame as a mouse in a chamber pot." On the next day he leaves the town, without having ever noticed that Frau Steinbach was in love with him from the beginning. But now he has disentangled the true *Imago* from the real Theuda and the spurious *Pseuda*. The purified *Imago* will be to him a glowing source of inspiration for the rest of his life.

Both the plot and the style of that novel appear curiously anachronistic today, but Spitteler's *Imago* must be understood in the light of the thinking at the time. We have seen that the notion of an imaginary picture projected onto a real person was a common theme in Romantic philosophy and fiction and that it had again become a current topic for discussion at the end of the nineteenth century.[210] Much was written about the *femmes inspiratrices* and the destructive effects of confusing the real person with the phantom. Jensen's novel, *Gradiva*, in 1903, had renewed the theme, in that the woman who was the object of the projection helped the hero of the story out of illusion through a kind of psychotherapy. This is also what Spitteler related in his novel with greater psychological acumen. We find here one of the links between the Romantic tradition and the new dynamic psychiatry. Spitteler's novel was greatly admired by psychoanalysts; they adopted the term *imago* to designate the picture an individual unconsciously builds of his father or mother independently of what either is really like. This notion later developed into the Jungian concept of *anima*. The title *Imago* was also to be given to a psychoanalytic journal, a collection of psychoanalytic books, and finally to the house that published the complete works of Freud.

In 1907 French occupation troops landed in Morocco and President Theodore Roosevelt sent the Great White Fleet around the world to show the American power. There were agricultural crises and riots in the south of France, new art shools were much discussed, and audacious young artists such as Picasso came into the limelight.

In Bern Dubois was immensely successful with his theories of the influence of the mind over the body; his books were constantly being reedited and translated. Zurich, in turn, emerged as a great center of psychotherapy. In February 1907, Jung went to Vienna to visit Freud, accompanied by a young colleague, Ludwig Binswanger. Freud, who is spite of the growth of his group, was unsatisfied with the reception given to his ideas in Vienna and was pleased to learn that they had been accepted in a university setting. Freud was much taken with Jung's personality and saw him as a potential successor. Jung thought he had now found the master for whom he had long been searching and was eager to propagate the Freudian concepts at the Burghölzli. From that day on, it seemed that psychoanalysis had two centers, Vienna and Zurich, and the entire staff of the Burghölzli was seized with an impassionate interest in Freud's ideas. A young physician, Dr. A. A. Brill, who came to work at the Burghölzli at that time later recalled his impressions of those days:

> In 1907 everybody at the Burghölzli was actively engaged in mastering Freud's psychoanalysis. Professor Eugen Bleuler, the Director who was the first orthodox psychiatrist to recognize the value of Freud's contribution, urged his assistants to master these new theories and to utilize Freud's techniques in their clinical work. Headed by Jung, all assistants in the Clinic worked with the Association experiments; for hours daily they examined test persons in order to find out, experimentally, whether Freud's views were correct. . . . It is quite impossible to describe today how I felt when I was accepted in the ranks of these ardent and enthusiastic workers. I am sure that no such group of psychiatric workers ever existed before or since then. Not only were the Freudian principles applied to the patients, but psychoanalysis seemed to obsess everybody at the clinic.[211]

In Vienna Freud was gathering more disciples each year and receiving foreign visitors. His pupils published original contributions, such as Alfred Adler's *Study of Organ Inferiority*.[212] A twenty-year-old youngster, Otto Rank, impressed the psychoanalytic group with his monograph, *The Artist*.[213]

The more psychoanalysis took the character of a movement, the more polemics arose around it. As an example, we shall take the First International Congress of Psychiatry and Neurology, which took place in Amsterdam from September 2 to 7, 1907, and presented the participants with an opportunity to air the rival trends in dynamic psychiatry.[214] One of the great discussions, on September 4, was devoted to modern theories of the genesis of hysteria, and the main report was entrusted to Janet. Janet restated his theory of subconscious fixed ideas and the narrowing of the field of consciousness resulting from mental dissociation, and concluded that hysteria belonged to a wider group of mental depressions. Following Janet, Aschaffenburg presented a criticism of Freud's theory of hysteria. Freud's theory, he said, did not explain why certain individuals became hysterical and others not, after suffering similar trauma; predisposition must play a role. Freud and Jung, he added, lay so much emphasis on sexuality that they promoted the appearance of sexual representations in patients.

The third speaker was Carl Gustav Jung, who began with a historical survey, and declared that "the theoretical presuppositions for the thinking work of the Freudian investigation reside, above all, in the findings of Janet's experiments." Jung gave a lengthy outline of the psychoanalytic technique, and stated that his own experience confirmed every one of Freud's points. According to Jones, who was present at the meeting, Jung "made the mistake of not timing his paper and also of refusing to obey the chairman's repeated signals to finish. Ultimately he was compelled to, whereupon, with a flushed, angry face, he strode out of the room."[215]

On the next day, September 5, there was a lively discussion on the nature of hysteria, and various views were aired.[216] Dupré, Auguste Marie, and Sollier defended their respective theories. Joire contended that hysteria resulted from modifications in the nervous potential and that he had invented an apparatus, the "sthenometer," that could demonstrate these modifications. Bezzola said he accepted the old Breuer-Freud theory, but not Freud's more recent psychoanalytic theory. Otto Gross and Ludwig Frank defended Freud's theory of hysteria whereupon Konrad Alt and Heilbronner attacked it. Alt declared, "If Freud's conceptions on the genesis of hysteria prevail, the poor hysterics would be despised outcasts as before. This would mean a great step backward, to the greatest detriment of the unfortunate patients." Janet declared, "The first work of Messrs. Breuer and Freud on hysteria in 1895 is, in my opinion, an interesting contribution to the work of French physicians who had, for fifteen years, analyzed the mental state of hysterics by means of hypnosis or automatic writing." Breuer and Freud had found cases similar to those of the French authors, Janet added, but Freud had unduly generalized from them. We all know, he concluded, that in hysteria we sometimes find sexual fixed ideas, but one should not ground a general theory for hysteria on these cases.

Dubois told of his method of treating phobias. Emotions, he said, always follow ideas, so the treatment should go to the root, namely, the erroneous idea the patient has allowed to creep into his mind. Van Renterghem gave a classification of psychotherapeutic methods in three groups: those directed to the affectivity of the patient (for example, to dissipate anxiety or to encourage); those addressed to his intelligence (explanations as to the causes of the illness, training, and reeducation); and those aimed at the imagination (varieties of suggestive treatment).

It was interesting to see how great the prestige of Janet was at this congress. He had been charged with the main report on hysteria; Jung credited him the basic ideas from which psychoanalysis originated, and a young English physician, Ernest Jones, in a paper on allochiria, referred to "Professor Janet's remarkable essay, which has not received the attention it deserves." Another salient feature at this congress was the marked animation of the discussions as soon as they touched on psychoanalysis. In a report about the congress, Conrad Alt stated that the Freudian theories found little support among the numerous German neurologists and psychiatrists who were there.[217] It was said that Janet called the Freudian hypothesis on hysteria a joke (*une plaisanterie*).[218]

The discussions on psychoanalysis at the Amsterdam Congress were a part of a wider controversy, the meaning of which has often been obscured by legend. One paper by Friedländer was quoted by Jones as having been "full of gross misunderstandings."[219] Actually Friedländer gave due credit to Freud's method and said, "I consider Breuer-Freud's *Studies* as one of the most valuable works on hysteria."[220] Friedländer, though, did not accept Jung's argument that only those who had used the psychoanalytic method had any right to question Freud; one way to disprove Freud was to cure hysteria by nonanalytic methods. Friedländer told of seven severely hysterical patients he had treated by a nonanalytic method and who had remained cured for as long as two decades. The same could be said about Weygandt's alleged fierce attacks on psychoanalysis.[221] Weygandt objected to the manner in which Freud's disciples compared their master to Galileo and refused to listen to any opinion that did not correspond to Freud's theories. Weygandt also objected to their argument that "only those who had used the psychoanalytic method have the right to discuss "because faulty methods give wrong findings, and repeating the faulty method will necessarily produce the same error over and over again." Weygandt also deemed certain psychoanalytic terms unscientific, for instance, "wish fulfillment." In a book review of Jung's *The Psychology of Dementia Praecox*, Isserlin wondered whether there was a causal connection between the test word and the answer, and whether the answer really revealed dissociated complexes.[222] This methodological criticism was termed by Jones "violent polemics."

In 1908 the Turkish Empire, "the sick man of Europe," showed that it was not yet dead. An event occurred that some considered the final death throe, others the first sign of recovery. A group of revolutionaries, the Young Turks, tired of the bloody despotism of Sultan Abdul Hamid II, carried off a *coup d'état,* whereupon the Sultan offered them a share in the government. The oppressed minorities of the Turkish Empire began to gather hope. The Bulgarians proclaimed their independence, and national agitation arose among the Armenians, who dreamed of emancipating themselves as the Greeks, Serbians, and Bulgarians had done. The Austrian-Hungarian government seized the opportunity to proclaim the annexation of the provinces of Bosnia and Herzegovina, which for three decades had nominally been under the Sultan's sovereignty, although in practice they had been administered by Austria-Hungary. This annexation increased political tension between Austria-Hungary on the one side and Serbia and Russia on the other. Tensions between Germany and France had not diminished. The rapprochement between France and England, inaugurated by King Edward VII, was taking shape, so that Germany felt itself more and more the victim of an encirclement.

People had the feeling of living under a general climate of violence and destructiveness. Anarchists continued their activity and King Carlos of

Portugal was assassinated. New trends appeared among the European intellectuals in the forms of antidemocratism, antiintellectualism, and futurism. The economist Georges Sorel published his *Reflections on Violence*, a negation of the liberalist faith in reason and progress.[223] The public was shocked by exhibitions of cubistic paintings. Many persons came to think of terrifying wars as the inescapable outcome of the international political situation. Karl Kraus predicted that the advent of aviation would unleash the collapse of the world.[224]

There had never before been more talk of psychotherapy, both in regard to mental hospitals and private practice. Two Americans, E. Ryan,[225] and R. C. Clarke,[226] who had visited German and Swiss institutions, marveled at the therapeutic achievements in the mental hospitals they visited in Berlin, Munich, Tübingen, and Zurich. Oberndorf, who studied in Germany in the same year, tells of a sanitarium near Berlin, Haus Schonow, where sports, gardening, and art therapy were in full operation.[227] Patients had pets (including a donkey) at their disposal. In Paris, Pierre Janet gave a survey of all methods of psychotherapy at the Collège de France, beginning with miraculous religious healings, and enlarging on hypnosis, suggestion, reeducation, and training.

Freud was now a psychotherapist of world renown with a large practice, and new disciples continued to come to him, such as Ferenczi and Brill. An informal meeting of persons interested in psychoanalysis was held in Salzburg on April 26, with forty-two participants, the majority being Austrians. Among the six papers was one by Freud, presenting excerpts from a case history of a celebrated patient, "the man with the rats." In later years this meeting came to be known as the First International Congress of Psychoanalysis.

Some of Freud's critics expressed benevolent skepticism and puzzlement. Such was Gruhle's review of Freud's paper on "Cultural Sexual Morals and Modern Nervousness."[228] After a detailed and objective summary of the paper, Gruhle added that it was up to everyone to draw his own conclusions: "Perhaps it is pleasant at times to wander along untrodden, fantastic paths that lead you far away into the realm of strange day-dreams." The more decided opposition against psychoanalysis came from persons who had previously received it with enthusiasm. Karl Kraus's celebrated journal, *Die Fackel*, which waged a vehement fight against conventional sexual morality and glorified the Marquis de Sade and Weininger, had lauded Freud's *Three Essays*. Now Karl Kraus ridiculed a psychoanalyst who claimed to detect masturbation fantasies in Goethe's poem, *The Apprentice Sorcerer*.[229] Kraus denied the healing power of psychoanalysis and compared psychoanalysts to meteorologists who would pretend not just to predict the weather, but to control it.

In psychiatric circles, polemics continued. On November 9, 1908, Abraham read a paper at the Psychiatric Association of Berlin on the

neurotic significance of marriage between close relatives.[230] In the traditional account it was an almost riotous meeting that led to "furious outbursts"
from Oppenheim against "such monstrous ideas," from Ziehen against
"such frivolous statements" and "nonsense," and from Braatz who cried out
that "German ideals were at stake, and something drastic should be
done to protect them."[231] According to the official record, however, the
meeting was far less stormy. Oppenheim, though rejecting the Oedipus
complex, said he had seen cases similar to Abraham's and agreed with
his interpretations. Ziehen actually said that Freud's concepts were
"nonsense" (*Unsinn*), but found Abraham's observations interesting and
generally true. Rothmann believed consanguineous marriages were common
among Jews because they had lived in isolated communities. In a concluding
word Abraham stated that he agreed with Oppenheim, not in regard to the
interpretation but as to the facts themselves.

The year 1909 brought further aggravation of tensions throughout Europe.
In Turkey, conservative elements rebelled against the Young Turks, whose
leaders were assassinated on March 31, but an army detachment commanded by Young Turks was able to seize power and depose Abdul
Hamid II, replacing him with his brother Mohammed V. The new Turkish
government decided to reorganize and modernize Turkey. The army was
placed under German military advisors. A fiercely nationalistic movement arose, the consequence of which was the massacre of Armenians in
Cilicia and Constantinople. The new government strove to revitalize Turkish
literature and culture. Throughout the world the public was fascinated by
the conquest of the North Pole by Perry, by Shackleton's exploration of the
South Polar regions, and by the first airplane flight across the English Channel
by Blériot.

The Sixth International Congress of Psychology took place in Geneva
from August 2 to 7 under the chairmanship of Claparède.[232] The main
theme of the congress was *The Subconscious,* and the main report was given
by the man who had coined the term, Pierre Janet. Janet's concern was to
distinguish the subconscious, which was a clinical concept, from the unconscious, a philosophical concept. The former term had been devised to
summarize the singular features presented by certain personality disturbances
in one particular neurosis, hysteria. There were no psychoanalysts present
to offer a rebuttal, but in subsequent publications they misinterpreted Janet
as having rejected his previous views and denied the existence of the unconscious.

In view of the ever-increasing interest in psychotherapy, attempts were
made to assess and compare the value of the existing methods. In America,
a collective work, edited by W. B. Parker, contained contributions on the
philosophy and history of psychotherapy, and a survey of various methods:
religious therapy of the Emmanuel movement, Dubois' moral cure, De-
jerine's isolation method, work therapy, analysis and modification of the

environment, and Cabot's "creative assertion" procedure.[233] The chapter on psychoanalysis was contributed by Brill.[234] In a concluding chapter, R. C. Cabot criticized the current fashion to consider Freud's work as the most scientific part of psychotherapy; in his opinion only Janet's work deserved this respect, though every method could be useful.[235]

Meanwhile the psychoanalytic movement was making great forward strides. Freud and Jung, among other scientists, received an invitation to participate in the ceremonies for the twentieth anniversary of the foundation of Clark University in Worcester, Massachusetts. A lively narrative of Freud's and Jung's visit to America has been written by Jones.[236] Accounts of the sessions are found in the Proceedings, and interesting sidelights were described in the New York and Boston newspapers.[237]

In the first days of September 1909, the *New York Times* announced that Cook had claimed to have reached the North Pole, that the Crown Prince of Abyssinia had offered a white elephant to President Roosevelt, that the first national aviation meeting on record had been held in Rheims, France, and that the steamer *George Washington* had arrived from Bremen on August 30. Curiously enough, the list of noted passengers did not include Freud and Jung; the psychologist William Stern, however, was mentioned.

The *Boston Evening Transcript* offered detailed accounts of the celebrations and lectures. On Monday, September 6, William Stern spoke on the psychology of witnesses, a new branch of applied psychology in which he had pioneered, and on the following day he spoke on the subject of school problems. Among other eminent scholars who talked on Tuesday, September 7, were Franz Boas and Sigmund Freud. The *Boston Evening Transcript* reported on September 8:

> Students of Dr. Freud's book on Psychic Analysis have doubtless fancied him as a cold and cheerless person, but that prepossession vanishes when one confronts the man, bent and grey, but wearing the kindly face that age could never stiffen . . . and hears his own stories of his patients. Dr. Freud is modest withal, and gives Dr. Breuer, his colleague, more credit than, perhaps, is due to a man who was willing to let a discovery sleep for ten years or so. The characteristic appeared once more when Dr. Freud—speaking in German, but, like Dr. Stern, with studied clearness—spoke of a case of his own. Dr. Franz Boas . . . who had generously yielded his place on the morning program, was enthusiastic about the sacrifice, and though Dr. Boas's friends consoled themselves that he was worth waiting for, they were glad of an early introduction to the Viennese, who seemed fairly entitled to the honour of an epoch-making discovery.

There were also learned lectures on biology, mathematics, and the Italian physician Volterra reported in French on the theories of Maxwell and Lorentz.

On Thursday, September 9, a wide range of scientific topics was discussed in the various sections. Titchener spoke on experimental psychology,

C. G. Jung spoke on the word association test, and Leo Bürgerstein of Vienna ("who has already become a favorite with Clark audiences"), on coeducation. Adolf Meyer gave a "striking essay" on the dynamic factors in dementia praecox, and Freud's lectures found enthusiastic listeners.

On Friday, September 10, the miscellany of lectures on scholarly topics continued. Freud emphasized that his theory was a "dynamic" one, in contrast with the "hereditary" theory of the Janet School. Jung kept his audience spellbound by telling how he used his word association test successfully in detecting crimes and in revealing hidden causes of illness. The scholarly atmosphere was disrupted in the afternoon when, at a conference on education, the anarchist Emma Goldman, accompanied by Ben Reitman, "the King of the Hoboes," broke in on the discussion.

On Saturday, September 11, the *Boston Evening Transcript* published a long interview with Sigmund Freud by Adelbert Albrecht.[238] According to the journalist, Freud predicted that the then much-discussed Emmanuel movement in the United States would die. As pioneers of psychotherapy, Freud mentioned Liébeault, Bernheim, and Moebius. He termed hypnosis "a failure and a method of doubtful ethical value." In regard to the psychoanalytic cure, Freud said that "I have been able to apply my method only to cases which were severe and given up as hopeless by other physicians. It is best suited to severe cases."

During their stay at Clark University, Freud and Jung were personal guests of its president, Stanley Hall. Freud declared, in his opening address, that this invitation to America was the first official recognition of his efforts, a rather surprising assertion in view of his established recognition by Bleuler and the Burghölzli staff.

At this time Jung had just resigned from his position as associated director at the Burghölzli. He now devoted himself to his private practice, to the direction of the newly founded International Psychoanalytic Association, and to the editorship of the *Jahrbuch*. It would seem that he had fully identified himself with the fate of the psychoanalytic movement.

Psychoanalytic literature was increasing from year to year. Freud published many papers, among which were two of his most famous case histories, the story of Little Hans, and that of the man with the rats. Freud's disciples were prolific writers, especially Stekel, Rank, and Abraham; and there were many others who are less well remembered today. Moreover, there was an abundance of literature about psychoanalysis, either in the form of impartial surveys, or as controversies in favor or against it.

Interesting in that regard is a paper read by Friedländer at the International Congress of Medicine in Budapest, because it shows what exactly the objections against psychoanalysis were:

First, instead of the quiet demonstrations usual with scientists in their discussions, psychoanalysts make dogmatic affirmations punctuated by emotional outbursts; psychoanalysts are unique in equating Freud with such men as Kepler, Newton, and Semmelweis, and for the vigor of their attacks on their adversaries. Second, instead of proving their assertions in a scientific manner, psychoanalysts content themselves with unverifiable statements. They say: "We know from psychoanalytic experience that . . ." and lay the burden of proof on others. Third, psychoanalysts do not accept any criticism nor even the expressing of the most justified of doubts, terming these "neurotic resistance." Friedländer quoted from Sadger: "The prudery of physicians in their discussions of sexual matters is due less to principle than to psychological background. . . . Rather than accept themselves as hysterics, they prefer to be neurasthenics. Even if they are neither, they might have to admit having a hysterical wife, mother, or sister. It goes against the grain to concede such things about one's close relatives or oneself, so they prefer to declare the whole theory invalid and condemn it à priori."[239] Friedländer agreed with Aschaffenburg that such argumentation was unacceptable among scientists. Fourth, psychoanalysts ignore what has been done before them, or by others, thereby claiming to be innovators. It is as if, before Freud, no hysterical patient was ever cured, and no psychotherapy ever practiced. Fifth, sexual theories of psychoanalysis, are presented as scientific fact, though unproven, as when Wulffen says: "All ethical powers in the interior of man, his sense of shame, his morality, his worship of God, his esthetics, his social feelings, originate from repressed sexuality." Wulffen reminds one of Weininger when he said: "Woman is a born sexual criminal; her strong sexuality when successfully repressed easily leads her to illness and hysteria, and when it is insufficiently repressed, to criminality; often it will lead her to both." Sixth, Friedländer objected to the practice of psychoanalysts of addressing themselves directly to a wide lay public, as if their theories had already been scientifically proven; by so doing, they make those who do not accept the theories appear ignorant and backward.[240]

Friedländer's arguments were supplemented with others by contemporary psychiatrists. One common complaint was the lack of statistics in psychoanalysis. Another was that psychoanalytic ideas were "ingenious" (*geistreich*) but not properly "scientific." A third was that far from being novel, psychoanalytic ideas were often a return to older, obsolete concepts (this is what Rieger meant when he talked of old wives' psychiatry, that is, psychiatry as it was before the introduction of modern nosology; Freud's sexual theory of hysteria was seen as a return to an already rejected theory). Finally, there was the argument of the *genius loci*. Aschaffenburg, Löwenfeld, and Friedländer explained the success of Freud's sexual theories by the fact that they fell on fertile ground in Vienna. Krafft-Ebing's *Psychopathia Sexualis* in 1886 had had an extraordinary success in Vienna with the lay public, and specific interest in sexual matters had increased since then, as shown by the fabulous success of Weininger's book, not to mention Schnitzler's and the works of other writers. Freud's patients were thus receptive to his specific type of questions. This argument of the "genius loci," later to be quoted by Ladame, and from him by Janet, has been misunderstood as referring to the general immorality of the Viennese milieu.

The First Prewar Period: 1910–1914

Until 1910 Europe had lived under the system of armed peace, but in spite of increasing political tensions it was hoped that the peace could be maintained. Now, it became evident that a general conflagration was inevitable. The Balkan Wars were seen by many as a prelude to the war between the great European powers. France, England, and Germany, were the prey of a nationalistic mass neurosis, and the desperate efforts of a handful of pacifists were quite inadequate to counteract it.[241] The expectation of war was reflected in the literature of the time and in the general outlook of the people's mentality.

Another ominous sign was the appearance of nihilistic trends such as the Futurist movement. An Italian poet, Filippo Tommaso Marinetti, preached the overthrowing of morality and traditional values, the destruction of academies, libraries and museums; he extolled the beauty of speed, of modern machines, danger, and war.[242] Marinetti and his followers sought to revolutionize painting, sculpture, music, and literature; they organized theatrical shows devised to shock and outrage the public that ended in brawls. They promoted an aggressive Italian nationalism; later they were to wage a campaign in favor of the intervention of Italy in World War I and the cause of Fascism. Marinetti found imitators throughout Europe, particularly in Russia.

This general tension, it would seem, was reflected in the history of dynamic psychiatry as well. It was a period of polemics and internal crises for the psychoanalytic movement.

The great event of 1910 was the death of King Edward VII, who was succeeded by George V. During the ten years of his reign, Edward had brought about a rapprochement with France, but the Germans accused him of being the author of the political encirclement of their country, so the situation was considerably more explosive when he died than at the time of his accession to the throne. In the same year a great apostle of peace, the eighty-two-year-old patriarch of European letters, Count Leo Tolstoy, died. His doctrine of nonviolence was to be applied later by his foremost disciple, Gandhi.

During the first decade of the twentieth century there had been many changes in dynamic psychiatry. When the jubilee of Bernheim was celebrated, he seemed to be a figure of the past and the address he gave was filled with bitterness.[243] All he had written during the previous twenty-eight years was now forgotten, he said. A Swiss, Dubois, was now considered the founder of psychotherapy and had "annexed" it (this was a simile to Germany's "annexation" of Alsace-Lorraine from France). Apparently, Bernheim did not realize what was going on in Vienna and Zurich.

Psychoanalysts were increasingly active, notably in the field of the interpretation of myths, literature, and anthropology. Freud published his celebrated essay on Leonardo da Vinci.[244] Jones published his interpretation of Hamlet.[245] The folklorist Friedrich Krauss whose periodical *Anthropophyteia* was devoted to the collecting of obscene jokes from all peoples and countries, asked Freud to give a psychoanalytic appraisal of that material.[246]

A second international meeting took place in Nuremberg on March 30 and 31. It was decided to form an International Psychoanalytic Association. Freud preferred to have a gentile at the head of the organization.[247] In spite of much opposition of the Viennese members, Jung was elected president. As a compensation, a new periodical, the *Zentralblatt für Psychoanalyse* was put under the joint editorship of Adler and Stekel.

A great part of the antagonism felt at that time toward psychoanalysis was due to the so-called "wild analysts," that is, people who without any preparation for that task started "analyzing" in ways that often proved detrimental to their patients. Hans Blüher who belonged to the Freudian group in Berlin has given a picture of the situation:

> In Berlin, [Blüher relates] as well as in Vienna and in Zurich, a psychoanalytic group consisted of two circles: a small medical one using a strictly medical terminology, and whose aim was the treatment of neurotic; and a much larger lay circle whose task was to attract public attention to neuroses and psychoanalysis. According to Blüher, this lay circle was the main driving force of the psychoanalytic movement; its adherents wrote a flood of would-be psychoanalytic literature. In their unrestrained way, they proclaimed that psychoanalysis could furnish a key to all possible problems of mankind, from the cure of individual neuroses to the abolition of war. So, although they attracted patients to psychoanalytic treatment, they brought the movement into disrepute.[248]

This is what caused Freud to write his well-known paper on "Wild Analysis."[249] Freud emphasized that no one should analyze if he had not received proper training. Freud now used the term *psychosexuality* for the first time. He explained that his concept of the libido not only included the instinctual sexual drives, but also encompassed the total meaning of the German word *lieben* (to love). "How much anger and spite would have been saved if that clarification had been given earlier," Oskar Pfister commented.[250]

The International Congress of Medical Psychology and Psychotherapy, which took place in Brussels from August 7 to 8, showed how the relationship between the psychotherapeutic schools had changed.[251] Janet, who had played a moderating role in the previous congresses, did not attend (his report on suggestion was read in absentia). The discussions often took the appearance of a conflict of the generations between the old (Forel, Bernheim, and Vogt) and the young (Seif, Jones, and Muthmann). At times it was as though the young would reply with a massive attack to anything the old would say. An example was Ernst Trömner's paper on "The

Process of Falling Asleep" and hypnagogic phenomena. Foremost in the discussion on this paper was Seif, who took exception with the author because he had not quoted Freud and Silberer, adding that "the material was ripe for a psychoanalytic working-through." Forel rose to protest, whereupon Muthmann, Jones, and Graeter energetically supported Seif. De Montet undertook to contradict Freud's theory, and then Trömner reminded the audience that his paper had been on the subject of falling asleep, rather than on dreams. In the discussion of one of the next papers, Vogt protested against Seif's pretention in forbidding him to speak of dreams and the unconscious: "I object that a man like myself who has collected his own dreams since the age of sixteen and has investigated the problems under discussion here since 1894, that is, almost as long as Freud has done and longer than any of his disciples, should be refused the right to discuss these questions by any Freudian!"

The Brussels Congress is typical of the kind of discussions that arose in almost every congress of that time in the German-speaking areas. The tone was sometimes dominated by the psychoanalysts, as in Brussels, sometimes by their adversaries. In a meeting of the psychiatrists and neurologists of southwest Germany in Baden-Baden, on May 8, Dr. Hoche made a memorable speech on "A Psychic Epidemic Among Physicians."

> A psychic epidemic, he said, is "the transmission of specific representations of a compelling power in a great number of heads, resulting in the loss of judgment and lucidity." Freud's followers, he said, did not belong to a "School" in the scientific sense but a kind of sect, that does not bring forth verifiable facts but articles of faith. Psychoanalysis shows all the features of a sect: the fanatical conviction of being superior to others, its jargon, the sharp intolerance of and tendency to vilify those of another belief, its high veneration for the Master, its tendency to proselytize, its readiness to accept the most monstrous improbabilities, and the fantastic overevaluation of what has already been accomplished and can be accomplished by adherents of the sect. As an explanation for these psychic epidemics, Hoche gave a lack of historical sense and philosophical education in in its victims and the thanklessness of curing nervous illnesses. The therapeutic successes resulted, he said, from the untiring attention given by the physicians to the patients. Hoche concluded that the Freudian movement was the "return, in a modernized form of a magical medicine, a kind of secret teaching . . ," and would bring to the history of medicine another example of psychic epidemics.[252]

In Zurich, Ludwig Frank applied a modification of the original Breuer-Freud cathartic method.[253] He had his patients lie on a couch and concentrate on the feelings that occurred in them. The patient would revive emotions from the past, often from forgotten episodes of his life, whereupon the memory of the events would occur in turn and be discussed with the therapist. Sometimes past emotions were abreacted without full knowledge of the facts, and this sufficed to bring about a cure. Forel proclaimed that this method was the only true, original psychoanalysis of Breuer, which Freud had since distorted.

The year 1911 brought European tensions almost to the breaking point, and the object of discord was again Morocco. By virtue of an agreement with England, France gave up her claims in Egypt in exchange for a free hand in Morocco. Germans, though, also had interests in Morocco, and to emphasize it, sent a warship to Agadir. After difficult negotiations, war was avoided, and Germany gave up her "rights" in Morocco in exchange for a piece of the French Congo, but both France and Germany felt they had been cheated, and the tension was hardly diminished. Italy objected to being left out in the partitioning of Africa, and seeing that the Turkish Empire was undergoing a severe internal crisis, Italy declared war on Turkey, and invaded Tripoli to acquire a new colony and thus avenge her defeat at Adua.

It seemed that there had never been so many psychotherapeutic schools. Janet in Paris and Dubois in Bern still enjoyed great prestige. Another therapist who acquired great fame at that time was Roger Vittoz who lived in Lausanne on the shore of Lake Geneva.[254] He submitted his patients to an ingenious system of mental training that consisted of graduated exercises of relaxation and concentration. Vittoz taught his subjects full awareness of all the sensations, and how to concentrate on one representation or idea, such as the idea of "rest," "control," "the infinite," and so on. Vittoz contended that by placing his hand on the subject's forehead, he could check the degree of control. He also taught a philosophy of life.[255] Patients came to Vittoz from all parts of the world, but he did not teach his method, and few practised it after his death.

To people of that time the great psychiatric event of the year 1911 was probably the appearance of Bleuler's book on dementia praecox, for which he had coined the new term "Schizophrenia":

This book, which was the fruit of twenty years of work, brought four innovations. First, it encompassed under the wider concept of "schizophrenia" not only the old dementia praecox, but a number of conditions, especially acute transient ones, which had been considered as separate entities. Second, he brought a dynamic concept of the illness, which seemed to have been inspired by Janet's concept of psychasthenia, that is the distinction of primary symptoms directly related to the disease process, and secondary symptoms deriving from the primary ones. Third, Bleuler proposed an interpretation of the content of schizophrenic hallucination and delusion, in which he followed Freud. Fourth, in contrast to the view that dementia praecox was incurable, Bleuler brought the optimistic concept that schizophrenia was an illness that could be stopped or made to recede at any point of its course. The intensive preoccupation of the Burghölzli physicians with their patients and the use of occupational therapy and other devices resulted in a remarkable increase in the number of therapeutic successes.[256]

The year 1911 was one of great expansion for the psychoanalytic movement, with the very successful International Congress at Weimar in September. But it was also a period of inner strife. Even after Adler's resignation in July the Viennese Society was (in Jones' words) "torn by jealousies and dissensions."

In 1911 a novel by Grete Meisel-Hess appeared, which is the first known work of fiction giving a picture of a psychoanalyst as the public could imagine one at that time.

The characters of that novel are a group of sophisticated intellectuals who spend their time with futile love affairs and lengthy discussions on any conceivable topic. A forty-year-old neurotic lady who has lived her best years in that circle realizes that she needs the help of a physician. She hears that a new method, psychoanalysis, is able to cure patients by bringing the unconscious life into the consciousness. Filled with intense feelings of curiosity and hope, she enters the house of the psychoanalyst. The maid, a tall, skinny old woman clad in black, leads her through a long suite of elegantly furnished rooms to the door of the great man's office.

The doctor, who sits at his desk, looks at her piercingly for a while and silently strokes his beard. Then he bids her to sit down, and with an encouraging gesture, invites her to tell her story. From now on the consultation evolves in four phases. The patient tells her whole story while the psychoanalyst listens quietly and takes notes. Then comes the second phase: the analyst explains to the patient that she has repressed painful sexual memories; thereupon he strives to drag out these repressed memories "by means of a special technique." He asks among others about her dreams. In the third phase the psychoanalyst turns into a gynecologist: since sexual causes are at the root of the neurosis, a thorough gynecological examination is necessary. Fortunately, the findings are satisfying. So that we may proceed to the fourth phase in which the psychoanalyst turns into a hypnotist. He has the patient sit in a comfortable armchair and the technique is described at length. Once the lady is in hypnotic sleep, the analyst keeps on stroking her forehead and gives her suggestions to the effect that she will lose all her complexes. When the séance is over the patient leaves the analyst with a feeling of exhilaration. No mention is made of the fee. The psychoanalytic treatment is terminated with this one session, and until the end of the novel the former patient is free from any neurotic symptom.[257]

The year 1912 was marked, above all, by the Balkan Wars. Greece, Serbia, and Bulgaria, the new Balkan States, attacked Turkey, claiming to liberate their nationals still under the Turkish yoke. It was the topic of the day, and much was said about "Macedonian atrocities." This war caused more tension between the other European powers, particularly between Russia and Austria-Hungary.

Another sensational event was the sinking of the *Titanic* on its maiden voyage on April 14, with a loss of more than fifteen hundred lives. The ship was considered the most modern and perfected ever built and had been advertised as unsinkable, but safety measures had been inadequate and lifeboats insufficient. Social prejudices were mirrored in the way passengers of the first and second class were rescued before those of the third. Thus a great number of poor immigrants and their children were sacrificed.[258] The superstitious saw this disaster as an ill omen for the future of European civilization. Much was written about the imminence of war. A German, Von Bernhardi, explained in his book, *Germany and the Next War*, that his country would have to face a host of enemies; victory would be gained only at the price of unheard-of efforts and sacrifices.[259] A group of scholars founded a *Gesellschaft für positivistische Philosophie* (Society for Positivist Philosophy), with headquarters in Berlin, with the aim of arriving at a unified, scientific conception of the universe, and thus to solve mankind's problems. Among the members of the society were Ernst Mach, Josef Popper, Albert Einstein, August Forel, and Sigmund Freud.

It was a period of feverish agitation among European youth. New literary, artistic, cultural, and political groups were flourishing everywhere, claiming to break with the past, to introduce new values, and polemicizing with each other. The polemics around and within the psychoanalytic movement must be understood in that context.

Josef Breuer was now completely ignored by the new generation. When his seventieth anniversary was celebrated on January 15, 1912, Sigmund Exner read an address and presented him with the documents of the *Breuer-Stiftung*, a foundation whose aim was to award prizes for research work and enable prominent scientists to lecture in Vienna. A subscription totaled an initial sum of 58,125 Crowns.[260] The list of subscribers included the names of the foremost Viennese scientists, writers, and artists. The name of Freud, however, is not to be found on this list.[261]

There was a great activity among psychoanalysts. A new periodical, *Imago*, was launched by Rank and Sachs. In its first issue was Freud's initial contribution to what was to become his *Totem and Taboo*. Freud's interest in ethnology was apparently stimulated by Jung's *Metamorphoses and Symbols of Libido*. During the previous few years there had been much interest in the problem of totemism. Frazer had published his *Totemism and Exogamy*.[262] Durkheim[263] contended that totemism was the original form of religion, and Thurnwald described it as a primitive way of thought.[264] Wundt sketched a vast picture of the evolution of mankind, which he said comprised four periods: a primitive period of savage life, a totemic period with tribal organization and exogamy, a "period of the heroes and the gods," and the modern period (with world religions, world powers, world culture, and world history).[265] It would seem, furthermore, than when he wrote *Totem and Taboo* Freud was also inspired by recent events: the uprising of the Young Turks (the thwarted sons) against Sultan Abdul Hamid II (the cruel old father), who kept a large harem guarded by eunuchs, furnished a model. After the revolution, social organization could be modernized and literature began to flourish in Turkey, just as in Freud's model in which human culture flourished after the murder of the old father. As a complement to *Totem and Taboo*, Otto Rank published a vast compilation of the incest motif in poetry and legend.[266]

Controversies around psychoanalysis raged more than ever. To understand their true meaning requires a thorough knowledge of the cultural background of the time. This is well illustrated by an example of a controversy that occurred in Zurich at the beginning of 1912.[267]

No mention of psychoanalysis is to be found in the *Neue Zürcher Zeitung* before February 8, 1911, when Dr. Karl Oetker published a review of a booklet *Die Psychanalyse* by Ludwig Frank.[268] This review, in which the name of Freud is not even mentioned, left the reader with the impression that "Psychanalysis" (sic) was a Swiss discovery; and it contained a materialistic profession of faith, including the assertion that at death the soul perished forever. Ten months later, on December 7, a certain "Dr. E.A." gave an account of a lecture by Dr. F. Riklin at a recent meeting of a Zurich philological society, the Gesellschaft für deutsche Sprache. Riklin said that psychoanalysis had proved able to cure neurotics by bringing repressed images back to consciousness, and interpreting dreams. Riklin added that it had been shown that dream and delusion symbols were identical with the universal myths of mankind so that the meaning of universal symbols and myths had been deciphered. The sun, for instance, was a symbol of masculine sexual energy, the serpent and the foot were phallic symbols, and gold was a symbol of excrement. All this was presented in the review not as hypotheses but as discoveries of absolute certainty. It would seem that it was this lecture and perhaps others of the same sort that caused the Kepler-Bund to devote an evening to the topic of psychoanalysis. The significance of that meeting would be lost without an explanation.

In those years, European culture was permeated with scientism, that is, the belief that only science could give answers to the great enigmas of the world. The dominant science at that time was natural science (as atomic physics is that of our day), with the theory of evolution in the foreground. Under that name, four different concepts were intermingled: that of transformism (as opposed to creationism or fixism), Darwin's original theory that evolution of species was achieved through natural selection under the impact of the struggle for existence, an array of pseudo-Darwinist doctrines called social Darwinism, and finally Haeckel's doctrine. No one can imagine today what an overwhelming role Haeckel's ideas played in the cultural life of his time. Haeckel had begun his career as a brilliant naturalist, developed into a philosopher of nature, and was now becoming more and more an enemy of religion. In his eyes science was equated with materialism, atheism, and the Haeckelian brand of transformism. Religion was equated with tradition, superstition, and antiscientific attitudes. Haeckel was the idol of many young men who had undergone a conversion to his doctrine. There was, for instance, the story of the dramatic conversion of young Goldschmidt: Having read Haeckel's history of creation, he believed he had found the key to all philosophical and scientific problems and began to propagate these views with the zeal of a missionary.[269]

Haeckel had now founded an association, the Monisten-Bund, which claimed to absorb religion into science and to be the religion of the future. It is not surprising that his activity met considerable resistance from the various churches. It was easy for his enemies to demonstrate that he constantly presented hypotheses as certainties, and he was accused of having falsified a number of illustrations in his books in order to make them conform to his doctrine. The fight against Haeckel was conducted from two quarters. The theologian Wasmann founded the Thomas-Bund to refute Haeckel in the name of religion, and the naturalist Dennert founded the Kepler-Bund, whose official purpose was to defeat pseudoscientific speculations in the name of science. It included several noted scientists among its members and had branches in the main German-speaking towns.

The Zurich branch of the Kepler-Bund organized a meeting on psychoanalysis. On the basis of an account by Oetker on Frank's book, that by "E. A." on Riklin's lecture, the Kepler Bund, apparently was under the impression that psychoanalysis was a materialistic and atheistic doctrine that taught fantastic speculations as if they were scientific truths. On January 2, 1912, the *Neue Zürcher Zeitung* reported on the meeting of the Kepler-Bund. Dr. Max Kesserling, specialist in nervous diseases in Zurich, had spoken "On the Theory and Practice of the Viennese Psychologist Freud." The speaker began by expressing his regret that Freud's teaching had met with so much success in Zurich among educators and pastors. Kesselring had attended a course of lectures by Freud in Vienna, and he said that Freud was imbued with the conviction that his teaching was true, that in his lectures he encouraged students to ask questions but gave them vague and unconvincing answers. After giving a historical survey of psychoanalysis, Kesselring declared himself definitely opposed to it. He read quotations from Freud that caused laughter from his audience. The reviewer regretted that Kesselring did not do justice to the kernel of truth contained in Freud's teachings. On the next day, January 3, 1912, the *Neue Zürcher Zeitung* published a short statement by Kesselring, declaring that he was not a member of the Kepler-Bund, and that his rejection of psychoanalysis was not based on philosophical opinion, but was the result of his unprejudiced studies. On January 5, a member of the Kepler-Bund confirmed that Dr. Kesselring was not a member and explained that the Kepler-Bund had a "neutral" attitude toward the subject under discussion. The only concern of the Kepler-Bund was to distinguish hypothesis from confirmed facts in scientific literature.

In its January 10 issue, the *Neue Zürcher Zeitung* published two letters; one signed "J. M." contended that the Kepler-Bund was actually a combat organization against monism and atheism. Obviously Freud's teaching was opposed to the ideas held by the Kepler-Bund, and when the Kepler-Bund invited Dr. Kesselring to speak about Freud, they knew in advance what his attitude would be. The second letter, signed "Dr. J.," said it was in bad taste to conduct such a discussion before a lay audience; why not, then, gynecological examinations? Even the best-educated public could not form an objective opinion on such matters. Moreover, he said the lecture lacked objectivity and contained a great number of untrue assertions.

In January 13 issue a certain "F." replied to "Dr. J." that the most recent *Raschers Jahrbuch* contained a long article by C. G. Jung about Freud's ideas, which was a masterpiece of vulgarization. He found it extremely rash that personal secrets that formerly were confided only to the priest should now be entrusted with no safeguards to the psychoanalyst. He added that he was being overwhelmed with extravagant psychoanalytic literature, that he had just received a work by Johann Michelsen in which Christ was interpreted as a symbol of the sex act, the ox in the stable as a symbol of castration, and every other item pertaining to the Nativity scene explained in a similar fashion.[270] "F. M." then quoted a few examples of sexual symbolism from Freud himself, as, for instance: if one dreams of a landscape one is certain of having visited before, the scene is symbolic of the mother's genitals, because that is the only place where a man can be sure he has already been. "F.M." concluded by pointing out the danger of the psychoanalyst believing he has an infallible secret, and that those who suffer from sexual distress cannot really be helped by psychoanalysis because the cause of the disorder is often social and economic, and in other cases the cure would demand a rejection of moral concepts. In the following issue of January 15, Dr. Kesselring protested against Jung's accusation that he had brought psychoanalysis to a lay public. In Zurich, educators and pastors did so constantly, as shown by the many articles in *Evangelische Freiheit, Berner Seminarblätter*, and in any case, psychoanalysts themselves had started the practice.

In the issue of January 17 there were again two letters. The first, by C. G. Jung, said that "the concept of sexuality used by Freud and myself has a much wider meaning than the vulgar one. . . . This can be read in Freud's and my own writings. . . ." and also that it was unjust to place Michelsen's book on the same level with Riklin's valuable works. The second letter was "F.M." 's reply to Jung. Theoretically, he said, Freud had a wide concept of sexuality but in practise he used the word in its narrow sense. "F.M." protested against those who criticized him for speaking about psycho-analysis without being a physician; one did not need, in fact, to be a physician to judge the immense danger of psychoanalysis, a pseudoscience that had found so many more fanatical adherents in Zurich than anywhere else and had unleashed a psychic epidemic.

On January 25, August Forel, in retirement near Lake Geneva, joined the exchange. He took exception with a criticism by "F.M." concerning hypnosis, and with Kesselring's contention that neurotic patients become psychotic after psychoanalytic treatment. He deplored that Breuer's fruitful teaching of cathartic therapy should have been distorted by Freud. One's concern should be not to polemicize about psychoanalysis but to study it seriously, as did Dr. Frank in Zurich. This letter was followed by Kesselring's reply: psychoanalysts constantly spoke of their successes and never of their failures. He gave two examples of neurotic patients who, following analysis, had become psychotic. Finally "F.M." replied to Forel that it was the psychoanalysts who addressed themselves to a wide lay public and wrote propaganda by means of numerous pamphlets and newspaper articles.

The January 27 issue contained a psychoanalysts' protest in somewhat vehement terms:

> The President of the International and of the Zurich Psychoanalytic Associations sees himself obliged to energetically reject the insulting and severely disparaging accusations formulated by a layman against medical specialists. The articles signed by F. M. give a completely distorted picture of psychoanalytic treatment owing to the ignorance of their author. No reasonable man would submit himself to such a disgusting method of treatment as depicted by F.M. The tone of these indictments makes any further discussion impossible.
>
> For the International Psychoanalytic Association: C. G. Jung, M.D., President, F. Riklin, M.D., Secretary.
>
> For the Zurich Psychoanalytic Association, Alph. Maeder, M.D., President, J.H.W. van Ophuijsen, Physician, Secretary.

This protest was followed, in the same issue, by "F.M." 's answer. "The Mrss. Psychoanalysts," he said, "identify themselves so much with their science that they take any criticism of it as a personal insult." He pointed out the thoroughly haughty tone of Dr. Jung, in calling him a reporter and a layman, and that there were physicians, too, who were opposed to psychoanalysis. Although Freud had made many interesting observations on neuroses, his method was faulty and unscientific. (The fact that his observations were made in half-Slavic Vienna was not irrelevant.) Psychoanalysts now analyzed not only the living but the dead: the entire spiritual life of mankind, religion, art, literature, and folklore. They cannot accept criticism from laymen, but they do not hesitate to encroach in fields where they themselves are laymen.

On January 28, F.M. continued his attack on psychoanalysis, calling it a positively dangerous method. Even in the best of cases, that is when it is practised by an extremely capable and conscientious physician, it reduces the individual to a sexual formula and pretends to cure him on that basis. What child would not suffer despair after being taught that he had incestuous wishes toward his mother? As for the adult, if his neurosis originated in repressed sexual wishes, what would the catharsis be? F.M. mentioned the case of a friend whom he had referred to an eminent nerve specialist, and who, in spite of warnings, went to a psychoanalyst. Unable to follow the psychoanalyst's advice in his home town, he disappeared and was never heard from again. If psychoanalysis is such a dangerous instrument in the hands of a conscientious physician, what disasters could it cause in the hands of the unscrupulous. Popularization of psychoanalytic concepts, furthermore, would mean the rejection of sexual morality on the grounds of scientific justification.

On January 31, the *Neue Zürcher Zeitung* published Kesselring's answer to Forel. He maintained that psychoanalysis could be dangerous, and that he was not the only one to have observed its disastrous effects on patients. It was an untenable attitude, he added, that psychoanalysts should speak only of their successes in their treatments while forbidding others to mention their failures. The fact that psychoanalysts were so sensitive betrayed their lack of objectivity, and made any constructive discussion impossible.

In the February 1 issue, Forel's answer to Fritz Marti (designated by his full name for the first time) appeared, in which Forel blamed Marti for lumping together hypnosis, Freudian psychoanalysis, and the new psychotherapies (meaning Ludwig Frank's perfecting of the old Breuer-Freud cathartic cure). "I must definitely declare that lucid researchers fully agree with Mr. F.M. with his condemnation of the one-sidedness of the Freudian school, its sanctifying sexual church, its infant sexuality, its Talmudic-exegetic-theological interpretations." It was Freud and Jung who had involved laymen in these matters. Fortunately there were a few men concerned with utilizing the kernel of truth contained in the Breuer-Freud research. Following this letter were a few lines by F.M., thanking Forel and declaring the discussion ended.

From the example of this Zurich controversy of 1912 one can surmise that the real nature of the opposition to psychoanalysis in those years was very different from the picture that is usually given of it today. The current stereotype is that "Freud's discoveries met fierce and fanatical resistance from those who could not accept his concept of sexuality, in view of the 'Victorian' prejudices of the times and of neurotic repression." Actually, objective examination of facts shows that the situation was quite different. In the controversies around psychoanalysis, at least five elements should be distinguished.

First, psychoanalytic concepts were presented to the public in a manner that was bound to produce two opposite types of reactions; one group was bound to be shocked and find these concepts distasteful and dangerous; and another group was to accept them enthusiastically as revelations. Wittgenstein has pointed this out quite clearly.[271] Clashes between these two groups were inevitable, and often took the form of a conflict of generations. Midway between these extreme attitudes was that of those lucid men who tried to think for themselves in order to select what was scientific in these theories. Men such as Oppenheim, Friedländer, Isserlin, who are usually considered today as early opponents of psychoanalysis, actually belonged to the group that attempted to make an objective appraisal. Their criticism has since been considerably amplified and "the kernel of truth" they accepted has been overlooked.

Second, under the heading psychoanalysis, a great number of trends were confused: there were many possible gradations between the writings of Freud, of his immediate circle, of the wider circle of lay analysts, and of eccentrics, such as Michelsen, who claimed to be psychoanalysts. How could the public recognize what pertained to genuine psychoanalysis? The same was true in regard to psychoanalytic therapy, which could be given by analysts of Freud's group or by irresponsible individuals. It was these same abuses that caused criticism of and opposition to psychoanalysis, which led Freud to write his essay on "Wild Analysis"

Third, psychoanalysis was received in two different ways. In Vienna, men such as Krafft-Ebing, Weininger, and Schnitzler had conditioned the public to accept Freud's sexual theories. In Zurich, another type of *genius loci* caused psychoanalysis to be accepted as a key to religious and educational problems, and to the understanding of myths and psychosis. It was inevitable that clashes should occur between these two diverging perspectives.

Fourth, psychoanalysis was commonly identified with materialistic philosophy and Haeckelian Monism. To be sure, psychoanalysis could equally well be used as an argument against atheism as for it. Rank and Sachs suggested that atheism was the extreme expression of the overcoming of the father.[272] The knowledge that Freud was an avowed atheist who termed religion a collective neurosis contributed to the misunderstanding. Hans Blüher relates in his Memoirs how the Berlin house of Dr. Heinrich Koerber, head of the local Monisten-Bund, was also the meeting place for young "modern" artists and writers, and Freudians.[273] To some extent the opposition to psychoanalysis was a part of the growing opposition to Haeckel and his Monisten-Bund.

Finally, the most important reason for the antagonism toward psychoanalysis was probably the manner in which it was promoted. Psychoanalysts, particularly the young disciples, proclaimed their findings without backing them up with proofs or statistics. They left the burden of proof to their adversaries, were intolerant to any kind of criticism, and used *ad hominem* arguments, saying that their adversaries were neurotic for instance. Psychoanalysis was at times used by men such as Michelsen to write things that seemed devised only to scandalize the devout reader, much in the fashion of the Futurists.[274]

The picture of these controversies would be incomplete without mentioning that they were equally vehement among psychoanalysts. Alphonse Maeder relates that once during a discussion about dreams in a psychoanalytic congress, he mentioned his own concept of the "prospective" function of dreams. This brought "a storm of opposition against me as if I had touched something sacred." He had not contradicted any of Freud's theories, but merely proposed to supplement them.[275] In the same period, conflicts raged between the Viennese Society and Stekel. Worst of all, Jung had begun on the evolution that was to separate him from Freud. In February 1912, the *Zentralblatt* published a condensed excerpt of a book by the French art historian Sartiaux under the signature of Freud:[276]

> Twenty centuries ago, in the town of Ephesus, the temple of Diana attracted numerous pilgrims, as Lourdes does today. In 54 A.D. the Apostle Saint Paul preached and made converts there for several years. Being persecuted, he founded his own community. This proved to be detrimental to the goldsmiths' commerce, and they organized uprising against Saint Paul with the cry "Great is the Diana of the Ephesians!" Saint Paul's community did not remain loyal to him, it fell under the influence of a man named John, who had come with Mary, and promoted the cult of the Mother of God. Again pilgrims flocked, and the goldsmiths found work again. Nineteen centuries later the same site was the object of the visions of Katharina Emmerich.[277]

Why did Freud publish this archaeological anecdote? One need not be well versed in hermeneutics to guess its allegoric meaning. Freud (Saint Paul) promoted a new teaching, and because of opposition to him, gathered a group of faithful disciples who became the object of violent persecutions because his teachings threatened certain interests. A disciple John (Jung) came to him, who at first was his ally but then introduced mystical tendencies, took his disciples away from him, and organized a dissident community, which gratified anew the "Merchants of the Temple."

The year 1913 brought an exacerbation of political conflicts in Europe to the point that, at times, a general war seemed imminent. The center of the conflict was in the Balkans. After Greece, Bulgaria, and Serbia had won victories over Turkey they began to tear each other to pieces in a second Balkan war, with Greece, Serbia, and Rumania allied against Bulgaria. These convulsions shook Austria-Hungary and Russia. In Russia there was a partial mobilization, and war was prevented only by a conference of ambassadors. Tension between France and Germany was heightened by frequent frontier incidents, and the French Parliament lengthened the period of compulsory military service from two years to three. Characteristically, Léon Daudet published a book with the title, *L'Avant-Guerre* (the Eve of War).

In that year conflicts were increasingly rife between the various dynamic psychiatric schools. In Paris, Janet was compiling his vast work on psychological healing. In Nancy, Bernheim's resignation was followed by an antipsychological reaction, much as had occurred in Paris after Charcot's death. In Bern, Dubois was still a luminary of psychotherapy, as was Vittoz in Lausanne, but both were isolated. In Zurich, Ludwig Frank was fighting hard to promote his own brand of cathartic treatment, and in that year he published a textbook on his method.[278] In Vienna the psychoanalytic movement was undergoing the most severe crisis it had ever known. It had already lost Alfred Adler, who now, as chief of a new school, published a textbook on his method.[279] Stekel, who had left the movement the year before, was promoting his own method of brief psychoanalytic treatment. And now it was Jung who severed relations with Freud after publishing his own non-Freudian views as a description of psychoanalysis. That year the war of dynamic psychiatric schools was waged on two main battlefields: the Seventeenth International Congress of Medicine in London and the Fourth Psychoanalytic Congress in Munich.

The Seventeenth International Congress of Medicine took place in London from August 7 to 12. Psychoanalysis was one of the topics discussed in Section XII. The reports and the discussions that followed are known, not only through the official proceedings, but through detailed accounts published in *The Times*.[280] On Thursday, August 7, Adolf Meyer gave a report on the Phipps Psychiatric Clinic, which had just opened in Baltimore under his direction. The discussion showed the amazement of his English colleagues with his ratio of ten physicians to ninety patients. Sir Thomas Clouston exclaimed: "We feel that our paymasters and our committees will need a great deal of education before they will provide the funds for carrying out such beneficent schemes as that!"

On Friday, August 8, Pierre Janet read his report on psychoanalysis.

The starting point of psychoanalysis, Janet said, resides in Charcot's observations on traumatic neuroses, which he (Janet himself) had extended to other neuroses, adding to them the concepts of the narrowing of the field of consciousness and the weakness of psychological tension. Thus from the beginning, Janet had seen a confirmation of his own observations in Freud's work. Freud claimed as novel the enormous amount of time he devoted to each patient, the thorough investigation of his life history, the minute observation of words, gestures, and so on, but Janet said he had always done the very same thing. The method of free association Janet called naïve, because the therapist was unknowingly suggesting the course of associations. As to the interpretation of dreams, Freud had no accurate method of recording dreams, and his methods of interpreting them were arbitrary; Freud called complex what Janet had called subconscious fixed ideas. Many of the so-called novel ideas of psychoanalysis were but renamed existing concepts, such as repression, which was Janet's narrowing of the field of consciousness. Even the word "psychoanalysis" was another one for Janet's "psychological analysis." Above all, Janet did not admit Freud's concept that sexuality was the essential and unique cause of neuroses; in Janet's experience, sexual disturbances were more the result than the cause of neuroses. Freud gave the word "libido" an immeasurably wide and vague meaning. Psychoanalysis could achieve therapeutic successes as well as any other method. In passing, Janet mentioned (without taking a stand) the curious opinion voiced by certain authors about the role of the *genius loci* in Vienna.[281] Janet concluded, in a conciliatory way, that Freud's writings contained " . . . a great number of precious studies about neuroses, the evolution of the mind in childhood, the various forms of sexual feelings. . . ." In later years, he said, the current exaggerations of psychoanalysis would be forgotten and it only would remembered that "psychoanalysis rendered great services to psychological analysis."

Obviously, Janet based his knowledge of Freud's teaching on the extant psychoanalytic literature in French and English. He had read the *Interpretation of Dreams* in Brill's translation, the abstracts of Freudian literature published by Brill and Acher, and certain publications of Maeder, Ferenczi, Sadger, Jung, Jones, and Putnam. Thus Janet's criticism was directed against early psychoanalysis rather than against its more recent developments.

Jung's defense of psychoanalysis, which followed, was given in English and began with a caustic remark against Janet: "Unfortunately, it is often the case that people believe themselves entitled to judge psychoanalysis when they are not even able to read German." Since Freud's theory was not yet, on the whole, very clear nor easily accessible, Jung offered a condensed version of psychoanalysis, with criticisms even more severe than those of Janet: "Therefore I propose to liberate the psychoanalytic theory from the purely sexual standpoint. In its place I should like to introduce an *energetic viewpoint* into the psychology of neuroses." Jung equated the libido and Bergson's *élan vital*. Neurosis is an act of adaptation that has failed, causing a damming up of energy and the substitution of lower parts of a function for its higher parts. (Incidentally, though Janet was not quoted, this was almost exactly his concept of neurosis.)

In the discussion that followed, no one replied to Jung. Nine persons participated in the discussion, of whom five were favorable to Freud, three against, and one neutral. Jones said that Janet's account contained a long series of misconceptions, distortions, and misstatements, and that he had understood nothing of psychoanalysis. Corriat said he had been an opponent of psychoanalysis, but had now come to understand the complete validity of its theory and its utmost value from the therapeutic standpoint. Forsyth said that Freud had given a "unique insight into the affective attributes of children." Eder wondered how Janet could state that psychoanalysis was absurd and at the same time contend that he was its real author. Savage said that one should not be impressed by Janet's eloquence, and should realize the importance of the infantile subconscious. Frankl-Hochwart of Vienna objected that there had been numerous cases where psychoanalytic treatment had failed, that it is often dangerous to stir up the sexual problems in patients, that lay analysts were dangerous, and that, above all, one should set up statistics of successful and failed cases. Walsh also stressed the danger of overemphasis on sexuality, and said that there was no therapeutic method that did not have its successes. Bérillon gave six criteria for acceptable psychotherapy, and found that none of the six was met by psychoanalysis. A divided opinion was expressed by T.A. Williams, "Psychoanalytic research for the origin of disease is a great advance over mere description." However, he said that he had doubts whether the disturbing complexes were really unconscious, that psychoanalysis did not cure faulty psychic habits, and that reorientation was preferable whenever it was effected consciously and rationally. He concluded that the therapeutic criterion was doubtful.

All accounts of this discussion confirm that it was somewhat stormy. In his autobiography, Jones said that Janet's report was "a slashing and satirical attack on Freud and his work . . . delivered with his inimitable theatrical skill," adding that "it was easy for me to demonstrate to the audience not only Janet's profound ignorance of psychoanalysis but also his lack of scruple in inventing, in the most unfair way, men of straw for his ridicule to play on."[282] Jones ascribed Janet's opposition to psychoanalysis to jealousy, because he felt himself surpassed by Freud. In his biography of Freud, Jones simply said, "In the first week of August there was a duel between Janet and myself at the International Congress of Medicine, which put an end to his pretentions of having founded psychoanalysis and then seeing it spoiled by Freud"; following this was Freud's letter of congratulations.[283] Contemporary accounts do not substantiate the story of the "duel." In the official proceedings of the congress, Jones' intervention is very short and it does not stand out from those of the other eight participants. The London *Times* in its detailed accounts of all meetings and discussions summarized only Dr. Coriat's forceful intervention in favor of psychoanalysis, and Dr. Walsh's contention that psychoanalysis was the latest in a series of psychic epidemics. No mention was made of Jones. Possibly Jones confused his verbal intervention at the congress with his rejoinder to Janet, which was later published in the *Journal for Abnormal Psychology*.

A complete appreciation of the events of that congress must necessarily consider the political atmosphere of the day. For several years in England there had been a campaign against anything that was "made in Germany." Wollenberg, one of the German psychiatrists who participated in the congress, later recalled that evidence for this anti-German feeling at the congress was that no German was invited to offer a toast at the closing banquet.[284]

Three weeks after the International Medical Congress in London, the psychoanalysts gathered for their Fourth International Congress in Munich, on September 7 and 8. It would seem that the participants at that congress were concerned not so much with scientific papers as with conflicts within the association. Freud and his close collaborators were anxious about the new turn that Jung and his followers were giving to psychoanalysis. In his capacity of president of the International Association, Jung was in the chair, but his term was on the verge of expiring. In spite of the strong opposition against him, Jung was reelected by thirty out of fifty-two votes.

Lou Andreas-Salome who came as a guest accompanied by the poet Rilke, noted her impressions in her diary.[285] She felt that Jung's attitude toward

Freud was unduly aggressive and dogmatic; Freud stood on the defensive and contained with difficulty his deep emotion when facing the break with the "son" he had loved so much.

One may assume that the conflict was tinged with emotional elements. Did not the relationship of Jung and Freud recall what had been that of Freud and Breuer eighteen years before? As for Jung, he was reenacting the conflict he had had with Bleuler in 1909, if not his still earlier conflict with his father. But the deeper reason for the conflict was the basic difference in outlook between the Zurich group and Freud. Bleuler and Jung had viewed their relationship with Freud as a collaboration between independent scientists working in the same field. They had accepted from psychoanalysis what they deemed to be true and stated their differences. In that same manner Breuer and Freud had stated the differences in their respective theories in the *Studies in Hysteria*. In 1908 Bleuler and Jung had explained their conflicting theories of schizophrenia in a joint article.[286] But Freud wanted disciples who would accept his teaching *en bloc* or develop it under his control, so the conflict was inevitable, and this is also the reason why Bleuler always declined to be a member of the International Psychoanalytic Association.

The true history of this episode has never been written as yet, nor has the true history of the polemics around psychoanalysis. The current version that Freud and his disciples were the victims of massive attacks by dishonest enemies does not stand before an objective examination of the available facts, nor does the story of alleged persecutions. There were lively, sometimes vehement, discussions in medical societies and congresses, but there is no record that anyone ever questioned Freud's sincerity or integrity. As to Jones' assertion that an Australian pastor, Reverend Donald Fraser, was forced to resign on account of his interest in psychoanalysis and that the Swedish linguist, Hans Sperber, had his career broken for the same reason, both definitely belong to legend: Reverend Donald Fraser voluntarily left the ministry to study medicine with the support of his community,[288] and Sperber was refused the Privat Dozentship for reasons which had nothing to do with his paper on the sexual origin of the language.[289] Characteristic of the legend is the way in which harmless jokes have been turned into heinous offenses. Jones, who was better acquainted with British humor than with Viennese *Witz*, gives as an example of shameless anti-Freudian insults jests that linked Freud's name with the word *Freudenmädchen* (harlot).[290] In fact, the joke was, "Why do certain women go to Freud, others to Jung? The former are *Freudenmädchen* (harlots), the latter *Jungfrauen* (virgins)."

The year 1914 began under black clouds. Europe was full of overt and covert conflicts. In Austria-Hungary the growing Czech nationalistic agitation brought a strong protest from the German-speaking groups against what they considered Slavic encroachment. Relations were tense between Austria and Serbia over Albania, which the Serbians had wished to annex, whereas Austria-Hungary had secured Albania's independence. The English were preoccupied by increasing nationalistic agitation in Ireland. The new President of France, Poincaré, went to Russia in June and at an official banquet assured the Russians of France's support in the event of conflict.

These were also months of acute crisis in the psychoanalytic movement. Jung found his position untenable and resigned from the International Association in March. Bleuler published a criticism of Freud's theories but did not sever his personal relationships with Freud. The Swiss Psychoanalytic Association was dissolved.

The great crisis caused Freud to write a history of the psychoanalytic movement as an *apologia pro domo*, brought with the usual inaccuracies of memory and polemic overtones regarding his relationship with Adler and Jung. In those months the journal *Imago* published an anonymous contribution "On the Moses of Michelangelo."[291] The anonymous contributor analyzed the pose and expression of that famous statue, and concluded that far from showing the anger of the Prophet about to break the stone tablets, it expressed the supreme effort made by the great leader to control his righteous anger. Years later it was revealed that the author had been none other than Freud. The consensus was that Freud had been projecting his own feelings. These months also brought one of the main novelties in psychoanalytic theory: Freud's *Introduction to Narcissism*.[292]

In spite of the crisis in the psychoanalytic movement, Freud's theories were acquiring an ever wider audience throughout the world. Psychoanalysis was becoming popular in Russia, where Freud's main works had been translated, and there were psychoanalytic groups in several large cities. It was also gaining ground in England and the United States. In France, Freud's ideas had been known to a limited number of persons, but in the midst of the strong chauvinism that permeated the country he was the object of vehement attacks, as before the Paris Psychotherapy Society on June 16, where Janet came to his defense.

Janet protested against the fact in a session devoted to Freud's work, one had heard nothing but criticisms; this was neither courteous nor just. The research of Freud and his school had acquired considerable development not only in Austria and Germany, but in other countries, including the United States; this would be impossible if these studies were devoid of value. Admitting the part of errors and exaggerations, the general theory served as a basis for valuable studies. Psychoanalysis had contributed numerous data to the knowledge of neuroses, of sexual psychology and psychopathology. "Let us acknowledge these merits; our unavoidable criticisms should not detract us to show our regards for the fine work and the important observations of our Viennese colleagues."[293]

But nationalistic feelings had mounted to such a pitch that scientific objectivity was impossible for years to come. It was in that tense atmosphere

that the news of the assassination at Sarajevo resounded twelve days later
as the death knell of Europe.

World War I: July 1914–November 1918

Henri Bergson relates that when on August 4, 1914, he unfolded a
newspaper and his eyes fell on a banner headline: *Germany Declares War
on France*, he had the sudden perception of an invisible presence, as if a
mythical figure had escaped from a book and had quietly taken a place in
his room.[294] As all those who had been children during the Franco-Prussian
War of 1870–1871, he had lived the twelve or fifteen years following that
war with the idea that a new war was imminent, and after that with a
complex feeling that a new war was both probable and impossible. Bergson
now realized that this event, whose expectation had filled his past forty-
three years with unrest, had now arrived, and in spite of his horror before
the catastrophe, he could not but marvel at the ease with which the abstract
idea of the war had become a living presence. This war, which we see in
retrospect as a thunderbolt out of the blue and as a dramatic interruption
of Europe's march toward happiness and prosperity, appeared to many
contemporaries as the inevitable outcome of a long series of conflicts,
threats, local wars, and rumors of war, if not as a liberation from intolerable
tensions.

In 1914 European civilization, in its expansion, was confronted with the
last remaining outpost of barbarity, the Turkish Empire. Only the rivalries
among the European powers had prevented the deathblow from being dealt
to the sick man, as Turkey was then commonly called. But from the dragon's
seed the new Balkan countries had arisen. Hardly were they liberated than
they started to oppress their own minorities and to fight with each other.
Secret terrorist organizations, formerly engaged in fighting the Turks, were
now employed as general political weapons. Young men who called themselves patriots were trained as terrorists to be used by nefarious political
interests.

The principle of nationalities, now extending to the Balkan countries,
was more than ever ruling over Europe, and each country had its particular
way of solving this problem. France had already assimilated its minorities
in the past, but Great Britain had difficulties with the Irish, Spain with the
Catalans, and Germany with its Alsatian, Danish, and Polish minorities.
Turkey resorted to periodic massacres, of which the Bulgarians and the
Armenians had been the latest victims. Russia, which had long been liberal,
was now attempting to "russify" its minorities. Austria-Hungary's situation
was the most difficult, as it was the only large multinational state in a period
of universal nationalism. It was exposed to agitation from within, and to
intrigues from Russia and Serbia. The problems of the Austrian-Hungarian
monarchy could hardly be understood in a time when the concepts of
"decolonization," "satellite states," and "supranational state," had not yet

been formulated. The Balkan countries, recently decolonized from the Turkish rule, fell prey to fanatical nationalism and interior strife. Serbia was a satellite of Russia, which practically directed her politics and used them against Austria-Hungary. The latter would today be called a supranational state, but in view of inner dissensions, it needed a thorough political reform.[295] The monarchy was the one binding force of the Empire, and the Crown Prince Francis Ferdinand was considered the only man who possessed the will and the ability to conduct the necessary reform.

The European public was so accustomed to murders of kings and heads of state by isolated anarchists or paranoiacs that it misunderstood the true meaning of the Sarajevo assassination, which in fact was a plot organized by the Serbian secret service.[296] We have already seen that in 1903 the pro-Austrian King of Serbia, Alexander III, and his wife, Queen Draga, as well as some of their supporters, had been assassinated. The new king, Peter, who was supported by Russia, initiated an anti-Austrian policy backed by the terrorists who had brought him to power. The annexation of Bosnia-Herzegovina by Austria-Hungary and the creation of a Bosnian Diet enraged the Serbian nationalists, who perpetrated a series of terrorist acts against Austrian civil servants and in 1912 even against the governor of Croatia. On June 28, 1914, a group of young Bosnian conspirators, who had been trained in Serbian terrorists' schools, furnished with arms from the Serbian Army, and helped across the frontier by Serbian agents, assassinated the Archduke Francis Ferdinand and his wife on a visit to Sarajevo. If ever there was a crime that could be called machiavellian, this was one: since the Archduke had decided to solve the problems of the Empire by giving equal status to the south Slavic groups in order to check the Serbian nationalists, his murder put an end to any hope of such readjustment, leaving a weary old emperor and an unprepared young man as heir presumptive. The Austrian-Hungarian government was now facing a tragic dilemma: either to leave unpunished the activities of a dangerous nest of terrorists who had sworn to destroy the Empire, or to resort to an armed intervention with the risk of a general war, in view of Russia's support of Serbia.[297] According to Somary:

> Western Europe did not at all understand what was the matter. . . . They erroneously assumed that a little nation was assaulted by imperialistic malice, and they instinctively took the part of David, whereas it was a case of the systematic undermining of a civilized empire through a Russian satellite, and the murder at Sarajevo was a typical partisan act.[298]

War was a deadly risk, even more so because only a year before it had been discovered that Colonel Alfred Redl, chief of the counterintelligence section of the Imperial Army, had been blackmailed into handing vital military information to the Russians. Moreover, Italy was turning away from her Austrian-Hungarian ally. The problem of whether the war would remain localized or not depended upon what Russia would do. Because of its rapid economic growth, social conflicts, and activities of revolutionary groups, Russia was ill-prepared for war. But a militarist party succeeded in obtaining a general mobilization, which also meant a threat to Germany. Germany was prepared for a war that its military and political leaders had long regarded as inevitable. Since the outcome was considered to depend on the rapidity of the first moves, and in order to secure the initial strategic advantage, Germany declared war on Russia and France, and violated Belgium's neutrality; whereupon Italy stepped out of her alliance with the Central Empires, and England declared war on Germany. Thus, in a few weeks, the infernal machine was set into motion.

Most of the peoples of Europe had long been conditioned to this war, which they began with a show of extraordinary patriotic enthusiasm. Austrians and Hungarians saw the struggle as the only means of survival for the Dual Monarchy. The Germans sought to free themselves from the encircling vise of neighboring nations and the invasion of Russian barbarism. The French saw it as a crusade for the freedom of the world and the liberation of Alsace-Lorraine. The war meant bankruptcy for the spiritual powers. Churches of all denominations took sides with their countries, and the Pope simply commended the combatants to God. The socialists, who had repeatedly proclaimed their opposition to war, joined the general movement within their respective countries with hardly less enthusiasm than the others. Pacifists were the minority everywhere, and those who refused to fight were quietly shot. Intellectuals participated with feverish enthusiasm in what has since been called the mobilization of consciences, that is, that fanatical nationalism that was intolerant of the least deviation of opinion. A small number of thinkers remained able to contemplate the catastrophe with lucidity. The French philosopher Alain foretold that this war would be a hecatomb of the elite, leaving the country at the mercy of the shrewd, the tyrants, and the slaves.[299] Anatole France, who in a written protest against the bombardment of Rheims Cathedral, expressed the hope that after the end of the war the French people would again admit the defeated enemy to their friendship, was copiously insulted and his house was stoned by the mob. Romain Rolland, another French writer who resided in Geneva, launched a manifesto praising the heroism of European youth and its sacrifices to a patriotic ideal, but castigating the statesmen who had unleashed the war and were doing nothing to stop it, and condemning the writers who were fanning the flame.[300] In the same vein the German novelist Hermann Hesse, while praising the combatants, denounced those who remained in the safety of their homes to write fiery incitations against the enemy.[301]

During the initial upheaval, each psychiatrist reacted according to his own character and background. Breuer predicted that Austria would either burn up or rise again from the conflagration as a young and strong Phoenix.[302]

Freud expressed patriotic Austrian feelings, and one wonders at Jones' surprise in that regard.[303] More unusual was the attitude of Janet, one of the very few who did not participate in the chauvinistic fever.[304] A curious episode is related by Moll in his autobiography.[305] A secret agent came to him and requested that Moll instruct him so that he might convincingly assume the identity of a physician. Moll told the man that this was impossible, but that he could show him how to impersonate a psychoanalyst. He thus taught him the rudiments and the jargon of the profession in a few days, and the man actually served his country throughout the war by "exercising" his new skill. In Switzerland, August Forel was so distressed by the catastrophe that he left his antialcoholic campaign and became involved in intensive pacifist activities.[306]

Those thousands of men who had gone to fight with such enthusiasm expected a short-lived war, assuming that modern weapons would necessarily bring it to a rapid conclusion. Very few foresaw that the fighting would last more than four years. The war began with a period of fiery enthusiasm and murderous attacks. Never, perhaps, in the history of mankind were such feats of heroism demanded from so many men, and never had human lives been wasted with such prodigality.

This initial period was followed by a standstill of the armies on the Western fronts, where they came to a kind of deadlock. This war of attrition was interspersed with fruitless attempts on both sides to break through the enemy lines. As in a kind of gigantic potlatch, the belligerents vied with each other to see who would throw more riches and more men into the brazier and acquire new allies. At that time the first grand-scale genocide of modern times took place. The Armenians, who had been incited by Allied agents to throw off the Turkish yoke with the promise of independence, fell prey to an organized and systematic massacre; almost two million of them were murdered in a gruesome manner.[307]

The spontaneous patriotic enthusiasm exhibited by the belligerent nations in the beginning had gradually been replaced by an ever-present, well-organized, and insidious propaganda. Around 1917 the populations were showing signs of weariness, and there were mutinies in the French Army. The Russian Empire was the first to crumble through the democratic revolution of Kerenski in March 1917 and through the Bolshevik Revolution of November 1917, followed by a separate peace with the Central Empires. Germany attempted to force the issue by intensifying her submarine war, which in turn elicited the intervention of the United States on the side of the Allies.

After the death of Emperor Francis Joseph, his successor, the young Charles, made vain attempts to obtain a separate peace. Germany tried desperately to attain victory before the United States Army could intervene efficaciously. But once more the decision was forced in the Near East, with the collapse of Turkey, followed by that of Bulgaria, Austria-Hungary, and finally Germany, with the armistice of November 11, 1918. For the English and particularly for the French it was a Pyrrhic victory acquired only through American intervention. By the end of 1918 all the people of Europe had set their unlimited hopes on President Wilson. The Allies saw in him the powerful defender who would support their claims at the peace conference; the Germans and Austrians were convinced that he would carry through a peace of justice and reconciliation.

During these four and one-half years, the life of the Western world had been thrown into confusion. The political, economic, social, and intellectual life of the belligerent nations was absorbed in the war. In that regard psychiatrists were no exception. Their most immediate concern was the treatment of war neuroses, and they were placed before problems they were ill prepared to meet. Treatment by electric stimulation, frequently successful with functional paralysis, was often used in a somewhat drastic manner, which earned it in France the name of *torpillage* ("torpedoing"). Babinski, who had overthrown Charcot's concept of hysteria, was faced with clinical disturbances very similar to the old hysteria that, however, resisted the therapeutic action of suggestion.[308] He called them physiopathic disturbances. Wagner-Jauregg distinguished, in regard to shell shock, the action of physical factors (noise, intense light, vibrations, and air pressure) and of two categories of psychogenic factors: the precipitating and the determining ones.[309] He pointed out that there were very few Germans, Austrians, Hungarians, and south Slavs among the patients with war neuroses, but in contrast there were many Czechs, and the worst cases of war neuroses occurred among soldiers from the Italian and Rumanian ethnic groups. (In other words, the incidence of war neuroses was proportionate to the lack of loyalty to the Dual Monarchy.) Psychoanalysts, to whom war neuroses were also a new field, had to revise and extend their theories.

Meanwhile psychiatry was making great progress. In 1917 Wagner-Jauregg published the first results of his research on the treatment of general paresis with malaria therapy. Von Economo gave the first description of epidemic encephalitis and its lesions. The mobilization of the American Army made it possible for the first time simultaneously to apply psychological tests to about two million individuals, and from then on psychological testing became a common procedure.

During the war years the great systems of dynamic psychiatry were reformulated by their authors. Janet was absorbed by the elaboration of his new psychology of tendencies. In 1916 Freud published his *Introductory Lectures to Psychoanalysis*, which was the first systematic survey of his theories. At the same time he gave a new development to psychoanalysis with his papers on metapsychology. It was thought that the increasing importance ascribed by Freud to aggressive drives was due to the war events. Alfred Adler, who like everyone else had at first shown ardent patriotism, gradually came to view the war with horror and to consider community feeling a basic component of human nature. For Jung the war years were the period of his creative neurosis; he published almost nothing during this time, but kept a group of disciples around him.

Of the four great dynamic systems, the only one that made tangible progress during the war was psychoanalysis. In 1918 a psychoanalytic publishing house (the Verlag) was founded in Vienna thanks to the generous gift of Anton von Freund, a wealthy Hungarian, who had been a patient of Freud. This was the powerful instrument by which the propagation of the movement was assured. In England psychoanalysis became increasingly popular, mainly through the work of Rivers. In America, Frink published his once famous book on morbid fears and compulsions.[310] Original contributions developed on the fringes of psychoanalysis, such as Silberer's writings on the symbolism of rebirth.[311] Hans Blüher contended that what held young men's associations together was a more or less unconscious homosexual bond; this was an early application of psychoanalysis to mass psychology.[312]

Circumstances compelled many men to think about the causes and the meaning of war. When Freud published his *Thoughts for the Times of War and Death* in 1915, he was following a current in which many distinguished thinkers were engaged. A leading German cardiologist, G. F. Nicolai, who was imprisoned for his pacifist ideas, wrote his *Biology of War*.[313] Others such as Arthur Schnitzler in Vienna, or the philosopher Alain in France, took notes that were to be later assembled in book form.

During the war, Zurich, the largest city of neutral Switzerland, kept its cosmopolitan character.[314] A group of young artists, poets, and musicians, who gathered around the Rumanian Tristan Tzara, in 1916 opened the "Cabaret Voltaire" in one of the oldest and narrowest streets of Zurich, the Spiegelgasse (the same street, incidentally, where Lenin lived). There these young people, who called themselves the Dadaists, recited poems of calculated absurdity, and expressed in all possible ways their contempt for the establishment, which had been unable to prevent the mass slaughter. Several of these men had escaped their military obligations in their respective countries.[315] A few Dadaists, such as Hans Arp, Hugo Ball, and Marcel Janco, were to become well known later as writers or artists. Friedrich Glauser became the foremost Swiss author of detective stories, and another Dadaist, Richard Hülsenbeck, was to end his career as a psychoanalyst in New York.

In Vienna the war events gave rise to divergent trends of thought. The initial enthusiasm had been rapidly reduced by the first defeats. The Serbian Army, well trained as a result of the Balkan Wars, proved tougher than expected. The Russian invasion of Galicia caused crowds of refugees, comprising many Jews of the poorer classes, to pour into Vienna. Italy and later Rumania declared war on Austria. Skillful propaganda provoked mass desertions among the Czechs and other less loyal minorities. Food and fuel were becoming scarce, while the cost of living was steadily rising. Emperor Francis Joseph's death was felt by many to be the death of the Empire. During the last months of the war opposition to the hostilities was voiced openly. A young physician who actively participated in the literary life, Jakob Moreno Levy, launched a new journal, *Daimon*, whose first issue opened on a lyrical manifesto: "Invitation to an Encounter," a disguised plea for peace that later was considered as a milestone in existentialist literature.[316] The entire hopes of the population were centered on President Wilson, who on January 8, 1918, had proclaimed his Fourteen Points for world peace. But the defeat and the dislocation of the centuries-old Hapsburg Empire were experienced by most Austrians as an unsurmountable catastrophe. This has been well expressed by Ernst Lothar in his Memoirs:

> The day of Austria-Hungary's ruin struck me and countless others in the heart. We knew with wounding clarity that something irreplaceable was dead, the like of which would never return. . . . The Empire was reduced to one-eighth of its size. In it there had been room for a little universe: The sea and the steppes, the glaciers and the wheat fields, the South, the West and the East, the Germanic, the Roman and the manifold Slav, the Magyar and even the Turk—the United States of Europe had existed here for generations when nowhere else it had been possible to bring them to live together. And this hundredfold Empire, with its languages, cultures, and temperaments, that brilliant mixture of contrasting color, it existed only here. . . .[317]

Lothar, who was acquainted with Freud, felt the need to consult him in his distress and according to his account asked Freud how one could exist without the country one has lived for. Freud, who knew that Lothar had lost his mother five months earlier, told him:

> I have been moved to hear of your mother's death, but you yourself continue to live. The mother is one's homeland. That one survives her is a biological fact, because the mother dies before her children. . . . The time always comes when an adult becomes an orphan. "The country exists no longer" you say. Perhaps the country you mean has never existed and you and I have been deceiving ourselves. The need for self-deceit is also a biological fact. It can happen that you notice at a certain point that a person who is close to you is not what you believed him to be. . . .

Lothar insisted that Austria was the only land where he could live, to which Freud replied:

> In how many countries have you lived as yet? . . . Like you, I come from Moravia, and, like you, I have an indomitable affection for Vienna and Austria, though perhaps, unlike you, I am acquainted with its seamy side.[318]

Thereupon Freud took a piece of paper upon which he had written:

Austria-Hungary is no more. I could not live anywhere else. Emigration is out of the question for me. I will continue to live with the trunk and imagine that it is the whole.

Freud concluded that it was a country that could make one die of rage, but where one would gladly end one's days.

In Vienna, in the midst of the disaster, there were also a few men who tried to make the best of a disastrous situation; their immediate concern was to save the youth and devise new methods for the education of the people.

Between the Two World Wars: November 1918–September 1939

The war had left France and England ruined and exhausted by their Pyrrhic victory, Russia the prey of revolution and civil war, and central Europe afflicted by famine and despair. Millions of men had fought with the conviction, instilled by an astute propaganda, that they were fighting the last war, a war that allegedly was being waged to insure peace and democracy forever. But those politicians who had been unable to prevent the war or to stop it when it had started showed themselves also incapable of securing a lasting peace, so that twenty years after the end of World War I, World War II broke out. The interval between wars was marked by countless vicissitudes that also put their stamp on the evolution of dynamic psychiatry.

The Year of the Failed Peace: 1919

The world was anxiously awaiting the promised peace that would bring a new order under the aegis of the League of Nations. But the peace treaties were drawn up in a manner that differed radically from the tradition of the Western world. The Congress of Vienna, where a lasting peace had been signed in 1815 after the Napoleonic Wars, had given defeated France equal status during the negotiations. The treaties of 1919 did not admit the defeated powers to the negotiations; moreover, Germany was forced to plead guilty, a demand that was unheard of in the history of diplomacy. No wonder that the peoples of central Europe who had placed their trust in President Wilson were infuriated, and if Freud kept an inveterate dislike of President Wilson, he was merely sharing a feeling that was widely held in Austria and central Europe.

The Treaty of Versailles, signed on June 28, 1919, returned Alsace-Lorraine to France and Polish Silesia to the resurrected state of Poland. After the disgraceful flight of the Kaiser to Holland, and a short-lived attempt at a Communist revolution, the democratic government of Weimar was established on unsure ground. Germany was no longer a world power, she had lost her navy, her colonies in Africa and the Pacific, and her establishments in China. German landowners in the Baltic countries were expropriated, German immigrants in the United States accelerated their Americanization, and German, until now the world's great cultural language, was replaced by English. Under the strain of material and spiritual misery, many Germans rebelled against the situation and accepted the legend that the defeat was due to the "stabbing in the back" (*Dolchstoss*) of the socialists, and started to think of revenge.

The population that had formed the Austrian-Hungarian Empire was now divided into three groups. Those of the first group were attributed to the so-called successor states that sided with the victors: Yugoslavia, Rumania, Poland, and Czechoslovakia. In the second group was Austria, deprived of the German-speaking peoples of Sudetenland that were given to Czechoslovakia, and of southern Tyrol that went to Italy; and Hungary, deprived of one-third of its Hungarian-speaking population. In the third group were the Slovenians, the Slovaks, and the Ruthenians that went to the successor states. The treaties that had given Alsace-Lorraine back to France had now created a dozen of new Alsace-Lorraines in central Europe and engendered undying hatreds. "The makers of the Peace Treaty had failed to realize that the breaking-up of the Hapsburg Empire had released races whose rivalries were a thousand years old, and who had been held together only by the traditions of the Monarchy."[319] Austria now found itself a country of six and one-half million inhabitants with a hypertrophic capital of two and one-half million. It was a period of acute distress in Austria. There was no food, no fuel, no transportation, and there was plundering, rioting, the black market, and moral dissolution everywhere.

In Russia the new Soviet government showed itself stronger than the Allies had expected, and Europe began to tremble before the specter of Bolshevism. Until then, Nihilism had been to most a rather abstract concept, or a thing that concerned only the Russians, but now it suddenly appeared as a terrible threat to the world.[320]

The Turkish Empire was also dismembered, particularly with the founding of the new Arabic States. The Armenians had been promised an independent state, but it was found that there were no Armenians left after the massacres. The Jews had been promised the founding of a "national home" in Palestine by the Balfour Declaration of November 2, 1917, but this promise was carried out half-heartedly by the British Mandate in Palestine.

The general mood was dominated by the impact of the war and the large-scale destruction. War novels began to appear by the dozens, and works were written on the decay of Europe, Western civilization, the White Race, and mankind as a whole. Oswald Spengler's *Decline of the West* enjoyed prodigious success in German.

Like Nietzsche, Spengler sees man as a beast of prey, though a creative predator, who has invented science, technology, and art in order to sever himself from Nature and become similar to God. According to Spengler, great cultures are biological forms of life that are born, grow, decay, and die, following an ineluctable pattern. There have been eight such cultures, and the eighth or the present one, namely Western culture, is already dying, soon to be replaced by the cultures of colored races. The only thing left to Western man is to die an honorable death at his last post.[321]

Spengler was criticized by biologists as well as historians for the numerous errors contained in his works. Some compared him to Freud because of his cultural pessimism and the importance he gave to the aggressive drives. The comparison is somewhat faulty because, in contrast to Spengler, Freud believed that libidinal drives neutralize aggressive drives to a certain extent.

The catastrophic mood of the period is reflected in the drama by Karl Kraus: *The Last Days of Mankind*.[322] Like Spengler's book, it had been written during the war years though it appeared later. It is a vast, apocalyptic vision picturing not only the end of Austria, but the destruction of human values, the defeat of mankind, and the disintegration of our planet viewed as a sin against cosmic harmony.

Several dynamic psychiatrists attempted to interpret contemporary events. As already seen, Alfred Adler published a pamphlet, *The Other Side*, in which he attempted to explain why the ordinary working man fought with such courage and endured so much misery for a cause that was not his own.[323] He concluded that, besides military pressure and deception through propaganda, his complete isolation had brought him to make the cause of his real enemy (namely his superiors) his own.

The psychoanalyst Paul Federn distinguished among the consequences of the Austrian revolution negative ones (such as strikes) and positive ones (such as the councils of workers).[324] He explained both in the light of Freud's concepts of the primeval horde and the rebellion of the sons. Old Emperor Francis Josef had been the father figure of the country. After his downfall, a fatherless society had appeared; some orphans rejected any kind of substitute, hence the strikes and revolts; others sought to create a new organization and a Society of Brothers.

In the midst of the disaster, heroic efforts were made to save the emotional health of the youth. Among these attempts were Aichhorn's celebrated experiment of therapeutic education in Oberhollabrunn, near Vienna. Unfortunately it is one of the least documented episodes in the history of education. It is not clear to what degree the experiment was imposed by current conditions and to what extent it was planned by Aichhorn. We have no contemporary account, no statistics, no follow-up; we do not even know how long it lasted. Aichhorn's collaborators remained anonymous, and the scarce data we have all come from Aichhorn's book published six years later. Aichhorn had been a public schoolteacher in Vienna. During the war he had been active in the organization of youth centers for boys where they were drilled in military fashion and instilled with patriotic feelings, as may be seen from the newsletter Aichhorn edited in connection with these activities.[325] When the Austrian-Hungarian Monarchy collapsed, Aichhorn was put in charge of a group of difficult boys. (According to Aichhorn's own account he had under his direct care a group of twelve delinquent or aggressive boys, mostly from broken homes.) They were lodged in old military barracks. At a time when Vienna was the prey of revolutionary agitation and riots, it is not surprising that these boys also revolted, demolishing the furniture, breaking in doors and windows, and beating one another. Aichhorn instructed his collaborators to interfere only when there was real danger. And, just as in Vienna itself, the revolutionary manifestations, though noisy, were becoming less dangerous, so the boys' aggressiveness was replaced by a kind of pseudoaggressiveness, followed by emotional outbursts. And then, just as there was a period of improvement throughout Austria in spite of prolonged instability, so these boys remained unstable for a long time and recovered only gradually. The findings of this experiment were later given a psychoanalytic interpretation.[326]

In spite of the extreme harshness of the times, the psychoanalytic movement was reorganized and contact reestablished with some foreign countries. Three American psychoanalysts went to Vienna for a training analysis with Freud.[327] Freud's disciples remained prolific writers. They published among others a collection of studies on war neuroses.[328]

In France, Janet was slowly constructing a new system of behavioral psychology, but he had a comparatively small audience. In 1919 he was able to publish his long-postponed book on mental healing,[329] but its belated appearance left the erroneous impression that his teachings had stagnated since the years before the war.

As for Jung, no one knew of his self-experiment and he was still working on his *Psychological Types*. Curiously enough, the first inkling of his new analytic psychology was given by the writer Hermann Hesse, in a novel, *Demian*.

Emil Sinclair has been brought up in a very religious setting. In his schooldays, he once boasted of being the author of some mischief committed by others, and this brought him to be bullied and blackmailed by a wicked comrade. He then meets an older boy, Max Demian, to whom he confides his secret, which results in the prompt liberation from an intolerable situation. A close friendship with Demian incites Sinclair to modify his vision of the world, to accept the existence and necessity of evil. But Sinclair goes too far and leads a dissolute student's life, until a brief encounter with a young lady, Beatrice, inspires him with a new ideal (though no words have been exchanged between them). Later he meets a learned and wise musician who teaches him how to interpret his dreams and spontaneous drawings. Both men agree on the notion that God is identical with the devil (or, rather, God and the devil are two aspects of one supreme Being, Abraxas). Still later, Sinclair meets Demian's mother, Eva, and recognizes in her the woman image he saw in a vision and painted. At this point, the World War breaks out. Demian appears to Sinclair and explains to him that from now on, when he will need help and counsel he will find it within his own deepest self.[330]

It is easy to recognize in the spiritual adventures of the hero the phases of Jungian therapy: confession of the pathogenic secret, assimilation of the shadow, confrontation with the anima, the old wise man, and the Self.[331]

The First Post War Period: 1920–1925

The Great War (as contemporaries called it) had caused about thirty million deaths, and countless other victims (not to mention those of famines and epidemics), but the greatest disaster resided in the "massacre of the elites," that is, of the vigorous young men between the ages of twenty and forty. The leaders of the postwar world belonged to the older generation that often was unable to understand and meet the new problems. The newer generation (that is, those who came of age just after the war) felt that they had nothing in common with their elders, were full of contempt for them, but showed themselves more able to protest than to act in a constructive way. The young as well as the old were faced with a general upheaval in all spheres of life. The supremacy of the white race, and particularly of Europe, was questioned. In Europe the French lived with the illusion that they had replaced Germany in her hegemony. The democratic liberal form of government was on the decline and a new type of state appeared, based on the absolute power of one party reinforced by the power of political police. Torture, which had disappeared during the nineteenth century, made a comeback and became a permanent institution in an increasing number of states.[332] Revolutionary and counterrevolutionary movements were threatening everywhere, and desperate attempts were made to find new solutions. At least there was a certain progress in regard to social legislation, such as a reduction in the number of working hours.

Most striking to contemporaries was perhaps the transformation in the mores, which some saw as a disastrous dissolution of values, and others as a welcome simplification of the style of life.[333] These changes were manifested in the manner of dress, speech, in letter writing, in social relationships, and even in the gestures and tone of voice. Education became less strict. Distances between social classes were reduced, and people from different backgrounds began to mix more freely. Relationships between the sexes became less formal. Young women were permitted to go out without a chaperone even at night, marriages of reason were in disfavor, "romantic" love was accepted as the norm, marriages were often concluded after a short courtship, the incidence of divorce grew, and divorced women no longer suffered social reprobation. Sports and traveling became popular, especially with the growth of the automobile industry. The theater was gradually displaced by the cinema, which reached a much larger audience, to which it brought the new ideal figures of the movie stars. Jazz music became immensely popular not only in America but also in Europe. The world was seized by a feverish desire for money and pleasure, thousands speculated at the Stock Exchange, and works of art and special book editions were used as objects for speculation. In Europe it was fashionable to imitate everything Anglo-Saxon. Whereas before the war the drinking of alcohol had been considered a vice of the working classes, it now became an elegant habit of the upper classes.[334]

There was a general iconoclastic trend and a search for new forms of expression. It was the heyday of expressionism and cubism, and the cinema was proclaimed the seventh art. The young literary generation was filled with sarcasm and contempt for the old masters. When Anatole France died in 1924, a group of young writers composed and diffused a vehement diatribe with the title: *Un Cadavre* (a corpse).[335] The new generation searched in the past for precursors and prophets of the new spirit of the times. Thus in France, the poet Lautréamont, who had died young and whose writings had been considered tainted with mental illness, was proclaimed the greatest French poet of the nineteenth century. The Marquis de Sade was hailed as a mighty genius, a profound philosopher and writer, and the true founder of sexual pathology.

Those features of the postwar period such as the contempt for the older generation, anti-intellectualism, and the affectation never to be shocked by anything favored the success of a movement that played a great part in the cultural life of the time, especially in France—the surrealist movement.[336] Surrealism has often been seen as a hoax invented by artists and encouraged by intellectual snobbery. However, there was more to it, and it satisfied an intellectual need of the time. It all began when Tristan Tzara and a few other Dadaists left Zurich and came to Paris to continue their activities. They were joined by others, but soon broke up into different groups. One of these took the name of Surrealists and gathered around André Breton, Philippe Soupault, Paul Eluard, and Louis Aragon. The history of their movement is a rather stormy one with the members constantly fighting among themselves. However, André Breton succeeded in maintaining himself as the leader of the movement for two decades and showed himself as the most creative.

The Surrealists had kept the negative attitude and the rejection of accepted values of Dadaism: family, country, religion, work, and even honor. Many of them joined, at least temporarily, the Communist party. However, their great concern was the exploration of the hidden realms of the mind, which the Romantics had called the night side of Nature, that is, the unconscious, dreams, mental illness, the fantastic, and the wonderful.

As a medical student, André Breton was mobilized to work in a military psychiatric unit. Among his patients there was a man who had stood on a trench embankment during battle and, like a policeman directing traffic, had "directed" the flight of the shells around him. The man was convinced that it was a simulated war, with fake weapons, and faked wounded and dead; a proof was that he had always escaped injury. Breton was impressed to see how a young and well-bred person, who appeared lucid, could live in a fantastic world to such a degree. Breton became interested in the work of Myers, Flournoy, Janet, and Freud, but after the war he gave up his medical studies, joined the Dadaists, and later founded his own literary movement. His aim was the rejuvenation of poetry and art by resorting to untapped sources of creativity. His first interest was in the intermediary state between dreaming and waking, in other words that hypnagogic state where scattered words and images occur to the mind. Once he heard the words: "There is a man cut in two by the window," and he saw the corresponding image. Breton seems to have been unaware that this type of dream had been thoroughly investigated by Herbert Silberer, who had shown that the hypnagogic image was a symbolic representation of the state of the dreamer who was halfway between the states of waking and dreaming. [337] Breton's attention was drawn to these mysterious sentences in which he saw the very essence of poetry. He distinguished this verbal automatism from the visual imagery, stating that though they can be mixed at times, they are two distinct sets of phenomena. However, verbal automatism was of more value to the poet than to others.

Breton then noted that there is in man, not only in the hypnagogic state but permanently, an "inner discourse" (*discours intérieur*), which can be perceived at any moment if sufficient attention is paid. This inner voice is quite different from what poets such as James Joyce called the interior monologue, which is rather an imitation of ordinary speech. Breton's inner discourse is intermittent and appears in short sentences and groups of words that are disconnected from one another. Moreover, there can be several simultaneous verbal streams, each carrying a flow of images that vie for supremacy.

The problem now was how to tap this inner discourse for creative purposes. For some time Breton working with Desnos tried automatic talking, that is to say whatever came to the mind at random (a method that, incidentally, had been used by Janet with his patients Madame D.). [338] But they soon found the method to be dangerous, and Breton resorted to automatic writing. That method, as used by the Surrealists, was different from the kind used by the spiritists, namely, a purely motor automatism, the subject being unconscious of the content of what he is putting on paper. As it was used by the Surrealists, automatic writing was an interior dictation (*dictée intérieure*), that is, the poet had to place himself in an oneiric climate so as to be able to listen to his inner discourse, which he recorded without changing a word. According to Breton, clear consciousness and visual images impeded interior dictation. For this, training is necessary and there is no guarantee that it will produce masterpieces. Actually, only a few among the literary works of the Surrealists originated from automatic writing.[339]

Breton came to the conclusion that there is a mysterious realm in the human mind, a kind of central point that links the conscious individual with his innermost self, and at the same time with unknown forces in the universe. The aim of Surrealism is to reconquer that central point so that the individual might recover the totality of his psychic energy and the unknown riches within him. From this center emanate all forms of artistic creativity: poetry, paintings, and sculpting, as well as new forms of art.

During the first two years the Surrealists made liberal use of automatic writing and hypnosis, but they soon became aware of the dangers of these practices. Breton tells of how an immoderate use of automatic writing sent him into hallucinatory states.[340] One of his associates, Desnos, fell more and more easily into deep somnambulic states in which he became agitated and dangerous to the point that once he pursued the poet Eluard with a knife in order to kill him. Another evening, at a Surrealist party, ten out of about thirty people fell into hypnotic somnambulism, and several of these were discovered attempting to hang themselves in a dark antechamber (one of them actually committed suicide later). This caused a temporary halt in the activities of the movement, which was reorganized by Breton in 1924.

Gradually the field of interest of Surrealism extended to painting, sculpture, photography, and the cinema, and it claimed to enrich mankind with a new form of esthetics. Surrealists looked for ancestry and allies, and listed Freud, Sade, and Lautréamont among their father figures. (They omitted in their long list of precursors the only direct ones, namely, the Futurists.) Surrealists were interested in all the manifestations of the marvelous, the fantastic, the uncanny, and unexplainable coincidences; Breton suspected that strange invisible beings played a role in human life. They were attentive to those ironies that suddenly betray the tragic character of life (this is what they called black humor or *humour noir*). Another of their great concerns was the *hasard objectif*, or those strange coincidences that seem to have been combined with ironic intent.

Surrealists furthered and invented new forms of art, and organized exhibitions of Surrealistic objects: including very precise and ingenious machines without any practical use; things that had been seen in dreams or resulting from the combination of creative inspiration, chance, and automatism.[341] Among the many other devices of the Surrealists we must mention their conscious imitation of mental illness, at least in writing. Breton and Eluard once published a series of five essays in which they imitated the verbal manifestations of feeble-mindedness, acute mania, general paresis, delusions of interpretation, and "dementia praecox."[342]

The Surrealist movement is related to the history of dynamic psychiatry in several ways. It is clear that its leader, André Breton, took a great deal from the first dynamic psychiatry, even though his technique of automatic writing had nothing in common with that of the spiritists, William James, or Janet. Nor was his dictation from the unconscious identical with Freud's method of free association. Had Breton taken his medical degree and remained active in psychiatry, he could very well, with these new methods, have become the founder of a new trend of dynamic psychiatry. This also explains his admiration for Freud and interest in psychoanalysis. He visited Freud in Vienna and exchanged a few letters with him.[343] At least two of Freud's papers appeared in French translation for the first time in Surrealist journals.[344] Freud, though, seemed to be puzzled and embarrassed by the interest showed in him by these men whose ideas and writings he failed to understand.[345] As might be expected, Surrealism also became an object of study for psychiatrists. Henry Ey contends that both psychopathological art and surrealistic art originate from the same unconscious creative source; however, the Surrealist goes consciously to this source and channels its inspiration, whereas the mental patient is overwhelmed by it.[346] In other words, as Ey concludes, the Surrealist "*makes* the marvellous," whereas the psychotic artist "*is* marvellous."

In 1920, when western Europe and America were on the way to renewed prosperity, Germany, and particularly Austria, was still in economic and financial distress. Worst of all was the deprecatory attitude of the Austrians toward their own country and their traditional culture. They had nothing but sarcasm and contempt for the days of the Dual Monarchy.

In socialist circles there had been fierce attacks against those military surgeons who had made use of electric stimulation in the treatment of war neuroses. The Austrian Parliament appointed a commission of inquiry under the chairmanship of Professor Löffler, an outstanding lawyer. Complaints were received from a number of former military patients, against half a dozen neuropsychiatrists, including Wagner-Jauregg.[347] The hearings took place from October 15 to 17, 1920, in the presence of many neuropsychiatrists and journalists.[348] The commission appointed Sigmund Freud and Emil Raimann to give an expert report on the electric treatment of war neurotics.

Wagner-Jauregg declared that Lieutenant Kauders (his main accuser) had been a simulator, and it had been no pleasure for him to make such a diagnosis. Wagner-Jauregg mentioned that he volunteered to serve as a neuropsychiatrist for the entire duration of the war, having neither uniform, nor military rank, nor salary, nor official recognition. He had examined and treated many thousands of soldiers and officers afflicted with all kinds of war neuroses. Only a fraction of these neuroses had originated at the battle line. None were observed among prisoners of war. Most cases were contracted at the rear and often in the fashion of epidemics, mostly among certain ethnic groups. "Among the Czechs the courageous ones held up their hands and surrendered to the enemy, although they knew that they would have to fight for the enemy; the less courageous took flight into illness. When the collapse came, a great number of neurotics ran away from the hospital. They had suddenly acquired the capacity to move." Many Czechs openly admitted that they had simulated, and there had even been schools for simulators. Wagner-Jauregg added that he first treated war neurotics with isolation and milk diet, and then he applied faradic treatment, "a treatment of hysterical conditions that had been known for a long time," with brilliant results, often after only one session.

Freud was next called to read his report.[349] He took exception with Wagner-Jauregg for having seen too much simulation, and pointed out that the term "flight into illness" had been introduced by him and accepted by medical science.[350] The number of simulators must have been slight. (Here Wagner-Jauregg interrupted: "What about the confessions!"). The role of the physicians should not be that of machine guns directed against runaway soldiers; they should be the defenders of the patients, and not of anyone else. The patient Kauders had been wounded (Wagner-Jauregg exclaimed: "No!"), and Wagner-Jauregg has wronged him by calling him a malingerer. "I therefore believe that the causes partly reside in Court Counselor Wagner. This is because he did not make use of my therapy. I do not demand of him that he be able to do so, I cannot ask it of him when even my pupils cannot do it." Freud added that in Germany psychoanalytic treatment had extraordinary success with Dr. Schnee and Dr. Siegel.

Wagner-Jauregg replied: "In regard to simulation, I can perhaps say without immodesty that I am somewhat more competent. No simulators come to Professor Freud for treatment, whereas I in my profession have many opportunities to treat simulators. Moreover, I have had a rich experience during the war, that Professor Freud has lacked." Wagner-Jauregg added that psychoanalysis could not be used during the war, and Freud himself admitted the language obstacle.[351] However, Freud said, "Psychoanalysis can be conducted also in war." Wagner-Jauregg replied, "But only in isolated cases." Freud then stated, "In masses, but shortened by hypnosis. It has given much trouble, but in particularly difficult cases it would have been rewarding."

On the following day, October 16, the other expert, Raimann, read his report, which—as might have been expected from a faithful disciple of Wagner-Jauregg—was entirely in his favor. Freud was also sharply criticized by Fuchs. Freud replied that Wagner-Jauregg's opinion "proves that he is a poor psychologist and is inclined to see malingerers everywhere" . . . "If these patients had also been examined psychoanalytically there would have been no such complaints."

Raimann then took exception with what Freud had said (namely: "I would have done it differently"): "Why in the subjunctive? Why did he not do it otherwise and show how one cures war neuroses psychoanalytically? He would have immediately been allotted a ward. . . . He has never seen war neuroses, and it requires some courage to give an expert report on these matters without knowing anything about them." Raimann added that at the Psychoanalytic Congress in 1918 two of Freud's closest pupils had admitted that psychoanalysis could not be applied in these cases, not to mention the question of money. Destitute patients cannot be analyzed. . . . "When someone cannot pay he thereby admits to be healthy."

Otto Pötzl sided with Freud and declared that from the theoretical point of view he was definitely an adherent of psychoanalysis, although he was of another opinion in regard to its practical application.

Fuchs testified that he had studied and applied psychoanalysis, but that he had never had the least results with that method. He had referred war neurotics to psychoanalysts and all of them had been sent back to him without being cured. "When Professor Freud says that his pupils were not equal to the task, why did he not go down into the arena himself?" he concluded sarcastically.

It is obvious that what had begun as a commission of inquiry soon took the character of a verbal joust between the partisans and the adversaries of psychoanalysis, with the latter having the upper hand. The commission concluded that there were no grounds for a trial. In the midst of the general contemporary turmoil the incident was soon forgotten. Later, when Freud's expert report was published, psychoanalysts had the impression that he had been extremely fair to Wagner-Jauregg, who, however, thought quite otherwise.[352] In his autobiography he claimed that the inquiry gave Freud an unexpected occasion to express his anger against him.[353]

Such polemics, however, did not impede the growth of the psychoanalytic movement. It was becoming fashionable for Englishmen and Americans to go to Vienna for didactic or therapeutic analysis. In Berlin the first Psychoanalytic Policlinic was opened by Max Eitingon. Freud was in a new creative phase and he published his essay *Beyond the Pleasure Principle.*

The year 1921 showed once more how difficult it was for Europe to recover from the effects of the war. Germany was requested by the commission of reparations to pay 132 billion gold marks, resulting in insolvable economic and financial problems. The Irish Rebellion forced Great Britain to allow the founding of the Republic of Ireland (Eire). Italy became prey to leftist subversive movements, while Mussolini was building up his Fascist movement. In Russia the Bolshevik government had great difficulties in organizing a purely Communist economy, so that Lenin decreed a "New Economic Policy" (N.E.P.) with a partial return to traditional methods. Austria was desperately struggling with a seemingly hopeless situation, to the point that separatist movements arose in certain provinces.

In psychiatry some of the masters of the former generation were moving toward other interests. Eugen Bleuler published his *Natural History of the*

Soul[354] which he had worked on for many years and which some people called his *Second Faust*.[355] To many it was a surprise to see the positivist scientist adopt some of the speculative concepts of Driesch and describe the development of consciousness out of the psychoid, a hypothetical, elementary form of psychic activity (Somewhat reminiscent of the organic unconscious of the German Romantics.) Forel, who besides his neuropsychiatric vocation, had been a passionate fighter for social reform all his life, and was also considered a world authority on the classification of ants, now published a vast work depicting the allegedly perfect social order of the ants, which he proposed as a model for mankind.[356]

In the academic year of 1920 to 1921 Janet gave a course on the psychology of religion that attracted enthusiastic listeners, including the American clergyman, Reverend Horton, who published his notes upon his return to the United States.[357] But Janet was consistently ignored by the new generation, who in France and elsewhere was beginning to turn toward Vienna.

One psychiatric event of that year was the reentry of Jung, with the publication of his *Psychological Types*. This book was the fruit of years of silent work pursued during the war and (as we know today) of Jung's self-experiment. It explained the basic principles of his system, which he was to develop for the next two or three decades. At the same time, this book treated a topic that happened to be of great interest among the younger psychiatric generation, namely, the study of psychological types and their correlations with various kinds of mental illness.

Characteristically, three psychiatrists, Jung, Kretschmer, and Rorschach, published, almost simultaneously, descriptions of systems centered around the distinction of two types. Jung's typology has been described in the preceding chapter.[358] For Kretschmer, manic-depressive illness and schizophrenia are the extreme degrees of two attitudes that he called cyclothymia and schizothymia.[359] Cyclothymic individuals are syntonic, which means that their whole personality vibrates in tune with their environment, whereas the schizothymic individuals are schizoid, that is, there is a kind of discordance in their reactions to their environment. Kretschmer also made a correlation between cyclothymia and individuals of the pyknic type, schizophrenia and individuals of the asthenic types; in other words, there is a correlation between psychological type, predisposition to mental illness, and constitutional biotype.

Hermann Rorschach, a young Swiss psychiatrist who had followed the development of Jung's typology with keen interest, integrated the notions of introversion and extratension into the framework of a psychological theory linked with the invention of a new and original projective test.[360] A man of artistic gifts and multifaceted interests. Rorschach had been Bleuler's pupil (although he never was on the Burghölzli staff) and published studies on the psychopathology of Swiss sects and various psychoanalytic topics.[361] He had tested schoolchildren with inkblots and compared the findings with those of the word association test. He was preoccupied with the problem of the translation of sensory images from one field of perception to another; for instance, visual into kinesthetic perceptions. Mourly Vold had shown that the inhibition of movements stimulates the appearance of kinesthetic dreams. This observation brought Rorschach to conceive introversion as the turning toward an inner world of kinesthetic images and creative activity. Conversely, extratension was the turning toward a world of color, emotions, and adjustment to reality. Rorschach combined these two functions into the more inclusive concept of *Erlebnistȳpus* (that is, the extent of introversion, extratension, and their proportion to each other). Further, he conceived *Erlebnistypus* as being the inmost, intimate capacity of resonance to life experiences, and at the same time a continuous elaboration of these new life experiences. In the same individual, *Erlebnistypus* is subject to daily fluctuations, but also to a slow, continuous autonomous process of evolution. The knowledge of *Erlebnistypus* could be investigated with the inkblot test. As compared to similar former tests (notably that of Hens), the main diagnostic element was not the content of the answers but the formal elements: number and proportion of whole and detail answers, of kinetic and color answers, and so on. Rorschach's book on his "Psychodiagnostic" was published in spite of difficult circumstances in the middle of 1921 and found acceptance among a small group of friends and colleagues.[362]

Freud's main achievement of that year was his *Group Psychology and Ego Analysis*.[363] The sixty-five-year-old Freud was now analyzing full-time, and in this one year he had no less than four new American analysands, among whom were Abraham Kardiner and Clarence Oberndorf.[364] The psychoanalytic atmosphere in Vienna was rather stormy at that time. In view of the ever increasing flow of foreigners coming to Vienna for analysis, there was a shortage of serious analysts and the situation was favorable for incompetent and insufficiently trained persons. There were rumors about rich Americans going to Vienna only to fall into the hands of dangerous quacks who charged high fees and just made matters worse.[365] The Psychoanalytic Publishing House (the *Verlag*) also had its good and bad periods. When it published a "psychoanalytic novel" by Groddeck, sharp criticisms were unleashed; some analysts found it in bad taste, pornographic, and unworthy of a scientific publishing house.[366]

Another work published by the Verlag in 1918 and reedited at that time unleashed a vivacious controversy. It was a diary written by an anonymous adolescent girl between her eleventh and her fourteenth year, and presented by Hermine von Hug-Helmuth with a foreword by Freud.[367] This work was said to be a hoax. To be sure, Cyril Burt[368] in England had pointed out the improbability that such a document could be the verbatim diary of an adolescent without additions, omissions, or other changes.[369]

In Russia the movement that had come to a standstill during the war and the revolution, was reorganized; a flourishing group was found in Moscow, and interest in psychoanalysis was awakening even in the Balkan countries. Thus a Bulgarian, Ivan Kinkel, published a psychoanalytic study of the foundations of religion.[370]

There was still much turmoil in the Western world in 1922, with conflicts between the Germans and the Allies, and between the Allies themselves. In Asia Minor the Greeks were defeated by the Turks. But there were definite signs of economic recovery. In Austria, Prelate Seippel became Prime Minister and gradually extricated the country from an apparently hopeless situation.

New trends were manifested in psychiatry. Wagner-Jauregg's treatment of general paresis by malaria became generally known and applied. It is difficult to realize today what a sensation this discovery aroused: general paresis was the archetype of the incurable and fatal mental illness, and physiological method was introduced in psychiatry: Klaesi, in Switzerland, worked out a new kind of prolonged sleep therapy using Somnifain, which was more effective than Otto Wolff's Trional cure.[371] Psychiatrists gradually came to admit that severe mental illness could be treated by physiological methods.

Psychoanalysis was emerging more and more as the major psychotherapeutic school. Hypnosis, suggestion, and the teachings of the first dynamic psychiatry were again considered obsolete, as they had been between 1860 and 1880. There was, however, a so-called Second Nancy School. A pharmacist of that town, Emile Coué, had devised a method of treatment of nervous disturbances by means of a training of the subconscious.[372] Patients came to him from many countries and he treated them in groups and free of charge.[373]

The first sign of a new and quite different approach was given when Ludwig Binswanger read a paper "On Phenomenology" at the Swiss Society for Neurology and Psychiatry.[374] A psychiatrist with a philosophical background, who was a disciple of Bleuler and was influenced by Freud, Binswanger pointed out the interest of Husserl's phenomenology as a method that could be applied to clinical psychiatry. This contribution did not attract much attention at the moment, but when Rorschach gave his last communication to the Swiss Psychoanalytic Society on February 18, 1922, it was clear that he was developing his method of test interpretation in the direction of phenomenology. Soon afterward, however, Rorschach died on April 2, 1922, at the age of thirty-seven, and his loss was tragically felt by his colleagues.

The year 1923 brought a sharpening of conflicts in Western Europe. Because of Germany's failure to pay the reparations, the French occupied the rich industrial centers of the Ruhr. This caused much political agitation in Germany and conflicts between France and England. Dictatorial governments seized power in a growing number of countries. Shortly after the establishment of Mussolini's Fascist dictatorship in Italy, Primo de Rivera seized power in Spain.

Psychology was developing rapidly and invading all fields of life in what came to be called the psychological revolution. This was particularly evident in Switzerland. In Geneva the pupils of Théodore Flournoy and Claparède were developing child psychology and the science of education. Jean Piaget published his *Language and Thought in the Child,* the first of a long series of monographs that were to renew our knowledge of child psychology and development.[375] In Zurich, a group of engineers gathered around Alfred Carrard and founded the "Institute for Applied Psychology" (*Institut für angewandte Psychologie*), making practical use of recent developments of psychology in the fields of vocational guidance, industrial psychology, and counseling. Particular emphasis was given to psychological testing and graphology.

The first paper on clinical phenomenology appeared in that year. Eugène Minkowski related the story of a depressed schizophrenic who announced daily that he would be executed in the evening.[376] But when Minkowski pointed out to him that although he had made this statement so many times it had never come about, the patient simply dismissed the argument and contended that he would be executed that same evening. Minkowski concluded that this patient experienced time in a quite different manner from normal people. The usual assumption would have been that the perception of time was distorted because of the delusions, but Minkowski advanced the idea that it was the reverse:

Isn't the disorder pertaining to the future a natural consequence of the delusional belief that execution is imminent? . . . Could we not, on the contrary, suppose the more basic disorder is the distorted attitude toward the future, whereas the delusion is only one of its manifestations?

This paper of Minkowski's was to mark the beginning of a new trend in psychiatric phenomenology. In that same year, Buber published a little book, *I and Thou,* that was to become one of the classics of existentialism.[377] Buber emphasized the difference between relations to a thing that I observe and to a person who addresses me and to whose address I respond. But though my relation to a person may be of "I and Thou," it often becomes a relation of "I and It."

The psychoanalytic movement was in full expansion, and at the same time was undergoing new changes. Its publishing house issued Freud's treatise, *The Ego and the Id,* in which he explained his new theory of the three "agencies" of human personality: the ego, the id, and the superego.[378]

The term *das Es* (the Id) has been borrowed by Freud from Groddeck, whose *Book of the Id* had just appeared and attracted attention.[379] It was a collection of letters allegedly written by a certain Patrick Troll to a woman, concerning the influence of the unconscious on our conscious life and the organism. Groddeck's description of the id reflected, to an extreme degree, the old Romantic concept of an irrational unconscious. He conceived of the id as impersonal and full of aggressive and murderous impulses, and believed each drive had its obverse. For instance, the young mother who loves her baby also unconsciously hates it. The pregnant woman's nausea, vomiting, and toothaches were symbolic manifestations of her wish to get rid of the child. A true epigone of Novalis, Carus, and Von Hartmann, Groddeck proclaimed that the id could shape physiological processes and cause illnesses.

Psychoanalysis was also spreading in Russia. In the foreword of the third volume of a new collection of translations from Freud, Ivan Ermakov acknowledged Freud's concept of child sexuality as one of the great psychological discoveries of our times, the knowledge of which was absolutely indispensable to every educator.[380]

In 1924 many observers felt that the Western world was well on its way to recovery in spite of the political turmoil in Germany. In Italy, after the murder of the socialist leader, Matteotti, the Fascists were strengthening their dictatorship. In Austria conditions were slowly returning to normal.

In dynamic psychiatry, psychoanalysis was definitely the dominant trend and was discussed everywhere in Western Europe, in the United States, and even in Russia. In Bulgaria, Ivan Kinkel wrote a psychoanalytic study of revolutionary movements (with particular emphasis on the French Revolution from 1789 to 1799).[381]

Much controversy developed around newer tendencies, and discussions were held as to whether they were deviant or not. At the very beginning of the year a joint book by Ferenczi and Rank pointed to new ways in psychoanalytic therapy and theory.[382] In the course of the same year, each one of them brought forth a separate contribution, both publications being remarkably bold.

Otto Rank's book *The Trauma of Birth* was nothing less than an attempt toward a reformulation of psychoanalytic theory and practice, based on the theory that every human being suffers at birth the greatest trauma of his life, tries vainly to overcome this trauma in all possible ways, and is unconsciously longing to return into his mother's womb.[383] The book was dedicated to Freud and purported to be a further development of psychoanalysis, based on Rank's analytic work with his patients. Freud had once expressed the opinion that the infant's anxiety during the process of birth was the prototype of all later anxiety. Rank developed the idea that not only anxiety, but the totality of the individual's psychic life can be related to the trauma of birth. In the dreams and fantasies of his patients, he said, the healing process was represented by birth symbols, transference proved to be a reenactment of the earliest fixation on the mother, and at the end of the analysis, the freeing from the analyst represented the separation from the mother at birth. A successful analysis was thus a related abreaction of the birth trauma. This theory entailed a new system of interpretation of dreams, a new code of universal symbols, a reformulation of the pleasure principle as the wish to return to the womb, and a new interpretation of normal and abnormal sexual life, neurosis, psychosis, and cultural life as a whole.

Rank's work came as a surprise to psychoanalysts. Freud himself seems to have been impressed by the theory but also greatly perplexed; he hesitated for several months, but finally rejected Rank's theory, and separated himself from him with regret. According to Edward Glover, some analysts rapidly discovered birth traumas in all their patients after the publication of Rank's book, but this ceased after Rank's theory was officially exploded.[384]

Ferenczi's theory was even bolder than that of Rank, but it aroused less controversy.[385] Intrauterine life, Ferenczi contended, is a reenactment of the existence of the earliest forms of life in the ocean. When an animal species emerged, ages ago, from the sea to pursue its evolution on dry land, it experienced a trauma of which the trauma of birth is but a repetition. Man is afflicted with the nostalgia, not just to return to his mother's womb (as Rank claimed), but to return to his primeval existence in the depths of the sea.[386]

In the year 1925 the Western world could have the impression that it had at last overcome the turmoil that had followed the Great War. In October the Locarno Pact, which aimed at the prevention of further aggression, was signed by the big powers and was considered "the end of the postwar period."

It was also a period of prosperity for psychiatry, psychology, and psychotherapy, particularly in the two cities of Zurich and Vienna which vied for the title, Capital of Psychology.

Zurich was not only the seat of the famed Burghölzli but also of the Institute for Applied Psychology, where practical psychologists were trained, and of Hans Hanselmann's Seminar for Therapeutic Education for the formation of specialized therapeutic teachers. Psychologists and psychotherapists abounded to such an extent in Zurich and its environment that its lake came to be known as the Lake of Psychology. Eugen Bleuler, the grand old man of Swiss psychiatry, was pursuing his interest in that elementary unconscious activity he called the psychoid.[387] His successor at the Burghölzli, Hans Maier, who in 1920 had founded the first Child Observation Center, had set the prototype of many similar instutions in Switzerland and elsewhere. Max Bircher-Benner, an outstanding dietitian and gifted psychotherapist, held discussion classes on problems of physical and mental health in his sanitarium. The Swiss Psychoanalytic Society had been revived in 1920 and its leading figure was Reverend Oskar Pfister, a pugnacious personality and prolific writer who published a flow of books and articles on the application of psychoanalysis to the education of normal and abnormal children, to the cure of souls (*Seelsorge*), and problems of art and philosophy. Jung, in Küsnacht, was enjoying increasing fame and gathered disciples around him in the *Psychologischer Club*. In 1925 he undertook his travels to Mount Elgon in Kenya. Not far from Zurich, in Kilchberg, by the lake shore, lived the German philosopher and psychologist Ludwig Klages, one of the founders of characterology and graphology.

The other city that claimed to be the capital of psychology was Vienna, of which an American visitor, Mrs. Stratton Parker, gave a lively description.[388] Freud, she said, was now an aging and sick man who limited his work to analyzing a few important persons and writing articles, and who was almost never to be seen even by his Viennese disciples. The headquarters of the Psychoanalytic Society in the Pelikangasse was a busy place with the sessions of the Psychoanalytic Society every Wednesday, and lectures on the other evenings. Mrs. Parker also speaks of the extraordinary activity displayed by Alfred Adler, his lectures before large audiences, mostly of the working classes, the clinics he held in the public schools devoted to the handling cases of difficult children, and his discussion evenings for teachers, institution workers, and doctors. There were also Dr. Schilder's lectures on psychiatry on Saturday evenings attended by hundreds of listeners, Dr. Lazar's clinics for difficult children, and the activity of the Stekel group.

The activity of the Freudian group in Vienna is shown by the fact that in the year 1925 two works appeared that are still considered as classics of psychoanalysis. One was Theodor Reik's *Compulsion to Confessing and Need for Punishment*.[389] A lawyer and lay analyst, Reik took up a problem that had puzzled criminologists such as Anselm Feuerbach and Hans Gross: Why do certain offenders give a confession unexpectedly when they could save their lives by keeping silent, and how is it that a criminal will forget an object on the site of his crime that will serve as evidence against him? As an explanation, Reik gave the need for punishment issued from the Oedipus complex. From the beginning the criminal drives were in conflict with the drives from the super-ego; once the criminal drives had been gratified by the crime, the need for punishment becomes relatively stronger and can manifest itself through unconscious self-betrayal (hence the object forgotten on the place of the crime), or the "unnecessary" confession. Reik emphasized the importance of the need for punishment and of the self-punitive drive in the life of the individual and in society. He concluded that many of the evils that afflict mankind could be understood in this light. Following the publication of Reik's book, the concept of self-punishment became one of the most popular of psychoanalysis.

The second classic of psychoanalysis that appeared in 1925 was Aichhorn's book, *Wayward Youth*, with a foreword by Freud.[390] It is not known why Aichhorn waited until that year to publish the story of the experiment in therapeutic education he had conducted in 1918–1919 in Oberhollabrunn.[391] In the meantime Aichhorn had undergone analytic training, and his book was less concerned with giving an account of his experiment than with providing a psychoanalytic interpretation.

In Soviet Russia, Freud's earlier works were reissued and new works were translated. A prominent Russian psychologist, Alexander Luria, published enthusiastic books and papers on psychoanalysis that he considered a "system of Monistic psychology," and "the fundamental materialistic basis for the construction of a truly Marxist psychology," including the fields of pedagogics and criminology ("the study of crime without psychoanalysis is but the headline of a chapter without content").[392] According to Morselli, psychoanalysis had become one of the great topics for discussion among intellectuals in Russia.[393]

In France, psychoanalysis met much opposition, and Freud's intervention in the case of Philippe Daudet was sharply criticized. The fourteen-year-old boy, the son of the writer and royalist leader, Léon Daudet, and grandson of Alphonse Daudet, had disappeared from home on November 20, 1923, and was found dead on November 23, from a ball shot in the skull. It was assumed that he had committed suicide, but a judicial investigation showed that the boy had been in close connection with an anarchist group. Léon Daudet was convinced that his son had been assassinated by the secret police, and conducted a violent press campaign against those whom he accused of having trapped and murdered his son.[394] Some time later the anarchist, André Gaucher, known for his vehement attacks against Léon Daudet, said that shortly before Philippe's mysterious death he had received a visit from an unknown adolescent who wanted to learn whether it was true that Léon Daudet was a pornographic writer, and that he, Gaucher, had shown him some significant excerpts from Léon Daudet's novels. Gaucher implied that this boy was Philippe Daudet, who, upset by the revelations about his father, could have committed suicide. Gaucher utilized the sensation caused by that story to launch a book against Léon Daudet, and tried to enroll Pierre Janet and Sigmund Freud in his campaign.[395] To Janet he sent, through an intermediary, an incomplete case history of Philippe Daudet, without giving any names, but he received only a short and evasive answer. To Freud he sent part of the manuscript of the book he was writing about Léon Daudet and received two letters. Freud said that he had met Léon Daudet several times in Paris in 1885 and 1886, but that he had never read anything of him. Alphonse Daudet had been syphilitic, Freud said, adding that he had found syphilis to be one of the main causes of predisposition to neurosis. Freud declared that "your Daudet would perhaps have been choked by his neurosis if he had not possessed a talent great enough to enable him to discharge his perversions into his literary production." Freud concluded that Philippe Daudet's case, as well as any other one, could be explained by psychoanalysis. Obviously Freud had been unaware that André Gaucher was a notorious anarchist who would hasten to utilize these two letters for his own questionable purposes. The German poet and journalist Tucholsky, reporting on that story, deplored that Sigmund Freud could have "given his papal blessing to that evil action."[396]

The Years of Failed Reconstruction: 1926–1929

The signing of the Locarno Pact in October 1925 had given millions of Europeans the impression that peace was now assured. Economic prosperity had returned in varying degrees in European countries, and had reached unprecedented heights in the United States. But the young people who had lived through the war were more disoriented than ever. There were, for instance, those Americans who lived as voluntary expatriates in Paris, the lost generation as described by Hemingway, or the Englishmen who appeared in Aldous Huxley's novels. In those countries where dictatorships were already established or just emerging, the same generation provided the leaders and the adherents for Fascist organizations. Emotional immaturity, irresponsibility, hopelessness, cynicism, and rebelliousness were the keynotes of this new malady, often as a cover for real but unavowed sufferings. The rejection of old moral standards and the all-pervading search for pleasure brought the French to call this period *les années folles* (the crazy years). They came to a close abruptly with the collapse of the New York Stock Exchange in October 1929.

To some contemporaries, the admission of Germany to the League of Nations in September 1926 appeared as a step toward the reconstruction of Europe, to others as a disquieting sign of her regaining lost power. Political observers noticed that democracy was losing ground, as when General Pilsudski seized power in Poland in May 1926. In France the leftist government, that had come to power in 1924 had brought the country to the brink of monetary catastrophe and in July 1926 the Parliament was obliged to call Poincaré to the rescue.

Pierre Janet, who for the previous twelve years had been absorbed with the construction of his great psychological synthesis, made a brilliant return in 1926 with the publication of *From Anguish to Ecstasy*, a volume that contained the story of his patient Madeleine and the first substantial account of his new system.[397] The course Janet gave at the Collège de France in 1925–1926 was also published,[398] and finally the lectures he delivered as an invited professor in Mexico, on the psychology of feelings, appeared in Spanish translation.[399] But these works did not attract much attention beyond French academic circles.

In Zurich, Jung, who had published almost nothing since the *Psychological Types* in 1921, brought forth a collection of previous articles that represented an overall view of his system[400] A characteristic feature of Zurich was the number and variety of independent psychotherapeutic schools existing side by side.

Freud's seventieth birthday was celebrated throughout the civilized world. In that year, Freud published *Inhibition, Symptom and Anxiety*, and *The Problem of Lay Analysis*. The psychoanalytic movement was confronted with the same problem that magnetism had faced a century earlier, namely, whether the right to practise the method should be restricted to physicians or extended to well-trained laymen.[401] Freud was definitely in favor of lay analysis. Psychoanalysis was developing steadily in many directions. Ernst Simmel opened a psychoanalytic sanitarium, Schloss Tegel, near Berlin. In Russia the psychoanalytic movement reached its peak, but because of the lack of communication with Soviet Russia, these developments were hardly even suspected in the Western world. In Paris, psychoanalysis had long been a fad among Surrealists and *avant-garde* writers; now it also attracted the attention of psychiatrists and psychologists, and a Psychoanalytic Society was founded in Paris in November 1926.[402]

Another salient event of 1926 was the great International Congress for Sexual Research in Berlin, from October 11 to 16, organized by Albert Moll. Its aim was to make a total survey of the present knowledge of sexology, and it was divided into various sections such as biology, psychology, sociology, and criminology, and each section was represented by a brilliant array of eminent specialists. Freud declined to attend, and his disciples followed his example. Alfred Adler was among the speakers. Moll himself gave a much commented upon lecture on the tendency of some homosexuals to present their Eros as something above ordinary sexuality.

The year 1927 was marked by the end of the military control of the Allies in Germany and many other political events, but for contemporaries its great moment was Charles A. Lindbergh's flight across the Atlantic in the *Spirit of St. Louis*, on May 20 to May 22. Now Europeans and Americans could say that their respective continents had been brought closer together.

Freud's main contribution of that year was his essay, *The Future of an Illusion*, in which he declared that religion was the equivalent of an infantile as well as a compulsive neurosis, a denial of reality, and a cultural defense that largely failed to attain its object.[403] Reverend Oskar Pfister, who had a tie of mutual friendship and respect with Freud, replied that with a paper: *The Illusion of a Future*, in which he tactfully but firmly indicated the weaknesses in Freud's argumentation and of his scientistic optimism.[404] To this Freud did not reply, and both men kept their positions as well as their feelings of respect and friendship for each other.

Two of Freud's disciples, Federn and Meng, had the idea of publishing a book illustrating the influence and relevance of psychoanalysis in the various branches of science and human activity.[405] Another of Freud's followers, Heinz Hartmann, wrote a systematic, basic account of the psychoanalytic doctrine.[406] In Berlin Franz Alexander undertook a reformulation of the theory of neurosis, referring to Freud's later works (*The Ego and the Id*; *Inhibition, Symptom and Anxiety*).[407] This was the first step toward what was to become the psychoanalytic theory of the ego. A quite different innovation was found in Wilhelm Reich's book, *The Function of Orgasm*, where he claimed to establish connections between sexuality, anxiety, and the vegetative system.[408]

Otto Rank, after modifying psychoanalytic theory, now devised his own therapeutic method.[409] He set in advance a term for the duration of the treatment. Resistance was now considered a manifestation of the patient's will to independence, and therefore a positive factor. Emphasis was placed on the immediate analytic situation rather than on the past, on "experiencing" rather than learning, on becoming aware of the patterns of reaction rather than analyzing individual experiences. Rank emphasized the will to self-determination in the patient, the creative aspects of his behavior, and the social aspects of analysis. This therapy could be considered as a mixture of Freudian, Adlerian, and Jungian principles.

In Vienna, Adler now brought out his book *Understanding Human Nature*, which was generally considered the best organized and clearest survey he had hitherto given of his system.[410] In Zurich, Ludwig Frank was having great therapeutic success with Breuer's and Freud's old cathartic method that he had perfected.[411] Bircher-Benner was also beginning to publish the result of his rich psychotherapeutic experience.[412] In Paris, Eugène Minkowski was leading the new trend of phenomenological psychiatry.[413] His book, *Schizophrenia*, inaugurated a new approach to that much-explored mental illness; Minkowski pointed out the prevalence of the experience of space over the experience of time in the inner universe of the patient and his "morbid geometricism."

Among international manifestations was the Wittenberg Symposium, held at Springfield, Ohio, from October 19 to 23, at the inauguration of the new psychological laboratory of Wittenberg College.[414] The guests were an impressive array of the world's most distinguished psychologists. Russia, who never sent delegates to international congresses, was represented by the aged Bechterev of Leningrad. Honorary degrees were conferred upon Pierre Janet and Alfred Adler.

In Russia the celebrated physiologist, Ivan Petrovitch Pavlov, who had begun studying experimental neuroses around 1921, was gradually becoming more interested in clinical psychiatry. It seems that this evolution was precipitated by a personal event. In 1927 Pavlov underwent an operation for gallstones, and during his convalescence he suffered from a heart neurosis, which he later described in a little-known paper.[415]

An account of the year 1927 would not be complete without mentioning Heidegger's book *Sein und Zeit* (Being and Time), a thoroughly new and original analysis of the structure of human existence.[416] As had happened with Husserl's *Logische Untersuchungen* in 1900, this philosophical work passed almost unnoticed in psychiatric circles. However, years later, Heidegger's work was to be the starting point of a new psychiatric trend, existential analysis.

One of the main events of 1928, the Briand-Kellogg Pact for the renunciation of war, was solemnly signed in Paris on August 27 by the representatives of fifteen states. Some saw it as a definite step toward peace, others as a meaningless ceremonial.

Freud, whose health was severely impaired, published an essay, *Dostoevsky and the Murder of the Father*, which is one of his few contributions to criminology.[417] He assumed that Dostoevsky's unsolved Oedipus complex had resulted in powerful parricidal tendencies in him that were diverted in various ways and directed against himself.

In Paris, Janet was increasingly active. He published the second volume of *From Anguish to Ecstasy* with a more extensive survey of his vast psychological synthesis. Moreover, since 1926 his lectures at the Collège de France were stenographed and published every year. But he found little audience among the younger generation.

During the same year in Zurich, Jung published two of his main books in German[418] and a volume of collected essays translated into English.[419]

There was an active interest in new psychological approaches. Von Gebsattel published a phenomenological study on melancholia that confirmed some of Minkowski's findings.[420] Among the new psychotherapeutic methods was Jacobson's technique of progressive relaxation, in Chicago, and Morita's therapy in Japan.[421]

The year 1929 began with Trotsky's banishment from Russia and with King Alexander's seizing power in Yugoslavia. The Lateran Agreement, signed by Pope Pius XI and Mussolini in February, ended a long conflict between the Papacy and the Italian government, and created the Vatican State. General elections in England brought the Labour party to power, while in Germany the agitation of the extremist parties became threatening. In the United States the unprecedented economic boom came to a sudden end with the crash of the New York Stock Exchange in October.

In Vienna, Freud published *Civilization and Its Discontents*, expressing the pessimistic opinion that civilization had been acquired at the cost of mankind's neurosis resulting from the repression of instinct. This theory, which was not new, fitted into the mood of the times.[422] A significant contribution to psychoanalytic criminology was Alexander's and Staub's book: *The Criminal and His Judges*.[423] The authors emphasized the old idea that criminal drives exist in every human being. In the psychology of punishment there is not only an inner demand for a violation of the law to be atoned for, but also the desire for revenge. Furthermore, the spectator's repressed criminal impulses are awakened by the example of the criminal and threaten to rise to expression, hence the need for the reenforcement of one's own repression and the severity of penal law.

There was a certain tension in the psychoanalytic movement because the

American Association was disinclined to accept the principle of lay analysis that Freud considered essential. Another, perhaps even more far-reaching event, was the rapid disappearance of psychoanalysis in Russia in the period of one or two years. The story of Russian psychoanalysis has actually never been written, nor do we know why exactly the Freudian theory, which had been considered materialistic, monistic, and compatible with Marxism, was suddenly discarded by Communist ideology. One of the last Russian statements in favor of psychoanalysis was to be found in Kannabikh's *History of Psychiatry*.[424] He considered Freud a foremost representative of the progressist rebellion against Kraepelin's "formal, static, impersonal" psychiatry, and contended that "thanks to him we have considerably progressed in our knowledge of many mechanisms of human behavior." On the other hand, psychoanalysis was progressing in other parts of the world. In Japan, where a few of Freud's writings had been adapted from English translations, Dr. Kenji Ohtsuki undertook a translation of Freud's *Complete Works* from the original German text.

Among the new psychotherapeutic methods, some were the revival and perfecting of older ones. Thus Krestnikoff, a Bulgarian psychiatrist, devised a new technique of cathartic therapy; he is said to have obtained brilliant therapeutic success, but because he was far removed from large university centers his method did not attract much attention.[425]

Hermann Simon's[426] "more active therapy" in mental hospitals was a perfecting of those methods that had been applied in Germany before World War I.[427] Simon's principle was that no mental patient should ever be considered "irresponsible" or be excused from work. Simon had originated an elaborate system of work and occupational therapy in the mental hospital of Gütersloh, Westphalia. At a time when there was neither insulin, electric-shock-therapy, nor tranquilizers, Simon caused symptoms of agitation, aggressiveness, emotional regression, and deterioration entirely to disappear from his institution. Hermann Simon's method was greatly admired, but was adopted in only a small number of other mental hospitals.

Another German psychiatrist, Hans Berger, published in that same year his first findings with a new method of brain physiological investigation, electroencephalography, which in that time aroused little interest.[428]

The Second Prewar Period: 1930–1939

The collapse of the Stock Exchange in New York in October 1929, set off a chain reaction that gradually affected all of America and Europe, bringing in its wake numerous bankruptcies of business concerns and banks, general unemployment, and countless individual tragedies. This was the background against which Hitler set up the propaganda causing him to appear as a savior in the eyes of millions of hopeless Germans. After he seized power in 1933, it seemed that the nations walked to their catastrophes with open eyes without being able to prevent it.

In 1930 the great economic depression dominated America and extended to Europe. The general elections in September in Germany were marked by the great advance of the Nazi party. The British Imperial conference took place from October 1 to November 14 and resulted in the adoption of the Westminster Statute, granting each one of the dominions its independence within the British Commonwealth.

There seem to have been remarkably few events in the chronicle of dynamic psychiatry apart from the fact that Freud was bestowed the Goethe Prize by the City of Frankfurt. His friends had made attempts to have him receive the Nobel Prize, but these efforts were in vain.

In 1931 storm clouds were definitely gathering over Europe. Austria's most important bank, the Kreditanstalt of Vienna, declared bankruptcy in May, and two months later the banks closed in Germany, whereupon the Germans declared that they were suspending their international payments. The Spanish Republic was proclaimed in April, and Manchuria was occupied by the Japanese in September. Ludwig Bauer, a political thinker, wrote an analysis of the situation and came to the conclusion that a new world war, more terrible than the first, was inevitable, except in the improbable event of the creation of a universal, supranational state.[429]

This deterioration of the political situation influenced the world of dynamic psychiatry. Several well-established analysts emigrated to America. Alfred Adler felt that the future of individual psychology no longer lay in Europe but in the United States, and permanently settled in New York.

Psychoanalysis was then the dominating trend in dynamic psychiatry. This was made quite obvious by the numerous celebrations on Freud's seventy-fifth birthday and the honors that were bestowed on him, as well as the addresses of congratulations he received from celebrities everywhere.

However, other schools were not remaining inactive, and new trends were gradually emerging. Ludwig Binswanger, who had been a student of Bleuler, then an adherent of psychoanalysis, and later a promoter of psychiatric phenomenology, now endeavored to reconstruct the inner world of experience of mental patients.[430] In 1931 he began to publish a subtle phenomenological analysis of manic patients, with particular emphasis on the manifestation of flight of ideas.

The year 1932 was marked by an aggravation of the depression and punctuated by political aggressions and threats of aggression. The Japanese created the puppet state of Manchukuo. In Germany Hindenburg was reelected president and seemed to be the last barrier to Hitler's access to power. Salazar became dictator in Portugal, and in South America the murderous Chaco War broke out between Paraguay and Bolivia. Roosevelt was elected President of the United States, and France refused to pay her debts to the United States.

In the general turmoil thousands of individual destinies were shaken. The Psychoanalytic Publishing House (the *Verlag*), which had been the supporting structure of the psychoanalytic movement, was now facing bankruptcy and was saved with difficulty. Some psychotherapists emigrated to America; many lost their patients. But all this did not impede the appearance of new trends and ideas. Melanie Klein, a child psychoanalyst who had moved to London, introduced new concepts about the early forms of the ego and the Oedipus complex, the prevalance of the mechanisms of projection and introjection in early childhood.[431] These ideas startled some of her colleagues, while others considered them the most brilliant development of psychoanalytic theory after Freud's own contributions.

A German psychiatrist, J. H. Schultz, published a textbook of autogenous training, a method inspired by Oskar Vogt's old techniques of self-hypnosis.[432] Autogenous training consists of a series of graduated exercises of relaxation and concentration under competent supervision; their aim is to increase the individual's control over his neuro-vegetative functions.

The year 1932 has remained famous in the annals of psychiatry as the year in which the term "group psychotherapy" was introduced by J. L. Moreno.[433] There had been many physicians and laymen who gathered patients and gave them lectures followed by discussions on problems of health and illness. Such had been J. H. Pratt's classes for tuberculosis patients in Boston. In Europe similar experiments had been conducted in Bircher-Benner's sanitarium, among antialcoholic organizations and elsewhere. But the new group psychotherapy was based on quite different principles, namely, on the dynamics of interpersonal relationships within the group situation. Moreno was to develop his concepts in the threefold direction of sociometry, psychodrama, and group therapy proper.

The fateful year 1933 brought the advent of Hitler to power. On January 30 his government came into office, and on February 27 a mysterious fire which the Communists were accused of having kindled destroyed the Reichstag building. On March 24, Hitler demanded and obtained full powers. The Communist party was banned. The slogan: "The Jews must leave" was launched, and a nationwide boycott of Jewish business was proclaimed. Thousands of terror-stricken Jews tried to cross the frontiers, but practically nothing had been prepared for their emigration and resettlement, so that many returned. A last attempt to save the peace was the Pact of Rome signed on July 15 between the four big western states (Germany, Italy, France, and England). But the situation continued to deteriorate steadily.

These political events had deep-reaching consequences for dynamic psychiatry. Since everything Jewish was systematically banned, Freud's psychoanalysis and Adler's individual psychology were outlawed in Germany, together with their institutions, organizations, and journals. The German Society for Psychotherapy was to be reorganized, and its president, Ernst Kretschmer, resigned his post. Attempts were made from all sides to save what could be saved, in psychoanalytic as well as larger psychotherapeutic and psychiatric circles. These attempts at compromise were made in good faith, since at that moment no one could imagine what turn the events were subsequently going to take. In a preceding chapter we have seen the role Jung played in this matter. He was not the only one who believed for some time that one could "talk with the Nazis."[434]

In that turmoil one could hardly expect psychoanalysts to make many original contributions. It was, however, in that year that Wilhelm Reich published his *Character Analysis*.[435] He asserted that in the course of psychoanalytic treatment, resistance expressed itself not only through the various psychological devices well known to the analysts but through specific types of muscular tension. The dissolving of psychic resistance is parallel to that of the "muscle armour." Reich also gave a typology of various types of neurotics, particularly the masochist.

The phenomenological approach was widened when Eugène Minkowski published his book, *Experienced Time*, a study of the varieties of the subjective experience of time found in many psychopathological conditions.[436]

In 1934, Hitler not only consolidated his power in Germany but tried to form an alliance with Fascist Italy. This was the object of the meeting of the two dictators in Venice on June 14 and 15. In France the Stavisky scandal caused riotous protest against corruption in the government. It was worse in Austria, where the socialist uprisings of February 1 to 16 were repressed without mercy and the socialist party was dissolved. On July 25, Chancellor Dollfuss, who had only recently escaped from an attempted murder, was assassinated by a group of Nazis. Assassination was increasingly becoming a political weapon. On October 9, King Alexander of Yugoslavia and the French Minister Barthou were assassinated in Marseilles by a group of Ustachi conspirators.

In view of the impending catastrophe, the best minds sought desperately for a solution. Einstein deplored the fact that scientists and intellectuals, who in the seventeenth century had formed a spiritual community, were now merely representatives of their various nationalist traditions. They had abandoned the responsibility of thinking on an international scale to the politicians.[437] He urged scientists to reconstitute a spiritual community that would assume the leadership of all the efforts against war.

Freud, who by now was a very old and sick man, was urged by his friends to leave Austria. But like so many of his contemporaries, he was strangely blind to the pervasiveness of the Nazi danger. He published complements and revisions of his teaching in the form of imaginary lectures under the title, *New Introductory Lectures to Psychoanalysis*.[438]

Jung was obviously in a creative mood and published, among others, a book with the characteristic title, *Reality of the Soul*.[439] One of his disciples, Gehrard Adler, sketched the history of modern psychotherapy, presenting Freud and Adler as the precursors of Jung.[440] In the United States, Moreno published one of his best-known works, *Who Shall Survive?*[441]

The year 1935 left a frightening memory on those who lived in Europe.

Individuals as well as nations felt powerless as if they were hypnotized in the face of the impending disaster that they were unable to avert. Hitler was enjoying immense popularity among a large segment of the German population, as being the man who had wiped out the shame of the Versailles Treaty and solved the problem of unemployment. In fact, Germany was feverishly rearming and preparing for war. On March 16, Hitler denounced the military restrictions of the Versailles Treaty. On September 15, the Nuremberg Laws were proclaimed "for the protection of German blood and German honor." The German Jews realized that emigration was their only hope for survival, but it was bound up with immense difficulties: prohibition to export capital, and above all the severe restrictions on visas for almost any country. Meanwhile the Italian troops invaded Ethiopia on October 3, whereupon the League of Nations Council declared Italy as an aggressor and decided to enforce economic sanctions.

In the midst of all these oppressive occurrences, it seems almost ironic that psychiatry should have made significant progress just during this period. We have seen that in 1929 Hans Berger had found a means to record the electroencephalogram of man. However, the true value of that discovery was to be appreciated only a few years later. In 1935, Gibbs, Davis, and Lennox registered and described the electroencephalogram during an epileptic attack, and Grey Walter was able to localize brain tumors by means of the EEG. Researchers enthusiastically began applying this new method that was expected to revolutionize our knowledge of brain physiology, neuropsychiatry, and criminology. Furthermore, Manfred Sakel in Vienna published the result of the research he had been conducting over several years on a new physiological treatment of schizophrenia with insulin shock therapy.[442] It was the first time that schizophrenia could be treated successfully with purely physiological methods, and it appeared as a vindication of the old organicist psychiatry against the newer dynamic trends.

The year 1936 was experienced by contemporaries as yet another step toward the inevitable disaster. Hitler denounced the Locarno Agreement and proceeded to remilitarize the Rhineland. France and Britain did not dare to intervene. In France the elections brought victory to the "Popular Front," and Léon Blum, the leader of the Socialist party, organized a new government. Belgium restated its neutrality, Italian troops entered Addis Ababa on May 5, whereupon Mussolini proclaimed the founding of the Italian Empire with the King of Italy as Emperor of Ethiopia. On July 17, General Franco instigated a military insurrection in Spanish Morocco, marking the beginning of the Spanish Civil War. The Western world was puzzled and shocked by the Moscow trials, where the old Bolshevik leaders publicly accused themselves of treason and requested punishment. However, a perhaps greater sensation was caused by Britain's king, Edward VIII, who, after having succeeded his father, George V, on January 20, abdicated on December 10, in order to marry the divorced Mrs. Simpson.

The success of physiological treatment of mental illness led psychiatrists to be more and more bold. Egaz Moniz attempted to treat psychotic conditions with lobotomy, and this was the beginning of what a few years later was to be called psychosurgery.[443]

In that year Janet's last book, *Intelligence before Language*, appeared, a study of the nonverbal forms of intelligence, comparing the animal, the infant, and the idiot.[444] Anna Freud published *The Ego and the Defense Mechanisms* a decisive step toward the new ego psychoanalysis.[445] She recapitulated the already known types of ego defenses (repression, reaction formation, isolation, undoing, introjection, and projection), described several varieties of denial, and added two new defense mechanisms, identification with the aggressor and altruistic yielding.

The year 1937 began with the second phase of the Moscow show trials. Political relationships became closer between France and England on the one hand and Germany and Italy on the other, whereas Soviet Russia's attitude remained inscrutable. Civil war raged in Spain, and experts analyzed it as a rehearsal for World War II.

Another new physiological treatment of mental illness was introduced by Von Meduna.[446] By means of metrazol injections, he produced epileptic attacks in schizophrenic patients, and many successes were recorded.

Sigmund Freud, who was now eighty-one years old and very ill, obstinately declined his friends' pressing invitations to leave Austria. Apparently he still believed that Chancellor Schuschnigg would save Austria from the Nazis. To the bewilderment of most of his friends and disciples, Freud published at that already tragic moment the first chapters of his essay on Moses.

Anong the vast amount of contemporary literature, one monograph passed almost unnoticed, namely, Szondi's *Analysis of Marriages.*[447] A Hungarian genetician well versed in psychoanalysis, Szondi compared heredity of the husband and the wife in a number of marriages, and contended that the matrimonial choice is unconsciously determined by similarities in the genetic-hereditary background. This biological phenomenon he called genotropism.

In 1938 the political situation deteriorated to the point where even to the blindest World War II seemed impossible to avert. In the presence of the Nazi agitation toward the annexation (*Anschluss*) of Austria to Germany, Chancellor Schuschnigg ordered a plebiscite that probably would have given the majority to the partisans of independence. On March 12, one day before the plebiscite, German troops occupied Austria, on the following day Nazi legislation legalized the act, and on March 14, Hitler made a triumphal appearance in Vienna. Germany and Austria were full of Jews who desperately attempted to get visas and emigration permits to foreign countries. Legal regulations in almost all the countries became more and more restrictive. Swindlers sold forged documents, and unscrupulous shipping companies embarked Jews on "errant ships" that were repelled from one land to the other (they were even greeted in Palestine with gunfire). Following the initiative of President Roosevelt, there was a conference to solve the problem of refugees in Evian, from July 6 to July 15, but the only result was the creation of an inefficient "Inter-Governmental Commission on Refugees."[448]

Meanwhile Nazi agitation had seized the German-speaking provinces of Bohemia. This was an occasion for new threats, and of the Munich Conference. In September 1938, Chamberlain and Daladier, the representatives of Great Britain and France, accepted the cession of the Sudetenland from Czechoslovakia to Germany. The flight of the Jews took panic proportions after November 7, when a young Polish Jew, Herszel Grynszpan, killed an official of the German embassy in Paris. This was used as a pretext for nationwide pogroms in Germany; moreover, a collective fine of one billion reichsmarks was imposed on the Jews.

The history of dynamic psychiatry of those years is largely a part of the tragic political events. After the Nazis occupied Vienna, they suppressed the psychoanalytic and individual psychological societies and destroyed all Freudian and Adlerian books, as they had already done in Germany. Those Jewish psychotherapists who had stayed behind now tried to leave. The gloomy atmosphere of Vienna in 1938, with the terrible difficulties encountered by those who attempted to flee, have been vividly described in a novel by Leopold Ehrlich-Hichler.[449] To those who have read it, the tribulations encountered by Freud before he could leave Vienna will not seem exceptional, moreover, he benefited from uncommon protection afforded him by the Princess Marie Bonaparte, by the American embassy, and by British and American associations. The details of Freud's exodus from Vienna and of the triumphant reception he was given in England were largely publicized, as if it were to divert public attention from certain painful issues.

The Nazis not only suppressed Jewish theories and institutions, they also attacked Christian religion and ethics and promoted a National-Socialist doctrine, which was a combination of various extrascientific theories. There were the racist theories devised in the nineteenth century by two Frenchmen, the Count of Gobineau and Vacher de Lapouge, and an Englishman, Houston Stewart Chamberlain.[450] These theories were now associated with pseudohistorical representations of the life and culture of the ancient Germans. There were also the pseudobiological theories of the struggle for life and the "life-space" (Lebensraum), with some remains of Haeckelian Monism. According to Jochen Besser, Nazi ideology was strongly influenced by theories of occultist and theosophical circles of the early twentieth century.[451] Noteworthy was the favor bestowed by the Nazis on Hörbiger's Glazial-Kosmogonie, alias Welt-Eis-Lehre (Cosmic Ice Theory). Hörbiger, an Austrian engineer, taught a complicated astronomic and cosmogonic system. Included in this system was the idea that ice was the main substance constituting the universe.[452] His system had prodigious success among the Nazis[453] and even found adherents in England.[454] The Nazis also favored a so-called Germanic medicine, which was a combination of Bircher-Benner's dietetics, naturist principles, traditional use of medicinal herbs, and popular medicine.

In spite of the dark clouds steadily gathering over the world and the spreading of obscurantism over Europe, scientific psychiatry pursued its progress. Two Italians, Cerletti and Bini, announced their discovery of a powerful therapeutic agent: electroshock therapy. This method, which had been devised to treat schizophrenia, later proved to be more successful in the treatment of severe depression.[455]

One of the new psychotherapeutic methods was Desoille's Directed Day-Dream.[456] The patient lying on a couch is invited to imagine that he is ascending into the air and to tell the psychiatrist of all that he feels and fancies is happening to him. The emerging feelings and productions of the subliminal imagination are then discussed between the patient and the therapist. In fact, this therapy is a variation of Jung's method of forced imagination. In the United States Sullivan defined psychiatry as the study of interpersonal relations and began to publish the basic principles of his system.[457]

Those few optimistic persons who had hoped that peace could still be saved had to lose this illusion in March 1939. On these new Ides of March the Germans occupied Bohemia and Moravia, and Hitler made a spectacular entry into Prague. In the same month the Spanish Civil War came to an end with the capitulation of Madrid and the flight of thousands of Republicans to France. As Toynbee described it, the world was now divided into three camps: the Western Powers (comprising England and the Commonwealth, France, and the reluctant United States), the anti-Comintern Powers (Germany, Italy, and Japan), and Soviet Russia.[458] The problem was to know to which of the two other groups Soviet Russia would become an ally. Efforts were made on both sides to gain Russia's support. The announcement, on August 23, that a treaty of nonaggression had been signed between Nazi Germany and Soviet Russia was the last signal that preceded the German ultimatum to Poland, soon followed by Great Britain's and France's declaration of war on Germany.

While the French were afraid of the impending war and the possible destruction of Paris, a group at the Sorbonne organized a celebration for the centennial of Théodule Ribot, which coincided with the fiftieth year of Janet's celebrated thesis, *L'Automatisme Psychologique*. It was the last public recognition the eighty-year-old Janet was to receive before his death. Circumstances were so dismal that the event passed unnoticed and the memorial book has become a bibliographic rarity.[459]

September 23, 1939, was marked by the death of two men who cordially detested each other: Sigmund Freud in London and Albert Moll in Berlin. Though the one died world famous and the other in total obscurity, curious parallels can be found in their biographies. Both were the sons of Jewish merchants. As young physicians both were interested in hypnotism and the exploration of the unconscious mind. Both then turned their interests toward sexual pathology, particularly to the evolutionary stages of the sexual instinct, termed by Moll *libido sexualis*, and by Freud (referring to Moll) *libido*. At the time of his death, Moll was living inconspicuously after the Nazis destroyed his books, including his recently published autobiography. Freud, in contrast, was placed in the limelight as a symbol of the struggle between Democracy and Fascism.

Before his death Freud expressed concern about the future of psychoanalysis. He saw it as being on the way toward suppression in Europe and distortion in America. He realized that the time had now come when the creation had emancipated itself from the creator and taken its independent course of life.

In fact deviant schools had already arisen, and others were to follow. Otto Rank had some success with the schools of social work and was now moving toward a kind of religious psychotherapy. Wilhelm Reich arrived in the United States in May 1939, where he was to found the Orgone Institute, with theories far removed from orthodox Freudian psychoanalysis. In that same year, Karen Horney published her *New Ways in Psychoanalysis*, the manifesto and first textbook of a deviant school that combined Adlerian teachings with Freudian terminology.[460]

In that same year 1939, Heinz Hartmann published a much noted paper on ego psychology, which marked a new metamorphosis of psychoanalysis.[461] Completing the evolution that had started with Freud's *Mass Psychology and Ego Analysis*, enlarged by Alexander's *Psychoanalysis of the Total Personality* and Anna Freud's *Ego and Defense Mechanisms*, Hartmann definitively put the ego in the focus of the psychoanalyst's interest and work. The emphasis of the technique shifted from the analysis of the content of the unconscious to the nature of the defense mechanisms, as to whether they were adequate to the patient's age, and to the external and internal conflicts he had to withstand. No doubt this new technique was appropriate to contemporary man's condition in a changing and distressing world.

World War II: 1939–1945

From 1939 to 1945 the fate of the world was at stake. In the general upheaval, dynamic psychiatry underwent new vicissitudes.

World War II differed from Word War I in several respects. The outbreak occurred without the popular enthusiasm that had marked the beginning of World War I. There was a bitter feeling of helplessness, similar to that of some populations in Austria-Hungary in August 1914.

New strategies, new tactics, and new weapons were devised, all of which culminated in the exploding of the atomic bomb. It was not so much a war between nations as between ideologies: Hitlerian racism, Soviet Russian Communism, and the Anglo-Saxon concept of democracy. World War II brought terrible devastation, the complete destruction of cities from Coventry to Dresden, extensive migrations, massacres of military and civilian populations, and genocide (after the two million Armenians in 1915–1916, there were now six million Jews). It aggravated the decline of the West and was followed by often painful processes of decolonization. However, the League of Nations was reconstructed on a sounder basis under the name of the United Nations Organization, and for the first time in history, a court was set up to judge war criminals. This war accelerated the change in the mores and ways of life that had accompanied and followed World War I. The generation that emerged in 1945 was as different from the preceding one as the 1919 generation had been from that of the Belle Epoque.

As soon as the war became a fact, it was obvious that it would be unusually cruel and merciless. Hitler had stated his aims in his declaration of August 22, 1939:

> ... Our strength is in our quickness and our brutality. Ghengis Khan had millions of women and children killed by his own will and with a gay heart. History sees in him only a great State-builder. What the weak European civilization thinks about me does not matter. . . . Thus, for the time being, I have sent to the East only my "Death's Head" units, with the order to kill without pity or mercy all men, women and children of the Polish race or language. Who still talks nowadays of the extermination of the Armenians?[462]

The German troops started their blitzkrieg in Poland, on the first of September 1939. On September 17, the Russians invaded the country from the east to take their share of the booty, so that in less than three weeks Poland had disappeared from the map. On the Western front it was a *drôle de guerre* (a crazy war): two gigantic armies stood face to face for eight months engaging in nothing but insignificant skirmishes. In November the Russians attacked Finland; in April 1940 the Germans rapidly occupied Denmark and Norway. On May 10, 1940, the Germans launched a blitzkrieg on Holland, Belgium, and France, with such unexpected impact that the French were obliged to sign an armistice on June 16. But from August to October the Germans lost the battle over England, and this saved the Western world. After a new pause, the Germans invaded Yugoslavia and Greece in April 1941, and on June 22 they attacked Russia. After many initial successes and a rapid advance the German Army was stopped outside of Moscow. This campaign was fought with unprecedented fierceness in the rigorous Russian winter.

The war took a new turn on December 7, 1941. The Japanese renewed a strategic move that had brought them victory in their war with Russia: as with the Russian fleet in 1904, they attacked the American fleet in Pearl Harbor before declaring war on the United States. Japan's declaration of war on the United States and England was followed by a swift invasion of Malaya, Indonesia, the Philippines, and the South Sea Islands. The Americans' colossal war effort enabled them to conduct war simultaneously in the Pacific and in Europe. The Japanese-occupied territories were reconquered one by one by the American General MacArthur, while General Eisenhower prepared the invasion of the Allies in Europe. In November 1942 the Allies landed in Algeria, in July 1943 in Sicily, and on June 6, 1944, in Normandy. Following the Anglo-American victories in Western Europe and the Russian victories in the East, the German armies capitulated on May 8, 1945, while Japan continued to resist. But on July 6, after a brief flight of an American squadron over Hiroshima, the shocked world learned of the atomic bomb. The war was over, and a new era had begun for mankind.

The fate of dynamic psychiatry was profoundly affected by these events. Among the four great pioneers two, Freud and Adler, had died in exile; another, Janet, was working on a book, *The Psychology of Belief* (that remained uncompleted), whereas the last one, Jung, seemed to concentrate his interest on mythology and alchemy. The major fact, however, was the massive emigration of central European psychotherapists to England and even more to the United States. As a result, the center of the psychoanalytic and the individual psychological associations were transferred to America; English supplanted German as their official language. After the destruction of the Psychoanalytic *Verlag* in Vienna, a new one, the Imago Publishing House, was founded in London and began the publication of Freud's *Sämtliche Werke*, to replace the destroyed collections of the *Gesammelte Werke*. More recent works, even those of German and Austrian therapists, were now being published directly in English. This transfer from the German to the English language did not occur without some semantic fluctuations. Certain shades of meaning in the German terminology were lost, whereas a term such as "frustration" enjoyed a popularity it did not possess in German.

The psychiatric chronicle of those years is relatively short.

In 1940 Freud's posthumous *Outline of Psychoanalysis* appeared. His book on Moses provoked much controversy and protest in Jewish circles. It seemed extraordinary that at a moment when the physical existence of the people of Israel was threatened, a Jew should publish a book contending that Moses was an Egyptian and had been killed by the Hebrews. Freud's attitude was contrasted with that of Bergson, who through personal conviction had become a Catholic but refused to be baptized so as to express solidarity with his people. Bergson indeed refused to be relieved from any of the indiginities imposed on the Jews; however, he died on January 3, 1941, before the deportation of the French Jews.

In 1941, psychoanalysis flourished more than ever in America, but the so-called neo-Freudian trends gained in importance. Karen Horney left the American Psychoanalytic Association and founded the American Institute of Psychoanalysis, for the propagation of her own teaching and therapy. Eric Fromm published his *Escape from Freedom*, inspired more by contemporary events than by psychoanalytic theory.[463]

In 1942, Binswanger, in Switzerland, published his *Basic Forms and Knowledge of Human Existence*, a formidable 726-page book in which he compiled and discussed his new system of *Daseinsanalyse* (existential analysis).[464] This system was inspired by Heidegger's *Daseinsanalytik*, but whereas the latter is a philosophical analysis of the structure of human existence in general, Binswanger's purpose is to analyze the "Being in the World" of individuals. By means of a system of phenomenological coordinates derived from Heidegger, Binswanger attempts to reconstruct the universe of inner experience, even of severely psychotic patients, and make it intelligible.

The search for new psychotherapies was going on as actively as ever. Carl R. Rogers in the United States published the first account of his method of psychotherapeutic counseling.[465] "Effective counseling," he said, "consists of a definitely structured, permissive relationship which allows the client to gain an understanding of himself to a degree which enables him to take positive steps in the light of his new orientation." In Switzerland, Marc Guillerey reported to the Psychiatric Association on the psychotherapeutic method he had been applying for the last fifteen years.[466] It was an original combination of Vittoz' technique of relaxation, concentration, and bodily awareness with Jung's technique of forced imagination.

In 1943 a new dynamic trend came to the foreground—psychosomatic medicine. Two classical works were published in that year, those of Weiss and English,[467] and of Flanders Dunbar.[468] To be sure, psychosomatic medicine already had a long history: primitive healing was to a large degree psychosomatic, as also were the cures performed by Gassner and Mesmer, by generations of magnetizers and hypnotists, by men such as Liébeault, Bernheim, Forel, and their followers. Romantic medicine was not alone in proclaiming that physical illness can originate from emotional causes. The same was taught by the great representatives of scientific medicine and by certain physiologists (Krehl in Germany, Cannon in the United States). Adolf Meyer had tried to correlate certain clinical conditions with certain consciously experienced emotions of the patients. The new pioneers of psychosomatic medicine now undertook to delineate the personality profile of the patients in various diseases: hypertension, coronary occlusion, rheumatism, diabetes, and the like. This was to be the starting point for new research and new theories which were to take an unexpected development in the following decades.

We may add that in the same year, in the laboratories of the pharmaceutical company Sandoz, in Basel, the chemist Albert Hofmann discovered by chance a substance which produced vivid hallucinations at infinitesimal doses.[469] This discovery did not attract much attention at the time, but the product was to become famous later under the designation of LSD[25].

In France, Sartre published *Being and Nothingness*. This elaborate and original work inspired by Heidegger contained, as we have seen earlier, a chapter devoted to "existential psychoanalysis," a psychotherapeutic method showing great similarities to the Adlerian approach.[470] In Spain, J. J. López Ibor brought the first account of his new and original theory of vital anxiety, a concept with deep-reaching implications for psychotherapy.[471]

The year 1944 was marked by the development of Binswanger's existential analysis and of Szondi's analysis of destiny.

Existential analysis had been known until then as a rather abstract theoretical system. With the publication of the case of Ellen West it entered into the field of clinical psychiatry and psychopathology.[472] This model case was for Binswanger what that of Madeleine had been for Janet, and that of the Wolf-Man for Freud. As Binswanger remarked, the case of Ellen West greatly resembled that of Janet's Nadia.[473] Both had been referred to a psychiatrist because they were obsessed by the fear of becoming fat; both deprived themselves of food but at times devoured greedily in secret. Janet soon recognized that Nadia's illness was no ordinary *anorexia nervosa*: her refusal of food was part of an obsession regarding her body and its functions, and this obsession in turn was connected with her fear that people would reject or despise her. In regard to Ellen West, Binswanger begins his analysis where Janet had stopped Nadia's study, that is the attempts to elucidate and reconstruct the evolution of the patient's *Dasein* with her universe of subjective experience. In that task, Binswanger was favored because Ellen West, a well-educated person, had a talent for self-expression in prose and in verse.

In dealing with a clinical case, the traditional procedure consists of a double reduction: from the patient's life history to the story of his illness, and from the clinical picture to its biological substratum (checking, for instance, whether Nadia or Ellen had endocrinic disturbances). Psychoanalysis would supplement with a reduction of the patient's vicissitudes of drives and object relations. Binswanger retains the framework of Kraepelinian nosology and occasionally resorts to psychoanalytic concepts, but his main concern is the unfolding of the patient's "Being in the World" with its metamorphoses since infancy.

Ellen West came from a wealthy Jewish family to which belonged distinguished persons, and in which there had been some cases of mental illness and suicide. At the age of nine months she refused milk and always showed difficulties in regard to food intake. She was a lively, boyish child, extremely stubborn and ambitious and she liked to read. Since adolescence she had kept a diary, wrote poetry, and expressed a kind of pantheistic enthusiasm for life and nature. She felt called to great achievements, to gain undying fame, and was longing for the love of a perfect man. She led the life of a rich cosmopolitan young lady with riding, traveling, and irregular studies, but was preoccupied with social problems, with the idea "to go to the people," and the hope for a great social revolution. (In fact Ellen West had much in common with Marie Bashkirtseff or Lou Andreas-Salomé; her behavior appears less erratic if one assumes that she was a Russian aristocrat of the Czarist time.)

At the age of twenty she began having a fear of becoming fat, and gradually it became an obsession that dominated her entire life. She imposed upon herself drastic diets and weight reducing cures, but at times she would throw herself on food and engulf great quantities of it to her shame.

At the age of about twenty-seven, she married a cousin who seems to have been an extremely devoted husband; she remained active in social welfare, but her physical condition altered. At thirty-two she underwent treatment with a psychoanalyst who brought her the insight that her goal was "the subjugation of all other people." One year later, a second analysis was apparently less successful; the analyst pursued it in spite of several suicidal attempts, and her condition worsened to the point that her internist intervened, stopping the treatment. Ellen West then entered Binswanger's sanitarium in Kreuzlingen, where she stayed two and a half months. Owing to her suicidal impulses, Binswanger could not take the responsibility of keeping her in the open part of the sanitarium. Two foremost psychiatrists called in consultation agreed with Binswanger that the patient was incurable. The husband, informed of this condition and of the danger, preferred to take her home. The patient's sufferings immediately subsided. In a festive mood, she ate to her heart's content for the first time in thirteen years, read poetry, wrote letters, and thereupon took poison and died on the following morning.

Binswanger's long thorough and subtle analysis of Ellen West's "Being in the World" cannot be summarized and must be read in the original or the English translation. Ellen West's fear of being fat and of gluttony were but the more conspicuous manifestations of a slow process of existential impoverishment and emptying. She had lost her footing in the world of practical action; her social welfare activities had been a means of filling the emptiness of her life. The patient constantly oscillated between two increasingly divergent worlds of subjective experience. One was an ideal, ethereal, spacious, light, warm, colorful, glowing world of effortless flying in which one does not need to eat. The other world, of which gluttony was the expression, was dominated by the process by which the individual's spontaneity and freedom of action yield to the hold of the surrounding world. It was a world of damp fog, dark clouds, of heaviness, sluggishness, withering and decay, a world of the tomb. From the point of view of temporality, Ellen West, who had not been able to build time, had no future, or rather the future was replaced by the ethereal world of daydream that had no roots in the patient's present or past. Neither did she have a past on which to build her present actions and her future; the past was replaced by that world of darkness, heaviness, and decay, whose full expression was death. The present was reduced to the instantaneous. The continuity of time was replaced by a succession of instants. The conflict and increasing discrepancy between the two worlds allowed no compromise, and thus came a point when the only act of freedom and authenticity left to Ellen West was suicide.

The year 1944 also saw the publication of Szondi's *Analysis of Destiny,* containing a theory that has often been misunderstood.[474] *Analysis of Destiny* (Schicksalsanalyse) can best be defined as a symthesis of psychiatric genetics and psychoanalysis. The genetic approach originated in the study of hereditary mental illness. The German school of psychiatric geneticians first engaged in the study of hereditary diseases (epilepsy, schizophrenia, and manic-depressive illness) and later arrived at the notion of "hereditary circles." A "hereditary circle" (*Erbkreis*) comprises not only negative manifestations (specific types of psychosis and character abnormalities), but also positive ones (specific endowments and talents), so that, in the same family, certain individuals can be afflicted with a psychosis, others favored with a particular talent, and others display only specific character features within the limits of normality. This leads to the assumption that in each hereditary circle lies a common denominator that has been called a root factor, or biological radical. What Szondi calls drive factors is a system of eight such biological radicals derived from psychiatric genetic research.

As for psychoanalysis, it has always admitted the existence of a biological substratum of the unconscious life. Freud had called predisposition a mixture of biological *anlage* and early environmental influences. Some analysts came to suspect that there were various kinds of predispositions. Abraham claimed that a marked development of oral and anal characteristics could be related to specific predisposing factors.[475] Other psychoanalysts talked of patients with a strong or weak ego, thus implying the existence of another kind of specific predisposition.

It is precisely this obscure realm of the biological predispositions underlying man's unconscious life that becomes the focus of Szondi's *Analysis of Destiny.* Here he finds again the eight biological radicals or factors that had resulted from psychiatric genetics.

We see how the two lines of research, namely, of psychiatric genetics and of psychoanalysis, crossed each other. The point of intersection lies in a hitherto almost unexplored realm of the human being that Szondi calls the family unconscious. For the geneticians it belongs to the genotype, that is to the hidden, latent, hereditary *anlagen.* For the psychologist it is, according to Szondi, a newly discovered layer of the unconscious, a field of destiny from which proceed the vital choices (choice in love, friendship, profession, illness, and even the manner of death), the sum of which constitutes our destiny. Szondi's fundamental hypothesis is that every man comes to the world with a bundle of destiny possibilities, which are determined by the formula of his genotype. As Freud had analyzed the mechanisms of dream-formation (displacement, and condensation), in order to interpret the dream for the dreamer, Szondi analyzes the mechanisms of destiny-formation in order to reconstruct the latent genetic structure of the individual. Among the main destiny mechanisms described by Szondi is genotropism: namely, that the love choice is unconsciously directed by similarities latent

to the gene formula. Another mechanism is operotropism, that is the unconscious tendency of an individual to choose an occupation through which
the positive hereditary factor confers a superiority upon him. Szondi found
a list of occupations characteristic for each one of his eight factors. Because
of the dual origin of *Analysis of Destiny*, the same manifestations can
receive a biological and a psychological interpretation. What for the
genetician are "positive manifestations of a biological radical" may be
"sublimation" for the psychoanalyst. Szondi distinguished three degrees of
sublimation: "socialization," that is, the channeling of drives in one's occupation, "sublimation proper" within the individual's character, and
"humanization," a superior form of sublimation extended to the benefit of
mankind.

The basic method in the analysis of destiny consists in establishing an
extremely thorough genealogy of the individual. To the difference of ordinary
psychiatric genetics one will not only record occurrences of psychosis,
neurosis, psychopathy, or criminality, but also the character structure and
the occupation of all persons included in that genealogy. Furthermore, the
genealogy established in that way will be confronted with that of the persons
with whom the individual is closely bound by destiny (this is the method
Szondi had applied in his *Analysis of Marriages*).

Since this method clearly was much too long and time-consuming, Szondi
thought of a shorter way of exploring the family unconscious to find the
genetic formula of his subjects. In 1944 Szondi had already devised and
applied for years the test he was later to publish. The test material consists
of a series of photographs of murderers, homosexuals, epileptics, and
other patients representative of the extreme negative manifestations in each
one of Szondi's eight factors. The testee is shown these sets in succession
and is invited to show what pictures he feels are the most sympathetic
and which are the most repulsive to him. A complex method of evaluation
is used to elucidate the subject's genetic formula and his personality structure
from his reactions.

From the beginning, Szondi's *Analysis of Destiny* met with enthusiastic
admiration and sharp criticism. His genetic suppositions were questioned,
particularly his system of eight factors grouped in four vectors. Actually, it
seems that in Szondi's mind this system is more a fictitious model, comparable
to the resonators devised by Helmholtz with which physicists analyze the
constitutive elements of a tone. The choice of the resonators is necessarily
arbitrary, but no physicist will deny their usefulness in analyzing a sound.
As years went by, Szondi was to emphasize his test, and still later his own
original psychotherapeutic method.

When the war came to an end in 1945, a flow of new publications was
the sure sign that the creative spirit was still alive. In France, the philosopher Merleau-Ponty published his *Phenomenology of Perception*, which
soon became one of the classics of phenomenology.[476] The French psychia-

trist, Henri Baruk, a Jew who had lived the past years in great danger and who had escaped almost miraculously, published *Moral Psychiatry*, a book in which he emphasized the persistence of the "moral personality" in the most regressed and demented of mental patients. He pointed out how in these patients the sense of justice was even increased and showed that a noticeable improvement could be obtained by taking into account the patient's feeling of dignity and need for justice. This concern for the inner-most personality of the patient was felt to be a reaction against the organicist and materialistic spirit that had dominated psychiatry since the middle of the nineteenth century.[477] Another aspect of that reaction was the success of existentialism in psychiatry as well as in philosophy in Western Europe.

Another innovation was Maeder's method of brief psychotherapy, a method that postulated from the patient a real and genuine wish for recovery and from the therapist a genuine wish to help his patient.[478] The therapist calls upon the self-healing tendencies in the patient, and the patient projects onto the therapist the archetype of the Healer image. Maeder's method was partly inspired by Jungian concepts, but his main emphasis is on self-regulation and self-healing processes. (These notions he had learned from the biologist Hans Driesch and from Théodore Flournoy.)

In America the main feature was the growing development of group therapy. Moreno had many followers and imitators and numerous techniques of group therapy were devised and applied.[479]

The war left the world with two major powers facing each other with increasing suspicion, the United States and Soviet Russia, each one with its allies, satellites, and zones of influence. Between these two colossi the debris of what had been the European countries were struggling to recover their identities. This situation was reflected in psychiatry. In Soviet Russia, Pavlovian psychiatry was now an official doctrine, whereas psychoanalysis and kindred teachings were prohibited. In the United States equal freedom was granted to all psychiatric schools (to the Pavlovian as well as to any other), but psychoanalysis was factually prevalent; the number of psycho-analysits continually increased, they occupied leading posts in the psychiatric departments of universities, and Freudian or pseudo-Freudian ideology pervaded cultural life.

The opposition between the two great world powers was also reflected in the controversies between Russian and American psychiatrists. Although no one questioned the achievements of Pavlov as a physiologist, they were regarded as insufficient to form the basis of a psychiatry. Knowledge acquired in experiments with animals in an artifical experimental setting could not be applied offhand to human beings; it could never provide an understand-ing of the mental patient's subjective condition. Pavlovian psychiatry was thus considered a psychiatry for robots rather than for humans and the technique of brainwashing its most original achievement. Russian psychia-trists, in turn, brandmarked psychoanalysis as idealistic (with the pejorative connotation of that word in Marxist terminology), as a pitiful manifestation of decaying capitalism, as a plutocratic therapy restricted to wealthy parasites, whereas the poor were deprived of the possibility of treatment.

As a further reflection of the political situation, Pavlovian psychiatry extended over Eastern Europe and the Balkan countries. In western and central Europe (where few prewar psychoanalysts remained) Freudianism sometimes took the appearance of a cultural importation from America. It became usual for the French to read Freud in English, and even the young Germans talked of the ego, the id, the superego, instead of using the original terms *Ich, Es, Ueberich.* On the other hand, the influence of existential philosophy and psychiatry was spreading, and Europe continued to be the cradle of new psychotherapeutic methods. The future of dynamic psychiatry looked promising and filled with possibilities, but as unpredictable as the future of mankind.

Notes

1. J. M. Charcot, "Sur les divers états nerveux déterminés par l'hynotisation chez les hystériques," *Comptes-Rendus hebdomadaires des séances de l'Académie des Sciences,* XCIV (1882) (I), 403–405.

2. Pierre Janet, *Les Médications psychologiques* (Paris: Alcan, 1919), I, 155.

3. A. Jaquet, *Ein halbes Jahrhundert Medizin* (Basel: Benno Schwabe, 1929), pp. 169–171.

4. Charles Richet, "Du Somnambulisme provoqué," *Journal de l'Anatomie et de la Physiologie normale et pathologique de l'homme et des animaux,* II (1875), 348–377.

5. Rudolf Heidenhain, *Der sog thierische Magnetismus; Physiologische Beobachtungen* (Leipzig: Breitkopf and Härtel, 1880).

6. See Chap. 2, p. 86.

7. Robert G. Hillman, "A Scientific Study of Mystery: The Role of the Medical and Popular Press in the Nancy-Salpêtrière Controversy on Hypnotism," *Bulletin of the History of Medicine,* XXXIX (1965), 163–182.

8. Jules Liégeois, "De la Suggestion hypnotique dans ses rapports avec le droit civil et le droit criminel," *Séances et travaux de l'Académie des sciences morales et politiques,* CXXII (1884), 155.

9. H. Bernheim, *De la Suggestion dans l'état hynotique et dans l'état de veille* (Paris: Doin, 1884).

10. See Chap. 2, pp. 90–91; Chap. 7, 437–442.

11. See Chap. 2, pp. 90–91.

12. Sigmund Freud, "Charcot," *Wiener medizinische Wochenschrift,* XLIII (1893), 1,513–1,520. Standard Edition, III, 11–23.

13. Paul Richer, *Etudes cliniques sur l'hystérie-épilepsie ou grande hystérie* (Delahaye et Lecrosnier, 1881).

14. Sigmund Freud, *Selbstdarstellung,* in Grote, *Die Medizin der Gegenwart* (1925), IV, 1–52 (quotation from p. 4). Standard Edition, XX, 7–74.

15. See Chap. 6, pp. 336–337.

16. Personal communication from Mme. Hélène Pichon-Janet.

17. See Chap. 6, p. 338.

18. Ernst Freud, who was kind enough to look, at the author's request, into the letters of Freud to his fiancée, told him that he found no mention of that meeting.

19. Ernest Jones, *The Life and Work of Sigmund Freud* (New York: Basic Books, 1953), I, 187.

20. This is shown by the two letters of Freud reproduced in French translation in André Gaucher, *L'Obsédé. Drame de la libido*. Avec lettres de Freud et de Pierre Janet (Paris: André Delpech, 1925).

21. Léon Daudet, "Le Moi et le Soi," in *L'Hérédo* (Paris: Nouvelle Librairie Nationale, 1917), pp. 1–38.

22. See Chap. 9, pp. 730–731.

23. See Chap. 7, pp. 437–442.

24. J. Delboeuf, "De l'Influence de l'imitation et de l'éducation dans le somnambulisme provoqué," *Revue philosophique*, XXII (1886) (II), 146–171.

25. Henri Bergson,"Simulation inconsciente dans l'état d'hypnotisme," *Revue philosophique*, XXII (1886) (II), 525–531.

26. See Chap. 6, p. 358.

27. H. Bernheim, *De la Suggestion et de ses applications à la thérapeutique* (Paris: Doin, 1886).

28. Enrico Morselli, *Il Magnetismo animale. La fascinazione e gli stati ipnotici* (Turin: Roux and Favale, 1886).

29. Frederick W. H. Myers, "Multiplex Personality," *The Nineteenth Century*, XXX (1886), 648–666.

30. E. Gurney, F. W. H. Myers, F. Podmore, *Phantasms of the Living*, 2 vols. (London: Society for Psychical Research, 1886).

31. Richard von Krafft-Ebing, *Psychopathia Sexualis. Eine Klinisch-Forensische Studie* (Stuttgart: Enke, 1886).

32. Benjamin Tarnowsky, *Die krankhaften Erscheinungen des Geschlechtssinnes; eine forensisch-psychiatrische Studie* (Berlin: Hirschwald, 1886).

33. Julius Wagner, "Ueber die Einwirkung fieberhafter Erkrankungen auf Psychosen," *Jahrbuch für Psychologie und Neurologie*, VII (1887), 94–130.

34. Gehrart Hauptmann, *Das Abenteuer meiner Jugend*, in *Sämtliche Werke* (n.p.: Propyläen-Verlag, 1962), VII, 451–1088. (See the description of Forel's Burghölzli, 1063–1067.)

35. Albert Moll, *Ein Leben als Arzt der Seele, Erinnerungen* (Dresden: Reissner, 1936), p. 31.

36. Dr. Crocq, *L'Hypnotisme scientifique* (2nd ed.; Paris: Société d'Editions Scientifiques, 1900).

37. Max Dessoir, *Bibliographie des modernen Hypnotismus* (Berlin: Düncker, 1888).

38. August Forel, *Der Hypnotismus und seine strafrechtliche Bedeutung* (Berlin and Leipzig: Guttentag, 1888).

39. Anon., "L'Affaire Chambige," *Revue des grands procès contemporains*, VII (1889), 21–101.

40. P. J. Moebius, "Ueber den Begriff der Hysterie," *Centralblatt für Nervenheilkunde*, XI (1888), 66–71.

41. Henri Bergson, *Les Données immédiates de la conscience* (Paris: Alcan, 1889).

42. See Chap. 6, pp. 358–364.

43. Brown-Sequard, "Des Effets produits chez l'homme par des injections sous-cutanées d'un liquide retiré des testicules frais de cobaye et de chien," *Comptes-rendus hebdomadaires des séances et mémoires de la société de biologie*, 9th series, I (1889), 415–419.

44. "Congrès international de Psychologie Physiologique," *Revue Philosophique*, XXVIII (1889) (II), 109–111, 539–546.

45. *Premier Congrès international de l'hypnotisme expérimental et thérapeutique*, Paris, August 8–12, 1889. C. R. publiés par Edgar Bérillon (Paris: Doin, 1890).

46. Briand, *Premier Congrès international de l'hypnotisme*, pp. 182–187.

47. Bourru and Burot, *Premier Congrès international de l'hypnotisme*, pp. 228–240.

48. *Congrès international de 1889. Le Magnétisme humain appliqué au soulagement et à la guérison des malades*. Rapport général (Paris: Georges Carré, 1890).

49. J. M. Charcot, *Leçons du mardi à la Salpêtrière. Policlinique, 1888–1889* (Paris: Progrès Médical, 1889), pp. 247–256.

50. A. A. Liebeault, *Le Sommeil provoqué et les états analogues* (Paris: Doin, 1889).
51. Albert Moll, *Der Hypnotismus* (Berlin: Kornfeld, 1889).
52. G. Anton; "Hypnotische Heilmethode und mitgetheilte Neurose," *Jahrbuch für Psychiatrie*, VIII (1889), 194–211.
53. See Chap. 3, pp. 145–146.
54. See Chap. 5, pp. 314–315.
55. Moritz Benedikt, "Aus der Pariser Kongresszeit. Erinnerungen und Betrachtungen," *Internationale Klinische Rundschau*, III (1889), 1531–1533, 1573–1576, 1611–1614, 1657–1659, 1699–1703, 1858–1860.
56. See Chap. 5, p. 301.
57. Adolf Strümpell, *Aus dem Leben eines deutschen Klinikers. Erinnerungen und Beobachtungen* (Leipzig: F. C. W. Vogel, 1925), pp. 217–219.
58. William James, *The Principles of Psychology*, 2 vols. (New York: H. Holt, 1890).
59. Anon., "Michel Eyraud et Gabrielle Bompard," *Revue des Grands Procès Contemporains*, IX (1891), 19–107.
60. H. Bernheim, *De la Suggestion* (Paris: Albin Michel, n.d.), pp. 170–171.
61. J. Grasset, "Le Roman d'une hystérique. Histoire vraie pouvant servir à l'étude médico-légale de l'hystérie et de l'hypnotisme," *Le Semaine Médicale*, X (1890), 57–58.
62. Georges Gilles de la Tourette, *Traité clinique et thérapeutique de l'hysterie d'après l'enseignement de la Salpêtriere* (Paris: Plon, 1891).
63. See Chap. 6, pp. 364–366.
64. "La Manifestation en l'honneur du Dr. Liébeault le 25 mai 1891," *Revue de l'Hynotisme*, V (1890–1891), 353–359.
65. Moritz Benedikt, "Ueber Neuralgien und neuralgische Affectionen und deren Behandlung," *Klinische Zeit und Streitfragen*, VI, No. 3 (1892), 67–106.
66. See Chap. 5, p. 301.
67. J. M. Charcot, "La Foi qui guérit," *Revue hebdomadaire*, I (1892); *Archives de Neurologia*, XXV (1893), 72–87.
68. J. M. Charcot, "Sur un Cas d'amnésie rétro-antérograde probablement d'origine hystérique," *Revue de Médicine*, XII (1892), 81–96. (With a follow-up by A. Souques, same journal, same year and volume, 267–400, 867–881.)
69. See Chap. 6, pp. 366–367.
70. See Chap. 6, p. 399.
71. Louis-Henri-Charles Laurent, *Des Etats seconds. Variations pathologiques du champ de la conscience*. Thèse Méd. Bordeaux, 1891–1892, No. 13 (Bordeaux: Cadoret, 1892).
72. *International Congress on Experimental Psychology. Second Session* (London: Williams & Norgate, 1892).
73. Adolf Strümpell, *Ueber die Entstehung und die Heilung von Krankheiten durch Vorstellungen* (Erlangen: F. Junge, 1892).
74. Marcel Prévost, *L'Automne d'une femme* (Paris: Lemerre, 1893).
75. Richard von Krafft-Ebing, *Hypnotische Experimente* (Stuttgart: Enke, 1893).
76. See Chap. 7, p. 485.
77. *Revue Neurologique*, I (1893), 36.
78. Heinrich Obersteiner, *Die Lehre vom Hypnotismus* (Vienna: Breitenstein, 1893), p. 44.
79. Frederic W. H. Myers, "The Subliminal Consciousness," *Proceedings of the Society for Psychical Research*, IX (1893–1894), 3–25.
80. J. Michell Clarke: "Critical Digest, Hysteria and Neurasthenia," *Brain*, XVII (1894), 119–178, 263–321.
81. J. Dallemagne, *Dégénérés et déséquilibrés* (Brussels: Lamertin, 1894), pp. 436, 445–446.
82. Pierre Janet, *Contribution à l'étude des accidents mentaux chez les hystériques*. Thèse méd. Paris, 1892–1893, No. 432 (Paris: Rueff, 1893), pp. 252–257.
83. Moritz Benedikt, *Hypnotismus und Suggestion. Eine Klinisch-psychologische Studie* (Leipzig and Vienna: Breitenstein, 1894), pp. 64–65.

84. See Chap. 2, pp. 96–97.

85. Auguste Motet, *Affaire Valroff. Double tentative de meurtre. Somnambulisme allégué* (Paris: Baillière, 1893).

86. A. Lyubimov, *Professor Sharko, Nautshno-biografitshesky etiud* (St. Petersburg: Tip. Suborina, 1894).

87. See Chap. 2, p. 100.

88. See Chap. 7, pp. 486, 538; Chap. 10, p. 753.

89. See Chap. 2, p. 98.

90. See Chap. 2, pp. 100–101.

91. See Chap. 6, pp. 367–370.

92. See Chap. 6, p. 372.

93. Gustave Le Bon, *Psychologie des foules* (Paris: Alcan, 1895). Eng. trans., *The Psychology of Peoples* (New York: Macmillan, 1898).

94. See Chap. 7, pp. 480–484.

95. Umpfenbach, *Zeitschrift für die Psychologie und Physiologie der Sinnesorgane,* X (1896), 308–309.

96. E. Bleuler, *Münchener medizinische Wochenschrift,* XLIII (1896), 524–525.

97. Adolf Strümpell, *Deutsche Zeitschrift für Nervenheilkunde,* VIII (1896), 159–161.

98. J. Michell Clarke, *Brain,* XIX (1896), 401–414.

99. Frederic W. H. Myers, "Hysteria and Genius," *Journal of the Society for Psychical Research,* VIII, No. 138 (April 1897), 50–59.

100. Havelock Ellis, "Hysteria in Relation to Sexual Emotions," *The Alienist and Neurologist,* XIX (1898), 599–615.

101. Johann Bressler, 'Culturhistorischer Beitrag zur Hysterie," *Allgemeine Zeitschrift für Psychiatrie,* LIII (1896–1897), 333–376.

102. See Chap. 1, pp. 18–22.

103. Paul Ranschburg and Ludwig Hajos, *Neue Beiträge zur Psychologie des Hysterischen Geisteszustandes. Kritisch-experimentelle Studien* (Leipzig and Vienna: Deuticke, 1897).

104. Richard von Krafft-Ebing, "Zur Suggestionsbehandlung der Hysteria Gravis," *Zeitschrift für Hypnotismus,* IV, No. 1 (1896), 27–31.

105. Richard von Krafft-Ebing, *Arbeiten aus dem Gesamtgebiet der Psichiatrie und Neuropathologie* (Leipzig: Barth, 1897), III, 193–211.

106. Alfred Freiherr von Berger, "Chirurgie der Seele" (1896). Partially reprinted in *Almanach der Psychoanalyse* (Vienna: Internationaler Psychoanalytiker Verlag, 1933), pp. 285–289.

107. Hugo von Hofmannsthal, *Elektra* (Berlin: Fischer, 1904).

108. Quoted by Walter Jens, *Hofmannsthal und die Griechen* (Tübingen: Niemayer, 1955), p. 155.

109. Hermann Bahr, *Dialog vom Tragischen* (Berlin: Fischer, 1904).

110. Theodor Herzl, *Der Judenstaat. Versuch einer modernen Lösung der Judenfrage* (Leipzig and Vienna: M. Breitenstein, 1896).

111. *III. Internationaler Congress für Psychologie in München vom 4. bis 7. August 1896* (Munich: J. F. Lehmann, 1897).

112. Theodor Lipps, *III. Internationaler Congress für Psychologie in München,* pp. 146–164.

113. Georg Hirth, *III. Internationaler Congress für Psychologie in München,* pp. 458–473.

114. See Chap. 3, pp. 154–155; Chap. 6, p. 374.

115. Albert Freiherr von Schrenck-Notzing, *Ueber Spaltung der Persönlichkeit (sogenanntes Doppel-Ich)* (Vienna: Hölder, 1896).

116. See Chap. 5, pp. 281–284.

117. Frederic W. H. Myers, "Hysteria and Genius," *Journal of the Society for Psychical Research,* VIII (1897), 50–59.

118. L. Löwenfeld, *Lehrbuch der gesamten Psychotherapie mit einer einleitenden, Darstellung der Hauptthatsachen der medicinischen Psychologie* (Wiesbaden: Bergmann, 1897).

119. See Chap. 6, p. 374.

120. Pierre Janet, "Traitement psychologique de l'hystérie," in *Traité de Thérapeutique*, Albert Robin, ed., fascicule 15, 2nd part (Paris: Rueff, 1898), pp. 140–216.

121. A. W. Van Renterghem, *Liébeault en zijne School* (Amsterdam: Van Rossen, 1898).

122. See Chap. 5, pp. 286–288.

123. Albert Moll, *Untersuchungen über die Libido sexualis* (Berlin: H. Kornfeld, 1898), Vol. I.

124. *Jahrbuch für sexuelle Zwischenstufen unter besonderer Berücksichtigung der Homosexualität* (Leipzig: Max Spohr, 1899).

125. Charles Féré, *L'Instinct sexuel. Evolution et dissolution* (Paris: Alcan, 1899).

126. E. Husserl, *Logische Untersuchungen* (Halle: Niemeyer, 1890), Vol. I.

127. See Chap. 6, pp. 342–343.

128. *IIe Congrès International de l'Hypnotisme*, Paris, August 12–16, 1900 (Paris: Revue de l'Hypnotisme, Vigot, 1902), p. 320. Comptes-Rendus publiés par Dr. Bérillon et Dr. Farez.

129. See Chap. 3, p. 173.

130. *IVe Congrès International de Psychologie*, Paris, August 20–26, 1900 (Paris: Alcan, 1901).

131. See Chap. 5, p. 308.

132. Paul Farez, "L'Hypnotisme et l'évocation du subconscient," *IVe Congrès International de Psychologie*, 1900 (Paris: Alcan, 1901), pp. 670–674.

133. *Le Figaro*, August 29, 1900.

134. See Chap. 5, pp. 315–317.

135. Anon. (D. Metzger), *Autour "des Indes à la planète Mars,"* Bâle et Genève Georg & Cie, ed. (Paris: Librairie Spirite, 1901).

136. Edouard Claparede, "Théodore Flournoy, Sa Vie et son oeuvre. 1854–1920," *Archives de Psychologie*, XVIII (1923), 1–125.

137. See Chap. 7, pp. 450–452, 490–493.

138. Ilse Bry and Alfred H. Rifkin, "Freud and the History of Ideas: Primary Sources, 1886–1910," *Science and Psychoanalysis*, V (1962), 6–36.

139. William Stern, *Zeitschrift für Psychologie und Physiologie der Sinnesorgane* XXVI (1901), 30–133.

140. Naecke, *Archiv für Kriminal-Anthropologie und Kriminalistik*, VII (901), 168–169.

141. W. Weygandt, *Zentralblatt für Nervenheilkunde*, XXIV (1901), 548–549.

142. Théodore Flournoy, *Archives de Psychologie*, II (1903), 72–73.

143. Henri Bergson, "Le Rêve," *Bulletin de l'Institut Psychologique International*, I (1901), 97–122; reprinted in *Revue scientifique*, 4th series, XV (1901), 705–713, and in *Revue de Philosophie*, I (1901), 486–489.

144. Emil Raimann, *Die hysterischen Geistesstörungen. Eine Klinische Studie* (Leipzig and Vienna: Deuticke, 1904).

145. In the same book, Raimann gives the highest praise to Breuer's and Freud's theory of hysteria. It is indeed extraordinary that Jones could consider this book a vitriolic attack against Freud.

146. Max Burckhardt, "Ein modernes Traumbuch," *Die Zeit*, XXII (January 6, 1900), No. 275, p. 911; and (January 13, 1900), No. 276, pp. 25–27.

147. *Die Umschau*, IV, No. 11 (March 10, 1900), 218–219.

148. "H. K. Träume und Traumdeutung," *Fremden-Blatt*, LIV, No. 67 (March 10, 1900), 13–14.

149. *Arbeiter-Zeitung*, XII, No. 289 (October 21, 1900).

150. *Neues Wiener Tagblatt*, January 29 and 30, 1902.

151. These last mentioned two reviews were discovered by Dr. Hans Beckh-Widmanstetter. The author is grateful to him and to K. R. Eissler for photocopies.

152. See Chap. 5, pp. 257–258.

153. J. Babinski, "Definition de l'hystérie,"*Revue Neurologique*, IX (1901), 1074–1080.

154. Sigmund Freud, *Ueber den Traum*, in Loewenfeld and Kurella, *Grenzfragen*

des Nerven- und Seelenlebens (Wiesbaden: Bergmann, 1901), pp. 307–344. Standard Edition, V, 633–686.

155. Ilse Bry and Alfred Rifkin, "Freud and the History of Ideas: Primary Sources," *Science and Psychoanalysis*, V (1962), 6–36.

156. Hermann Kornfeld, *Psychiatrische Wochenschrift*, II (1900–1901), 430–431.

157. Ziehen, *Jahresbericht über die Leistungen und Fortschritte auf dem Gebiete der Neurologie und Psychiatrie*, V (1901), 829.

158. Moebius, *Schmidt's Jahrbücher der in- und ausländischen gesammten Medizin*, CCLXIX (1901), 271.

159. Liepmann, *Monatsschrift für Psychiatrie und Neurologie*, X (1901), 237–239.

160. Giessler, *Zeitschrift für Psychologie und Physiologie der Sinnesorgane*, XXIX (1902), 228–230.

161. O. Kohnstamm, *Fortschritte der Medizin*, XX (1902), 45–46.

162. A. Pick, *Prager Medizinische Wochenschrift*, XXVI (1901), 145.

163. Voss, *St. Petersburger Medizinische Wochenschrift*, XXVI (1901), 325.

164. See Chap. 7, pp. 494–495.

165. *Jahresbericht über die Leistungen und Fortschritte auf dem Gebiete der Neurologie und Psychiatrie*, V (1901).

166. Hermann Rohleder, *Vorlesungen über Sexualtrieb und Sexualleben des Menschen* (Berlin: Fischer, 1901).

167. Albert Moll, "Ueber eine wenig beachtete Gefahr der Prügelstrafe bei Kindern," *Zeitschrift für Psychologie und Physiologie der Sinnesorgane*, XXVIII (1902), 203–204.

168. Heinrich Schurtz, *Altersklassen und Männerbünde. Eine Darstellung der Grundformen der Gesellschaft* (Berlin: G. Reimer, 1902).

169. Theodor Dunin, *Grundsätze der Behandlung der Neurasthenie und Hysterie* (Berlin: Hirschwald, 1902).

170. *Congrès des Médecins Aliénistes et Neurologistes de France*, 12th session, Grenoble, 1902, II (Paris: Masson, 1902).

171. See Chap. 9, pp. 689–691.

172. Théodore Flournoy, "Nouvelles Observations sur un cas de somnambulisme avec glossolalie," *Archives de Psychologie*, I (1902), 101–255.

173. *XIVe Congrès International de Médicine, Madrid, 23–30 avril 1903*. Volume général (1904), p. 295.

174. See Chap. 6, pp. 374–377.

175. Frederic W. H. Myers, *Human Personality and Its Survival of Bodily Death*, 2 vols. (London: Longmans, Green & Co., 1903).

176. See Chap. 5, pp. 313–314.

177. Otto Weininger, *Geschlecht und Charakter* (Vienna: Braumüller, 1903).

178. Among the widespread literature about Weininger, see notably, David Abrahamsen, *The Mind and Death of a Genius* (New York: Columbia University Press, 1946).

179. See Chap. 7, pp. 503–504.

180. Paul Daniel Schreber, *Denkwürdigkeiten eines Nervenkranken* (Leipzig: Oswald Mutze, 1903).

181. Wilhelm Jensen, *Gradiva; ein pompeianisches Phantasiestück* (Dresden and Leipzig: Reissner, 1903).

182. See Chap. 5, pp. 292–293.

183. See Chap. 5, p. 293.

184. See Chap. 3, pp. 123–124.

185. See Chap. 6, p. 344.

186. It is not clear from the proceedings of the Congress whether this was an exhibit of books or just a recommended list.

187. Jean Camus and Philippe Pagniez, *Isolement et psychothérapie* (Paris: Alcan, 1904), pp. 5–82.

188. Paul Dubois, *Les Psychonévroses et leur traitement moral* (Paris: Masson, 1904).

189. See Chap. 7, pp. 494–496.

190. Sigmund Freud, "Die Freudsche psychoanalytische Methode," in L. Löwenfeld,

Die psychischen Zwangserscheinungen auf klinischer Grundlage dargestellt (Wiesbaden: Bergmann, 1904), pp. 545–551. Standard Edition, VII, 249–254.

191. Willy Hellpach, *Grundlinien einer Psychologie der Hysterie* (Leipzig: Wilhelm Engelmann, 1904).

192. Emil Raimann, *Die hysterischen Geistesstörungen. Eine Klinische Studie* (Leipzig and Vienna: Deuticke, 1904).

193. Edouard Claparède, *Psychologie de l'enfant et pédagogie expérimentale* (Geneva: Kündig, 1905).

194. Alfred Binet and Théodore Simon, "Méthodes nouvelles pour le diagnostic du niveau intellectuel des anormaux," *L'Année psychologique*, XI (1905), 191–244.

195. August Forel, *Die sexuelle Frage* (Munich: Reinhardt, 1905).

196. Ilse Bry and Alfred H. Rifkin, "Freud and the History of Ideas: Primary Sources, 1886–1910," *Science and Psychoanalysis*, V (1962), 6–36.

197. *Medizinische Klinik*, II (1906), 740.

198. *Archiv für Kriminal-Anthropologie und Kriminalistik*, XXIV (1906), 166.

199. *Wiener klinische Rundschau*, XX (1906), 189–190.

200. *Psychological Bulletin*, III (1906), 280–283.

201. *Jahrbuch für sexuelle Zwischenstufen*, VIII (1906), 729–748.

202. Otto Soyka, "Zwei Bücher," *Die Fackel*, No. 191 (December 21, 1905), 6–11.

203. See William James' experience of the earthquake (Chap. 9, p. 706).

204. Eugen Bleuler, *Affektivität, Suggestibilität, Paranoia* (Halle: Marhold, 1906).

205. Eugen Bleuler, "Freud'sche Mechanismen in der Symptomatologie von Psychosen," *Psychiatrisch-Neurologische Wochenschrift*, VIII (1906–1907), 316–318, 323–325, 338–340.

206. See Chap. 9, pp. 691–694.

207. Gustav Aschaffenburg, "Die Beziehungen des sexuellen Leben zur Entstehung von Nerven- und Geisteskrankheiten," *Münchener medizinische Wochenschrift*, LIII (1906), 1793–1798.

208. Adolf Meyer, "Fundamental Conceptions of Dementia Praecox," *British Medical Journal*, II (1906), 757–760.

209. Carl Spitteler, *Imago* (Jena: Diederichs, 1906).

210. See Chap. 5, pp. 292–294.

211. A. A. Brill, translator's Introduction to C. G. Jung, *The Psychology of Dementia Praecox*, Nervous and Mental Disease Monographs, 1936.

212. See Chap. 8, pp. 603–606.

213. Otto Rank, *Der Künstler; Ansätze zu einer Sexualpsychologie* (Vienna: Heller, 1907).

214. *Premier Congrès International de Psychiatrie, de Neurologie, de Psychologie, et de l'Assistance des Aliénés*. Amsterdam, September 2–7, 1907 (Amsterdam: De Bussy, 1908).

215. Ernest Jones, *The Life and Work of Sigmund Freud* (New York: Basic Books, 1955), II, 186.

216. The account of the meeting by Jones implies that the session was nothing but a concentrated attack on Freud's theories. The official proceedings leave a quite different impression: most speakers were only interested in defending their own theories; among the others, as many were for as against Freud.

217. *Monatsschrift für Neurologie und Psychiatrie*, XXII (1907), 562–572.

218. This supposed assertion of Janet's is not to be found in the proceedings of the Congress. It may have been an offhand remark during an intermission. It was nonetheless distorted in later accounts: Janet (the saying went) had declared publicly that psychoanalysis (not just its theory of hysteria) was a *mauvaise plaisanterie* (a practical joke).

219. Ernest Jones, *The Life and Work of Sigmund Freud* (New York: Basic Books, 1955), II, 119.

220. A. A. Friedländer, "Ueber Hysterie und die Freudsche psychoanalytische Behandlung derselben," *Monatsschrift für Psychiatrie und Neurologie*, XXII (1907), Ergänzungsheft, 45–54.

221. W. Weygandt, "Kritische Bemerkungen zur Psychologie der Dementia Praecox," *Monatsschrift für Psychiatrie und Neurologie*, XXII (1907), 289–302.

222. M. Isserlin, *Centralblatt für Nervenheilkunde und Psychiatrie*, XVIII (1907), 329–343.

223. Georges Sorel, *Réflexions sur la violence* (Paris: Librairie de "Pages Libres," 1908).

224. Karl Kraus, "Apocalypse (Offener Brief an das Publikum)," *Die Fackel*, X, No. 261/262 (October 13, 1908), 1–14.

225. Edward Ryan, "A Visit to the Psychiatric Clinics and Asylums of the Old Land," *American Journal of Insanity*, LXV (1908–1909), 347–356.

226. R. C. Clarke, "Notes on Some of the Psychiatric Clinics and Asylums of Germany," *American Journal of Insanity*, LXV (1908–1909), 357–376.

227. Clarence P. Oberndorf, *A History of Psychoanalysis in America* (New York: Grune and Stratton, 1953), p. 75.

228. H. W. Gruhle, *Zentralblatt für Nervenheilkunde*, XXXI (XIX) (1908), 885–887.

229. Karl Kraus, "Tagebuch," *Die Fackel*, X, No. 256 (June 5, 1908), 15–32.

230. Karl Abraham, "Verwandtenehe und Neurose," *Zentralblatt für Nervenheilkunde*, XXXII (1909), 87–90.

231. Ernest Jones, *The Life and Work of Sigmund Freud* (New York: Basic Books, 1955), II, 128.

232. *VIe Congrès International de Psychologie, 1909, Rapports et Comptes-Rendus*, Edouard Claparède, ed. (Geneva: Kündig, 1910).

233. W. B. Parker, ed., *Psychotherapy: A Course of Reading in Sound Psychology, Sound Medicine, and Sound Religion*, 3 vols. (New York: Centre Publishing Co., 1909).

234. A. A. Brill, "Freud's Method of Psychotherapy," *Psychotherapy*, II, No. 4, 36–47.

235. Richard C. Cabot, "The Literature of Psychotherapy," *Psychotherapy*, III, No. 4 (1909), 18–25.

236. Ernest Jones, *The Life and Work of Sigmund Freud* (New York: Basic Books, 1955), II, 54–59.

237. *Lectures and Addresses Delivered before the Departments of Psychology and Pedagogy in Celebration of the Twentieth Anniversary of the Opening of Clarke University, September 1909*, 2 vols. (Worcester, Mass., 1910).

238. See Chap. 7, p. 460.

239. A. Friedländer, "Hysterie und Moderne Psychoanalyse," *Congrès International de Médecine*, Budapest (1909), Sect. XII, pp. 146–172.

240. J. I. Sadger, "Die Bedeutung der psychoanalytischen Methode nach Freud," *Centralblatt für Nervenheilkunde und Psychiatrie*, XXX (XVIII) (1907), 45–52 (quotation from p. 50).

241. Caroline E. Playne, *The Neuroses of the Nations* (London: Allen and Unwin, 1928).

242. F. T. Marinetti, "Le Futurisme," *Le Figaro*, No. 51 (February 20, 1909).

243. Anon., *Jubilé du Professeur Bernheim. 12 novembre 1910* (Nancy, 1910).

244. See Chap. 7, pp. 530–531.

245. Ernest Jones, "The Oedipus Complex as an Explanation of Hamlet's Mystery: A Study in Motive," *American Journal of Psychology*, XXI (1910), 72–113.

246. Sigmund Freud, "Brief an Dr. Friedrich Krauss," *Anthropophyteia*, VII (1910), 472–473. Standard Edition, XI, 221–227.

247. It is noteworthy that, at the same time, Ludwig Zamenhof, the creator of Esperanto, wanted to leave the direction of his organization to a non-Jew. See *Israelitisches Wochenblatt*, XI (1912), 541–542.

248. Hans Blüher, *Traktat über die Heilkunde* (Stuttgart: Klett, 1926). (Quoted from the 3rd edition, 1950, pp. 99–107.)

249. Sigmund Freud, "Ueber 'wilde' Psychoanalyse," *Zentralblatt für Psychoanalyse*, I (1910), 91–95. Standard Edition, XI, 221–227.

250. Oskar Pfister, *Die psychanalytische Methode* (Leipzig and Berlin: Klinkhardt, 1913), pp. 59–60.

251. *Journal für Psychologie und Neurologie*, XVII, Ergänzungscheft (1910–1911), 307–433.

252. Alfred Hoche, "Eine psychische Epidemie unter Aertzten," *Medizinische Klinik*, VI (1910), 1007–1010.

253. Ludwig Frank, *Die Psychanalyse* (Munich: E. Reinhardt, 1910).

254. Roger Vittoz, *Traitement des psychonévroses par la rééducation du contrôle cérébral* (Paris: Baillière, 1911).

255. Further details about Vittoz' method may be found in the medical dissertation of Robert Dupond, *La Cure des psychonévroses par la méthode du Dr. Vittoz* (Paris: Jouve, 1934), and in a booklet written by an admirer, Henriette Lefebvre, *Un Sauveur, le Docteur Vittoz* (Paris: Jouve, n.d.).

256. E. Bleuler, *Dementia Praecox, oder Gruppe der Schizophrenien*, in Aschaffenburg, *Handbuch der Psychiatrie, Spezieller Teil*, 4. Abt., 1. Hälfte (Vienna: Deuticke, 1911). (See Chap. 5, pp. 287–288).

257. Grete Meisel-Hess, *Die Intellektuellen* (Berlin: Oesterheld, 1911), pp. 341–346.

258. At one of the hearings after the shipwreck, a third-class passenger gave evidence under oath that during the rescue operations a gate separating the steerage from the upper deck was locked in their faces. Those third-class passengers who escaped did so by breaking the lock. *Titanic Disaster. Hearings before a Subcommittee on Commerce*. United States Senate, 62nd Congress, 2nd session. Document No. 726 (Washington: Government Printing Office, 1912), p. 1,021.

259. Friedrich von Bernhardi, *Deutschland und der nächste Krieg* (Stuttgart: Cottas Nachfolger, 1912). Eng. trans. *Germany and the Next War* (London: E. Arnold, 1912).

260. It has not been possible to find out whether any part of the foundation funds were disbursed. The Breuer-Stiftung was one of the many victims of the postwar inflation. When the Austrian currency was stabilized in 1922, 10,000 crowns became one shilling (one seventh of a dollar).

261. The author is grateful to Mrs. Käthe Breuer, who showed him these documents, and to Mr. George H. Bryant, Josef Breuer's grandson, for complementary information.

262. Sir James Frazer, *Totemism and Exogany, A Treatise on Certain Early Forms of Superstition and Society*, 4 vols. (London: Macmillan Co., 1910).

263. Emile Durkheim, *Les Formes élémentaires de la vie religieuse, le système totémique en Australie* (Paris: Alcan, 1912).

264. Richard Thurnwald, "Die Denkart als Wurzel des Totemismus," *Korrespondenzblatt der deutschen Gesellschaft für Anthropologie, Ethnologie, und Urgeschichte* (1911), pp. 173–179.

265. Wilhelm Wundt, *Elemente der Völkerpsychologie* (Leipzig: Alfred Kröner, 1912).

266. Otto Rank, *Das Inzest-Motiv in Dichtung und Sage* (Leipzig and Vienna: Deuticke, 1912).

267. The author is grateful to Dr. Gustav Morf who drew his attention to the interest of that episode, and to the Archive Department of the *Neue Zürcher Zeitung*, Zurich, for their help.

268. See Chap. 10, p. 806.

269. Richard B. Goldschmidt, *Portraits from Memory: Recollections of a Zoologist* (Seattle: University of Washington Press, 1956), p. 35.

270. Johann Michelsen, *Ein Wort an geistigen Adel deutscher Nation* (Munich: Bonsels, 1911).

271. Norman Malcolm, *Ludwig Wittgenstein: A Memoir* (London: Oxford University Press, 1958).

272. Otto Rank and Hanns Sachs, *Die Bedeutung der Psychoanalyse für die Geitesswissenschaften* (Wiesbaden: Bergmann, 1913), p. 68.

273. Hans Blüher, *Werke und Tage. Geschichte eines Denkers* (Munich: Paul List, 1953), p. 252.

274. In the same year Marinetti published a novel in French verses, *Le Monoplan du Pape, roman politique en vers libres* (Paris: Sansot, 1912), with the "shocking" story of the Pope kidnapped and traveling by airplane. Little could he guess that many young readers would live long enough to see a Pope flying to Jerusalem and New York.

275. Dr. Alphonse Maeder, Personal communication.

276. Sigmund Freud, "Gross ist die Diana der Epheser," *Zentralblatt für Psycho-analyse,* II (1912), 158–159. Standard Edition, XII, 342–344.

277. See Chap. 2, p. 78.

278. Ludwig Frank, *Affektstörungen* (Berlin: J. Springer, 1913).

279. See Chap. 7, pp. 606–608.

280. *17th International Congress of Medicine,* London, 1913, Sect. 12, Parts I and II (London: Henry Frowde, 1913).

281. This has given rise to one of the most tenacious legends in the history of dynamic psychiatry: Janet is reputed to have insulted Freud, and to have said that "psychoanalysis could arise only in such an immoral place as Vienna." It is sufficient to refer to the text of Janet's report to find that he was quoting Ladame, who in turn had quoted Friedländer's opinion of the *genius loci,* that is, the particular interest of the Viennese public in sexual pathology following the publications of Krafft-Ebing and others.

282. Ernest Jones, *Free Associations: Memories of a Psycho-Analyst* (London: Hogarth Press, 1959), p. 241.

283. Ernest Jones, *The Life and Work of Sigmund Freud* (New York: Basic Books, 1955), II, 99.

284. Robert Wollenberg, *Erinnerungen eines alten Psychiaters* (Stuttgart: Enke, 1931), p. 126.

285. Lou Andreas-Salomé, *In der Schule bei Freud. Tagebuch eines Jahres 1912–1913* (Zurich: Max Niehans, 1958), p. 190.

286. See Chap. 9, p. 693.

287. Ernest Jones, *The Life and Work of Sigmund Freud* (New York: Basic Books, 1955), II, 109.

288. The author is most grateful to Mrs. Paula Hammet, of Melbourne, who inquired in that matter on his behalf and brought evidence from persons who had been acquainted with Reverend Donald Fraser's family.

289. Professor Birger Strandell kindly made investigations into the archives of the University of Uppsala and procured for the author a photocopy of the Faculty Council's discussion of Sperber's candidacy. Sperber's thesis was rejected after a long discussion in which he had only one supporter. Among the opponents only one made a casual, derogatory remark about Sperber's article on the sexual origin of the language. Actually this paper played no role whatever in the rejection of Sperber's thesis.

290. Ernest Jones, *Free Associations: Memories of a Psychoanalyst* (London: Hogarth Press, 1959), p. 225.

291. See Chap. 7, pp. 529–530.

292. See Chap. 7, pp. 510–511.

293. See Chap. 6, p. 344.

294. Henri Bergson, *Les Deux Sources de la morale et de la religion* (Paris: Alcan, 1932), pp. 166–167.

295. Robert A. Kann, *The Multinational Empire,* 2 vols. (New York: Oregon Books, 1964).

296. Z. A. B. Zerman, *The Break-Up of the Hapsburg Empire, 1914–1918* (London: Oxford University Press, 1961), p. 24.

297. In so doing, the Austrian-Hungarian government was following the political practice of the times. Two months previously the U. S. government had sent an expedition against the Mexicans at Vera Cruz, following a much less grievous act of aggression. To give a parallel to the Austro-Serbian situation, one should imagine what would have happened if President Wilson had been assassinated in Santa Fe by a group of terrorists from New Mexico, armed, trained, and directed by the Mexican secret police with the occult support of a major power.

298. Felix Somary, *Erinnerungen aus meinem Leben* (Zurich: Manasse-Verlag, 1959), p. 114.

299. Quoted by Georges Pascal, *Pour Connaître la pensée d'Alain,* 3rd ed. (Paris: Bordas, 1957), pp. 176–177.

300. Romain Rolland, "Au-dessus de la mêlée," *Journal de Genève* (September 22–23, 1914), supp., p. 5.

301. Hermann Hesse, "O Freunde, nicht diese Töne!" No. 1487, *Neue Zurcher Zeitung* (November 3, 1914), pp. 1–2.
302. Josef Breuer, Letter to Maria Ebner-Eschenbach, June 28, 1914. (Kindly communicated by Mrs. Käthe Breuer.)
303. Ernest Jones, *The Life and Work of Sigmund Freud* (New York: Basic Books, 1955), II, 192.
304. See Chap. 6, p. 345.
305. Albert Moll, *Ein Leben als Arzt der Seele. Erinnerungen* (Dresden: Carl Reissner, 1936), pp. 192–193.
306. August Forel, *Rückblick auf mein Leben* (Zurich: Europa-Verlag, 1935), pp. 263–270.
307. See, among others, the official documents compiled under the title, *The Memoirs of Naim Bey. Turkish Official Documents Relating to the Deportations and Massacres of Armenians* (London: Hodder and Stoughton, 1920).
308. Joseph Babinski and Eugène Froment, *Hystérie-pithiatisme et troubles nerveux d'origine réflexe en neurologie de guerre* (Paris: Masson, 1917).
309. J. Wagner-Jauregg, "Erfahrungen über Kriegsneurosen." Reprint from *Wiener Medizinische Wochenschrift* (1916–1917).
310. Horace W. Frink, *Morbid Fears and Compulsions: Their Psychology and Psychoanalytic Treatment* (New York: Dodd Mead, 1918).
311. Herbert Silberer, *Durch Tod zum Leben* (Leipzig, Heims, 1915).
312. Hans Blüher, *Die Rolle der Erotik in der Männergesellschaft* (Jena: Diederich, 1917–1919).
313. Georg Friedrich Nicolai, *Die Biologie des Krieges. Betrachtungen eines deutschen Naturforschers* (Zurich: Orell-Füssli, 1917). Eng. trans. *The Biology of War* (New York: The Century Co., 1919).
314. See the special issue of the Swiss magazine *Du*, XXVI (September 1966), "Zürich, 1914–1918."
315. According to Friedrich Glauser, Tristan Tzara went so far as to simulate mental illness before a Rumanian medical commission; he simply answered "Da, Da" (yes, yes) to each question asked by the experts.
316. Jakob Moreno Levy, "Einladung zu einer Begegnung," *Daimon, eine Monatsschrift*, No. 1 (February 1918), pp. 3–21.
317. Ernst Lothar, *Das Wunder des Ueberlebens, Erinnerungen und Erlebnisse* (Hamburg-Wirn: Paul Zsolnay, 1960), pp. 36–37.
318. *"Ich habe wie Sie eine unbändige Zuneigung zu Wien und Oesterreich."* Incidentally, this is further evidence against the legend according to which Freud deeply hated Vienna during his entire life.
319. Malcolm Bullock, *Austria, 1918–1938: A Study in Failure* (London: Macmillan Co., 1939), p. 67.
320. Characteristic in that regard was a pamphlet by Hermann Hesse, *Blick ins Chaos* (Bern: Verlag Seldwyla, 1921).
321. Oswald Spengler, *Der Untergang des Abendlandes; Umriss einer Morphologie der Weltgeschichte*, 2 vols. (Munich: Beck, 1919, 1922).
322. Karl Kraus, *Die Letzten Tage der Menschheit* (1926), in *Werke* (Munich: Kösel-Verlag, 1957), Vol. V.
323. See Chap. 8, p. 588.
324. Paul Federn, "Zur Psychologie der Revolution: die Vaterlose Gesellschaft," *Der Aufstieg. Neue Zeit—und Streitschriften*, No. 12/13 (Leipzig and Vienna: Anzengruber Verlag, 1919).
325. A. Aichhorn, editor, *Saatkörnlein. Mitteilungen Zum Ausbau des Hortbetriebes der Wiener städtischen Knabenhorte* (Erstes Heft: Vienna, 1917).
326. See Chap. 10, pp. 846–847.
327. Clarence P. Oberndorf, *A History of Psychoanalysis in America* (New York: Grune and Stratton, 1953), p. 1.
328. Sandor Ferenczi et al., *Zur Psychoanalyse der Kriegsneurosen* (Vienna: Internationaler Psychoanalytischer Verlag, 1919). (Foreword by Freud.)
329. See Chap. 6, pp. 345, 377–386.
330. Hermann Hesse, *Demian, die Geschichte einer Jugend, von Emil Sinclair*

(Berlin: S. Fischer, 1919). Eng. trans., *Demian* (New York: Boni and Liveright, 1923).

331. Hermann Hesse had a Jungian analysis in 1916 and 1917 with Dr. Josef Lang in Lucerne, and later, in 1920, "therapeutic talks" with Jung himself. *Demian* was written in 1917 and published two years later. (Information kindly provided by Frau Ninon Hesse in a letter of March 15, 1964.)

332. Alec Mellor, *La Torture, son histoire, son abolition, sa réapparition au XXe siècle* (Tours: Mame, 1961).

333. See, for instance, Maurice Sachs, *Au Temps du boeuf sur le toit* (Paris: Nouvelle Revue Critique, 1939), pp. 108–127.

334. It is characteristic that in Marcel Proust's novels there is no mention of alcoholic drinks, whereas in those of Hemingway and other postwar writers, alcohol plays a considerable role.

335. Philippe Soupault, Paul Eluard, Pierre Drieu La Rochelle, Joseph Delteil, André Breton, and Louis Aragon, *Un Cadavre* (Paris, 1924). Partially reprinted in Marcel Nadeau, *Histoire du surréalisme. II. Documents surréalistes* (Paris: Editions du Seuil, 1948), pp. 11–15.

336. Among the widespread literature devoted to surrealism, see particularly: Maurice Nadeau, *Histoire du surréalisme*, 2 vols. (Paris: Editions du Seuil, 1945, 1948). M. Carrouges, *André Breton et les données fondamentales du surréalisme* (Paris: Gallimard, 1950). Yves Duplessis, "Que-sais-je?" *Le surréalisme* (Paris: Presses Universitaires de France, 1958), No. 432.

337. Herbert Silberer, "Bericht über eine Methode, gewisse symbolische Halluzinations-Erscheinungen hervorzurufen und zu beobachten," *Jahrbuch für psychoanalytische und psychopathologische Forschungen*, I (1909), 513–525.

338. See Chap. 6, p. 366.

339. One of the best known of them was that of André Breton and Philippe Soupault, *Les Champs magnétiques* (Paris: Au Sans-Pareil, 1921).

340. André Breton, *Entretiens, 1913–1952, avec André Parinaud* (Paris: Nouvelle Revue Française, 1952), pp. 89–91.

341. This was not as new as the Surrealists believed. During the mental epidemics called Ghost Dance Religion, American Indians systematically made objects they had seen in visions and dreams. See James Mooney, *The Ghost Dance Religion and the Sioux Outbreak of 1890*, Fourteenth Annual Report of the Bureau of Ethnology for 1892–1893, part II, Washington, 1896.

342. André Breton and Paul Eluard, *L'Immaculée Conception* (Paris: Corti, 1930),

343. See Chap. 7, p. 460.

344. A part of Freud's paper on lay analysis appeared in *La Révolution surréaliste*, III, No. 9/10 (October 1927), 25–32. A part of his essay on "Jokes and the Unconscious" appeared in *Variétés*, special issue (June 1929), pp. 3–6, under the title "L'Humour."

345. As to Jung, he is reported to have said of Dadaist productions, "It's too idiotic to be schizophrenic."

346. Henri Ey, "La Psychiatrie devant le surréalisme," *L'Evolution Psychiatrique*, (1948), No. 4, pp. 3–52.

347. This episode has been termed, quite wrongly, the Wagner-Jauregg trial. Actually it was an administrative inquiry that had to hear not only Wagner-Jauregg but several other former military neuropsychiatrists.

348. The author is most grateful to Renée Giklhorn, who lent him the manuscript of her unpublished book: *Der Wagner-Jauregg "Prozess,"* a detailed account of the inquiry, including the text of the main documents and the stenogram of the discussions. The account given by Jones conveys an inaccurate impression of the debates, because it tells only of Freud's written report, not of his verbal interventions during the discussions.

349. Freud's expert report was published first in English translation in the Standard Edition, XVII, 210–215.

350. In fact, the concept of "flight into illness" had been formulated almost in the same terms by Ideler (See Chap. 4, p. 213) and had been current in Romantic medicine.

351. Let it be recalled that no less than eleven languages were spoken in the armies of the multinational empire.

352. Ernest Jones, *The Life and Work of Sigmund Freud* (New York: Basic Books, 1957), III, 21–24.

353. Julius Wagner-Jauregg, *Lebenserinnerungen.* Von L. Schönbauer and M. Jantsch, eds. (Vienna: Springer, 1950), pp. 71–73.

354. Eugen Bleuler, *Naturgeschichte der Seele und ihres Bewusstwerdens* (Berlin: Springer, 1921).

355. Meaning that like Goethe with his *Second Faust,* Bleuler wrote it toward the end of his life, and that this work was profound and obscure.

356. August Forel, *Le Monde social des fourmis,* 5 vols. (Geneva: Kündig, 1921).

357. See Chap. 6, pp. 394–400.

358. See Chap. 9, pp. 700–703.

359. Ernst Kretschmer, *Körperbau und Charakter* (Berlin: Springer, 1921), pp. 189–192. *Medizinische Psychologie* (Leipzig: Thieme, 1922), pp. 149–156.

360. H. F. Ellenberger, "The Life and Work of Hermann Rorschach (1884–1922), *Bulletin of the Menninger Clinic,* XVIII (1954), 173–219.

361. Hermann Rorschach, *Gesammelte Aufsätze* (Bern: Huber, 1965).

362. Hermann Rorschach, *Psychodiagnostik. Methodik und Ergebnisse eines wahnehmungsdiagnostischen Experiments. (Deutenlassen von Zufallsformen)* (Bern: Bircher, 1921).

363. See Chap. 7, pp. 527–528.

364. C. P. Oberndorf, *A History of Psychoanalysis in America* (New York: Grune and Stratton, 1953), p. 138.

365. George Seldes, *Can These Things Be!* (New York: Brewer, Warren and Putnam, 1931), pp. 409–423.

366. Georg Groddeck, *Der Seelensucher. Ein psychoanalytischer Roman* (Vienna: Internationaler Psychoanalytischer Verlag, 1921).

367. Hermine von Hug-Helmuth, *Tagebuch eines halbwüchsigen Mädchens* (Vienna: Internationaler Psychoanalytischer Verlag, 1918).

368. Cyril Burt, *British Journal of Psychology,* Medical Section, I (1920–1921), 353–357.

369. Not only were literary qualities and logical coherence above the level of those of an adolescent, Cyril Burt said, but the personal trivialities that usually fill young people's diaries were strangely absent from it. Moreover, she went to much trouble to describe and explain the personalities and relationships of the persons she spoke of. Certain entries were so long that she could not have written for less than five hours in one day, although it was an allegedly secret diary written under conditions where privacy was impossible. And one wondered why she took the trouble of copying the full text of long letters, rather than just annexing them to the diary.

370. Ivan Kinkel, *Kem veprosa za psikhologicheskite osnovi i proizkhoda na religiata* (Sofia, 1921).

371. Jakob Klaesi, "Ueber die therapeutische Anwendung der Dauernarkose mittels Somnifens bei Schizophrenen," *Zeitschrift für die gesamte Neurologie und Psytriatrie,* LXXIV (1922), 557–592.

372. Emile Coué, *La Maîtrise de soi par l'autosuggestion consciente,* nouvelle edition (Nancy: chez l'auteur, 1922).

373. Ella Boyce Kirk, *My Pilgrimage to Nancy* (New York: American Library Service, 1922).

374. Ludwig Binswanger, "Ueber Phänomenologie," *Schweizer Archiv für Neurologie und Psychiatrie,* XII (1923), 327–330.

375. Jean Piaget, *Le Langage et la pensée chez l'enfant* (Neuchâtel: Delachaux et Niestlé, 1923). Eng. trans., *The Language and Thought of the Child* (New York: Harcourt Brace and Co., 1926).

376. Eugène Minkowski, "Etude psychologique et analyse phénoménologique d'un cas de mélancolie schizophrénique," *Journal de psychologie normale et pathologique,* XX (1923), 543–558. Eng. trans., Rollo May, Ernst Angel, and Henri F. Ellenberger,

eds., *Existence* (New York: Basic Books, 1958), pp. 127–138.

377. Martin Buber, *Ich und Du* (Leipzig: Insel-Verlag, 1923). Eng. trans., *I And Thou*, 2nd ed. (New York: Scribner, 1958).

378. See Chap. 7, pp. 515–517.

379. Georg Groddeck, *Das Buch vom Es; Psychoanalytische Briefe and eine Freundin* (Vienna: Internationaler Psychoanalytischer Verlag, 1923). Eng. trans., *The Book of the Id* (New York: Funk and Wagnalls, 1950).

380. Ivan Dm. Ermakov, ed., *Psikhologicheskaya i psikhoanaliticheskaya biblioteka*, III, *Osnovnie psikhologicheskie teorii v psikhoanalize* (1923).

381. Ivan Kinkel, "Sotsialna psikhopatiya v revolutsionnit dvizheniya," *Annuaire de l'Université de Sofia*, XIX (1924).

382. Sandor Ferenczi and Otto Rank, *Entwicklungsziele der Psychoanalyse* (Vienna: Internationaler Psychoanalytischer Verlag, 1924).

383. Otto Rank, *Das Trauma der Geburt und seine Bedeutung für die Psychoanalyse* (Vienna: Internationaler Psychoanalytischer Verlag, 1924). Eng. trans., *The Trauma of Birth* (New York: Harcourt, Brace and Co., 1929).

384. Edward Glover, "The Therapeutic Effect of Inexact Interpretations: A Contribution to the Theory of Suggestion," *International Journal of Psychoanalysis*, XII (1931), 397–411.

385. Sandor Ferenczi, *Versuch einer Genitaltheorie* (Vienna: Internationaler Psychoanalytischer Verlag, 1924).

386. Incidentally, a similar theory was expressed by the neurotic Ellida in Ibsen's play *The Lady from the Sea (Fruen fra havet, 1888)*, trans. by Eleanor Marx-Aveling (London: Unwin, 1890).

387. Eugen Bleuler, *Die Psychoide, das Princip der organischen Entwicklung* (Berlin: Springer, 1925).

388. Cornelia Stratton Parker, "The Capital of Psychology," *The Survey* (New York), LIV (September), 551–555.

389. Theodor Reik, *Geständniszwang und Strafbedürfnis. Probleme der Psychoanalyse und der Kriminologie* (Vienna: *Internationaler Psychoanalytischer Verlag*, 1925).

390. August Aichhorn, *Verwahrloste Jugend, die Psychoanalyse in der Fürsorgeerziehung. Zehn Vorträge zur ersten Einführung*. Mit eine Geleitwort von Prof. Dr. Sigmund Freud (Leipzig: Internationale Psychoanalytische Bibliothek, 1925), No. 19. Eng. trans., *Wayward Youth* (New York: Meridian Books, 1955).

391. See Chap. 10, pp. 831–832.

392. Alexander R. Luria, "Psikhoanaliz kak sistema monisticheskoi psikhologii," in *Psikhologii i Marxisma* (1925), pp. 47–80.

393. Enrico Morselli, *La psicanalisi* (Turin: Bocca, 1926), I, p. 19.

394. Léon Daudet's version of the case can be found in his book *La Police politique, ses moyens et ses crimes* (Paris: Denoel et Steel, 1934), pp. 170–324.

395. André Gaucher, *L'Obsédé, Drame de la libido*. Avec lettres de Freud et de Pierre Janet (Paris: Delpeuch, 1925).

396. Kurt Tucholsky, "Herr Maurras vor Gericht," in *Gesammelte Werke* (Hamburf: Rohwolt Verlag, n.d.), II, 217–223.

397. Pierre Janet, *De l'Angoisse à l'extase, Etudes sur les croyances et les sentiments*, I (Paris: Alcan, 1926). (See also Chap. 6, pp. 395–396).

398. Pierre Janet, *Les Stades de l'évolution psychologique* (Paris: Maloine, 1926).

399. Pierre Janet, *Psicología de los sentimientos* (México, DF: Sociedad de Edición y Librería Franco-Americana, 1926).

400. C. G. Jung, *Das Unbewusste im normalen und kranken Seelenleben* (Zurich: Rascher, 1926).

401. See Chap. 3, p. 156.

402. At the "Bureau des Recherches Surréalistes" (Office for Surrealistic Research) in Paris, a copy of Freud's *Introductory Lectures to Psychoanalysis* was on exhibit, surrounded with forks "as an invitation to devour the book." See André Masson, "Le Peintre et ses fantasmes," *Les Etudes Philosophiques*, II, No. 4 (1956), 634–636.

403. Sigmund Freud, *Die Zukunft einer Illusion* (Vienna: Internationaler Psychoanalytischer Verlag, 1927). Standard Edition, XXI, 5–56.

404. Oskar Pfister, "Die Illusion einer Zukunft, Eine freundschaftliche Auseinandersetzung mit Sigmund Freud," *Imago*, XIV (1928), 149–184.

405. Federn-Meng, *Das Psychoanalytische Volksbuch* (Stuttgart: Hippokrates-Verlag, 1927).

406. Heinz Hartmann, *Die Grundlagen der Psychoanalyse* (Leipzig: Thieme, 1927).

407. Franz Alexander, *Psychoanalyse der Gesamtpersönlichkeit; neun Vorlesungen über die Anwendung von Freud's Ichteorie auf die Neurosenlehre* (Vienna: Internationaler Psychoanalytischer Verlag, 1927).

408. Wilhelm Reich, *Die Funktion des Orgasmus. Zur Psychopathologie und zur Soziologie des Geschlechtslebens* (Vienna: Internationaler Psychoanalytischer Verlag, 1927).

409. Otto Rank, *Die Technik der Psychoanalyse* (Leipzig and Vienna: Deuticke, 1926), Vol. I.

410. See Chap. 8, pp. 608–616.

411. Ludwig Frank, *Die Psychokathartische Behandlung nervöser Störungen* (Leipzig: Thieme, 1927).

412. Max Bircher-Benner, *Der Menschenseele Not, Erkrankung und Gesundung,* 2 vols. (Zurich: Wendepunkt-Verlag, 1927–1933).

413. Eugène Minkowski, *La Schizophrénie* (Paris: Payot, 1927).

414. Martin L. Reymert, ed., *Feelings and Emotions. The Wittenberg Symposium* (Worcester: Clark University Press, 1928).

415. M. K. Petrova, "Posleoperatsionnyi nevroz serdtsa, tchastyu analizirovannyi samim patsientom-fiziologom I. P. P. *Klinitcheskaya Meditsina*, VIII (1930), 937–940. The author is much obliged to Professor P. Kupalov, of Leningrad, who sent him a photostat of this article, which is not to be found in Pavlov's *Collected Works*.

416. Martin Heidegger, *Sein und Zeit* (Tübingen: Niemayer, 1927).

417. See Chap. 7, p. 532.

418. C. G. Jung, *Beziehungen zwischen dem Ich und dem Unbewussten* (Darmstad: Reichel, 1928). *Ueber die Energetik der Seele* (Zurich: Rascher, 1928). (See Chap. 8, p. 000).

419. C. G. Jung, *Contributions to Analytical Psychology*, trans. by C. F. Baynes and H. G. Baynes (London: Kegan Paul, 1928).

420. V. E. Freiherr von Gebsattel, "Zeitbezogenes Zwangsdenken in der Melancholie (Versuche einer konstruktiv-genetischen Betrachtung der Melancholiesymptome)," *Nervenarzt*, I (1928), 275–287.

421. Edmund Jacobson, *Progressive Relaxation* (Chicago: University of Chicago Press, 1928).

422. See Chap. 7, pp. 528–529.

423. Franz Alexander and Hugo Staub, *Der Verbrecher und seine Richter* (Vienna: Internationaler Psychoanalytischer Verein, 1929). A revised and augmented English translation has been published: *The Criminal, the Judge and the Public: A Psychological Analysis* (New York: Macmillan, 1931).

424. Yuriy V. Kannabikh, *Istoriya psikhiatrii* (Leningrad: Gos. Med. Izd., 1929), pp. 455–458, 470–471.

425. Nicolaus Krestnikoff, "Die heilende Wirkung hervorgerufener Reproduktionen von pathogenen affektiven Erlebnissen," *Archiv für Psychiatrie und Nervenkrankheiten*, LXXXVIII (1929), 369–410.

426. Hermann Simon, *Aktivere Krankenbehandlung in der Irrenanstalt* (Berlin: De Gruyter, 1929).

427. See Chap. 10, p. 799.

428. Hans Berger, "Ueber das Elektrenkephalogramm des Menschen," *Archiv für Psychiatrie und Nervenkrankheiten*, LXXXVII (1929), 527–570.

429. Ludwig Bauer, *Morgen wieder Krieg. Untersuchung der Gegenwart, Blick in die Zukunft* (Berlin: Rowohlt, 1931).

430. Ludwig Binswanger, Über Ideenflucht, *Schweizer Archiv für Neurologie und Psychiatrie*, XXVII (1931), 203–217; XXVIII (1932), 18–72; XXVIII (1932), 183–202; XXIX (1932), 1 and 193; XXX (1932), 68–85.

431. Melanie Klein, *The Psychoanalysis of Children* (London: Hogarth Press, 1932).

432. J. H. Schultz, *Das autogene Training (konzentrative Selbstentspannung)* (Leipzig:, Thieme, 1932). Eng. trans., *Autogenic Training* (New York: Grune and Stratton, 1959).

433. J. L. Moreno, *Group Method and Group Psychotherapy* (New York: Beacon House, 1932).

434. Let it be recalled that as late as July 19, 1936, Ernest Jones had a meeting in Basel with Dr. M. H. Göring, Böhm, and Müller-Braunschweig; he obtained promises from Göring guaranteeing the freedom to practice psychoanalysis. See Ernest Jones, *The Life and Work of Sigmund Freud* (New York: Basic Books, 1952), III.

435. Wilhelm Reich, *Charakteranalyse* (Copenhagen: Sexpol Verlag, 1933). Eng. trans., *Character Analysis* (New York: Orgone Institute Press, 1945).

436. Eugène Minkowski, *Le Temps vécu. Etudes phénoménologiques et psychopathologiques* (Paris: D'Artrey, 1933).

437. Albert Einstein, *Mein Weltbild* (Amsterdam: Querido, 1934), pp. 36–69, 72.

438. Sigmund Freud, *Neue Folge der Vorlesungen zur Einführung in die Psychoanalyse* (Vienna: Internationaler Psychoanalytischer Verlag, 1934). Standard Edition, XXII, 5–182.

439. C. G. Jung, *Wirklichkeit der Seele* (Zurich: Rascher, 1934).

440. Gerhard Adler, *Entdeckung der Seele von Sigmund Freud und Alfred Adler zu C. G. Jung* (Zurich: Rascher, 1934).

441. J. L. Moreno, *Who Shall Survive?* (Washington: Nervous and Mental Disease Co., 1934).

442. Manfred Sakel, *Neue Behandlungsmethode der Schizophrenie* (Vienna and Leipzig: Perles, 1935).

443. Egaz Moniz, "Les Premières Tentatives opératoires dans le traitement de certaines psychoses," *L'Encéphale*, XXXI, No. 2 (1936), 1–29.

444. Pierre Janet, *L'Intelligence avant le langage* (Paris: Flammarion, 1936). (See Chap. 6, p. 390.)

445. See Chap. 7, p. 517.

446. L. J. von Meduna, *Die Konvulsionstherapie der Schizophrenie* (Halle: Carl Marhold, 1937).

447. L. Szondi, "Analysis of Marriages," *Acta Psychologica*, III (1938), 1–80.

448. Mark Wischnitzer, *To Dwell in Safety, The Story of Jewish Emigration Since 1800* (Philadelphia: Jewish Publication Society of America, 1948).

449. Leopold Ehrlich-Hichler, *"1938"—Ein Wiener Roman* (Vienna: Europäischer Verlag, n.d.).

450. See Chap. 5, p. 281.

451. Quoted by Annemarie Wettley, *August Forel* (Salzburg: Otto Müller, 1953), pp. 116–117.

452. Hans Wolfgang, *Hörbiger. Ein Schicksal* (Leipzig: Koehler and Amelang, 1930).

453. Ironically, the headquarters of the Hörbiger Institute came to be located in the house that had belonged to Alfred Adler in Salmannsdorf.

454. H. S. Bellamy ,*A Life History of Our Earth. Based on the Geological Application of Hoerbiger's Theory* (London: Faber and Faber, n.d.).

455. Ugo Cerletti and L. Bini, "L'elettroshock," *Archivio generale di neurologia, psichiatria e psicoanalisi*, XIX (1938), 266–268.

456. Robert Desoille, *Exploration de l'affectivité subconsciente par la méthode du rêve éveillé* (Paris: d'Artrey, 1938).

457. Harry Stack Sullivan, "Introduction to the Study of Interpersonal Relations," *Psychiatry*, I (1938), 121–134.

458. Arnold Toynbee and Frank T. Ashton-Gwatkin, *The World in March, 1939* (London and New York: Oxford University Press, 1952).

459. *Le Centenaire de Théodore Ribot et Jubilé de la Psychologie Scientifique Française* (Agen: Imprimerie Française, 1939). Neither the Bibliothèque Nationale in Paris, nor the Collège de France possesses a copy. (See Chap. 6, p. 346).

460. See Chap. 8, pp. 639–640.

461. See Chap. 7, p. 518.

462. Quoted from the translation given by *The Times* (London), November 24,

1945. See Hrant Pasdermadjian, *Histoire de l'Arménie depuis les Origines jusqu'au Traité de Lausanne* (Paris: Samuelian, 1949), p. 456.

463. Erich Fromm, *Escape from Freedom* (New York: Farrer and Rinehart, 1941).

464. Ludwig Binswanger, *Grundformen und Erkenntnis menschlichen Daseins* (Zurich: Niehans, 1942).

465. Carl R. Rogers, *Counseling and Psychotherapy: Newer Concepts in Practice* (Boston: Houghton Mifflin, 1942).

466. Marc Guillerey, "Médecine psychologique," in Alexis Carrel and Auguste Lumière, *Médecines officielles et médecines hérétiques* (Paris: Plon, 1943).

467. Edward Weiss, and O. Spurgeon English, *Psychosomatic Medicine* (Philadelphia: W. B. Saunders Co., 1943).

468. Flanders Dunbar, *Psychosomatic Diagnosis* (New York: P. Hoeber, 1943).

469. The importance of this discovery from the psychiatric viewpoint was shown by W. A. Stoll, "Lysergsäure-diäthylamid, ein Phantastikum aus der Mutterkorngruppe." *Schweizer Archiv für Neurologie und Psychiatrie*, LX (1947), 279–323. See also B. Holmstedt and Liljestrand, *Readings in Pharmacology* (New York: Pergamon Press, 1963), p. 209.

470. See Chap. 8, p. 642.

471. J. J. López Ibor, "Psicopatología de la angustia," reprint from *Revista Clínica Española* (1943). López Ibor's theory of anxiety was developed and expounded in his book *La Angustia Vital* (Madrid: Paz Montalvo, 1950).

472. Ludwig Binswanger, "Der Fall Ellen West," *Schweizer Archiv für Neurologie und Psychiatrie*, LIII (1944), pp. 255–277; LIV, 69–117, 330–360; LV, 16–40. Eng. trans. in Rollo May, Ernst Angel, and H. F. Ellenberger, eds. *Existence* (New York: Basic Books, 1958), pp. 237–364.

473. Pierre Janet, *Les Obsessions et la psychasthénie* (Paris: Alcan, 1903), I, 33–41.

474. Leopold Szondi, *Schicksalsanalyse* (Basel: Benno Schwabe, 1944).

475. Karl Abraham, *Klinische Beiträge zur Psychoanalyse* (Vienna: Internationaler Psychoanalytischer Verlag, 1921), 231–258. *Psychoanalytische Studien zur Charakterbildung* (1925).

476. Maurice Merleau-Ponty, *Phénoménologie de la perception* (Paris: Gallimard, 1945).

477. Henri Baruk, *Psychiatrie morale expérimentale, individuelle et sociale* (Paris: Presses Universitaires de France, 1945).

478. Alphonse Maeder, *Wege zur seelischen Heilung* (Zurich: Rascher, 1945).

479. J. L. Moreno, *Group Therapy* (New York: Beacon House, 1945).

11

Conclusion

THROUGHOUT THIS SURVEY of the origin and development of dynamic psychiatry, we remained as much as possible on the ground of historical facts. We shall now try to analyze the factors that caused and directed that evolution in order to find an answer to the problem that was the starting point of our inquiry (as stated in the Introduction).

These factors may be grouped in several categories pertaining to the socioeconomic and political background, the cultural trends, the personality of the pioneers, the role of the patients, and the occurrence of a variety of events.

In the first place, let us view the evolution of dynamic psychiatry against the socioeconomic and political background, notably that of economic history and class struggle. Mesmer's victory over Gassner was that of the aristocracy over the clergy.[1] Mesmer's Société de l'Harmonie was mainly composed of members of the French nobility shortly before its downfall. The "crises" elicited around Mesmer's *baquet* were identical to the *vapeurs*, the fashionable ailment of the ladies of the society. The shift from Mesmer to Puységur meant a shift from "magnetism for the aristocrats" to a "magnetism for the people," with corresponding changes in doctrine and therapeutic practices.[2] But the growing power of the new ruling class, bourgeoisie, was followed by the shift from magnetism to hypnotism. Whereas the rapport between the magnetizer and his patient reflected the paternalistic and symbiotic relationship between the nobleman and his subject, the rapport between the hypnotizer and the hypnotized reflected the authoritarian attitude of the bourgeois master toward his dependents; the bargaining therapy of the old magnetizers and their handling of the patients' pathogenic secrets were thus replaced by the imparting of hypnotic commands.[3] Speaking of Bleuler, we noted that the origin of his work on schizophrenia can be traced back to the political struggles between the farmers and the city aristocracy of Zurich. In that perspective, the genesis of Bleuler's concept of schizophrenia would appear as a byproduct, as it were, of the victory of the farmers' party over the city patricians.[4] The failed Revolution of 1848, whose implications for dynamic psychiatry we have noted, brought forth a reinforcement of the domination of the bourgeois class.[5] Meanwhile, the Industrial Revolution had led to the constitution of a powerful industrial and commercial upper class on one side, and of a numerous and destitute proletariat on the other side. Darwin's theories were distorted in order to provide the upper bourgeoisie with an ideology of blind and merciless competition, whereas Marx furnished an ideology for the working class and its allies.[6] The failed revolutionary attempt of the Paris Commune in 1871 unleashed a wave of antidemocratic feeling. Dupréel has shown that Gustave Le Bon's theory of the "psychology of crowds" was an expression of that trend, and yet it was taken as indisputable scientific truth and utilized as such by many authors, including Freud.[7] At the same time, that is, by the end of the nineteenth century, the upper classes could no longer be content with the existing method of hypnotic and suggestive therapy and demanded a new, nonauthoritarian psychotherapy that would explain to the patient what was going on in his own mind.[8] We have seen also how the great social and political upheavals caused by World War I led to deep-reaching changes within the new dynamic psychiatric systems.[9] Freudian concepts were distorted so as to furnish an ideology to the hedonistic-utilitarian world of mass consumption born from the technological revolution of the twentieth century, in the same way as distorted Darwinian concepts had furnished an ideology to the world of ferocious competition wrought by the Industrial Revolution.[10]

The socioeconomic structure is the ground upon which cultural trends originate and develop. In Chapter 4 we reviewed those cultural movements that succeeded each other in the Western world after the Renaissance, namely those of Baroque, Enlightenment, Romanticism, and Positivism. Mesmer's victory over Gassner was not only the victory of the aristocracy over the clergy, but also that of Enlightenment over the declining Baroque, and it is ironic that Mesmer's teachings were taken over and developed by the Romantics.[11] The Enlightenment inspired the psychiatric work of Pinel and Esquirol, and Mesmer considered himself a representative of the same trend. But Romanticism appropriated and reinterpreted magnetism, and extended its influence over medicine and psychiatry; we have seen that many of the concepts that are considered characteristic of Freud's psychoanalysis and Jung's analytic psychology permeated the work of Romantic psychiatrists.[12] Then around 1850, Romanticism was checked by Positivism, the cultural trend that forwarded organicist psychiatry and prevailed throughout the second half of the nineteenth century.[13] By the end of the nineteenth century and the beginning of the twentieth a revival of Romanticism exerted an unmistakable influence on the incipient new dynamic schools.[14] It is no wonder that many of Freud's and Jung's ideas are similar to the teachings of the old Romantic psychiatrists. Janet, in contrast, is definitely a late representative of the Enlightenment, as is Adler to a lesser extent. In that light the rivalries between Janet, Freud, Adler, Jung and their disciples may be understood as belated waves of the struggles of the Enlightenment and Romanticism at the end of the eighteenth and the beginning of the nineteenth century.

Like the artist and the writer, the dynamic psychiatrist mainly draws from his specific talents and sensitivities to determine his way of perceiving the world. Each dynamic psychiatrist has his own specific feeling for psychic reality, and his theories are also influenced by the events of his life. Janet was an active and nonemotional man, hence his interest in founding a kind of behavioral psychology.[15] His detached, mildly humorous, and benevolent attitude is reflected in his rational psychotherapy; the laborious and thrifty customs of his ancestors is reflected in his theory of the "budget of psychological forces." Since Janet did not remember his dreams, he could not possibly have written an *Interpretation of Dreams*, as did Freud, who was a good dreamer. The unsolved religious crisis of his adolescence caused him to come back repeatedly to the psychology of religion. Freud, as we have seen, shared with the great writers a deep interest in the secret aspects of people's lives and personalities, and a superior command of language.[16] The notion of the Oedipus complex and of its central place in human destiny was obviously derived from his own life history, and is also the reason why neither Adler nor Jung could accept it, since they had experienced quite different family situations in early childhood. As to Adler, his foremost talent was that quick sense of exact observation that makes the great clinician, what the Germans call the clinical look (*der klinische Blick*).[17] Transposed into the field of psychology, it was the ability of making at first sight an accurate evaluation of a normal or sick individual's style of life, and consequently to become the founder of a system of pragmatic psychology. Events of his childhood led Adler to attribute a basic importance to the situation of the individual in the siblings' row, even more than to the early relationships with parental figures. In Jung's case, the striking feature is the contrast between the practical abilities of a man well adjusted to material reality and a rare gift for psychological (if not parapsychological) intuition.[18] This contrast is reflected in Jung's typological system, and his psychotherapy, which includes the bringing back of patients to awareness and the synthetic-hermeneutic method for the furthering of individuation. As in Janet's case, the unsolved religious crisis of Jung's adolescence exerted a lasting influence on the development of his psychological system.

Furthermore, a student of the mind may be confronted with his own neurosis or neurotic elements in his personality. A basic distinction must be made, however, between those psychiatrists who merely took their own neurosis as an object of study and those whose life work was the outcome of a creative illness.

It would not be difficult to find many examples for the first group. Robert Burton described his own condition in his sad but vigorous description of the "scholar's melancholy."[19] George Cheyne gave a classical description of hypochondriasis based on several case histories, of which the longest and most interesting is his own.[20] Bénédict-Augustin Morel enhanced his description of the *délire émotif* (later called phobia) with the vivid story of his own case.[21] As to Janet, there is some reason to assume that certain features of his description of psychasthenia were taken from his personal experience. According to Phyllis Bottome, Adler was afflicted at an early age with rickets, and this would account for his theories of organ inferiority, inferiority complex, and compensation. Pavlov himself gave a short but significant account of the heart neurosis he suffered after being operated on in 1927, and it seems that his interest in psychiatry was greatly stimulated by this event.[22]

The common neurosis that provides a psychiatrist with a topic for reflection and perhaps incites him to efforts at self-healing should not be confused with the manifestation of the creative illness. It is our hypothesis that Freud's and Jung's systems originated mostly from their respective creative illness (of which their self-analysis was but one aspect). The main features of creative illness have already been described in former chapters.[23] Let us recall them briefly.

This rare condition begins after a long period of restless intellectual work and preoccupation. The main symptoms are depression, exhaustion, irritability, sleeplessness, and headaches. In short, it presents the picture of a severe neurosis, sometimes of a psychosis. There can be oscillations in the intensity of the symptoms but throughout the patient remains obsessed by a prevailing idea or the pursuit of some difficult aim. He lives in utter spiritual isolation and has the feeling that nobody can help him, hence his attempts at self-healing. But usually he will feel that these attempts intensify his sufferings. The illness may last three or more years. The recovery occurs spontaneously and rapidly; it is marked by feelings of euphoria, and is followed by a transformation of the personality. The subject is convinced that he has gained access to a new spiritual world, or that he has attained a new spiritual truth that he will reveal to the world. Examples of this illness can be found among Siberian and Alaskan shamans, among mystics of all religions, and among certain creative writers and philosophers. A well-documented example is that of Fechner, and it seems probable that Nietzsche, too, conceived his most original ideas during the agony of a creative illness.[24]

The clinical aspect of a creative illness differs from one individual to the other. Above all, a sharp line of distinction should be drawn between two categories, the illness of the pathfinder and that of the follower. The first shaman, who perhaps thousands of years ago found a means of sending himself into a trance to explore the world of the spirits, was a model for generations of shamans after him. He was the pathfinder, and they were the followers. Many individuals underwent a creative neurosis that no one repeated after them, because, like Fechner, they never thought of encouraging others to do so. However, it is not enough to describe the way and to encourage others to follow it. Thus Rudolf Steiner wrote a precise account of his method to obtain cognizance of superior spiritual worlds, but it seems that none of those who tried it ever succeeded.[25] In order to have followers, the pathfinder should not only teach the theory but provide a practical guide for others to follow that theory. Thus the shaman-apprentice must see an old shaman, at regular intervals, whose instruction he will put into practice step by step throughout his initiatory malady. Similar considerations apply to the mystics of most religions. Here too, the need of a spiritual guide is universally emphasized. Even more so, the follower must find the appropriate guide. Mystics such as Saint Teresa of Avila and Saint John of the Cross insisted upon the importance of finding the right director of conscience in order to avoid harmful experiences.

In regard to dynamic psychiatry, we surmise that Mesmer underwent a creative neurosis from which he emerged with the conviction of having made the epoch-making discovery of animal magnetism. However, he was only able to communicate it theoretically to his disciples, but not to initiate them to his own secret path. And this, by contrast, reveals the full originality of Freud and Jung. Both of them underwent a creative illness in a spontaneous and original form, and both of them made it a model to be followed by their disciples under the name of training analysis. Jung promoted the training analysis, and Freudians accepted it for didactic value, but the Jungian school later came to consider it as being a kind of initiatory malady comparable to that of the shaman.

We do not need to rerelate the story of the creative illness of Freud[26] and Jung.[27] Among the characteristic features of the creative illness, however, is the subject's conviction, after his recovery, that whatever he has discovered is a universal truth. This is how Mesmer came to proclaim the truth of animal magnetism, Fechner the principle of pleasure, Nietzsche the eternal return, Freud the Oedipus complex and the infantile sexual root of neurosis, and Jung the anima and the process of individuation. Those who have known Freud report that he talked of the Oedipus complex and the libido as absolute truths that could not suffer any doubt. But Jung also spoke of the collective unconscious, the anima, and the self with the quiet certitude of the man who knows.

We are thus led to make a distinction between two groups of dynamic systems. To the first group belong those of Janet and Adler. Even if Janet made use of his own experience of psychasthenia, and Adler of his personal experience of organ inferiority, their main discoveries were obtained by means of objective clinical research. In the second group are the systems of Freud and Jung. Here the basic tenets originated from within, that is, from the experience of a creative illness.

This distinction, in turn, brings a difficult question: What is the heuristic value of a creative illness? Is the certitude of having discovered a universal truth sufficient proof of the validity of that discovery? This question belongs to the more general problem of the validity of dynamic psychological experiences. One of its aspects is the specific character of the creative illness: it is a strictly personal experience for its pathfinder, but it sets a model for the follower, and this conformity of pattern will tend to be transmitted from one initiated to the other within the same school. The shaman apprentice will never come to the Nirvana experience of a Tibetan monk, nor will the yogi travel in the land of the spirits like the shaman. The same kind of specificity had been noted in regard to the various schools of hypnotism, and is also true for the new dynamic schools.[28] Persons analyzed by a psychoanalyst will have "Freudian" dreams and become conscious of their Oedipus complex, while those analyzed by Jungians will have archetypical dreams and be confronted with their anima. Involuntarily, one is reminded of Tarde's dictum that "genius is the capacity to engender one's own progeny."[29]

In addition to their own personalities, the most important source of achievement for dynamic psychiatrists lies in their relationship with their patients, the role of the latter being manifested in two different ways. The first one is the relationship between psychiatric theories and the class of patients to which the psychiatrist has access. As mentioned elsewhere, I. Wassermann held that the difference between Freud's psychoanalysis and Adler's individual psychology derived from the difference in the concepts communicated to them by their patients; in the wealthy group to which Freud's patients belonged the prevailing concern revolved around amorous problems; for Adler's patients the problems of material existence and their drive to success were much more anxiety-inspiring.[30] Freud's long researches in the field of neuroanatomy would also explain his emphasis on conceptual models inspired by brain physiology. The wide divergences between Freud's and Jung's concepts of the unconscious may be related to the fact that they did not deal with the same type of patients. Freud, who worked with neurotic, and had not much experience of psychoses, came upon the unconscious of repressed drives and memories; Jung, who worked for nine years with severe schizophrenics, was bound to find the collective unconscious and the archetypes.

There is another, probably more important aspect of the relationships of the dynamic psychiatrist with his patients. Sometimes a psychotherapist, who has taken a patient as a special object of study, finds himself engaged in a prolonged, difficult, and ambiguous relationship. This patient is usually a hysterical woman. What the psychiatrist comes to learn from the patient is sometimes quite different from what he had expected, and the true findings may be better understood by one of his successors than by himself.[31] Since the role of patients in the history of dynamic psychiatry has been all too neglected, it is appropriate briefly to recall a few typical episodes.

While treating his young patient, Fräulein Oesterlin, Mesmer acquired the conviction that a therapeutic effect did not originate from the magnets, but from a magnetic fluid emanating from his own person.[32] Then he believed to have cured Maria Theresia Paradis from her blindness and she herself believed for a short time that she could see again; today we see in that story a typical instance of suggestion, transference, and counter-transference, but Mesmer misunderstood the case, suspected a plot against him, and left Vienna.[33] Puységur was far more fortunate. Not only did he observe in Victor Race the first example of a perfect crisis, but he learned from him how magnetic sleep could be used for therapeutic purposes, that Mesmer's fluid theory was fallacious, and that a magnetizer should not use a patient for demonstrations as if he were an inert instrument.[34] Apparently, these teachings were not lost. When reading the story of Despine and Estelle, one realizes how much experience Despine needed to become aware of his patient's tricks and to utilize the rapport to lead her skillfully out of her illness.[35] As to Justinus Kerner, he did not fall so blindly into the snares of Friedericke Hauffe as is often said. He rather looked upon her with a mixture of wonder and criticism. He did not encourage her supposed therapeutic talents; he was proud to show her to celebrities of philosophy and theology, and if he made his seeress famous, the publication of her story procured fame to Kerner.[36] A more extraordinary example of involvement between therapist and patient may be found in the struggle of Pastor Blumhardt with his possessed parishioner, Gottliebin Dittus. For two years, Blumhardt fought a desperate fight against the powers of darkness; the more he fought, the more severe became Gottliebin's symptoms. After achieving his final victory Blumhardt's personality had undergone a great change.[37]

It is unfortunate that the teachings of Puységur and the old magnetizers had been so completely forgotten in the last decades of the nineteenth century, as shown by the examples of Charcot and Breuer. We have seen how Charcot utilized Blanche Wittman and other hysterical women for what he believed to be experimental studies.[38] The case of Breuer's celebrated patient Anna O. (Bertha Pappenheim) actually belonged to those great magnetic diseases that were so much sought after by the early magnetizers. She had unique symptoms, directed her cure, explained it to the physician, and prophesied the date of its termination. Because she chose for her self-directed therapy the procedure of catharsis (which a recent book had made fashionable), Breuer believed that he had discovered the key to the psychogenesis and treatment of hysteria. It was a theoretical misconstruction and a therapeutic failure, which, however, stimulated Freud toward the inception of psychoanalysis.[39] But it was given to Janet to rediscover the findings of the old magnetizers, notably the therapeutic utilization of the rapport. Janet learned from Léonie that another personality, which emerged under deep hypnosis, was but the reenactment of former hypnotic experiments performed upon her. He was thereby able to understand the error of Charcot's three stages of hypnosis.[40] Léonie's capacity of being hypnotized at a distance imbued Janet with an invincible distrust in regard to parapsychology. This in turn may explain Janet's extreme caution when he later had to deal with Madeleine, that patient who at intervals showed the stigmata of the Passion and oscillated between anguish and ecstasy.[41]

Flournoy's findings with "Hélène Smith" were rich and manifold. He demonstrated the importance of forgotten childhood memories, the reversion to various stages of childhood in the patient's fantasies, and that these were the expression of secret wishes. But though he understood the nature of the medium's feelings toward him he was not cautious enough. The publication of his book antagonized her, she restricted her activities to a sterile autistic life, and Flournoy came to understand the danger of carrying on prolonged studies of that kind upon one subject.[42] Jung's medium, Helene Preiswerk, combined certain features of the Seeress of Prevorst, and of Hélène Smith. Jung benefited from the experience of Kerner and Flournoy, though he understood only later the role played by the feelings of the patient toward himself. Jung's discovery was that the mediumistic humbug was a desperate attempt of the young lady to overcome the obstacles that hindered the development of her personality, and this was the first germ of his later concept of individuation.[43] Actually, it is noteworthy that Mesmer's former patient, Maria Theresia Paradis, though blind, was to achieve a brilliant career as a musician, that Gottliebin Dittus entered Blumhardt's household and became his assistant, that Blanche Wittman became a radiologist's assistant and died a martyr of science, that Bertha Pappenheim became a pioneer in social welfare, and that Helene Preiswerk successfully operated a dressmaker's shop in Basel.

As to Freud, it must be recalled that the method of free association was partly suggested to him by one of his patients, Elisabeth von R., and that his Wolf-Man played a historical role in the development of psychoanalysis.[44] Freud learned a great deal from him and was so grateful that he later treated him gratis and collected money to support him for several years. But the Wolf-Man conceived an intensive attachment to Freud, with paranoid delusions, which necessitated a further, prolonged treatment.[45] We thus see that the history of dynamic psychiatry is inseparable from the contributions of a gallery of eminent patients whose role has been strangely overlooked.

Throughout the present book we have encountered a variety of other sources of the achievements of dynamic psychiatrists. "No man is an island," not even the pioneer undergoing a creative illness with the feeling of utmost isolation. Creative minds are indissolubly bound to their social environment, and also to a more restricted specific human context that comprises their masters, colleagues, friends, pupils, critics, and even adversaries. It is impossible to distinguish in a man's thought what is truly his and what has been suggested by those around him or what he has read. The power of cryptomnesia should never be underestimated, nor that of the stimulation produced by contemporary events. We have referred in that regard to the revolution of the Young Turks in 1908 to 1909 and the way it is reflected in Freud's *Totem and Taboo*.[46] Sometimes the psychologist seeking a new path will find the lead toward a solution in a recent book. Freud was inspired by Frazer's book on totemism,[47] Jung was inspired by Frobenius' *Epoch of the Sun God*,[48] and Adler was inspired by Vaihinger's *Philosophy of the as If*.[49] The publication of Schreber's *Memoirs* incited Jung to depart from Freud's theory of the libido, but inspired Freud's theory of paranoia.[50] Even a novel can be thought-provoking, as were Jensen's *Gradiva*[51] and Spitteler's *Imago*.[52]

Another, often overlooked, aspect of the process in dynamic psychiatry is the adoption of ideas that were current in another branch of knowledge. Once transferred into the psychiatric field and formulated in another terminology, they present the appearance of new discoveries. The possibility of awakening the sexual instinct in the infant, and the amorous attraction of the little boy toward his mother, were well known to Catholic educators, and these notions had been popularized by Michelet, but when proclaimed by Freud they appeared as startling novelties.[53] The notion that homosexuality was in most cases due to psychological causes and not physical constitution was well known to educators before it imposed itself on psychiatrists. Similarly, the psychosexual theory of hysteria was current among gynecologists before it prevailed among neuropsychiatrists. Criminal investigators knew the meaning of parapraxes and utilized them before it became an established part of psychoanalysis.[54] Long before Moreno had introduced psychodrama as a therapeutic procedure, reconstructions of crimes was in practice, which not infrequently resulted in a confession by the murderers.

Progress is sometimes merely the picking up of an old, abandoned idea. Certain concepts of the new dynamic psychiatry, far from being shocking in their novelty, appeared old-fashioned. Such was the concept of the flight into illness, which had been proclaimed by the old Romantic psychiatrists and was still alive in the popular mind, as was the idea that the stereotyped movements of a psychotic could have a psychological meaning. In a novel by Edmond de Goncourt an unfortunate woman undergoes so many sufferings that she takes flight into a severe psychosis.[55] We see her sitting in a corner of the asylum, ceaselessly making circular movements with her hand. The author explains that in her delusions she imagines herself gathering flowers falling from a cherry tree, as she did in her happy childhood years. Psychiatrists reading that novel must have smiled about that obsolete Romantic fancy, but when Bleuler and Jung came to teach similar ideas, it appeared as an illuminating novelty.

Whatever its novelty and originality, a creative work is almost always a part of a contemporary trend; it crystallizes a great number of insights that lay scattered around. Freud's *Interpretation of Dreams* appeared at a time when public interest had been aroused by a flow of literature on dreams; his *Three Essays on the Sexual Theory* was published in 1905 in the midst of a flood of writings on sexual pathology that started around 1880; *Totem and Taboo* also appeared during a contemporary trend that brought historians, ethnologists, and psychologists to view totemism as one decisive phase in a hypothetical reconstruction of the history of mankind. It is extremely difficult to ascertain to what extent an epoch-making work really inaugurates a cultural revolution, or is not rather the embodiment of an already existing trend.

We are thus brought back to the paradox that was the starting point of our inquiry, namely, the fact that dynamic psychiatry underwent a seemingly incoherent succession of vicissitudes with phases of rejection and revival, in contrast to the consistent course of evolution of the physical sciences. At this point we must note that further basic differences distinguish dynamic psychiatry from the other sciences.

Modern science is a unified body of knowledge in which each separate science has its autonomy and is defined by its object and by its specific methodology; the field of dynamic psychiatry, in contrast, is not clearly delineated, it tends to invade the field of other sciences, if not to revolutionize them. Freud insisted that "the founder of psychoanalysis must be the person best qualified to judge what was psychoanalysis and what was not."[56] Such a point of view is foreign to modern science; nobody would imagine Pasteur, for example, declaring that he was the one to decide what was and what was not bacteriology, whereas it would be perfectly normal if Heidegger would assert that he is the one to define what is and what is not Heideggerian philosophy.

Within a unified science the term "school" merely designates the temporary grouping of a few pupils around a master working along a new trend, not yet fully incorporated into the general body of knowledge. Such was, for instance, Pasteur's "school" before his discoveries became common knowledge. Among the founders of modern dynamic psychiatry we note that only one, Janet, remained faithful to the tradition of unified science. Although he was a cofounder of a psychological society and of a psychological journal and although he created a powerful psychological synthesis, it never occurred to him to found a "movement" or a "school." He expected his teachings to be integrated into the discipline of psychology, as Pasteur expected his discoveries to be integrated into medicine. Speaking of Freud, Adler and Jung we note, in contrast, that with them the word "school" has assumed the meaning it had in connection with the "philosophical schools" of Greco-Roman antiquity.[57] That return from the concept of unified science to that of independent "schools" is an extraordinary novelty that does not seem to have attracted the attention it deserves.

All these paradoxes cover another deeper one, namely, the contrast between the commitments of dynamic psychiatry and of experimental psychology. Modern science is based on experimentation, quantification, and measurement, not only in physics, but in the total realm of the human soul. In that perspective, dynamic psychiatry is no doubt open to criticism. Who has ever been able to measure the libido, ego strength, the superego, the anima, individuation, and the like? The very existence of these entities has never been demonstrated. But to those psychiatrists who devote themselves exclusively to dealing with their patients in the immediate psychotherapeutic situation, these terms are not abstract conceptualizations; they are living realities whose existence is much more tangible than the statistics and computations of experimental researchers. Jung, who spent years developing the word association test, later declared: "Whosoever wants to know about the human soul will learn nothing, or almost nothing, from experimental psychology."[58] Hans Kunz explained why the Freudians did not accept the objections of epistemologists: "Because the psychoanalysts have experienced the truth of psycho-analysis in a way which widely transcends in forcefulness and convincingness the usual evidence of logically formulated insights . . . , they could hardly give up their convictions on the grounds of the incomparably smaller evidence of formal logics."[59]

Actually, we have to deal with two conceptions of reality facing each other, and it would seem that the realm of psychic life can be approached from two sides, both legitimate: either with the accurate technique of measurement, quantification, and experimentation of the research specialist, or with the immediate, nonquantifiable approach of the dynamic psychotherapist.

The dynamic psychotherapist is thus dealing with what Jung calls psychic existences or psychic realities. But what exactly are psychic realities? We are only concerned here with those that are discovered in the process of creative illness and in the daily work of depth psychologists. Even so, there are many kinds of psychic realities, and they often are contradictory and incompatible with each other, though endowed with the same character of certainty for those who are working with them. It would be vain, for instance, to attempt a reduction of Jung's analytic psychology into Freud's psychoanalysis or vice versa, no less than to attempt to reduce any of these two into the conceptual framework of experimental psychology. And many other dynamic systems are conceivable.[60]

The coexistence of two mutually incompatible approaches to the cognition of the human psyche shocks the scientist's yearning for unity. Shall we keep the principle of the unity of science by sacrificing the autonomy of the new dynamic systems, or keep these systems (and possibly further ones that will arise in their wake) and consider the ideal of unified science as a noble dream? A way out of this dilemma could be provided by the combined effort of psychologists and philosophers. In our survey of the exploration of the unconscious, we noticed that psychologists have been mainly interested in its conservative, dissolutive, and creative aspects, whereas little attention was devoted after Flournoy to the mythopoetic unconscious.[61] A renewed investigation of that still largely unexplored field could shed a new light on many obscure problems. On the other hand, one would wish that philosophers extend their reflections upon the notion of psychic reality and define its structure (as Heidegger did for the structure of human existence in contrast to that of material and manufactured objects). We might then hope to reach a higher synthesis and devise a conceptual framework that would do justice to the rigorous demands of experimental psychology and to the psychic realities experienced by the explorers of the unconscious.

Notes

1. See Chap. 2, pp. 55–57.
2. See Chap. 4, pp. 188–191.
3. See Chap. 4, pp. 191–192.
4. See Chap. 5, pp. 286–287.
5. See Chap. 4, pp. 223–226; Chap. 2, pp. 83–85.
6. See Chap. 4, pp. 228–240.
7. See Chap. 7, p. 528.
8. See Chap. 5, p. 321.
9. See Chap. 10, pp. 826–827.
10. See Chap. 7, pp. 548–549.
11. See Chap. 2, pp. 77–88.
12. See Chap. 4, pp. 210–215.
13. See Chap. 4, pp. 225–228.
14. See Chap. 5, pp. 278–284.
15. See Chap. 6, pp. 400–401.
16. See Chap. 7, p. 535.
17. See Chap. 8, p. 625.
18. See Chap. 9, p. 727.
19. Robert Burton, *The Anatomy of Melancholy* (Oxford: John Lichfield, 1621).
20. George Cheyne, *The English Malady* (London: Strahan, 1735).
21. B. A. Morel, "Du Délire émotif," *Archives générales de médecine,* 6th series, VII (1866), 385–402, 530–551, 700–707.
22. See Chap. 10, p. 850.
23. See Chap. 7, pp. 447–448.
24. See Chap. 4, p. 216.
25. See Chap. 9, p. 684–686.
26. See Chap. 7, pp. 448–450.
27. See Chap. 9, pp. 670–673.
28. See Chap. 3, p. 172.
29. Gabriel Tarde, *La Philosophie pénale* (Lyon: Storck, 1890), pp. 165–166.
30. See Chap. 8, p. 626.

31. H. F. Ellenberger, "La Psychiatrie et son histoire inconnue," *L'Union médicale du Canada*, XC (1961), 281–289.

32. See Chap. 2, p. 59.

33. See Chap. 2, pp. 60–61.

34. See Chap. 2, pp. 70–72.

35. See Chap. 3, pp. 129–131.

36. See Chap. 2, pp. 79–81.

37. See Chap. 1, pp. 18–22.

38. See Chap. 2, pp. 98–99.

39. See Chap. 7, pp. 480–484.

40. See Chap. 6, pp. 337–339; 358–359.

41. See Chap. 6, pp. 395–396.

42. See Chap. 5, pp. 315–317; Chap. 10, p. 787.

43. See Chap. 9, p. 690.

44. See Chap. 7, p. 487.

45. See Chap. 7, p. 543–544.

46. See Chap. 7, p. 527.

47. See Chap. 10, p. 809.

48. See Chap. 9, p. 730.

49. See Chap. 8, pp. 606, 630

50. See Chap. 7, pp. 531–532.

51. See Chap. 10, p. 790.

52. See Chap. 10, pp. 794–795.

53. See Chap. 5, p. 296.

54. See Chap. 7, p. 495.

55. Edmond de Goncourt, *La Fille Elisa* (Paris: Charpentier, 1873).

56. Ernest Jones, *The Life and Work of Sigmund Freud* (New York: Basic Books, 1955), II, 362.

57. See Chap. 1, pp. 41–42.

58. See Chap. 9, p. 694.

59. Hanz Kunz, "Die existentielle Bedeutung der Psychoanalyse in ihrer Konsequenz für deren Kritik," *Der Nervenarzt*, III (1930), 657–668.

60. Potential systems of dynamic psychiatry were conceived, for instance, by Arthur Schnitzler (Chap. 7, p. 473), Léon Daudet (Chap. 9, p. 731), and André Breton (Chap. 10, p. 835–837).

61. See Chap. 5, p. 318.

ACKNOWLEDGMENTS

The author wishes to make the following acknowledgments: American Jewish Committee, for Stanley Edgar Hyman, "Freud and Boas: Secular Rabbis?" reprinted from *Commentary* (March 1954), pp. 264–267, © 1954, by the American Jewish Committee. *American Journal of Psychiatry* for excerpts from Ernest Harms, "Pierre M. F. Janet: 1859–1947", CXV (1959), pp. 1036–1037. *American Journal of Psychotherapy* for H. F. Ellenberger, "Charcot and the Salpêtrière School", *American Journal of Psychotherapy,* XIX (April 1965), pp. 253–267. Association for Research on Nervous and Mental Disease, New York, for excerpts from A. Brill's translator's introduction to C. G. Jung, *The Psychology of Dementia Praecox,* Nervous and Mental Disease Monograph Series, No. 3 (1936). Bailliere, Tindall and Cassel Ltd., London, for excerpts from Siegfried Bernfeld, "Sigmund Freud, M.D.", *International Journal of Psychoanalysis* XXXII (1951), pp. 204–217. Grune and Stratton, Inc. for Ilse Bry and Alfred Rifkin, "Freud and the History of Ideas", in Jules H. Masserman, ed. *Science and Psychoanalysis* (V) (New York: Grune and Stratton, 1962). *Journal of the History of Behavioral Sciences* for excerpts from H. F. Ellenberger, "The Pathogenic Secret and Its Therapy", *Journal of the History of Behavioral Sciences* II (January 1966), pp. 29–42. Liveright Publishers, New York, for excerpts from Fritz Wittels' *Freud and His Time* (New York: Liveright, 1931), p. 17. The Menninger Foundation for excerpts from H. F. Ellenberger, "Fechner and Freud" and "The Ancestry of Dynamic Psychiatry", *Bulletin of the Menninger Clinic* XX (1956), pp. 201–214; 288–299, © 1956; and "The Unconscious Before Freud", XXI (1957), pp. 3–15, © 1957 by the Menninger Foundation.

NAME INDEX

Both indexes in this book were prepared by Mrs. Margaret Karaivan.

Abraham, Karl, 427, 493, 533, 544, 695, 799–800, 802, 866
Ach, Narziss, 313
Achilles (Janet's patient), 22, 341, 369–370, 394, 406, 409, 771, 777
Ackerknecht, Erwin, 39, 40, 48, 247, 739
Adler, Alexandra, 583, 584, 590, 653
Adler, Alfred: associates:
Bachofen, 223, 611, 629; Benedikt, 582, 619, 626; Bleuler, 608; Darwin, 236, 629; Freud, 452, 454, 456, 510, 513, 517, 543, 544, 547, 557, 571–576, 579–581, 583–586, 590–593, 595–596, 598, 603–605, 607–609, 613, 618–621, 626–628, 634, 637–641, 645–648, 699, 821, 855, 891; Jahn (*see* Jahn); Janet, 406, 594, 608, 632; Jung, 592, 645, 698, 709, 715, 719, 728, 855; Krafft–Ebing, 581, 626; Marx, 238, 603, 609, 610, 611, 629–630; Nietzsche, 276, 278, 603, 608, 609, 630, 633, 638; Smuts (*see* Smuts); Stekel, 584, 596–599; Vaihinger, 606–608, 630–631; Wagner–Jauregg, 585–586; biographic studies on, 580, 582–583, 634; childhood and youth, 579–580, 591–592; citizen of Vienna, 590; collective denial of his work, 645–648; contemporaries, 596–599; conversion to Protestantism, 573, 583–584, 595; country-house, 577, 589, 590, 597; death and burial, 571, 577–578, 591, 647–648, 862; family background, 572–580; first memories, 592; on the French Revolution, 618–619; Hungarian citizenship, 579, 582; individual psychology, 589, 592, 608–619; individual psychological movement, 267, 456, 596, 637, 817, 846, 854, 858; influence, 636–648: on existential psychiatry, 641–642; on neo-psychoanalysis, 638–641, 860; on psychoanalysis, 637–638, 641; on psychology, 642–644; Jewish background, 424, 572–574, 579–580, 595, 597; later development of his theories, 624–625; lecturing tours, 589, 590–591; legend, 583, 646–648; life-frame, 571–572; marriage and children, 583, 584, 590, 594–595, 626; medical vocation and studies, 573, 581–582; military life, 582, 583; participation in congresses, 849, 850; and patients, 891; personality, 591–596, 888; philosophical opinions, 624; pre-psychoanalytic period, 583, 599–603; Privat-Dozent, application for, 585–586, 593; psychoanalytic period, 452, 454, 603–606, 805, 807; psychotherapy, 619–623; religious opinions, 595, 624–625; settling in U.S., 590, 594, 595, 853; sibling constellation, 576–579, 592, 625, 888; on social medicine, 582, 591, 599–603; socialistic opinions, 583, 587–589, 591, 595, 601; sources, 625–636, 888, 894; therapeutic educational institutions, 589, 621–623; theories, 182:
basic axioms, 609–610; community feeling, 278, 608–611, 622, 623, 628, 629, 635–636, 644–645; compensation, 236, 517, 604–605, 629, 639, 641, 889; course of human life, 615–616; crime, 618, 623–624, 644;

Beard, George M., 97, 242–244, 262, 404
Beauchamp, Miss (Morton Prince's patient), 139–140, 147, 780
Beaunis, Henri–Etienne, 88
Bebel, August, 222, 223, 239, 292, 611, 629
Beccaria, Cesare, 197
Bechterev, Vladimir, 88, 268, 850
Beckh–Widmanstetter, Hans, 574, 580, 581, 582, 648–650, 663, 873
Beer, Hermann, 574–575
Beer–Hofmann, Richard, 283
Beethoven, Ludwig van, 206, 575
Benedetti, Gaetano, 21, 22
Benedikt, Moritz: associates:
  Charcot, 94, 269, 436, 440; Krafft–Ebing, 267, 299, 767; *see also* Adler, Freud;
  concept of fantasy life, 489, 523, 536, 762:
    hypnosis, 171, 267, 751; hysteria, 144, 301, 440, 489, 764, 768; pathogenic secret, 46, 301, 486, 518, 536, 714, 767;
  data about his contemporaries, 265, 299, 431, 570; Jewish background, 423, 464, 573; life and career, 269–270; use of the word libido, 303, 777
Benoit, Pierre, 709, 730
Bentham, Jeremy, 630
Ber of Bolechow, 421
Bergasse, Nicolas, 62, 64, 65, 66, 68, 73
Berger, Alfred von, 773
Berger, Hans, 852, 856
Bergson, Henri, 168, 172, 205, 262, 321, 336, 343, 354–355, 376, 394, 400, 405, 560, 624, 683, 726, 755, 758–759, 784, 785, 818, 822, 862
Bérillon, Edgar, 757, 780, 818
Bernays, Jacob, 484
Bernays, Martha (*see* Freud)
Berne, Eric, 643
Bernfeld, Siegfried, 250, 426, 427, 429, 430, 433, 494, 552, 663
Bernhardi, Friedrich von, 809
Bernheim, Hippolyte: associates:
  Liébeault, 86–87, 751, 755; *see also* Charcot, Freud;
  decline of his school, 89, 804, 805; head of Nancy School, 87–89, 110, 285, 749, 757, 771, 775, 777, 778, 791; illusions about his work, 98, 107, 158, 339; Jubilee and resignation, 804, 816; life and career, 87; as a novel character, 100; participation to congresses, 340, 760–761, 805; personality, 87; rapport,

overlooks role of, 153; theory of hypnosis, 87, 471, 751, 760:
  of hypnotically induced crime, 164, 751, 763; ideodynamism, 148–150, 151, 178, 290, 760; post-hypnotic amnesia, 89, 114, 518, 538; post-hypnotic suggestion, 114, 538; suggested memories, 118, 164; unconscious simulation, 172;
therapeutic methods:
  hypnosis, 110, 171, 314, 760; patient directed therapy, 151; psychosomatic cures, 863; suggestion in waking state, 120, 770; use of word "psychotherapy", 321; works, 755
Bersot, Ernest, 335, 356
Bertha Pappenheim (*see* Anna O.)
Berthelot, Marcellin, 719
Bertrand, Alexandre, 76, 82, 86, 114, 119, 155, 187, 339, 359, 403
Bezzola, D., 797
Bichat, Xavier, 540
Bierer, Joshua, 623, 653
Billy, André, 283, 321
Binder, Hans, 141
Binet, Alfred, 141, 143–145, 166, 298, 301, 318, 343, 354–356, 375, 405, 691, 702–703, 727, 757, 759, 761, 772, 780, 791–793
Binswanger, Ludwig, 309, 455, 529–530, 641–642, 795, 842, 853, 863, 864–865
Binz, Carl, 310
Biran, Maine de (*see* Maine de Biran)
Bircher (Birche–Benner), Max, 132–133, 845, 850, 854, 859
Bittel, Karl, 57
Bjerre, Poul, 150
Blanche, Emile–Antoine, 769
Blanche Wittmann, (Charcot's patient), 98–99, 100, 775, 892, 893
Bleuler, Eugen, 285–288; associates:
  Binswanger, 842, 853; Charcot, 286; Forel, 116, 285–287; Janet, 287, 347, 377, 406, 807; Romantic psychiatrists, 215, 537, 895; Rorschach, 840; *see also* Adler, Freud, Jung;
Burghölzli, director of, 287, 666–667, 777, 787, 793, 796; depth psychology, coins the term, 562; hypnosis, subjective experience in, 116; life and background, 286, 324; mediumistic experiments, 674; organodynamic psychiatry, 242, 287; patients, devotion to, 286–287, 521,

315, 775
Felkin, G. W., 37
Féré, Charles, 299, 355, 778
Ferenzi, Sandor, 414, 452, 455, 493, 520, 544, 799, 818, 844, 845
Ferstel, baroness Marie von, 453–454
Feuchtersleben, Ernst Freiherr von, 210
Feuerbach, Anselm Ritter von, 176, 846
Feuerbach, Ludwig, 237
Fichte, Johann Gottlieb, 159, 264, 517, 728
Fierz, H. K., 733
Flammarion, Camille, 163, 761
Flaubert, Gustave, 144, 161, 189, 271, 466, 507, 635
Flechsig, Paul, 434, 531
Fleischl von Marxow, Ernst von, 423, 431, 433, 435
Fliess, Wilhelm, 427, 444-449, 451–455, 458, 459, 465, 477, 484, 488, 493, 502, 545, 546, 673, 789
Flournoy, Théodore, 315–317, 357; and Freud (*see* Freud); influence of his work, 791, 835, 843, 868; and Jung (*see* Jung); life and work, 315; observations on Hélène Smith (*see* Hélène Smith); on Miss Miller, 696; theories:
    on cryptomnesia, 170, 317, 781; on mediums, 121, 315, 350; on multiple personality, 141, 732; on mythopoetic unconscious, 150, 318, 350, 897; on spiritism, 85, 399
Foerster, Friedrich Wilhelm, 542
Forel, Auguste, 285–286; ants, studies on, 285, 840; associates:
    Bechterev, 268; Bernheim, 88, 285; Meyer, 222; Meynert, 434; *see also* Bleuler, Freud;
Burghölzli, director of, 285, 286, 757, 777; dynamic concepts, shift to, 480; hypnotism:
    illusions about, 171; utilization of, 88, 116, 285, 761;
influence, 791; life and personality, 285–286, 468; medical vocation, 285, 430; neurological research, 268, 475; participation in congresses, 340, 805–806; participation in Zurich polemics, 812–814; philosophical ideas, 809; sexual problems, on, 502, 792, 793; theories:
    hypnotic resistance, 490, 757; hypnotically induced crime, 757; hysteria, 774;
therapy of alcoholism, 285:

case of amnesia, 125–126; psychosomatic illness, 285, 863; World War I, 825
Fouillée, Alfred, 168, 361, 401
Fourier, Charles, 504
France, Anatole (Anatole-François Thibaut), 282, 758, 824, 834
Frank, Ludwig, 797, 806, 810, 811, 813, 814, 850
Frankl, Ludwig August, 103
Frankl, Viktor, 637, 641, 651
Franklin, Benjamin, 58, 65, 183
Franz, S. I., 135–136
Fraser, Rev. Donald, 820
Frazer, Sir James, 7, 263, 525, 526, 809, 894
Freeland, L. S., 29
Freud, Amalia, 425, 426, 428, 429, 433
Freud, Anna, 443, 517, 619
Freud, Emanuel, 425, 426–428
Freud, Ernst, 443, 456, 457
Freud, Jacob, 422–426, 428–430, 445–446, 451–452, 468, 551
Freud, Jean-Martin, 427, 443, 456, 458, 558, 679, 680
Freud, Joseph, 426, 451
Freud, Martha, née Bernays, 433, 437, 443, 458, 468
Freud, Sigmund: *see also* psychoanalysis, Wednesday psychoanalytic Association; America, opinions on, 460, 829; apartment on Berggasse, 443, 460–461; birthdays:
    50th, 455; 70th, 849; 75th, 853; 80th, 457;
cancer and operations, 456, 457, 460, 463, 845, 851; childhood and youth, 428–430, 451–452, 457–458, 581; cocain research, 434–436, 442, 451; contemporaries, 469–474; creative illness, 210, 444–450, 527, 672–673, 687, 736, 889–891; criticism of his theories, 344, 675, 792–794, 796–803, 805–806, 810–821; cultural background, 194, 263, 727; death and funeral, 419, 457, 859–860; disciples, 544, 796; engagement, 433–436, 458, 468; England, emigration to, 419, 457, 858; fame, 450, 454–455, 780, 791–793, 799, 821, 844, 853; family background, 419–427; feeling of isolation, 448, 455, 468; Freiberg, ceremony in, 456; Goethe Prize award, 456, 853; hostility against, 267, 448–456, 462, 468, 470, 508, 678, 771–773, 792–793, 819–820; influence, 546–550,

SUBJECT INDEX

acedia, 398
affluent society, 548–549
aggressive drives, 274–277, 513, 527, 534, 544, 598, 605, 638
alchemy, alchemists, 226, 263, 339, 696, 719–720, 730, 862
Alcoholics Anonymous, 733
alcoholism, 243, 285, 321, 344–345, 379, 384, 397, 617, 624, 643, 692, 733, 834
Alsace, 73, 87, 89, 199, 258–259, 332, 333, 335, 345, 757, 804, 822, 830
analysis, complex (*see* Jung, analytic psychology); of destiny, 866–867; dialectic, 239, 240, 319; existential, 779, 850–851, 863–865; lay, 849; psychological (*see* Janet); self-analysis (*see* Freud, Jung); training, 520, 544, 719, 732, 890; wild, 519, 805, 815, 841
anarchism, anarchists, 222, 228, 254, 762, 764, 767, 770, 777, 779, 798, 847–848
anima, animus (*see* Jung, theories)
animal magnetism, 57–83, chap. 3 & 4 (passim), 761, 890
anthroposophy, 207, 684–687
antisemitism, 423–424, 427, 451, 454, 463–464, 467, 533, 544, 547–548, 573, 675–677, 771, 773, 775, 853–854
anxiety, theories of: Horney, 640; López Ibor, 864; Neumann, 214, 215, 536; Rank, 844; Stekel, 596; *see also* Freud
anxiety neurosis (*see* Freud, theories)
aphasia, 97, 121, 290, 476, 764
archetypes (*see* Jung, theories): Divine Child, 712, 718, 734; God, 724–725; Magna Mater, 223, 710, 718, 730; Old Wise Man, 223, 278, 710, 718; Savior, 22, 38, 718, 868; self,

710, 712, 725; soul, 708–709, 717–718; spirit, 709–710; Virgin Mother, 293, 294; Wotan, 722
aristocracy, 184–185, 255, 256, 261, 775, 886, 887
Armenians, 260, 770, 798, 800, 822, 825, 830, 861
art, mediumistic, 163–164; psychology of, 95, 221, 529, 796, *see also* beauty
associations, free, 519, 539, 728, 837
Associations and Societies, 196, 226, 269; Académie des Sciences, 335, 750; Académie des Sciences Morales et Politiques, 349, 354; British Medico-Psychological Association, 299; German Society for Psychotherapy, 674–677, 854; International Psychoanalytic Association, 455, 457, 669–670, 677, 802, 805, 813, 819, 820, 821; International Psychological Institute, 342–343, 779; International Society of Psychotherapy, 675; Kepler–Bund, 810–811; Monisten–Bund, 548, 811; Psychiatric Association of Berlin, 799; Psychologischer Club of Zurich, 673, 674, 846; Société des Amis Réunis de Strasbourg, 72; Société de l'Harmonie, 65–66, 73, 188, 191, 199; Société de Neurologie, 349, 785; Société de Psychologie, 349, 350; Société de Psychologie Physiologique, 338, 341, 342, 754; Société de Psycho-thérapie de Paris, 344, 821; Society for Individual Psychology, 585; Society for Psychical Research, 85, 121, 308, 313, 338, 534, 673, 755; Swiss Society of Applied Psychology, 347, 675; Viennese Psychoanalytic Society, 455, 584–585, 807, 816, 846; Vien-